SHOWCASE PRESENTS

VOLUME ONE

BATMAN CREATED BY BOB KANE

SHOWCASE PRESENTS BATMAN VOL. ONE

Published by DC Comics. Cover and compilation copyright © 2006 DC Comics.
All Rights Reserved. Originally published in single magazine form in
DETECTIVE COMICS 327-342 and BATMAN #164-174 © 1964, 1965 DC Comics.
All Rights Reserved. All characters, their distinctive likenesses and related
elements featured in this publication are trademarks of DC Comics.
The stories, characters and incidents featured in this publication are entirely fictional.
DC Comics does not read or accept unsolicited submissions of stories, ideas or artwork.
DC Comics, 1700 Broadway, New York, NY 10019.
A Warner Bros. Entertainment Company.
Printed in Canada. First Printing.
ISBN: 1-4012-1086-4.
ISBN13: 978-1-4012-1086-1.
Cover illustration by Carmine Infantino & Joe Giella.
Front cover colored by Alex Sinclair.
Special thanks to Mark Waid for loan of source material.

TABLE OF CONTENTS

ALL COVERS AND STORIES INKED BY **JOE GIELLA** UNLESS OTHERWISE NOTED.

UNTIL THE 1970s IT WAS NOT COMMON PRACTICE IN THE COMIC BOOK INDUSTRY TO CREDIT ALL STORIES.
IN THE PREPARATION OF THIS COLLECTION WE HAVE USED OUR BEST EFFORTS TO REVIEW ANY
SURVIVING RECORDS AND CONSULT ANY AVAILABLE DATABASES AND KNOWLEDGEABLE PARTIES.
WE REGRET THE INNATE LIMITATIONS OF THIS PROCESS AND ANY MISSING OR MISASSIGNED
ATTRIBUTIONS THAT MAY OCCUR. ANY ADDITIONAL INFORMATION ON CREDITS SHOULD BE DIRECTED TO:
EDITOR, COLLECTED EDITIONS, C/O DC COMICS.

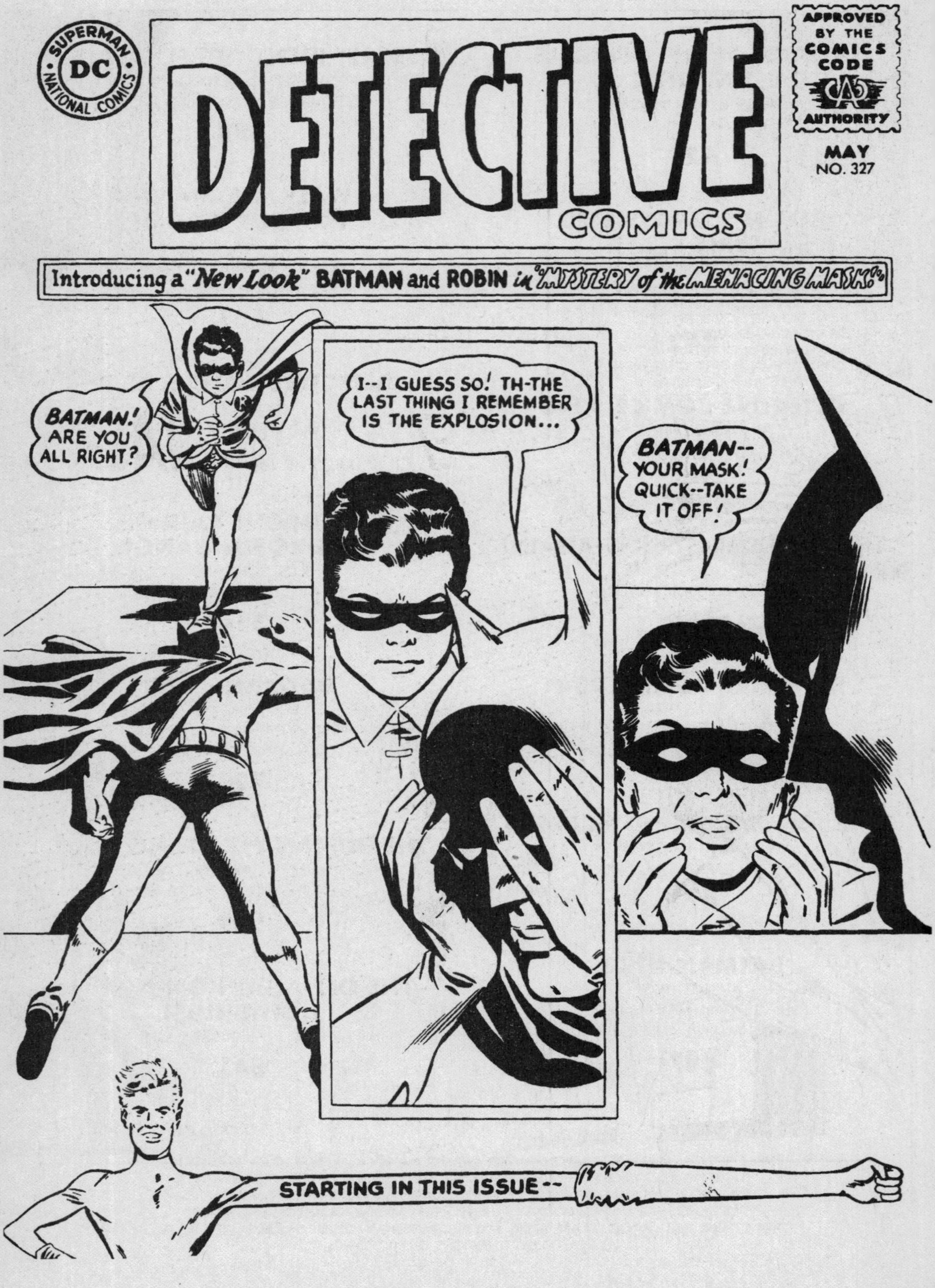
SUPERMAN DC NATIONAL COMICS
DETECTIVE COMICS
APPROVED BY THE COMICS CODE AUTHORITY
MAY NO. 327
Introducing a "New Look" BATMAN and ROBIN in "MYSTERY of the MENACING MASK!"
BATMAN! ARE YOU ALL RIGHT?
I--I GUESS SO! TH-THE LAST THING I REMEMBER IS THE EXPLOSION...
BATMAN-- YOUR MASK! QUICK--TAKE IT OFF!
STARTING IN THIS ISSUE--

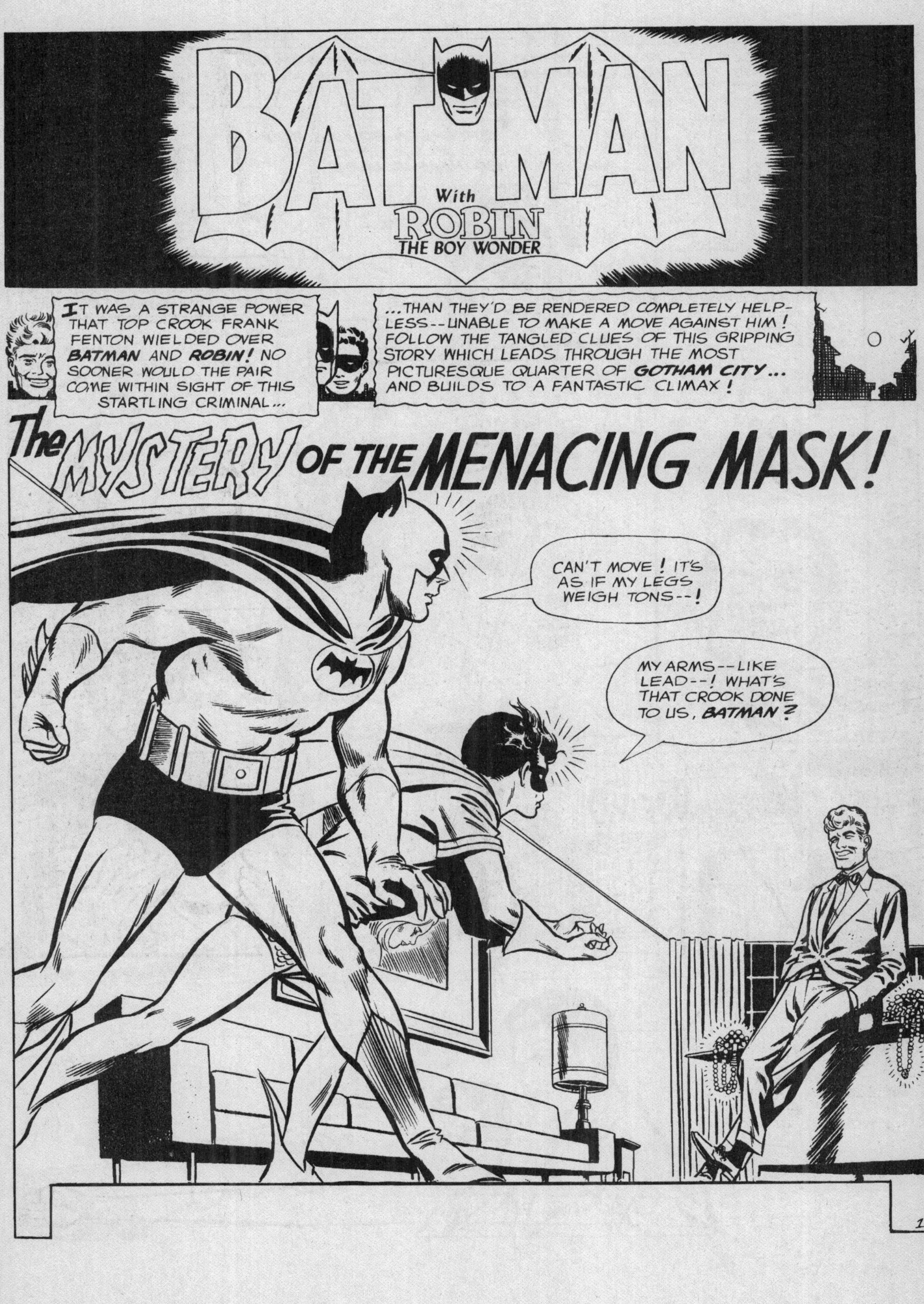
BATMAN
With ROBIN THE BOY WONDER
IT WAS A STRANGE POWER THAT TOP CROOK FRANK FENTON WIELDED OVER BATMAN AND ROBIN! NO SOONER WOULD THE PAIR COME WITHIN SIGHT OF THIS STARTLING CRIMINAL...
...THAN THEY'D BE RENDERED COMPLETELY HELP-LESS--UNABLE TO MAKE A MOVE AGAINST HIM! FOLLOW THE TANGLED CLUES OF THIS GRIPPING STORY WHICH LEADS THROUGH THE MOST PICTURESQUE QUARTER OF GOTHAM CITY... AND BUILDS TO A FANTASTIC CLIMAX!
The MYSTERY OF THE MENACING MASK!
CAN'T MOVE! IT'S AS IF MY LEGS WEIGH TONS--!
MY ARMS--LIKE LEAD--! WHAT'S THAT CROOK DONE TO US, BATMAN?
1

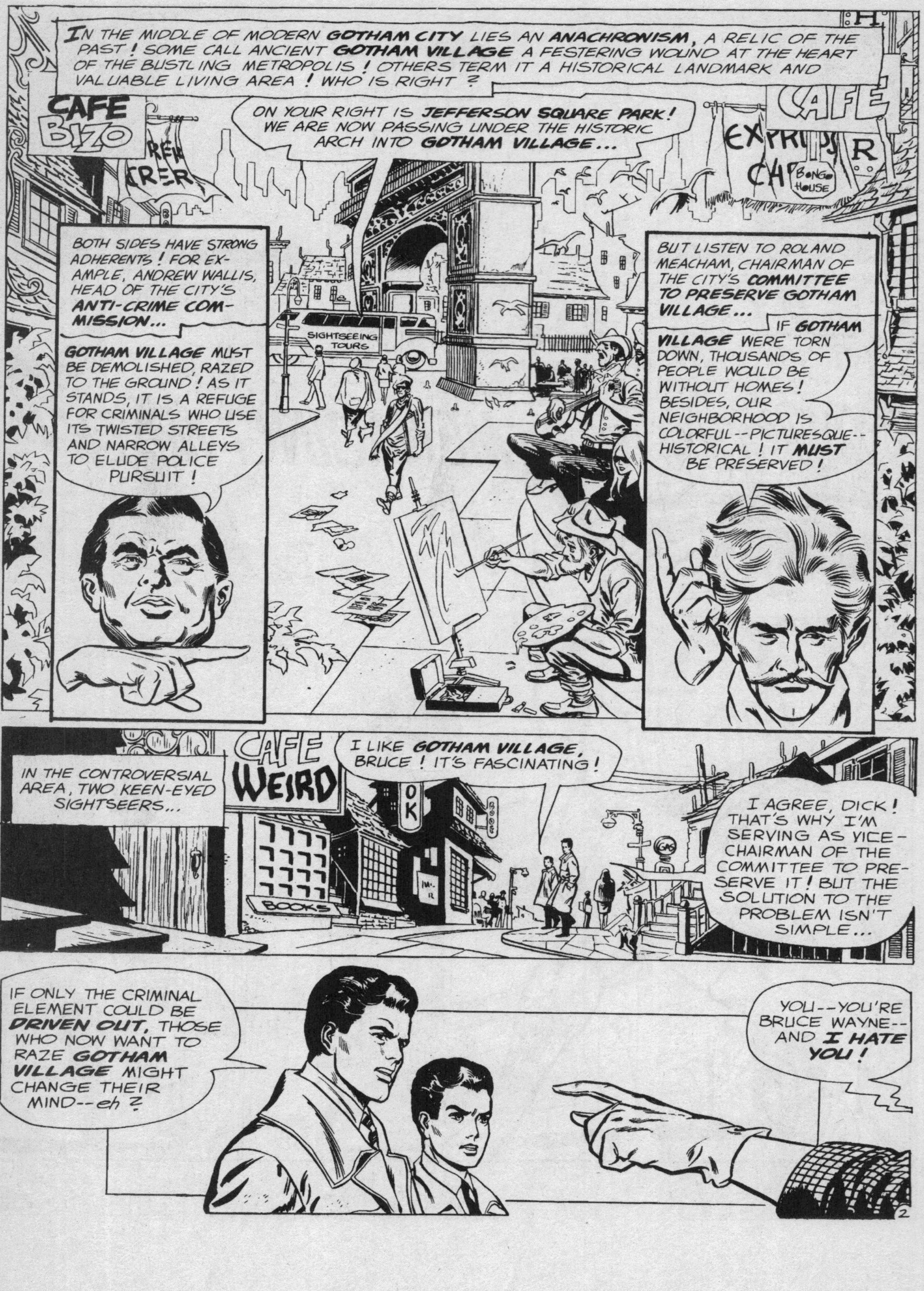
IN THE MIDDLE OF MODERN GOTHAM CITY LIES AN ANACHRONISM, A RELIC OF THE PAST! SOME CALL ANCIENT GOTHAM VILLAGE A FESTERING WOUND AT THE HEART OF THE BUSTLING METROPOLIS! OTHERS TERM IT A HISTORICAL LANDMARK AND VALUABLE LIVING AREA! WHO IS RIGHT?
CAFE BIZO
CAFE
ON YOUR RIGHT IS JEFFERSON SQUARE PARK! WE ARE NOW PASSING UNDER THE HISTORIC ARCH INTO GOTHAM VILLAGE...
BONGO HOUSE
SIGHTSEEING TOURS
BOTH SIDES HAVE STRONG ADHERENTS! FOR EXAMPLE, ANDREW WALLIS, HEAD OF THE CITY'S ANTI-CRIME COMMISSION...
GOTHAM VILLAGE MUST BE DEMOLISHED, RAZED TO THE GROUND! AS IT STANDS, IT IS A REFUGE FOR CRIMINALS WHO USE ITS TWISTED STREETS AND NARROW ALLEYS TO ELUDE POLICE PURSUIT!
BUT LISTEN TO ROLAND MEACHAM, CHAIRMAN OF THE CITY'S COMMITTEE TO PRESERVE GOTHAM VILLAGE...
IF GOTHAM VILLAGE WERE TORN DOWN, THOUSANDS OF PEOPLE WOULD BE WITHOUT HOMES! BESIDES, OUR NEIGHBORHOOD IS COLORFUL--PICTURESQUE--HISTORICAL! IT MUST BE PRESERVED!
IN THE CONTROVERSIAL AREA, TWO KEEN-EYED SIGHTSEERS...
CAFE WEIRD
BOOKS
I LIKE GOTHAM VILLAGE, BRUCE! IT'S FASCINATING!
I AGREE, DICK! THAT'S WHY I'M SERVING AS VICE-CHAIRMAN OF THE COMMITTEE TO PRESERVE IT! BUT THE SOLUTION TO THE PROBLEM ISN'T SIMPLE...
IF ONLY THE CRIMINAL ELEMENT COULD BE DRIVEN OUT, THOSE WHO NOW WANT TO RAZE GOTHAM VILLAGE MIGHT CHANGE THEIR MIND--eh?
YOU--YOU'RE BRUCE WAYNE--AND I HATE YOU!
2

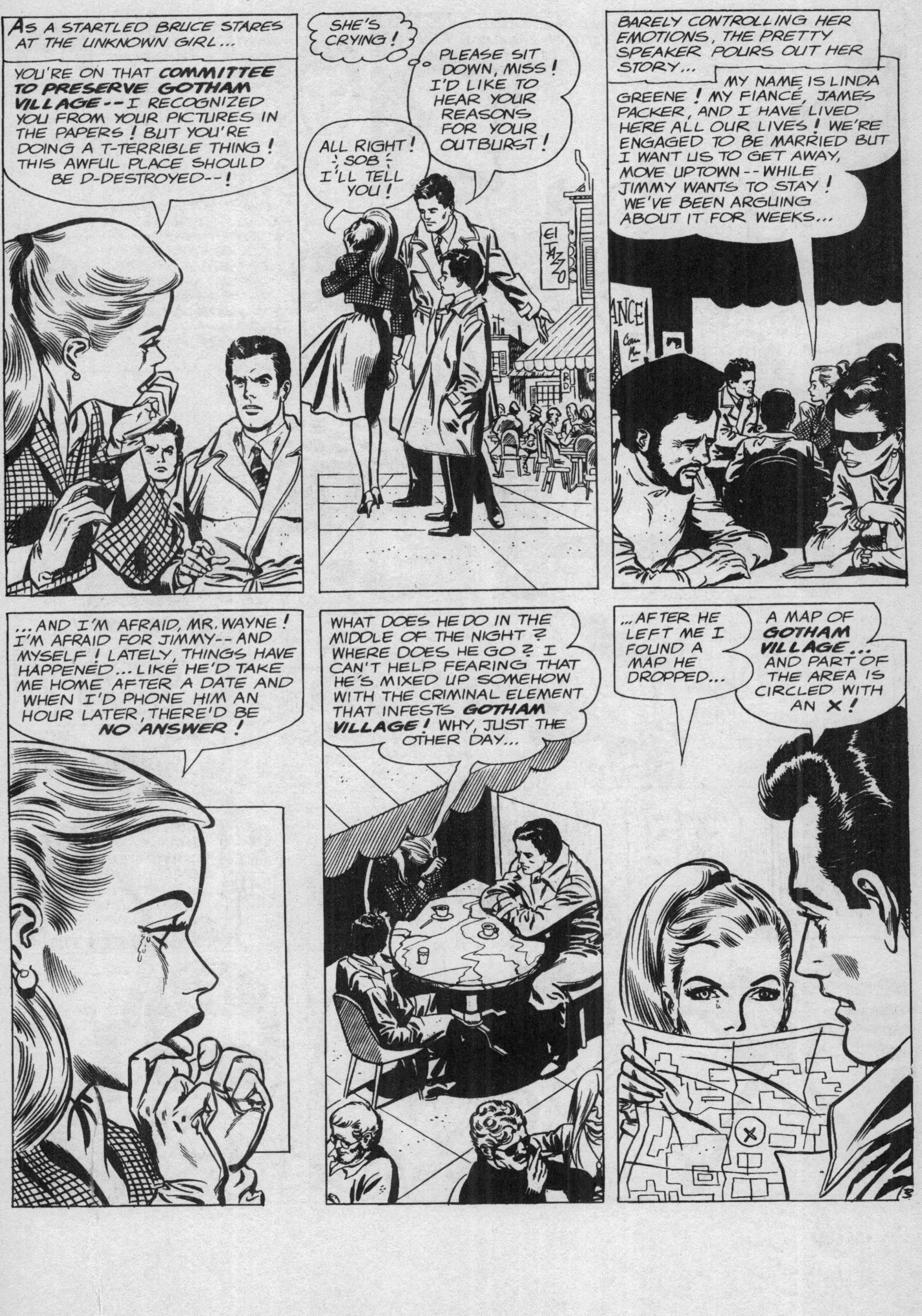
AS A STARTLED BRUCE STARES AT THE UNKNOWN GIRL...
YOU'RE ON THAT COMMITTEE TO PRESERVE GOTHAM VILLAGE--I RECOGNIZED YOU FROM YOUR PICTURES IN THE PAPERS! BUT YOU'RE DOING A T-TERRIBLE THING! THIS AWFUL PLACE SHOULD BE D-DESTROYED--!
SHE'S CRYING!
PLEASE SIT DOWN, MISS! I'D LIKE TO HEAR YOUR REASONS FOR YOUR OUTBURST!
ALL RIGHT! SOB I'LL TELL YOU!
El Jazzo
BARELY CONTROLLING HER EMOTIONS, THE PRETTY SPEAKER POURS OUT HER STORY...
MY NAME IS LINDA GREENE! MY FIANCÉ, JAMES PACKER, AND I HAVE LIVED HERE ALL OUR LIVES! WE'RE ENGAGED TO BE MARRIED BUT I WANT US TO GET AWAY, MOVE UPTOWN--WHILE JIMMY WANTS TO STAY! WE'VE BEEN ARGUING ABOUT IT FOR WEEKS...
...AND I'M AFRAID, MR. WAYNE! I'M AFRAID FOR JIMMY--AND MYSELF! LATELY, THINGS HAVE HAPPENED...LIKE HE'D TAKE ME HOME AFTER A DATE AND WHEN I'D PHONE HIM AN HOUR LATER, THERE'D BE NO ANSWER!
WHAT DOES HE DO IN THE MIDDLE OF THE NIGHT? WHERE DOES HE GO? I CAN'T HELP FEARING THAT HE'S MIXED UP SOMEHOW WITH THE CRIMINAL ELEMENT THAT INFESTS GOTHAM VILLAGE! WHY, JUST THE OTHER DAY...
...AFTER HE LEFT ME I FOUND A MAP HE DROPPED...
A MAP OF GOTHAM VILLAGE... AND PART OF THE AREA IS CIRCLED WITH AN X!
8

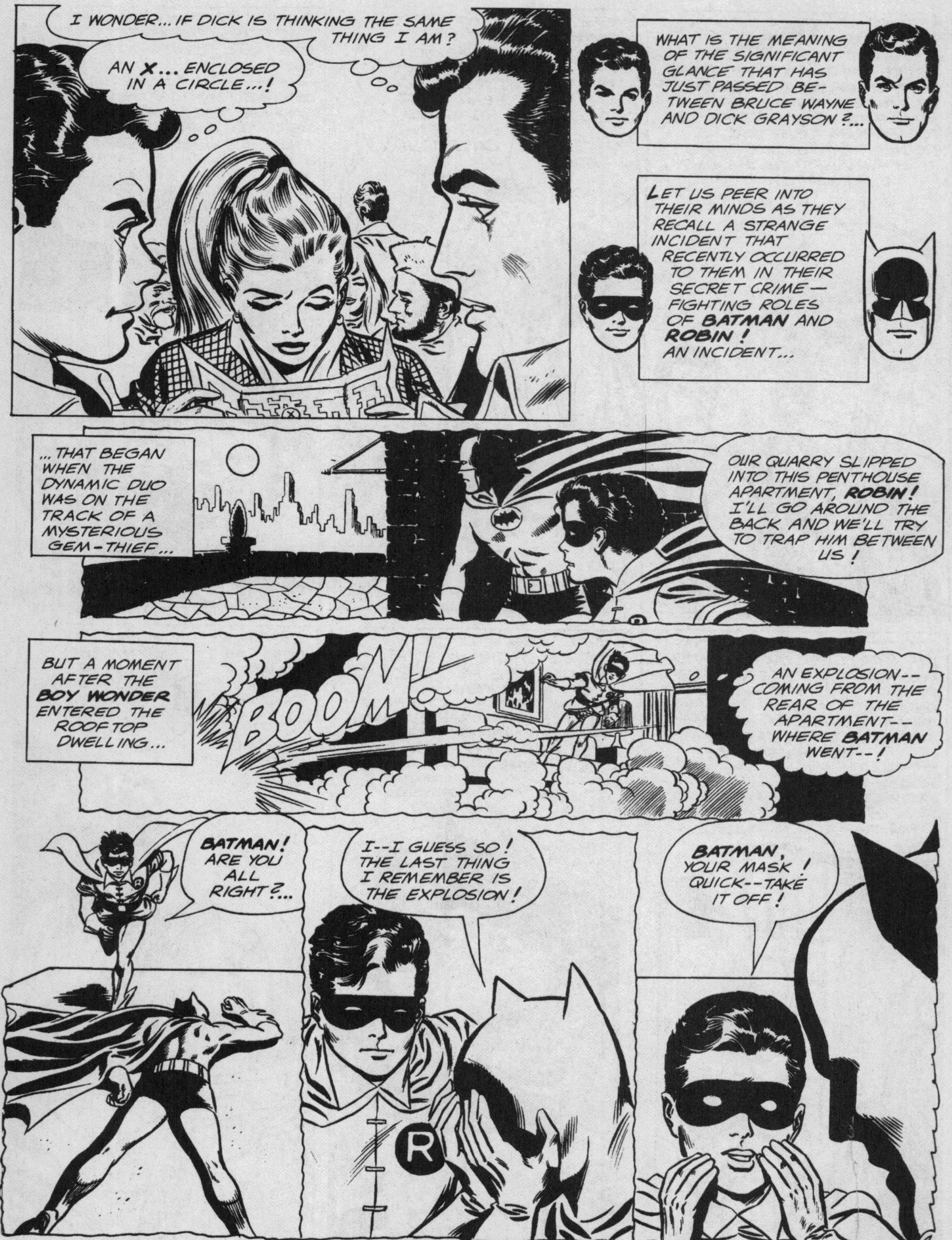
I WONDER... IF DICK IS THINKING THE SAME THING I AM?
AN X... ENCLOSED IN A CIRCLE...!
WHAT IS THE MEANING OF THE SIGNIFICANT GLANCE THAT HAS JUST PASSED BETWEEN BRUCE WAYNE AND DICK GRAYSON?...
LET US PEER INTO THEIR MINDS AS THEY RECALL A STRANGE INCIDENT THAT RECENTLY OCCURRED TO THEM IN THEIR SECRET CRIME-FIGHTING ROLES OF BATMAN AND ROBIN! AN INCIDENT...
...THAT BEGAN WHEN THE DYNAMIC DUO WAS ON THE TRACK OF A MYSTERIOUS GEM-THIEF...
OUR QUARRY SLIPPED INTO THIS PENTHOUSE APARTMENT, ROBIN! I'LL GO AROUND THE BACK AND WE'LL TRY TO TRAP HIM BETWEEN US!
BUT A MOMENT AFTER THE BOY WONDER ENTERED THE ROOFTOP DWELLING...
BOOM
AN EXPLOSION--COMING FROM THE REAR OF THE APARTMENT--WHERE BATMAN WENT--!
BATMAN! ARE YOU ALL RIGHT?...
I--I GUESS SO! THE LAST THING I REMEMBER IS THE EXPLOSION!
BATMAN, YOUR MASK! QUICK--TAKE IT OFF!
4

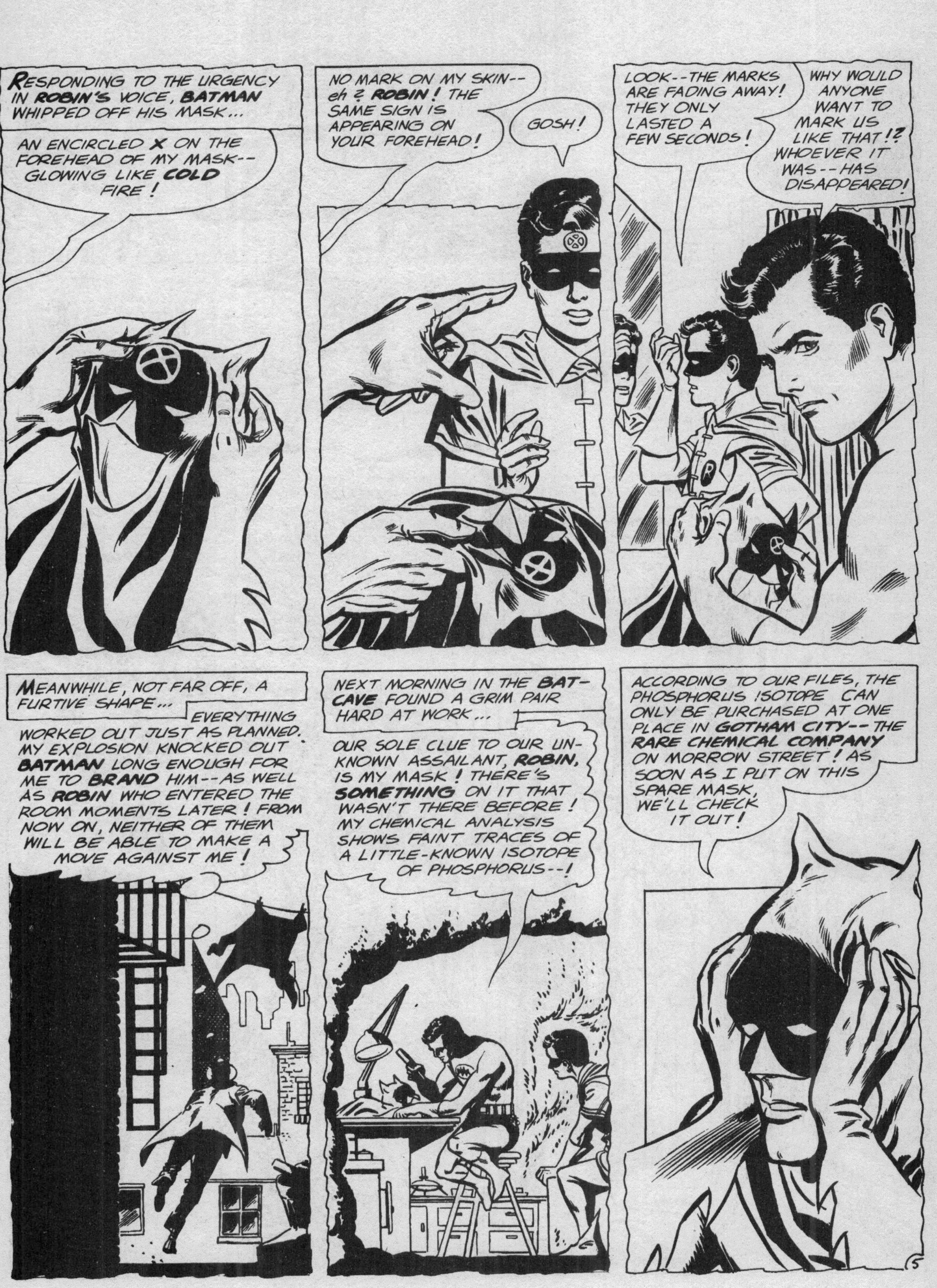
RESPONDING TO THE URGENCY IN ROBIN'S VOICE, BATMAN WHIPPED OFF HIS MASK...
AN ENCIRCLED X ON THE FOREHEAD OF MY MASK--GLOWING LIKE COLD FIRE!
NO MARK ON MY SKIN--eh? ROBIN! THE SAME SIGN IS APPEARING ON YOUR FOREHEAD!
GOSH!
LOOK--THE MARKS ARE FADING AWAY! THEY ONLY LASTED A FEW SECONDS!
WHY WOULD ANYONE WANT TO MARK US LIKE THAT!? WHOEVER IT WAS--HAS DISAPPEARED!
MEANWHILE, NOT FAR OFF, A FURTIVE SHAPE...
EVERYTHING WORKED OUT JUST AS PLANNED. MY EXPLOSION KNOCKED OUT BATMAN LONG ENOUGH FOR ME TO BRAND HIM--AS WELL AS ROBIN WHO ENTERED THE ROOM MOMENTS LATER! FROM NOW ON, NEITHER OF THEM WILL BE ABLE TO MAKE A MOVE AGAINST ME!
NEXT MORNING IN THE BAT-CAVE FOUND A GRIM PAIR HARD AT WORK...
OUR SOLE CLUE TO OUR UNKNOWN ASSAILANT, ROBIN, IS MY MASK! THERE'S SOMETHING ON IT THAT WASN'T THERE BEFORE! MY CHEMICAL ANALYSIS SHOWS FAINT TRACES OF A LITTLE-KNOWN ISOTOPE OF PHOSPHORUS--!
ACCORDING TO OUR FILES, THE PHOSPHORUS ISOTOPE CAN ONLY BE PURCHASED AT ONE PLACE IN GOTHAM CITY--THE RARE CHEMICAL COMPANY ON MORROW STREET! AS SOON AS I PUT ON THIS SPARE MASK, WE'LL CHECK IT OUT!
5

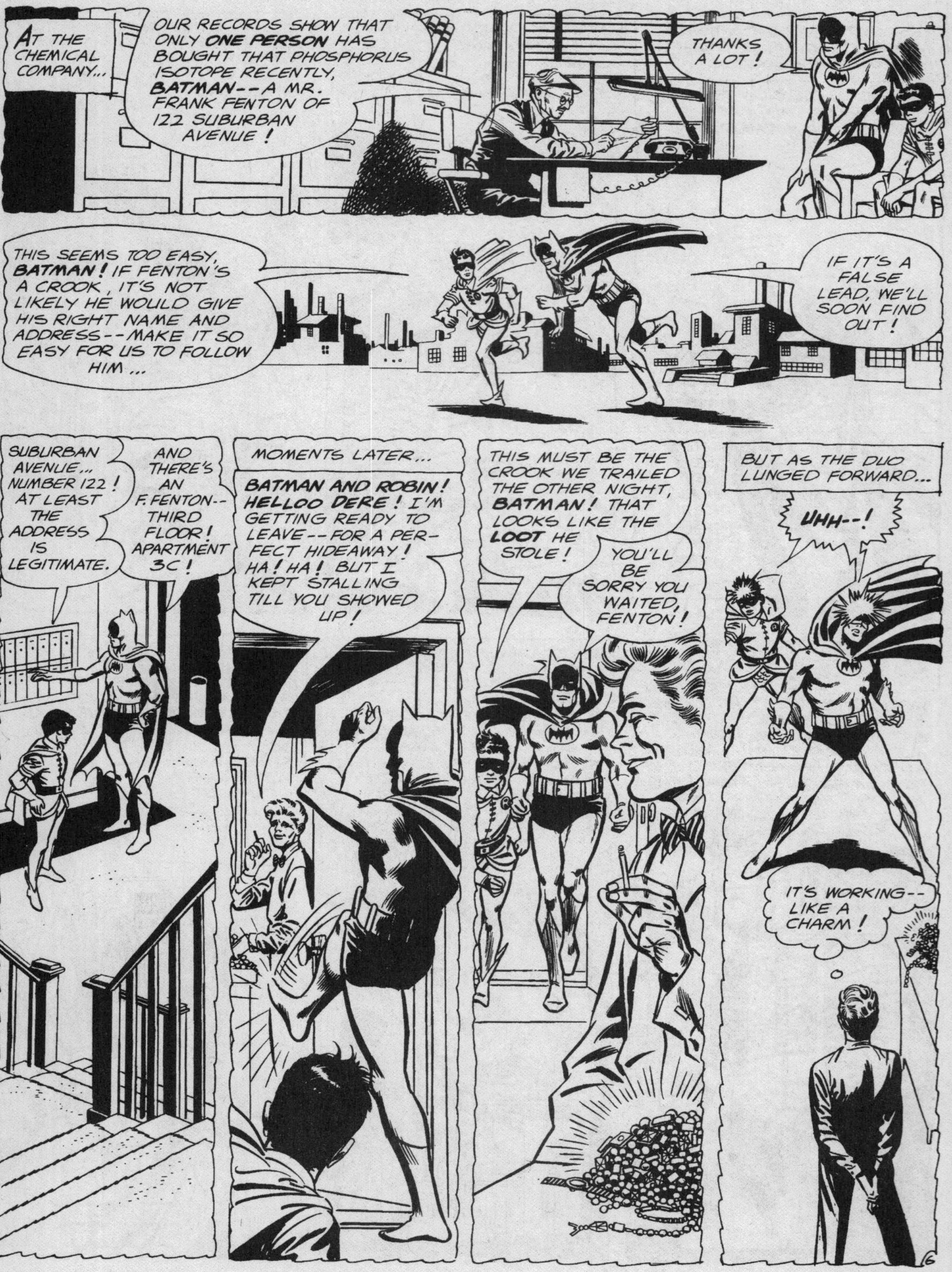
AT THE CHEMICAL COMPANY...
OUR RECORDS SHOW THAT ONLY ONE PERSON HAS BOUGHT THAT PHOSPHORUS ISOTOPE RECENTLY, BATMAN--A MR. FRANK FENTON OF 122 SUBURBAN AVENUE!
THANKS A LOT!
THIS SEEMS TOO EASY, BATMAN! IF FENTON'S A CROOK, IT'S NOT LIKELY HE WOULD GIVE HIS RIGHT NAME AND ADDRESS--MAKE IT SO EASY FOR US TO FOLLOW HIM...
IF IT'S A FALSE LEAD, WE'LL SOON FIND OUT!
SUBURBAN AVENUE... NUMBER 122! AT LEAST THE ADDRESS IS LEGITIMATE.
AND THERE'S AN F. FENTON--THIRD FLOOR! APARTMENT 3C!
MOMENTS LATER...
BATMAN AND ROBIN! HELLOO DERE! I'M GETTING READY TO LEAVE--FOR A PERFECT HIDEAWAY! HA! HA! BUT I KEPT STALLING TILL YOU SHOWED UP!
THIS MUST BE THE CROOK WE TRAILED THE OTHER NIGHT, BATMAN! THAT LOOKS LIKE THE LOOT HE STOLE!
YOU'LL BE SORRY YOU WAITED, FENTON!
BUT AS THE DUO LUNGED FORWARD...
UHH--!
IT'S WORKING--LIKE A CHARM!
6

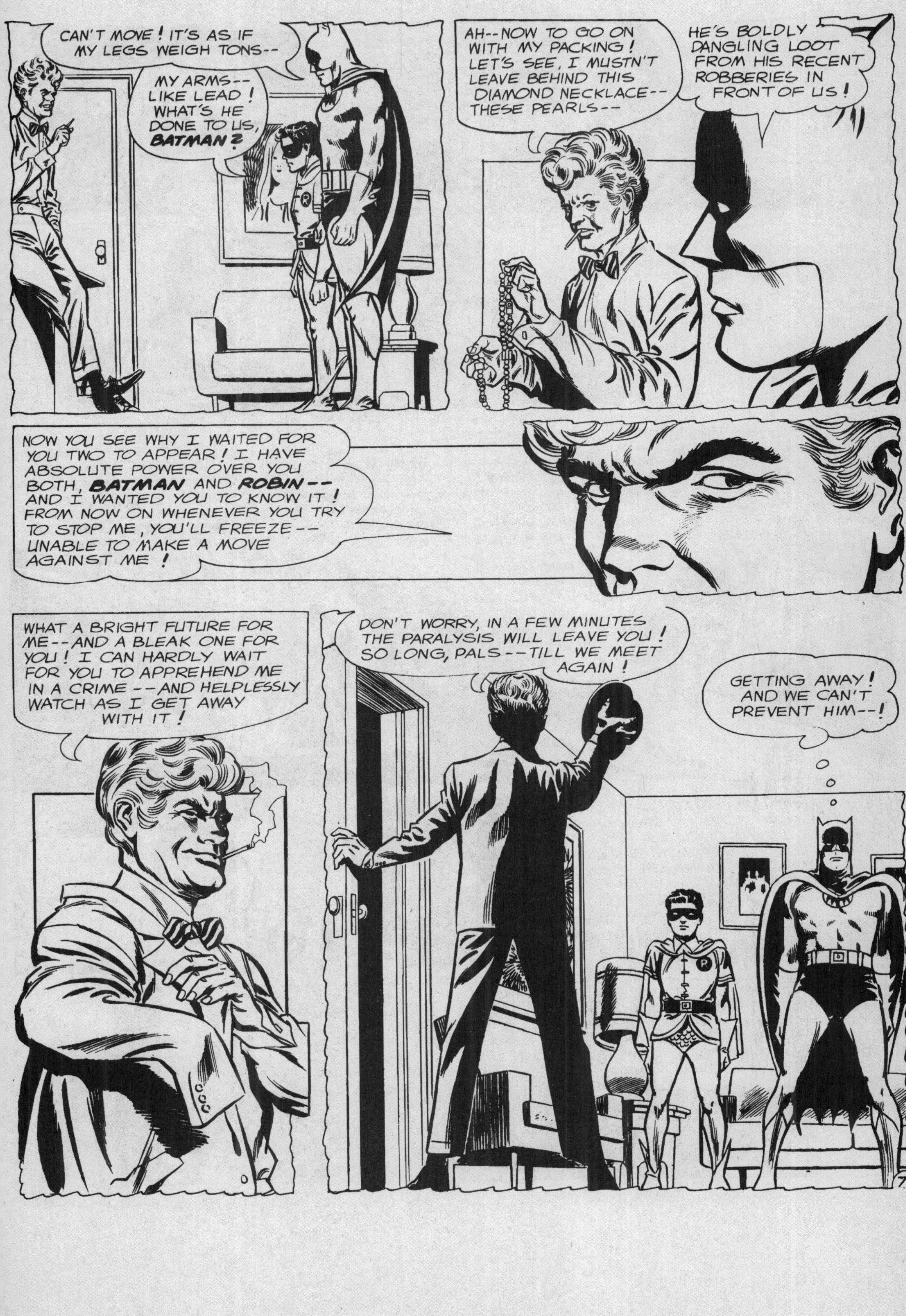
CAN'T MOVE! IT'S AS IF MY LEGS WEIGH TONS--
MY ARMS--LIKE LEAD! WHAT'S HE DONE TO US, BATMAN?
AH--NOW TO GO ON WITH MY PACKING! LET'S SEE, I MUSTN'T LEAVE BEHIND THIS DIAMOND NECKLACE--THESE PEARLS--
HE'S BOLDLY DANGLING LOOT FROM HIS RECENT ROBBERIES IN FRONT OF US!
NOW YOU SEE WHY I WAITED FOR YOU TWO TO APPEAR! I HAVE ABSOLUTE POWER OVER YOU BOTH, BATMAN AND ROBIN--AND I WANTED YOU TO KNOW IT! FROM NOW ON WHENEVER YOU TRY TO STOP ME, YOU'LL FREEZE--UNABLE TO MAKE A MOVE AGAINST ME!
WHAT A BRIGHT FUTURE FOR ME--AND A BLEAK ONE FOR YOU! I CAN HARDLY WAIT FOR YOU TO APPREHEND ME IN A CRIME--AND HELPLESSLY WATCH AS I GET AWAY WITH IT!
DON'T WORRY, IN A FEW MINUTES THE PARALYSIS WILL LEAVE YOU! SO LONG, PALS--TILL WE MEET AGAIN!
GETTING AWAY! AND WE CAN'T PREVENT HIM--!
7

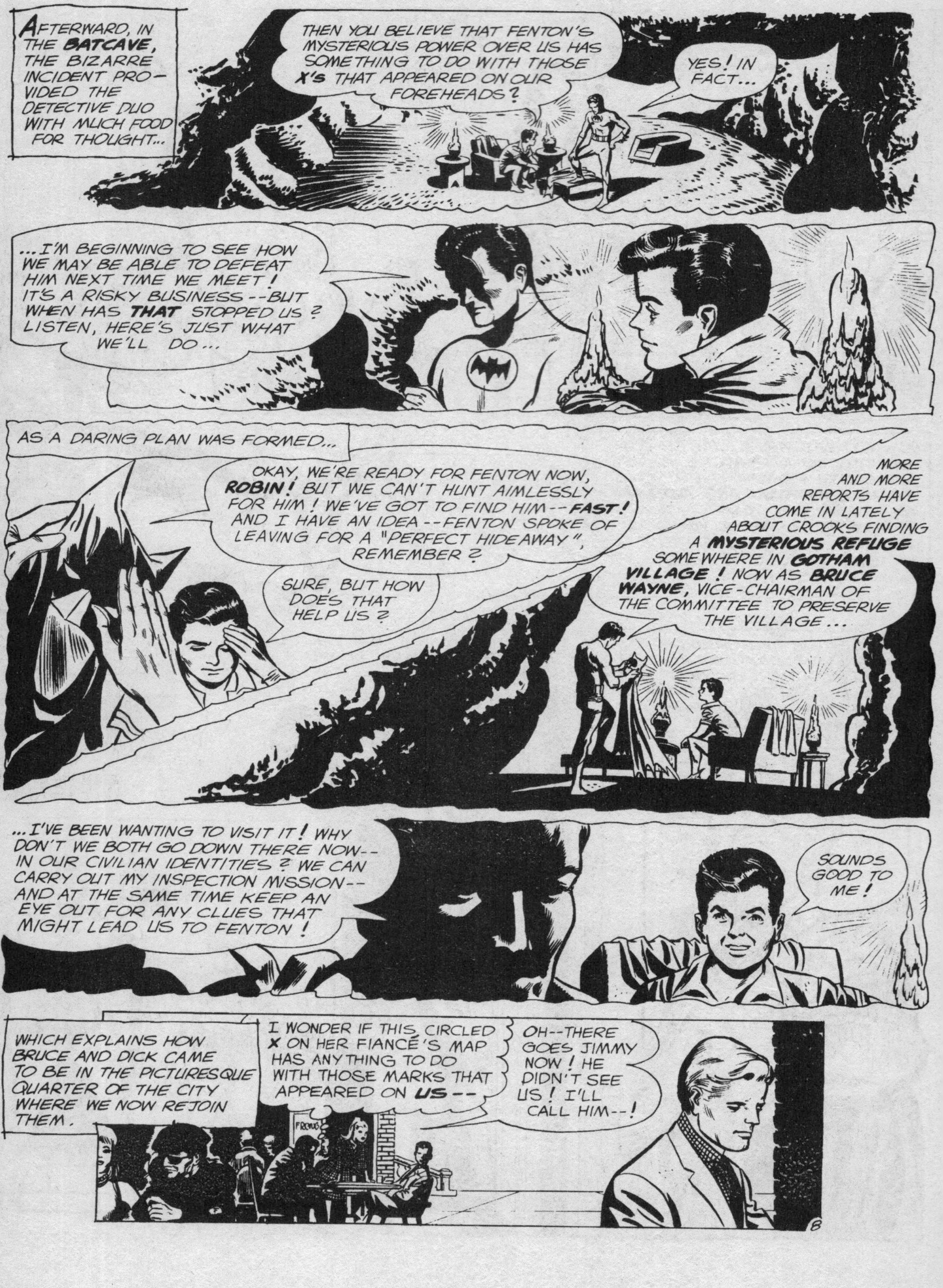
AFTERWARD, IN THE BATCAVE, THE BIZARRE INCIDENT PROVIDED THE DETECTIVE DUO WITH MUCH FOOD FOR THOUGHT...
THEN YOU BELIEVE THAT FENTON'S MYSTERIOUS POWER OVER US HAS SOMETHING TO DO WITH THOSE X'S THAT APPEARED ON OUR FOREHEADS?
YES! IN FACT...
...I'M BEGINNING TO SEE HOW WE MAY BE ABLE TO DEFEAT HIM NEXT TIME WE MEET! IT'S A RISKY BUSINESS--BUT WHEN HAS THAT STOPPED US? LISTEN, HERE'S JUST WHAT WE'LL DO...
AS A DARING PLAN WAS FORMED...
OKAY, WE'RE READY FOR FENTON NOW, ROBIN! BUT WE CAN'T HUNT AIMLESSLY FOR HIM! WE'VE GOT TO FIND HIM--FAST! AND I HAVE AN IDEA--FENTON SPOKE OF LEAVING FOR A "PERFECT HIDEAWAY", REMEMBER?
SURE, BUT HOW DOES THAT HELP US?
MORE AND MORE REPORTS HAVE COME IN LATELY ABOUT CROOKS FINDING A MYSTERIOUS REFUGE SOMEWHERE IN GOTHAM VILLAGE! NOW AS BRUCE WAYNE, VICE-CHAIRMAN OF THE COMMITTEE TO PRESERVE THE VILLAGE...
...I'VE BEEN WANTING TO VISIT IT! WHY DON'T WE BOTH GO DOWN THERE NOW--IN OUR CIVILIAN IDENTITIES? WE CAN CARRY OUT MY INSPECTION MISSION--AND AT THE SAME TIME KEEP AN EYE OUT FOR ANY CLUES THAT MIGHT LEAD US TO FENTON!
SOUNDS GOOD TO ME!
WHICH EXPLAINS HOW BRUCE AND DICK CAME TO BE IN THE PICTURESQUE QUARTER OF THE CITY WHERE WE NOW REJOIN THEM.
I WONDER IF THIS CIRCLED X ON HER FIANCÉ'S MAP HAS ANYTHING TO DO WITH THOSE MARKS THAT APPEARED ON US--
OH--THERE GOES JIMMY NOW! HE DIDN'T SEE US! I'LL CALL HIM--!
8

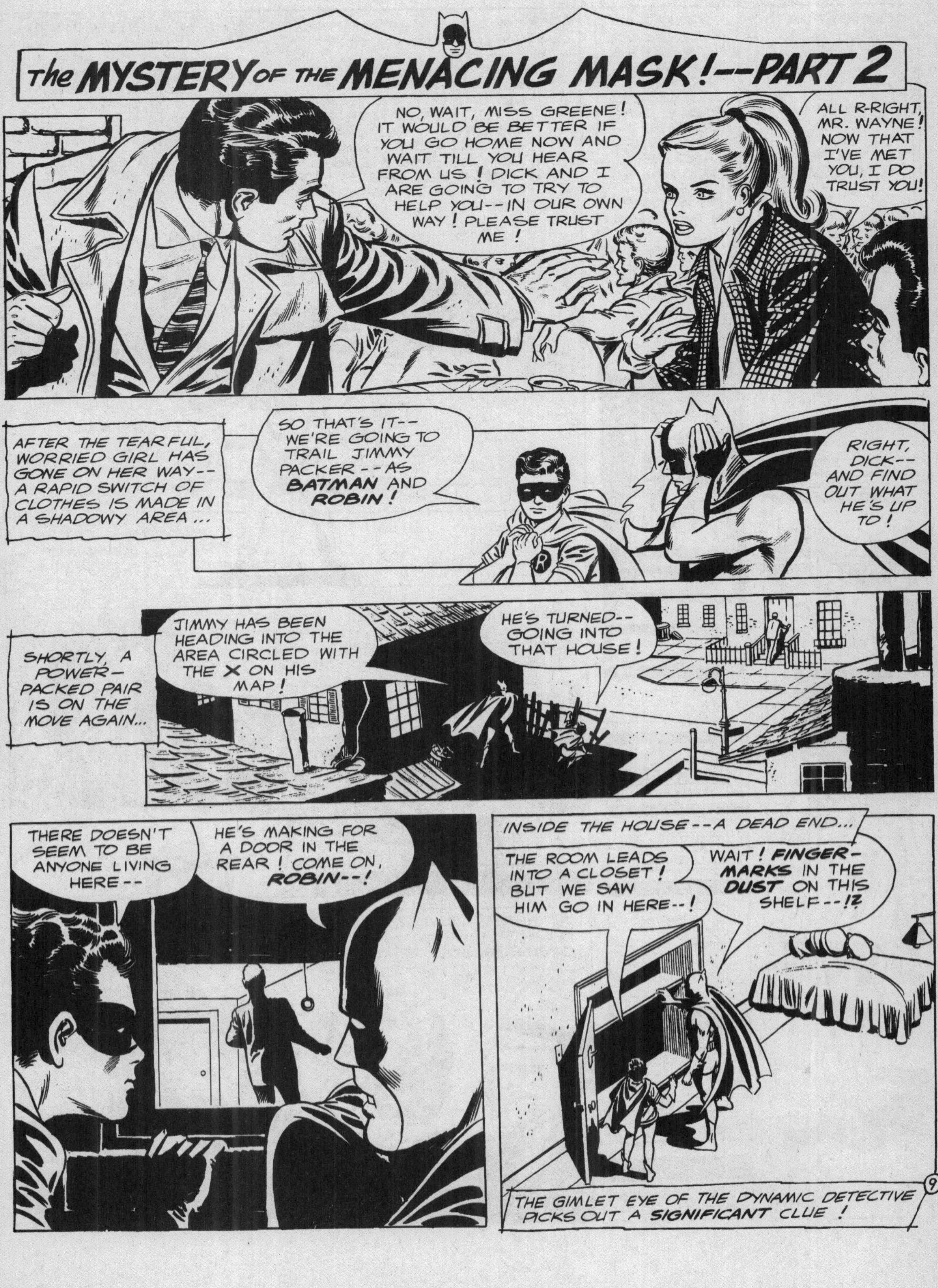
the MYSTERY OF THE MENACING MASK!--PART 2
NO, WAIT, MISS GREENE! IT WOULD BE BETTER IF YOU GO HOME NOW AND WAIT TILL YOU HEAR FROM US! DICK AND I ARE GOING TO TRY TO HELP YOU--IN OUR OWN WAY! PLEASE TRUST ME!
ALL R-RIGHT, MR. WAYNE! NOW THAT I'VE MET YOU, I DO TRUST YOU!
AFTER THE TEARFUL, WORRIED GIRL HAS GONE ON HER WAY--A RAPID SWITCH OF CLOTHES IS MADE IN A SHADOWY AREA...
SO THAT'S IT--WE'RE GOING TO TRAIL JIMMY PACKER--AS BATMAN AND ROBIN!
RIGHT, DICK--AND FIND OUT WHAT HE'S UP TO!
SHORTLY, A POWER-PACKED PAIR IS ON THE MOVE AGAIN...
JIMMY HAS BEEN HEADING INTO THE AREA CIRCLED WITH THE X ON HIS MAP!
HE'S TURNED--GOING INTO THAT HOUSE!
THERE DOESN'T SEEM TO BE ANYONE LIVING HERE--
HE'S MAKING FOR A DOOR IN THE REAR! COME ON, ROBIN--!
INSIDE THE HOUSE--A DEAD END...
THE ROOM LEADS INTO A CLOSET! BUT WE SAW HIM GO IN HERE--!
WAIT! FINGER-MARKS IN THE DUST ON THIS SHELF--!?
THE GIMLET EYE OF THE DYNAMIC DETECTIVE PICKS OUT A SIGNIFICANT CLUE!
9

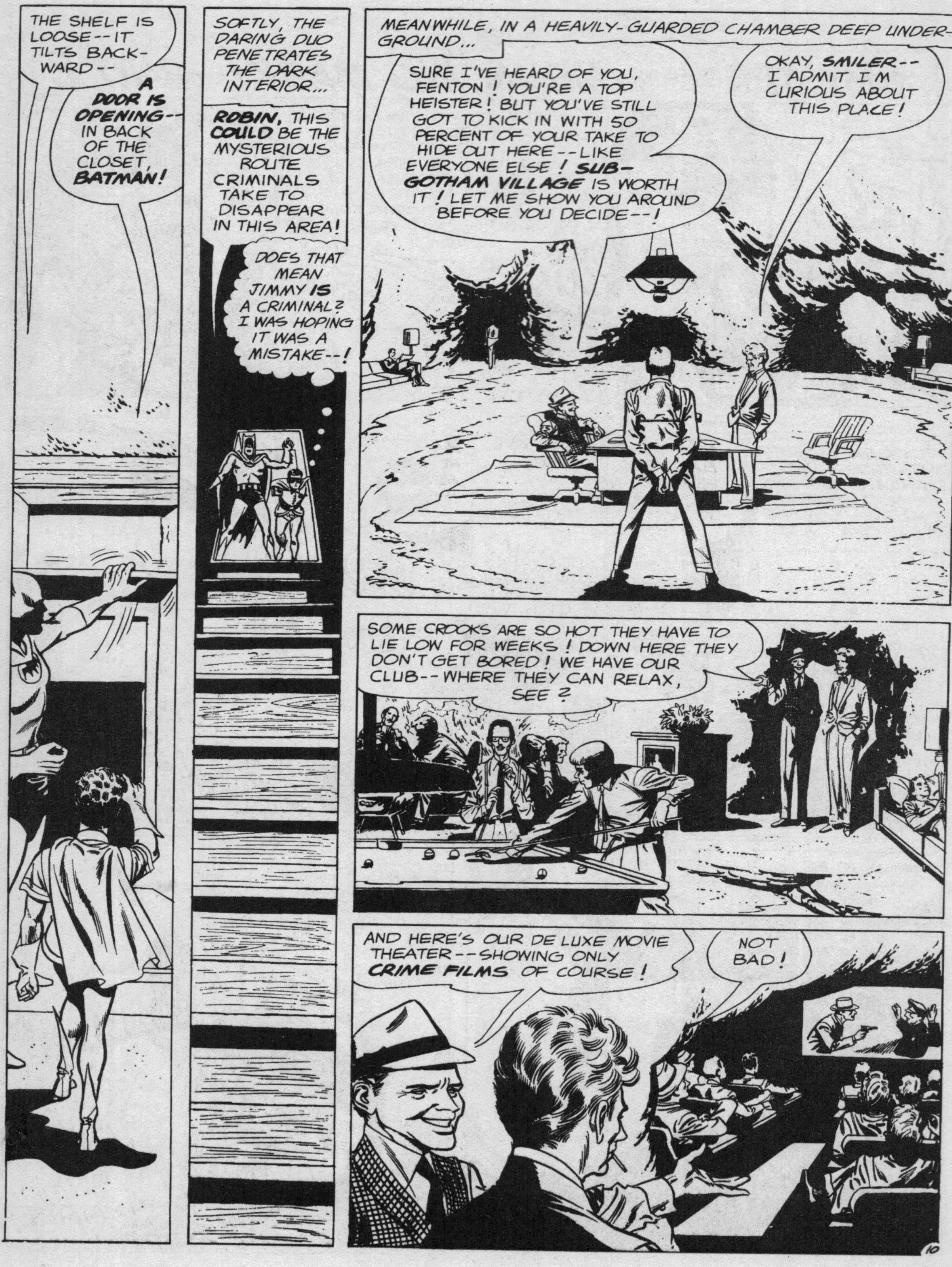
THE SHELF IS LOOSE--IT TILTS BACKWARD--
A DOOR IS OPENING--IN BACK OF THE CLOSET, BATMAN!
SOFTLY, THE DARING DUO PENETRATES THE DARK INTERIOR...
ROBIN, THIS COULD BE THE MYSTERIOUS ROUTE CRIMINALS TAKE TO DISAPPEAR IN THIS AREA!
DOES THAT MEAN JIMMY IS A CRIMINAL? I WAS HOPING IT WAS A MISTAKE--!
MEANWHILE, IN A HEAVILY-GUARDED CHAMBER DEEP UNDERGROUND...
SURE I'VE HEARD OF YOU, FENTON! YOU'RE A TOP HEISTER! BUT YOU'VE STILL GOT TO KICK IN WITH 50 PERCENT OF YOUR TAKE TO HIDE OUT HERE--LIKE EVERYONE ELSE! SUB-GOTHAM VILLAGE IS WORTH IT! LET ME SHOW YOU AROUND BEFORE YOU DECIDE--!
OKAY, SMILER--I ADMIT I'M CURIOUS ABOUT THIS PLACE!
SOME CROOKS ARE SO HOT THEY HAVE TO LIE LOW FOR WEEKS! DOWN HERE THEY DON'T GET BORED! WE HAVE OUR CLUB--WHERE THEY CAN RELAX, SEE?
AND HERE'S OUR DE LUXE MOVIE THEATER--SHOWING ONLY CRIME FILMS OF COURSE!
NOT BAD!
10

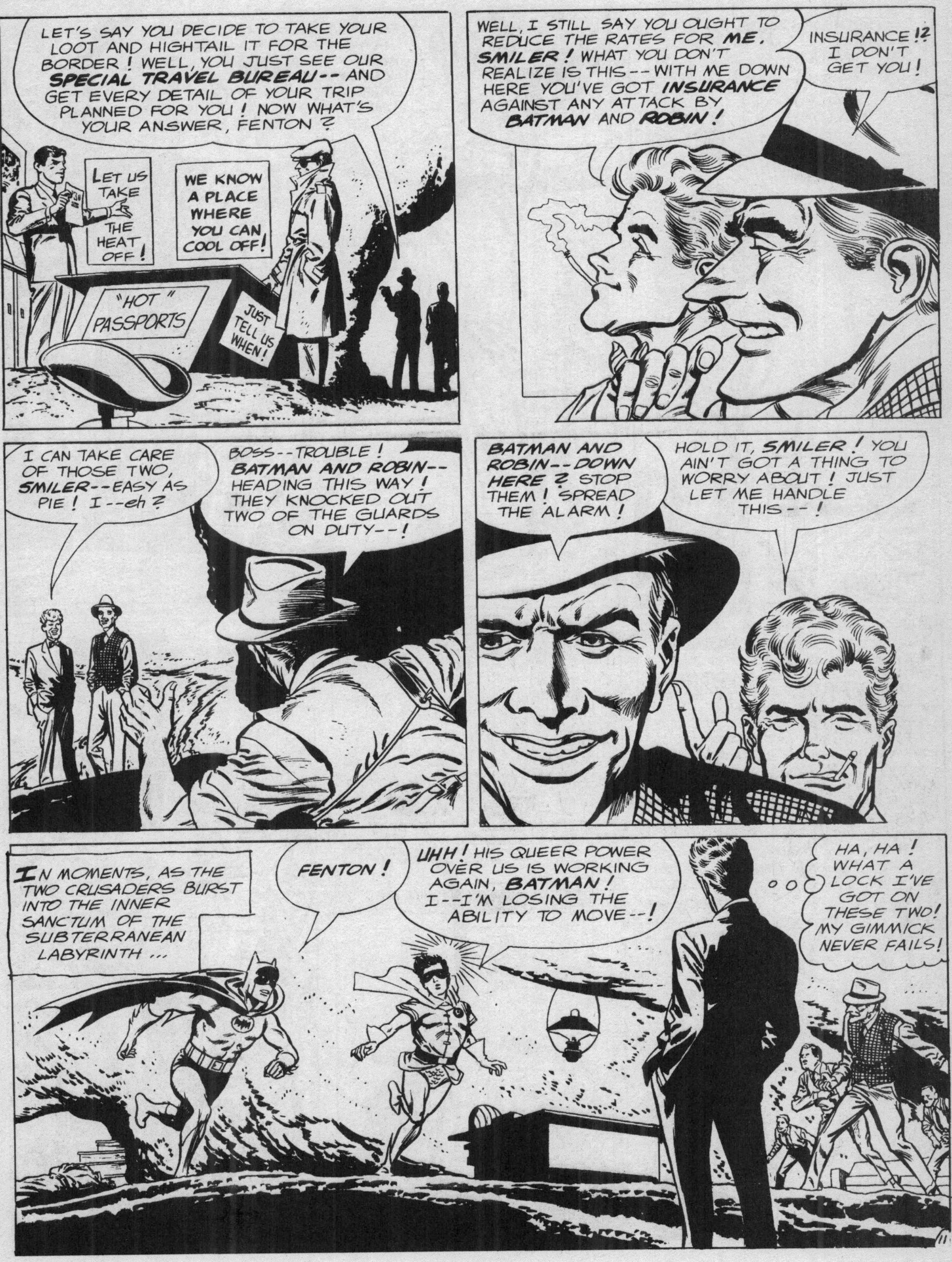
LET'S SAY YOU DECIDE TO TAKE YOUR LOOT AND HIGHTAIL IT FOR THE BORDER! WELL, YOU JUST SEE OUR SPECIAL TRAVEL BUREAU-- AND GET EVERY DETAIL OF YOUR TRIP PLANNED FOR YOU! NOW WHAT'S YOUR ANSWER, FENTON?
LET US TAKE THE HEAT OFF!
WE KNOW A PLACE WHERE YOU CAN COOL OFF!
"HOT" PASSPORTS
JUST TELL US WHEN!
WELL, I STILL SAY YOU OUGHT TO REDUCE THE RATES FOR ME, SMILER! WHAT YOU DON'T REALIZE IS THIS-- WITH ME DOWN HERE YOU'VE GOT INSURANCE AGAINST ANY ATTACK BY BATMAN AND ROBIN!
INSURANCE!? I DON'T GET YOU!
I CAN TAKE CARE OF THOSE TWO, SMILER--EASY AS PIE! I--eh?
BOSS--TROUBLE! BATMAN AND ROBIN-- HEADING THIS WAY! THEY KNOCKED OUT TWO OF THE GUARDS ON DUTY--!
BATMAN AND ROBIN--DOWN HERE? STOP THEM! SPREAD THE ALARM!
HOLD IT, SMILER! YOU AIN'T GOT A THING TO WORRY ABOUT! JUST LET ME HANDLE THIS--!
IN MOMENTS, AS THE TWO CRUSADERS BURST INTO THE INNER SANCTUM OF THE SUBTERRANEAN LABYRINTH ...
FENTON!
UHH! HIS QUEER POWER OVER US IS WORKING AGAIN, BATMAN! I--I'M LOSING THE ABILITY TO MOVE--!
HA, HA! WHAT A LOCK I'VE GOT ON THESE TWO! MY GIMMICK NEVER FAILS!
11

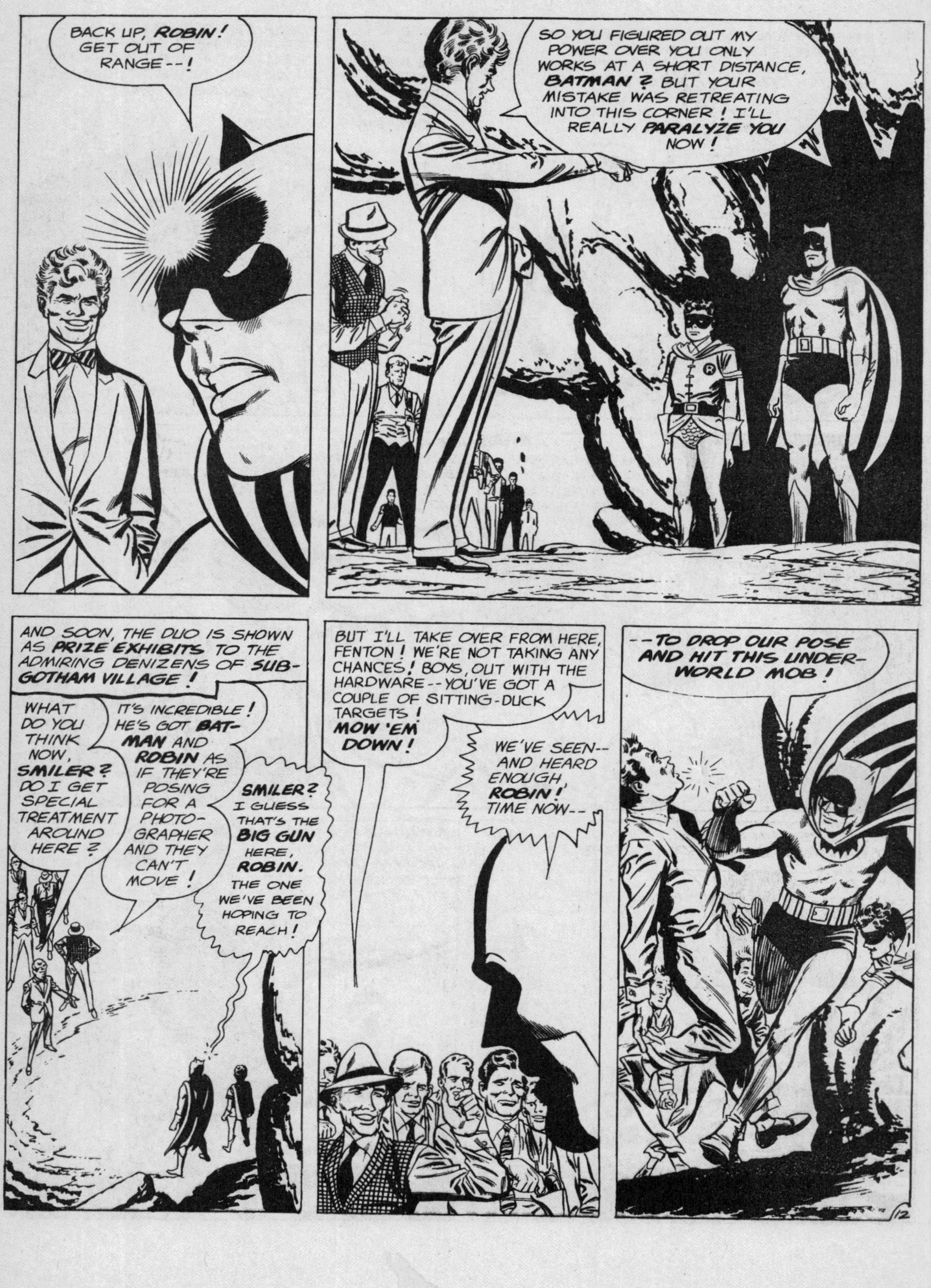
BACK UP, ROBIN! GET OUT OF RANGE--!
SO YOU FIGURED OUT MY POWER OVER YOU ONLY WORKS AT A SHORT DISTANCE, BATMAN? BUT YOUR MISTAKE WAS RETREATING INTO THIS CORNER! I'LL REALLY PARALYZE YOU NOW!
AND SOON, THE DUO IS SHOWN AS PRIZE EXHIBITS TO THE ADMIRING DENIZENS OF SUB-GOTHAM VILLAGE!
WHAT DO YOU THINK NOW, SMILER? DO I GET SPECIAL TREATMENT AROUND HERE?
IT'S INCREDIBLE! HE'S GOT BATMAN AND ROBIN AS IF THEY'RE POSING FOR A PHOTOGRAPHER AND THEY CAN'T MOVE!
SMILER? I GUESS THAT'S THE BIG GUN HERE, ROBIN. THE ONE WE'VE BEEN HOPING TO REACH!
BUT I'LL TAKE OVER FROM HERE, FENTON! WE'RE NOT TAKING ANY CHANCES! BOYS, OUT WITH THE HARDWARE--YOU'VE GOT A COUPLE OF SITTING-DUCK TARGETS! MOW 'EM DOWN!
WE'VE SEEN--AND HEARD ENOUGH, ROBIN! TIME NOW--
--TO DROP OUR POSE AND HIT THIS UNDERWORLD MOB!
12

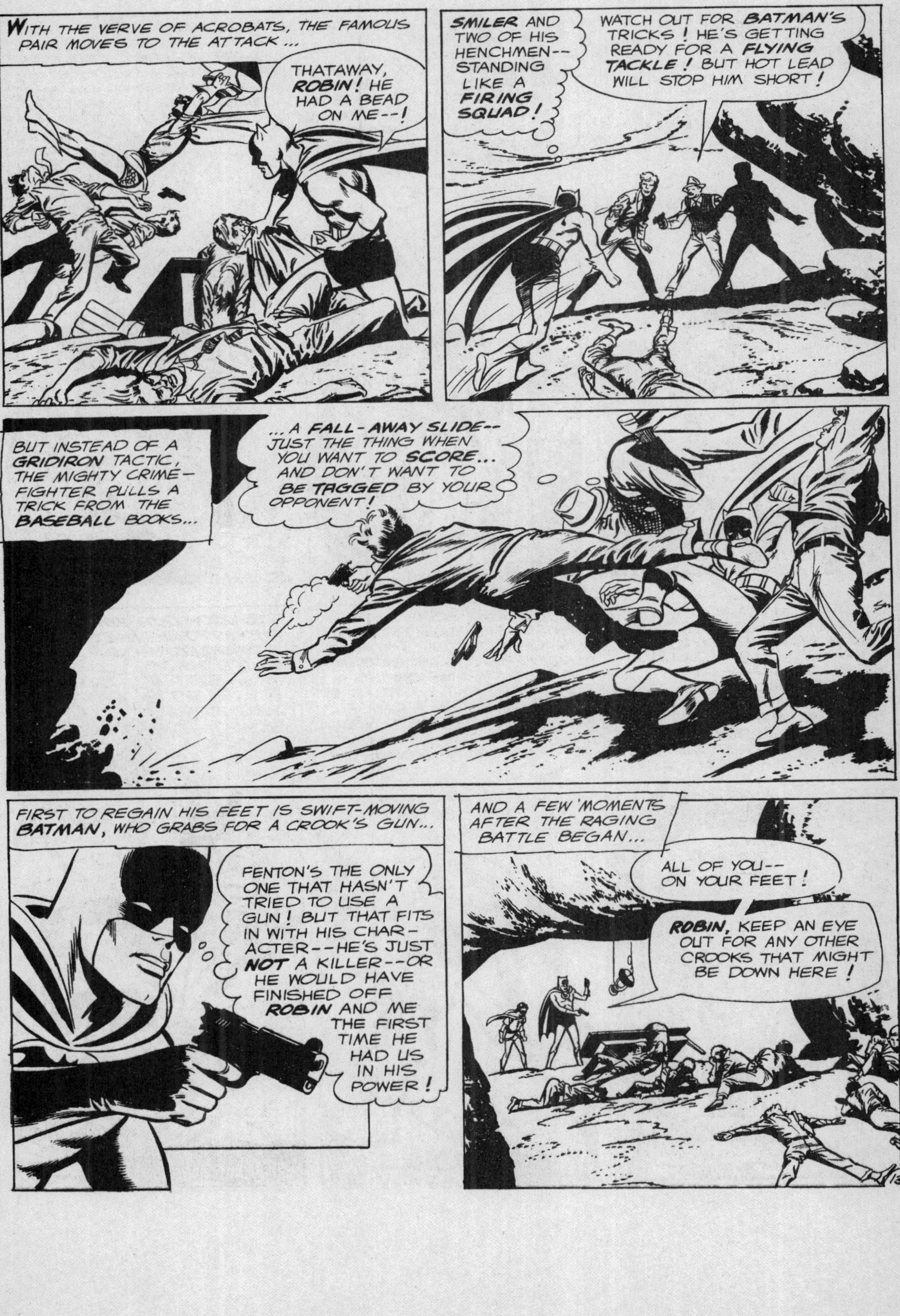
WITH THE VERVE OF ACROBATS, THE FAMOUS PAIR MOVES TO THE ATTACK ...
THATAWAY, ROBIN! HE HAD A BEAD ON ME--!
SMILER AND TWO OF HIS HENCHMEN--STANDING LIKE A FIRING SQUAD!
WATCH OUT FOR BATMAN'S TRICKS! HE'S GETTING READY FOR A FLYING TACKLE! BUT HOT LEAD WILL STOP HIM SHORT!
BUT INSTEAD OF A GRIDIRON TACTIC, THE MIGHTY CRIME-FIGHTER PULLS A TRICK FROM THE BASEBALL BOOKS...
... A FALL-AWAY SLIDE-- JUST THE THING WHEN YOU WANT TO SCORE... AND DON'T WANT TO BE TAGGED BY YOUR OPPONENT!
FIRST TO REGAIN HIS FEET IS SWIFT-MOVING BATMAN, WHO GRABS FOR A CROOK'S GUN...
FENTON'S THE ONLY ONE THAT HASN'T TRIED TO USE A GUN! BUT THAT FITS IN WITH HIS CHARACTER--HE'S JUST NOT A KILLER--OR HE WOULD HAVE FINISHED OFF ROBIN AND ME THE FIRST TIME HE HAD US IN HIS POWER!
AND A FEW MOMENTS AFTER THE RAGING BATTLE BEGAN...
ALL OF YOU-- ON YOUR FEET!
ROBIN, KEEP AN EYE OUT FOR ANY OTHER CROOKS THAT MIGHT BE DOWN HERE!
13

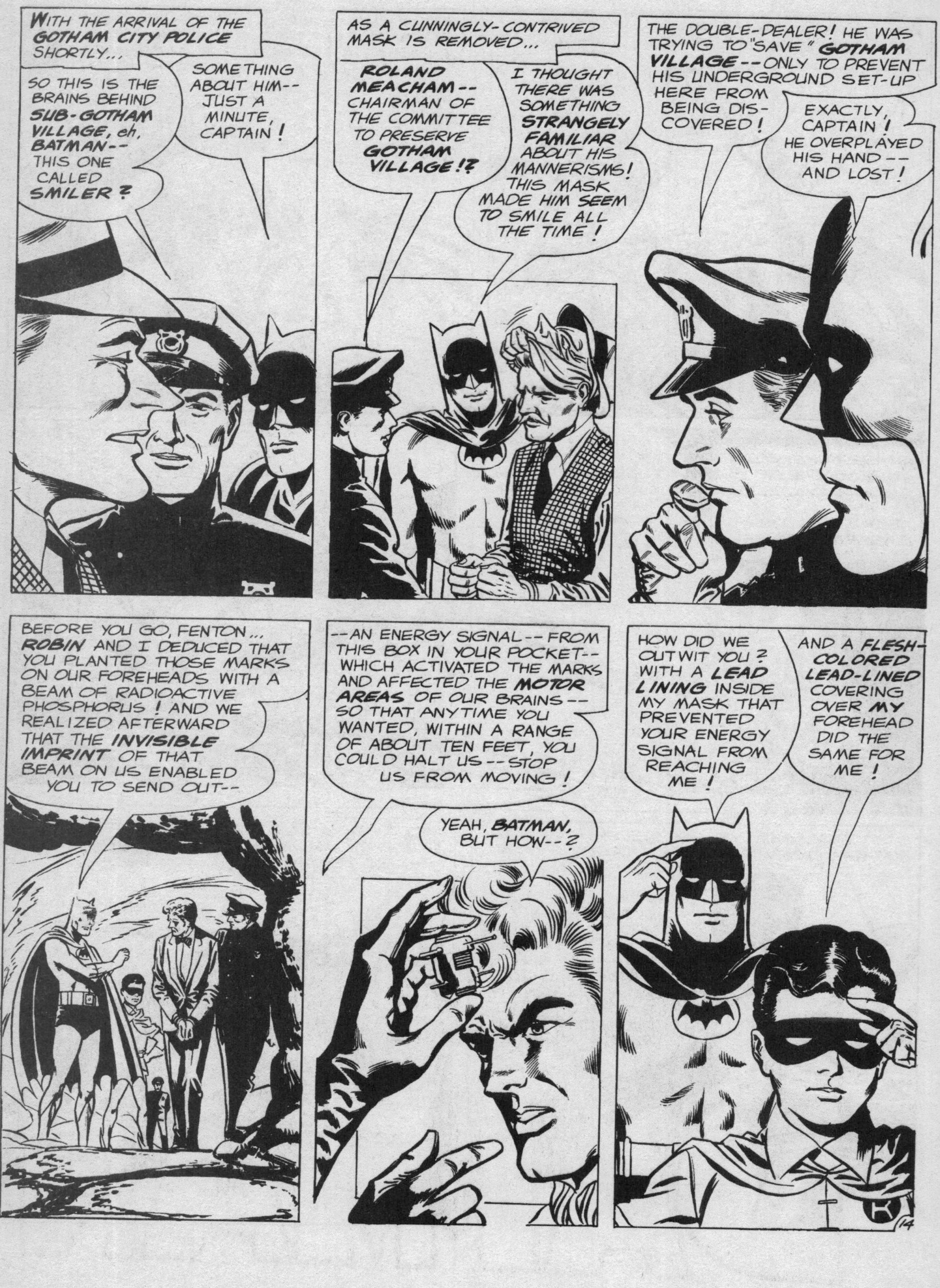
WITH THE ARRIVAL OF THE GOTHAM CITY POLICE SHORTLY...
SO THIS IS THE BRAINS BEHIND SUB-GOTHAM VILLAGE, eh, BATMAN-- THIS ONE CALLED SMILER?
SOMETHING ABOUT HIM-- JUST A MINUTE, CAPTAIN!
AS A CUNNINGLY-CONTRIVED MASK IS REMOVED...
ROLAND MEACHAM-- CHAIRMAN OF THE COMMITTEE TO PRESERVE GOTHAM VILLAGE!?
I THOUGHT THERE WAS SOMETHING STRANGELY FAMILIAR ABOUT HIS MANNERISMS! THIS MASK MADE HIM SEEM TO SMILE ALL THE TIME!
THE DOUBLE-DEALER! HE WAS TRYING TO "SAVE" GOTHAM VILLAGE--ONLY TO PREVENT HIS UNDERGROUND SET-UP HERE FROM BEING DISCOVERED!
EXACTLY, CAPTAIN! HE OVERPLAYED HIS HAND--AND LOST!
BEFORE YOU GO, FENTON... ROBIN AND I DEDUCED THAT YOU PLANTED THOSE MARKS ON OUR FOREHEADS WITH A BEAM OF RADIOACTIVE PHOSPHORUS! AND WE REALIZED AFTERWARD THAT THE INVISIBLE IMPRINT OF THAT BEAM ON US ENABLED YOU TO SEND OUT--
--AN ENERGY SIGNAL--FROM THIS BOX IN YOUR POCKET--WHICH ACTIVATED THE MARKS AND AFFECTED THE MOTOR AREAS OF OUR BRAINS--SO THAT ANYTIME YOU WANTED, WITHIN A RANGE OF ABOUT TEN FEET, YOU COULD HALT US--STOP US FROM MOVING!
YEAH, BATMAN, BUT HOW--?
HOW DID WE OUTWIT YOU? WITH A LEAD LINING INSIDE MY MASK THAT PREVENTED YOUR ENERGY SIGNAL FROM REACHING ME!
AND A FLESH-COLORED LEAD-LINED COVERING OVER MY FOREHEAD DID THE SAME FOR ME!
14

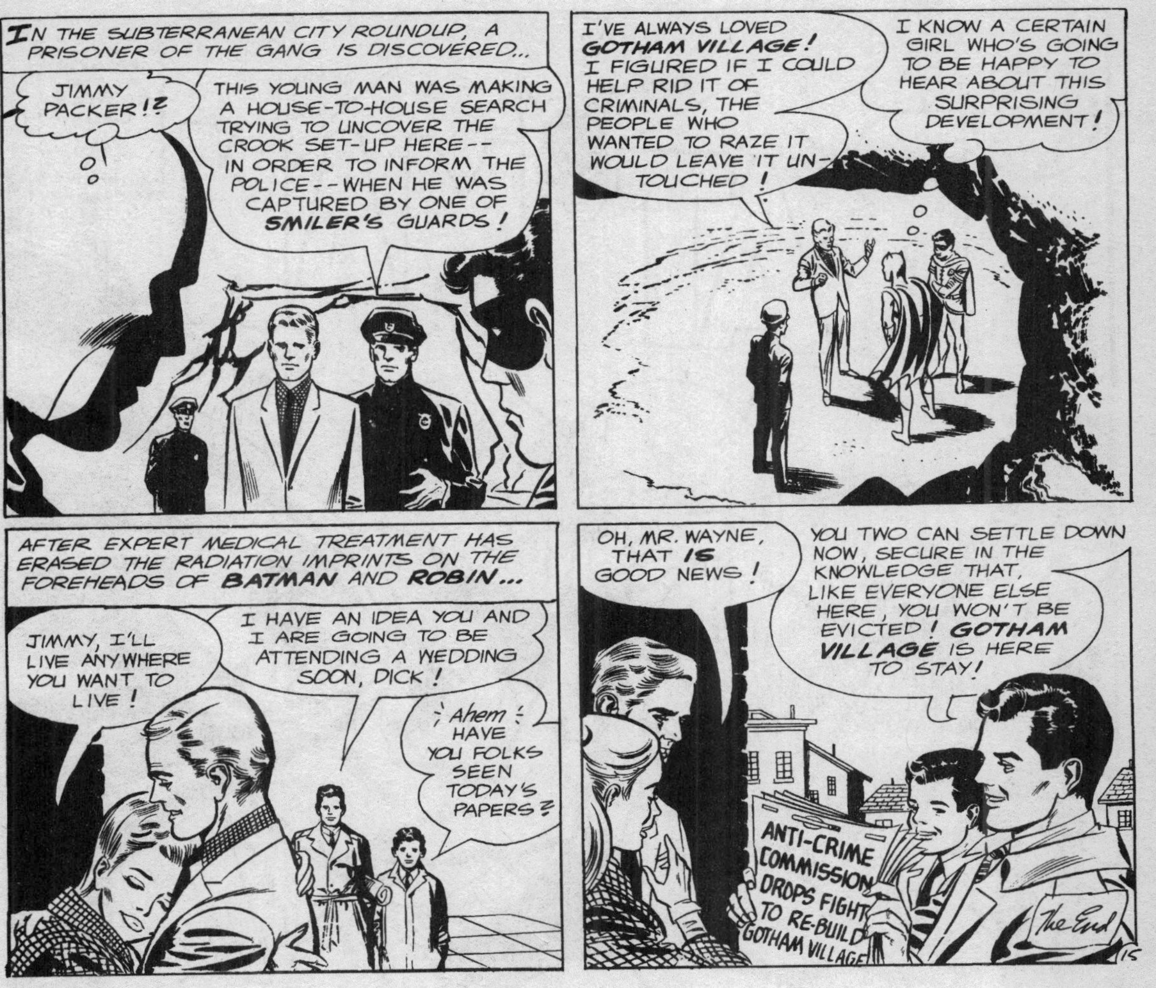
IN THE SUBTERRANEAN CITY ROUNDUP, A PRISONER OF THE GANG IS DISCOVERED...
JIMMY PACKER!?
THIS YOUNG MAN WAS MAKING A HOUSE-TO-HOUSE SEARCH TRYING TO UNCOVER THE CROOK SET-UP HERE-- IN ORDER TO INFORM THE POLICE--WHEN HE WAS CAPTURED BY ONE OF SMILER'S GUARDS!
I'VE ALWAYS LOVED GOTHAM VILLAGE! I FIGURED IF I COULD HELP RID IT OF CRIMINALS, THE PEOPLE WHO WANTED TO RAZE IT WOULD LEAVE IT UN-TOUCHED!
I KNOW A CERTAIN GIRL WHO'S GOING TO BE HAPPY TO HEAR ABOUT THIS SURPRISING DEVELOPMENT!
AFTER EXPERT MEDICAL TREATMENT HAS ERASED THE RADIATION IMPRINTS ON THE FOREHEADS OF BATMAN AND ROBIN...
JIMMY, I'LL LIVE ANYWHERE YOU WANT TO LIVE!
I HAVE AN IDEA YOU AND I ARE GOING TO BE ATTENDING A WEDDING SOON, DICK!
Ahem HAVE YOU FOLKS SEEN TODAY'S PAPERS?
OH, MR. WAYNE, THAT IS GOOD NEWS!
YOU TWO CAN SETTLE DOWN NOW, SECURE IN THE KNOWLEDGE THAT, LIKE EVERYONE ELSE HERE, YOU WON'T BE EVICTED! GOTHAM VILLAGE IS HERE TO STAY!
ANTI-CRIME COMMISSION DROPS FIGHT TO RE-BUILD GOTHAM VILLAGE
The End
15

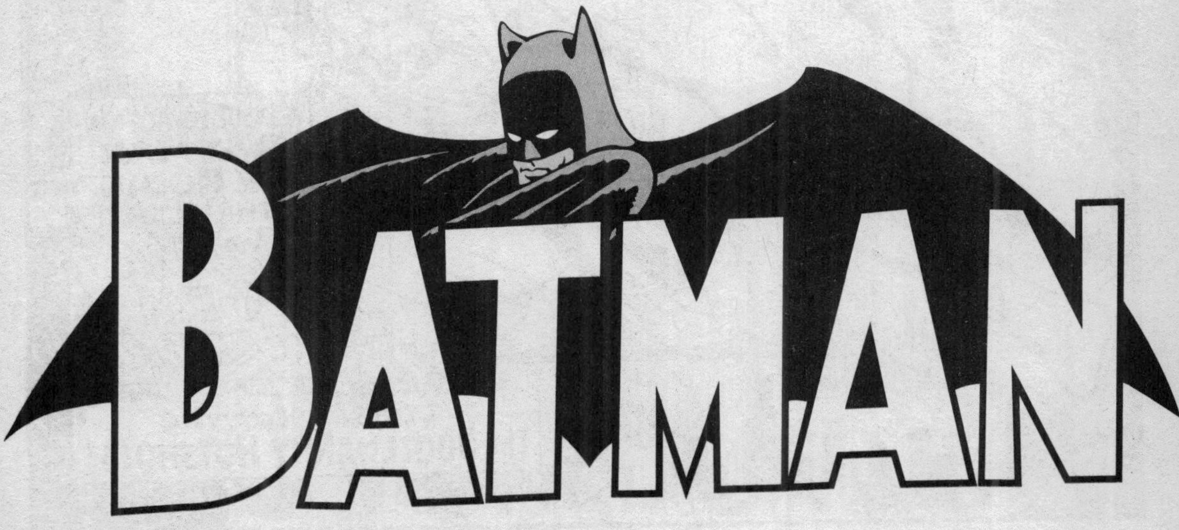
BATMAN

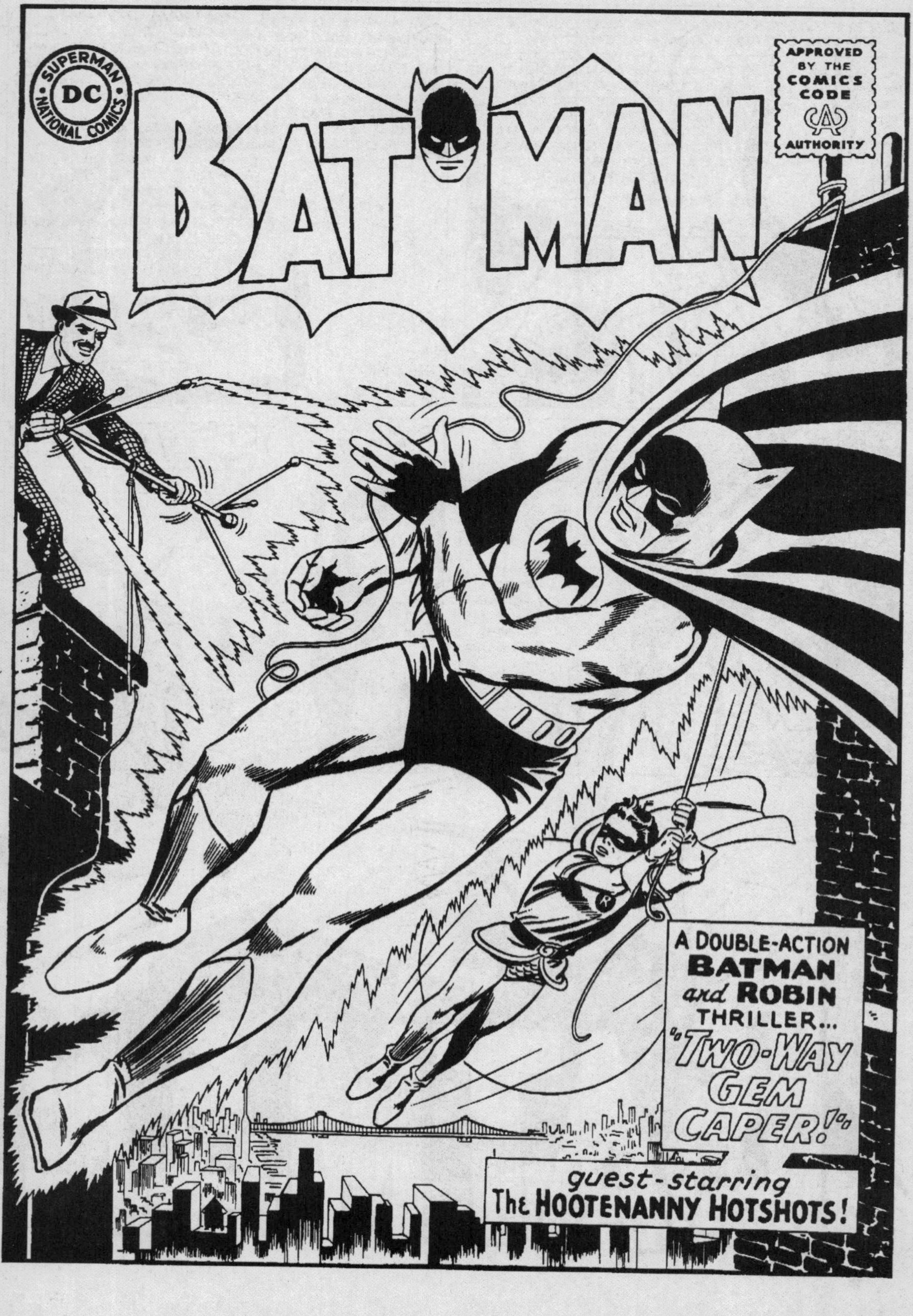
SUPERMAN DC NATIONAL COMICS
APPROVED BY THE COMICS CODE AUTHORITY
BATMAN
A DOUBLE-ACTION BATMAN and ROBIN THRILLER... "TWO-WAY GEM CAPER!"
guest-starring The HOOTENANNY HOTSHOTS!

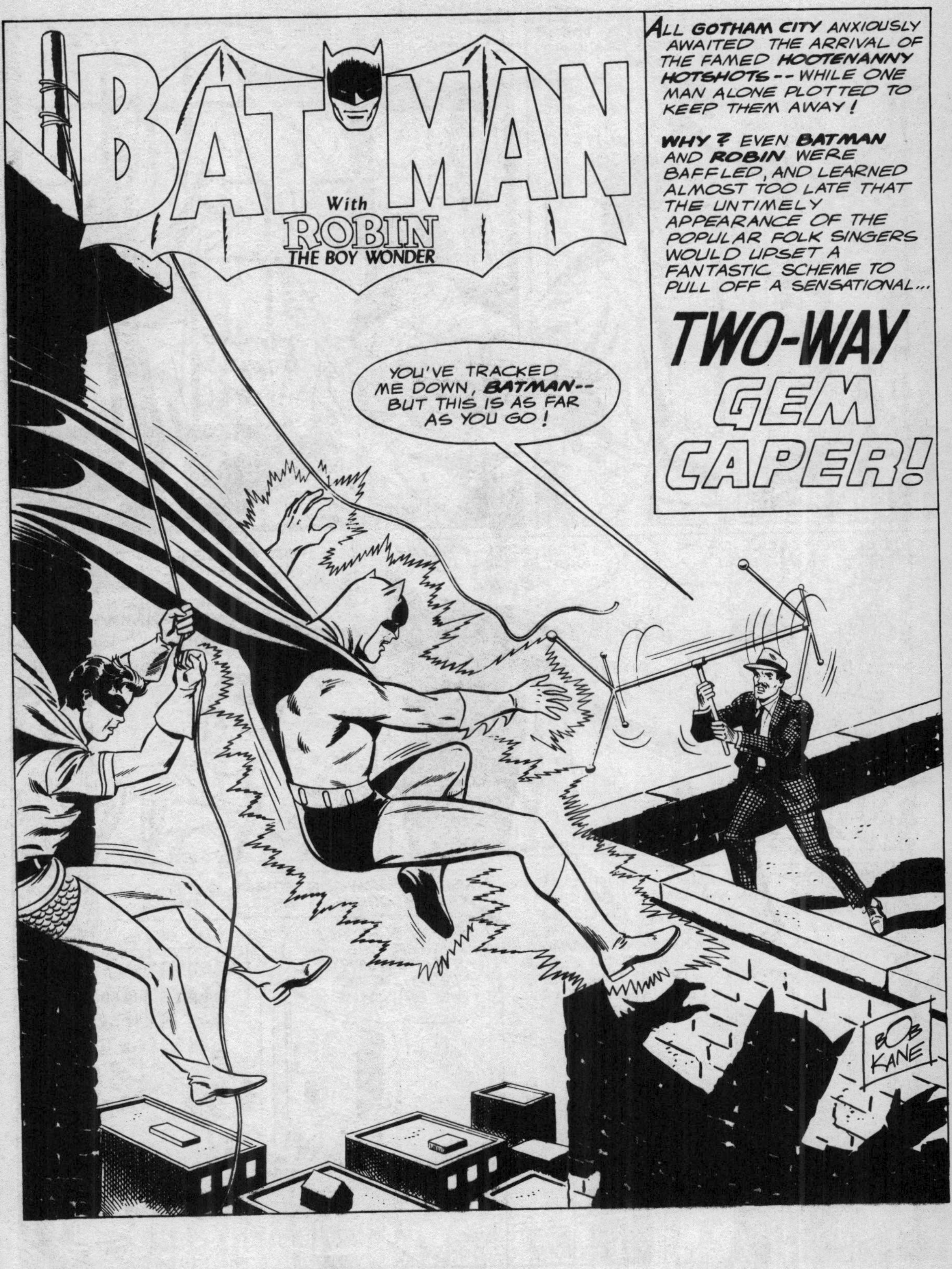
BATMAN
With ROBIN THE BOY WONDER
ALL GOTHAM CITY ANXIOUSLY AWAITED THE ARRIVAL OF THE FAMED HOOTENANNY HOTSHOTS -- WHILE ONE MAN ALONE PLOTTED TO KEEP THEM AWAY!
WHY? EVEN BATMAN AND ROBIN WERE BAFFLED, AND LEARNED ALMOST TOO LATE THAT THE UNTIMELY APPEARANCE OF THE POPULAR FOLK SINGERS WOULD UPSET A FANTASTIC SCHEME TO PULL OFF A SENSATIONAL...
TWO-WAY GEM CAPER!
YOU'VE TRACKED ME DOWN, BATMAN-- BUT THIS IS AS FAR AS YOU GO!
BOB KANE

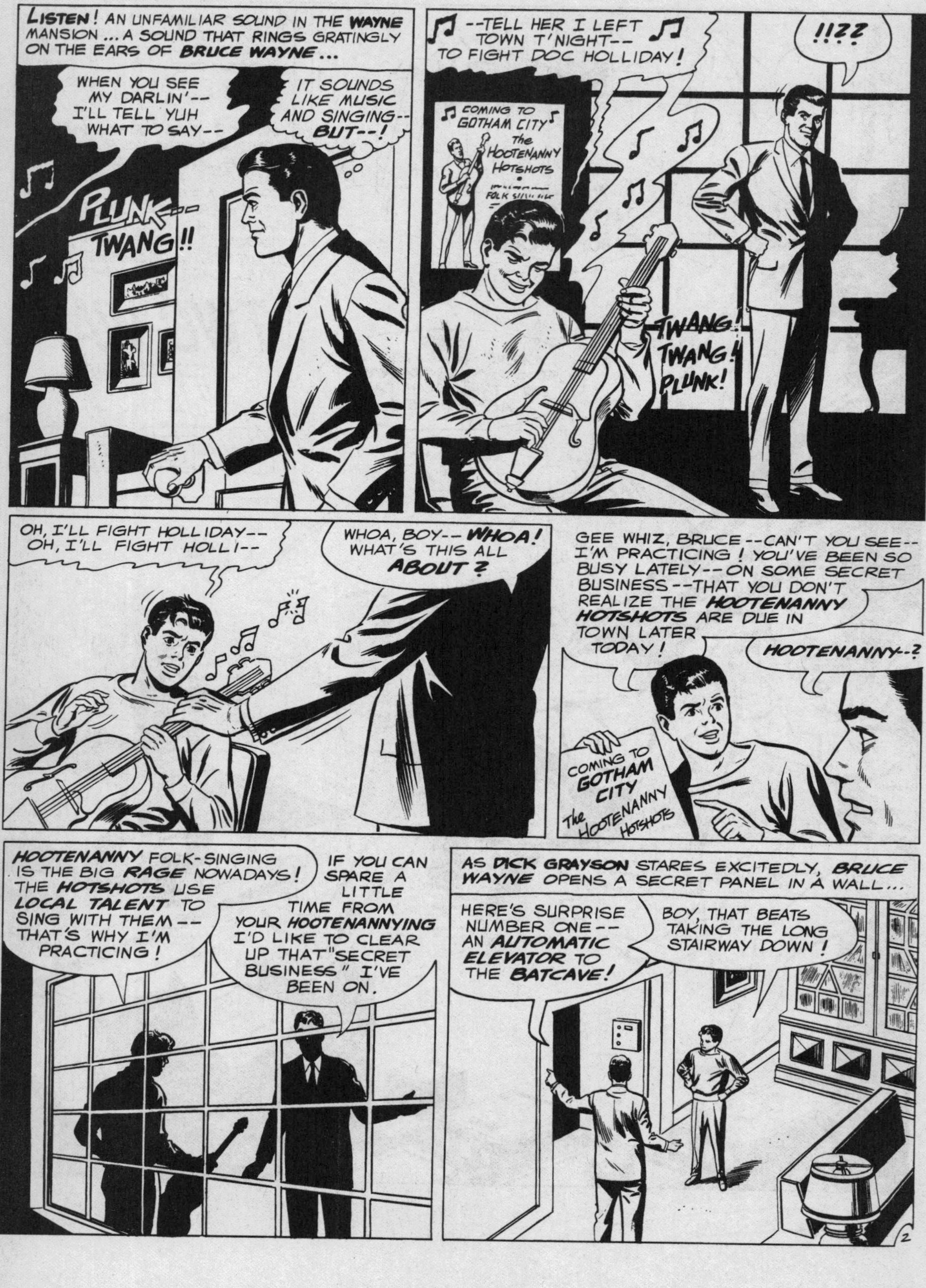
LISTEN! AN UNFAMILIAR SOUND IN THE WAYNE MANSION ... A SOUND THAT RINGS GRATINGLY ON THE EARS OF BRUCE WAYNE...
WHEN YOU SEE MY DARLIN'-- I'LL TELL YUH WHAT TO SAY--
IT SOUNDS LIKE MUSIC AND SINGING-- BUT--!
PLUNK-- TWANG!!
--TELL HER I LEFT TOWN T'NIGHT-- TO FIGHT DOC HOLLIDAY!
!!??
COMING TO GOTHAM CITY the HOOTENANNY HOTSHOTS
TWANG! TWANG! PLUNK!
OH, I'LL FIGHT HOLLIDAY-- OH, I'LL FIGHT HOLLI--
WHOA, BOY-- WHOA! WHAT'S THIS ALL ABOUT?
GEE WHIZ, BRUCE --CAN'T YOU SEE-- I'M PRACTICING! YOU'VE BEEN SO BUSY LATELY-- ON SOME SECRET BUSINESS --THAT YOU DON'T REALIZE THE HOOTENANNY HOTSHOTS ARE DUE IN TOWN LATER TODAY!
HOOTENANNY--?
COMING TO GOTHAM CITY The HOOTENANNY HOTSHOTS
HOOTENANNY FOLK-SINGING IS THE BIG RAGE NOWADAYS! THE HOTSHOTS USE LOCAL TALENT TO SING WITH THEM -- THAT'S WHY I'M PRACTICING!
IF YOU CAN SPARE A LITTLE TIME FROM YOUR HOOTENANNYING I'D LIKE TO CLEAR UP THAT "SECRET BUSINESS" I'VE BEEN ON.
AS DICK GRAYSON STARES EXCITEDLY, BRUCE WAYNE OPENS A SECRET PANEL IN A WALL...
HERE'S SURPRISE NUMBER ONE -- AN AUTOMATIC ELEVATOR TO THE BATCAVE!
BOY, THAT BEATS TAKING THE LONG STAIRWAY DOWN!
2

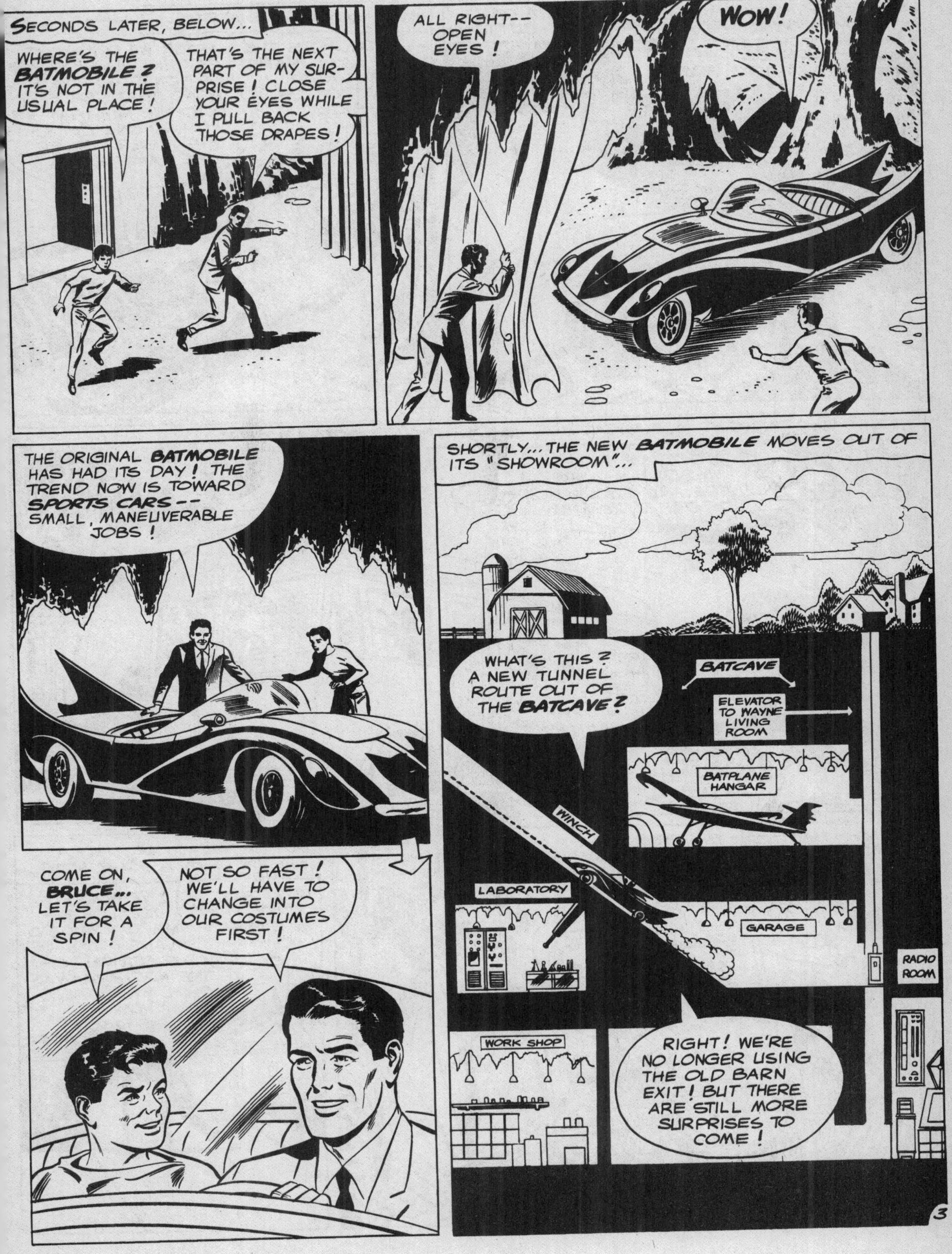
SECONDS LATER, BELOW...
WHERE'S THE BATMOBILE? IT'S NOT IN THE USUAL PLACE!
THAT'S THE NEXT PART OF MY SURPRISE! CLOSE YOUR EYES WHILE I PULL BACK THOSE DRAPES!
ALL RIGHT-- OPEN EYES!
WOW!
THE ORIGINAL BATMOBILE HAS HAD ITS DAY! THE TREND NOW IS TOWARD SPORTS CARS-- SMALL, MANEUVERABLE JOBS!
COME ON, BRUCE... LET'S TAKE IT FOR A SPIN!
NOT SO FAST! WE'LL HAVE TO CHANGE INTO OUR COSTUMES FIRST!
SHORTLY... THE NEW BATMOBILE MOVES OUT OF ITS "SHOWROOM"...
WHAT'S THIS? A NEW TUNNEL ROUTE OUT OF THE BATCAVE?
BATCAVE
ELEVATOR TO WAYNE LIVING ROOM
BATPLANE HANGAR
WINCH
LABORATORY
GARAGE
RADIO ROOM
WORK SHOP
RIGHT! WE'RE NO LONGER USING THE OLD BARN EXIT! BUT THERE ARE STILL MORE SURPRISES TO COME!
3

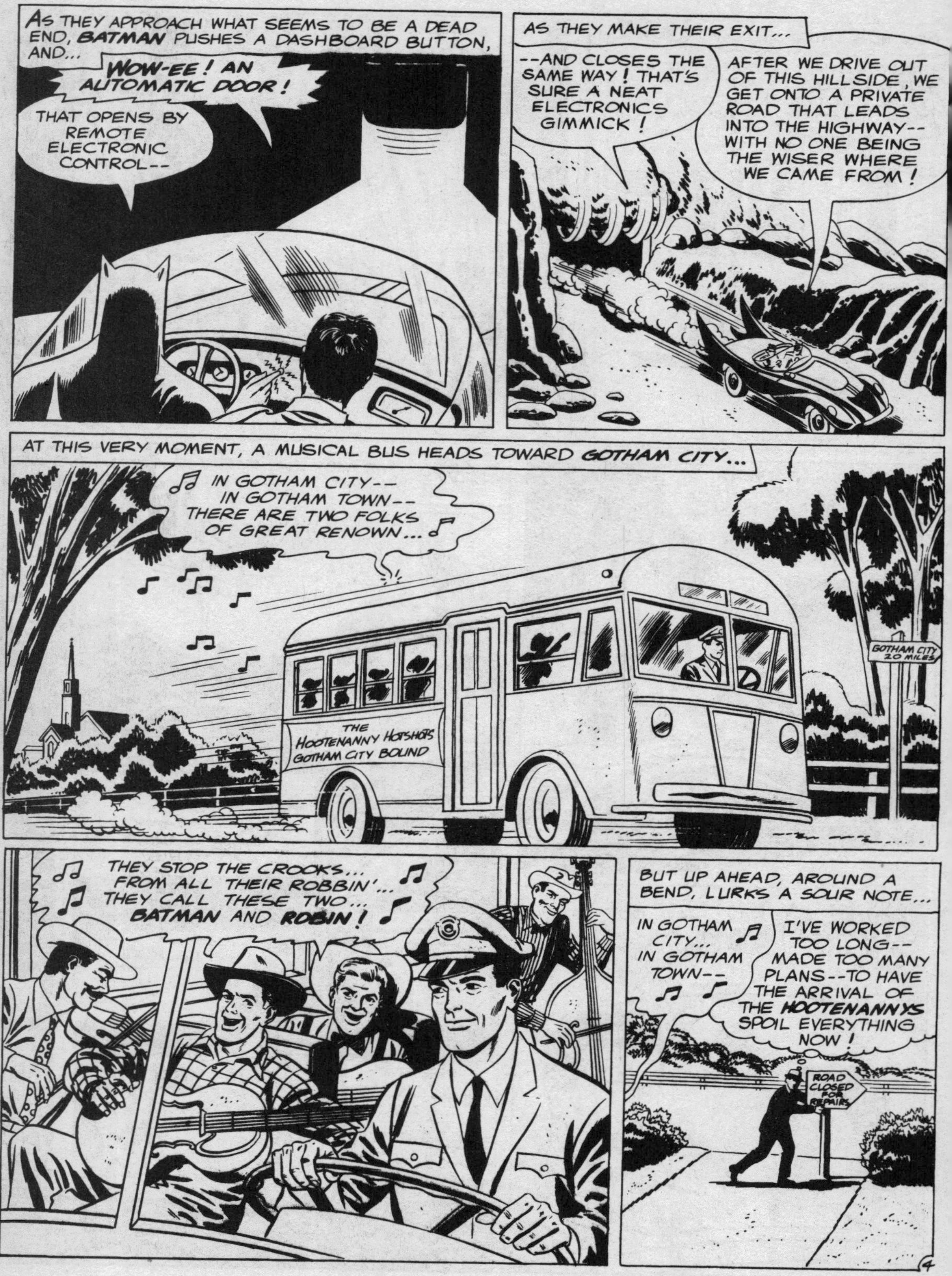
AS THEY APPROACH WHAT SEEMS TO BE A DEAD END, BATMAN PUSHES A DASHBOARD BUTTON, AND...
WOW-EE! AN AUTOMATIC DOOR!
THAT OPENS BY REMOTE ELECTRONIC CONTROL--
AS THEY MAKE THEIR EXIT...
--AND CLOSES THE SAME WAY! THAT'S SURE A NEAT ELECTRONICS GIMMICK!
AFTER WE DRIVE OUT OF THIS HILLSIDE, WE GET ONTO A PRIVATE ROAD THAT LEADS INTO THE HIGHWAY-- WITH NO ONE BEING THE WISER WHERE WE CAME FROM!
AT THIS VERY MOMENT, A MUSICAL BUS HEADS TOWARD GOTHAM CITY...
IN GOTHAM CITY-- IN GOTHAM TOWN-- THERE ARE TWO FOLKS OF GREAT RENOWN...
THE HOOTENANNY HOTSHOTS GOTHAM CITY BOUND
GOTHAM CITY 20 MILES
THEY STOP THE CROOKS... FROM ALL THEIR ROBBIN'... THEY CALL THESE TWO... BATMAN AND ROBIN!
BUT UP AHEAD, AROUND A BEND, LURKS A SOUR NOTE...
IN GOTHAM CITY... IN GOTHAM TOWN--
I'VE WORKED TOO LONG-- MADE TOO MANY PLANS--TO HAVE THE ARRIVAL OF THE HOOTENANNYS SPOIL EVERYTHING NOW!
ROAD CLOSED FOR REPAIRS
4

IN EXPECTING THE UNEXPECTED, MY EVERY MOVE WAS MADE WITH "PLAN A" BACKED UP BY AN ALTERNATE "PLAN B"-- BUT EVEN I DIDN'T FIGURE ON A LAST-MINUTE APPEARANCE OF THE HOOTENANNYS IN GOTHAM SQUARE!

CLOSED FOR REPAIR

THEY'RE SCHEDULED TO BE THERE AT 8:30--THE EXACT TIME MY BIG JOB MUST BE PULLED! THERE'LL BE A CROWD--NO TRAFFIC-- AND MY CAPER WILL BE STOPPED COLD--UNLESS I DO SOMETHING ABOUT IT!

MOMENTS LATER...

HOLD IT! YOU CAN'T GET THROUGH HERE!

I'VE GOT TO! MY PASSENGERS ARE DUE IN GOTHAM CITY AT 8:30! AND A DETOUR WILL MAKE US LATE!

ROAD CLOSED Repair

THAT'S WHY I'M HERE! I'M ON GOTHAM CITY'S HOOTENANNY GREETING COMMITTEE! MY JOB IS TO GUIDE YOU INTO TOWN OVER ANOTHER ROAD--SO YOU WON'T BE LATE FOR THE CELEBRATION! LET'S ROLL!

LATER, WHEN THE BATMOBILE BRAKES TO A HALT...

VERY ODD! A SIGN FACING THE CLIFFSDALE ROAD SAYING THE MAIN HIGH- WAY IS UNDER REPAIR-- BUT WE JUST DROVE OVER IT, AND IT'S IN PERFECT SHAPE! SOMETHING'S WRONG HERE!

ROAD CLOSED FOR REPAIRS

AFTER REMOVING THE PUZZLING SIGN...

I JUST THOUGHT-- THE HOOTENANNY HOTSHOTS ARE TRAVELING THIS WAY FROM CLIFFS- DALE--WHERE THEY JUST PUT ON A SHOW!

LOOKS LIKE THEY'VE ALREADY PASSED HERE, ROBIN! THE FRESH TIRE TRACKS ON THIS DIRT ROAD SEEM TO HAVE BEEN MADE BY A BUS!

5

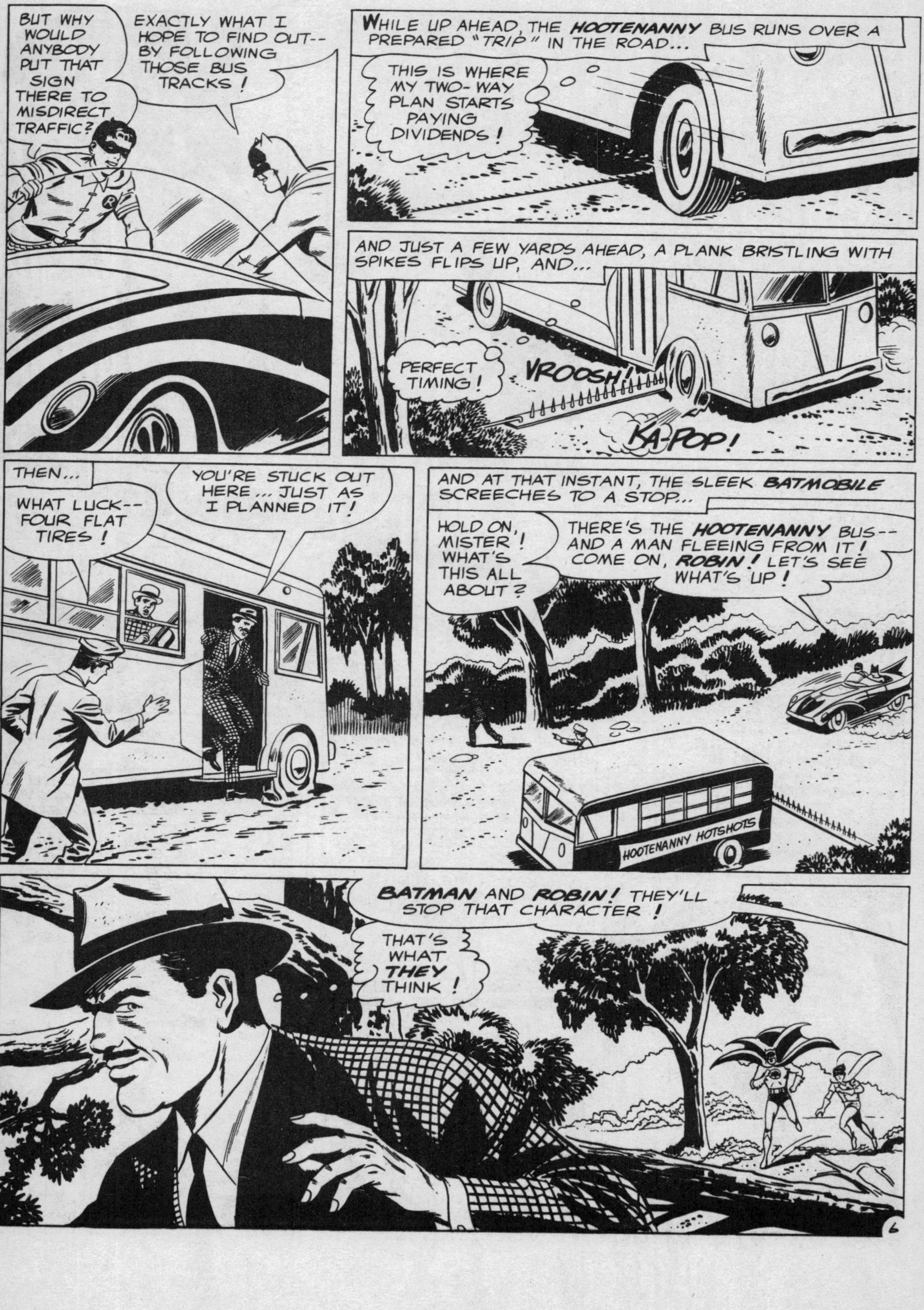
BUT WHY WOULD ANYBODY PUT THAT SIGN THERE TO MISDIRECT TRAFFIC?
EXACTLY WHAT I HOPE TO FIND OUT-- BY FOLLOWING THOSE BUS TRACKS!
WHILE UP AHEAD, THE HOOTENANNY BUS RUNS OVER A PREPARED "TRIP" IN THE ROAD...
THIS IS WHERE MY TWO-WAY PLAN STARTS PAYING DIVIDENDS!
AND JUST A FEW YARDS AHEAD, A PLANK BRISTLING WITH SPIKES FLIPS UP, AND...
PERFECT TIMING!
VROOSH!
KA-POP!
THEN...
WHAT LUCK-- FOUR FLAT TIRES!
YOU'RE STUCK OUT HERE... JUST AS I PLANNED IT!
AND AT THAT INSTANT, THE SLEEK BATMOBILE SCREECHES TO A STOP...
HOLD ON, MISTER! WHAT'S THIS ALL ABOUT?
THERE'S THE HOOTENANNY BUS-- AND A MAN FLEEING FROM IT! COME ON, ROBIN! LET'S SEE WHAT'S UP!
HOOTENANNY HOTSHOTS
BATMAN AND ROBIN! THEY'LL STOP THAT CHARACTER!
THAT'S WHAT THEY THINK!
6

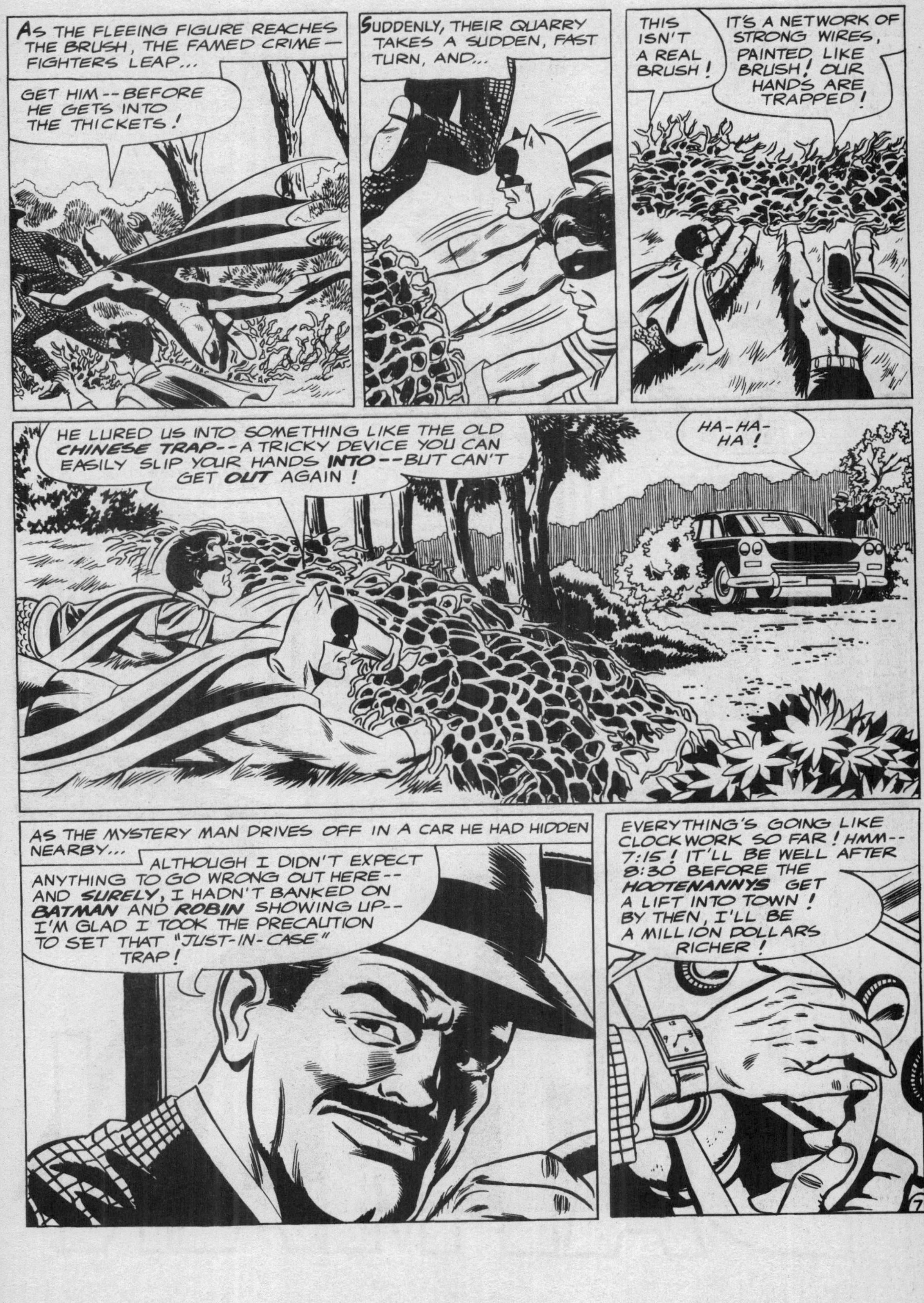
AS THE FLEEING FIGURE REACHES THE BRUSH, THE FAMED CRIME-FIGHTERS LEAP...
GET HIM -- BEFORE HE GETS INTO THE THICKETS!
SUDDENLY, THEIR QUARRY TAKES A SUDDEN, FAST TURN, AND...
THIS ISN'T A REAL BRUSH!
IT'S A NETWORK OF STRONG WIRES, PAINTED LIKE BRUSH! OUR HANDS ARE TRAPPED!
HE LURED US INTO SOMETHING LIKE THE OLD CHINESE TRAP-- A TRICKY DEVICE YOU CAN EASILY SLIP YOUR HANDS INTO--BUT CAN'T GET OUT AGAIN!
HA-HA-HA!
AS THE MYSTERY MAN DRIVES OFF IN A CAR HE HAD HIDDEN NEARBY...
ALTHOUGH I DIDN'T EXPECT ANYTHING TO GO WRONG OUT HERE-- AND SURELY, I HADN'T BANKED ON BATMAN AND ROBIN SHOWING UP-- I'M GLAD I TOOK THE PRECAUTION TO SET THAT "JUST-IN-CASE" TRAP!
EVERYTHING'S GOING LIKE CLOCKWORK SO FAR! HMM-- 7:15! IT'LL BE WELL AFTER 8:30 BEFORE THE HOOTENANNYS GET A LIFT INTO TOWN! BY THEN, I'LL BE A MILLION DOLLARS RICHER!
7

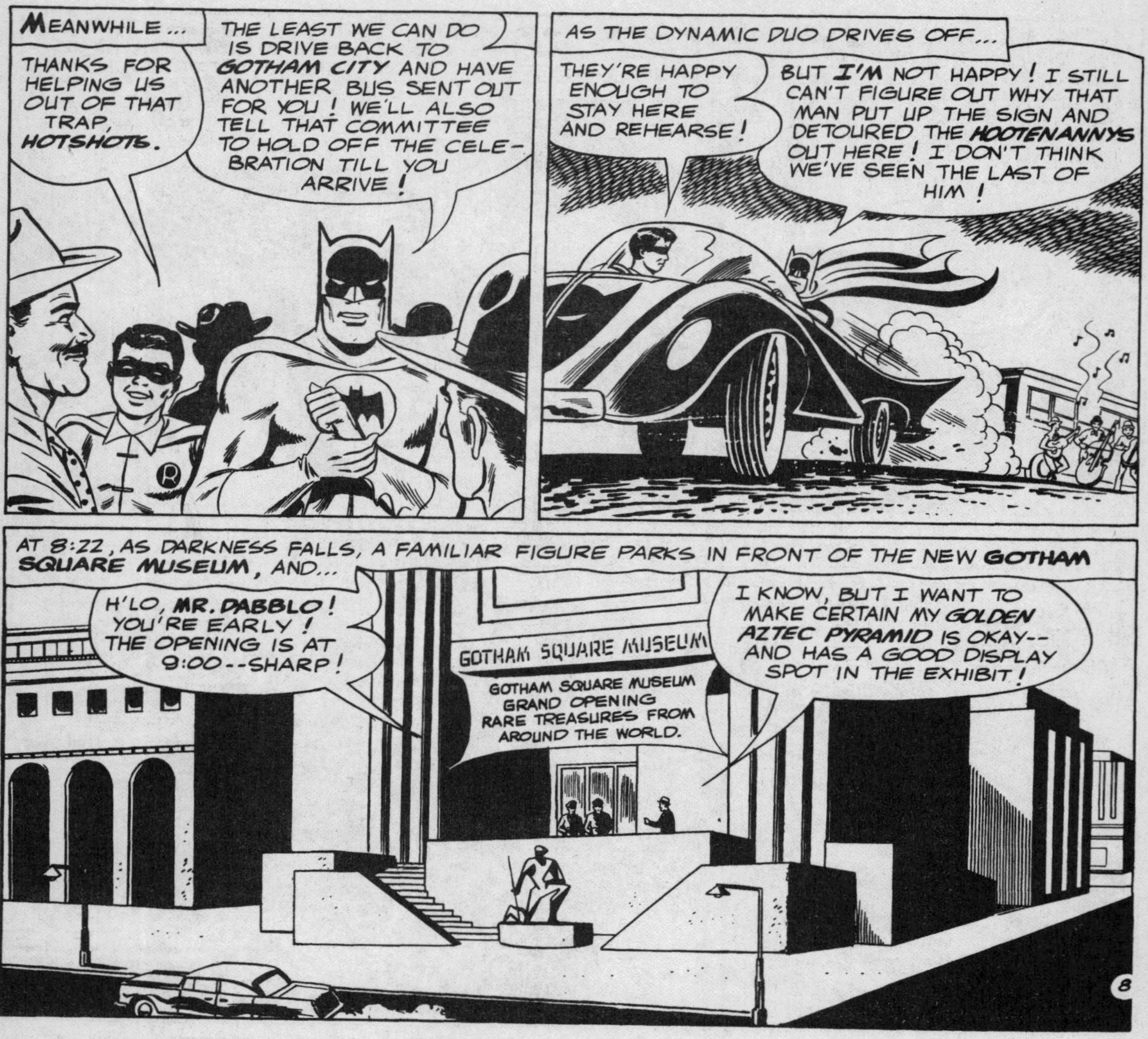
MEANWHILE...
THANKS FOR HELPING US OUT OF THAT TRAP, HOTSHOTS.
THE LEAST WE CAN DO IS DRIVE BACK TO GOTHAM CITY AND HAVE ANOTHER BUS SENT OUT FOR YOU! WE'LL ALSO TELL THAT COMMITTEE TO HOLD OFF THE CELE-BRATION TILL YOU ARRIVE!
AS THE DYNAMIC DUO DRIVES OFF...
THEY'RE HAPPY ENOUGH TO STAY HERE AND REHEARSE!
BUT I'M NOT HAPPY! I STILL CAN'T FIGURE OUT WHY THAT MAN PUT UP THE SIGN AND DETOURED THE HOOTENANNYS OUT HERE! I DON'T THINK WE'VE SEEN THE LAST OF HIM!
AT 8:22, AS DARKNESS FALLS, A FAMILIAR FIGURE PARKS IN FRONT OF THE NEW GOTHAM SQUARE MUSEUM, AND...
H'LO, MR. DABBLO! YOU'RE EARLY! THE OPENING IS AT 9:00--SHARP!
GOTHAM SQUARE MUSEUM
GOTHAM SQUARE MUSEUM GRAND OPENING RARE TREASURES FROM AROUND THE WORLD.
I KNOW, BUT I WANT TO MAKE CERTAIN MY GOLDEN AZTEC PYRAMID IS OKAY--AND HAS A GOOD DISPLAY SPOT IN THE EXHIBIT!
8

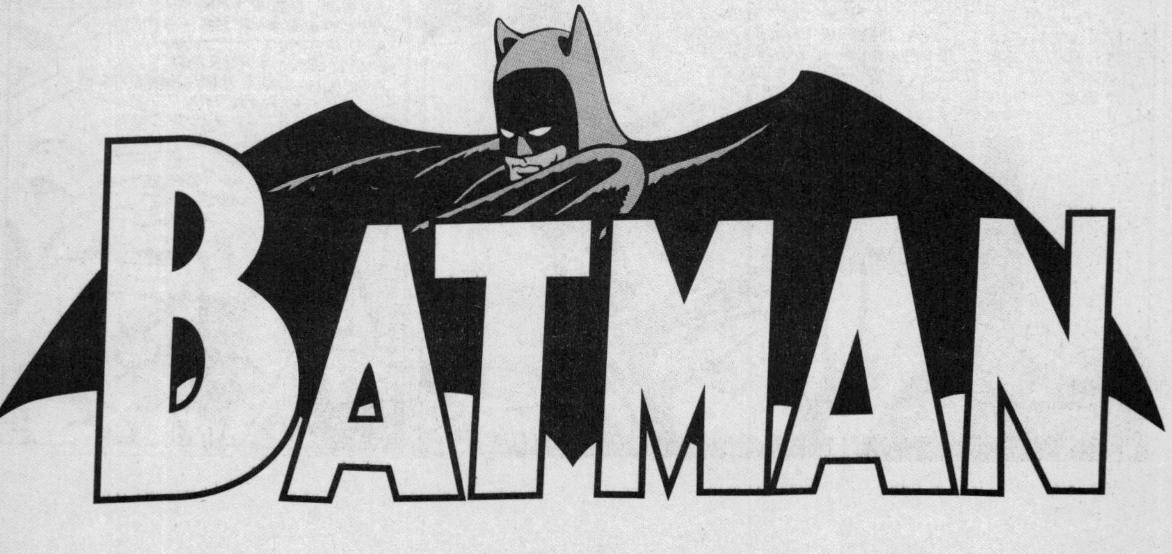
BATMAN

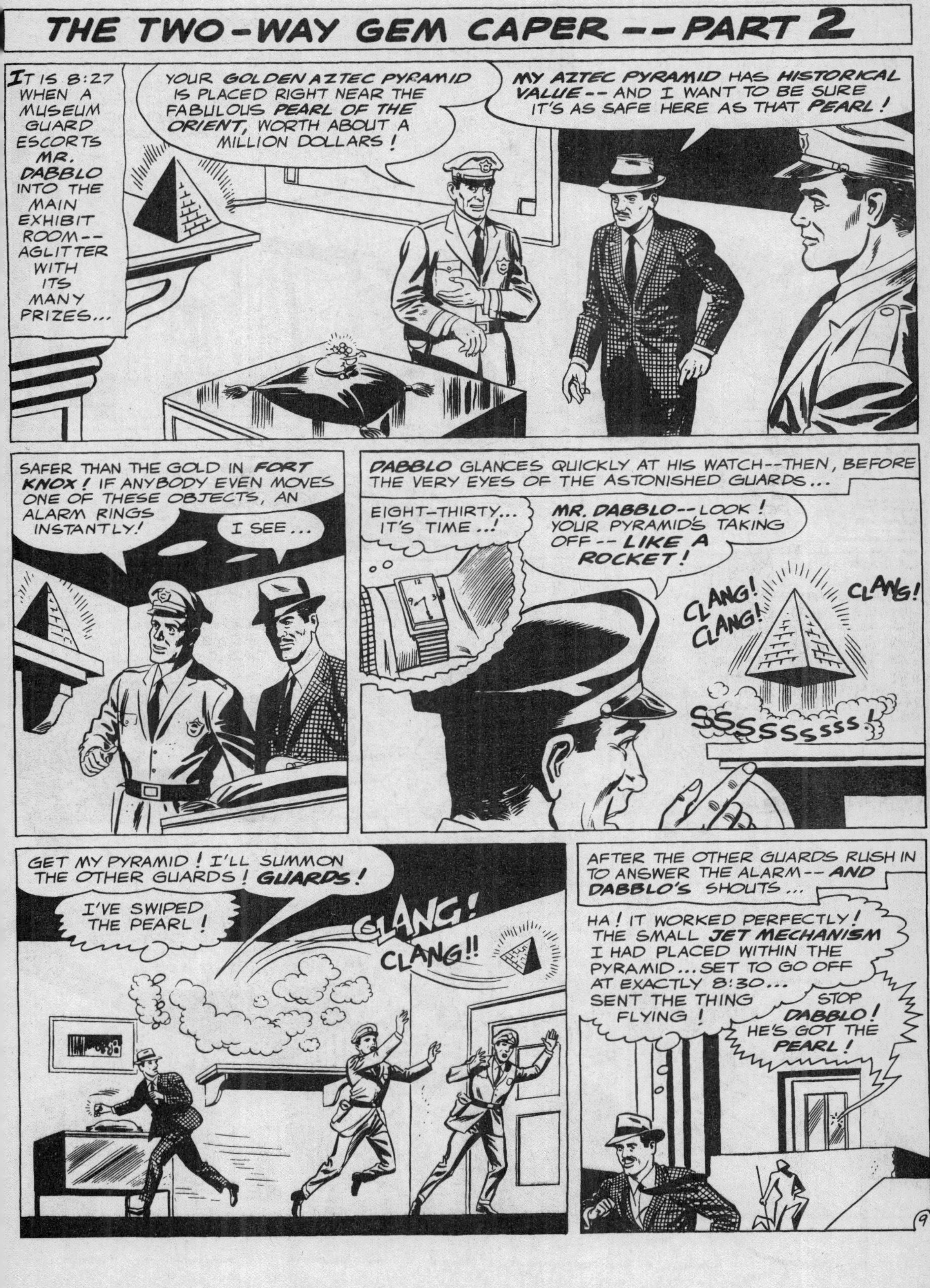
THE TWO-WAY GEM CAPER --PART 2
IT IS 8:27 WHEN A MUSEUM GUARD ESCORTS MR. DABBLO INTO THE MAIN EXHIBIT ROOM--AGLITTER WITH ITS MANY PRIZES...
YOUR GOLDEN AZTEC PYRAMID IS PLACED RIGHT NEAR THE FABULOUS PEARL OF THE ORIENT, WORTH ABOUT A MILLION DOLLARS!
MY AZTEC PYRAMID HAS HISTORICAL VALUE--AND I WANT TO BE SURE IT'S AS SAFE HERE AS THAT PEARL!
SAFER THAN THE GOLD IN FORT KNOX! IF ANYBODY EVEN MOVES ONE OF THESE OBJECTS, AN ALARM RINGS INSTANTLY!
I SEE...
DABBLO GLANCES QUICKLY AT HIS WATCH--THEN, BEFORE THE VERY EYES OF THE ASTONISHED GUARDS...
EIGHT-THIRTY... IT'S TIME...!
MR. DABBLO--LOOK! YOUR PYRAMID'S TAKING OFF--LIKE A ROCKET!
CLANG! CLANG!
CLANG!
SSSSSSSSS!
GET MY PYRAMID! I'LL SUMMON THE OTHER GUARDS! GUARDS!
I'VE SWIPED THE PEARL!
CLANG!
CLANG!!
AFTER THE OTHER GUARDS RUSH IN TO ANSWER THE ALARM--AND DABBLO'S SHOUTS...
HA! IT WORKED PERFECTLY! THE SMALL JET MECHANISM I HAD PLACED WITHIN THE PYRAMID...SET TO GO OFF AT EXACTLY 8:30... SENT THE THING FLYING!
STOP DABBLO! HE'S GOT THE PEARL!
9

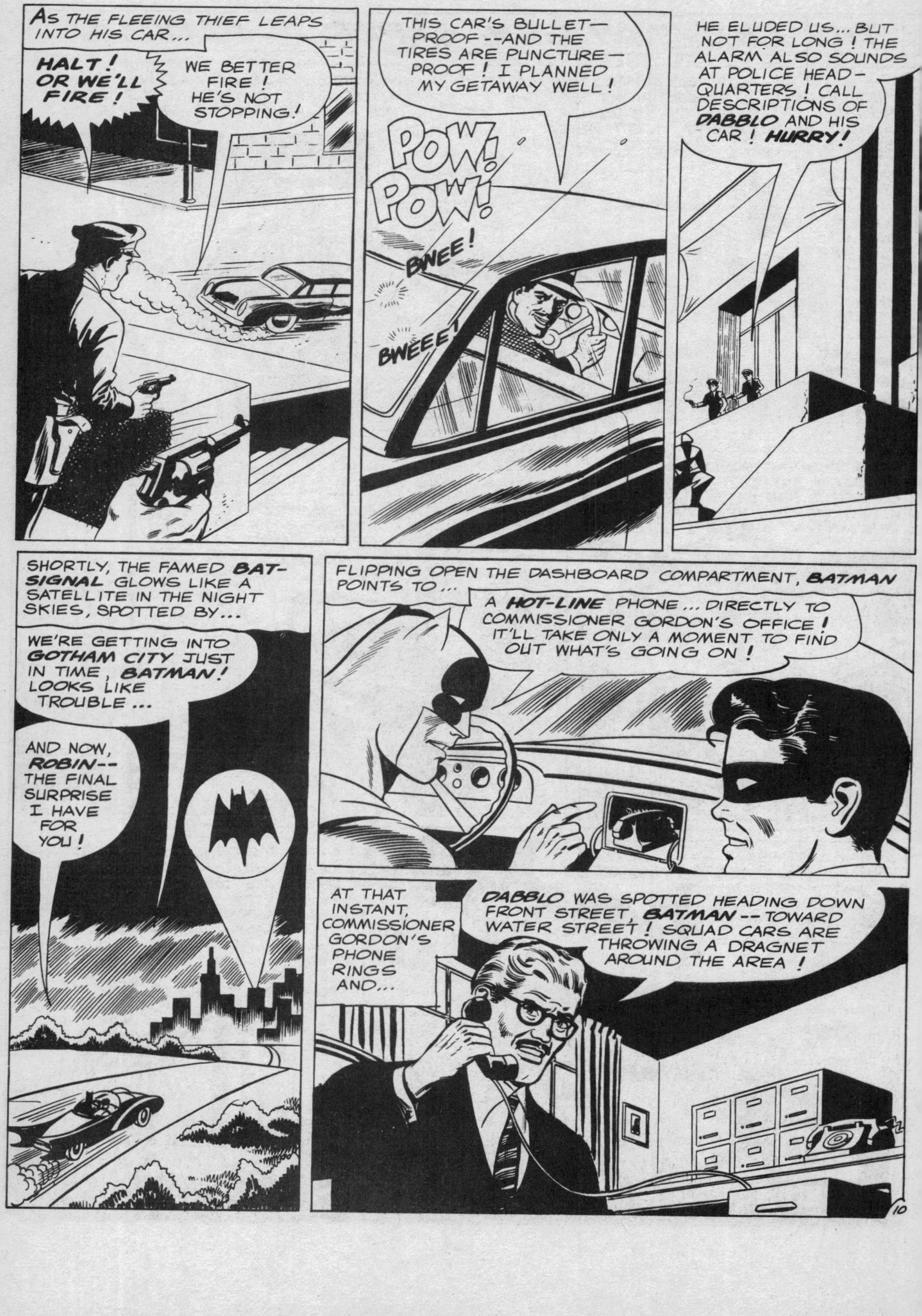
AS THE FLEEING THIEF LEAPS INTO HIS CAR...
HALT! OR WE'LL FIRE!
WE BETTER FIRE! HE'S NOT STOPPING!
THIS CAR'S BULLET-PROOF --AND THE TIRES ARE PUNCTURE-PROOF! I PLANNED MY GETAWAY WELL!
POW! POW!
BWEE!
BWEEE!
HE ELUDED US... BUT NOT FOR LONG! THE ALARM ALSO SOUNDS AT POLICE HEAD-QUARTERS! CALL DESCRIPTIONS OF DABBLO AND HIS CAR! HURRY!
SHORTLY, THE FAMED BAT-SIGNAL GLOWS LIKE A SATELLITE IN THE NIGHT SKIES, SPOTTED BY...
WE'RE GETTING INTO GOTHAM CITY JUST IN TIME, BATMAN! LOOKS LIKE TROUBLE...
AND NOW, ROBIN-- THE FINAL SURPRISE I HAVE FOR YOU!
FLIPPING OPEN THE DASHBOARD COMPARTMENT, BATMAN POINTS TO...
A HOT-LINE PHONE... DIRECTLY TO COMMISSIONER GORDON'S OFFICE! IT'LL TAKE ONLY A MOMENT TO FIND OUT WHAT'S GOING ON!
AT THAT INSTANT, COMMISSIONER GORDON'S PHONE RINGS AND,...
DABBLO WAS SPOTTED HEADING DOWN FRONT STREET, BATMAN -- TOWARD WATER STREET! SQUAD CARS ARE THROWING A DRAGNET AROUND THE AREA!
10

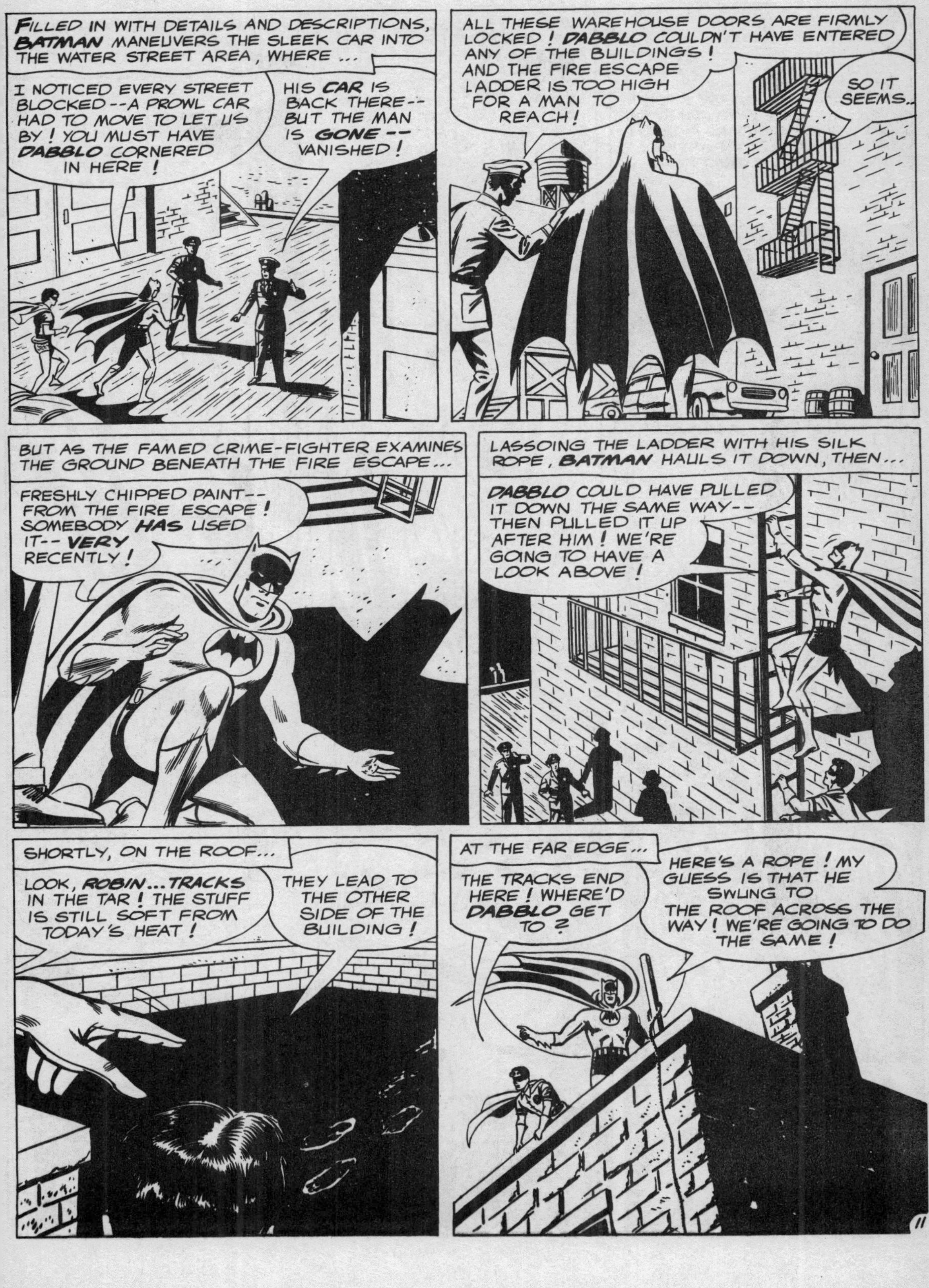
FILLED IN WITH DETAILS AND DESCRIPTIONS, BATMAN MANEUVERS THE SLEEK CAR INTO THE WATER STREET AREA, WHERE ...
I NOTICED EVERY STREET BLOCKED--A PROWL CAR HAD TO MOVE TO LET US BY! YOU MUST HAVE DABBLO CORNERED IN HERE!
HIS CAR IS BACK THERE--BUT THE MAN IS GONE--VANISHED!
ALL THESE WAREHOUSE DOORS ARE FIRMLY LOCKED! DABBLO COULDN'T HAVE ENTERED ANY OF THE BUILDINGS! AND THE FIRE ESCAPE LADDER IS TOO HIGH FOR A MAN TO REACH!
SO IT SEEMS...
BUT AS THE FAMED CRIME-FIGHTER EXAMINES THE GROUND BENEATH THE FIRE ESCAPE...
FRESHLY CHIPPED PAINT--FROM THE FIRE ESCAPE! SOMEBODY HAS USED IT--VERY RECENTLY!
LASSOING THE LADDER WITH HIS SILK ROPE, BATMAN HAULS IT DOWN, THEN...
DABBLO COULD HAVE PULLED IT DOWN THE SAME WAY--THEN PULLED IT UP AFTER HIM! WE'RE GOING TO HAVE A LOOK ABOVE!
SHORTLY, ON THE ROOF...
LOOK, ROBIN...TRACKS IN THE TAR! THE STUFF IS STILL SOFT FROM TODAY'S HEAT!
THEY LEAD TO THE OTHER SIDE OF THE BUILDING!
AT THE FAR EDGE...
THE TRACKS END HERE! WHERE'D DABBLO GET TO?
HERE'S A ROPE! MY GUESS IS THAT HE SWUNG TO THE ROOF ACROSS THE WAY! WE'RE GOING TO DO THE SAME!
11

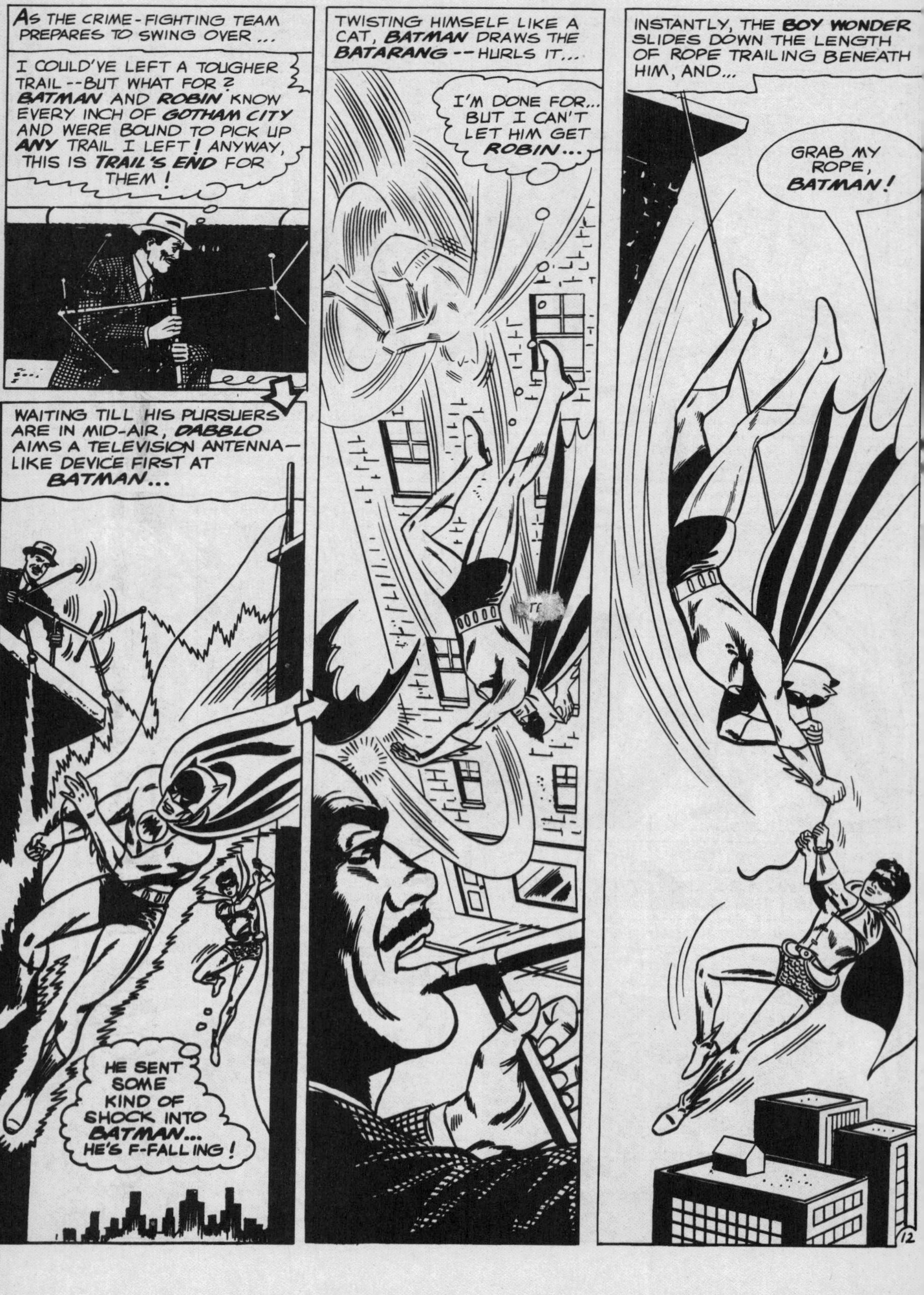
AS THE CRIME-FIGHTING TEAM PREPARES TO SWING OVER ...
I COULD'VE LEFT A TOUGHER TRAIL --BUT WHAT FOR? BATMAN AND ROBIN KNOW EVERY INCH OF GOTHAM CITY AND WERE BOUND TO PICK UP ANY TRAIL I LEFT! ANYWAY, THIS IS TRAIL'S END FOR THEM!
WAITING TILL HIS PURSUERS ARE IN MID-AIR, DABBLO AIMS A TELEVISION ANTENNA-LIKE DEVICE FIRST AT BATMAN...
HE SENT SOME KIND OF SHOCK INTO BATMAN... HE'S F-FALLING!
TWISTING HIMSELF LIKE A CAT, BATMAN DRAWS THE BATARANG --HURLS IT...
I'M DONE FOR... BUT I CAN'T LET HIM GET ROBIN...
INSTANTLY, THE BOY WONDER SLIDES DOWN THE LENGTH OF ROPE TRAILING BENEATH HIM, AND...
GRAB MY ROPE, BATMAN!
12

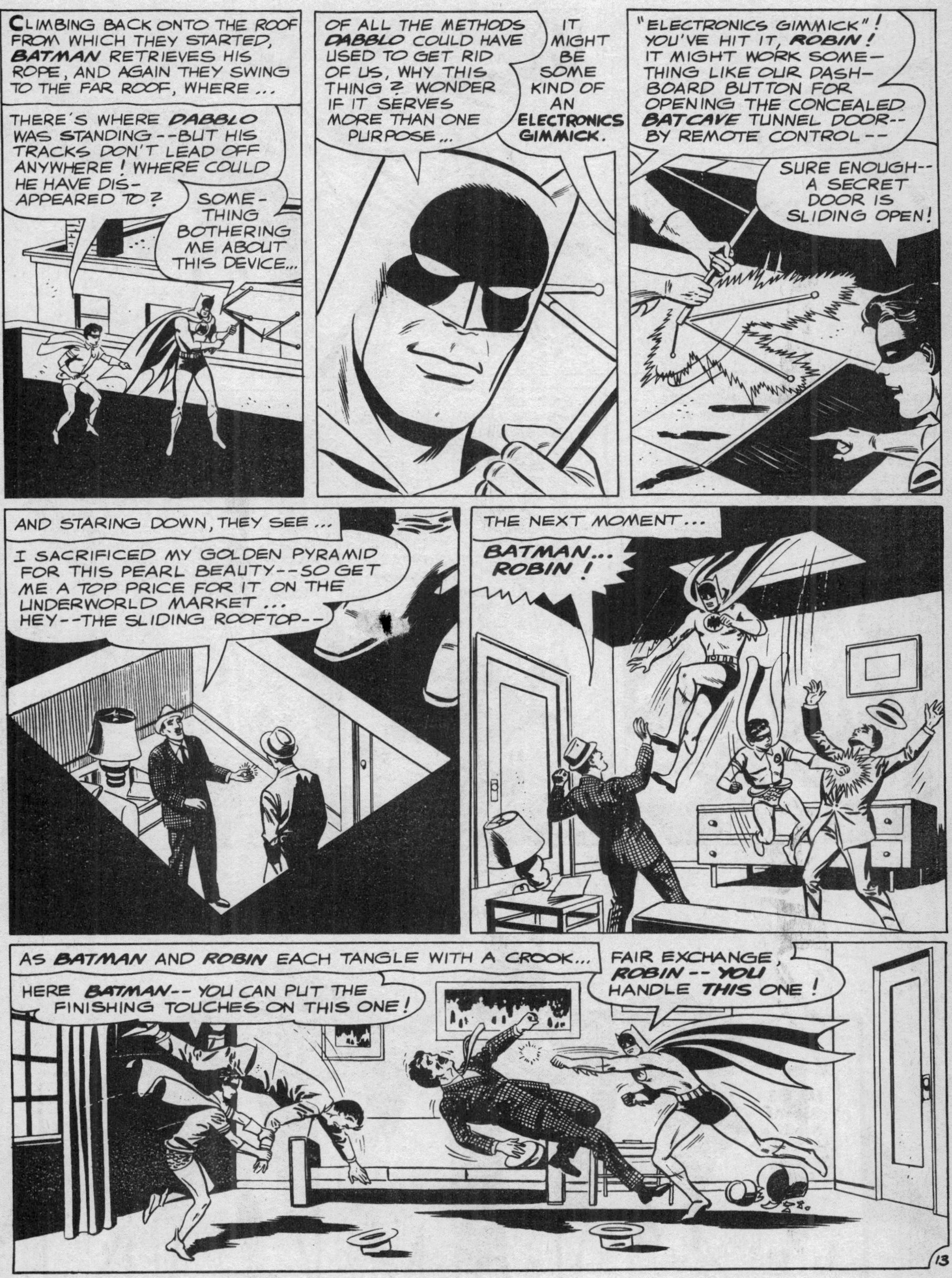
CLIMBING BACK ONTO THE ROOF FROM WHICH THEY STARTED, BATMAN RETRIEVES HIS ROPE, AND AGAIN THEY SWING TO THE FAR ROOF, WHERE ...
THERE'S WHERE DABBLO WAS STANDING--BUT HIS TRACKS DON'T LEAD OFF ANYWHERE! WHERE COULD HE HAVE DISAPPEARED TO?
SOMETHING BOTHERING ME ABOUT THIS DEVICE...
OF ALL THE METHODS DABBLO COULD HAVE USED TO GET RID OF US, WHY THIS THING? WONDER IF IT SERVES MORE THAN ONE PURPOSE...
IT MIGHT BE SOME KIND OF AN ELECTRONICS GIMMICK.
"ELECTRONICS GIMMICK"! YOU'VE HIT IT, ROBIN! IT MIGHT WORK SOMETHING LIKE OUR DASHBOARD BUTTON FOR OPENING THE CONCEALED BATCAVE TUNNEL DOOR--BY REMOTE CONTROL--
SURE ENOUGH--A SECRET DOOR IS SLIDING OPEN!
AND STARING DOWN, THEY SEE ...
I SACRIFICED MY GOLDEN PYRAMID FOR THIS PEARL BEAUTY--SO GET ME A TOP PRICE FOR IT ON THE UNDERWORLD MARKET ... HEY--THE SLIDING ROOFTOP--
THE NEXT MOMENT...
BATMAN... ROBIN!
AS BATMAN AND ROBIN EACH TANGLE WITH A CROOK...
HERE BATMAN--YOU CAN PUT THE FINISHING TOUCHES ON THIS ONE!
FAIR EXCHANGE, ROBIN--YOU HANDLE THIS ONE!
13

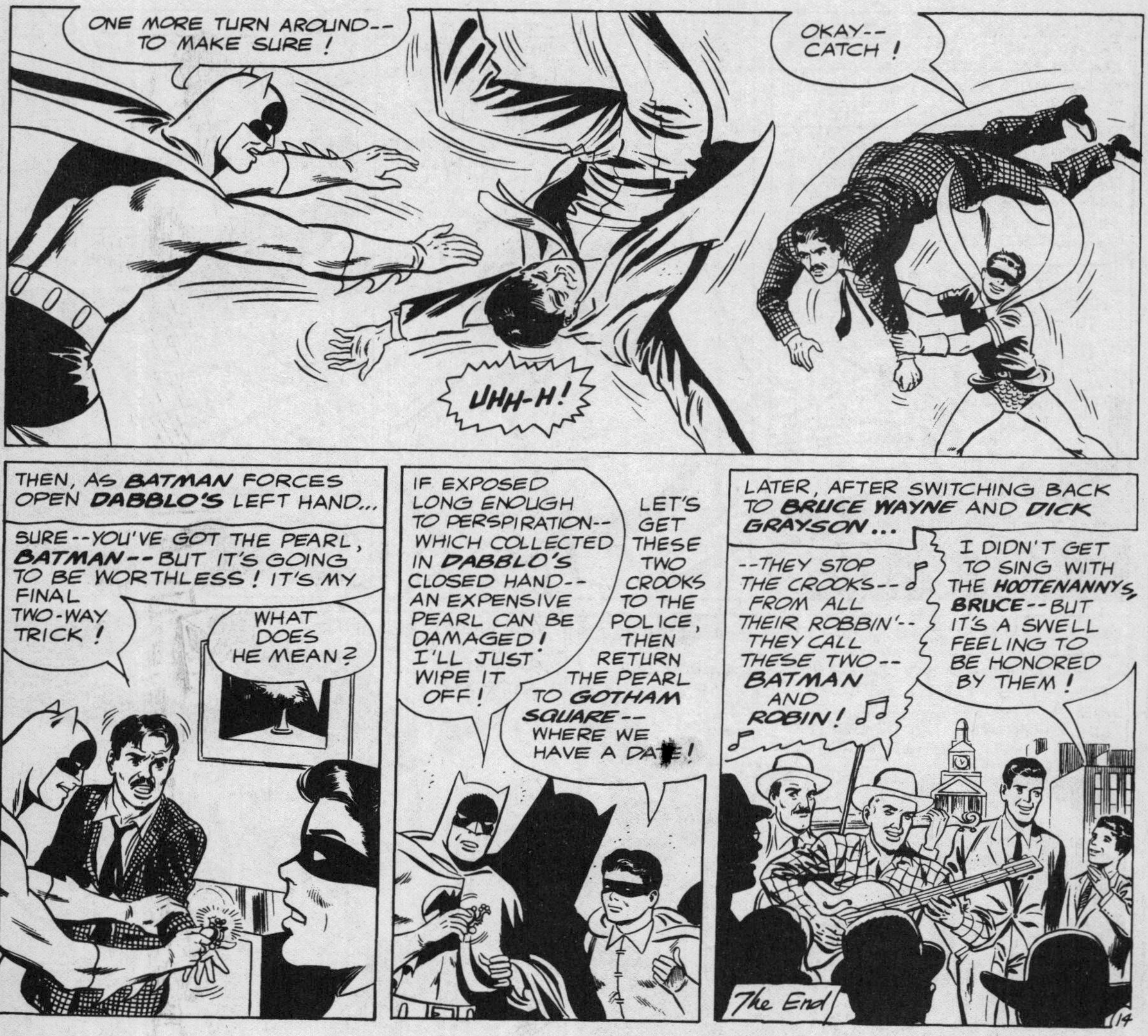
ONE MORE TURN AROUND-- TO MAKE SURE!
UHH-H!
OKAY-- CATCH!
THEN, AS BATMAN FORCES OPEN DABBLO'S LEFT HAND...
SURE--YOU'VE GOT THE PEARL, BATMAN--BUT IT'S GOING TO BE WORTHLESS! IT'S MY FINAL TWO-WAY TRICK!
WHAT DOES HE MEAN?
IF EXPOSED LONG ENOUGH TO PERSPIRATION--WHICH COLLECTED IN DABBLO'S CLOSED HAND--AN EXPENSIVE PEARL CAN BE DAMAGED! I'LL JUST WIPE IT OFF!
LET'S GET THESE TWO CROOKS TO THE POLICE, THEN RETURN THE PEARL TO GOTHAM SQUARE--WHERE WE HAVE A DATE!
LATER, AFTER SWITCHING BACK TO BRUCE WAYNE AND DICK GRAYSON...
--THEY STOP THE CROOKS--FROM ALL THEIR ROBBIN'--THEY CALL THESE TWO--BATMAN AND ROBIN!
I DIDN'T GET TO SING WITH THE HOOTENANNYS, BRUCE--BUT IT'S A SWELL FEELING TO BE HONORED BY THEM!
The End
14

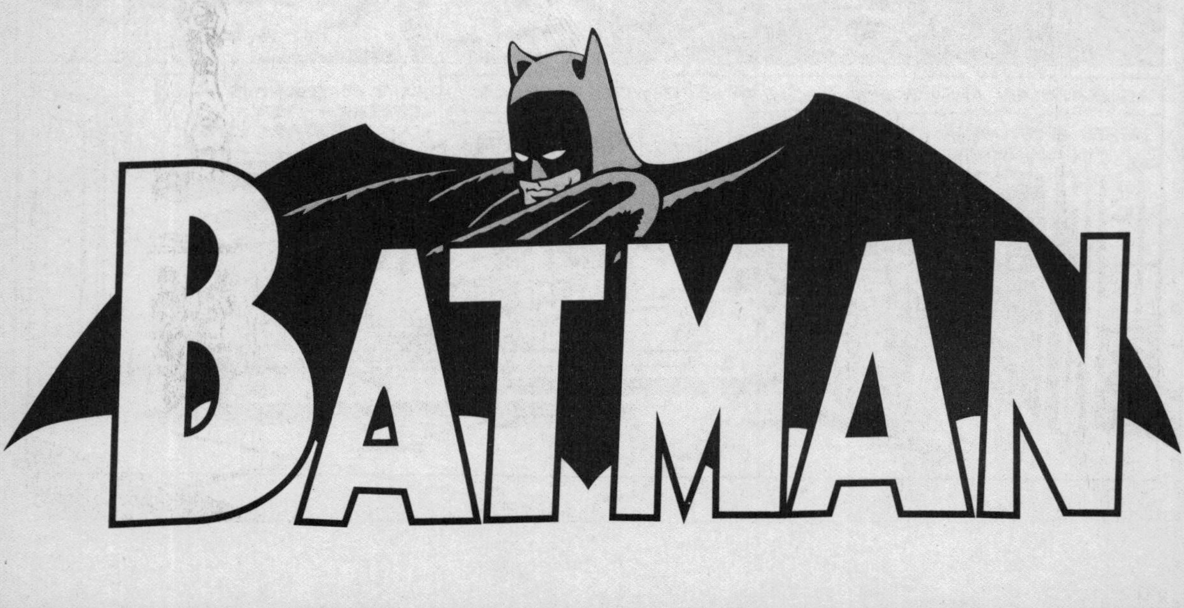
BATMAN

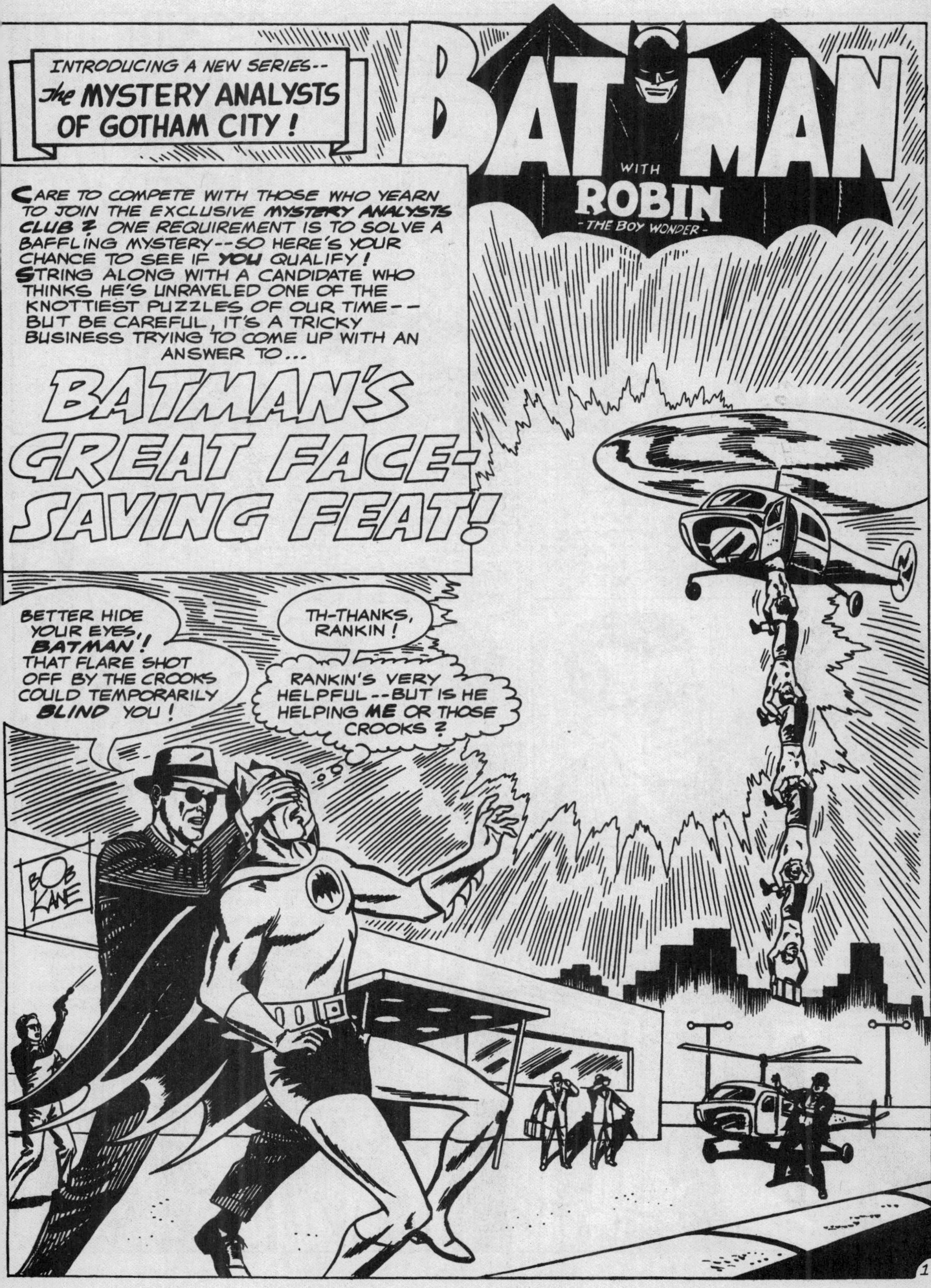
INTRODUCING A NEW SERIES-- The MYSTERY ANALYSTS OF GOTHAM CITY!
BATMAN
WITH
ROBIN
-THE BOY WONDER-
CARE TO COMPETE WITH THOSE WHO YEARN TO JOIN THE EXCLUSIVE MYSTERY ANALYSTS CLUB? ONE REQUIREMENT IS TO SOLVE A BAFFLING MYSTERY--SO HERE'S YOUR CHANCE TO SEE IF YOU QUALIFY! STRING ALONG WITH A CANDIDATE WHO THINKS HE'S UNRAVELED ONE OF THE KNOTTIEST PUZZLES OF OUR TIME--BUT BE CAREFUL, IT'S A TRICKY BUSINESS TRYING TO COME UP WITH AN ANSWER TO...
BATMAN'S GREAT FACE-SAVING FEAT!
BETTER HIDE YOUR EYES, BATMAN! THAT FLARE SHOT OFF BY THE CROOKS COULD TEMPORARILY BLIND YOU!
TH-THANKS, RANKIN!
RANKIN'S VERY HELPFUL--BUT IS HE HELPING ME OR THOSE CROOKS?
BOB KANE
1

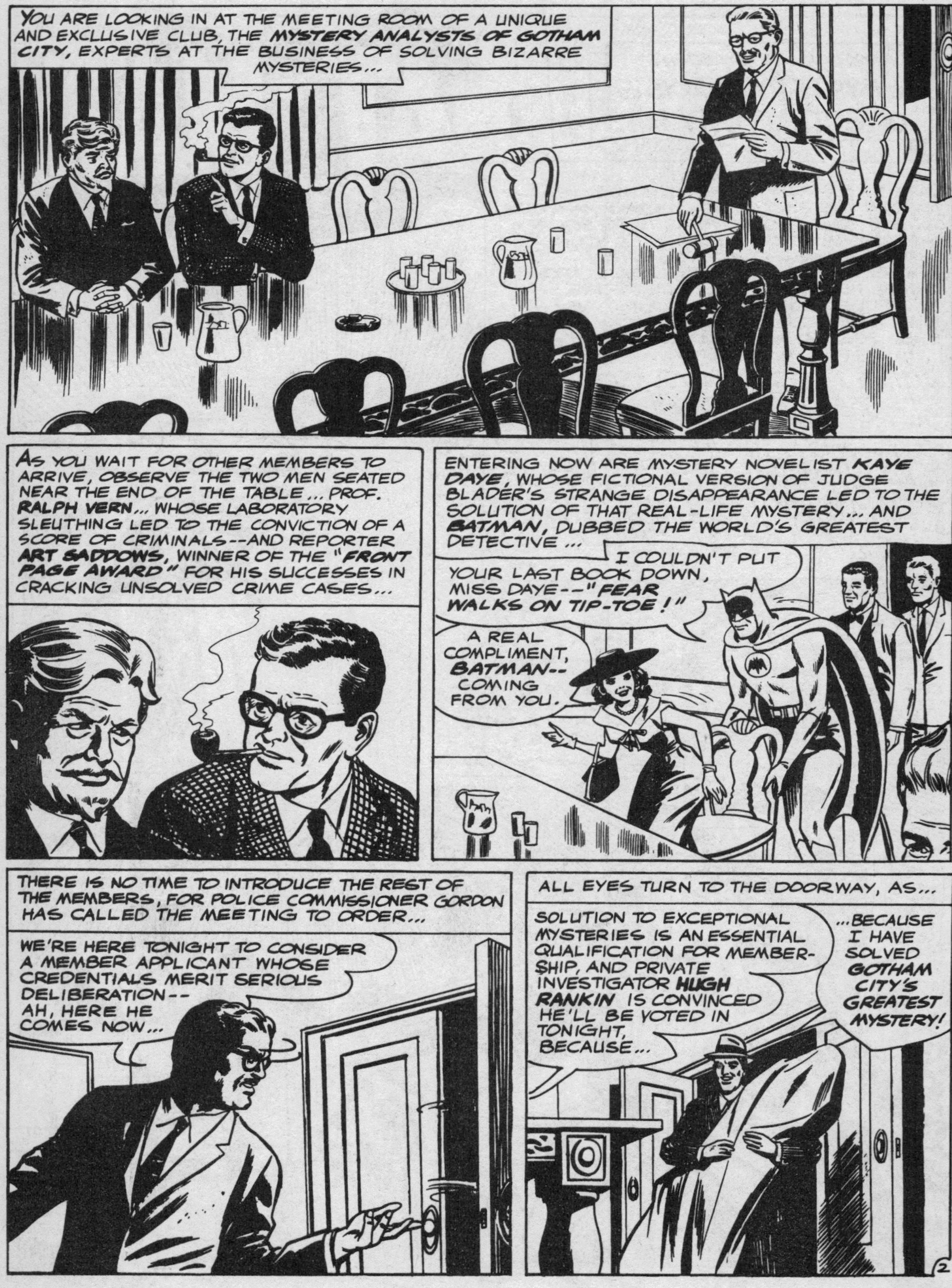
YOU ARE LOOKING IN AT THE MEETING ROOM OF A UNIQUE AND EXCLUSIVE CLUB, THE MYSTERY ANALYSTS OF GOTHAM CITY, EXPERTS AT THE BUSINESS OF SOLVING BIZARRE MYSTERIES...
AS YOU WAIT FOR OTHER MEMBERS TO ARRIVE, OBSERVE THE TWO MEN SEATED NEAR THE END OF THE TABLE... PROF. RALPH VERN... WHOSE LABORATORY SLEUTHING LED TO THE CONVICTION OF A SCORE OF CRIMINALS--AND REPORTER ART SADDOWS, WINNER OF THE "FRONT PAGE AWARD" FOR HIS SUCCESSES IN CRACKING UNSOLVED CRIME CASES...
ENTERING NOW ARE MYSTERY NOVELIST KAYE DAYE, WHOSE FICTIONAL VERSION OF JUDGE BLADER'S STRANGE DISAPPEARANCE LED TO THE SOLUTION OF THAT REAL-LIFE MYSTERY... AND BATMAN, DUBBED THE WORLD'S GREATEST DETECTIVE...
I COULDN'T PUT YOUR LAST BOOK DOWN, MISS DAYE--"FEAR WALKS ON TIP-TOE!"
A REAL COMPLIMENT, BATMAN-- COMING FROM YOU.
THERE IS NO TIME TO INTRODUCE THE REST OF THE MEMBERS, FOR POLICE COMMISSIONER GORDON HAS CALLED THE MEETING TO ORDER...
WE'RE HERE TONIGHT TO CONSIDER A MEMBER APPLICANT WHOSE CREDENTIALS MERIT SERIOUS DELIBERATION-- AH, HERE HE COMES NOW...
ALL EYES TURN TO THE DOORWAY, AS...
SOLUTION TO EXCEPTIONAL MYSTERIES IS AN ESSENTIAL QUALIFICATION FOR MEMBERSHIP, AND PRIVATE INVESTIGATOR HUGH RANKIN IS CONVINCED HE'LL BE VOTED IN TONIGHT, BECAUSE...
...BECAUSE I HAVE SOLVED GOTHAM CITY'S GREATEST MYSTERY!
2

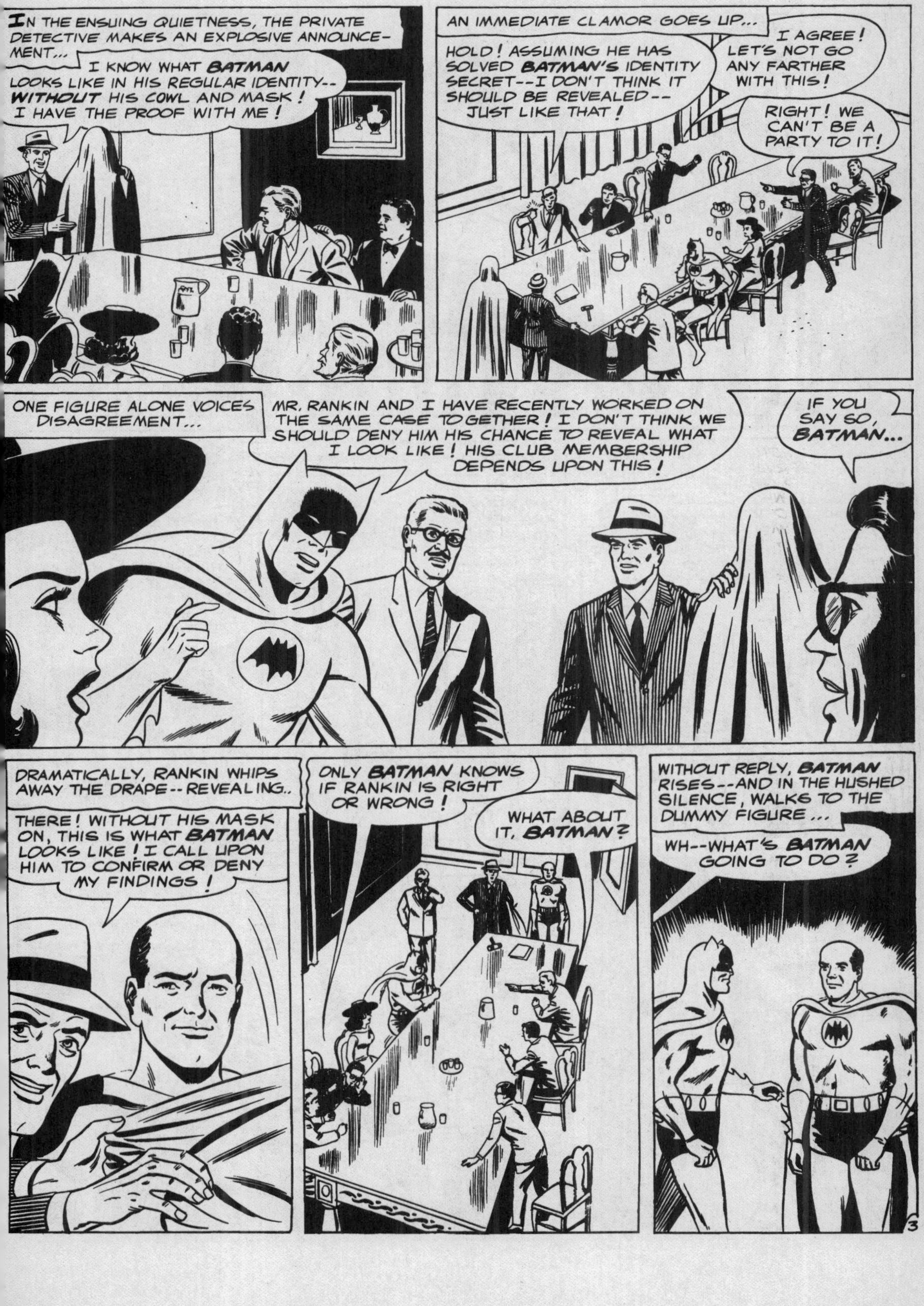
IN THE ENSUING QUIETNESS, THE PRIVATE DETECTIVE MAKES AN EXPLOSIVE ANNOUNCEMENT...
I KNOW WHAT BATMAN LOOKS LIKE IN HIS REGULAR IDENTITY-- WITHOUT HIS COWL AND MASK! I HAVE THE PROOF WITH ME!
AN IMMEDIATE CLAMOR GOES UP...
HOLD! ASSUMING HE HAS SOLVED BATMAN'S IDENTITY SECRET--I DON'T THINK IT SHOULD BE REVEALED-- JUST LIKE THAT!
I AGREE! LET'S NOT GO ANY FARTHER WITH THIS!
RIGHT! WE CAN'T BE A PARTY TO IT!
ONE FIGURE ALONE VOICES DISAGREEMENT...
MR. RANKIN AND I HAVE RECENTLY WORKED ON THE SAME CASE TOGETHER! I DON'T THINK WE SHOULD DENY HIM HIS CHANCE TO REVEAL WHAT I LOOK LIKE! HIS CLUB MEMBERSHIP DEPENDS UPON THIS!
IF YOU SAY SO, BATMAN...
DRAMATICALLY, RANKIN WHIPS AWAY THE DRAPE--REVEALING..
THERE! WITHOUT HIS MASK ON, THIS IS WHAT BATMAN LOOKS LIKE! I CALL UPON HIM TO CONFIRM OR DENY MY FINDINGS!
ONLY BATMAN KNOWS IF RANKIN IS RIGHT OR WRONG!
WHAT ABOUT IT, BATMAN?
WITHOUT REPLY, BATMAN RISES--AND IN THE HUSHED SILENCE, WALKS TO THE DUMMY FIGURE...
WH--WHAT'S BATMAN GOING TO DO?
3

BEFORE THE STUNNED AUDIENCE, THE CRIME-FIGHTER BEGINS TO...

H-HE'S LIFTING HIS MASK!

LOOK! RANKIN WAS RIGHT! IT'S AN EXACT LIKENESS!

SHOCKED AT FIRST BY THE SENSATIONAL REVELATION, THE OTHER MEMBERS GATHER EXCITEDLY AROUND THE PRIVATE DETECTIVE...

YOU MUST TELL US -- IN **DETAIL** -- HOW YOU KNEW **BATMAN'S** MASKED FEATURES SO THOROUGHLY THAT YOU WERE ABLE TO CONSTRUCT A LOOK-ALIKE FIGURE OF HIM!

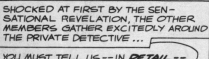

IN THRILLING DETAIL, RANKIN UNFOLDS HIS STARTLING STORY. THEN...

TELL US, **BATMAN**, WHO ARE YOU IN THIS OTHER IDENTITY?

THAT MUCH AT LEAST WILL REMAIN **MY** SECRET!

CLAP! CLAP!

JUST PRIOR TO THE SECRET VOTING, A CUSTOMARY REMINDER IS MADE...

REMEMBER, A **WHITE** BALL MEANS ACCEPTANCE OF THE CANDIDATE -- WHILE EVEN A **SINGLE** BLACK BALL MEANS REJECTION!

HOW CAN RANKIN MISS -- AFTER THE DISCOVERY HE'S MADE?

BUT FOLLOWING THE BALLOTING -- TO THE ASTONISHMENT OF NEARLY EVERYONE THERE...

ONE LONE **BLACK BALL**! RANKIN HAS BEEN REJECTED!

BUT WHY... AND BY WHOM?

4

PUZZLED MEMBERS SEARCH IN VAIN FOR THE MOTIVE BEHIND THE MYSTERIOUS BLACK-BALLER...
RANKIN LOOKED LIKE A SHOO-IN! WHY WAS HE BLACK-BALLED?
WHOEVER VOTED AGAINST HIM MUST HAVE HAD A GOOD REASON!
LATER, WHEN BRUCE (BATMAN) WAYNE ARRIVES HOME TO TELL DICK GRAYSON OF THE INTRIGUING EVENT AT THE CLUB...
I KNOW YOU CAST THE BLACK BALL--BECAUSE RANKIN WAS WRONG! BUT HOW DID YOU EVER MANAGE TO DISGUISE YOUR FACE TO THE EXACT LIKENESS OF RANKIN'S DUMMY?
THAT'S THE STORY I'VE BEEN HOLDING OFF TELLING YOU, DICK--TILL I HAD ALL THE FACTS!
"IT ALL BEGAN THAT NIGHT WHEN, AS BATMAN AND ROBIN, WE WERE PATROLLING THE ROOFTOPS IN SEARCH OF THE NEW SENSATIONAL GANG, THE TRAPEZE TEN..."
OVER THERE, ROBIN--ON THAT DERRICK! IT'S SOME OF THE GANG!
"YOU'LL REMEMBER THAT THE GANG HAD TURNED A DERRICK FROM A CONSTRUCTION SITE TO WHERE IT REARED UP NEAR THE GOTHAM INSURANCE BUILDING NEXT DOOR, AND..."
HURRY--THIS JOB MUST GO OFF LIKE CLOCKWORK!
"WHEN WE REACHED AN ADJACENT ROOF..."
THE INSURANCE COMPANY'S SAFES ARE ON THAT FLOOR, ROBIN--WHERE THE CROOKS CAUGHT THE LEDGE WITH A GRAPPLING HOOK! GET TO THE DERRICK--SO THEY CAN'T ESCAPE DOWN IT...
5

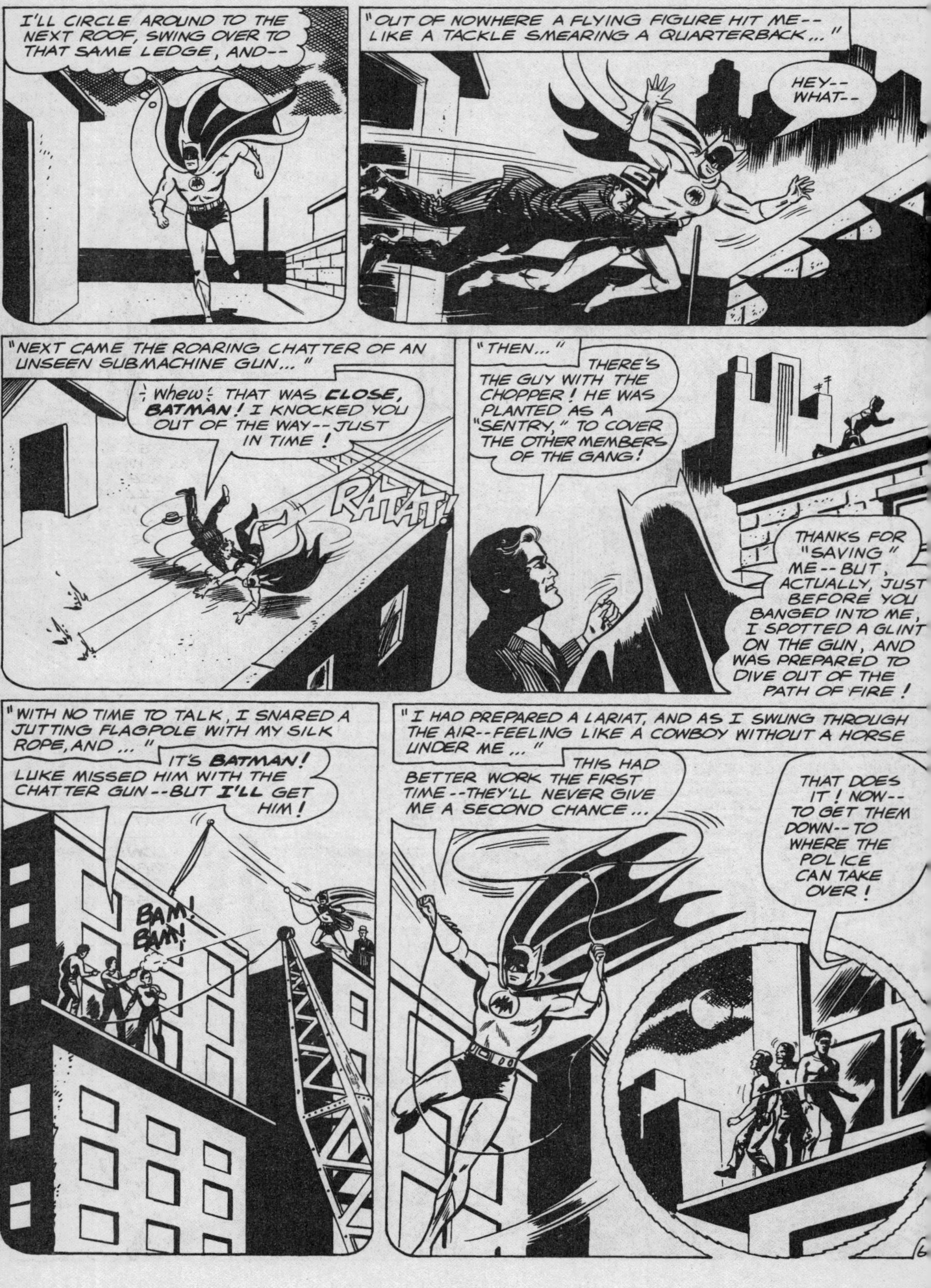
I'LL CIRCLE AROUND TO THE NEXT ROOF, SWING OVER TO THAT SAME LEDGE, AND--
"OUT OF NOWHERE A FLYING FIGURE HIT ME-- LIKE A TACKLE SMEARING A QUARTERBACK..."
HEY-- WHAT--
"NEXT CAME THE ROARING CHATTER OF AN UNSEEN SUBMACHINE GUN..."
Whew! THAT WAS CLOSE, BATMAN! I KNOCKED YOU OUT OF THE WAY--JUST IN TIME!
RATAT!
"THEN..."
THERE'S THE GUY WITH THE CHOPPER! HE WAS PLANTED AS A "SENTRY," TO COVER THE OTHER MEMBERS OF THE GANG!
THANKS FOR "SAVING" ME--BUT, ACTUALLY, JUST BEFORE YOU BANGED INTO ME, I SPOTTED A GLINT ON THE GUN, AND WAS PREPARED TO DIVE OUT OF THE PATH OF FIRE!
"WITH NO TIME TO TALK, I SNARED A JUTTING FLAGPOLE WITH MY SILK ROPE, AND..."
IT'S BATMAN! LUKE MISSED HIM WITH THE CHATTER GUN--BUT I'LL GET HIM!
BAM! BAM!
"I HAD PREPARED A LARIAT, AND AS I SWUNG THROUGH THE AIR--FEELING LIKE A COWBOY WITHOUT A HORSE UNDER ME..."
THIS HAD BETTER WORK THE FIRST TIME--THEY'LL NEVER GIVE ME A SECOND CHANCE...
THAT DOES IT! NOW-- TO GET THEM DOWN--TO WHERE THE POLICE CAN TAKE OVER!
6

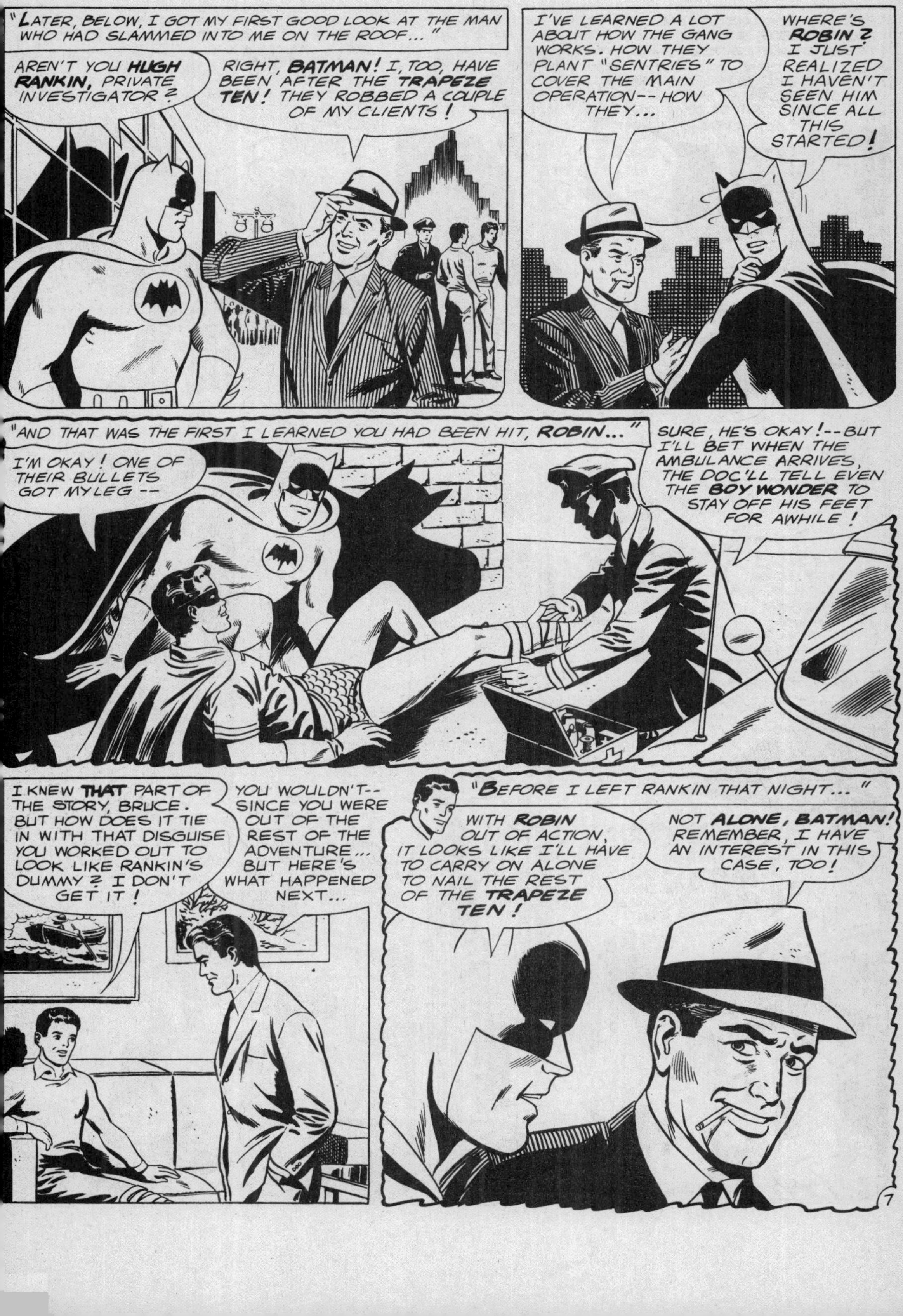
"LATER, BELOW, I GOT MY FIRST GOOD LOOK AT THE MAN WHO HAD SLAMMED INTO ME ON THE ROOF..."
AREN'T YOU HUGH RANKIN, PRIVATE INVESTIGATOR?
RIGHT, BATMAN! I, TOO, HAVE BEEN AFTER THE TRAPEZE TEN! THEY ROBBED A COUPLE OF MY CLIENTS!
I'VE LEARNED A LOT ABOUT HOW THE GANG WORKS. HOW THEY PLANT "SENTRIES" TO COVER THE MAIN OPERATION--HOW THEY...
WHERE'S ROBIN? I JUST REALIZED I HAVEN'T SEEN HIM SINCE ALL THIS STARTED!
"AND THAT WAS THE FIRST I LEARNED YOU HAD BEEN HIT, ROBIN..."
I'M OKAY! ONE OF THEIR BULLETS GOT MY LEG--
SURE, HE'S OKAY!--BUT I'LL BET WHEN THE AMBULANCE ARRIVES, THE DOC'LL TELL EVEN THE BOY WONDER TO STAY OFF HIS FEET FOR AWHILE!
I KNEW THAT PART OF THE STORY, BRUCE. BUT HOW DOES IT TIE IN WITH THAT DISGUISE YOU WORKED OUT TO LOOK LIKE RANKIN'S DUMMY? I DON'T GET IT!
YOU WOULDN'T--SINCE YOU WERE OUT OF THE REST OF THE ADVENTURE... BUT HERE'S WHAT HAPPENED NEXT...
"BEFORE I LEFT RANKIN THAT NIGHT..."
WITH ROBIN OUT OF ACTION, IT LOOKS LIKE I'LL HAVE TO CARRY ON ALONE TO NAIL THE REST OF THE TRAPEZE TEN!
NOT ALONE, BATMAN! REMEMBER, I HAVE AN INTEREST IN THIS CASE, TOO!
7

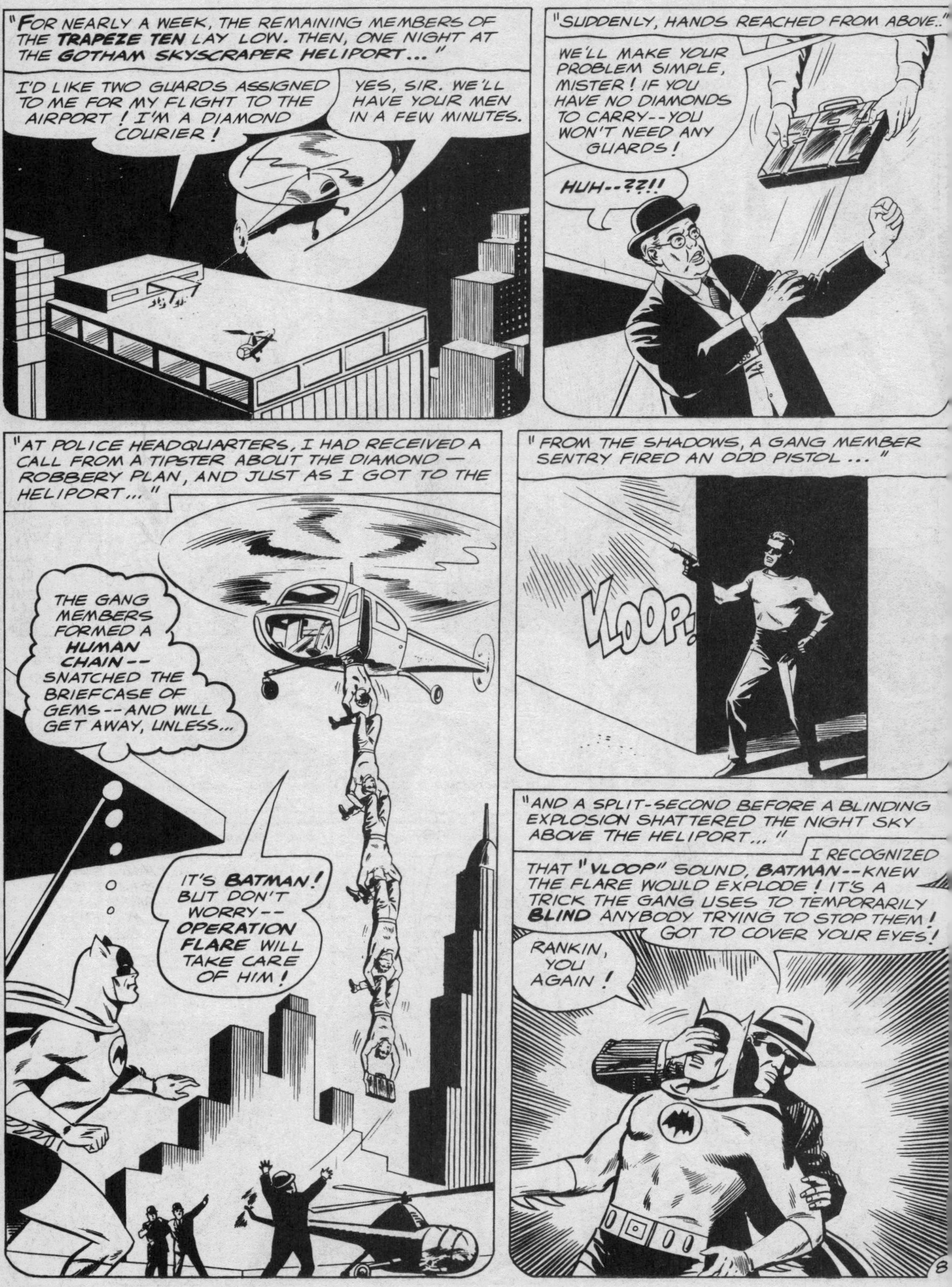
"FOR NEARLY A WEEK, THE REMAINING MEMBERS OF THE TRAPEZE TEN LAY LOW. THEN, ONE NIGHT AT THE GOTHAM SKYSCRAPER HELIPORT..."
I'D LIKE TWO GUARDS ASSIGNED TO ME FOR MY FLIGHT TO THE AIRPORT! I'M A DIAMOND COURIER!
YES, SIR. WE'LL HAVE YOUR MEN IN A FEW MINUTES.
"SUDDENLY, HANDS REACHED FROM ABOVE."
WE'LL MAKE YOUR PROBLEM SIMPLE, MISTER! IF YOU HAVE NO DIAMONDS TO CARRY--YOU WON'T NEED ANY GUARDS!
HUH--??!!
"AT POLICE HEADQUARTERS, I HAD RECEIVED A CALL FROM A TIPSTER ABOUT THE DIAMOND-ROBBERY PLAN, AND JUST AS I GOT TO THE HELIPORT..."
THE GANG MEMBERS FORMED A HUMAN CHAIN--SNATCHED THE BRIEFCASE OF GEMS--AND WILL GET AWAY, UNLESS...
IT'S BATMAN! BUT DON'T WORRY--OPERATION FLARE WILL TAKE CARE OF HIM!
"FROM THE SHADOWS, A GANG MEMBER SENTRY FIRED AN ODD PISTOL..."
VLOOP!
"AND A SPLIT-SECOND BEFORE A BLINDING EXPLOSION SHATTERED THE NIGHT SKY ABOVE THE HELIPORT..."
I RECOGNIZED THAT "VLOOP" SOUND, BATMAN--KNEW THE FLARE WOULD EXPLODE! IT'S A TRICK THE GANG USES TO TEMPORARILY BLIND ANYBODY TRYING TO STOP THEM! GOT TO COVER YOUR EYES!
RANKIN, YOU AGAIN!
8

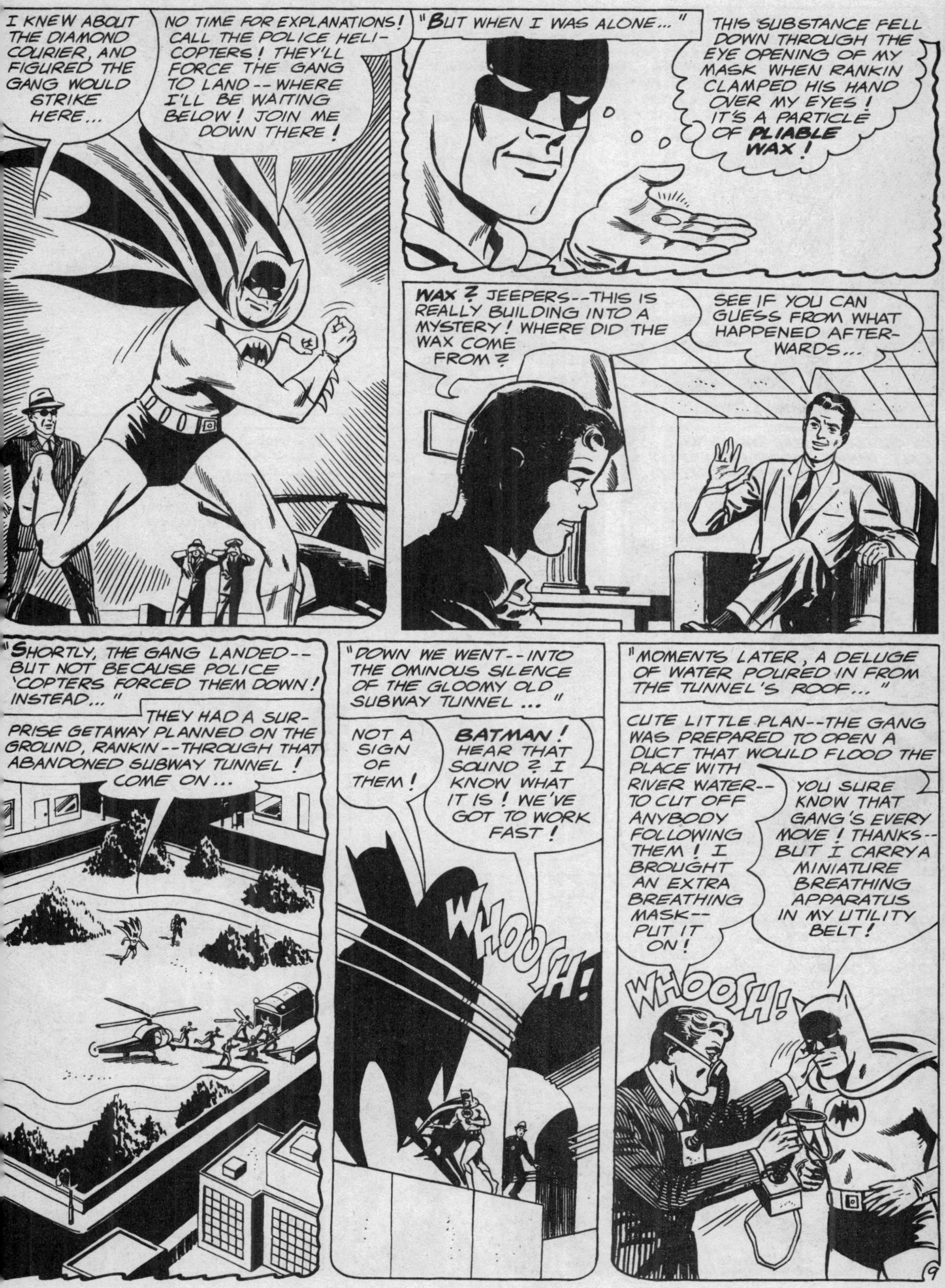
I KNEW ABOUT THE DIAMOND COURIER, AND FIGURED THE GANG WOULD STRIKE HERE...
NO TIME FOR EXPLANATIONS! CALL THE POLICE HELI-COPTERS! THEY'LL FORCE THE GANG TO LAND--WHERE I'LL BE WAITING BELOW! JOIN ME DOWN THERE!
"BUT WHEN I WAS ALONE..."
THIS SUBSTANCE FELL DOWN THROUGH THE EYE OPENING OF MY MASK WHEN RANKIN CLAMPED HIS HAND OVER MY EYES! IT'S A PARTICLE OF PLIABLE WAX!
WAX? JEEPERS--THIS IS REALLY BUILDING INTO A MYSTERY! WHERE DID THE WAX COME FROM?
SEE IF YOU CAN GUESS FROM WHAT HAPPENED AFTER-WARDS...
"SHORTLY, THE GANG LANDED--BUT NOT BECAUSE POLICE 'COPTERS FORCED THEM DOWN! INSTEAD..."
THEY HAD A SUR-PRISE GETAWAY PLANNED ON THE GROUND, RANKIN--THROUGH THAT ABANDONED SUBWAY TUNNEL! COME ON...
"DOWN WE WENT--INTO THE OMINOUS SILENCE OF THE GLOOMY OLD SUBWAY TUNNEL..."
NOT A SIGN OF THEM!
BATMAN! HEAR THAT SOUND? I KNOW WHAT IT IS! WE'VE GOT TO WORK FAST!
WHOOSH!
"MOMENTS LATER, A DELUGE OF WATER POURED IN FROM THE TUNNEL'S ROOF..."
CUTE LITTLE PLAN--THE GANG WAS PREPARED TO OPEN A DUCT THAT WOULD FLOOD THE PLACE WITH RIVER WATER--TO CUT OFF ANYBODY FOLLOWING THEM! I BROUGHT AN EXTRA BREATHING MASK--PUT IT ON!
YOU SURE KNOW THAT GANG'S EVERY MOVE! THANKS--BUT I CARRY A MINIATURE BREATHING APPARATUS IN MY UTILITY BELT!
WHOOSH!
9

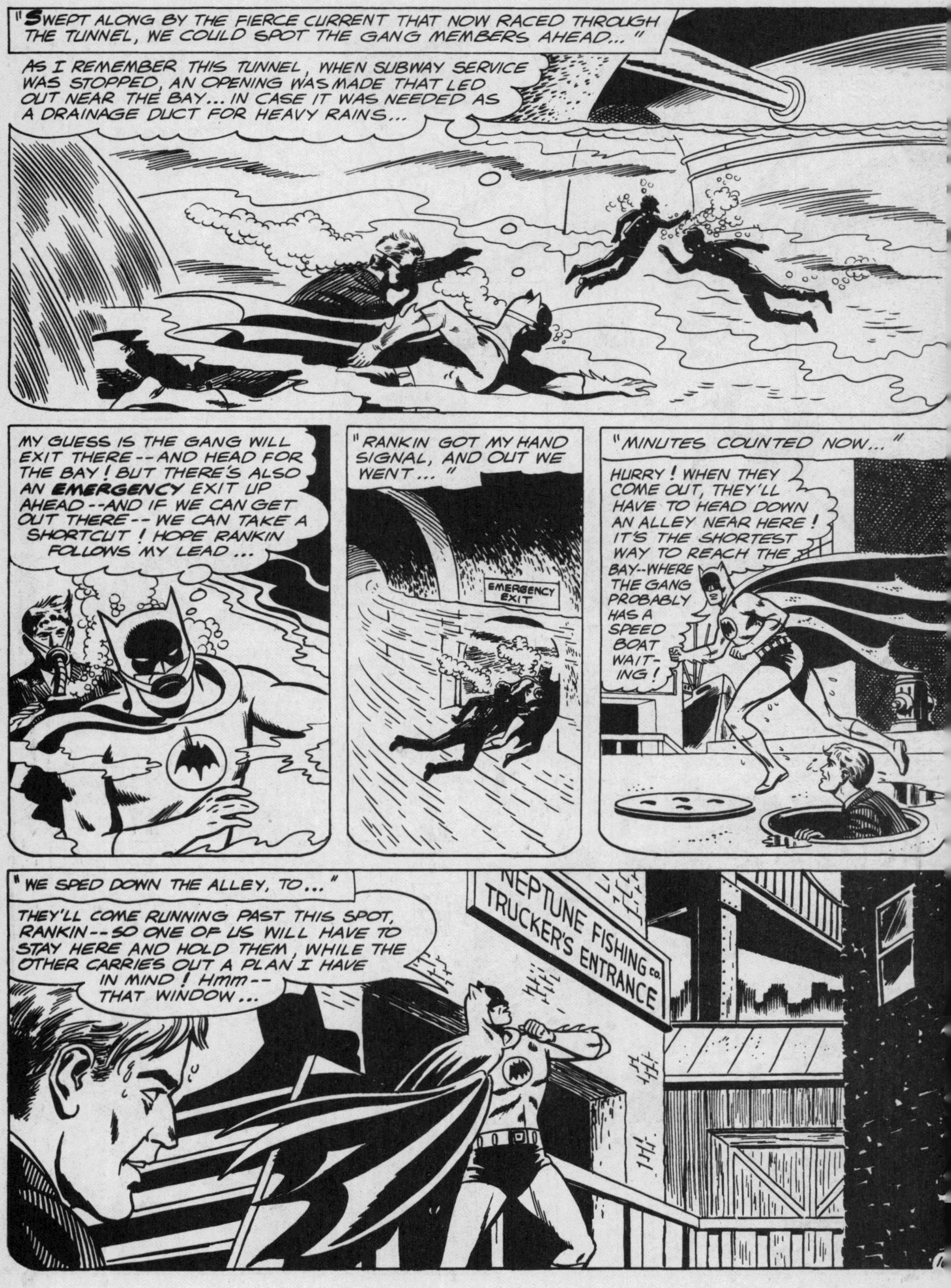
"SWEPT ALONG BY THE FIERCE CURRENT THAT NOW RACED THROUGH THE TUNNEL, WE COULD SPOT THE GANG MEMBERS AHEAD..."
AS I REMEMBER THIS TUNNEL, WHEN SUBWAY SERVICE WAS STOPPED, AN OPENING WAS MADE THAT LED OUT NEAR THE BAY... IN CASE IT WAS NEEDED AS A DRAINAGE DUCT FOR HEAVY RAINS...
MY GUESS IS THE GANG WILL EXIT THERE--AND HEAD FOR THE BAY! BUT THERE'S ALSO AN EMERGENCY EXIT UP AHEAD--AND IF WE CAN GET OUT THERE--WE CAN TAKE A SHORTCUT! HOPE RANKIN FOLLOWS MY LEAD...
"RANKIN GOT MY HAND SIGNAL, AND OUT WE WENT..."
EMERGENCY EXIT
"MINUTES COUNTED NOW..."
HURRY! WHEN THEY COME OUT, THEY'LL HAVE TO HEAD DOWN AN ALLEY NEAR HERE! IT'S THE SHORTEST WAY TO REACH THE BAY--WHERE THE GANG PROBABLY HAS A SPEED BOAT WAITING!
"WE SPED DOWN THE ALLEY, TO..."
THEY'LL COME RUNNING PAST THIS SPOT, RANKIN--SO ONE OF US WILL HAVE TO STAY HERE AND HOLD THEM, WHILE THE OTHER CARRIES OUT A PLAN I HAVE IN MIND! Hmm--THAT WINDOW...
NEPTUNE FISHING CO.
TRUCKER'S ENTRANCE

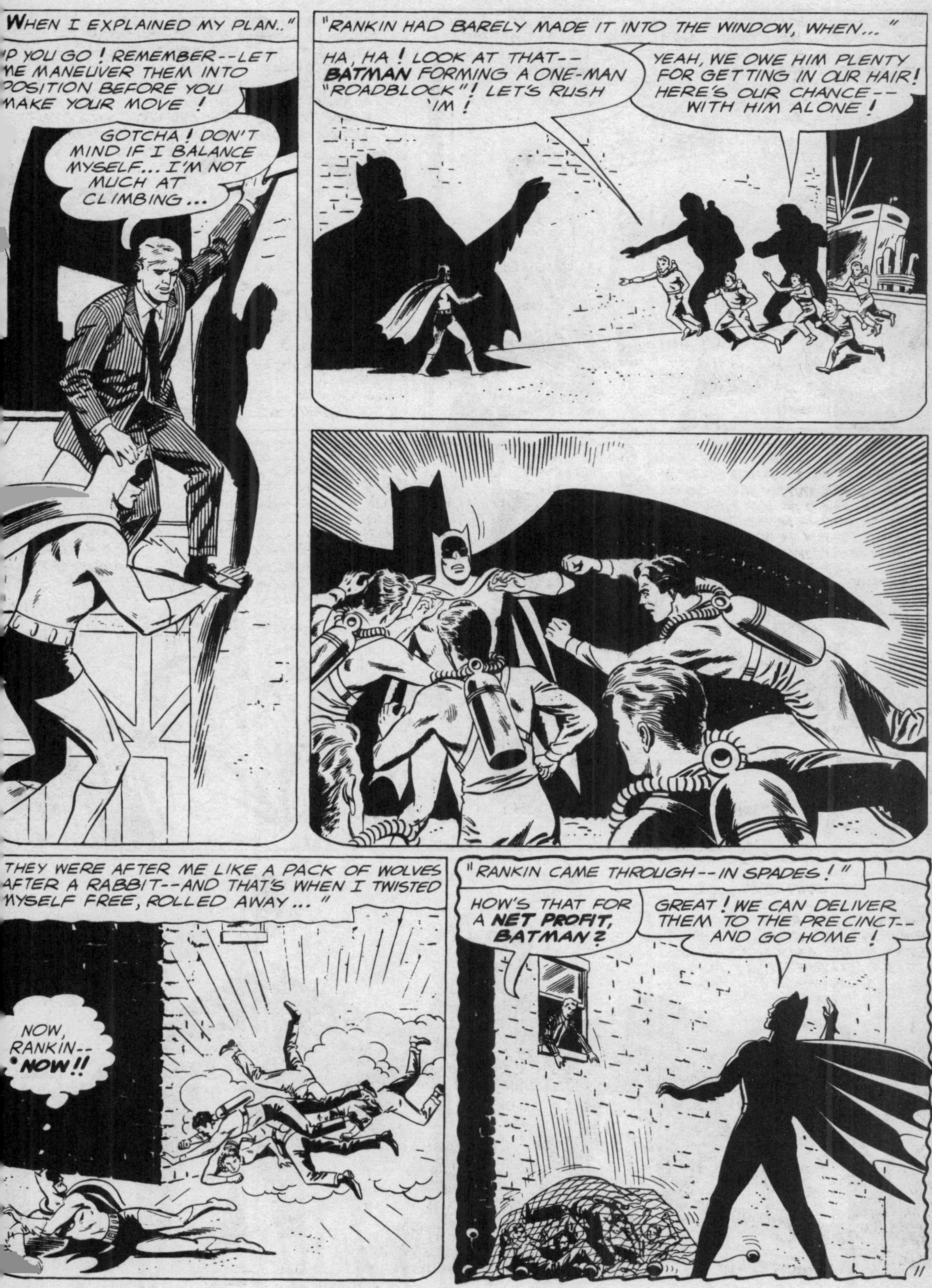
WHEN I EXPLAINED MY PLAN.."
P YOU GO! REMEMBER--LET ME MANEUVER THEM INTO POSITION BEFORE YOU MAKE YOUR MOVE!
GOTCHA! DON'T MIND IF I BALANCE MYSELF... I'M NOT MUCH AT CLIMBING...
"RANKIN HAD BARELY MADE IT INTO THE WINDOW, WHEN..."
HA, HA! LOOK AT THAT-- BATMAN FORMING A ONE-MAN "ROADBLOCK"! LET'S RUSH 'IM!
YEAH, WE OWE HIM PLENTY FOR GETTING IN OUR HAIR! HERE'S OUR CHANCE-- WITH HIM ALONE!
THEY WERE AFTER ME LIKE A PACK OF WOLVES AFTER A RABBIT--AND THAT'S WHEN I TWISTED MYSELF FREE, ROLLED AWAY..."
NOW, RANKIN-- NOW!!
"RANKIN CAME THROUGH--IN SPADES!"
HOW'S THAT FOR A NET PROFIT, BATMAN?
GREAT! WE CAN DELIVER THEM TO THE PRECINCT-- AND GO HOME!
11

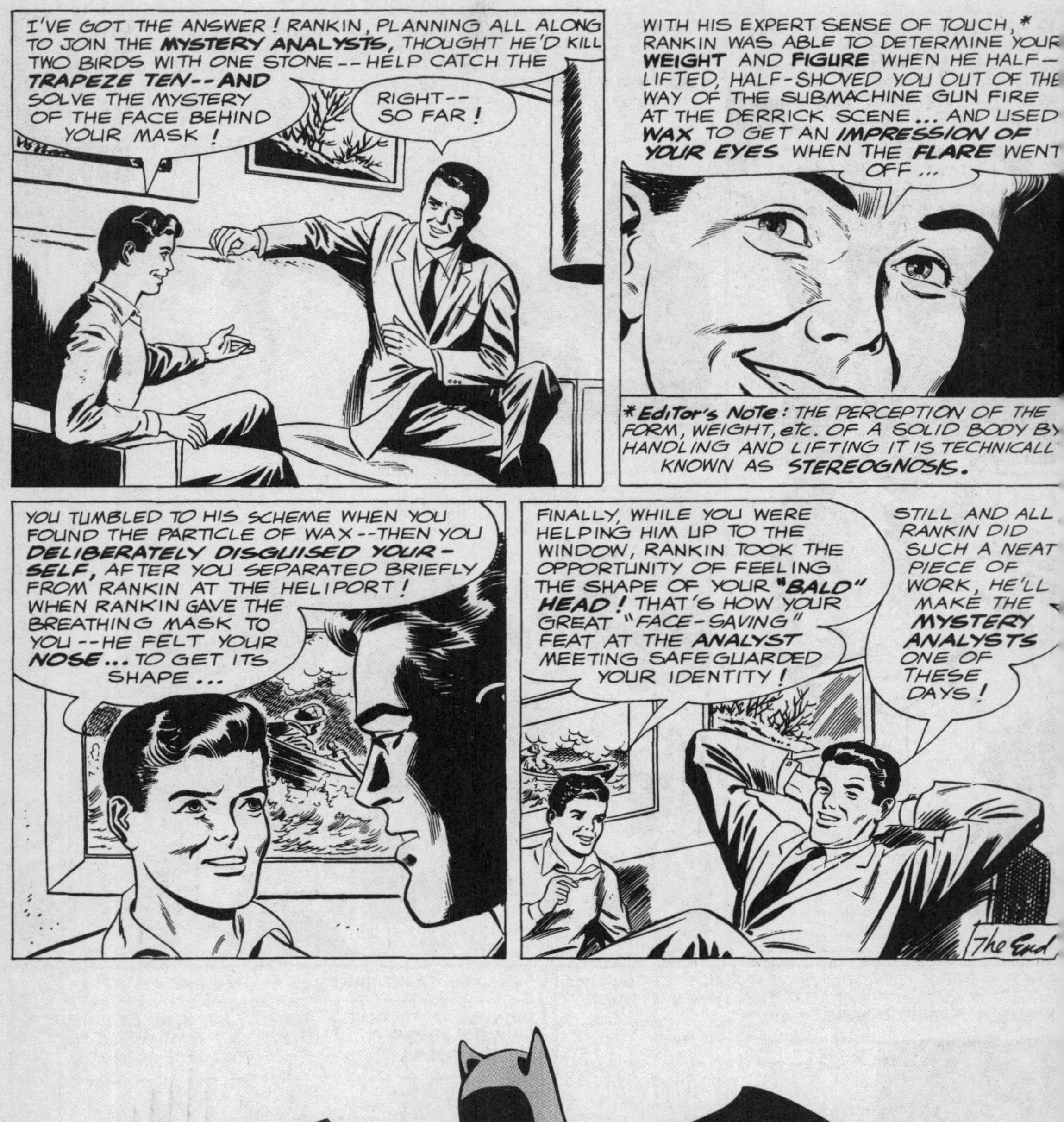
I'VE GOT THE ANSWER! RANKIN, PLANNING ALL ALONG TO JOIN THE MYSTERY ANALYSTS, THOUGHT HE'D KILL TWO BIRDS WITH ONE STONE -- HELP CATCH THE TRAPEZE TEN -- AND SOLVE THE MYSTERY OF THE FACE BEHIND YOUR MASK!
RIGHT -- SO FAR!
WITH HIS EXPERT SENSE OF TOUCH,* RANKIN WAS ABLE TO DETERMINE YOUR WEIGHT AND FIGURE WHEN HE HALF-LIFTED, HALF-SHOVED YOU OUT OF THE WAY OF THE SUBMACHINE GUN FIRE AT THE DERRICK SCENE... AND USED WAX TO GET AN IMPRESSION OF YOUR EYES WHEN THE FLARE WENT OFF...
*Editor's Note: THE PERCEPTION OF THE FORM, WEIGHT, etc. OF A SOLID BODY BY HANDLING AND LIFTING IT IS TECHNICALLY KNOWN AS STEREOGNOSIS.
YOU TUMBLED TO HIS SCHEME WHEN YOU FOUND THE PARTICLE OF WAX -- THEN YOU DELIBERATELY DISGUISED YOURSELF, AFTER YOU SEPARATED BRIEFLY FROM RANKIN AT THE HELIPORT! WHEN RANKIN GAVE THE BREATHING MASK TO YOU -- HE FELT YOUR NOSE... TO GET ITS SHAPE...
FINALLY, WHILE YOU WERE HELPING HIM UP TO THE WINDOW, RANKIN TOOK THE OPPORTUNITY OF FEELING THE SHAPE OF YOUR "BALD" HEAD! THAT'S HOW YOUR GREAT "FACE-SAVING" FEAT AT THE ANALYST MEETING SAFEGUARDED YOUR IDENTITY!
STILL AND ALL, RANKIN DID SUCH A NEAT PIECE OF WORK, HE'LL MAKE THE MYSTERY ANALYSTS ONE OF THESE DAYS!
The End

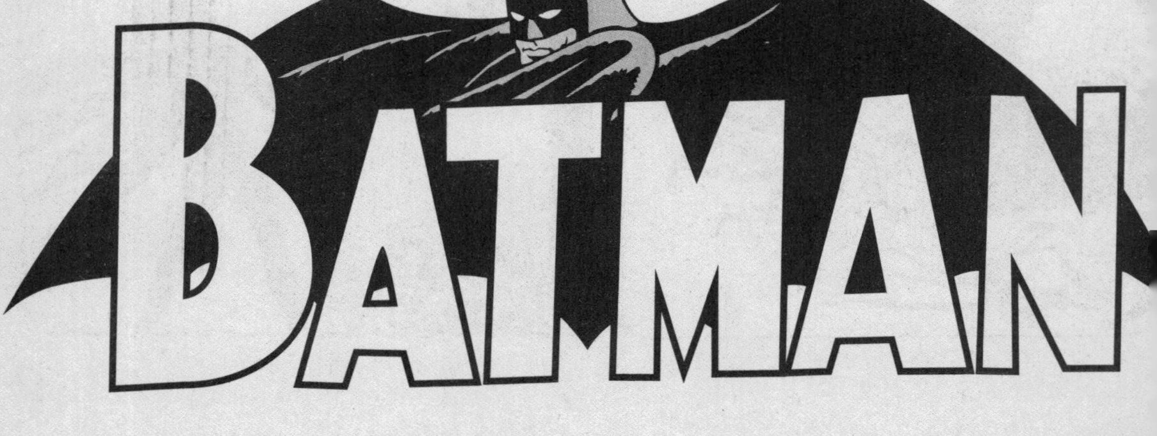
BATMAN

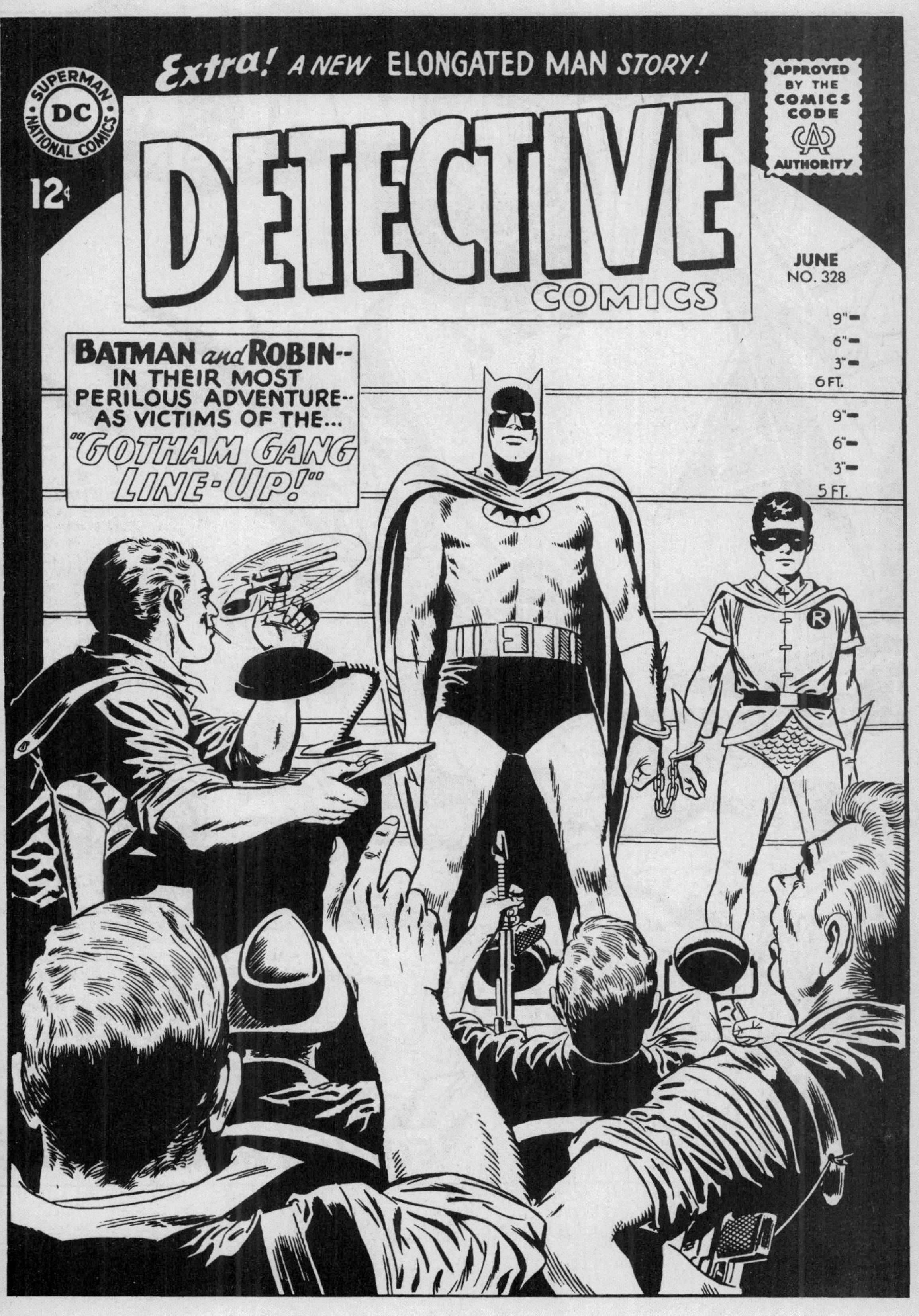
Extra! A NEW ELONGATED MAN STORY!
SUPERMAN DC NATIONAL COMICS
12¢
APPROVED BY THE COMICS CODE AUTHORITY
DETECTIVE COMICS
JUNE NO. 328
BATMAN and ROBIN-- IN THEIR MOST PERILOUS ADVENTURE-- AS VICTIMS OF THE... "GOTHAM GANG LINE-UP!"
9" 6" 3" 6 FT.
9" 6" 3" 5 FT.

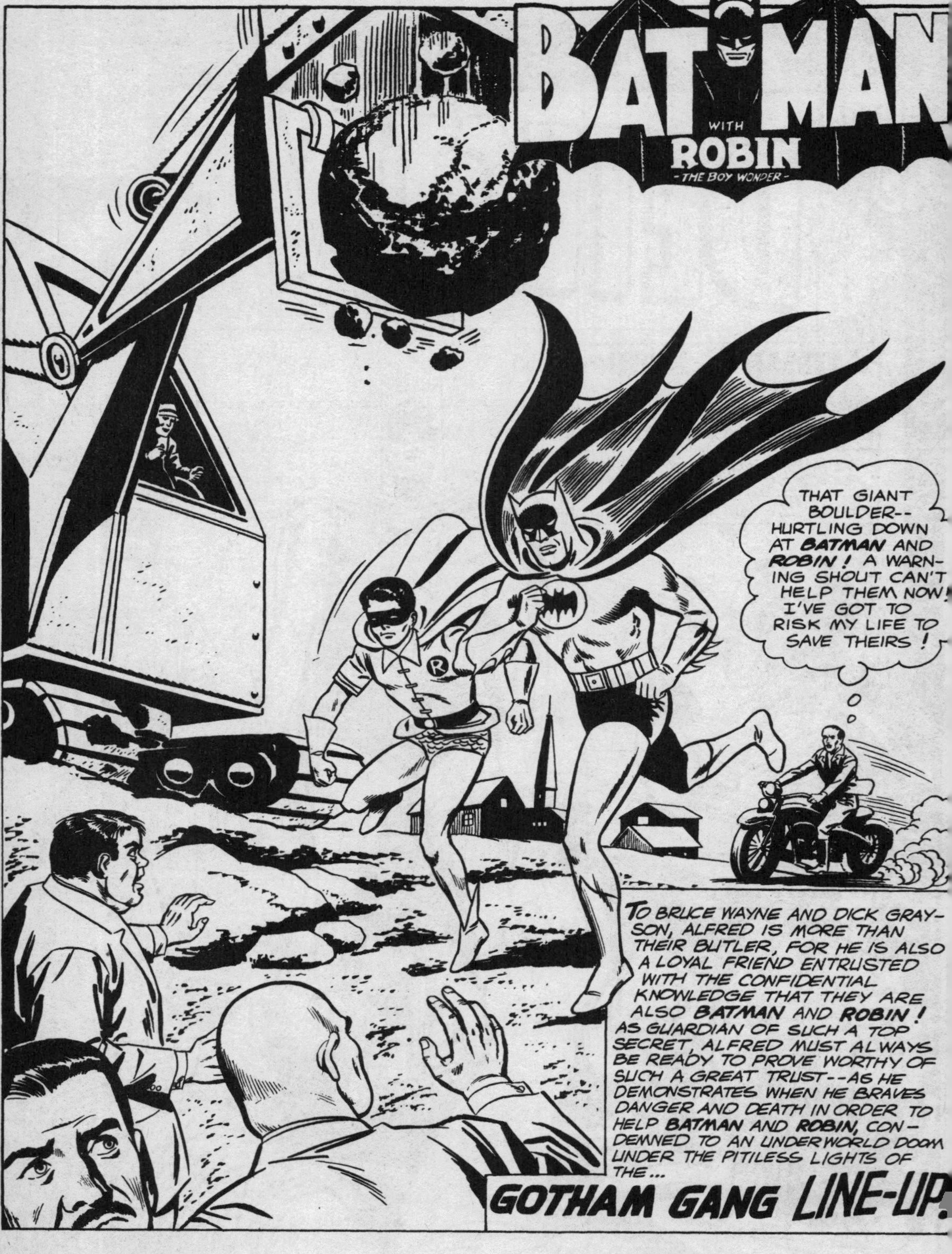
BATMAN
WITH
ROBIN
-THE BOY WONDER-
THAT GIANT BOULDER-- HURTLING DOWN AT BATMAN AND ROBIN! A WARNING SHOUT CAN'T HELP THEM NOW! I'VE GOT TO RISK MY LIFE TO SAVE THEIRS!
TO BRUCE WAYNE AND DICK GRAYSON, ALFRED IS MORE THAN THEIR BUTLER, FOR HE IS ALSO A LOYAL FRIEND ENTRUSTED WITH THE CONFIDENTIAL KNOWLEDGE THAT THEY ARE ALSO BATMAN AND ROBIN! AS GUARDIAN OF SUCH A TOP SECRET, ALFRED MUST ALWAYS BE READY TO PROVE WORTHY OF SUCH A GREAT TRUST--AS HE DEMONSTRATES WHEN HE BRAVES DANGER AND DEATH IN ORDER TO HELP BATMAN AND ROBIN, CONDEMNED TO AN UNDERWORLD DOOM UNDER THE PITILESS LIGHTS OF THE...
GOTHAM GANG LINE-UP!

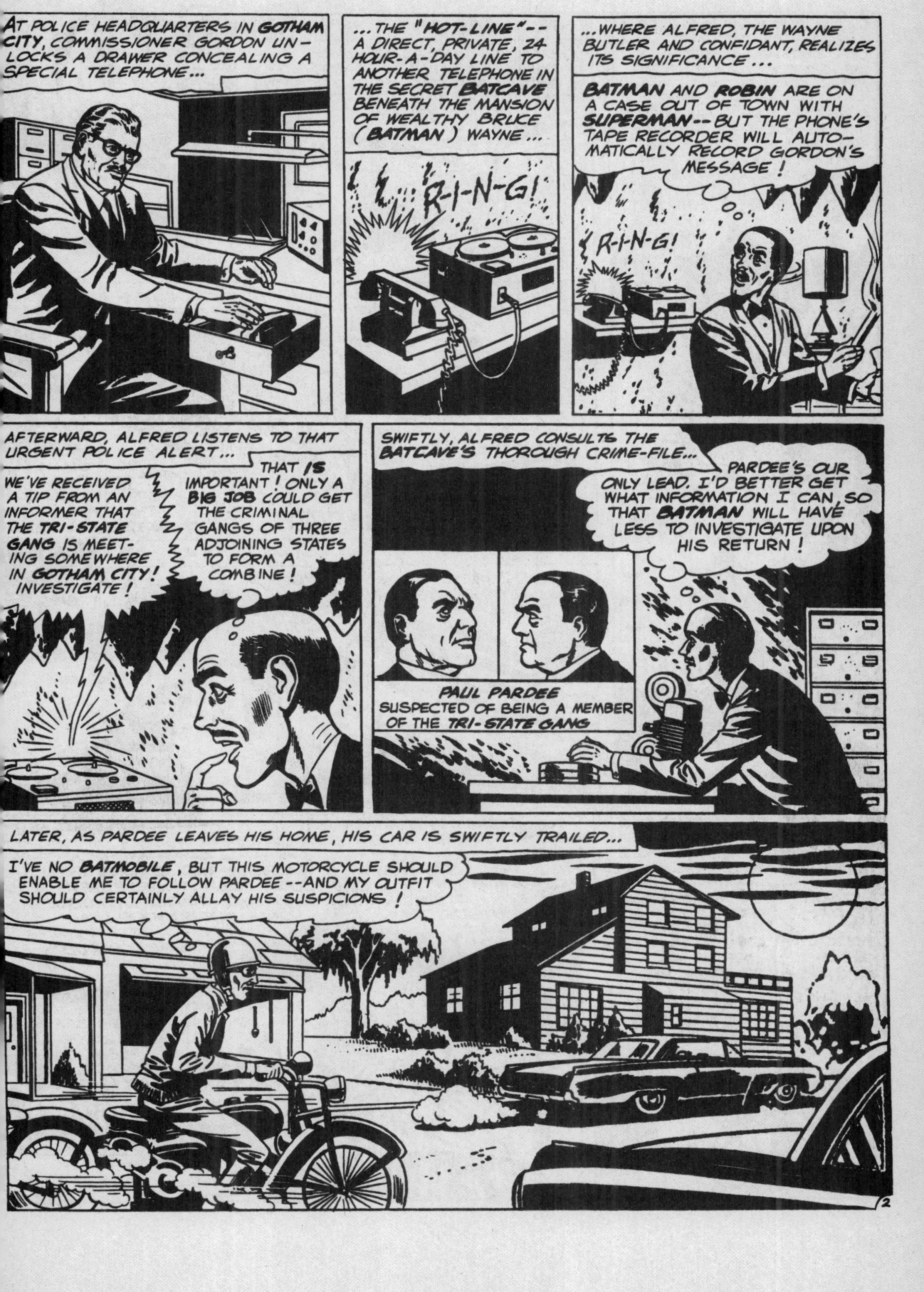
AT POLICE HEADQUARTERS IN GOTHAM CITY, COMMISSIONER GORDON UNLOCKS A DRAWER CONCEALING A SPECIAL TELEPHONE...
...THE "HOT-LINE"--A DIRECT, PRIVATE, 24-HOUR-A-DAY LINE TO ANOTHER TELEPHONE IN THE SECRET BATCAVE BENEATH THE MANSION OF WEALTHY BRUCE (BATMAN) WAYNE...
R-I-N-G!
...WHERE ALFRED, THE WAYNE BUTLER AND CONFIDANT, REALIZES ITS SIGNIFICANCE...
BATMAN AND ROBIN ARE ON A CASE OUT OF TOWN WITH SUPERMAN--BUT THE PHONE'S TAPE RECORDER WILL AUTOMATICALLY RECORD GORDON'S MESSAGE!
R-I-N-G!
AFTERWARD, ALFRED LISTENS TO THAT URGENT POLICE ALERT...
WE'VE RECEIVED A TIP FROM AN INFORMER THAT THE TRI-STATE GANG IS MEETING SOMEWHERE IN GOTHAM CITY! INVESTIGATE!
THAT IS IMPORTANT! ONLY A BIG JOB COULD GET THE CRIMINAL GANGS OF THREE ADJOINING STATES TO FORM A COMBINE!
SWIFTLY, ALFRED CONSULTS THE BATCAVE'S THOROUGH CRIME-FILE...
PARDEE'S OUR ONLY LEAD. I'D BETTER GET WHAT INFORMATION I CAN, SO THAT BATMAN WILL HAVE LESS TO INVESTIGATE UPON HIS RETURN!
PAUL PARDEE
SUSPECTED OF BEING A MEMBER OF THE TRI-STATE GANG
LATER, AS PARDEE LEAVES HIS HOME, HIS CAR IS SWIFTLY TRAILED...
I'VE NO BATMOBILE, BUT THIS MOTORCYCLE SHOULD ENABLE ME TO FOLLOW PARDEE--AND MY OUTFIT SHOULD CERTAINLY ALLAY HIS SUSPICIONS!
2

LATER, *BATMAN* AND *ROBIN* ARRIVE HOME TO FIND GORDON'S RECORDED MESSAGE--AND A MEMO FROM ALFRED...

ALFRED'S GONE TO CHECK ON PARDEE! BUT THAT WAS TWO HOURS AGO, ACCORDING TO THE TIME ON THIS NOTE!

HE SHOULD HAVE RETURNED BY NOW! WE'D BETTER FIND OUT WHY HE HASN'T!

SHORTLY, AT PARDEE'S HOME...

NO SIGN OF ALFRED OR PARDEE IN THE HOUSE AND THE GARAGE IS EMPTY! TOO BAD ALFRED DIDN'T THINK TO LEAVE A TRAIL FOR US TO FOLLOW...

MAYBE HE *DID*-- BUT IN SUCH A WAY THAT IT WOULD NOT BE SEEN BY ANYONE BUT US...

PLAYING A HUNCH, *BATMAN* AIMS THE *BATMOBILE'S* MOVABLE HEADLIGHTS ON THE ROAD-- AND PEERS THROUGH THE CAR'S WINDSHIELD...

I UNDERESTIMATED ALFRED! HE TRAILED PARDEE ON A MOTORCYCLE WHOSE TIRES WERE PREVIOUSLY COATED WITH A SPECIAL *INFRARED* CHEMICAL!

RIGHT! ALFRED KNEW OUR HEADLIGHTS ILLUMINATE THE INFRARED WHICH CAN ONLY BE VIEWED THROUGH OUR *BATMOBILE'S* SPECIAL-FILTER WINDSHIELD.

SOMETIME LATER, THE TRAIL COMES TO AN END AT...

THE OLD GOTHAM PRISON! IT'S BEEN DESERTED FOR YEARS!

MAYBE NOT! IT COULD HAVE BEEN TURNED INTO THE *TRI-STATE GANG'S* SECRET HEADQUARTERS!

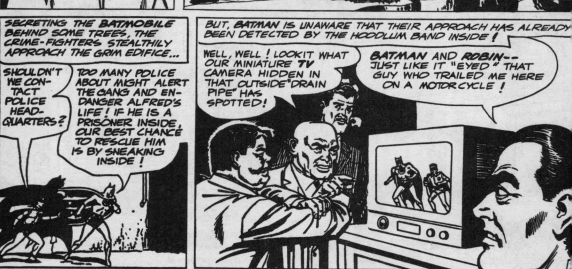

SECRETING THE BATMOBILE BEHIND SOME TREES, THE CRIME-FIGHTERS STEALTHILY APPROACH THE GRIM EDIFICE...

SHOULDN'T WE CON- TACT POLICE HEAD- QUARTERS?

TOO MANY POLICE ABOUT MIGHT ALERT THE GANG AND EN- DANGER ALFRED'S LIFE! IF HE IS A PRISONER INSIDE, OUR BEST CHANCE TO RESCUE HIM IS BY SNEAKING INSIDE!

BUT, BATMAN IS UNAWARE THAT THEIR APPROACH HAS ALREADY BEEN DETECTED BY THE HOODLUM BAND INSIDE!

WELL, WELL! LOOKIT WHAT OUR MINIATURE *TV* CAMERA HIDDEN IN THAT OUTSIDE "DRAIN PIPE" HAS SPOTTED!

BATMAN AND *ROBIN*-- JUST LIKE IT "EYED" THAT GUY WHO TRAILED ME HERE ON A MOTORCYCLE!

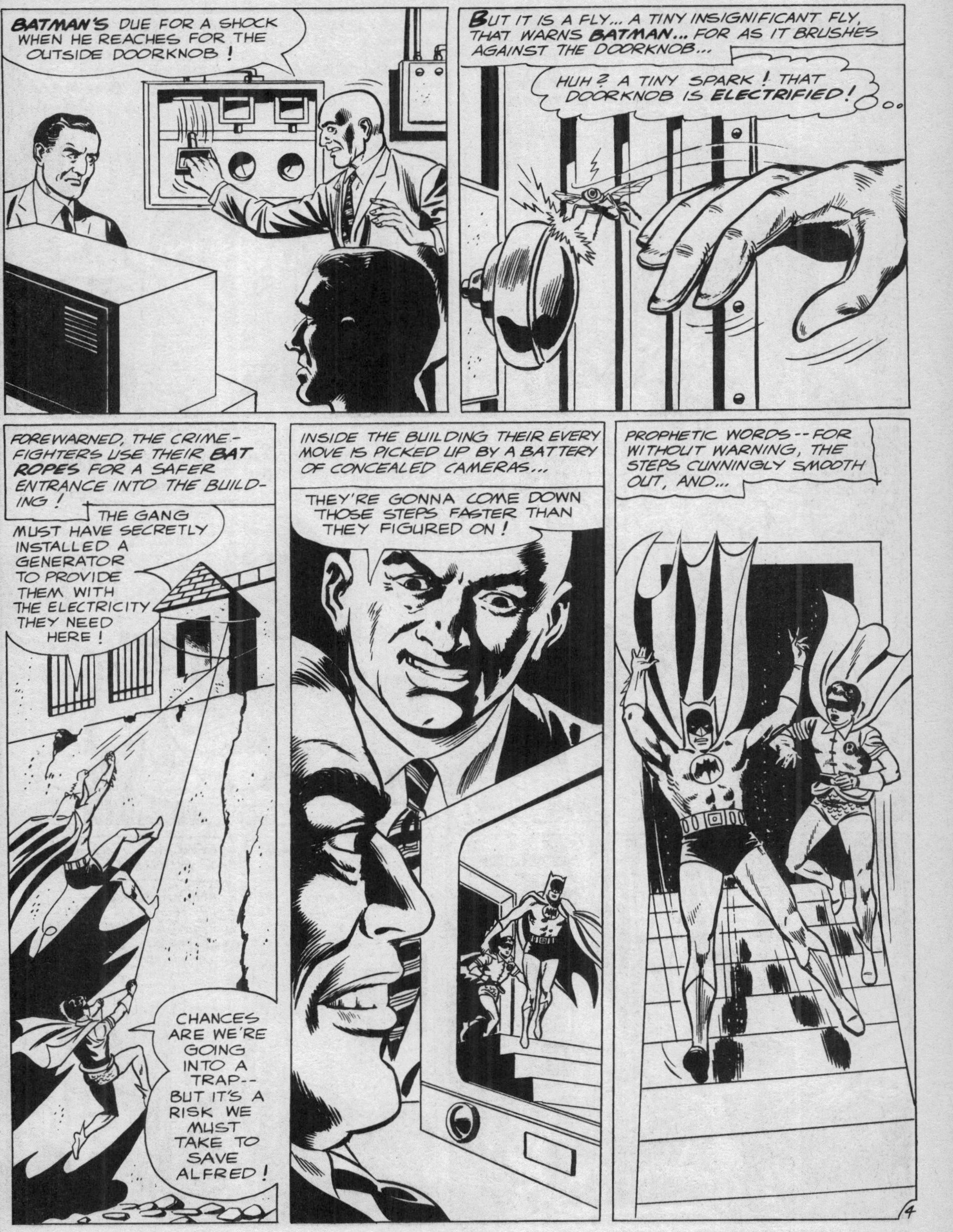
BATMAN'S DUE FOR A SHOCK WHEN HE REACHES FOR THE OUTSIDE DOORKNOB!
BUT IT IS A FLY... A TINY INSIGNIFICANT FLY, THAT WARNS BATMAN... FOR AS IT BRUSHES AGAINST THE DOORKNOB...
HUH? A TINY SPARK! THAT DOORKNOB IS ELECTRIFIED!
FOREWARNED, THE CRIME-FIGHTERS USE THEIR BAT ROPES FOR A SAFER ENTRANCE INTO THE BUILDING!
THE GANG MUST HAVE SECRETLY INSTALLED A GENERATOR TO PROVIDE THEM WITH THE ELECTRICITY THEY NEED HERE!
CHANCES ARE WE'RE GOING INTO A TRAP-- BUT IT'S A RISK WE MUST TAKE TO SAVE ALFRED!
INSIDE THE BUILDING THEIR EVERY MOVE IS PICKED UP BY A BATTERY OF CONCEALED CAMERAS...
THEY'RE GONNA COME DOWN THOSE STEPS FASTER THAN THEY FIGURED ON!
PROPHETIC WORDS--FOR WITHOUT WARNING, THE STEPS CUNNINGLY SMOOTH OUT, AND...
4

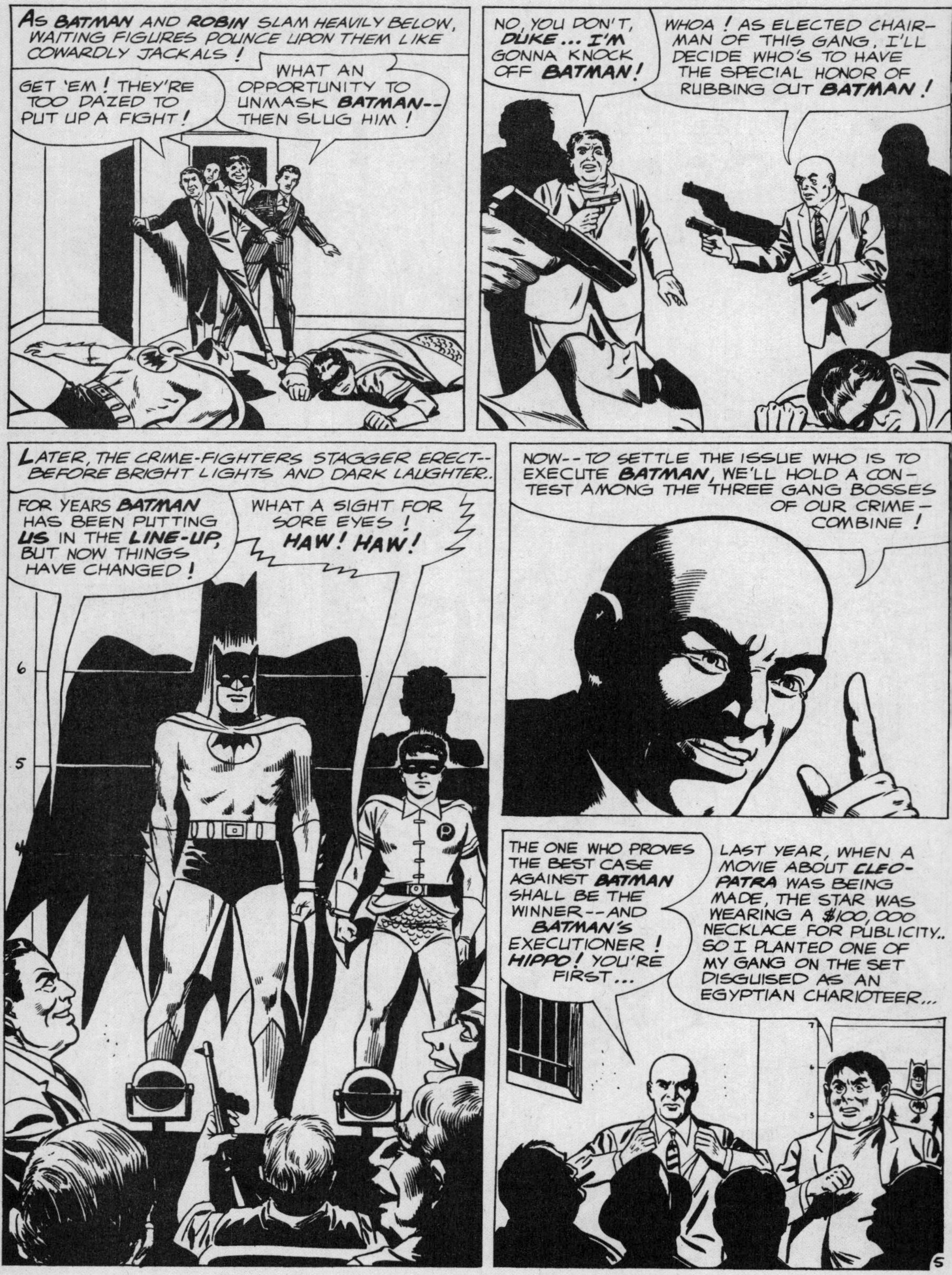
AS BATMAN AND ROBIN SLAM HEAVILY BELOW, WAITING FIGURES POUNCE UPON THEM LIKE COWARDLY JACKALS!
GET 'EM! THEY'RE TOO DAZED TO PUT UP A FIGHT!
WHAT AN OPPORTUNITY TO UNMASK BATMAN-- THEN SLUG HIM!
NO, YOU DON'T, DUKE... I'M GONNA KNOCK OFF BATMAN!
WHOA! AS ELECTED CHAIRMAN OF THIS GANG, I'LL DECIDE WHO'S TO HAVE THE SPECIAL HONOR OF RUBBING OUT BATMAN!
LATER, THE CRIME-FIGHTERS STAGGER ERECT-- BEFORE BRIGHT LIGHTS AND DARK LAUGHTER..
FOR YEARS BATMAN HAS BEEN PUTTING US IN THE LINE-UP, BUT NOW THINGS HAVE CHANGED!
WHAT A SIGHT FOR SORE EYES! HAW! HAW!
NOW--TO SETTLE THE ISSUE WHO IS TO EXECUTE BATMAN, WE'LL HOLD A CONTEST AMONG THE THREE GANG BOSSES OF OUR CRIME-COMBINE!
THE ONE WHO PROVES THE BEST CASE AGAINST BATMAN SHALL BE THE WINNER--AND BATMAN'S EXECUTIONER! HIPPO! YOU'RE FIRST...
LAST YEAR, WHEN A MOVIE ABOUT CLEOPATRA WAS BEING MADE, THE STAR WAS WEARING A $100,000 NECKLACE FOR PUBLICITY.. SO I PLANTED ONE OF MY GANG ON THE SET DISGUISED AS AN EGYPTIAN CHARIOTEER...
5

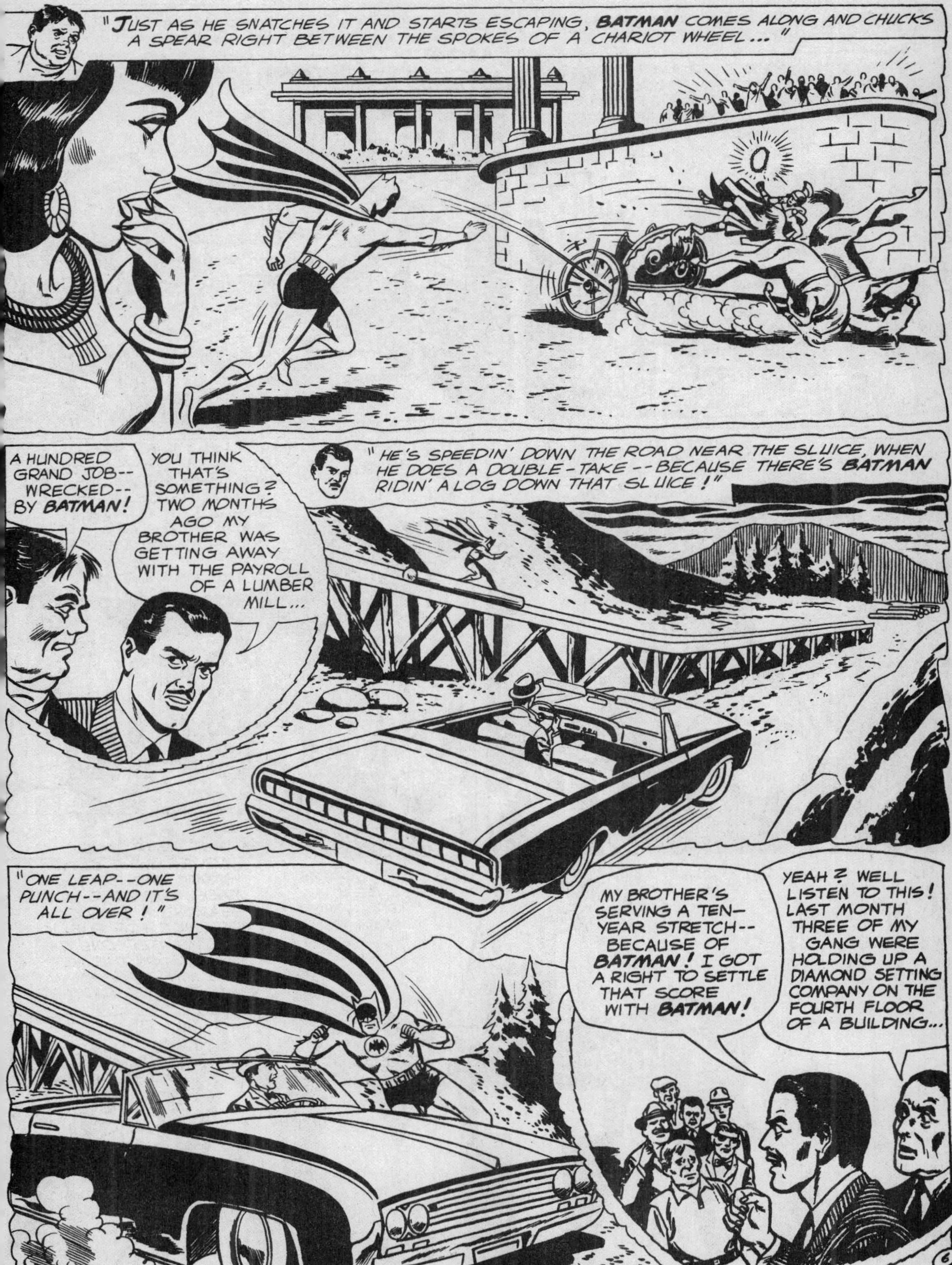
"JUST AS HE SNATCHES IT AND STARTS ESCAPING, BATMAN COMES ALONG AND CHUCKS A SPEAR RIGHT BETWEEN THE SPOKES OF A CHARIOT WHEEL..."
A HUNDRED GRAND JOB-- WRECKED-- BY BATMAN!
YOU THINK THAT'S SOMETHING? TWO MONTHS AGO MY BROTHER WAS GETTING AWAY WITH THE PAYROLL OF A LUMBER MILL...
"HE'S SPEEDIN' DOWN THE ROAD NEAR THE SLUICE, WHEN HE DOES A DOUBLE-TAKE--BECAUSE THERE'S BATMAN RIDIN' A LOG DOWN THAT SLUICE!"
"ONE LEAP--ONE PUNCH--AND IT'S ALL OVER!"
MY BROTHER'S SERVING A TEN-YEAR STRETCH--BECAUSE OF BATMAN! I GOT A RIGHT TO SETTLE THAT SCORE WITH BATMAN!
YEAH? WELL LISTEN TO THIS! LAST MONTH THREE OF MY GANG WERE HOLDING UP A DIAMOND SETTING COMPANY ON THE FOURTH FLOOR OF A BUILDING...
6

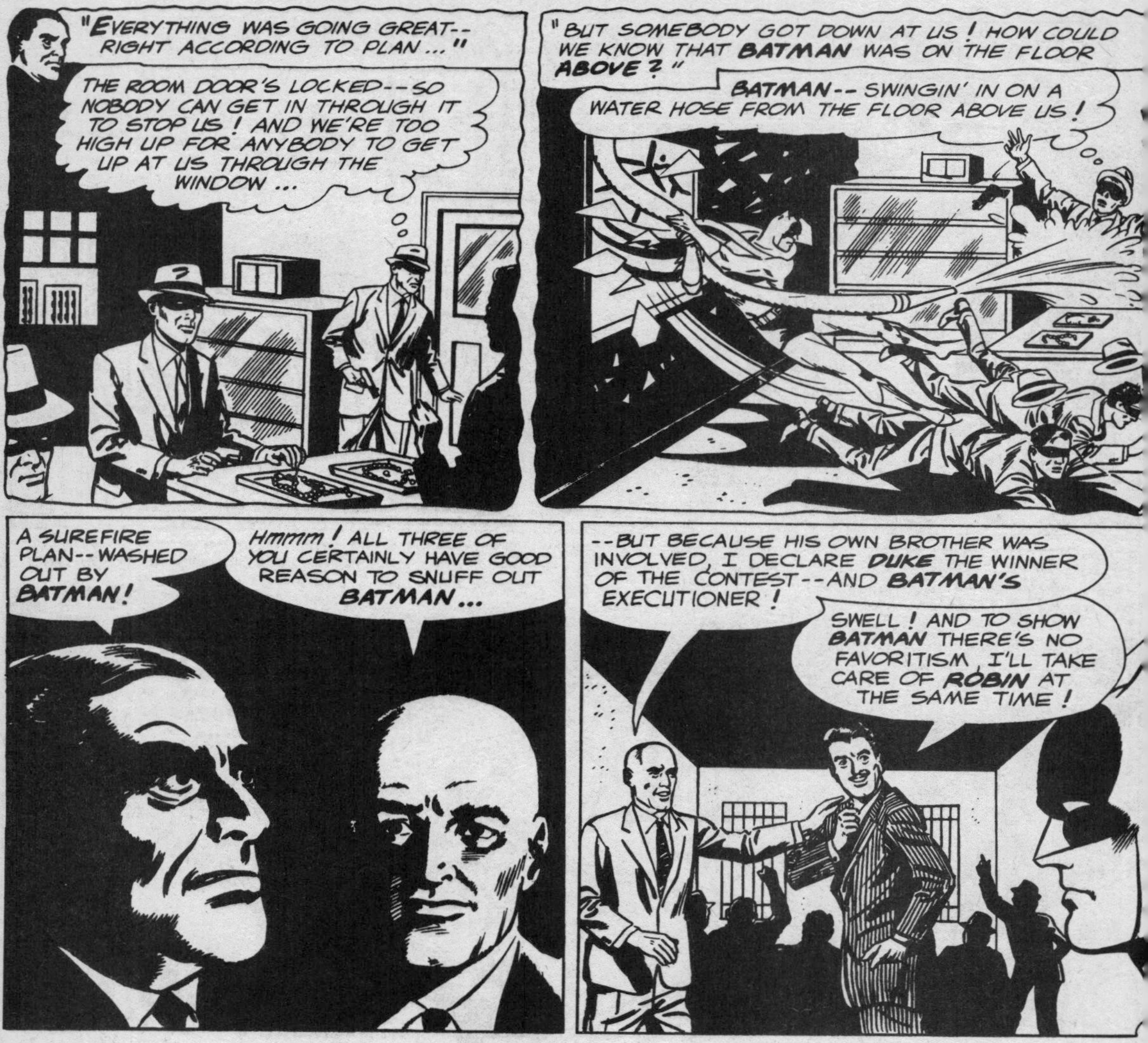
"EVERYTHING WAS GOING GREAT--RIGHT ACCORDING TO PLAN ..."
THE ROOM DOOR'S LOCKED--SO NOBODY CAN GET IN THROUGH IT TO STOP US! AND WE'RE TOO HIGH UP FOR ANYBODY TO GET UP AT US THROUGH THE WINDOW ...
"BUT SOMEBODY GOT DOWN AT US! HOW COULD WE KNOW THAT BATMAN WAS ON THE FLOOR ABOVE?"
BATMAN-- SWINGIN' IN ON A WATER HOSE FROM THE FLOOR ABOVE US!
A SUREFIRE PLAN--WASHED OUT BY BATMAN!
Hmmm! ALL THREE OF YOU CERTAINLY HAVE GOOD REASON TO SNUFF OUT BATMAN...
--BUT BECAUSE HIS OWN BROTHER WAS INVOLVED, I DECLARE DUKE THE WINNER OF THE CONTEST--AND BATMAN'S EXECUTIONER!
SWELL! AND TO SHOW BATMAN THERE'S NO FAVORITISM, I'LL TAKE CARE OF ROBIN AT THE SAME TIME!

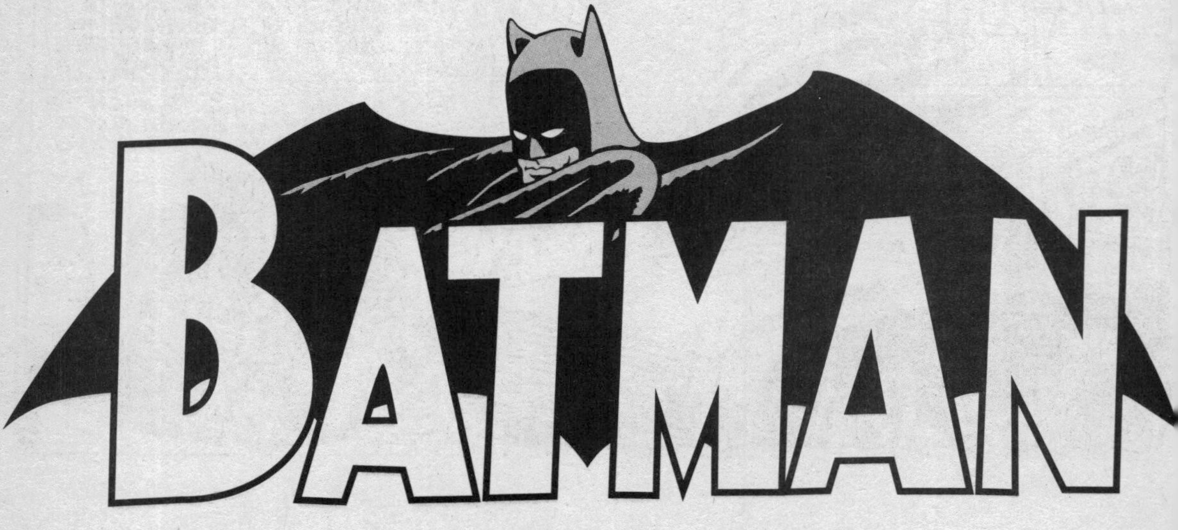
BATMAN

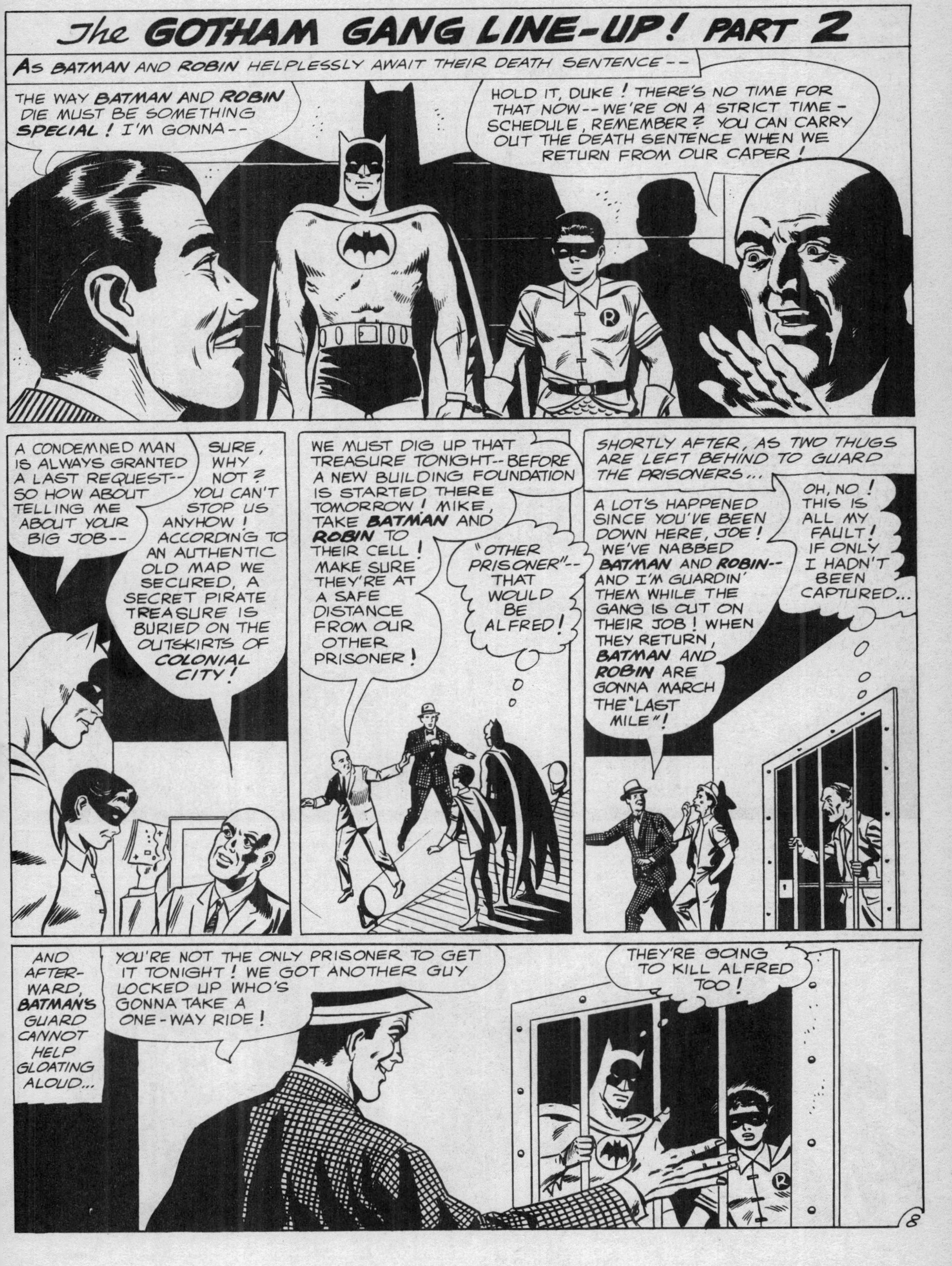
The GOTHAM GANG LINE-UP! PART 2
AS BATMAN AND ROBIN HELPLESSLY AWAIT THEIR DEATH SENTENCE--
THE WAY BATMAN AND ROBIN DIE MUST BE SOMETHING SPECIAL! I'M GONNA--
HOLD IT, DUKE! THERE'S NO TIME FOR THAT NOW--WE'RE ON A STRICT TIME-SCHEDULE, REMEMBER? YOU CAN CARRY OUT THE DEATH SENTENCE WHEN WE RETURN FROM OUR CAPER!
A CONDEMNED MAN IS ALWAYS GRANTED A LAST REQUEST--SO HOW ABOUT TELLING ME ABOUT YOUR BIG JOB--
SURE, WHY NOT? YOU CAN'T STOP US ANYHOW! ACCORDING TO AN AUTHENTIC OLD MAP WE SECURED, A SECRET PIRATE TREASURE IS BURIED ON THE OUTSKIRTS OF COLONIAL CITY!
WE MUST DIG UP THAT TREASURE TONIGHT--BEFORE A NEW BUILDING FOUNDATION IS STARTED THERE TOMORROW! MIKE, TAKE BATMAN AND ROBIN TO THEIR CELL! MAKE SURE THEY'RE AT A SAFE DISTANCE FROM OUR OTHER PRISONER!
"OTHER PRISONER"--THAT WOULD BE ALFRED!
SHORTLY AFTER, AS TWO THUGS ARE LEFT BEHIND TO GUARD THE PRISONERS...
A LOT'S HAPPENED SINCE YOU'VE BEEN DOWN HERE, JOE! WE'VE NABBED BATMAN AND ROBIN--AND I'M GUARDIN' THEM WHILE THE GANG IS OUT ON THEIR JOB! WHEN THEY RETURN, BATMAN AND ROBIN ARE GONNA MARCH THE "LAST MILE"!
OH, NO! THIS IS ALL MY FAULT! IF ONLY I HADN'T BEEN CAPTURED...
AND AFTERWARD, BATMAN'S GUARD CANNOT HELP GLOATING ALOUD...
YOU'RE NOT THE ONLY PRISONER TO GET IT TONIGHT! WE GOT ANOTHER GUY LOCKED UP WHO'S GONNA TAKE A ONE-WAY RIDE!
THEY'RE GOING TO KILL ALFRED TOO!
8

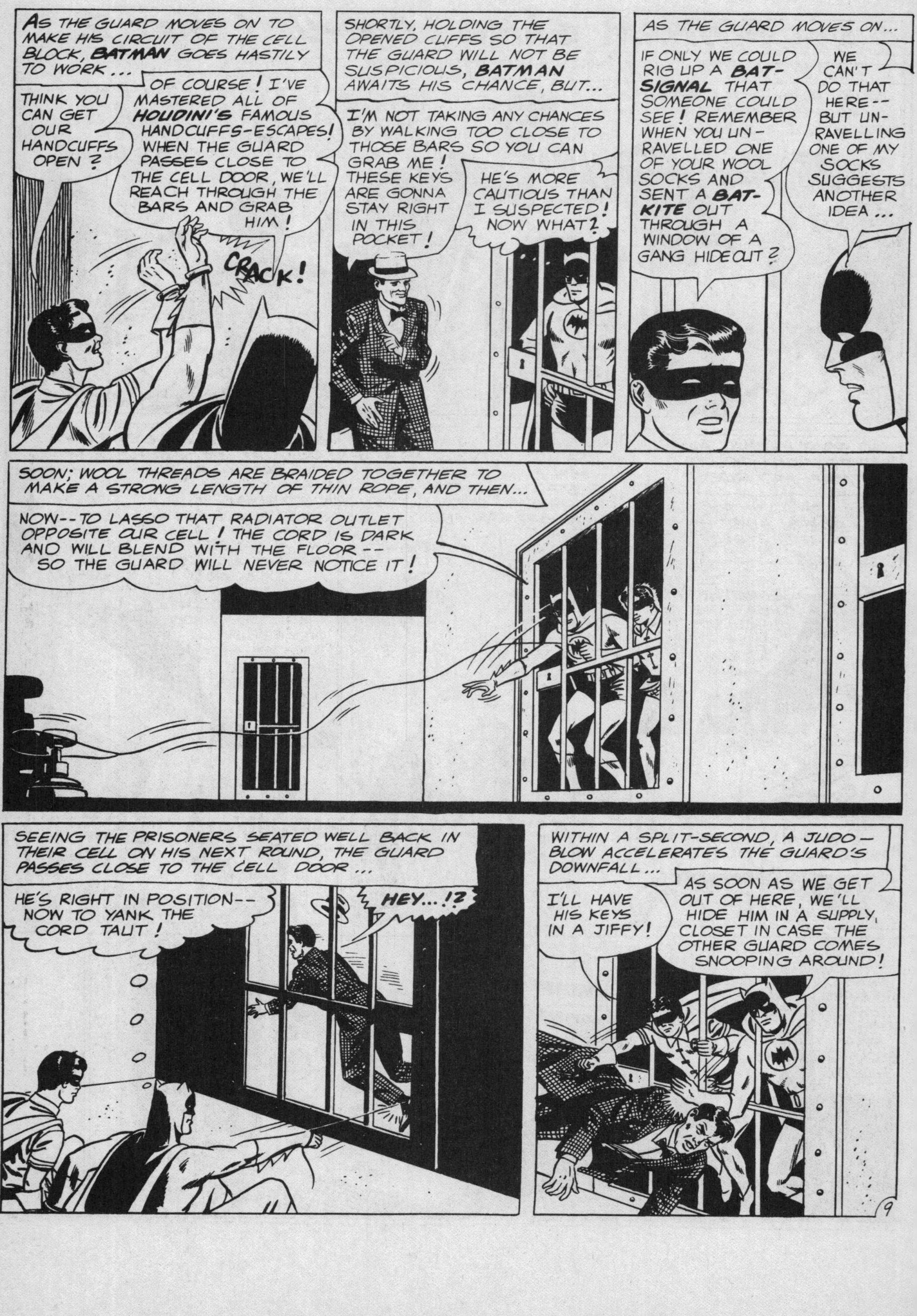
AS THE GUARD MOVES ON TO MAKE HIS CIRCUIT OF THE CELL BLOCK, BATMAN GOES HASTILY TO WORK ...
THINK YOU CAN GET OUR HANDCUFFS OPEN ?
OF COURSE ! I'VE MASTERED ALL OF HOUDINI'S FAMOUS HANDCUFFS-ESCAPES! WHEN THE GUARD PASSES CLOSE TO THE CELL DOOR, WE'LL REACH THROUGH THE BARS AND GRAB HIM !
CRACK!
SHORTLY, HOLDING THE OPENED CUFFS SO THAT THE GUARD WILL NOT BE SUSPICIOUS, BATMAN AWAITS HIS CHANCE, BUT...
I'M NOT TAKING ANY CHANCES BY WALKING TOO CLOSE TO THOSE BARS SO YOU CAN GRAB ME ! THESE KEYS ARE GONNA STAY RIGHT IN THIS POCKET !
HE'S MORE CAUTIOUS THAN I SUSPECTED ! NOW WHAT ?
AS THE GUARD MOVES ON...
IF ONLY WE COULD RIG UP A BAT-SIGNAL THAT SOMEONE COULD SEE ! REMEMBER WHEN YOU UN-RAVELLED ONE OF YOUR WOOL SOCKS AND SENT A BAT-KITE OUT THROUGH A WINDOW OF A GANG HIDEOUT ?
WE CAN'T DO THAT HERE-- BUT UN-RAVELLING ONE OF MY SOCKS SUGGESTS ANOTHER IDEA ...
SOON; WOOL THREADS ARE BRAIDED TOGETHER TO MAKE A STRONG LENGTH OF THIN ROPE, AND THEN...
NOW--TO LASSO THAT RADIATOR OUTLET OPPOSITE OUR CELL ! THE CORD IS DARK AND WILL BLEND WITH THE FLOOR -- SO THE GUARD WILL NEVER NOTICE IT !
SEEING THE PRISONERS SEATED WELL BACK IN THEIR CELL ON HIS NEXT ROUND, THE GUARD PASSES CLOSE TO THE CELL DOOR ...
HE'S RIGHT IN POSITION-- NOW TO YANK THE CORD TAUT !
HEY... !?
WITHIN A SPLIT-SECOND, A JUDO-BLOW ACCELERATES THE GUARD'S DOWNFALL ...
I'LL HAVE HIS KEYS IN A JIFFY!
AS SOON AS WE GET OUT OF HERE, WE'LL HIDE HIM IN A SUPPLY CLOSET IN CASE THE OTHER GUARD COMES SNOOPING AROUND!
9

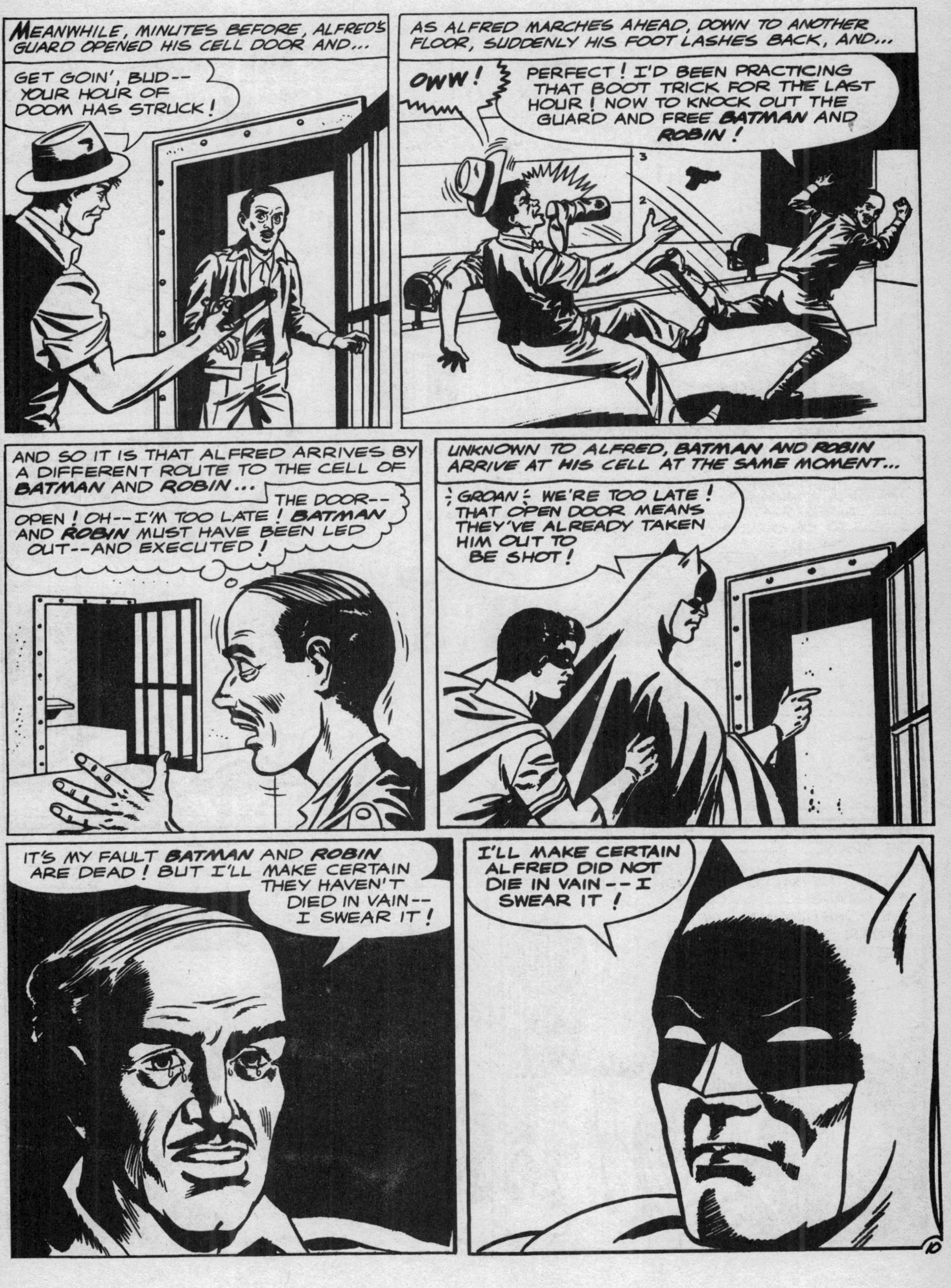
MEANWHILE, MINUTES BEFORE, ALFRED'S GUARD OPENED HIS CELL DOOR AND...
GET GOIN', BUD-- YOUR HOUR OF DOOM HAS STRUCK!
AS ALFRED MARCHES AHEAD, DOWN TO ANOTHER FLOOR, SUDDENLY HIS FOOT LASHES BACK, AND...
OWW!
PERFECT! I'D BEEN PRACTICING THAT BOOT TRICK FOR THE LAST HOUR! NOW TO KNOCK OUT THE GUARD AND FREE BATMAN AND ROBIN!
AND SO IT IS THAT ALFRED ARRIVES BY A DIFFERENT ROUTE TO THE CELL OF BATMAN AND ROBIN...
THE DOOR-- OPEN! OH--I'M TOO LATE! BATMAN AND ROBIN MUST HAVE BEEN LED OUT--AND EXECUTED!
UNKNOWN TO ALFRED, BATMAN AND ROBIN ARRIVE AT HIS CELL AT THE SAME MOMENT...
GROAN WE'RE TOO LATE! THAT OPEN DOOR MEANS THEY'VE ALREADY TAKEN HIM OUT TO BE SHOT!
IT'S MY FAULT BATMAN AND ROBIN ARE DEAD! BUT I'LL MAKE CERTAIN THEY HAVEN'T DIED IN VAIN-- I SWEAR IT!
I'LL MAKE CERTAIN ALFRED DID NOT DIE IN VAIN-- I SWEAR IT!
10

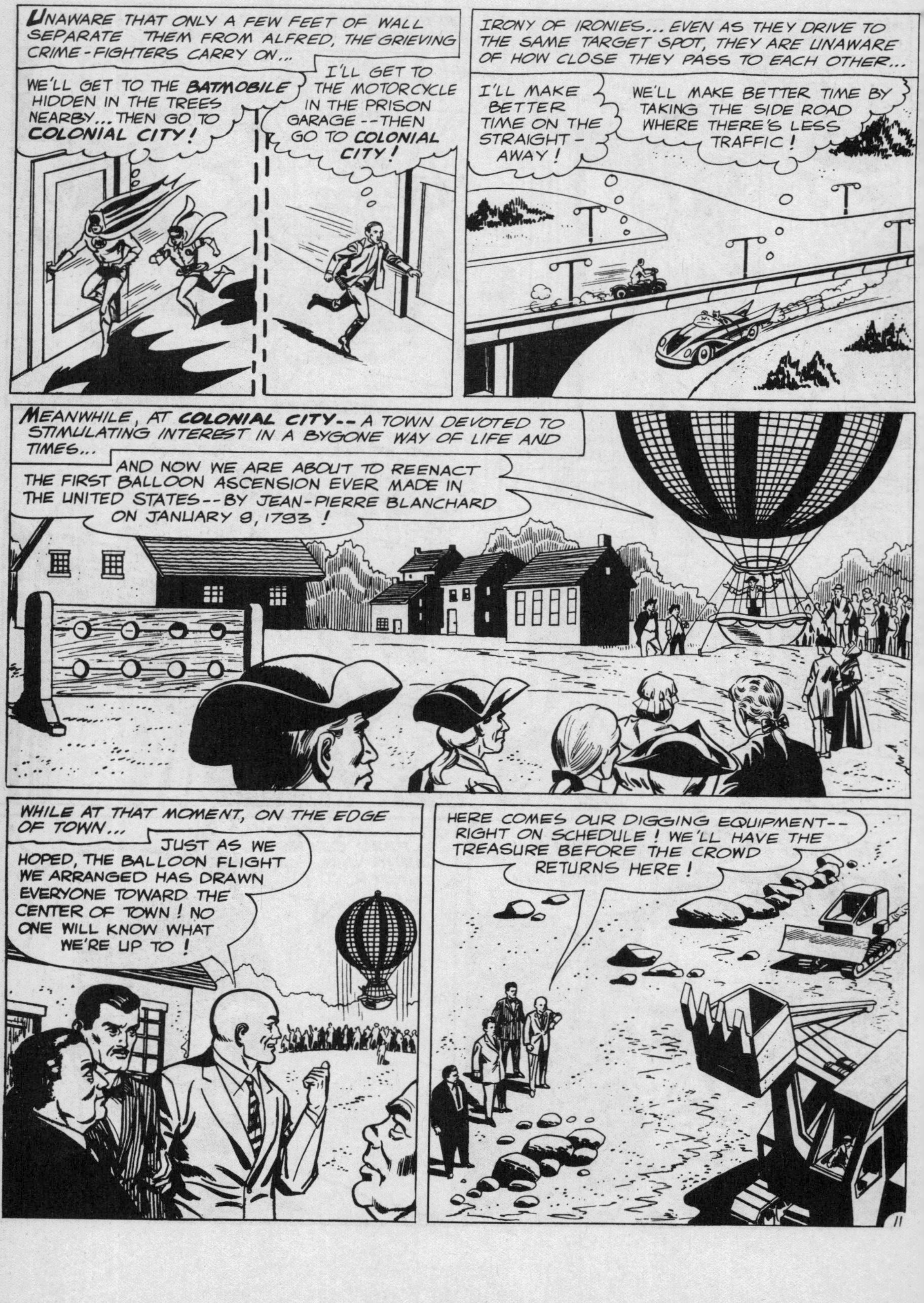
UNAWARE THAT ONLY A FEW FEET OF WALL SEPARATE THEM FROM ALFRED, THE GRIEVING CRIME-FIGHTERS CARRY ON...
WE'LL GET TO THE BATMOBILE HIDDEN IN THE TREES NEARBY... THEN GO TO COLONIAL CITY!
I'LL GET TO THE MOTORCYCLE IN THE PRISON GARAGE--THEN GO TO COLONIAL CITY!
IRONY OF IRONIES... EVEN AS THEY DRIVE TO THE SAME TARGET SPOT, THEY ARE UNAWARE OF HOW CLOSE THEY PASS TO EACH OTHER...
I'LL MAKE BETTER TIME ON THE STRAIGHT-AWAY!
WE'LL MAKE BETTER TIME BY TAKING THE SIDE ROAD WHERE THERE'S LESS TRAFFIC!
MEANWHILE, AT COLONIAL CITY-- A TOWN DEVOTED TO STIMULATING INTEREST IN A BYGONE WAY OF LIFE AND TIMES...
AND NOW WE ARE ABOUT TO REENACT THE FIRST BALLOON ASCENSION EVER MADE IN THE UNITED STATES--BY JEAN-PIERRE BLANCHARD ON JANUARY 9, 1793!
WHILE AT THAT MOMENT, ON THE EDGE OF TOWN...
JUST AS WE HOPED, THE BALLOON FLIGHT WE ARRANGED HAS DRAWN EVERYONE TOWARD THE CENTER OF TOWN! NO ONE WILL KNOW WHAT WE'RE UP TO!
HERE COMES OUR DIGGING EQUIPMENT--RIGHT ON SCHEDULE! WE'LL HAVE THE TREASURE BEFORE THE CROWD RETURNS HERE!
11

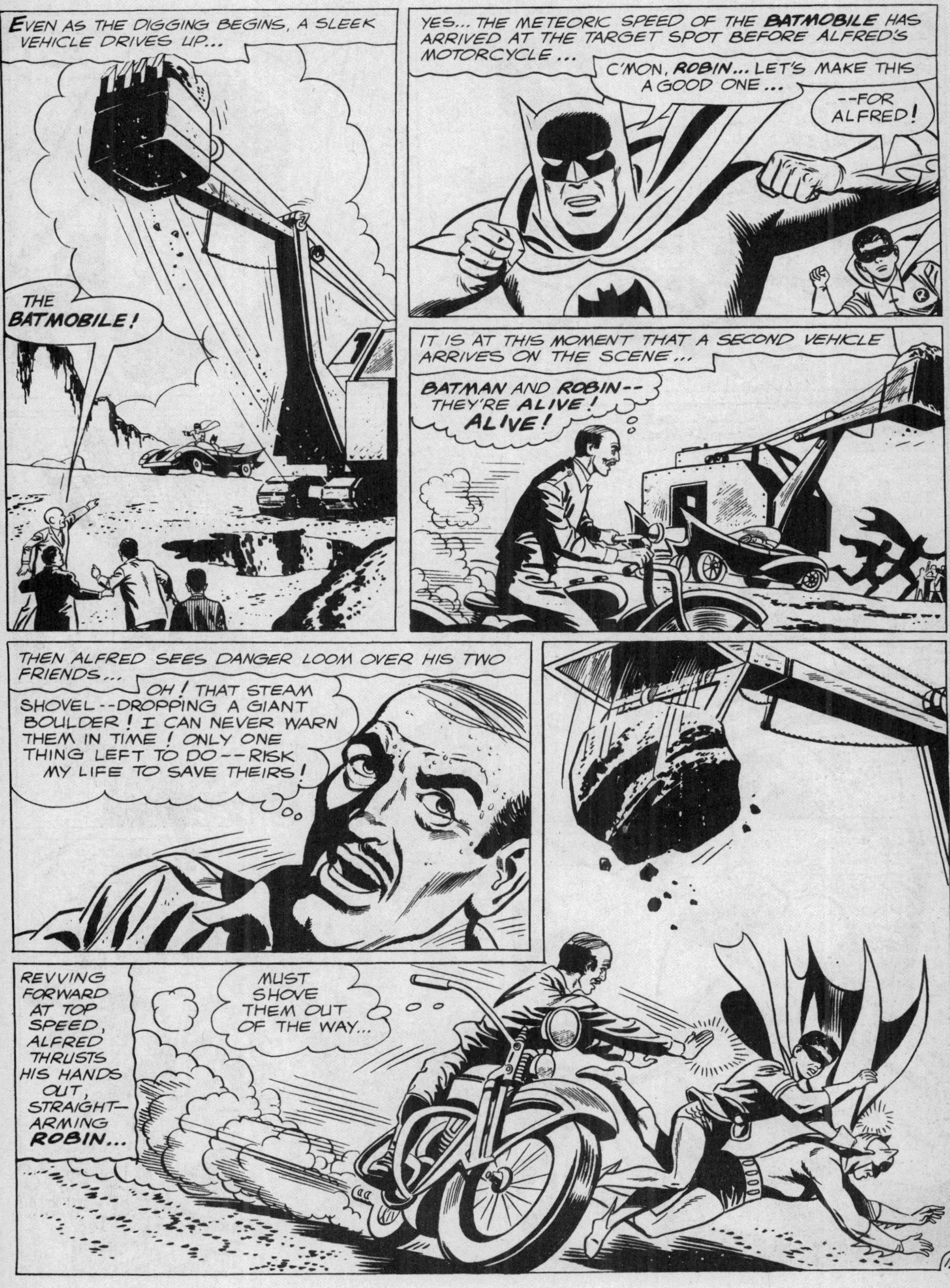
EVEN AS THE DIGGING BEGINS, A SLEEK VEHICLE DRIVES UP...
THE BATMOBILE!
YES... THE METEORIC SPEED OF THE BATMOBILE HAS ARRIVED AT THE TARGET SPOT BEFORE ALFRED'S MOTORCYCLE...
C'MON, ROBIN... LET'S MAKE THIS A GOOD ONE...
--FOR ALFRED!
IT IS AT THIS MOMENT THAT A SECOND VEHICLE ARRIVES ON THE SCENE...
BATMAN AND ROBIN-- THEY'RE ALIVE! ALIVE!
THEN ALFRED SEES DANGER LOOM OVER HIS TWO FRIENDS...
OH! THAT STEAM SHOVEL--DROPPING A GIANT BOULDER! I CAN NEVER WARN THEM IN TIME! ONLY ONE THING LEFT TO DO--RISK MY LIFE TO SAVE THEIRS!
REVVING FORWARD AT TOP SPEED, ALFRED THRUSTS HIS HANDS OUT, STRAIGHT-ARMING ROBIN...
MUST SHOVE THEM OUT OF THE WAY...
12

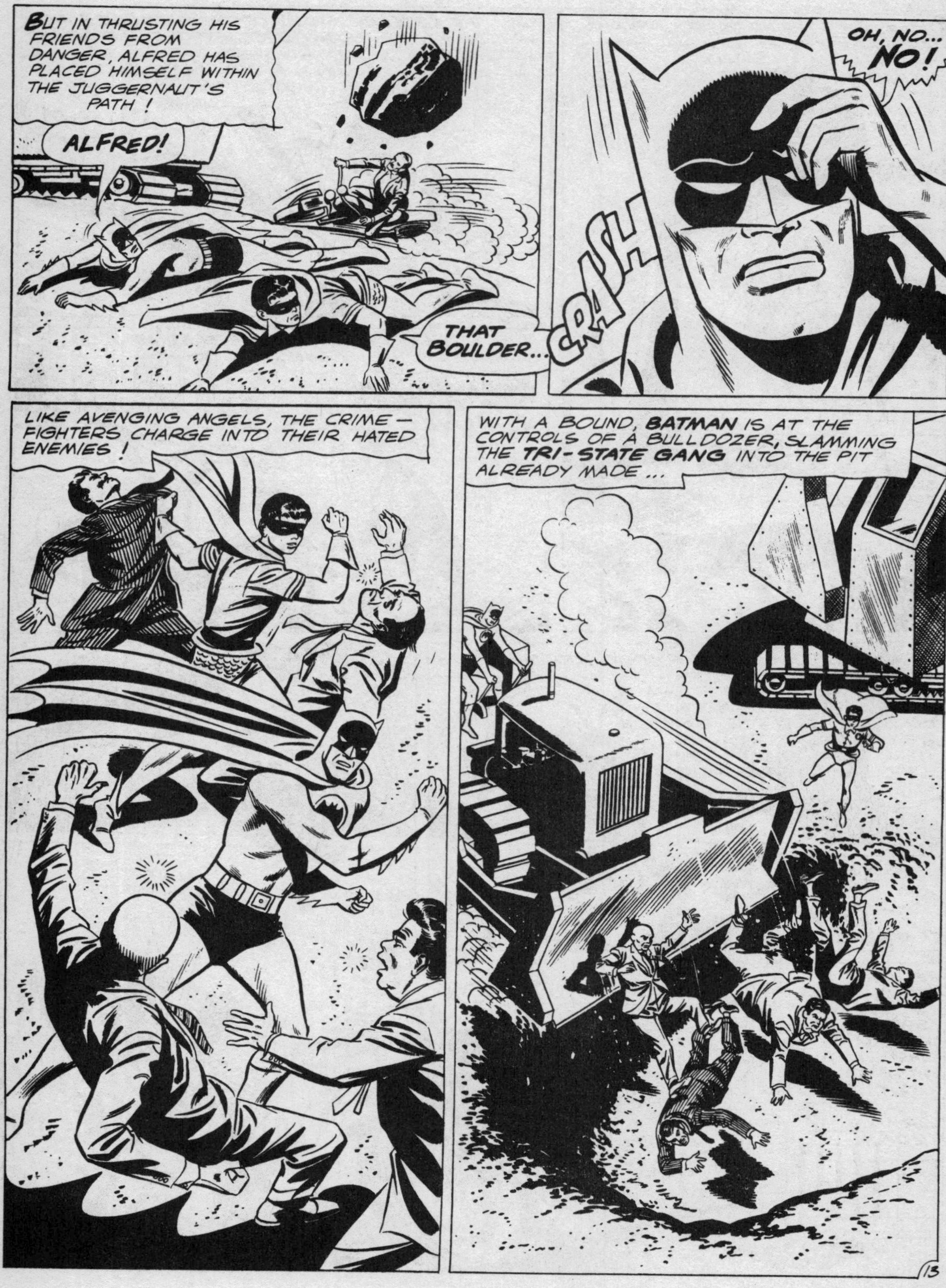
BUT IN THRUSTING HIS FRIENDS FROM DANGER, ALFRED HAS PLACED HIMSELF WITHIN THE JUGGERNAUT'S PATH !
ALFRED!
THAT BOULDER...
CRASH
OH, NO... NO!
LIKE AVENGING ANGELS, THE CRIME-FIGHTERS CHARGE INTO THEIR HATED ENEMIES !
WITH A BOUND, BATMAN IS AT THE CONTROLS OF A BULLDOZER, SLAMMING THE TRI-STATE GANG INTO THE PIT ALREADY MADE ...
13

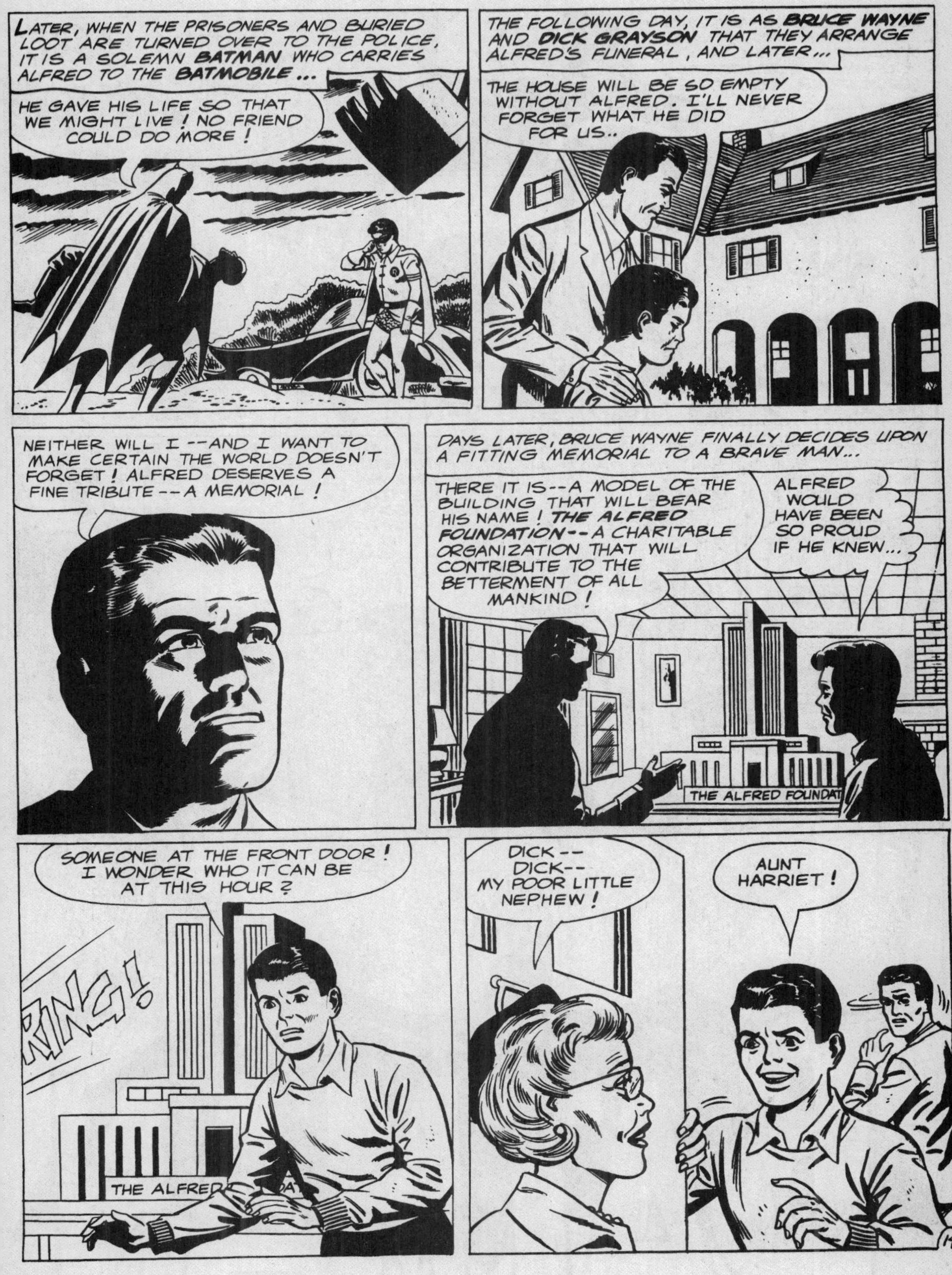
LATER, WHEN THE PRISONERS AND BURIED LOOT ARE TURNED OVER TO THE POLICE, IT IS A SOLEMN BATMAN WHO CARRIES ALFRED TO THE BATMOBILE...
HE GAVE HIS LIFE SO THAT WE MIGHT LIVE! NO FRIEND COULD DO MORE!
THE FOLLOWING DAY, IT IS AS BRUCE WAYNE AND DICK GRAYSON THAT THEY ARRANGE ALFRED'S FUNERAL, AND LATER...
THE HOUSE WILL BE SO EMPTY WITHOUT ALFRED. I'LL NEVER FORGET WHAT HE DID FOR US..
NEITHER WILL I --AND I WANT TO MAKE CERTAIN THE WORLD DOESN'T FORGET! ALFRED DESERVES A FINE TRIBUTE -- A MEMORIAL!
DAYS LATER, BRUCE WAYNE FINALLY DECIDES UPON A FITTING MEMORIAL TO A BRAVE MAN...
THERE IT IS--A MODEL OF THE BUILDING THAT WILL BEAR HIS NAME! THE ALFRED FOUNDATION--A CHARITABLE ORGANIZATION THAT WILL CONTRIBUTE TO THE BETTERMENT OF ALL MANKIND!
ALFRED WOULD HAVE BEEN SO PROUD IF HE KNEW...
THE ALFRED FOUNDAT
SOMEONE AT THE FRONT DOOR! I WONDER WHO IT CAN BE AT THIS HOUR?
RING!
THE ALFRED
DICK-- DICK-- MY POOR LITTLE NEPHEW!
AUNT HARRIET!
14

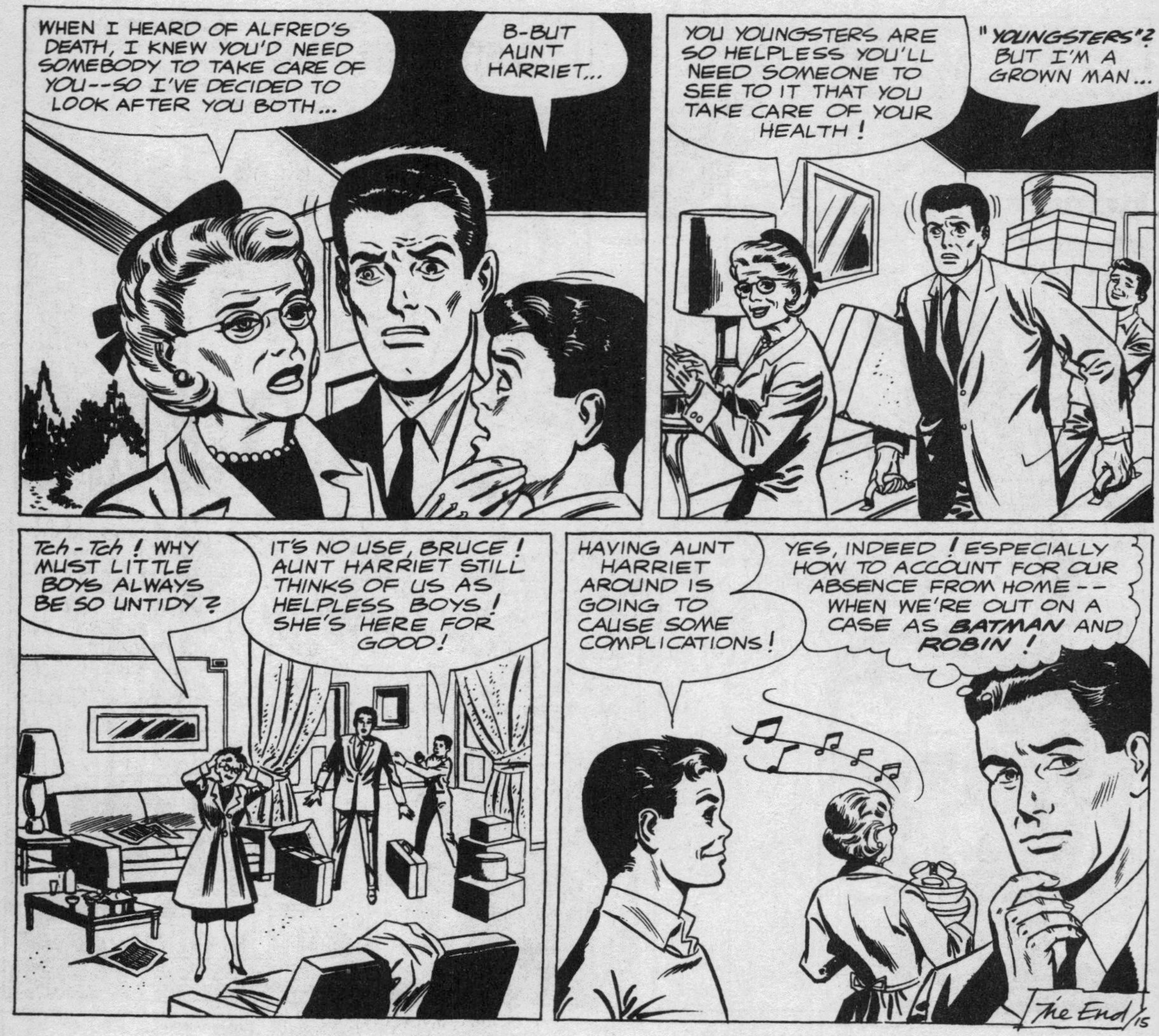
WHEN I HEARD OF ALFRED'S DEATH, I KNEW YOU'D NEED SOMEBODY TO TAKE CARE OF YOU--SO I'VE DECIDED TO LOOK AFTER YOU BOTH...
B-BUT AUNT HARRIET...
YOU YOUNGSTERS ARE SO HELPLESS YOU'LL NEED SOMEONE TO SEE TO IT THAT YOU TAKE CARE OF YOUR HEALTH!
"YOUNGSTERS"? BUT I'M A GROWN MAN...
Tch-Tch! WHY MUST LITTLE BOYS ALWAYS BE SO UNTIDY?
IT'S NO USE, BRUCE! AUNT HARRIET STILL THINKS OF US AS HELPLESS BOYS! SHE'S HERE FOR GOOD!
HAVING AUNT HARRIET AROUND IS GOING TO CAUSE SOME COMPLICATIONS!
YES, INDEED! ESPECIALLY HOW TO ACCOUNT FOR OUR ABSENCE FROM HOME--WHEN WE'RE OUT ON A CASE AS BATMAN AND ROBIN!
The End
15

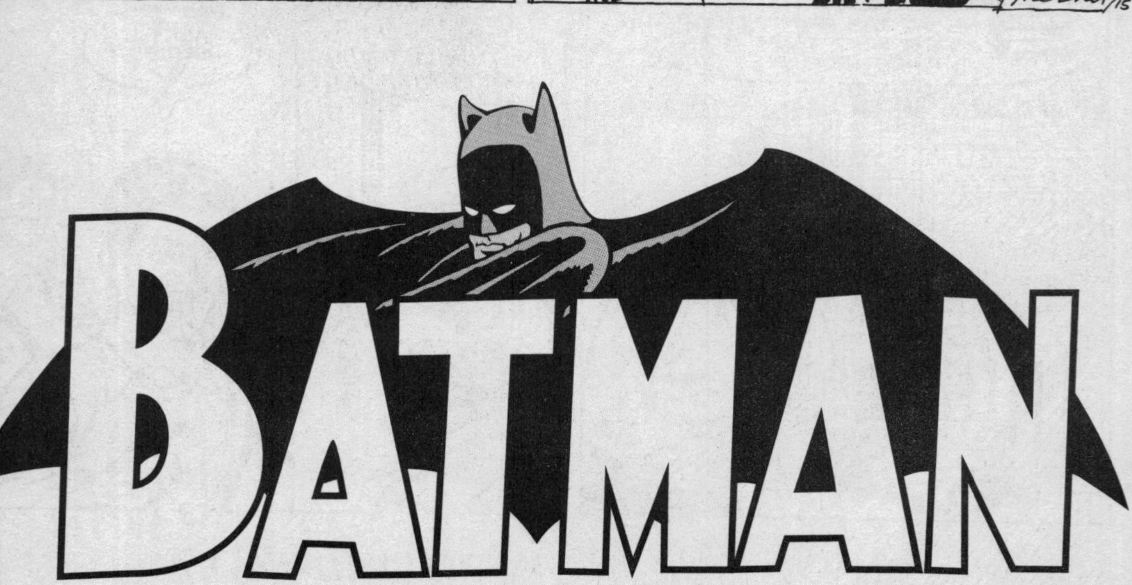
BATMAN

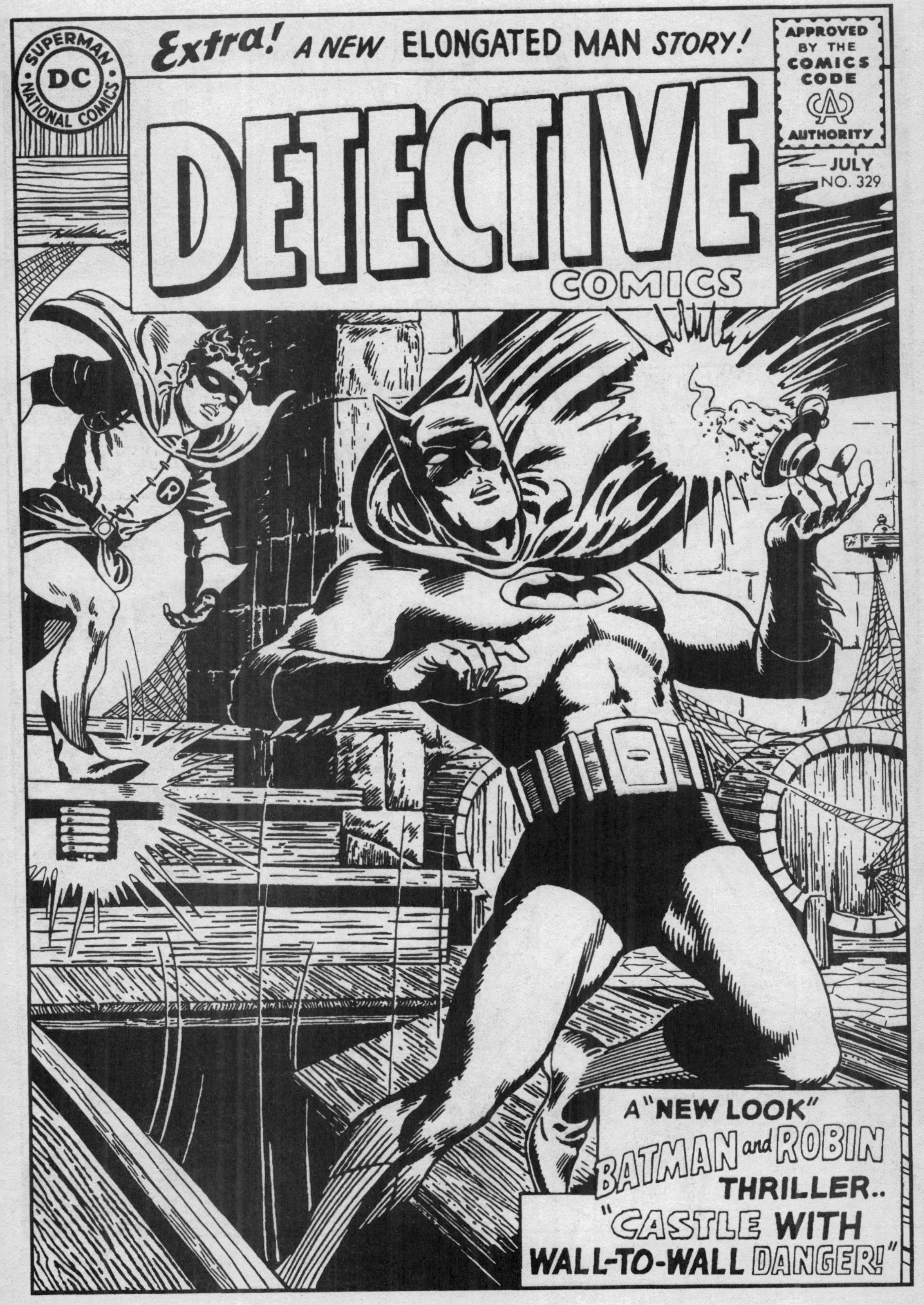
Extra! A NEW ELONGATED MAN STORY!
SUPERMAN DC NATIONAL COMICS
APPROVED BY THE COMICS CODE AUTHORITY
DETECTIVE COMICS
JULY NO. 329
A "NEW LOOK" BATMAN and ROBIN THRILLER.. "CASTLE WITH WALL-TO-WALL DANGER!"

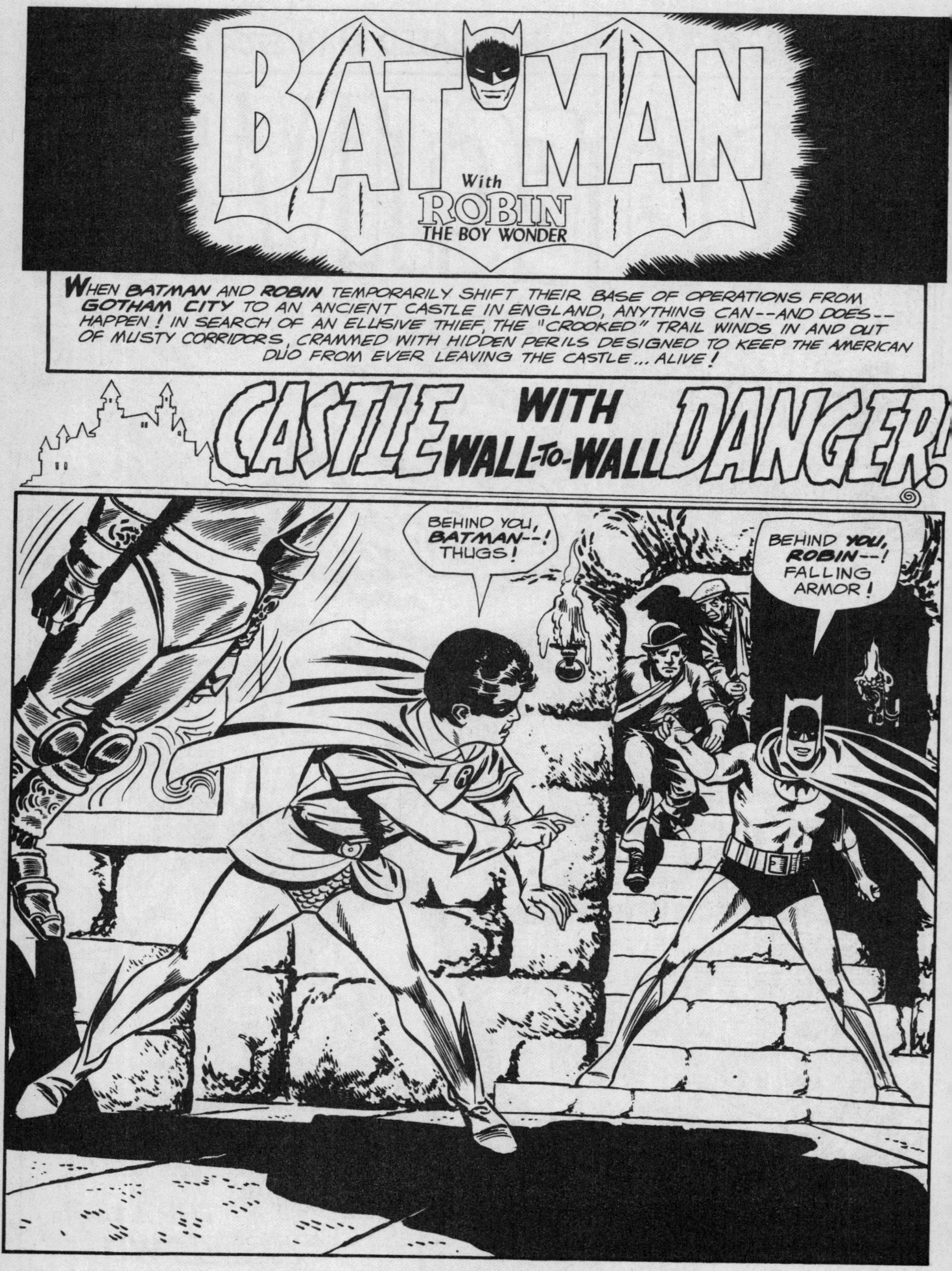
BATMAN
With
ROBIN
THE BOY WONDER
WHEN BATMAN AND ROBIN TEMPORARILY SHIFT THEIR BASE OF OPERATIONS FROM GOTHAM CITY TO AN ANCIENT CASTLE IN ENGLAND, ANYTHING CAN--AND DOES--HAPPEN! IN SEARCH OF AN ELUSIVE THIEF, THE "CROOKED" TRAIL WINDS IN AND OUT OF MUSTY CORRIDORS, CRAMMED WITH HIDDEN PERILS DESIGNED TO KEEP THE AMERICAN DUO FROM EVER LEAVING THE CASTLE... ALIVE!
CASTLE WITH WALL-TO-WALL DANGER!
BEHIND YOU, BATMAN--! THUGS!
BEHIND YOU, ROBIN--! FALLING ARMOR!

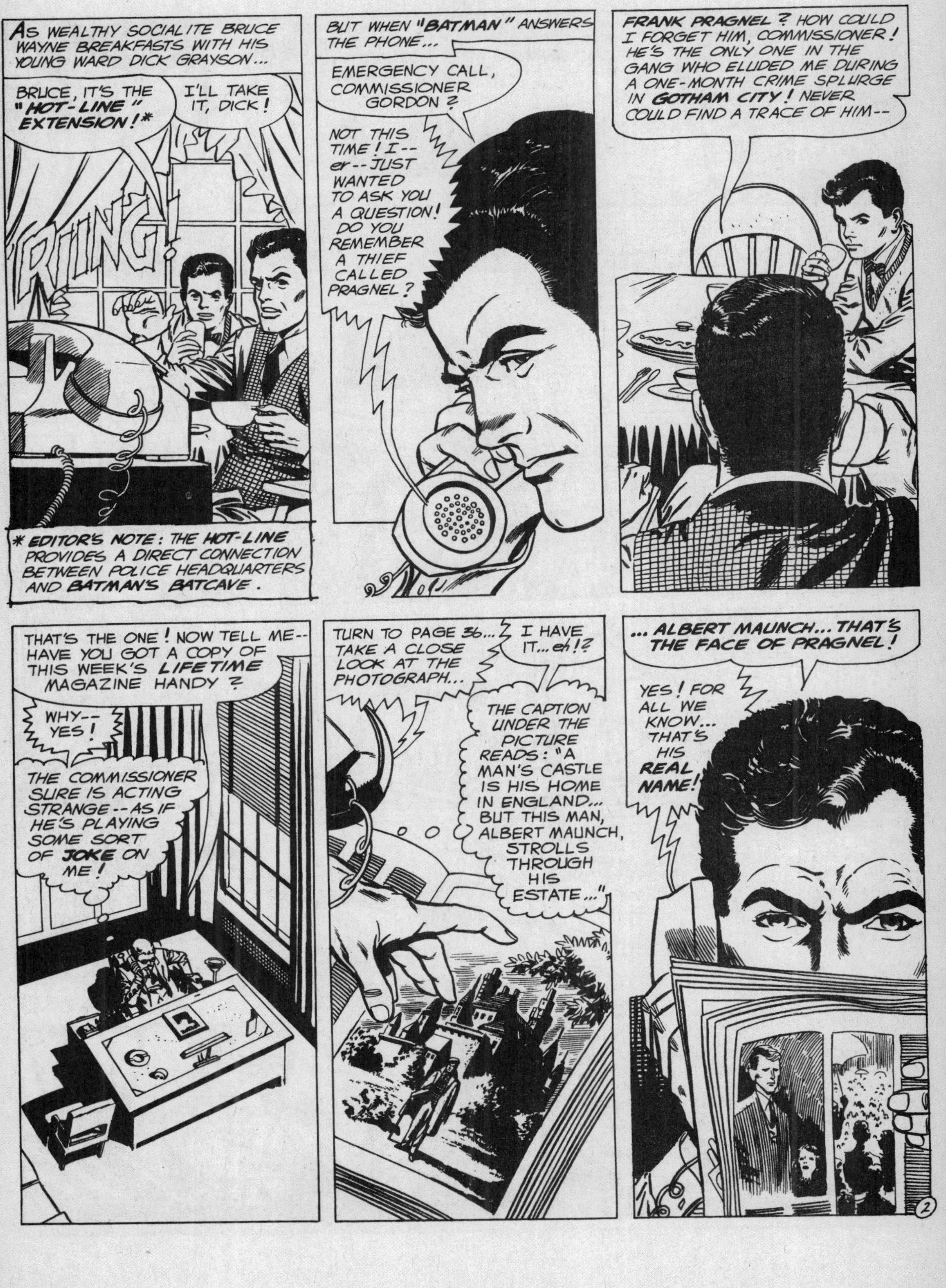
AS WEALTHY SOCIALITE BRUCE WAYNE BREAKFASTS WITH HIS YOUNG WARD DICK GRAYSON...
BRUCE, IT'S THE "HOT-LINE" EXTENSION!*
I'LL TAKE IT, DICK!
R-R-RING!
* EDITOR'S NOTE: THE HOT-LINE PROVIDES A DIRECT CONNECTION BETWEEN POLICE HEADQUARTERS AND BATMAN'S BATCAVE.
BUT WHEN "BATMAN" ANSWERS THE PHONE...
EMERGENCY CALL, COMMISSIONER GORDON?
NOT THIS TIME! I-- er--JUST WANTED TO ASK YOU A QUESTION! DO YOU REMEMBER A THIEF CALLED PRAGNEL?
FRANK PRAGNEL? HOW COULD I FORGET HIM, COMMISSIONER! HE'S THE ONLY ONE IN THE GANG WHO ELUDED ME DURING A ONE-MONTH CRIME SPLURGE IN GOTHAM CITY! NEVER COULD FIND A TRACE OF HIM--
THAT'S THE ONE! NOW TELL ME-- HAVE YOU GOT A COPY OF THIS WEEK'S LIFETIME MAGAZINE HANDY?
WHY-- YES!
THE COMMISSIONER SURE IS ACTING STRANGE--AS IF HE'S PLAYING SOME SORT OF JOKE ON ME!
TURN TO PAGE 36... TAKE A CLOSE LOOK AT THE PHOTOGRAPH...
I HAVE IT... eh!?
THE CAPTION UNDER THE PICTURE READS: "A MAN'S CASTLE IS HIS HOME IN ENGLAND... BUT THIS MAN, ALBERT MAUNCH, STROLLS THROUGH HIS ESTATE..."
...ALBERT MAUNCH...THAT'S THE FACE OF PRAGNEL!
YES! FOR ALL WE KNOW... THAT'S HIS REAL NAME!
2

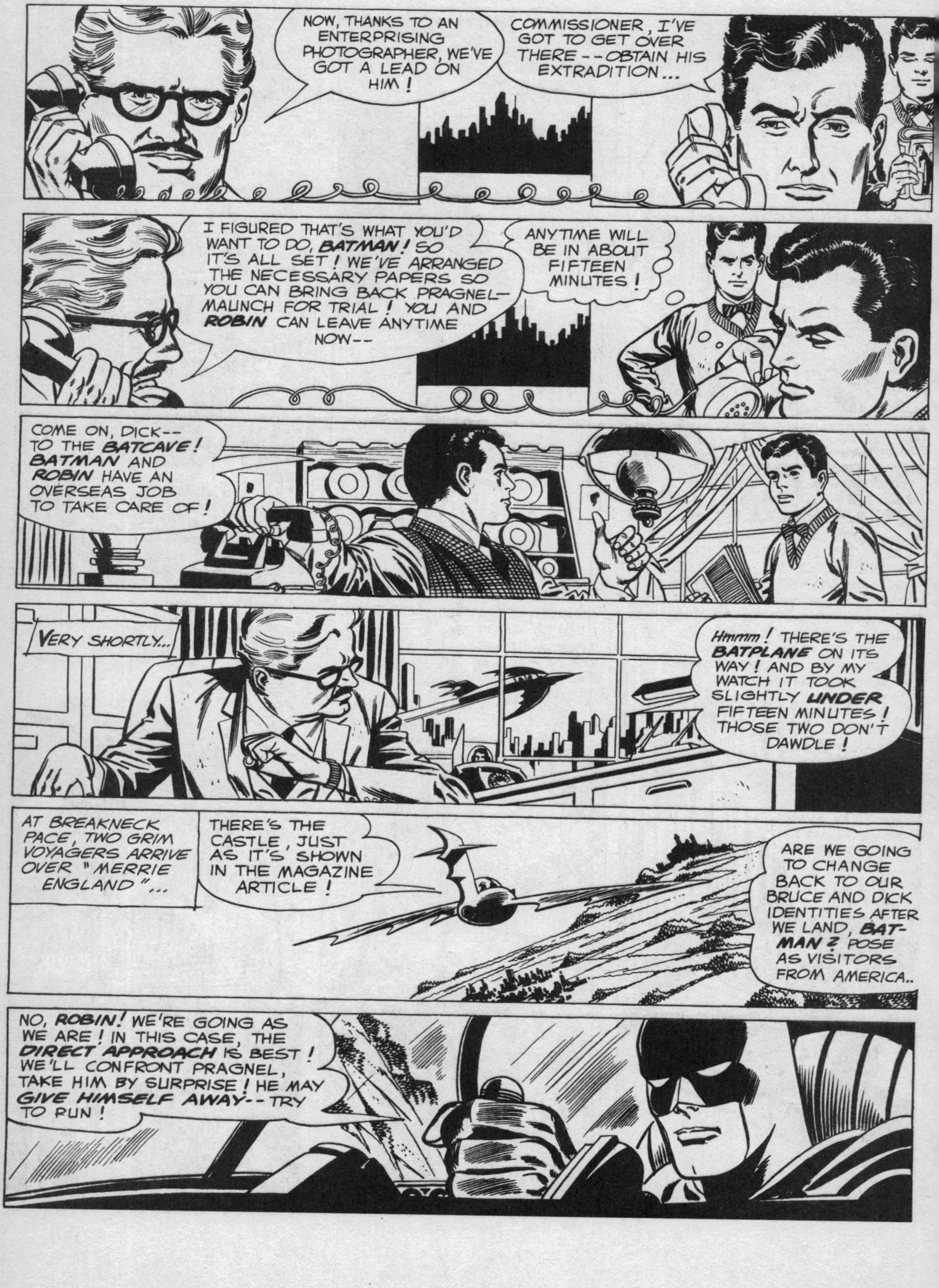
NOW, THANKS TO AN ENTERPRISING PHOTOGRAPHER, WE'VE GOT A LEAD ON HIM!
COMMISSIONER, I'VE GOT TO GET OVER THERE--OBTAIN HIS EXTRADITION...
I FIGURED THAT'S WHAT YOU'D WANT TO DO, BATMAN! SO IT'S ALL SET! WE'VE ARRANGED THE NECESSARY PAPERS SO YOU CAN BRING BACK PRAGNEL-MAUNCH FOR TRIAL! YOU AND ROBIN CAN LEAVE ANYTIME NOW--
ANYTIME WILL BE IN ABOUT FIFTEEN MINUTES!
COME ON, DICK--TO THE BATCAVE! BATMAN AND ROBIN HAVE AN OVERSEAS JOB TO TAKE CARE OF!
VERY SHORTLY...
Hmmm! THERE'S THE BATPLANE ON ITS WAY! AND BY MY WATCH IT TOOK SLIGHTLY UNDER FIFTEEN MINUTES! THOSE TWO DON'T DAWDLE!
AT BREAKNECK PACE, TWO GRIM VOYAGERS ARRIVE OVER "MERRIE ENGLAND"...
THERE'S THE CASTLE, JUST AS IT'S SHOWN IN THE MAGAZINE ARTICLE!
ARE WE GOING TO CHANGE BACK TO OUR BRUCE AND DICK IDENTITIES AFTER WE LAND, BATMAN? POSE AS VISITORS FROM AMERICA..
NO, ROBIN! WE'RE GOING AS WE ARE! IN THIS CASE, THE DIRECT APPROACH IS BEST! WE'LL CONFRONT PRAGNEL, TAKE HIM BY SURPRISE! HE MAY GIVE HIMSELF AWAY--TRY TO RUN!

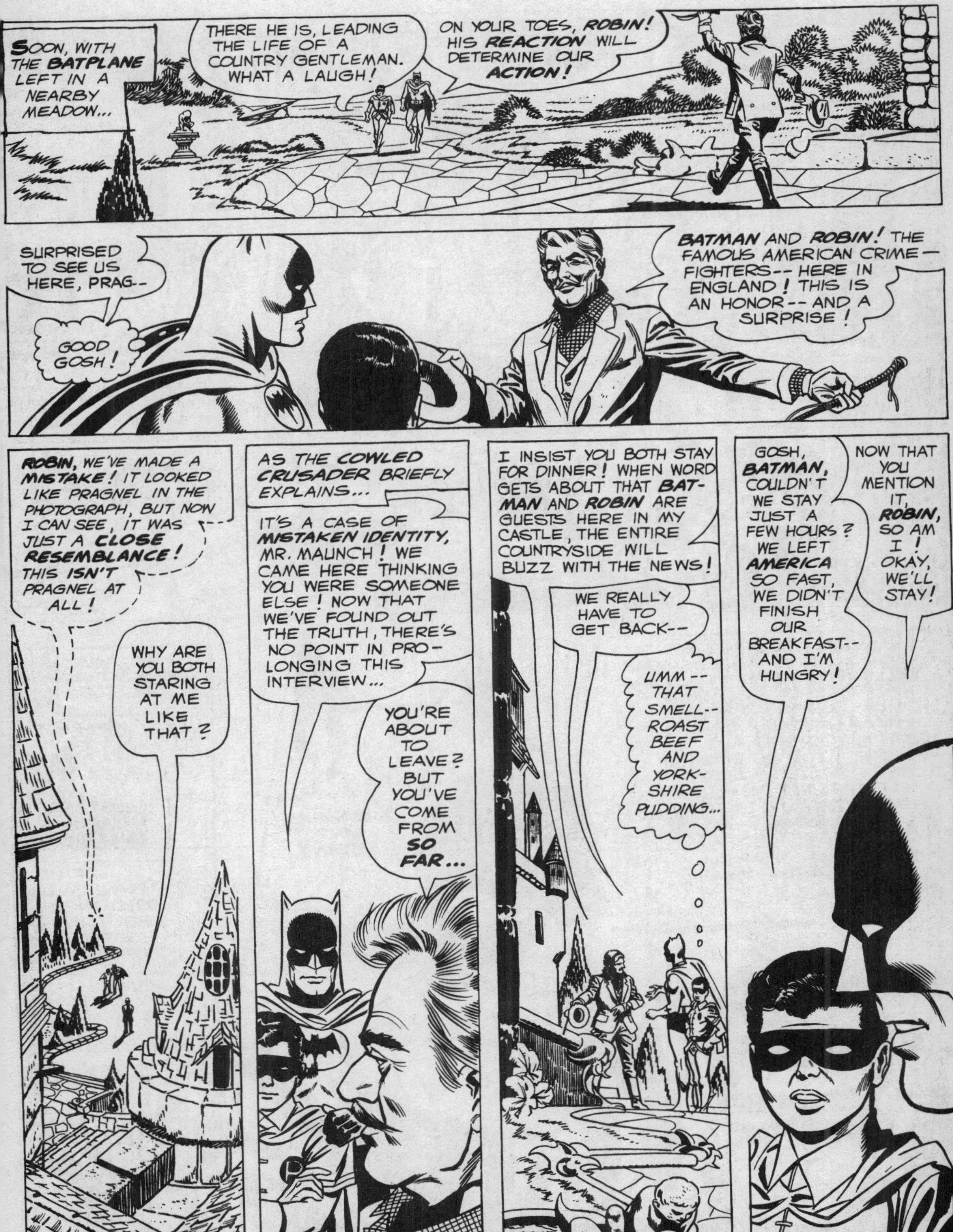
SOON, WITH THE BATPLANE LEFT IN A NEARBY MEADOW...
THERE HE IS, LEADING THE LIFE OF A COUNTRY GENTLEMAN. WHAT A LAUGH!
ON YOUR TOES, ROBIN! HIS REACTION WILL DETERMINE OUR ACTION!
SURPRISED TO SEE US HERE, PRAG--
GOOD GOSH!
BATMAN AND ROBIN! THE FAMOUS AMERICAN CRIME-FIGHTERS-- HERE IN ENGLAND! THIS IS AN HONOR-- AND A SURPRISE!
ROBIN, WE'VE MADE A MISTAKE! IT LOOKED LIKE PRAGNEL IN THE PHOTOGRAPH, BUT NOW I CAN SEE, IT WAS JUST A CLOSE RESEMBLANCE! THIS ISN'T PRAGNEL AT ALL!
WHY ARE YOU BOTH STARING AT ME LIKE THAT?
AS THE COWLED CRUSADER BRIEFLY EXPLAINS...
IT'S A CASE OF MISTAKEN IDENTITY, MR. MAUNCH! WE CAME HERE THINKING YOU WERE SOMEONE ELSE! NOW THAT WE'VE FOUND OUT THE TRUTH, THERE'S NO POINT IN PRO-LONGING THIS INTERVIEW...
YOU'RE ABOUT TO LEAVE? BUT YOU'VE COME FROM SO FAR...
I INSIST YOU BOTH STAY FOR DINNER! WHEN WORD GETS ABOUT THAT BATMAN AND ROBIN ARE GUESTS HERE IN MY CASTLE, THE ENTIRE COUNTRYSIDE WILL BUZZ WITH THE NEWS!
WE REALLY HAVE TO GET BACK--
UMM -- THAT SMELL-- ROAST BEEF AND YORK-SHIRE PUDDING...
GOSH, BATMAN, COULDN'T WE STAY JUST A FEW HOURS? WE LEFT AMERICA SO FAST, WE DIDN'T FINISH OUR BREAKFAST-- AND I'M HUNGRY!
NOW THAT YOU MENTION IT, ROBIN, SO AM I! OKAY, WE'LL STAY!
4

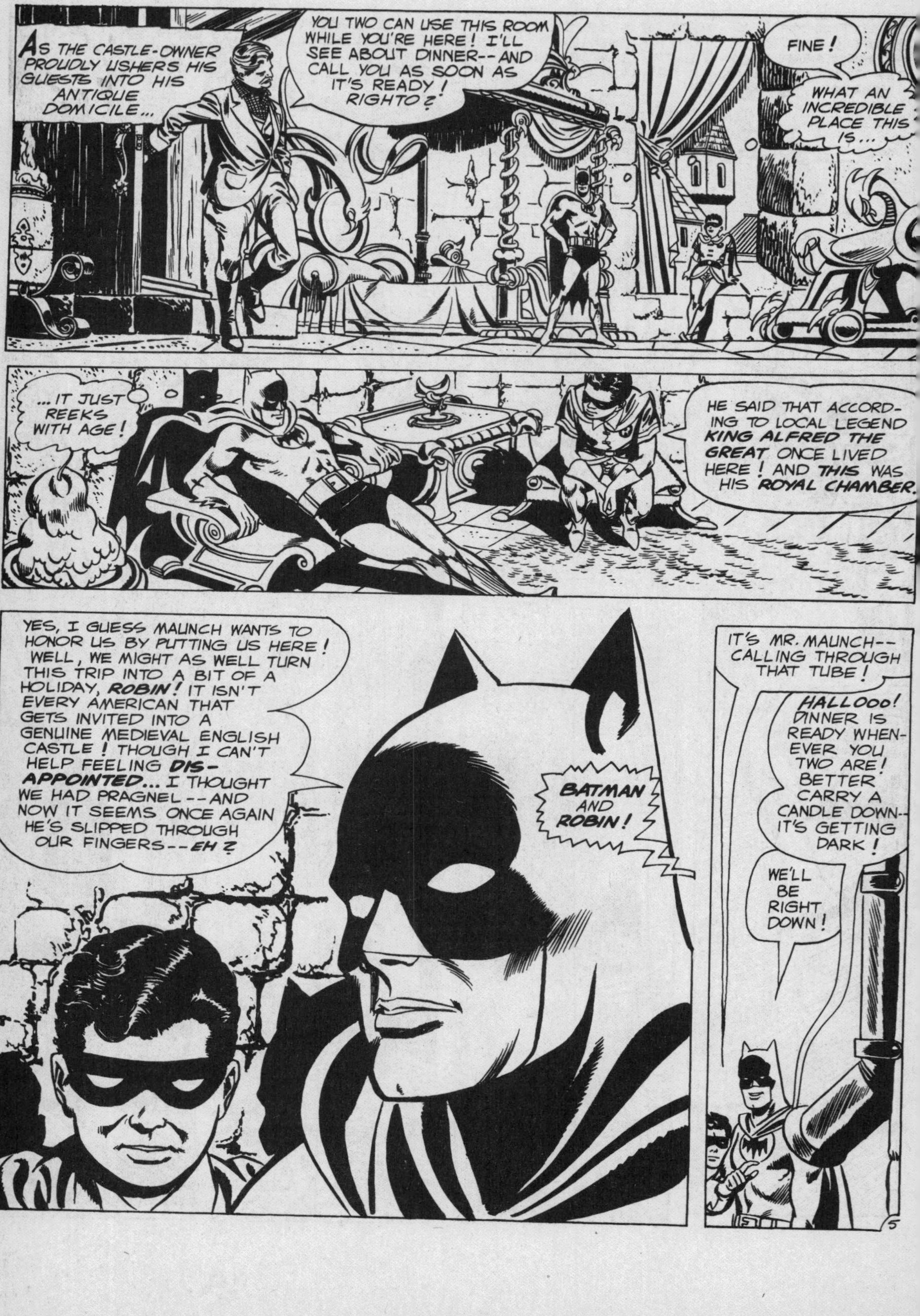
AS THE CASTLE-OWNER PROUDLY USHERS HIS GUESTS INTO HIS ANTIQUE DOMICILE...
YOU TWO CAN USE THIS ROOM WHILE YOU'RE HERE! I'LL SEE ABOUT DINNER--AND CALL YOU AS SOON AS IT'S READY! RIGHTO?
FINE!
WHAT AN INCREDIBLE PLACE THIS IS...
...IT JUST REEKS WITH AGE!
HE SAID THAT ACCORDING TO LOCAL LEGEND KING ALFRED THE GREAT ONCE LIVED HERE! AND THIS WAS HIS ROYAL CHAMBER.
YES, I GUESS MAUNCH WANTS TO HONOR US BY PUTTING US HERE! WELL, WE MIGHT AS WELL TURN THIS TRIP INTO A BIT OF A HOLIDAY, ROBIN! IT ISN'T EVERY AMERICAN THAT GETS INVITED INTO A GENUINE MEDIEVAL ENGLISH CASTLE! THOUGH I CAN'T HELP FEELING DISAPPOINTED... I THOUGHT WE HAD PRAGNEL--AND NOW IT SEEMS ONCE AGAIN HE'S SLIPPED THROUGH OUR FINGERS--EH?
BATMAN AND ROBIN!
IT'S MR. MAUNCH--CALLING THROUGH THAT TUBE!
HALLOOO! DINNER IS READY WHENEVER YOU TWO ARE! BETTER CARRY A CANDLE DOWN--IT'S GETTING DARK!
WE'LL BE RIGHT DOWN!
5

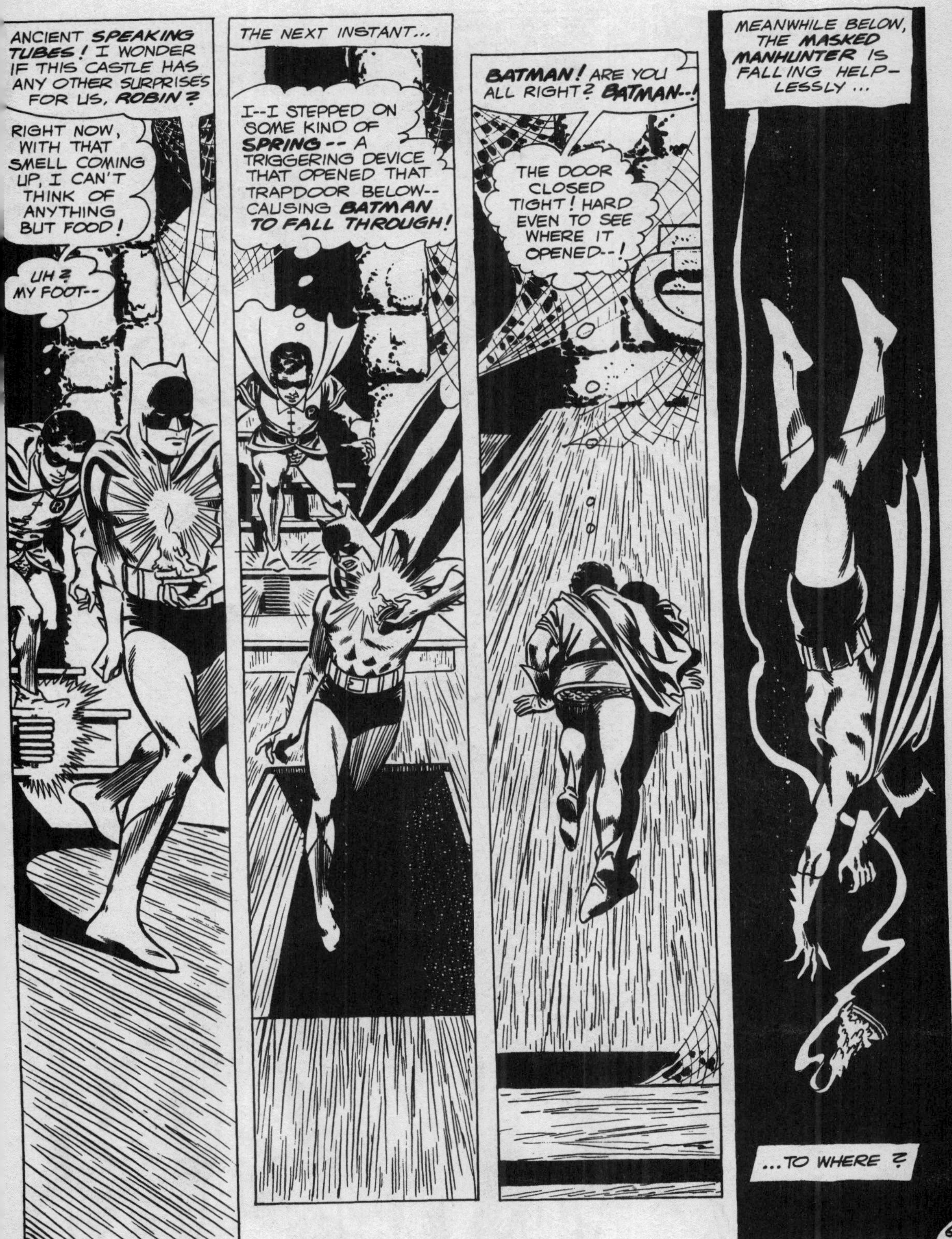
ANCIENT SPEAKING TUBES! I WONDER IF THIS CASTLE HAS ANY OTHER SURPRISES FOR US, ROBIN?
RIGHT NOW, WITH THAT SMELL COMING UP, I CAN'T THINK OF ANYTHING BUT FOOD!
UH? MY FOOT--
THE NEXT INSTANT...
I--I STEPPED ON SOME KIND OF SPRING-- A TRIGGERING DEVICE THAT OPENED THAT TRAPDOOR BELOW-- CAUSING BATMAN TO FALL THROUGH!
BATMAN! ARE YOU ALL RIGHT? BATMAN--!
THE DOOR CLOSED TIGHT! HARD EVEN TO SEE WHERE IT OPENED--!
MEANWHILE BELOW, THE MASKED MANHUNTER IS FALLING HELP-LESSLY ...
...TO WHERE?
6

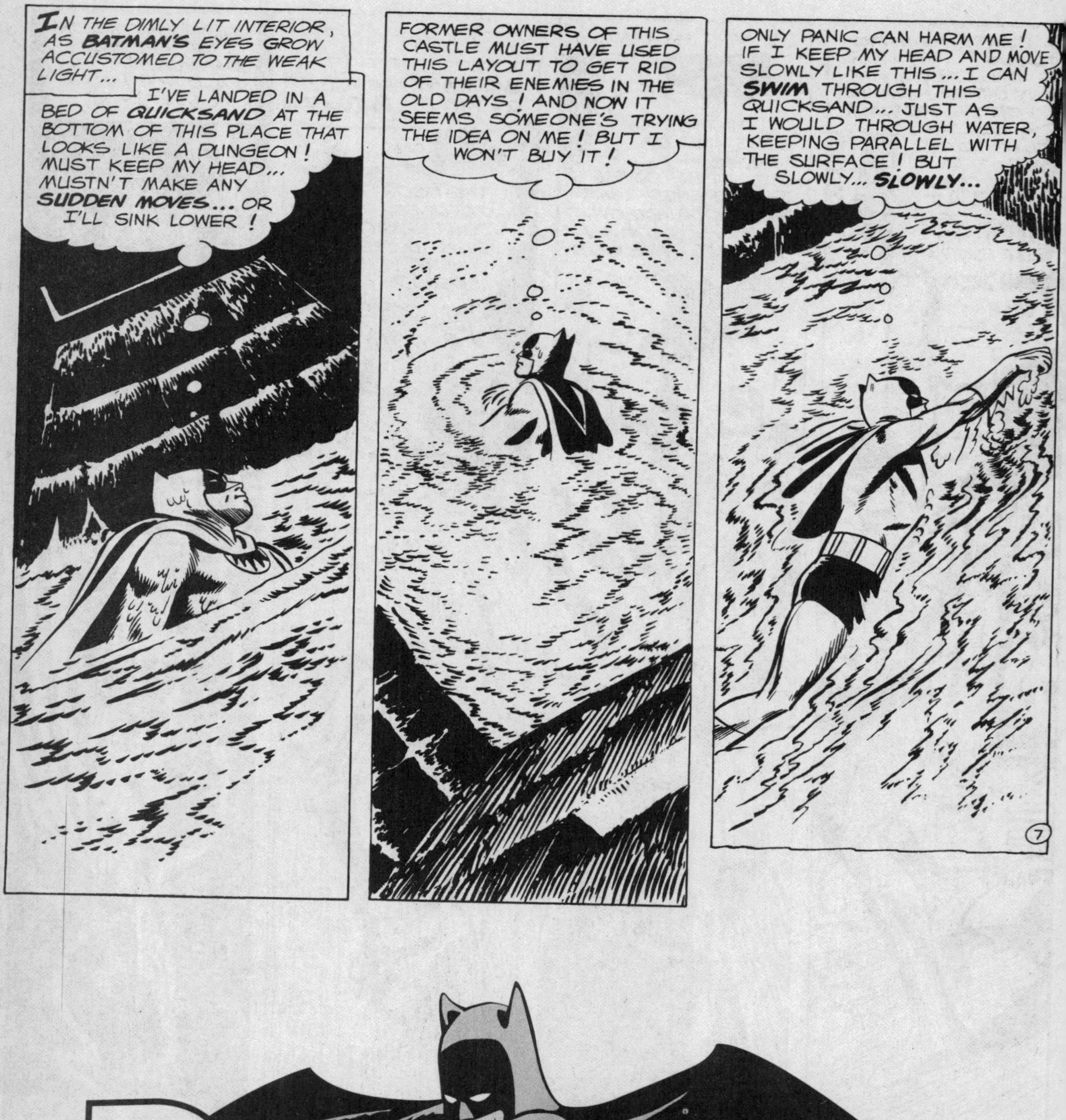
IN THE DIMLY LIT INTERIOR, AS BATMAN'S EYES GROW ACCUSTOMED TO THE WEAK LIGHT...
I'VE LANDED IN A BED OF QUICKSAND AT THE BOTTOM OF THIS PLACE THAT LOOKS LIKE A DUNGEON! MUST KEEP MY HEAD... MUSTN'T MAKE ANY SUDDEN MOVES... OR I'LL SINK LOWER!
FORMER OWNERS OF THIS CASTLE MUST HAVE USED THIS LAYOUT TO GET RID OF THEIR ENEMIES IN THE OLD DAYS! AND NOW IT SEEMS SOMEONE'S TRYING THE IDEA ON ME! BUT I WON'T BUY IT!
ONLY PANIC CAN HARM ME! IF I KEEP MY HEAD AND MOVE SLOWLY LIKE THIS... I CAN SWIM THROUGH THIS QUICKSAND... JUST AS I WOULD THROUGH WATER, KEEPING PARALLEL WITH THE SURFACE! BUT SLOWLY... SLOWLY...
7

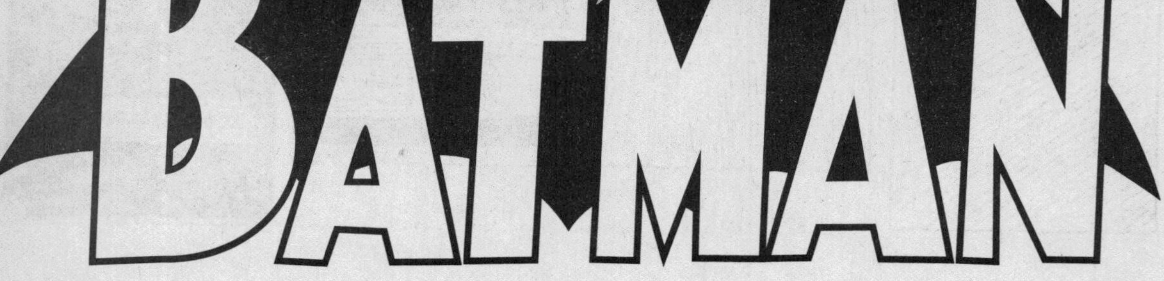
BATMAN

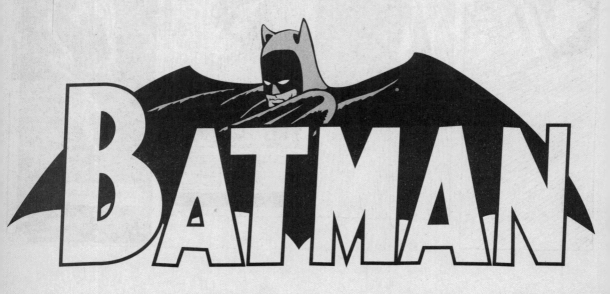

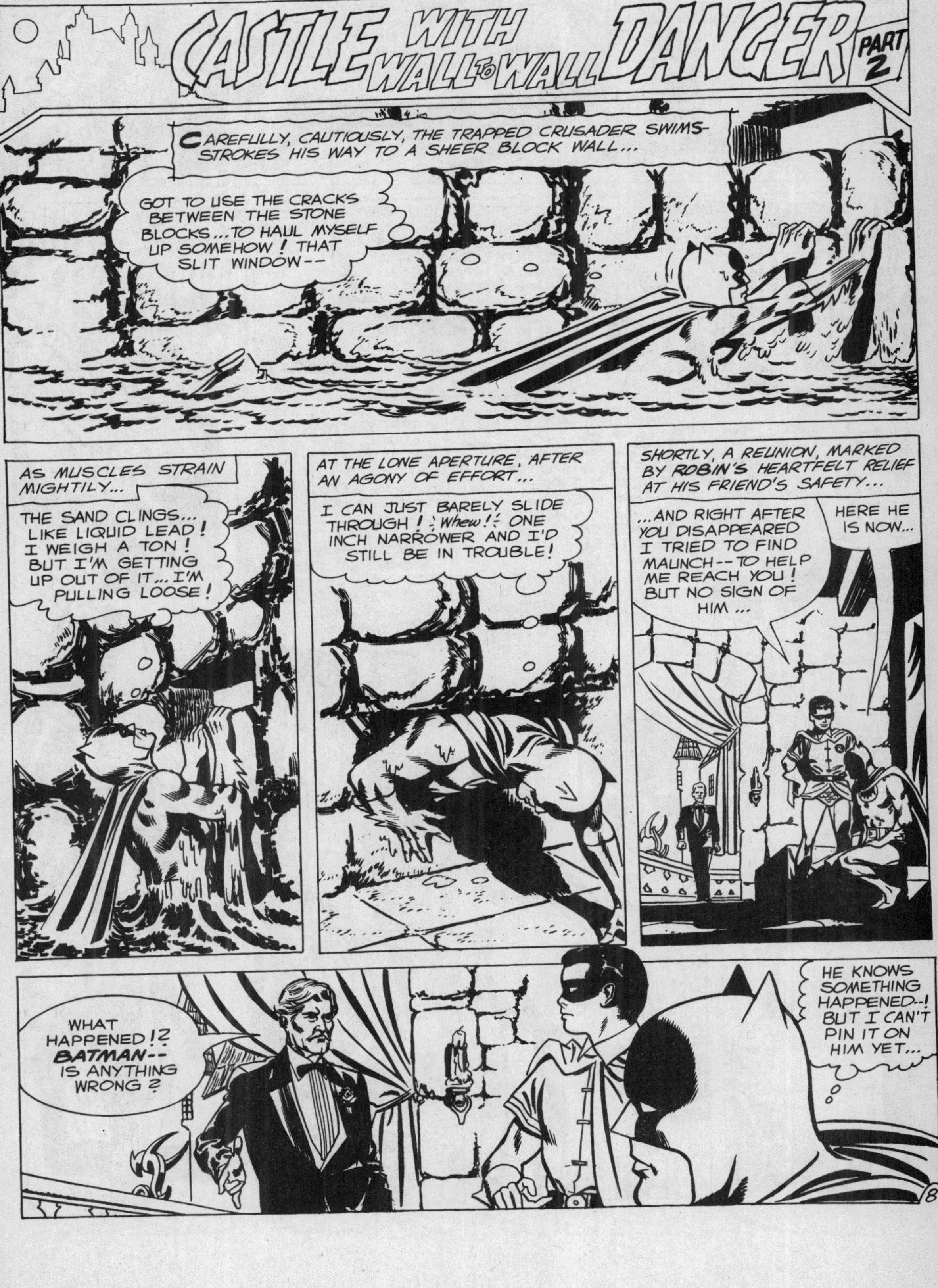
CASTLE WITH WALL TO WALL DANGER PART 2
CAREFULLY, CAUTIOUSLY, THE TRAPPED CRUSADER SWIMS-STROKES HIS WAY TO A SHEER BLOCK WALL...
GOT TO USE THE CRACKS BETWEEN THE STONE BLOCKS...TO HAUL MYSELF UP SOMEHOW! THAT SLIT WINDOW--
AS MUSCLES STRAIN MIGHTILY...
THE SAND CLINGS... LIKE LIQUID LEAD! I WEIGH A TON! BUT I'M GETTING UP OUT OF IT... I'M PULLING LOOSE!
AT THE LONE APERTURE, AFTER AN AGONY OF EFFORT...
I CAN JUST BARELY SLIDE THROUGH! Whew! ONE INCH NARROWER AND I'D STILL BE IN TROUBLE!
SHORTLY, A REUNION, MARKED BY ROBIN'S HEARTFELT RELIEF AT HIS FRIEND'S SAFETY...
...AND RIGHT AFTER YOU DISAPPEARED I TRIED TO FIND MAUNCH--TO HELP ME REACH YOU! BUT NO SIGN OF HIM...
HERE HE IS NOW...
WHAT HAPPENED!? BATMAN-- IS ANYTHING WRONG?
HE KNOWS SOMETHING HAPPENED--! BUT I CAN'T PIN IT ON HIM YET...
8

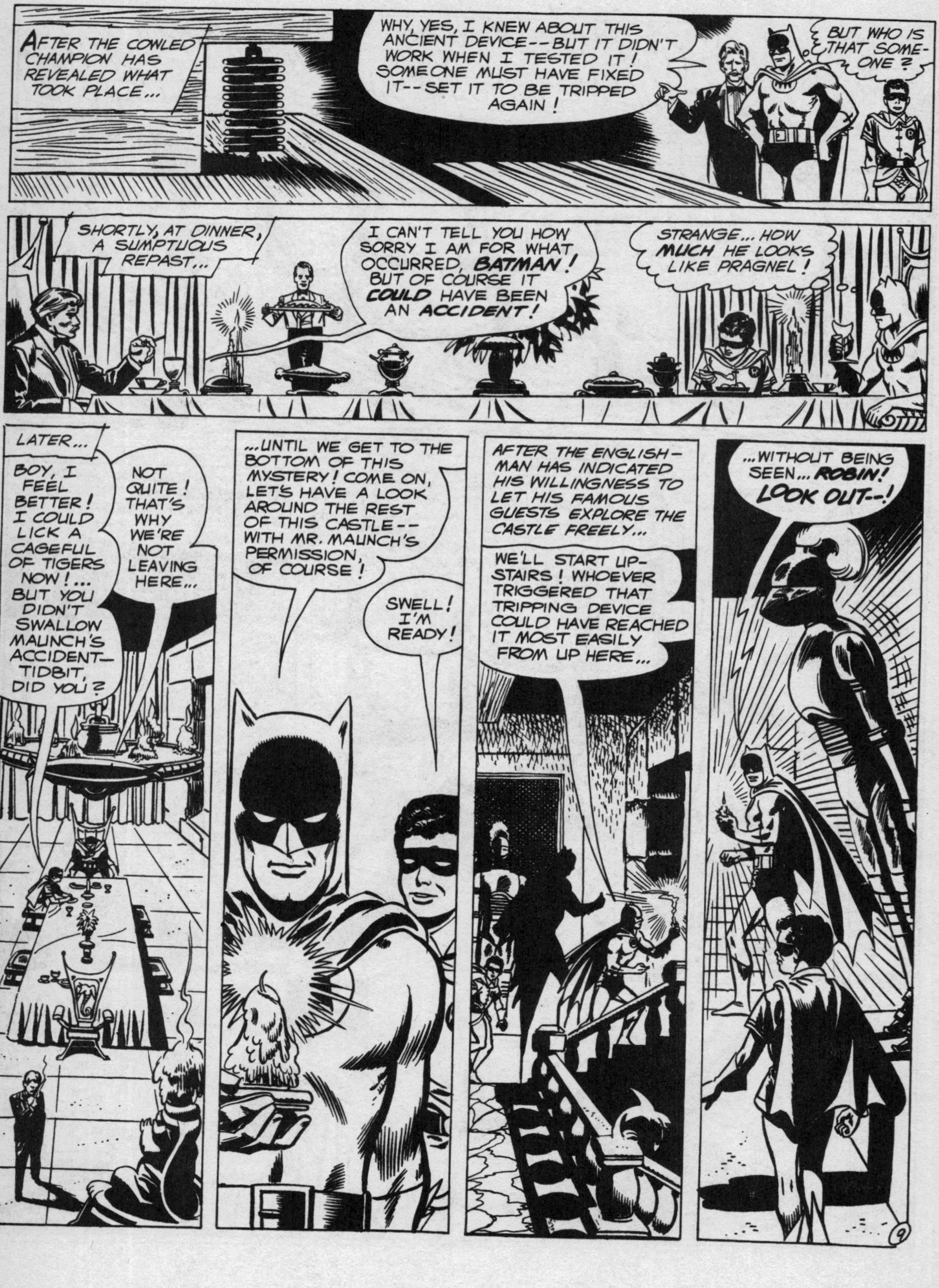
AFTER THE COWLED CHAMPION HAS REVEALED WHAT TOOK PLACE...
WHY, YES, I KNEW ABOUT THIS ANCIENT DEVICE--BUT IT DIDN'T WORK WHEN I TESTED IT! SOMEONE MUST HAVE FIXED IT--SET IT TO BE TRIPPED AGAIN!
BUT WHO IS THAT SOME-ONE?
SHORTLY, AT DINNER, A SUMPTUOUS REPAST...
I CAN'T TELL YOU HOW SORRY I AM FOR WHAT OCCURRED, BATMAN! BUT OF COURSE IT COULD HAVE BEEN AN ACCIDENT!
STRANGE... HOW MUCH HE LOOKS LIKE PRAGNEL!
LATER...
BOY, I FEEL BETTER! I COULD LICK A CAGEFUL OF TIGERS NOW!... BUT YOU DIDN'T SWALLOW MAUNCH'S ACCIDENT-TIDBIT, DID YOU?
NOT QUITE! THAT'S WHY WE'RE NOT LEAVING HERE...
...UNTIL WE GET TO THE BOTTOM OF THIS MYSTERY! COME ON, LET'S HAVE A LOOK AROUND THE REST OF THIS CASTLE--WITH MR. MAUNCH'S PERMISSION, OF COURSE!
SWELL! I'M READY!
AFTER THE ENGLISH-MAN HAS INDICATED HIS WILLINGNESS TO LET HIS FAMOUS GUESTS EXPLORE THE CASTLE FREELY...
WE'LL START UP-STAIRS! WHOEVER TRIGGERED THAT TRIPPING DEVICE COULD HAVE REACHED IT MOST EASILY FROM UP HERE...
...WITHOUT BEING SEEN... ROBIN! LOOK OUT--!
9

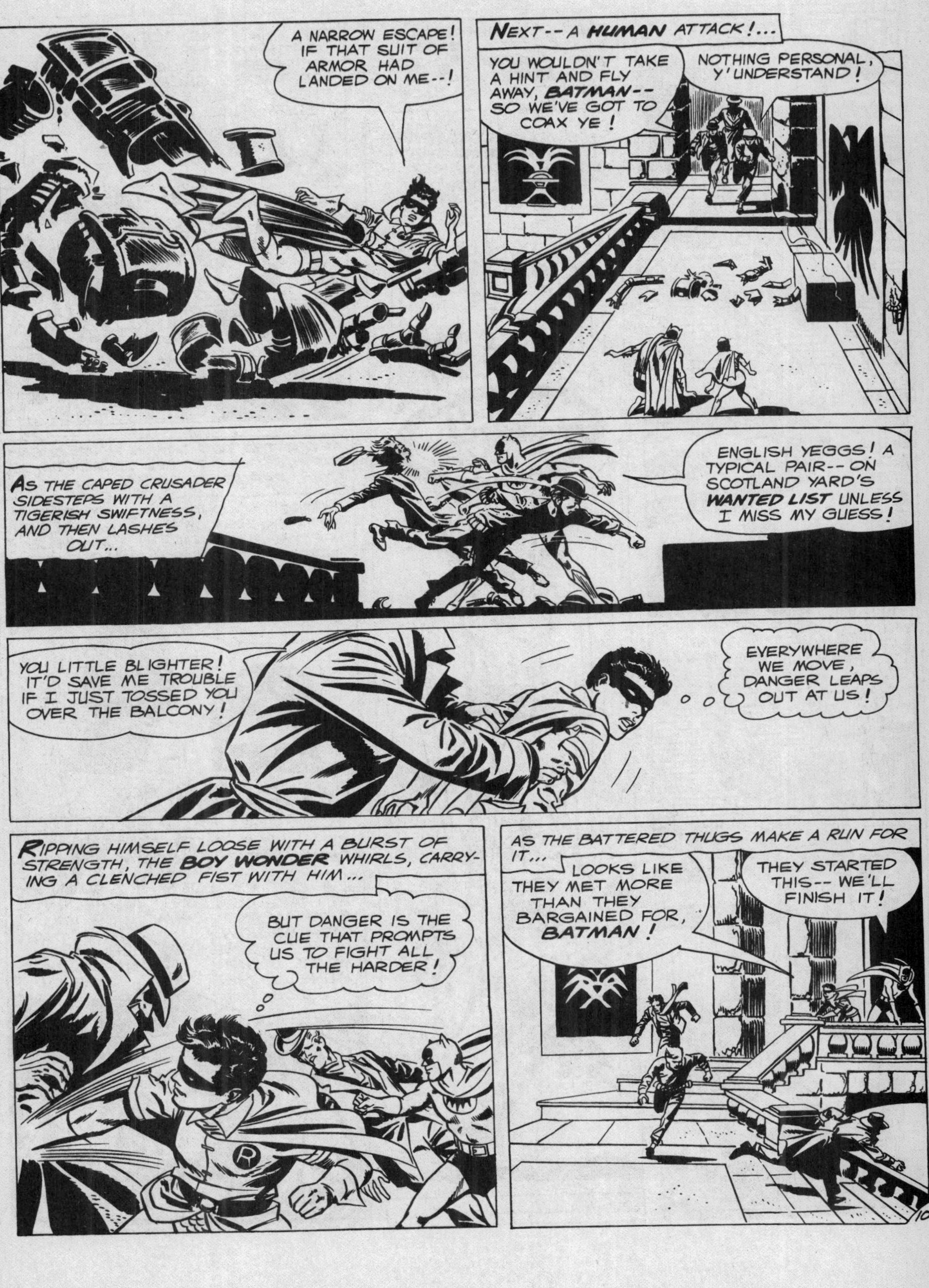
A NARROW ESCAPE! IF THAT SUIT OF ARMOR HAD LANDED ON ME--!
NEXT--A HUMAN ATTACK!...
YOU WOULDN'T TAKE A HINT AND FLY AWAY, BATMAN-- SO WE'VE GOT TO COAX YE!
NOTHING PERSONAL, Y'UNDERSTAND!
AS THE CAPED CRUSADER SIDESTEPS WITH A TIGERISH SWIFTNESS, AND THEN LASHES OUT...
ENGLISH YEGGS! A TYPICAL PAIR-- ON SCOTLAND YARD'S WANTED LIST UNLESS I MISS MY GUESS!
YOU LITTLE BLIGHTER! IT'D SAVE ME TROUBLE IF I JUST TOSSED YOU OVER THE BALCONY!
EVERYWHERE WE MOVE, DANGER LEAPS OUT AT US!
RIPPING HIMSELF LOOSE WITH A BURST OF STRENGTH, THE BOY WONDER WHIRLS, CARRYING A CLENCHED FIST WITH HIM...
BUT DANGER IS THE CUE THAT PROMPTS US TO FIGHT ALL THE HARDER!
AS THE BATTERED THUGS MAKE A RUN FOR IT...
LOOKS LIKE THEY MET MORE THAN THEY BARGAINED FOR, BATMAN!
THEY STARTED THIS-- WE'LL FINISH IT!
10

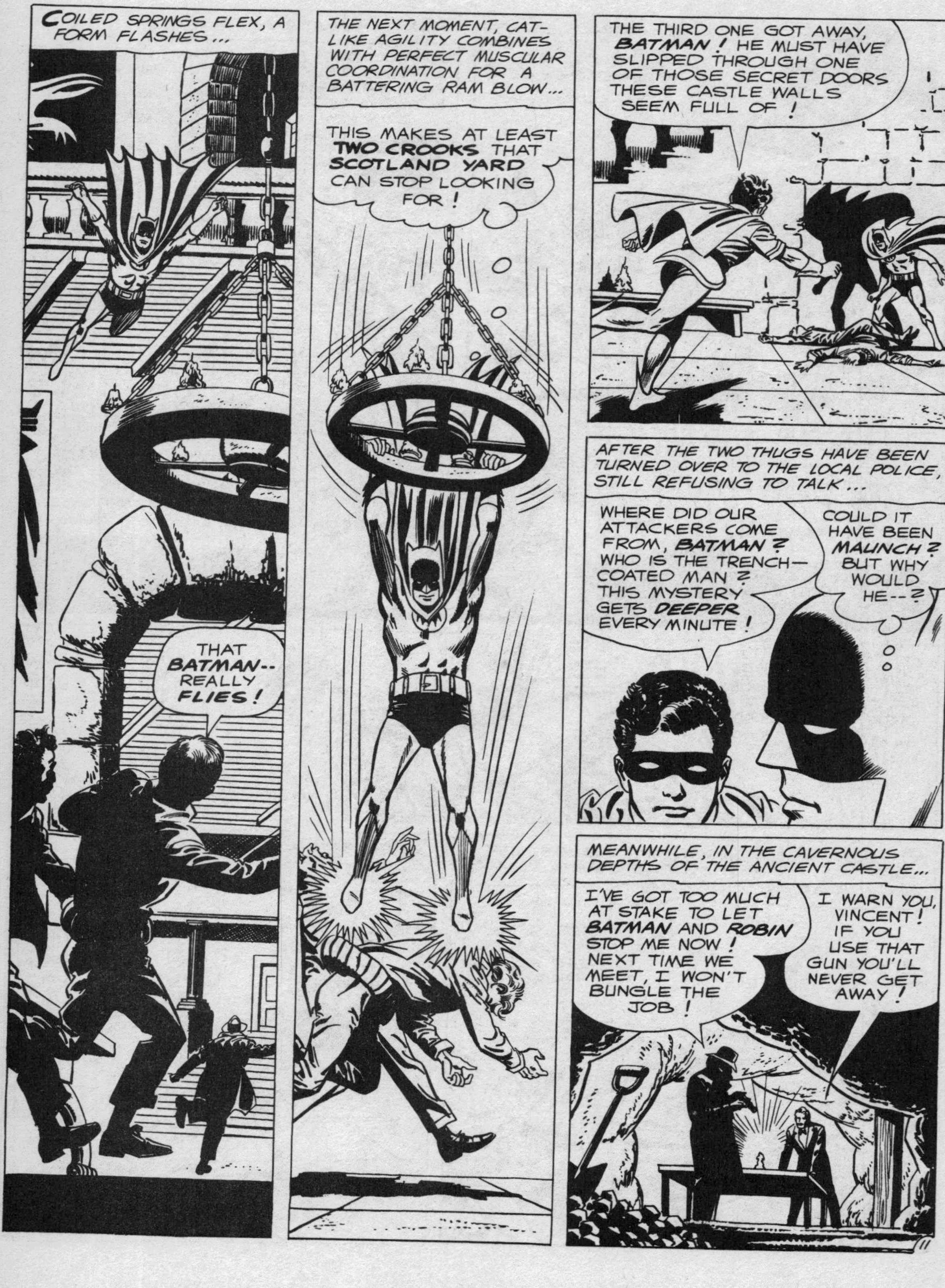
COILED SPRINGS FLEX, A FORM FLASHES...
THAT BATMAN-- REALLY FLIES!
THE NEXT MOMENT, CAT-LIKE AGILITY COMBINES WITH PERFECT MUSCULAR COORDINATION FOR A BATTERING RAM BLOW...
THIS MAKES AT LEAST TWO CROOKS THAT SCOTLAND YARD CAN STOP LOOKING FOR!
THE THIRD ONE GOT AWAY, BATMAN! HE MUST HAVE SLIPPED THROUGH ONE OF THOSE SECRET DOORS THESE CASTLE WALLS SEEM FULL OF!
AFTER THE TWO THUGS HAVE BEEN TURNED OVER TO THE LOCAL POLICE, STILL REFUSING TO TALK...
WHERE DID OUR ATTACKERS COME FROM, BATMAN? WHO IS THE TRENCH-COATED MAN? THIS MYSTERY GETS DEEPER EVERY MINUTE!
COULD IT HAVE BEEN MAUNCH? BUT WHY WOULD HE--?
MEANWHILE, IN THE CAVERNOUS DEPTHS OF THE ANCIENT CASTLE...
I'VE GOT TOO MUCH AT STAKE TO LET BATMAN AND ROBIN STOP ME NOW! NEXT TIME WE MEET, I WON'T BUNGLE THE JOB!
I WARN YOU, VINCENT! IF YOU USE THAT GUN YOU'LL NEVER GET AWAY!
11

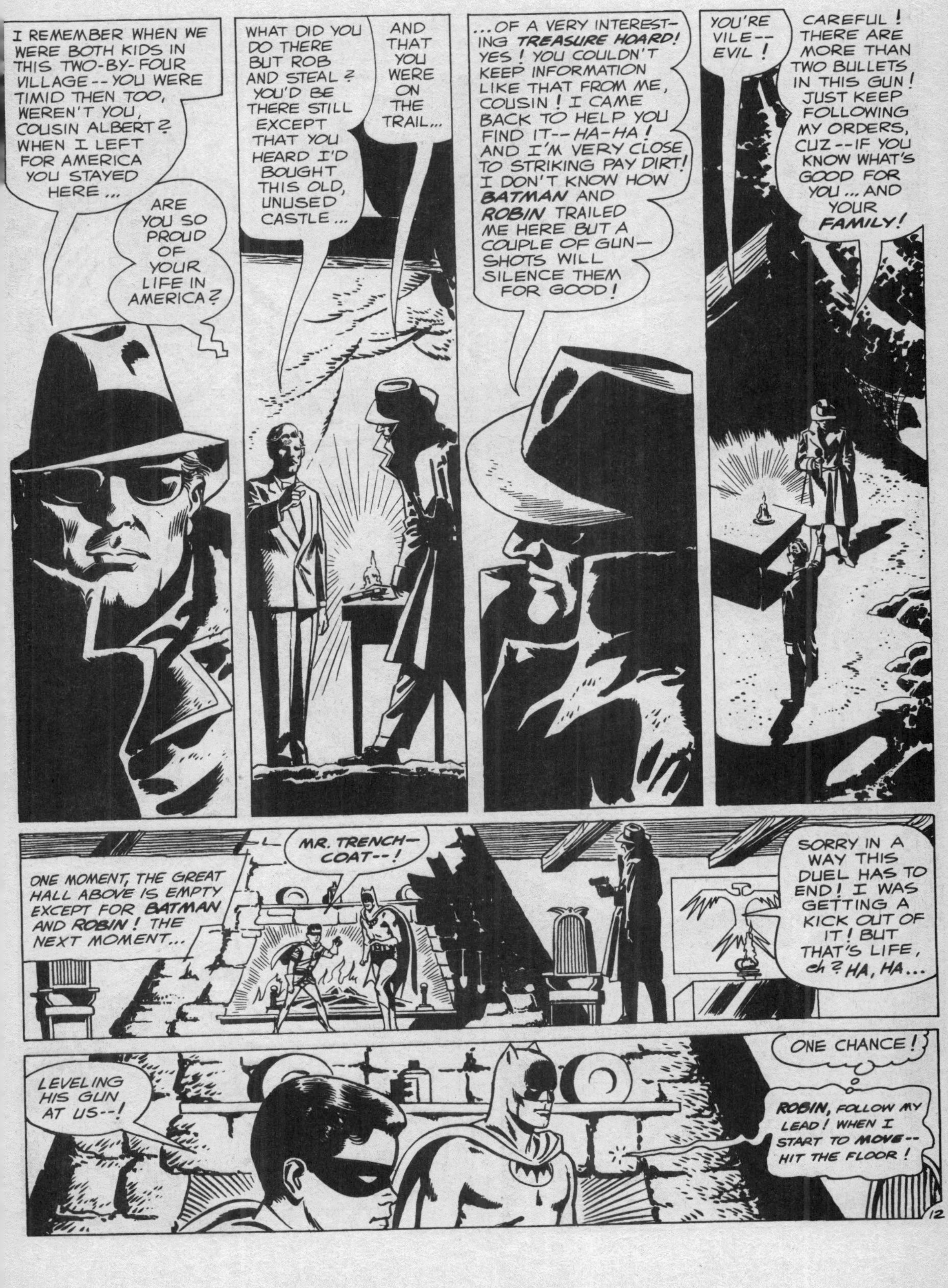
I REMEMBER WHEN WE WERE BOTH KIDS IN THIS TWO-BY-FOUR VILLAGE--YOU WERE TIMID THEN TOO, WEREN'T YOU, COUSIN ALBERT? WHEN I LEFT FOR AMERICA YOU STAYED HERE...
ARE YOU SO PROUD OF YOUR LIFE IN AMERICA?
WHAT DID YOU DO THERE BUT ROB AND STEAL? YOU'D BE THERE STILL EXCEPT THAT YOU HEARD I'D BOUGHT THIS OLD, UNUSED CASTLE...
AND THAT YOU WERE ON THE TRAIL...
...OF A VERY INTERESTING TREASURE HOARD! YES! YOU COULDN'T KEEP INFORMATION LIKE THAT FROM ME, COUSIN! I CAME BACK TO HELP YOU FIND IT--HA-HA! AND I'M VERY CLOSE TO STRIKING PAY DIRT! I DON'T KNOW HOW BATMAN AND ROBIN TRAILED ME HERE BUT A COUPLE OF GUN-SHOTS WILL SILENCE THEM FOR GOOD!
YOU'RE VILE--EVIL!
CAREFUL! THERE ARE MORE THAN TWO BULLETS IN THIS GUN! JUST KEEP FOLLOWING MY ORDERS, CUZ--IF YOU KNOW WHAT'S GOOD FOR YOU... AND YOUR FAMILY!
ONE MOMENT, THE GREAT HALL ABOVE IS EMPTY EXCEPT FOR BATMAN AND ROBIN! THE NEXT MOMENT...
MR. TRENCH-COAT--!
SORRY IN A WAY THIS DUEL HAS TO END! I WAS GETTING A KICK OUT OF IT! BUT THAT'S LIFE, eh? HA, HA...
LEVELING HIS GUN AT US--!
ONE CHANCE!
ROBIN, FOLLOW MY LEAD! WHEN I START TO MOVE--HIT THE FLOOR!
12

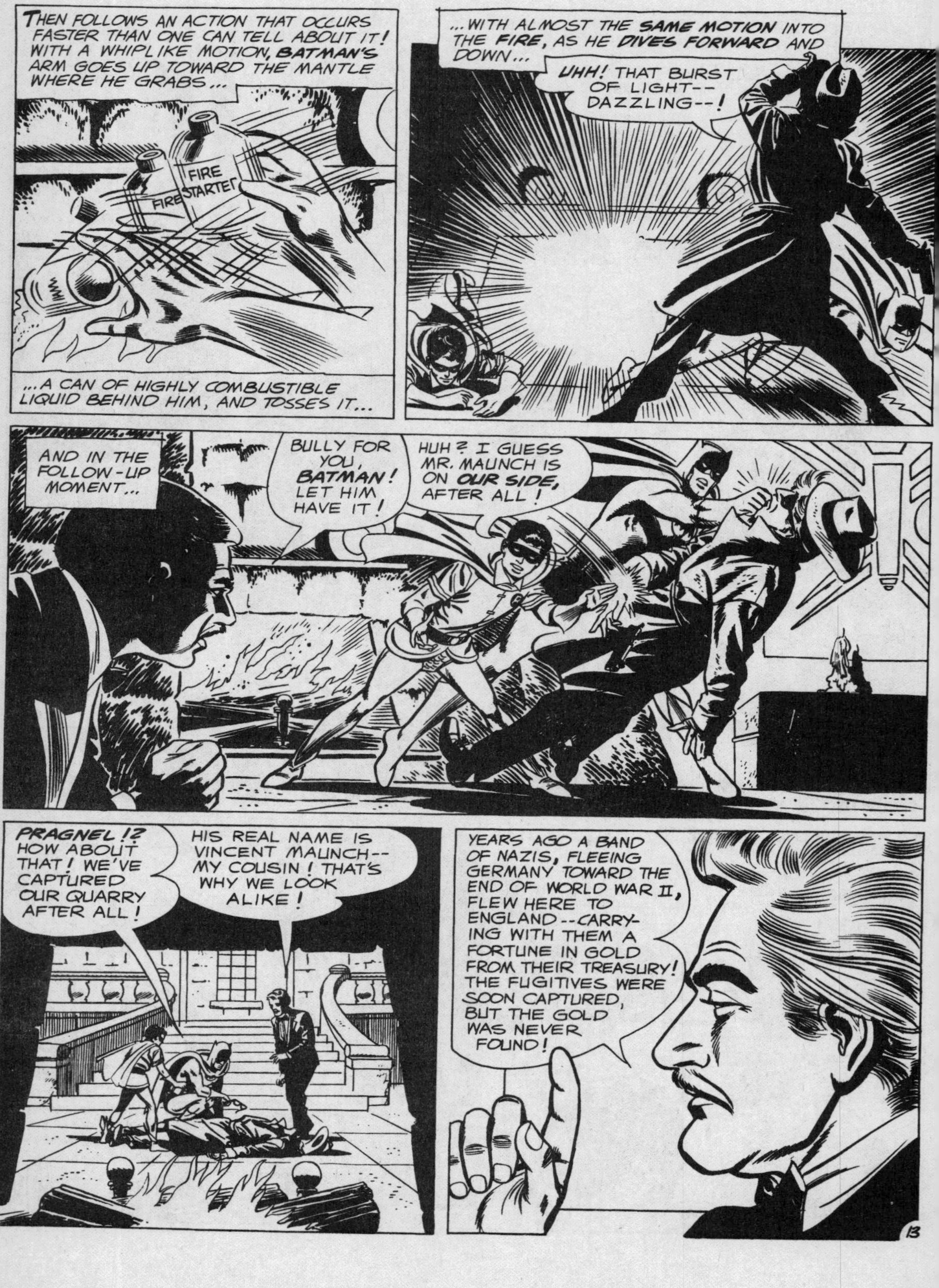
THEN FOLLOWS AN ACTION THAT OCCURS FASTER THAN ONE CAN TELL ABOUT IT! WITH A WHIPLIKE MOTION, BATMAN'S ARM GOES UP TOWARD THE MANTLE WHERE HE GRABS...
FIRE STARTER
FIRE
...A CAN OF HIGHLY COMBUSTIBLE LIQUID BEHIND HIM, AND TOSSES IT...
...WITH ALMOST THE SAME MOTION INTO THE FIRE, AS HE DIVES FORWARD AND DOWN...
UHH! THAT BURST OF LIGHT--DAZZLING--!
AND IN THE FOLLOW-UP MOMENT...
BULLY FOR YOU, BATMAN! LET HIM HAVE IT!
HUH? I GUESS MR. MAUNCH IS ON OUR SIDE, AFTER ALL!
PRAGNEL!? HOW ABOUT THAT! WE'VE CAPTURED OUR QUARRY AFTER ALL!
HIS REAL NAME IS VINCENT MAUNCH--MY COUSIN! THAT'S WHY WE LOOK ALIKE!
YEARS AGO A BAND OF NAZIS, FLEEING GERMANY TOWARD THE END OF WORLD WAR II, FLEW HERE TO ENGLAND--CARRYING WITH THEM A FORTUNE IN GOLD FROM THEIR TREASURY! THE FUGITIVES WERE SOON CAPTURED, BUT THE GOLD WAS NEVER FOUND!
13

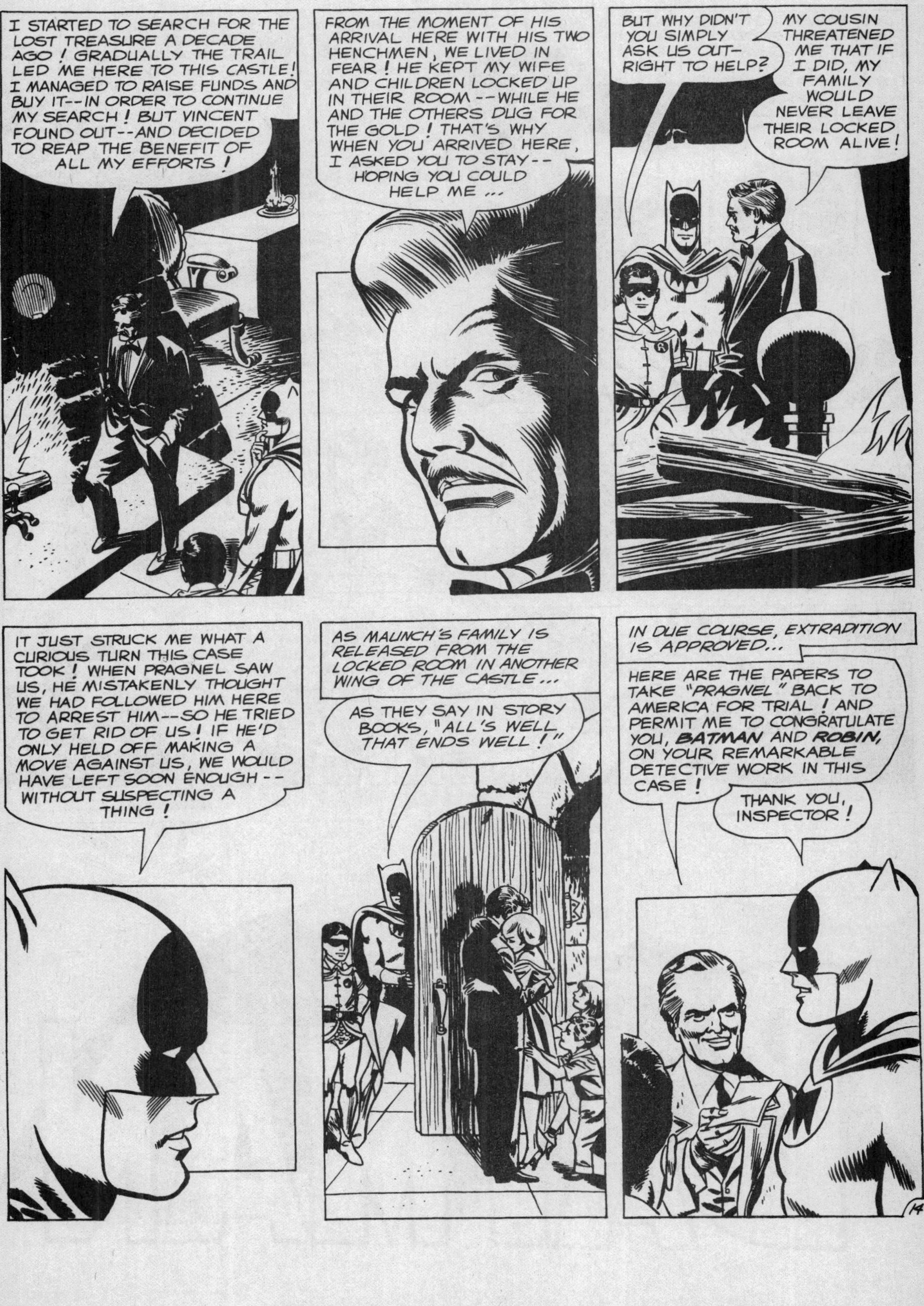
I STARTED TO SEARCH FOR THE LOST TREASURE A DECADE AGO! GRADUALLY THE TRAIL LED ME HERE TO THIS CASTLE! I MANAGED TO RAISE FUNDS AND BUY IT--IN ORDER TO CONTINUE MY SEARCH! BUT VINCENT FOUND OUT--AND DECIDED TO REAP THE BENEFIT OF ALL MY EFFORTS!
FROM THE MOMENT OF HIS ARRIVAL HERE WITH HIS TWO HENCHMEN, WE LIVED IN FEAR! HE KEPT MY WIFE AND CHILDREN LOCKED UP IN THEIR ROOM --WHILE HE AND THE OTHERS DUG FOR THE GOLD! THAT'S WHY WHEN YOU ARRIVED HERE, I ASKED YOU TO STAY-- HOPING YOU COULD HELP ME ...
BUT WHY DIDN'T YOU SIMPLY ASK US OUT-RIGHT TO HELP?
MY COUSIN THREATENED ME THAT IF I DID, MY FAMILY WOULD NEVER LEAVE THEIR LOCKED ROOM ALIVE!
IT JUST STRUCK ME WHAT A CURIOUS TURN THIS CASE TOOK! WHEN PRAGNEL SAW US, HE MISTAKENLY THOUGHT WE HAD FOLLOWED HIM HERE TO ARREST HIM--SO HE TRIED TO GET RID OF US! IF HE'D ONLY HELD OFF MAKING A MOVE AGAINST US, WE WOULD HAVE LEFT SOON ENOUGH-- WITHOUT SUSPECTING A THING!
AS MAUNCH'S FAMILY IS RELEASED FROM THE LOCKED ROOM IN ANOTHER WING OF THE CASTLE...
AS THEY SAY IN STORY BOOKS, "ALL'S WELL THAT ENDS WELL!"
IN DUE COURSE, EXTRADITION IS APPROVED...
HERE ARE THE PAPERS TO TAKE "PRAGNEL" BACK TO AMERICA FOR TRIAL! AND PERMIT ME TO CONGRATULATE YOU, BATMAN AND ROBIN, ON YOUR REMARKABLE DETECTIVE WORK IN THIS CASE!
THANK YOU, INSPECTOR!
14

ODD, *ROBIN!* WE'VE SELDOM DONE LESS *DEDUCTION* ON A CASE! IT SEEMS TO ME THAT MAINLY WE HAD TO *THINK FAST* AND *ACT FAST*--

HOW TRUE...

...BUT WHO AM I TO ARGUE WITH *SCOTLAND YARD*?

RIGHT! LET'S GO, *PRAGNEL!* NEXT STOP-- *GOTHAM CITY!*

WEEKS LATER...

TREASURE COMES TO LIGHT IN ENGLAND! NAZI GOLD LONG BURIED FOUND!

DICK! MAUNCH FOUND THE *TREASURE!* AND ACCORDING TO THIS NEWS REPORT HE HAS MADE OUT A CHECK FOR *$50,000* TO BE PAID TO THE FAVORITE CHARITY OF *BATMAN* AND *ROBIN*-- IN GRATITUDE FOR WHAT THEY DID FOR HIM AND HIS FAMILY!

GOSH! HE SURE IS A SWELL GUY, BRUCE!

AS DECENT AND HONEST--AS HIS *COUSIN* IS DISHONEST! AND WITH PRAGNEL FINALLY IN JAIL, I GUESS THEY *BOTH* NOW HAVE WHAT THEY DESERVE!

The End

15

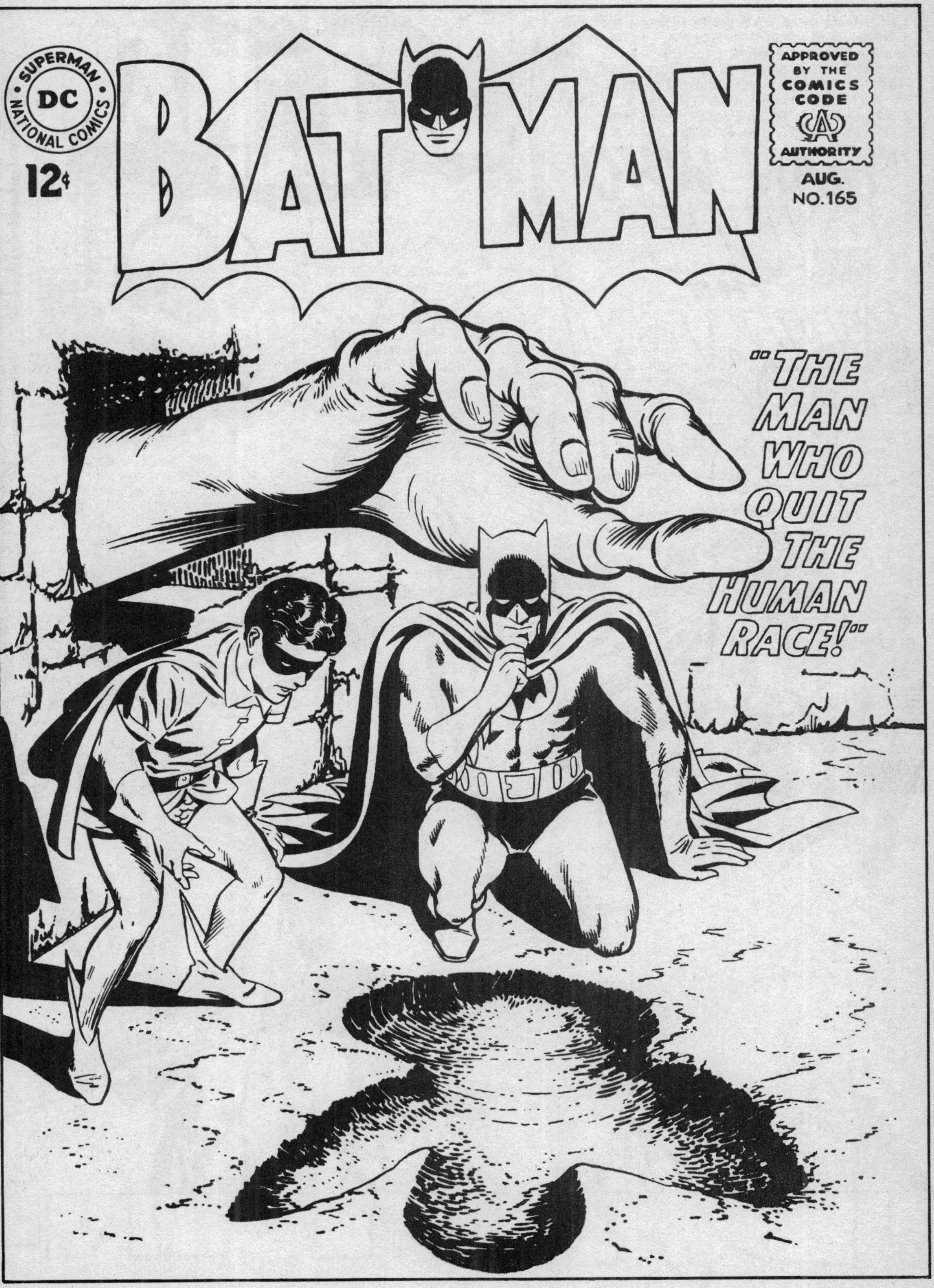
SUPERMAN DC NATIONAL COMICS
12¢
BATMAN
APPROVED BY THE COMICS CODE AUTHORITY
AUG.
NO.165
"THE MAN WHO QUIT THE HUMAN RACE!"

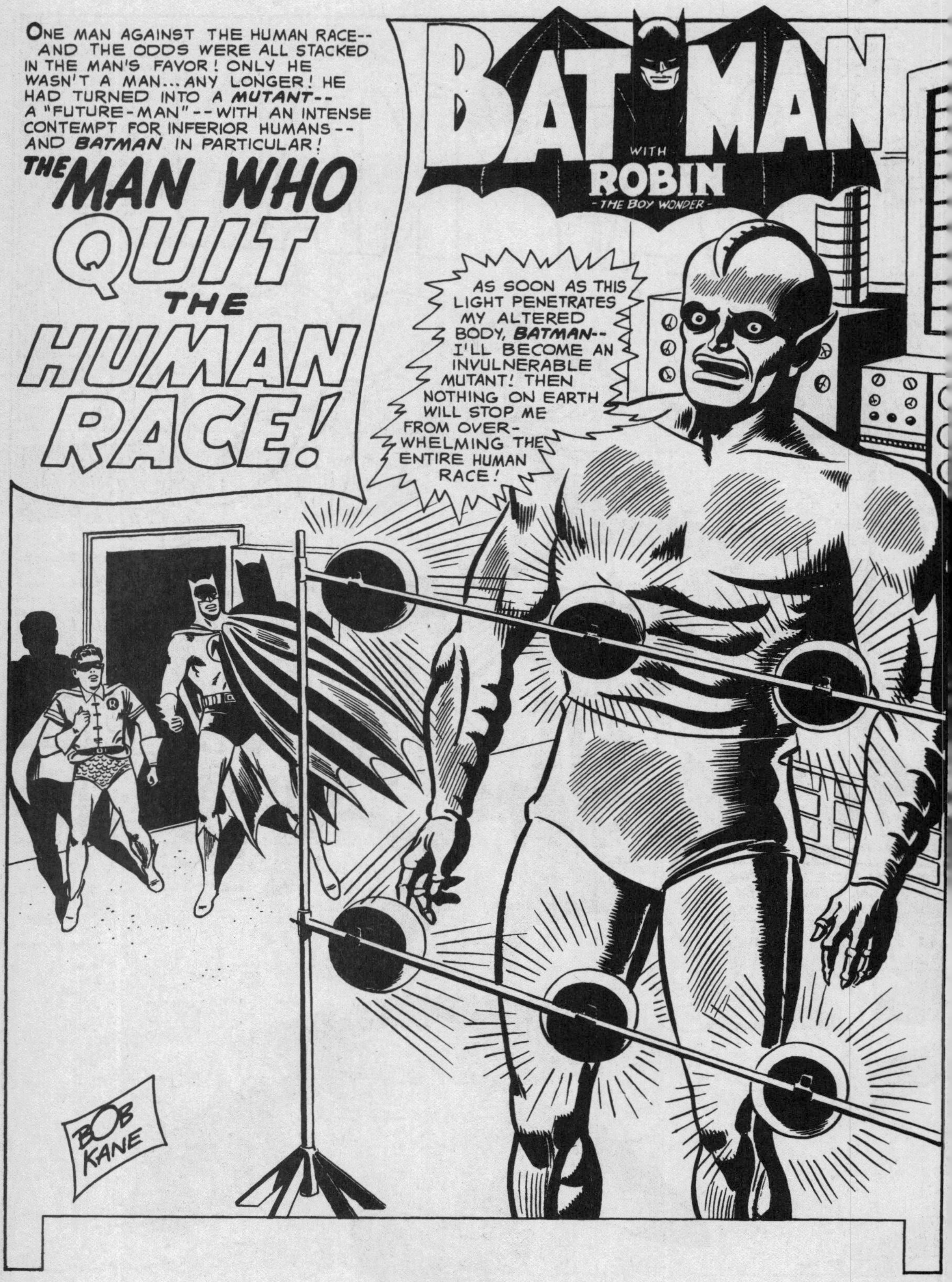
ONE MAN AGAINST THE HUMAN RACE-- AND THE ODDS WERE ALL STACKED IN THE MAN'S FAVOR! ONLY HE WASN'T A MAN... ANY LONGER! HE HAD TURNED INTO A MUTANT-- A "FUTURE-MAN"-- WITH AN INTENSE CONTEMPT FOR INFERIOR HUMANS-- AND BATMAN IN PARTICULAR!
THE MAN WHO QUIT THE HUMAN RACE!
BATMAN WITH ROBIN -THE BOY WONDER-
AS SOON AS THIS LIGHT PENETRATES MY ALTERED BODY, BATMAN-- I'LL BECOME AN INVULNERABLE MUTANT! THEN NOTHING ON EARTH WILL STOP ME FROM OVER-WHELMING THE ENTIRE HUMAN RACE!
BOB KANE

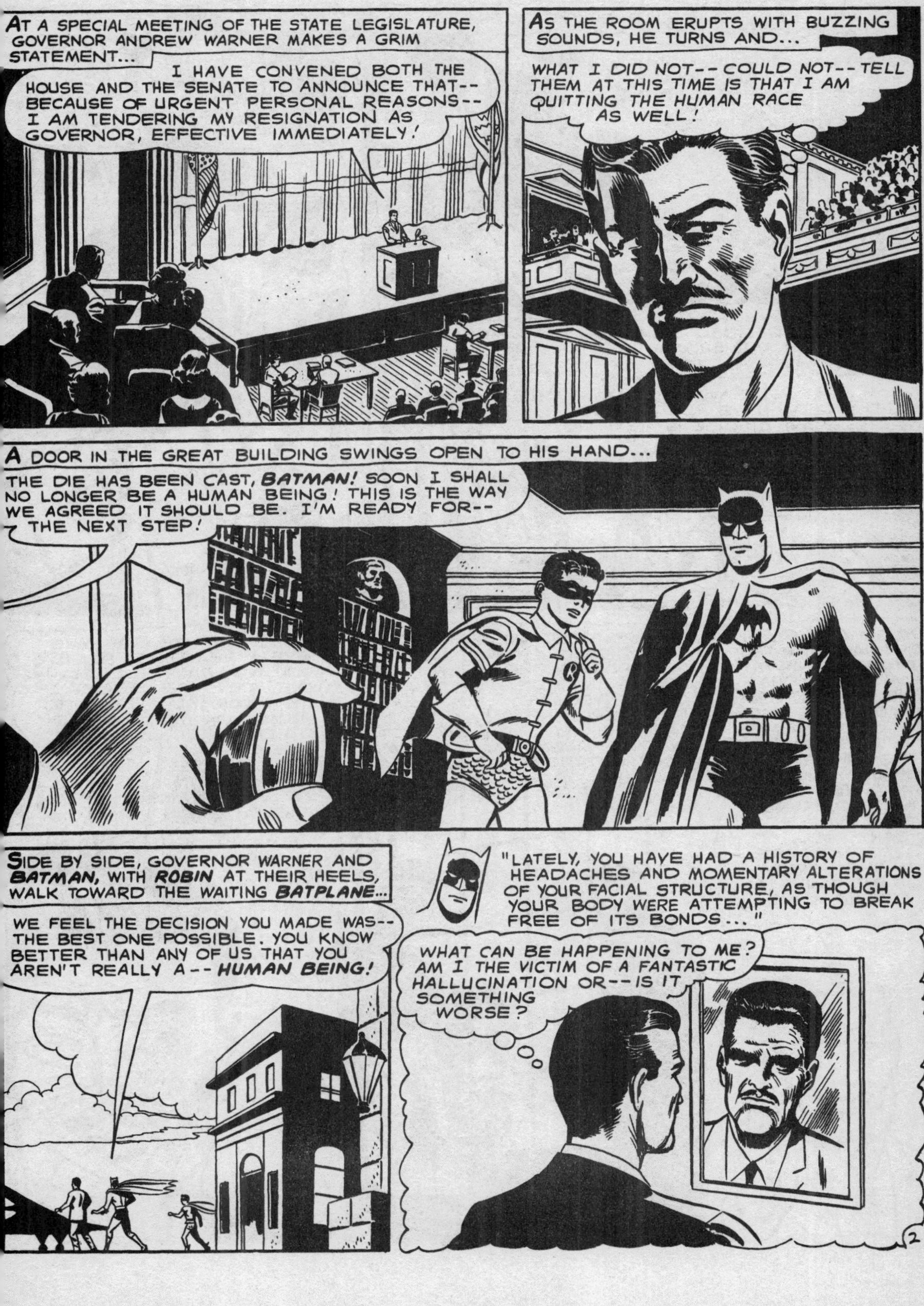
AT A SPECIAL MEETING OF THE STATE LEGISLATURE, GOVERNOR ANDREW WARNER MAKES A GRIM STATEMENT...
I HAVE CONVENED BOTH THE HOUSE AND THE SENATE TO ANNOUNCE THAT-- BECAUSE OF URGENT PERSONAL REASONS-- I AM TENDERING MY RESIGNATION AS GOVERNOR, EFFECTIVE IMMEDIATELY!
AS THE ROOM ERUPTS WITH BUZZING SOUNDS, HE TURNS AND...
WHAT I DID NOT-- COULD NOT-- TELL THEM AT THIS TIME IS THAT I AM QUITTING THE HUMAN RACE AS WELL!
A DOOR IN THE GREAT BUILDING SWINGS OPEN TO HIS HAND...
THE DIE HAS BEEN CAST, BATMAN! SOON I SHALL NO LONGER BE A HUMAN BEING! THIS IS THE WAY WE AGREED IT SHOULD BE. I'M READY FOR-- THE NEXT STEP!
SIDE BY SIDE, GOVERNOR WARNER AND BATMAN, WITH ROBIN AT THEIR HEELS, WALK TOWARD THE WAITING BATPLANE...
WE FEEL THE DECISION YOU MADE WAS-- THE BEST ONE POSSIBLE. YOU KNOW BETTER THAN ANY OF US THAT YOU AREN'T REALLY A-- HUMAN BEING!
"LATELY, YOU HAVE HAD A HISTORY OF HEADACHES AND MOMENTARY ALTERATIONS OF YOUR FACIAL STRUCTURE, AS THOUGH YOUR BODY WERE ATTEMPTING TO BREAK FREE OF ITS BONDS..."
WHAT CAN BE HAPPENING TO ME? AM I THE VICTIM OF A FANTASTIC HALLUCINATION OR-- IS IT SOMETHING WORSE?
2

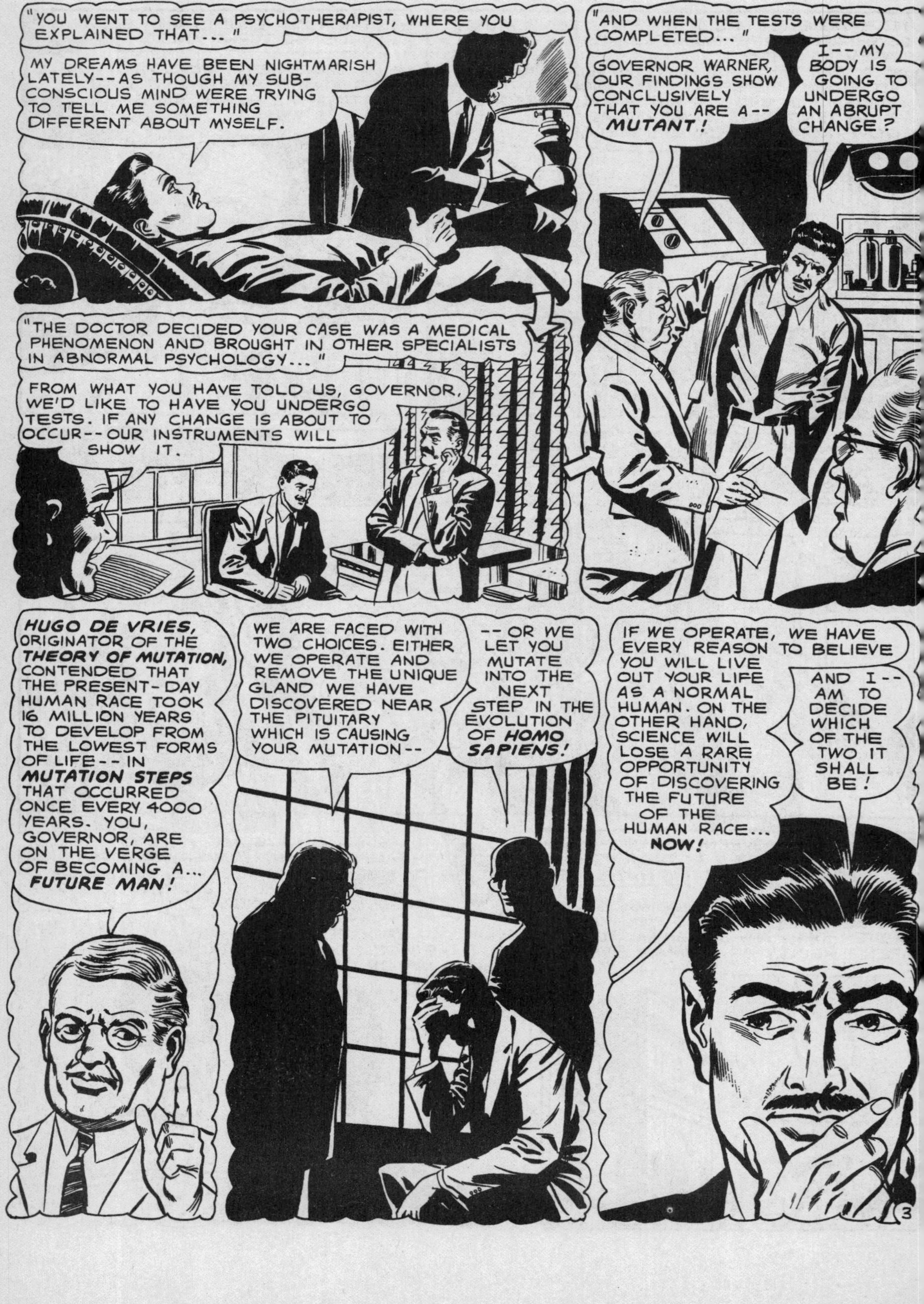
"YOU WENT TO SEE A PSYCHOTHERAPIST, WHERE YOU EXPLAINED THAT... "
MY DREAMS HAVE BEEN NIGHTMARISH LATELY--AS THOUGH MY SUB-CONSCIOUS MIND WERE TRYING TO TELL ME SOMETHING DIFFERENT ABOUT MYSELF.
"THE DOCTOR DECIDED YOUR CASE WAS A MEDICAL PHENOMENON AND BROUGHT IN OTHER SPECIALISTS IN ABNORMAL PSYCHOLOGY... "
FROM WHAT YOU HAVE TOLD US, GOVERNOR, WE'D LIKE TO HAVE YOU UNDERGO TESTS. IF ANY CHANGE IS ABOUT TO OCCUR--OUR INSTRUMENTS WILL SHOW IT.
"AND WHEN THE TESTS WERE COMPLETED... "
GOVERNOR WARNER, OUR FINDINGS SHOW CONCLUSIVELY THAT YOU ARE A-- **MUTANT!**
I--MY BODY IS GOING TO UNDERGO AN ABRUPT CHANGE?
HUGO DE VRIES, ORIGINATOR OF THE **THEORY OF MUTATION,** CONTENDED THAT THE PRESENT-DAY HUMAN RACE TOOK 16 MILLION YEARS TO DEVELOP FROM THE LOWEST FORMS OF LIFE--IN **MUTATION STEPS** THAT OCCURRED ONCE EVERY 4000 YEARS. YOU, GOVERNOR, ARE ON THE VERGE OF BECOMING A... **FUTURE MAN!**
WE ARE FACED WITH TWO CHOICES. EITHER WE OPERATE AND REMOVE THE UNIQUE GLAND WE HAVE DISCOVERED NEAR THE PITUITARY WHICH IS CAUSING YOUR MUTATION--
--OR WE LET YOU MUTATE INTO THE NEXT STEP IN THE EVOLUTION OF **HOMO SAPIENS!**
IF WE OPERATE, WE HAVE EVERY REASON TO BELIEVE YOU WILL LIVE OUT YOUR LIFE AS A NORMAL HUMAN. ON THE OTHER HAND, SCIENCE WILL LOSE A RARE OPPORTUNITY OF DISCOVERING THE FUTURE OF THE HUMAN RACE... **NOW!**
AND I--AM TO DECIDE WHICH OF THE TWO IT SHALL BE!
3

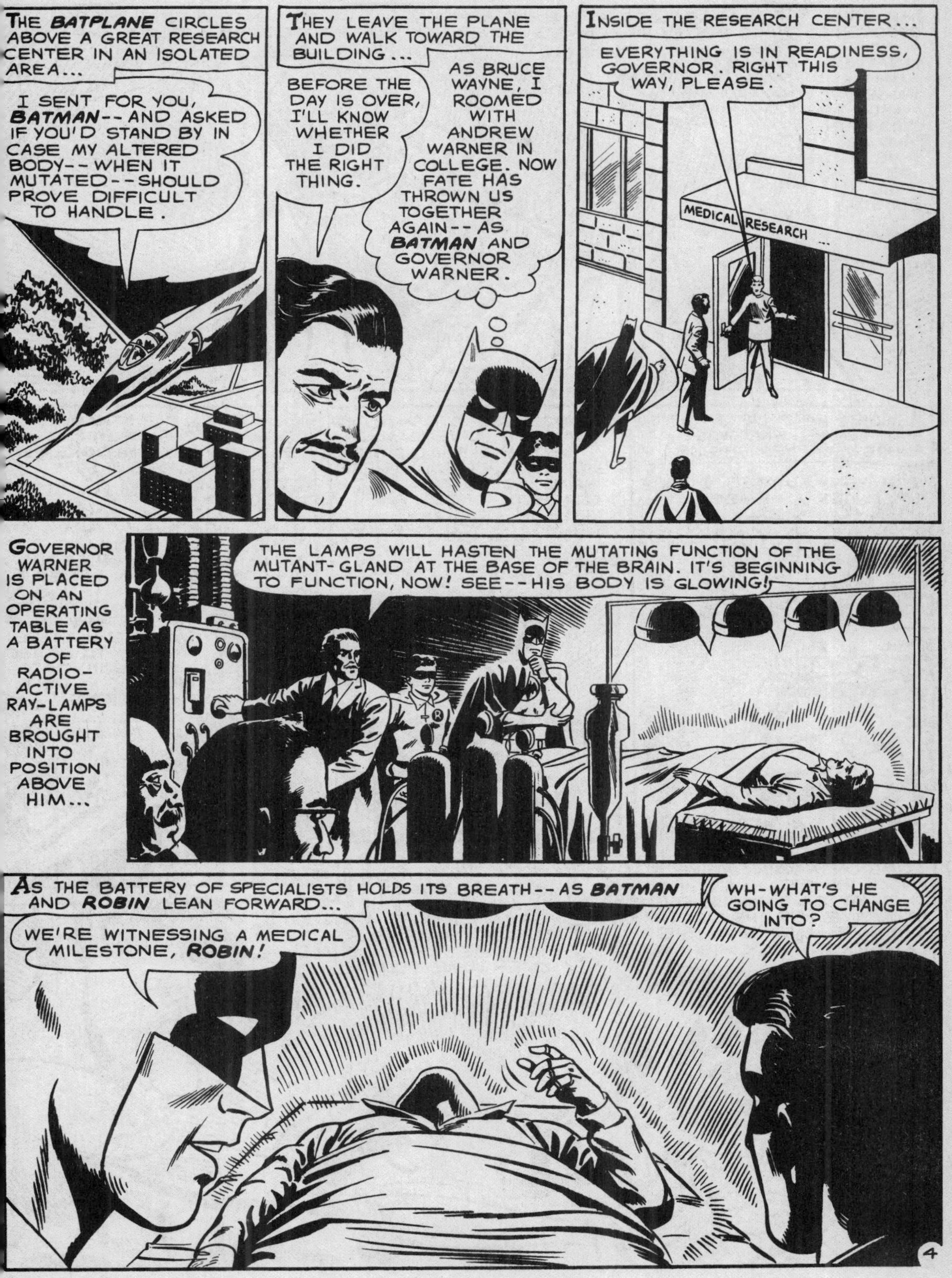
THE BATPLANE CIRCLES ABOVE A GREAT RESEARCH CENTER IN AN ISOLATED AREA...
I SENT FOR YOU, BATMAN--AND ASKED IF YOU'D STAND BY IN CASE MY ALTERED BODY--WHEN IT MUTATED--SHOULD PROVE DIFFICULT TO HANDLE.
THEY LEAVE THE PLANE AND WALK TOWARD THE BUILDING...
BEFORE THE DAY IS OVER, I'LL KNOW WHETHER I DID THE RIGHT THING.
AS BRUCE WAYNE, I ROOMED WITH ANDREW WARNER IN COLLEGE. NOW FATE HAS THROWN US TOGETHER AGAIN--AS BATMAN AND GOVERNOR WARNER.
INSIDE THE RESEARCH CENTER...
EVERYTHING IS IN READINESS, GOVERNOR. RIGHT THIS WAY, PLEASE.
MEDICAL RESEARCH
GOVERNOR WARNER IS PLACED ON AN OPERATING TABLE AS A BATTERY OF RADIO-ACTIVE RAY-LAMPS ARE BROUGHT INTO POSITION ABOVE HIM...
THE LAMPS WILL HASTEN THE MUTATING FUNCTION OF THE MUTANT-GLAND AT THE BASE OF THE BRAIN. IT'S BEGINNING TO FUNCTION, NOW! SEE--HIS BODY IS GLOWING!
AS THE BATTERY OF SPECIALISTS HOLDS ITS BREATH--AS BATMAN AND ROBIN LEAN FORWARD...
WE'RE WITNESSING A MEDICAL MILESTONE, ROBIN!
WH-WHAT'S HE GOING TO CHANGE INTO?
4

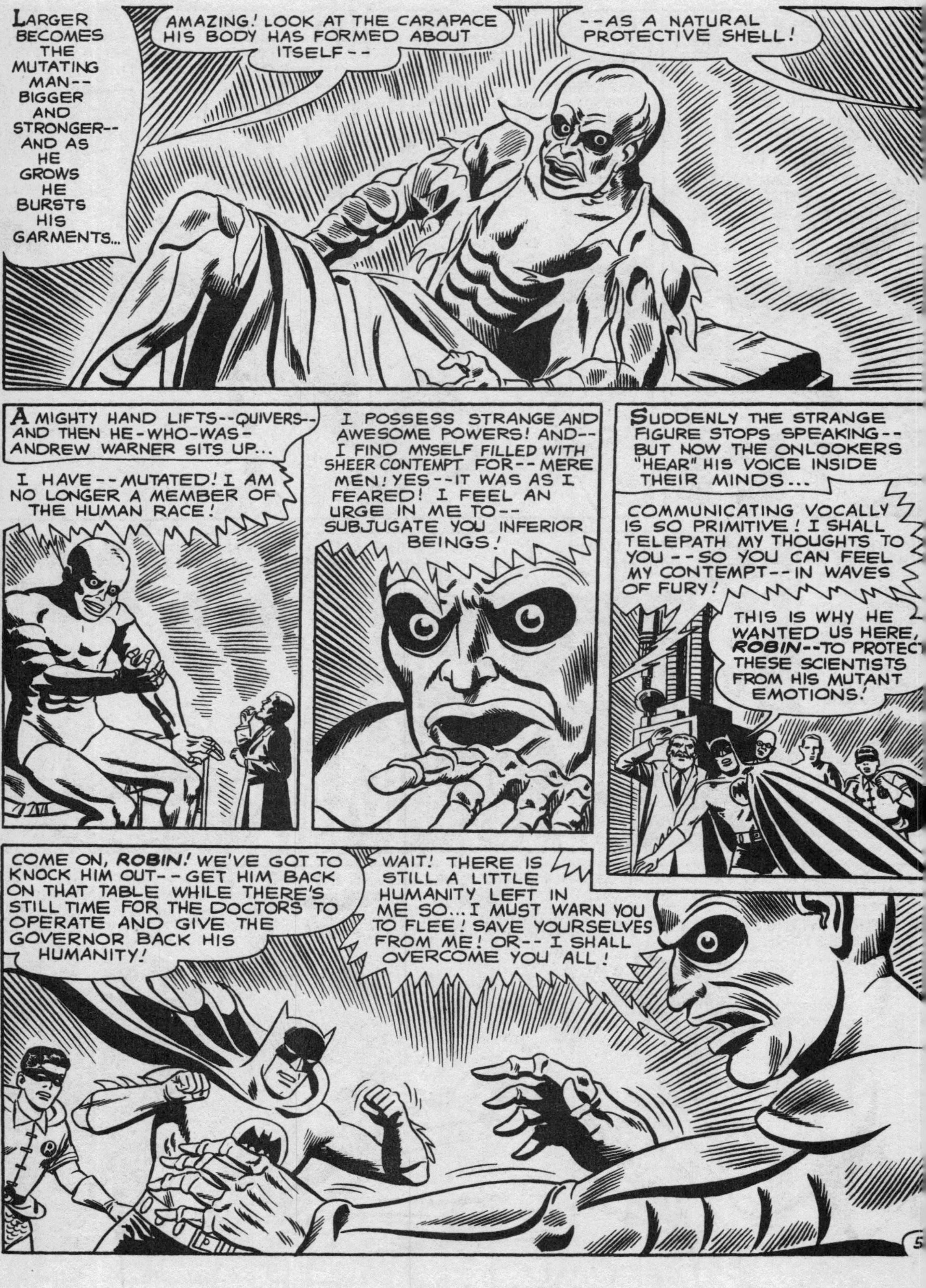
LARGER BECOMES THE MUTATING MAN--BIGGER AND STRONGER--AND AS HE GROWS HE BURSTS HIS GARMENTS...
AMAZING! LOOK AT THE CARAPACE HIS BODY HAS FORMED ABOUT ITSELF--
--AS A NATURAL PROTECTIVE SHELL!
A MIGHTY HAND LIFTS--QUIVERS--AND THEN HE-WHO-WAS-ANDREW WARNER SITS UP...
I HAVE--MUTATED! I AM NO LONGER A MEMBER OF THE HUMAN RACE!
I POSSESS STRANGE AND AWESOME POWERS! AND--I FIND MYSELF FILLED WITH SHEER CONTEMPT FOR--MERE MEN! YES--IT WAS AS I FEARED! I FEEL AN URGE IN ME TO--SUBJUGATE YOU INFERIOR BEINGS!
SUDDENLY THE STRANGE FIGURE STOPS SPEAKING--BUT NOW THE ONLOOKERS "HEAR" HIS VOICE INSIDE THEIR MINDS...
COMMUNICATING VOCALLY IS SO PRIMITIVE! I SHALL TELEPATH MY THOUGHTS TO YOU--SO YOU CAN FEEL MY CONTEMPT--IN WAVES OF FURY!
THIS IS WHY HE WANTED US HERE, ROBIN--TO PROTECT THESE SCIENTISTS FROM HIS MUTANT EMOTIONS!
COME ON, ROBIN! WE'VE GOT TO KNOCK HIM OUT--GET HIM BACK ON THAT TABLE WHILE THERE'S STILL TIME FOR THE DOCTORS TO OPERATE AND GIVE THE GOVERNOR BACK HIS HUMANITY!
WAIT! THERE IS STILL A LITTLE HUMANITY LEFT IN ME SO...I MUST WARN YOU TO FLEE! SAVE YOURSELVES FROM ME! OR--I SHALL OVERCOME YOU ALL!

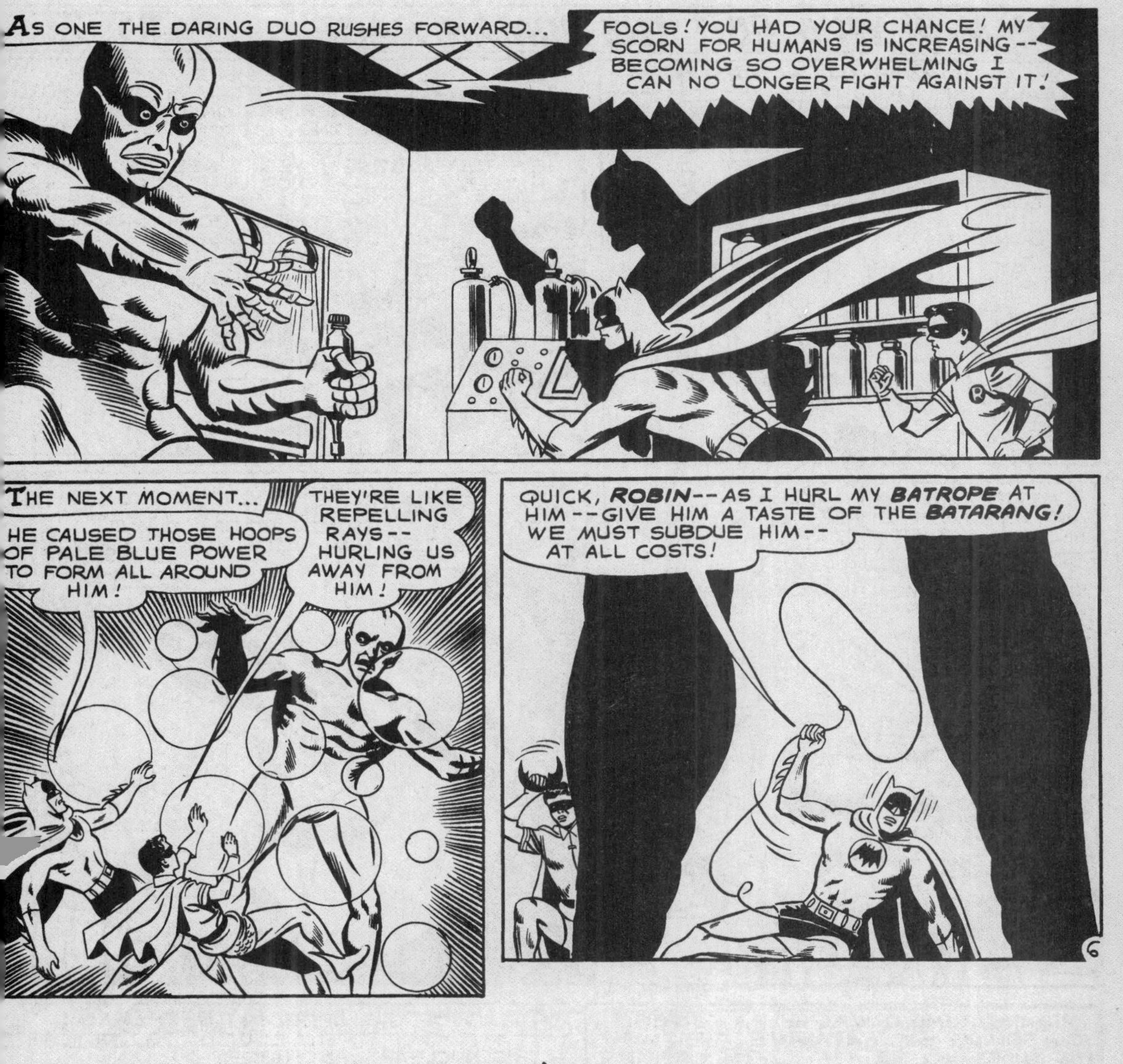
AS ONE THE DARING DUO RUSHES FORWARD...
FOOLS! YOU HAD YOUR CHANCE! MY SCORN FOR HUMANS IS INCREASING-- BECOMING SO OVERWHELMING I CAN NO LONGER FIGHT AGAINST IT!
THE NEXT MOMENT...
HE CAUSED THOSE HOOPS OF PALE BLUE POWER TO FORM ALL AROUND HIM!
THEY'RE LIKE REPELLING RAYS-- HURLING US AWAY FROM HIM!
QUICK, ROBIN--AS I HURL MY BATROPE AT HIM--GIVE HIM A TASTE OF THE BATARANG! WE MUST SUBDUE HIM-- AT ALL COSTS!
6

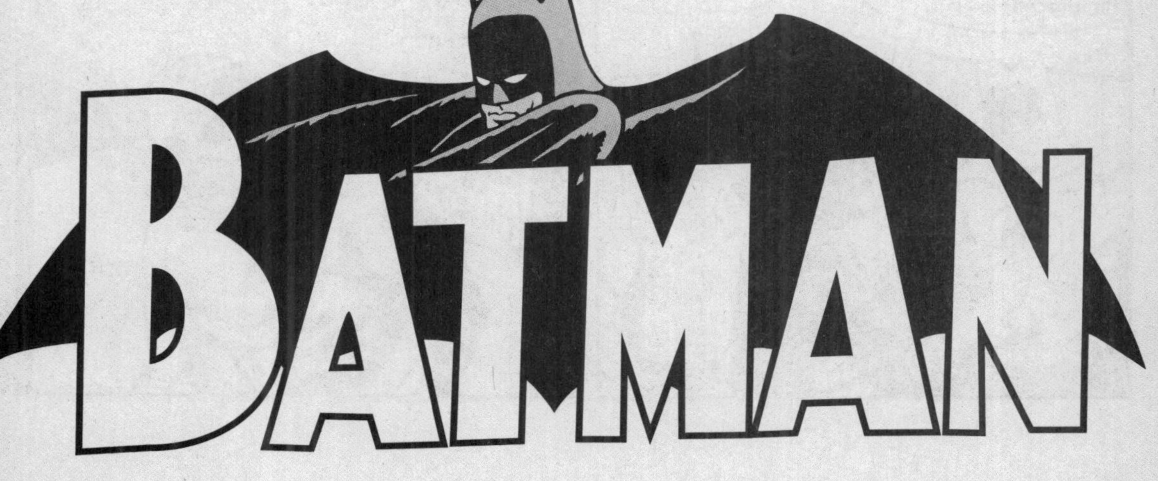
BATMAN

THE MAN WHO QUIT THE HUMAN RACE   PART 2

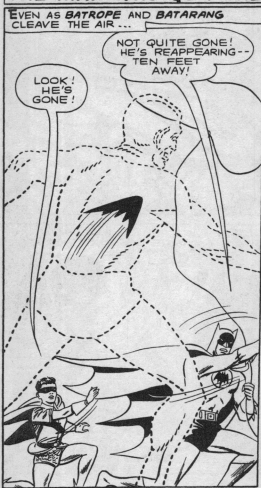

EVEN AS *BATROPE* AND *BATARANG* CLEAVE THE AIR...

LOOK! HE'S GONE!

NOT QUITE GONE! HE'S REAPPEARING-- TEN FEET AWAY!

BEFORE THE INCREDULOUS EYES OF THE DYNAMIC DUO, THE MUTATED MAN ONCE MORE FADES OUT AND REAPPEARS ON THE LAWN OUTSIDE THE BUILDING...

HE'S TELEPORTING HIMSELF!

YES! I NEED NOT RUN NOR LEAP TO GO WHERE I WANT! I CAN TELEPORT MYSELF BODILY ACROSS SMALL DISTANCES TO GET WHERE I'M GOING!

HE'S TRAVELING FASTER-- AND FURTHER AWAY--APPEARING ON THAT CAR AND ON THAT FARAWAY GREEN ROOF! I MUST KEEP AFTER HIM-- BUT HOW?

THIS INSTRUMENT WILL HELP YOU FOLLOW HIM, *BATMAN!* IT'S TUNED TO THE PULSATIONS OF THE MUTATION GLAND IN HIS HEAD!

SWELL! THEN WE CAN CATCH UP TO HIM IN THE *BATPLANE!*

AHEAD OF THE SPEEDING *BATPLANE*...

THIS NUCLEAR LABORATORY BUILDING WILL HAVE ALL I NEED TO COMPLETE MY MUTATION. AS SOON AS I BATHE IN GAMMA RAYS-- I'LL LOSE THE LAST OF MY HUMANITY!

NUCLEAR LAB B-9 DANGER

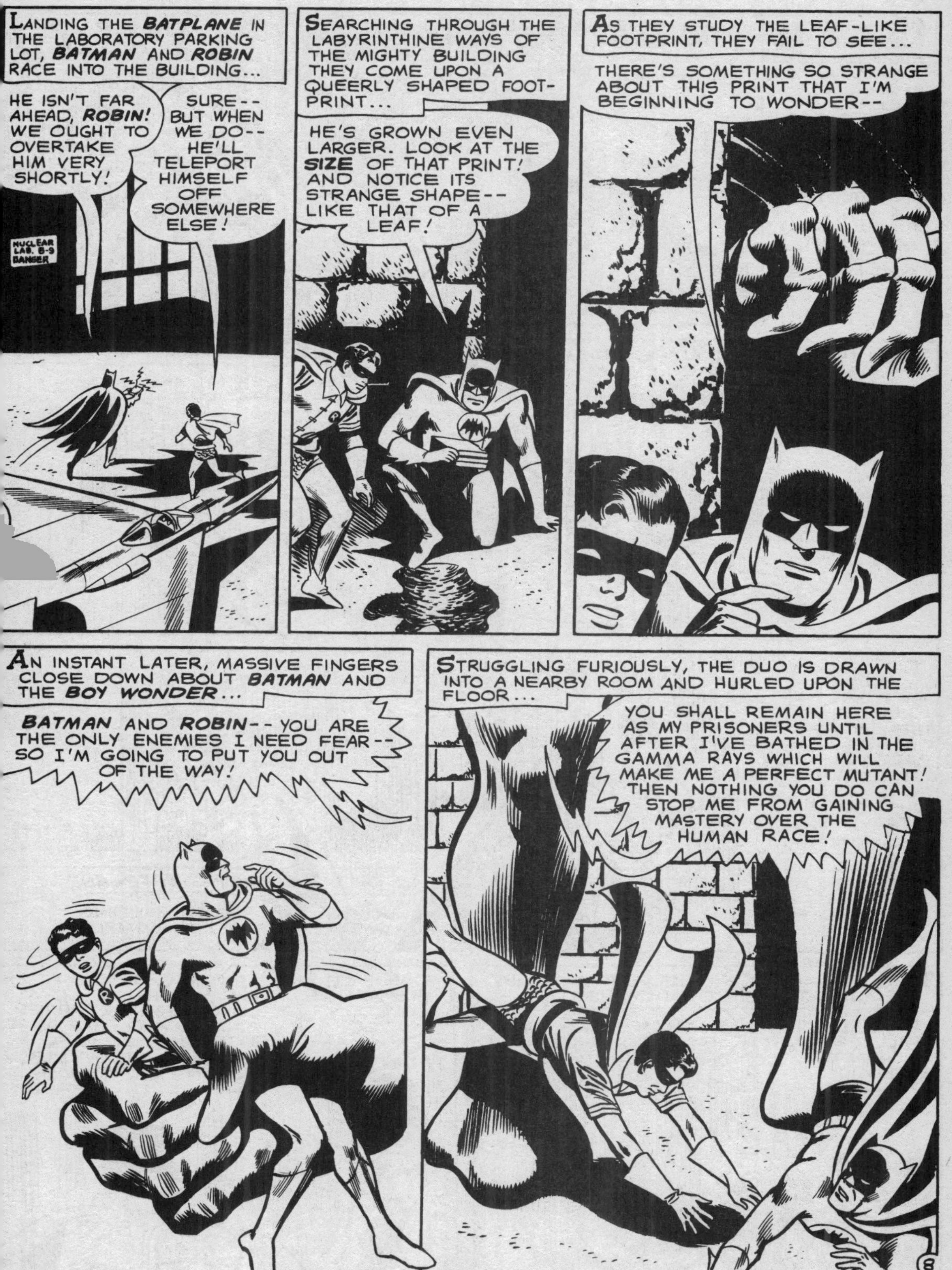
LANDING THE BATPLANE IN THE LABORATORY PARKING LOT, BATMAN AND ROBIN RACE INTO THE BUILDING...
HE ISN'T FAR AHEAD, ROBIN! WE OUGHT TO OVERTAKE HIM VERY SHORTLY!
SURE-- BUT WHEN WE DO-- HE'LL TELEPORT HIMSELF OFF SOMEWHERE ELSE!
NUCLEAR LAB. B-9 DANGER
SEARCHING THROUGH THE LABYRINTHINE WAYS OF THE MIGHTY BUILDING THEY COME UPON A QUEERLY SHAPED FOOT-PRINT...
HE'S GROWN EVEN LARGER. LOOK AT THE SIZE OF THAT PRINT! AND NOTICE ITS STRANGE SHAPE-- LIKE THAT OF A LEAF!
AS THEY STUDY THE LEAF-LIKE FOOTPRINT, THEY FAIL TO SEE...
THERE'S SOMETHING SO STRANGE ABOUT THIS PRINT THAT I'M BEGINNING TO WONDER--
AN INSTANT LATER, MASSIVE FINGERS CLOSE DOWN ABOUT BATMAN AND THE BOY WONDER...
BATMAN AND ROBIN-- YOU ARE THE ONLY ENEMIES I NEED FEAR-- SO I'M GOING TO PUT YOU OUT OF THE WAY!
STRUGGLING FURIOUSLY, THE DUO IS DRAWN INTO A NEARBY ROOM AND HURLED UPON THE FLOOR...
YOU SHALL REMAIN HERE AS MY PRISONERS UNTIL AFTER I'VE BATHED IN THE GAMMA RAYS WHICH WILL MAKE ME A PERFECT MUTANT! THEN NOTHING YOU DO CAN STOP ME FROM GAINING MASTERY OVER THE HUMAN RACE!
8

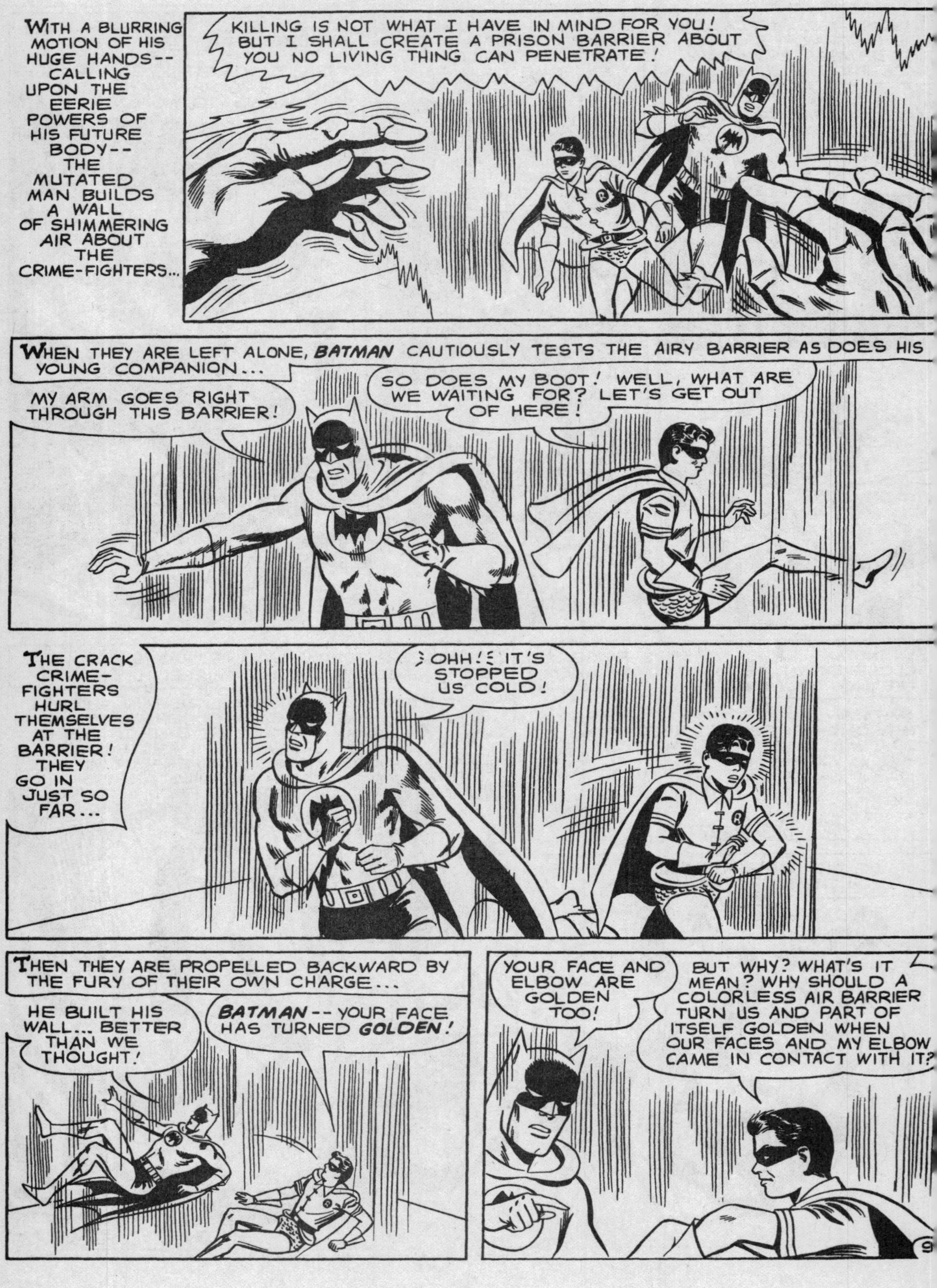
WITH A BLURRING MOTION OF HIS HUGE HANDS-- CALLING UPON THE EERIE POWERS OF HIS FUTURE BODY-- THE MUTATED MAN BUILDS A WALL OF SHIMMERING AIR ABOUT THE CRIME-FIGHTERS...
KILLING IS NOT WHAT I HAVE IN MIND FOR YOU! BUT I SHALL CREATE A PRISON BARRIER ABOUT YOU NO LIVING THING CAN PENETRATE!
WHEN THEY ARE LEFT ALONE, BATMAN CAUTIOUSLY TESTS THE AIRY BARRIER AS DOES HIS YOUNG COMPANION...
MY ARM GOES RIGHT THROUGH THIS BARRIER!
SO DOES MY BOOT! WELL, WHAT ARE WE WAITING FOR? LET'S GET OUT OF HERE!
THE CRACK CRIME-FIGHTERS HURL THEMSELVES AT THE BARRIER! THEY GO IN JUST SO FAR...
OHH! IT'S STOPPED US COLD!
THEN THEY ARE PROPELLED BACKWARD BY THE FURY OF THEIR OWN CHARGE...
HE BUILT HIS WALL... BETTER THAN WE THOUGHT!
BATMAN -- YOUR FACE HAS TURNED GOLDEN!
YOUR FACE AND ELBOW ARE GOLDEN TOO!
BUT WHY? WHAT'S IT MEAN? WHY SHOULD A COLORLESS AIR BARRIER TURN US AND PART OF ITSELF GOLDEN WHEN OUR FACES AND MY ELBOW CAME IN CONTACT WITH IT?
9

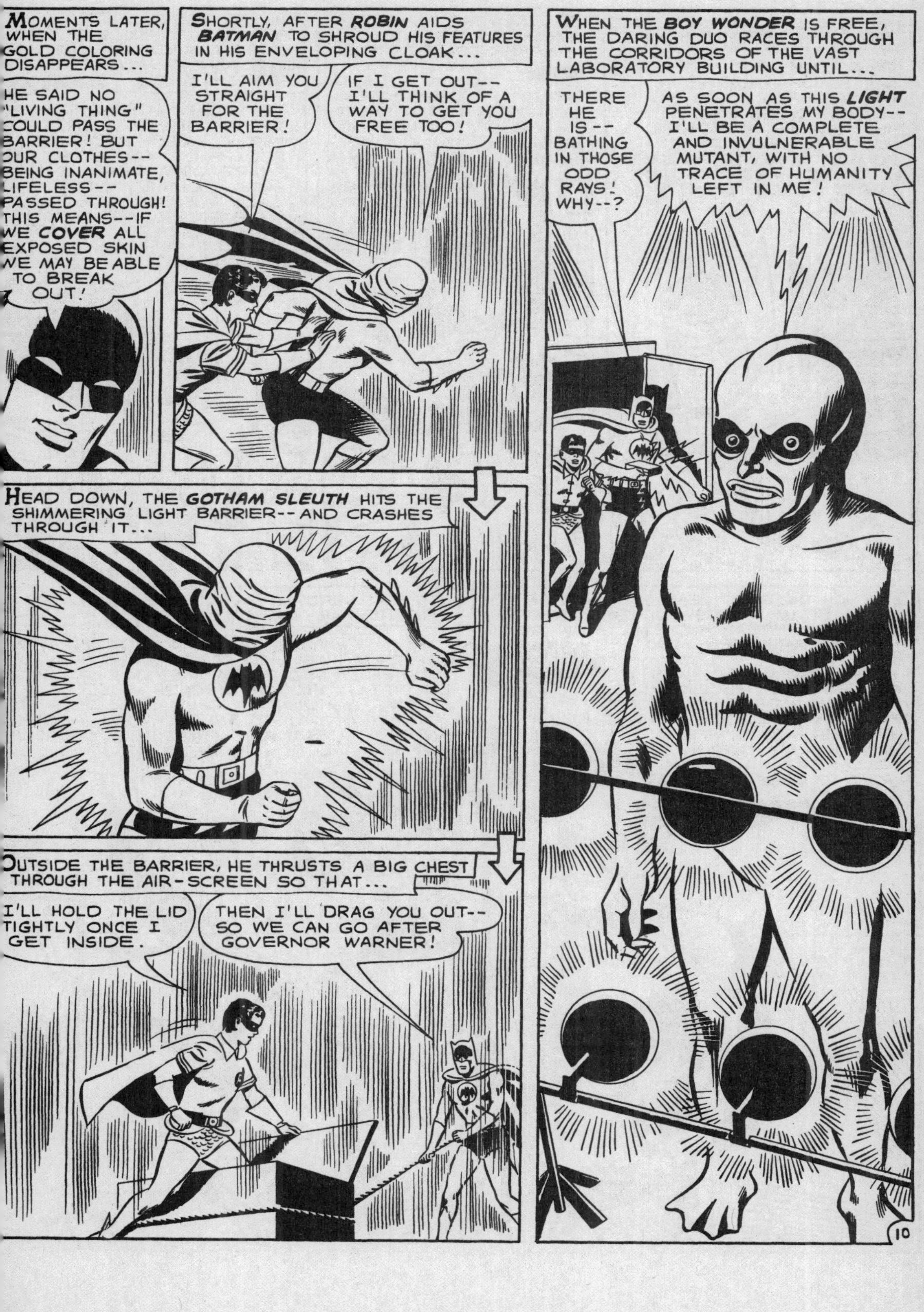
MOMENTS LATER, WHEN THE GOLD COLORING DISAPPEARS...
HE SAID NO "LIVING THING" COULD PASS THE BARRIER! BUT OUR CLOTHES-- BEING INANIMATE, LIFELESS-- PASSED THROUGH! THIS MEANS--IF WE COVER ALL EXPOSED SKIN WE MAY BE ABLE TO BREAK OUT!
SHORTLY, AFTER ROBIN AIDS BATMAN TO SHROUD HIS FEATURES IN HIS ENVELOPING CLOAK...
I'LL AIM YOU STRAIGHT FOR THE BARRIER!
IF I GET OUT-- I'LL THINK OF A WAY TO GET YOU FREE TOO!
HEAD DOWN, THE GOTHAM SLEUTH HITS THE SHIMMERING LIGHT BARRIER--AND CRASHES THROUGH IT...
OUTSIDE THE BARRIER, HE THRUSTS A BIG CHEST THROUGH THE AIR-SCREEN SO THAT...
I'LL HOLD THE LID TIGHTLY ONCE I GET INSIDE.
THEN I'LL DRAG YOU OUT-- SO WE CAN GO AFTER GOVERNOR WARNER!
WHEN THE BOY WONDER IS FREE, THE DARING DUO RACES THROUGH THE CORRIDORS OF THE VAST LABORATORY BUILDING UNTIL...
THERE HE IS-- BATHING IN THOSE ODD RAYS! WHY--?
AS SOON AS THIS LIGHT PENETRATES MY BODY-- I'LL BE A COMPLETE AND INVULNERABLE MUTANT, WITH NO TRACE OF HUMANITY LEFT IN ME!
10

FOR A MOMENT, *BATMAN* STANDS FROZEN IN THOUGHT, THEN...

OF COURSE! THE LAST FEW TRACES OF HUMANITY IN WARNER HAVE BEEN LEAVING CLUES BEHIND HIM--FOR ME TO UNDERSTAND! BUT UNTIL THIS MOMENT I NEVER REALIZED WHAT THEY MEANT! *GOLD! LEAF! GREEN! LIGHT!*

QUICKLY, THE CAPED CRUSADER TURNS TO ANOTHER CORNER OF THE LABORATORY...

THAT SOUNDS LIKE GIBBERISH TO ME.

THE GOVERNOR'S MUTANT PART FORBID HIM TO HELP ME-- BUT THE HUMAN PART OF HIS MIND LEFT ME CLUES TELLING ME HOW TO DEFEAT HIM--WITHOUT THE MUTATED SECTION REVEALING IT!

THE DYNAMIC DUO LIFTS A FRAGILE RECTANGLE OF THINLY BEATEN GOLD LEAF, HOLDING IT BEFORE A POWERFUL SEARCHLIGHT...

HE TELEPORTED ONTO *GREEN* GRASS, A *GREEN* CAR, A *GREEN* ROOF. HIS FOOTPRINT WAS IN THE SHAPE OF A *LEAF.* OUR FACES TURNED *GOLD* WHEN WE CONTACTED HIS AIR-BARRIER! AND, FINALLY, HE EMPHASIZED THAT *LIGHT* WOULD MAKE HIM INVULNERABLE!

SO?

THROUGH THE GOLD LEAF THE BRILLIANT LIGHT-BEAM PASSES--CAUSING A GREEN BEAM TO APPEAR AND FALL UPON THE MASSIVE MUTATED MAN...

YEARS AGO WHEN I WAS IN COLLEGE AS BRUCE WAYNE, ANDREW WARNER AND I TOOK PART IN A PHYSICS EXPERIMENT IN WHICH--BY SHINING A BRIGHT LIGHT THROUGH GOLD LEAF--A *GREEN* LIGHT EMERGED!

AS THAT VERDANT BRILLIANCE COATS THE FUTURE MAN-- HE COLLAPSES...

BUT GOVERNOR WARNER DOESN'T KNOW YOU'RE BRUCE WAYNE!

TRUE--BUT AS A *MUTATED MAN* ABLE TO TELEPATH HIS THOUGHTS AND PERHAPS EVEN READ MINDS HE SAW THROUGH MY SECRET IDENTITY TO MY TRUE SELF! IT WAS TO *BRUCE WAYNE*-- NOT *BATMAN*--THAT HE ADDRESSED THOSE CLUES!

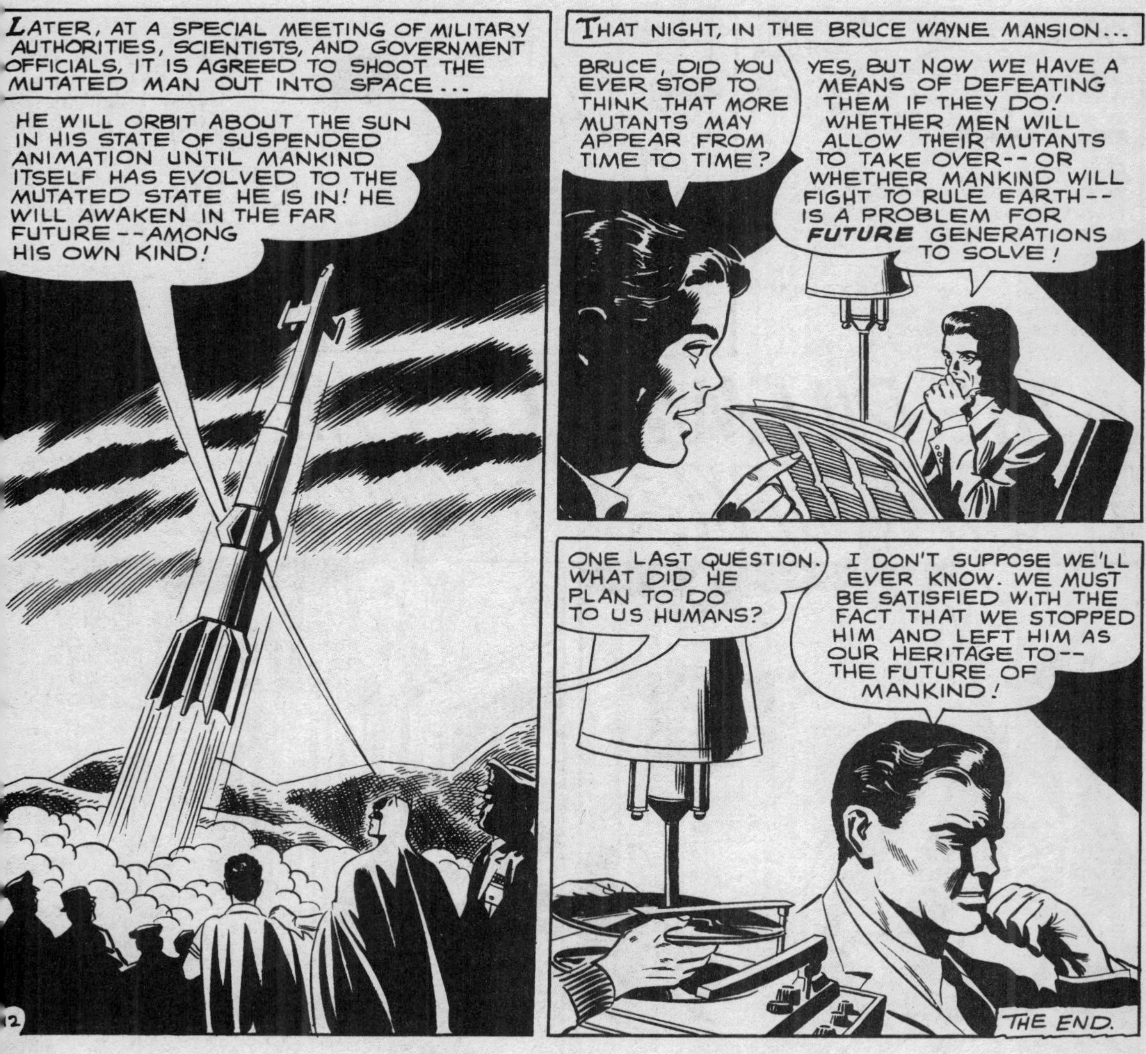
LATER, AT A SPECIAL MEETING OF MILITARY AUTHORITIES, SCIENTISTS, AND GOVERNMENT OFFICIALS, IT IS AGREED TO SHOOT THE MUTATED MAN OUT INTO SPACE...
HE WILL ORBIT ABOUT THE SUN IN HIS STATE OF SUSPENDED ANIMATION UNTIL MANKIND ITSELF HAS EVOLVED TO THE MUTATED STATE HE IS IN! HE WILL AWAKEN IN THE FAR FUTURE--AMONG HIS OWN KIND!
THAT NIGHT, IN THE BRUCE WAYNE MANSION...
BRUCE, DID YOU EVER STOP TO THINK THAT MORE MUTANTS MAY APPEAR FROM TIME TO TIME?
YES, BUT NOW WE HAVE A MEANS OF DEFEATING THEM IF THEY DO! WHETHER MEN WILL ALLOW THEIR MUTANTS TO TAKE OVER--OR WHETHER MANKIND WILL FIGHT TO RULE EARTH--IS A PROBLEM FOR FUTURE GENERATIONS TO SOLVE!
ONE LAST QUESTION. WHAT DID HE PLAN TO DO TO US HUMANS?
I DON'T SUPPOSE WE'LL EVER KNOW. WE MUST BE SATISFIED WITH THE FACT THAT WE STOPPED HIM AND LEFT HIM AS OUR HERITAGE TO--THE FUTURE OF MANKIND!
THE END.

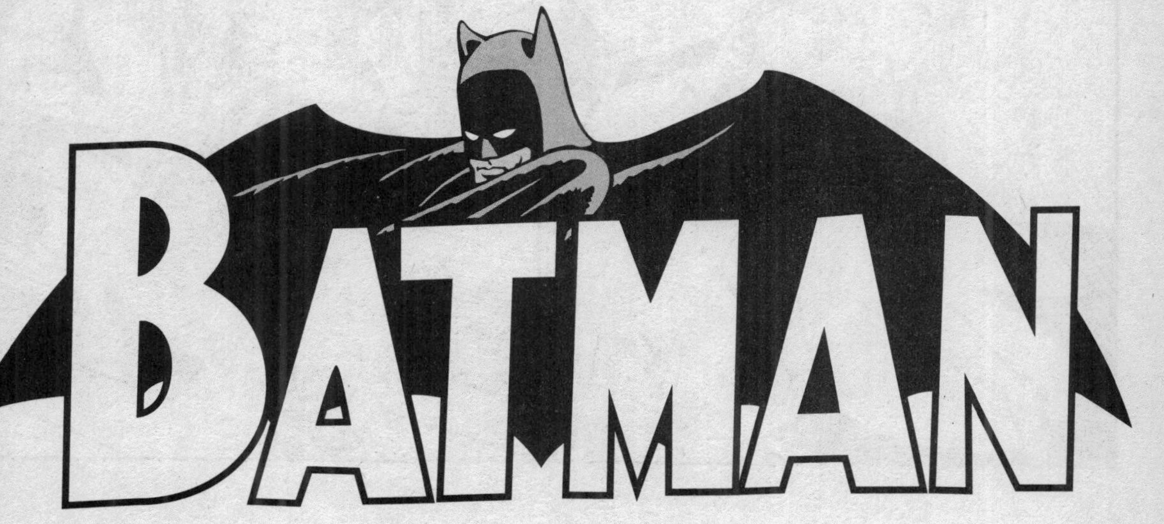
BATMAN

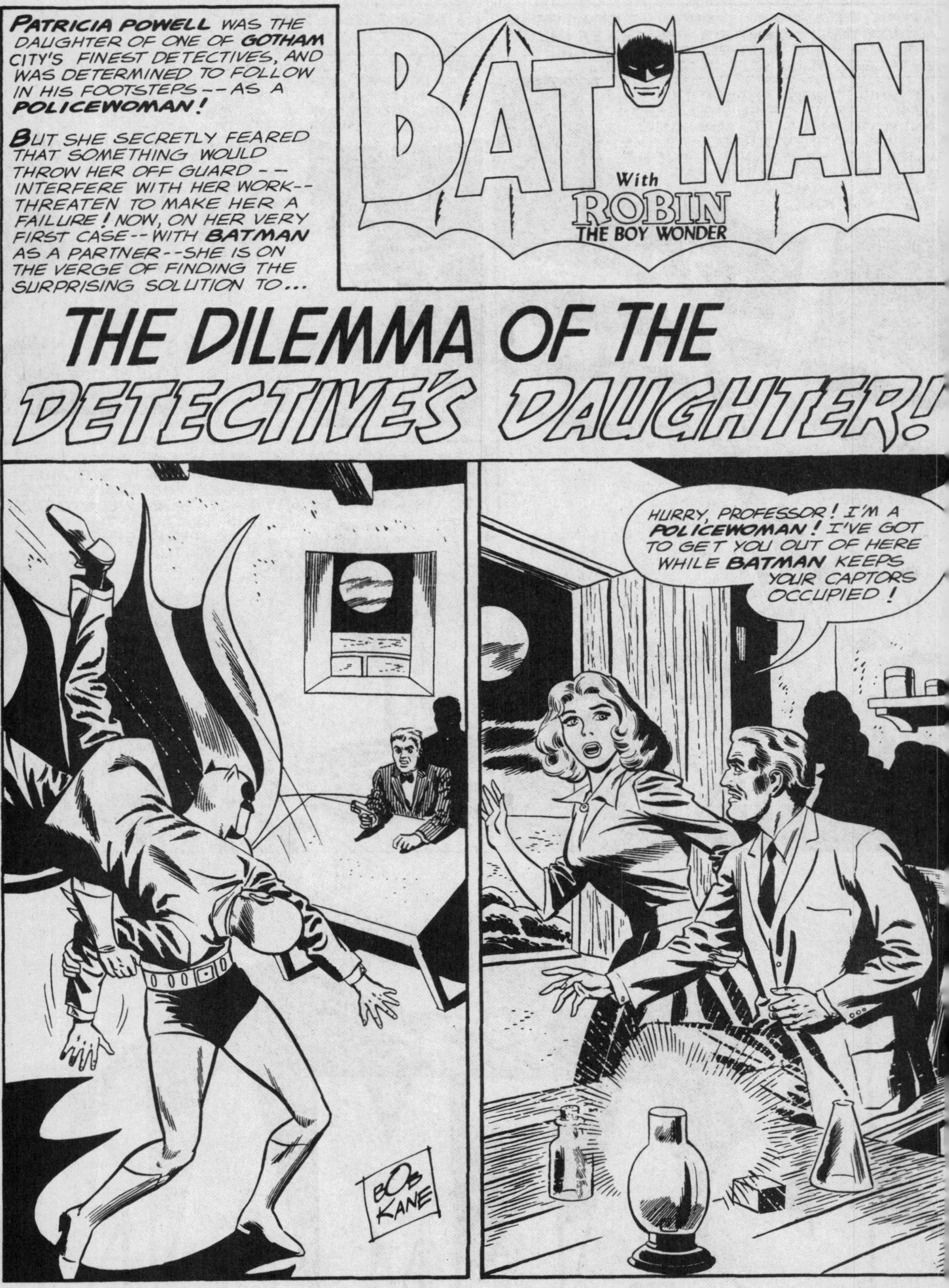
PATRICIA POWELL WAS THE DAUGHTER OF ONE OF GOTHAM CITY'S FINEST DETECTIVES, AND WAS DETERMINED TO FOLLOW IN HIS FOOTSTEPS--AS A POLICEWOMAN!
BUT SHE SECRETLY FEARED THAT SOMETHING WOULD THROW HER OFF GUARD--INTERFERE WITH HER WORK--THREATEN TO MAKE HER A FAILURE! NOW, ON HER VERY FIRST CASE--WITH BATMAN AS A PARTNER--SHE IS ON THE VERGE OF FINDING THE SURPRISING SOLUTION TO...
BATMAN
With ROBIN THE BOY WONDER
THE DILEMMA OF THE DETECTIVE'S DAUGHTER!
BOB KANE
HURRY, PROFESSOR! I'M A POLICEWOMAN! I'VE GOT TO GET YOU OUT OF HERE WHILE BATMAN KEEPS YOUR CAPTORS OCCUPIED!

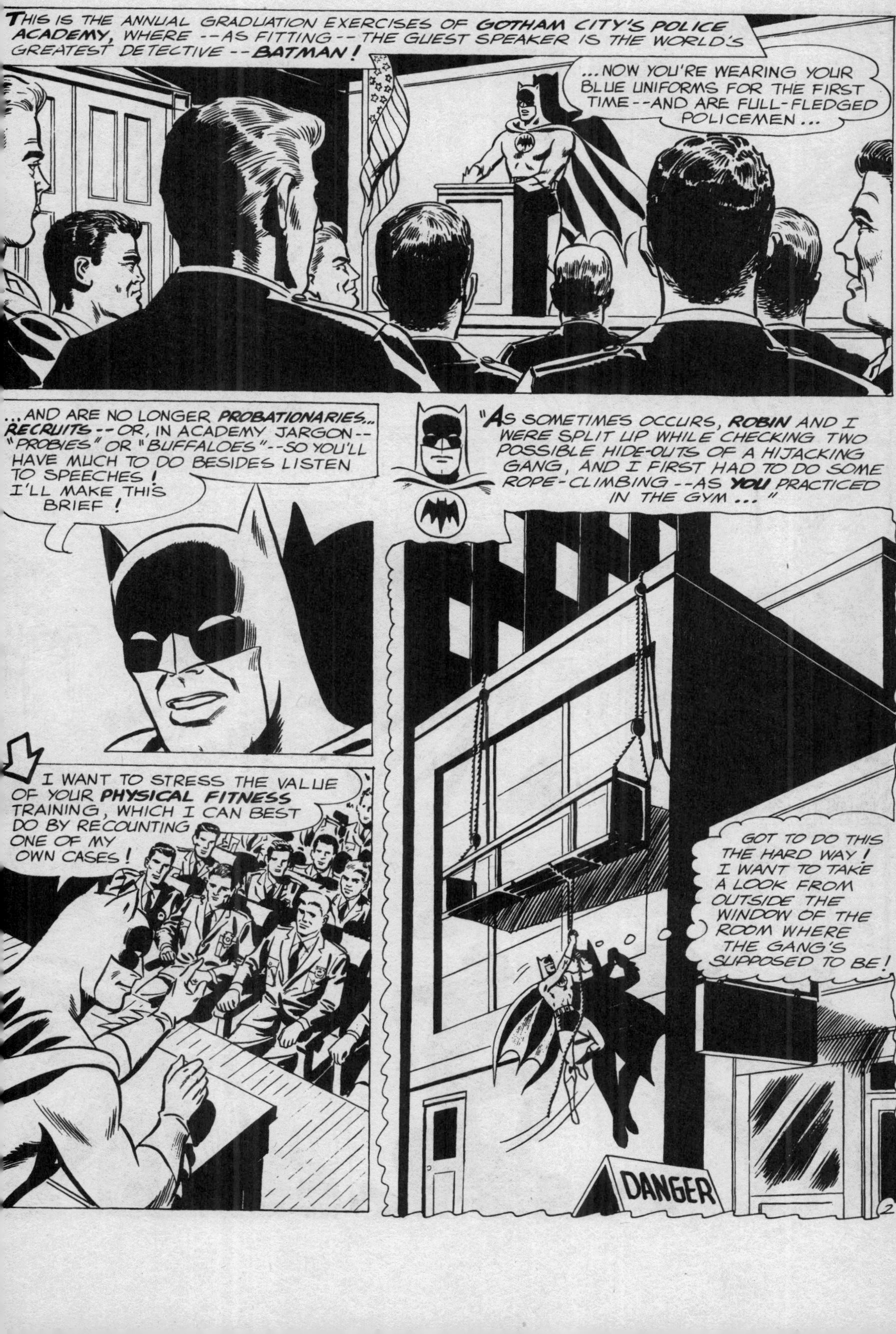
THIS IS THE ANNUAL GRADUATION EXERCISES OF GOTHAM CITY'S POLICE ACADEMY, WHERE --AS FITTING-- THE GUEST SPEAKER IS THE WORLD'S GREATEST DETECTIVE --BATMAN!
...NOW YOU'RE WEARING YOUR BLUE UNIFORMS FOR THE FIRST TIME--AND ARE FULL-FLEDGED POLICEMEN...
...AND ARE NO LONGER PROBATIONARIES... RECRUITS--OR, IN ACADEMY JARGON--"PROBIES" OR "BUFFALOES"--SO YOU'LL HAVE MUCH TO DO BESIDES LISTEN TO SPEECHES! I'LL MAKE THIS BRIEF!
I WANT TO STRESS THE VALUE OF YOUR PHYSICAL FITNESS TRAINING, WHICH I CAN BEST DO BY RECOUNTING ONE OF MY OWN CASES!
"AS SOMETIMES OCCURS, ROBIN AND I WERE SPLIT UP WHILE CHECKING TWO POSSIBLE HIDE-OUTS OF A HIJACKING GANG, AND I FIRST HAD TO DO SOME ROPE-CLIMBING--AS YOU PRACTICED IN THE GYM..."
GOT TO DO THIS THE HARD WAY! I WANT TO TAKE A LOOK FROM OUTSIDE THE WINDOW OF THE ROOM WHERE THE GANG'S SUPPOSED TO BE!
DANGER
2

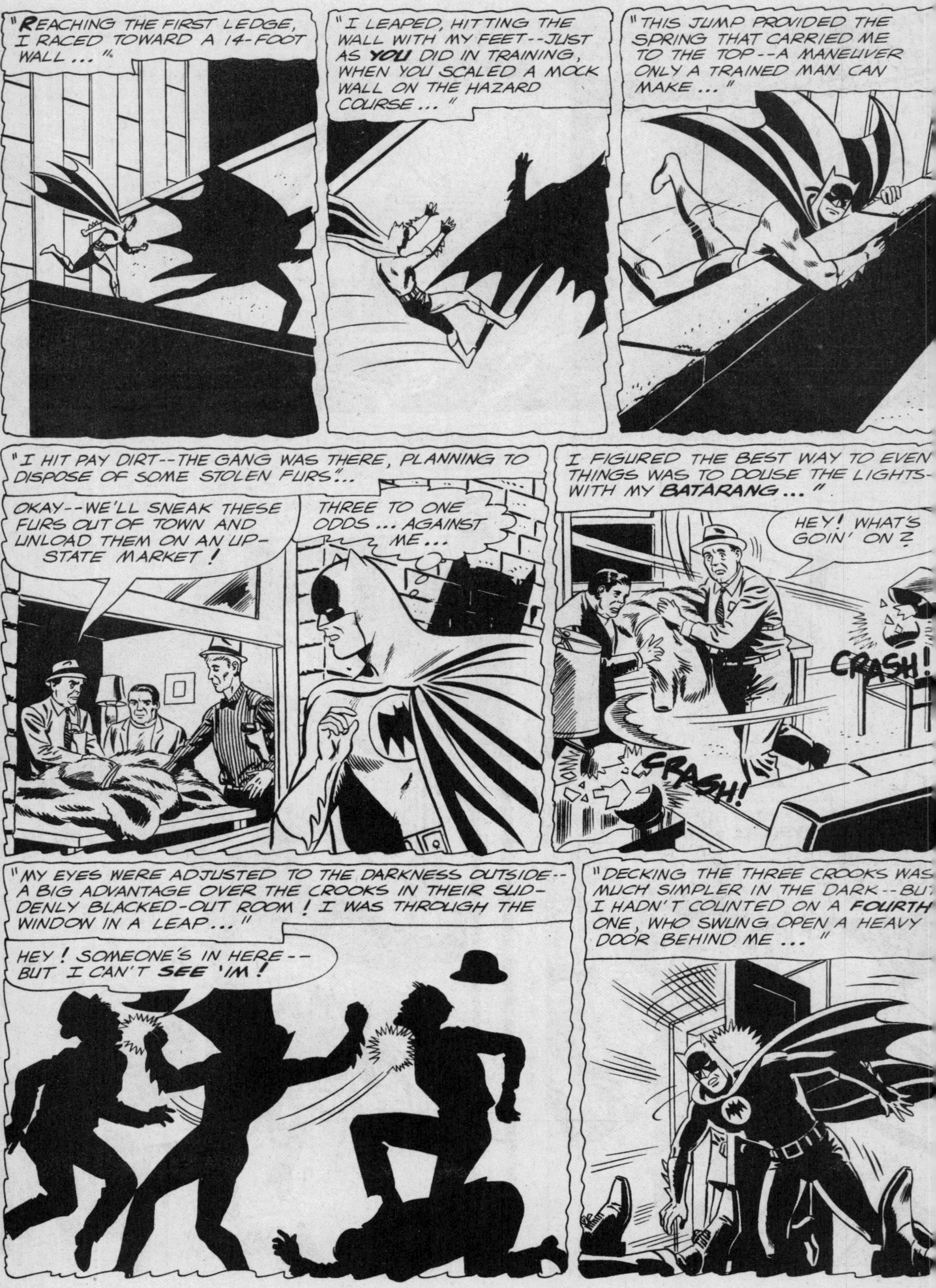
"REACHING THE FIRST LEDGE, I RACED TOWARD A 14-FOOT WALL ..."
"I LEAPED, HITTING THE WALL WITH MY FEET--JUST AS YOU DID IN TRAINING, WHEN YOU SCALED A MOCK WALL ON THE HAZARD COURSE ..."
"THIS JUMP PROVIDED THE SPRING THAT CARRIED ME TO THE TOP--A MANEUVER ONLY A TRAINED MAN CAN MAKE ..."
"I HIT PAY DIRT--THE GANG WAS THERE, PLANNING TO DISPOSE OF SOME STOLEN FURS"...
OKAY--WE'LL SNEAK THESE FURS OUT OF TOWN AND UNLOAD THEM ON AN UP-STATE MARKET!
THREE TO ONE ODDS ... AGAINST ME...
I FIGURED THE BEST WAY TO EVEN THINGS WAS TO DOUSE THE LIGHTS-WITH MY BATARANG ..."
HEY! WHAT'S GOIN' ON?
CRASH!
CRASH!
"MY EYES WERE ADJUSTED TO THE DARKNESS OUTSIDE--A BIG ADVANTAGE OVER THE CROOKS IN THEIR SUDDENLY BLACKED-OUT ROOM! I WAS THROUGH THE WINDOW IN A LEAP ..."
HEY! SOMEONE'S IN HERE--BUT I CAN'T SEE 'IM!
"DECKING THE THREE CROOKS WAS MUCH SIMPLER IN THE DARK--BUT I HADN'T COUNTED ON A FOURTH ONE, WHO SWUNG OPEN A HEAVY DOOR BEHIND ME ..."

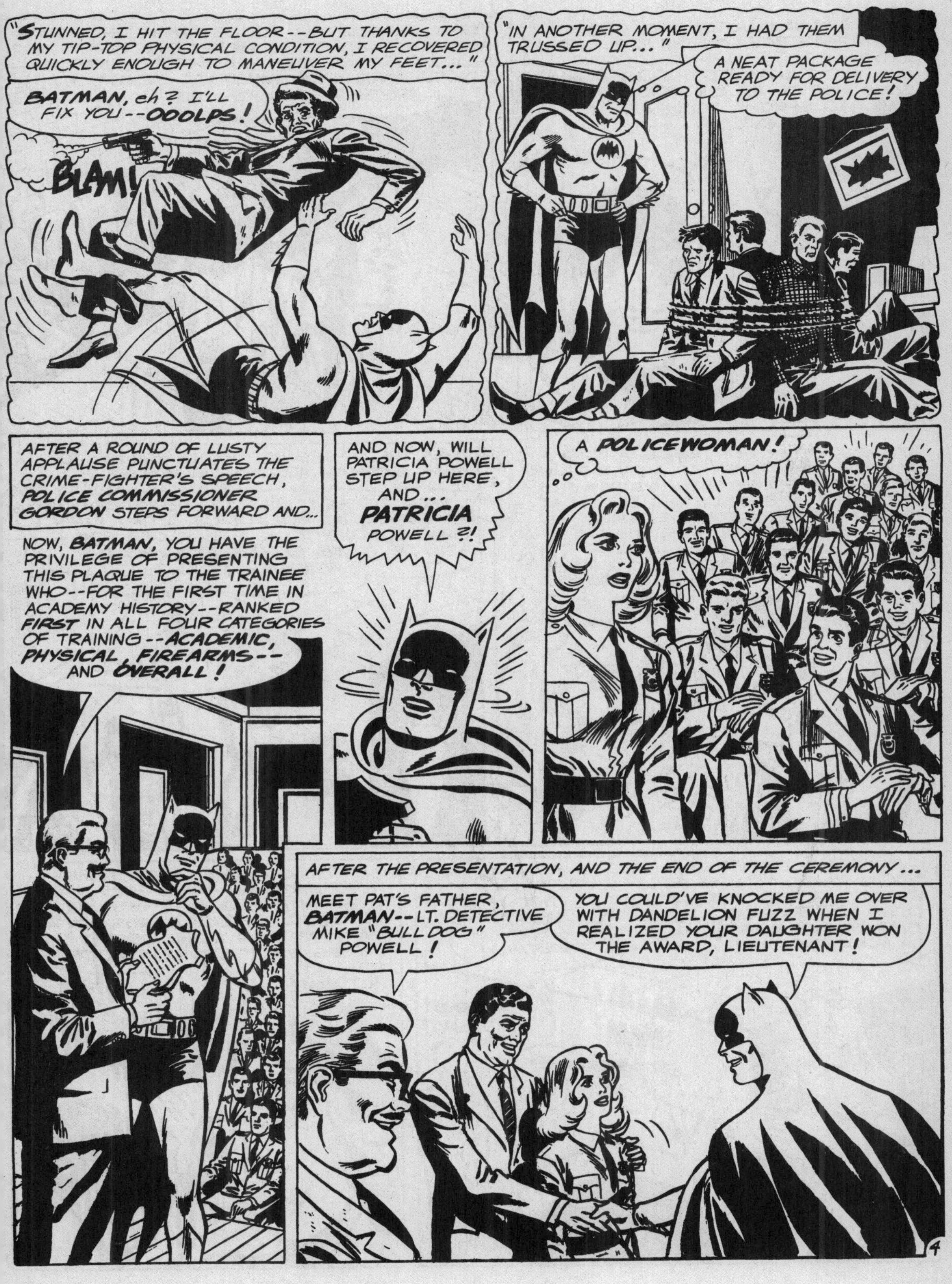
"STUNNED, I HIT THE FLOOR--BUT THANKS TO MY TIP-TOP PHYSICAL CONDITION, I RECOVERED QUICKLY ENOUGH TO MANEUVER MY FEET..."
BATMAN, eh? I'LL FIX YOU--OOOLPS!
BLAM!
"IN ANOTHER MOMENT, I HAD THEM TRUSSED UP..."
A NEAT PACKAGE READY FOR DELIVERY TO THE POLICE!
AFTER A ROUND OF LUSTY APPLAUSE PUNCTUATES THE CRIME-FIGHTER'S SPEECH, POLICE COMMISSIONER GORDON STEPS FORWARD AND...
NOW, BATMAN, YOU HAVE THE PRIVILEGE OF PRESENTING THIS PLAQUE TO THE TRAINEE WHO--FOR THE FIRST TIME IN ACADEMY HISTORY--RANKED FIRST IN ALL FOUR CATEGORIES OF TRAINING--ACADEMIC, PHYSICAL, FIREARMS--AND OVERALL!
AND NOW, WILL PATRICIA POWELL STEP UP HERE, AND... PATRICIA POWELL?!
A POLICEWOMAN!
AFTER THE PRESENTATION, AND THE END OF THE CEREMONY...
MEET PAT'S FATHER, BATMAN--LT. DETECTIVE MIKE "BULLDOG" POWELL!
YOU COULD'VE KNOCKED ME OVER WITH DANDELION FUZZ WHEN I REALIZED YOUR DAUGHTER WON THE AWARD, LIEUTENANT!
4

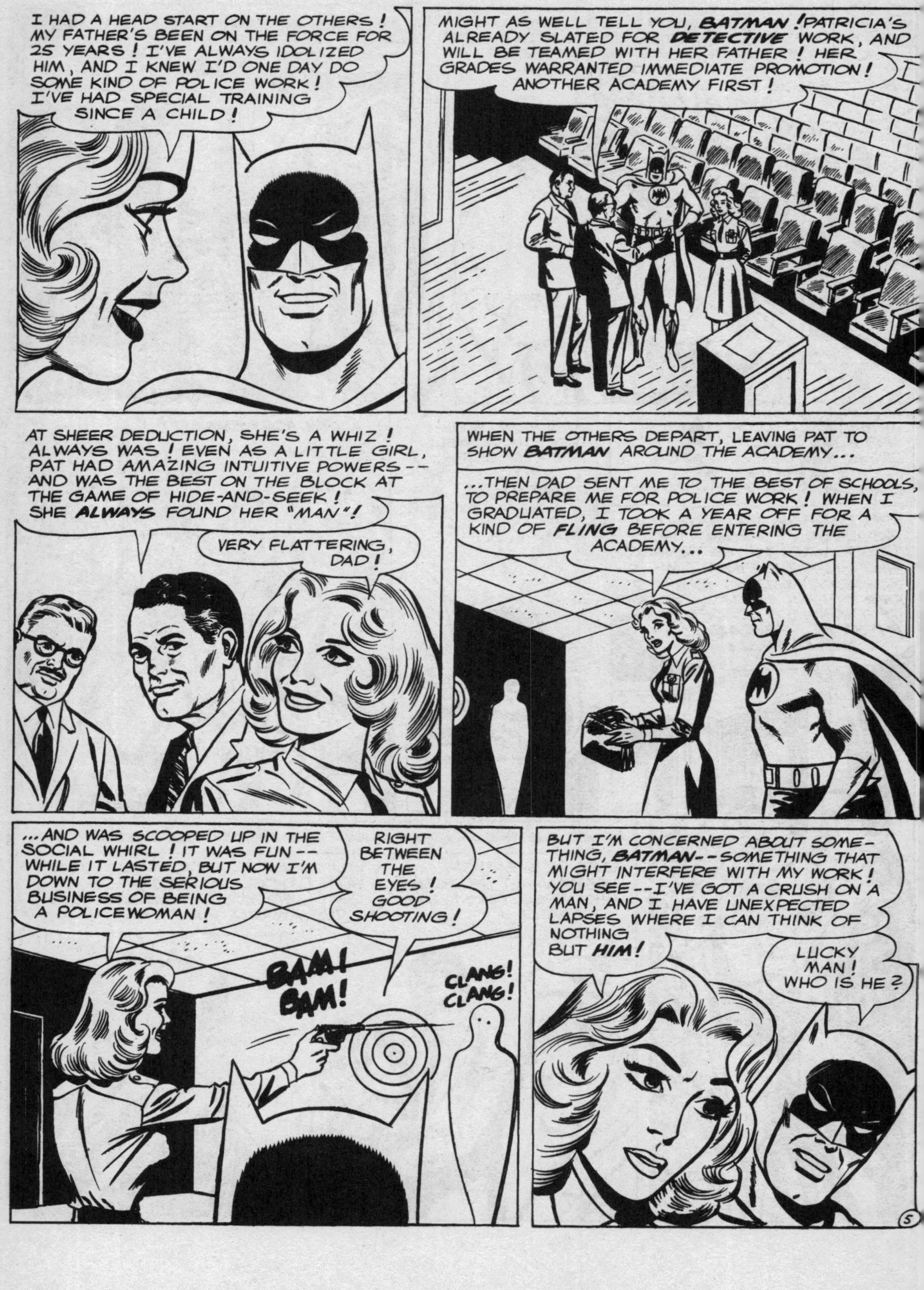
I HAD A HEAD START ON THE OTHERS! MY FATHER'S BEEN ON THE FORCE FOR 25 YEARS! I'VE ALWAYS IDOLIZED HIM, AND I KNEW I'D ONE DAY DO SOME KIND OF POLICE WORK! I'VE HAD SPECIAL TRAINING SINCE A CHILD!
MIGHT AS WELL TELL YOU, BATMAN! PATRICIA'S ALREADY SLATED FOR DETECTIVE WORK, AND WILL BE TEAMED WITH HER FATHER! HER GRADES WARRANTED IMMEDIATE PROMOTION! ANOTHER ACADEMY FIRST!
AT SHEER DEDUCTION, SHE'S A WHIZ! ALWAYS WAS! EVEN AS A LITTLE GIRL, PAT HAD AMAZING INTUITIVE POWERS-- AND WAS THE BEST ON THE BLOCK AT THE GAME OF HIDE-AND-SEEK! SHE ALWAYS FOUND HER "MAN"!
VERY FLATTERING, DAD!
WHEN THE OTHERS DEPART, LEAVING PAT TO SHOW BATMAN AROUND THE ACADEMY...
...THEN DAD SENT ME TO THE BEST OF SCHOOLS, TO PREPARE ME FOR POLICE WORK! WHEN I GRADUATED, I TOOK A YEAR OFF FOR A KIND OF FLING BEFORE ENTERING THE ACADEMY...
...AND WAS SCOOPED UP IN THE SOCIAL WHIRL! IT WAS FUN-- WHILE IT LASTED, BUT NOW I'M DOWN TO THE SERIOUS BUSINESS OF BEING A POLICEWOMAN!
RIGHT BETWEEN THE EYES! GOOD SHOOTING!
BAM! BAM!
CLANG! CLANG!
BUT I'M CONCERNED ABOUT SOMETHING, BATMAN--SOMETHING THAT MIGHT INTERFERE WITH MY WORK! YOU SEE--I'VE GOT A CRUSH ON A MAN, AND I HAVE UNEXPECTED LAPSES WHERE I CAN THINK OF NOTHING BUT HIM!
LUCKY MAN! WHO IS HE?
5

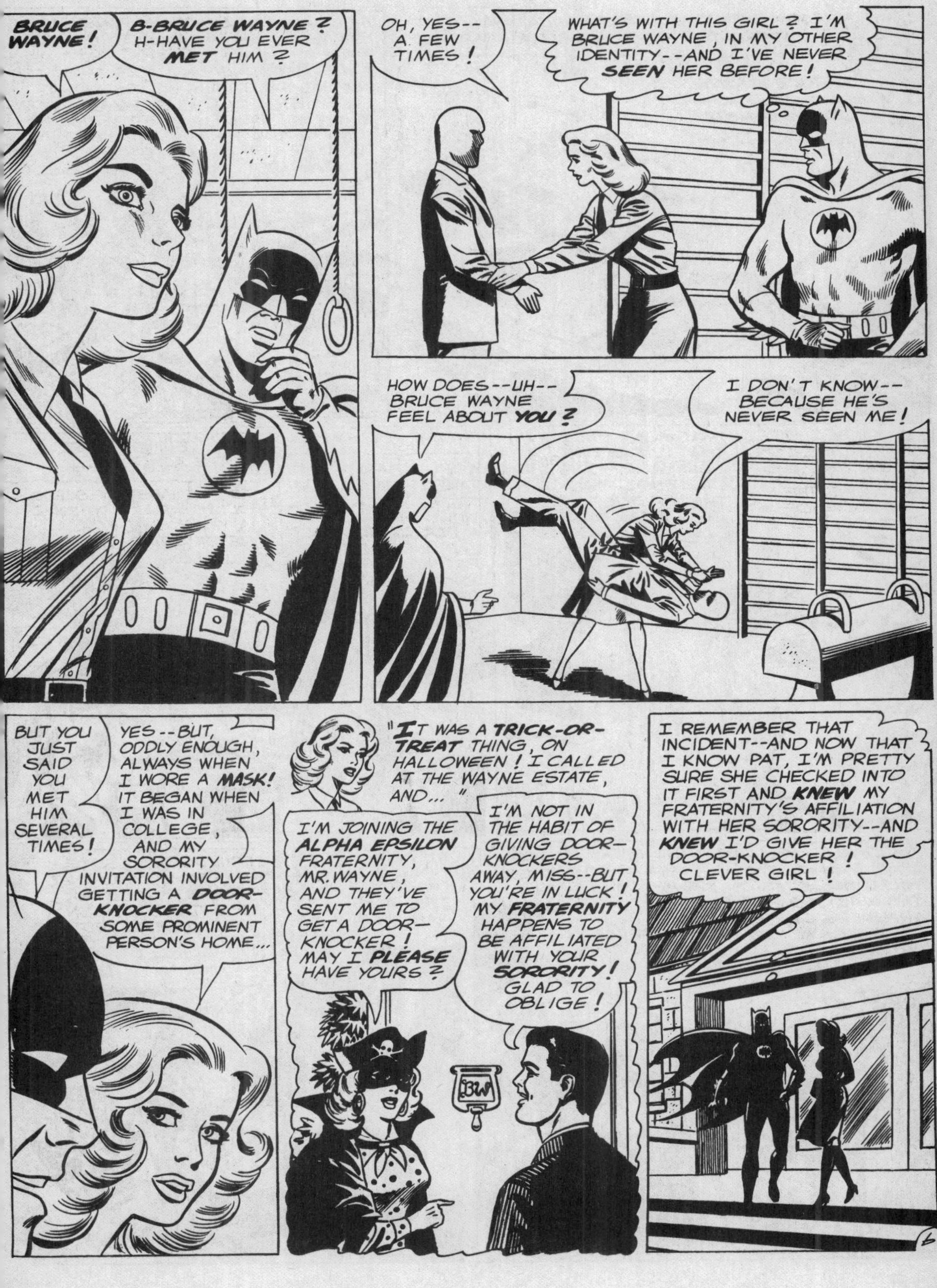
BRUCE WAYNE!
B-BRUCE WAYNE? H-HAVE YOU EVER MET HIM?
OH, YES-- A FEW TIMES!
WHAT'S WITH THIS GIRL? I'M BRUCE WAYNE, IN MY OTHER IDENTITY--AND I'VE NEVER SEEN HER BEFORE!
HOW DOES--UH-- BRUCE WAYNE FEEL ABOUT YOU?
I DON'T KNOW-- BECAUSE HE'S NEVER SEEN ME!
BUT YOU JUST SAID YOU MET HIM SEVERAL TIMES!
YES--BUT, ODDLY ENOUGH, ALWAYS WHEN I WORE A MASK! IT BEGAN WHEN I WAS IN COLLEGE, AND MY SORORITY INVITATION INVOLVED GETTING A DOOR-KNOCKER FROM SOME PROMINENT PERSON'S HOME...
"IT WAS A TRICK-OR-TREAT THING, ON HALLOWEEN! I CALLED AT THE WAYNE ESTATE, AND..."
I'M JOINING THE ALPHA EPSILON FRATERNITY, MR. WAYNE, AND THEY'VE SENT ME TO GET A DOOR-KNOCKER! MAY I PLEASE HAVE YOURS?
I'M NOT IN THE HABIT OF GIVING DOOR-KNOCKERS AWAY, MISS--BUT YOU'RE IN LUCK! MY FRATERNITY HAPPENS TO BE AFFILIATED WITH YOUR SORORITY! GLAD TO OBLIGE!
BW
I REMEMBER THAT INCIDENT--AND NOW THAT I KNOW PAT, I'M PRETTY SURE SHE CHECKED INTO IT FIRST AND KNEW MY FRATERNITY'S AFFILIATION WITH HER SORORITY--AND KNEW I'D GIVE HER THE DOOR-KNOCKER! CLEVER GIRL!
6

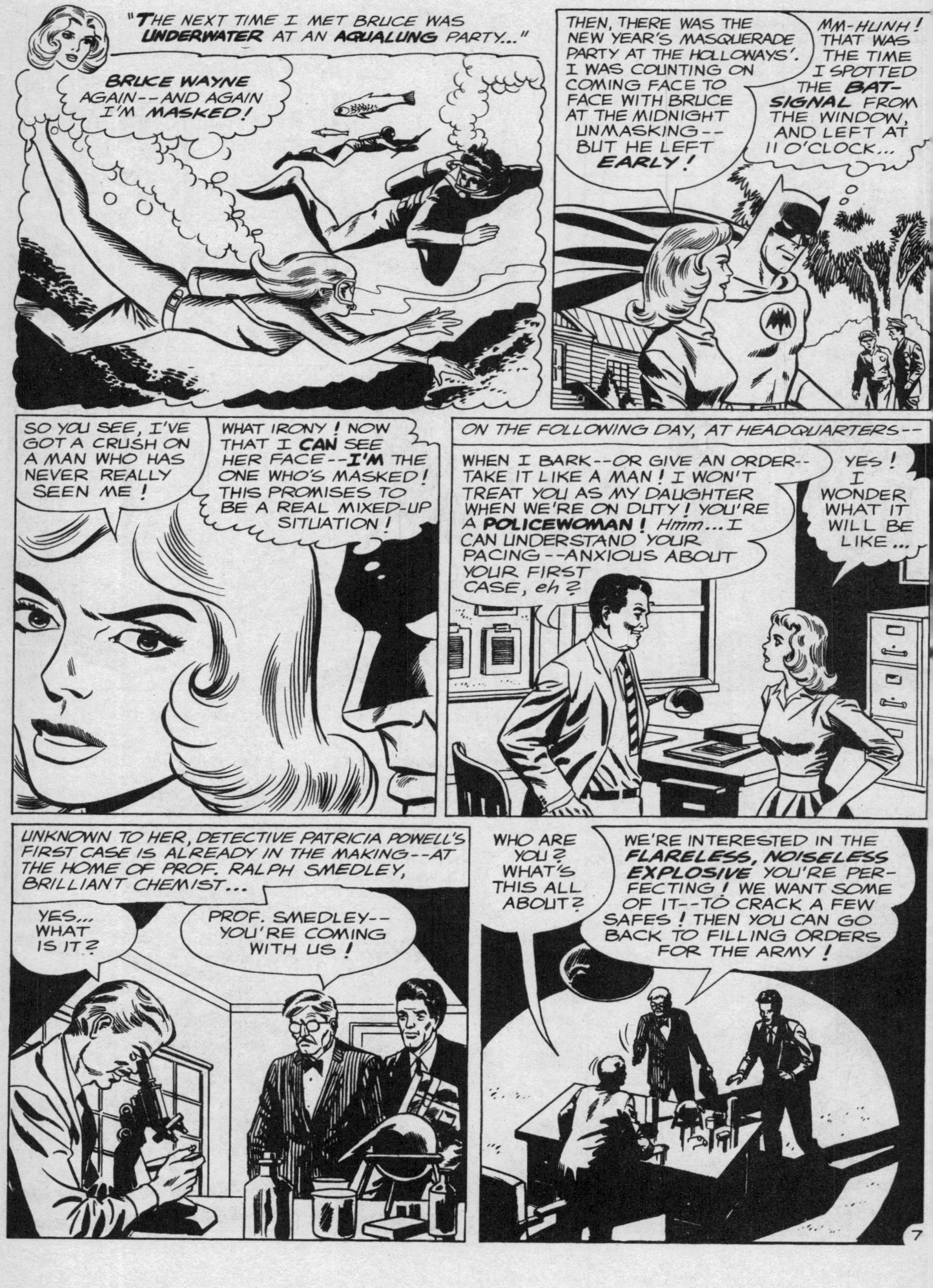
"THE NEXT TIME I MET BRUCE WAS UNDERWATER AT AN AQUALUNG PARTY..."
BRUCE WAYNE AGAIN--AND AGAIN I'M MASKED!
THEN, THERE WAS THE NEW YEAR'S MASQUERADE PARTY AT THE HOLLOWAYS'. I WAS COUNTING ON COMING FACE TO FACE WITH BRUCE AT THE MIDNIGHT UNMASKING--BUT HE LEFT EARLY!
MM-HUNH! THAT WAS THE TIME I SPOTTED THE BAT-SIGNAL FROM THE WINDOW, AND LEFT AT 11 O'CLOCK...
SO YOU SEE, I'VE GOT A CRUSH ON A MAN WHO HAS NEVER REALLY SEEN ME!
WHAT IRONY! NOW THAT I CAN SEE HER FACE--I'M THE ONE WHO'S MASKED! THIS PROMISES TO BE A REAL MIXED-UP SITUATION!
ON THE FOLLOWING DAY, AT HEADQUARTERS--
WHEN I BARK--OR GIVE AN ORDER--TAKE IT LIKE A MAN! I WON'T TREAT YOU AS MY DAUGHTER WHEN WE'RE ON DUTY! YOU'RE A POLICEWOMAN! Hmm...I CAN UNDERSTAND YOUR PACING--ANXIOUS ABOUT YOUR FIRST CASE, eh?
YES! I WONDER WHAT IT WILL BE LIKE...
UNKNOWN TO HER, DETECTIVE PATRICIA POWELL'S FIRST CASE IS ALREADY IN THE MAKING--AT THE HOME OF PROF. RALPH SMEDLEY, BRILLIANT CHEMIST...
YES... WHAT IS IT?
PROF. SMEDLEY--YOU'RE COMING WITH US!
WHO ARE YOU? WHAT'S THIS ALL ABOUT?
WE'RE INTERESTED IN THE FLARELESS, NOISELESS EXPLOSIVE YOU'RE PERFECTING! WE WANT SOME OF IT--TO CRACK A FEW SAFES! THEN YOU CAN GO BACK TO FILLING ORDERS FOR THE ARMY!
7

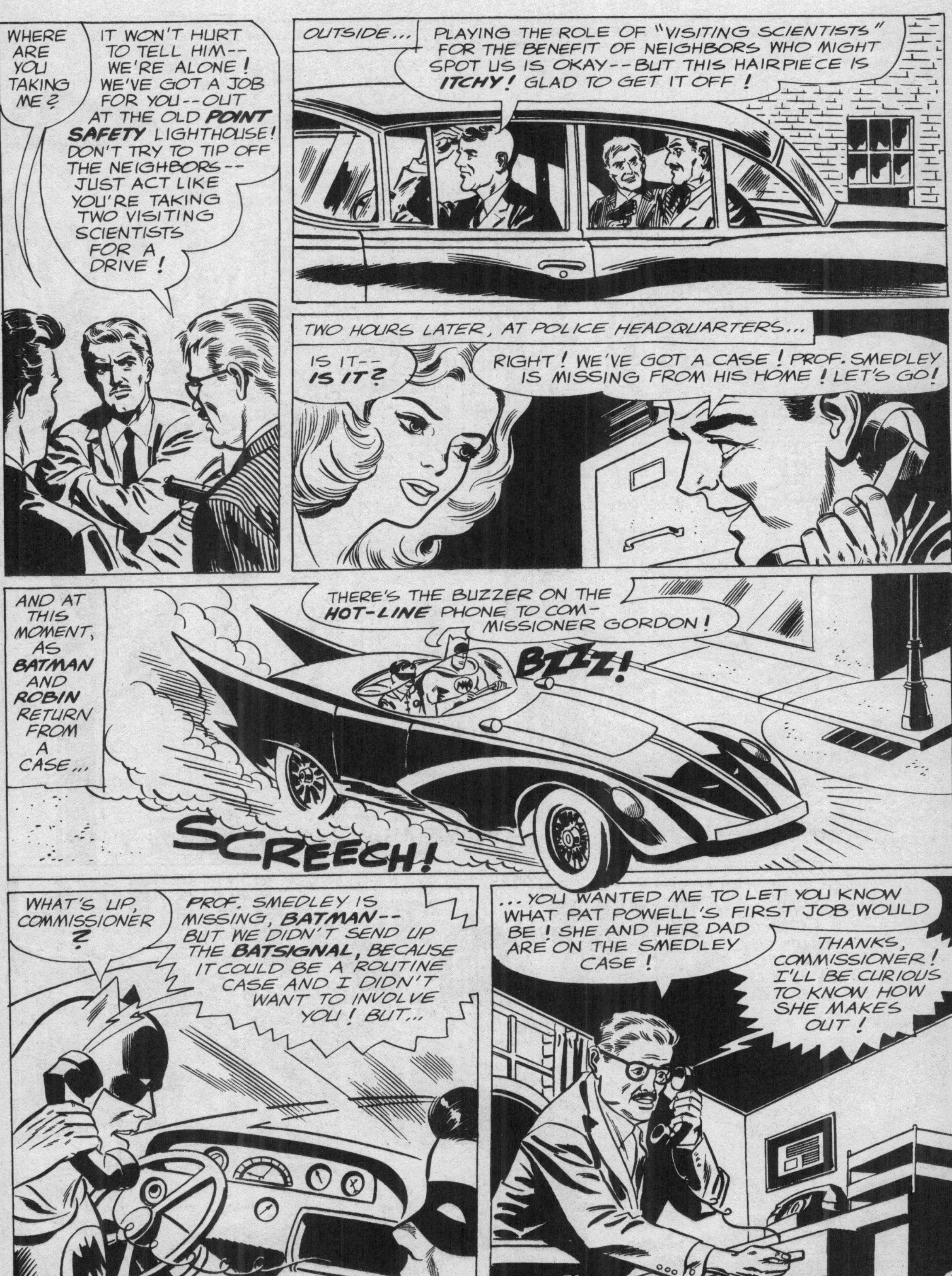
WHERE ARE YOU TAKING ME?
IT WON'T HURT TO TELL HIM--WE'RE ALONE! WE'VE GOT A JOB FOR YOU--OUT AT THE OLD POINT SAFETY LIGHTHOUSE! DON'T TRY TO TIP OFF THE NEIGHBORS--JUST ACT LIKE YOU'RE TAKING TWO VISITING SCIENTISTS FOR A DRIVE!
OUTSIDE...
PLAYING THE ROLE OF "VISITING SCIENTISTS" FOR THE BENEFIT OF NEIGHBORS WHO MIGHT SPOT US IS OKAY--BUT THIS HAIRPIECE IS ITCHY! GLAD TO GET IT OFF!
TWO HOURS LATER, AT POLICE HEADQUARTERS...
IS IT--IS IT?
RIGHT! WE'VE GOT A CASE! PROF. SMEDLEY IS MISSING FROM HIS HOME! LET'S GO!
AND AT THIS MOMENT, AS BATMAN AND ROBIN RETURN FROM A CASE...
THERE'S THE BUZZER ON THE HOT-LINE PHONE TO COMMISSIONER GORDON!
BZZZ!
SCREECH!
WHAT'S UP, COMMISSIONER?
PROF. SMEDLEY IS MISSING, BATMAN--BUT WE DIDN'T SEND UP THE BATSIGNAL, BECAUSE IT COULD BE A ROUTINE CASE AND I DIDN'T WANT TO INVOLVE YOU! BUT...
...YOU WANTED ME TO LET YOU KNOW WHAT PAT POWELL'S FIRST JOB WOULD BE! SHE AND HER DAD ARE ON THE SMEDLEY CASE!
THANKS, COMMISSIONER! I'LL BE CURIOUS TO KNOW HOW SHE MAKES OUT!
8

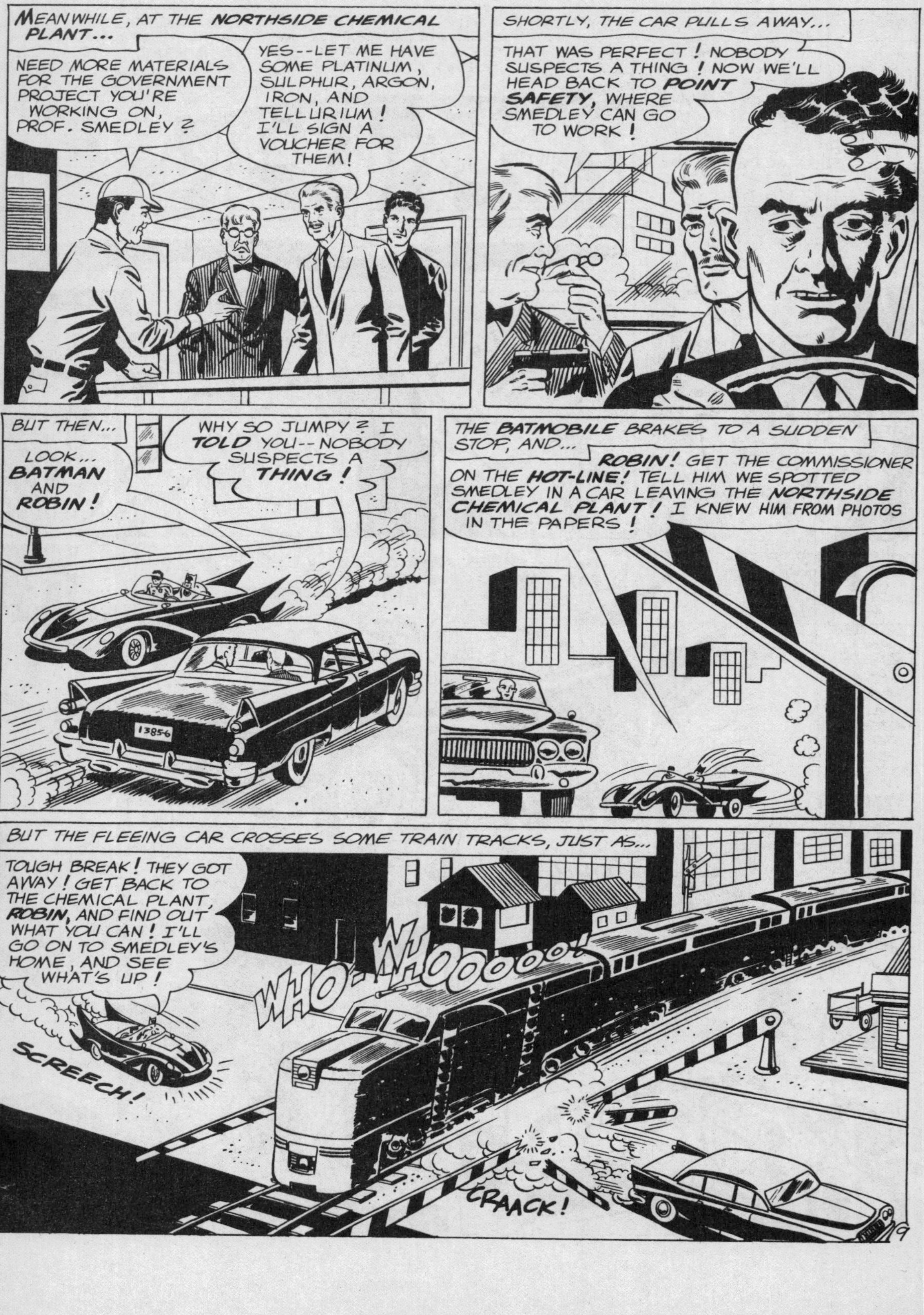
MEANWHILE, AT THE NORTHSIDE CHEMICAL PLANT...
NEED MORE MATERIALS FOR THE GOVERNMENT PROJECT YOU'RE WORKING ON, PROF. SMEDLEY ?
YES--LET ME HAVE SOME PLATINUM, SULPHUR, ARGON, IRON, AND TELLURIUM ! I'LL SIGN A VOUCHER FOR THEM !
SHORTLY, THE CAR PULLS AWAY...
THAT WAS PERFECT ! NOBODY SUSPECTS A THING ! NOW WE'LL HEAD BACK TO POINT SAFETY, WHERE SMEDLEY CAN GO TO WORK !
BUT THEN...
LOOK... BATMAN AND ROBIN !
WHY SO JUMPY ? I TOLD YOU--NOBODY SUSPECTS A THING !
1385-6
THE BATMOBILE BRAKES TO A SUDDEN STOP, AND...
ROBIN ! GET THE COMMISSIONER ON THE HOT-LINE ! TELL HIM WE SPOTTED SMEDLEY IN A CAR LEAVING THE NORTHSIDE CHEMICAL PLANT ! I KNEW HIM FROM PHOTOS IN THE PAPERS !
BUT THE FLEEING CAR CROSSES SOME TRAIN TRACKS, JUST AS...
TOUGH BREAK ! THEY GOT AWAY ! GET BACK TO THE CHEMICAL PLANT, ROBIN, AND FIND OUT WHAT YOU CAN ! I'LL GO ON TO SMEDLEY'S HOME, AND SEE WHAT'S UP !
WHO-WHOOOOOO !
SCREECH !
CRAACK !
9

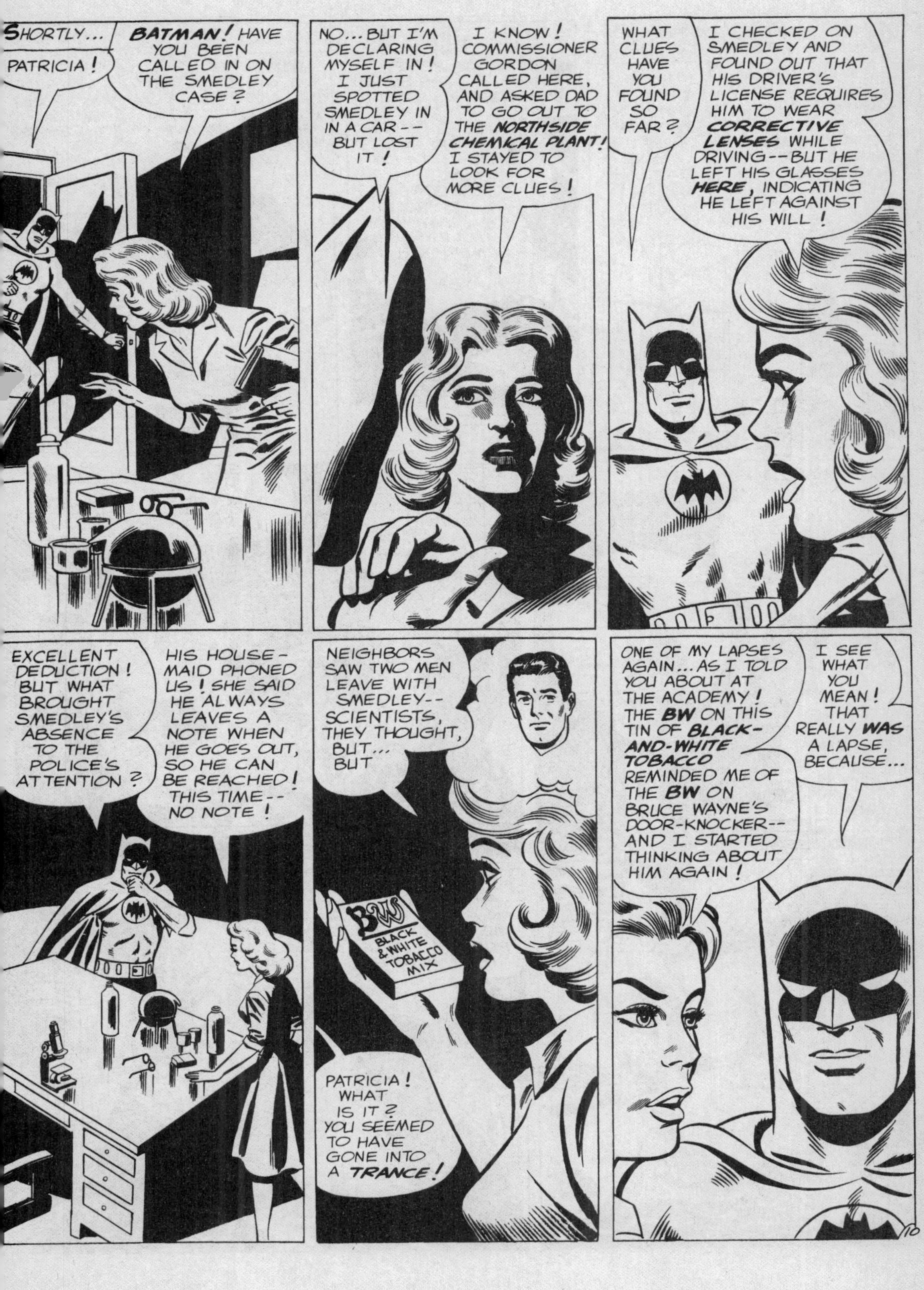
SHORTLY...
PATRICIA!
BATMAN! HAVE YOU BEEN CALLED IN ON THE SMEDLEY CASE?
NO... BUT I'M DECLARING MYSELF IN! I JUST SPOTTED SMEDLEY IN IN A CAR -- BUT LOST IT!
I KNOW! COMMISSIONER GORDON CALLED HERE, AND ASKED DAD TO GO OUT TO THE NORTHSIDE CHEMICAL PLANT! I STAYED TO LOOK FOR MORE CLUES!
WHAT CLUES HAVE YOU FOUND SO FAR?
I CHECKED ON SMEDLEY AND FOUND OUT THAT HIS DRIVER'S LICENSE REQUIRES HIM TO WEAR CORRECTIVE LENSES WHILE DRIVING -- BUT HE LEFT HIS GLASSES HERE, INDICATING HE LEFT AGAINST HIS WILL!
EXCELLENT DEDUCTION! BUT WHAT BROUGHT SMEDLEY'S ABSENCE TO THE POLICE'S ATTENTION?
HIS HOUSE-MAID PHONED US! SHE SAID HE ALWAYS LEAVES A NOTE WHEN HE GOES OUT, SO HE CAN BE REACHED! THIS TIME -- NO NOTE!
NEIGHBORS SAW TWO MEN LEAVE WITH SMEDLEY -- SCIENTISTS, THEY THOUGHT, BUT... BUT
BW
BLACK & WHITE TOBACCO MIX
PATRICIA! WHAT IS IT? YOU SEEMED TO HAVE GONE INTO A TRANCE!
ONE OF MY LAPSES AGAIN... AS I TOLD YOU ABOUT AT THE ACADEMY! THE BW ON THIS TIN OF BLACK-AND-WHITE TOBACCO REMINDED ME OF THE BW ON BRUCE WAYNE'S DOOR-KNOCKER -- AND I STARTED THINKING ABOUT HIM AGAIN!
I SEE WHAT YOU MEAN! THAT REALLY WAS A LAPSE, BECAUSE...
10

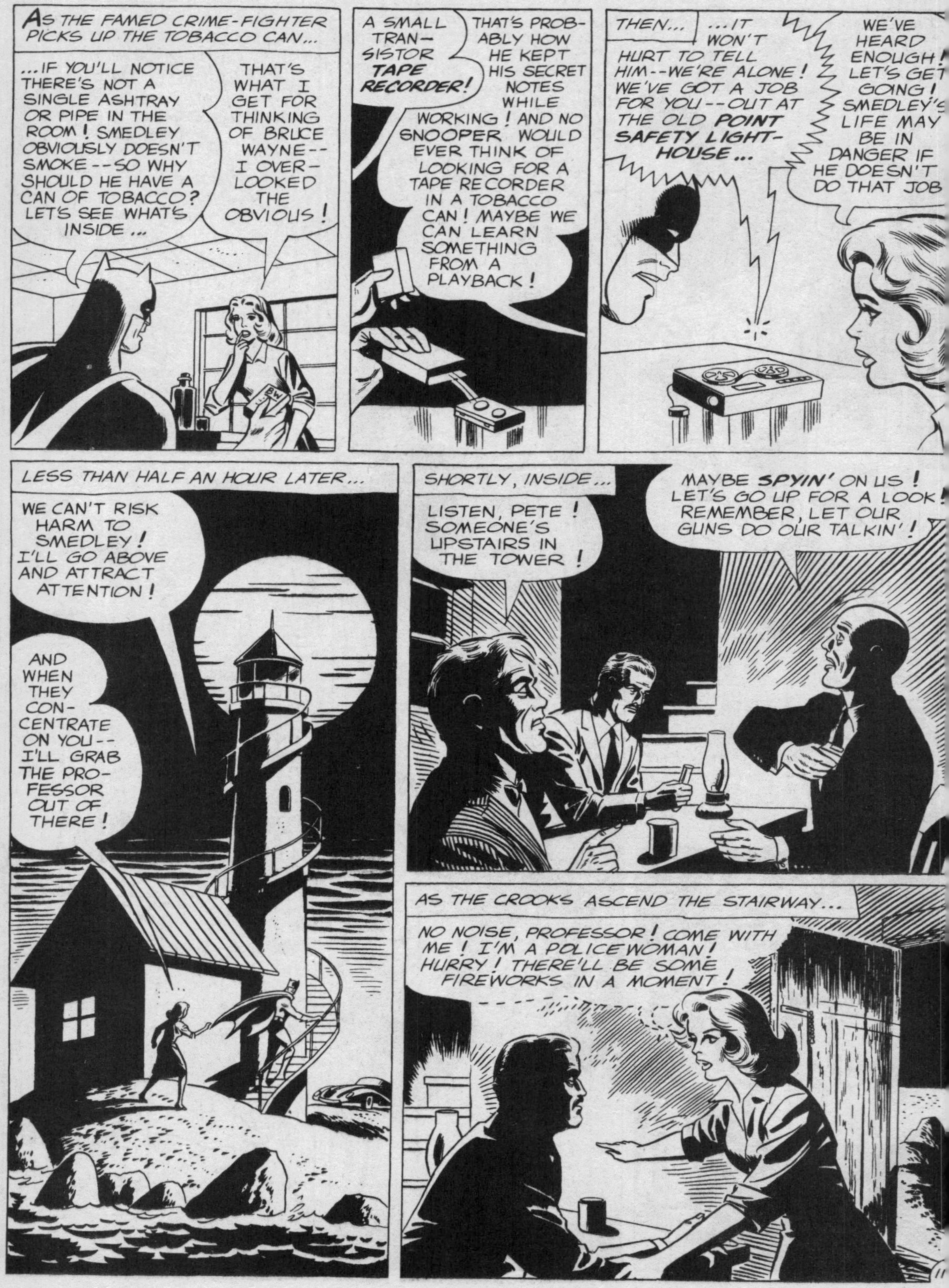
AS THE FAMED CRIME-FIGHTER PICKS UP THE TOBACCO CAN...
...IF YOU'LL NOTICE THERE'S NOT A SINGLE ASHTRAY OR PIPE IN THE ROOM! SMEDLEY OBVIOUSLY DOESN'T SMOKE--SO WHY SHOULD HE HAVE A CAN OF TOBACCO? LET'S SEE WHAT'S INSIDE...
THAT'S WHAT I GET FOR THINKING OF BRUCE WAYNE--I OVERLOOKED THE OBVIOUS!
BW
A SMALL TRANSISTOR TAPE RECORDER!
THAT'S PROBABLY HOW HE KEPT HIS SECRET NOTES WHILE WORKING! AND NO SNOOPER WOULD EVER THINK OF LOOKING FOR A TAPE RECORDER IN A TOBACCO CAN! MAYBE WE CAN LEARN SOMETHING FROM A PLAYBACK!
THEN...
...IT WON'T HURT TO TELL HIM--WE'RE ALONE! WE'VE GOT A JOB FOR YOU--OUT AT THE OLD POINT SAFETY LIGHTHOUSE...
WE'VE HEARD ENOUGH! LET'S GET GOING! SMEDLEY'S LIFE MAY BE IN DANGER IF HE DOESN'T DO THAT JOB
LESS THAN HALF AN HOUR LATER...
WE CAN'T RISK HARM TO SMEDLEY! I'LL GO ABOVE AND ATTRACT ATTENTION!
AND WHEN THEY CONCENTRATE ON YOU--I'LL GRAB THE PROFESSOR OUT OF THERE!
SHORTLY, INSIDE...
LISTEN, PETE! SOMEONE'S UPSTAIRS IN THE TOWER!
MAYBE SPYIN' ON US! LET'S GO UP FOR A LOOK! REMEMBER, LET OUR GUNS DO OUR TALKIN'!
AS THE CROOKS ASCEND THE STAIRWAY...
NO NOISE, PROFESSOR! COME WITH ME! I'M A POLICE WOMAN! HURRY! THERE'LL BE SOME FIREWORKS IN A MOMENT!

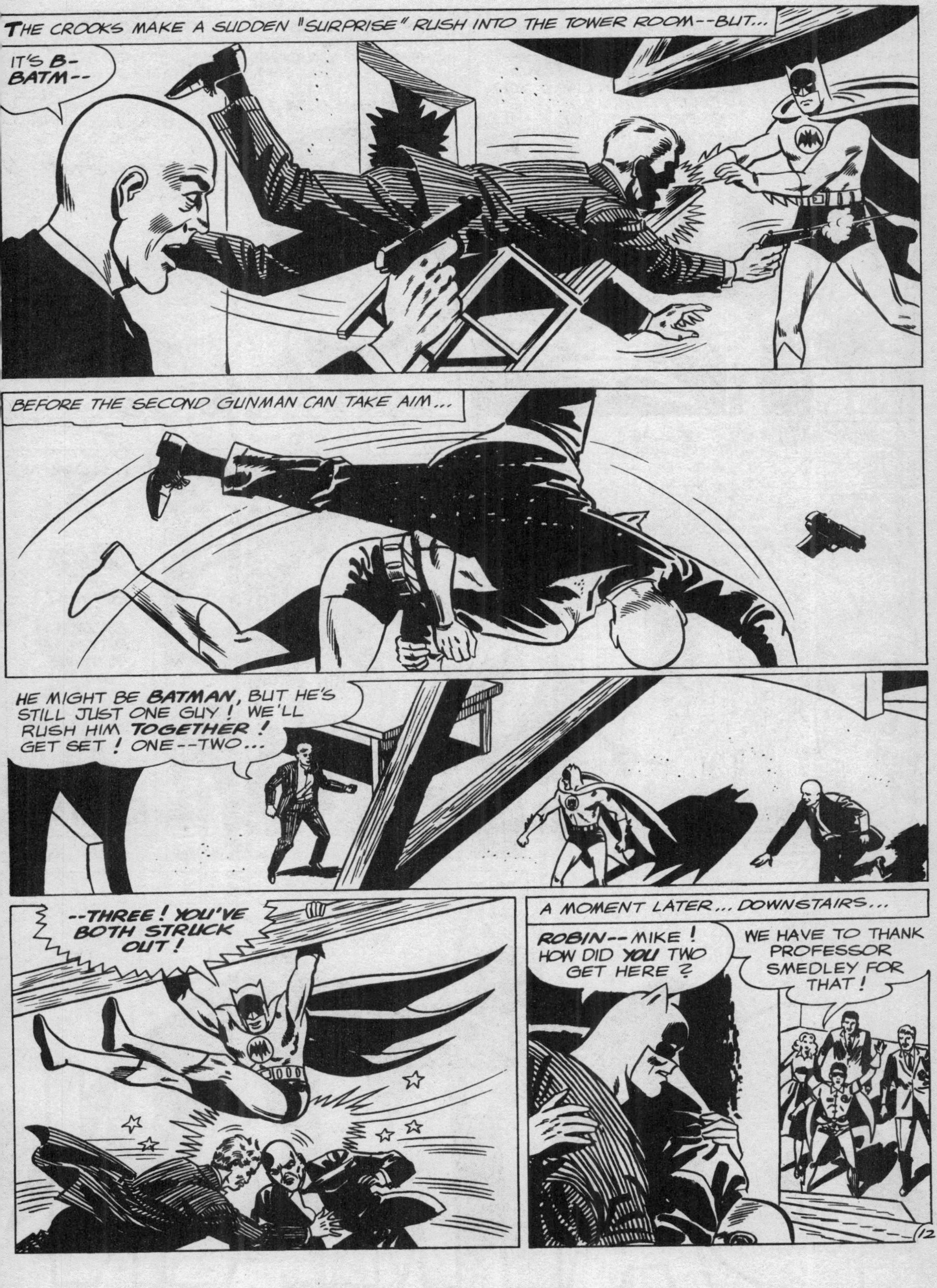
THE CROOKS MAKE A SUDDEN "SURPRISE" RUSH INTO THE TOWER ROOM--BUT...
IT'S B-BATM--
BEFORE THE SECOND GUNMAN CAN TAKE AIM...
HE MIGHT BE BATMAN, BUT HE'S STILL JUST ONE GUY! WE'LL RUSH HIM TOGETHER! GET SET! ONE--TWO...
--THREE! YOU'VE BOTH STRUCK OUT!
A MOMENT LATER... DOWNSTAIRS...
ROBIN--MIKE! HOW DID YOU TWO GET HERE?
WE HAVE TO THANK PROFESSOR SMEDLEY FOR THAT!
12

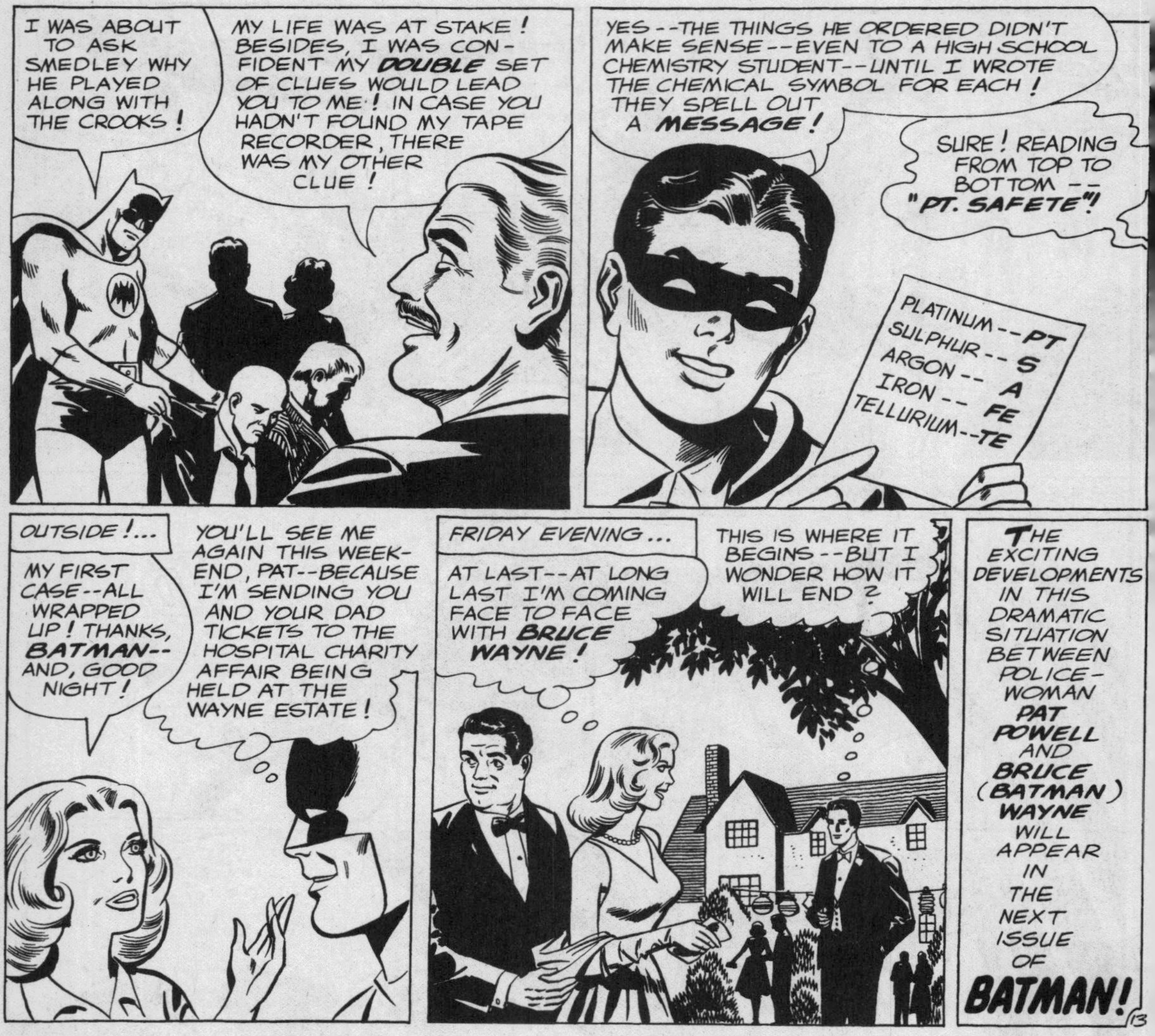
I WAS ABOUT TO ASK SMEDLEY WHY HE PLAYED ALONG WITH THE CROOKS!
MY LIFE WAS AT STAKE! BESIDES, I WAS CONFIDENT MY DOUBLE SET OF CLUES WOULD LEAD YOU TO ME! IN CASE YOU HADN'T FOUND MY TAPE RECORDER, THERE WAS MY OTHER CLUE!
YES--THE THINGS HE ORDERED DIDN'T MAKE SENSE--EVEN TO A HIGH SCHOOL CHEMISTRY STUDENT--UNTIL I WROTE THE CHEMICAL SYMBOL FOR EACH! THEY SPELL OUT A MESSAGE!
SURE! READING FROM TOP TO BOTTOM--"PT. SAFETE"!
PLATINUM--PT
SULPHUR--S
ARGON--A
IRON--FE
TELLURIUM--TE
OUTSIDE!...
MY FIRST CASE--ALL WRAPPED UP! THANKS, BATMAN--AND, GOOD NIGHT!
YOU'LL SEE ME AGAIN THIS WEEK-END, PAT--BECAUSE I'M SENDING YOU AND YOUR DAD TICKETS TO THE HOSPITAL CHARITY AFFAIR BEING HELD AT THE WAYNE ESTATE!
FRIDAY EVENING...
AT LAST--AT LONG LAST I'M COMING FACE TO FACE WITH BRUCE WAYNE!
THIS IS WHERE IT BEGINS--BUT I WONDER HOW IT WILL END?
THE EXCITING DEVELOPMENTS IN THIS DRAMATIC SITUATION BETWEEN POLICE-WOMAN PAT POWELL AND BRUCE (BATMAN) WAYNE WILL APPEAR IN THE NEXT ISSUE OF BATMAN!
13

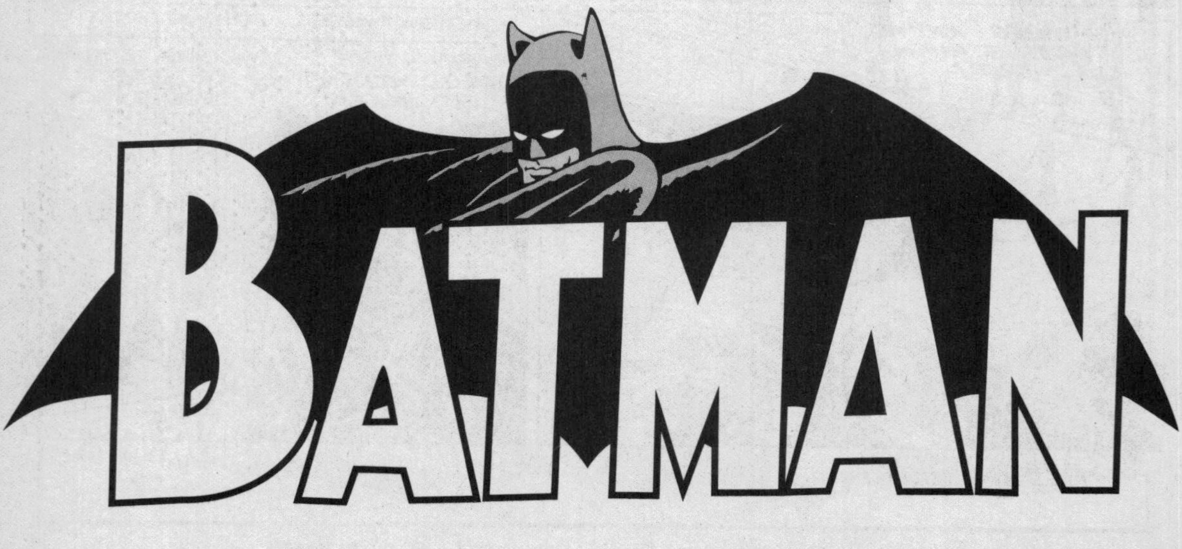
BATMAN

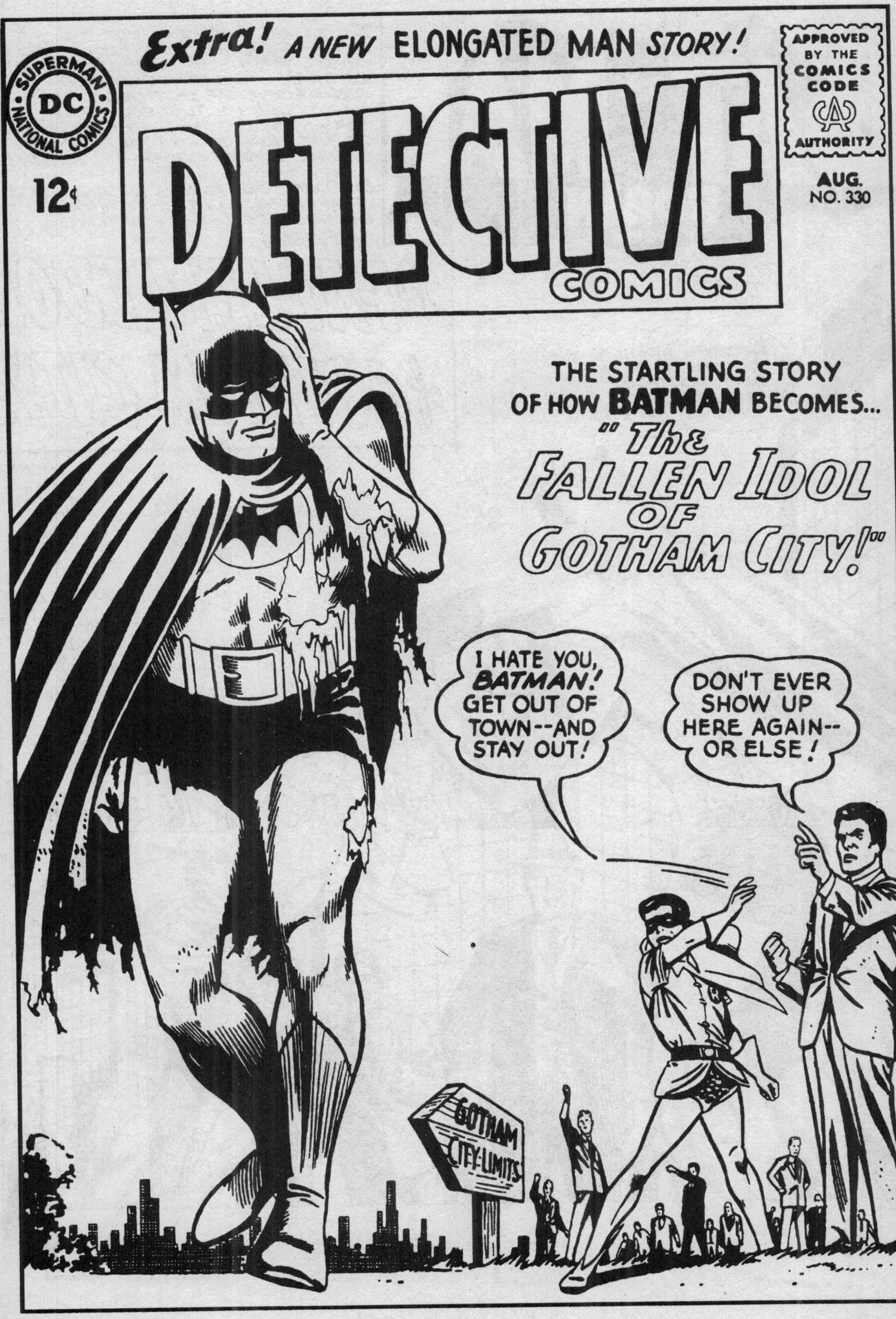
Extra! A NEW ELONGATED MAN STORY!
SUPERMAN DC NATIONAL COMICS
12¢
DETECTIVE COMICS
APPROVED BY THE COMICS CODE AUTHORITY
AUG. NO. 330
THE STARTLING STORY OF HOW BATMAN BECOMES... "The FALLEN IDOL OF GOTHAM CITY!"
I HATE YOU, BATMAN! GET OUT OF TOWN--AND STAY OUT!
DON'T EVER SHOW UP HERE AGAIN--OR ELSE!
GOTHAM CITY-LIMITS

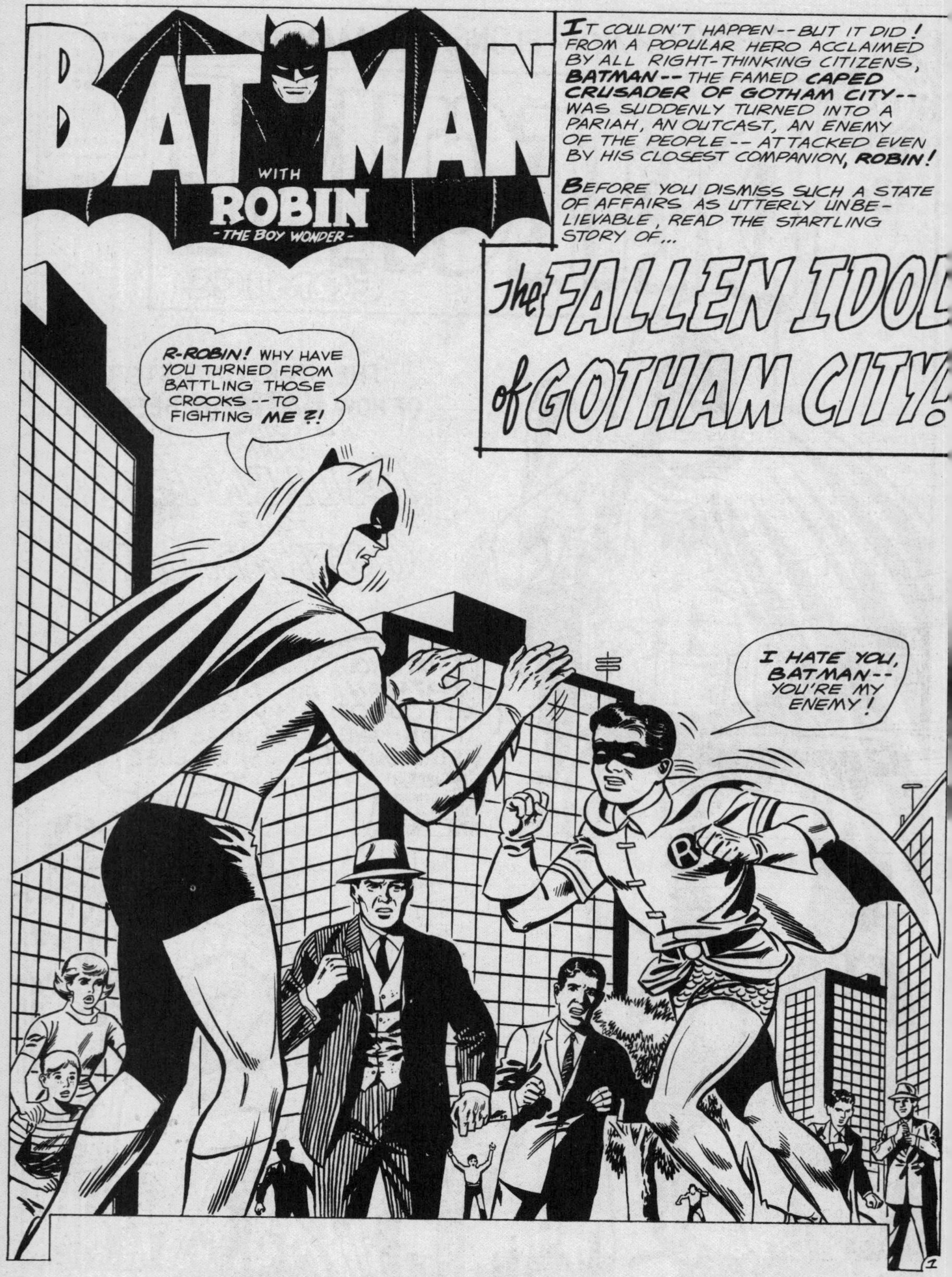
BATMAN
WITH ROBIN
-THE BOY WONDER-
IT COULDN'T HAPPEN--BUT IT DID! FROM A POPULAR HERO ACCLAIMED BY ALL RIGHT-THINKING CITIZENS, BATMAN--THE FAMED CAPED CRUSADER OF GOTHAM CITY--WAS SUDDENLY TURNED INTO A PARIAH, AN OUTCAST, AN ENEMY OF THE PEOPLE--ATTACKED EVEN BY HIS CLOSEST COMPANION, ROBIN!
BEFORE YOU DISMISS SUCH A STATE OF AFFAIRS AS UTTERLY UNBELIEVABLE, READ THE STARTLING STORY OF...
The FALLEN IDOL of GOTHAM CITY!
R-ROBIN! WHY HAVE YOU TURNED FROM BATTLING THOSE CROOKS--TO FIGHTING ME ?!
I HATE YOU, BATMAN--YOU'RE MY ENEMY!
1

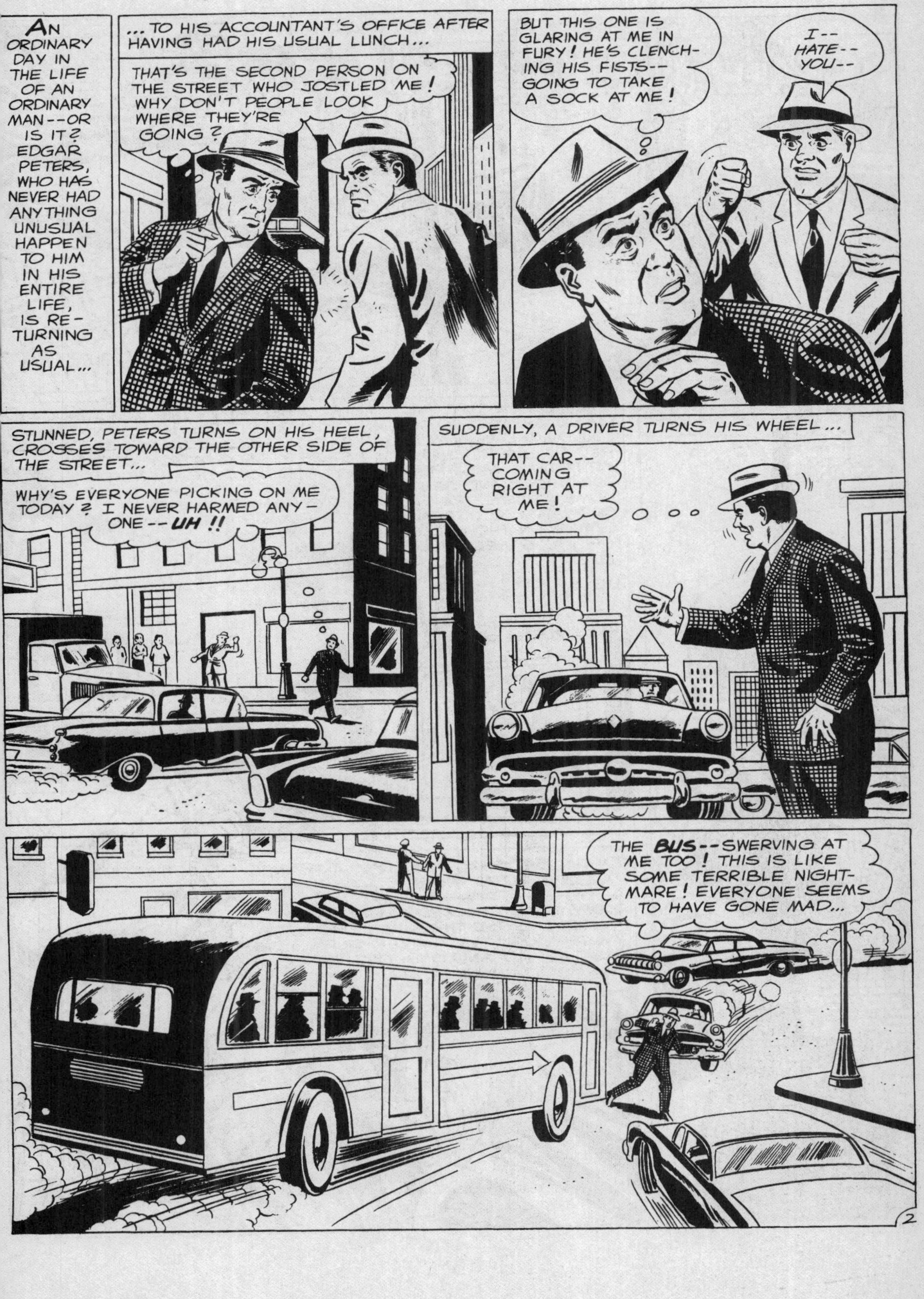
AN ORDINARY DAY IN THE LIFE OF AN ORDINARY MAN--OR IS IT? EDGAR PETERS, WHO HAS NEVER HAD ANYTHING UNUSUAL HAPPEN TO HIM IN HIS ENTIRE LIFE, IS RETURNING AS USUAL...
...TO HIS ACCOUNTANT'S OFFICE AFTER HAVING HAD HIS USUAL LUNCH...
THAT'S THE SECOND PERSON ON THE STREET WHO JOSTLED ME! WHY DON'T PEOPLE LOOK WHERE THEY'RE GOING?
BUT THIS ONE IS GLARING AT ME IN FURY! HE'S CLENCHING HIS FISTS--GOING TO TAKE A SOCK AT ME!
I--HATE--YOU--
STUNNED, PETERS TURNS ON HIS HEEL, CROSSES TOWARD THE OTHER SIDE OF THE STREET...
WHY'S EVERYONE PICKING ON ME TODAY? I NEVER HARMED ANYONE--UH!!
SUDDENLY, A DRIVER TURNS HIS WHEEL...
THAT CAR--COMING RIGHT AT ME!
THE BUS--SWERVING AT ME TOO! THIS IS LIKE SOME TERRIBLE NIGHTMARE! EVERYONE SEEMS TO HAVE GONE MAD...
2

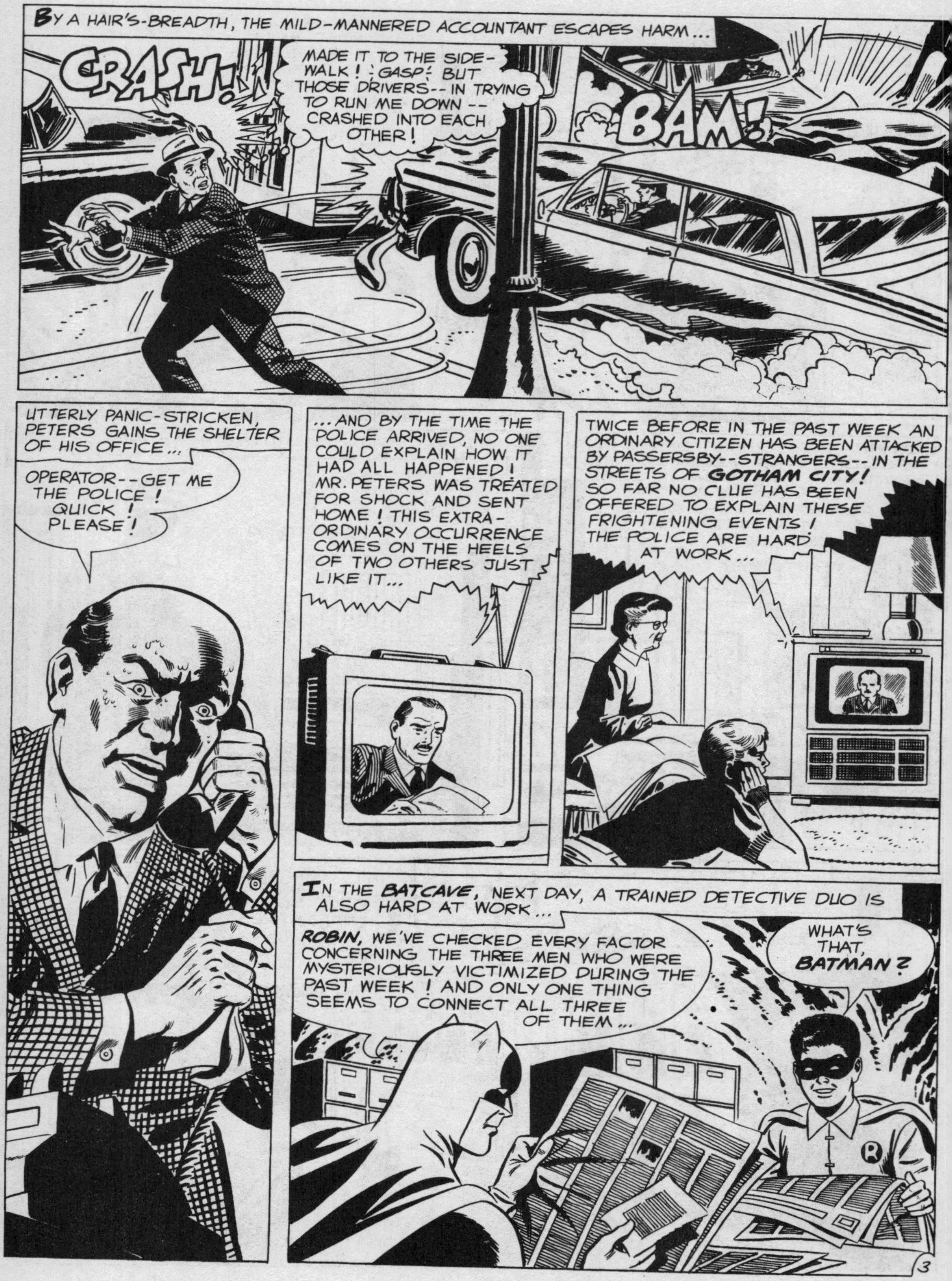
BY A HAIR'S-BREADTH, THE MILD-MANNERED ACCOUNTANT ESCAPES HARM...
CRASH!
MADE IT TO THE SIDE-WALK! GASP! BUT THOSE DRIVERS-- IN TRYING TO RUN ME DOWN -- CRASHED INTO EACH OTHER!
BAM!
UTTERLY PANIC-STRICKEN, PETERS GAINS THE SHELTER OF HIS OFFICE...
OPERATOR--GET ME THE POLICE! QUICK! PLEASE!
...AND BY THE TIME THE POLICE ARRIVED, NO ONE COULD EXPLAIN HOW IT HAD ALL HAPPENED! MR. PETERS WAS TREATED FOR SHOCK AND SENT HOME! THIS EXTRA-ORDINARY OCCURRENCE COMES ON THE HEELS OF TWO OTHERS JUST LIKE IT...
TWICE BEFORE IN THE PAST WEEK AN ORDINARY CITIZEN HAS BEEN ATTACKED BY PASSERSBY--STRANGERS--IN THE STREETS OF GOTHAM CITY! SO FAR NO CLUE HAS BEEN OFFERED TO EXPLAIN THESE FRIGHTENING EVENTS! THE POLICE ARE HARD AT WORK...
IN THE BATCAVE, NEXT DAY, A TRAINED DETECTIVE DUO IS ALSO HARD AT WORK...
ROBIN, WE'VE CHECKED EVERY FACTOR CONCERNING THE THREE MEN WHO WERE MYSTERIOUSLY VICTIMIZED DURING THE PAST WEEK! AND ONLY ONE THING SEEMS TO CONNECT ALL THREE OF THEM...
WHAT'S THAT, BATMAN?
3

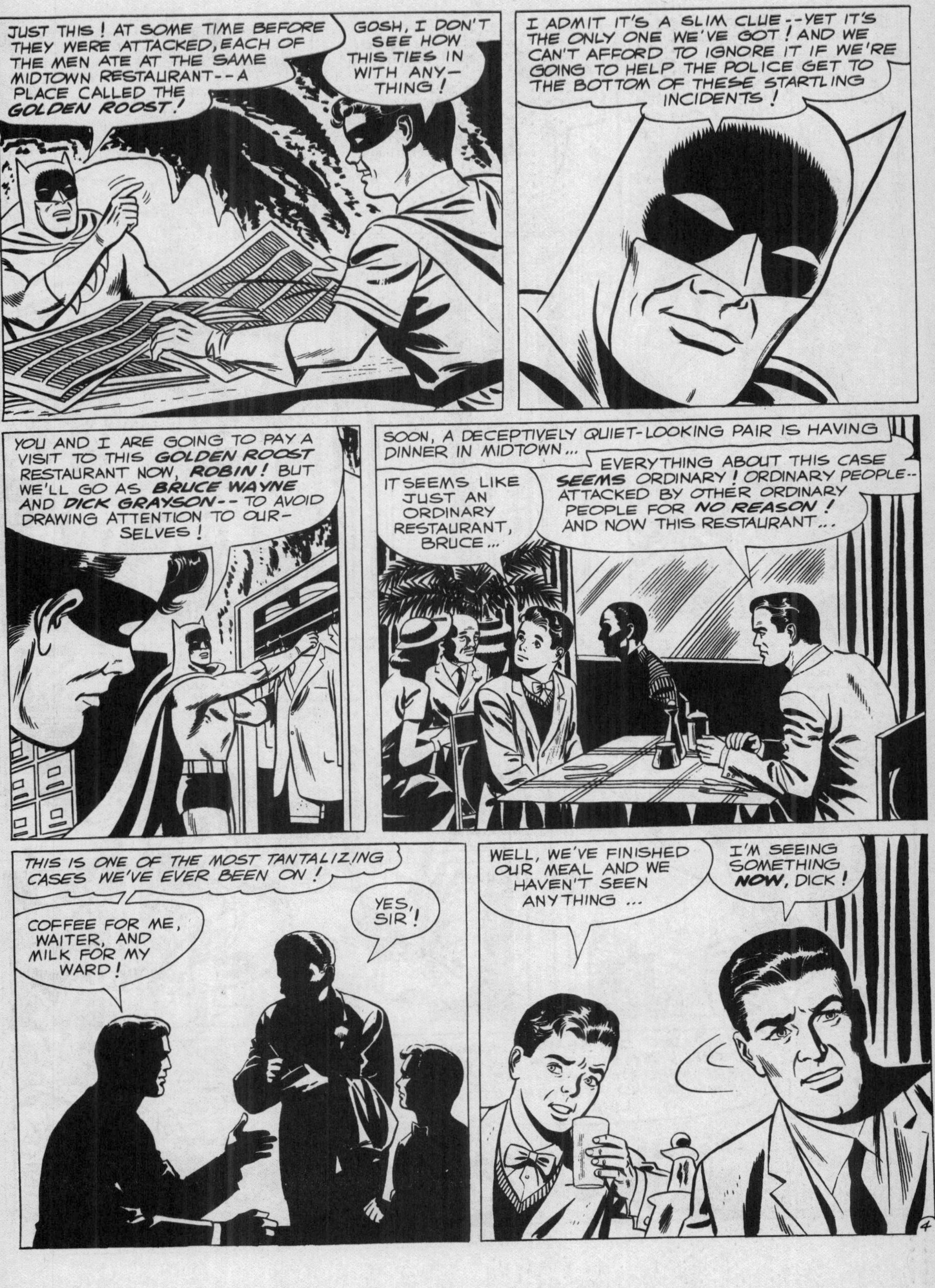
JUST THIS! AT SOME TIME BEFORE THEY WERE ATTACKED, EACH OF THE MEN ATE AT THE SAME MIDTOWN RESTAURANT--A PLACE CALLED THE GOLDEN ROOST!
GOSH, I DON'T SEE HOW THIS TIES IN WITH ANY-THING!
I ADMIT IT'S A SLIM CLUE--YET IT'S THE ONLY ONE WE'VE GOT! AND WE CAN'T AFFORD TO IGNORE IT IF WE'RE GOING TO HELP THE POLICE GET TO THE BOTTOM OF THESE STARTLING INCIDENTS!
YOU AND I ARE GOING TO PAY A VISIT TO THIS GOLDEN ROOST RESTAURANT NOW, ROBIN! BUT WE'LL GO AS BRUCE WAYNE AND DICK GRAYSON--TO AVOID DRAWING ATTENTION TO OUR-SELVES!
SOON, A DECEPTIVELY QUIET-LOOKING PAIR IS HAVING DINNER IN MIDTOWN...
IT SEEMS LIKE JUST AN ORDINARY RESTAURANT, BRUCE...
EVERYTHING ABOUT THIS CASE SEEMS ORDINARY! ORDINARY PEOPLE--ATTACKED BY OTHER ORDINARY PEOPLE FOR NO REASON! AND NOW THIS RESTAURANT...
THIS IS ONE OF THE MOST TANTALIZING CASES WE'VE EVER BEEN ON!
COFFEE FOR ME, WAITER, AND MILK FOR MY WARD!
YES, SIR!
WELL, WE'VE FINISHED OUR MEAL AND WE HAVEN'T SEEN ANYTHING ...
I'M SEEING SOMETHING NOW, DICK!
4

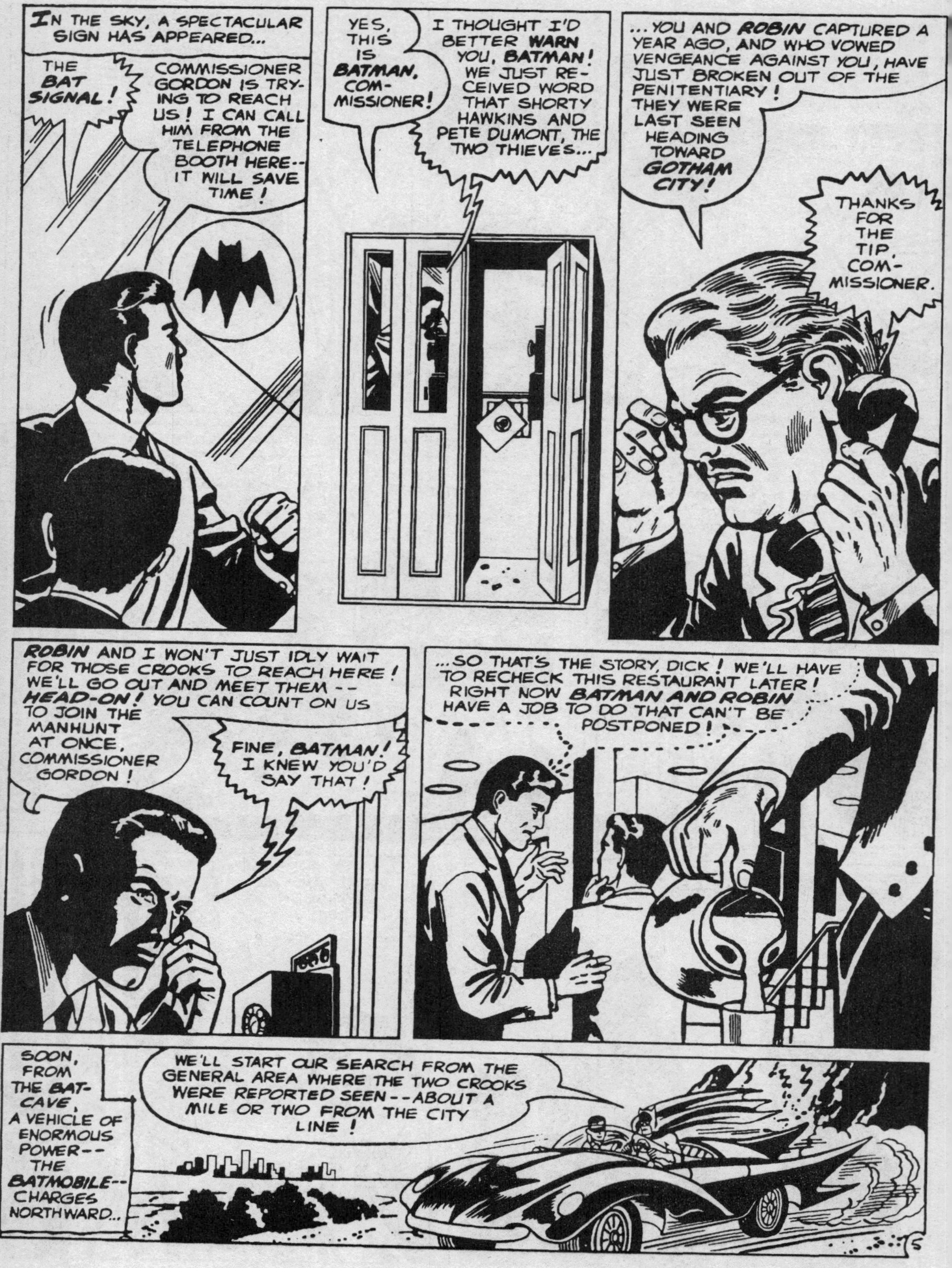
IN THE SKY, A SPECTACULAR SIGN HAS APPEARED...
THE BAT SIGNAL!
COMMISSIONER GORDON IS TRYING TO REACH US! I CAN CALL HIM FROM THE TELEPHONE BOOTH HERE-- IT WILL SAVE TIME!
YES, THIS IS BATMAN, COMMISSIONER!
I THOUGHT I'D BETTER WARN YOU, BATMAN! WE JUST RECEIVED WORD THAT SHORTY HAWKINS AND PETE DUMONT, THE TWO THIEVES...
...YOU AND ROBIN CAPTURED A YEAR AGO, AND WHO VOWED VENGEANCE AGAINST YOU, HAVE JUST BROKEN OUT OF THE PENITENTIARY! THEY WERE LAST SEEN HEADING TOWARD GOTHAM CITY!
THANKS FOR THE TIP, COMMISSIONER.
ROBIN AND I WON'T JUST IDLY WAIT FOR THOSE CROOKS TO REACH HERE! WE'LL GO OUT AND MEET THEM -- HEAD-ON! YOU CAN COUNT ON US TO JOIN THE MANHUNT AT ONCE, COMMISSIONER GORDON!
FINE, BATMAN! I KNEW YOU'D SAY THAT!
...SO THAT'S THE STORY, DICK! WE'LL HAVE TO RECHECK THIS RESTAURANT LATER! RIGHT NOW BATMAN AND ROBIN HAVE A JOB TO DO THAT CAN'T BE POSTPONED!
SOON, FROM THE BAT-CAVE, A VEHICLE OF ENORMOUS POWER-- THE BATMOBILE-- CHARGES NORTHWARD...
WE'LL START OUR SEARCH FROM THE GENERAL AREA WHERE THE TWO CROOKS WERE REPORTED SEEN--ABOUT A MILE OR TWO FROM THE CITY LINE!
5

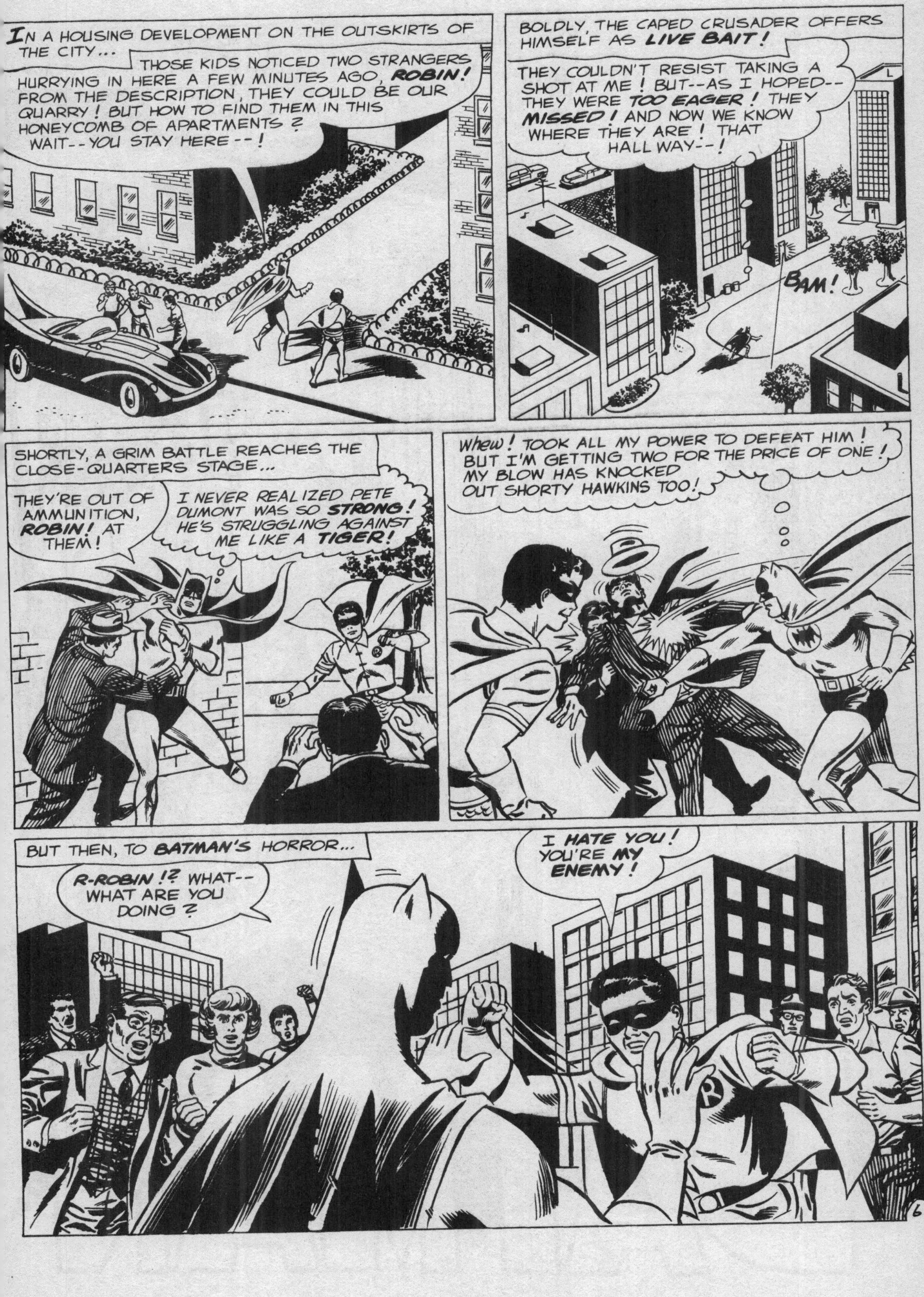
IN A HOUSING DEVELOPMENT ON THE OUTSKIRTS OF THE CITY...
THOSE KIDS NOTICED TWO STRANGERS HURRYING IN HERE A FEW MINUTES AGO, ROBIN! FROM THE DESCRIPTION, THEY COULD BE OUR QUARRY! BUT HOW TO FIND THEM IN THIS HONEYCOMB OF APARTMENTS ? WAIT--YOU STAY HERE--!
BOLDLY, THE CAPED CRUSADER OFFERS HIMSELF AS LIVE BAIT!
THEY COULDN'T RESIST TAKING A SHOT AT ME! BUT--AS I HOPED--THEY WERE TOO EAGER! THEY MISSED! AND NOW WE KNOW WHERE THEY ARE! THAT HALL WAY--!
BAM!
SHORTLY, A GRIM BATTLE REACHES THE CLOSE-QUARTERS STAGE...
THEY'RE OUT OF AMMUNITION, ROBIN! AT THEM!
I NEVER REALIZED PETE DUMONT WAS SO STRONG! HE'S STRUGGLING AGAINST ME LIKE A TIGER!
Whew! TOOK ALL MY POWER TO DEFEAT HIM! BUT I'M GETTING TWO FOR THE PRICE OF ONE! MY BLOW HAS KNOCKED OUT SHORTY HAWKINS TOO!
BUT THEN, TO BATMAN'S HORROR...
R-ROBIN!? WHAT--WHAT ARE YOU DOING ?
I HATE YOU! YOU'RE MY ENEMY!
6

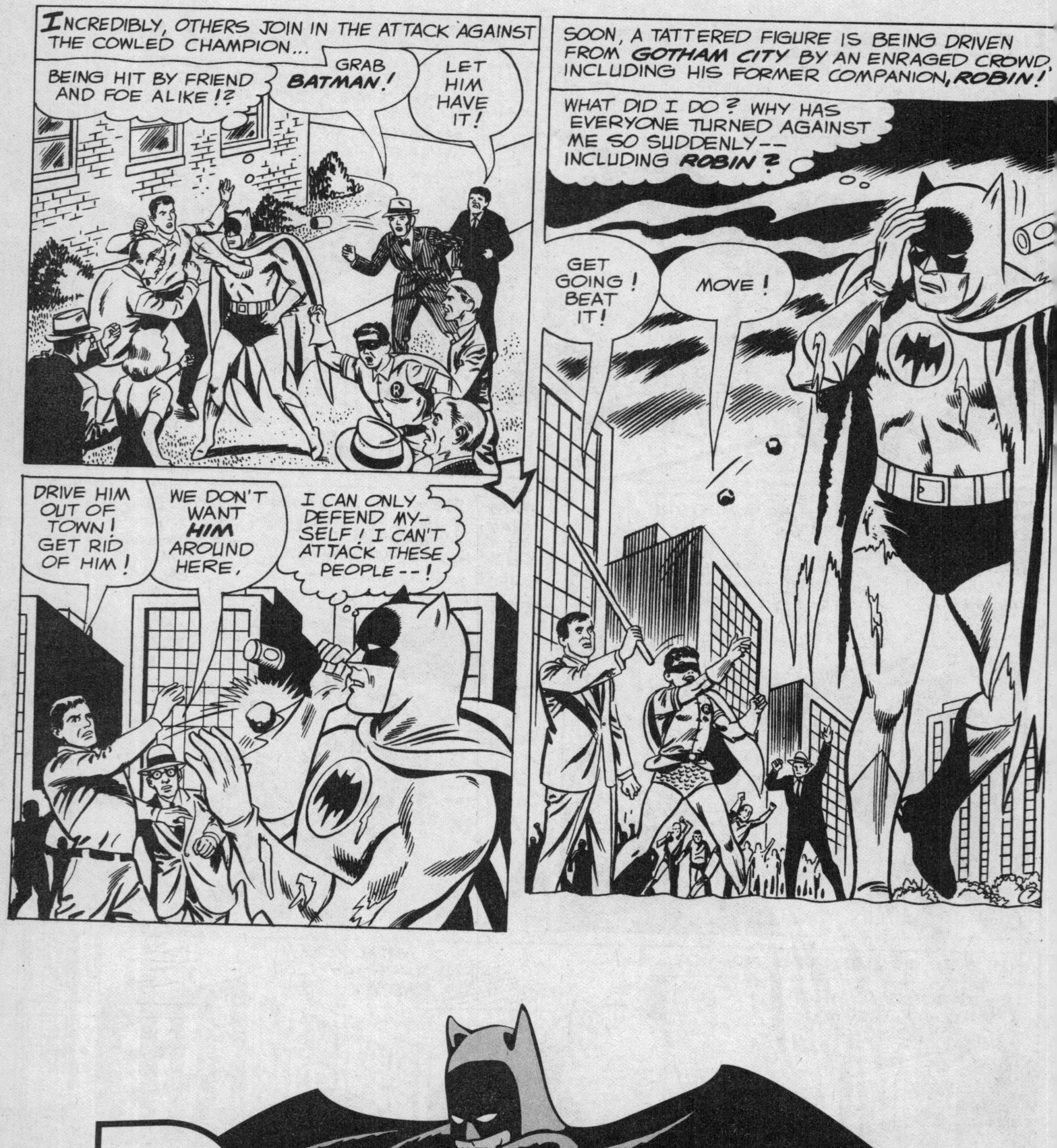
INCREDIBLY, OTHERS JOIN IN THE ATTACK AGAINST THE COWLED CHAMPION...
BEING HIT BY FRIEND AND FOE ALIKE !?
GRAB BATMAN!
LET HIM HAVE IT!
DRIVE HIM OUT OF TOWN! GET RID OF HIM!
WE DON'T WANT HIM AROUND HERE,
I CAN ONLY DEFEND MYSELF! I CAN'T ATTACK THESE PEOPLE--!
SOON, A TATTERED FIGURE IS BEING DRIVEN FROM GOTHAM CITY BY AN ENRAGED CROWD, INCLUDING HIS FORMER COMPANION, ROBIN!
WHAT DID I DO? WHY HAS EVERYONE TURNED AGAINST ME SO SUDDENLY-- INCLUDING ROBIN?
GET GOING! BEAT IT!
MOVE!

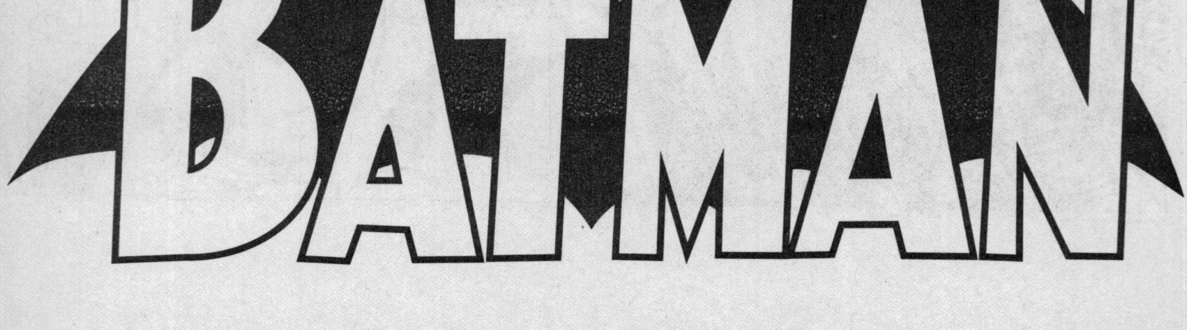
BATMAN

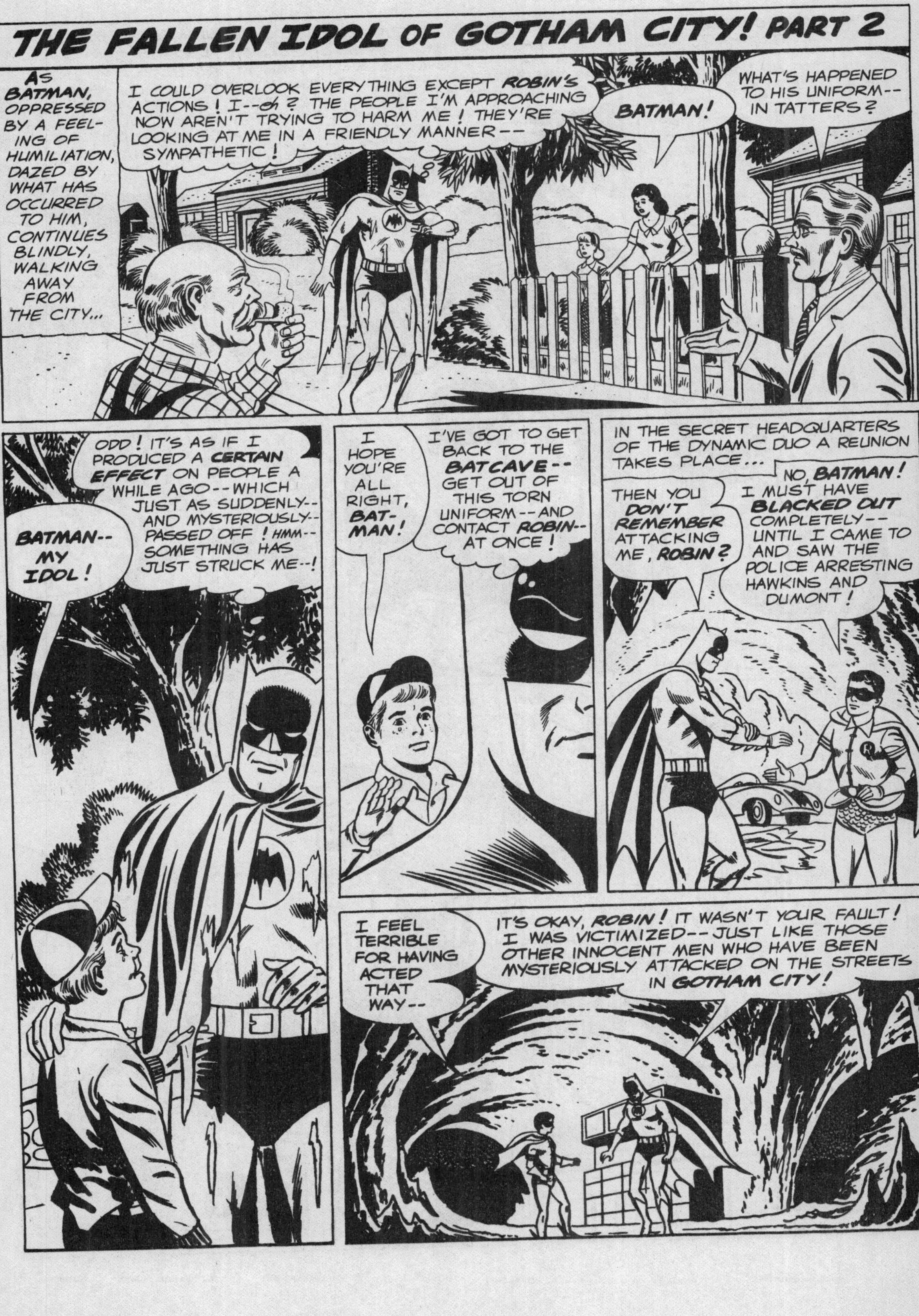
THE FALLEN IDOL OF GOTHAM CITY! PART 2
AS BATMAN, OPPRESSED BY A FEELING OF HUMILIATION, DAZED BY WHAT HAS OCCURRED TO HIM, CONTINUES BLINDLY, WALKING AWAY FROM THE CITY...
I COULD OVERLOOK EVERYTHING EXCEPT ROBIN'S ACTIONS! I--oh? THE PEOPLE I'M APPROACHING NOW AREN'T TRYING TO HARM ME! THEY'RE LOOKING AT ME IN A FRIENDLY MANNER--SYMPATHETIC!
BATMAN!
WHAT'S HAPPENED TO HIS UNIFORM--IN TATTERS?
ODD! IT'S AS IF I PRODUCED A CERTAIN EFFECT ON PEOPLE A WHILE AGO--WHICH JUST AS SUDDENLY--AND MYSTERIOUSLY--PASSED OFF! HMM--SOMETHING HAS JUST STRUCK ME--!
BATMAN--MY IDOL!
I HOPE YOU'RE ALL RIGHT, BATMAN!
I'VE GOT TO GET BACK TO THE BATCAVE--GET OUT OF THIS TORN UNIFORM--AND CONTACT ROBIN--AT ONCE!
IN THE SECRET HEADQUARTERS OF THE DYNAMIC DUO A REUNION TAKES PLACE...
THEN YOU DON'T REMEMBER ATTACKING ME, ROBIN?
NO, BATMAN! I MUST HAVE BLACKED OUT COMPLETELY--UNTIL I CAME TO AND SAW THE POLICE ARRESTING HAWKINS AND DUMONT!
I FEEL TERRIBLE FOR HAVING ACTED THAT WAY--
IT'S OKAY, ROBIN! IT WASN'T YOUR FAULT! I WAS VICTIMIZED--JUST LIKE THOSE OTHER INNOCENT MEN WHO HAVE BEEN MYSTERIOUSLY ATTACKED ON THE STREETS IN GOTHAM CITY!
8

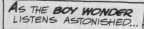

AS THE *BOY WONDER* LISTENS ASTONISHED...

IT ALL ADDS UP! BEFORE THE ASSAULT ON ME, YOU AND I ATE IN THAT RESTAURANT WHICH WAS THE *ONLY LINK* CONNECTING THE PREVIOUS VICTIMS! AND NOT ONLY THAT! IF YOU REMEMBER-- WE TWO HAD THE SAME DINNER--

--EXCEPT THAT AT THE END YOU HAD *MILK* AND I HAD *COFFEE*.. WHICH MAY BE THE REASON WHY THE THING HAPPENED TO *ME* AND NOT TO *YOU!*

WHAT'S OUR NEXT MOVE?

WE'RE GOING BACK TO THE *GOLDEN ROOST!* BUT THIS TIME WE'RE GOING IN SUCH A WAY THAT WE'LL *REALLY* BE ABLE TO INVESTIGATE THE PLACE-- WITH COMMISSIONER GORDON'S COOPERATION! NOW HERE'S WHAT WE'RE GOING TO DO...

THAT EVENING, IN FRONT OF THE *GOLDEN ROOST*...

GETCHA PAPERS! LATE PAPERS! READ ALL ABOUT THE *ATTACK ON BATMAN!*

GOTHAM
CROWD ATTACKS BATMAN

AND INSIDE...

FOOD INSPECTOR! I'LL WANT TO CHECK THE *CLEANLINESS* OF YOUR EMPLOYEES...

ALWAYS SOMETHING!

WELL, ALL RIGHT!

A NEWSBOY? A FOOD INSPECTOR? CAN YOU *GUESS* WHO THEY REALLY ARE, READER?

9

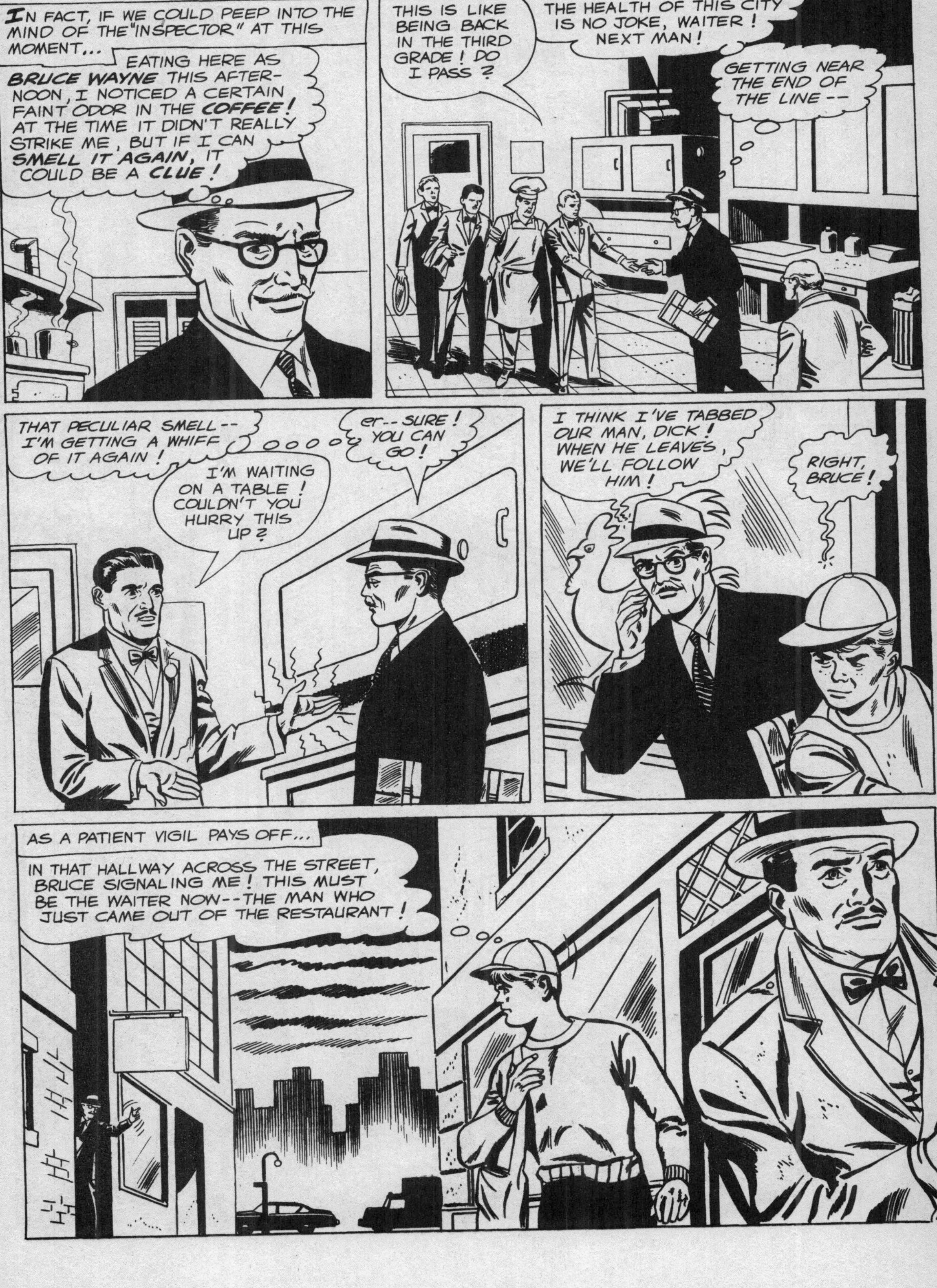
IN FACT, IF WE COULD PEEP INTO THE MIND OF THE "INSPECTOR" AT THIS MOMENT...
EATING HERE AS BRUCE WAYNE THIS AFTERNOON, I NOTICED A CERTAIN FAINT ODOR IN THE COFFEE! AT THE TIME IT DIDN'T REALLY STRIKE ME, BUT IF I CAN SMELL IT AGAIN, IT COULD BE A CLUE!
THIS IS LIKE BEING BACK IN THE THIRD GRADE! DO I PASS?
THE HEALTH OF THIS CITY IS NO JOKE, WAITER! NEXT MAN!
GETTING NEAR THE END OF THE LINE--
THAT PECULIAR SMELL-- I'M GETTING A WHIFF OF IT AGAIN!
er-- SURE! YOU CAN GO!
I'M WAITING ON A TABLE! COULDN'T YOU HURRY THIS UP?
I THINK I'VE TABBED OUR MAN, DICK! WHEN HE LEAVES, WE'LL FOLLOW HIM!
RIGHT, BRUCE!
AS A PATIENT VIGIL PAYS OFF...
IN THAT HALLWAY ACROSS THE STREET, BRUCE SIGNALING ME! THIS MUST BE THE WAITER NOW--THE MAN WHO JUST CAME OUT OF THE RESTAURANT!
10

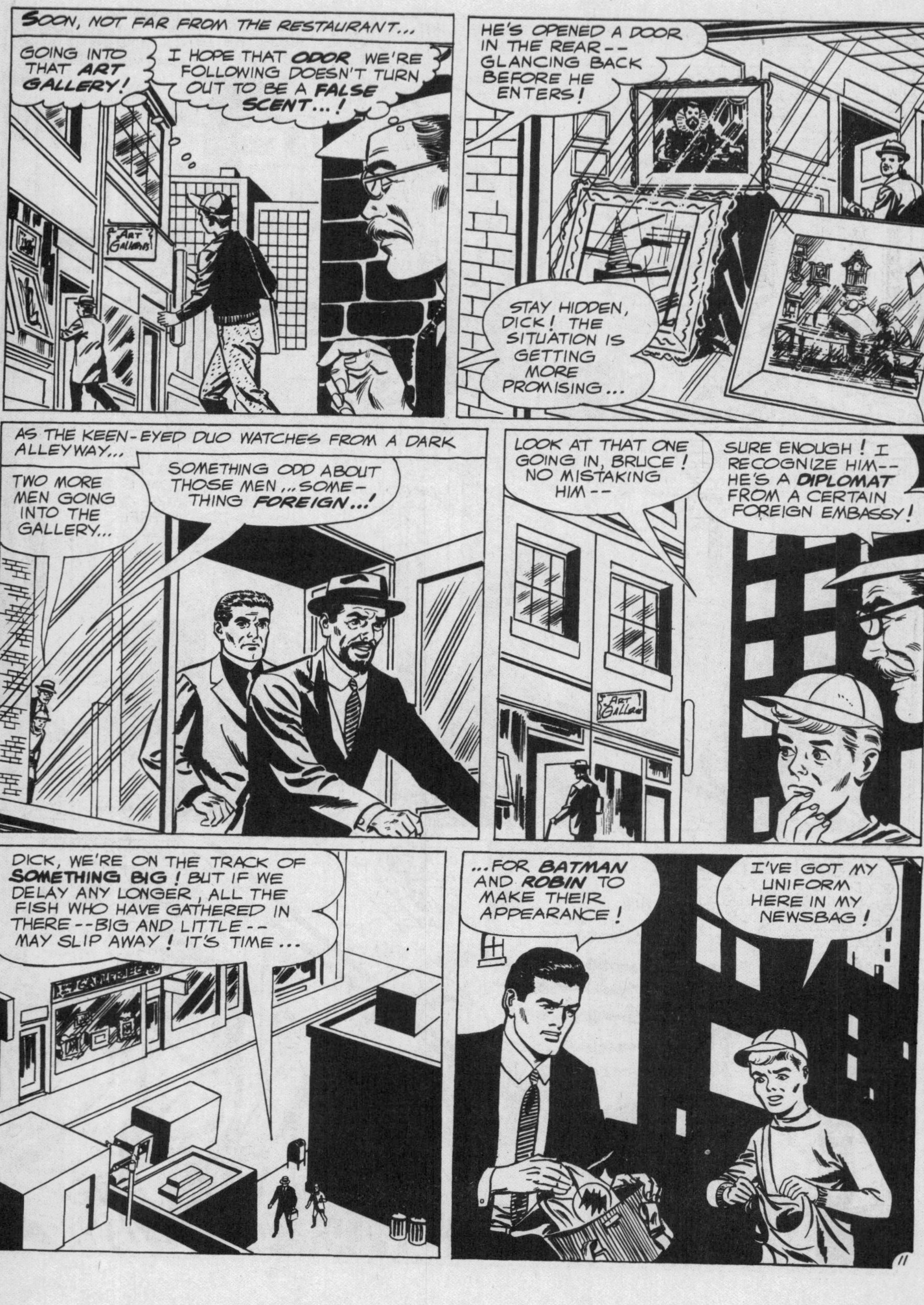
SOON, NOT FAR FROM THE RESTAURANT...
GOING INTO THAT ART GALLERY!
I HOPE THAT ODOR WE'RE FOLLOWING DOESN'T TURN OUT TO BE A FALSE SCENT...!
ART GALLERY
HE'S OPENED A DOOR IN THE REAR-- GLANCING BACK BEFORE HE ENTERS!
STAY HIDDEN, DICK! THE SITUATION IS GETTING MORE PROMISING...
AS THE KEEN-EYED DUO WATCHES FROM A DARK ALLEYWAY...
TWO MORE MEN GOING INTO THE GALLERY...
SOMETHING ODD ABOUT THOSE MEN... SOMETHING FOREIGN...!
LOOK AT THAT ONE GOING IN, BRUCE! NO MISTAKING HIM--
SURE ENOUGH! I RECOGNIZE HIM-- HE'S A DIPLOMAT FROM A CERTAIN FOREIGN EMBASSY!
DICK, WE'RE ON THE TRACK OF SOMETHING BIG! BUT IF WE DELAY ANY LONGER, ALL THE FISH WHO HAVE GATHERED IN THERE--BIG AND LITTLE-- MAY SLIP AWAY! IT'S TIME...
...FOR BATMAN AND ROBIN TO MAKE THEIR APPEARANCE!
I'VE GOT MY UNIFORM HERE IN MY NEWSBAG!
11

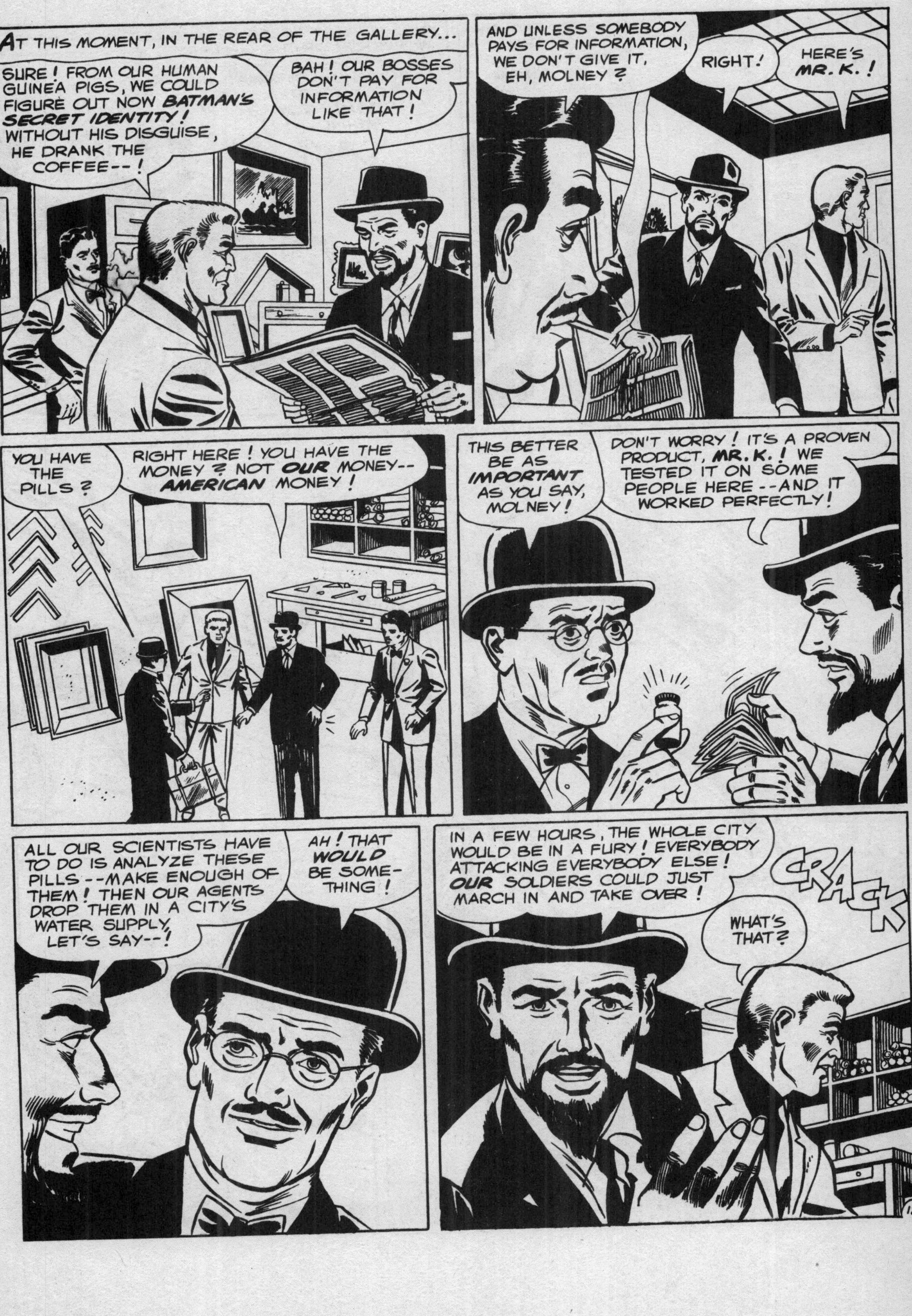
AT THIS MOMENT, IN THE REAR OF THE GALLERY...
SURE! FROM OUR HUMAN GUINEA PIGS, WE COULD FIGURE OUT NOW BATMAN'S SECRET IDENTITY! WITHOUT HIS DISGUISE, HE DRANK THE COFFEE--!
BAH! OUR BOSSES DON'T PAY FOR INFORMATION LIKE THAT!
AND UNLESS SOMEBODY PAYS FOR INFORMATION, WE DON'T GIVE IT, EH, MOLNEY?
RIGHT!
HERE'S MR. K.!
YOU HAVE THE PILLS?
RIGHT HERE! YOU HAVE THE MONEY? NOT OUR MONEY--AMERICAN MONEY!
THIS BETTER BE AS IMPORTANT AS YOU SAY, MOLNEY!
DON'T WORRY! IT'S A PROVEN PRODUCT, MR. K.! WE TESTED IT ON SOME PEOPLE HERE--AND IT WORKED PERFECTLY!
ALL OUR SCIENTISTS HAVE TO DO IS ANALYZE THESE PILLS--MAKE ENOUGH OF THEM! THEN OUR AGENTS DROP THEM IN A CITY'S WATER SUPPLY, LET'S SAY--!
AH! THAT WOULD BE SOMETHING!
IN A FEW HOURS, THE WHOLE CITY WOULD BE IN A FURY! EVERYBODY ATTACKING EVERYBODY ELSE! OUR SOLDIERS COULD JUST MARCH IN AND TAKE OVER!
CRACK
WHAT'S THAT?
12

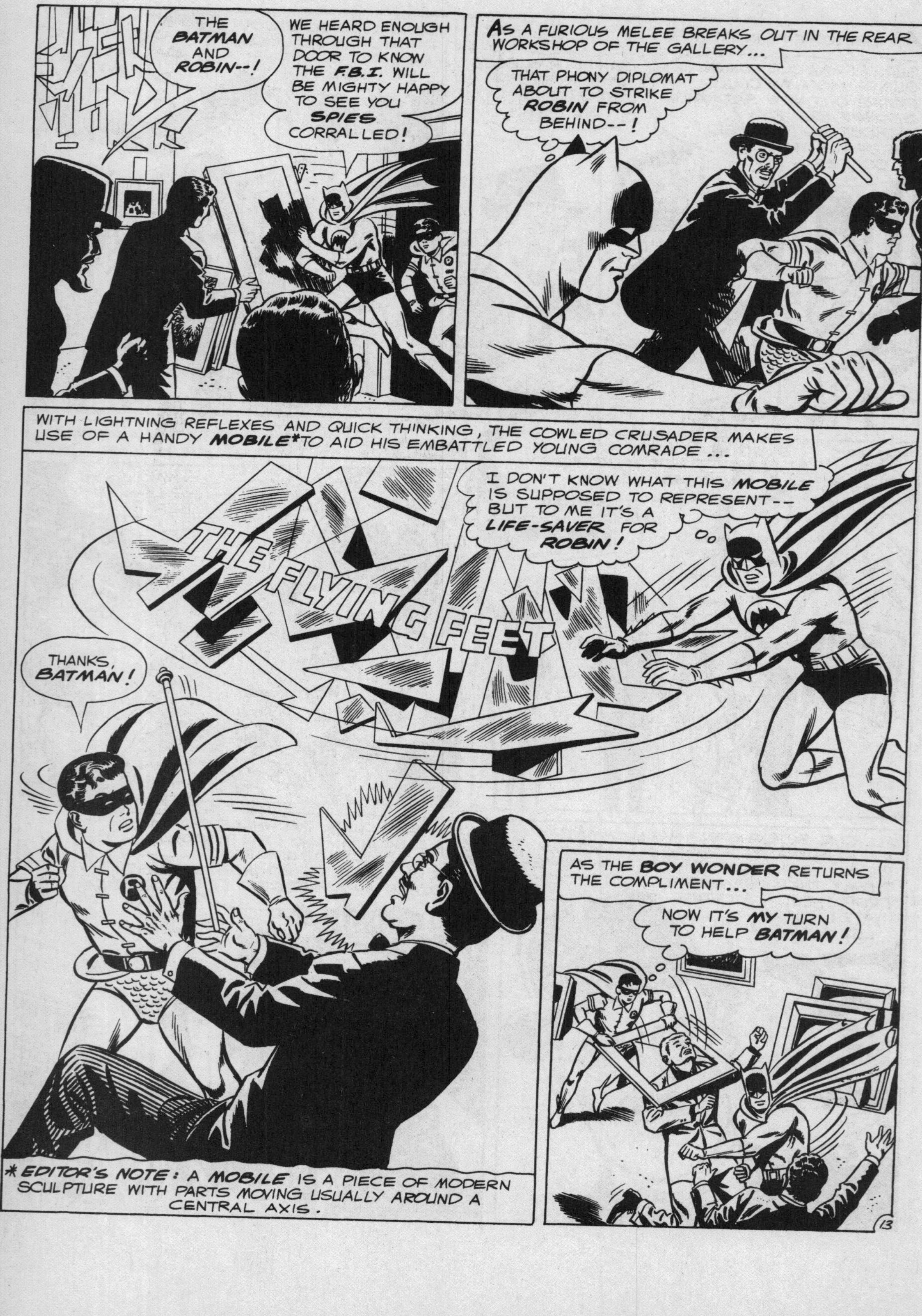

THE BATMAN AND ROBIN--!
WE HEARD ENOUGH THROUGH THAT DOOR TO KNOW THE F.B.I. WILL BE MIGHTY HAPPY TO SEE YOU SPIES CORRALLED!
AS A FURIOUS MELEE BREAKS OUT IN THE REAR WORKSHOP OF THE GALLERY...
THAT PHONY DIPLOMAT ABOUT TO STRIKE ROBIN FROM BEHIND--!
WITH LIGHTNING REFLEXES AND QUICK THINKING, THE COWLED CRUSADER MAKES USE OF A HANDY MOBILE* TO AID HIS EMBATTLED YOUNG COMRADE...
I DON'T KNOW WHAT THIS MOBILE IS SUPPOSED TO REPRESENT-- BUT TO ME IT'S A LIFE-SAVER FOR ROBIN!
THE FLYING FEET
THANKS, BATMAN!
* EDITOR'S NOTE: A MOBILE IS A PIECE OF MODERN SCULPTURE WITH PARTS MOVING USUALLY AROUND A CENTRAL AXIS.
AS THE BOY WONDER RETURNS THE COMPLIMENT...
NOW IT'S MY TURN TO HELP BATMAN!
13

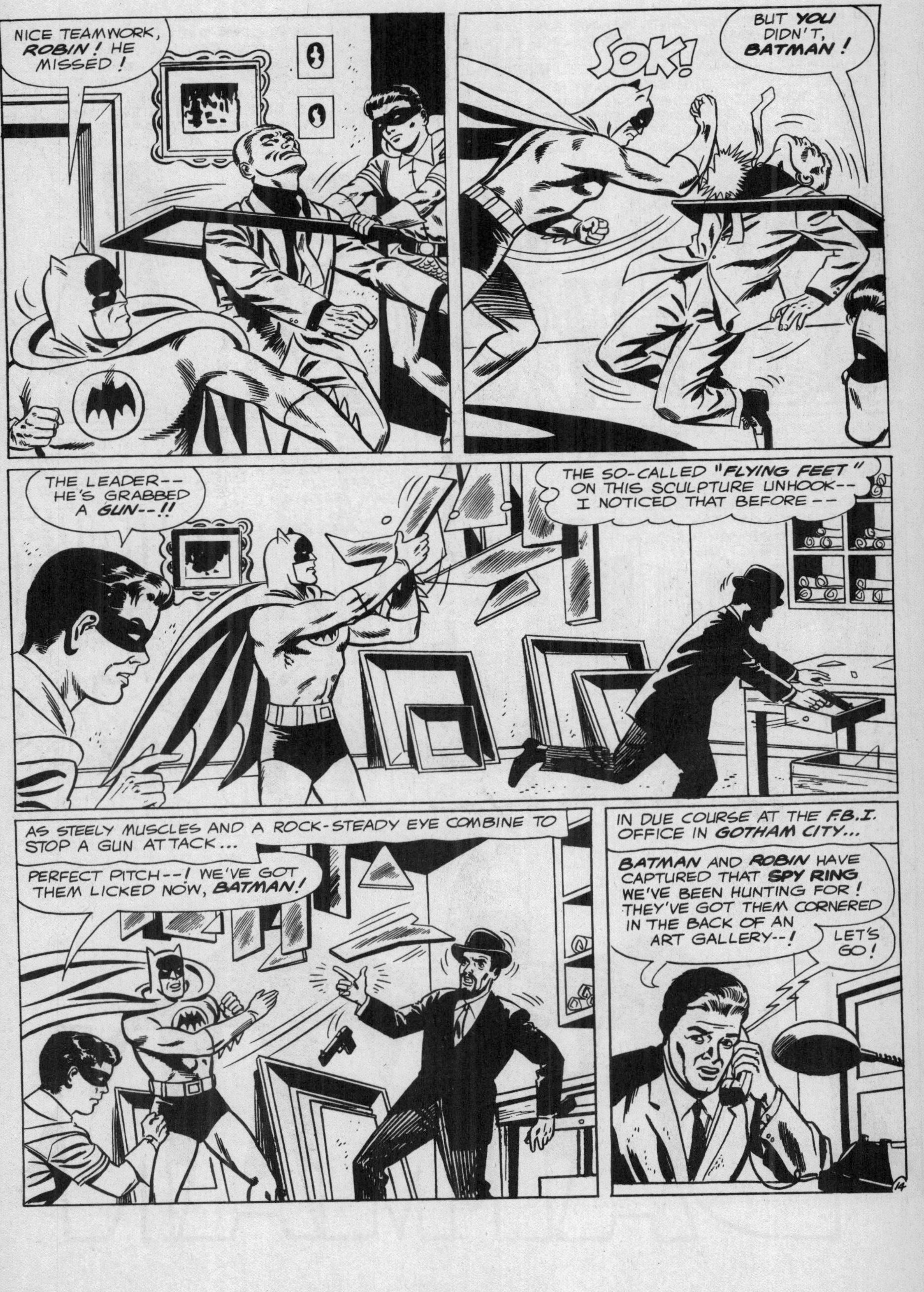
NICE TEAMWORK, ROBIN! HE MISSED!
SOK!
BUT YOU DIDN'T, BATMAN!
THE LEADER-- HE'S GRABBED A GUN--!!
THE SO-CALLED "FLYING FEET" ON THIS SCULPTURE UNHOOK-- I NOTICED THAT BEFORE--
AS STEELY MUSCLES AND A ROCK-STEADY EYE COMBINE TO STOP A GUN ATTACK...
PERFECT PITCH--! WE'VE GOT THEM LICKED NOW, BATMAN!
IN DUE COURSE AT THE F.B.I. OFFICE IN GOTHAM CITY...
BATMAN AND ROBIN HAVE CAPTURED THAT SPY RING WE'VE BEEN HUNTING FOR! THEY'VE GOT THEM CORNERED IN THE BACK OF AN ART GALLERY--!
LET'S GO!
14

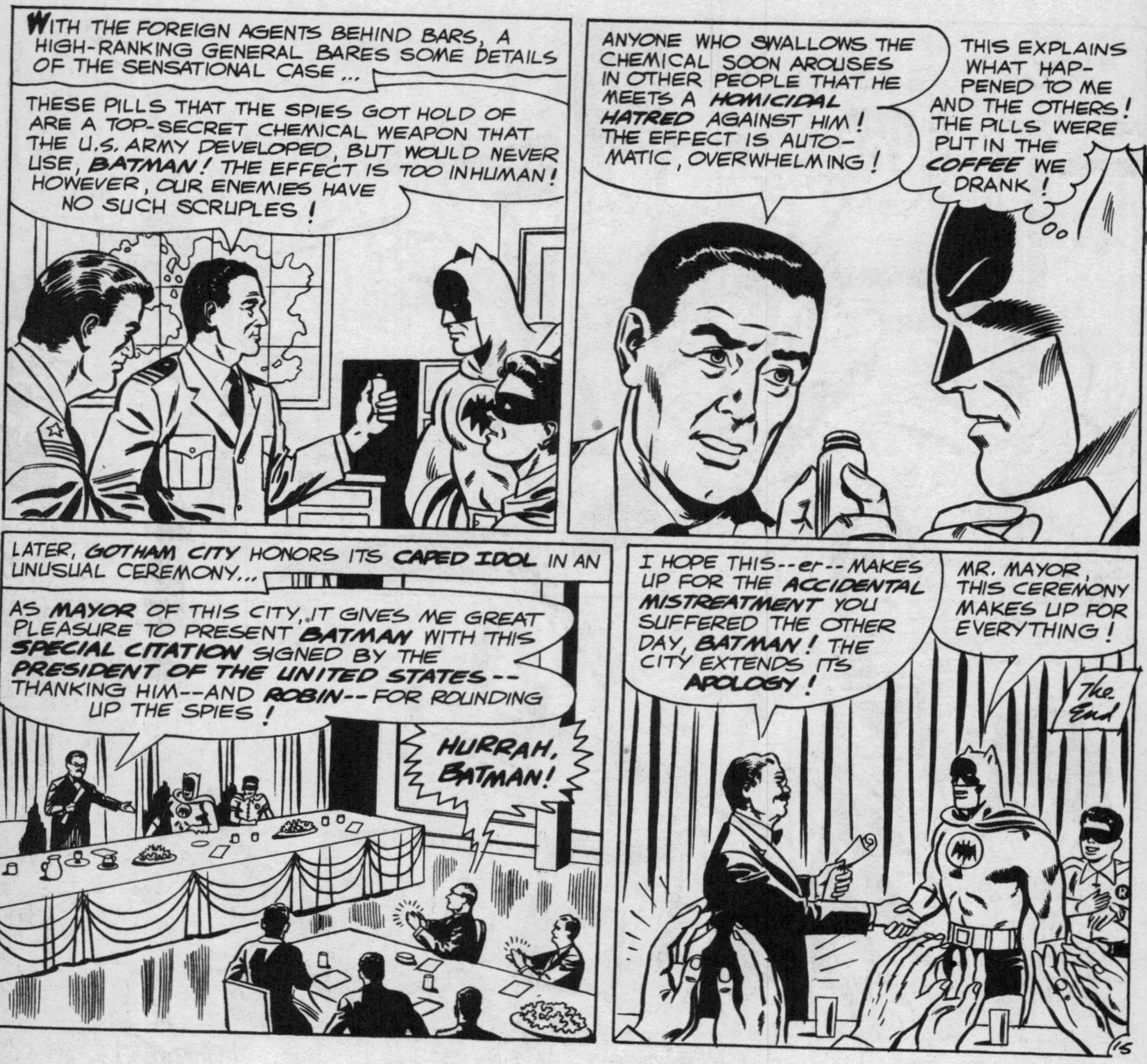
WITH THE FOREIGN AGENTS BEHIND BARS, A HIGH-RANKING GENERAL BARES SOME DETAILS OF THE SENSATIONAL CASE ...
THESE PILLS THAT THE SPIES GOT HOLD OF ARE A TOP-SECRET CHEMICAL WEAPON THAT THE U.S. ARMY DEVELOPED, BUT WOULD NEVER USE, BATMAN! THE EFFECT IS TOO INHUMAN! HOWEVER, OUR ENEMIES HAVE NO SUCH SCRUPLES!
ANYONE WHO SWALLOWS THE CHEMICAL SOON AROUSES IN OTHER PEOPLE THAT HE MEETS A HOMICIDAL HATRED AGAINST HIM! THE EFFECT IS AUTO-MATIC, OVERWHELMING!
THIS EXPLAINS WHAT HAP-PENED TO ME AND THE OTHERS! THE PILLS WERE PUT IN THE COFFEE WE DRANK!
LATER, GOTHAM CITY HONORS ITS CAPED IDOL IN AN UNUSUAL CEREMONY...
AS MAYOR OF THIS CITY, IT GIVES ME GREAT PLEASURE TO PRESENT BATMAN WITH THIS SPECIAL CITATION SIGNED BY THE PRESIDENT OF THE UNITED STATES-- THANKING HIM--AND ROBIN-- FOR ROUNDING UP THE SPIES!
HURRAH, BATMAN!
I HOPE THIS--er--MAKES UP FOR THE ACCIDENTAL MISTREATMENT YOU SUFFERED THE OTHER DAY, BATMAN! THE CITY EXTENDS ITS APOLOGY!
MR. MAYOR, THIS CEREMONY MAKES UP FOR EVERYTHING!
The End
15

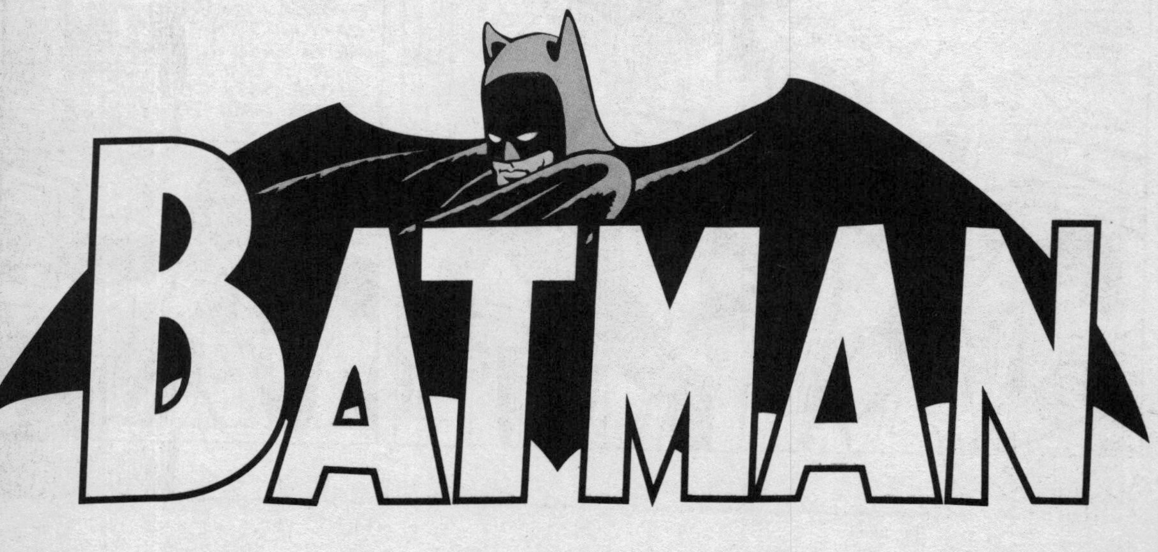
BATMAN

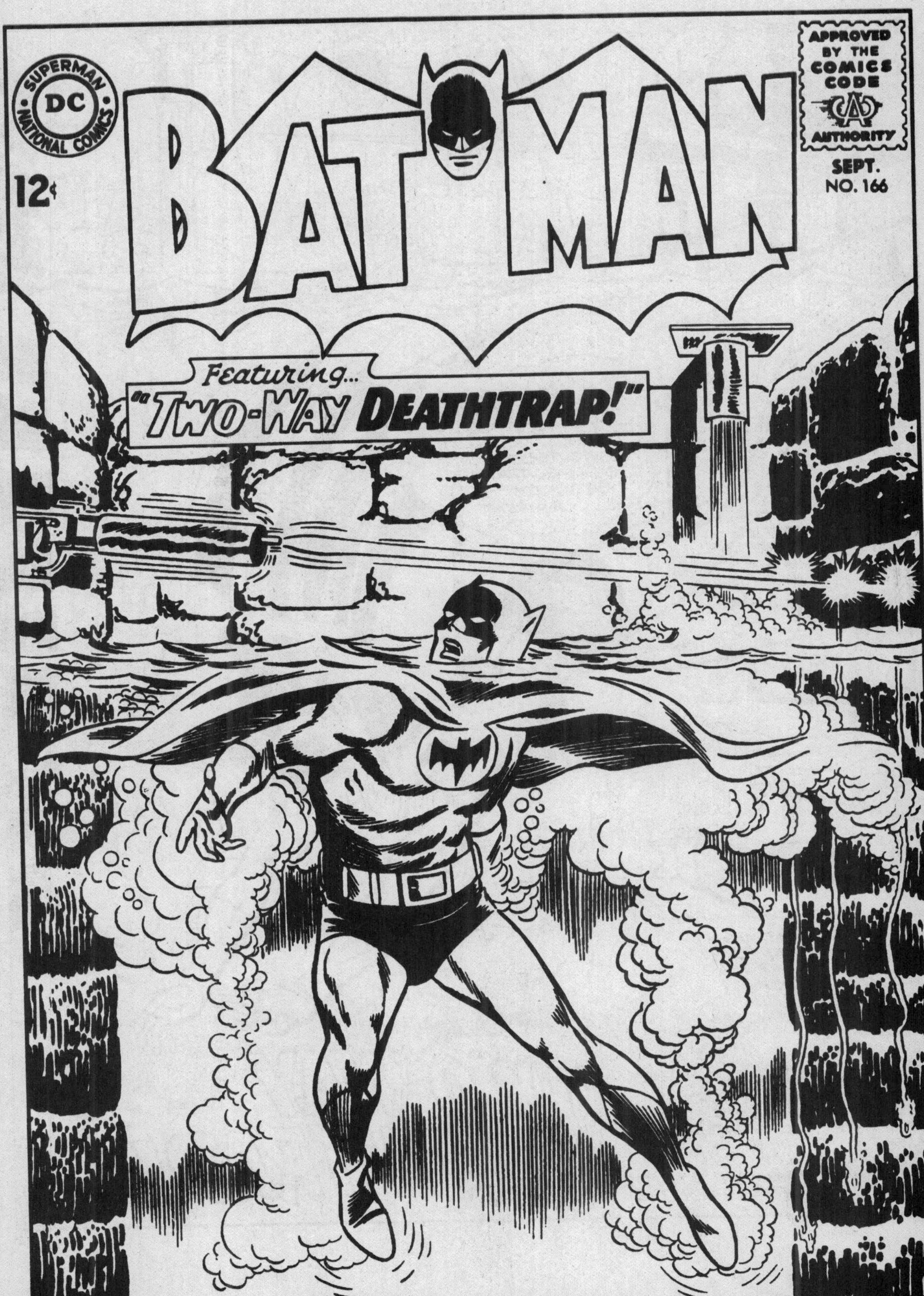
SUPERMAN
DC
NATIONAL COMICS
12¢
BATMAN
APPROVED BY THE COMICS CODE AUTHORITY
SEPT.
NO. 166
Featuring...
"TWO-WAY DEATHTRAP!"

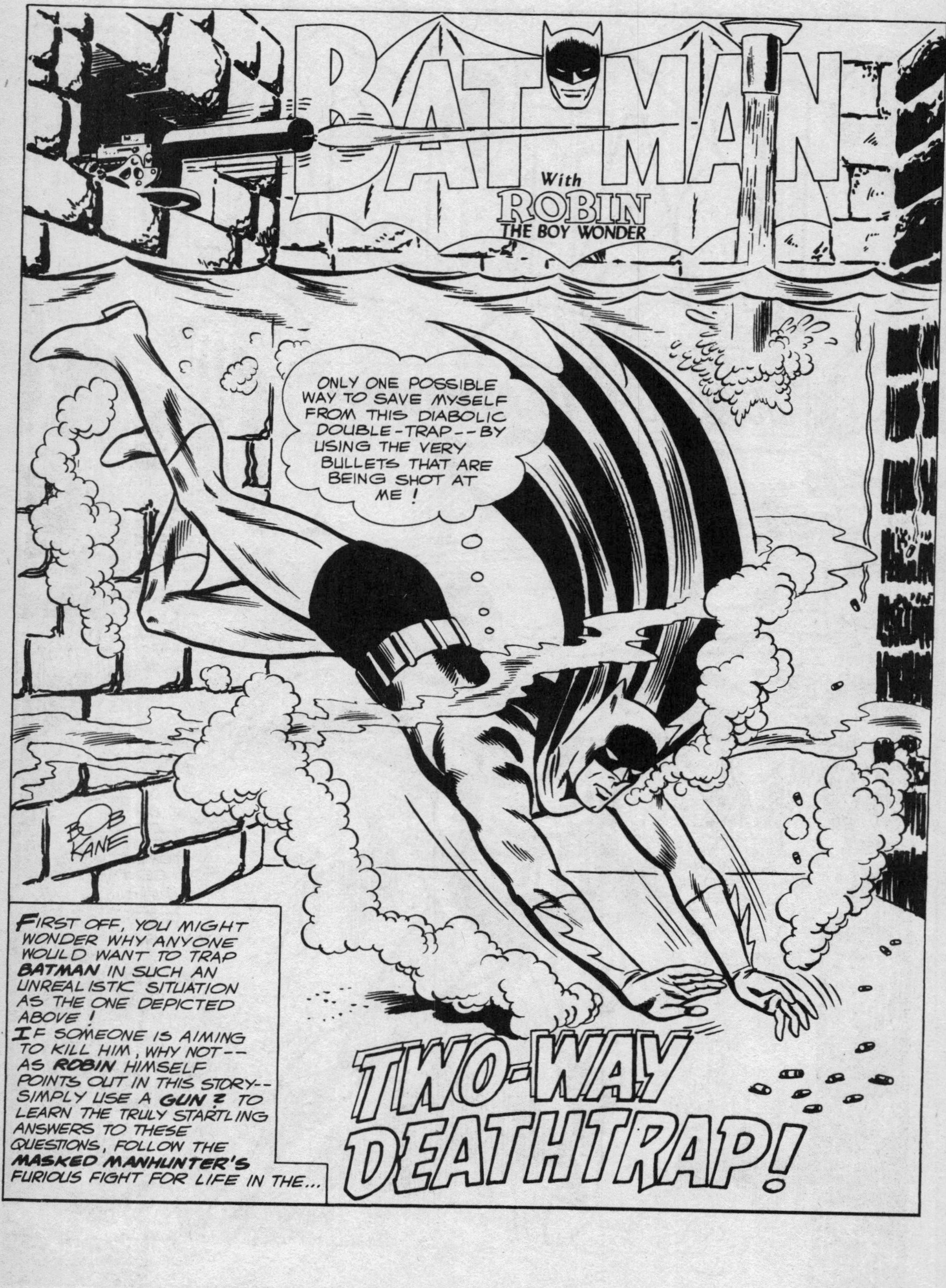
BATMAN
With ROBIN THE BOY WONDER
ONLY ONE POSSIBLE WAY TO SAVE MYSELF FROM THIS DIABOLIC DOUBLE-TRAP--BY USING THE VERY BULLETS THAT ARE BEING SHOT AT ME!
BOB KANE
FIRST OFF, YOU MIGHT WONDER WHY ANYONE WOULD WANT TO TRAP BATMAN IN SUCH AN UNREALISTIC SITUATION AS THE ONE DEPICTED ABOVE! IF SOMEONE IS AIMING TO KILL HIM, WHY NOT--AS ROBIN HIMSELF POINTS OUT IN THIS STORY--SIMPLY USE A GUN? TO LEARN THE TRULY STARTLING ANSWERS TO THESE QUESTIONS, FOLLOW THE MASKED MANHUNTER'S FURIOUS FIGHT FOR LIFE IN THE...
TWO-WAY DEATHTRAP!

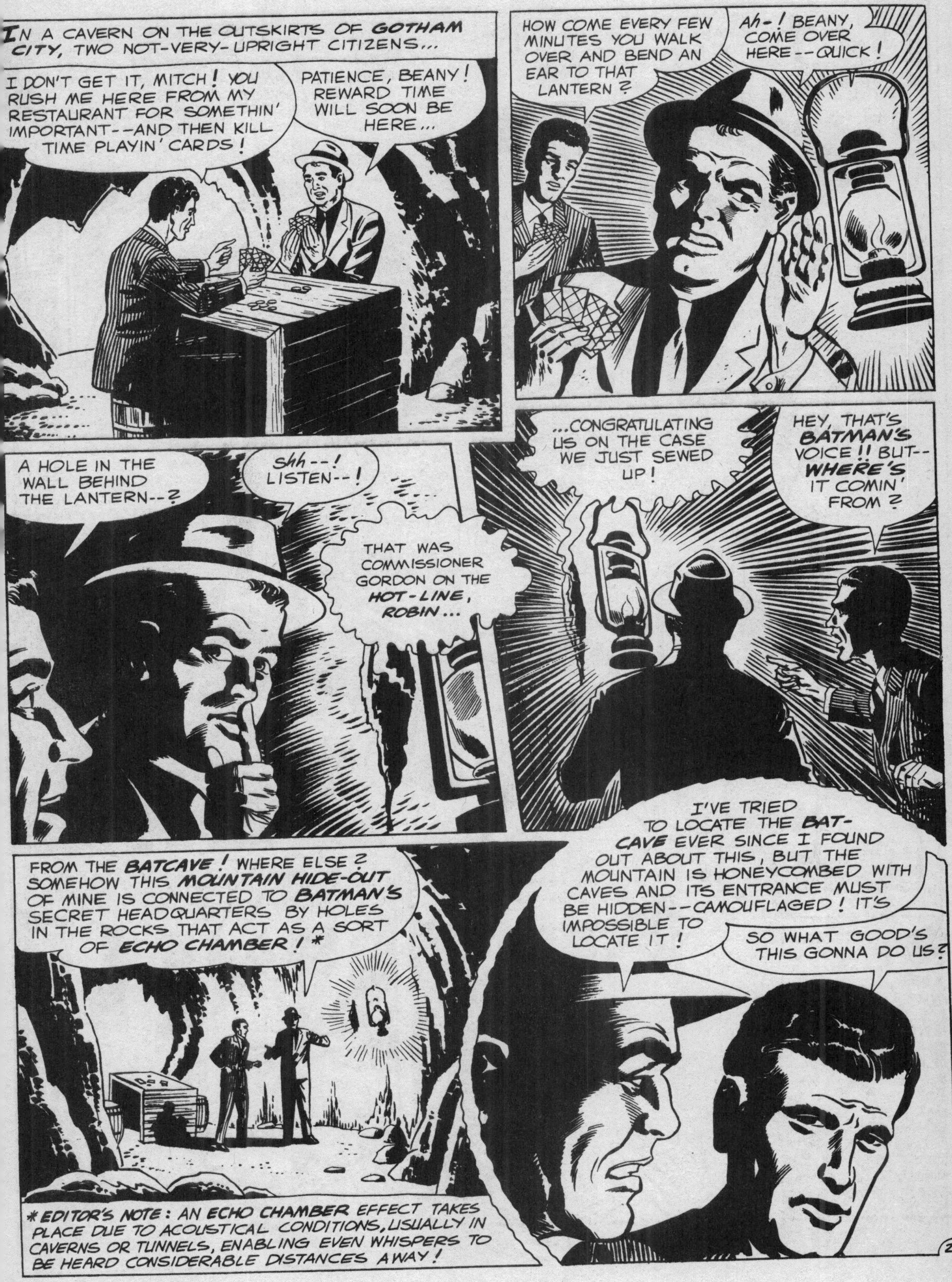
IN A CAVERN ON THE OUTSKIRTS OF GOTHAM CITY, TWO NOT-VERY-UPRIGHT CITIZENS...
I DON'T GET IT, MITCH! YOU RUSH ME HERE FROM MY RESTAURANT FOR SOMETHIN' IMPORTANT--AND THEN KILL TIME PLAYIN' CARDS!
PATIENCE, BEANY! REWARD TIME WILL SOON BE HERE...
HOW COME EVERY FEW MINUTES YOU WALK OVER AND BEND AN EAR TO THAT LANTERN?
Ah-! BEANY, COME OVER HERE--QUICK!
A HOLE IN THE WALL BEHIND THE LANTERN--?
Shh--! LISTEN--!
THAT WAS COMMISSIONER GORDON ON THE HOT-LINE, ROBIN...
...CONGRATULATING US ON THE CASE WE JUST SEWED UP!
HEY, THAT'S BATMAN'S VOICE!! BUT--WHERE'S IT COMIN' FROM?
FROM THE BATCAVE! WHERE ELSE? SOMEHOW THIS MOUNTAIN HIDE-OUT OF MINE IS CONNECTED TO BATMAN'S SECRET HEADQUARTERS BY HOLES IN THE ROCKS THAT ACT AS A SORT OF ECHO CHAMBER!*
*EDITOR'S NOTE: AN ECHO CHAMBER EFFECT TAKES PLACE DUE TO ACOUSTICAL CONDITIONS, USUALLY IN CAVERNS OR TUNNELS, ENABLING EVEN WHISPERS TO BE HEARD CONSIDERABLE DISTANCES AWAY!
I'VE TRIED TO LOCATE THE BAT-CAVE EVER SINCE I FOUND OUT ABOUT THIS, BUT THE MOUNTAIN IS HONEYCOMBED WITH CAVES AND ITS ENTRANCE MUST BE HIDDEN--CAMOUFLAGED! IT'S IMPOSSIBLE TO LOCATE IT!
SO WHAT GOOD'S THIS GONNA DO US?
2

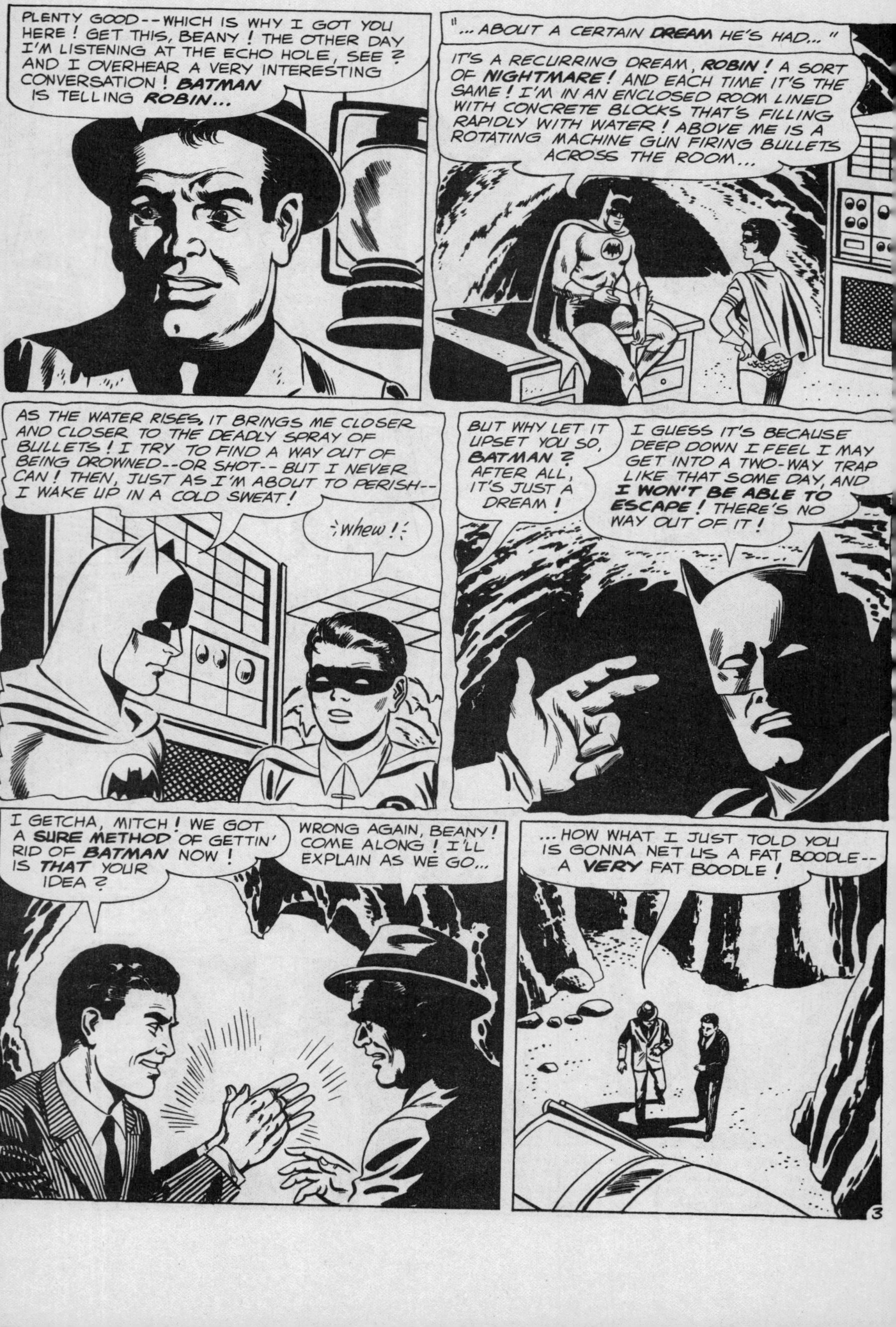
PLENTY GOOD--WHICH IS WHY I GOT YOU HERE! GET THIS, BEANY! THE OTHER DAY I'M LISTENING AT THE ECHO HOLE, SEE? AND I OVERHEAR A VERY INTERESTING CONVERSATION! BATMAN IS TELLING ROBIN...
"...ABOUT A CERTAIN DREAM HE'S HAD..."
IT'S A RECURRING DREAM, ROBIN! A SORT OF NIGHTMARE! AND EACH TIME IT'S THE SAME! I'M IN AN ENCLOSED ROOM LINED WITH CONCRETE BLOCKS THAT'S FILLING RAPIDLY WITH WATER! ABOVE ME IS A ROTATING MACHINE GUN FIRING BULLETS ACROSS THE ROOM...
AS THE WATER RISES, IT BRINGS ME CLOSER AND CLOSER TO THE DEADLY SPRAY OF BULLETS! I TRY TO FIND A WAY OUT OF BEING DROWNED--OR SHOT--BUT I NEVER CAN! THEN, JUST AS I'M ABOUT TO PERISH--I WAKE UP IN A COLD SWEAT!
whew!
BUT WHY LET IT UPSET YOU SO, BATMAN? AFTER ALL, IT'S JUST A DREAM!
I GUESS IT'S BECAUSE DEEP DOWN I FEEL I MAY GET INTO A TWO-WAY TRAP LIKE THAT SOME DAY, AND I WON'T BE ABLE TO ESCAPE! THERE'S NO WAY OUT OF IT!
I GETCHA, MITCH! WE GOT A SURE METHOD OF GETTIN' RID OF BATMAN NOW! IS THAT YOUR IDEA?
WRONG AGAIN, BEANY! COME ALONG! I'LL EXPLAIN AS WE GO...
...HOW WHAT I JUST TOLD YOU IS GONNA NET US A FAT BOODLE--A VERY FAT BOODLE!
3

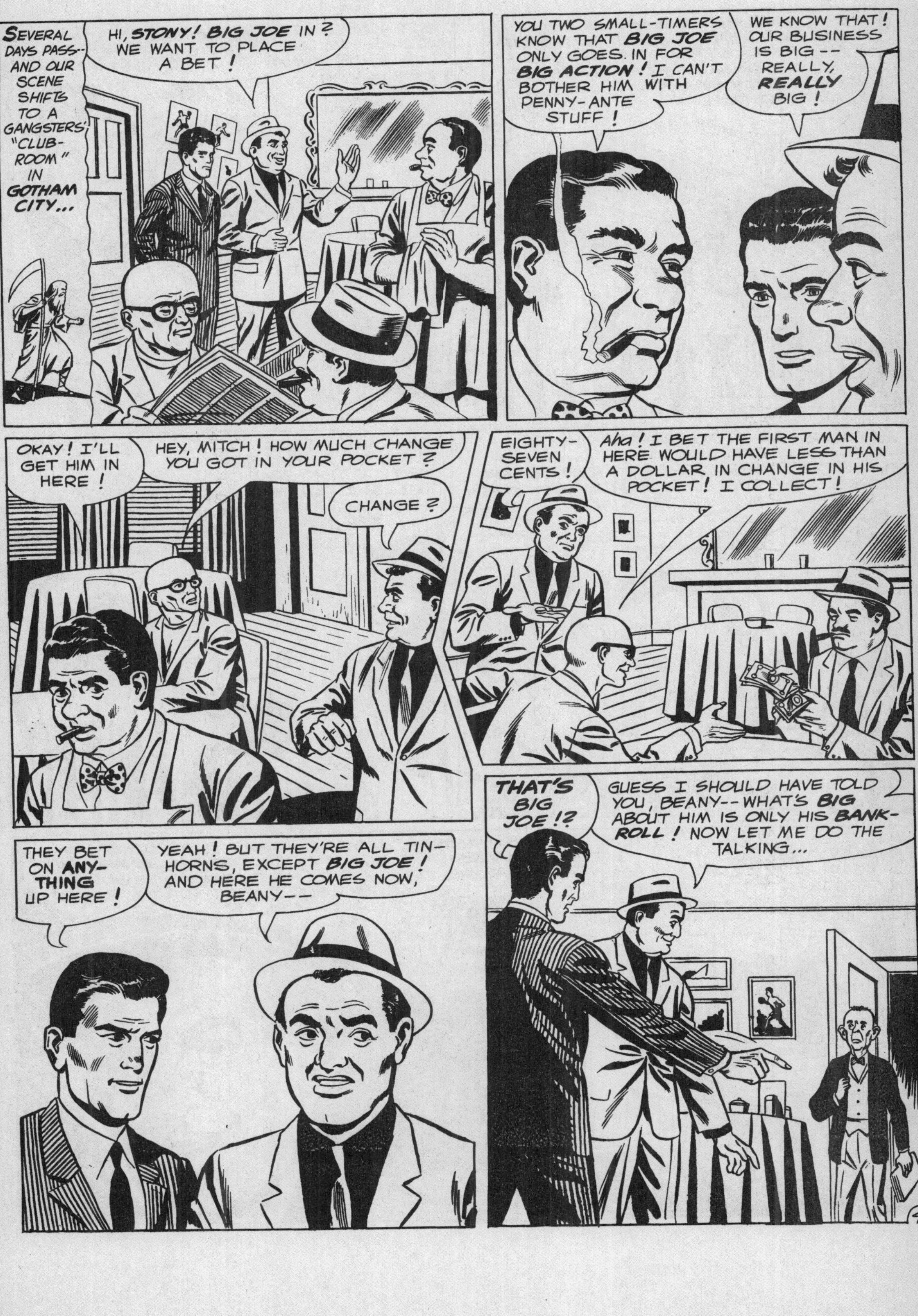
SEVERAL DAYS PASS--AND OUR SCENE SHIFTS TO A GANGSTERS' "CLUB-ROOM" IN GOTHAM CITY...
HI, STONY! BIG JOE IN? WE WANT TO PLACE A BET!
YOU TWO SMALL-TIMERS KNOW THAT BIG JOE ONLY GOES IN FOR BIG ACTION! I CAN'T BOTHER HIM WITH PENNY-ANTE STUFF!
WE KNOW THAT! OUR BUSINESS IS BIG -- REALLY, REALLY BIG!
OKAY! I'LL GET HIM IN HERE!
HEY, MITCH! HOW MUCH CHANGE YOU GOT IN YOUR POCKET?
CHANGE?
EIGHTY-SEVEN CENTS!
Aha! I BET THE FIRST MAN IN HERE WOULD HAVE LESS THAN A DOLLAR IN CHANGE IN HIS POCKET! I COLLECT!
THEY BET ON ANY-THING UP HERE!
YEAH! BUT THEY'RE ALL TIN-HORNS, EXCEPT BIG JOE! AND HERE HE COMES NOW, BEANY--
THAT'S BIG JOE!?
GUESS I SHOULD HAVE TOLD YOU, BEANY--WHAT'S BIG ABOUT HIM IS ONLY HIS BANK-ROLL! NOW LET ME DO THE TALKING...
4

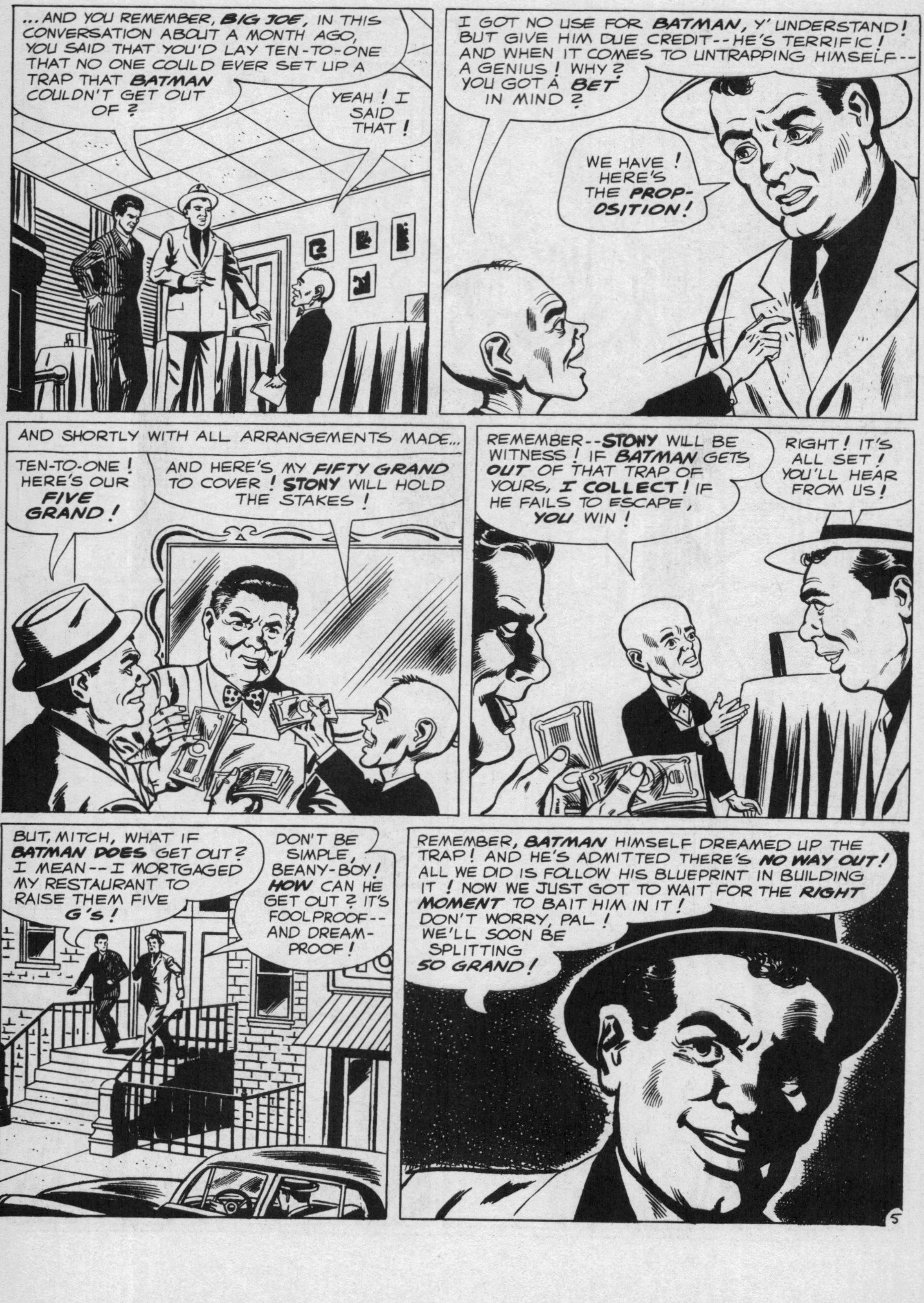
...AND YOU REMEMBER, BIG JOE, IN THIS CONVERSATION ABOUT A MONTH AGO, YOU SAID THAT YOU'D LAY TEN-TO-ONE THAT NO ONE COULD EVER SET UP A TRAP THAT BATMAN COULDN'T GET OUT OF?
YEAH! I SAID THAT!
I GOT NO USE FOR BATMAN, Y' UNDERSTAND! BUT GIVE HIM DUE CREDIT--HE'S TERRIFIC! AND WHEN IT COMES TO UNTRAPPING HIMSELF--A GENIUS! WHY? YOU GOT A BET IN MIND?
WE HAVE! HERE'S THE PROPOSITION!
AND SHORTLY WITH ALL ARRANGEMENTS MADE...
TEN-TO-ONE! HERE'S OUR FIVE GRAND!
AND HERE'S MY FIFTY GRAND TO COVER! STONY WILL HOLD THE STAKES!
REMEMBER--STONY WILL BE WITNESS! IF BATMAN GETS OUT OF THAT TRAP OF YOURS, I COLLECT! IF HE FAILS TO ESCAPE, YOU WIN!
RIGHT! IT'S ALL SET! YOU'LL HEAR FROM US!
BUT, MITCH, WHAT IF BATMAN DOES GET OUT? I MEAN--I MORTGAGED MY RESTAURANT TO RAISE THEM FIVE G'S!
DON'T BE SIMPLE, BEANY-BOY! HOW CAN HE GET OUT? IT'S FOOLPROOF--AND DREAM-PROOF!
REMEMBER, BATMAN HIMSELF DREAMED UP THE TRAP! AND HE'S ADMITTED THERE'S NO WAY OUT! ALL WE DID IS FOLLOW HIS BLUEPRINT IN BUILDING IT! NOW WE JUST GOT TO WAIT FOR THE RIGHT MOMENT TO BAIT HIM IN IT! DON'T WORRY, PAL! WE'LL SOON BE SPLITTING 50 GRAND!
5

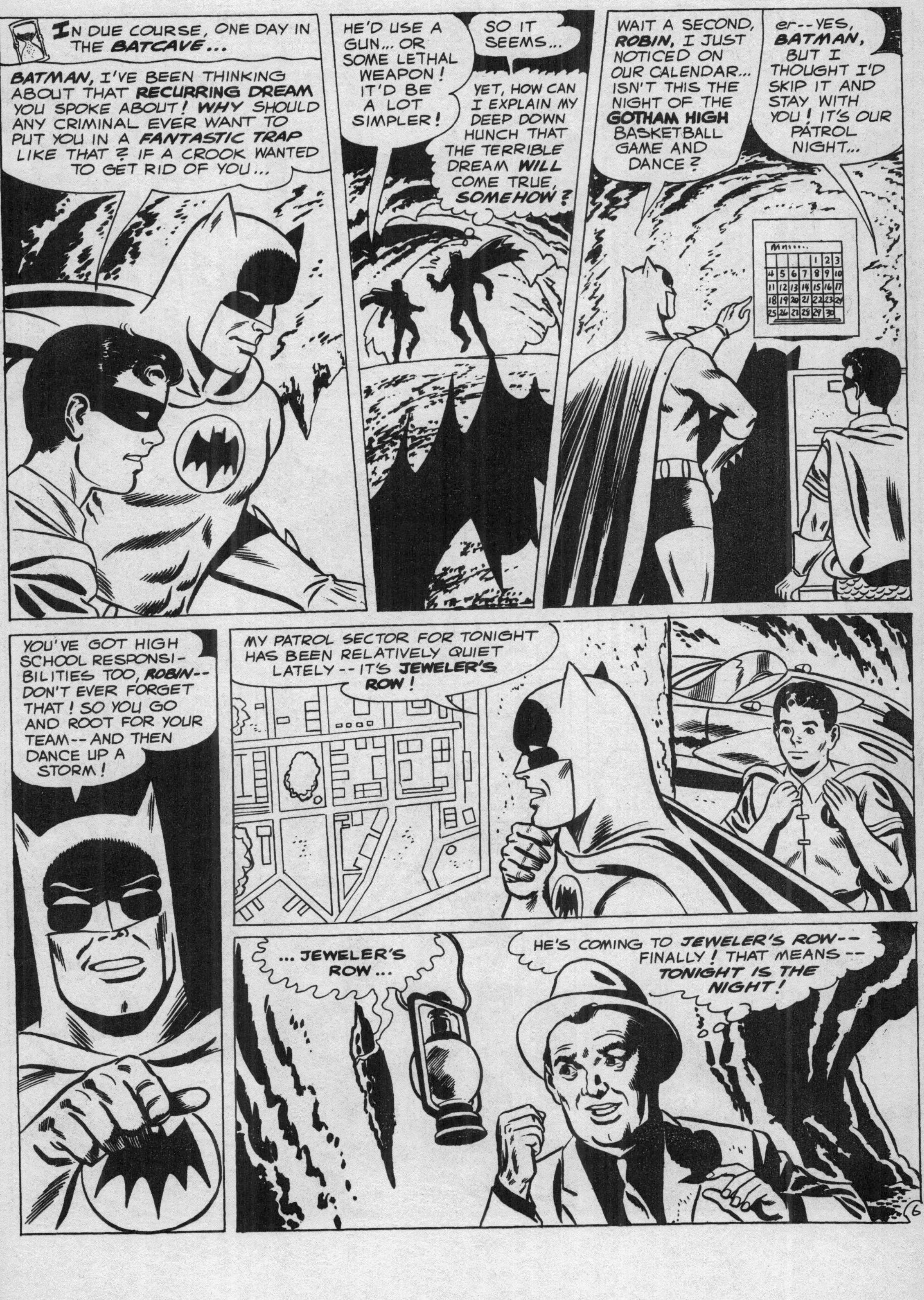
IN DUE COURSE, ONE DAY IN THE BATCAVE...
BATMAN, I'VE BEEN THINKING ABOUT THAT RECURRING DREAM YOU SPOKE ABOUT! WHY SHOULD ANY CRIMINAL EVER WANT TO PUT YOU IN A FANTASTIC TRAP LIKE THAT? IF A CROOK WANTED TO GET RID OF YOU...
HE'D USE A GUN... OR SOME LETHAL WEAPON! IT'D BE A LOT SIMPLER!
SO IT SEEMS...
YET, HOW CAN I EXPLAIN MY DEEP DOWN HUNCH THAT THE TERRIBLE DREAM WILL COME TRUE, SOMEHOW?
WAIT A SECOND, ROBIN, I JUST NOTICED ON OUR CALENDAR... ISN'T THIS THE NIGHT OF THE GOTHAM HIGH BASKETBALL GAME AND DANCE?
er--YES, BATMAN, BUT I THOUGHT I'D SKIP IT AND STAY WITH YOU! IT'S OUR PATROL NIGHT...
YOU'VE GOT HIGH SCHOOL RESPONSIBILITIES TOO, ROBIN-- DON'T EVER FORGET THAT! SO YOU GO AND ROOT FOR YOUR TEAM--AND THEN DANCE UP A STORM!
MY PATROL SECTOR FOR TONIGHT HAS BEEN RELATIVELY QUIET LATELY--IT'S JEWELER'S ROW!
... JEWELER'S ROW ...
HE'S COMING TO JEWELER'S ROW-- FINALLY! THAT MEANS-- TONIGHT IS THE NIGHT!
6

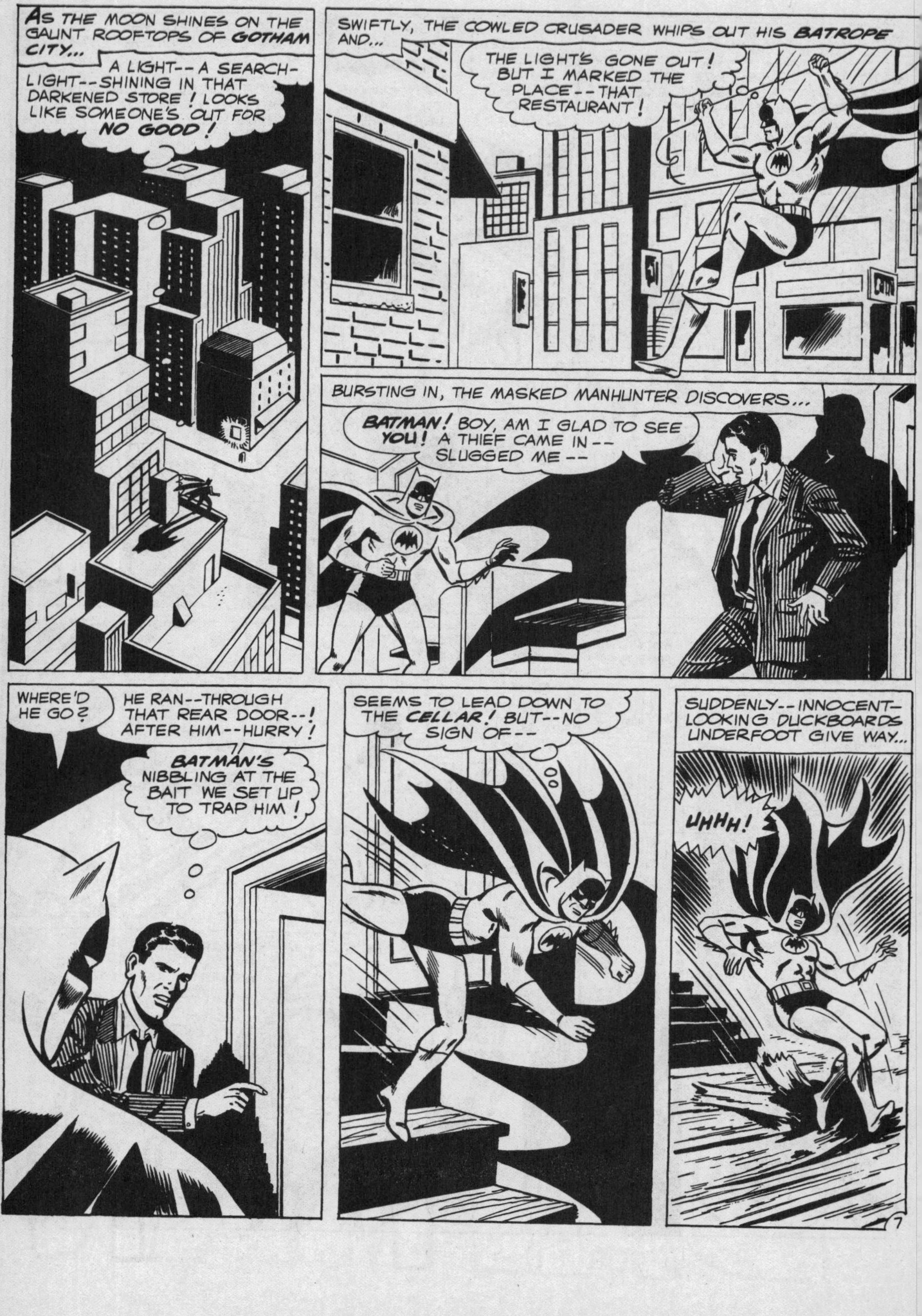
AS THE MOON SHINES ON THE GAUNT ROOFTOPS OF GOTHAM CITY...
A LIGHT--A SEARCH-LIGHT--SHINING IN THAT DARKENED STORE! LOOKS LIKE SOMEONE'S OUT FOR NO GOOD!
SWIFTLY, THE COWLED CRUSADER WHIPS OUT HIS BATROPE AND...
THE LIGHT'S GONE OUT! BUT I MARKED THE PLACE--THAT RESTAURANT!
BURSTING IN, THE MASKED MANHUNTER DISCOVERS...
BATMAN! BOY, AM I GLAD TO SEE YOU! A THIEF CAME IN--SLUGGED ME--
WHERE'D HE GO?
HE RAN--THROUGH THAT REAR DOOR--! AFTER HIM--HURRY!
BATMAN'S NIBBLING AT THE BAIT WE SET UP TO TRAP HIM!
SEEMS TO LEAD DOWN TO THE CELLAR! BUT--NO SIGN OF--
SUDDENLY--INNOCENT-LOOKING DUCKBOARDS UNDERFOOT GIVE WAY...
UHHH!
7

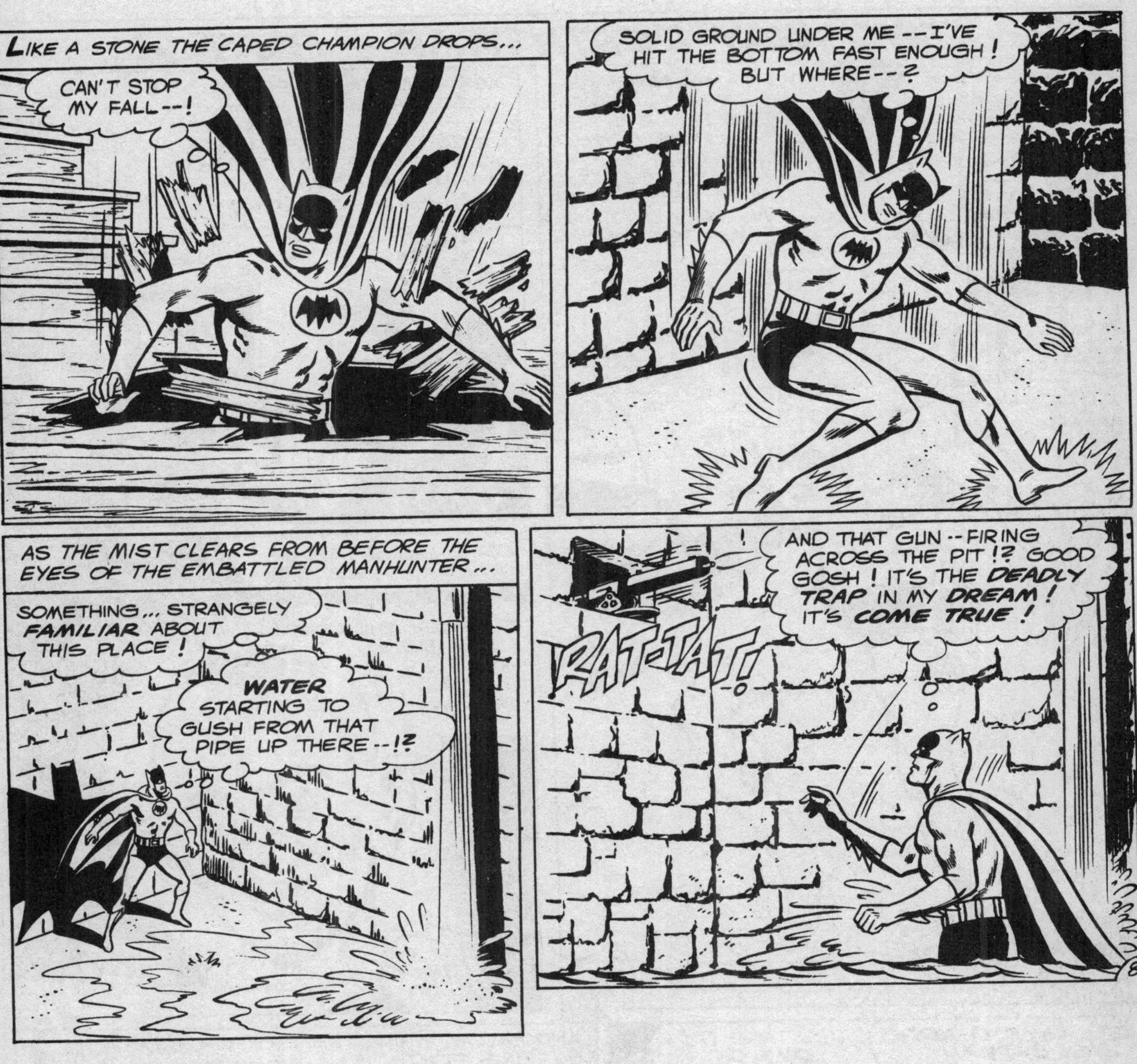
LIKE A STONE THE CAPED CHAMPION DROPS...
CAN'T STOP MY FALL--!
SOLID GROUND UNDER ME--I'VE HIT THE BOTTOM FAST ENOUGH! BUT WHERE--?
AS THE MIST CLEARS FROM BEFORE THE EYES OF THE EMBATTLED MANHUNTER...
SOMETHING... STRANGELY FAMILIAR ABOUT THIS PLACE!
WATER STARTING TO GUSH FROM THAT PIPE UP THERE--!?
RAT-TAT!
AND THAT GUN--FIRING ACROSS THE PIT!? GOOD GOSH! IT'S THE DEADLY TRAP IN MY DREAM! IT'S COME TRUE!
8

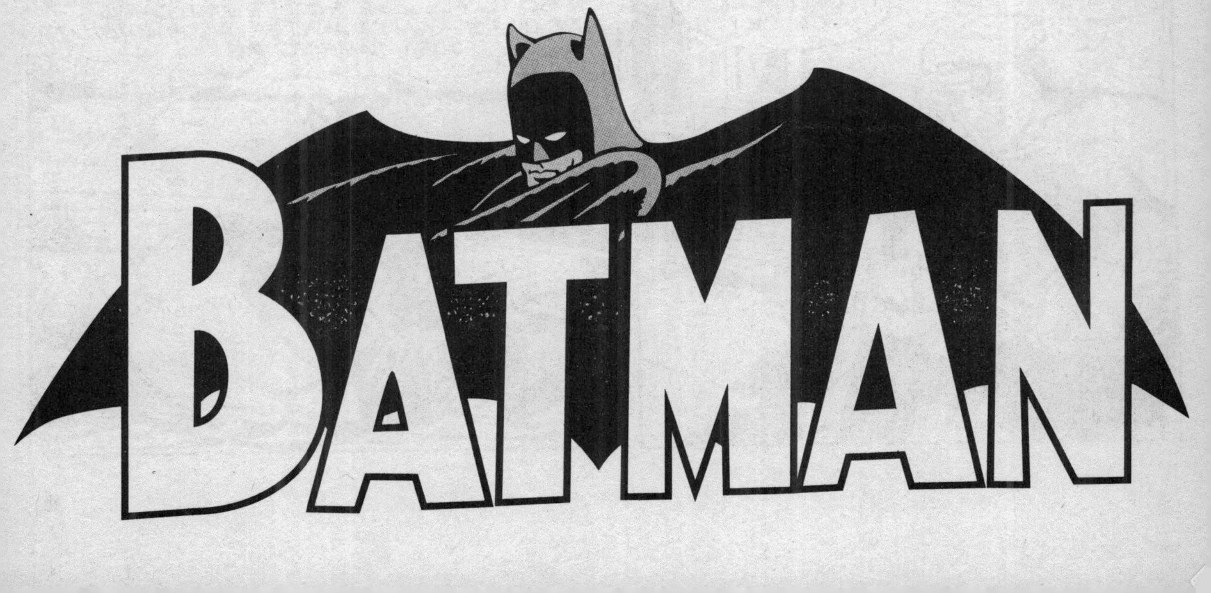
BATMAN

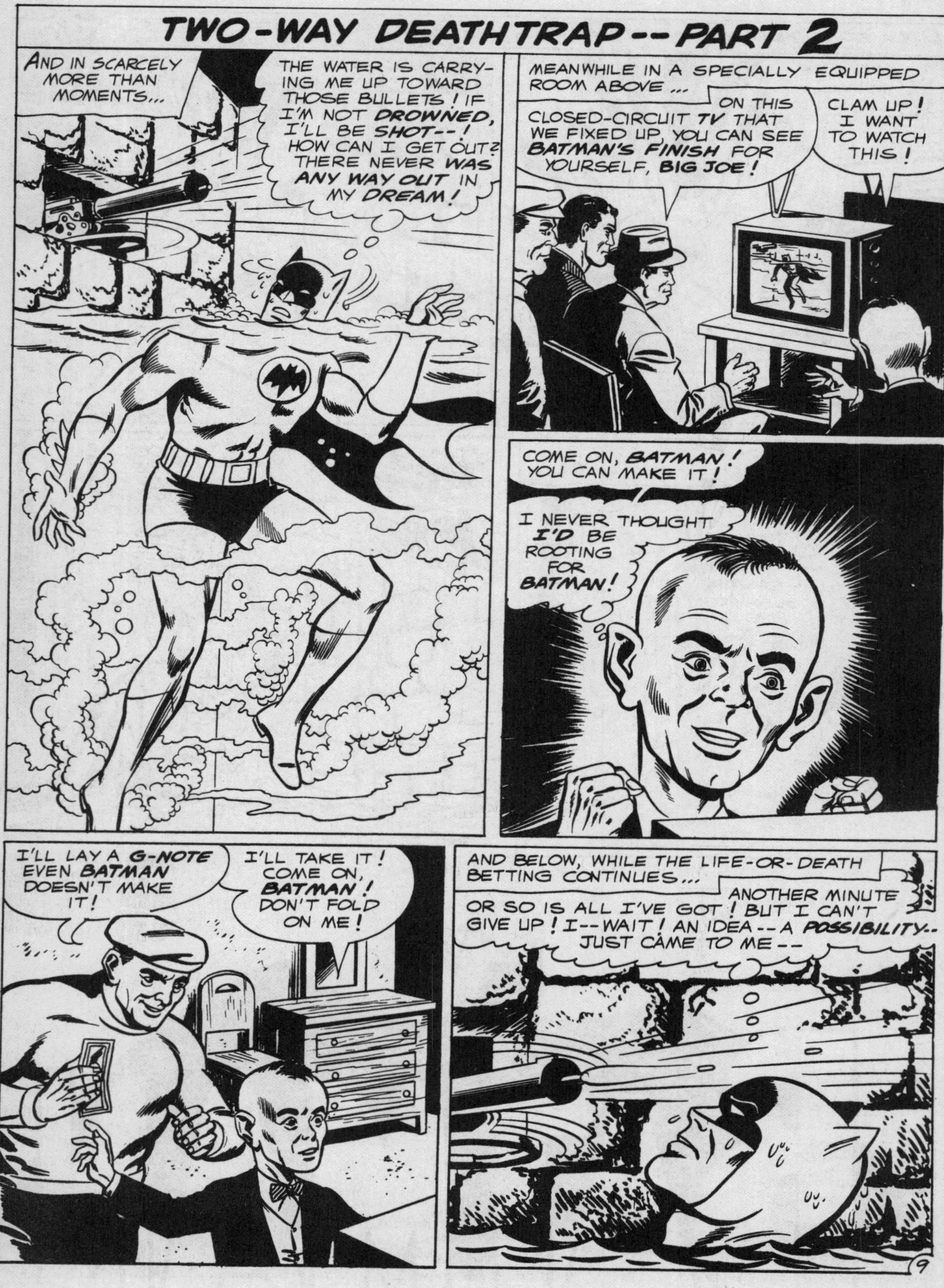
TWO-WAY DEATHTRAP--PART 2
AND IN SCARCELY MORE THAN MOMENTS...
THE WATER IS CARRYING ME UP TOWARD THOSE BULLETS! IF I'M NOT DROWNED, I'LL BE SHOT--! HOW CAN I GET OUT? THERE NEVER WAS ANY WAY OUT IN MY DREAM!
MEANWHILE IN A SPECIALLY EQUIPPED ROOM ABOVE...
ON THIS CLOSED-CIRCUIT TV THAT WE FIXED UP, YOU CAN SEE BATMAN'S FINISH FOR YOURSELF, BIG JOE!
CLAM UP! I WANT TO WATCH THIS!
COME ON, BATMAN! YOU CAN MAKE IT!
I NEVER THOUGHT I'D BE ROOTING FOR BATMAN!
I'LL LAY A G-NOTE EVEN BATMAN DOESN'T MAKE IT!
I'LL TAKE IT! COME ON, BATMAN! DON'T FOLD ON ME!
AND BELOW, WHILE THE LIFE-OR-DEATH BETTING CONTINUES...
ANOTHER MINUTE OR SO IS ALL I'VE GOT! BUT I CAN'T GIVE UP! I--WAIT! AN IDEA--A POSSIBILITY--JUST CAME TO ME--
9

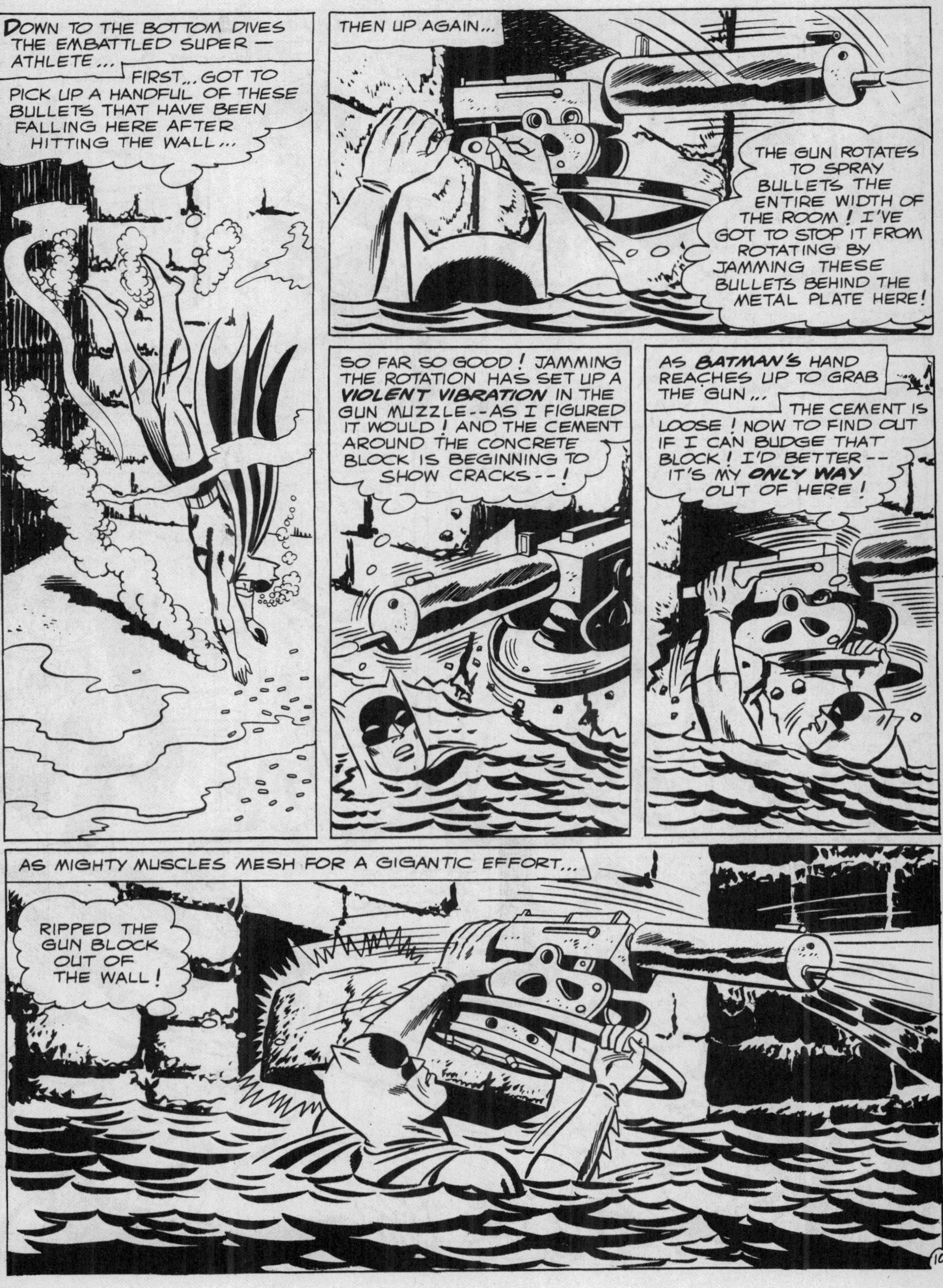
DOWN TO THE BOTTOM DIVES THE EMBATTLED SUPER—ATHLETE...
FIRST... GOT TO PICK UP A HANDFUL OF THESE BULLETS THAT HAVE BEEN FALLING HERE AFTER HITTING THE WALL...
THEN UP AGAIN...
THE GUN ROTATES TO SPRAY BULLETS THE ENTIRE WIDTH OF THE ROOM! I'VE GOT TO STOP IT FROM ROTATING BY JAMMING THESE BULLETS BEHIND THE METAL PLATE HERE!
SO FAR SO GOOD! JAMMING THE ROTATION HAS SET UP A VIOLENT VIBRATION IN THE GUN MUZZLE--AS I FIGURED IT WOULD! AND THE CEMENT AROUND THE CONCRETE BLOCK IS BEGINNING TO SHOW CRACKS--!
AS BATMAN'S HAND REACHES UP TO GRAB THE GUN...
THE CEMENT IS LOOSE! NOW TO FIND OUT IF I CAN BUDGE THAT BLOCK! I'D BETTER-- IT'S MY ONLY WAY OUT OF HERE!
AS MIGHTY MUSCLES MESH FOR A GIGANTIC EFFORT...
RIPPED THE GUN BLOCK OUT OF THE WALL!
10

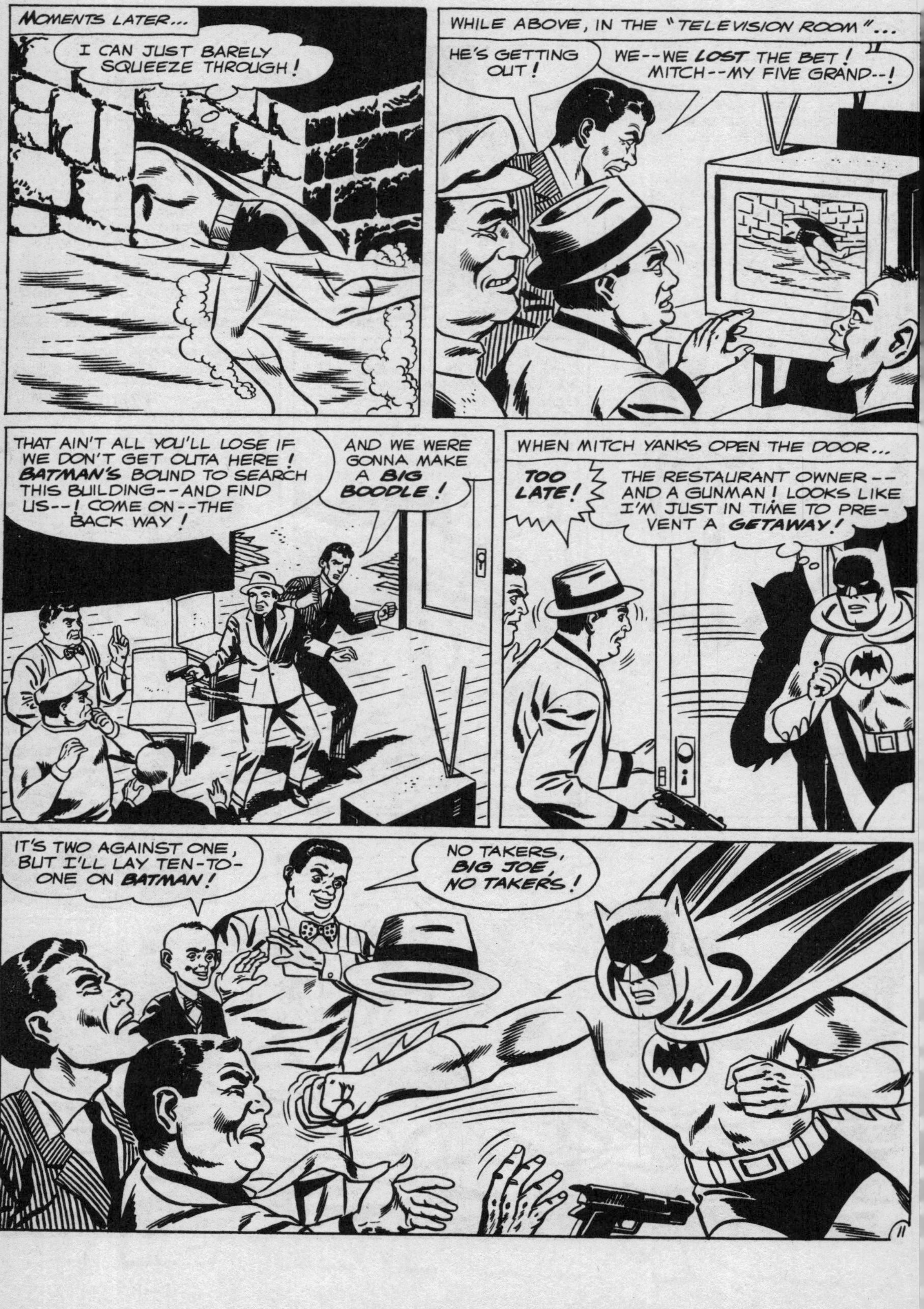
MOMENTS LATER...
I CAN JUST BARELY SQUEEZE THROUGH!
WHILE ABOVE, IN THE "TELEVISION ROOM"...
HE'S GETTING OUT!
WE--WE LOST THE BET! MITCH--MY FIVE GRAND--!
THAT AIN'T ALL YOU'LL LOSE IF WE DON'T GET OUTA HERE! BATMAN'S BOUND TO SEARCH THIS BUILDING--AND FIND US--! COME ON--THE BACK WAY!
AND WE WERE GONNA MAKE A BIG BOODLE!
WHEN MITCH YANKS OPEN THE DOOR...
TOO LATE!
THE RESTAURANT OWNER--AND A GUNMAN! LOOKS LIKE I'M JUST IN TIME TO PREVENT A GETAWAY!
IT'S TWO AGAINST ONE, BUT I'LL LAY TEN-TO-ONE ON BATMAN!
NO TAKERS, BIG JOE, NO TAKERS!
11

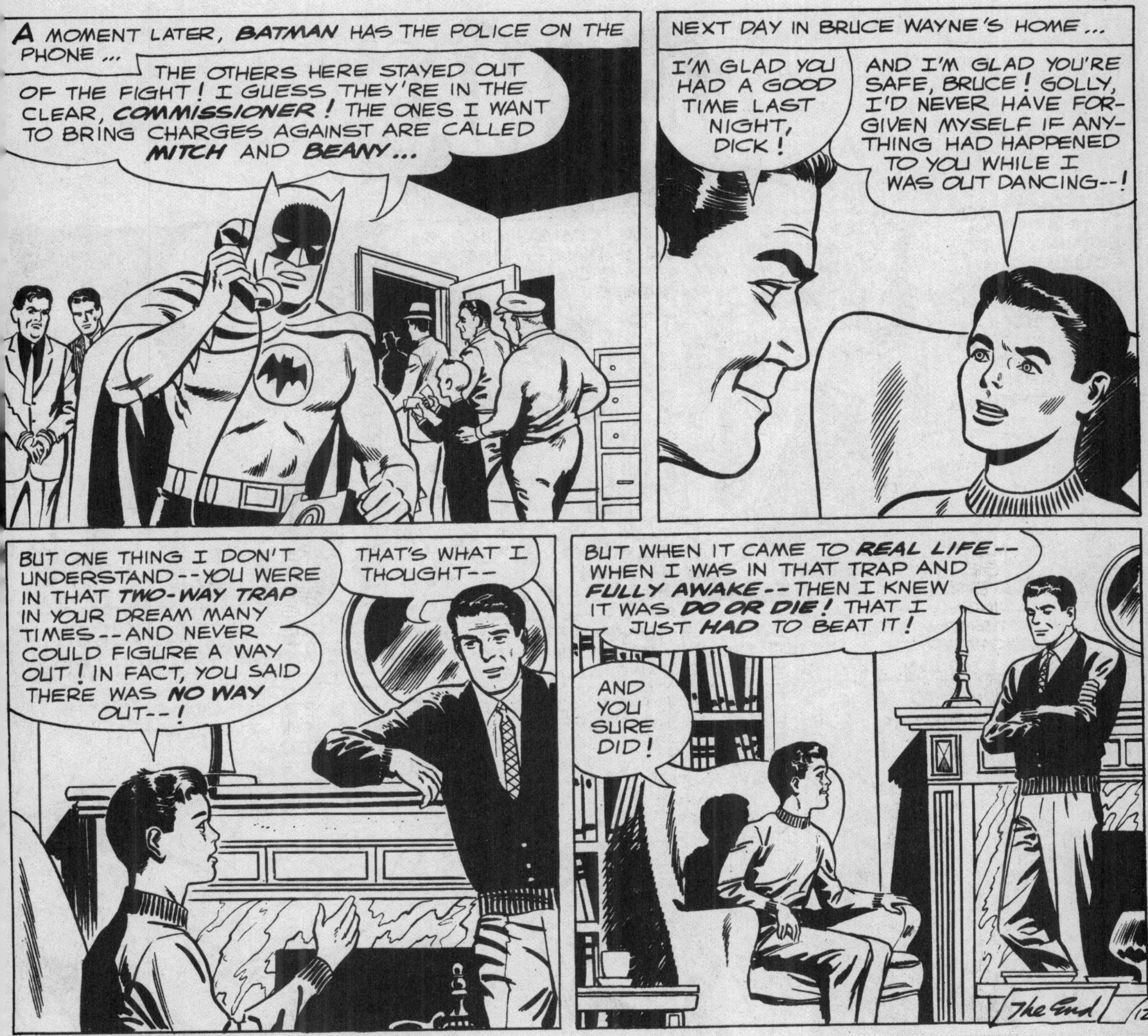
A MOMENT LATER, BATMAN HAS THE POLICE ON THE PHONE ...
THE OTHERS HERE STAYED OUT OF THE FIGHT! I GUESS THEY'RE IN THE CLEAR, COMMISSIONER! THE ONES I WANT TO BRING CHARGES AGAINST ARE CALLED MITCH AND BEANY...
NEXT DAY IN BRUCE WAYNE'S HOME ...
I'M GLAD YOU HAD A GOOD TIME LAST NIGHT, DICK!
AND I'M GLAD YOU'RE SAFE, BRUCE! GOLLY, I'D NEVER HAVE FOR-GIVEN MYSELF IF ANY-THING HAD HAPPENED TO YOU WHILE I WAS OUT DANCING--!
BUT ONE THING I DON'T UNDERSTAND--YOU WERE IN THAT TWO-WAY TRAP IN YOUR DREAM MANY TIMES--AND NEVER COULD FIGURE A WAY OUT! IN FACT, YOU SAID THERE WAS NO WAY OUT--!
THAT'S WHAT I THOUGHT--
BUT WHEN IT CAME TO REAL LIFE--WHEN I WAS IN THAT TRAP AND FULLY AWAKE--THEN I KNEW IT WAS DO OR DIE! THAT I JUST HAD TO BEAT IT!
AND YOU SURE DID!
The End
12

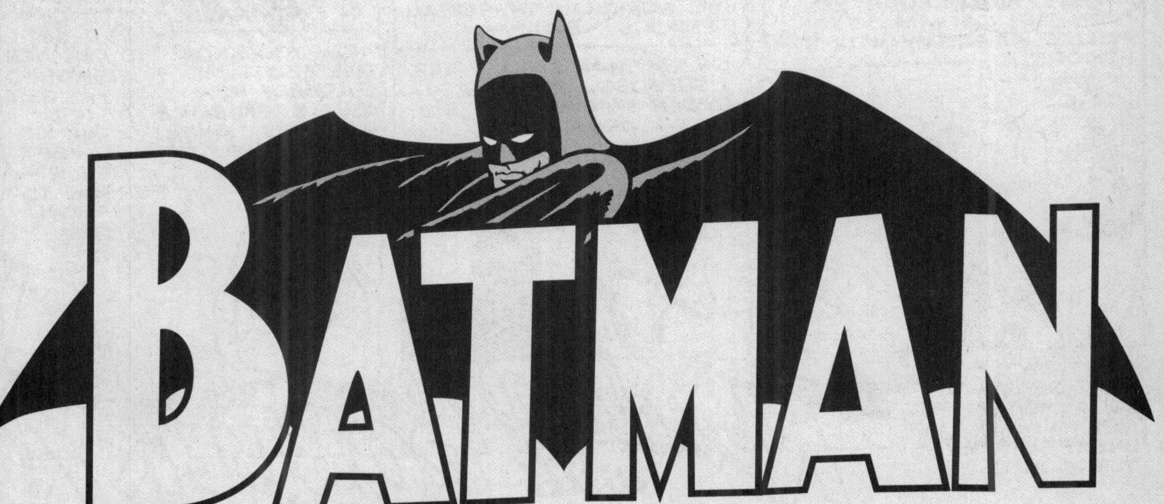
BATMAN

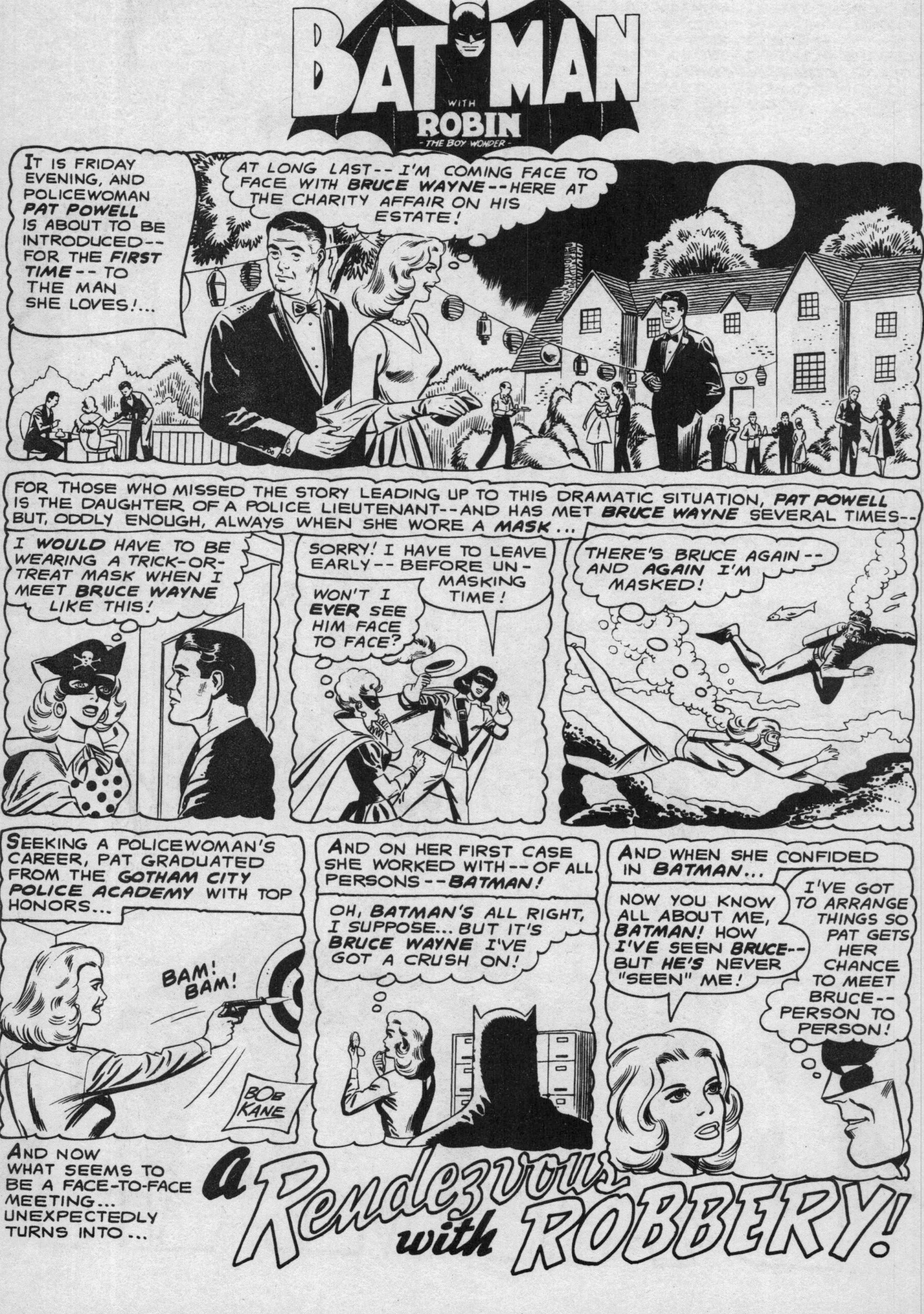
BATMAN WITH ROBIN -THE BOY WONDER-
IT IS FRIDAY EVENING, AND POLICEWOMAN PAT POWELL IS ABOUT TO BE INTRODUCED-- FOR THE FIRST TIME -- TO THE MAN SHE LOVES!...
AT LONG LAST-- I'M COMING FACE TO FACE WITH BRUCE WAYNE--HERE AT THE CHARITY AFFAIR ON HIS ESTATE!
FOR THOSE WHO MISSED THE STORY LEADING UP TO THIS DRAMATIC SITUATION, PAT POWELL IS THE DAUGHTER OF A POLICE LIEUTENANT--AND HAS MET BRUCE WAYNE SEVERAL TIMES-- BUT, ODDLY ENOUGH, ALWAYS WHEN SHE WORE A MASK...
I WOULD HAVE TO BE WEARING A TRICK-OR-TREAT MASK WHEN I MEET BRUCE WAYNE LIKE THIS!
SORRY! I HAVE TO LEAVE EARLY-- BEFORE UN-MASKING TIME!
WON'T I EVER SEE HIM FACE TO FACE?
THERE'S BRUCE AGAIN-- AND AGAIN I'M MASKED!
SEEKING A POLICEWOMAN'S CAREER, PAT GRADUATED FROM THE GOTHAM CITY POLICE ACADEMY WITH TOP HONORS...
BAM! BAM!
BOB KANE
AND ON HER FIRST CASE SHE WORKED WITH -- OF ALL PERSONS --BATMAN!
OH, BATMAN'S ALL RIGHT, I SUPPOSE... BUT IT'S BRUCE WAYNE I'VE GOT A CRUSH ON!
AND WHEN SHE CONFIDED IN BATMAN...
NOW YOU KNOW ALL ABOUT ME, BATMAN! HOW I'VE SEEN BRUCE-- BUT HE'S NEVER "SEEN" ME!
I'VE GOT TO ARRANGE THINGS SO PAT GETS HER CHANCE TO MEET BRUCE-- PERSON TO PERSON!
AND NOW WHAT SEEMS TO BE A FACE-TO-FACE MEETING... UNEXPECTEDLY TURNS INTO...
a Rendezvous with ROBBERY!

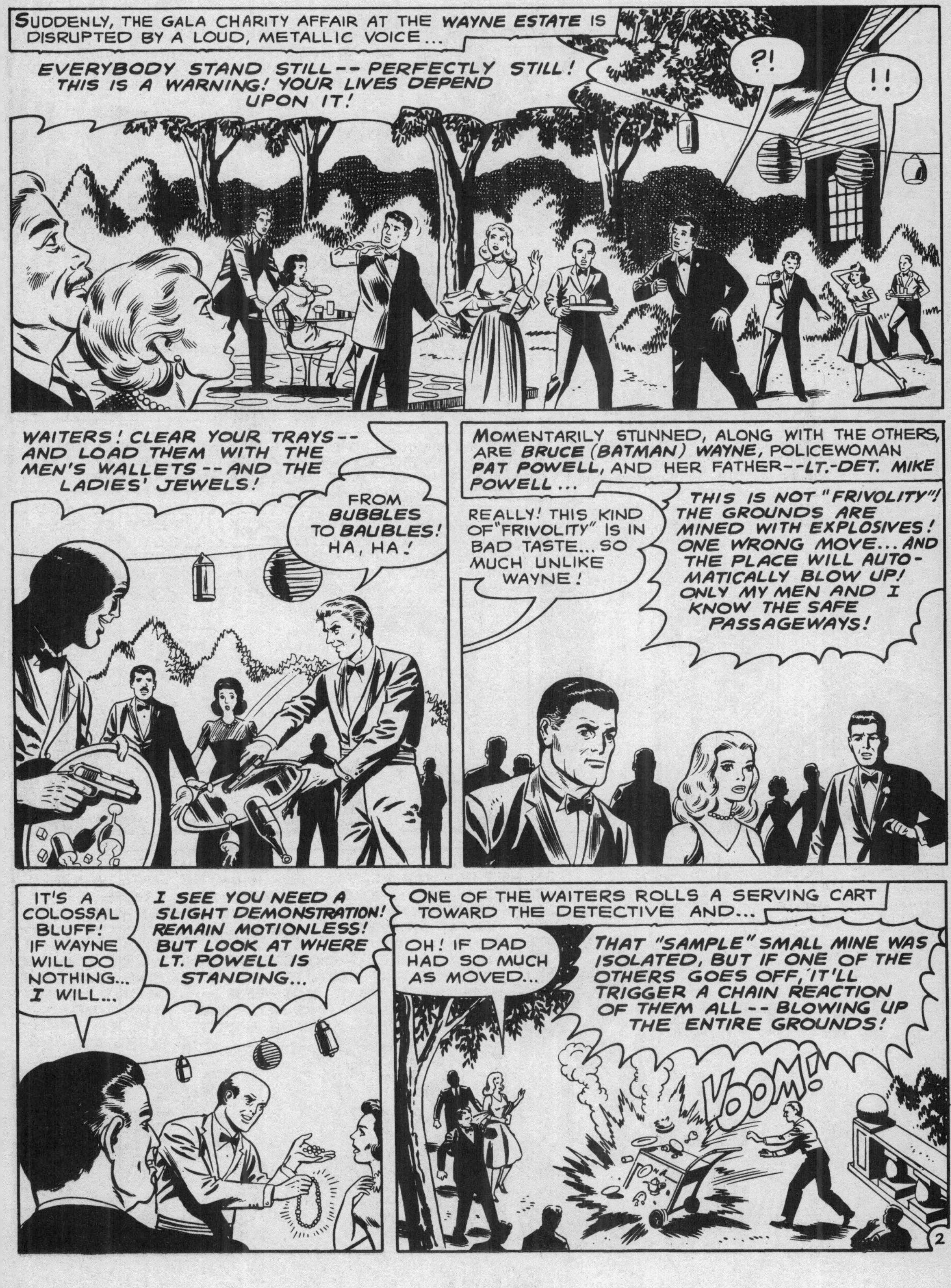
SUDDENLY, THE GALA CHARITY AFFAIR AT THE WAYNE ESTATE IS DISRUPTED BY A LOUD, METALLIC VOICE...
EVERYBODY STAND STILL--PERFECTLY STILL! THIS IS A WARNING! YOUR LIVES DEPEND UPON IT!
?!
!!
WAITERS! CLEAR YOUR TRAYS--AND LOAD THEM WITH THE MEN'S WALLETS--AND THE LADIES' JEWELS!
FROM BUBBLES TO BAUBLES! HA, HA!
MOMENTARILY STUNNED, ALONG WITH THE OTHERS, ARE BRUCE (BATMAN) WAYNE, POLICEWOMAN PAT POWELL, AND HER FATHER--LT.-DET. MIKE POWELL...
REALLY! THIS KIND OF "FRIVOLITY" IS IN BAD TASTE... SO MUCH UNLIKE WAYNE!
THIS IS NOT "FRIVOLITY"! THE GROUNDS ARE MINED WITH EXPLOSIVES! ONE WRONG MOVE... AND THE PLACE WILL AUTOMATICALLY BLOW UP! ONLY MY MEN AND I KNOW THE SAFE PASSAGEWAYS!
IT'S A COLOSSAL BLUFF! IF WAYNE WILL DO NOTHING... I WILL...
I SEE YOU NEED A SLIGHT DEMONSTRATION! REMAIN MOTIONLESS! BUT LOOK AT WHERE LT. POWELL IS STANDING...
ONE OF THE WAITERS ROLLS A SERVING CART TOWARD THE DETECTIVE AND...
OH! IF DAD HAD SO MUCH AS MOVED...
THAT "SAMPLE" SMALL MINE WAS ISOLATED, BUT IF ONE OF THE OTHERS GOES OFF, IT'LL TRIGGER A CHAIN REACTION OF THEM ALL--BLOWING UP THE ENTIRE GROUNDS!
VOOM!
2

THEN, APPEARING FROM THE SHADOWS, AN IMMACULATELY DRESSED MAN, MASKED...

AS YOUR WALLETS AND JEWELS ARE BEING REMOVED, PLEASE DON'T GET ANY FOOLISH NOTIONS...

WHEN THE LAST GRAINS OF SAND FROM THIS HOURGLASS RUN OUT, YOU CAN MAKE A MOVE -- THE MINES AUTOMATICALLY WILL BE RENDERED HARMLESS! BY THEN, WE'LL BE FAR AWAY!

AS THE CROOKS DEPART WITH THEIR LOOT...

WHAT A THING TO HAPPEN TO ME! HERE I AM, SECRETLY BATMAN, AND CAN'T RISK MAKING A MOVE TO HELP MY GUESTS!

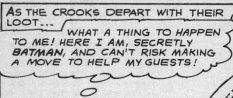

FINALLY, WHEN THE LAST GRAINS OF SAND SPILL INTO THE BOTTOM CONTAINER OF THE HOURGLASS, PAT POWELL ONCE MORE MOVES TOWARD BRUCE WAYNE -- BUT --

NO MORE TIME FOR SOCIAL ACTIVITIES, DETECTIVE POWELL! LET'S MOVE! WE'VE GOT A CASE ON OUR HANDS!

SO CLOSE -- SO VERY CLOSE -- BUT AGAIN I MISS MEETING BRUCE!

DON'T WORRY, PAT -- BATMAN'S ALSO GOING TO BE ON THIS CASE! AND WHEN IT'S WRAPPED UP, WELL... LET'S SEE WHAT HAPPENS! WE'RE BOUND TO MEET... SOMETIME!

AFTER EXCUSING HIS GUESTS, AND POSTPONING THE CHARITY BALL FOR A LATER DATE, BRUCE WAYNE ENTERS HIS HOUSE AND TAKES AN ELEVATOR DOWN TO THE BATCAVE WITH DICK GRAYSON...

HOW COULD CROOKED WAITERS GET ON THE ESTATE? YOU'VE USED THE SAME CATERER MANY TIMES -- AND HE ALWAYS SCREENS THE MEN HE HIRES!

RIGHT -- AND WE'RE GOING TO FIND OUT WHAT WENT WRONG THIS TIME! WE'RE SEEING THE CATERER TONIGHT!

3

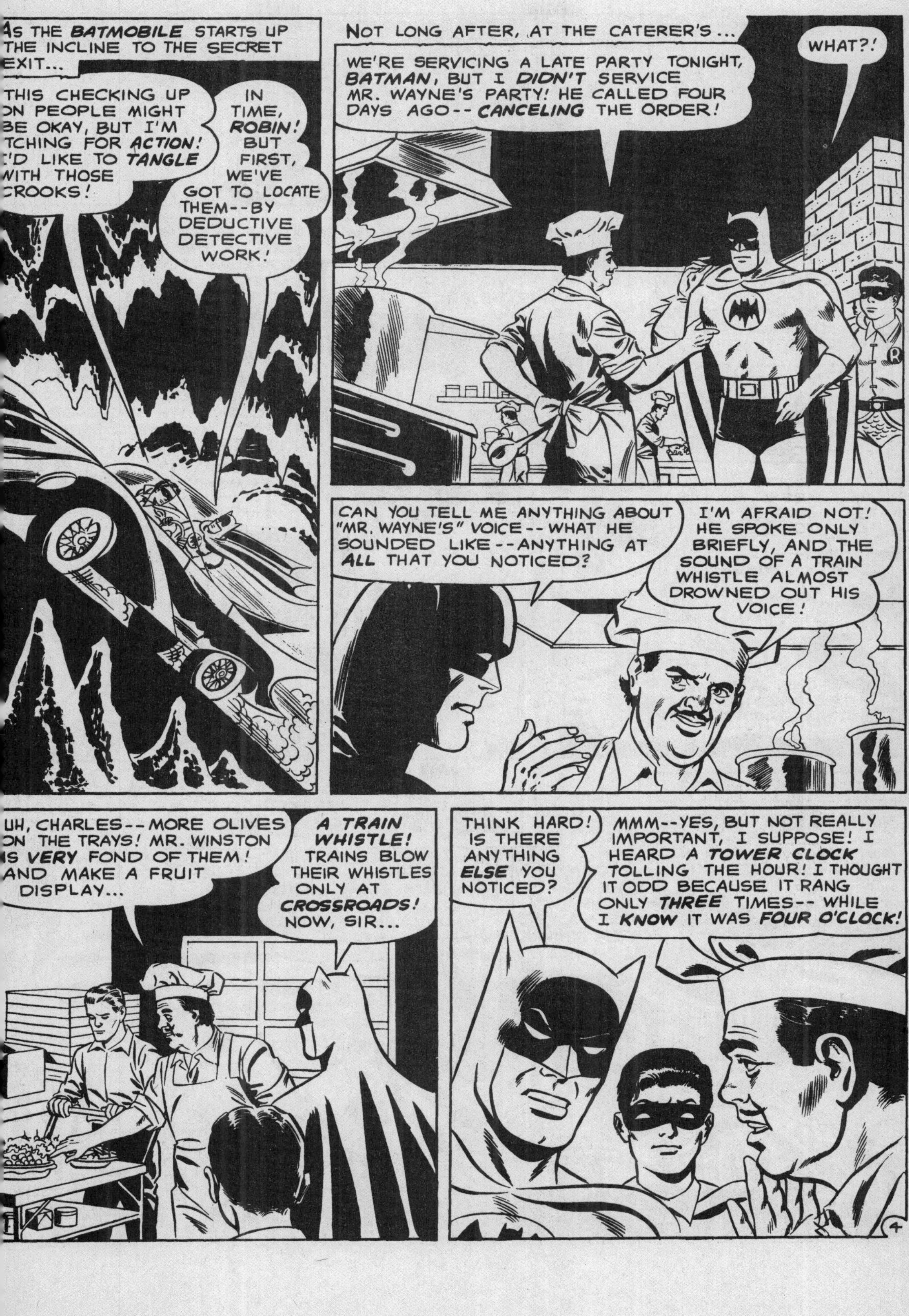
AS THE BATMOBILE STARTS UP THE INCLINE TO THE SECRET EXIT...
THIS CHECKING UP ON PEOPLE MIGHT BE OKAY, BUT I'M ITCHING FOR ACTION! I'D LIKE TO TANGLE WITH THOSE CROOKS!
IN TIME, ROBIN! BUT FIRST, WE'VE GOT TO LOCATE THEM--BY DEDUCTIVE DETECTIVE WORK!
NOT LONG AFTER, AT THE CATERER'S...
WE'RE SERVICING A LATE PARTY TONIGHT, BATMAN, BUT I DIDN'T SERVICE MR. WAYNE'S PARTY! HE CALLED FOUR DAYS AGO--CANCELING THE ORDER!
WHAT?!
CAN YOU TELL ME ANYTHING ABOUT "MR. WAYNE'S" VOICE--WHAT HE SOUNDED LIKE--ANYTHING AT ALL THAT YOU NOTICED?
I'M AFRAID NOT! HE SPOKE ONLY BRIEFLY, AND THE SOUND OF A TRAIN WHISTLE ALMOST DROWNED OUT HIS VOICE!
UH, CHARLES--MORE OLIVES ON THE TRAYS! MR. WINSTON IS VERY FOND OF THEM! AND MAKE A FRUIT DISPLAY...
A TRAIN WHISTLE! TRAINS BLOW THEIR WHISTLES ONLY AT CROSSROADS! NOW, SIR...
THINK HARD! IS THERE ANYTHING ELSE YOU NOTICED?
MMM--YES, BUT NOT REALLY IMPORTANT, I SUPPOSE! I HEARD A TOWER CLOCK TOLLING THE HOUR! I THOUGHT IT ODD BECAUSE IT RANG ONLY THREE TIMES--WHILE I KNOW IT WAS FOUR O'CLOCK!
4

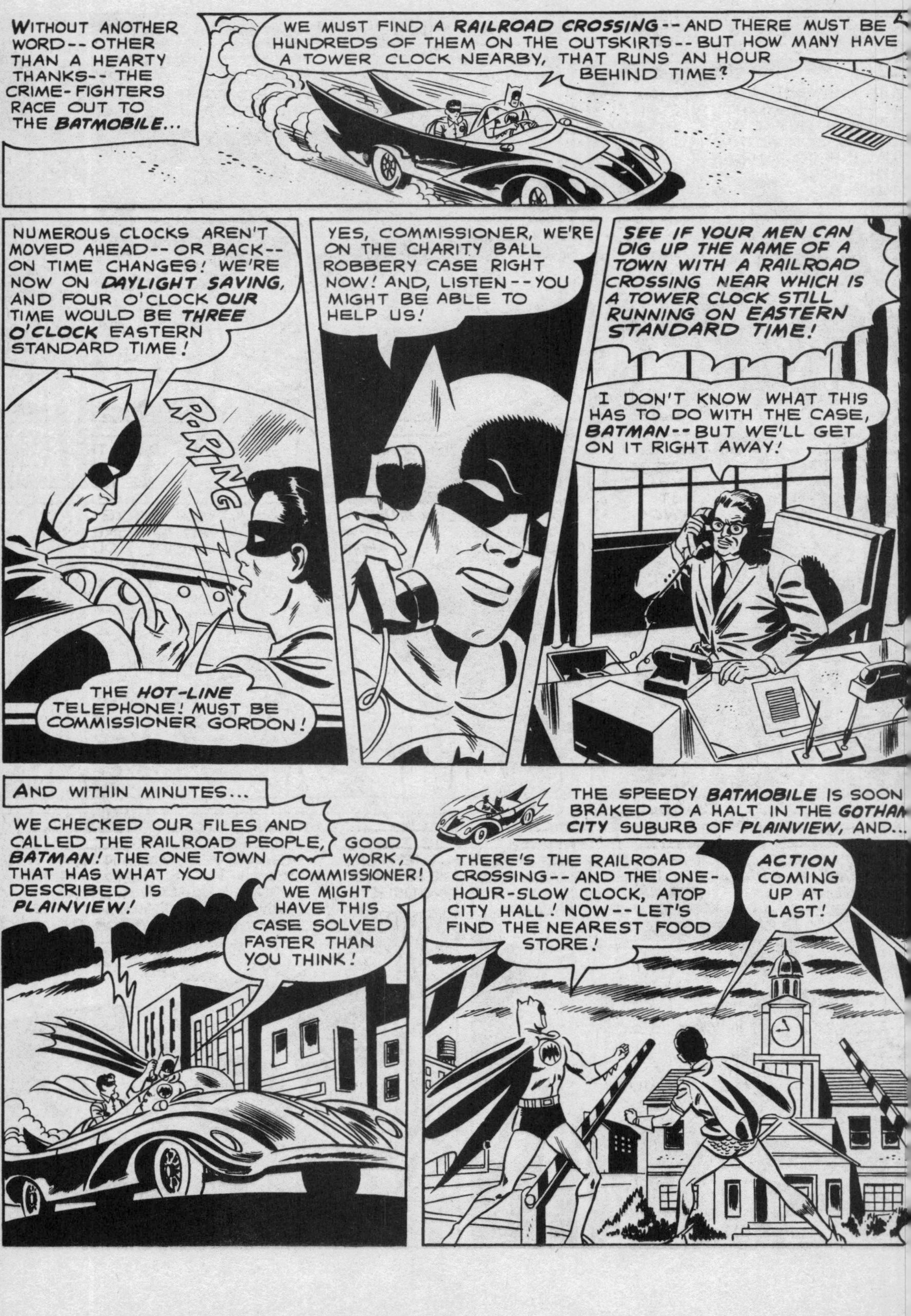
WITHOUT ANOTHER WORD-- OTHER THAN A HEARTY THANKS-- THE CRIME-FIGHTERS RACE OUT TO THE BATMOBILE...
WE MUST FIND A RAILROAD CROSSING-- AND THERE MUST BE HUNDREDS OF THEM ON THE OUTSKIRTS-- BUT HOW MANY HAVE A TOWER CLOCK NEARBY, THAT RUNS AN HOUR BEHIND TIME?
NUMEROUS CLOCKS AREN'T MOVED AHEAD-- OR BACK-- ON TIME CHANGES! WE'RE NOW ON DAYLIGHT SAVING, AND FOUR O'CLOCK OUR TIME WOULD BE THREE O'CLOCK EASTERN STANDARD TIME!
R-RING
THE HOT-LINE TELEPHONE! MUST BE COMMISSIONER GORDON!
YES, COMMISSIONER, WE'RE ON THE CHARITY BALL ROBBERY CASE RIGHT NOW! AND, LISTEN-- YOU MIGHT BE ABLE TO HELP US!
SEE IF YOUR MEN CAN DIG UP THE NAME OF A TOWN WITH A RAILROAD CROSSING NEAR WHICH IS A TOWER CLOCK STILL RUNNING ON EASTERN STANDARD TIME!
I DON'T KNOW WHAT THIS HAS TO DO WITH THE CASE, BATMAN-- BUT WE'LL GET ON IT RIGHT AWAY!
AND WITHIN MINUTES...
WE CHECKED OUR FILES AND CALLED THE RAILROAD PEOPLE, BATMAN! THE ONE TOWN THAT HAS WHAT YOU DESCRIBED IS PLAINVIEW!
GOOD WORK, COMMISSIONER! WE MIGHT HAVE THIS CASE SOLVED FASTER THAN YOU THINK!
THE SPEEDY BATMOBILE IS SOON BRAKED TO A HALT IN THE GOTHAM CITY SUBURB OF PLAINVIEW, AND...
THERE'S THE RAILROAD CROSSING-- AND THE ONE-HOUR-SLOW CLOCK, ATOP CITY HALL! NOW-- LET'S FIND THE NEAREST FOOD STORE!
ACTION COMING UP AT LAST!

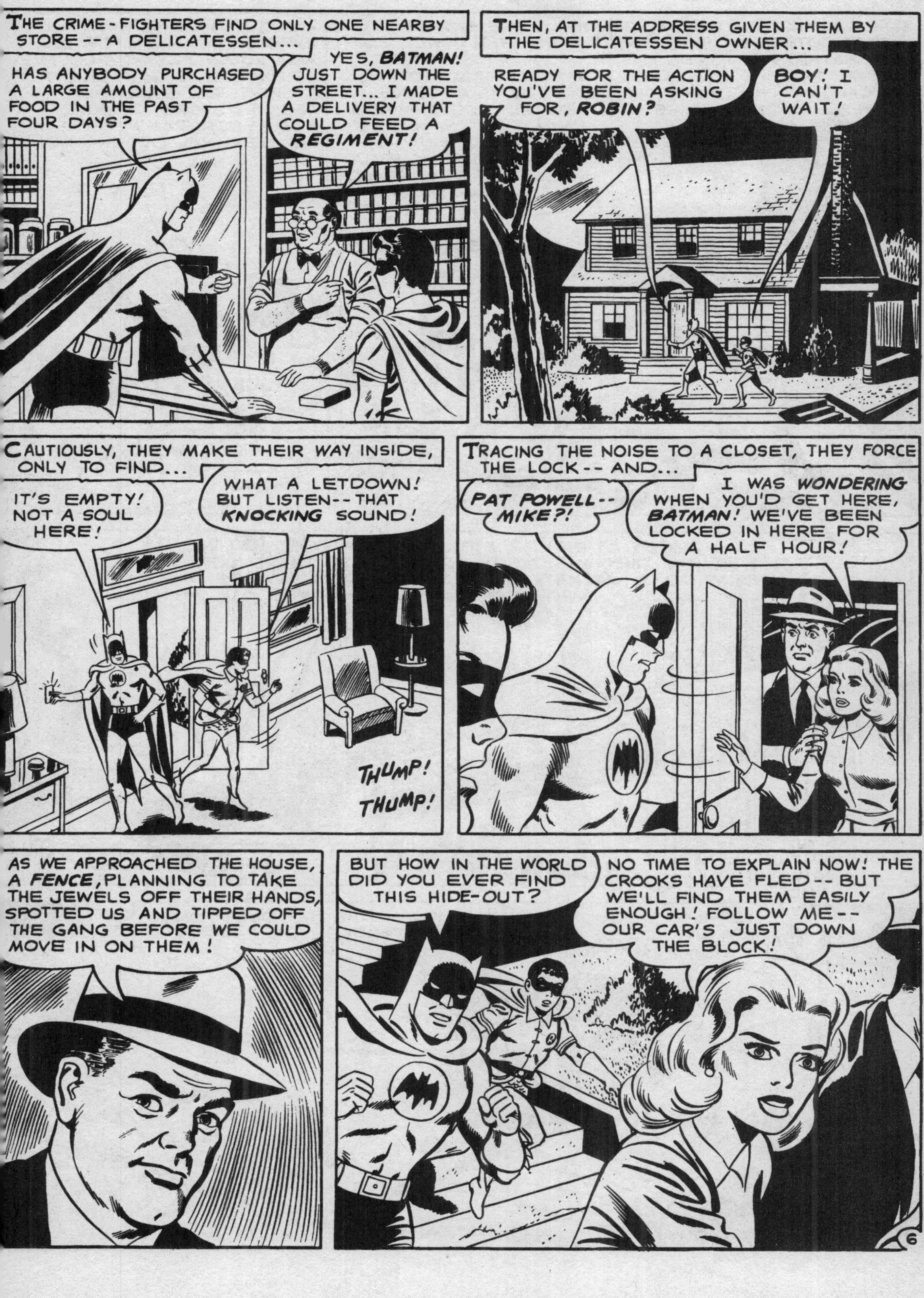
THE CRIME-FIGHTERS FIND ONLY ONE NEARBY STORE -- A DELICATESSEN...
HAS ANYBODY PURCHASED A LARGE AMOUNT OF FOOD IN THE PAST FOUR DAYS?
YES, BATMAN! JUST DOWN THE STREET... I MADE A DELIVERY THAT COULD FEED A REGIMENT!
THEN, AT THE ADDRESS GIVEN THEM BY THE DELICATESSEN OWNER...
READY FOR THE ACTION YOU'VE BEEN ASKING FOR, ROBIN?
BOY! I CAN'T WAIT!
CAUTIOUSLY, THEY MAKE THEIR WAY INSIDE, ONLY TO FIND...
IT'S EMPTY! NOT A SOUL HERE!
WHAT A LETDOWN! BUT LISTEN--THAT KNOCKING SOUND!
THUMP! THUMP!
TRACING THE NOISE TO A CLOSET, THEY FORCE THE LOCK -- AND...
PAT POWELL-- MIKE?!
I WAS WONDERING WHEN YOU'D GET HERE, BATMAN! WE'VE BEEN LOCKED IN HERE FOR A HALF HOUR!
AS WE APPROACHED THE HOUSE, A FENCE, PLANNING TO TAKE THE JEWELS OFF THEIR HANDS, SPOTTED US AND TIPPED OFF THE GANG BEFORE WE COULD MOVE IN ON THEM!
BUT HOW IN THE WORLD DID YOU EVER FIND THIS HIDE-OUT?
NO TIME TO EXPLAIN NOW! THE CROOKS HAVE FLED -- BUT WE'LL FIND THEM EASILY ENOUGH! FOLLOW ME -- OUR CAR'S JUST DOWN THE BLOCK!
6

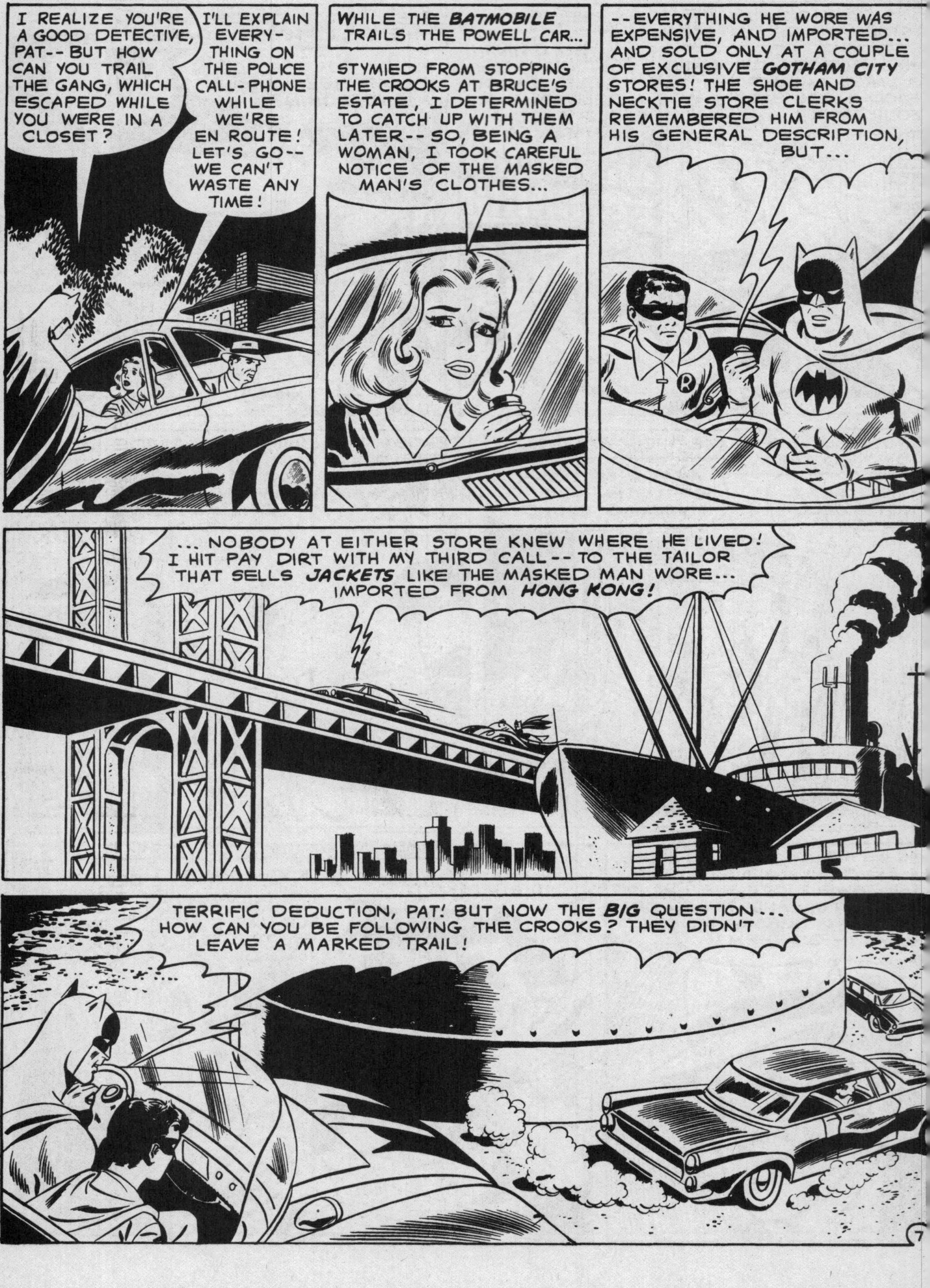
I REALIZE YOU'RE A GOOD DETECTIVE, PAT-- BUT HOW CAN YOU TRAIL THE GANG, WHICH ESCAPED WHILE YOU WERE IN A CLOSET?
I'LL EXPLAIN EVERYTHING ON THE POLICE CALL-PHONE WHILE WE'RE EN ROUTE! LET'S GO-- WE CAN'T WASTE ANY TIME!
WHILE THE BATMOBILE TRAILS THE POWELL CAR...
STYMIED FROM STOPPING THE CROOKS AT BRUCE'S ESTATE, I DETERMINED TO CATCH UP WITH THEM LATER-- SO, BEING A WOMAN, I TOOK CAREFUL NOTICE OF THE MASKED MAN'S CLOTHES...
--EVERYTHING HE WORE WAS EXPENSIVE, AND IMPORTED... AND SOLD ONLY AT A COUPLE OF EXCLUSIVE GOTHAM CITY STORES! THE SHOE AND NECKTIE STORE CLERKS REMEMBERED HIM FROM HIS GENERAL DESCRIPTION, BUT...
... NOBODY AT EITHER STORE KNEW WHERE HE LIVED! I HIT PAY DIRT WITH MY THIRD CALL-- TO THE TAILOR THAT SELLS JACKETS LIKE THE MASKED MAN WORE... IMPORTED FROM HONG KONG!
TERRIFIC DEDUCTION, PAT! BUT NOW THE BIG QUESTION... HOW CAN YOU BE FOLLOWING THE CROOKS? THEY DIDN'T LEAVE A MARKED TRAIL!
7

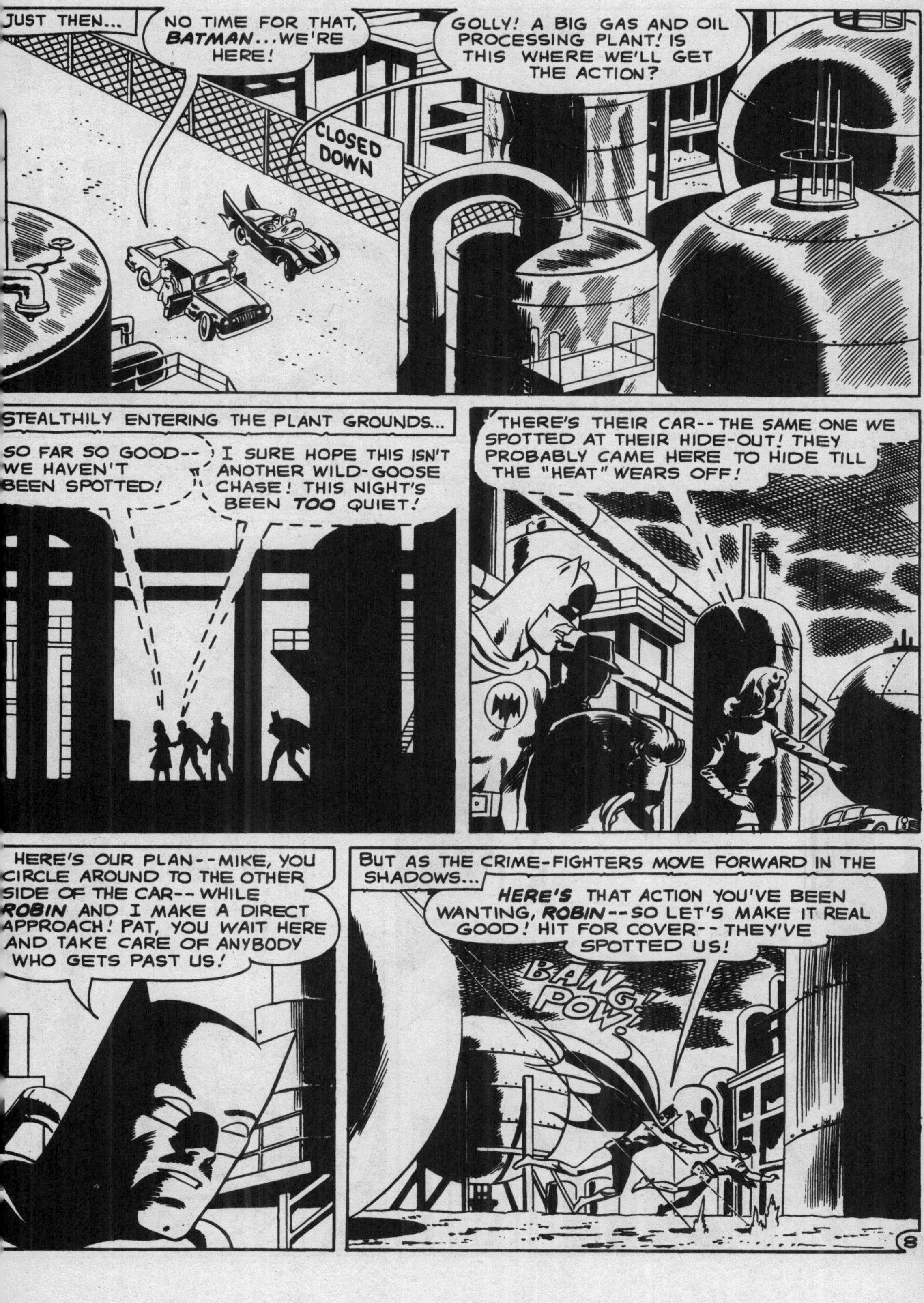
JUST THEN...
NO TIME FOR THAT, BATMAN...WE'RE HERE!
GOLLY! A BIG GAS AND OIL PROCESSING PLANT! IS THIS WHERE WE'LL GET THE ACTION?
CLOSED DOWN
STEALTHILY ENTERING THE PLANT GROUNDS...
SO FAR SO GOOD-- WE HAVEN'T BEEN SPOTTED!
I SURE HOPE THIS ISN'T ANOTHER WILD-GOOSE CHASE! THIS NIGHT'S BEEN TOO QUIET!
THERE'S THEIR CAR--THE SAME ONE WE SPOTTED AT THEIR HIDE-OUT! THEY PROBABLY CAME HERE TO HIDE TILL THE "HEAT" WEARS OFF!
HERE'S OUR PLAN--MIKE, YOU CIRCLE AROUND TO THE OTHER SIDE OF THE CAR-- WHILE ROBIN AND I MAKE A DIRECT APPROACH! PAT, YOU WAIT HERE AND TAKE CARE OF ANYBODY WHO GETS PAST US!
BUT AS THE CRIME-FIGHTERS MOVE FORWARD IN THE SHADOWS...
HERE'S THAT ACTION YOU'VE BEEN WANTING, ROBIN--SO LET'S MAKE IT REAL GOOD! HIT FOR COVER-- THEY'VE SPOTTED US!
BANG! POW!
8

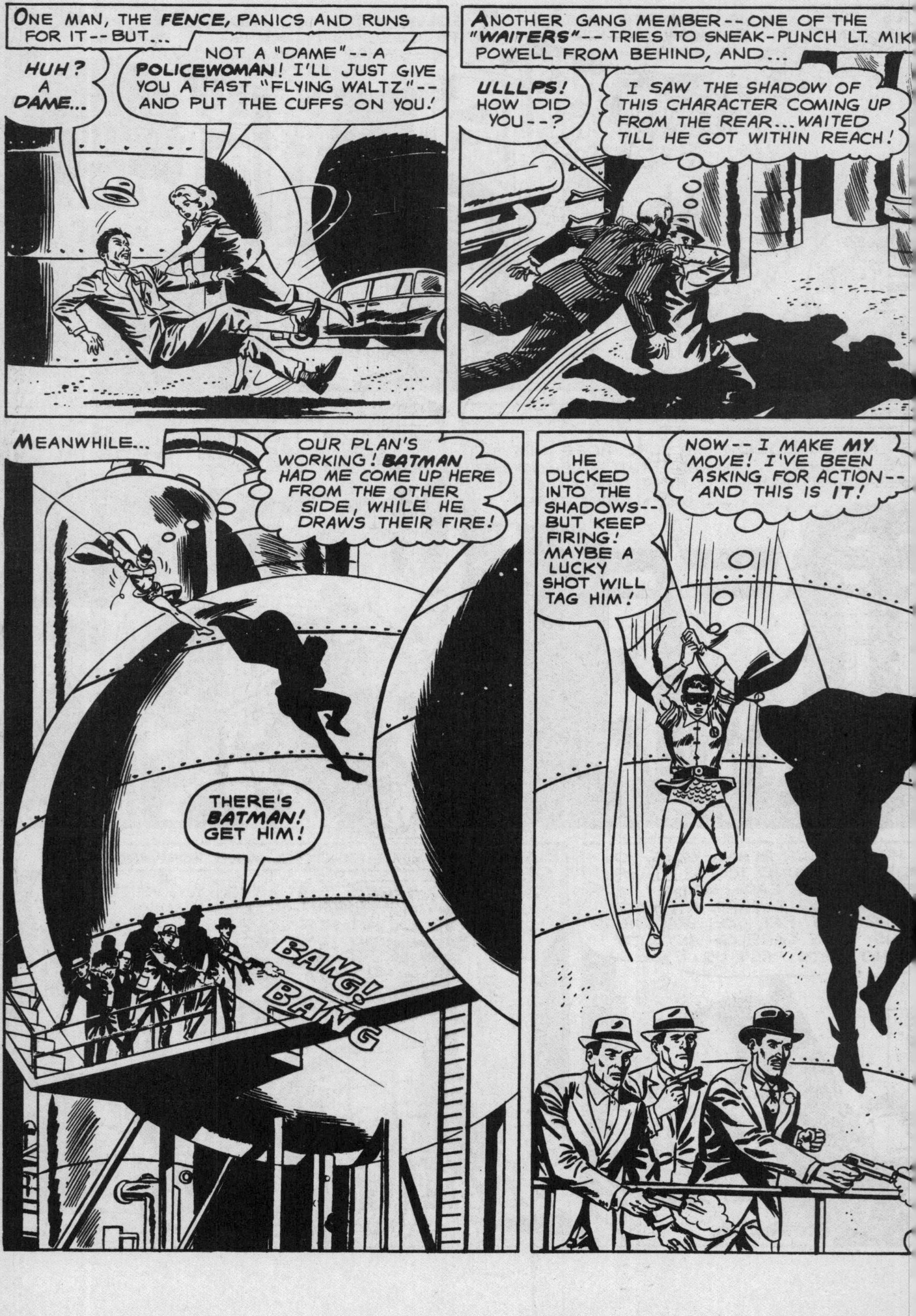
ONE MAN, THE FENCE, PANICS AND RUNS FOR IT--BUT...
HUH? A DAME...
NOT A "DAME"--A POLICEWOMAN! I'LL JUST GIVE YOU A FAST "FLYING WALTZ"--AND PUT THE CUFFS ON YOU!
ANOTHER GANG MEMBER--ONE OF THE "WAITERS"--TRIES TO SNEAK-PUNCH LT. MIK POWELL FROM BEHIND, AND...
ULLLPS! HOW DID YOU--?
I SAW THE SHADOW OF THIS CHARACTER COMING UP FROM THE REAR...WAITED TILL HE GOT WITHIN REACH!
MEANWHILE...
OUR PLAN'S WORKING! BATMAN HAD ME COME UP HERE FROM THE OTHER SIDE, WHILE HE DRAWS THEIR FIRE!
THERE'S BATMAN! GET HIM!
BANG! BANG
HE DUCKED INTO THE SHADOWS--BUT KEEP FIRING! MAYBE A LUCKY SHOT WILL TAG HIM!
NOW--I MAKE MY MOVE! I'VE BEEN ASKING FOR ACTION--AND THIS IS IT!

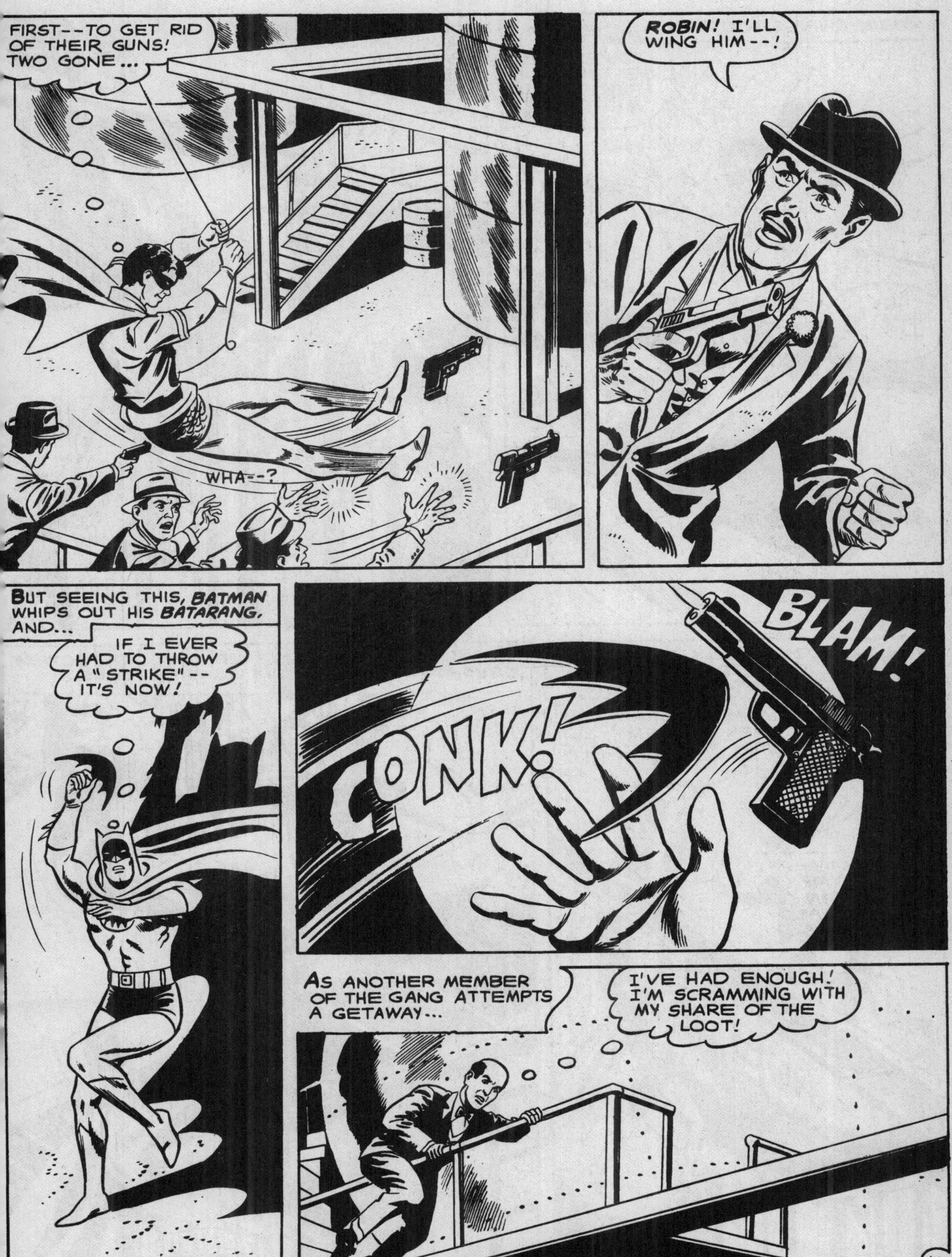
FIRST--TO GET RID OF THEIR GUNS! TWO GONE...
WHA--?
ROBIN! I'LL WING HIM--!
BUT SEEING THIS, BATMAN WHIPS OUT HIS BATARANG, AND...
IF I EVER HAD TO THROW A "STRIKE"-- IT'S NOW!
BLAM!
CONK!
AS ANOTHER MEMBER OF THE GANG ATTEMPTS A GETAWAY...
I'VE HAD ENOUGH! I'M SCRAMMING WITH MY SHARE OF THE LOOT!
10

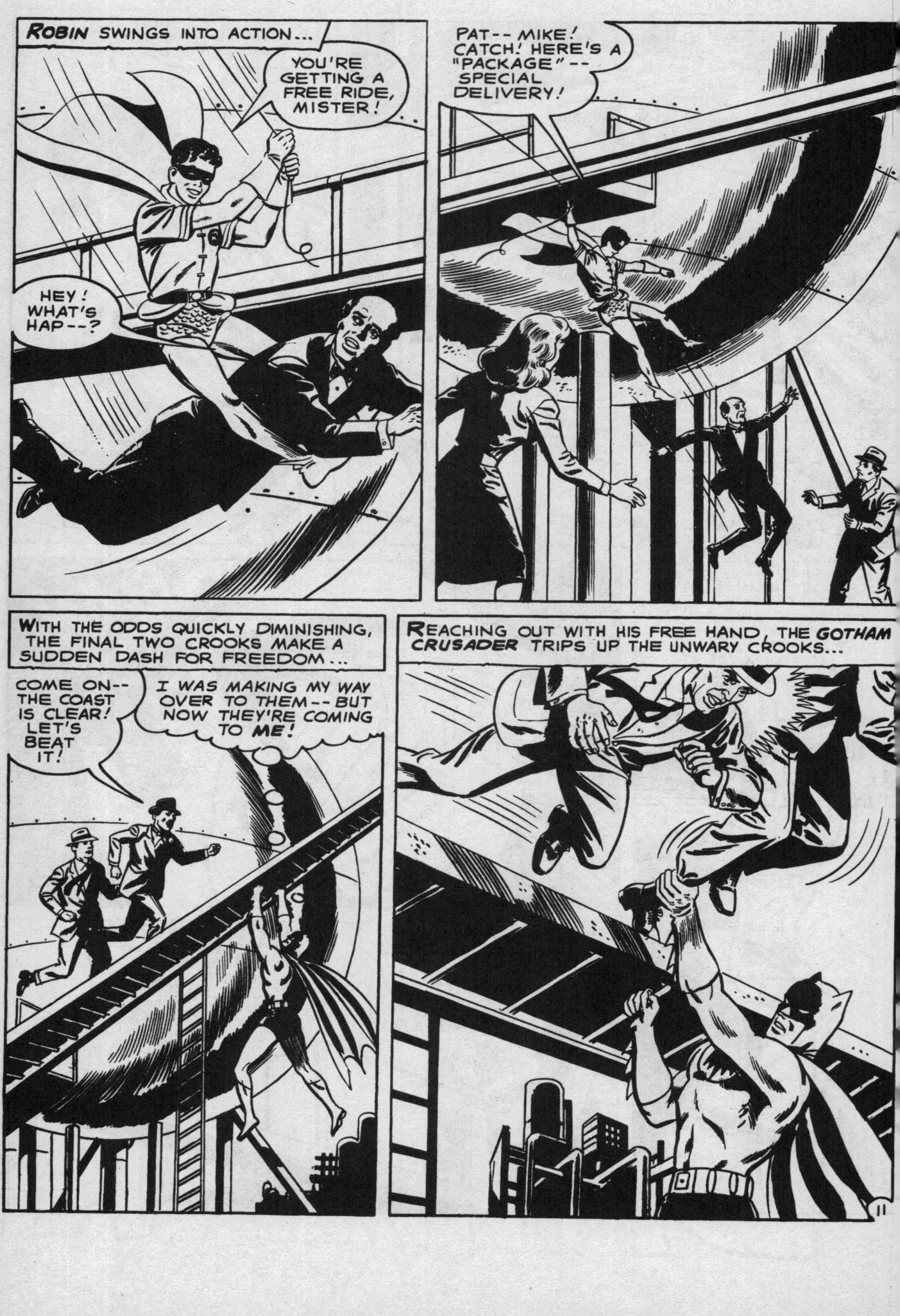
ROBIN SWINGS INTO ACTION...
YOU'RE GETTING A FREE RIDE, MISTER!
HEY! WHAT'S HAP--?
PAT--MIKE! CATCH! HERE'S A "PACKAGE"-- SPECIAL DELIVERY!
WITH THE ODDS QUICKLY DIMINISHING, THE FINAL TWO CROOKS MAKE A SUDDEN DASH FOR FREEDOM...
COME ON-- THE COAST IS CLEAR! LET'S BEAT IT!
I WAS MAKING MY WAY OVER TO THEM--BUT NOW THEY'RE COMING TO ME!
REACHING OUT WITH HIS FREE HAND, THE GOTHAM CRUSADER TRIPS UP THE UNWARY CROOKS...
11

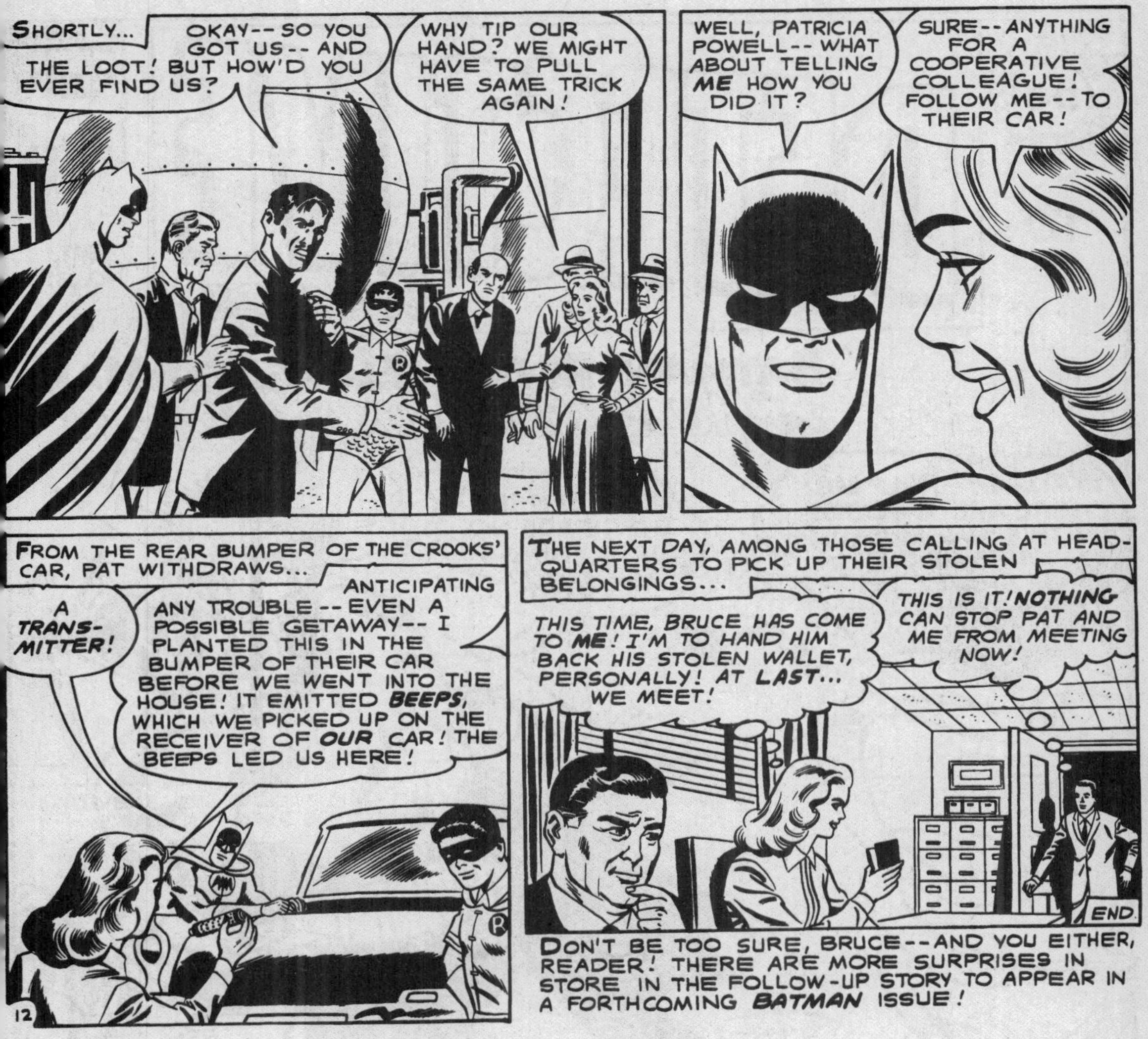
SHORTLY...
OKAY-- SO YOU GOT US-- AND THE LOOT! BUT HOW'D YOU EVER FIND US?
WHY TIP OUR HAND? WE MIGHT HAVE TO PULL THE SAME TRICK AGAIN!
WELL, PATRICIA POWELL-- WHAT ABOUT TELLING ME HOW YOU DID IT?
SURE-- ANYTHING FOR A COOPERATIVE COLLEAGUE! FOLLOW ME-- TO THEIR CAR!
FROM THE REAR BUMPER OF THE CROOKS' CAR, PAT WITHDRAWS...
A TRANS-MITTER!
ANTICIPATING ANY TROUBLE-- EVEN A POSSIBLE GETAWAY-- I PLANTED THIS IN THE BUMPER OF THEIR CAR BEFORE WE WENT INTO THE HOUSE! IT EMITTED BEEPS, WHICH WE PICKED UP ON THE RECEIVER OF OUR CAR! THE BEEPS LED US HERE!
12
THE NEXT DAY, AMONG THOSE CALLING AT HEAD-QUARTERS TO PICK UP THEIR STOLEN BELONGINGS...
THIS TIME, BRUCE HAS COME TO ME! I'M TO HAND HIM BACK HIS STOLEN WALLET, PERSONALLY! AT LAST... WE MEET!
THIS IS IT! NOTHING CAN STOP PAT AND ME FROM MEETING NOW!
END.
DON'T BE TOO SURE, BRUCE-- AND YOU EITHER, READER! THERE ARE MORE SURPRISES IN STORE IN THE FOLLOW-UP STORY TO APPEAR IN A FORTHCOMING BATMAN ISSUE!

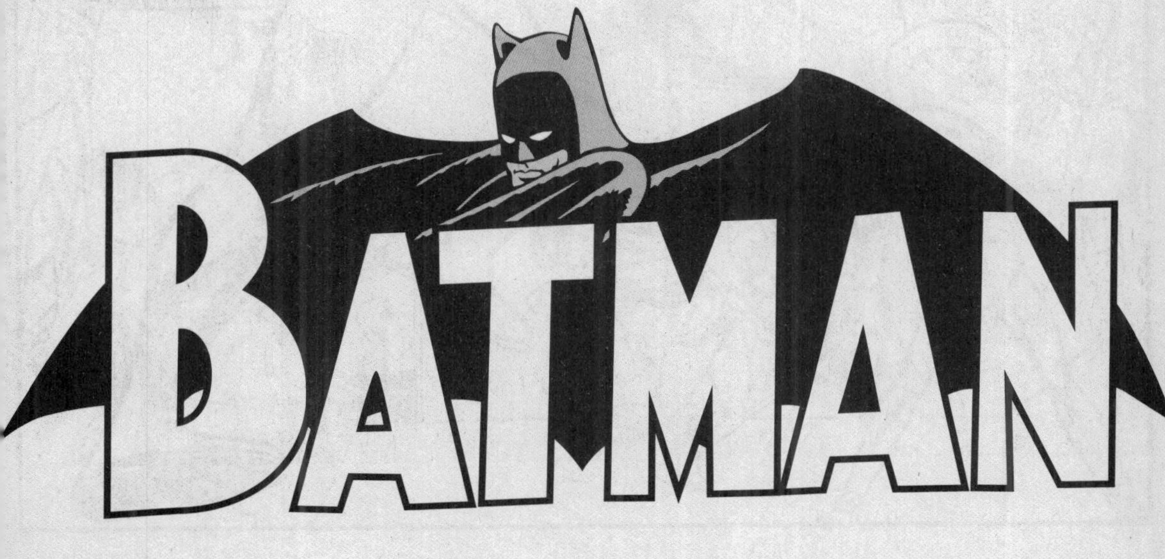
BATMAN

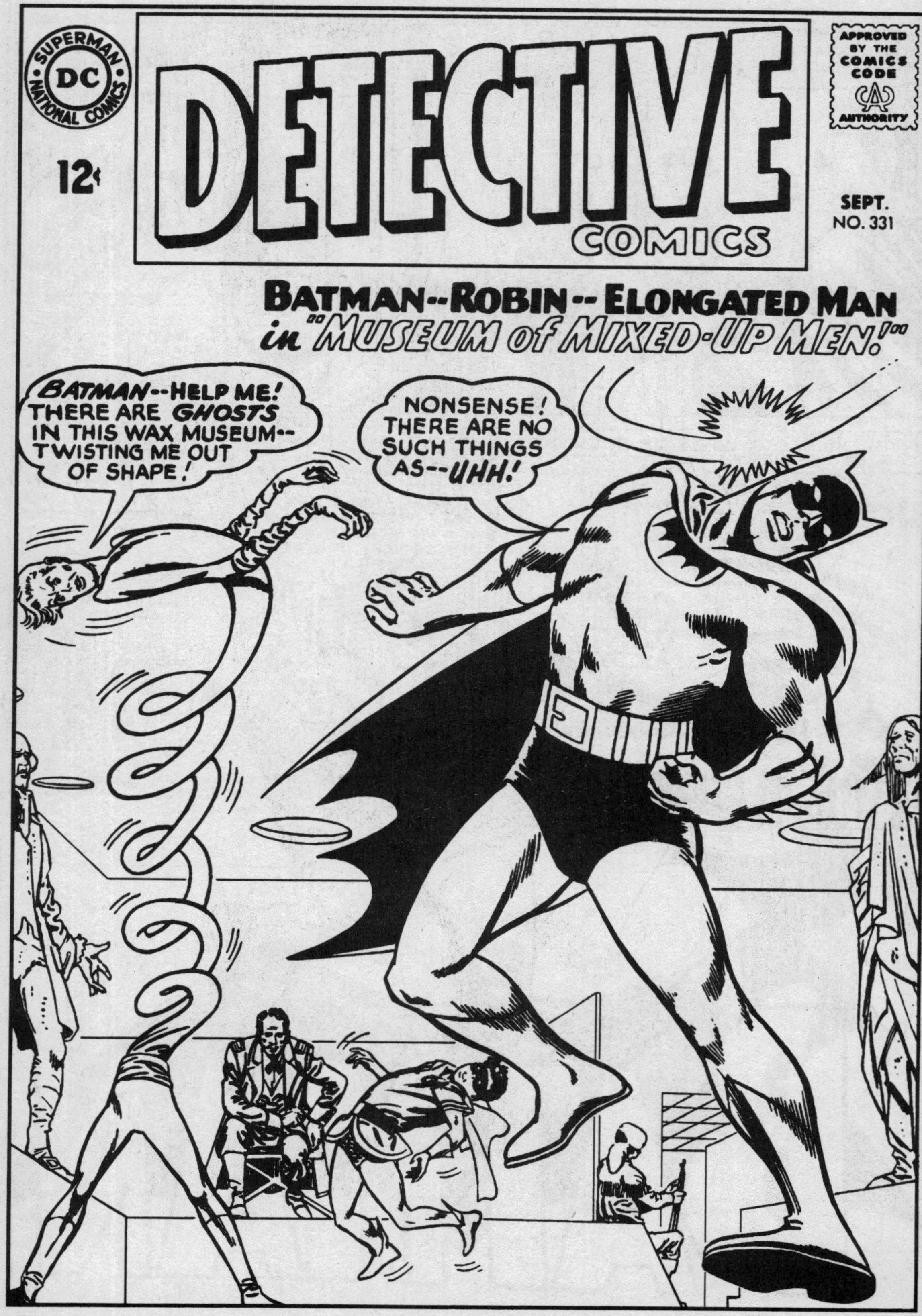
SUPERMAN DC NATIONAL COMICS
12¢
DETECTIVE COMICS
APPROVED BY THE COMICS CODE AUTHORITY
SEPT. NO. 331
BATMAN--ROBIN--ELONGATED MAN
in "MUSEUM of MIXED-UP MEN!"
BATMAN--HELP ME! THERE ARE GHOSTS IN THIS WAX MUSEUM--TWISTING ME OUT OF SHAPE!
NONSENSE! THERE ARE NO SUCH THINGS AS--UHH!

BAT·MAN With ROBIN THE BOY WONDER

Special Guest Star The ELONGATED Man

THE FACE OF A MAN IS HIS MOST IMPORTANT POSSESSION. ROB HIM OF THAT AND YOU ROB HIM OF HIS IDENTITY!

THIS WAS THE CLEVER SCHEME OF GANG LEADER "BOSS" BARRON -- WHO STAMPED HIS MOBSTERS WITH THE FACES OF LAW-ABIDING CITIZENS AND SENT THEM OUT TO LOOT!

ONLY THE COMBINED TALENTS OF BATMAN, ROBIN, AND THE ELONGATED MAN CAN HOPE TO SOLVE THE PUZZLING CASE OF THE

MUSEUM OF MIXED-UP MEN!

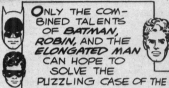

YOU'RE THE ELONGATED MAN, SEE? YOU CAN STRETCH YOUR ARM -- LIKE THIS! YOU'VE GOT TO HELP BATMAN AND ME CAPTURE THIS GANG OF CROOKS!

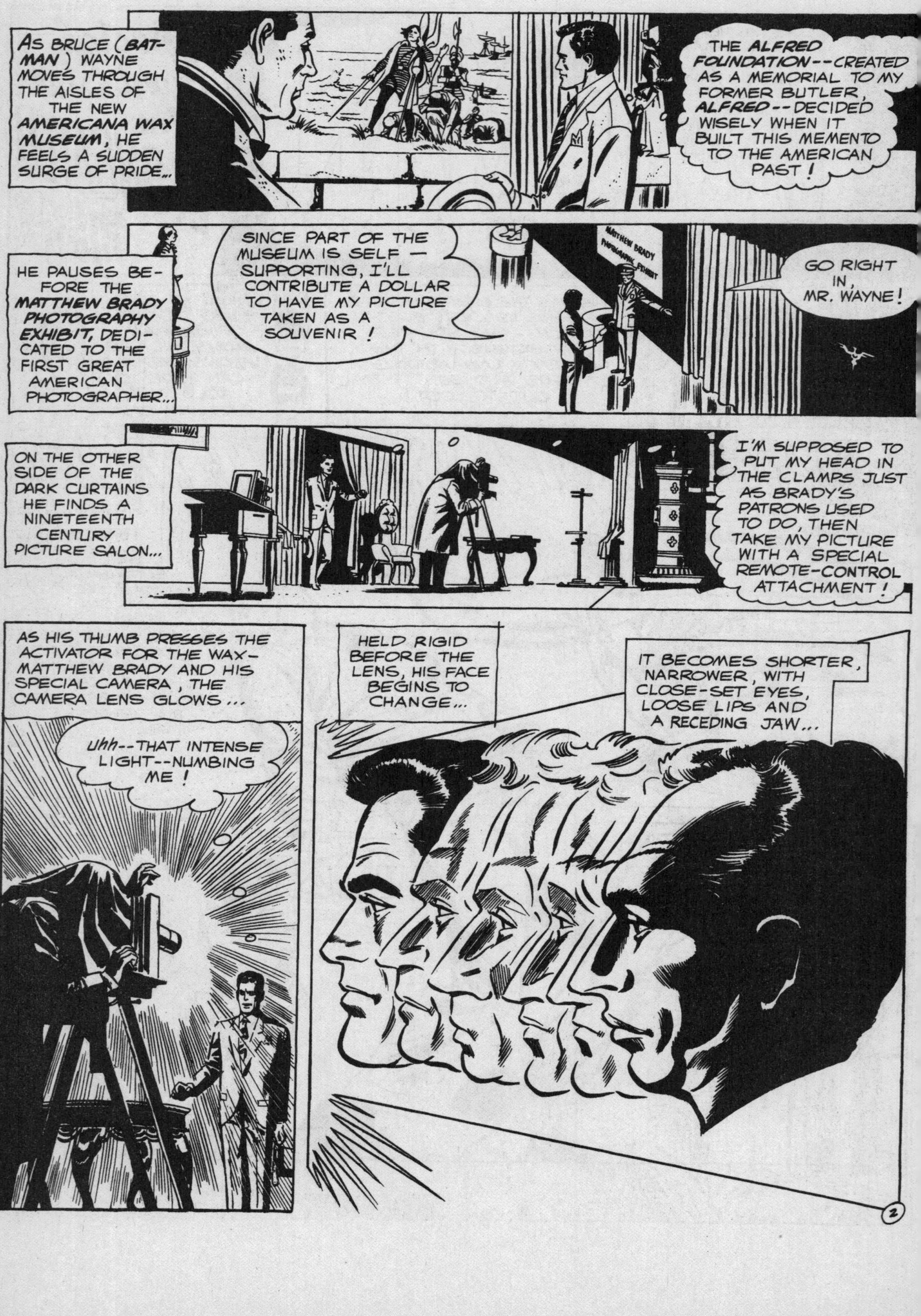
AS BRUCE (BATMAN) WAYNE MOVES THROUGH THE AISLES OF THE NEW AMERICANA WAX MUSEUM, HE FEELS A SUDDEN SURGE OF PRIDE...
THE ALFRED FOUNDATION--CREATED AS A MEMORIAL TO MY FORMER BUTLER, ALFRED--DECIDED WISELY WHEN IT BUILT THIS MEMENTO TO THE AMERICAN PAST!
HE PAUSES BEFORE THE MATTHEW BRADY PHOTOGRAPHY EXHIBIT, DEDICATED TO THE FIRST GREAT AMERICAN PHOTOGRAPHER...
SINCE PART OF THE MUSEUM IS SELF-SUPPORTING, I'LL CONTRIBUTE A DOLLAR TO HAVE MY PICTURE TAKEN AS A SOUVENIR!
GO RIGHT IN, MR. WAYNE!
ON THE OTHER SIDE OF THE DARK CURTAINS HE FINDS A NINETEENTH CENTURY PICTURE SALON...
I'M SUPPOSED TO PUT MY HEAD IN THE CLAMPS JUST AS BRADY'S PATRONS USED TO DO, THEN TAKE MY PICTURE WITH A SPECIAL REMOTE-CONTROL ATTACHMENT!
AS HIS THUMB PRESSES THE ACTIVATOR FOR THE WAX-MATTHEW BRADY AND HIS SPECIAL CAMERA, THE CAMERA LENS GLOWS...
Uhh--THAT INTENSE LIGHT--NUMBING ME!
HELD RIGID BEFORE THE LENS, HIS FACE BEGINS TO CHANGE...
IT BECOMES SHORTER, NARROWER, WITH CLOSE-SET EYES, LOOSE LIPS AND A RECEDING JAW...
2

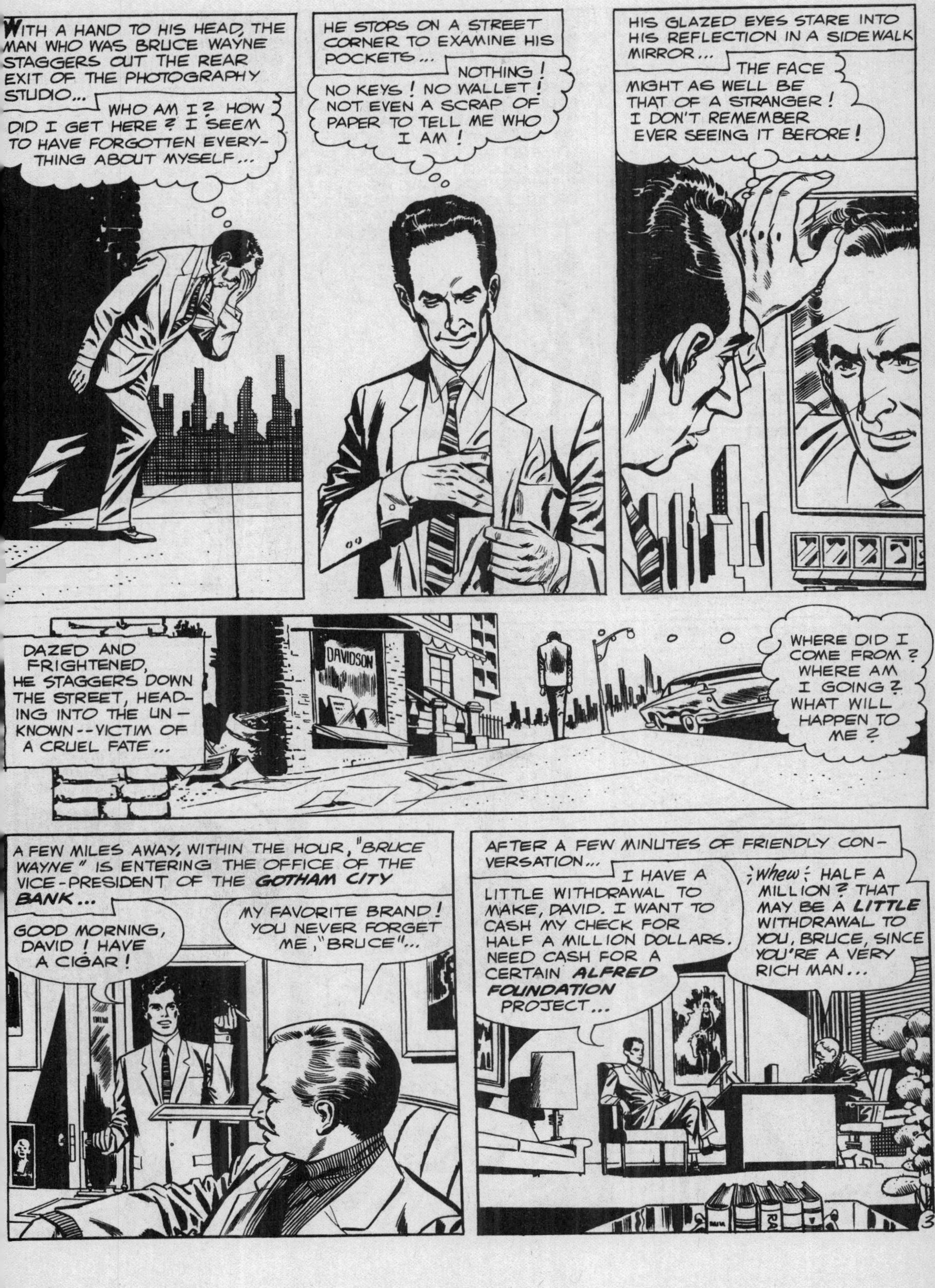
WITH A HAND TO HIS HEAD, THE MAN WHO WAS BRUCE WAYNE STAGGERS OUT THE REAR EXIT OF THE PHOTOGRAPHY STUDIO...
WHO AM I? HOW DID I GET HERE? I SEEM TO HAVE FORGOTTEN EVERYTHING ABOUT MYSELF...
HE STOPS ON A STREET CORNER TO EXAMINE HIS POCKETS...
NOTHING! NO KEYS! NO WALLET! NOT EVEN A SCRAP OF PAPER TO TELL ME WHO I AM!
HIS GLAZED EYES STARE INTO HIS REFLECTION IN A SIDEWALK MIRROR...
THE FACE MIGHT AS WELL BE THAT OF A STRANGER! I DON'T REMEMBER EVER SEEING IT BEFORE!
DAZED AND FRIGHTENED, HE STAGGERS DOWN THE STREET, HEADING INTO THE UNKNOWN--VICTIM OF A CRUEL FATE...
DAVIDSON
WHERE DID I COME FROM? WHERE AM I GOING? WHAT WILL HAPPEN TO ME?
A FEW MILES AWAY, WITHIN THE HOUR, "BRUCE WAYNE" IS ENTERING THE OFFICE OF THE VICE-PRESIDENT OF THE GOTHAM CITY BANK...
GOOD MORNING, DAVID! HAVE A CIGAR!
MY FAVORITE BRAND! YOU NEVER FORGET ME, "BRUCE"...
AFTER A FEW MINUTES OF FRIENDLY CONVERSATION...
I HAVE A LITTLE WITHDRAWAL TO MAKE, DAVID. I WANT TO CASH MY CHECK FOR HALF A MILLION DOLLARS. NEED CASH FOR A CERTAIN ALFRED FOUNDATION PROJECT...
WHEW! HALF A MILLION? THAT MAY BE A LITTLE WITHDRAWAL TO YOU, BRUCE, SINCE YOU'RE A VERY RICH MAN...
3

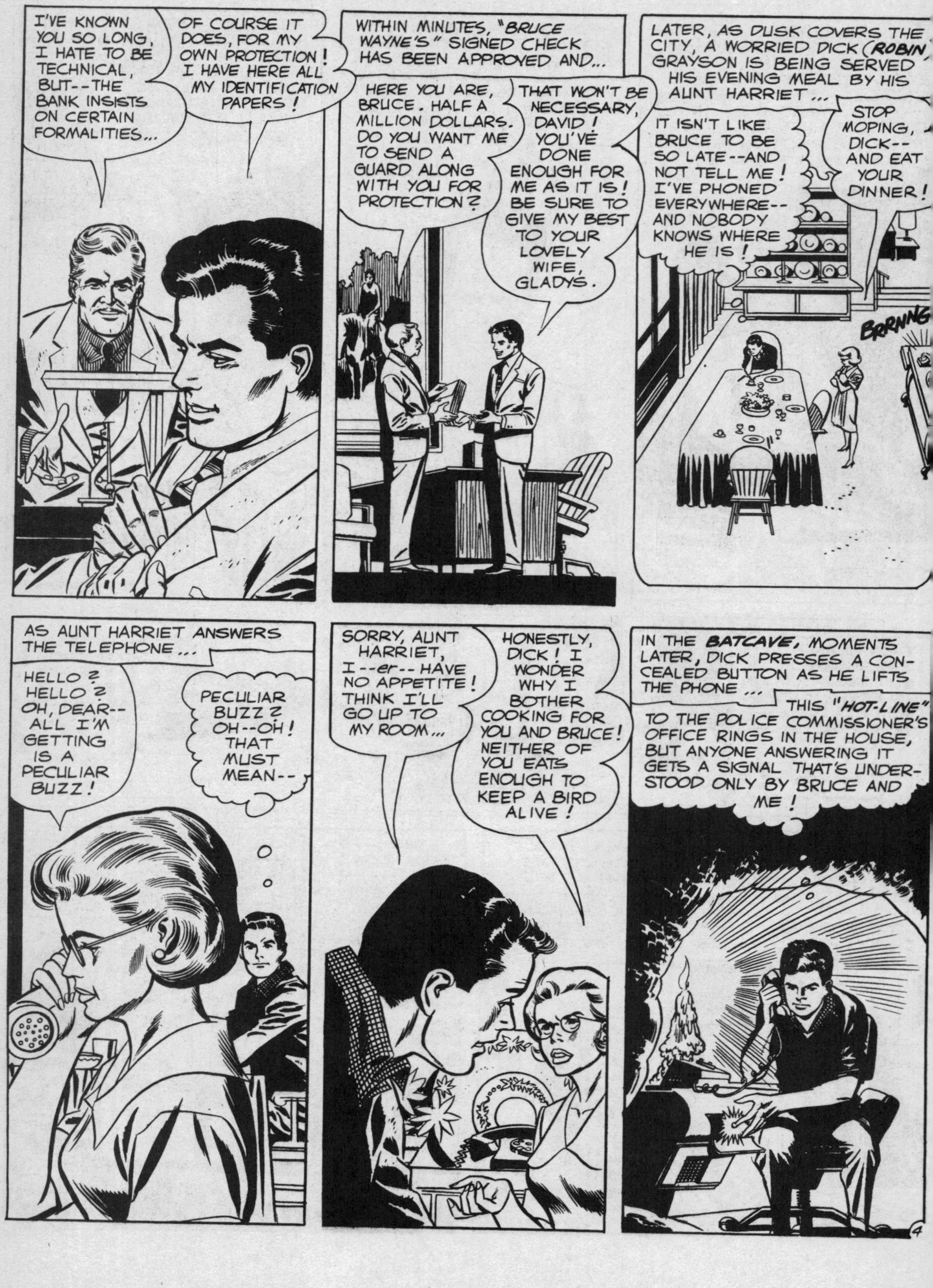
I'VE KNOWN YOU SO LONG, I HATE TO BE TECHNICAL, BUT--THE BANK INSISTS ON CERTAIN FORMALITIES...
OF COURSE IT DOES, FOR MY OWN PROTECTION! I HAVE HERE ALL MY IDENTIFICATION PAPERS!
WITHIN MINUTES, "BRUCE WAYNE'S" SIGNED CHECK HAS BEEN APPROVED AND...
HERE YOU ARE, BRUCE. HALF A MILLION DOLLARS. DO YOU WANT ME TO SEND A GUARD ALONG WITH YOU FOR PROTECTION?
THAT WON'T BE NECESSARY, DAVID! YOU'VE DONE ENOUGH FOR ME AS IT IS! BE SURE TO GIVE MY BEST TO YOUR LOVELY WIFE, GLADYS.
LATER, AS DUSK COVERS THE CITY, A WORRIED DICK (ROBIN) GRAYSON IS BEING SERVED HIS EVENING MEAL BY HIS AUNT HARRIET...
IT ISN'T LIKE BRUCE TO BE SO LATE--AND NOT TELL ME! I'VE PHONED EVERYWHERE--AND NOBODY KNOWS WHERE HE IS!
STOP MOPING, DICK--AND EAT YOUR DINNER!
BRRNNG
AS AUNT HARRIET ANSWERS THE TELEPHONE...
HELLO? HELLO? OH, DEAR--ALL I'M GETTING IS A PECULIAR BUZZ!
PECULIAR BUZZ? OH--OH! THAT MUST MEAN--
SORRY, AUNT HARRIET, I--er--HAVE NO APPETITE! THINK I'LL GO UP TO MY ROOM...
HONESTLY, DICK! I WONDER WHY I BOTHER COOKING FOR YOU AND BRUCE! NEITHER OF YOU EATS ENOUGH TO KEEP A BIRD ALIVE!
IN THE BATCAVE, MOMENTS LATER, DICK PRESSES A CONCEALED BUTTON AS HE LIFTS THE PHONE...
THIS "HOT-LINE" TO THE POLICE COMMISSIONER'S OFFICE RINGS IN THE HOUSE, BUT ANYONE ANSWERING IT GETS A SIGNAL THAT'S UNDERSTOOD ONLY BY BRUCE AND ME!
4

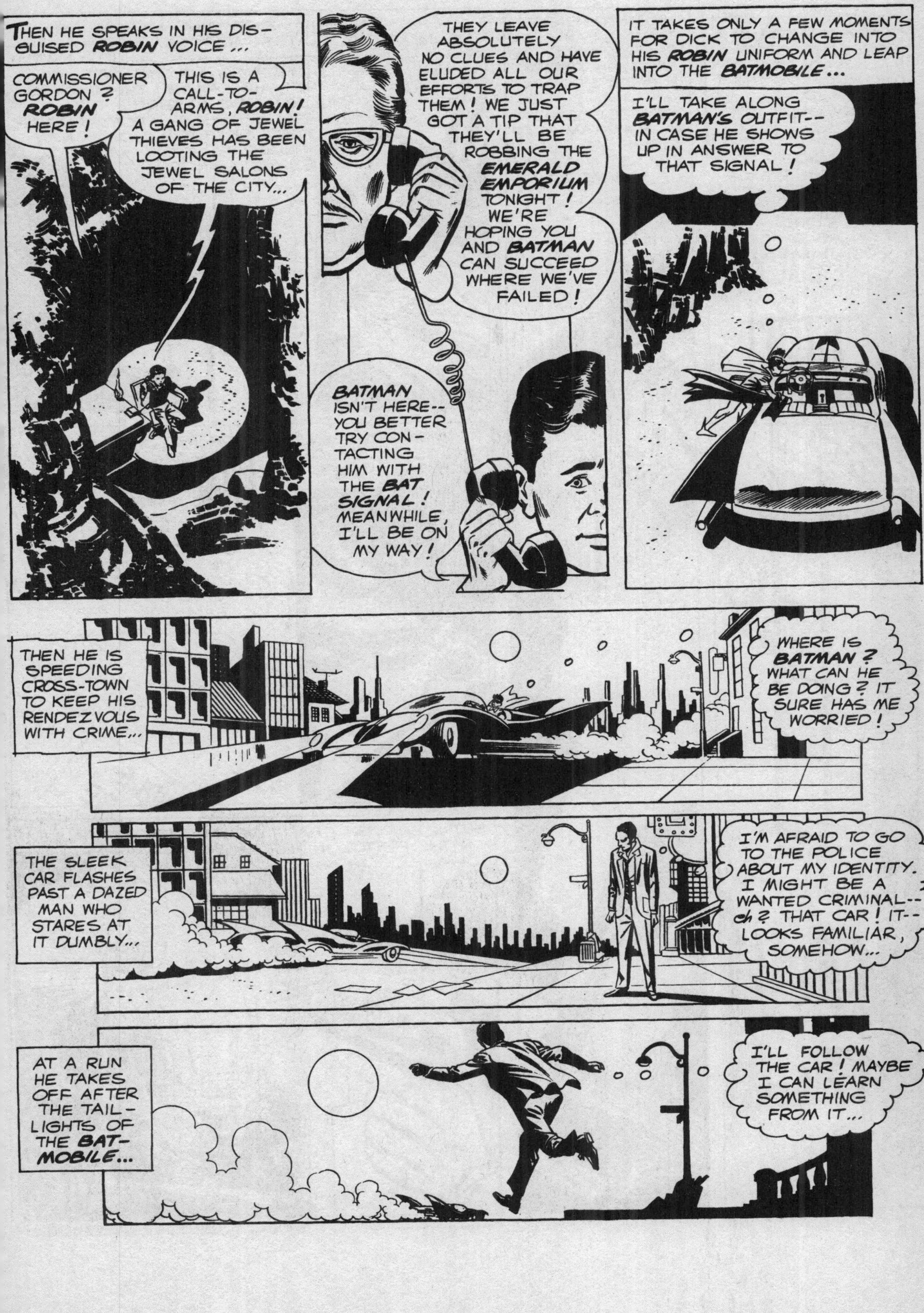
THEN HE SPEAKS IN HIS DISGUISED ROBIN VOICE...
COMMISSIONER GORDON? ROBIN HERE!
THIS IS A CALL-TO-ARMS, ROBIN! A GANG OF JEWEL THIEVES HAS BEEN LOOTING THE JEWEL SALONS OF THE CITY...
THEY LEAVE ABSOLUTELY NO CLUES AND HAVE ELUDED ALL OUR EFFORTS TO TRAP THEM! WE JUST GOT A TIP THAT THEY'LL BE ROBBING THE EMERALD EMPORIUM TONIGHT! WE'RE HOPING YOU AND BATMAN CAN SUCCEED WHERE WE'VE FAILED!
BATMAN ISN'T HERE--YOU BETTER TRY CONTACTING HIM WITH THE BAT SIGNAL! MEANWHILE, I'LL BE ON MY WAY!
IT TAKES ONLY A FEW MOMENTS FOR DICK TO CHANGE INTO HIS ROBIN UNIFORM AND LEAP INTO THE BATMOBILE...
I'LL TAKE ALONG BATMAN'S OUTFIT--IN CASE HE SHOWS UP IN ANSWER TO THAT SIGNAL!
THEN HE IS SPEEDING CROSS-TOWN TO KEEP HIS RENDEZVOUS WITH CRIME...
WHERE IS BATMAN? WHAT CAN HE BE DOING? IT SURE HAS ME WORRIED!
THE SLEEK CAR FLASHES PAST A DAZED MAN WHO STARES AT IT DUMBLY...
I'M AFRAID TO GO TO THE POLICE ABOUT MY IDENTITY. I MIGHT BE A WANTED CRIMINAL--eh? THAT CAR! IT--LOOKS FAMILIAR, SOMEHOW...
AT A RUN HE TAKES OFF AFTER THE TAIL-LIGHTS OF THE BAT-MOBILE...
I'LL FOLLOW THE CAR! MAYBE I CAN LEARN SOMETHING FROM IT...

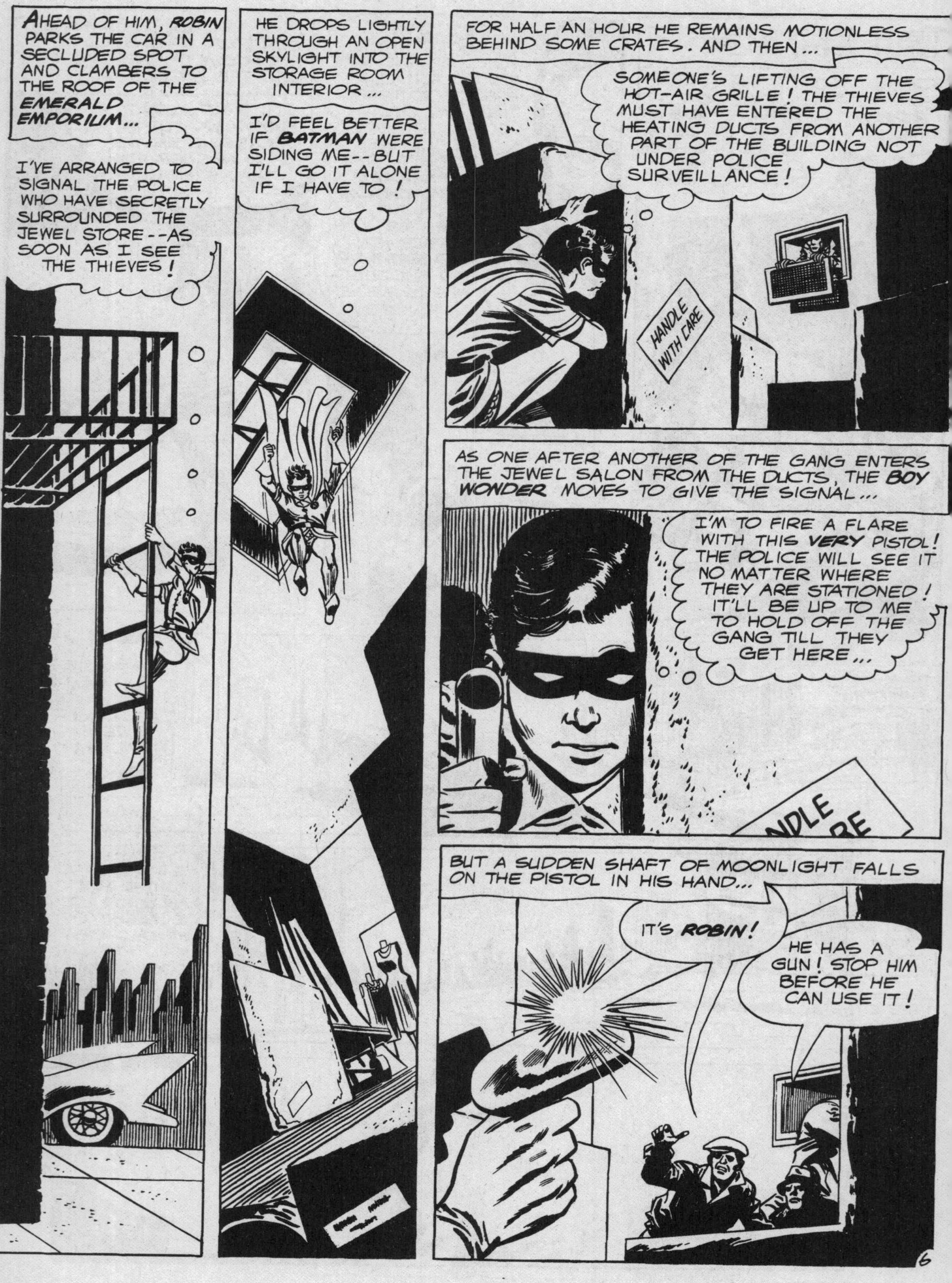
AHEAD OF HIM, ROBIN PARKS THE CAR IN A SECLUDED SPOT AND CLAMBERS TO THE ROOF OF THE EMERALD EMPORIUM...
I'VE ARRANGED TO SIGNAL THE POLICE WHO HAVE SECRETLY SURROUNDED THE JEWEL STORE--AS SOON AS I SEE THE THIEVES!
HE DROPS LIGHTLY THROUGH AN OPEN SKYLIGHT INTO THE STORAGE ROOM INTERIOR...
I'D FEEL BETTER IF BATMAN WERE SIDING ME--BUT I'LL GO IT ALONE IF I HAVE TO!
FOR HALF AN HOUR HE REMAINS MOTIONLESS BEHIND SOME CRATES. AND THEN...
SOMEONE'S LIFTING OFF THE HOT-AIR GRILLE! THE THIEVES MUST HAVE ENTERED THE HEATING DUCTS FROM ANOTHER PART OF THE BUILDING NOT UNDER POLICE SURVEILLANCE!
HANDLE WITH CARE
AS ONE AFTER ANOTHER OF THE GANG ENTERS THE JEWEL SALON FROM THE DUCTS, THE BOY WONDER MOVES TO GIVE THE SIGNAL...
I'M TO FIRE A FLARE WITH THIS VERY PISTOL! THE POLICE WILL SEE IT NO MATTER WHERE THEY ARE STATIONED! IT'LL BE UP TO ME TO HOLD OFF THE GANG TILL THEY GET HERE...
BUT A SUDDEN SHAFT OF MOONLIGHT FALLS ON THE PISTOL IN HIS HAND...
IT'S ROBIN!
HE HAS A GUN! STOP HIM BEFORE HE CAN USE IT!
6

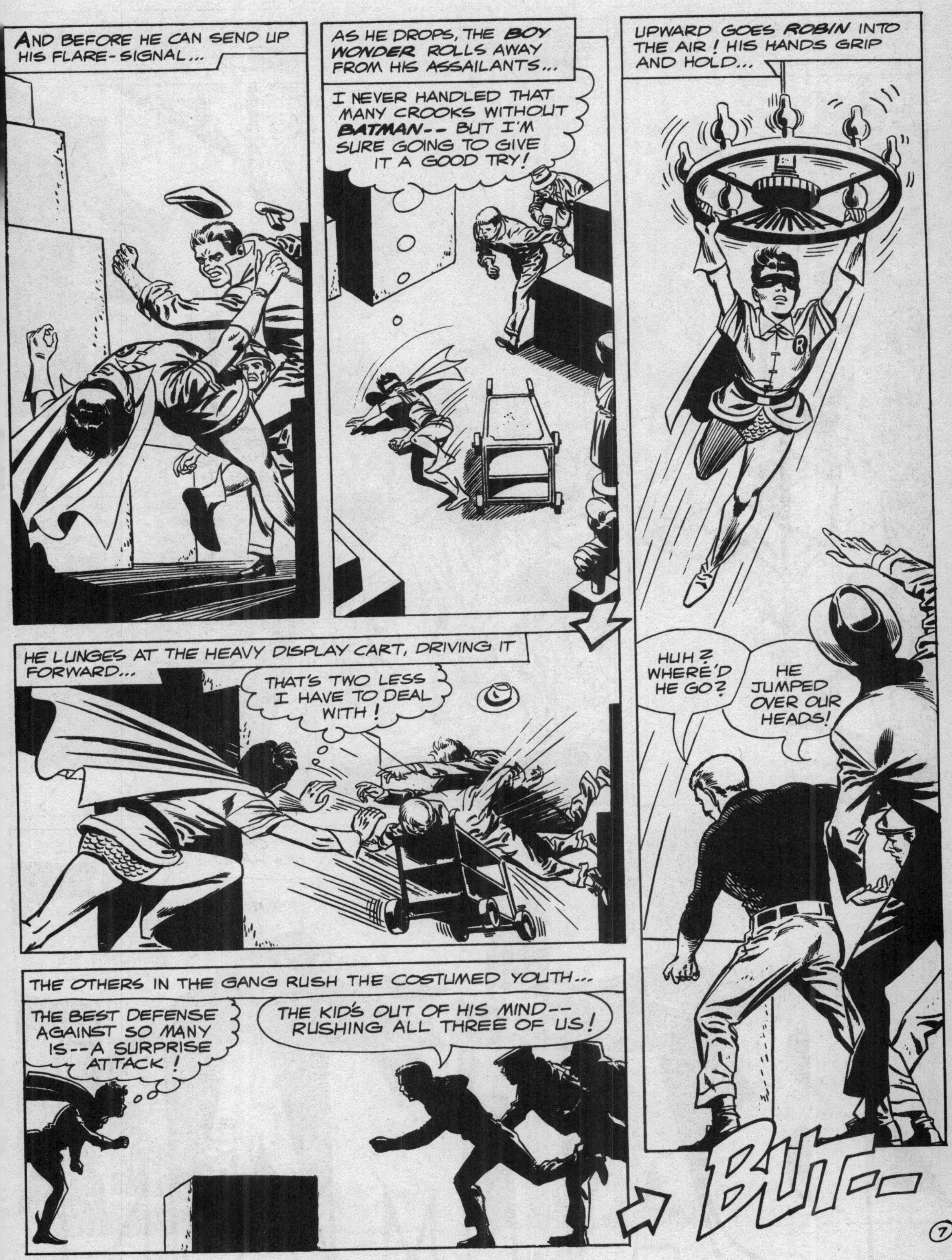
AND BEFORE HE CAN SEND UP HIS FLARE-SIGNAL...
AS HE DROPS, THE BOY WONDER ROLLS AWAY FROM HIS ASSAILANTS...
I NEVER HANDLED THAT MANY CROOKS WITHOUT BATMAN-- BUT I'M SURE GOING TO GIVE IT A GOOD TRY!
HE LUNGES AT THE HEAVY DISPLAY CART, DRIVING IT FORWARD...
THAT'S TWO LESS I HAVE TO DEAL WITH!
THE OTHERS IN THE GANG RUSH THE COSTUMED YOUTH...
THE BEST DEFENSE AGAINST SO MANY IS--A SURPRISE ATTACK!
THE KID'S OUT OF HIS MIND-- RUSHING ALL THREE OF US!
UPWARD GOES ROBIN INTO THE AIR! HIS HANDS GRIP AND HOLD...
HUH? WHERE'D HE GO?
HE JUMPED OVER OUR HEADS!
BUT--
7

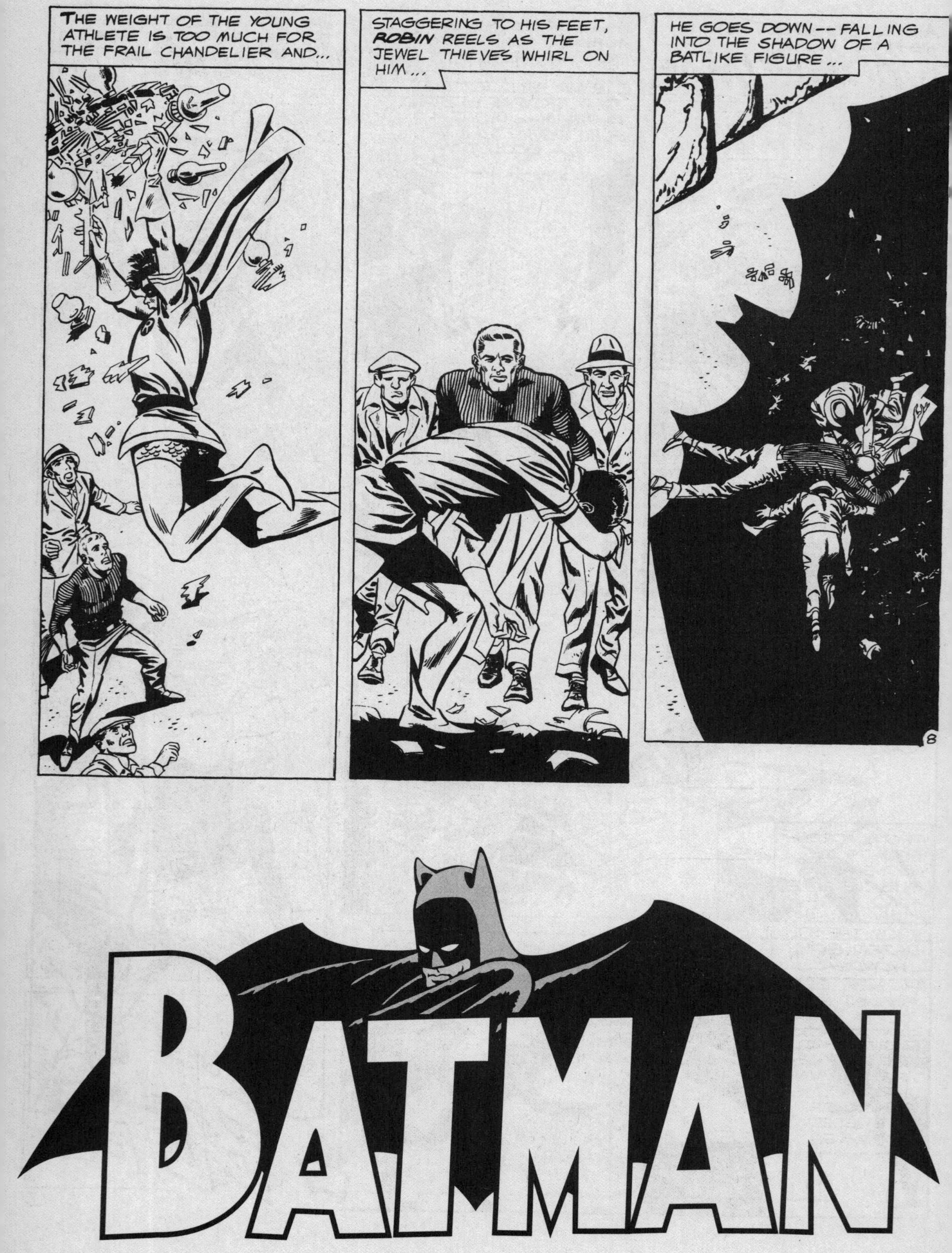
THE WEIGHT OF THE YOUNG ATHLETE IS TOO MUCH FOR THE FRAIL CHANDELIER AND...
STAGGERING TO HIS FEET, ROBIN REELS AS THE JEWEL THIEVES WHIRL ON HIM...
HE GOES DOWN -- FALLING INTO THE SHADOW OF A BATLIKE FIGURE...
8

BATMAN

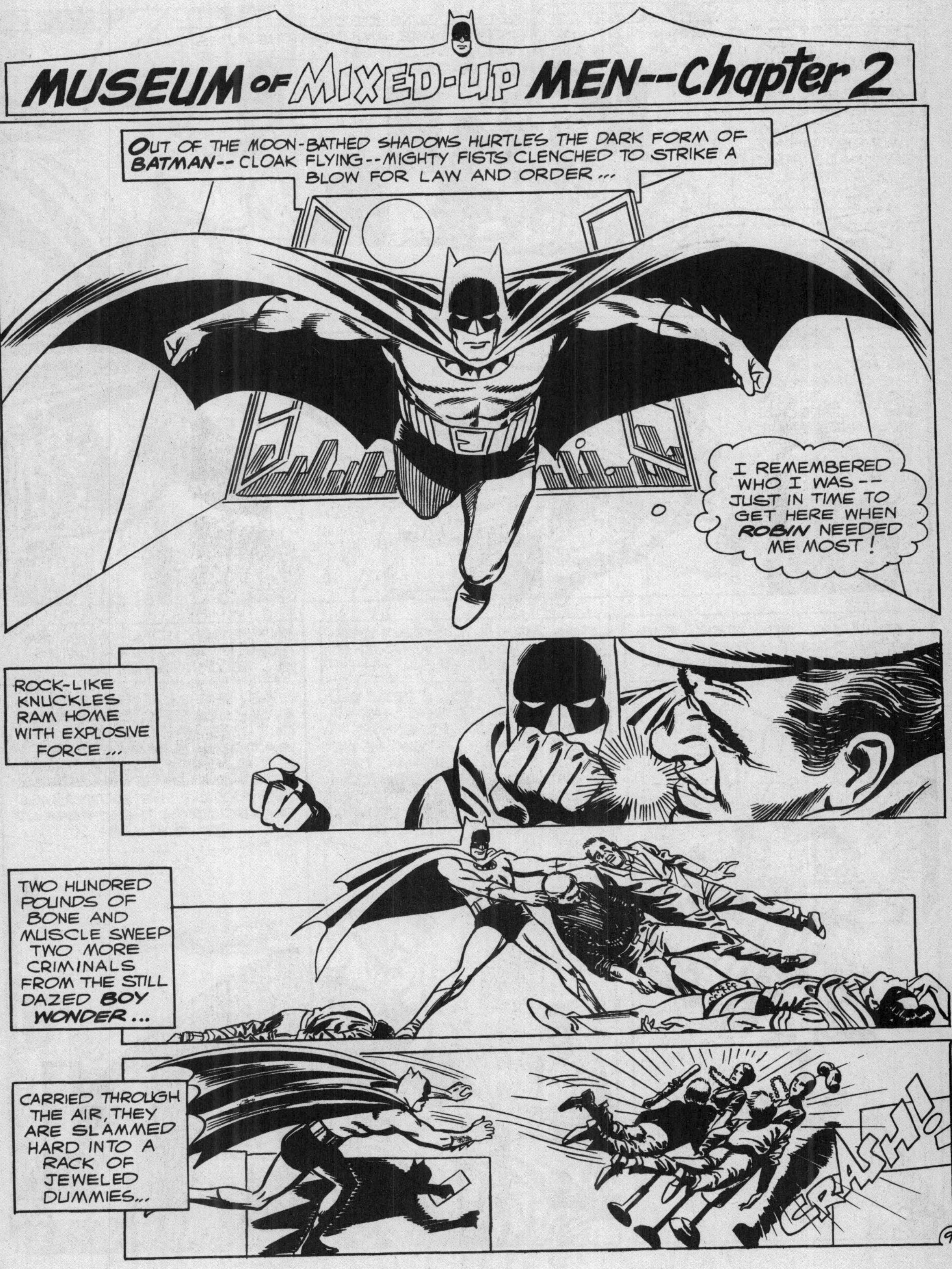
MUSEUM OF MIXED-UP MEN--Chapter 2
OUT OF THE MOON-BATHED SHADOWS HURTLES THE DARK FORM OF BATMAN-- CLOAK FLYING--MIGHTY FISTS CLENCHED TO STRIKE A BLOW FOR LAW AND ORDER...
I REMEMBERED WHO I WAS -- JUST IN TIME TO GET HERE WHEN ROBIN NEEDED ME MOST!
ROCK-LIKE KNUCKLES RAM HOME WITH EXPLOSIVE FORCE...
TWO HUNDRED POUNDS OF BONE AND MUSCLE SWEEP TWO MORE CRIMINALS FROM THE STILL DAZED BOY WONDER...
CARRIED THROUGH THE AIR, THEY ARE SLAMMED HARD INTO A RACK OF JEWELED DUMMIES...
CRASH!
9

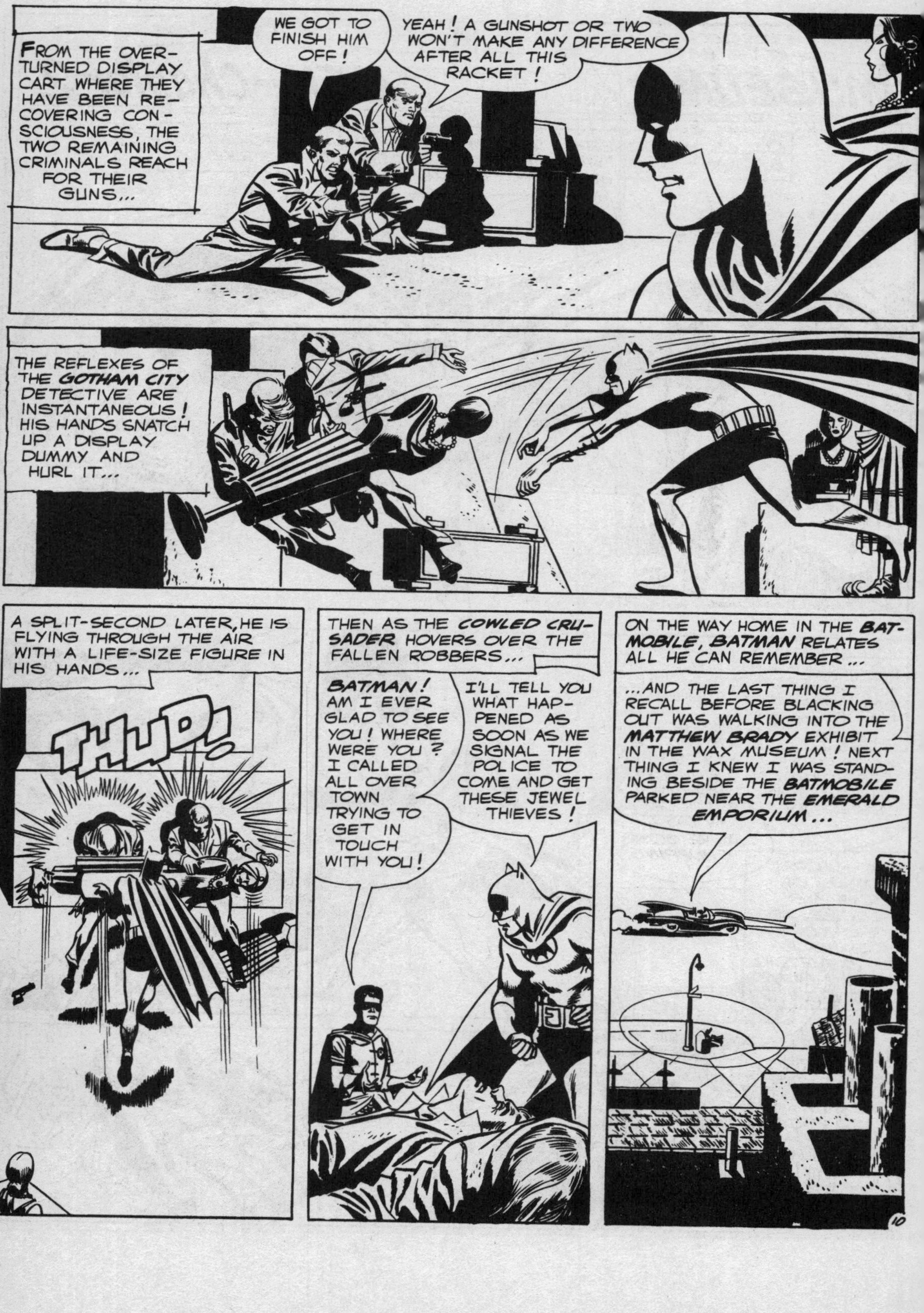
FROM THE OVER-TURNED DISPLAY CART WHERE THEY HAVE BEEN RE-COVERING CON-SCIOUSNESS, THE TWO REMAINING CRIMINALS REACH FOR THEIR GUNS...
WE GOT TO FINISH HIM OFF!
YEAH! A GUNSHOT OR TWO WON'T MAKE ANY DIFFERENCE AFTER ALL THIS RACKET!
THE REFLEXES OF THE GOTHAM CITY DETECTIVE ARE INSTANTANEOUS! HIS HANDS SNATCH UP A DISPLAY DUMMY AND HURL IT...
A SPLIT-SECOND LATER, HE IS FLYING THROUGH THE AIR WITH A LIFE-SIZE FIGURE IN HIS HANDS...
THUD!
THEN AS THE COWLED CRU-SADER HOVERS OVER THE FALLEN ROBBERS...
BATMAN! AM I EVER GLAD TO SEE YOU! WHERE WERE YOU? I CALLED ALL OVER TOWN TRYING TO GET IN TOUCH WITH YOU!
I'LL TELL YOU WHAT HAP-PENED AS SOON AS WE SIGNAL THE POLICE TO COME AND GET THESE JEWEL THIEVES!
ON THE WAY HOME IN THE BAT-MOBILE, BATMAN RELATES ALL HE CAN REMEMBER...
...AND THE LAST THING I RECALL BEFORE BLACKING OUT WAS WALKING INTO THE MATTHEW BRADY EXHIBIT IN THE WAX MUSEUM! NEXT THING I KNEW I WAS STAND-ING BESIDE THE BATMOBILE PARKED NEAR THE EMERALD EMPORIUM...
10

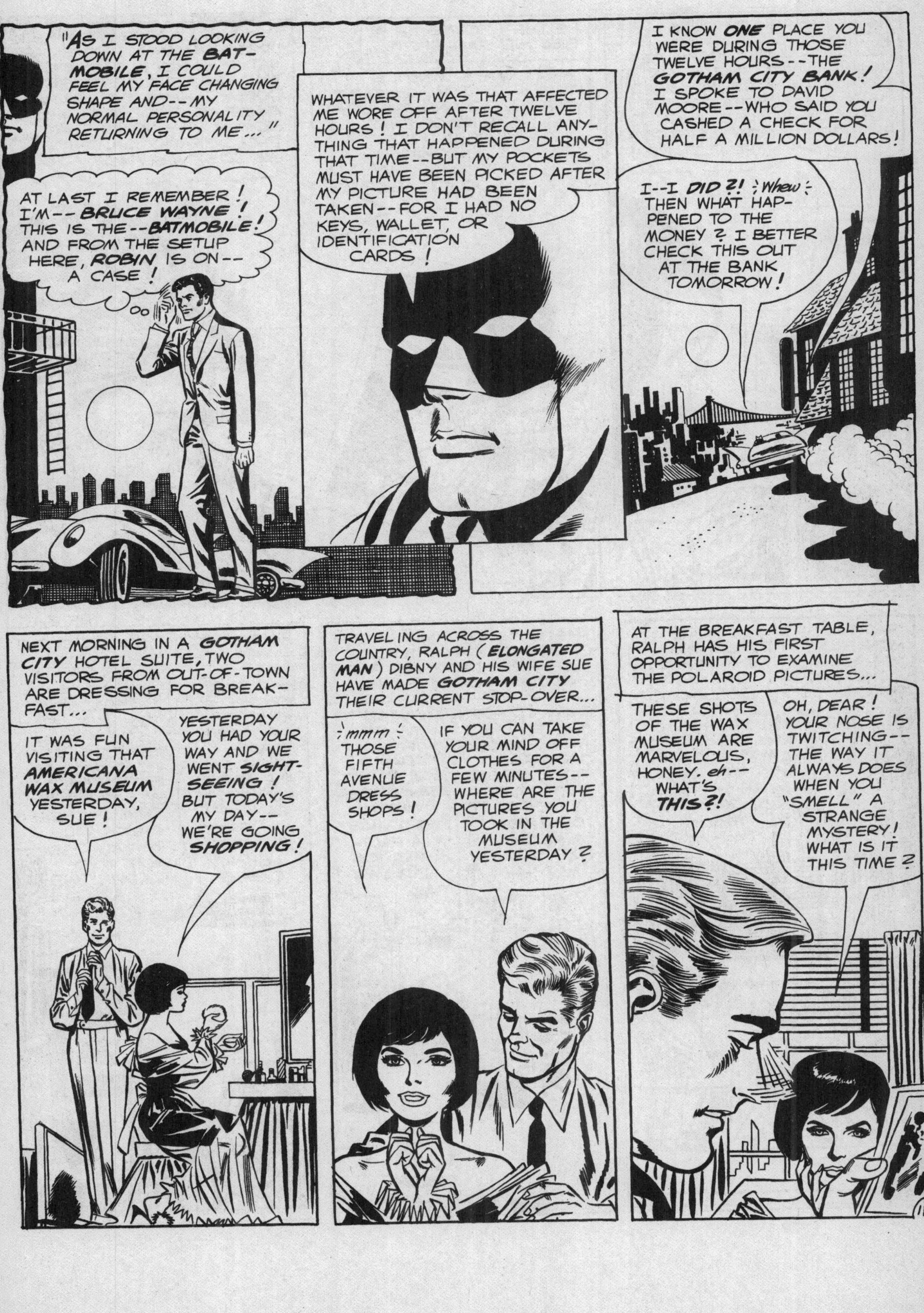
"AS I STOOD LOOKING DOWN AT THE BATMOBILE, I COULD FEEL MY FACE CHANGING SHAPE AND-- MY NORMAL PERSONALITY RETURNING TO ME..."
AT LAST I REMEMBER! I'M-- BRUCE WAYNE! THIS IS THE--BATMOBILE! AND FROM THE SETUP HERE, ROBIN IS ON-- A CASE!
WHATEVER IT WAS THAT AFFECTED ME WORE OFF AFTER TWELVE HOURS! I DON'T RECALL ANYTHING THAT HAPPENED DURING THAT TIME--BUT MY POCKETS MUST HAVE BEEN PICKED AFTER MY PICTURE HAD BEEN TAKEN--FOR I HAD NO KEYS, WALLET, OR IDENTIFICATION CARDS!
I KNOW ONE PLACE YOU WERE DURING THOSE TWELVE HOURS--THE GOTHAM CITY BANK! I SPOKE TO DAVID MOORE--WHO SAID YOU CASHED A CHECK FOR HALF A MILLION DOLLARS!
I--I DID?! Whew THEN WHAT HAPPENED TO THE MONEY? I BETTER CHECK THIS OUT AT THE BANK TOMORROW!
NEXT MORNING IN A GOTHAM CITY HOTEL SUITE, TWO VISITORS FROM OUT-OF-TOWN ARE DRESSING FOR BREAKFAST...
IT WAS FUN VISITING THAT AMERICANA WAX MUSEUM YESTERDAY, SUE!
YESTERDAY YOU HAD YOUR WAY AND WE WENT SIGHT-SEEING! BUT TODAY'S MY DAY-- WE'RE GOING SHOPPING!
TRAVELING ACROSS THE COUNTRY, RALPH (ELONGATED MAN) DIBNY AND HIS WIFE SUE HAVE MADE GOTHAM CITY THEIR CURRENT STOP-OVER...
mmm THOSE FIFTH AVENUE DRESS SHOPS!
IF YOU CAN TAKE YOUR MIND OFF CLOTHES FOR A FEW MINUTES-- WHERE ARE THE PICTURES YOU TOOK IN THE MUSEUM YESTERDAY?
AT THE BREAKFAST TABLE, RALPH HAS HIS FIRST OPPORTUNITY TO EXAMINE THE POLAROID PICTURES...
THESE SHOTS OF THE WAX MUSEUM ARE MARVELOUS, HONEY. eh-- WHAT'S THIS?!
OH, DEAR! YOUR NOSE IS TWITCHING-- THE WAY IT ALWAYS DOES WHEN YOU "SMELL" A STRANGE MYSTERY! WHAT IS IT THIS TIME?
11

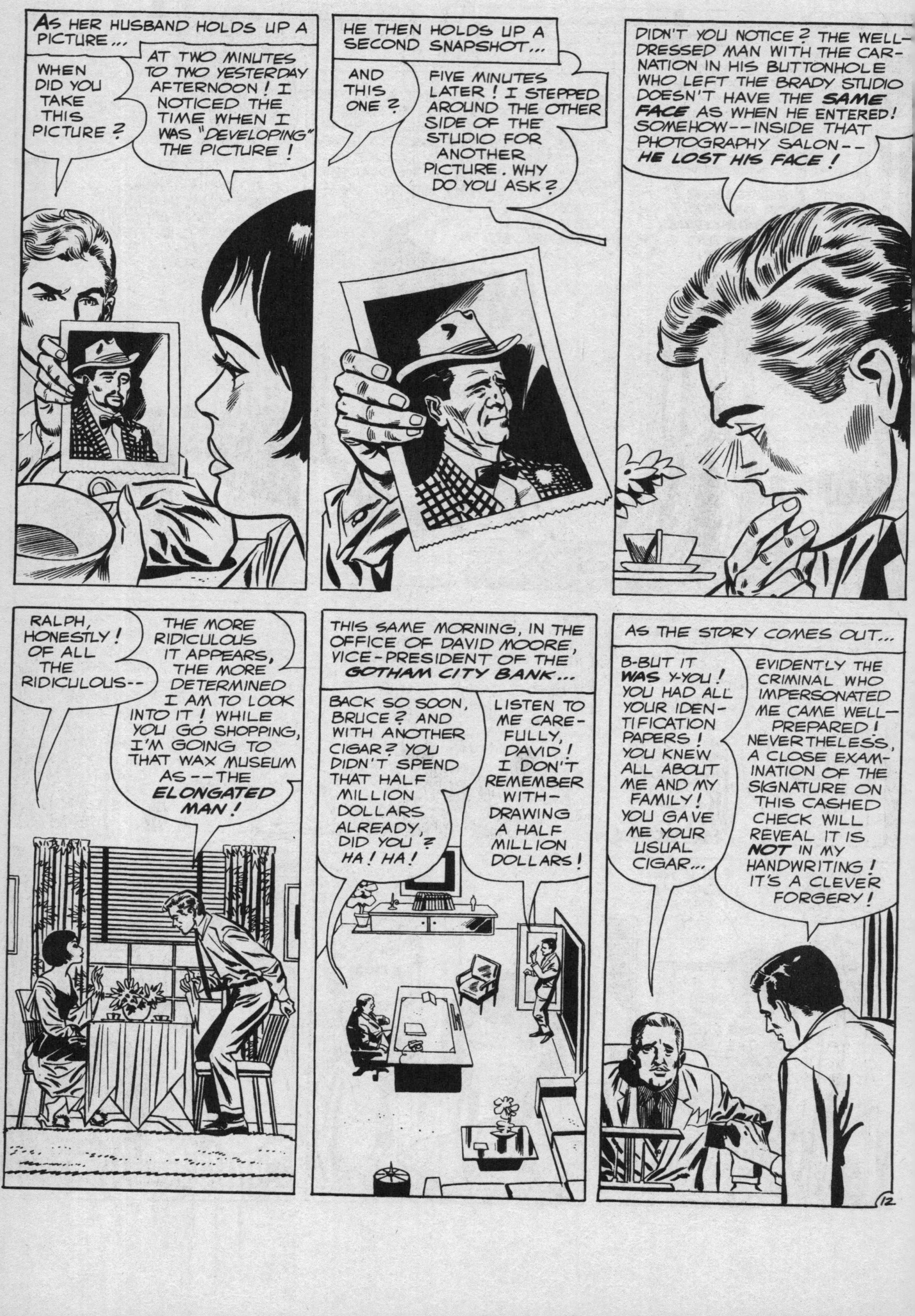
AS HER HUSBAND HOLDS UP A PICTURE...
WHEN DID YOU TAKE THIS PICTURE?
AT TWO MINUTES TO TWO YESTERDAY AFTERNOON! I NOTICED THE TIME WHEN I WAS "DEVELOPING" THE PICTURE!
HE THEN HOLDS UP A SECOND SNAPSHOT...
AND THIS ONE?
FIVE MINUTES LATER! I STEPPED AROUND THE OTHER SIDE OF THE STUDIO FOR ANOTHER PICTURE. WHY DO YOU ASK?
DIDN'T YOU NOTICE? THE WELL-DRESSED MAN WITH THE CARNATION IN HIS BUTTONHOLE WHO LEFT THE BRADY STUDIO DOESN'T HAVE THE **SAME FACE** AS WHEN HE ENTERED! SOMEHOW--INSIDE THAT PHOTOGRAPHY SALON--**HE LOST HIS FACE!**
RALPH, HONESTLY! OF ALL THE RIDICULOUS--
THE MORE RIDICULOUS IT APPEARS, THE MORE DETERMINED I AM TO LOOK INTO IT! WHILE YOU GO SHOPPING, I'M GOING TO THAT WAX MUSEUM AS--THE **ELONGATED MAN!**
THIS SAME MORNING, IN THE OFFICE OF DAVID MOORE, VICE-PRESIDENT OF THE **GOTHAM CITY BANK...**
BACK SO SOON, BRUCE? AND WITH ANOTHER CIGAR? YOU DIDN'T SPEND THAT HALF MILLION DOLLARS ALREADY, DID YOU? HA! HA!
LISTEN TO ME CAREFULLY, DAVID! I DON'T REMEMBER WITHDRAWING A HALF MILLION DOLLARS!
AS THE STORY COMES OUT...
B-BUT IT **WAS** Y-YOU! YOU HAD ALL YOUR IDENTIFICATION PAPERS! YOU KNEW ALL ABOUT ME AND MY FAMILY! YOU GAVE ME YOUR USUAL CIGAR...
EVIDENTLY THE CRIMINAL WHO IMPERSONATED ME CAME WELL-PREPARED! NEVERTHELESS, A CLOSE EXAMINATION OF THE SIGNATURE ON THIS CASHED CHECK WILL REVEAL IT IS **NOT** IN MY HANDWRITING! IT'S A CLEVER FORGERY!
12

I JUST CAN'T UNDERSTAND IT! WE'LL CONDUCT A THOROUGH INVESTIGATION-- BELIEVE ME!

I'M GOING TO CARRY ON MY OWN INVESTIGATION-- AS *BATMAN*!

SUDDENLY A BELLOW RINGS OUT IN THE HUSHED CORRIDORS OF THE SEDATE *GOTHAM CITY BANK*...

I'VE BEEN ROBBED! A MILLION DOLLARS' WORTH!

GOOD GOSH! WHAT HAPPENED, MR. LURIE?

SOMEBODY BROKE INTO MY SAFE DEPOSIT BOX YESTERDAY AFTERNOON AND REMOVED THE STOCKS AND BONDS IN IT WORTH A MILLION DOLLARS!

B-BUT IT WAS *YOU*, SIR! *YOU* OPENED THE BOX! *YOU* TOOK AWAY THE SECURITIES!

MOMENTS LATER, STILL RED WITH ANGER AND OUTRAGE, MILLIONAIRE CRAWFORD LURIE STARES AT PAPERS PROVING HE EMPTIED HIS OWN SAFE DEPOSIT BOX...

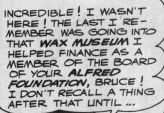

INCREDIBLE! I WASN'T HERE! THE LAST I REMEMBER WAS GOING INTO THAT *WAX MUSEUM* I HELPED FINANCE AS A MEMBER OF THE BOARD OF YOUR *ALFRED FOUNDATION*, BRUCE! I DON'T RECALL A THING AFTER THAT UNTIL ...

DID YOU SAY-- THE *WAX MUSEUM*?

YES, THE *MATTHEW BRADY* STUDIO PART OF IT! AFTER THAT-- MY MIND BLANKED OUT FOR ABOUT TWELVE HOURS!

ODD! THE SAME THING THAT HAPPENED TO ME YESTERDAY!

13

FORTUNATELY, BEING A FARSIGHTED MAN, I HAD A DUPLICATE SAFE DEPOSIT KEY MADE SO I WAS ABLE TO GET INTO MY BOX TODAY! OTHERWISE I WOULDN'T HAVE DISCOVERED THE ROBBERY!

I BETTER MAKE A PHONE CALL!

AS CHAIRMAN OF THE *ALFRED FOUNDATION*, I'M GOING TO SHUT DOWN THE WAX MUSEUM UNTIL WE GET TO THE BOTTOM OF THIS!

SOON *BATMAN* AND *ROBIN* ARE RACING TOWARD THE WAX MUSEUM...

IT'S CLOSED NOW, *ROBIN*! WE'LL BE THE ONLY ONES IN THERE--

--EXCEPT THE CROOKS CAUSING THE FACIAL CHANGE-OVERS, I HOPE!

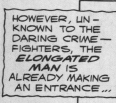

HOWEVER, UNKNOWN TO THE DARING CRIME-FIGHTERS, THE *ELONGATED MAN* IS ALREADY MAKING AN ENTRANCE...

LUCKILY THERE WAS NO KEY IN THE REAR DOOR--SO I COULD COME IN THROUGH THE KEYHOLE!

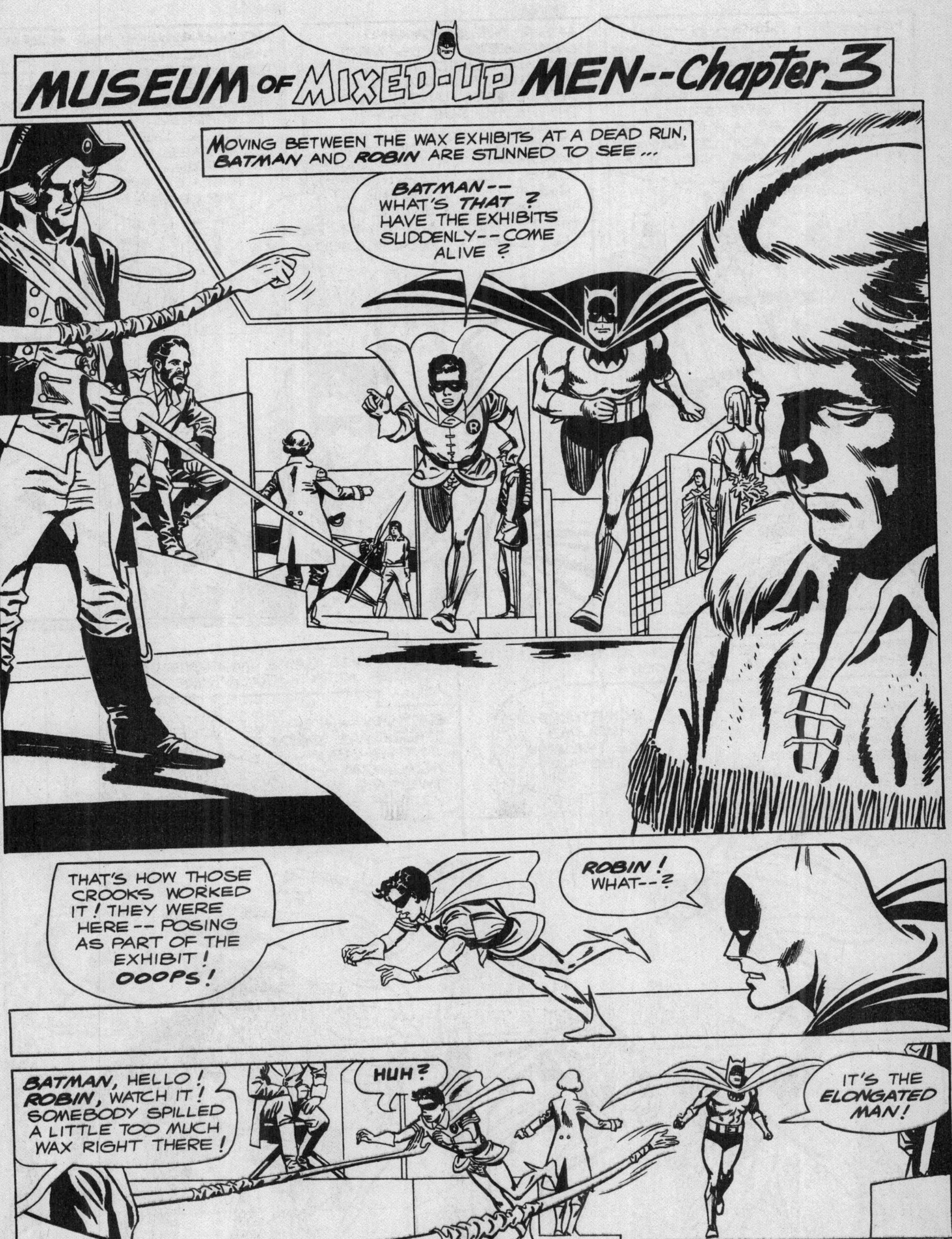
MUSEUM OF MIXED-UP MEN--Chapter 3
MOVING BETWEEN THE WAX EXHIBITS AT A DEAD RUN, BATMAN AND ROBIN ARE STUNNED TO SEE...
BATMAN-- WHAT'S THAT? HAVE THE EXHIBITS SUDDENLY--COME ALIVE?
THAT'S HOW THOSE CROOKS WORKED IT! THEY WERE HERE -- POSING AS PART OF THE EXHIBIT! OOOPS!
ROBIN! WHAT--?
BATMAN, HELLO! ROBIN, WATCH IT! SOMEBODY SPILLED A LITTLE TOO MUCH WAX RIGHT THERE!
HUH?
IT'S THE ELONGATED MAN!
15

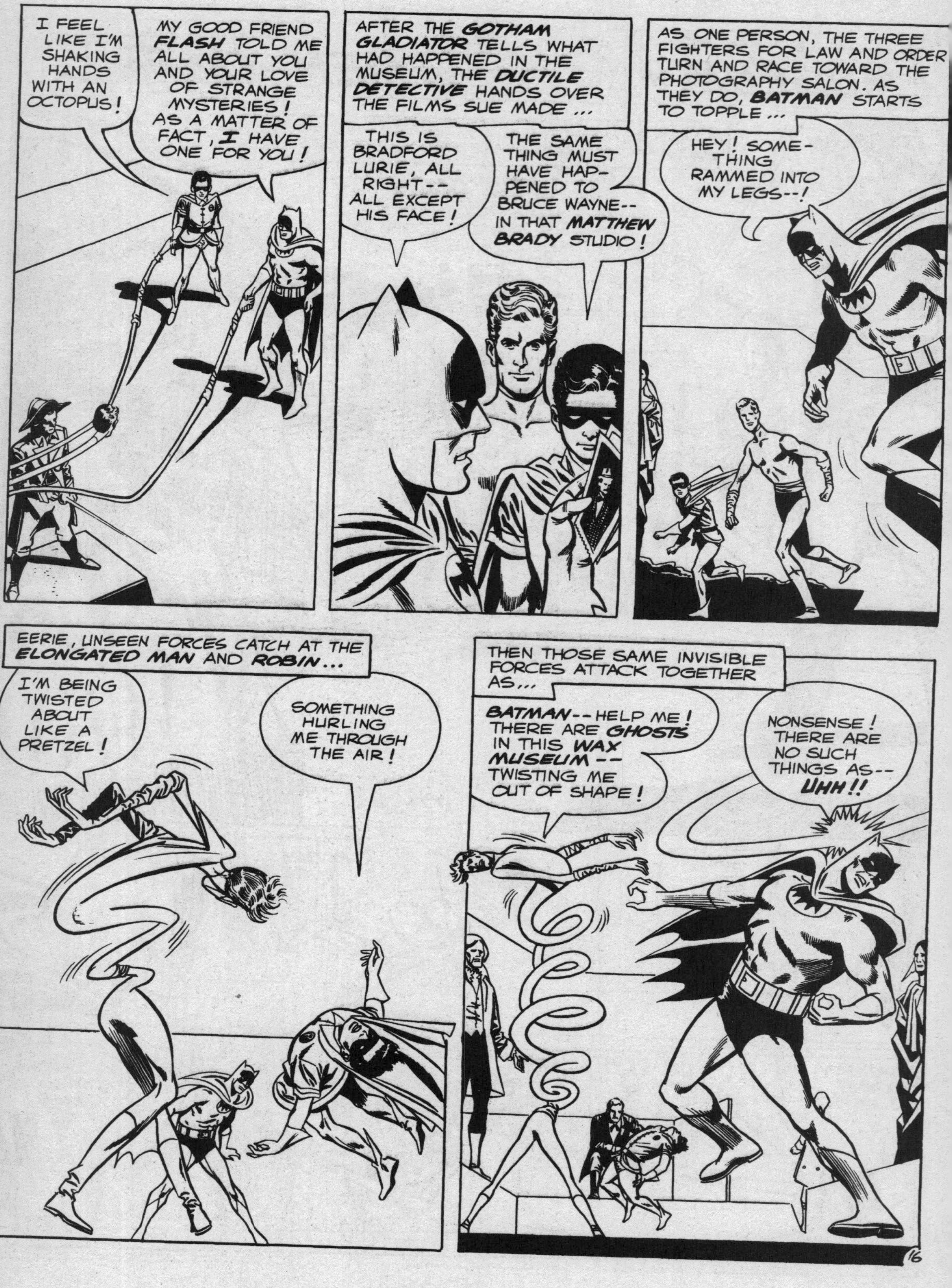
I FEEL LIKE I'M SHAKING HANDS WITH AN OCTOPUS!
MY GOOD FRIEND FLASH TOLD ME ALL ABOUT YOU AND YOUR LOVE OF STRANGE MYSTERIES! AS A MATTER OF FACT, I HAVE ONE FOR YOU!
AFTER THE GOTHAM GLADIATOR TELLS WHAT HAD HAPPENED IN THE MUSEUM, THE DUCTILE DETECTIVE HANDS OVER THE FILMS SUE MADE ...
THIS IS BRADFORD LURIE, ALL RIGHT-- ALL EXCEPT HIS FACE!
THE SAME THING MUST HAVE HAPPENED TO BRUCE WAYNE-- IN THAT MATTHEW BRADY STUDIO!
AS ONE PERSON, THE THREE FIGHTERS FOR LAW AND ORDER TURN AND RACE TOWARD THE PHOTOGRAPHY SALON. AS THEY DO, BATMAN STARTS TO TOPPLE ...
HEY! SOME-THING RAMMED INTO MY LEGS--!
EERIE, UNSEEN FORCES CATCH AT THE ELONGATED MAN AND ROBIN ...
I'M BEING TWISTED ABOUT LIKE A PRETZEL!
SOMETHING HURLING ME THROUGH THE AIR!
THEN THOSE SAME INVISIBLE FORCES ATTACK TOGETHER AS...
BATMAN--HELP ME! THERE ARE GHOSTS IN THIS WAX MUSEUM-- TWISTING ME OUT OF SHAPE!
NONSENSE! THERE ARE NO SUCH THINGS AS-- UHH!!
16

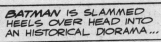

THE *ELONGATED MAN* RISES SO SWIFTLY IN HIS SPIRALLING ASCENT THAT...

THUNK!

BATMAN IS SLAMMED HEELS OVER HEAD INTO AN HISTORICAL DIORAMA...

WHILE *ROBIN* BANGS HARD INTO AN UNSYMPATHETIC GEORGE WASHINGTON...

BATMAN IS THE FIRST TO RECOVER, THANKS TO HIS SUPERB PHYSICAL CONDITION...

I MUST GET INTO THAT *MATTHEW BRADY* STUDIO-- LEARN WHAT'S GOING ON...

BUT--NO SOONER DOES HE SWEEP ASIDE THE HEAVY CURTAIN AND LURCH INTO THE PHOTOGRAPHY SALON THAN...

THE CAMERA LENS IS GLOWING AND-- HOLDING ME MOTIONLESS! IT'S GOING TO--STEAL MY FACE AND REVEAL THE SECRET OF MY DOUBLE IDENTITY!

17

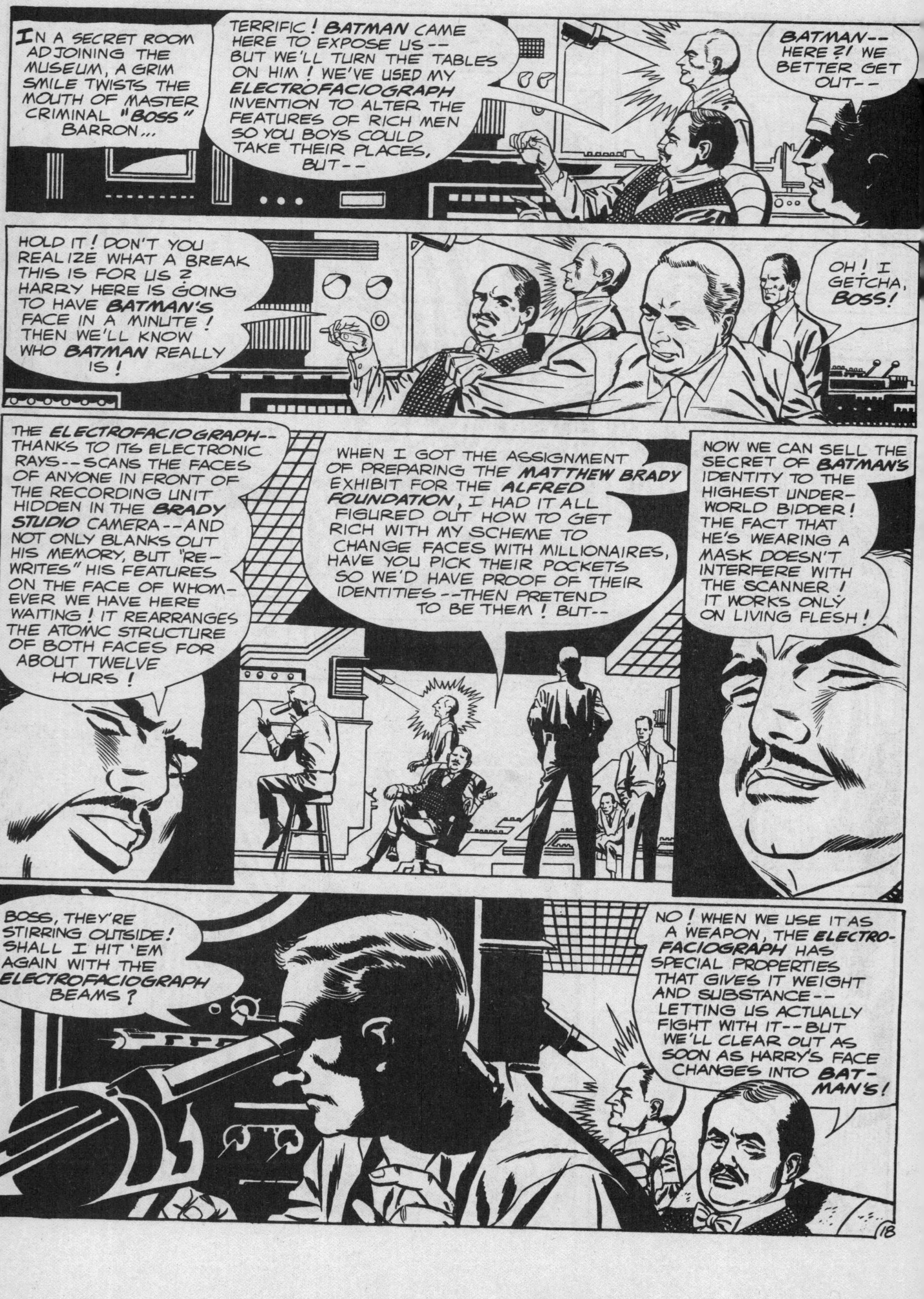
IN A SECRET ROOM ADJOINING THE MUSEUM, A GRIM SMILE TWISTS THE MOUTH OF MASTER CRIMINAL "BOSS" BARRON...
TERRIFIC! BATMAN CAME HERE TO EXPOSE US--BUT WE'LL TURN THE TABLES ON HIM! WE'VE USED MY ELECTROFACIOGRAPH INVENTION TO ALTER THE FEATURES OF RICH MEN SO YOU BOYS COULD TAKE THEIR PLACES, BUT--
BATMAN--HERE?! WE BETTER GET OUT--
HOLD IT! DON'T YOU REALIZE WHAT A BREAK THIS IS FOR US? HARRY HERE IS GOING TO HAVE BATMAN'S FACE IN A MINUTE! THEN WE'LL KNOW WHO BATMAN REALLY IS!
OH! I GETCHA, BOSS!
THE ELECTROFACIOGRAPH--THANKS TO ITS ELECTRONIC RAYS--SCANS THE FACES OF ANYONE IN FRONT OF THE RECORDING UNIT HIDDEN IN THE BRADY STUDIO CAMERA--AND NOT ONLY BLANKS OUT HIS MEMORY, BUT "RE-WRITES" HIS FEATURES ON THE FACE OF WHOMEVER WE HAVE HERE WAITING! IT REARRANGES THE ATOMIC STRUCTURE OF BOTH FACES FOR ABOUT TWELVE HOURS!
WHEN I GOT THE ASSIGNMENT OF PREPARING THE MATTHEW BRADY EXHIBIT FOR THE ALFRED FOUNDATION, I HAD IT ALL FIGURED OUT HOW TO GET RICH WITH MY SCHEME TO CHANGE FACES WITH MILLIONAIRES, HAVE YOU PICK THEIR POCKETS SO WE'D HAVE PROOF OF THEIR IDENTITIES--THEN PRETEND TO BE THEM! BUT--
NOW WE CAN SELL THE SECRET OF BATMAN'S IDENTITY TO THE HIGHEST UNDERWORLD BIDDER! THE FACT THAT HE'S WEARING A MASK DOESN'T INTERFERE WITH THE SCANNER! IT WORKS ONLY ON LIVING FLESH!
BOSS, THEY'RE STIRRING OUTSIDE! SHALL I HIT 'EM AGAIN WITH THE ELECTROFACIOGRAPH BEAMS?
NO! WHEN WE USE IT AS A WEAPON, THE ELECTROFACIOGRAPH HAS SPECIAL PROPERTIES THAT GIVES IT WEIGHT AND SUBSTANCE--LETTING US ACTUALLY FIGHT WITH IT--BUT WE'LL CLEAR OUT AS SOON AS HARRY'S FACE CHANGES INTO BATMAN'S!
18

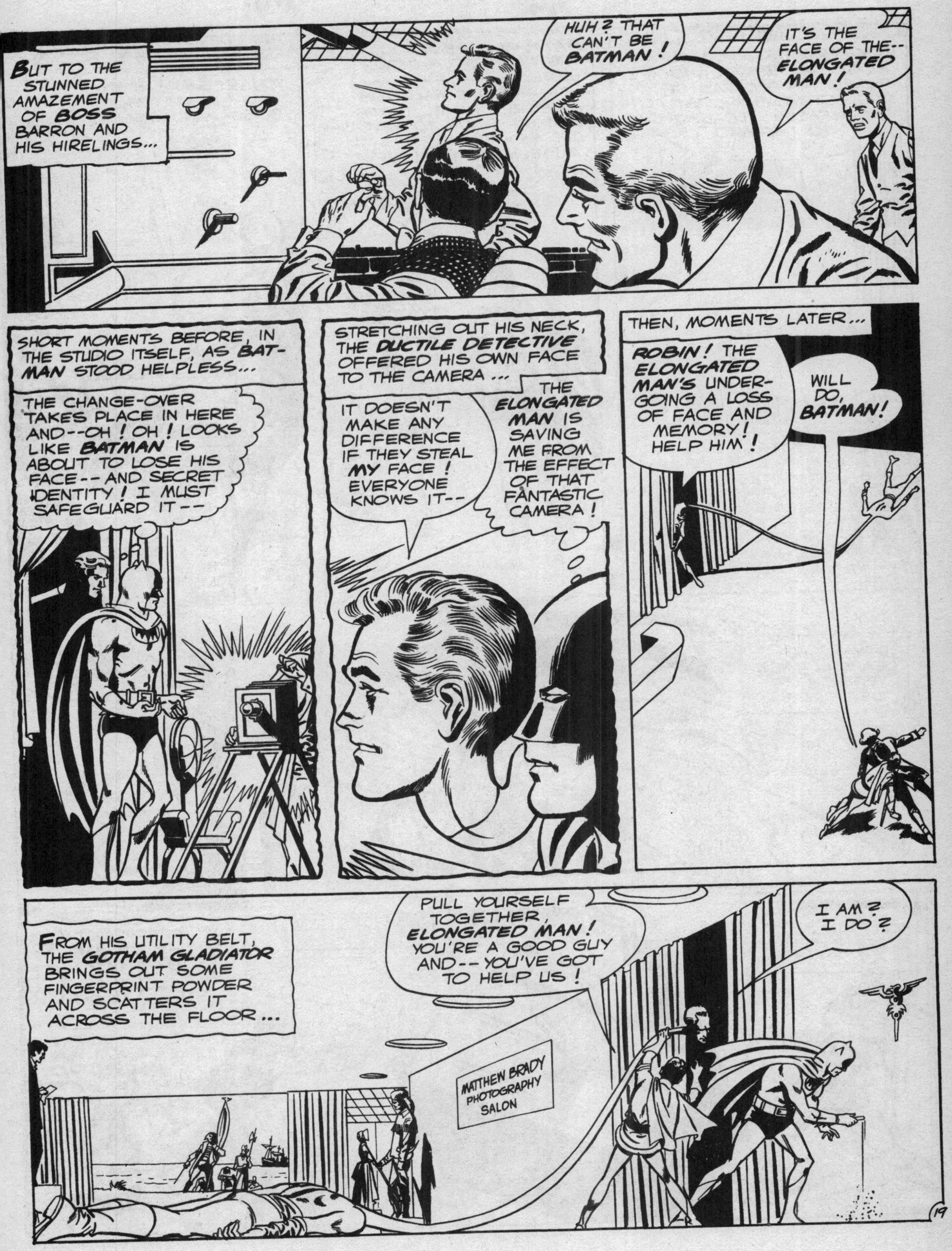
BUT TO THE STUNNED AMAZEMENT OF BOSS BARRON AND HIS HIRELINGS...
HUH? THAT CAN'T BE BATMAN!
IT'S THE FACE OF THE-- ELONGATED MAN!
SHORT MOMENTS BEFORE, IN THE STUDIO ITSELF, AS BATMAN STOOD HELPLESS...
THE CHANGE-OVER TAKES PLACE IN HERE AND--OH! OH! LOOKS LIKE BATMAN IS ABOUT TO LOSE HIS FACE-- AND SECRET IDENTITY! I MUST SAFEGUARD IT--
STRETCHING OUT HIS NECK, THE DUCTILE DETECTIVE OFFERED HIS OWN FACE TO THE CAMERA...
IT DOESN'T MAKE ANY DIFFERENCE IF THEY STEAL MY FACE! EVERYONE KNOWS IT--
THE ELONGATED MAN IS SAVING ME FROM THE EFFECT OF THAT FANTASTIC CAMERA!
THEN, MOMENTS LATER...
ROBIN! THE ELONGATED MAN'S UNDERGOING A LOSS OF FACE AND MEMORY! HELP HIM!
WILL DO, BATMAN!
FROM HIS UTILITY BELT, THE GOTHAM GLADIATOR BRINGS OUT SOME FINGERPRINT POWDER AND SCATTERS IT ACROSS THE FLOOR...
PULL YOURSELF TOGETHER, ELONGATED MAN! YOU'RE A GOOD GUY AND-- YOU'VE GOT TO HELP US!
I AM? I DO?
MATTHEW BRADY PHOTOGRAPHY SALON
19

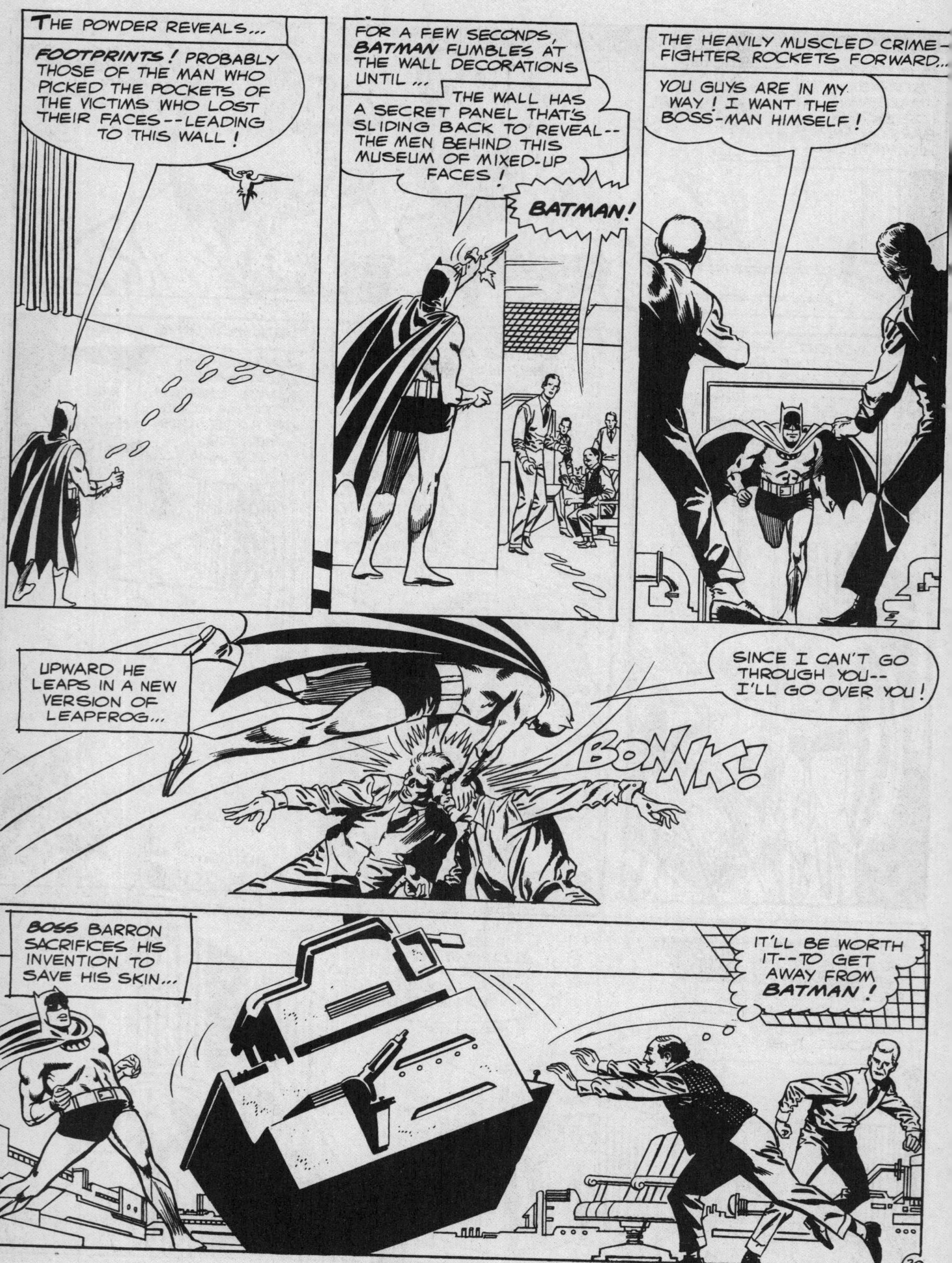
THE POWDER REVEALS...
FOOTPRINTS! PROBABLY THOSE OF THE MAN WHO PICKED THE POCKETS OF THE VICTIMS WHO LOST THEIR FACES--LEADING TO THIS WALL!
FOR A FEW SECONDS, BATMAN FUMBLES AT THE WALL DECORATIONS UNTIL ...
THE WALL HAS A SECRET PANEL THAT'S SLIDING BACK TO REVEAL-- THE MEN BEHIND THIS MUSEUM OF MIXED-UP FACES!
BATMAN!
THE HEAVILY MUSCLED CRIME-FIGHTER ROCKETS FORWARD...
YOU GUYS ARE IN MY WAY! I WANT THE BOSS-MAN HIMSELF!
UPWARD HE LEAPS IN A NEW VERSION OF LEAPFROG...
SINCE I CAN'T GO THROUGH YOU-- I'LL GO OVER YOU!
BONNK!
BOSS BARRON SACRIFICES HIS INVENTION TO SAVE HIS SKIN...
IT'LL BE WORTH IT--TO GET AWAY FROM BATMAN!
20

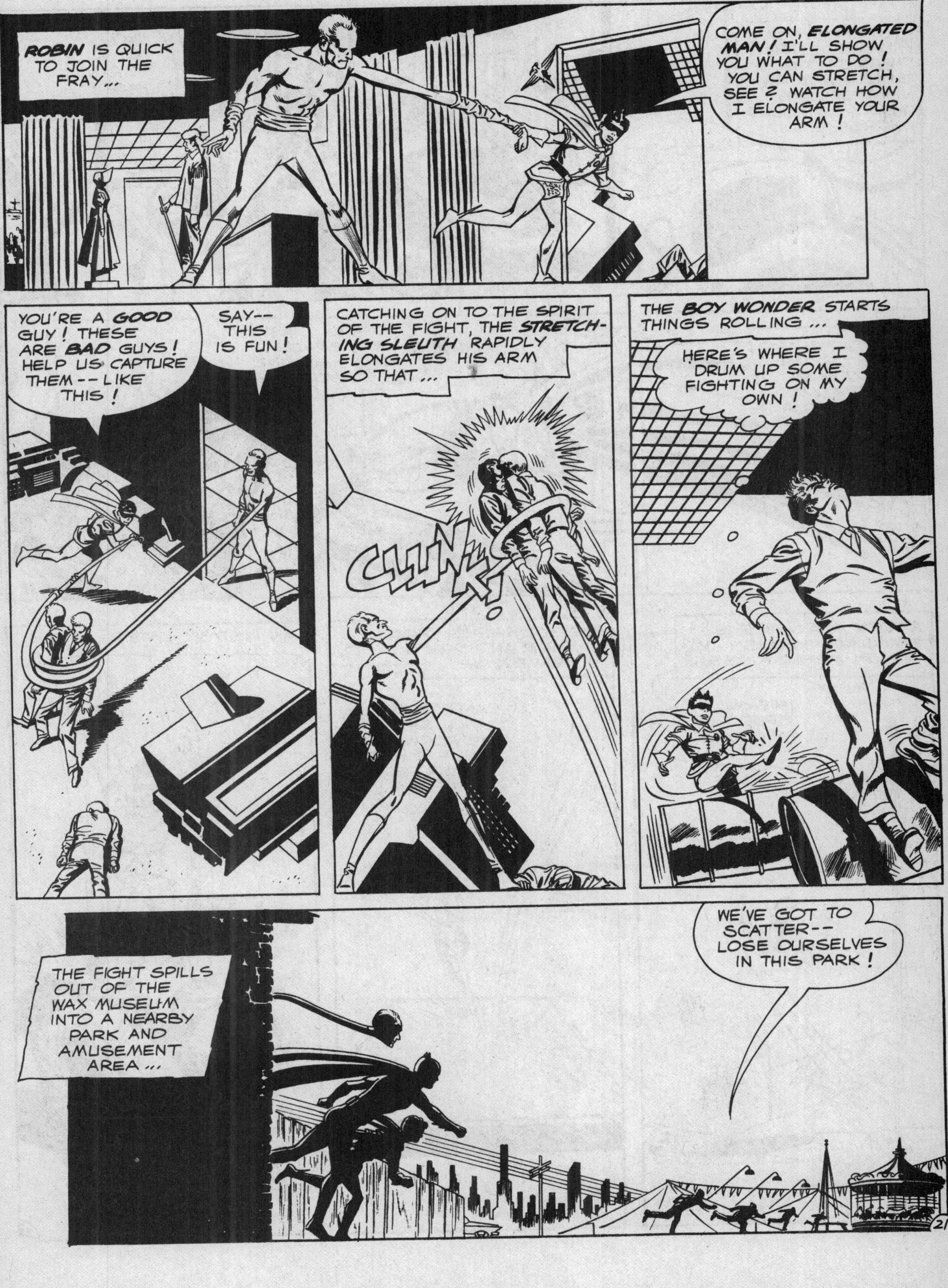
ROBIN IS QUICK TO JOIN THE FRAY...
COME ON, ELONGATED MAN! I'LL SHOW YOU WHAT TO DO! YOU CAN STRETCH, SEE? WATCH HOW I ELONGATE YOUR ARM!
YOU'RE A GOOD GUY! THESE ARE BAD GUYS! HELP US CAPTURE THEM--LIKE THIS!
SAY--THIS IS FUN!
CATCHING ON TO THE SPIRIT OF THE FIGHT, THE STRETCHING SLEUTH RAPIDLY ELONGATES HIS ARM SO THAT...
CLUNK!
THE BOY WONDER STARTS THINGS ROLLING...
HERE'S WHERE I DRUM UP SOME FIGHTING ON MY OWN!
THE FIGHT SPILLS OUT OF THE WAX MUSEUM INTO A NEARBY PARK AND AMUSEMENT AREA...
WE'VE GOT TO SCATTER--LOSE OURSELVES IN THIS PARK!
21

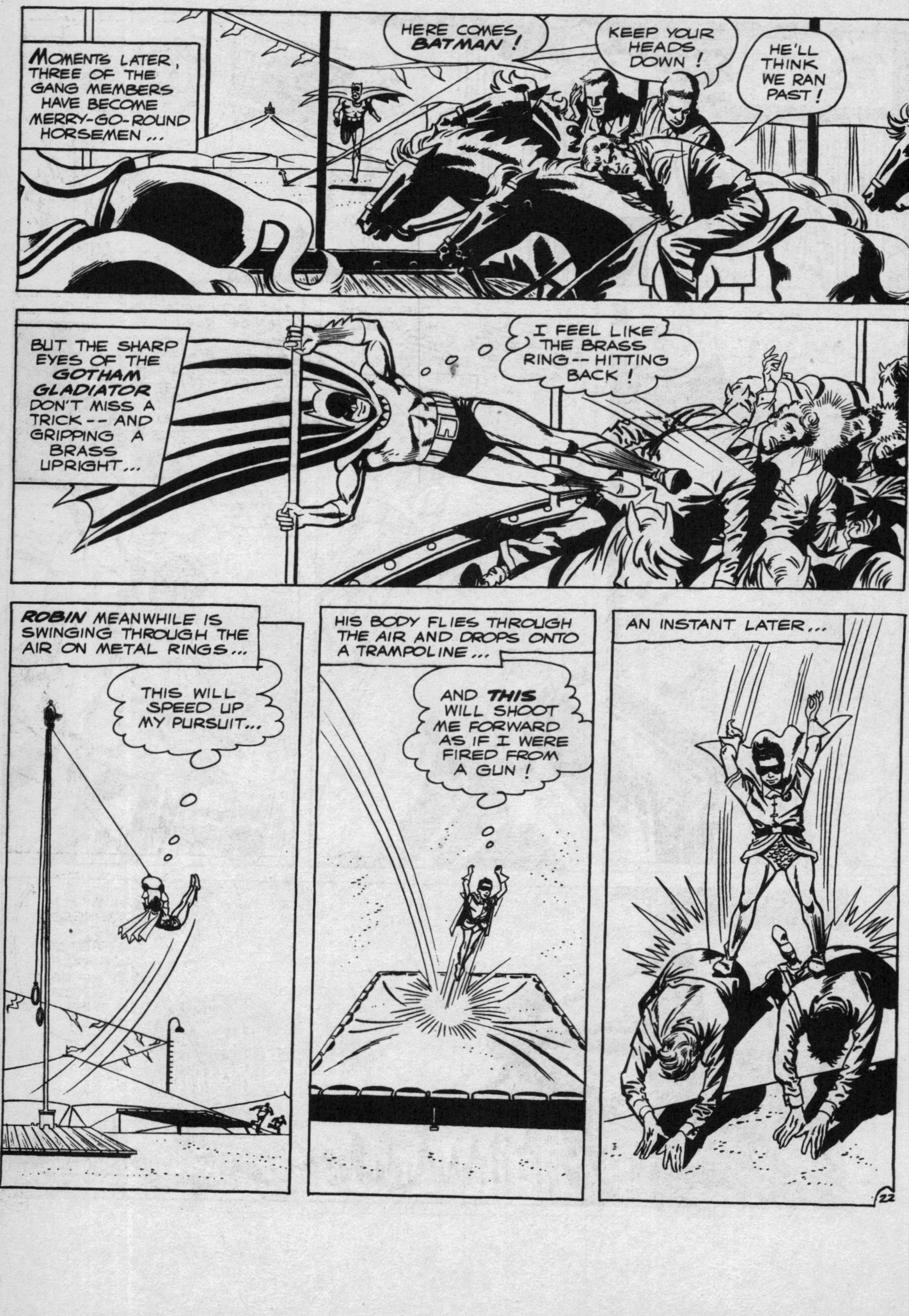
MOMENTS LATER, THREE OF THE GANG MEMBERS HAVE BECOME MERRY-GO-ROUND HORSEMEN...
HERE COMES, BATMAN!
KEEP YOUR HEADS DOWN!
HE'LL THINK WE RAN PAST!
BUT THE SHARP EYES OF THE GOTHAM GLADIATOR DON'T MISS A TRICK-- AND GRIPPING A BRASS UPRIGHT...
I FEEL LIKE THE BRASS RING-- HITTING BACK!
ROBIN MEANWHILE IS SWINGING THROUGH THE AIR ON METAL RINGS...
THIS WILL SPEED UP MY PURSUIT...
HIS BODY FLIES THROUGH THE AIR AND DROPS ONTO A TRAMPOLINE...
AND THIS WILL SHOOT ME FORWARD AS IF I WERE FIRED FROM A GUN!
AN INSTANT LATER...
22

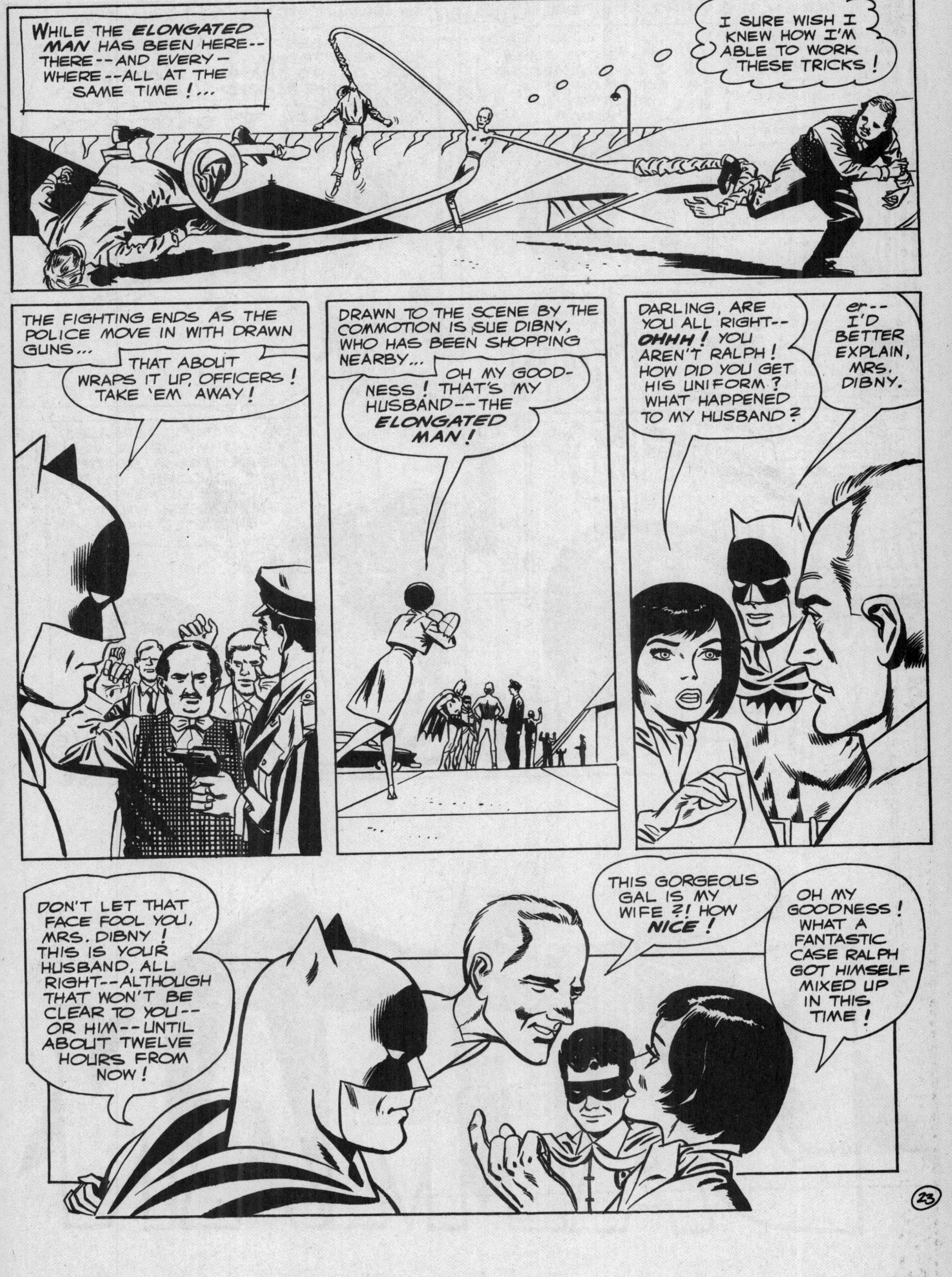
WHILE THE ELONGATED MAN HAS BEEN HERE-- THERE--AND EVERY- WHERE--ALL AT THE SAME TIME!...
I SURE WISH I KNEW HOW I'M ABLE TO WORK THESE TRICKS!
THE FIGHTING ENDS AS THE POLICE MOVE IN WITH DRAWN GUNS...
THAT ABOUT WRAPS IT UP, OFFICERS! TAKE 'EM AWAY!
DRAWN TO THE SCENE BY THE COMMOTION IS SUE DIBNY, WHO HAS BEEN SHOPPING NEARBY...
OH MY GOOD- NESS! THAT'S MY HUSBAND--THE ELONGATED MAN!
DARLING, ARE YOU ALL RIGHT-- OHHH! YOU AREN'T RALPH! HOW DID YOU GET HIS UNIFORM? WHAT HAPPENED TO MY HUSBAND?
er-- I'D BETTER EXPLAIN, MRS. DIBNY.
DON'T LET THAT FACE FOOL YOU, MRS. DIBNY! THIS IS YOUR HUSBAND, ALL RIGHT--ALTHOUGH THAT WON'T BE CLEAR TO YOU-- OR HIM--UNTIL ABOUT TWELVE HOURS FROM NOW!
THIS GORGEOUS GAL IS MY WIFE?! HOW NICE!
OH MY GOODNESS! WHAT A FANTASTIC CASE RALPH GOT HIMSELF MIXED UP IN THIS TIME!
23

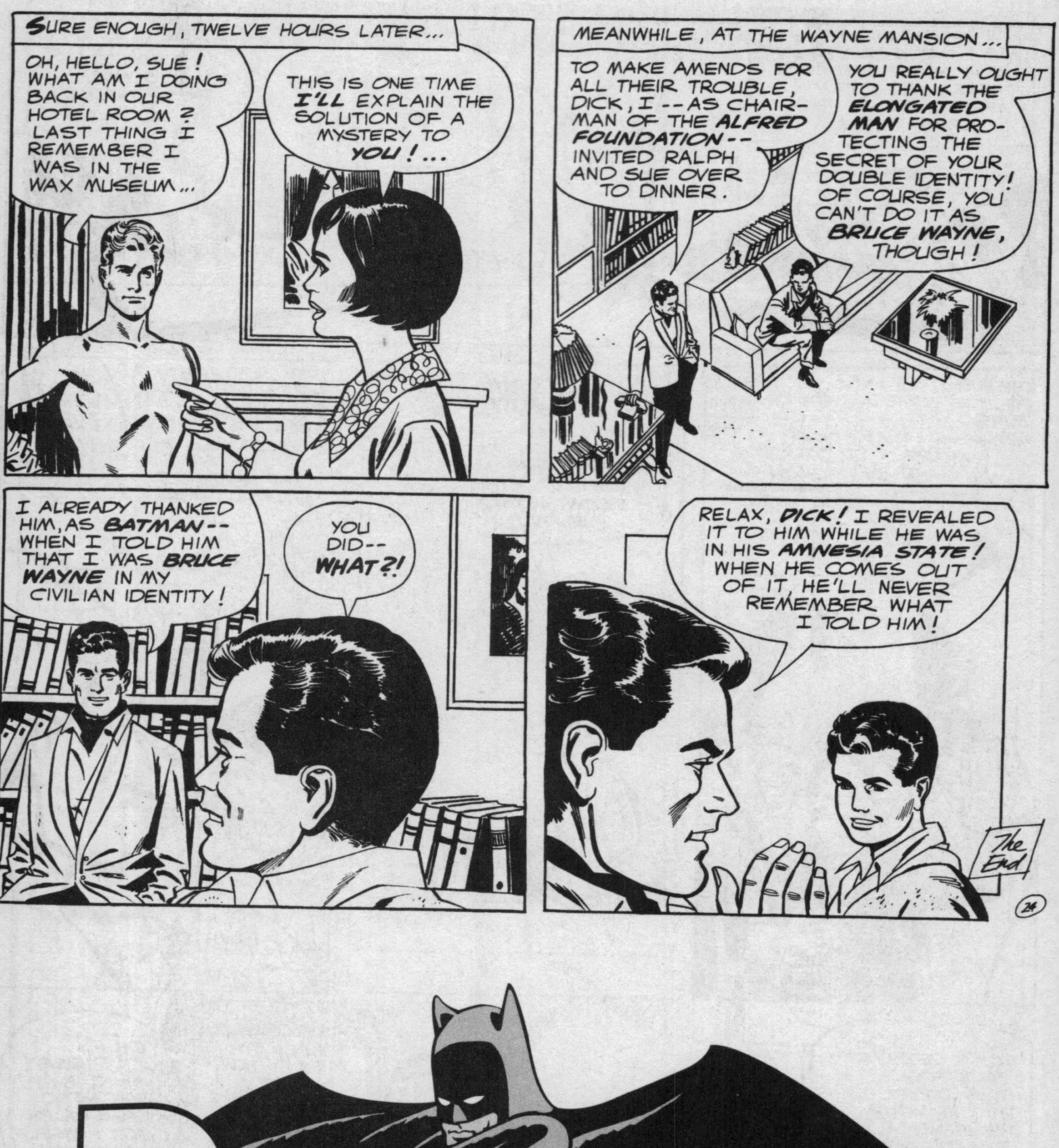
SURE ENOUGH, TWELVE HOURS LATER...
OH, HELLO, SUE! WHAT AM I DOING BACK IN OUR HOTEL ROOM? LAST THING I REMEMBER I WAS IN THE WAX MUSEUM...
THIS IS ONE TIME I'LL EXPLAIN THE SOLUTION OF A MYSTERY TO YOU!...
MEANWHILE, AT THE WAYNE MANSION...
TO MAKE AMENDS FOR ALL THEIR TROUBLE, DICK, I -- AS CHAIRMAN OF THE ALFRED FOUNDATION -- INVITED RALPH AND SUE OVER TO DINNER.
YOU REALLY OUGHT TO THANK THE ELONGATED MAN FOR PROTECTING THE SECRET OF YOUR DOUBLE IDENTITY! OF COURSE, YOU CAN'T DO IT AS BRUCE WAYNE, THOUGH!
I ALREADY THANKED HIM, AS BATMAN -- WHEN I TOLD HIM THAT I WAS BRUCE WAYNE IN MY CIVILIAN IDENTITY!
YOU DID-- WHAT?!
RELAX, DICK! I REVEALED IT TO HIM WHILE HE WAS IN HIS AMNESIA STATE! WHEN HE COMES OUT OF IT, HE'LL NEVER REMEMBER WHAT I TOLD HIM!
The End
24

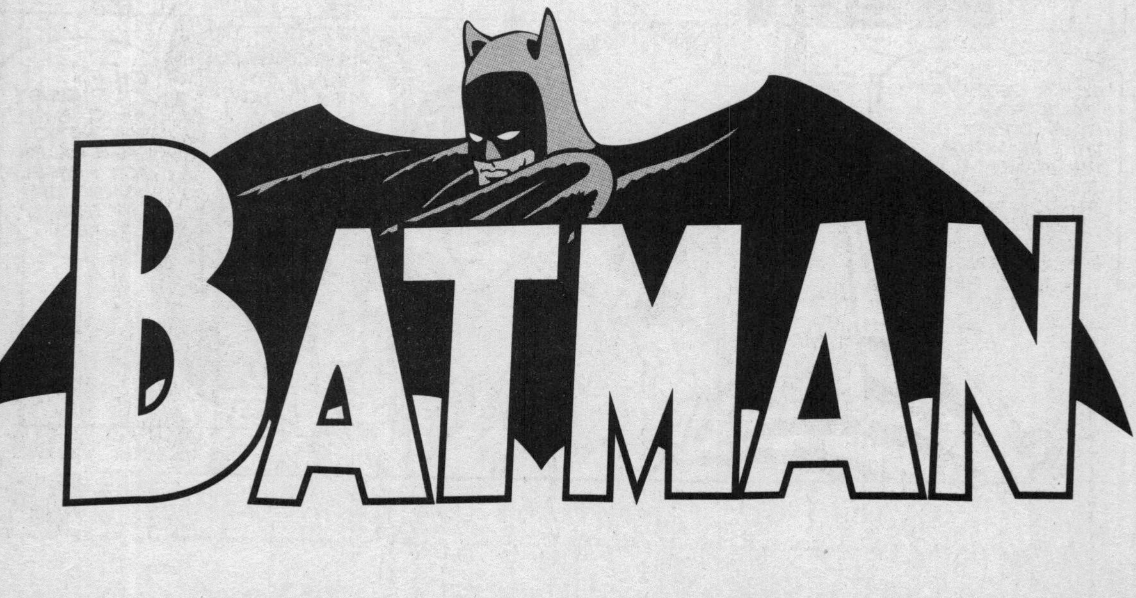
BATMAN

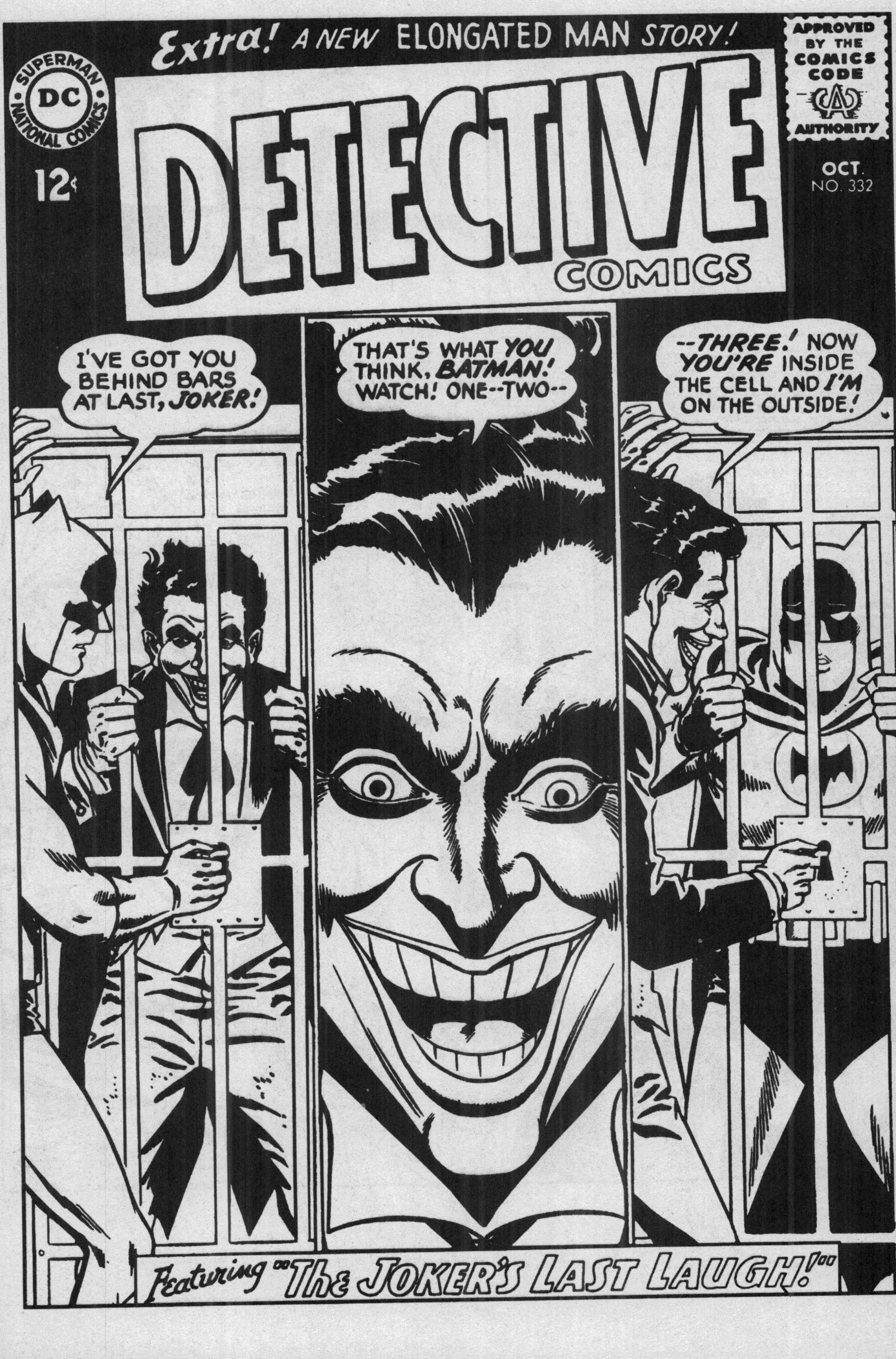
Extra! A NEW ELONGATED MAN STORY!
SUPERMAN DC NATIONAL COMICS
12¢
DETECTIVE COMICS
APPROVED BY THE COMICS CODE AUTHORITY
OCT. NO. 332
I'VE GOT YOU BEHIND BARS AT LAST, JOKER!
THAT'S WHAT YOU THINK, BATMAN! WATCH! ONE--TWO--
--THREE! NOW YOU'RE INSIDE THE CELL AND I'M ON THE OUTSIDE!
Featuring "The JOKER'S LAST LAUGH!"

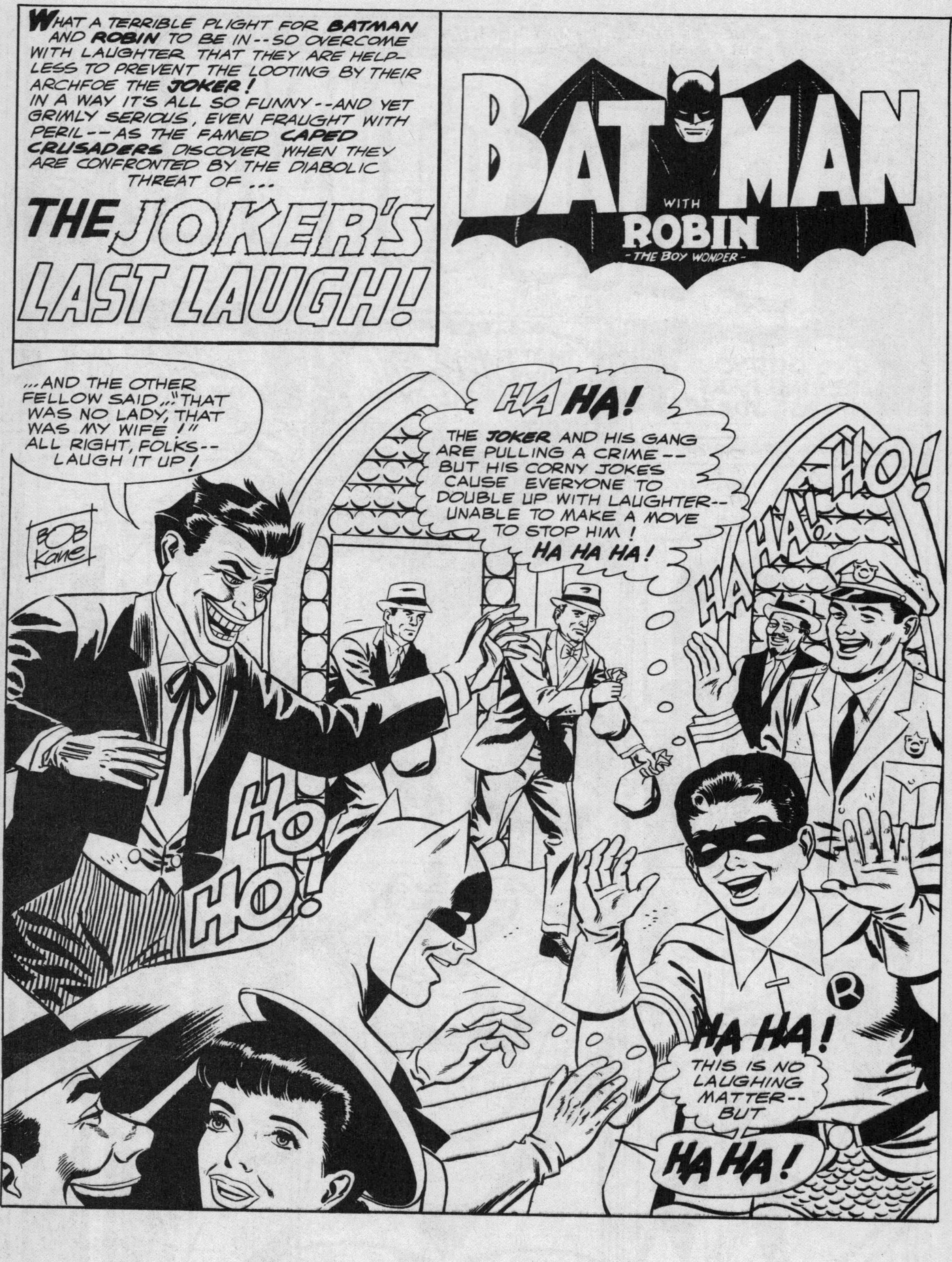
WHAT A TERRIBLE PLIGHT FOR BATMAN AND ROBIN TO BE IN--SO OVERCOME WITH LAUGHTER THAT THEY ARE HELPLESS TO PREVENT THE LOOTING BY THEIR ARCHFOE THE JOKER! IN A WAY IT'S ALL SO FUNNY--AND YET GRIMLY SERIOUS, EVEN FRAUGHT WITH PERIL--AS THE FAMED CAPED CRUSADERS DISCOVER WHEN THEY ARE CONFRONTED BY THE DIABOLIC THREAT OF ...
THE JOKER'S LAST LAUGH!
BATMAN WITH ROBIN THE BOY WONDER
...AND THE OTHER FELLOW SAID..."THAT WAS NO LADY, THAT WAS MY WIFE!" ALL RIGHT, FOLKS--LAUGH IT UP!
BOB KANE
HA HA! THE JOKER AND HIS GANG ARE PULLING A CRIME--BUT HIS CORNY JOKES CAUSE EVERYONE TO DOUBLE UP WITH LAUGHTER--UNABLE TO MAKE A MOVE TO STOP HIM! HA HA HA!
HA HA HO HO!
HO HO!
HA HA! THIS IS NO LAUGHING MATTER--BUT HA HA!

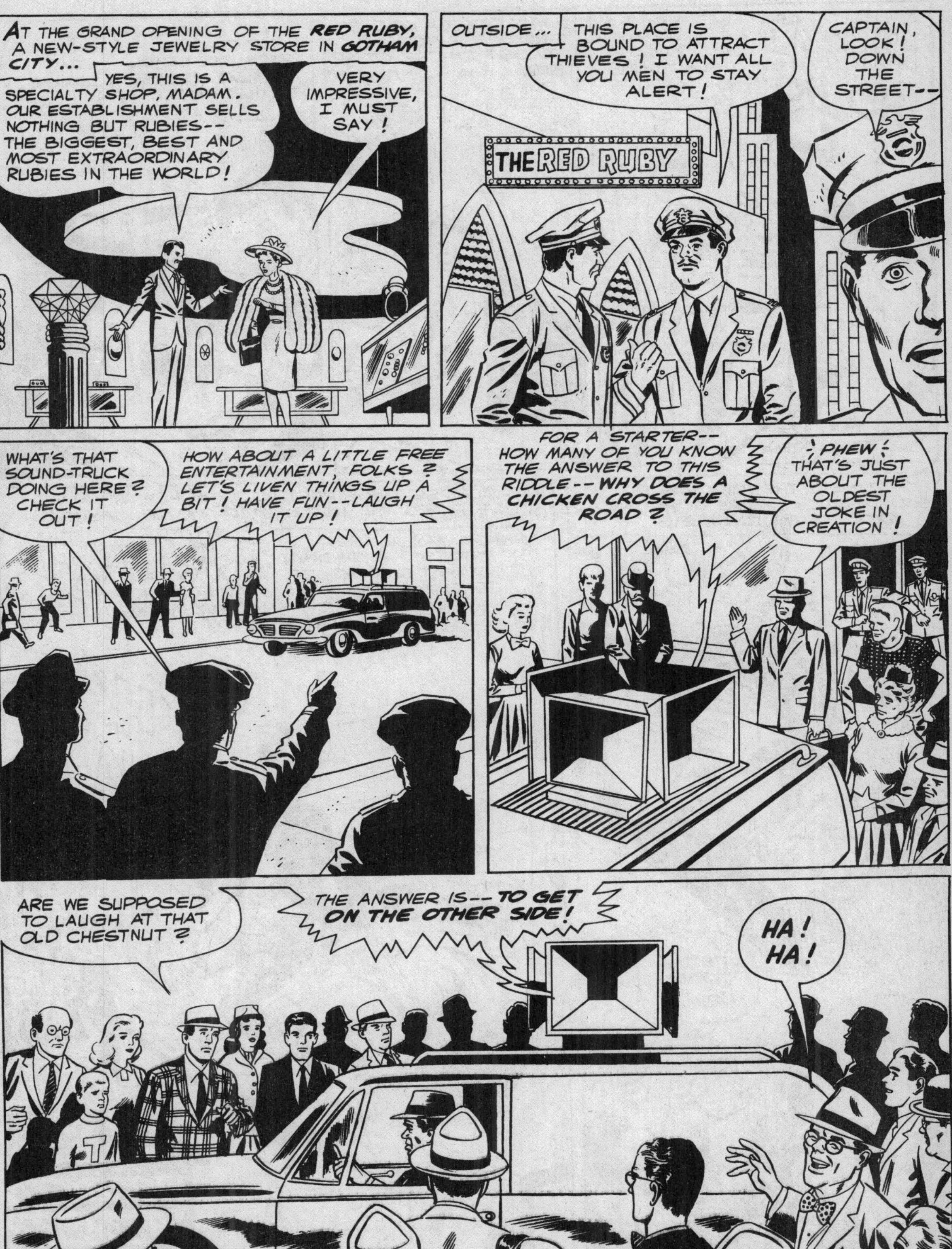
AT THE GRAND OPENING OF THE RED RUBY, A NEW-STYLE JEWELRY STORE IN GOTHAM CITY...
YES, THIS IS A SPECIALTY SHOP, MADAM. OUR ESTABLISHMENT SELLS NOTHING BUT RUBIES-- THE BIGGEST, BEST AND MOST EXTRAORDINARY RUBIES IN THE WORLD!
VERY IMPRESSIVE, I MUST SAY!
OUTSIDE...
THIS PLACE IS BOUND TO ATTRACT THIEVES! I WANT ALL YOU MEN TO STAY ALERT!
THE RED RUBY
CAPTAIN, LOOK! DOWN THE STREET--
WHAT'S THAT SOUND-TRUCK DOING HERE? CHECK IT OUT!
HOW ABOUT A LITTLE FREE ENTERTAINMENT, FOLKS? LET'S LIVEN THINGS UP A BIT! HAVE FUN--LAUGH IT UP!
FOR A STARTER-- HOW MANY OF YOU KNOW THE ANSWER TO THIS RIDDLE--WHY DOES A CHICKEN CROSS THE ROAD?
PHEW! THAT'S JUST ABOUT THE OLDEST JOKE IN CREATION!
ARE WE SUPPOSED TO LAUGH AT THAT OLD CHESTNUT?
THE ANSWER IS-- TO GET ON THE OTHER SIDE!
HA! HA!
2

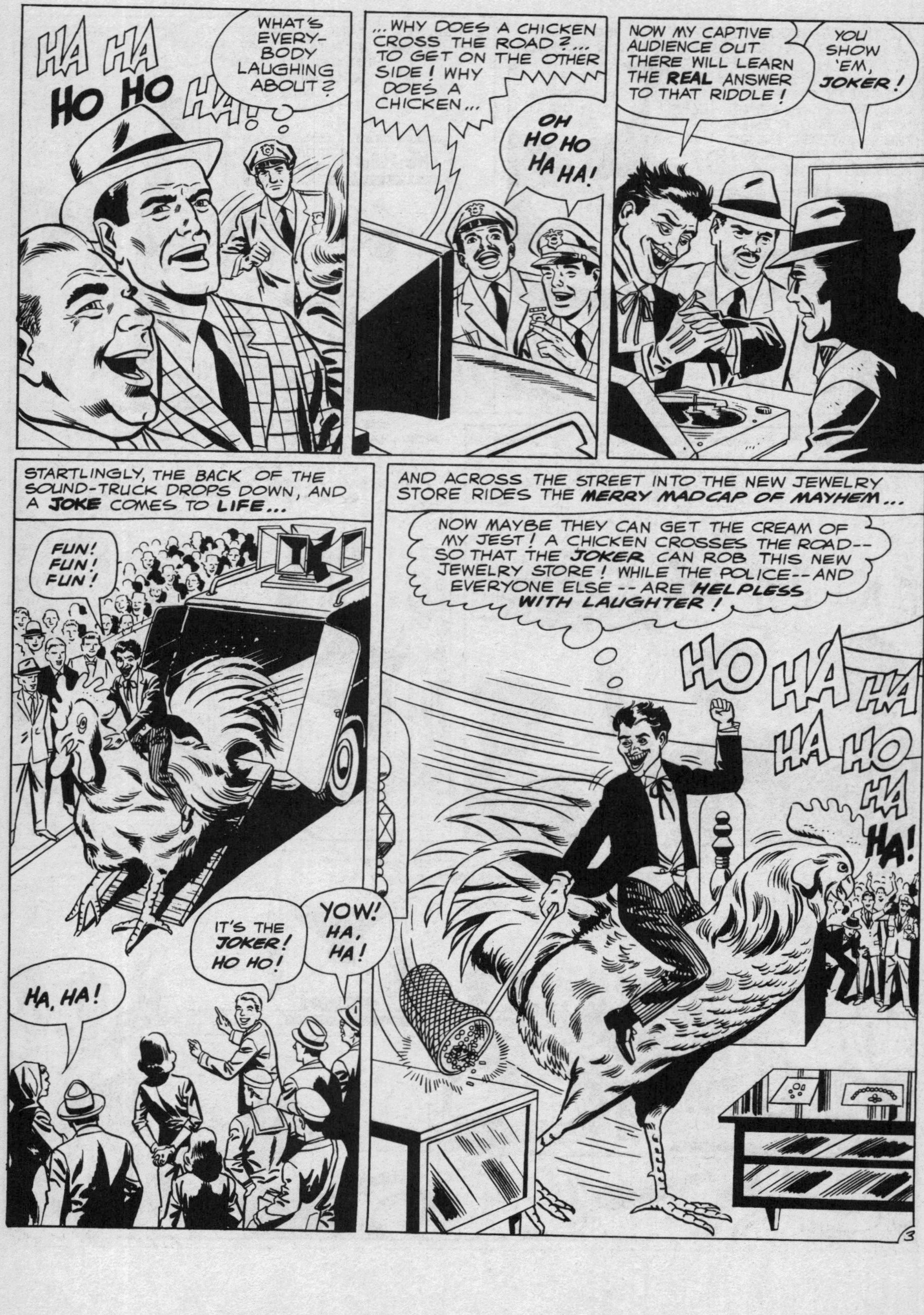
HA HA HO HO HA!
WHAT'S EVERYBODY LAUGHING ABOUT?
...WHY DOES A CHICKEN CROSS THE ROAD?... TO GET ON THE OTHER SIDE! WHY DOES A CHICKEN...
OH HO HO HA HA!
NOW MY CAPTIVE AUDIENCE OUT THERE WILL LEARN THE **REAL** ANSWER TO THAT RIDDLE!
YOU SHOW 'EM, JOKER!
STARTLINGLY, THE BACK OF THE SOUND-TRUCK DROPS DOWN, AND A **JOKE** COMES TO **LIFE**...
FUN! FUN! FUN!
IT'S THE JOKER! HO HO!
YOW! HA, HA!
HA, HA!
AND ACROSS THE STREET INTO THE NEW JEWELRY STORE RIDES THE ***MERRY MADCAP OF MAYHEM***...
NOW MAYBE THEY CAN GET THE CREAM OF MY JEST! A CHICKEN CROSSES THE ROAD-- SO THAT THE **JOKER** CAN ROB THIS NEW JEWELRY STORE! WHILE THE POLICE--AND EVERYONE ELSE--ARE **HELPLESS WITH LAUGHTER**!
HO HA HA HA HO HA HA!
3

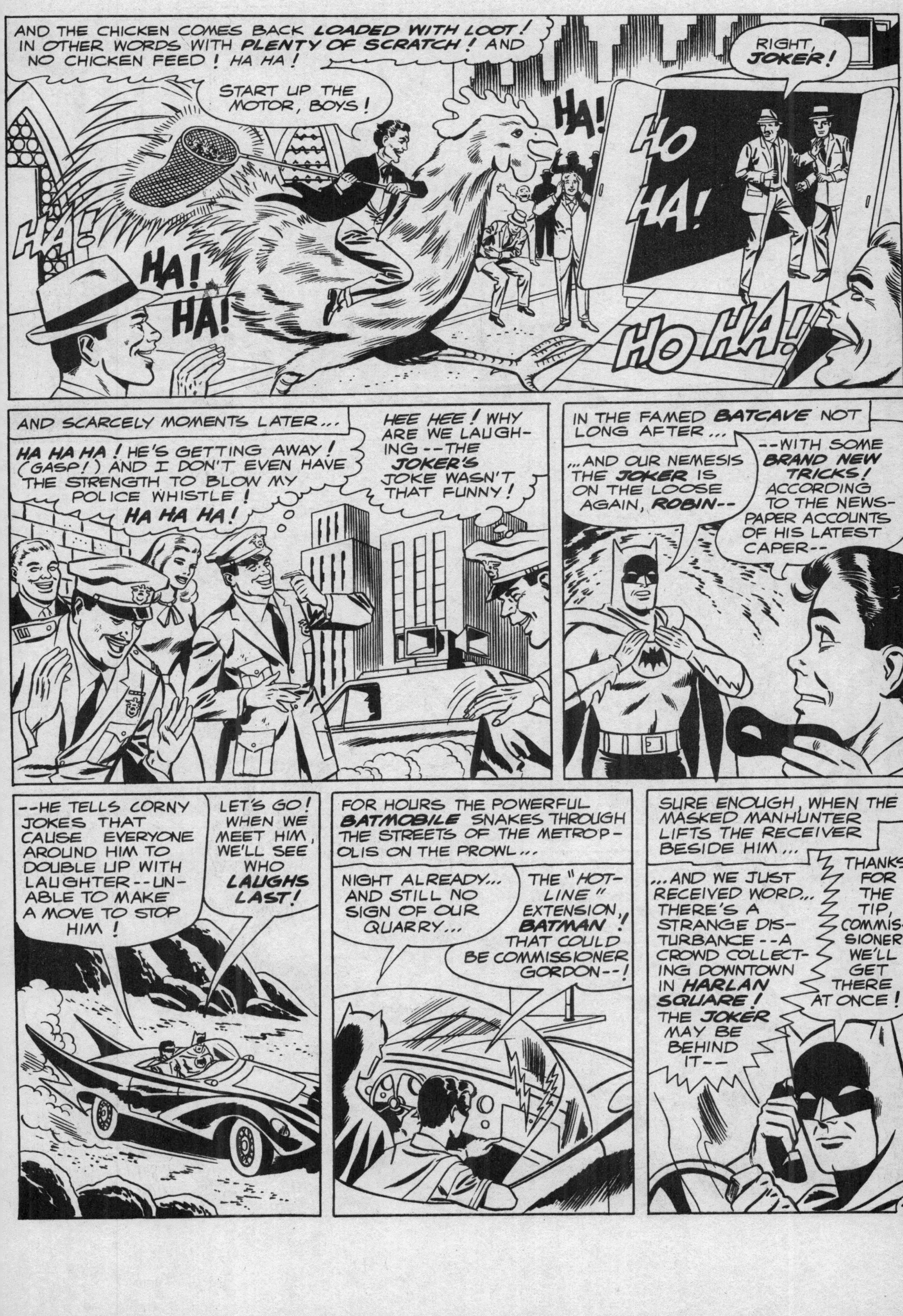
AND THE CHICKEN COMES BACK LOADED WITH LOOT! IN OTHER WORDS WITH PLENTY OF SCRATCH! AND NO CHICKEN FEED! HA HA!
START UP THE MOTOR, BOYS!
RIGHT, JOKER!
HA!
HO HA!
HA! HA! HA!
HO HA!
AND SCARCELY MOMENTS LATER...
HA HA HA! HE'S GETTING AWAY! (GASP!) AND I DON'T EVEN HAVE THE STRENGTH TO BLOW MY POLICE WHISTLE! HA HA HA!
HEE HEE! WHY ARE WE LAUGHING--THE JOKER'S JOKE WASN'T THAT FUNNY!
IN THE FAMED BATCAVE NOT LONG AFTER...
...AND OUR NEMESIS THE JOKER IS ON THE LOOSE AGAIN, ROBIN--
--WITH SOME BRAND NEW TRICKS! ACCORDING TO THE NEWSPAPER ACCOUNTS OF HIS LATEST CAPER--
--HE TELLS CORNY JOKES THAT CAUSE EVERYONE AROUND HIM TO DOUBLE UP WITH LAUGHTER--UNABLE TO MAKE A MOVE TO STOP HIM!
LET'S GO! WHEN WE MEET HIM, WE'LL SEE WHO LAUGHS LAST!
FOR HOURS THE POWERFUL BATMOBILE SNAKES THROUGH THE STREETS OF THE METROPOLIS ON THE PROWL...
NIGHT ALREADY... AND STILL NO SIGN OF OUR QUARRY...
THE "HOT-LINE" EXTENSION, BATMAN! THAT COULD BE COMMISSIONER GORDON--!
SURE ENOUGH, WHEN THE MASKED MANHUNTER LIFTS THE RECEIVER BESIDE HIM...
...AND WE JUST RECEIVED WORD... THERE'S A STRANGE DISTURBANCE--A CROWD COLLECTING DOWNTOWN IN HARLAN SQUARE! THE JOKER MAY BE BEHIND IT--
THANKS FOR THE TIP, COMMISSIONER! WE'LL GET THERE AT ONCE!
4

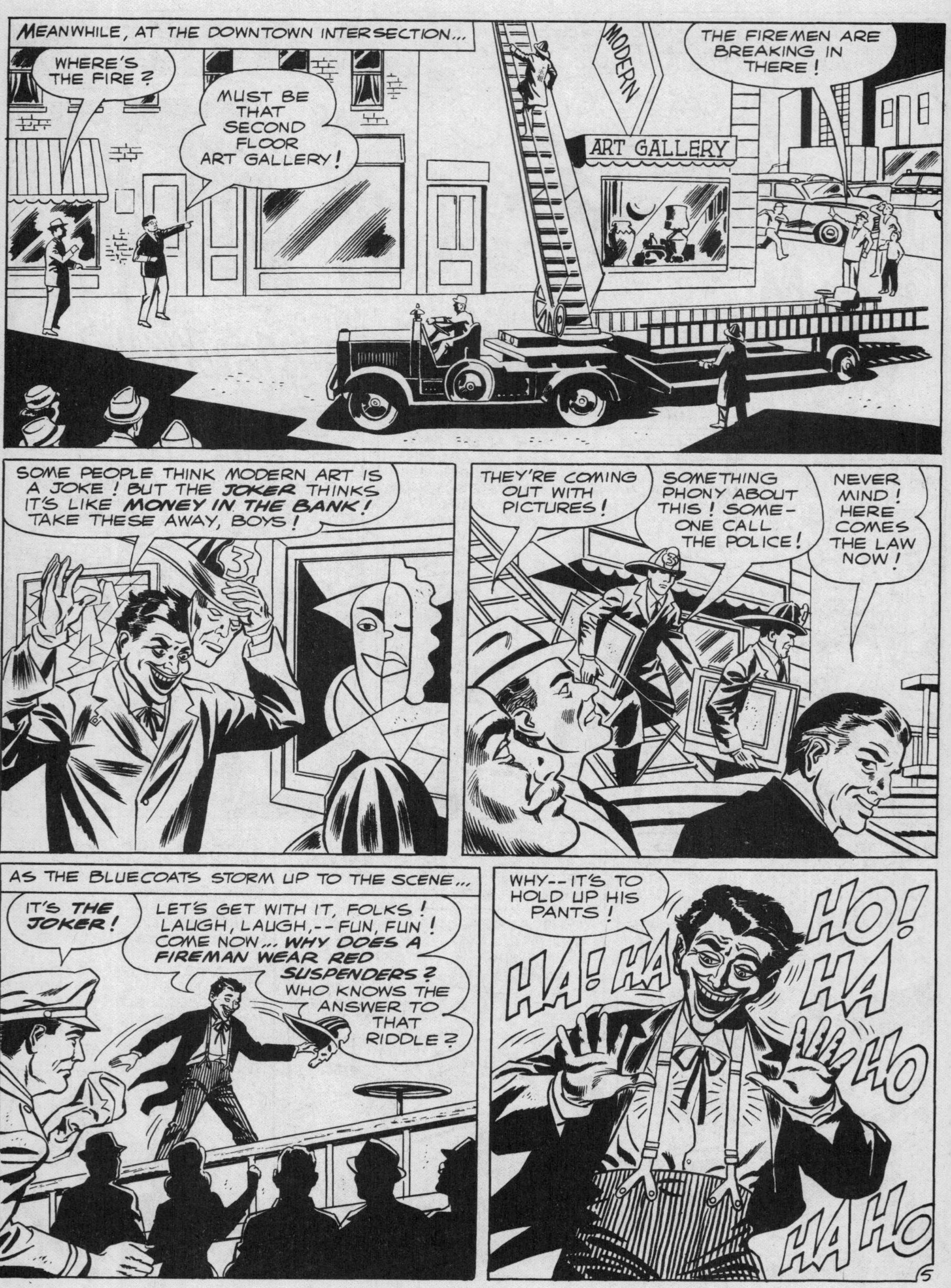
MEANWHILE, AT THE DOWNTOWN INTERSECTION...
WHERE'S THE FIRE?
MUST BE THAT SECOND FLOOR ART GALLERY!
MODERN
ART GALLERY
THE FIREMEN ARE BREAKING IN THERE!
SOME PEOPLE THINK MODERN ART IS A JOKE! BUT THE JOKER THINKS IT'S LIKE MONEY IN THE BANK! TAKE THESE AWAY, BOYS!
THEY'RE COMING OUT WITH PICTURES!
SOMETHING PHONY ABOUT THIS! SOME-ONE CALL THE POLICE!
NEVER MIND! HERE COMES THE LAW NOW!
AS THE BLUECOATS STORM UP TO THE SCENE...
IT'S THE JOKER!
LET'S GET WITH IT, FOLKS! LAUGH, LAUGH,--FUN, FUN! COME NOW... WHY DOES A FIREMAN WEAR RED SUSPENDERS? WHO KNOWS THE ANSWER TO THAT RIDDLE?
WHY--IT'S TO HOLD UP HIS PANTS!
HA! HA
HO! HA
HA HO
HA HO

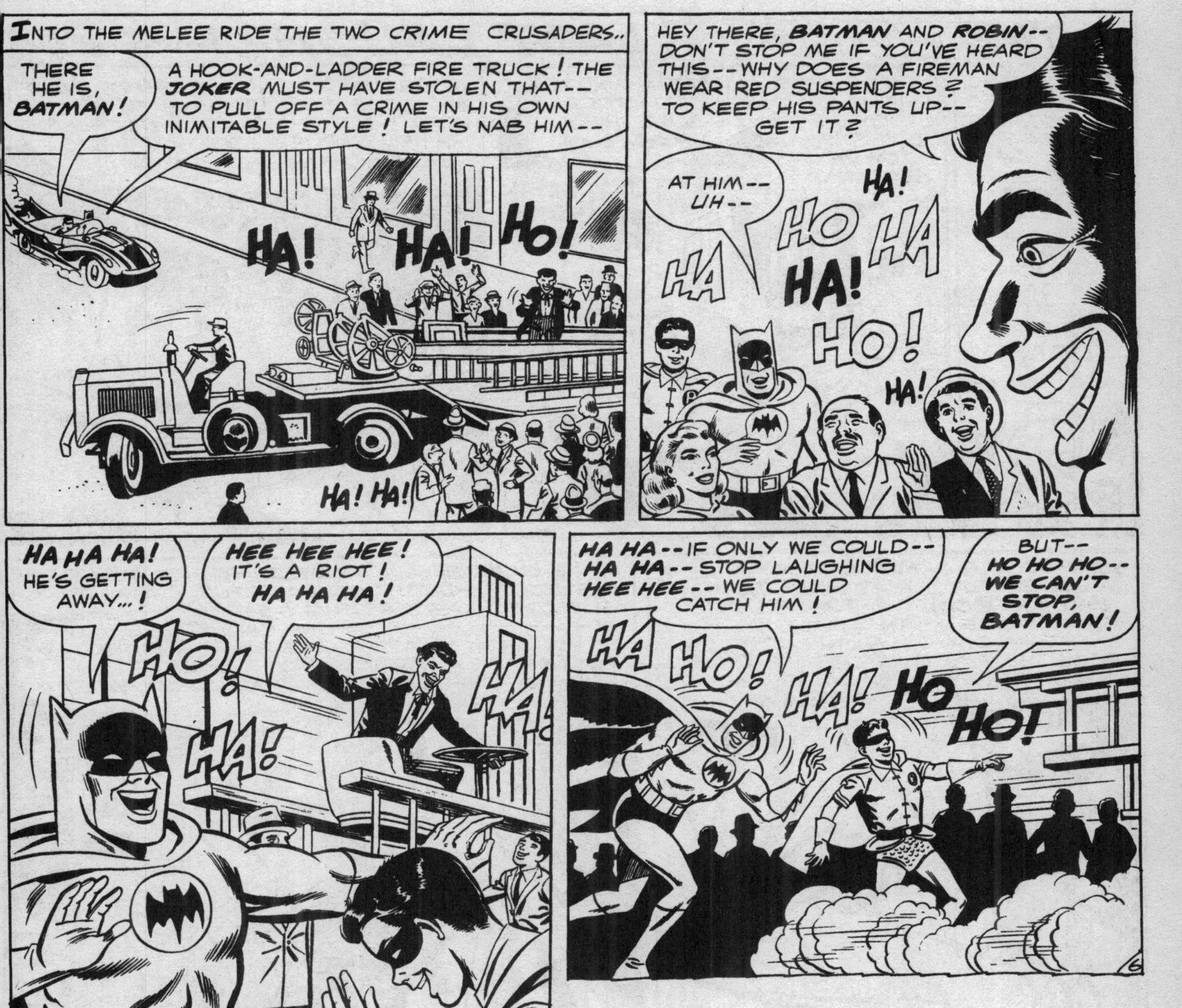
INTO THE MELEE RIDE THE TWO CRIME CRUSADERS..
THERE HE IS, BATMAN!
A HOOK-AND-LADDER FIRE TRUCK! THE JOKER MUST HAVE STOLEN THAT-- TO PULL OFF A CRIME IN HIS OWN INIMITABLE STYLE! LET'S NAB HIM--
HA! HA! HO!
HA! HA!
HEY THERE, BATMAN AND ROBIN-- DON'T STOP ME IF YOU'VE HEARD THIS--WHY DOES A FIREMAN WEAR RED SUSPENDERS? TO KEEP HIS PANTS UP-- GET IT?
AT HIM-- UH--
HA HO HA! HA HA! HO! HA!
HA HA HA! HE'S GETTING AWAY...!
HEE HEE HEE! IT'S A RIOT! HA HA HA!
HO! HA! HA!
HA HA--IF ONLY WE COULD-- HA HA-- STOP LAUGHING HEE HEE-- WE COULD CATCH HIM!
BUT-- HO HO HO-- WE CAN'T STOP, BATMAN!
HA HO! HA! HO HO!
6

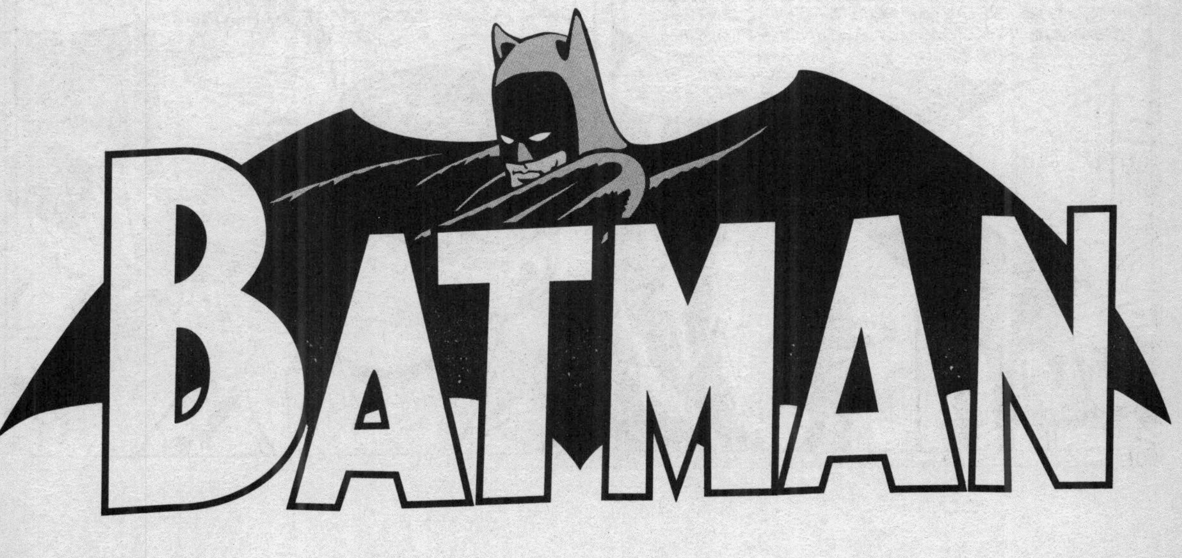
BATMAN

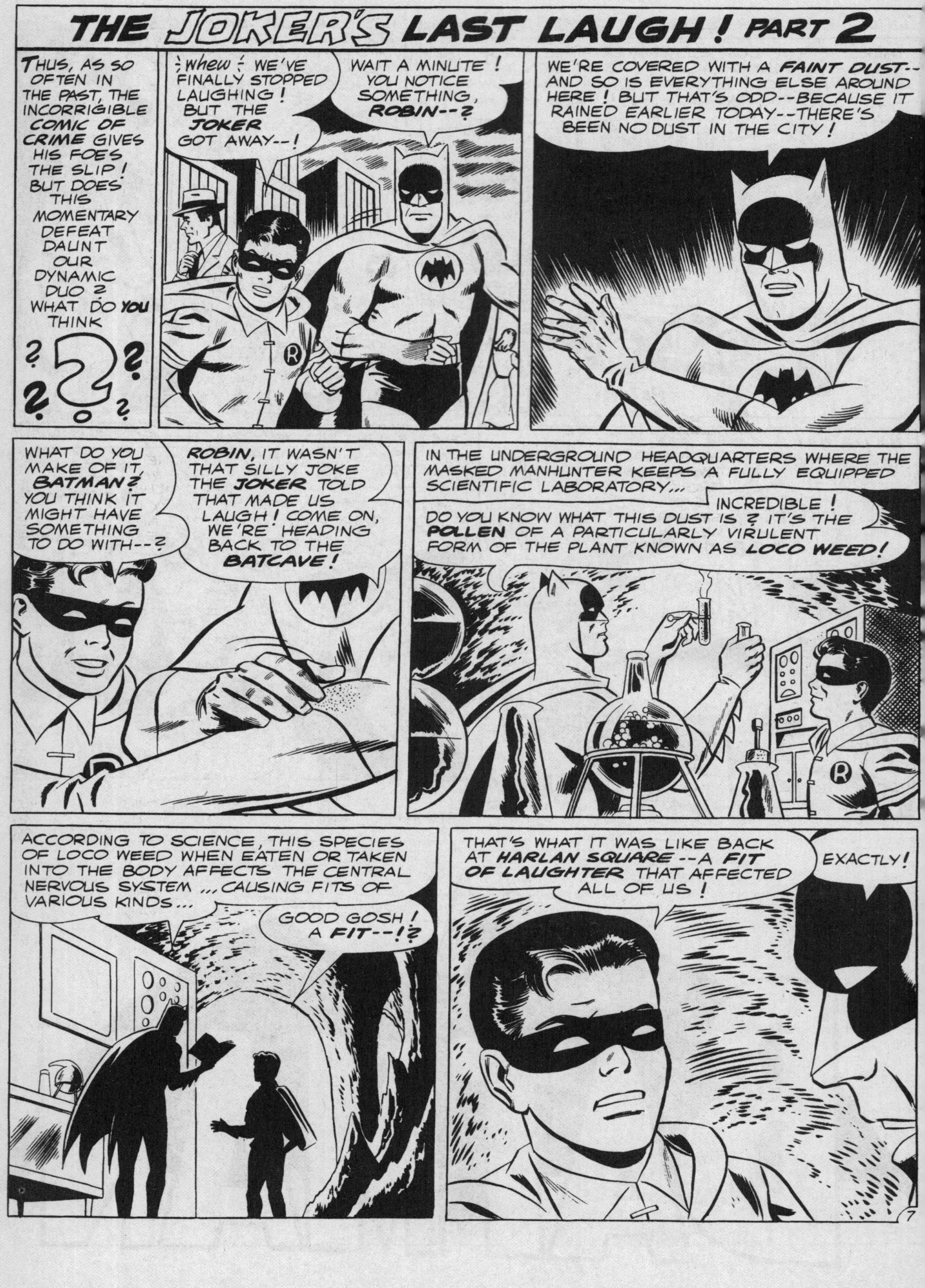
THE JOKER'S LAST LAUGH! PART 2
THUS, AS SO OFTEN IN THE PAST, THE INCORRIGIBLE COMIC OF CRIME GIVES HIS FOES THE SLIP! BUT DOES THIS MOMENTARY DEFEAT DAUNT OUR DYNAMIC DUO? WHAT DO YOU THINK
? ? ? ? ?
WHEW! WE'VE FINALLY STOPPED LAUGHING! BUT THE JOKER GOT AWAY--!
WAIT A MINUTE! YOU NOTICE SOMETHING, ROBIN--?
WE'RE COVERED WITH A FAINT DUST--AND SO IS EVERYTHING ELSE AROUND HERE! BUT THAT'S ODD--BECAUSE IT RAINED EARLIER TODAY--THERE'S BEEN NO DUST IN THE CITY!
WHAT DO YOU MAKE OF IT, BATMAN? YOU THINK IT MIGHT HAVE SOMETHING TO DO WITH--?
ROBIN, IT WASN'T THAT SILLY JOKE THE JOKER TOLD THAT MADE US LAUGH! COME ON, WE'RE HEADING BACK TO THE BATCAVE!
IN THE UNDERGROUND HEADQUARTERS WHERE THE MASKED MANHUNTER KEEPS A FULLY EQUIPPED SCIENTIFIC LABORATORY...
INCREDIBLE! DO YOU KNOW WHAT THIS DUST IS? IT'S THE POLLEN OF A PARTICULARLY VIRULENT FORM OF THE PLANT KNOWN AS LOCO WEED!
ACCORDING TO SCIENCE, THIS SPECIES OF LOCO WEED WHEN EATEN OR TAKEN INTO THE BODY AFFECTS THE CENTRAL NERVOUS SYSTEM ... CAUSING FITS OF VARIOUS KINDS...
GOOD GOSH! A FIT--!?
THAT'S WHAT IT WAS LIKE BACK AT HARLAN SQUARE--A FIT OF LAUGHTER THAT AFFECTED ALL OF US!
EXACTLY!
7

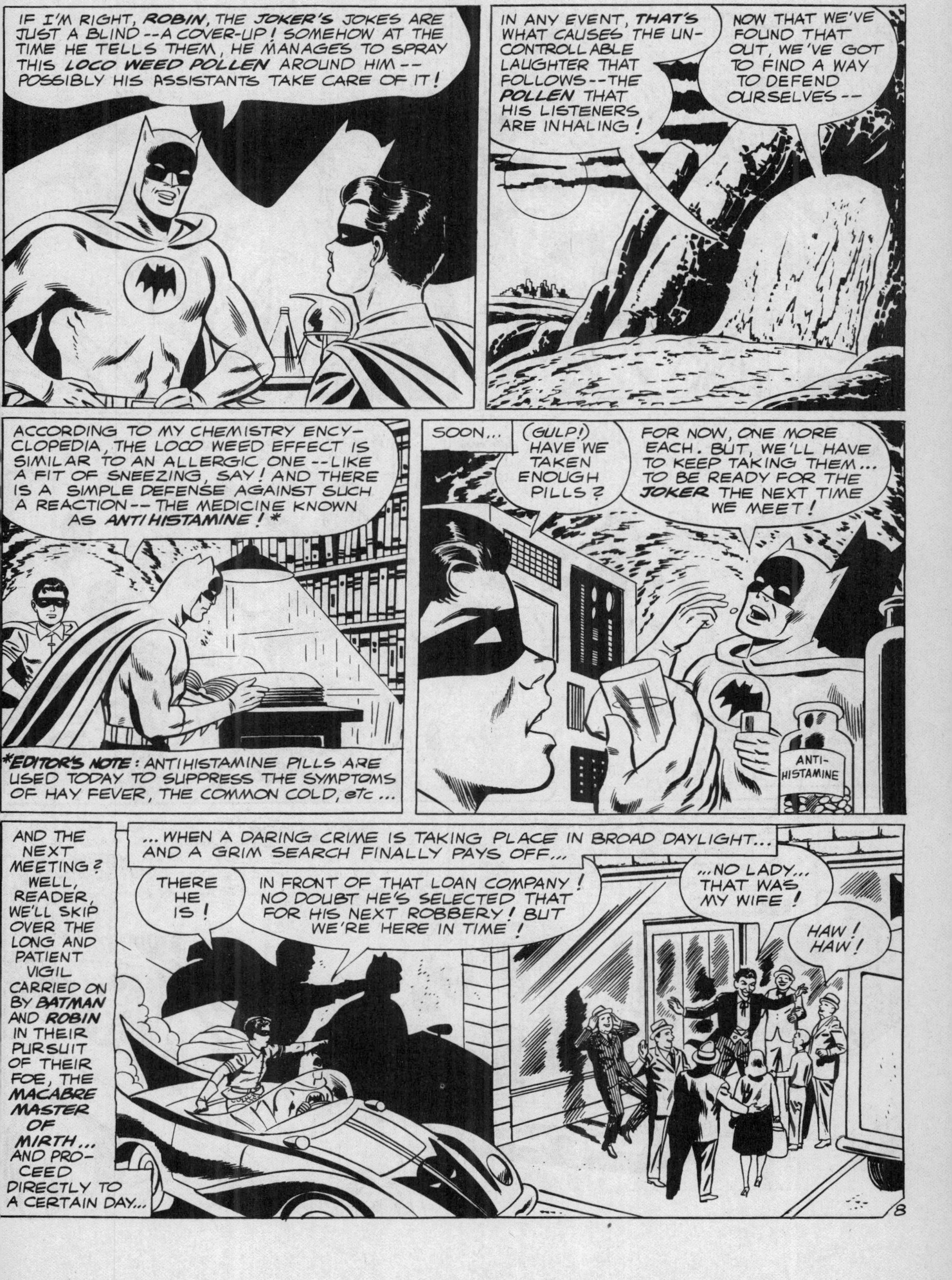
IF I'M RIGHT, ROBIN, THE JOKER'S JOKES ARE JUST A BLIND--A COVER-UP! SOMEHOW AT THE TIME HE TELLS THEM, HE MANAGES TO SPRAY THIS LOCO WEED POLLEN AROUND HIM--POSSIBLY HIS ASSISTANTS TAKE CARE OF IT!
IN ANY EVENT, THAT'S WHAT CAUSES THE UN-CONTROLLABLE LAUGHTER THAT FOLLOWS--THE POLLEN THAT HIS LISTENERS ARE INHALING!
NOW THAT WE'VE FOUND THAT OUT, WE'VE GOT TO FIND A WAY TO DEFEND OURSELVES--
ACCORDING TO MY CHEMISTRY ENCY-CLOPEDIA, THE LOCO WEED EFFECT IS SIMILAR TO AN ALLERGIC ONE--LIKE A FIT OF SNEEZING, SAY! AND THERE IS A SIMPLE DEFENSE AGAINST SUCH A REACTION--THE MEDICINE KNOWN AS ANTIHISTAMINE!*
*EDITOR'S NOTE: ANTIHISTAMINE PILLS ARE USED TODAY TO SUPPRESS THE SYMPTOMS OF HAY FEVER, THE COMMON COLD, etc...
SOON...
(GULP!) HAVE WE TAKEN ENOUGH PILLS?
FOR NOW, ONE MORE EACH. BUT, WE'LL HAVE TO KEEP TAKING THEM... TO BE READY FOR THE JOKER THE NEXT TIME WE MEET!
ANTI-HISTAMINE
AND THE NEXT MEETING? WELL, READER, WE'LL SKIP OVER THE LONG AND PATIENT VIGIL CARRIED ON BY BATMAN AND ROBIN IN THEIR PURSUIT OF THEIR FOE, THE MACABRE MASTER OF MIRTH... AND PRO-CEED DIRECTLY TO A CERTAIN DAY...
...WHEN A DARING CRIME IS TAKING PLACE IN BROAD DAYLIGHT... AND A GRIM SEARCH FINALLY PAYS OFF...
THERE HE IS!
IN FRONT OF THAT LOAN COMPANY! NO DOUBT HE'S SELECTED THAT FOR HIS NEXT ROBBERY! BUT WE'RE HERE IN TIME!
...NO LADY... THAT WAS MY WIFE!
HAW! HAW!
8

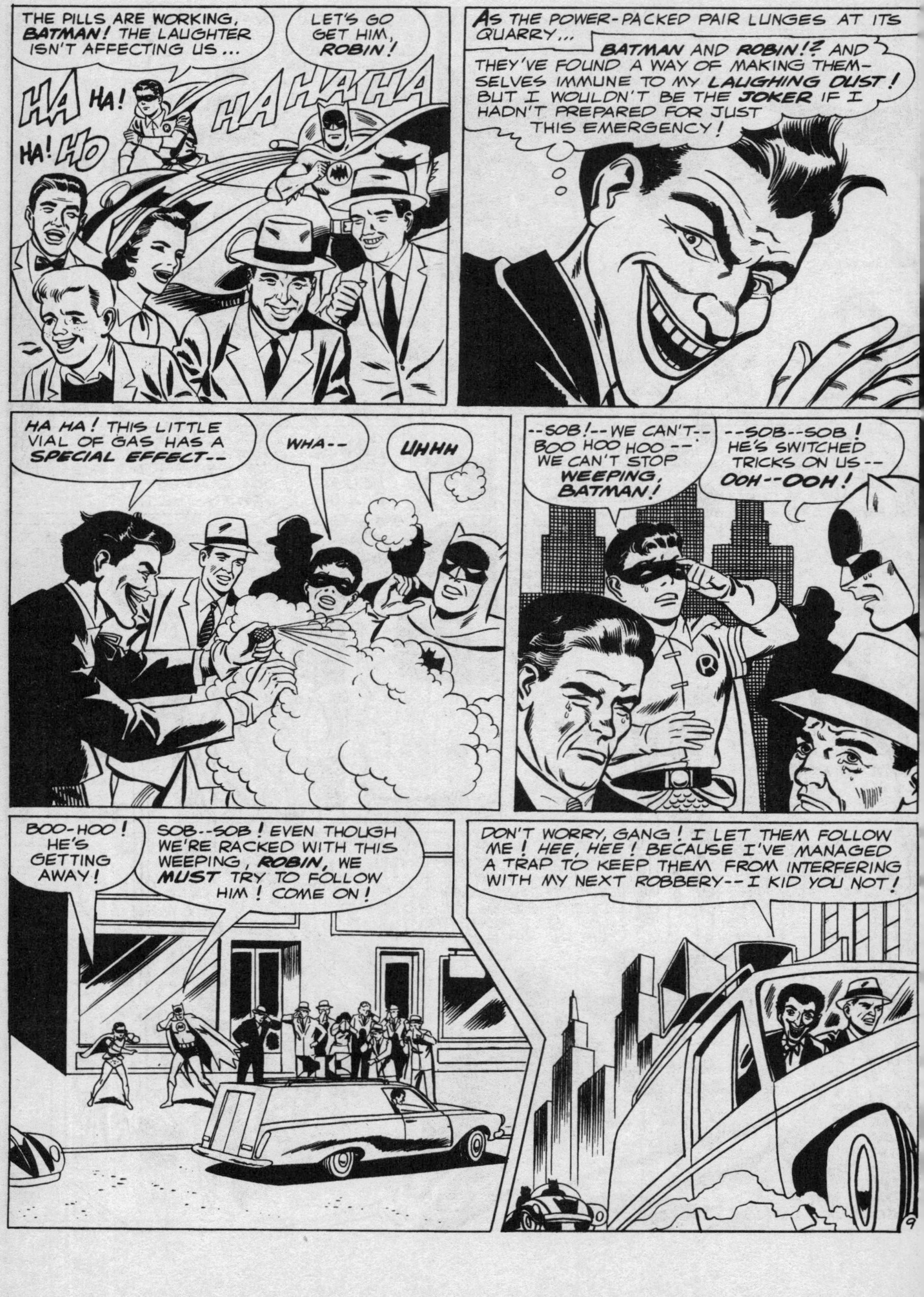
THE PILLS ARE WORKING, BATMAN! THE LAUGHTER ISN'T AFFECTING US...
LET'S GO GET HIM, ROBIN!
HA HA! HA! HO
HAHAHAHA
AS THE POWER-PACKED PAIR LUNGES AT ITS QUARRY...
BATMAN AND ROBIN!? AND THEY'VE FOUND A WAY OF MAKING THEMSELVES IMMUNE TO MY LAUGHING DUST! BUT I WOULDN'T BE THE JOKER IF I HADN'T PREPARED FOR JUST THIS EMERGENCY!
HA HA! THIS LITTLE VIAL OF GAS HAS A SPECIAL EFFECT--
WHA--
UHHH
--SOB!--WE CAN'T--BOO HOO HOO--WE CAN'T STOP WEEPING, BATMAN!
--SOB--SOB! HE'S SWITCHED TRICKS ON US--OOH--OOH!
BOO-HOO! HE'S GETTING AWAY!
SOB--SOB! EVEN THOUGH WE'RE RACKED WITH THIS WEEPING, ROBIN, WE MUST TRY TO FOLLOW HIM! COME ON!
DON'T WORRY, GANG! I LET THEM FOLLOW ME! HEE, HEE! BECAUSE I'VE MANAGED A TRAP TO KEEP THEM FROM INTERFERING WITH MY NEXT ROBBERY--I KID YOU NOT!
9

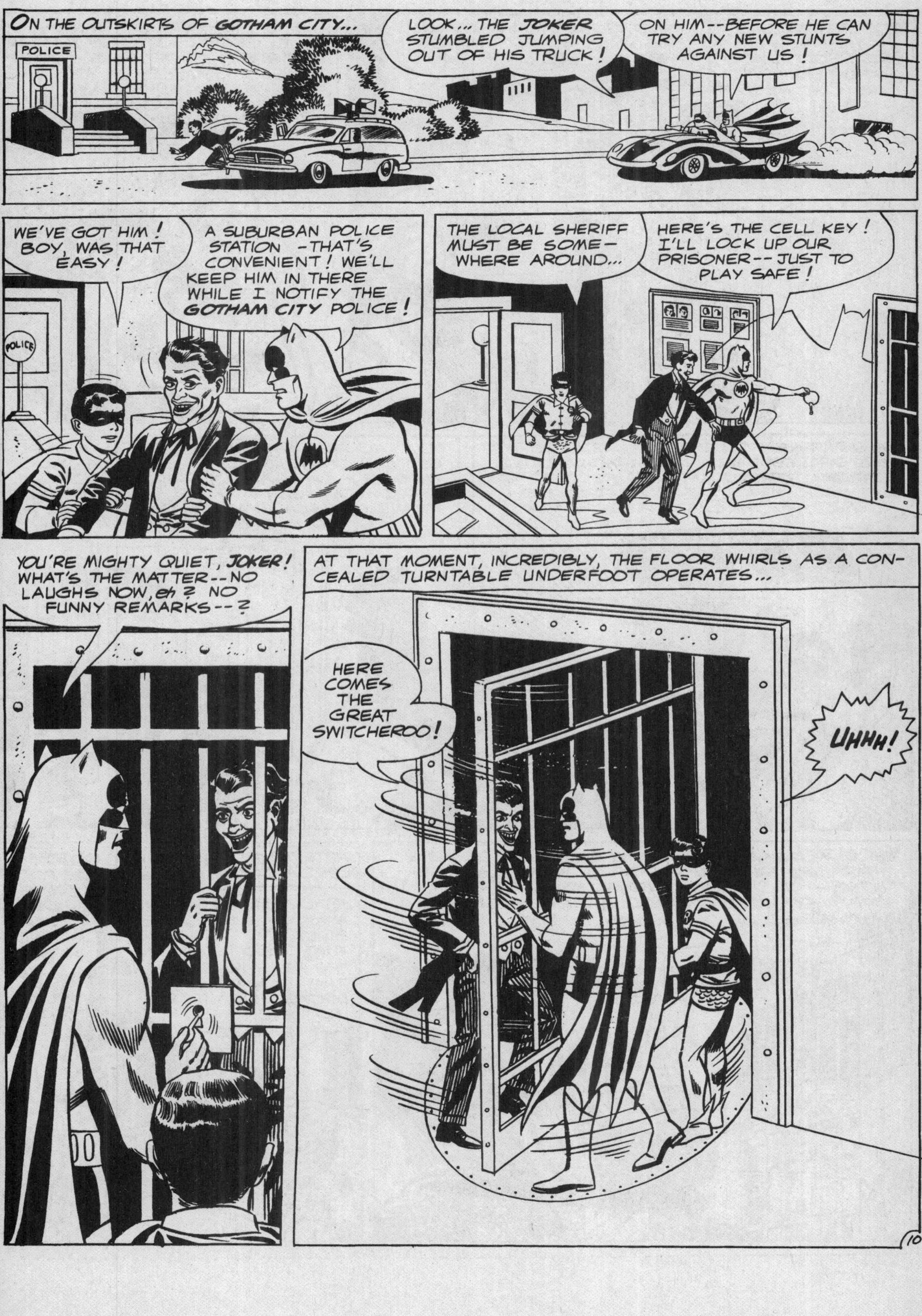
ON THE OUTSKIRTS OF GOTHAM CITY...
POLICE
LOOK... THE JOKER STUMBLED JUMPING OUT OF HIS TRUCK!
ON HIM--BEFORE HE CAN TRY ANY NEW STUNTS AGAINST US!
WE'VE GOT HIM! BOY, WAS THAT EASY!
A SUBURBAN POLICE STATION -THAT'S CONVENIENT! WE'LL KEEP HIM IN THERE WHILE I NOTIFY THE GOTHAM CITY POLICE!
POLICE
THE LOCAL SHERIFF MUST BE SOME-WHERE AROUND...
HERE'S THE CELL KEY! I'LL LOCK UP OUR PRISONER-- JUST TO PLAY SAFE!
YOU'RE MIGHTY QUIET, JOKER! WHAT'S THE MATTER--NO LAUGHS NOW, eh? NO FUNNY REMARKS--?
AT THAT MOMENT, INCREDIBLY, THE FLOOR WHIRLS AS A CON-CEALED TURNTABLE UNDERFOOT OPERATES...
HERE COMES THE GREAT SWITCHEROO!
UHHH!
10

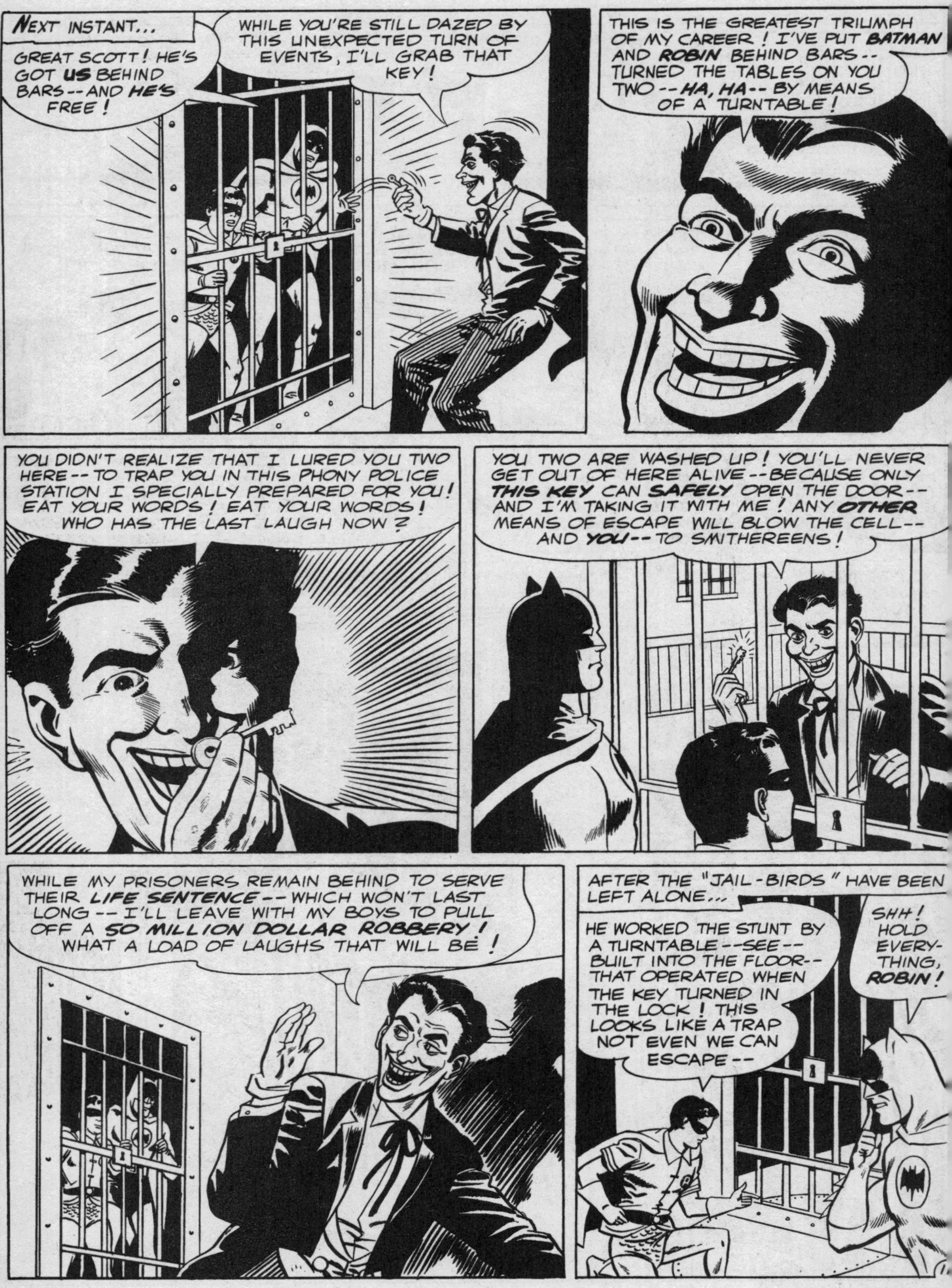
NEXT INSTANT...
GREAT SCOTT! HE'S GOT US BEHIND BARS--AND HE'S FREE!
WHILE YOU'RE STILL DAZED BY THIS UNEXPECTED TURN OF EVENTS, I'LL GRAB THAT KEY!
THIS IS THE GREATEST TRIUMPH OF MY CAREER! I'VE PUT BATMAN AND ROBIN BEHIND BARS--TURNED THE TABLES ON YOU TWO--HA, HA--BY MEANS OF A TURNTABLE!
YOU DIDN'T REALIZE THAT I LURED YOU TWO HERE--TO TRAP YOU IN THIS PHONY POLICE STATION I SPECIALLY PREPARED FOR YOU! EAT YOUR WORDS! EAT YOUR WORDS! WHO HAS THE LAST LAUGH NOW?
YOU TWO ARE WASHED UP! YOU'LL NEVER GET OUT OF HERE ALIVE--BECAUSE ONLY THIS KEY CAN SAFELY OPEN THE DOOR--AND I'M TAKING IT WITH ME! ANY OTHER MEANS OF ESCAPE WILL BLOW THE CELL--AND YOU--TO SMITHEREENS!
WHILE MY PRISONERS REMAIN BEHIND TO SERVE THEIR LIFE SENTENCE--WHICH WON'T LAST LONG--I'LL LEAVE WITH MY BOYS TO PULL OFF A 50 MILLION DOLLAR ROBBERY! WHAT A LOAD OF LAUGHS THAT WILL BE!
AFTER THE "JAIL-BIRDS" HAVE BEEN LEFT ALONE...
HE WORKED THE STUNT BY A TURNTABLE--SEE--BUILT INTO THE FLOOR--THAT OPERATED WHEN THE KEY TURNED IN THE LOCK! THIS LOOKS LIKE A TRAP NOT EVEN WE CAN ESCAPE--
SHH! HOLD EVERYTHING, ROBIN!

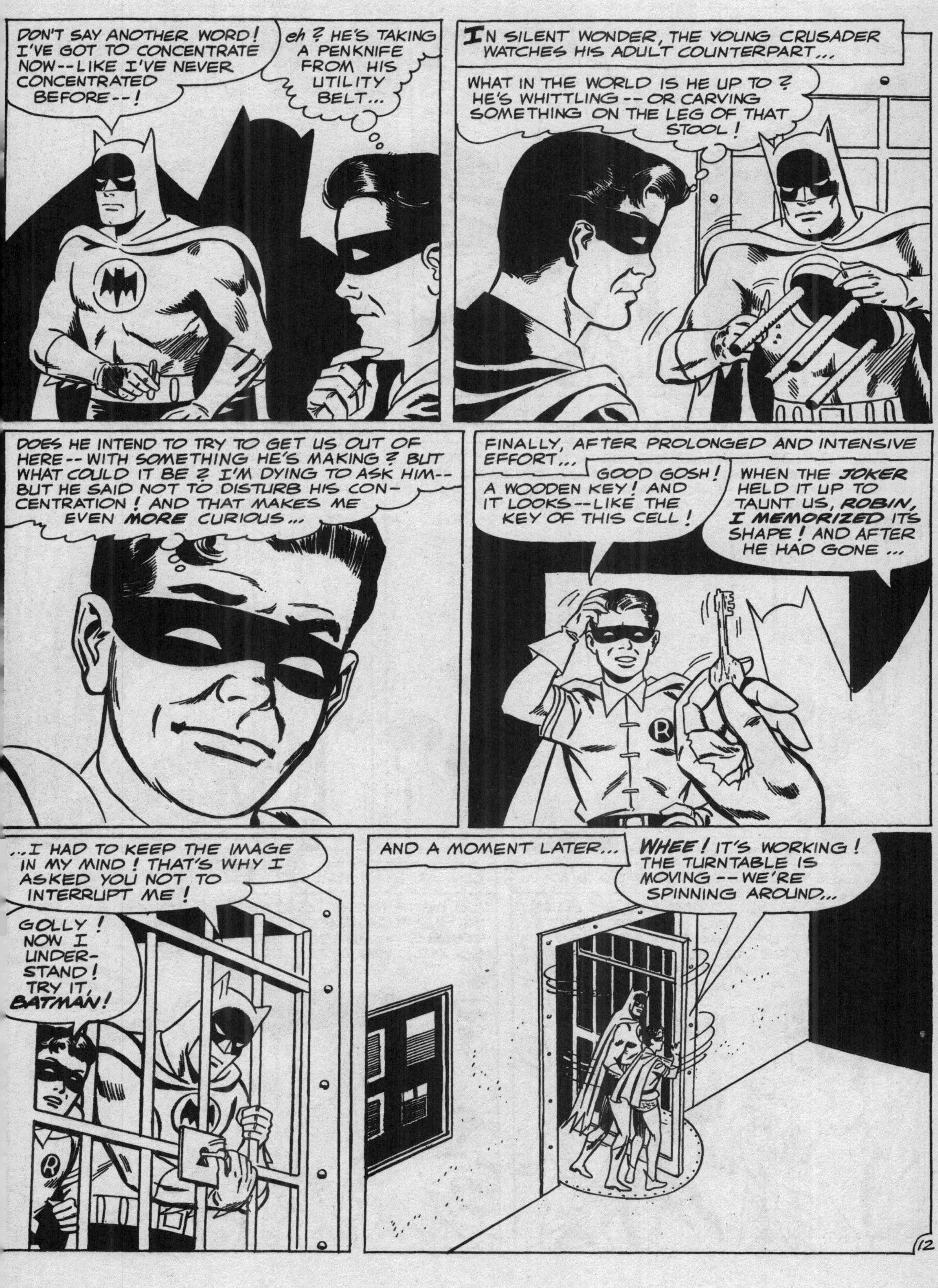
DON'T SAY ANOTHER WORD! I'VE GOT TO CONCENTRATE NOW--LIKE I'VE NEVER CONCENTRATED BEFORE--!
eh? HE'S TAKING A PENKNIFE FROM HIS UTILITY BELT...
IN SILENT WONDER, THE YOUNG CRUSADER WATCHES HIS ADULT COUNTERPART...
WHAT IN THE WORLD IS HE UP TO? HE'S WHITTLING--OR CARVING SOMETHING ON THE LEG OF THAT STOOL!
DOES HE INTEND TO TRY TO GET US OUT OF HERE--WITH SOMETHING HE'S MAKING? BUT WHAT COULD IT BE? I'M DYING TO ASK HIM--BUT HE SAID NOT TO DISTURB HIS CONCENTRATION! AND THAT MAKES ME EVEN MORE CURIOUS...
FINALLY, AFTER PROLONGED AND INTENSIVE EFFORT...
GOOD GOSH! A WOODEN KEY! AND IT LOOKS--LIKE THE KEY OF THIS CELL!
WHEN THE JOKER HELD IT UP TO TAUNT US, ROBIN, I MEMORIZED ITS SHAPE! AND AFTER HE HAD GONE...
...I HAD TO KEEP THE IMAGE IN MY MIND! THAT'S WHY I ASKED YOU NOT TO INTERRUPT ME!
GOLLY! NOW I UNDERSTAND! TRY IT, BATMAN!
AND A MOMENT LATER...
WHEE! IT'S WORKING! THE TURNTABLE IS MOVING--WE'RE SPINNING AROUND...
12

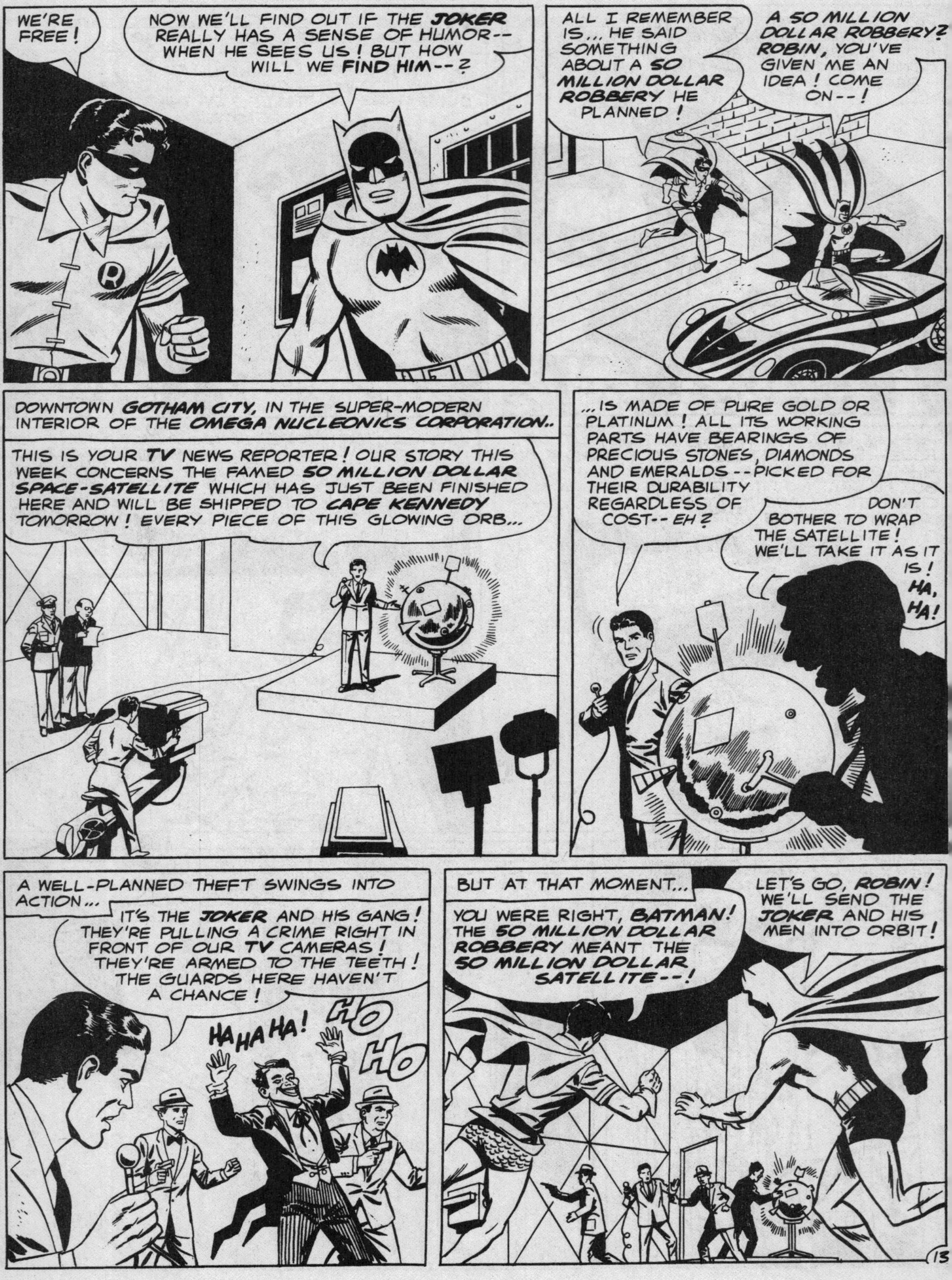
WE'RE FREE!
NOW WE'LL FIND OUT IF THE JOKER REALLY HAS A SENSE OF HUMOR-- WHEN HE SEES US! BUT HOW WILL WE FIND HIM--?
ALL I REMEMBER IS... HE SAID SOMETHING ABOUT A 50 MILLION DOLLAR ROBBERY HE PLANNED!
A 50 MILLION DOLLAR ROBBERY? ROBIN, YOU'VE GIVEN ME AN IDEA! COME ON--!
DOWNTOWN GOTHAM CITY, IN THE SUPER-MODERN INTERIOR OF THE OMEGA NUCLEONICS CORPORATION..
THIS IS YOUR TV NEWS REPORTER! OUR STORY THIS WEEK CONCERNS THE FAMED 50 MILLION DOLLAR SPACE-SATELLITE WHICH HAS JUST BEEN FINISHED HERE AND WILL BE SHIPPED TO CAPE KENNEDY TOMORROW! EVERY PIECE OF THIS GLOWING ORB...
...IS MADE OF PURE GOLD OR PLATINUM! ALL ITS WORKING PARTS HAVE BEARINGS OF PRECIOUS STONES, DIAMONDS AND EMERALDS--PICKED FOR THEIR DURABILITY REGARDLESS OF COST--EH?
DON'T BOTHER TO WRAP THE SATELLITE! WE'LL TAKE IT AS IT IS! HA, HA!
A WELL-PLANNED THEFT SWINGS INTO ACTION...
IT'S THE JOKER AND HIS GANG! THEY'RE PULLING A CRIME RIGHT IN FRONT OF OUR TV CAMERAS! THEY'RE ARMED TO THE TEETH! THE GUARDS HERE HAVEN'T A CHANCE!
HA HA HA!
HO HO
BUT AT THAT MOMENT...
YOU WERE RIGHT, BATMAN! THE 50 MILLION DOLLAR ROBBERY MEANT THE 50 MILLION DOLLAR SATELLITE--!
LET'S GO, ROBIN! WE'LL SEND THE JOKER AND HIS MEN INTO ORBIT!
13

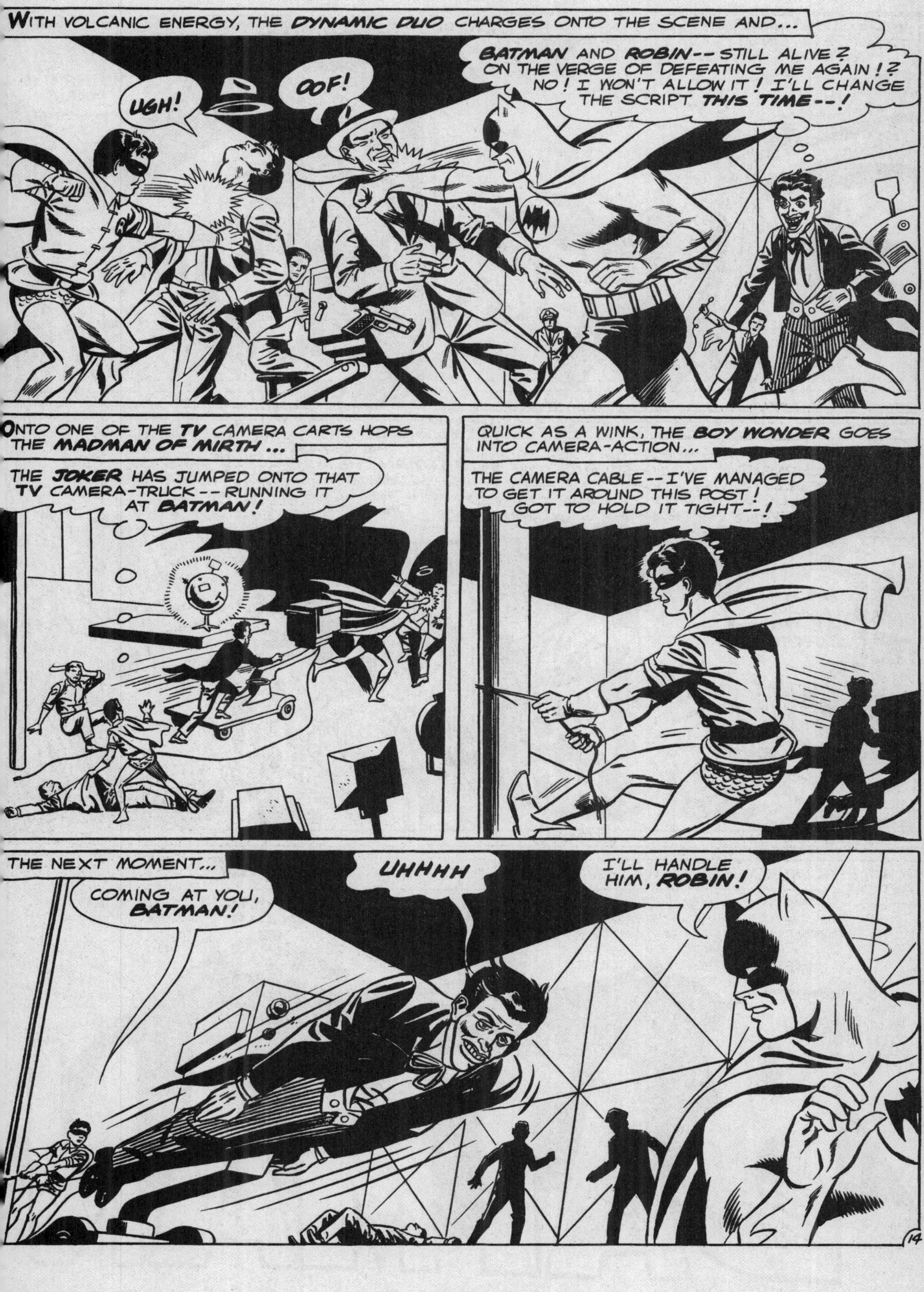
WITH VOLCANIC ENERGY, THE DYNAMIC DUO CHARGES ONTO THE SCENE AND...
UGH!
OOF!
BATMAN AND ROBIN-- STILL ALIVE? ON THE VERGE OF DEFEATING ME AGAIN!? NO! I WON'T ALLOW IT! I'LL CHANGE THE SCRIPT THIS TIME--!
ONTO ONE OF THE TV CAMERA CARTS HOPS THE MADMAN OF MIRTH...
THE JOKER HAS JUMPED ONTO THAT TV CAMERA-TRUCK-- RUNNING IT AT BATMAN!
QUICK AS A WINK, THE BOY WONDER GOES INTO CAMERA-ACTION...
THE CAMERA CABLE-- I'VE MANAGED TO GET IT AROUND THIS POST! GOT TO HOLD IT TIGHT--!
THE NEXT MOMENT...
COMING AT YOU, BATMAN!
UHHHH
I'LL HANDLE HIM, ROBIN!
14

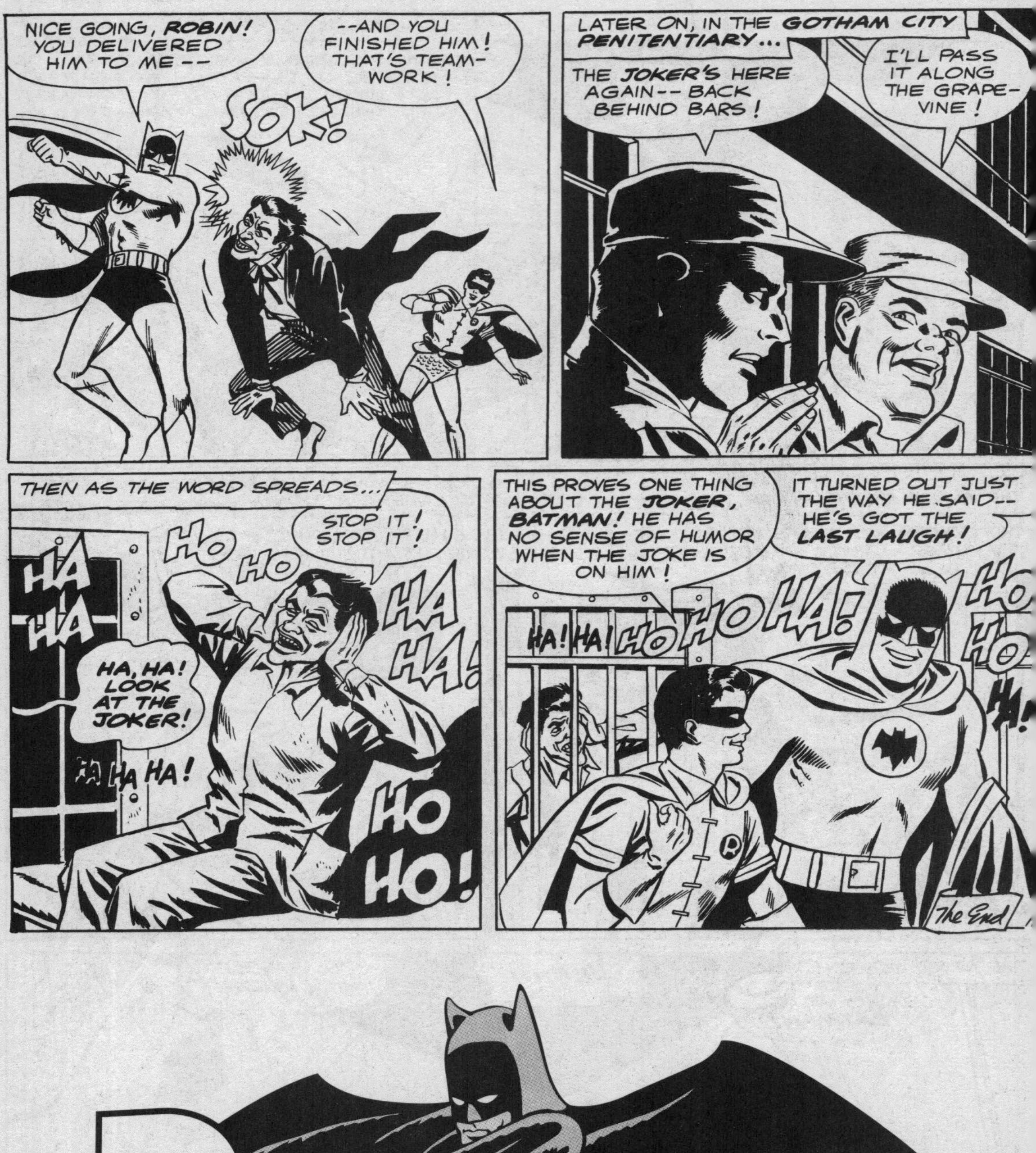
NICE GOING, ROBIN! YOU DELIVERED HIM TO ME --
SOK!
--AND YOU FINISHED HIM! THAT'S TEAM-WORK!
LATER ON, IN THE GOTHAM CITY PENITENTIARY...
THE JOKER'S HERE AGAIN-- BACK BEHIND BARS!
I'LL PASS IT ALONG THE GRAPE-VINE!
THEN AS THE WORD SPREADS...
HA HA
HO HO
STOP IT! STOP IT!
HA HA!
HA, HA! LOOK AT THE JOKER!
HA HA HA!
HO HO!
THIS PROVES ONE THING ABOUT THE JOKER, BATMAN! HE HAS NO SENSE OF HUMOR WHEN THE JOKE IS ON HIM!
IT TURNED OUT JUST THE WAY HE SAID-- HE'S GOT THE LAST LAUGH!
HA! HA! HO HO HO HA!
HO HO HA!
The End

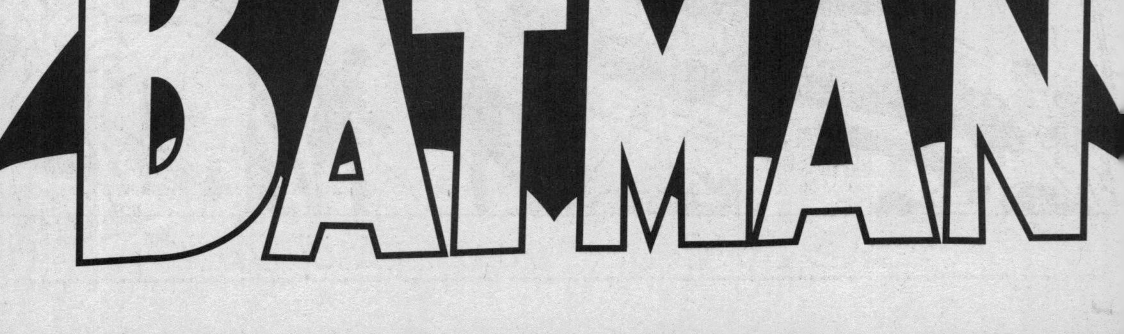
BATMAN

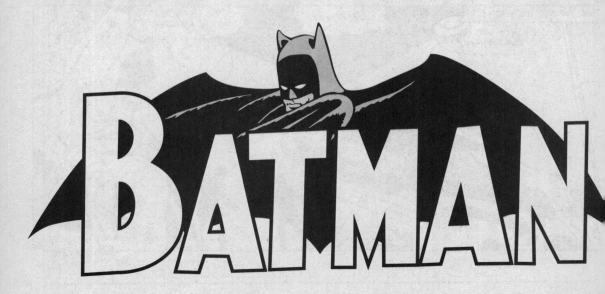

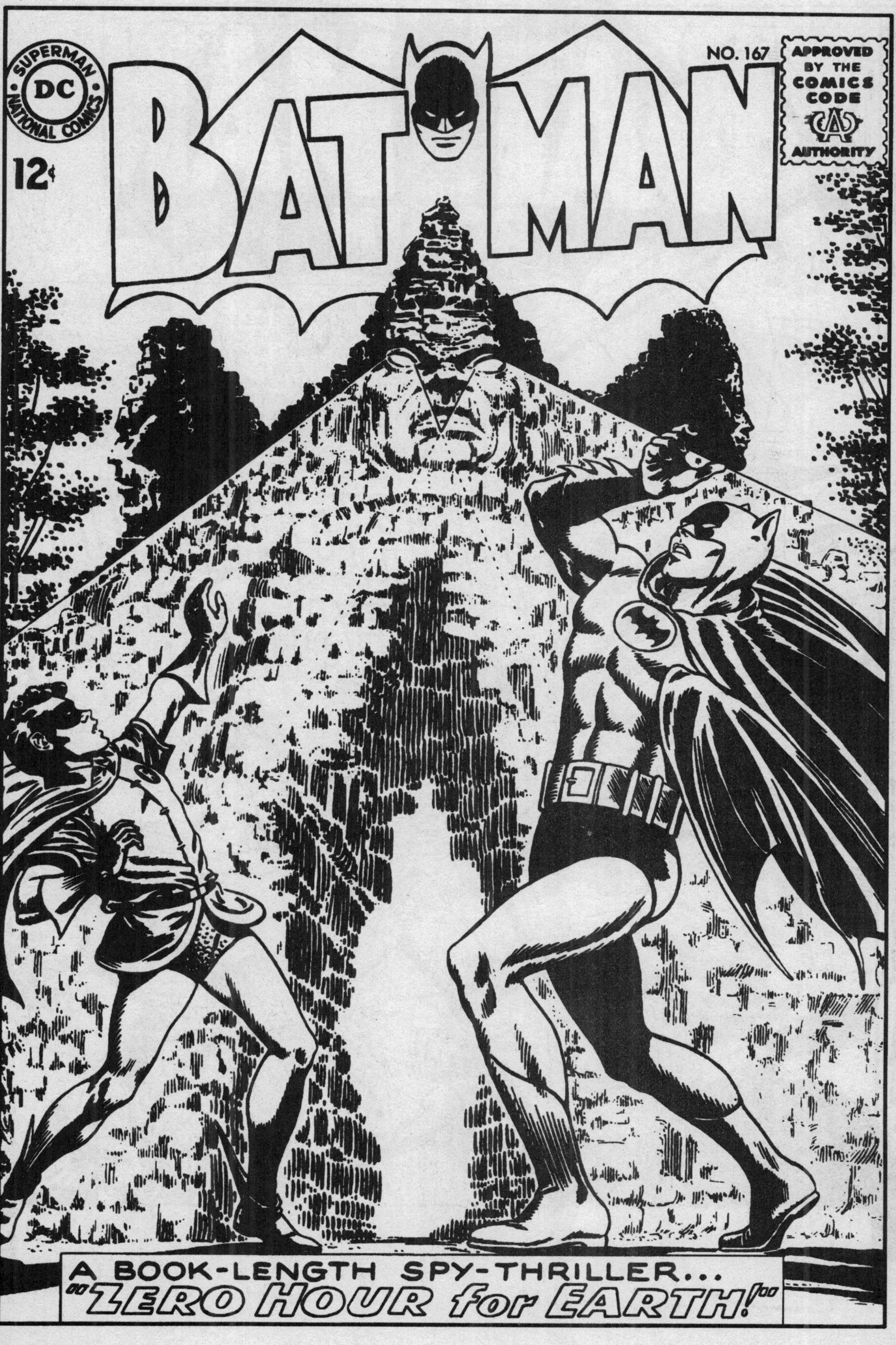
SUPERMAN
DC
NATIONAL COMICS
12¢
BATMAN
NO. 167
APPROVED BY THE COMICS CODE AUTHORITY
A BOOK-LENGTH SPY-THRILLER...
"ZERO HOUR for EARTH!"

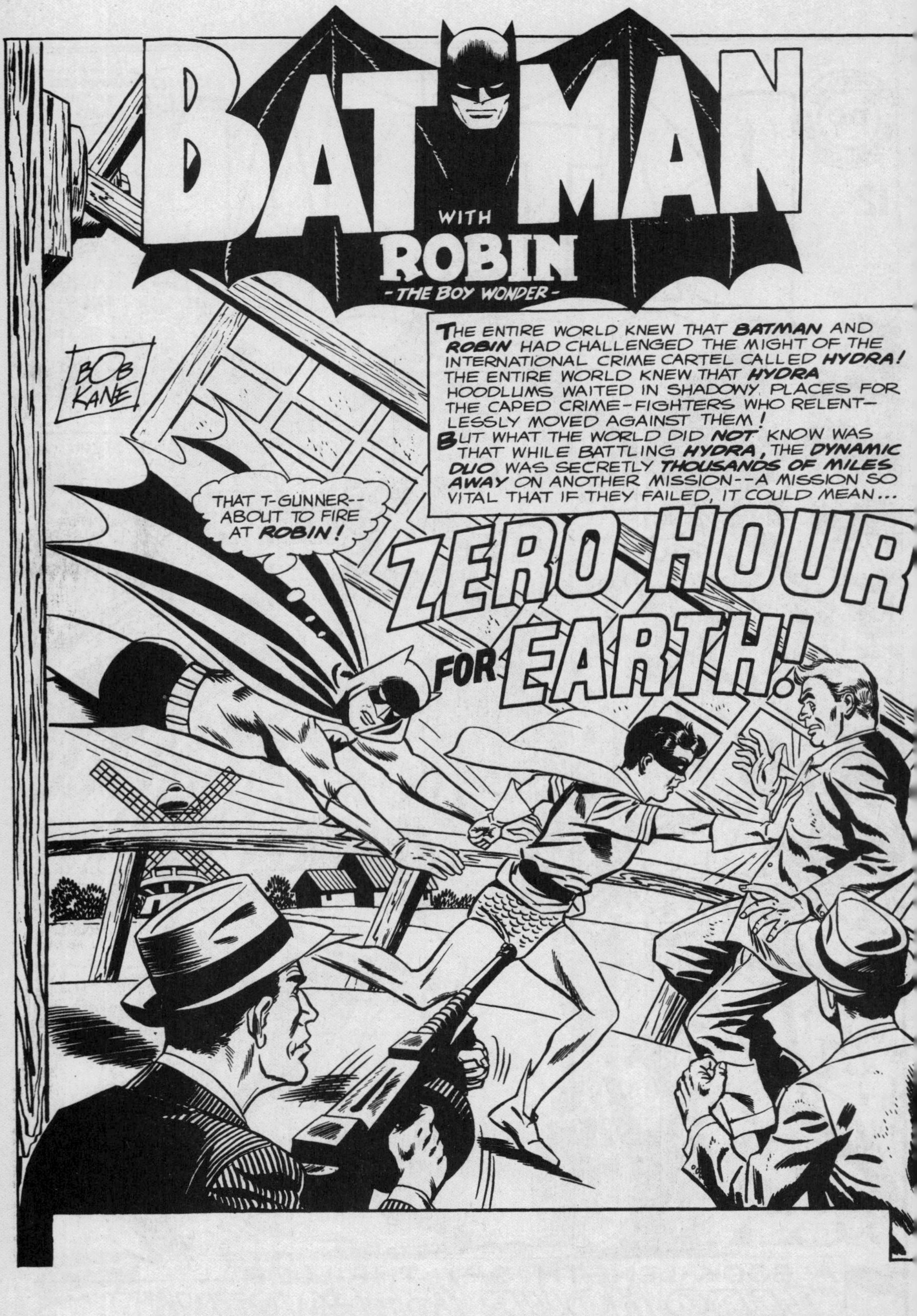
BATMAN
WITH
ROBIN
-THE BOY WONDER-
BOB KANE
THE ENTIRE WORLD KNEW THAT BATMAN AND ROBIN HAD CHALLENGED THE MIGHT OF THE INTERNATIONAL CRIME CARTEL CALLED HYDRA! THE ENTIRE WORLD KNEW THAT HYDRA HOODLUMS WAITED IN SHADOWY PLACES FOR THE CAPED CRIME-FIGHTERS WHO RELENTLESSLY MOVED AGAINST THEM!
BUT WHAT THE WORLD DID NOT KNOW WAS THAT WHILE BATTLING HYDRA, THE DYNAMIC DUO WAS SECRETLY THOUSANDS OF MILES AWAY ON ANOTHER MISSION--A MISSION SO VITAL THAT IF THEY FAILED, IT COULD MEAN...
THAT T-GUNNER-- ABOUT TO FIRE AT ROBIN!
ZERO HOUR FOR EARTH!

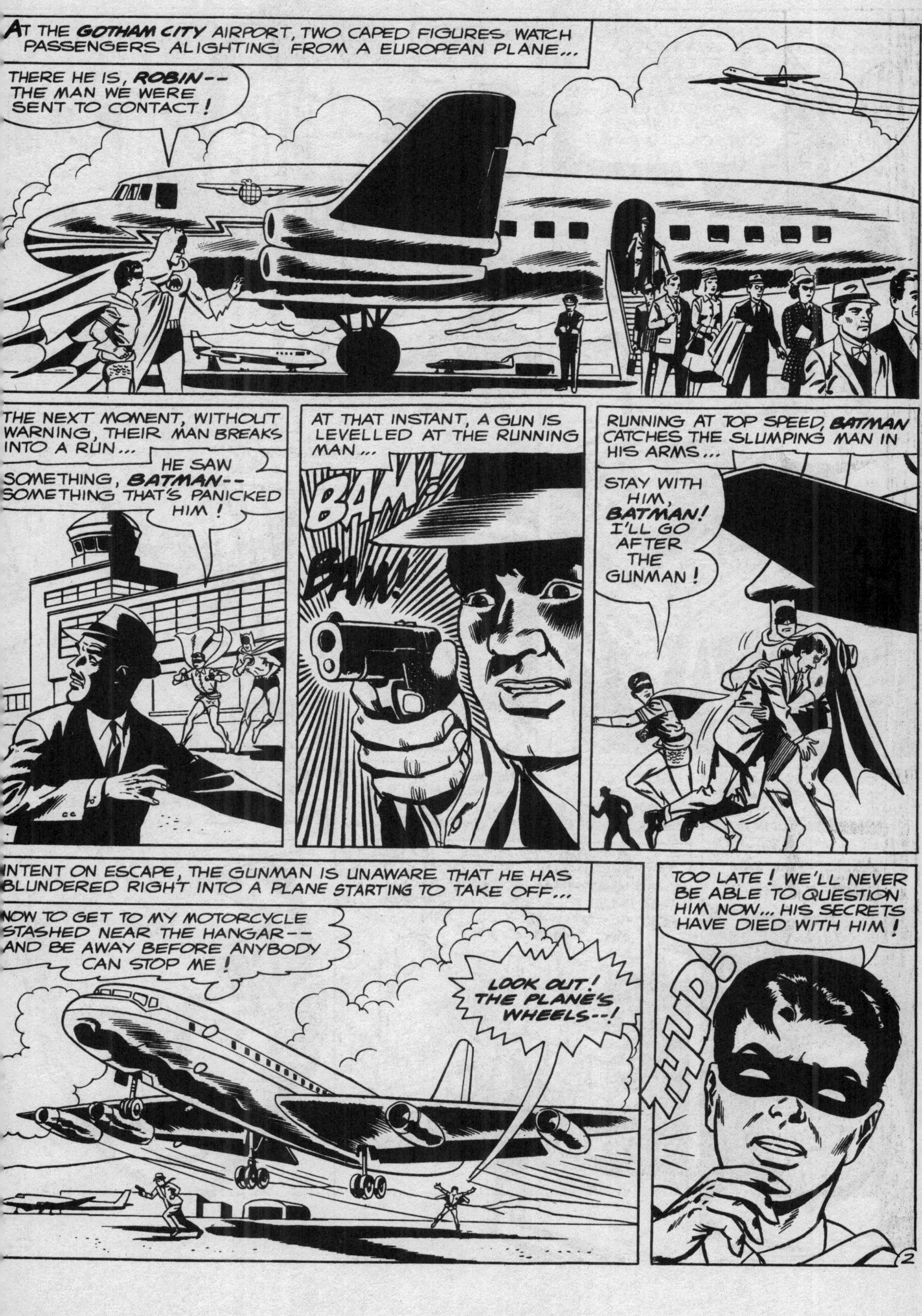
AT THE GOTHAM CITY AIRPORT, TWO CAPED FIGURES WATCH PASSENGERS ALIGHTING FROM A EUROPEAN PLANE...
THERE HE IS, ROBIN-- THE MAN WE WERE SENT TO CONTACT!
THE NEXT MOMENT, WITHOUT WARNING, THEIR MAN BREAKS INTO A RUN...
HE SAW SOMETHING, BATMAN-- SOMETHING THAT'S PANICKED HIM!
AT THAT INSTANT, A GUN IS LEVELLED AT THE RUNNING MAN...
BAM!
BAM!
RUNNING AT TOP SPEED, BATMAN CATCHES THE SLUMPING MAN IN HIS ARMS...
STAY WITH HIM, BATMAN! I'LL GO AFTER THE GUNMAN!
INTENT ON ESCAPE, THE GUNMAN IS UNAWARE THAT HE HAS BLUNDERED RIGHT INTO A PLANE STARTING TO TAKE OFF...
NOW TO GET TO MY MOTORCYCLE STASHED NEAR THE HANGAR-- AND BE AWAY BEFORE ANYBODY CAN STOP ME!
LOOK OUT! THE PLANE'S WHEELS--!
TOO LATE! WE'LL NEVER BE ABLE TO QUESTION HIM NOW... HIS SECRETS HAVE DIED WITH HIM!
THUD!
2

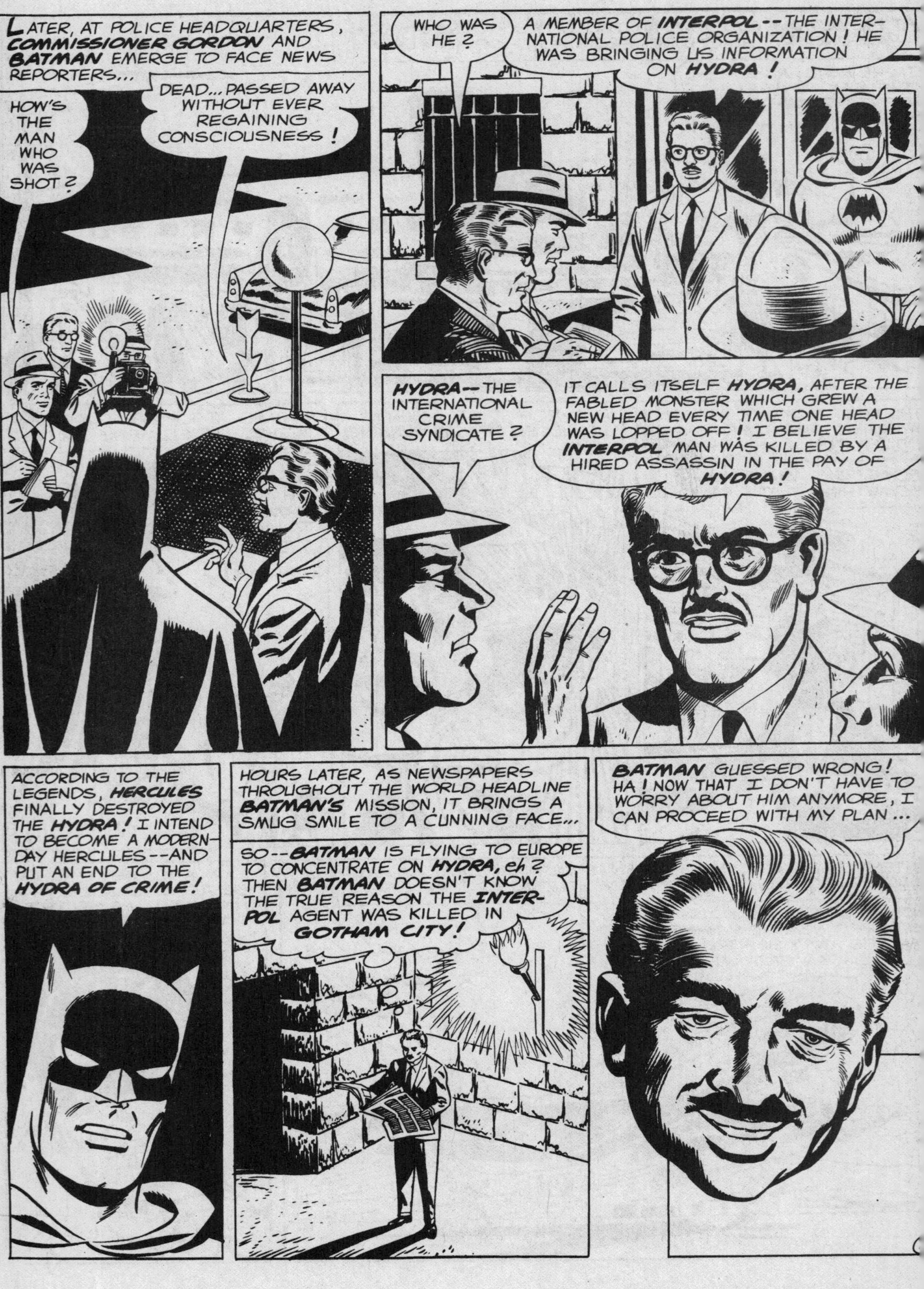
LATER, AT POLICE HEADQUARTERS, COMMISSIONER GORDON AND BATMAN EMERGE TO FACE NEWS REPORTERS...
HOW'S THE MAN WHO WAS SHOT?
DEAD... PASSED AWAY WITHOUT EVER REGAINING CONSCIOUSNESS!
WHO WAS HE?
A MEMBER OF INTERPOL--THE INTERNATIONAL POLICE ORGANIZATION! HE WAS BRINGING US INFORMATION ON HYDRA!
HYDRA--THE INTERNATIONAL CRIME SYNDICATE?
IT CALLS ITSELF HYDRA, AFTER THE FABLED MONSTER WHICH GREW A NEW HEAD EVERY TIME ONE HEAD WAS LOPPED OFF! I BELIEVE THE INTERPOL MAN WAS KILLED BY A HIRED ASSASSIN IN THE PAY OF HYDRA!
ACCORDING TO THE LEGENDS, HERCULES FINALLY DESTROYED THE HYDRA! I INTEND TO BECOME A MODERN-DAY HERCULES--AND PUT AN END TO THE HYDRA OF CRIME!
HOURS LATER, AS NEWSPAPERS THROUGHOUT THE WORLD HEADLINE BATMAN'S MISSION, IT BRINGS A SMUG SMILE TO A CUNNING FACE...
SO--BATMAN IS FLYING TO EUROPE TO CONCENTRATE ON HYDRA, eh? THEN BATMAN DOESN'T KNOW THE TRUE REASON THE INTERPOL AGENT WAS KILLED IN GOTHAM CITY!
BATMAN GUESSED WRONG! HA! NOW THAT I DON'T HAVE TO WORRY ABOUT HIM ANYMORE, I CAN PROCEED WITH MY PLAN...

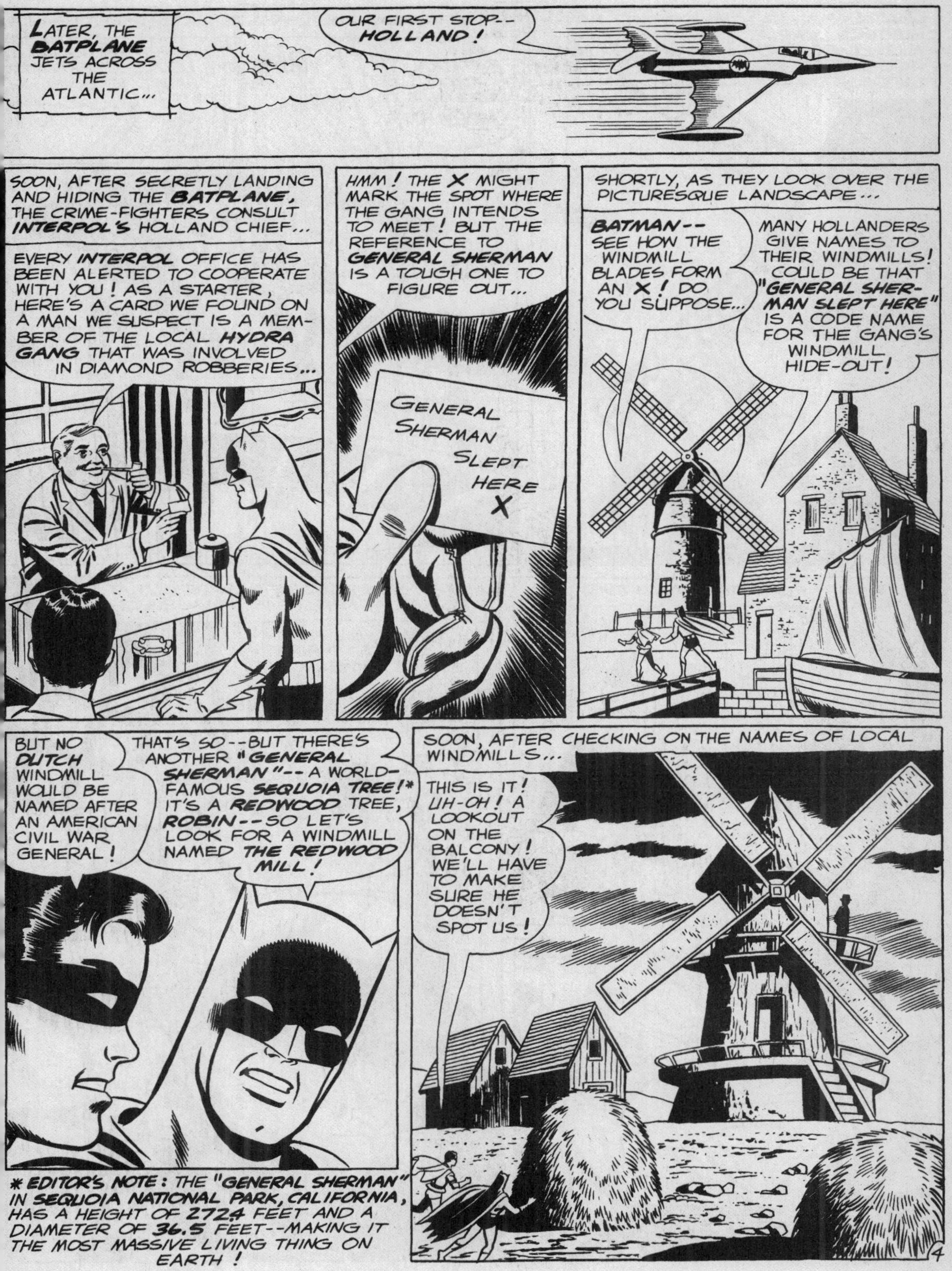
LATER, THE BATPLANE JETS ACROSS THE ATLANTIC...
OUR FIRST STOP-- HOLLAND!
SOON, AFTER SECRETLY LANDING AND HIDING THE BATPLANE, THE CRIME-FIGHTERS CONSULT INTERPOL'S HOLLAND CHIEF...
EVERY INTERPOL OFFICE HAS BEEN ALERTED TO COOPERATE WITH YOU! AS A STARTER, HERE'S A CARD WE FOUND ON A MAN WE SUSPECT IS A MEMBER OF THE LOCAL HYDRA GANG THAT WAS INVOLVED IN DIAMOND ROBBERIES...
HMM! THE X MIGHT MARK THE SPOT WHERE THE GANG INTENDS TO MEET! BUT THE REFERENCE TO GENERAL SHERMAN IS A TOUGH ONE TO FIGURE OUT...
GENERAL SHERMAN SLEPT HERE X
SHORTLY, AS THEY LOOK OVER THE PICTURESQUE LANDSCAPE...
BATMAN-- SEE HOW THE WINDMILL BLADES FORM AN X! DO YOU SUPPOSE...
MANY HOLLANDERS GIVE NAMES TO THEIR WINDMILLS! COULD BE THAT "GENERAL SHERMAN SLEPT HERE" IS A CODE NAME FOR THE GANG'S WINDMILL HIDE-OUT!
BUT NO DUTCH WINDMILL WOULD BE NAMED AFTER AN AMERICAN CIVIL WAR GENERAL!
THAT'S SO--BUT THERE'S ANOTHER "GENERAL SHERMAN"-- A WORLD-FAMOUS SEQUOIA TREE!* IT'S A REDWOOD TREE, ROBIN--SO LET'S LOOK FOR A WINDMILL NAMED THE REDWOOD MILL!
*EDITOR'S NOTE: THE "GENERAL SHERMAN" IN SEQUOIA NATIONAL PARK, CALIFORNIA, HAS A HEIGHT OF 272.4 FEET AND A DIAMETER OF 36.5 FEET--MAKING IT THE MOST MASSIVE LIVING THING ON EARTH!
SOON, AFTER CHECKING ON THE NAMES OF LOCAL WINDMILLS...
THIS IS IT! UH-OH! A LOOKOUT ON THE BALCONY! WE'LL HAVE TO MAKE SURE HE DOESN'T SPOT US!
4

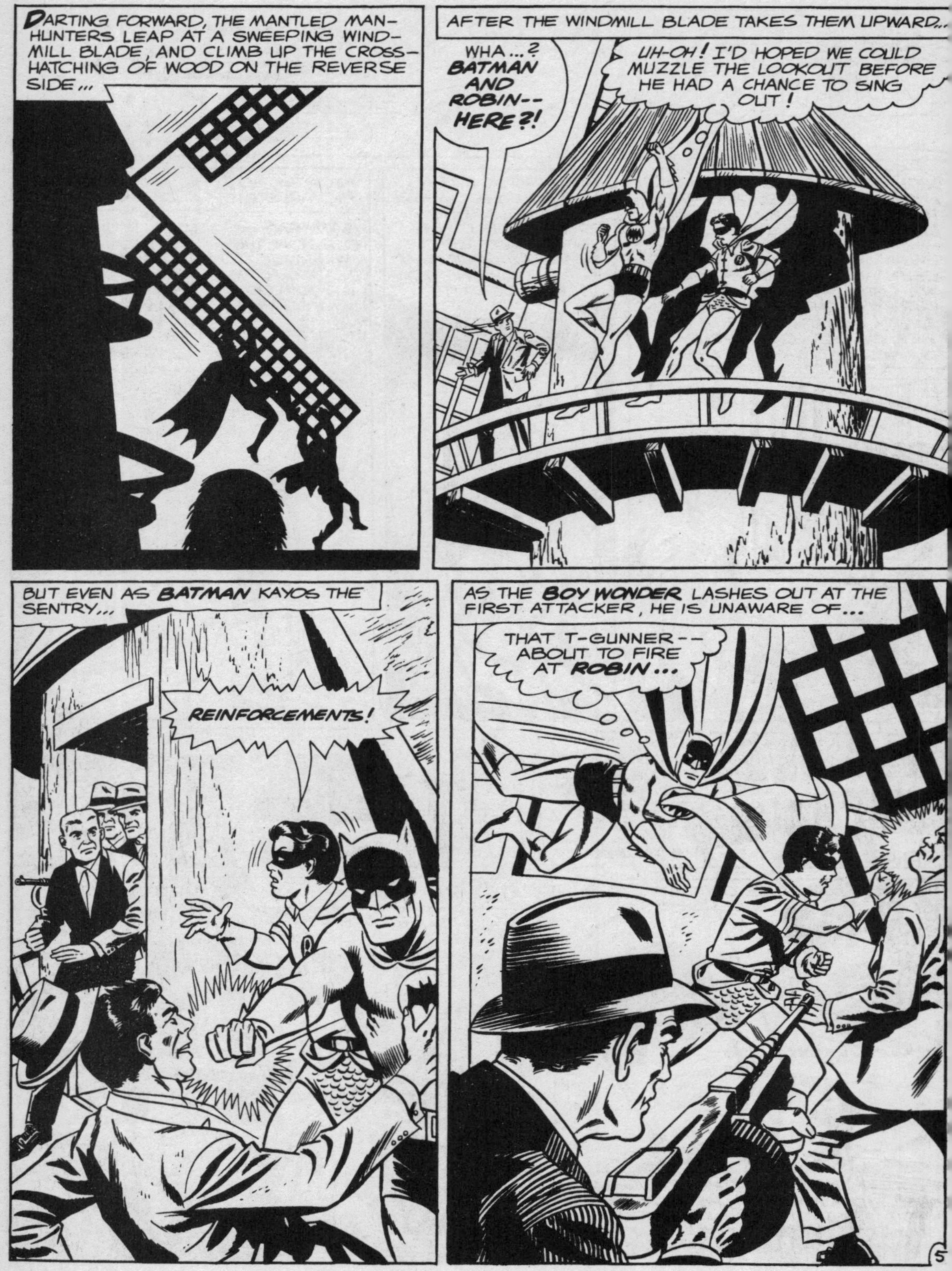
DARTING FORWARD, THE MANTLED MAN-HUNTERS LEAP AT A SWEEPING WIND-MILL BLADE, AND CLIMB UP THE CROSS-HATCHING OF WOOD ON THE REVERSE SIDE...
AFTER THE WINDMILL BLADE TAKES THEM UPWARD...
WHA...? BATMAN AND ROBIN--HERE?!
UH-OH! I'D HOPED WE COULD MUZZLE THE LOOKOUT BEFORE HE HAD A CHANCE TO SING OUT!
BUT EVEN AS BATMAN KAYOS THE SENTRY...
REINFORCEMENTS!
AS THE BOY WONDER LASHES OUT AT THE FIRST ATTACKER, HE IS UNAWARE OF...
THAT T-GUNNER--ABOUT TO FIRE AT ROBIN...
5

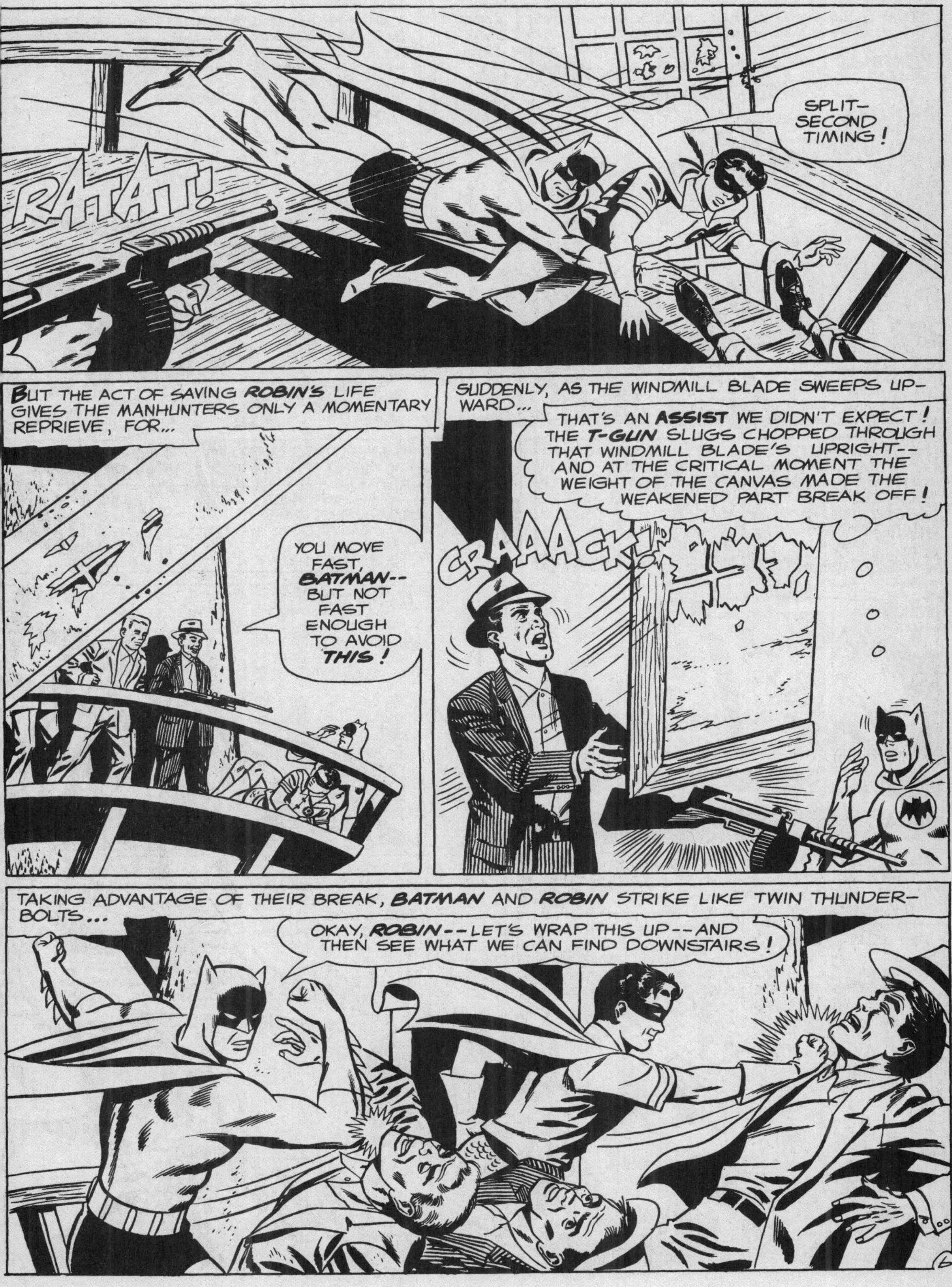
RATATAT!
SPLIT-SECOND TIMING!
BUT THE ACT OF SAVING ROBIN'S LIFE GIVES THE MANHUNTERS ONLY A MOMENTARY REPRIEVE, FOR...
YOU MOVE FAST, BATMAN-- BUT NOT FAST ENOUGH TO AVOID THIS!
SUDDENLY, AS THE WINDMILL BLADE SWEEPS UPWARD...
THAT'S AN ASSIST WE DIDN'T EXPECT! THE T-GUN SLUGS CHOPPED THROUGH THAT WINDMILL BLADE'S UPRIGHT-- AND AT THE CRITICAL MOMENT THE WEIGHT OF THE CANVAS MADE THE WEAKENED PART BREAK OFF!
CRAAACK!
TAKING ADVANTAGE OF THEIR BREAK, BATMAN AND ROBIN STRIKE LIKE TWIN THUNDERBOLTS...
OKAY, ROBIN--LET'S WRAP THIS UP--AND THEN SEE WHAT WE CAN FIND DOWNSTAIRS!
6

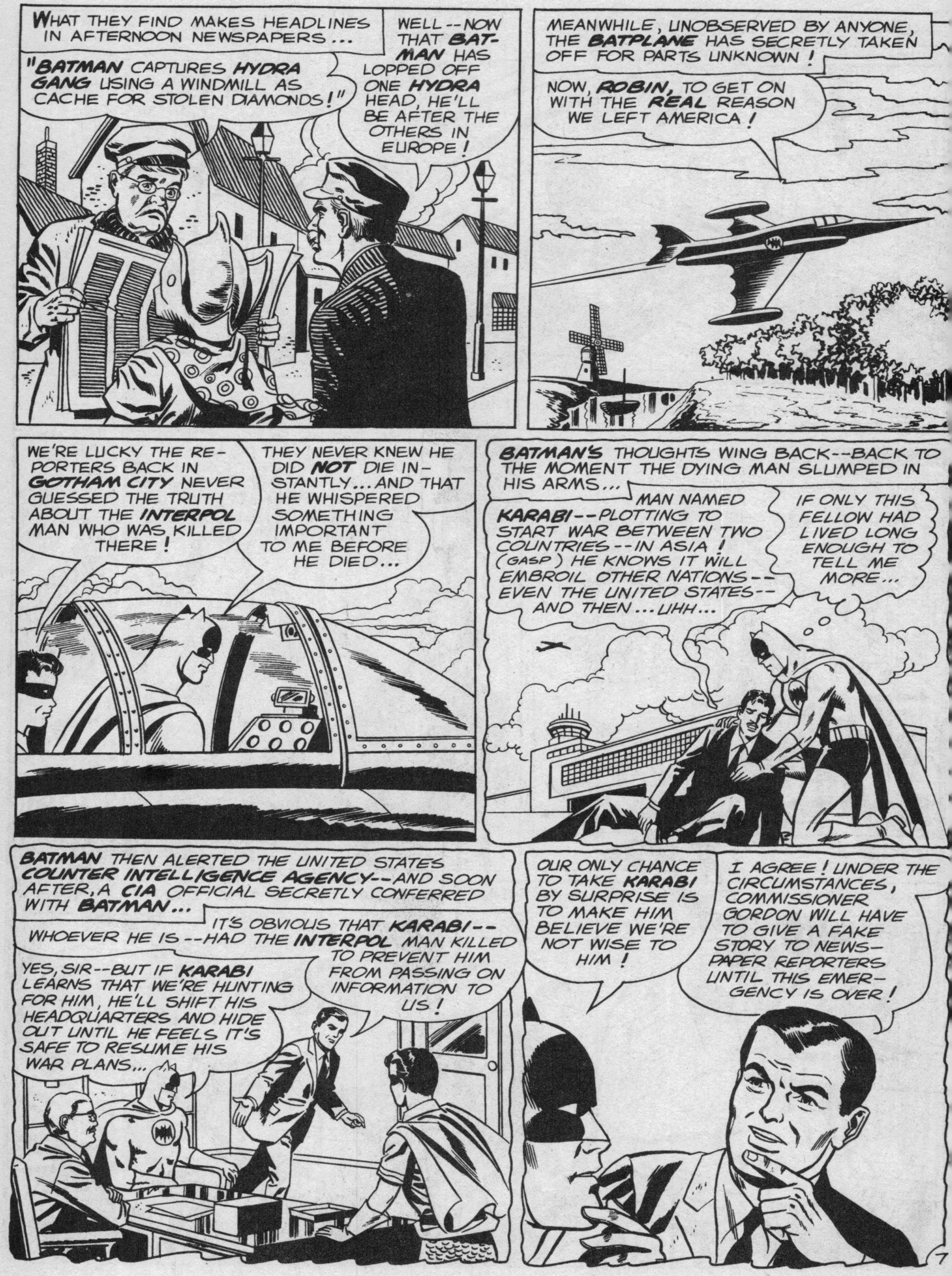
WHAT THEY FIND MAKES HEADLINES IN AFTERNOON NEWSPAPERS...
"BATMAN CAPTURES HYDRA GANG USING A WINDMILL AS CACHE FOR STOLEN DIAMONDS!"
WELL--NOW THAT BATMAN HAS LOPPED OFF ONE HYDRA HEAD, HE'LL BE AFTER THE OTHERS IN EUROPE!
MEANWHILE, UNOBSERVED BY ANYONE, THE BATPLANE HAS SECRETLY TAKEN OFF FOR PARTS UNKNOWN!
NOW, ROBIN, TO GET ON WITH THE REAL REASON WE LEFT AMERICA!
WE'RE LUCKY THE REPORTERS BACK IN GOTHAM CITY NEVER GUESSED THE TRUTH ABOUT THE INTERPOL MAN WHO WAS KILLED THERE!
THEY NEVER KNEW HE DID NOT DIE INSTANTLY...AND THAT HE WHISPERED SOMETHING IMPORTANT TO ME BEFORE HE DIED...
BATMAN'S THOUGHTS WING BACK--BACK TO THE MOMENT THE DYING MAN SLUMPED IN HIS ARMS...
MAN NAMED KARABI--PLOTTING TO START WAR BETWEEN TWO COUNTRIES--IN ASIA! (GASP) HE KNOWS IT WILL EMBROIL OTHER NATIONS--EVEN THE UNITED STATES--AND THEN...UHH...
IF ONLY THIS FELLOW HAD LIVED LONG ENOUGH TO TELL ME MORE...
BATMAN THEN ALERTED THE UNITED STATES COUNTER INTELLIGENCE AGENCY--AND SOON AFTER, A CIA OFFICIAL SECRETLY CONFERRED WITH BATMAN...
IT'S OBVIOUS THAT KARABI--WHOEVER HE IS--HAD THE INTERPOL MAN KILLED TO PREVENT HIM FROM PASSING ON INFORMATION TO US!
YES, SIR--BUT IF KARABI LEARNS THAT WE'RE HUNTING FOR HIM, HE'LL SHIFT HIS HEADQUARTERS AND HIDE OUT UNTIL HE FEELS IT'S SAFE TO RESUME HIS WAR PLANS...
OUR ONLY CHANCE TO TAKE KARABI BY SURPRISE IS TO MAKE HIM BELIEVE WE'RE NOT WISE TO HIM!
I AGREE! UNDER THE CIRCUMSTANCES, COMMISSIONER GORDON WILL HAVE TO GIVE A FAKE STORY TO NEWSPAPER REPORTERS UNTIL THIS EMERGENCY IS OVER!
7

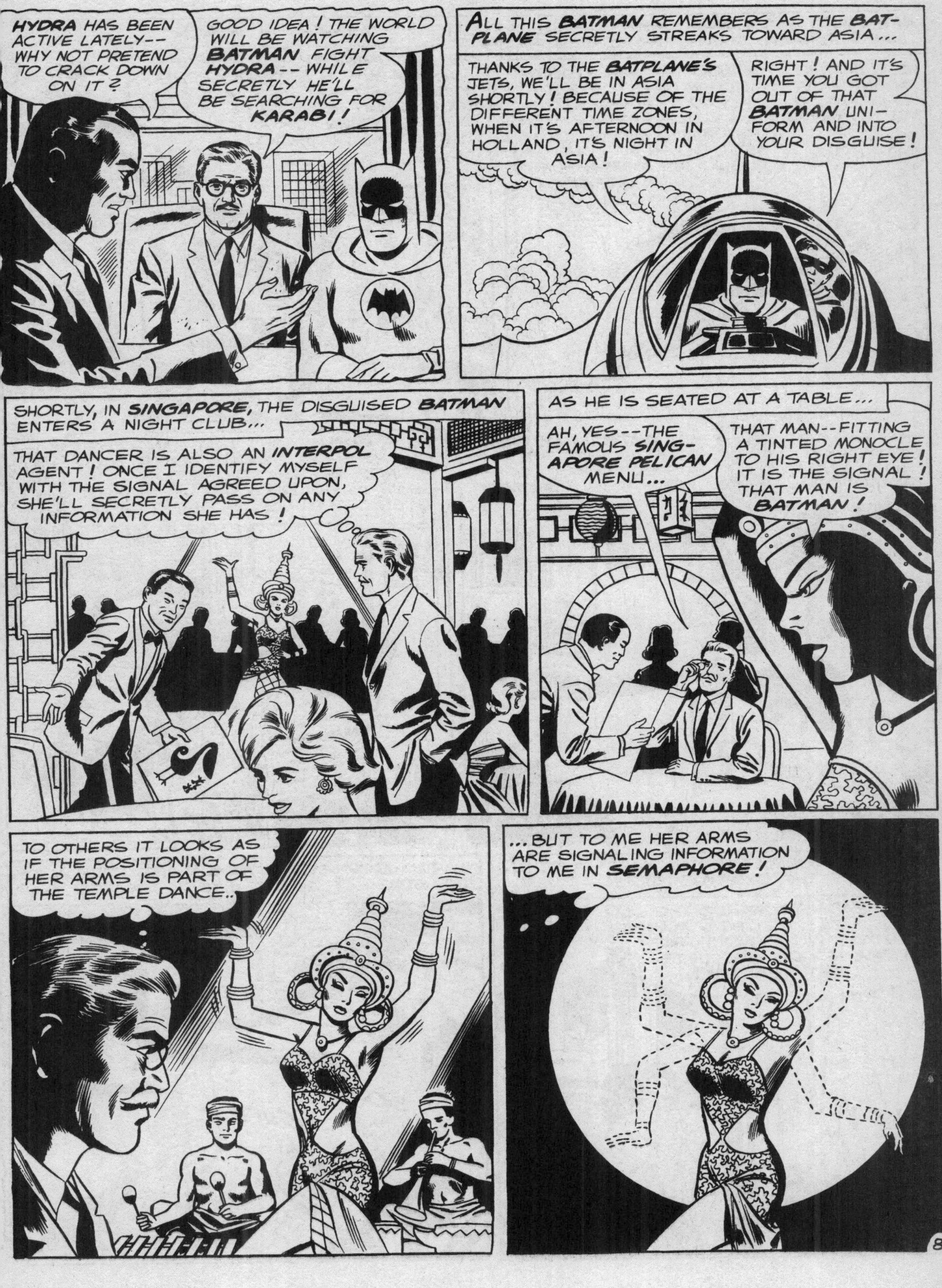
HYDRA HAS BEEN ACTIVE LATELY-- WHY NOT PRETEND TO CRACK DOWN ON IT?
GOOD IDEA! THE WORLD WILL BE WATCHING BATMAN FIGHT HYDRA-- WHILE SECRETLY HE'LL BE SEARCHING FOR KARABI!
ALL THIS BATMAN REMEMBERS AS THE BATPLANE SECRETLY STREAKS TOWARD ASIA...
THANKS TO THE BATPLANE'S JETS, WE'LL BE IN ASIA SHORTLY! BECAUSE OF THE DIFFERENT TIME ZONES, WHEN IT'S AFTERNOON IN HOLLAND, IT'S NIGHT IN ASIA!
RIGHT! AND IT'S TIME YOU GOT OUT OF THAT BATMAN UNIFORM AND INTO YOUR DISGUISE!
SHORTLY, IN SINGAPORE, THE DISGUISED BATMAN ENTERS A NIGHT CLUB...
THAT DANCER IS ALSO AN INTERPOL AGENT! ONCE I IDENTIFY MYSELF WITH THE SIGNAL AGREED UPON, SHE'LL SECRETLY PASS ON ANY INFORMATION SHE HAS!
AS HE IS SEATED AT A TABLE...
AH, YES--THE FAMOUS SINGAPORE PELICAN MENU...
THAT MAN--FITTING A TINTED MONOCLE TO HIS RIGHT EYE! IT IS THE SIGNAL! THAT MAN IS BATMAN!
TO OTHERS IT LOOKS AS IF THE POSITIONING OF HER ARMS IS PART OF THE TEMPLE DANCE..
...BUT TO ME HER ARMS ARE SIGNALING INFORMATION TO ME IN SEMAPHORE!
8

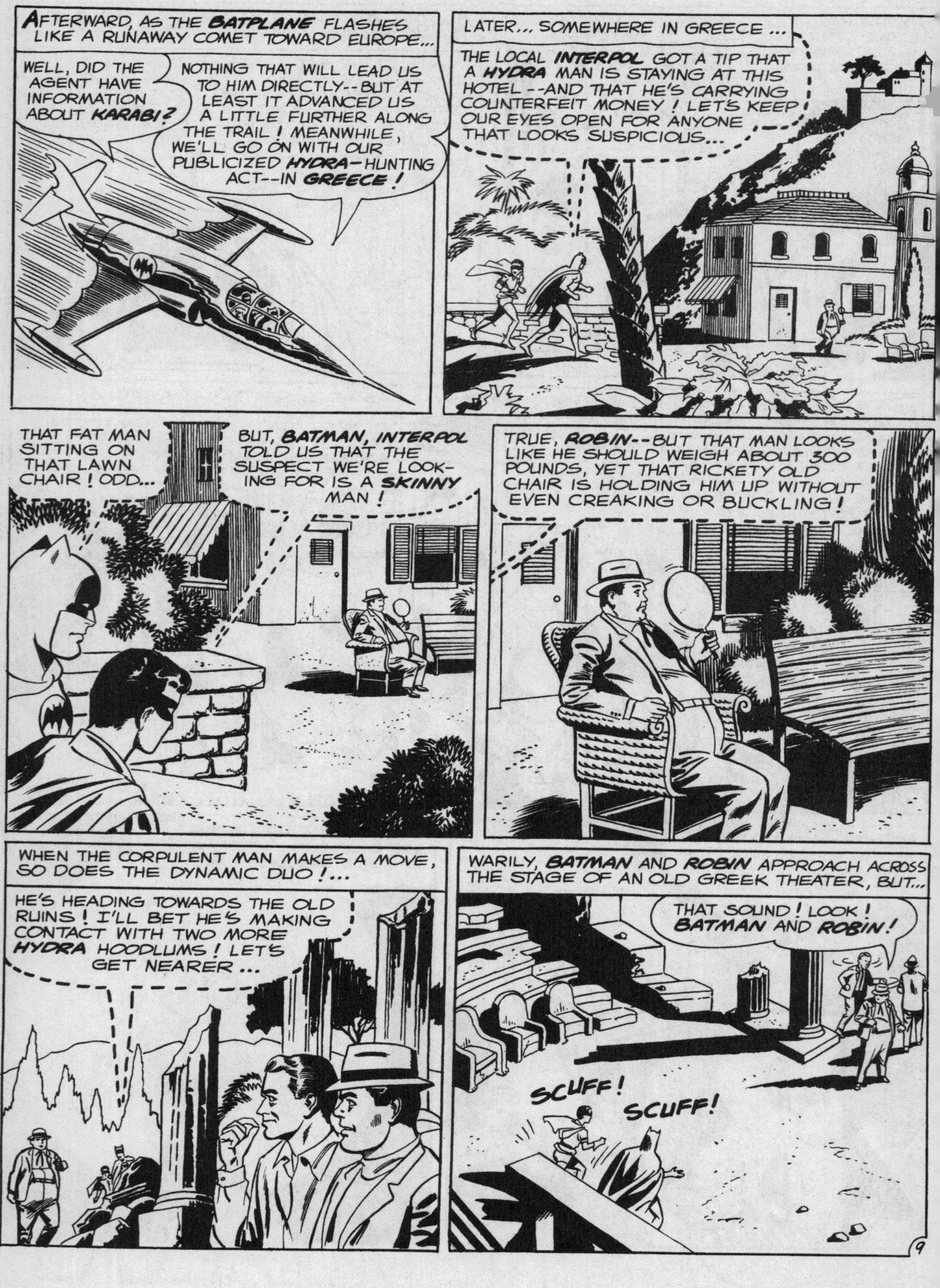
AFTERWARD, AS THE BATPLANE FLASHES LIKE A RUNAWAY COMET TOWARD EUROPE...
WELL, DID THE AGENT HAVE INFORMATION ABOUT KARABI?
NOTHING THAT WILL LEAD US TO HIM DIRECTLY--BUT AT LEAST IT ADVANCED US A LITTLE FURTHER ALONG THE TRAIL! MEANWHILE, WE'LL GO ON WITH OUR PUBLICIZED HYDRA-HUNTING ACT--IN GREECE!
LATER... SOMEWHERE IN GREECE...
THE LOCAL INTERPOL GOT A TIP THAT A HYDRA MAN IS STAYING AT THIS HOTEL--AND THAT HE'S CARRYING COUNTERFEIT MONEY! LET'S KEEP OUR EYES OPEN FOR ANYONE THAT LOOKS SUSPICIOUS...
THAT FAT MAN SITTING ON THAT LAWN CHAIR! ODD...
BUT, BATMAN, INTERPOL TOLD US THAT THE SUSPECT WE'RE LOOKING FOR IS A SKINNY MAN!
TRUE, ROBIN--BUT THAT MAN LOOKS LIKE HE SHOULD WEIGH ABOUT 300 POUNDS, YET THAT RICKETY OLD CHAIR IS HOLDING HIM UP WITHOUT EVEN CREAKING OR BUCKLING!
WHEN THE CORPULENT MAN MAKES A MOVE, SO DOES THE DYNAMIC DUO!...
HE'S HEADING TOWARDS THE OLD RUINS! I'LL BET HE'S MAKING CONTACT WITH TWO MORE HYDRA HOODLUMS! LET'S GET NEARER...
WARILY, BATMAN AND ROBIN APPROACH ACROSS THE STAGE OF AN OLD GREEK THEATER, BUT...
THAT SOUND! LOOK! BATMAN AND ROBIN!
SCUFF!
SCUFF!
9

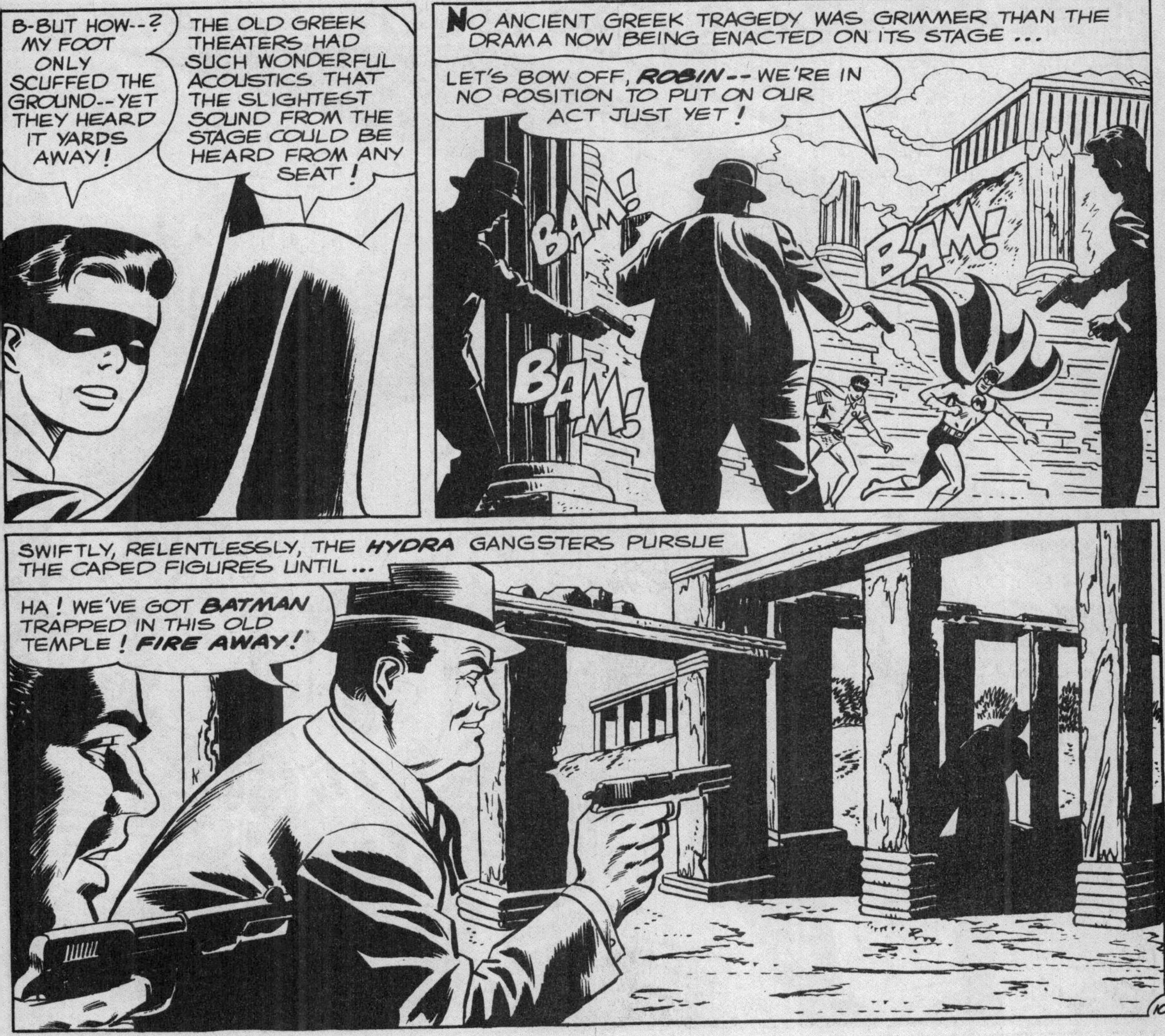
B-BUT HOW--? MY FOOT ONLY SCUFFED THE GROUND--YET THEY HEARD IT YARDS AWAY!
THE OLD GREEK THEATERS HAD SUCH WONDERFUL ACOUSTICS THAT THE SLIGHTEST SOUND FROM THE STAGE COULD BE HEARD FROM ANY SEAT!
NO ANCIENT GREEK TRAGEDY WAS GRIMMER THAN THE DRAMA NOW BEING ENACTED ON ITS STAGE ...
LET'S BOW OFF, ROBIN--WE'RE IN NO POSITION TO PUT ON OUR ACT JUST YET!
BAM!
BAM!
BAM!
SWIFTLY, RELENTLESSLY, THE HYDRA GANGSTERS PURSUE THE CAPED FIGURES UNTIL ...
HA! WE'VE GOT BATMAN TRAPPED IN THIS OLD TEMPLE! FIRE AWAY!
10

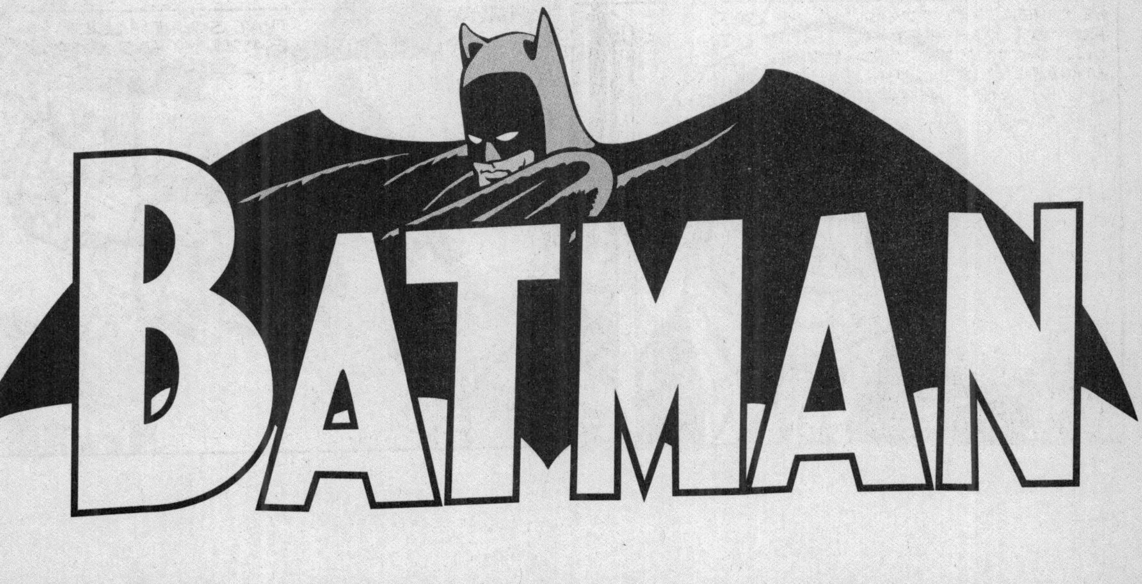
BATMAN

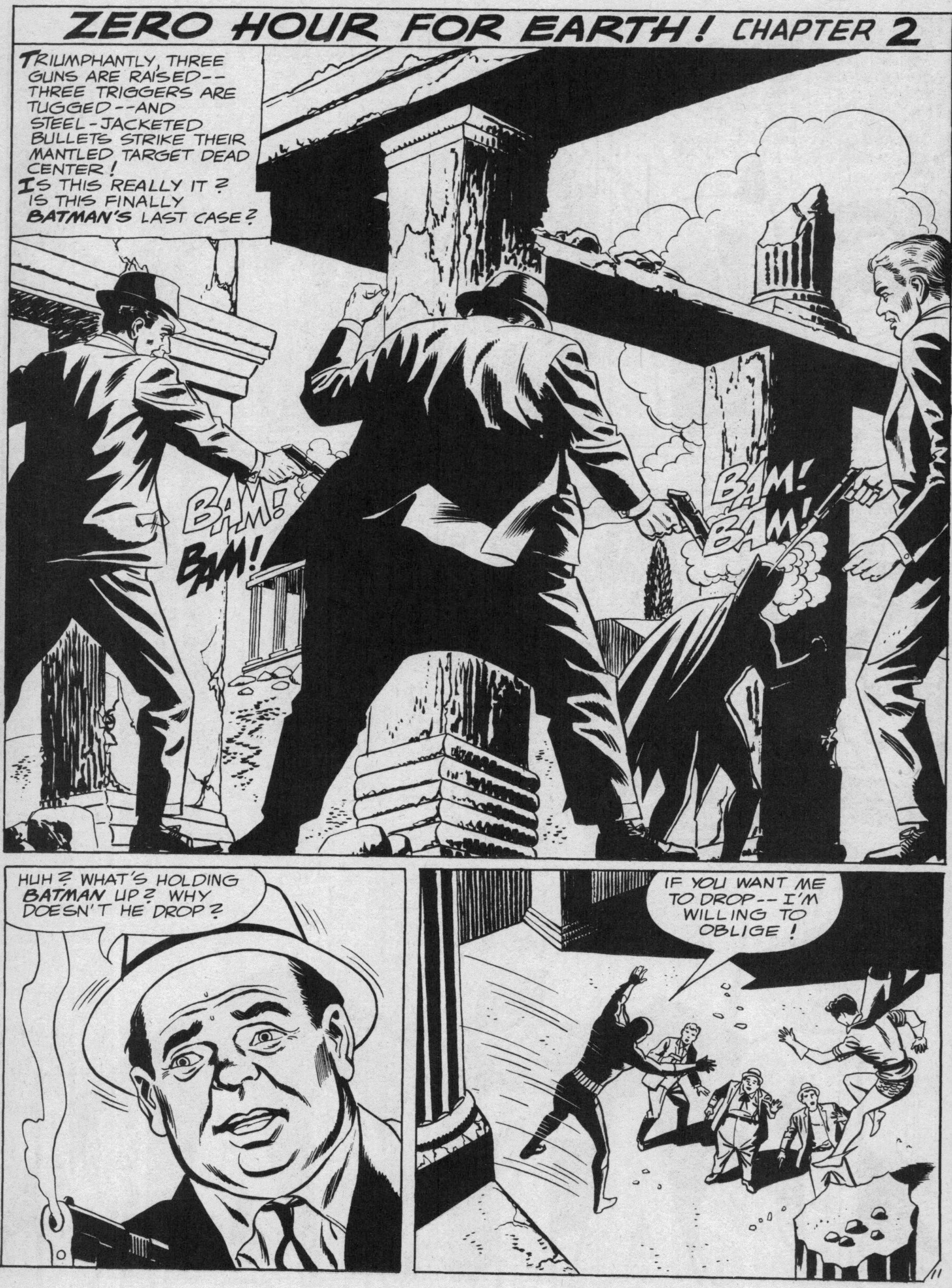
ZERO HOUR FOR EARTH! CHAPTER 2
TRIUMPHANTLY, THREE GUNS ARE RAISED-- THREE TRIGGERS ARE TUGGED--AND STEEL-JACKETED BULLETS STRIKE THEIR MANTLED TARGET DEAD CENTER! IS THIS REALLY IT? IS THIS FINALLY BATMAN'S LAST CASE?
BAM! BAM!
BAM! BAM!
HUH? WHAT'S HOLDING BATMAN UP? WHY DOESN'T HE DROP?
IF YOU WANT ME TO DROP-- I'M WILLING TO OBLIGE!
11

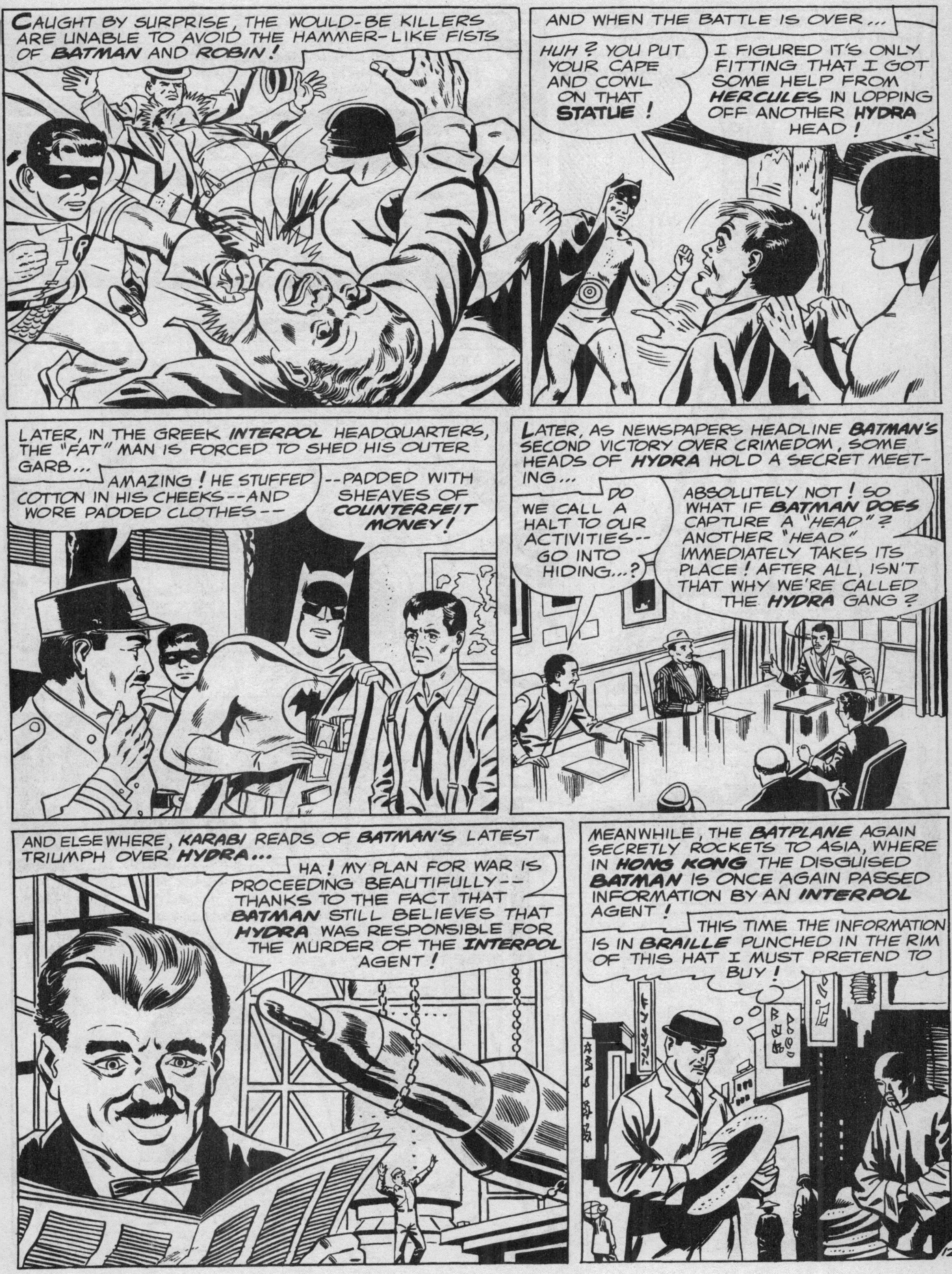
CAUGHT BY SURPRISE, THE WOULD-BE KILLERS ARE UNABLE TO AVOID THE HAMMER-LIKE FISTS OF BATMAN AND ROBIN!
AND WHEN THE BATTLE IS OVER...
HUH? YOU PUT YOUR CAPE AND COWL ON THAT STATUE!
I FIGURED IT'S ONLY FITTING THAT I GOT SOME HELP FROM HERCULES IN LOPPING OFF ANOTHER HYDRA HEAD!
LATER, IN THE GREEK INTERPOL HEADQUARTERS, THE "FAT" MAN IS FORCED TO SHED HIS OUTER GARB...
AMAZING! HE STUFFED COTTON IN HIS CHEEKS--AND WORE PADDED CLOTHES--
--PADDED WITH SHEAVES OF COUNTERFEIT MONEY!
LATER, AS NEWSPAPERS HEADLINE BATMAN'S SECOND VICTORY OVER CRIMEDOM, SOME HEADS OF HYDRA HOLD A SECRET MEETING...
DO WE CALL A HALT TO OUR ACTIVITIES--GO INTO HIDING...?
ABSOLUTELY NOT! SO WHAT IF BATMAN DOES CAPTURE A "HEAD"? ANOTHER "HEAD" IMMEDIATELY TAKES ITS PLACE! AFTER ALL, ISN'T THAT WHY WE'RE CALLED THE HYDRA GANG?
AND ELSEWHERE, KARABI READS OF BATMAN'S LATEST TRIUMPH OVER HYDRA...
HA! MY PLAN FOR WAR IS PROCEEDING BEAUTIFULLY--THANKS TO THE FACT THAT BATMAN STILL BELIEVES THAT HYDRA WAS RESPONSIBLE FOR THE MURDER OF THE INTERPOL AGENT!
MEANWHILE, THE BATPLANE AGAIN SECRETLY ROCKETS TO ASIA, WHERE IN HONG KONG THE DISGUISED BATMAN IS ONCE AGAIN PASSED INFORMATION BY AN INTERPOL AGENT!
THIS TIME THE INFORMATION IS IN BRAILLE PUNCHED IN THE RIM OF THIS HAT I MUST PRETEND TO BUY!
12

AND SO, AS PRECIOUS TIME PASSES, *BATMAN* CONTINUES PLAYING HIS DUAL ROLE--HOUNDING *HYDRA* IN EUROPE...

...AND AMASSING INFORMATION IN ASIA!

LUCKILY THE DARK *BATPLANE* BLENDS WITH THE DARK NIGHT-SKY! NOBODY BELOW CAN POSSIBLY SPOT US!

UNTIL AT LAST, SOMEWHERE IN SOUTHEASTERN ASIA...

EACH SCRAP OF INFORMATION I'VE COLLECTED MEANS NOTHING BY ITSELF--BUT TOGETHER THEY ADD UP TO *KARABI'S* INSANE PLAN FOR WORLD POWER!

KARABI INTENDS TO SECRETLY FIRE A NUCLEAR MISSILE FROM COUNTRY *A** TO COUNTRY *B**! HE KNOWS *B* WILL ACCUSE *A* OF AGGRESSION-- AND WAR WILL BREAK OUT...

**EDITOR'S NOTE :* FOR SECURITY REASONS, WE CANNOT REVEAL THE TRUE NAMES OF THE ACTUAL COUNTRIES INVOLVED.

THAT ERUPTION OF WAR WILL ONLY BE THE BEGINNING ! LIKE A CHAIN RE-ACTION, IT WILL INEVITABLY SPREAD, INVOLVING MORE COUNTRIES, NATIONS...EVEN THE UNITED STATES !

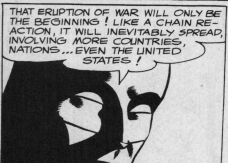

THEN *KARABI* INTENDS TO FORM A GROUP OF MAL-CONTENTS THAT WILL FORM THE NUCLEUS OF A BAND LIKE HITLER'S *S.S. ELITE* -- AND WITH THEM, WILL TRY TO SEIZE AS MUCH POWER AS HE CAN !

GOOD GOSH ! WE MUST STOP HIM BEFORE HE TURNS THE ENTIRE WORLD INTO ONE GREAT BATTLE-GROUND !

13

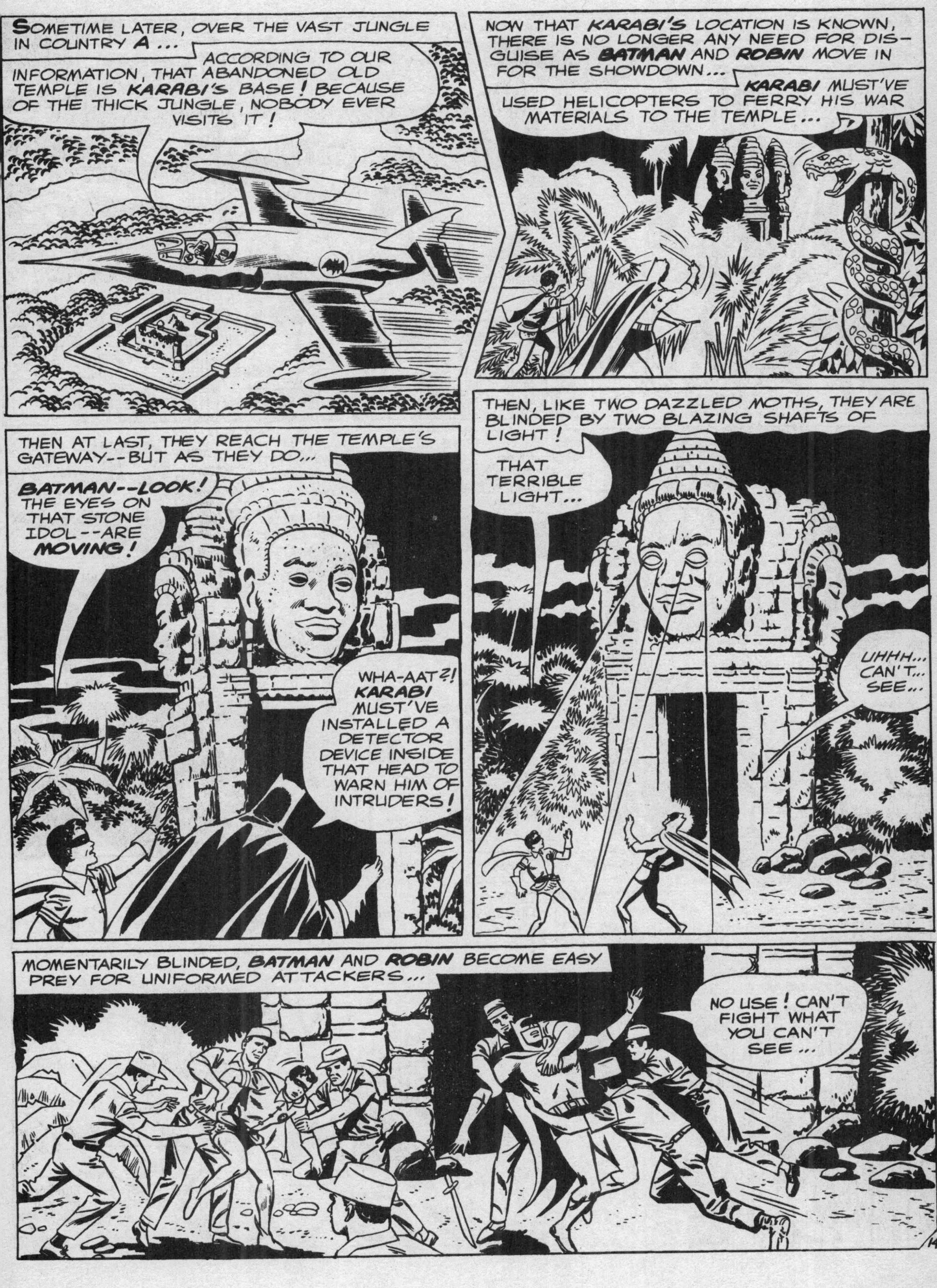
SOMETIME LATER, OVER THE VAST JUNGLE IN COUNTRY A ...
ACCORDING TO OUR INFORMATION, THAT ABANDONED OLD TEMPLE IS KARABI'S BASE! BECAUSE OF THE THICK JUNGLE, NOBODY EVER VISITS IT!
NOW THAT KARABI'S LOCATION IS KNOWN, THERE IS NO LONGER ANY NEED FOR DISGUISE AS BATMAN AND ROBIN MOVE IN FOR THE SHOWDOWN...
KARABI MUST'VE USED HELICOPTERS TO FERRY HIS WAR MATERIALS TO THE TEMPLE...
THEN AT LAST, THEY REACH THE TEMPLE'S GATEWAY--BUT AS THEY DO,..
BATMAN--LOOK! THE EYES ON THAT STONE IDOL--ARE MOVING!
WHA-AAT?! KARABI MUST'VE INSTALLED A DETECTOR DEVICE INSIDE THAT HEAD TO WARN HIM OF INTRUDERS!
THEN, LIKE TWO DAZZLED MOTHS, THEY ARE BLINDED BY TWO BLAZING SHAFTS OF LIGHT!
THAT TERRIBLE LIGHT...
UHHH... CAN'T... SEE...
MOMENTARILY BLINDED, BATMAN AND ROBIN BECOME EASY PREY FOR UNIFORMED ATTACKERS...
NO USE! CAN'T FIGHT WHAT YOU CAN'T SEE...
14

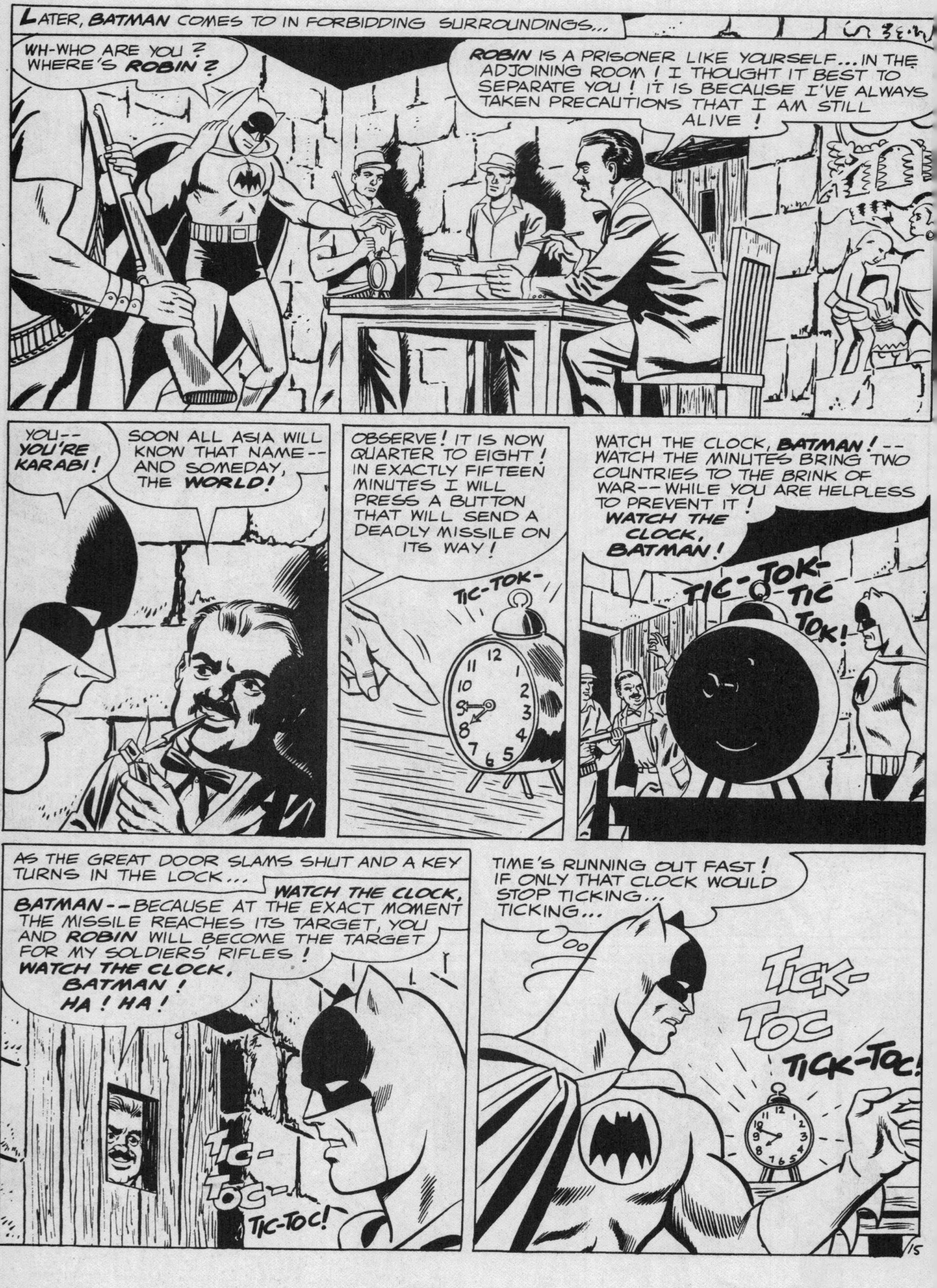
LATER, BATMAN COMES TO IN FORBIDDING SURROUNDINGS...
WH-WHO ARE YOU ? WHERE'S ROBIN ?
ROBIN IS A PRISONER LIKE YOURSELF... IN THE ADJOINING ROOM ! I THOUGHT IT BEST TO SEPARATE YOU ! IT IS BECAUSE I'VE ALWAYS TAKEN PRECAUTIONS THAT I AM STILL ALIVE !
YOU-- YOU'RE KARABI !
SOON ALL ASIA WILL KNOW THAT NAME-- AND SOMEDAY, THE WORLD !
OBSERVE ! IT IS NOW QUARTER TO EIGHT ! IN EXACTLY FIFTEEN MINUTES I WILL PRESS A BUTTON THAT WILL SEND A DEADLY MISSILE ON ITS WAY !
TIC-TOK-
WATCH THE CLOCK, BATMAN ! -- WATCH THE MINUTES BRING TWO COUNTRIES TO THE BRINK OF WAR-- WHILE YOU ARE HELPLESS TO PREVENT IT ! WATCH THE CLOCK, BATMAN !
TIC-TOK- TIC TOK !
AS THE GREAT DOOR SLAMS SHUT AND A KEY TURNS IN THE LOCK...
WATCH THE CLOCK, BATMAN-- BECAUSE AT THE EXACT MOMENT THE MISSILE REACHES ITS TARGET, YOU AND ROBIN WILL BECOME THE TARGET FOR MY SOLDIERS' RIFLES ! WATCH THE CLOCK, BATMAN ! HA ! HA !
TIC-TOC-- TIC-TOC !
TIME'S RUNNING OUT FAST ! IF ONLY THAT CLOCK WOULD STOP TICKING... TICKING...
TICK-TOC TICK-TOC !
/15

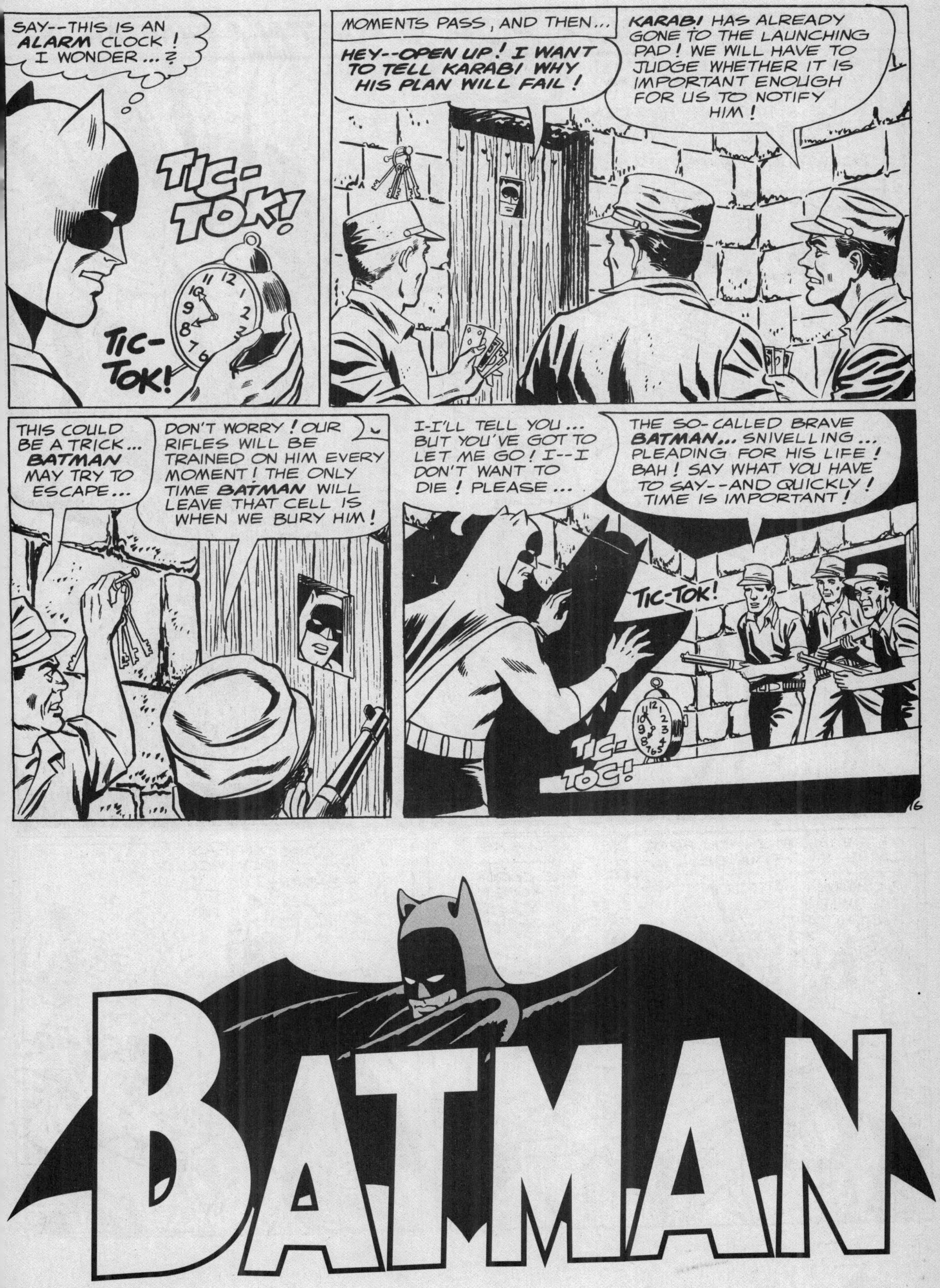
SAY--THIS IS AN ALARM CLOCK! I WONDER...?
TIC-TOK!
TIC-TOK!
MOMENTS PASS, AND THEN...
HEY--OPEN UP! I WANT TO TELL KARABI WHY HIS PLAN WILL FAIL!
KARABI HAS ALREADY GONE TO THE LAUNCHING PAD! WE WILL HAVE TO JUDGE WHETHER IT IS IMPORTANT ENOUGH FOR US TO NOTIFY HIM!
THIS COULD BE A TRICK... BATMAN MAY TRY TO ESCAPE...
DON'T WORRY! OUR RIFLES WILL BE TRAINED ON HIM EVERY MOMENT! THE ONLY TIME BATMAN WILL LEAVE THAT CELL IS WHEN WE BURY HIM!
I-I'LL TELL YOU... BUT YOU'VE GOT TO LET ME GO! I--I DON'T WANT TO DIE! PLEASE...
THE SO-CALLED BRAVE BATMAN... SNIVELLING... PLEADING FOR HIS LIFE! BAH! SAY WHAT YOU HAVE TO SAY--AND QUICKLY! TIME IS IMPORTANT!
TIC-TOK!
TIC-TOC!
16

BATMAN

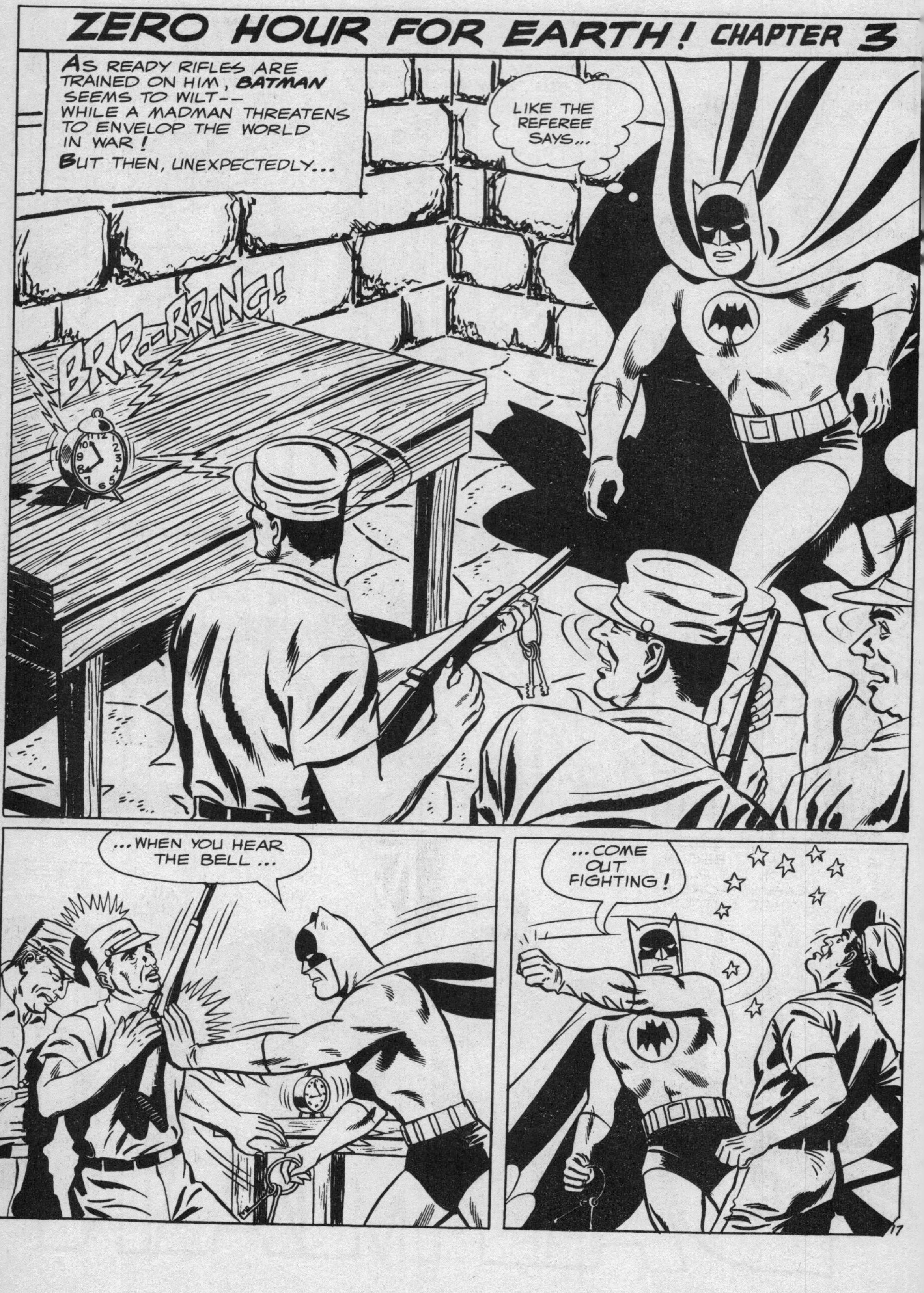
ZERO HOUR FOR EARTH! CHAPTER 3
AS READY RIFLES ARE TRAINED ON HIM, BATMAN SEEMS TO WILT-- WHILE A MADMAN THREATENS TO ENVELOP THE WORLD IN WAR! BUT THEN, UNEXPECTEDLY...
LIKE THE REFEREE SAYS...
BRR--RRING!
...WHEN YOU HEAR THE BELL...
...COME OUT FIGHTING!
17

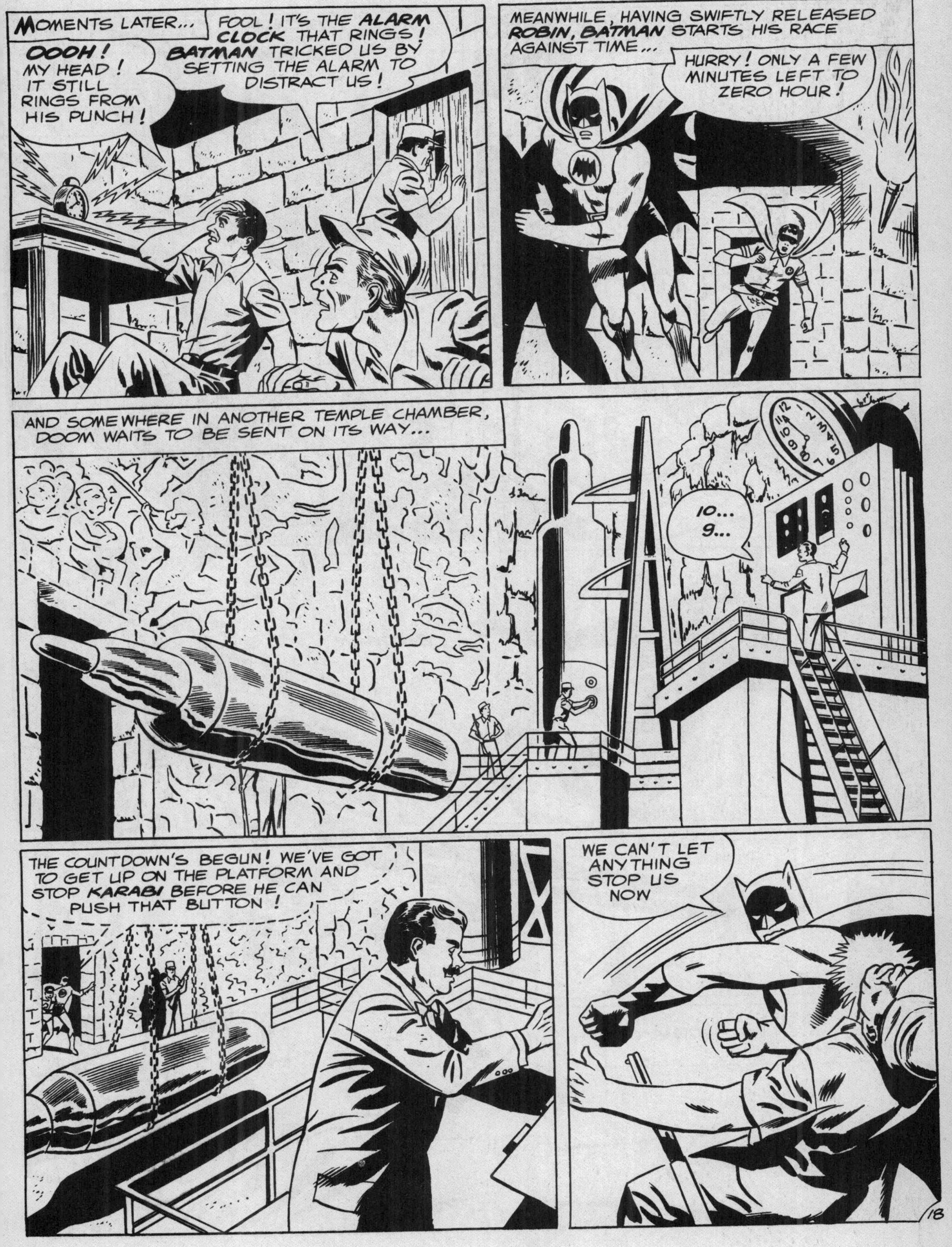
MOMENTS LATER...
OOOH! MY HEAD! IT STILL RINGS FROM HIS PUNCH!
FOOL! IT'S THE ALARM CLOCK THAT RINGS! BATMAN TRICKED US BY SETTING THE ALARM TO DISTRACT US!
MEANWHILE, HAVING SWIFTLY RELEASED ROBIN, BATMAN STARTS HIS RACE AGAINST TIME...
HURRY! ONLY A FEW MINUTES LEFT TO ZERO HOUR!
AND SOMEWHERE IN ANOTHER TEMPLE CHAMBER, DOOM WAITS TO BE SENT ON ITS WAY...
10... 9...
THE COUNTDOWN'S BEGUN! WE'VE GOT TO GET UP ON THE PLATFORM AND STOP KARABI BEFORE HE CAN PUSH THAT BUTTON!
WE CAN'T LET ANYTHING STOP US NOW
18

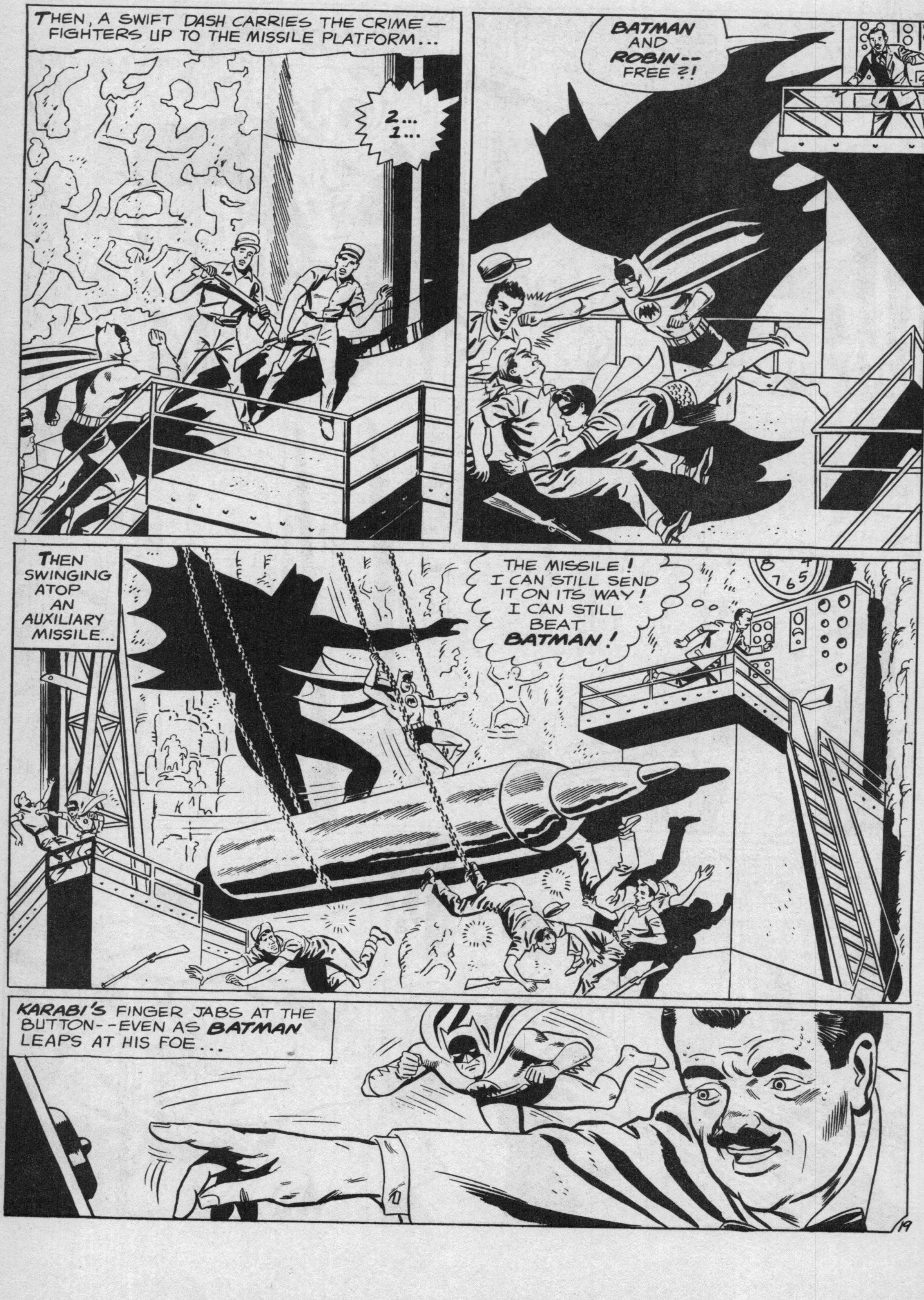
THEN, A SWIFT DASH CARRIES THE CRIME-FIGHTERS UP TO THE MISSILE PLATFORM...
2... 1...
BATMAN AND ROBIN-- FREE ?!
THEN SWINGING ATOP AN AUXILIARY MISSILE...
THE MISSILE! I CAN STILL SEND IT ON ITS WAY! I CAN STILL BEAT BATMAN!
KARABI'S FINGER JABS AT THE BUTTON--EVEN AS BATMAN LEAPS AT HIS FOE...
19

RIGHT ON THE BUTTON! BUT NOT THE ONE ON THE CONTROL PANEL!

LATER, AFTER *KARABI* AND HIS FOLLOWERS HAVE BEEN IMPRISONED...

THANKS TO YOU, A TERRIBLE WAR HAS BEEN AVERTED! OUR PEOPLE WILL BE ETERNALLY GRATEFUL!

THANK YOU, SIR-- AND NOW, IF YOU DON'T MIND, I'LL TAKE *KARABI'S* PAPERS THAT WE FOUND IN HIS HEAD- QUARTERS, AND TURN THEM OVER TO THE *U.N.!*

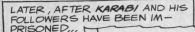

AFTERWARD, AS *BATMAN* CHECKS *KARABI'S DIARY* IN THE *BAT- PLANE*...

ACCORDING TO *KARABI'S* LAST ENTRY, HE *HAD* INTENDED TO DEPOSIT HIS CAMPAIGN MONEY UNDER AN ASSUMED NAME IN A SWISS BANK-- BUT HE CHANGED HIS MIND WHEN AN UNDER- WORLD TIPSTER TOLD HIM THAT BANK WOULD BE ROBBED...

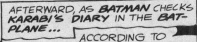

...ROBBED BY A *TOP HYDRA "HEAD"! KARABI'S* DIARY EVEN TELLS HOW THE ROBBERY IS TO BE DONE! GREAT SCOTT! IT'S TO BE ROBBED LATE THIS AFTERNOON!

THEN WE'RE TOO LATE-- IT'S ALREADY NIGHT- TIME!

IN REPLY, *BATMAN* SENDS THE *BAT- PLANE* ROCKETING SKYWARD...

YOU'RE FORGETTING THE *TIME ZONE* DIFFERENTIAL, *ROBIN*-- EVEN THOUGH IT'S NIGHT HERE IN ASIA, IT'S STILL DAY IN SWITZERLAND! THE *BAT- PLANE'S* JET WILL GET US BACK IN TIME TO INTERCEPT THE *HYDRA* ROBBERY!

WITHIN HOURS, THE CAPED CRIME-FIGHTERS ARE DARTING ACROSS A STREET IN A SWISS CITY...

THE *HYDRA* GANG IS USING THAT CURIO SHOP AS A COVER--WHILE THEY TUNNEL FROM THE SHOP BASEMENT INTO THE ADJOINING BANK'S UNDERGROUND VAULT!

20

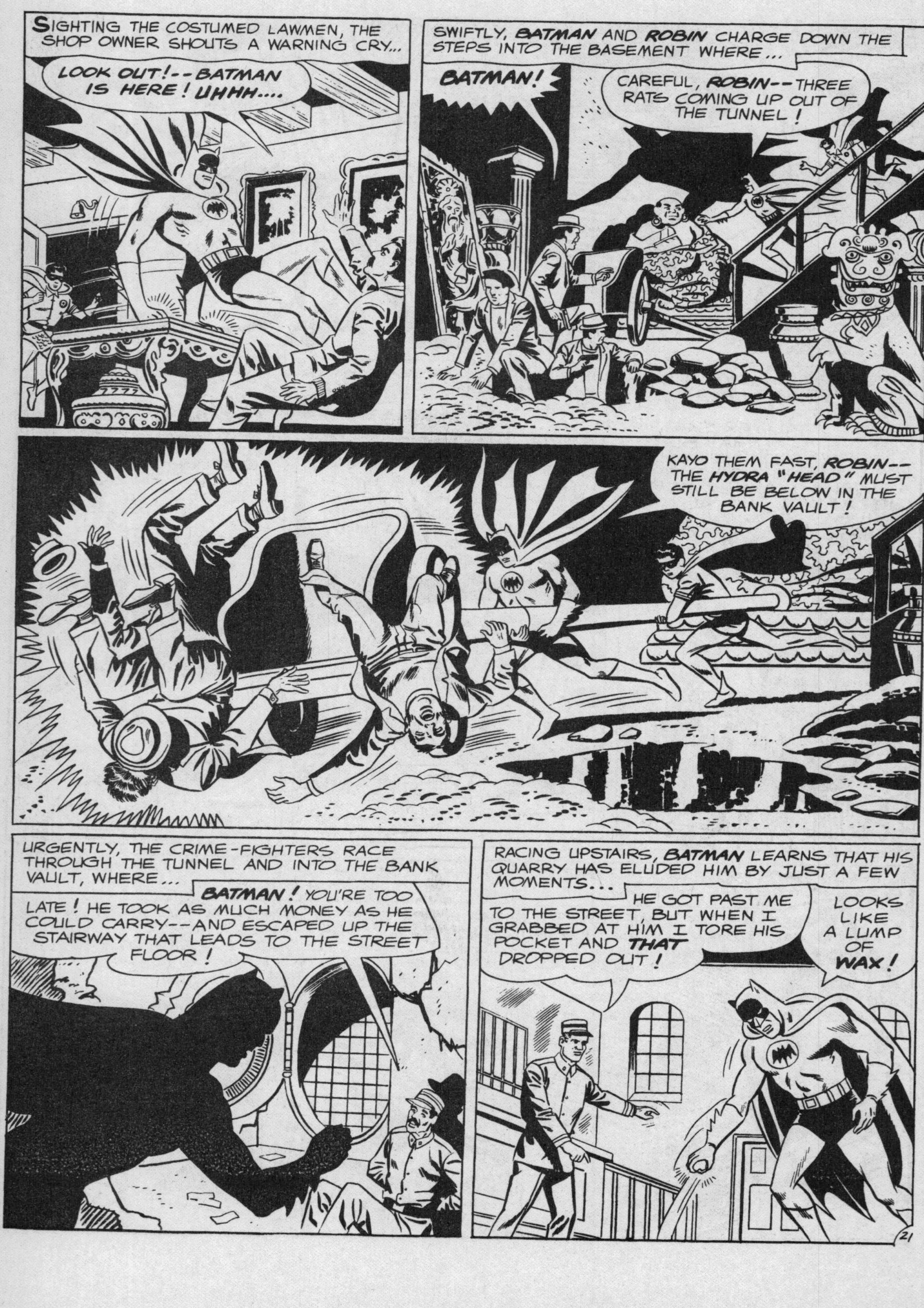
SIGHTING THE COSTUMED LAWMEN, THE SHOP OWNER SHOUTS A WARNING CRY...
LOOK OUT!--BATMAN IS HERE! UHHH....
SWIFTLY, BATMAN AND ROBIN CHARGE DOWN THE STEPS INTO THE BASEMENT WHERE...
BATMAN!
CAREFUL, ROBIN--THREE RATS COMING UP OUT OF THE TUNNEL!
KAYO THEM FAST, ROBIN-- THE HYDRA "HEAD" MUST STILL BE BELOW IN THE BANK VAULT!
URGENTLY, THE CRIME-FIGHTERS RACE THROUGH THE TUNNEL AND INTO THE BANK VAULT, WHERE...
BATMAN! YOU'RE TOO LATE! HE TOOK AS MUCH MONEY AS HE COULD CARRY--AND ESCAPED UP THE STAIRWAY THAT LEADS TO THE STREET FLOOR!
RACING UPSTAIRS, BATMAN LEARNS THAT HIS QUARRY HAS ELUDED HIM BY JUST A FEW MOMENTS...
HE GOT PAST ME TO THE STREET, BUT WHEN I GRABBED AT HIM I TORE HIS POCKET AND THAT DROPPED OUT!
LOOKS LIKE A LUMP OF WAX!
21

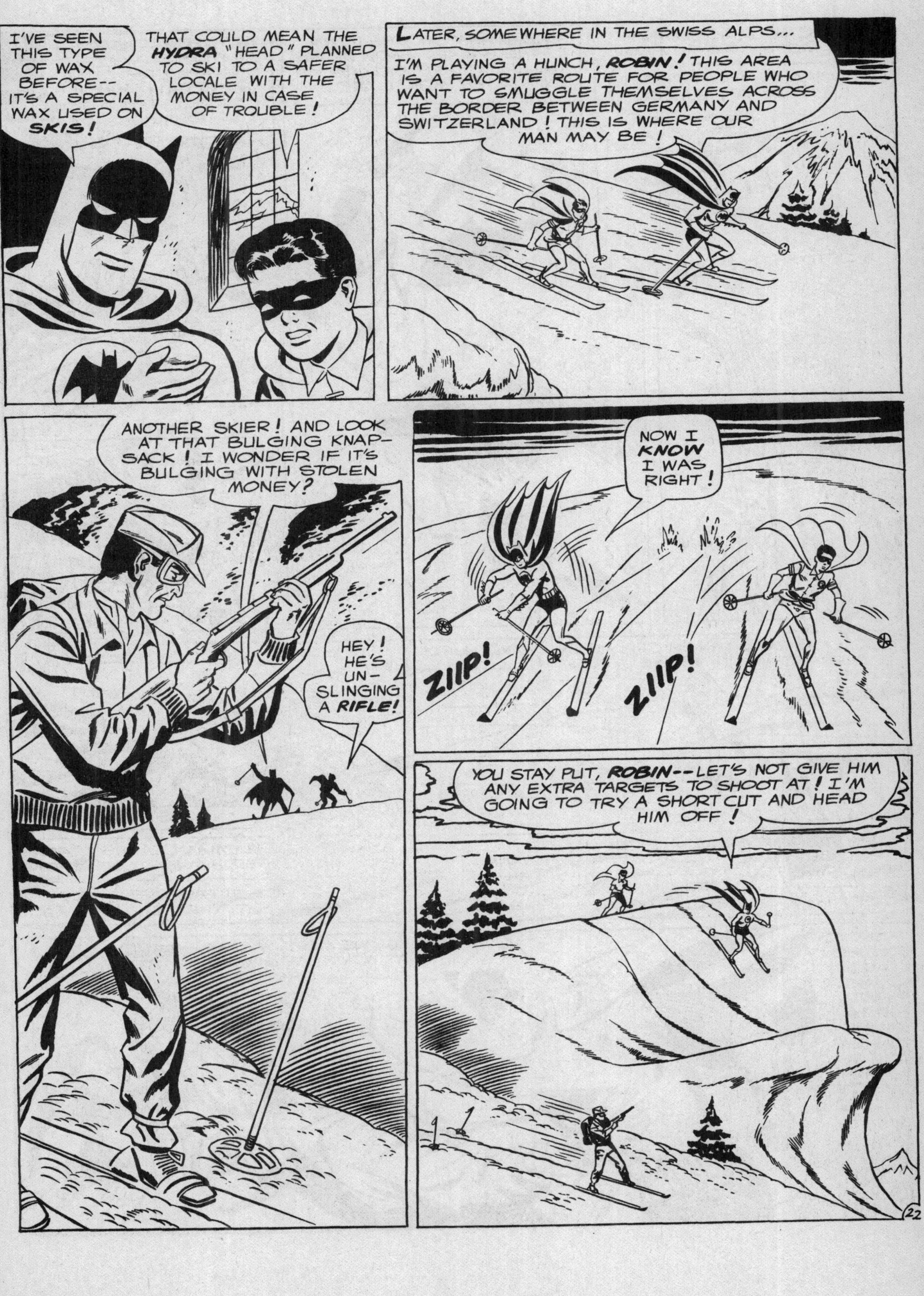
I'VE SEEN THIS TYPE OF WAX BEFORE-- IT'S A SPECIAL WAX USED ON SKIS!
THAT COULD MEAN THE HYDRA "HEAD" PLANNED TO SKI TO A SAFER LOCALE WITH THE MONEY IN CASE OF TROUBLE!
LATER, SOMEWHERE IN THE SWISS ALPS...
I'M PLAYING A HUNCH, ROBIN! THIS AREA IS A FAVORITE ROUTE FOR PEOPLE WHO WANT TO SMUGGLE THEMSELVES ACROSS THE BORDER BETWEEN GERMANY AND SWITZERLAND! THIS IS WHERE OUR MAN MAY BE!
ANOTHER SKIER! AND LOOK AT THAT BULGING KNAPSACK! I WONDER IF IT'S BULGING WITH STOLEN MONEY?
HEY! HE'S UN-SLINGING A RIFLE!
NOW I KNOW I WAS RIGHT!
ZIIP!
ZIIP!
YOU STAY PUT, ROBIN--LET'S NOT GIVE HIM ANY EXTRA TARGETS TO SHOOT AT! I'M GOING TO TRY A SHORT CUT AND HEAD HIM OFF!
22

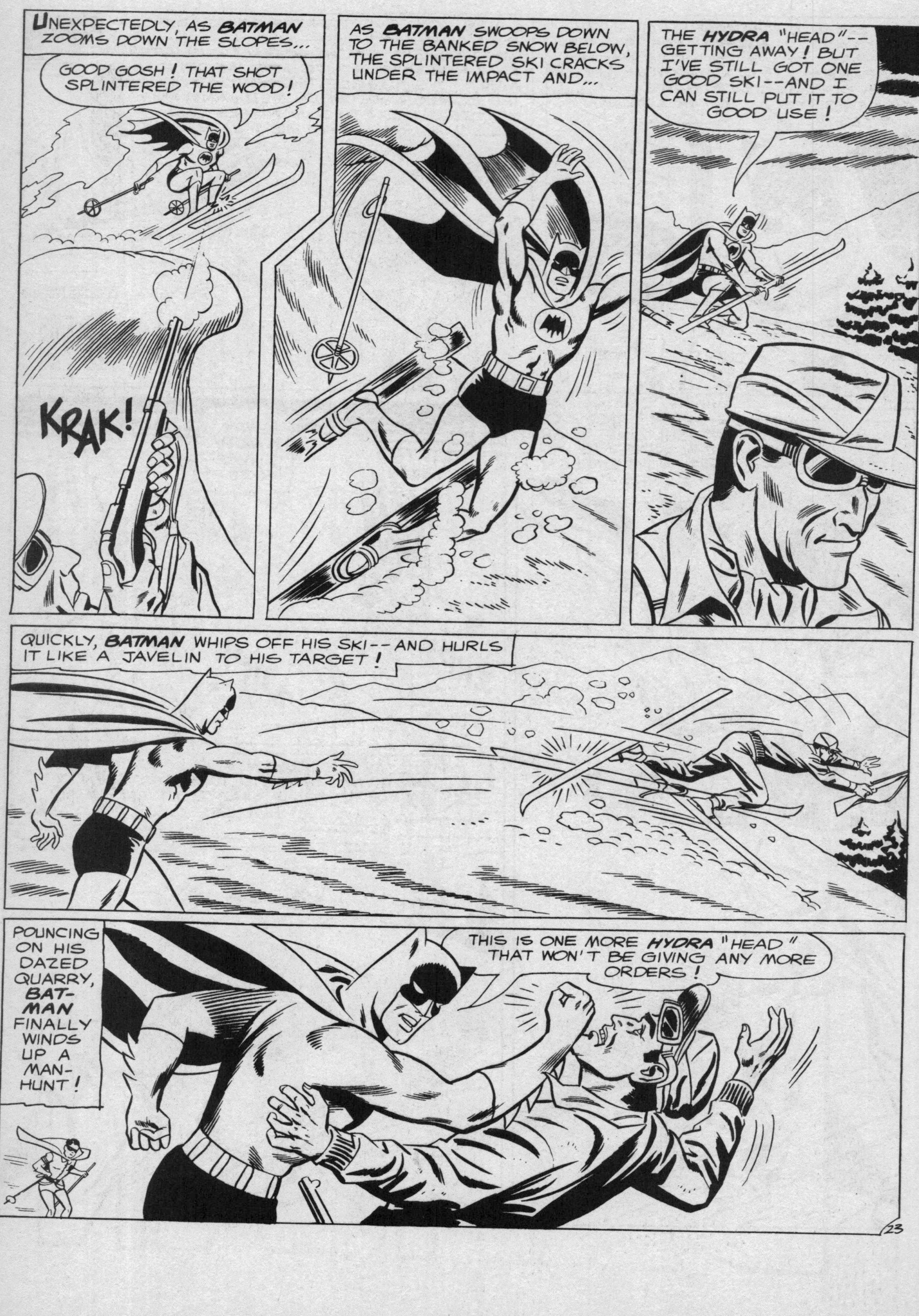
UNEXPECTEDLY, AS BATMAN ZOOMS DOWN THE SLOPES...
GOOD GOSH! THAT SHOT SPLINTERED THE WOOD!
KRAK!
AS BATMAN SWOOPS DOWN TO THE BANKED SNOW BELOW, THE SPLINTERED SKI CRACKS UNDER THE IMPACT AND...
THE HYDRA "HEAD"-- GETTING AWAY! BUT I'VE STILL GOT ONE GOOD SKI--AND I CAN STILL PUT IT TO GOOD USE!
QUICKLY, BATMAN WHIPS OFF HIS SKI--AND HURLS IT LIKE A JAVELIN TO HIS TARGET!
POUNCING ON HIS DAZED QUARRY, BATMAN FINALLY WINDS UP A MAN-HUNT!
THIS IS ONE MORE HYDRA "HEAD" THAT WON'T BE GIVING ANY MORE ORDERS!
23

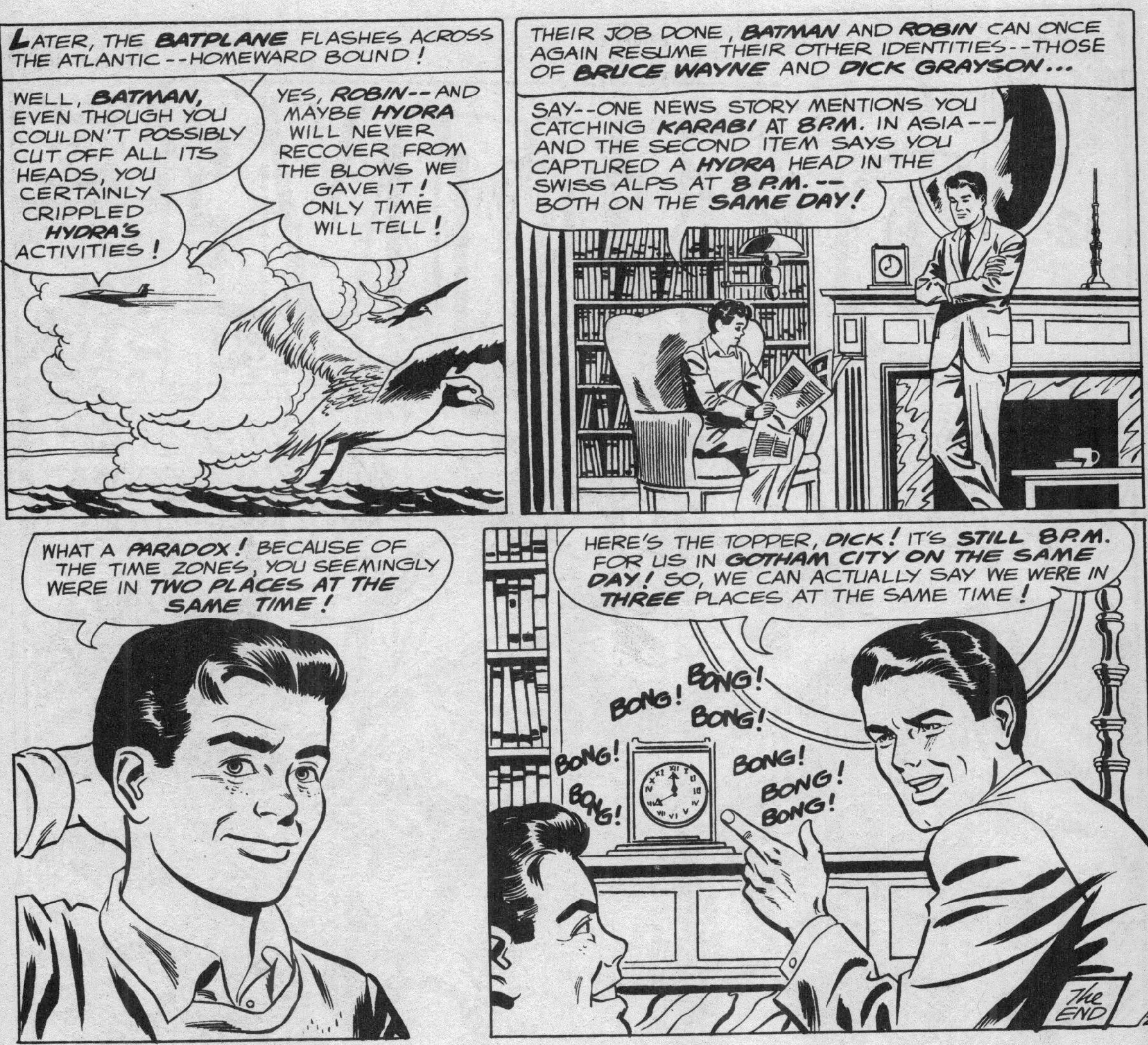
LATER, THE BATPLANE FLASHES ACROSS THE ATLANTIC--HOMEWARD BOUND!
WELL, BATMAN, EVEN THOUGH YOU COULDN'T POSSIBLY CUT OFF ALL ITS HEADS, YOU CERTAINLY CRIPPLED HYDRA'S ACTIVITIES!
YES, ROBIN--AND MAYBE HYDRA WILL NEVER RECOVER FROM THE BLOWS WE GAVE IT! ONLY TIME WILL TELL!
THEIR JOB DONE, BATMAN AND ROBIN CAN ONCE AGAIN RESUME THEIR OTHER IDENTITIES--THOSE OF BRUCE WAYNE AND DICK GRAYSON...
SAY--ONE NEWS STORY MENTIONS YOU CATCHING KARABI AT 8 P.M. IN ASIA--AND THE SECOND ITEM SAYS YOU CAPTURED A HYDRA HEAD IN THE SWISS ALPS AT 8 P.M.--BOTH ON THE SAME DAY!
WHAT A PARADOX! BECAUSE OF THE TIME ZONES, YOU SEEMINGLY WERE IN TWO PLACES AT THE SAME TIME!
HERE'S THE TOPPER, DICK! IT'S STILL 8 P.M. FOR US IN GOTHAM CITY ON THE SAME DAY! SO, WE CAN ACTUALLY SAY WE WERE IN THREE PLACES AT THE SAME TIME!
BONG! BONG! BONG! BONG! BONG! BONG! BONG! BONG!
THE END
24

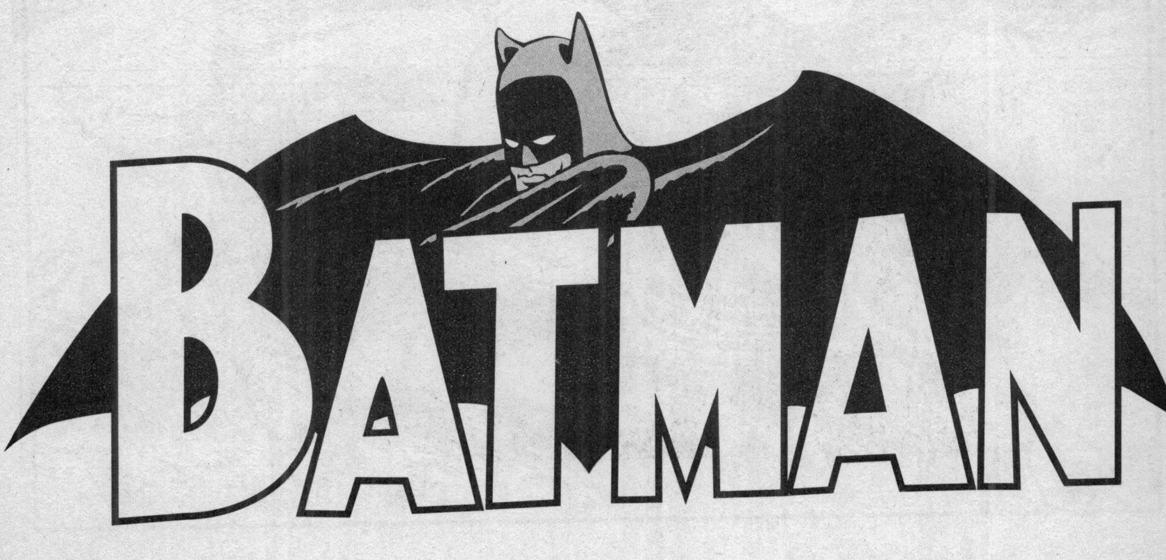
BATMAN

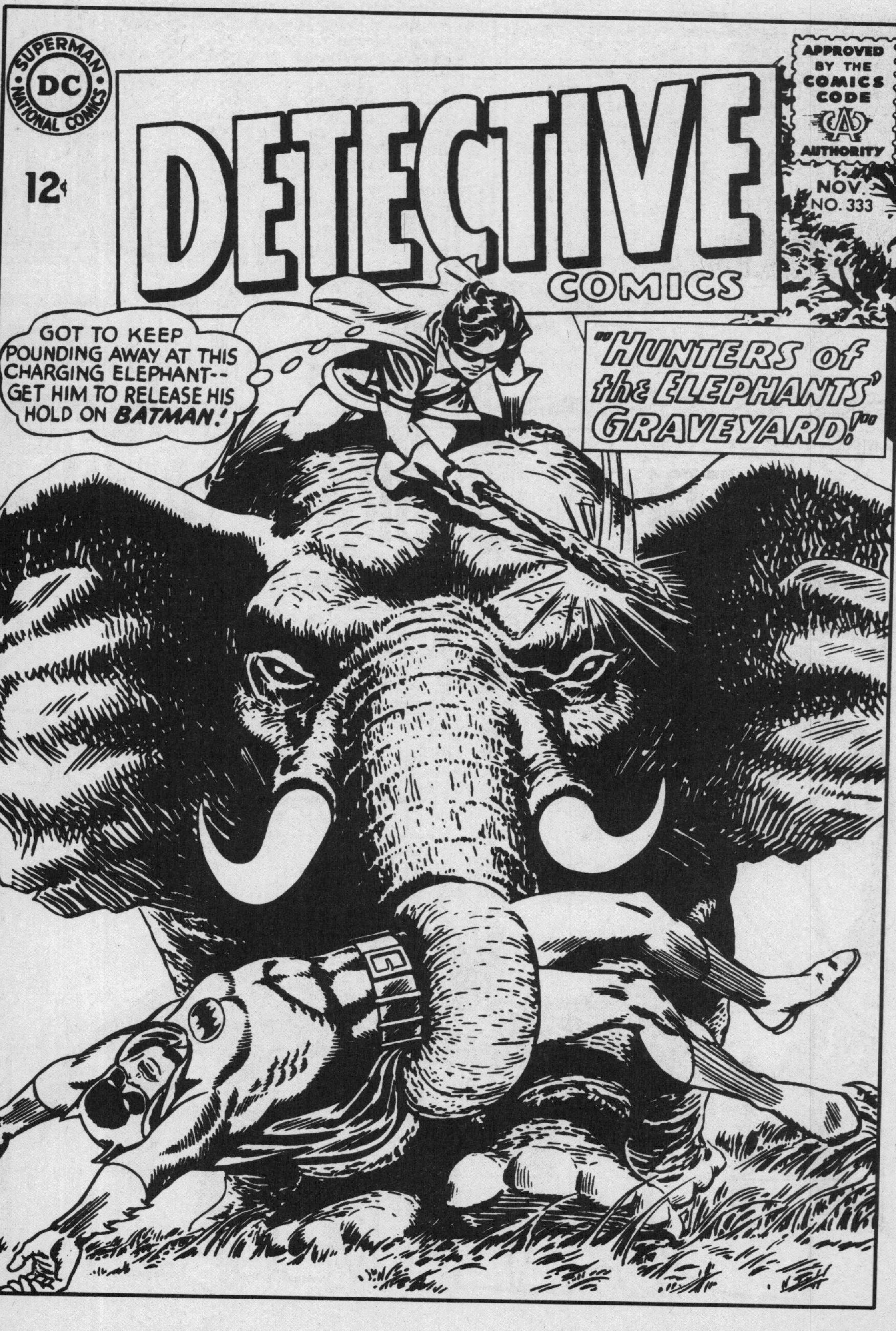
SUPERMAN DC NATIONAL COMICS
12¢
DETECTIVE COMICS
APPROVED BY THE COMICS CODE AUTHORITY
NOV. NO. 333
GOT TO KEEP POUNDING AWAY AT THIS CHARGING ELEPHANT-- GET HIM TO RELEASE HIS HOLD ON BATMAN!
"HUNTERS of the ELEPHANTS' GRAVEYARD!"

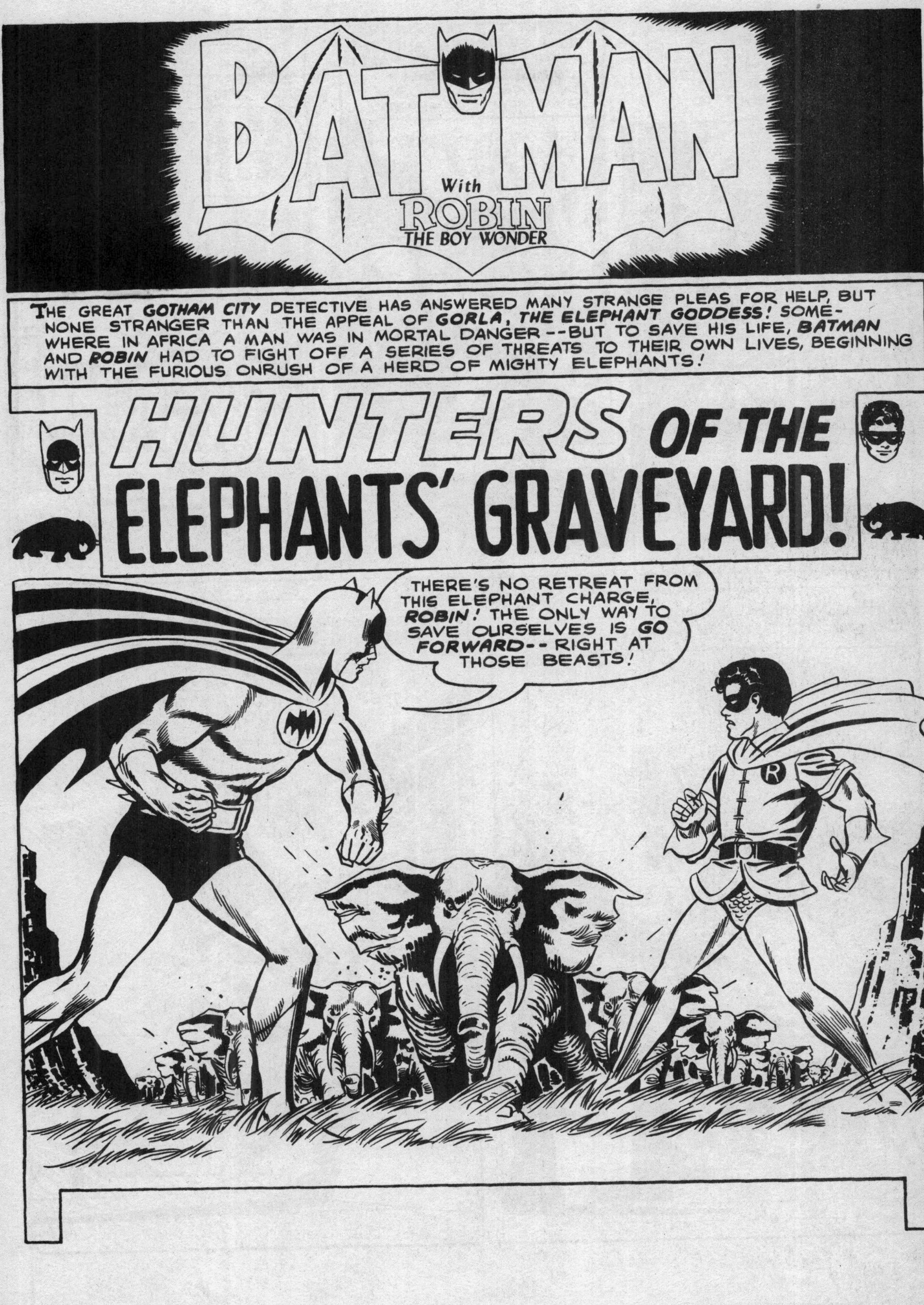
BATMAN
With ROBIN THE BOY WONDER
THE GREAT GOTHAM CITY DETECTIVE HAS ANSWERED MANY STRANGE PLEAS FOR HELP, BUT NONE STRANGER THAN THE APPEAL OF GORLA, THE ELEPHANT GODDESS! SOMEWHERE IN AFRICA A MAN WAS IN MORTAL DANGER --BUT TO SAVE HIS LIFE, BATMAN AND ROBIN HAD TO FIGHT OFF A SERIES OF THREATS TO THEIR OWN LIVES, BEGINNING WITH THE FURIOUS ONRUSH OF A HERD OF MIGHTY ELEPHANTS!
HUNTERS OF THE ELEPHANTS' GRAVEYARD!
THERE'S NO RETREAT FROM THIS ELEPHANT CHARGE, ROBIN! THE ONLY WAY TO SAVE OURSELVES IS GO FORWARD-- RIGHT AT THOSE BEASTS!

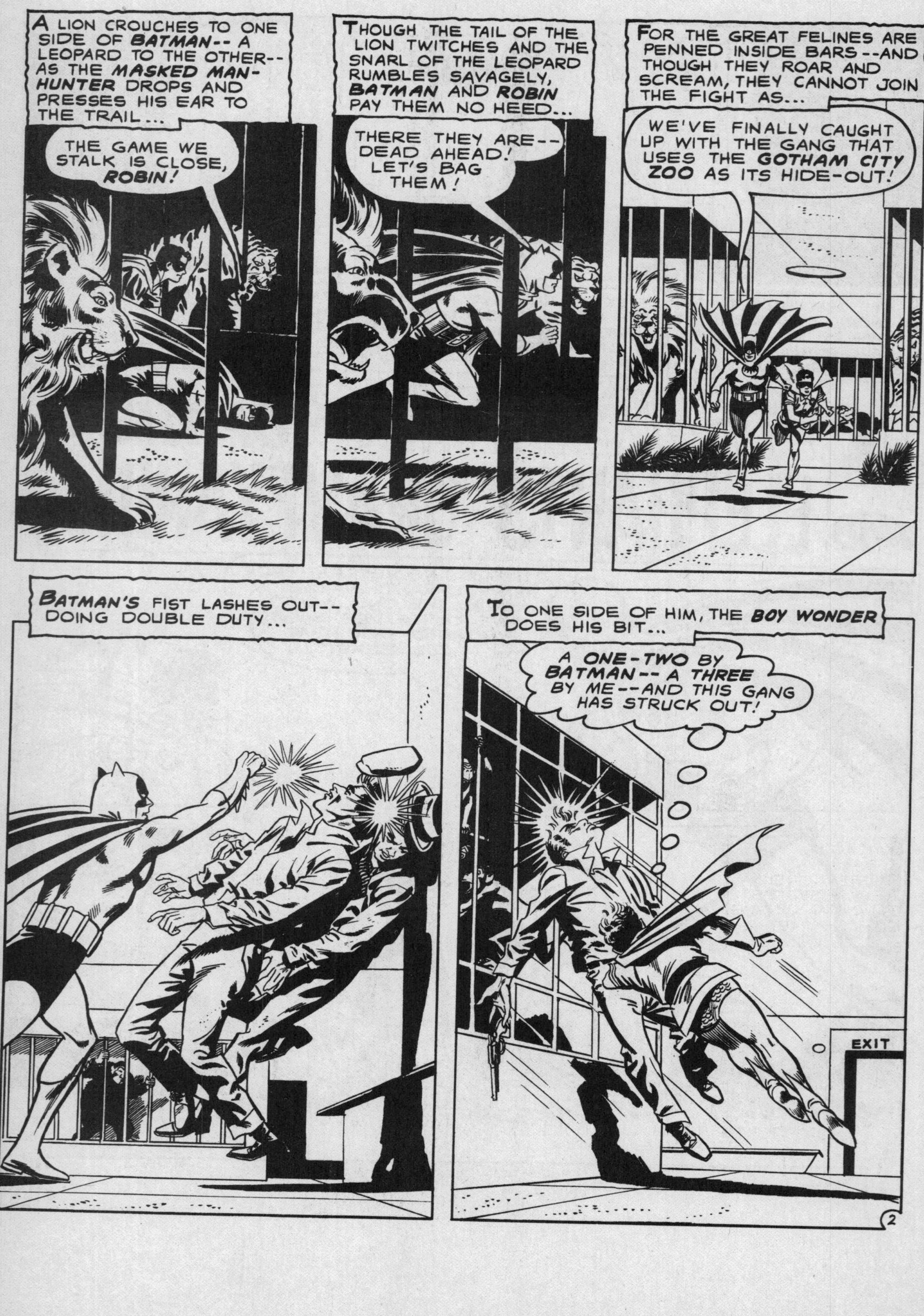
A LION CROUCHES TO ONE SIDE OF BATMAN-- A LEOPARD TO THE OTHER-- AS THE MASKED MAN-HUNTER DROPS AND PRESSES HIS EAR TO THE TRAIL...
THE GAME WE STALK IS CLOSE, ROBIN!
THOUGH THE TAIL OF THE LION TWITCHES AND THE SNARL OF THE LEOPARD RUMBLES SAVAGELY, BATMAN AND ROBIN PAY THEM NO HEED...
THERE THEY ARE-- DEAD AHEAD! LET'S BAG THEM!
FOR THE GREAT FELINES ARE PENNED INSIDE BARS--AND THOUGH THEY ROAR AND SCREAM, THEY CANNOT JOIN THE FIGHT AS...
WE'VE FINALLY CAUGHT UP WITH THE GANG THAT USES THE GOTHAM CITY ZOO AS ITS HIDE-OUT!
BATMAN'S FIST LASHES OUT-- DOING DOUBLE DUTY...
TO ONE SIDE OF HIM, THE BOY WONDER DOES HIS BIT...
A ONE-TWO BY BATMAN-- A THREE BY ME--AND THIS GANG HAS STRUCK OUT!
EXIT
2

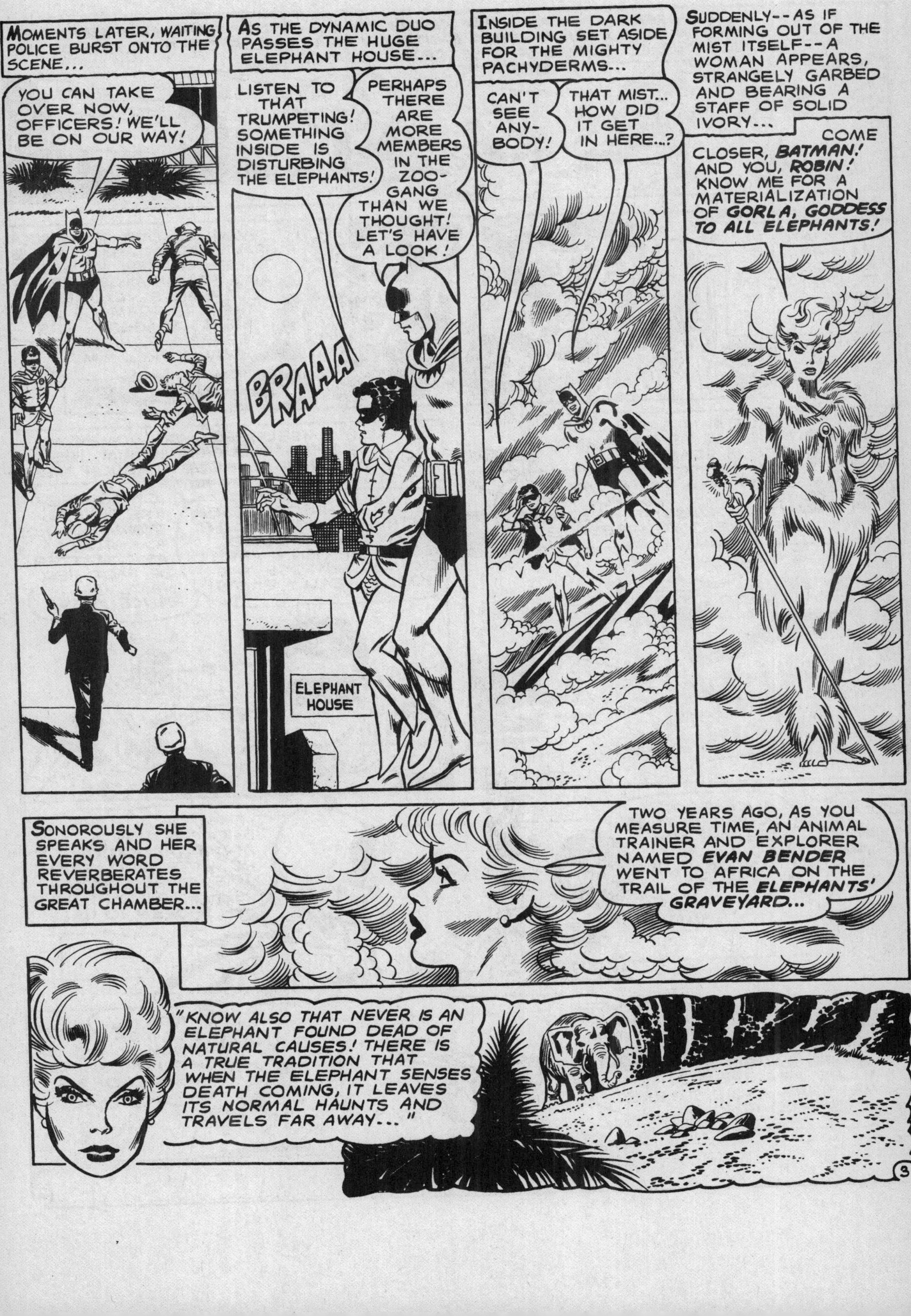
MOMENTS LATER, WAITING POLICE BURST ONTO THE SCENE...
YOU CAN TAKE OVER NOW, OFFICERS! WE'LL BE ON OUR WAY!
AS THE DYNAMIC DUO PASSES THE HUGE ELEPHANT HOUSE...
LISTEN TO THAT TRUMPETING! SOMETHING INSIDE IS DISTURBING THE ELEPHANTS!
PERHAPS THERE ARE MORE MEMBERS IN THE ZOO-GANG THAN WE THOUGHT! LET'S HAVE A LOOK!
BRAAA
ELEPHANT HOUSE
INSIDE THE DARK BUILDING SET ASIDE FOR THE MIGHTY PACHYDERMS...
CAN'T SEE ANY-BODY!
THAT MIST... HOW DID IT GET IN HERE...?
SUDDENLY--AS IF FORMING OUT OF THE MIST ITSELF--A WOMAN APPEARS, STRANGELY GARBED AND BEARING A STAFF OF SOLID IVORY...
COME CLOSER, BATMAN! AND YOU, ROBIN! KNOW ME FOR A MATERIALIZATION OF GORLA, GODDESS TO ALL ELEPHANTS!
SONOROUSLY SHE SPEAKS AND HER EVERY WORD REVERBERATES THROUGHOUT THE GREAT CHAMBER...
TWO YEARS AGO, AS YOU MEASURE TIME, AN ANIMAL TRAINER AND EXPLORER NAMED EVAN BENDER WENT TO AFRICA ON THE TRAIL OF THE ELEPHANTS' GRAVEYARD...
"KNOW ALSO THAT NEVER IS AN ELEPHANT FOUND DEAD OF NATURAL CAUSES! THERE IS A TRUE TRADITION THAT WHEN THE ELEPHANT SENSES DEATH COMING, IT LEAVES ITS NORMAL HAUNTS AND TRAVELS FAR AWAY..."
3

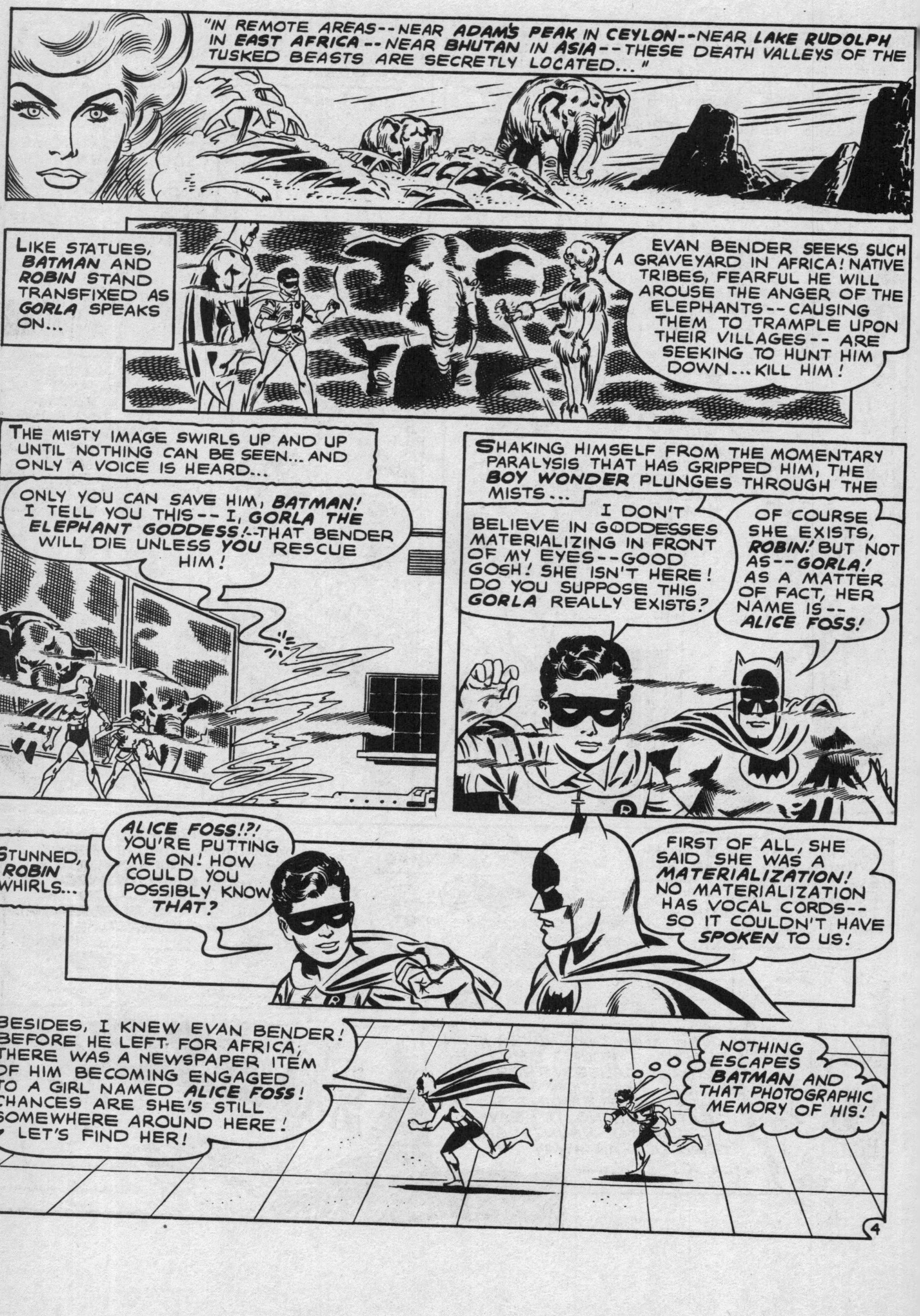
"IN REMOTE AREAS--NEAR ADAM'S PEAK IN CEYLON--NEAR LAKE RUDOLPH IN EAST AFRICA--NEAR BHUTAN IN ASIA--THESE DEATH VALLEYS OF THE TUSKED BEASTS ARE SECRETLY LOCATED..."
LIKE STATUES, BATMAN AND ROBIN STAND TRANSFIXED AS GORLA SPEAKS ON...
EVAN BENDER SEEKS SUCH A GRAVEYARD IN AFRICA! NATIVE TRIBES, FEARFUL HE WILL AROUSE THE ANGER OF THE ELEPHANTS--CAUSING THEM TO TRAMPLE UPON THEIR VILLAGES--ARE SEEKING TO HUNT HIM DOWN... KILL HIM!
THE MISTY IMAGE SWIRLS UP AND UP UNTIL NOTHING CAN BE SEEN... AND ONLY A VOICE IS HEARD...
ONLY YOU CAN SAVE HIM, BATMAN! I TELL YOU THIS--I, GORLA THE ELEPHANT GODDESS!--THAT BENDER WILL DIE UNLESS YOU RESCUE HIM!
SHAKING HIMSELF FROM THE MOMENTARY PARALYSIS THAT HAS GRIPPED HIM, THE BOY WONDER PLUNGES THROUGH THE MISTS...
I DON'T BELIEVE IN GODDESSES MATERIALIZING IN FRONT OF MY EYES--GOOD GOSH! SHE ISN'T HERE! DO YOU SUPPOSE THIS GORLA REALLY EXISTS?
OF COURSE SHE EXISTS, ROBIN! BUT NOT AS--GORLA! AS A MATTER OF FACT, HER NAME IS--ALICE FOSS!
STUNNED, ROBIN WHIRLS...
ALICE FOSS!?! YOU'RE PUTTING ME ON! HOW COULD YOU POSSIBLY KNOW THAT?
FIRST OF ALL, SHE SAID SHE WAS A MATERIALIZATION! NO MATERIALIZATION HAS VOCAL CORDS--SO IT COULDN'T HAVE SPOKEN TO US!
BESIDES, I KNEW EVAN BENDER! BEFORE HE LEFT FOR AFRICA, THERE WAS A NEWSPAPER ITEM OF HIM BECOMING ENGAGED TO A GIRL NAMED ALICE FOSS! CHANCES ARE SHE'S STILL SOMEWHERE AROUND HERE! LET'S FIND HER!
NOTHING ESCAPES BATMAN AND THAT PHOTOGRAPHIC MEMORY OF HIS!
4

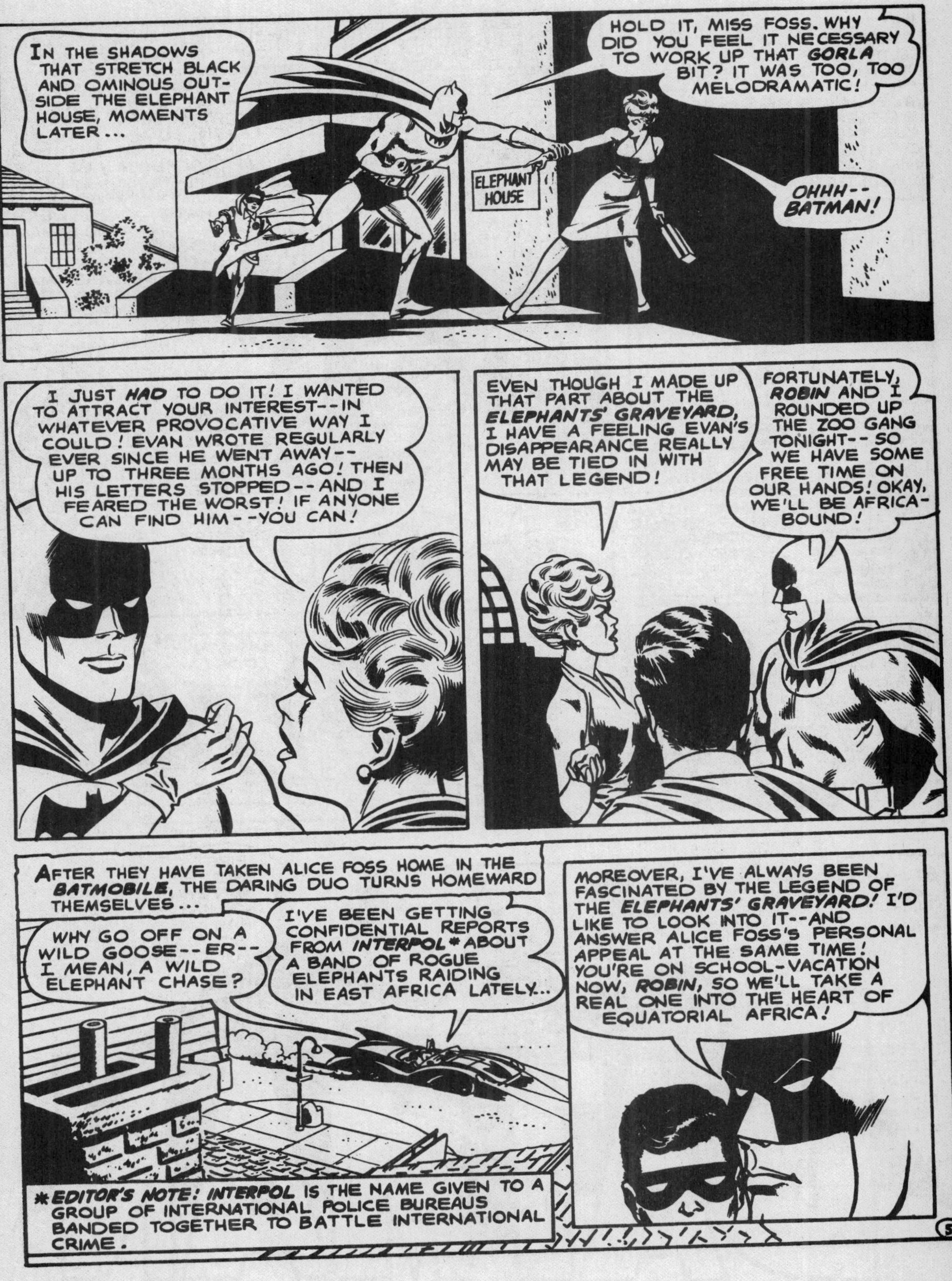
IN THE SHADOWS THAT STRETCH BLACK AND OMINOUS OUTSIDE THE ELEPHANT HOUSE, MOMENTS LATER...
HOLD IT, MISS FOSS. WHY DID YOU FEEL IT NECESSARY TO WORK UP THAT GORLA BIT? IT WAS TOO, TOO MELODRAMATIC!
ELEPHANT HOUSE
OHHH--BATMAN!
I JUST HAD TO DO IT! I WANTED TO ATTRACT YOUR INTEREST--IN WHATEVER PROVOCATIVE WAY I COULD! EVAN WROTE REGULARLY EVER SINCE HE WENT AWAY--UP TO THREE MONTHS AGO! THEN HIS LETTERS STOPPED--AND I FEARED THE WORST! IF ANYONE CAN FIND HIM--YOU CAN!
EVEN THOUGH I MADE UP THAT PART ABOUT THE ELEPHANTS' GRAVEYARD, I HAVE A FEELING EVAN'S DISAPPEARANCE REALLY MAY BE TIED IN WITH THAT LEGEND!
FORTUNATELY, ROBIN AND I ROUNDED UP THE ZOO GANG TONIGHT--SO WE HAVE SOME FREE TIME ON OUR HANDS! OKAY, WE'LL BE AFRICA-BOUND!
AFTER THEY HAVE TAKEN ALICE FOSS HOME IN THE BATMOBILE, THE DARING DUO TURNS HOMEWARD THEMSELVES...
WHY GO OFF ON A WILD GOOSE--ER--I MEAN, A WILD ELEPHANT CHASE?
I'VE BEEN GETTING CONFIDENTIAL REPORTS FROM INTERPOL* ABOUT A BAND OF ROGUE ELEPHANTS RAIDING IN EAST AFRICA LATELY...
*EDITOR'S NOTE: INTERPOL IS THE NAME GIVEN TO A GROUP OF INTERNATIONAL POLICE BUREAUS BANDED TOGETHER TO BATTLE INTERNATIONAL CRIME.
MOREOVER, I'VE ALWAYS BEEN FASCINATED BY THE LEGEND OF THE ELEPHANTS' GRAVEYARD! I'D LIKE TO LOOK INTO IT--AND ANSWER ALICE FOSS'S PERSONAL APPEAL AT THE SAME TIME! YOU'RE ON SCHOOL-VACATION NOW, ROBIN, SO WE'LL TAKE A REAL ONE INTO THE HEART OF EQUATORIAL AFRICA!
5

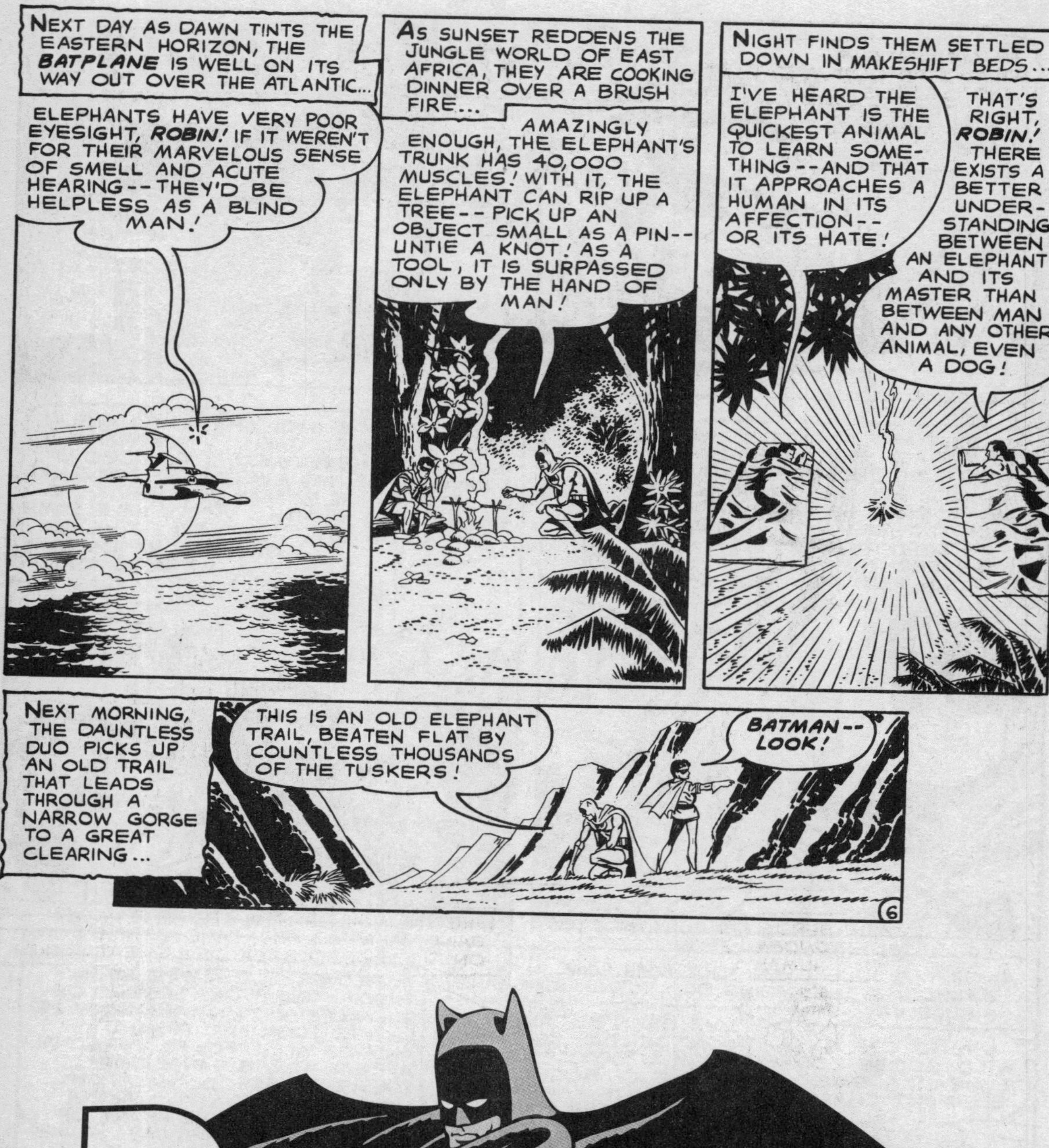
NEXT DAY AS DAWN TINTS THE EASTERN HORIZON, THE BATPLANE IS WELL ON ITS WAY OUT OVER THE ATLANTIC...
ELEPHANTS HAVE VERY POOR EYESIGHT, ROBIN! IF IT WEREN'T FOR THEIR MARVELOUS SENSE OF SMELL AND ACUTE HEARING--THEY'D BE HELPLESS AS A BLIND MAN!
AS SUNSET REDDENS THE JUNGLE WORLD OF EAST AFRICA, THEY ARE COOKING DINNER OVER A BRUSH FIRE...
AMAZINGLY ENOUGH, THE ELEPHANT'S TRUNK HAS 40,000 MUSCLES! WITH IT, THE ELEPHANT CAN RIP UP A TREE--PICK UP AN OBJECT SMALL AS A PIN--UNTIE A KNOT! AS A TOOL, IT IS SURPASSED ONLY BY THE HAND OF MAN!
NIGHT FINDS THEM SETTLED DOWN IN MAKESHIFT BEDS...
I'VE HEARD THE ELEPHANT IS THE QUICKEST ANIMAL TO LEARN SOME-THING--AND THAT IT APPROACHES A HUMAN IN ITS AFFECTION--OR ITS HATE!
THAT'S RIGHT, ROBIN! THERE EXISTS A BETTER UNDER-STANDING BETWEEN AN ELEPHANT AND ITS MASTER THAN BETWEEN MAN AND ANY OTHER ANIMAL, EVEN A DOG!
NEXT MORNING, THE DAUNTLESS DUO PICKS UP AN OLD TRAIL THAT LEADS THROUGH A NARROW GORGE TO A GREAT CLEARING...
THIS IS AN OLD ELEPHANT TRAIL, BEATEN FLAT BY COUNTLESS THOUSANDS OF THE TUSKERS!
BATMAN--LOOK!
6

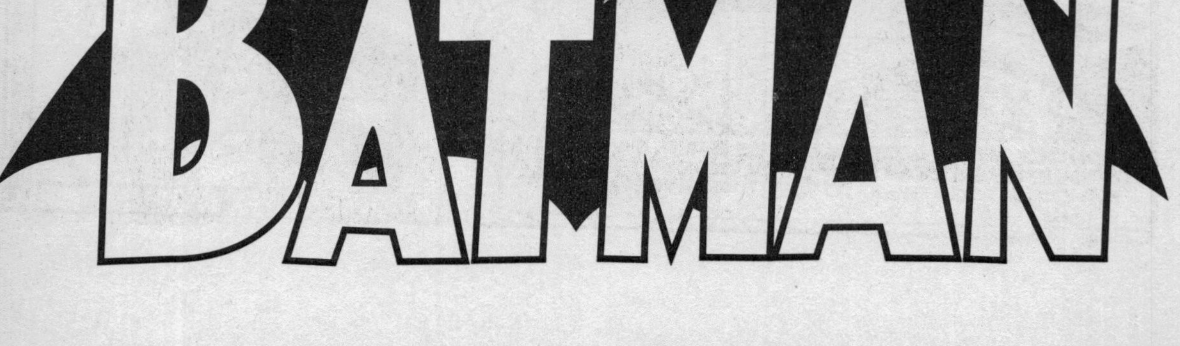
BATMAN

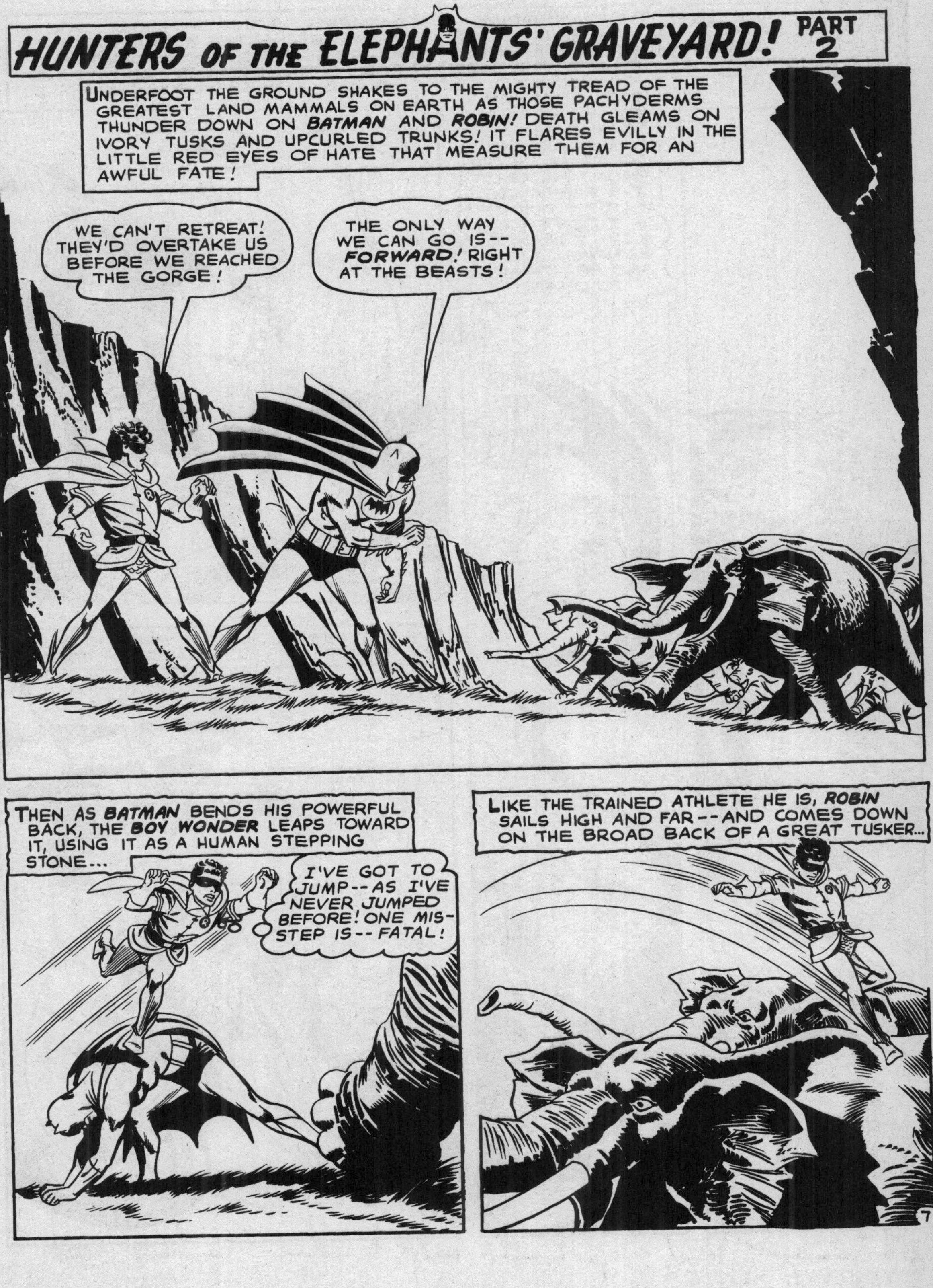
HUNTERS OF THE ELEPHANTS' GRAVEYARD! PART 2
UNDERFOOT THE GROUND SHAKES TO THE MIGHTY TREAD OF THE GREATEST LAND MAMMALS ON EARTH AS THOSE PACHYDERMS THUNDER DOWN ON BATMAN AND ROBIN! DEATH GLEAMS ON IVORY TUSKS AND UPCURLED TRUNKS! IT FLARES EVILLY IN THE LITTLE RED EYES OF HATE THAT MEASURE THEM FOR AN AWFUL FATE!
WE CAN'T RETREAT! THEY'D OVERTAKE US BEFORE WE REACHED THE GORGE!
THE ONLY WAY WE CAN GO IS-- FORWARD! RIGHT AT THE BEASTS!
THEN AS BATMAN BENDS HIS POWERFUL BACK, THE BOY WONDER LEAPS TOWARD IT, USING IT AS A HUMAN STEPPING STONE...
I'VE GOT TO JUMP--AS I'VE NEVER JUMPED BEFORE! ONE MIS-STEP IS--FATAL!
LIKE THE TRAINED ATHLETE HE IS, ROBIN SAILS HIGH AND FAR--AND COMES DOWN ON THE BROAD BACK OF A GREAT TUSKER...
7

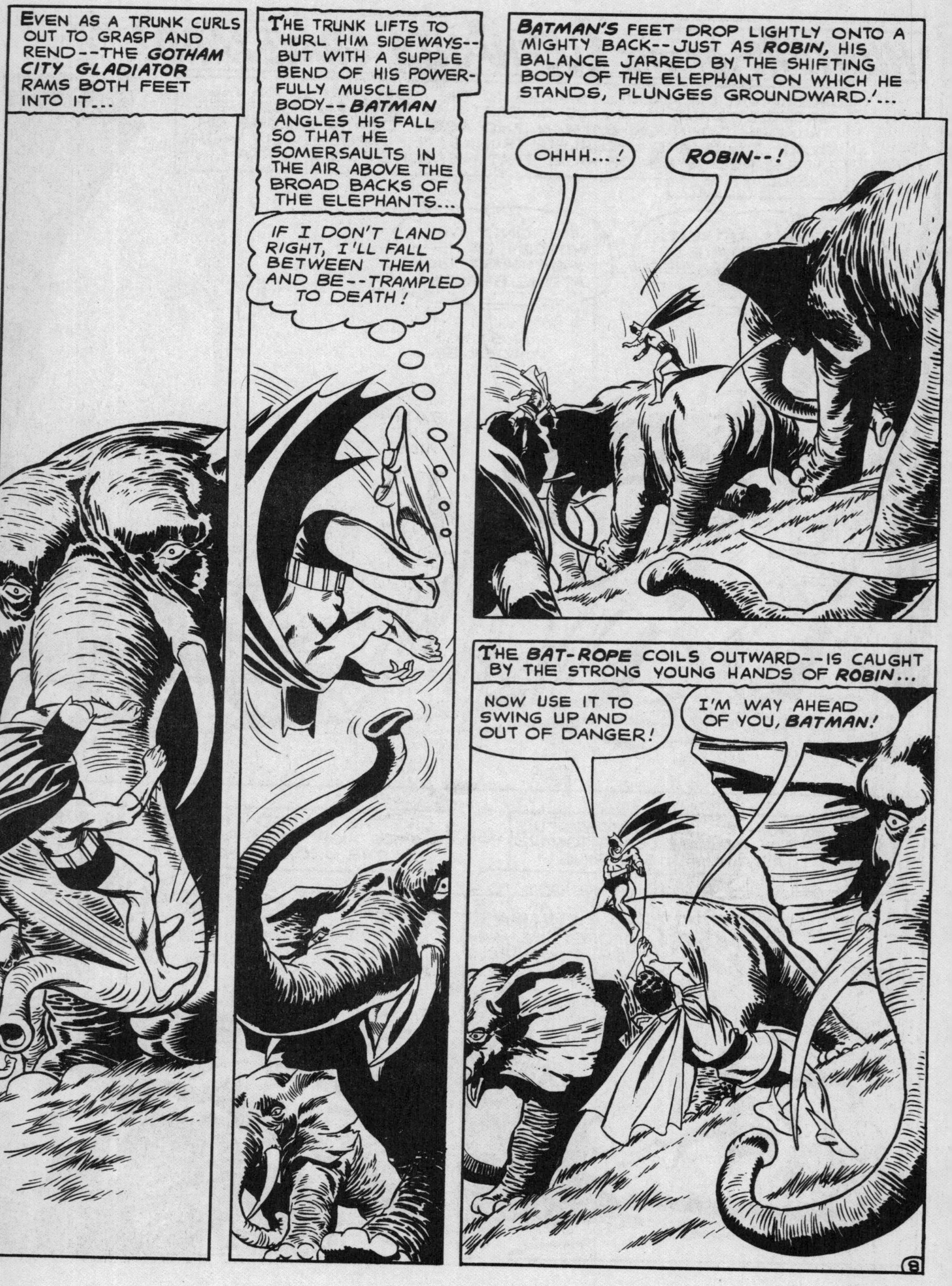
EVEN AS A TRUNK CURLS OUT TO GRASP AND REND--THE GOTHAM CITY GLADIATOR RAMS BOTH FEET INTO IT...
THE TRUNK LIFTS TO HURL HIM SIDEWAYS--BUT WITH A SUPPLE BEND OF HIS POWERFULLY MUSCLED BODY--BATMAN ANGLES HIS FALL SO THAT HE SOMERSAULTS IN THE AIR ABOVE THE BROAD BACKS OF THE ELEPHANTS...
IF I DON'T LAND RIGHT, I'LL FALL BETWEEN THEM AND BE--TRAMPLED TO DEATH!
BATMAN'S FEET DROP LIGHTLY ONTO A MIGHTY BACK--JUST AS ROBIN, HIS BALANCE JARRED BY THE SHIFTING BODY OF THE ELEPHANT ON WHICH HE STANDS, PLUNGES GROUNDWARD!...
OHHH...!
ROBIN--!
THE BAT-ROPE COILS OUTWARD--IS CAUGHT BY THE STRONG YOUNG HANDS OF ROBIN...
NOW USE IT TO SWING UP AND OUT OF DANGER!
I'M WAY AHEAD OF YOU, BATMAN!
8

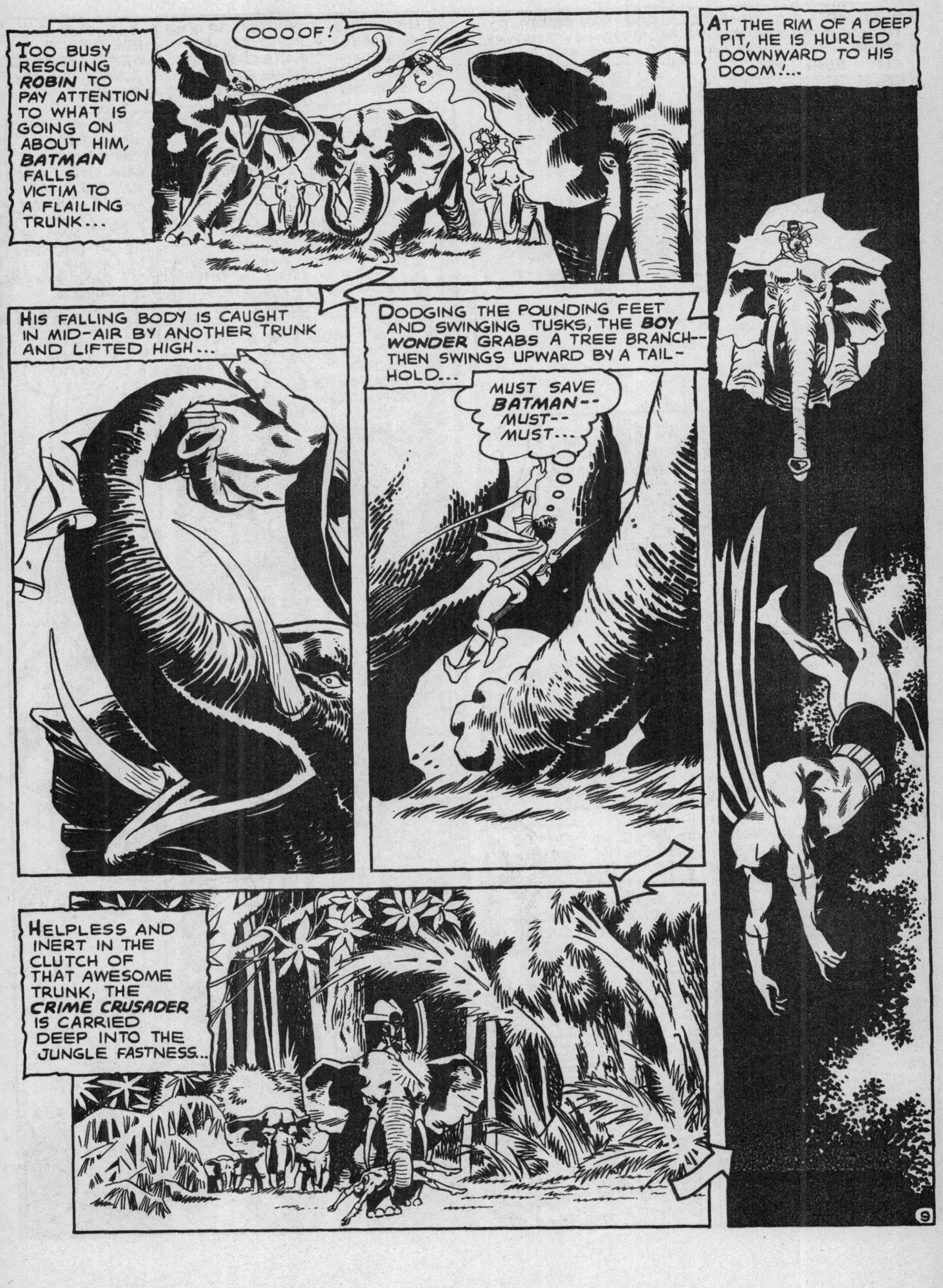

TOO BUSY RESCUING ROBIN TO PAY ATTENTION TO WHAT IS GOING ON ABOUT HIM, BATMAN FALLS VICTIM TO A FLAILING TRUNK...
OOOOF!
HIS FALLING BODY IS CAUGHT IN MID-AIR BY ANOTHER TRUNK AND LIFTED HIGH...
DODGING THE POUNDING FEET AND SWINGING TUSKS, THE BOY WONDER GRABS A TREE BRANCH--THEN SWINGS UPWARD BY A TAIL-HOLD...
MUST SAVE BATMAN-- MUST-- MUST...
AT THE RIM OF A DEEP PIT, HE IS HURLED DOWNWARD TO HIS DOOM!...
HELPLESS AND INERT IN THE CLUTCH OF THAT AWESOME TRUNK, THE CRIME CRUSADER IS CARRIED DEEP INTO THE JUNGLE FASTNESS...
9

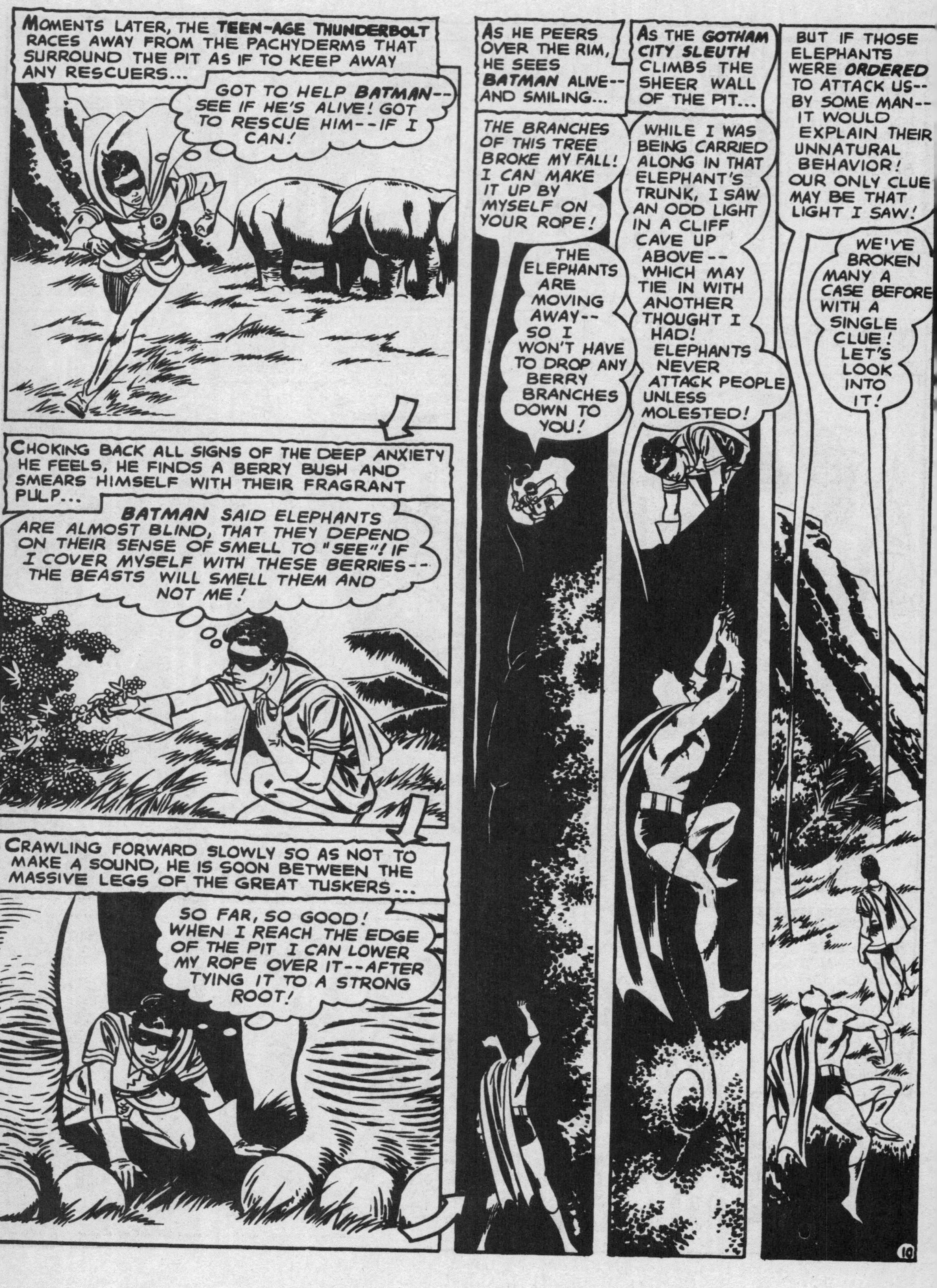
MOMENTS LATER, THE TEEN-AGE THUNDERBOLT RACES AWAY FROM THE PACHYDERMS THAT SURROUND THE PIT AS IF TO KEEP AWAY ANY RESCUERS...
GOT TO HELP BATMAN-- SEE IF HE'S ALIVE! GOT TO RESCUE HIM--IF I CAN!
CHOKING BACK ALL SIGNS OF THE DEEP ANXIETY HE FEELS, HE FINDS A BERRY BUSH AND SMEARS HIMSELF WITH THEIR FRAGRANT PULP...
BATMAN SAID ELEPHANTS ARE ALMOST BLIND, THAT THEY DEPEND ON THEIR SENSE OF SMELL TO "SEE"! IF I COVER MYSELF WITH THESE BERRIES-- THE BEASTS WILL SMELL THEM AND NOT ME!
CRAWLING FORWARD SLOWLY SO AS NOT TO MAKE A SOUND, HE IS SOON BETWEEN THE MASSIVE LEGS OF THE GREAT TUSKERS...
SO FAR, SO GOOD! WHEN I REACH THE EDGE OF THE PIT I CAN LOWER MY ROPE OVER IT--AFTER TYING IT TO A STRONG ROOT!
AS HE PEERS OVER THE RIM, HE SEES BATMAN ALIVE-- AND SMILING...
THE BRANCHES OF THIS TREE BROKE MY FALL! I CAN MAKE IT UP BY MYSELF ON YOUR ROPE!
THE ELEPHANTS ARE MOVING AWAY-- SO I WON'T HAVE TO DROP ANY BERRY BRANCHES DOWN TO YOU!
AS THE GOTHAM CITY SLEUTH CLIMBS THE SHEER WALL OF THE PIT...
WHILE I WAS BEING CARRIED ALONG IN THAT ELEPHANT'S TRUNK, I SAW AN ODD LIGHT IN A CLIFF CAVE UP ABOVE-- WHICH MAY TIE IN WITH ANOTHER THOUGHT I HAD! ELEPHANTS NEVER ATTACK PEOPLE UNLESS MOLESTED!
BUT IF THOSE ELEPHANTS WERE ORDERED TO ATTACK US-- BY SOME MAN-- IT WOULD EXPLAIN THEIR UNNATURAL BEHAVIOR! OUR ONLY CLUE MAY BE THAT LIGHT I SAW!
WE'VE BROKEN MANY A CASE BEFORE WITH A SINGLE CLUE! LET'S LOOK INTO IT!
10

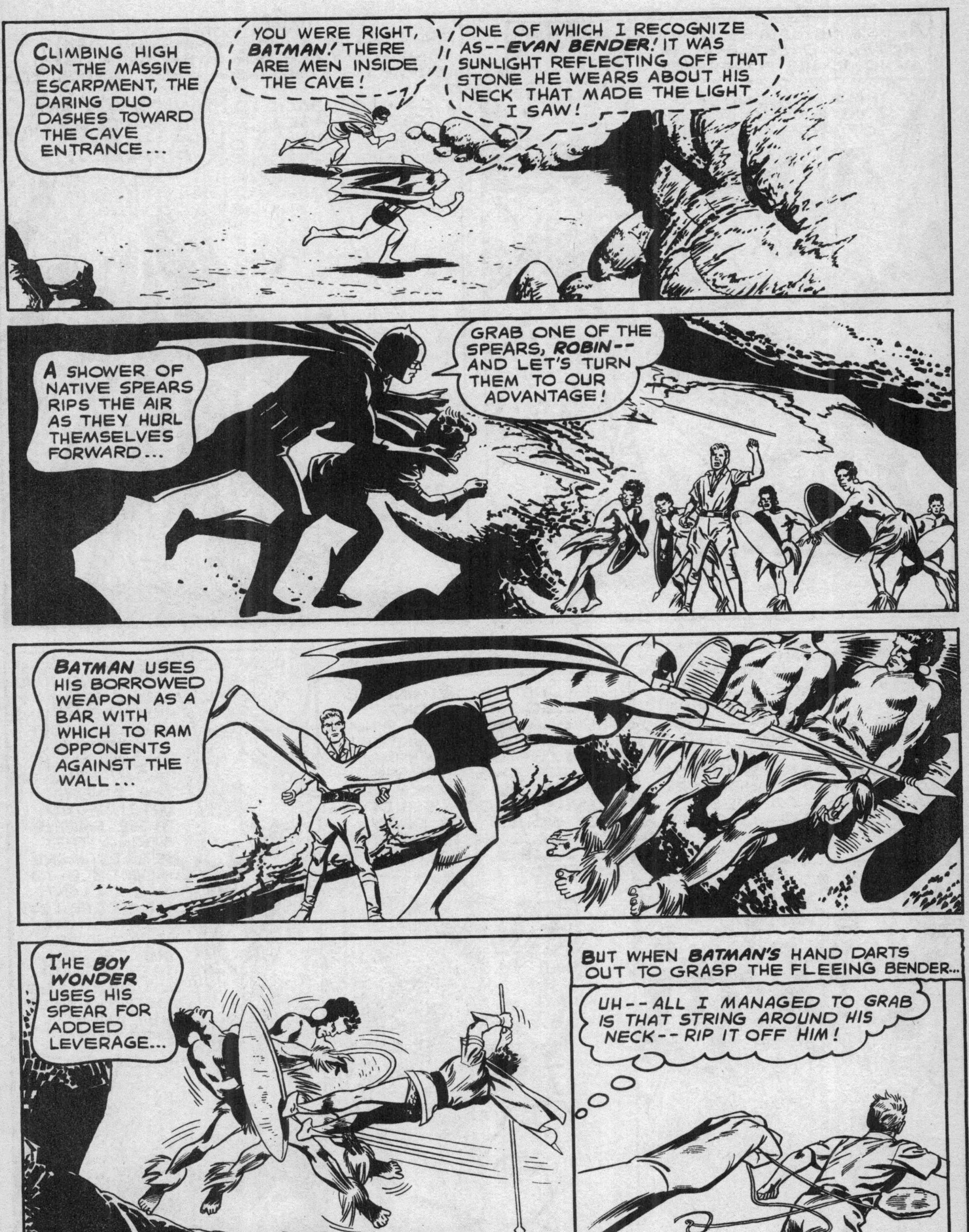
CLIMBING HIGH ON THE MASSIVE ESCARPMENT, THE DARING DUO DASHES TOWARD THE CAVE ENTRANCE...
YOU WERE RIGHT, BATMAN! THERE ARE MEN INSIDE THE CAVE!
ONE OF WHICH I RECOGNIZE AS--EVAN BENDER! IT WAS SUNLIGHT REFLECTING OFF THAT STONE HE WEARS ABOUT HIS NECK THAT MADE THE LIGHT I SAW!
A SHOWER OF NATIVE SPEARS RIPS THE AIR AS THEY HURL THEMSELVES FORWARD...
GRAB ONE OF THE SPEARS, ROBIN--AND LET'S TURN THEM TO OUR ADVANTAGE!
BATMAN USES HIS BORROWED WEAPON AS A BAR WITH WHICH TO RAM OPPONENTS AGAINST THE WALL...
THE BOY WONDER USES HIS SPEAR FOR ADDED LEVERAGE...
BUT WHEN BATMAN'S HAND DARTS OUT TO GRASP THE FLEEING BENDER...
UH--ALL I MANAGED TO GRAB IS THAT STRING AROUND HIS NECK--RIP IT OFF HIM!
11

As YELPING NATIVES ATTACK *BATMAN* AND *ROBIN*, A DAZED EVAN BENDER LIFTS A HAND TO HIS FOREHEAD...

THANK GOODNESS-- I'VE GAINED CONTROL OF MYSELF AGAIN!

BATTLING WITH FURIOUS COURAGE, *BATMAN* AND *ROBIN* ARE BORNE BACKWARD BY SUPERIOR NUMBERS-- WHEN UNEXPECTEDLY...

STOP! GO BACK TO THE VILLAGE! DON'T HARM THESE MEN!

WHAT'S HAPPENED TO BENDER? HE--LOOKS *DIFFERENT!*

I *AM* DIFFERENT! I'M MYSELF FOR THE FIRST TIME IN-- THREE MONTHS! YOU SEE THAT ODD MINERAL? IT GAVE ME CONTROL OVER THOSE ELEPHANTS THAT ATTACKED YOU! I ALSO MADE THEM STORM THROUGH DIAMOND MINES AND IVORY STOREHOUSES SO THESE NATIVES COULD COME IN AND LOOT THEM!

BUT-- JUST AS THE MINERAL ENABLED ME TO CONTROL THE BEASTS, SO THE MINERAL GAVE BIG-GAME HUNTER "RED" LOFTUS AN HYPNOTIC CONTROL OVER ME! HE *FORCED* ME TO MAKE THE ELEPHANTS DO HIS BIDDING! THEY WOULD NOT OBEY *HIM* SINCE HE HATED THE BIG BEASTS AND THEY *SENSED* IT!

HOW DID THIS MINERAL WORK?

ELEPHANTS SENSE FEAR AND HATE BY *SMELL!* HUMAN EMOTIONS *DO* GIVE OFF CERTAIN ODORS, YOU KNOW! SOMEHOW THE MINERAL *INTENSIFIED* THOSE SMELLS-- MAKING THE BEASTS MORE SUSCEPTIBLE TO HATE OR LOVE! OUT OF THE LOVE I BORE THEM, THEY OBEYED *ME,* THOUGH THEY WOULD NOT OBEY "RED" LOFTUS-- WHOM THEY KNEW HATED THEM!

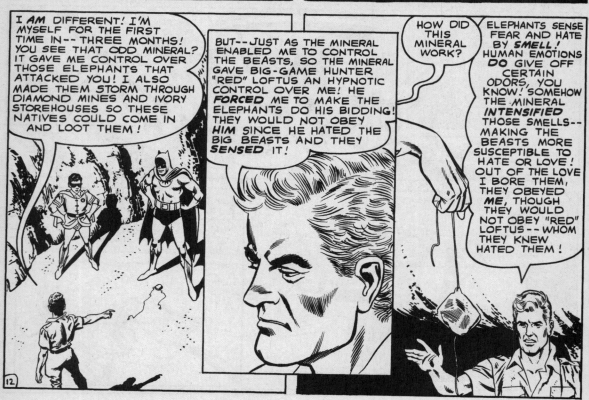

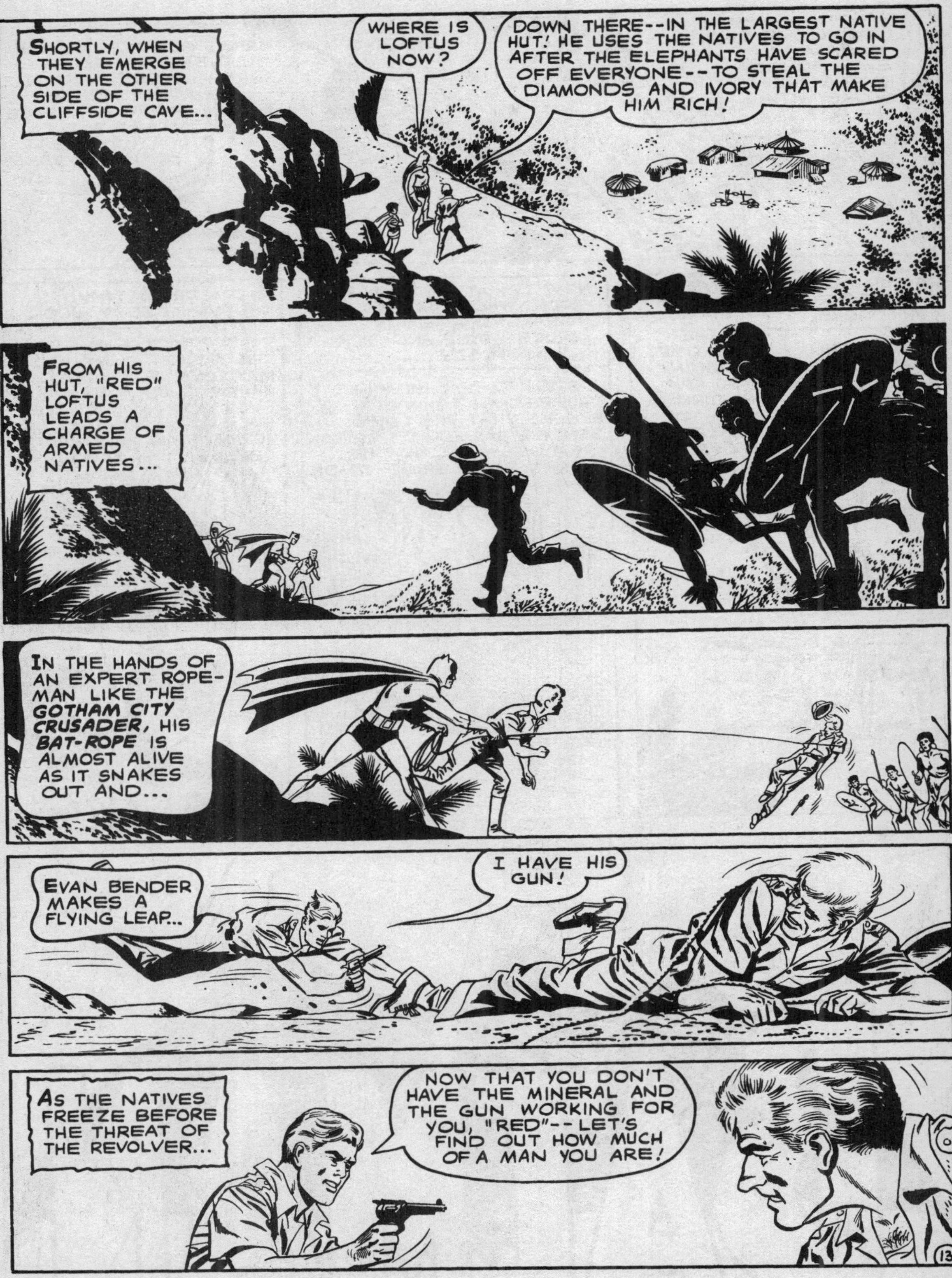
SHORTLY, WHEN THEY EMERGE ON THE OTHER SIDE OF THE CLIFFSIDE CAVE...
WHERE IS LOFTUS NOW?
DOWN THERE--IN THE LARGEST NATIVE HUT! HE USES THE NATIVES TO GO IN AFTER THE ELEPHANTS HAVE SCARED OFF EVERYONE--TO STEAL THE DIAMONDS AND IVORY THAT MAKE HIM RICH!
FROM HIS HUT, "RED" LOFTUS LEADS A CHARGE OF ARMED NATIVES...
IN THE HANDS OF AN EXPERT ROPE-MAN LIKE THE GOTHAM CITY CRUSADER, HIS BAT-ROPE IS ALMOST ALIVE AS IT SNAKES OUT AND...
EVAN BENDER MAKES A FLYING LEAP...
I HAVE HIS GUN!
AS THE NATIVES FREEZE BEFORE THE THREAT OF THE REVOLVER...
NOW THAT YOU DON'T HAVE THE MINERAL AND THE GUN WORKING FOR YOU, "RED"--LET'S FIND OUT HOW MUCH OF A MAN YOU ARE!
13

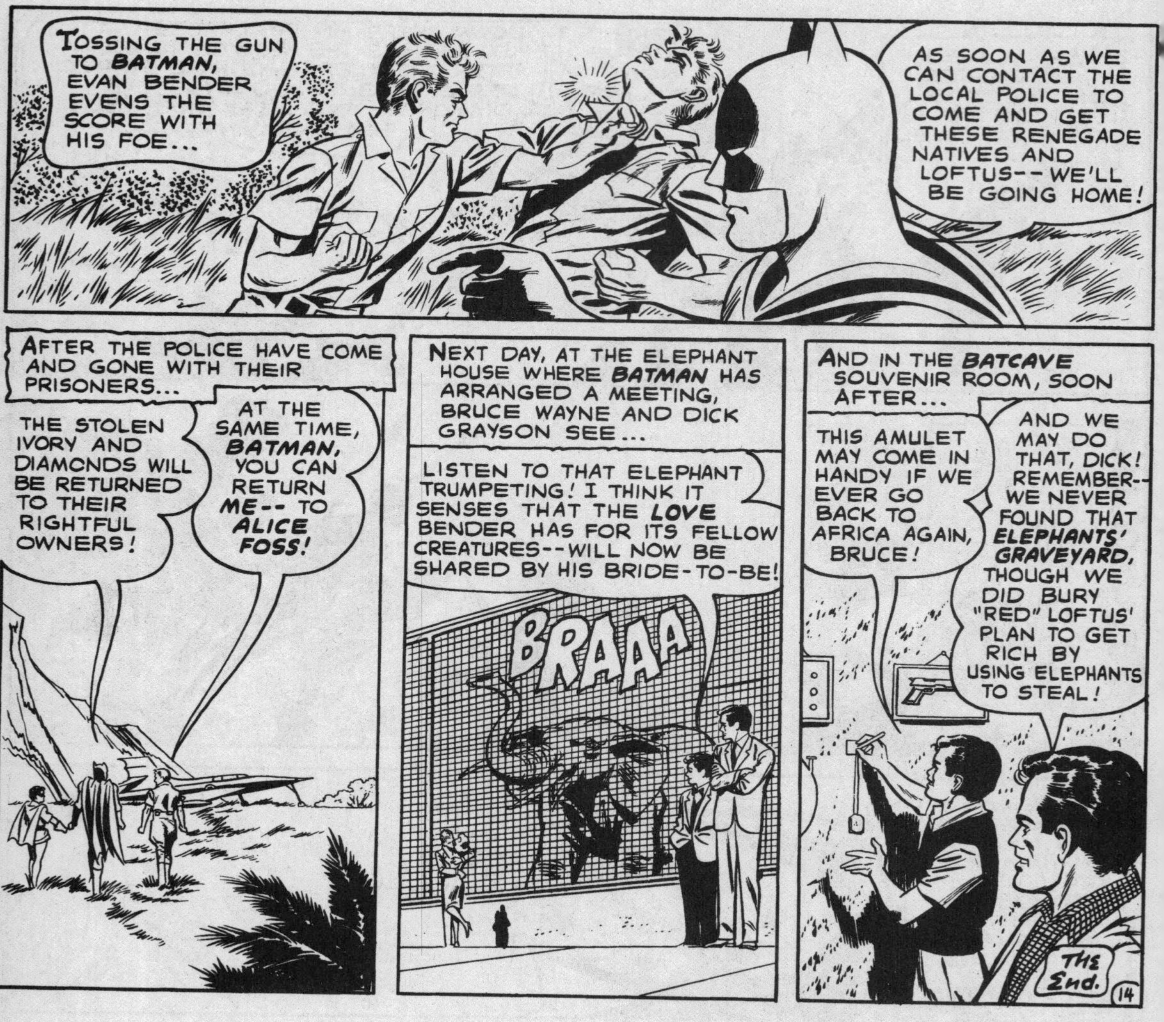
TOSSING THE GUN TO BATMAN, EVAN BENDER EVENS THE SCORE WITH HIS FOE...
AS SOON AS WE CAN CONTACT THE LOCAL POLICE TO COME AND GET THESE RENEGADE NATIVES AND LOFTUS--WE'LL BE GOING HOME!
AFTER THE POLICE HAVE COME AND GONE WITH THEIR PRISONERS...
THE STOLEN IVORY AND DIAMONDS WILL BE RETURNED TO THEIR RIGHTFUL OWNERS!
AT THE SAME TIME, BATMAN, YOU CAN RETURN ME-- TO ALICE FOSS!
NEXT DAY, AT THE ELEPHANT HOUSE WHERE BATMAN HAS ARRANGED A MEETING, BRUCE WAYNE AND DICK GRAYSON SEE...
LISTEN TO THAT ELEPHANT TRUMPETING! I THINK IT SENSES THAT THE LOVE BENDER HAS FOR ITS FELLOW CREATURES--WILL NOW BE SHARED BY HIS BRIDE-TO-BE!
BRAAA
AND IN THE BATCAVE SOUVENIR ROOM, SOON AFTER...
THIS AMULET MAY COME IN HANDY IF WE EVER GO BACK TO AFRICA AGAIN, BRUCE!
AND WE MAY DO THAT, DICK! REMEMBER-- WE NEVER FOUND THAT ELEPHANTS' GRAVEYARD, THOUGH WE DID BURY "RED" LOFTUS' PLAN TO GET RICH BY USING ELEPHANTS TO STEAL!
THE End.
14

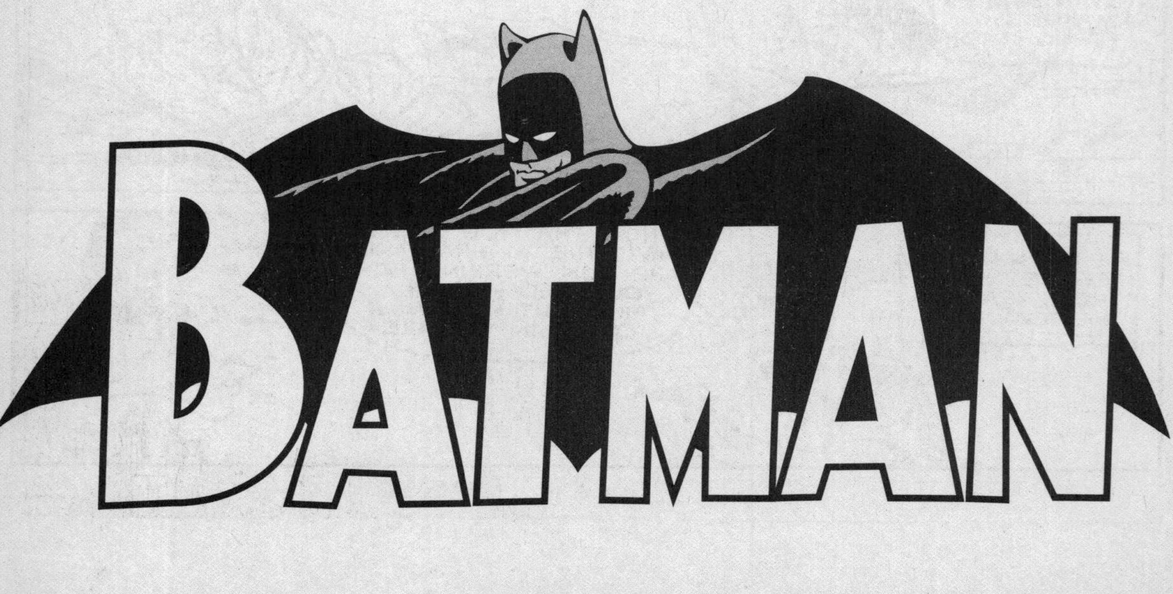
BATMAN

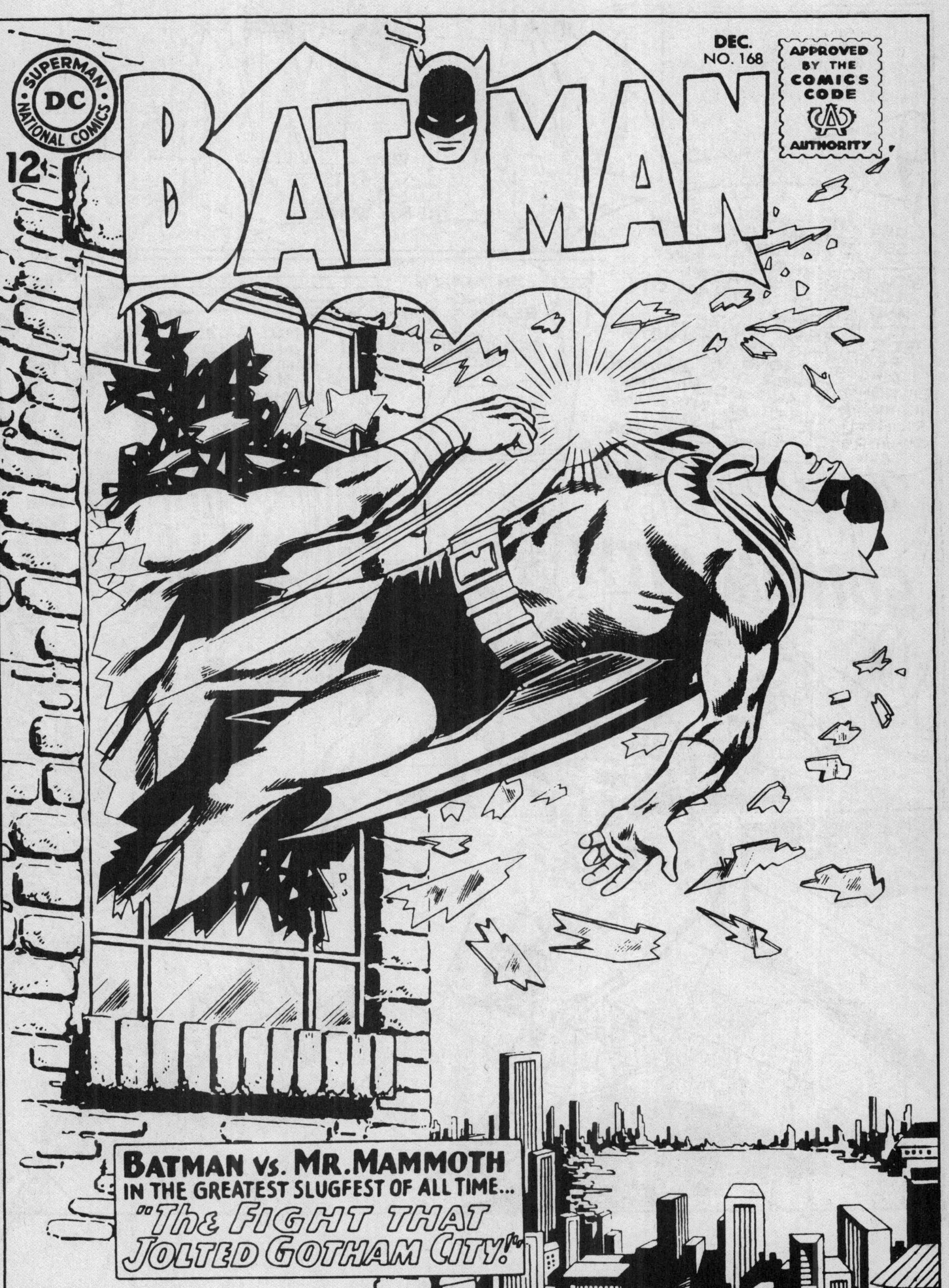
SUPERMAN
DC
NATIONAL COMICS
12¢
BATMAN
DEC.
NO. 168
APPROVED BY THE COMICS CODE AUTHORITY
BATMAN vs. MR. MAMMOTH
IN THE GREATEST SLUGFEST OF ALL TIME...
"THE FIGHT THAT JOLTED GOTHAM CITY!"

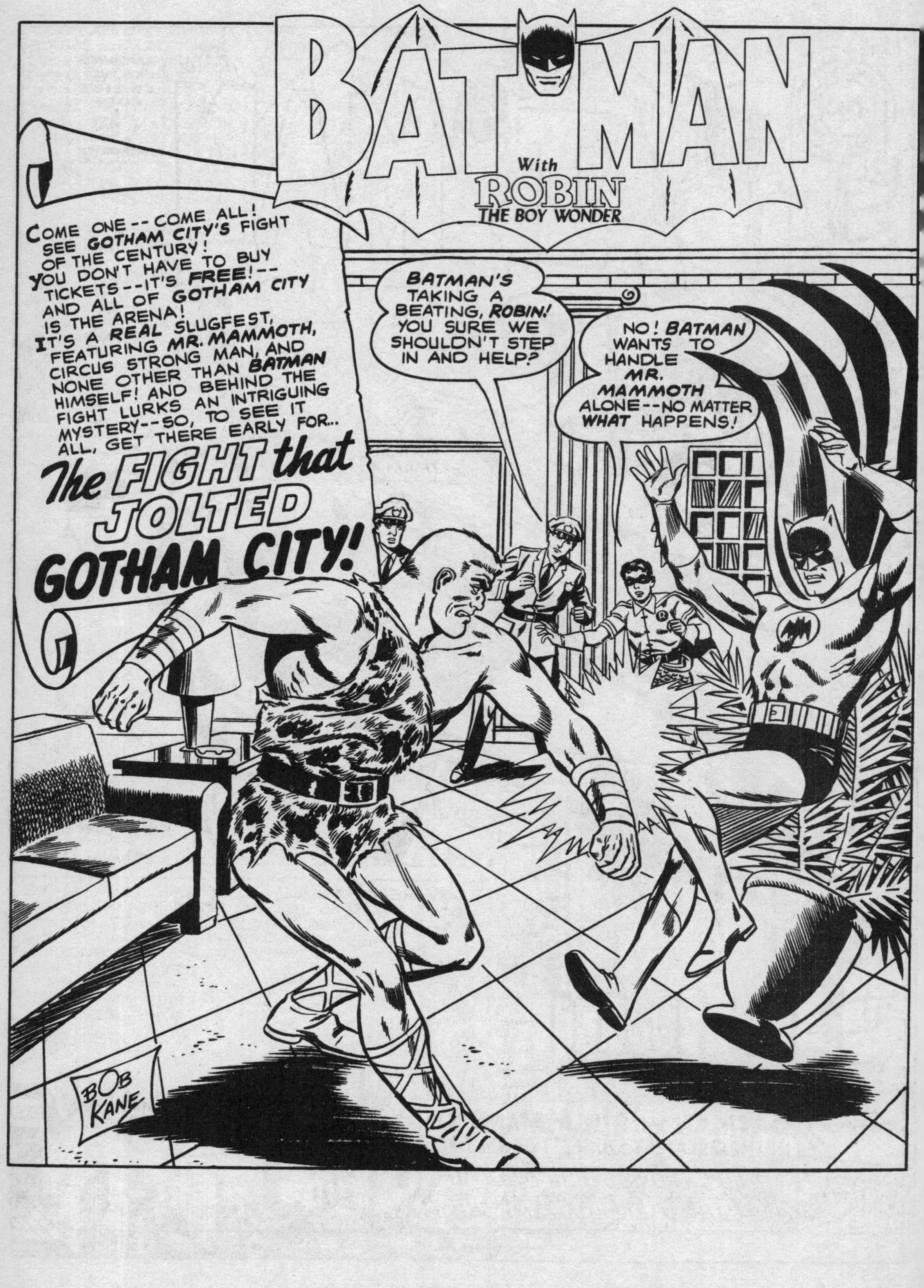
BATMAN
With ROBIN THE BOY WONDER
COME ONE -- COME ALL! SEE GOTHAM CITY'S FIGHT OF THE CENTURY! YOU DON'T HAVE TO BUY TICKETS -- IT'S FREE! -- AND ALL OF GOTHAM CITY IS THE ARENA! IT'S A REAL SLUGFEST, FEATURING MR. MAMMOTH, CIRCUS STRONG MAN, AND NONE OTHER THAN BATMAN HIMSELF! AND BEHIND THE FIGHT LURKS AN INTRIGUING MYSTERY -- SO, TO SEE IT ALL, GET THERE EARLY FOR...
The FIGHT that JOLTED GOTHAM CITY!
BATMAN'S TAKING A BEATING, ROBIN! YOU SURE WE SHOULDN'T STEP IN AND HELP?
NO! BATMAN WANTS TO HANDLE MR. MAMMOTH ALONE -- NO MATTER WHAT HAPPENS!
BOB KANE

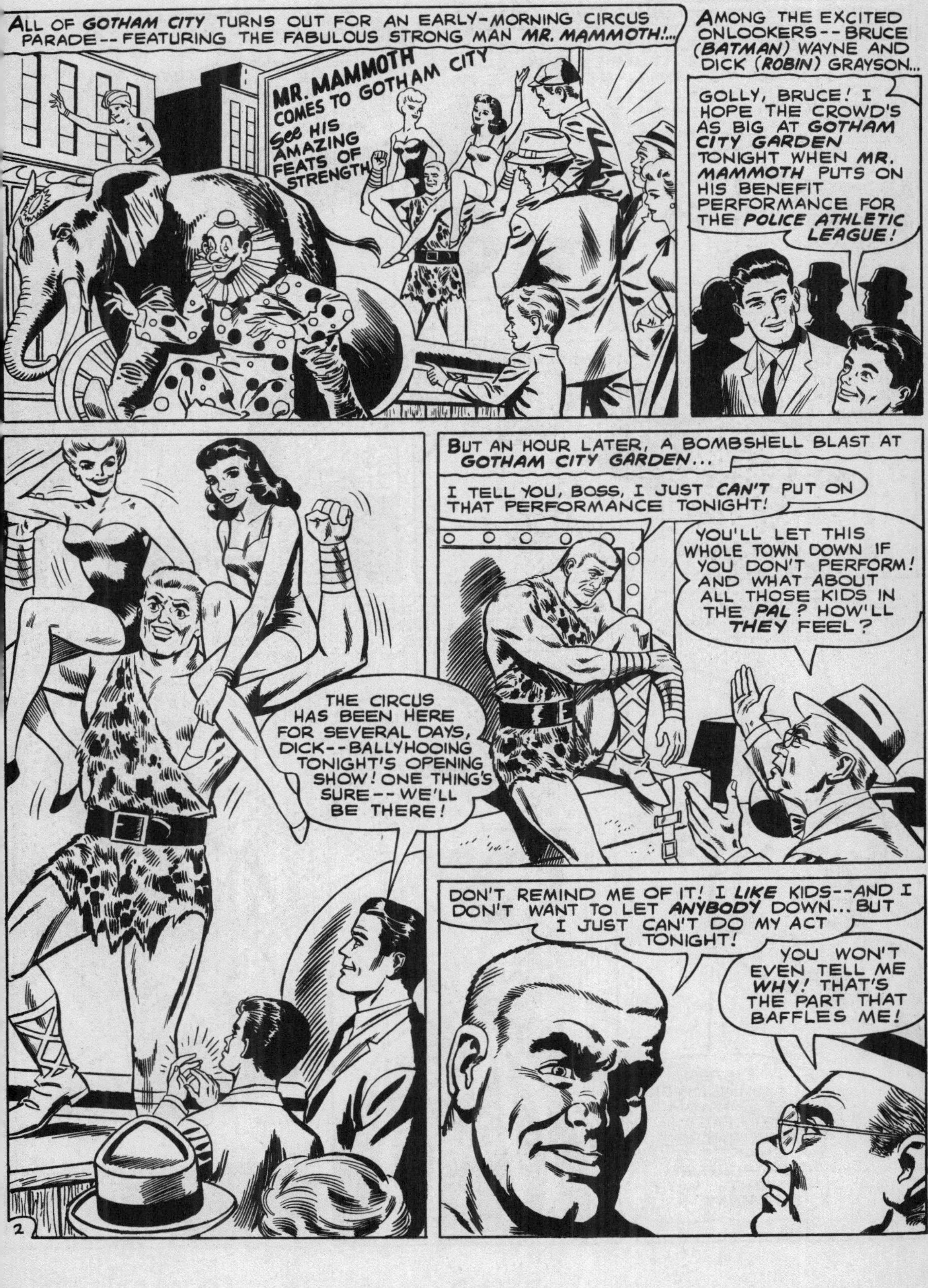
ALL OF GOTHAM CITY TURNS OUT FOR AN EARLY-MORNING CIRCUS PARADE--FEATURING THE FABULOUS STRONG MAN MR. MAMMOTH!...
MR. MAMMOTH COMES TO GOTHAM CITY
See HIS AMAZING FEATS OF STRENGTH
AMONG THE EXCITED ONLOOKERS--BRUCE (BATMAN) WAYNE AND DICK (ROBIN) GRAYSON...
GOLLY, BRUCE! I HOPE THE CROWD'S AS BIG AT GOTHAM CITY GARDEN TONIGHT WHEN MR. MAMMOTH PUTS ON HIS BENEFIT PERFORMANCE FOR THE POLICE ATHLETIC LEAGUE!
THE CIRCUS HAS BEEN HERE FOR SEVERAL DAYS, DICK--BALLYHOOING TONIGHT'S OPENING SHOW! ONE THING'S SURE--WE'LL BE THERE!
2
BUT AN HOUR LATER, A BOMBSHELL BLAST AT GOTHAM CITY GARDEN...
I TELL YOU, BOSS, I JUST CAN'T PUT ON THAT PERFORMANCE TONIGHT!
YOU'LL LET THIS WHOLE TOWN DOWN IF YOU DON'T PERFORM! AND WHAT ABOUT ALL THOSE KIDS IN THE PAL? HOW'LL THEY FEEL?
DON'T REMIND ME OF IT! I LIKE KIDS--AND I DON'T WANT TO LET ANYBODY DOWN... BUT I JUST CAN'T DO MY ACT TONIGHT!
YOU WON'T EVEN TELL ME WHY! THAT'S THE PART THAT BAFFLES ME!

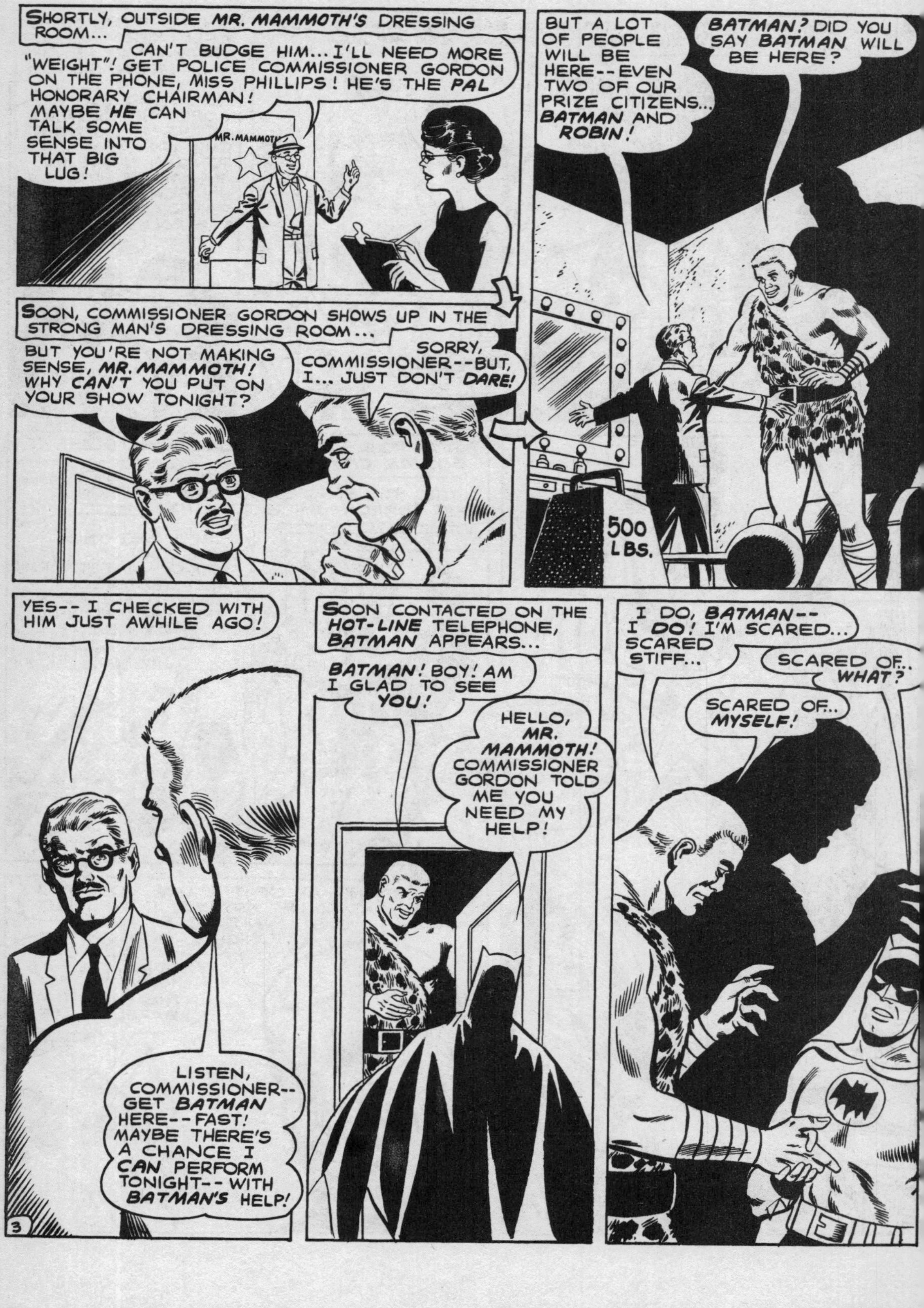
SHORTLY, OUTSIDE MR. MAMMOTH'S DRESSING ROOM...
CAN'T BUDGE HIM... I'LL NEED MORE "WEIGHT"! GET POLICE COMMISSIONER GORDON ON THE PHONE, MISS PHILLIPS! HE'S THE PAL HONORARY CHAIRMAN! MAYBE HE CAN TALK SOME SENSE INTO THAT BIG LUG!
MR. MAMMOTH
BUT A LOT OF PEOPLE WILL BE HERE--EVEN TWO OF OUR PRIZE CITIZENS... BATMAN AND ROBIN!
BATMAN? DID YOU SAY BATMAN WILL BE HERE?
500 LBS.
SOON, COMMISSIONER GORDON SHOWS UP IN THE STRONG MAN'S DRESSING ROOM...
BUT YOU'RE NOT MAKING SENSE, MR. MAMMOTH! WHY CAN'T YOU PUT ON YOUR SHOW TONIGHT?
SORRY, COMMISSIONER--BUT, I... JUST DON'T DARE!
YES--I CHECKED WITH HIM JUST AWHILE AGO!
LISTEN, COMMISSIONER--GET BATMAN HERE--FAST! MAYBE THERE'S A CHANCE I CAN PERFORM TONIGHT--WITH BATMAN'S HELP!
3
SOON CONTACTED ON THE HOT-LINE TELEPHONE, BATMAN APPEARS...
BATMAN! BOY! AM I GLAD TO SEE YOU!
HELLO, MR. MAMMOTH! COMMISSIONER GORDON TOLD ME YOU NEED MY HELP!
I DO, BATMAN--I DO! I'M SCARED... SCARED STIFF...
SCARED OF.. WHAT?
SCARED OF.. MYSELF!

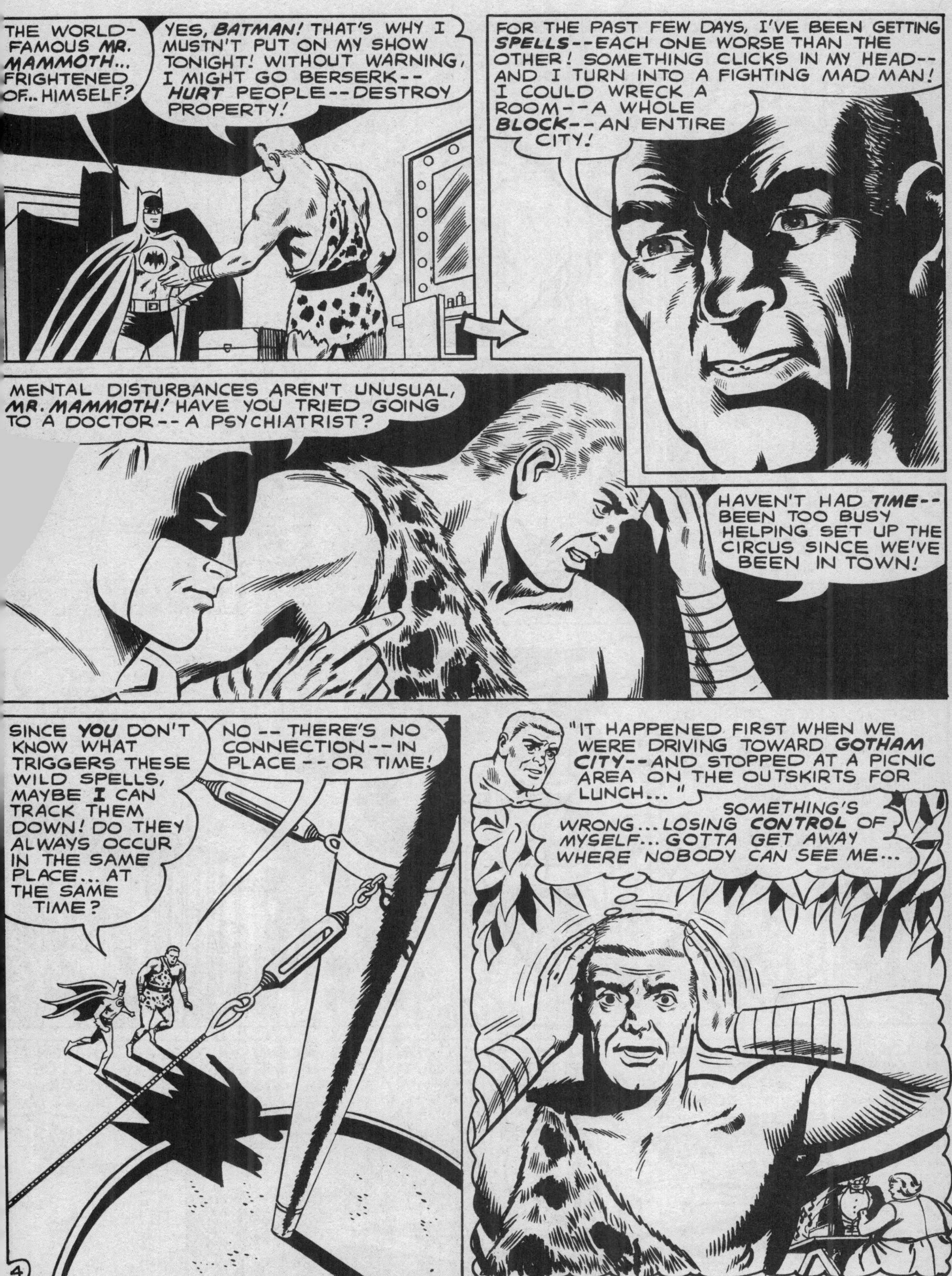
THE WORLD-FAMOUS MR. MAMMOTH... FRIGHTENED OF... HIMSELF?
YES, BATMAN! THAT'S WHY I MUSTN'T PUT ON MY SHOW TONIGHT! WITHOUT WARNING, I MIGHT GO BERSERK--HURT PEOPLE--DESTROY PROPERTY!
FOR THE PAST FEW DAYS, I'VE BEEN GETTING SPELLS--EACH ONE WORSE THAN THE OTHER! SOMETHING CLICKS IN MY HEAD--AND I TURN INTO A FIGHTING MAD MAN! I COULD WRECK A ROOM--A WHOLE BLOCK--AN ENTIRE CITY!
MENTAL DISTURBANCES AREN'T UNUSUAL, MR. MAMMOTH! HAVE YOU TRIED GOING TO A DOCTOR--A PSYCHIATRIST?
HAVEN'T HAD TIME--BEEN TOO BUSY HELPING SET UP THE CIRCUS SINCE WE'VE BEEN IN TOWN!
SINCE YOU DON'T KNOW WHAT TRIGGERS THESE WILD SPELLS, MAYBE I CAN TRACK THEM DOWN! DO THEY ALWAYS OCCUR IN THE SAME PLACE... AT THE SAME TIME?
NO--THERE'S NO CONNECTION--IN PLACE--OR TIME!
4
"IT HAPPENED FIRST WHEN WE WERE DRIVING TOWARD GOTHAM CITY--AND STOPPED AT A PICNIC AREA ON THE OUTSKIRTS FOR LUNCH..."
SOMETHING'S WRONG... LOSING CONTROL OF MYSELF... GOTTA GET AWAY WHERE NOBODY CAN SEE ME...

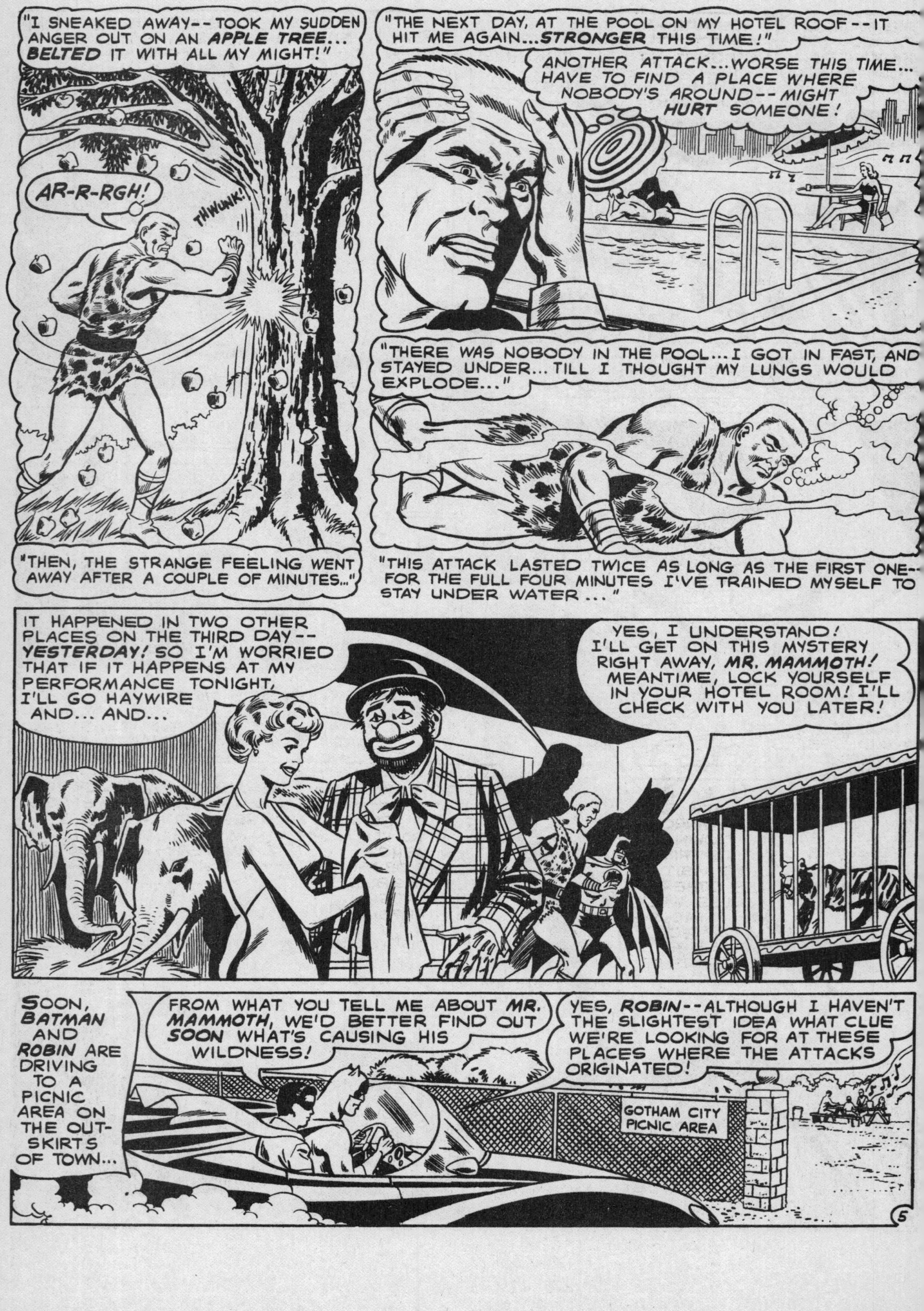
"I SNEAKED AWAY--TOOK MY SUDDEN ANGER OUT ON AN APPLE TREE... BELTED IT WITH ALL MY MIGHT!"
AR-R-RGH!
THWUNK!
"THEN, THE STRANGE FEELING WENT AWAY AFTER A COUPLE OF MINUTES..."
"THE NEXT DAY, AT THE POOL ON MY HOTEL ROOF--IT HIT ME AGAIN...STRONGER THIS TIME!"
ANOTHER ATTACK...WORSE THIS TIME... HAVE TO FIND A PLACE WHERE NOBODY'S AROUND--MIGHT HURT SOMEONE!
"THERE WAS NOBODY IN THE POOL...I GOT IN FAST, AND STAYED UNDER...TILL I THOUGHT MY LUNGS WOULD EXPLODE..."
"THIS ATTACK LASTED TWICE AS LONG AS THE FIRST ONE--FOR THE FULL FOUR MINUTES I'VE TRAINED MYSELF TO STAY UNDER WATER..."
IT HAPPENED IN TWO OTHER PLACES ON THE THIRD DAY--YESTERDAY! SO I'M WORRIED THAT IF IT HAPPENS AT MY PERFORMANCE TONIGHT, I'LL GO HAYWIRE AND... AND...
YES, I UNDERSTAND! I'LL GET ON THIS MYSTERY RIGHT AWAY, MR. MAMMOTH! MEANTIME, LOCK YOURSELF IN YOUR HOTEL ROOM! I'LL CHECK WITH YOU LATER!
SOON, BATMAN AND ROBIN ARE DRIVING TO A PICNIC AREA ON THE OUT-SKIRTS OF TOWN...
FROM WHAT YOU TELL ME ABOUT MR. MAMMOTH, WE'D BETTER FIND OUT SOON WHAT'S CAUSING HIS WILDNESS!
YES, ROBIN--ALTHOUGH I HAVEN'T THE SLIGHTEST IDEA WHAT CLUE WE'RE LOOKING FOR AT THESE PLACES WHERE THE ATTACKS ORIGINATED!
GOTHAM CITY PICNIC AREA
5

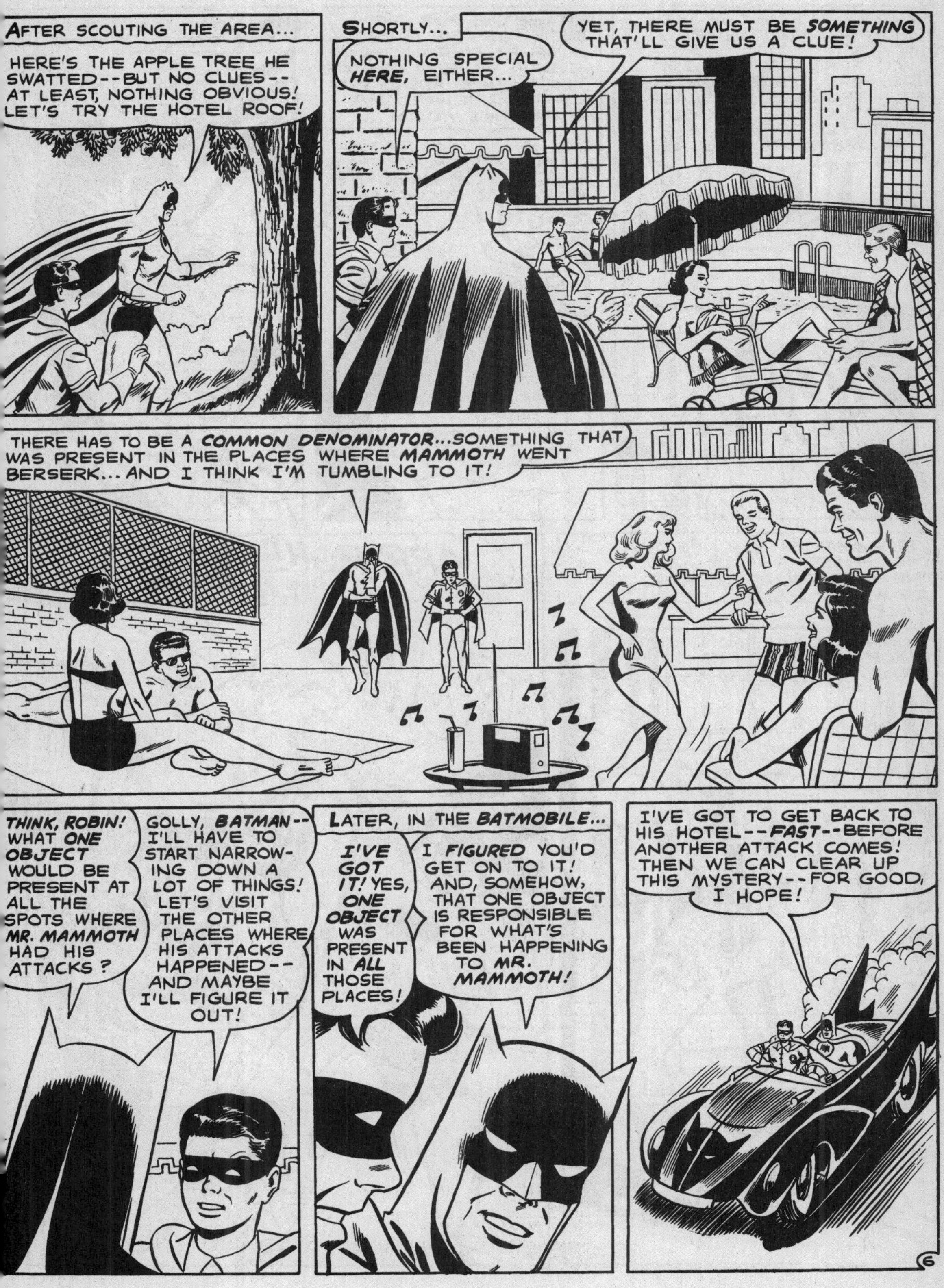
AFTER SCOUTING THE AREA...
HERE'S THE APPLE TREE HE SWATTED--BUT NO CLUES--AT LEAST, NOTHING OBVIOUS! LET'S TRY THE HOTEL ROOF!
SHORTLY...
NOTHING SPECIAL HERE, EITHER...
YET, THERE MUST BE SOMETHING THAT'LL GIVE US A CLUE!
THERE HAS TO BE A COMMON DENOMINATOR...SOMETHING THAT WAS PRESENT IN THE PLACES WHERE MAMMOTH WENT BERSERK... AND I THINK I'M TUMBLING TO IT!
THINK, ROBIN! WHAT ONE OBJECT WOULD BE PRESENT AT ALL THE SPOTS WHERE MR. MAMMOTH HAD HIS ATTACKS?
GOLLY, BATMAN--I'LL HAVE TO START NARROWING DOWN A LOT OF THINGS! LET'S VISIT THE OTHER PLACES WHERE HIS ATTACKS HAPPENED--AND MAYBE I'LL FIGURE IT OUT!
LATER, IN THE BATMOBILE...
I'VE GOT IT! YES, ONE OBJECT WAS PRESENT IN ALL THOSE PLACES!
I FIGURED YOU'D GET ON TO IT! AND, SOMEHOW, THAT ONE OBJECT IS RESPONSIBLE FOR WHAT'S BEEN HAPPENING TO MR. MAMMOTH!
I'VE GOT TO GET BACK TO HIS HOTEL--FAST--BEFORE ANOTHER ATTACK COMES! THEN WE CAN CLEAR UP THIS MYSTERY--FOR GOOD, I HOPE!
6

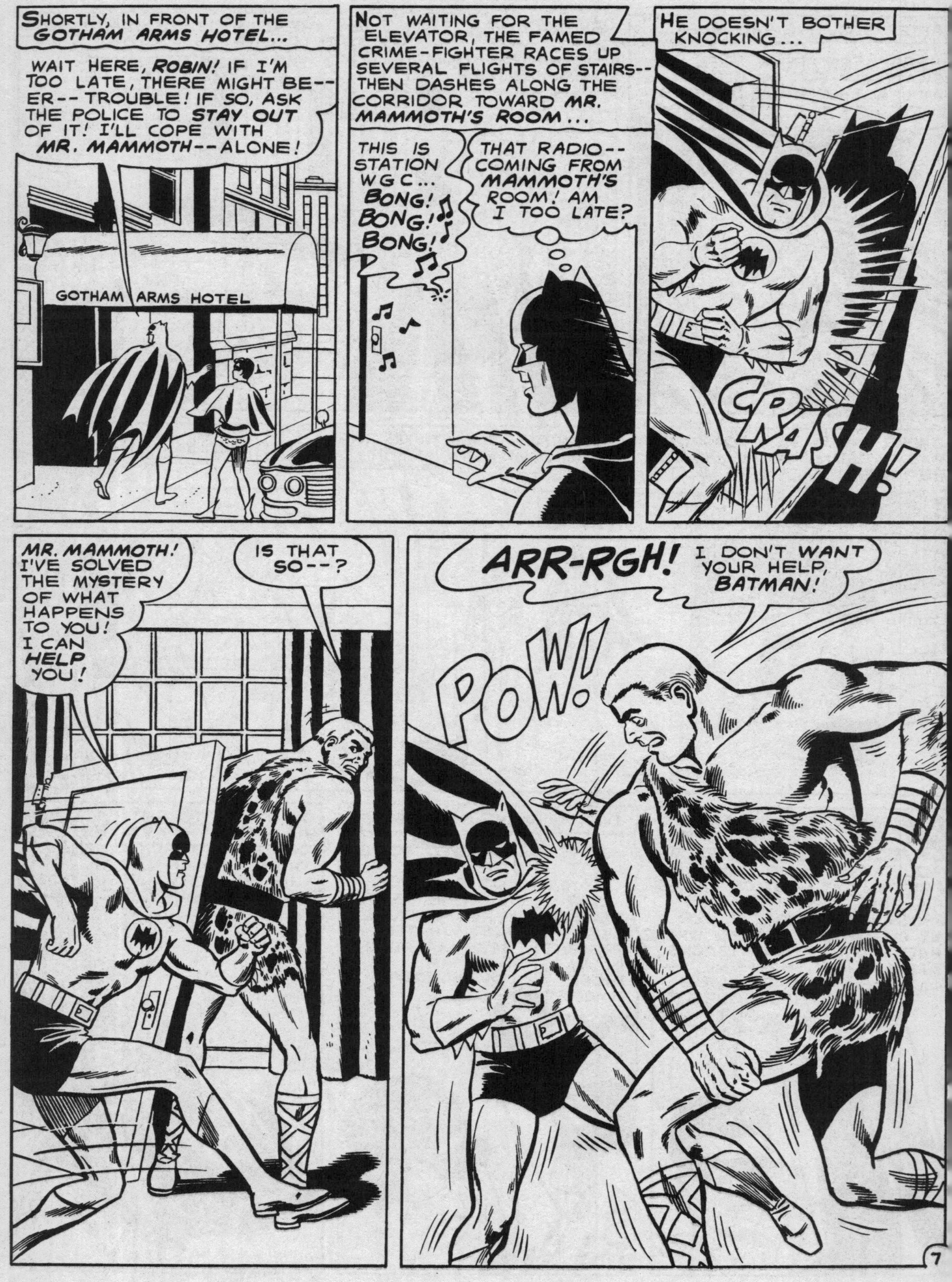
SHORTLY, IN FRONT OF THE GOTHAM ARMS HOTEL...
WAIT HERE, ROBIN! IF I'M TOO LATE, THERE MIGHT BE-- ER-- TROUBLE! IF SO, ASK THE POLICE TO STAY OUT OF IT! I'LL COPE WITH MR. MAMMOTH--ALONE!
GOTHAM ARMS HOTEL
NOT WAITING FOR THE ELEVATOR, THE FAMED CRIME-FIGHTER RACES UP SEVERAL FLIGHTS OF STAIRS-- THEN DASHES ALONG THE CORRIDOR TOWARD MR. MAMMOTH'S ROOM...
THIS IS STATION WGC... BONG! BONG! BONG!
THAT RADIO-- COMING FROM MAMMOTH'S ROOM! AM I TOO LATE?
HE DOESN'T BOTHER KNOCKING...
CRASH!
MR. MAMMOTH! I'VE SOLVED THE MYSTERY OF WHAT HAPPENS TO YOU! I CAN HELP YOU!
IS THAT SO--?
ARR-RGH! I DON'T WANT YOUR HELP, BATMAN!
POW!
7

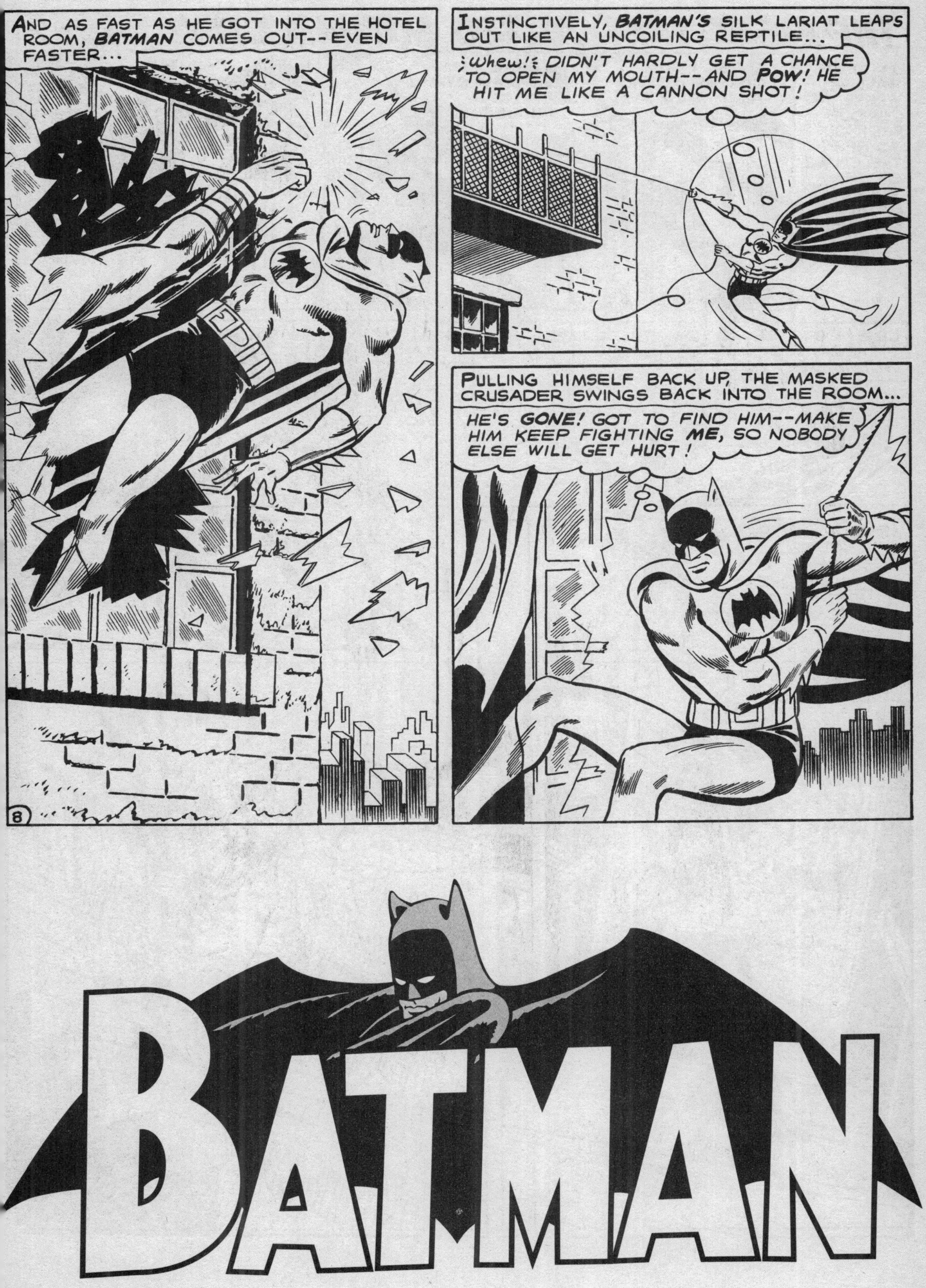
AND AS FAST AS HE GOT INTO THE HOTEL ROOM, BATMAN COMES OUT--EVEN FASTER...
8
INSTINCTIVELY, BATMAN'S SILK LARIAT LEAPS OUT LIKE AN UNCOILING REPTILE...
WHEW! DIDN'T HARDLY GET A CHANCE TO OPEN MY MOUTH--AND POW! HE HIT ME LIKE A CANNON SHOT!
PULLING HIMSELF BACK UP, THE MASKED CRUSADER SWINGS BACK INTO THE ROOM...
HE'S GONE! GOT TO FIND HIM--MAKE HIM KEEP FIGHTING ME, SO NOBODY ELSE WILL GET HURT!

BATMAN

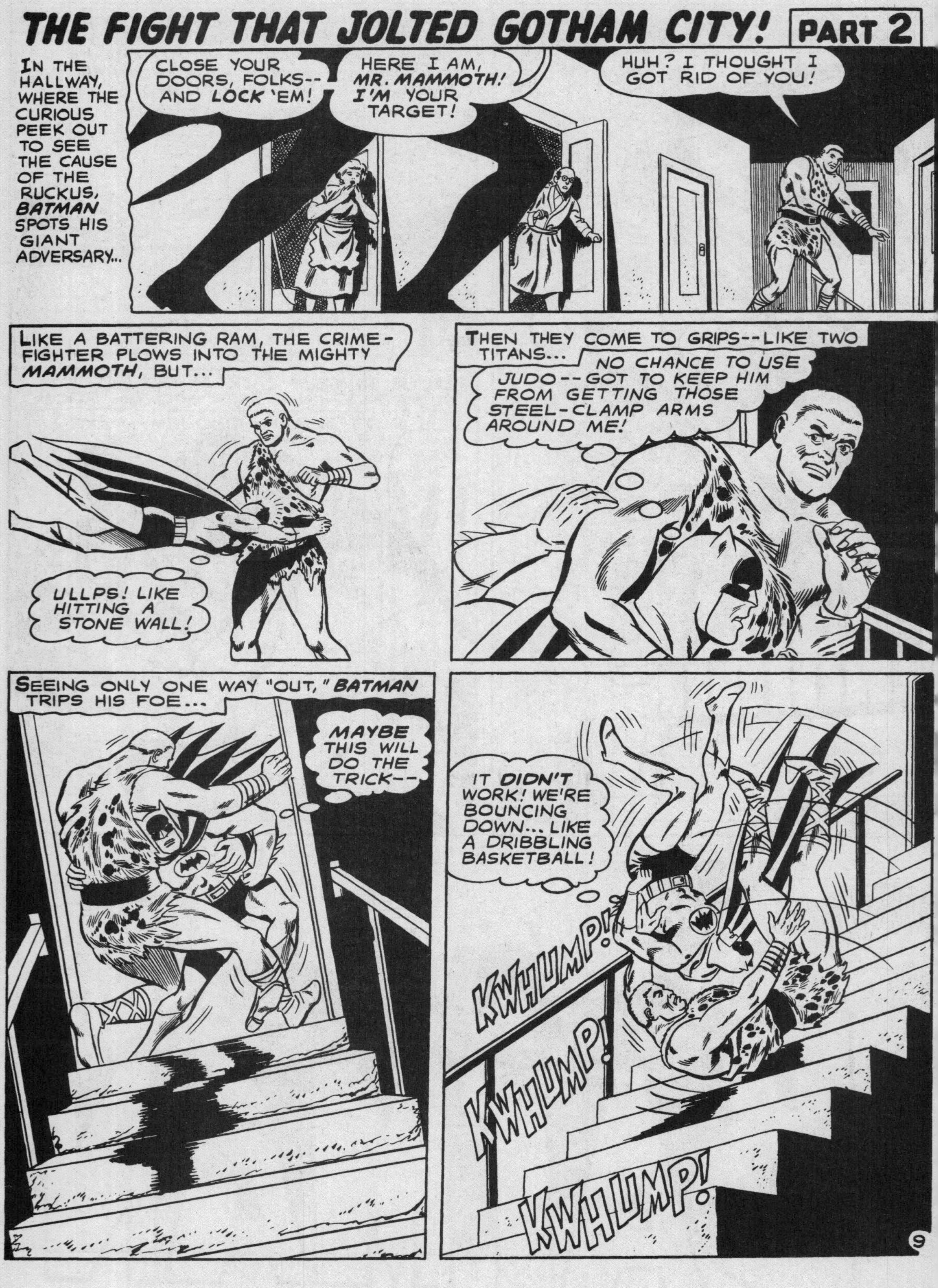
THE FIGHT THAT JOLTED GOTHAM CITY! PART 2
IN THE HALLWAY, WHERE THE CURIOUS PEEK OUT TO SEE THE CAUSE OF THE RUCKUS, BATMAN SPOTS HIS GIANT ADVERSARY...
CLOSE YOUR DOORS, FOLKS-- AND LOCK 'EM!
HERE I AM, MR. MAMMOTH! I'M YOUR TARGET!
HUH? I THOUGHT I GOT RID OF YOU!
LIKE A BATTERING RAM, THE CRIME-FIGHTER PLOWS INTO THE MIGHTY MAMMOTH, BUT...
ULLPS! LIKE HITTING A STONE WALL!
THEN THEY COME TO GRIPS--LIKE TWO TITANS...
NO CHANCE TO USE JUDO--GOT TO KEEP HIM FROM GETTING THOSE STEEL-CLAMP ARMS AROUND ME!
SEEING ONLY ONE WAY "OUT," BATMAN TRIPS HIS FOE...
MAYBE THIS WILL DO THE TRICK--
IT DIDN'T WORK! WE'RE BOUNCING DOWN... LIKE A DRIBBLING BASKETBALL!
KWHUMP!
KWHUMP!
KWHUMP!
9

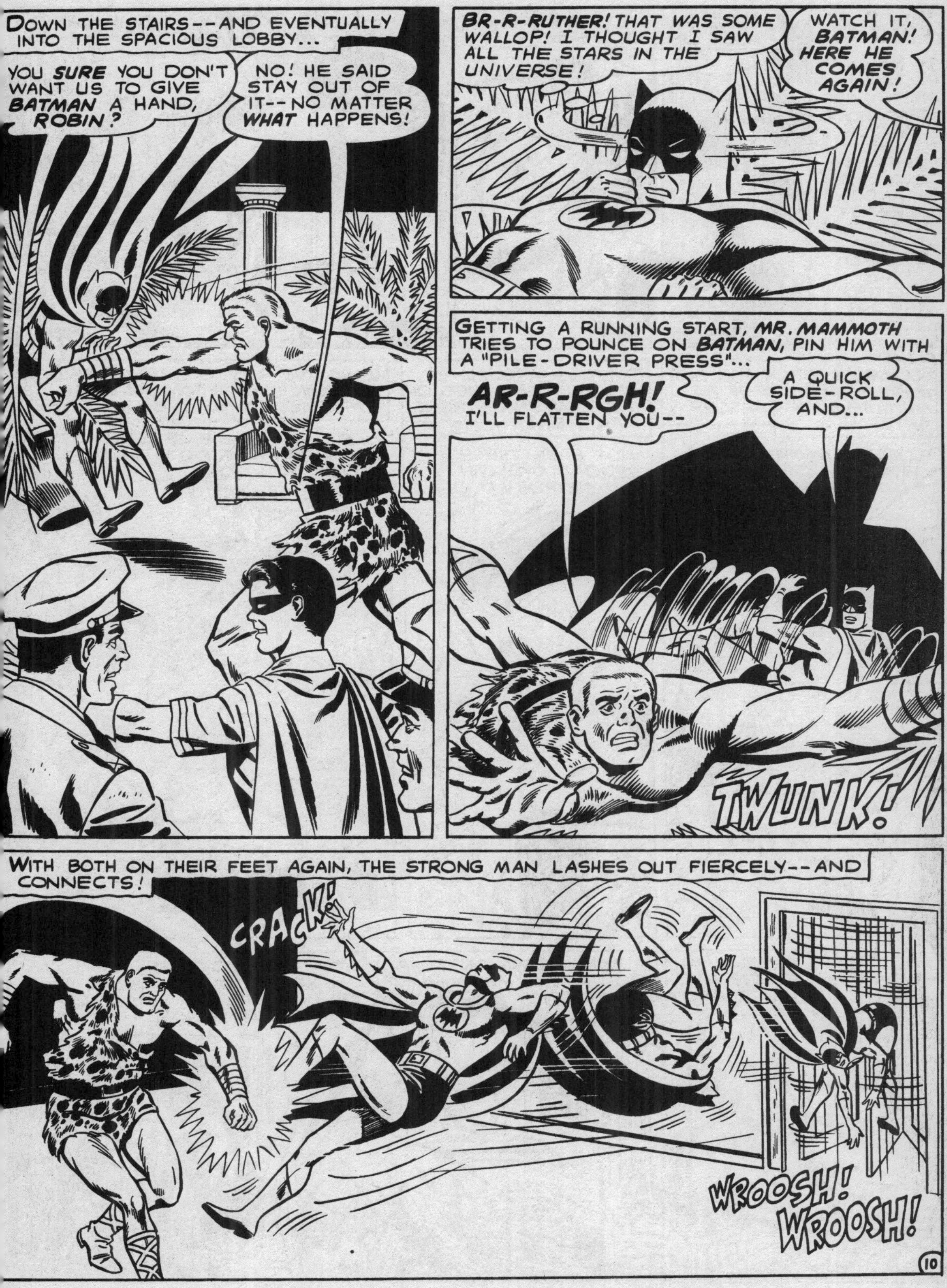
DOWN THE STAIRS--AND EVENTUALLY INTO THE SPACIOUS LOBBY...
YOU SURE YOU DON'T WANT US TO GIVE BATMAN A HAND, ROBIN?
NO! HE SAID STAY OUT OF IT--NO MATTER WHAT HAPPENS!
BR-R-RUTHER! THAT WAS SOME WALLOP! I THOUGHT I SAW ALL THE STARS IN THE UNIVERSE!
WATCH IT, BATMAN! HERE HE COMES AGAIN!
GETTING A RUNNING START, MR. MAMMOTH TRIES TO POUNCE ON BATMAN, PIN HIM WITH A "PILE-DRIVER PRESS"...
AR-R-RGH! I'LL FLATTEN YOU--
A QUICK SIDE-ROLL, AND...
TWUNK!
WITH BOTH ON THEIR FEET AGAIN, THE STRONG MAN LASHES OUT FIERCELY--AND CONNECTS!
CRACK!
WROOSH! WROOSH!
10

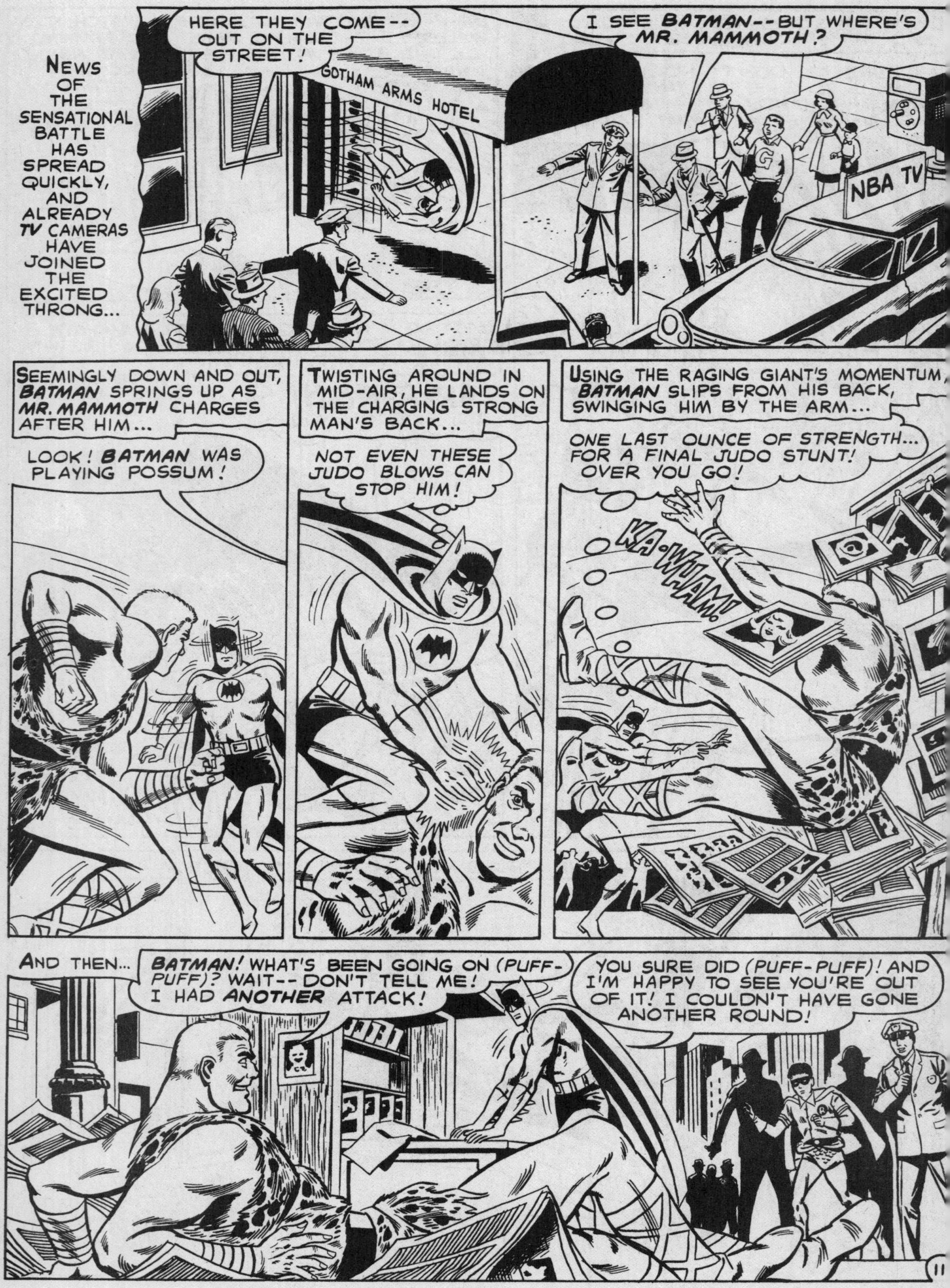
NEWS OF THE SENSATIONAL BATTLE HAS SPREAD QUICKLY, AND ALREADY TV CAMERAS HAVE JOINED THE EXCITED THRONG...
HERE THEY COME-- OUT ON THE STREET!
GOTHAM ARMS HOTEL
I SEE BATMAN--BUT WHERE'S MR. MAMMOTH?
NBA TV
SEEMINGLY DOWN AND OUT, BATMAN SPRINGS UP AS MR. MAMMOTH CHARGES AFTER HIM...
LOOK! BATMAN WAS PLAYING POSSUM!
TWISTING AROUND IN MID-AIR, HE LANDS ON THE CHARGING STRONG MAN'S BACK...
NOT EVEN THESE JUDO BLOWS CAN STOP HIM!
USING THE RAGING GIANT'S MOMENTUM, BATMAN SLIPS FROM HIS BACK, SWINGING HIM BY THE ARM...
ONE LAST OUNCE OF STRENGTH... FOR A FINAL JUDO STUNT! OVER YOU GO!
KA-WHAM!
AND THEN...
BATMAN! WHAT'S BEEN GOING ON (PUFF-PUFF)? WAIT-- DON'T TELL ME! I HAD ANOTHER ATTACK!
YOU SURE DID (PUFF-PUFF)! AND I'M HAPPY TO SEE YOU'RE OUT OF IT! I COULDN'T HAVE GONE ANOTHER ROUND!
11

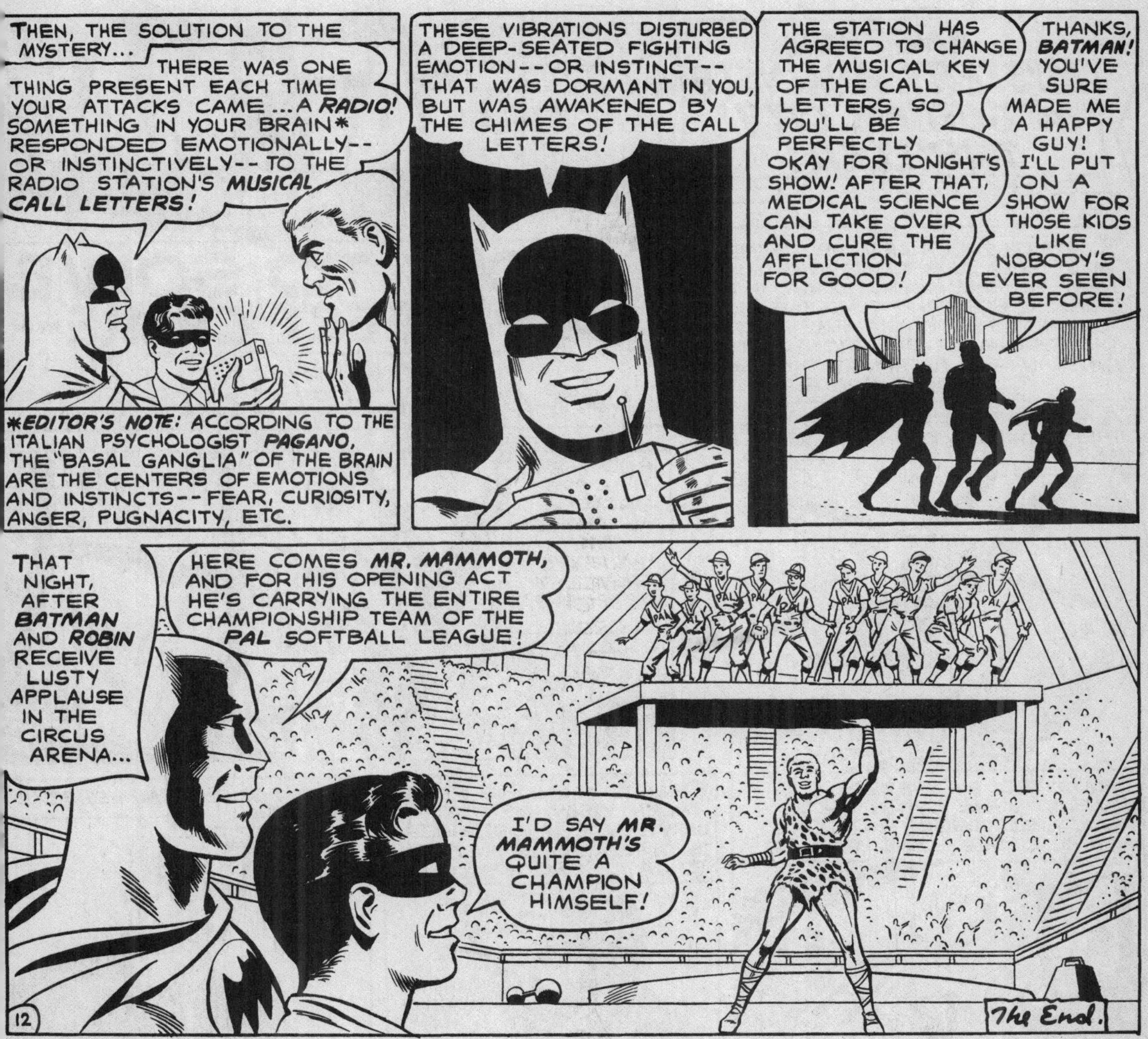
THEN, THE SOLUTION TO THE MYSTERY...
THERE WAS ONE THING PRESENT EACH TIME YOUR ATTACKS CAME ...A RADIO! SOMETHING IN YOUR BRAIN* RESPONDED EMOTIONALLY-- OR INSTINCTIVELY-- TO THE RADIO STATION'S MUSICAL CALL LETTERS!
*EDITOR'S NOTE: ACCORDING TO THE ITALIAN PSYCHOLOGIST PAGANO, THE "BASAL GANGLIA" OF THE BRAIN ARE THE CENTERS OF EMOTIONS AND INSTINCTS--FEAR, CURIOSITY, ANGER, PUGNACITY, ETC.
THESE VIBRATIONS DISTURBED A DEEP-SEATED FIGHTING EMOTION--OR INSTINCT--THAT WAS DORMANT IN YOU, BUT WAS AWAKENED BY THE CHIMES OF THE CALL LETTERS!
THE STATION HAS AGREED TO CHANGE THE MUSICAL KEY OF THE CALL LETTERS, SO YOU'LL BE PERFECTLY OKAY FOR TONIGHT'S SHOW! AFTER THAT, MEDICAL SCIENCE CAN TAKE OVER AND CURE THE AFFLICTION FOR GOOD!
THANKS, BATMAN! YOU'VE SURE MADE ME A HAPPY GUY! I'LL PUT ON A SHOW FOR THOSE KIDS LIKE NOBODY'S EVER SEEN BEFORE!
THAT NIGHT, AFTER BATMAN AND ROBIN RECEIVE LUSTY APPLAUSE IN THE CIRCUS ARENA...
HERE COMES MR. MAMMOTH, AND FOR HIS OPENING ACT HE'S CARRYING THE ENTIRE CHAMPIONSHIP TEAM OF THE PAL SOFTBALL LEAGUE!
I'D SAY MR. MAMMOTH'S QUITE A CHAMPION HIMSELF!
12
The End.

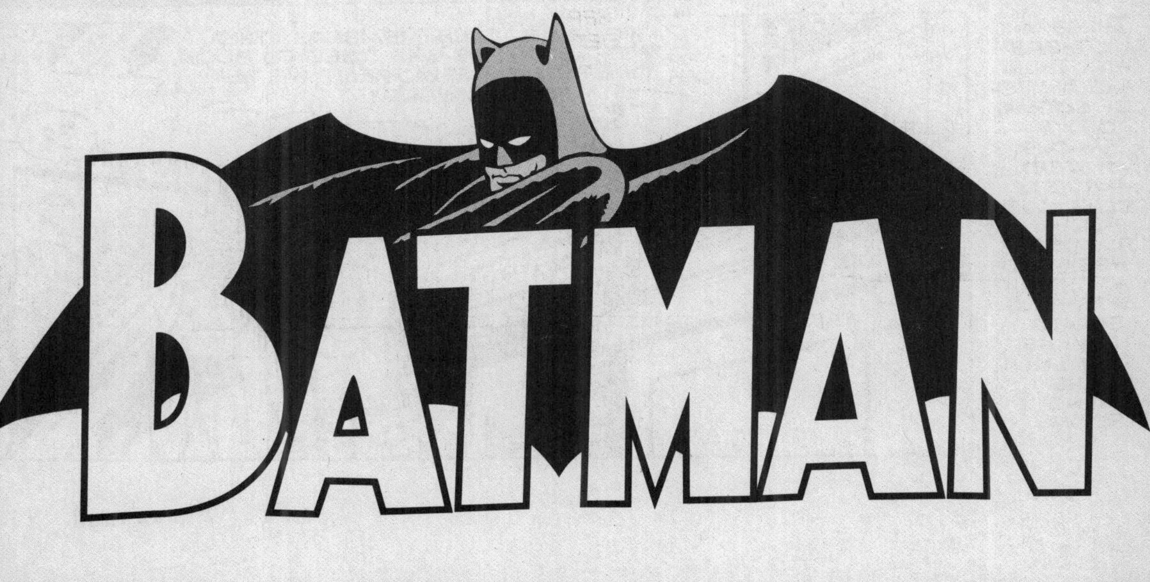
BATMAN

ANOTHER "MYSTERY ANALYSTS of GOTHAM CITY" THRILLER!

BAT MAN

WITH ROBIN
- THE BOY WONDER -

HOW TO SOLVE A PERFECT CRIME-- in REVERSE!

To apprehend a criminal, there must be a clue to his identity--but what happens when you *know* the criminal, but can't find the clue to pin the guilt on him? That is the turnabout situation confronting *Batman* and *Robin*, as they set out to demonstrate ...

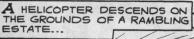

A helicopter descends on the grounds of a rambling estate...

And from it steps *Batman*, heralded the *world's greatest detective*...

...Followed by mystery novelist *Kaye Daye*, whose fiction strikingly parallels actual cases--and *solves* them!

Serious--thinking *Prof. Ralph Vern*, of State University, whose hobby is tinkering in a lab--to catch crooks!

And *Police Commissioner Gordon*...

These, and others with them, are members of *Gotham City's* famous *Mystery Analysts Club*, out for a "business" week-end at their sprawling estate. Now, as they enter the living room...

Welcome, club members! This tape recorder was timed to begin operation the moment we set foot in here!

!!

??

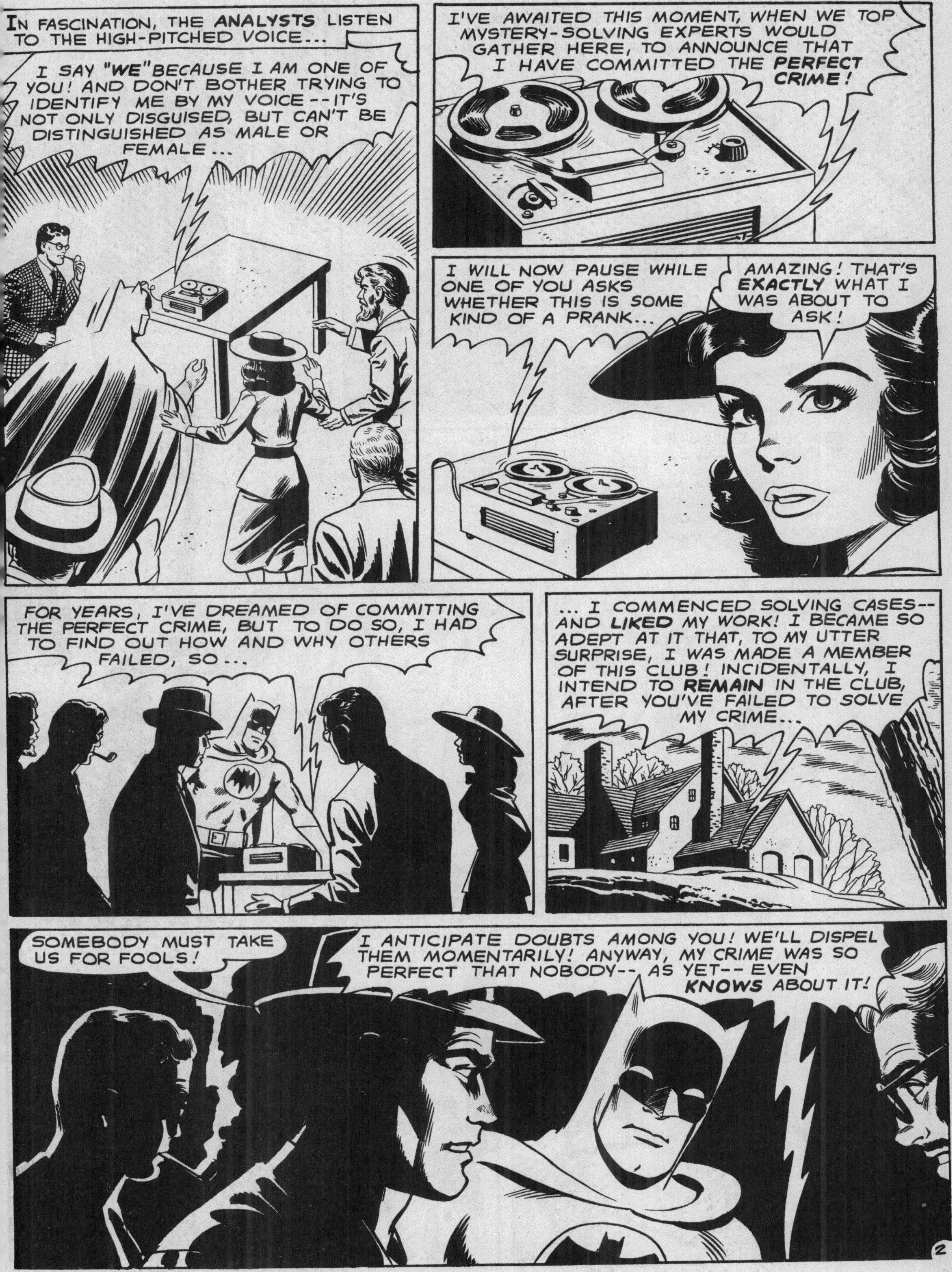
IN FASCINATION, THE ANALYSTS LISTEN TO THE HIGH-PITCHED VOICE...
I SAY "WE" BECAUSE I AM ONE OF YOU! AND DON'T BOTHER TRYING TO IDENTIFY ME BY MY VOICE--IT'S NOT ONLY DISGUISED, BUT CAN'T BE DISTINGUISHED AS MALE OR FEMALE...
I'VE AWAITED THIS MOMENT, WHEN WE TOP MYSTERY-SOLVING EXPERTS WOULD GATHER HERE, TO ANNOUNCE THAT I HAVE COMMITTED THE PERFECT CRIME!
I WILL NOW PAUSE WHILE ONE OF YOU ASKS WHETHER THIS IS SOME KIND OF A PRANK...
AMAZING! THAT'S EXACTLY WHAT I WAS ABOUT TO ASK!
FOR YEARS, I'VE DREAMED OF COMMITTING THE PERFECT CRIME, BUT TO DO SO, I HAD TO FIND OUT HOW AND WHY OTHERS FAILED, SO...
... I COMMENCED SOLVING CASES-- AND LIKED MY WORK! I BECAME SO ADEPT AT IT THAT, TO MY UTTER SURPRISE, I WAS MADE A MEMBER OF THIS CLUB! INCIDENTALLY, I INTEND TO REMAIN IN THE CLUB, AFTER YOU'VE FAILED TO SOLVE MY CRIME...
SOMEBODY MUST TAKE US FOR FOOLS!
I ANTICIPATE DOUBTS AMONG YOU! WE'LL DISPEL THEM MOMENTARILY! ANYWAY, MY CRIME WAS SO PERFECT THAT NOBODY-- AS YET-- EVEN KNOWS ABOUT IT!
2

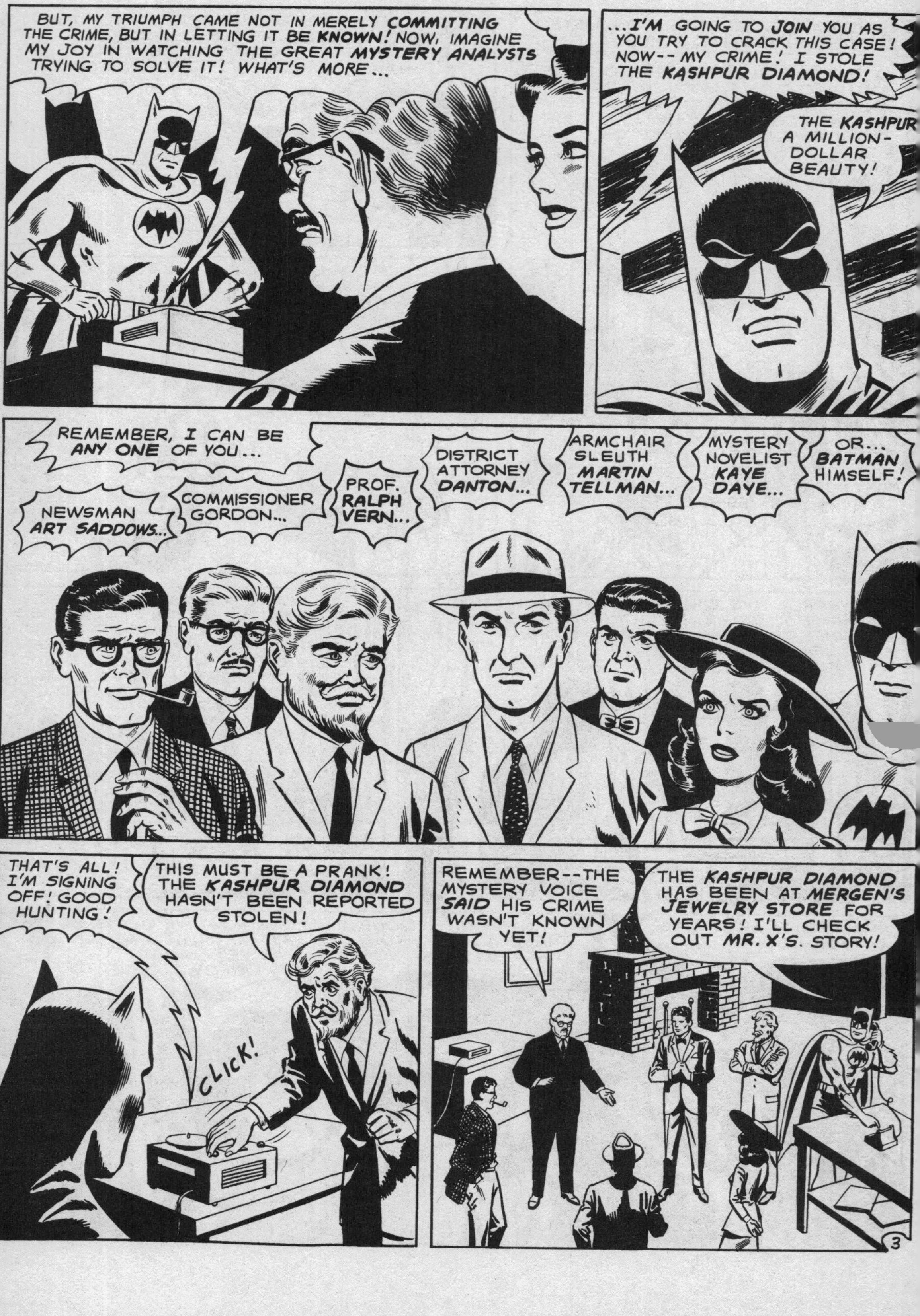
BUT, MY TRIUMPH CAME NOT IN MERELY COMMITTING THE CRIME, BUT IN LETTING IT BE KNOWN! NOW, IMAGINE MY JOY IN WATCHING THE GREAT MYSTERY ANALYSTS TRYING TO SOLVE IT! WHAT'S MORE...
...I'M GOING TO JOIN YOU AS YOU TRY TO CRACK THIS CASE! NOW-- MY CRIME! I STOLE THE KASHPUR DIAMOND!
THE KASHPUR A MILLION-DOLLAR BEAUTY!
REMEMBER, I CAN BE ANY ONE OF YOU...
NEWSMAN ART SADDOWS...
COMMISSIONER GORDON...
PROF. RALPH VERN...
DISTRICT ATTORNEY DANTON...
ARMCHAIR SLEUTH MARTIN TELLMAN...
MYSTERY NOVELIST KAYE DAYE...
OR... BATMAN HIMSELF!
THAT'S ALL! I'M SIGNING OFF! GOOD HUNTING!
THIS MUST BE A PRANK! THE KASHPUR DIAMOND HASN'T BEEN REPORTED STOLEN!
CLICK!
REMEMBER--THE MYSTERY VOICE SAID HIS CRIME WASN'T KNOWN YET!
THE KASHPUR DIAMOND HAS BEEN AT MERGEN'S JEWELRY STORE FOR YEARS! I'LL CHECK OUT MR. X'S STORY!
3

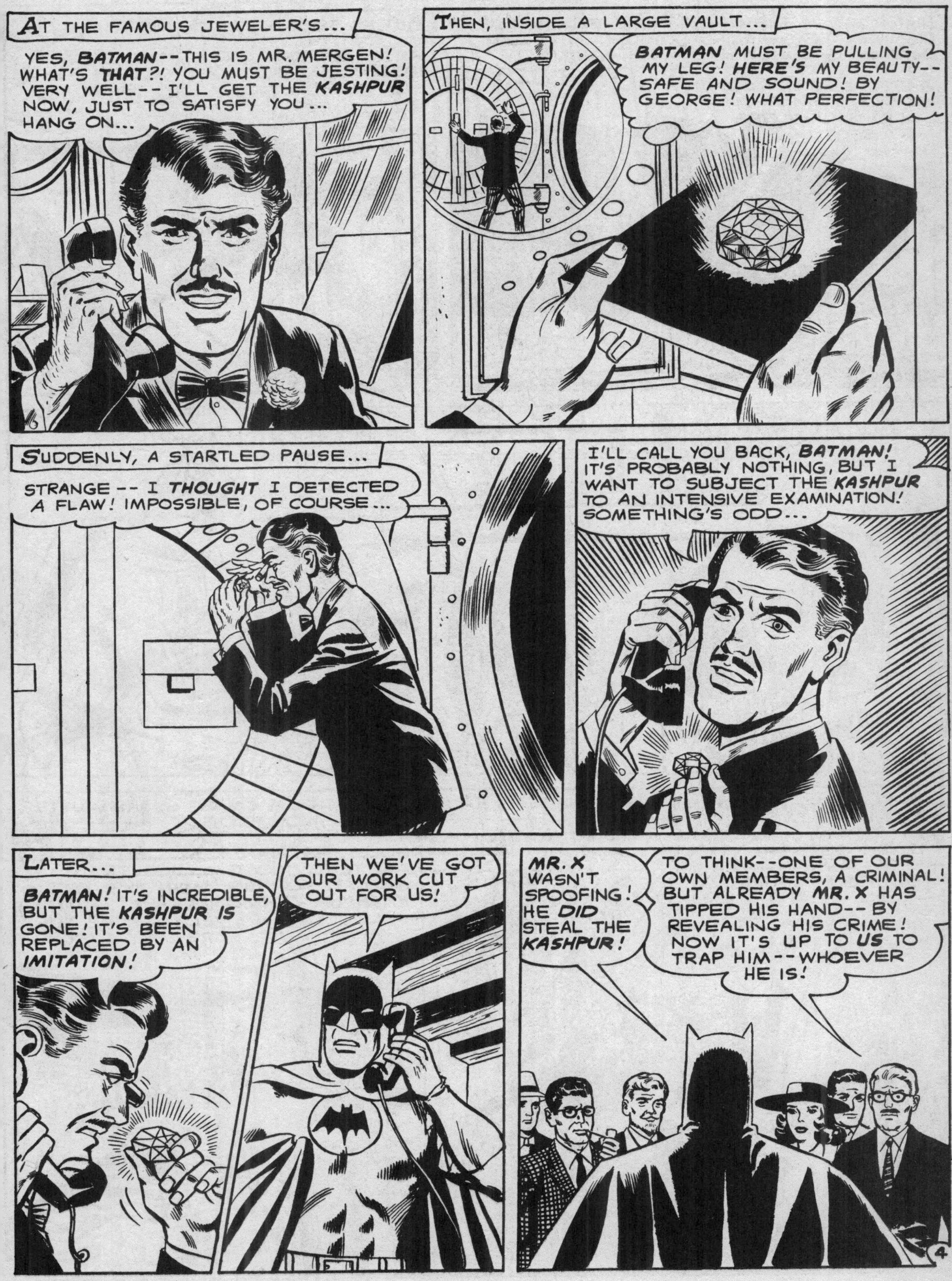
AT THE FAMOUS JEWELER'S...
YES, BATMAN--THIS IS MR. MERGEN! WHAT'S THAT?! YOU MUST BE JESTING! VERY WELL--I'LL GET THE KASHPUR NOW, JUST TO SATISFY YOU... HANG ON...
THEN, INSIDE A LARGE VAULT...
BATMAN MUST BE PULLING MY LEG! HERE'S MY BEAUTY--SAFE AND SOUND! BY GEORGE! WHAT PERFECTION!
SUDDENLY, A STARTLED PAUSE...
STRANGE--I THOUGHT I DETECTED A FLAW! IMPOSSIBLE, OF COURSE...
I'LL CALL YOU BACK, BATMAN! IT'S PROBABLY NOTHING, BUT I WANT TO SUBJECT THE KASHPUR TO AN INTENSIVE EXAMINATION! SOMETHING'S ODD...
LATER...
BATMAN! IT'S INCREDIBLE, BUT THE KASHPUR IS GONE! IT'S BEEN REPLACED BY AN IMITATION!
THEN WE'VE GOT OUR WORK CUT OUT FOR US!
MR. X WASN'T SPOOFING! HE DID STEAL THE KASHPUR!
TO THINK--ONE OF OUR OWN MEMBERS, A CRIMINAL! BUT ALREADY MR. X HAS TIPPED HIS HAND--BY REVEALING HIS CRIME! NOW IT'S UP TO US TO TRAP HIM--WHOEVER HE IS!
4

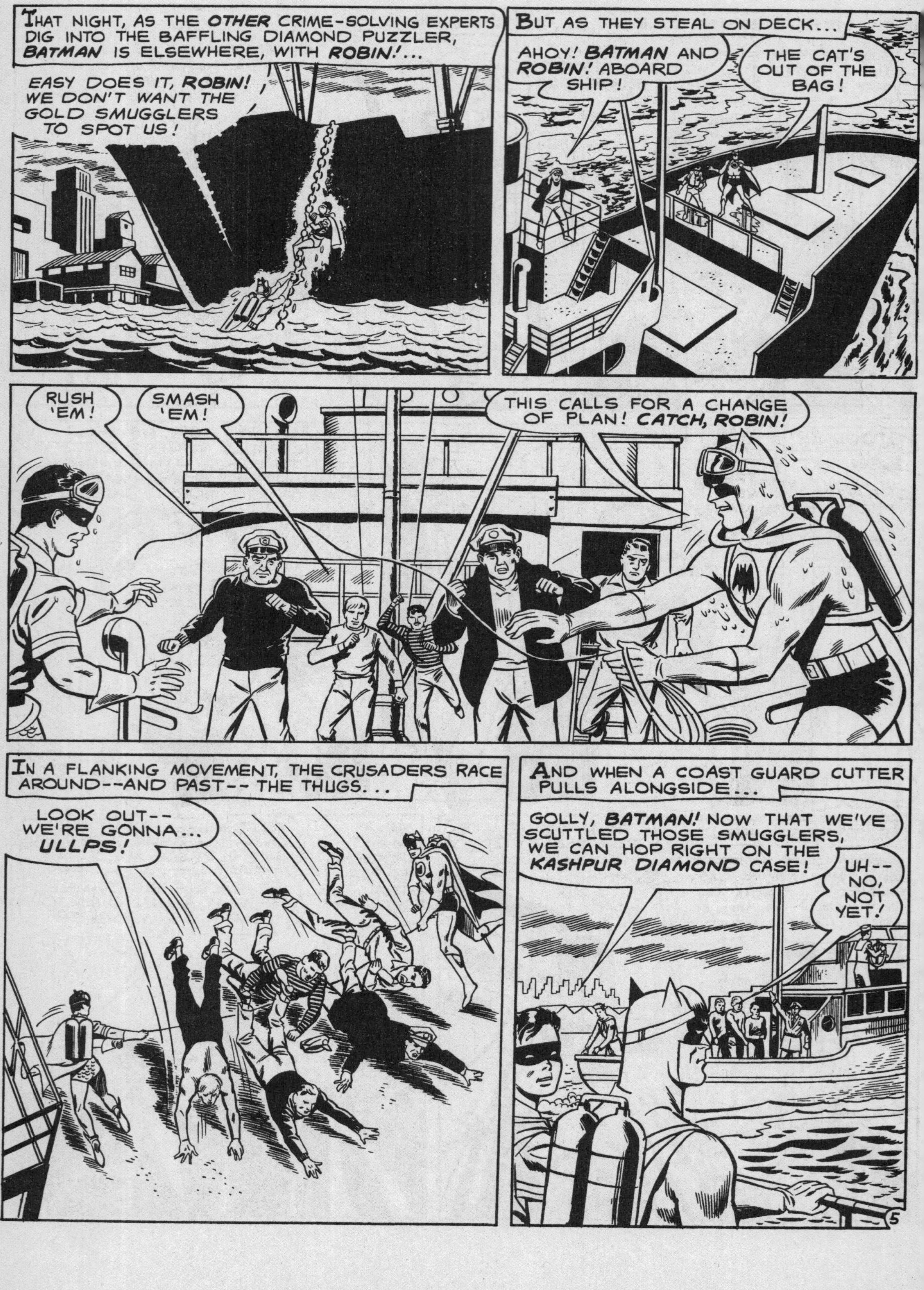
THAT NIGHT, AS THE OTHER CRIME-SOLVING EXPERTS DIG INTO THE BAFFLING DIAMOND PUZZLER, BATMAN IS ELSEWHERE, WITH ROBIN!...
EASY DOES IT, ROBIN! WE DON'T WANT THE GOLD SMUGGLERS TO SPOT US!
BUT AS THEY STEAL ON DECK...
AHOY! BATMAN AND ROBIN! ABOARD SHIP!
THE CAT'S OUT OF THE BAG!
RUSH 'EM!
SMASH 'EM!
THIS CALLS FOR A CHANGE OF PLAN! CATCH, ROBIN!
IN A FLANKING MOVEMENT, THE CRUSADERS RACE AROUND--AND PAST-- THE THUGS...
LOOK OUT-- WE'RE GONNA... ULLPS!
AND WHEN A COAST GUARD CUTTER PULLS ALONGSIDE...
GOLLY, BATMAN! NOW THAT WE'VE SCUTTLED THOSE SMUGGLERS, WE CAN HOP RIGHT ON THE KASHPUR DIAMOND CASE!
UH-- NO, NOT YET!
5

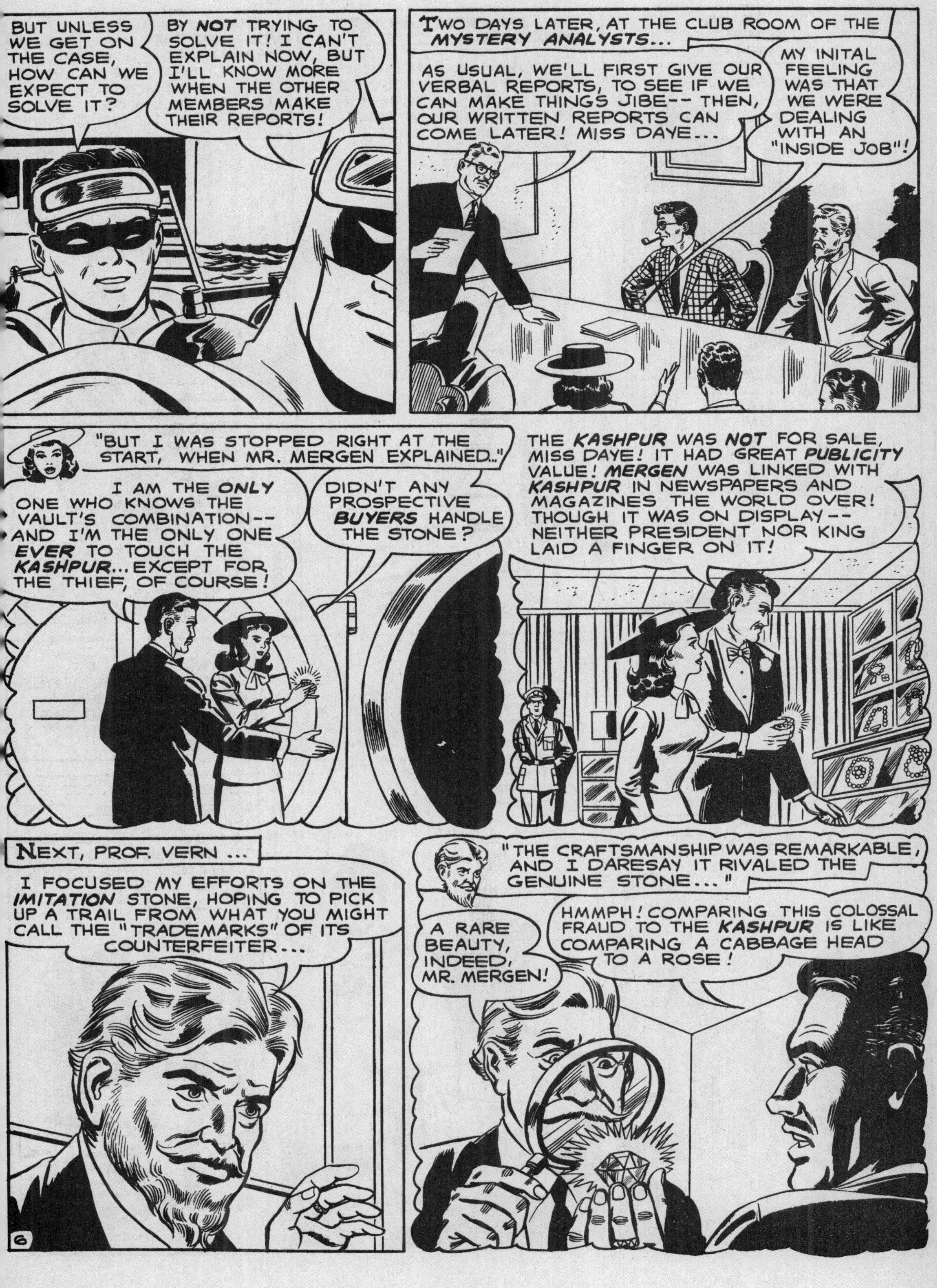
BUT UNLESS WE GET ON THE CASE, HOW CAN WE EXPECT TO SOLVE IT?
BY NOT TRYING TO SOLVE IT! I CAN'T EXPLAIN NOW, BUT I'LL KNOW MORE WHEN THE OTHER MEMBERS MAKE THEIR REPORTS!
TWO DAYS LATER, AT THE CLUB ROOM OF THE MYSTERY ANALYSTS...
AS USUAL, WE'LL FIRST GIVE OUR VERBAL REPORTS, TO SEE IF WE CAN MAKE THINGS JIBE-- THEN, OUR WRITTEN REPORTS CAN COME LATER! MISS DAYE...
MY INITAL FEELING WAS THAT WE WERE DEALING WITH AN "INSIDE JOB"!
"BUT I WAS STOPPED RIGHT AT THE START, WHEN MR. MERGEN EXPLAINED..."
I AM THE ONLY ONE WHO KNOWS THE VAULT'S COMBINATION-- AND I'M THE ONLY ONE EVER TO TOUCH THE KASHPUR... EXCEPT FOR THE THIEF, OF COURSE!
DIDN'T ANY PROSPECTIVE BUYERS HANDLE THE STONE?
THE KASHPUR WAS NOT FOR SALE, MISS DAYE! IT HAD GREAT PUBLICITY VALUE! MERGEN WAS LINKED WITH KASHPUR IN NEWSPAPERS AND MAGAZINES THE WORLD OVER! THOUGH IT WAS ON DISPLAY-- NEITHER PRESIDENT NOR KING LAID A FINGER ON IT!
NEXT, PROF. VERN ...
I FOCUSED MY EFFORTS ON THE IMITATION STONE, HOPING TO PICK UP A TRAIL FROM WHAT YOU MIGHT CALL THE "TRADEMARKS" OF ITS COUNTERFEITER...
6
"THE CRAFTSMANSHIP WAS REMARKABLE, AND I DARESAY IT RIVALED THE GENUINE STONE..."
A RARE BEAUTY, INDEED, MR. MERGEN!
HMMPH! COMPARING THIS COLOSSAL FRAUD TO THE KASHPUR IS LIKE COMPARING A CABBAGE HEAD TO A ROSE!

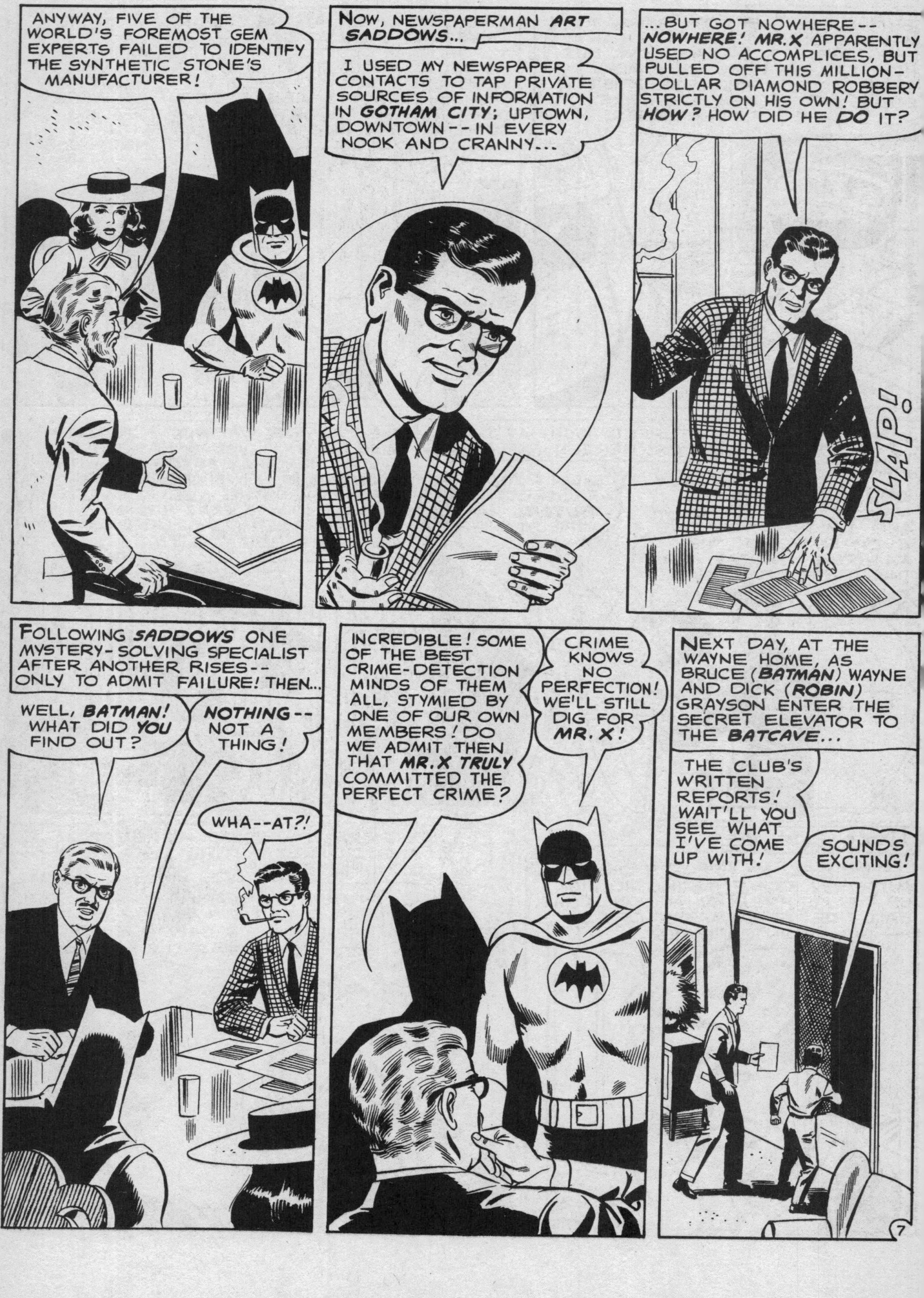

ANYWAY, FIVE OF THE WORLD'S FOREMOST GEM EXPERTS FAILED TO IDENTIFY THE SYNTHETIC STONE'S MANUFACTURER!
NOW, NEWSPAPERMAN ART SADDOWS...
I USED MY NEWSPAPER CONTACTS TO TAP PRIVATE SOURCES OF INFORMATION IN GOTHAM CITY; UPTOWN, DOWNTOWN--IN EVERY NOOK AND CRANNY...
...BUT GOT NOWHERE--NOWHERE! MR. X APPARENTLY USED NO ACCOMPLICES, BUT PULLED OFF THIS MILLION-DOLLAR DIAMOND ROBBERY STRICTLY ON HIS OWN! BUT HOW? HOW DID HE DO IT?
SLAP!
FOLLOWING SADDOWS ONE MYSTERY-SOLVING SPECIALIST AFTER ANOTHER RISES--ONLY TO ADMIT FAILURE! THEN...
WELL, BATMAN! WHAT DID YOU FIND OUT?
NOTHING--NOT A THING!
WHA--AT?!
INCREDIBLE! SOME OF THE BEST CRIME-DETECTION MINDS OF THEM ALL, STYMIED BY ONE OF OUR OWN MEMBERS! DO WE ADMIT THEN THAT MR. X TRULY COMMITTED THE PERFECT CRIME?
CRIME KNOWS NO PERFECTION! WE'LL STILL DIG FOR MR. X!
NEXT DAY, AT THE WAYNE HOME, AS BRUCE (BATMAN) WAYNE AND DICK (ROBIN) GRAYSON ENTER THE SECRET ELEVATOR TO THE BATCAVE...
THE CLUB'S WRITTEN REPORTS! WAIT'LL YOU SEE WHAT I'VE COME UP WITH!
SOUNDS EXCITING!
7

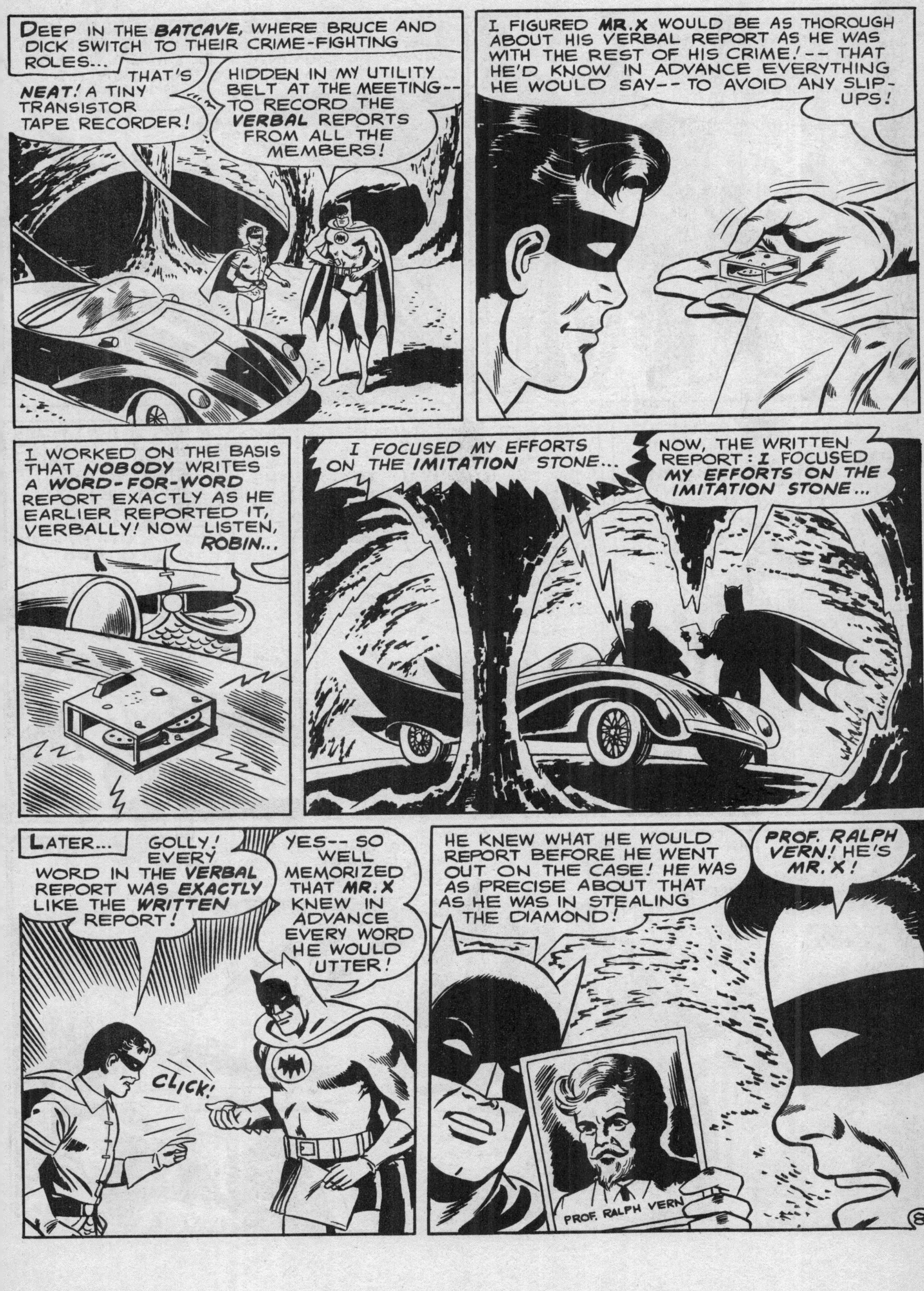
DEEP IN THE BATCAVE, WHERE BRUCE AND DICK SWITCH TO THEIR CRIME-FIGHTING ROLES...
THAT'S NEAT! A TINY TRANSISTOR TAPE RECORDER!
HIDDEN IN MY UTILITY BELT AT THE MEETING-- TO RECORD THE VERBAL REPORTS FROM ALL THE MEMBERS!
I FIGURED MR. X WOULD BE AS THOROUGH ABOUT HIS VERBAL REPORT AS HE WAS WITH THE REST OF HIS CRIME! -- THAT HE'D KNOW IN ADVANCE EVERYTHING HE WOULD SAY-- TO AVOID ANY SLIP-UPS!
I WORKED ON THE BASIS THAT NOBODY WRITES A WORD-FOR-WORD REPORT EXACTLY AS HE EARLIER REPORTED IT, VERBALLY! NOW LISTEN, ROBIN...
I FOCUSED MY EFFORTS ON THE IMITATION STONE...
NOW, THE WRITTEN REPORT: I FOCUSED MY EFFORTS ON THE IMITATION STONE...
LATER...
GOLLY! EVERY WORD IN THE VERBAL REPORT WAS EXACTLY LIKE THE WRITTEN REPORT!
YES-- SO WELL MEMORIZED THAT MR. X KNEW IN ADVANCE EVERY WORD HE WOULD UTTER!
CLICK!
HE KNEW WHAT HE WOULD REPORT BEFORE HE WENT OUT ON THE CASE! HE WAS AS PRECISE ABOUT THAT AS HE WAS IN STEALING THE DIAMOND!
PROF. RALPH VERN! HE'S MR. X!
PROF. RALPH VERN
8

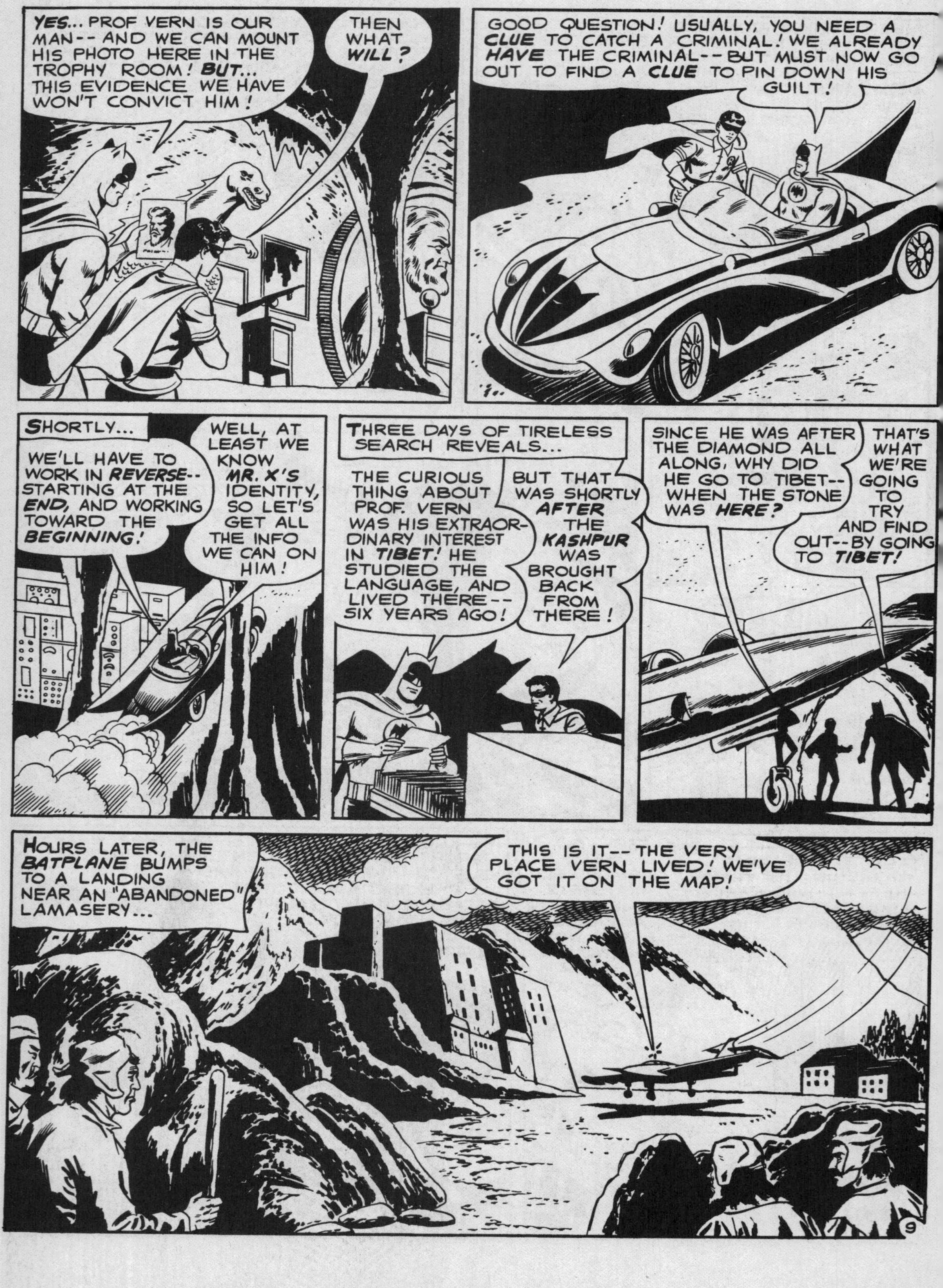
YES... PROF VERN IS OUR MAN-- AND WE CAN MOUNT HIS PHOTO HERE IN THE TROPHY ROOM! BUT... THIS EVIDENCE WE HAVE WON'T CONVICT HIM!
THEN WHAT WILL?
GOOD QUESTION! USUALLY, YOU NEED A CLUE TO CATCH A CRIMINAL! WE ALREADY HAVE THE CRIMINAL-- BUT MUST NOW GO OUT TO FIND A CLUE TO PIN DOWN HIS GUILT!
SHORTLY...
WE'LL HAVE TO WORK IN REVERSE-- STARTING AT THE END, AND WORKING TOWARD THE BEGINNING!
WELL, AT LEAST WE KNOW MR. X'S IDENTITY, SO LET'S GET ALL THE INFO WE CAN ON HIM!
THREE DAYS OF TIRELESS SEARCH REVEALS...
THE CURIOUS THING ABOUT PROF. VERN WAS HIS EXTRAORDINARY INTEREST IN TIBET! HE STUDIED THE LANGUAGE, AND LIVED THERE-- SIX YEARS AGO!
BUT THAT WAS SHORTLY AFTER THE KASHPUR WAS BROUGHT BACK FROM THERE!
SINCE HE WAS AFTER THE DIAMOND ALL ALONG, WHY DID HE GO TO TIBET-- WHEN THE STONE WAS HERE?
THAT'S WHAT WE'RE GOING TO TRY AND FIND OUT--BY GOING TO TIBET!
HOURS LATER, THE BATPLANE BUMPS TO A LANDING NEAR AN "ABANDONED" LAMASERY...
THIS IS IT-- THE VERY PLACE VERN LIVED! WE'VE GOT IT ON THE MAP!
9

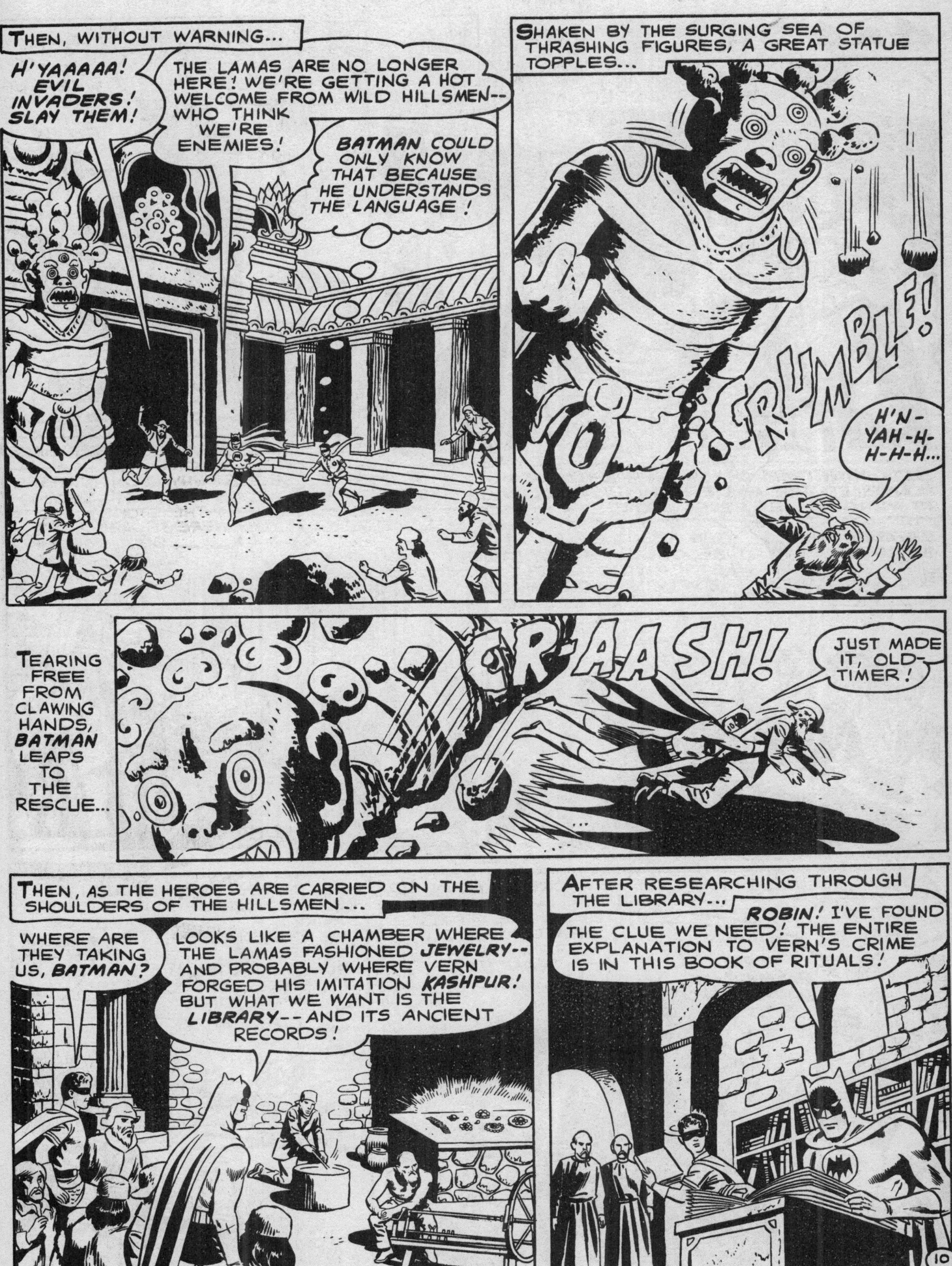
THEN, WITHOUT WARNING...
H'YAAAAA! EVIL INVADERS! SLAY THEM!
THE LAMAS ARE NO LONGER HERE! WE'RE GETTING A HOT WELCOME FROM WILD HILLSMEN-- WHO THINK WE'RE ENEMIES!
BATMAN COULD ONLY KNOW THAT BECAUSE HE UNDERSTANDS THE LANGUAGE!
SHAKEN BY THE SURGING SEA OF THRASHING FIGURES, A GREAT STATUE TOPPLES...
CRUMBLE!
H'N-YAH-H-H-H-H...
TEARING FREE FROM CLAWING HANDS, BATMAN LEAPS TO THE RESCUE...
CR-AASH!
JUST MADE IT, OLD-TIMER!
THEN, AS THE HEROES ARE CARRIED ON THE SHOULDERS OF THE HILLSMEN...
WHERE ARE THEY TAKING US, BATMAN?
LOOKS LIKE A CHAMBER WHERE THE LAMAS FASHIONED JEWELRY-- AND PROBABLY WHERE VERN FORGED HIS IMITATION KASHPUR! BUT WHAT WE WANT IS THE LIBRARY-- AND ITS ANCIENT RECORDS!
AFTER RESEARCHING THROUGH THE LIBRARY...
ROBIN! I'VE FOUND THE CLUE WE NEED! THE ENTIRE EXPLANATION TO VERN'S CRIME IS IN THIS BOOK OF RITUALS!
10

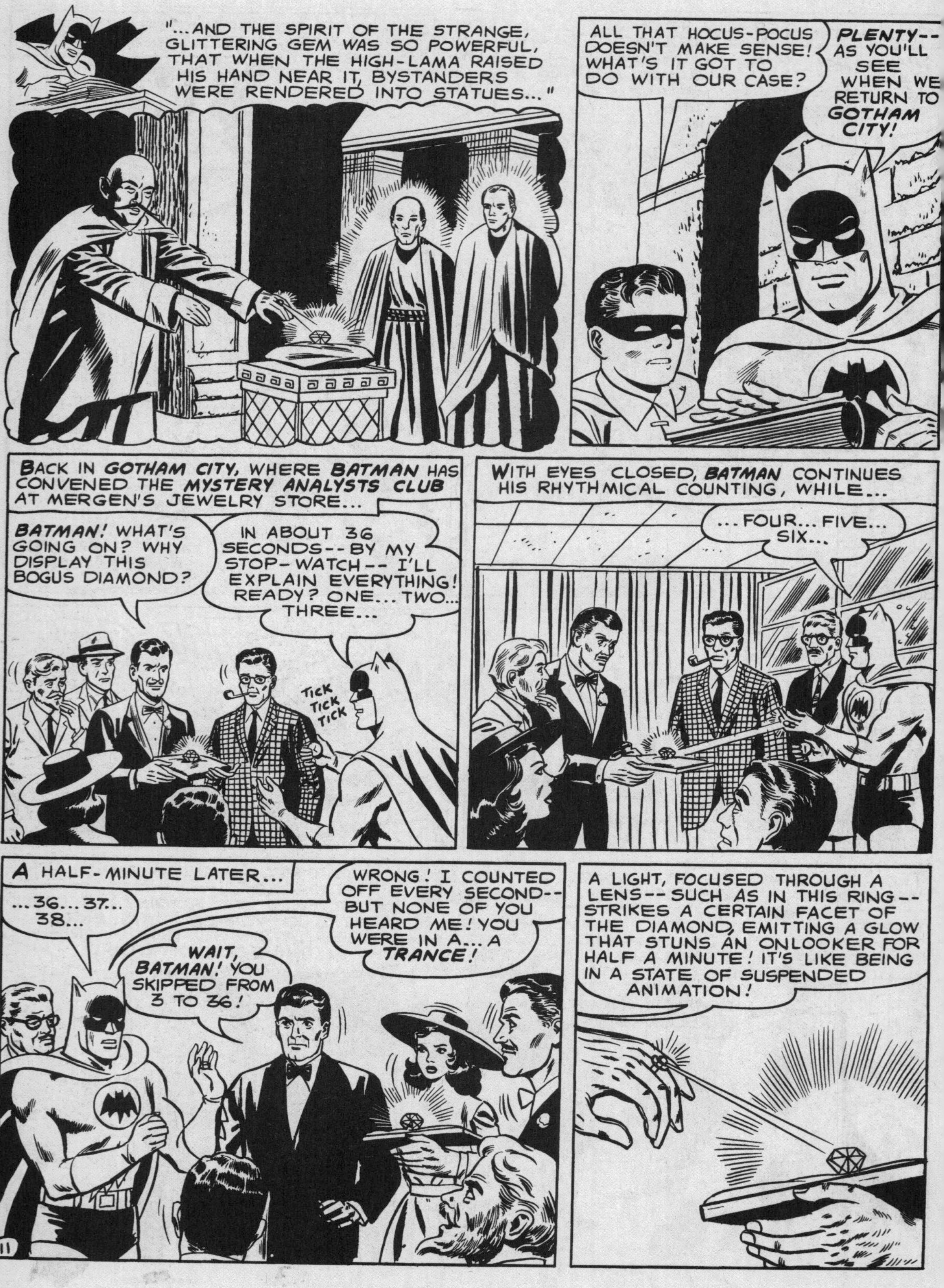
"...AND THE SPIRIT OF THE STRANGE, GLITTERING GEM WAS SO POWERFUL, THAT WHEN THE HIGH-LAMA RAISED HIS HAND NEAR IT, BYSTANDERS WERE RENDERED INTO STATUES..."
ALL THAT HOCUS-POCUS DOESN'T MAKE SENSE! WHAT'S IT GOT TO DO WITH OUR CASE?
PLENTY-- AS YOU'LL SEE WHEN WE RETURN TO GOTHAM CITY!
BACK IN GOTHAM CITY, WHERE BATMAN HAS CONVENED THE MYSTERY ANALYSTS CLUB AT MERGEN'S JEWELRY STORE...
BATMAN! WHAT'S GOING ON? WHY DISPLAY THIS BOGUS DIAMOND?
IN ABOUT 36 SECONDS--BY MY STOP-WATCH-- I'LL EXPLAIN EVERYTHING! READY? ONE... TWO... THREE...
TICK TICK TICK
WITH EYES CLOSED, BATMAN CONTINUES HIS RHYTHMICAL COUNTING, WHILE...
...FOUR... FIVE... SIX...
A HALF-MINUTE LATER...
...36... 37... 38...
WAIT, BATMAN! YOU SKIPPED FROM 3 TO 36!
WRONG! I COUNTED OFF EVERY SECOND-- BUT NONE OF YOU HEARD ME! YOU WERE IN A... A TRANCE!
A LIGHT, FOCUSED THROUGH A LENS--SUCH AS IN THIS RING-- STRIKES A CERTAIN FACET OF THE DIAMOND, EMITTING A GLOW THAT STUNS AN ONLOOKER FOR HALF A MINUTE! IT'S LIKE BEING IN A STATE OF SUSPENDED ANIMATION!
11

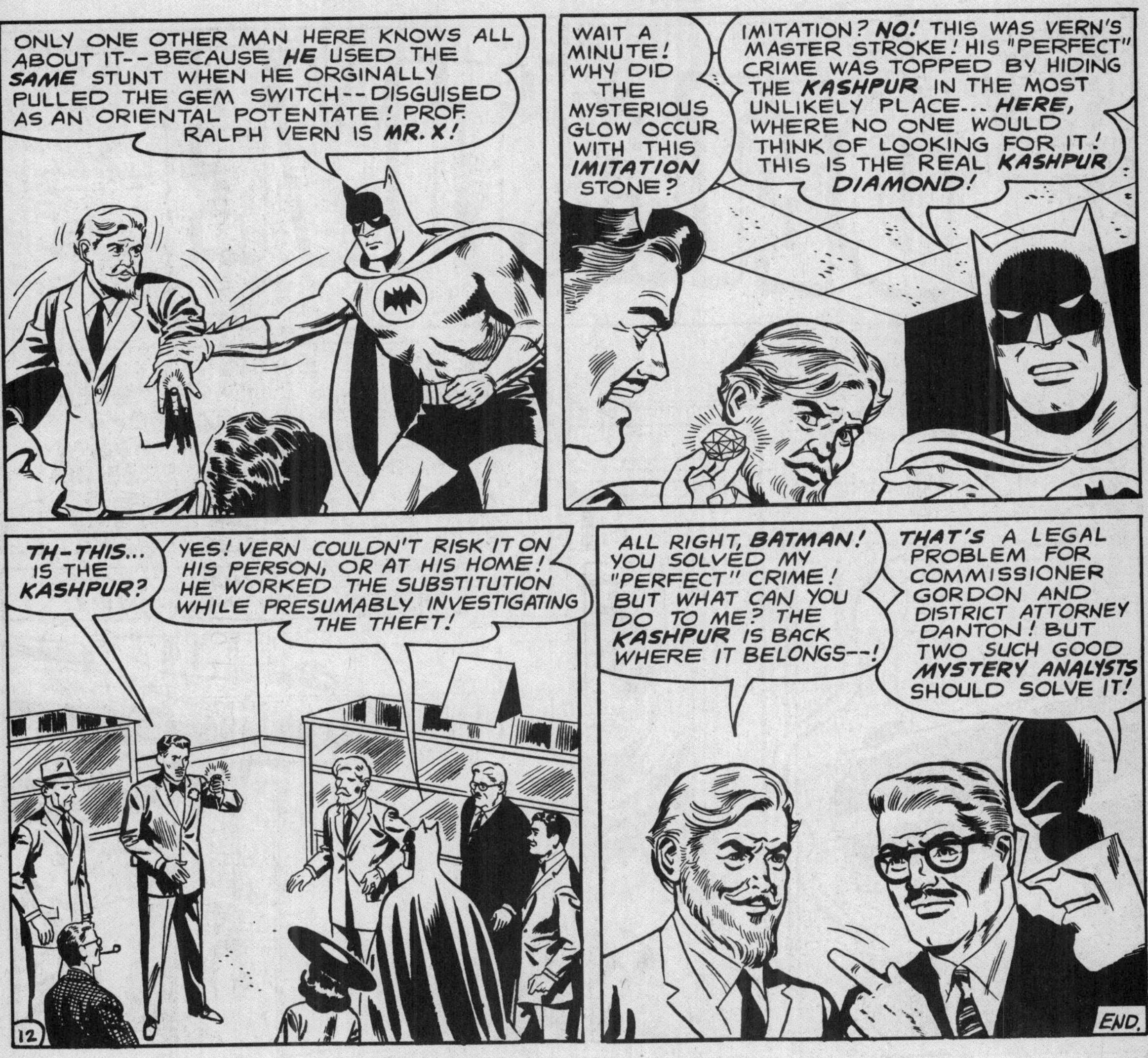
ONLY ONE OTHER MAN HERE KNOWS ALL ABOUT IT--BECAUSE HE USED THE SAME STUNT WHEN HE ORGINALLY PULLED THE GEM SWITCH--DISGUISED AS AN ORIENTAL POTENTATE! PROF. RALPH VERN IS MR. X!
WAIT A MINUTE! WHY DID THE MYSTERIOUS GLOW OCCUR WITH THIS IMITATION STONE?
IMITATION? NO! THIS WAS VERN'S MASTER STROKE! HIS "PERFECT" CRIME WAS TOPPED BY HIDING THE KASHPUR IN THE MOST UNLIKELY PLACE... HERE, WHERE NO ONE WOULD THINK OF LOOKING FOR IT! THIS IS THE REAL KASHPUR DIAMOND!
TH-THIS... IS THE KASHPUR?
YES! VERN COULDN'T RISK IT ON HIS PERSON, OR AT HIS HOME! HE WORKED THE SUBSTITUTION WHILE PRESUMABLY INVESTIGATING THE THEFT!
12
ALL RIGHT, BATMAN! YOU SOLVED MY "PERFECT" CRIME! BUT WHAT CAN YOU DO TO ME? THE KASHPUR IS BACK WHERE IT BELONGS--!
THAT'S A LEGAL PROBLEM FOR COMMISSIONER GORDON AND DISTRICT ATTORNEY DANTON! BUT TWO SUCH GOOD MYSTERY ANALYSTS SHOULD SOLVE IT!
END.

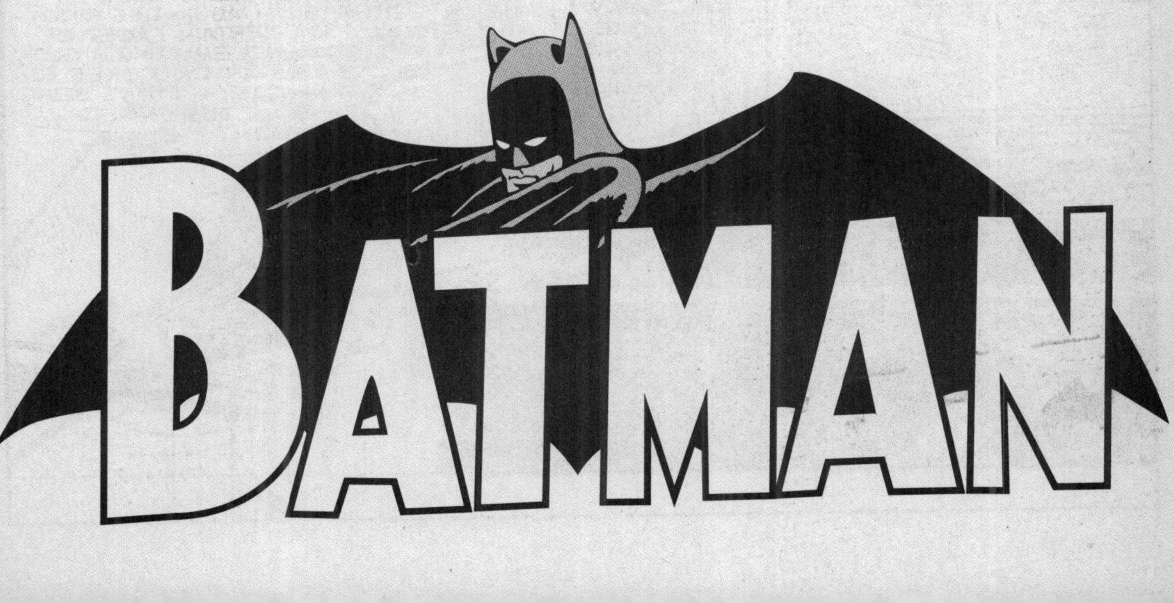
BATMAN

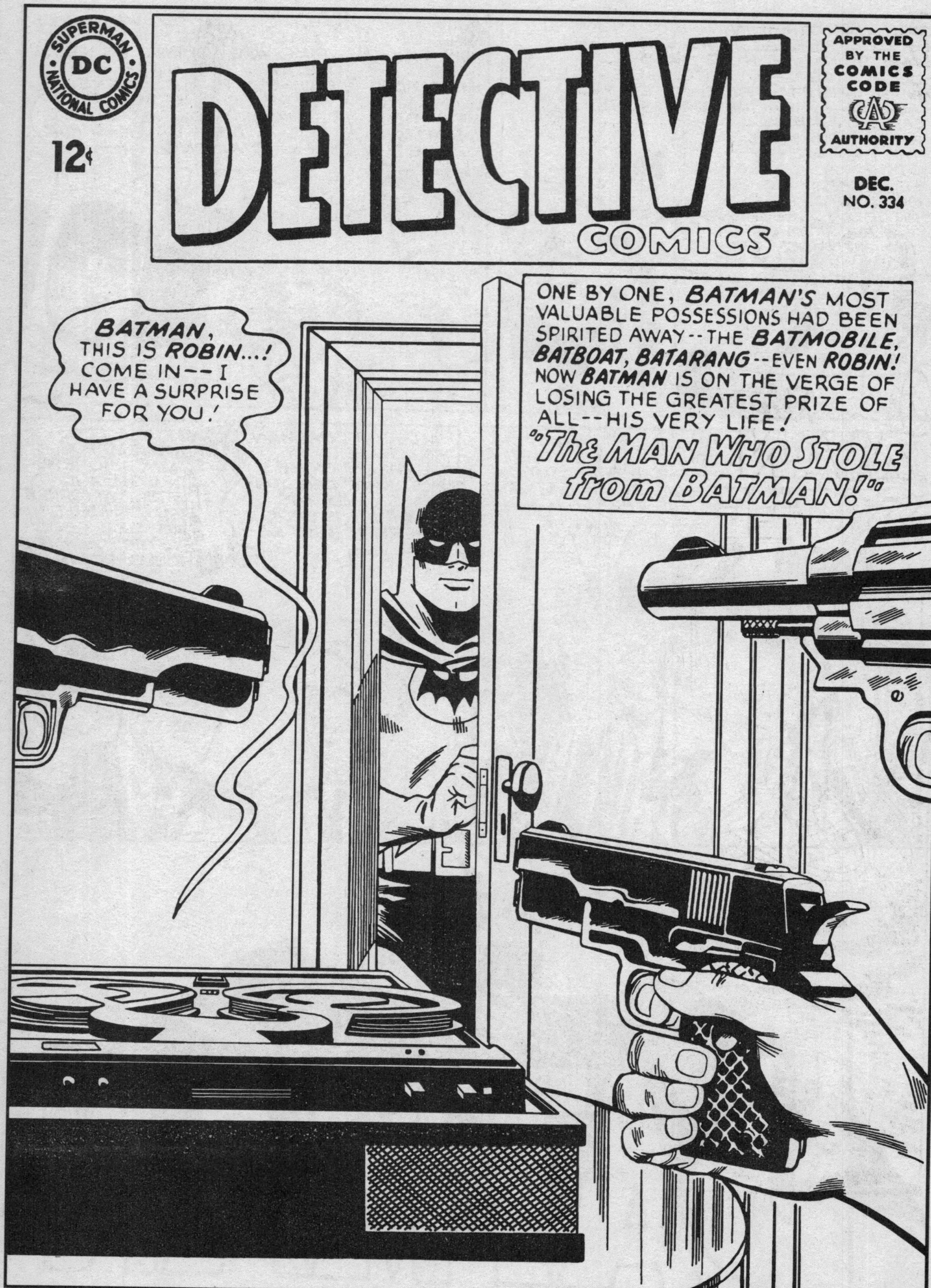
SUPERMAN DC NATIONAL COMICS
12¢
DETECTIVE COMICS
APPROVED BY THE COMICS CODE AUTHORITY
DEC. NO. 334
ONE BY ONE, BATMAN'S MOST VALUABLE POSSESSIONS HAD BEEN SPIRITED AWAY--THE BATMOBILE, BATBOAT, BATARANG--EVEN ROBIN! NOW BATMAN IS ON THE VERGE OF LOSING THE GREATEST PRIZE OF ALL--HIS VERY LIFE!
"The MAN WHO STOLE from BATMAN!"
BATMAN, THIS IS ROBIN...! COME IN-- I HAVE A SURPRISE FOR YOU!

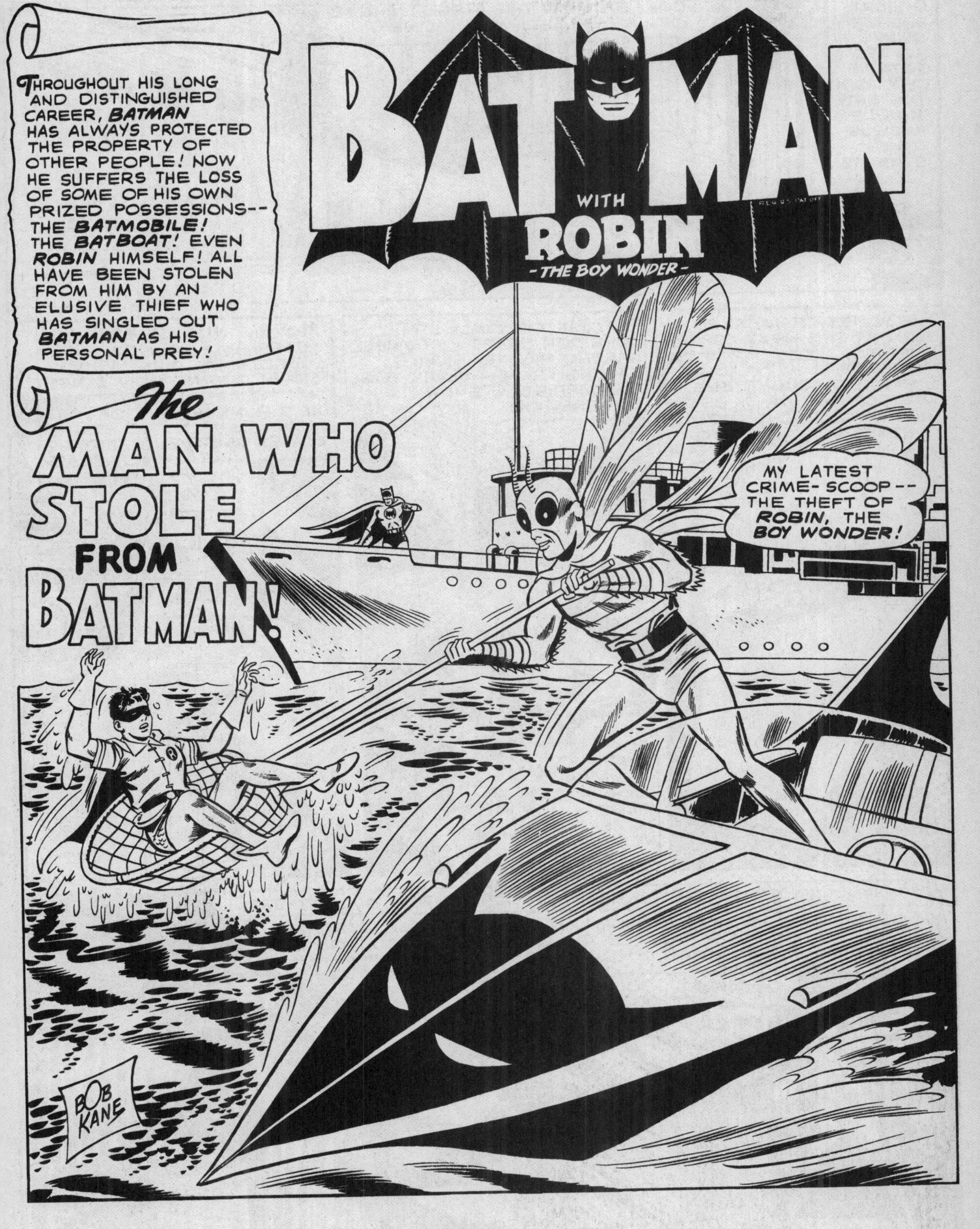
THROUGHOUT HIS LONG AND DISTINGUISHED CAREER, BATMAN HAS ALWAYS PROTECTED THE PROPERTY OF OTHER PEOPLE! NOW HE SUFFERS THE LOSS OF SOME OF HIS OWN PRIZED POSSESSIONS-- THE BATMOBILE! THE BATBOAT! EVEN ROBIN HIMSELF! ALL HAVE BEEN STOLEN FROM HIM BY AN ELUSIVE THIEF WHO HAS SINGLED OUT BATMAN AS HIS PERSONAL PREY!
BATMAN
WITH
ROBIN
-THE BOY WONDER-
REG. U.S. PAT. OFF.
The MAN WHO STOLE FROM BATMAN!
MY LATEST CRIME-SCOOP -- THE THEFT OF ROBIN, THE BOY WONDER!
BOB KANE

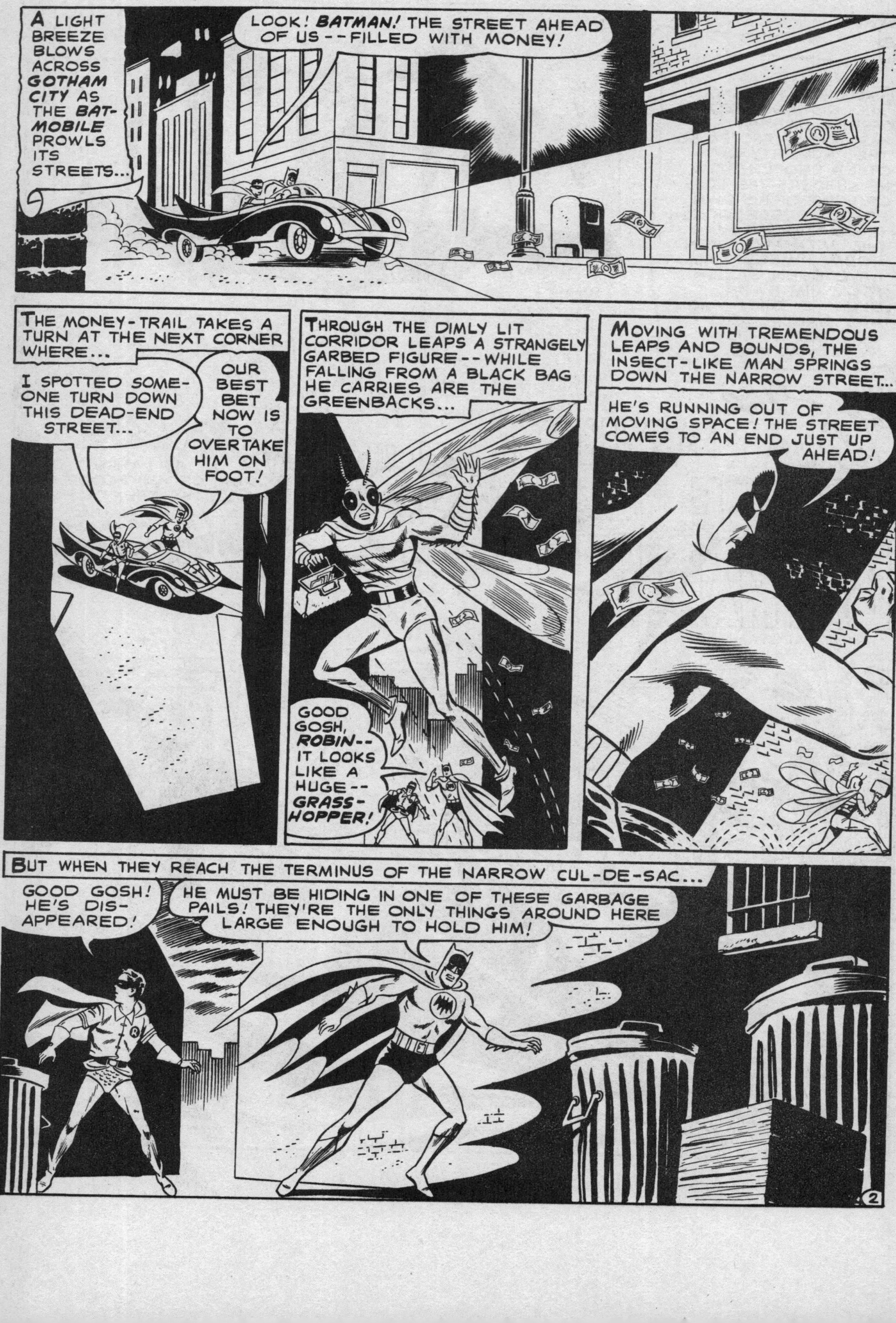
A LIGHT BREEZE BLOWS ACROSS GOTHAM CITY AS THE BAT-MOBILE PROWLS ITS STREETS...
LOOK! BATMAN! THE STREET AHEAD OF US--FILLED WITH MONEY!
THE MONEY-TRAIL TAKES A TURN AT THE NEXT CORNER WHERE...
I SPOTTED SOME-ONE TURN DOWN THIS DEAD-END STREET...
OUR BEST BET NOW IS TO OVERTAKE HIM ON FOOT!
THROUGH THE DIMLY LIT CORRIDOR LEAPS A STRANGELY GARBED FIGURE--WHILE FALLING FROM A BLACK BAG HE CARRIES ARE THE GREENBACKS...
GOOD GOSH, ROBIN--IT LOOKS LIKE A HUGE--GRASS-HOPPER!
MOVING WITH TREMENDOUS LEAPS AND BOUNDS, THE INSECT-LIKE MAN SPRINGS DOWN THE NARROW STREET...
HE'S RUNNING OUT OF MOVING SPACE! THE STREET COMES TO AN END JUST UP AHEAD!
BUT WHEN THEY REACH THE TERMINUS OF THE NARROW CUL-DE-SAC...
GOOD GOSH! HE'S DIS-APPEARED!
HE MUST BE HIDING IN ONE OF THESE GARBAGE PAILS! THEY'RE THE ONLY THINGS AROUND HERE LARGE ENOUGH TO HOLD HIM!
2

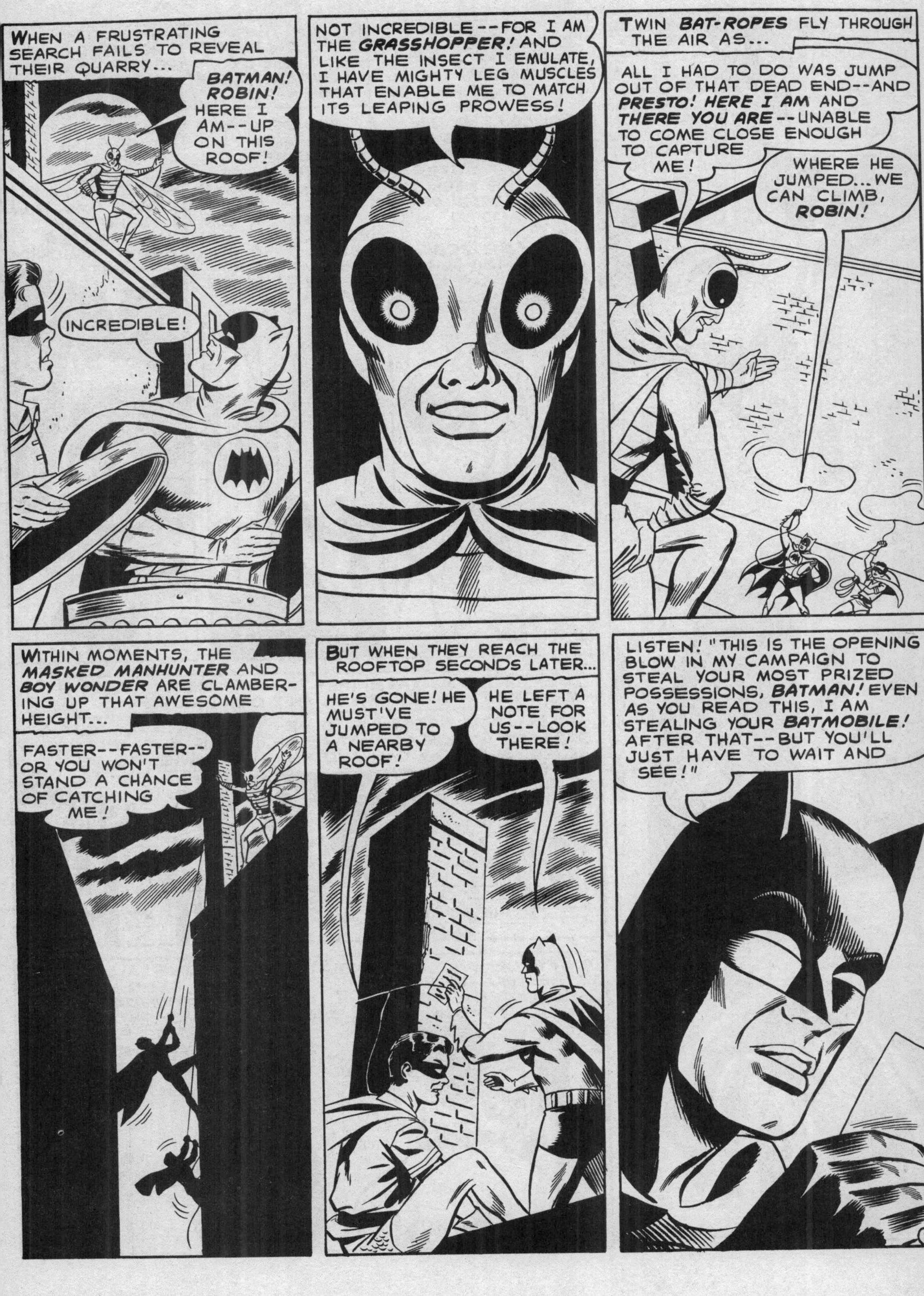
WHEN A FRUSTRATING SEARCH FAILS TO REVEAL THEIR QUARRY...
BATMAN! ROBIN! HERE I AM--UP ON THIS ROOF!
INCREDIBLE!
NOT INCREDIBLE--FOR I AM THE GRASSHOPPER! AND LIKE THE INSECT I EMULATE, I HAVE MIGHTY LEG MUSCLES THAT ENABLE ME TO MATCH ITS LEAPING PROWESS!
TWIN BAT-ROPES FLY THROUGH THE AIR AS...
ALL I HAD TO DO WAS JUMP OUT OF THAT DEAD END--AND PRESTO! HERE I AM AND THERE YOU ARE--UNABLE TO COME CLOSE ENOUGH TO CAPTURE ME!
WHERE HE JUMPED...WE CAN CLIMB, ROBIN!
WITHIN MOMENTS, THE MASKED MANHUNTER AND BOY WONDER ARE CLAMBERING UP THAT AWESOME HEIGHT...
FASTER--FASTER--OR YOU WON'T STAND A CHANCE OF CATCHING ME!
BUT WHEN THEY REACH THE ROOFTOP SECONDS LATER...
HE'S GONE! HE MUST'VE JUMPED TO A NEARBY ROOF!
HE LEFT A NOTE FOR US--LOOK THERE!
LISTEN! "THIS IS THE OPENING BLOW IN MY CAMPAIGN TO STEAL YOUR MOST PRIZED POSSESSIONS, BATMAN! EVEN AS YOU READ THIS, I AM STEALING YOUR BATMOBILE! AFTER THAT--BUT YOU'LL JUST HAVE TO WAIT AND SEE!"
3

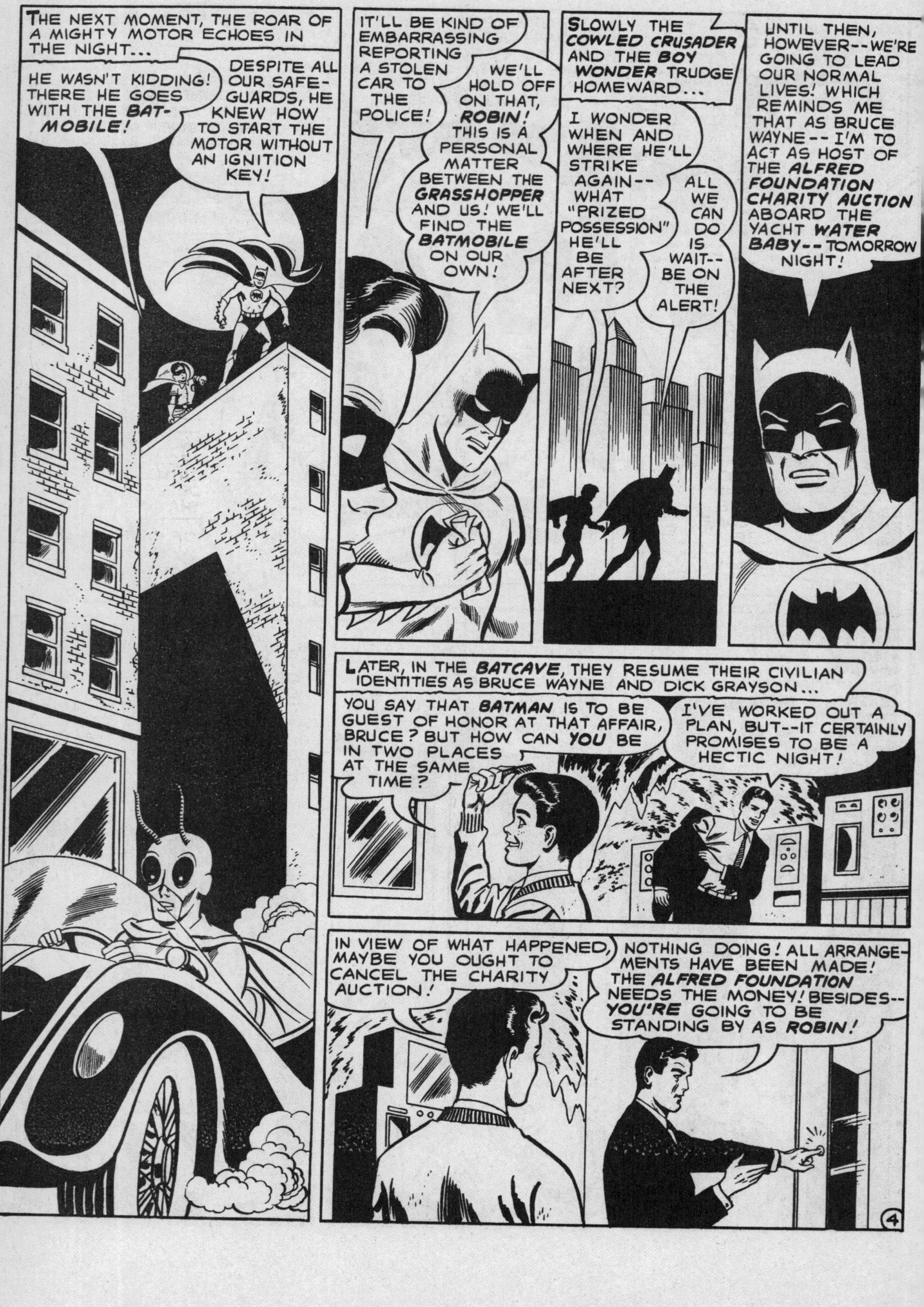
THE NEXT MOMENT, THE ROAR OF A MIGHTY MOTOR ECHOES IN THE NIGHT...
HE WASN'T KIDDING! THERE HE GOES WITH THE BAT-MOBILE!
DESPITE ALL OUR SAFE-GUARDS, HE KNEW HOW TO START THE MOTOR WITHOUT AN IGNITION KEY!
IT'LL BE KIND OF EMBARRASSING REPORTING A STOLEN CAR TO THE POLICE!
WE'LL HOLD OFF ON THAT, ROBIN! THIS IS A PERSONAL MATTER BETWEEN THE GRASSHOPPER AND US! WE'LL FIND THE BATMOBILE ON OUR OWN!
SLOWLY THE COWLED CRUSADER AND THE BOY WONDER TRUDGE HOMEWARD...
I WONDER WHEN AND WHERE HE'LL STRIKE AGAIN-- WHAT "PRIZED POSSESSION" HE'LL BE AFTER NEXT?
ALL WE CAN DO IS WAIT-- BE ON THE ALERT!
UNTIL THEN, HOWEVER--WE'RE GOING TO LEAD OUR NORMAL LIVES! WHICH REMINDS ME THAT AS BRUCE WAYNE-- I'M TO ACT AS HOST OF THE ALFRED FOUNDATION CHARITY AUCTION ABOARD THE YACHT WATER BABY-- TOMORROW NIGHT!
LATER, IN THE BATCAVE, THEY RESUME THEIR CIVILIAN IDENTITIES AS BRUCE WAYNE AND DICK GRAYSON...
YOU SAY THAT BATMAN IS TO BE GUEST OF HONOR AT THAT AFFAIR, BRUCE? BUT HOW CAN YOU BE IN TWO PLACES AT THE SAME TIME?
I'VE WORKED OUT A PLAN, BUT--IT CERTAINLY PROMISES TO BE A HECTIC NIGHT!
IN VIEW OF WHAT HAPPENED, MAYBE YOU OUGHT TO CANCEL THE CHARITY AUCTION!
NOTHING DOING! ALL ARRANGE-MENTS HAVE BEEN MADE! THE ALFRED FOUNDATION NEEDS THE MONEY! BESIDES-- YOU'RE GOING TO BE STANDING BY AS ROBIN!
4

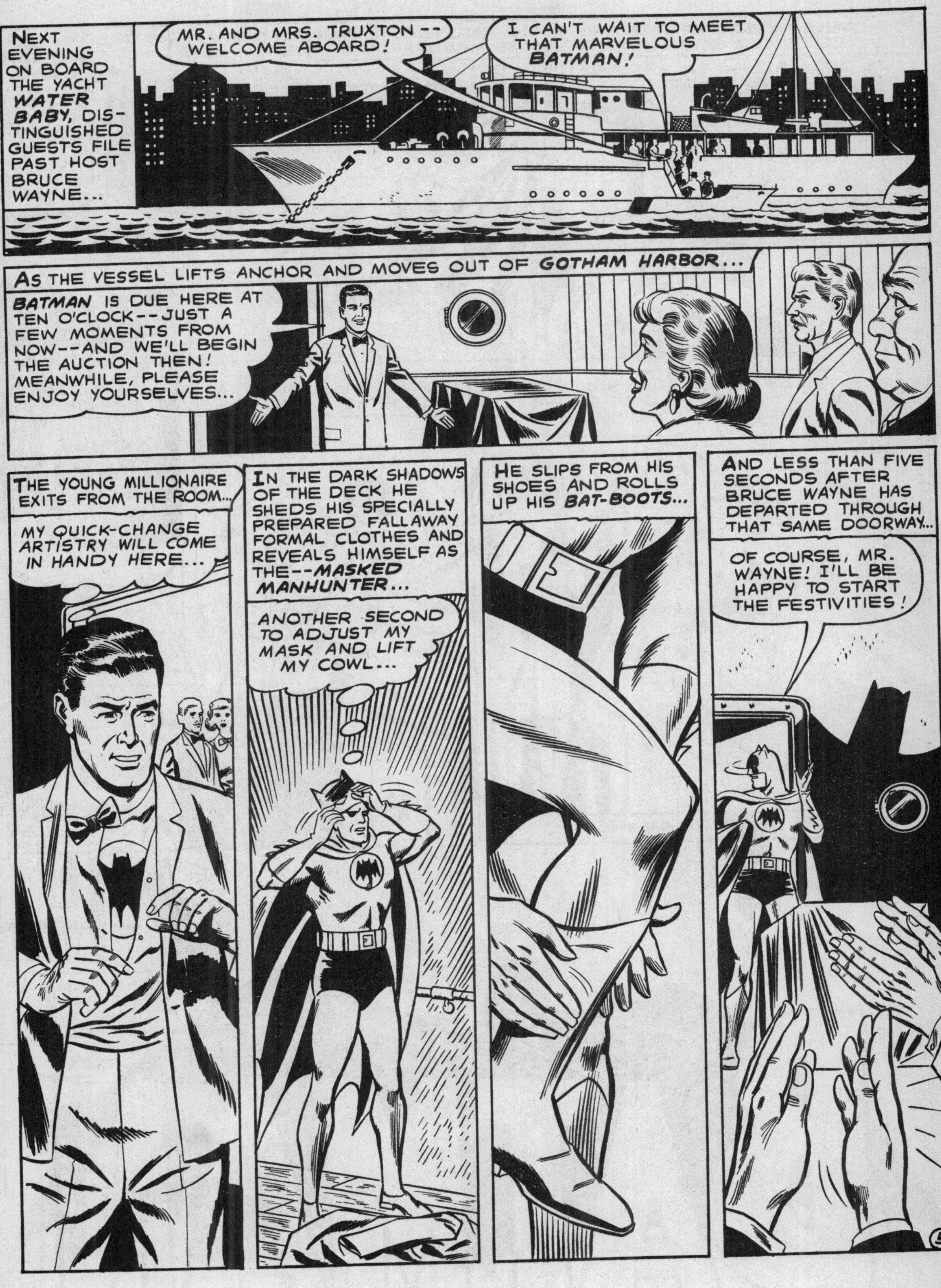
NEXT EVENING ON BOARD THE YACHT WATER BABY, DISTINGUISHED GUESTS FILE PAST HOST BRUCE WAYNE...
MR. AND MRS. TRUXTON -- WELCOME ABOARD!
I CAN'T WAIT TO MEET THAT MARVELOUS BATMAN!
AS THE VESSEL LIFTS ANCHOR AND MOVES OUT OF GOTHAM HARBOR...
BATMAN IS DUE HERE AT TEN O'CLOCK--JUST A FEW MOMENTS FROM NOW--AND WE'LL BEGIN THE AUCTION THEN! MEANWHILE, PLEASE ENJOY YOURSELVES...
THE YOUNG MILLIONAIRE EXITS FROM THE ROOM...
MY QUICK-CHANGE ARTISTRY WILL COME IN HANDY HERE...
IN THE DARK SHADOWS OF THE DECK HE SHEDS HIS SPECIALLY PREPARED FALLAWAY FORMAL CLOTHES AND REVEALS HIMSELF AS THE--MASKED MANHUNTER...
ANOTHER SECOND TO ADJUST MY MASK AND LIFT MY COWL...
HE SLIPS FROM HIS SHOES AND ROLLS UP HIS BAT-BOOTS...
AND LESS THAN FIVE SECONDS AFTER BRUCE WAYNE HAS DEPARTED THROUGH THAT SAME DOORWAY...
OF COURSE, MR. WAYNE! I'LL BE HAPPY TO START THE FESTIVITIES!
5

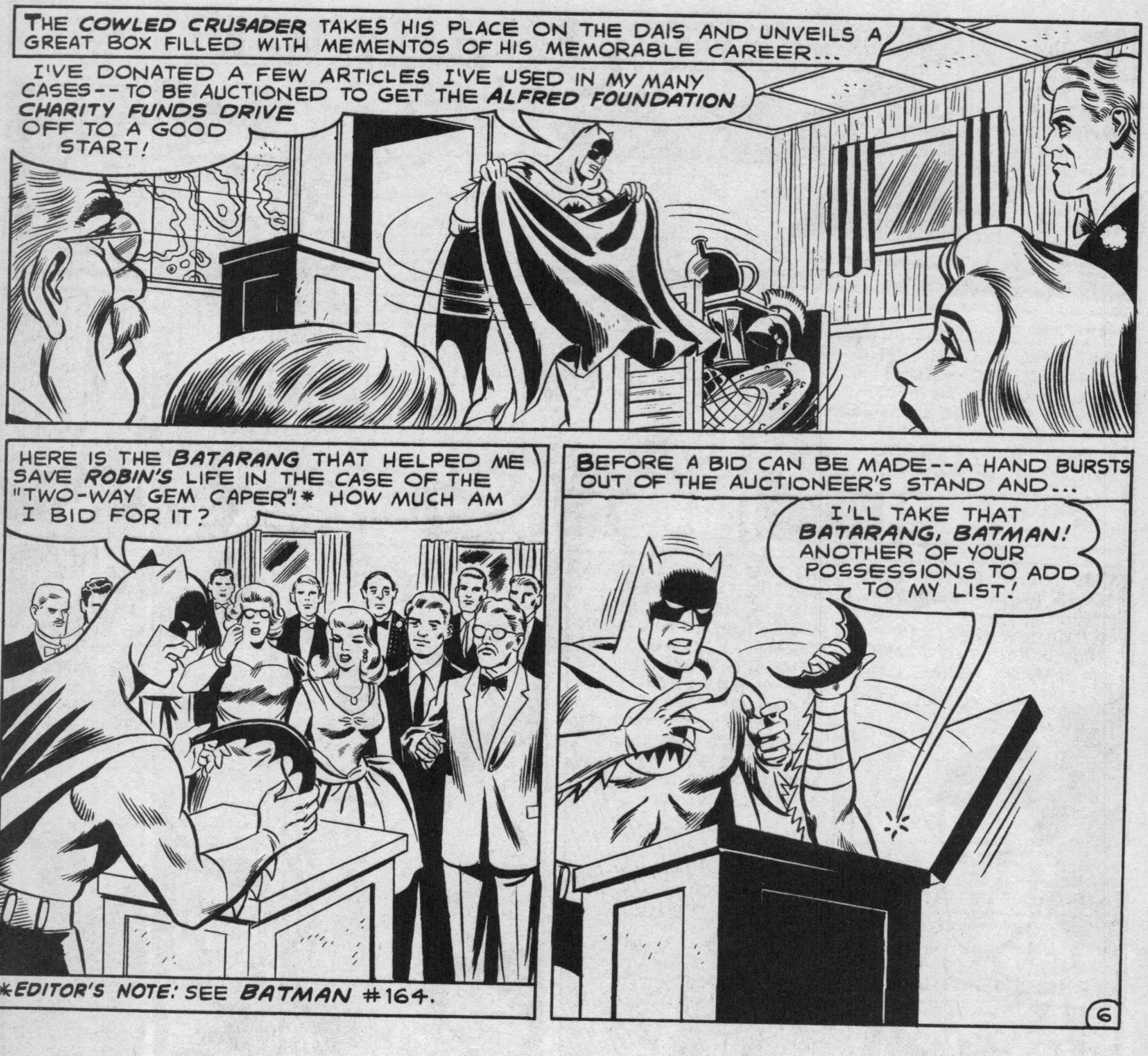
THE COWLED CRUSADER TAKES HIS PLACE ON THE DAIS AND UNVEILS A GREAT BOX FILLED WITH MEMENTOS OF HIS MEMORABLE CAREER...
I'VE DONATED A FEW ARTICLES I'VE USED IN MY MANY CASES--TO BE AUCTIONED TO GET THE ALFRED FOUNDATION CHARITY FUNDS DRIVE OFF TO A GOOD START!
HERE IS THE BATARANG THAT HELPED ME SAVE ROBIN'S LIFE IN THE CASE OF THE "TWO-WAY GEM CAPER"!* HOW MUCH AM I BID FOR IT?
*EDITOR'S NOTE: SEE BATMAN #164.
BEFORE A BID CAN BE MADE--A HAND BURSTS OUT OF THE AUCTIONEER'S STAND AND...
I'LL TAKE THAT BATARANG, BATMAN! ANOTHER OF YOUR POSSESSIONS TO ADD TO MY LIST!
6

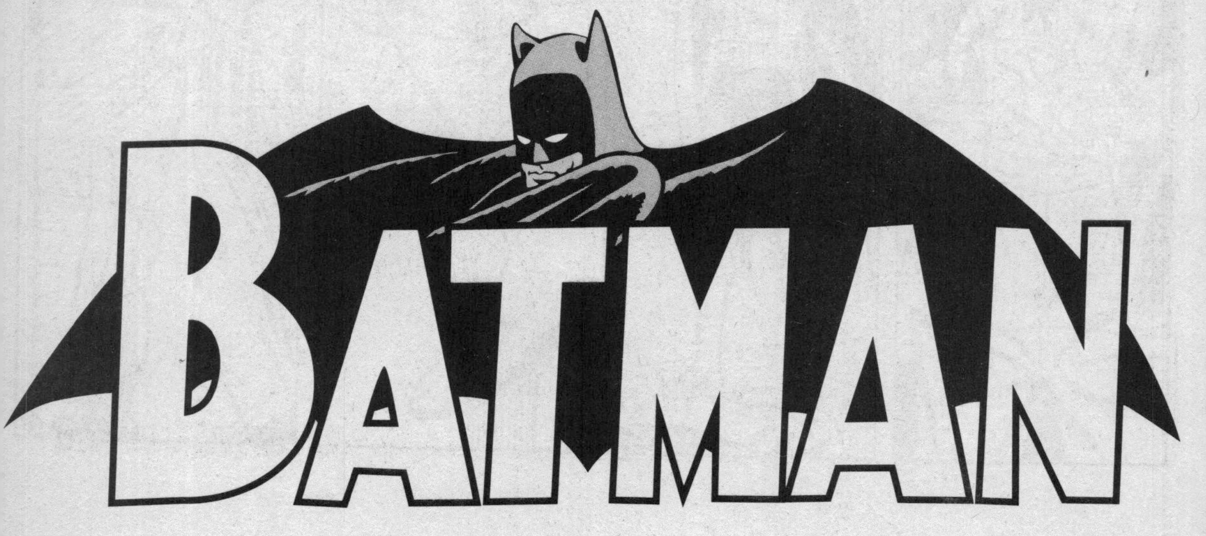
BATMAN

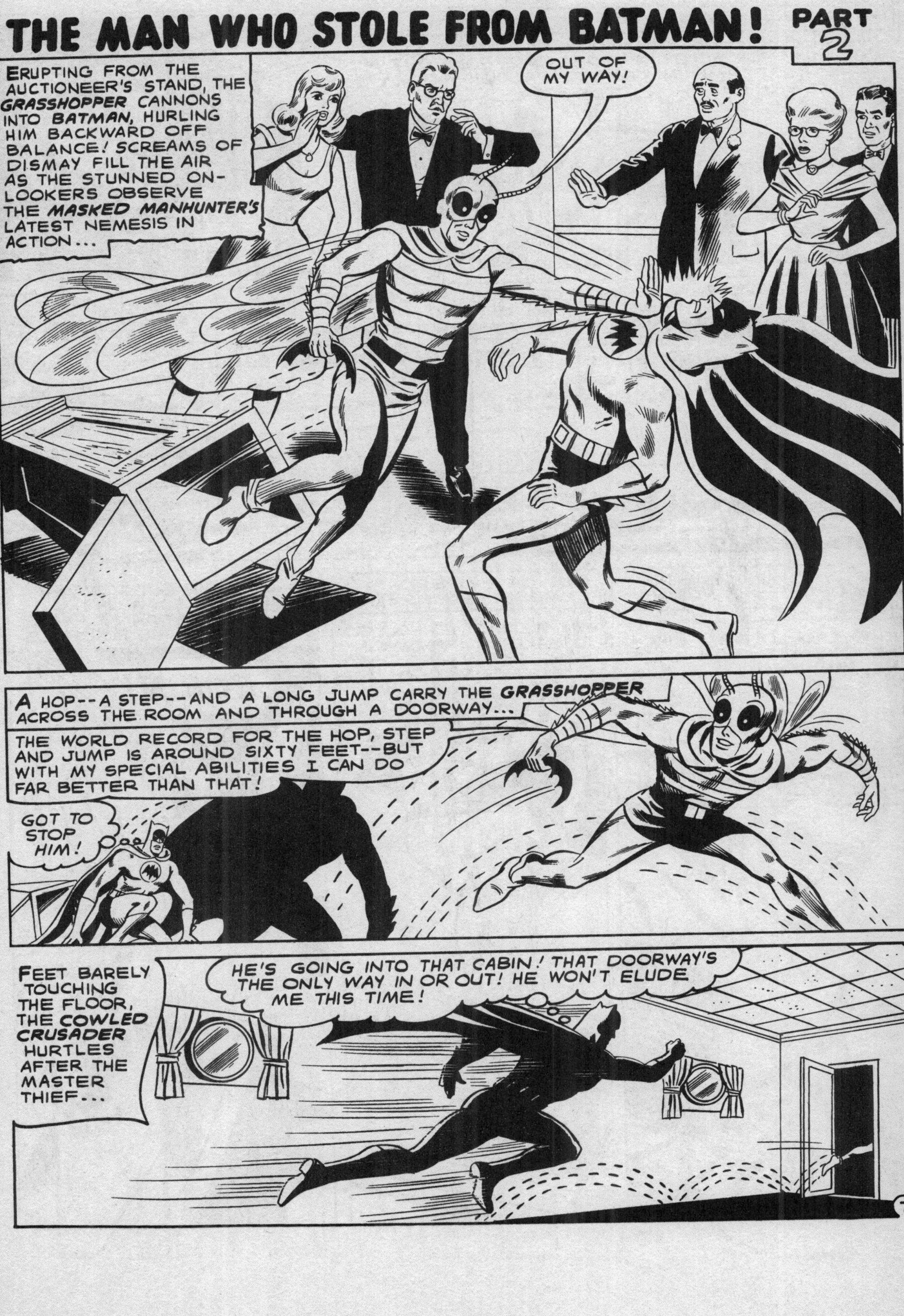
THE MAN WHO STOLE FROM BATMAN! PART 2
ERUPTING FROM THE AUCTIONEER'S STAND, THE GRASSHOPPER CANNONS INTO BATMAN, HURLING HIM BACKWARD OFF BALANCE! SCREAMS OF DISMAY FILL THE AIR AS THE STUNNED ONLOOKERS OBSERVE THE MASKED MANHUNTER'S LATEST NEMESIS IN ACTION...
OUT OF MY WAY!
A HOP--A STEP--AND A LONG JUMP CARRY THE GRASSHOPPER ACROSS THE ROOM AND THROUGH A DOORWAY...
THE WORLD RECORD FOR THE HOP, STEP AND JUMP IS AROUND SIXTY FEET--BUT WITH MY SPECIAL ABILITIES I CAN DO FAR BETTER THAN THAT!
GOT TO STOP HIM!
FEET BARELY TOUCHING THE FLOOR, THE COWLED CRUSADER HURTLES AFTER THE MASTER THIEF...
HE'S GOING INTO THAT CABIN! THAT DOORWAY'S THE ONLY WAY IN OR OUT! HE WON'T ELUDE ME THIS TIME!
7

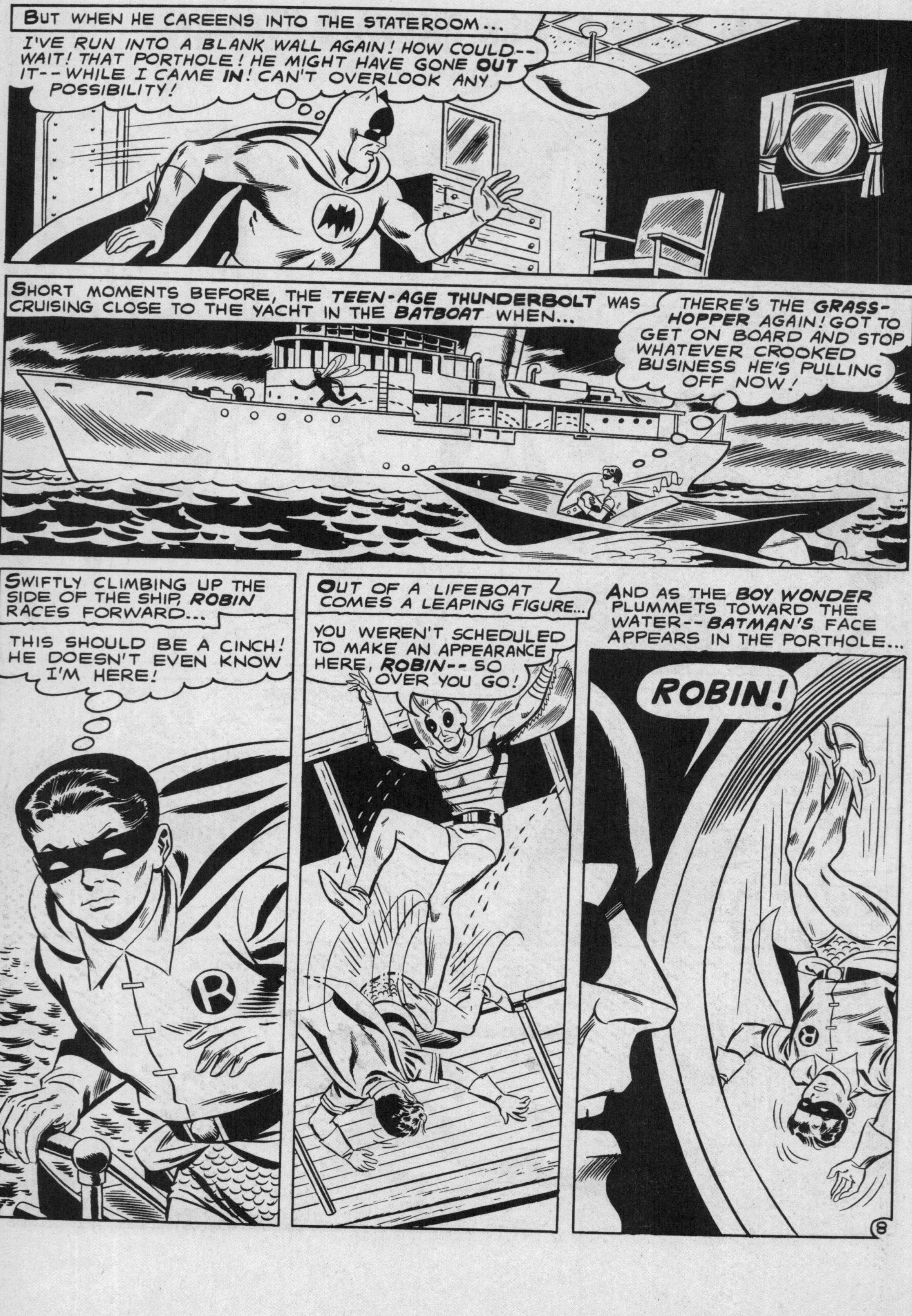
BUT WHEN HE CAREENS INTO THE STATEROOM...
I'VE RUN INTO A BLANK WALL AGAIN! HOW COULD-- WAIT! THAT PORTHOLE! HE MIGHT HAVE GONE OUT IT--WHILE I CAME IN! CAN'T OVERLOOK ANY POSSIBILITY!
SHORT MOMENTS BEFORE, THE TEEN-AGE THUNDERBOLT WAS CRUISING CLOSE TO THE YACHT IN THE BATBOAT WHEN...
THERE'S THE GRASS-HOPPER AGAIN! GOT TO GET ON BOARD AND STOP WHATEVER CROOKED BUSINESS HE'S PULLING OFF NOW!
SWIFTLY CLIMBING UP THE SIDE OF THE SHIP, ROBIN RACES FORWARD...
THIS SHOULD BE A CINCH! HE DOESN'T EVEN KNOW I'M HERE!
OUT OF A LIFEBOAT COMES A LEAPING FIGURE...
YOU WEREN'T SCHEDULED TO MAKE AN APPEARANCE HERE, ROBIN--SO OVER YOU GO!
AND AS THE BOY WONDER PLUMMETS TOWARD THE WATER--BATMAN'S FACE APPEARS IN THE PORTHOLE...
ROBIN!
8

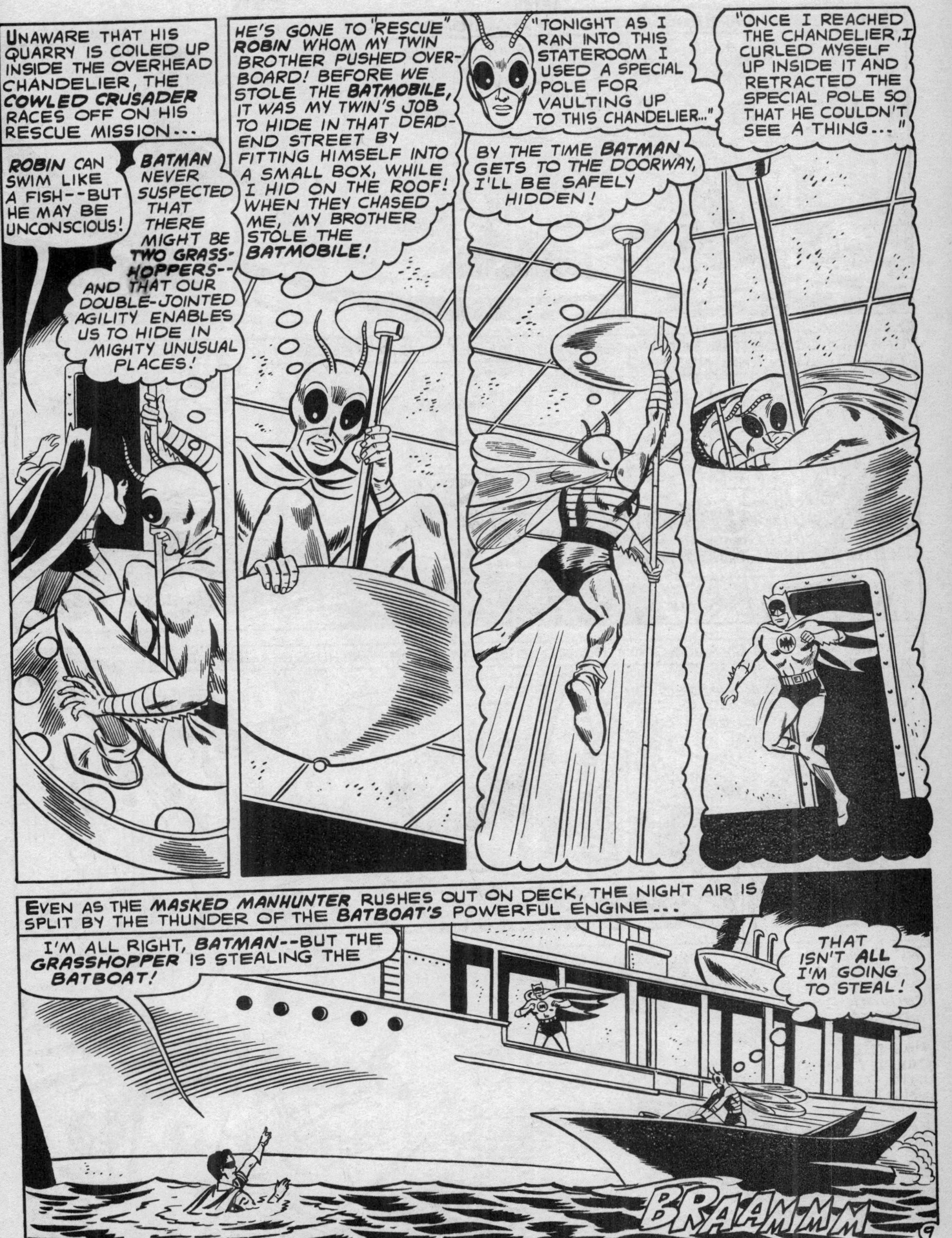
UNAWARE THAT HIS QUARRY IS COILED UP INSIDE THE OVERHEAD CHANDELIER, THE COWLED CRUSADER RACES OFF ON HIS RESCUE MISSION...
ROBIN CAN SWIM LIKE A FISH--BUT HE MAY BE UNCONSCIOUS!
BATMAN NEVER SUSPECTED THAT THERE MIGHT BE TWO GRASS-HOPPERS--AND THAT OUR DOUBLE-JOINTED AGILITY ENABLES US TO HIDE IN MIGHTY UNUSUAL PLACES!
HE'S GONE TO "RESCUE" ROBIN WHOM MY TWIN BROTHER PUSHED OVER-BOARD! BEFORE WE STOLE THE BATMOBILE, IT WAS MY TWIN'S JOB TO HIDE IN THAT DEAD-END STREET BY FITTING HIMSELF INTO A SMALL BOX, WHILE I HID ON THE ROOF! WHEN THEY CHASED ME, MY BROTHER STOLE THE BATMOBILE!
"TONIGHT AS I RAN INTO THIS STATEROOM I USED A SPECIAL POLE FOR VAULTING UP TO THIS CHANDELIER..."
BY THE TIME BATMAN GETS TO THE DOORWAY, I'LL BE SAFELY HIDDEN!
"ONCE I REACHED THE CHANDELIER, I CURLED MYSELF UP INSIDE IT AND RETRACTED THE SPECIAL POLE SO THAT HE COULDN'T SEE A THING..."
EVEN AS THE MASKED MANHUNTER RUSHES OUT ON DECK, THE NIGHT AIR IS SPLIT BY THE THUNDER OF THE BATBOAT'S POWERFUL ENGINE...
I'M ALL RIGHT, BATMAN--BUT THE GRASSHOPPER IS STEALING THE BATBOAT!
THAT ISN'T ALL I'M GOING TO STEAL!
BRAAMMM
9

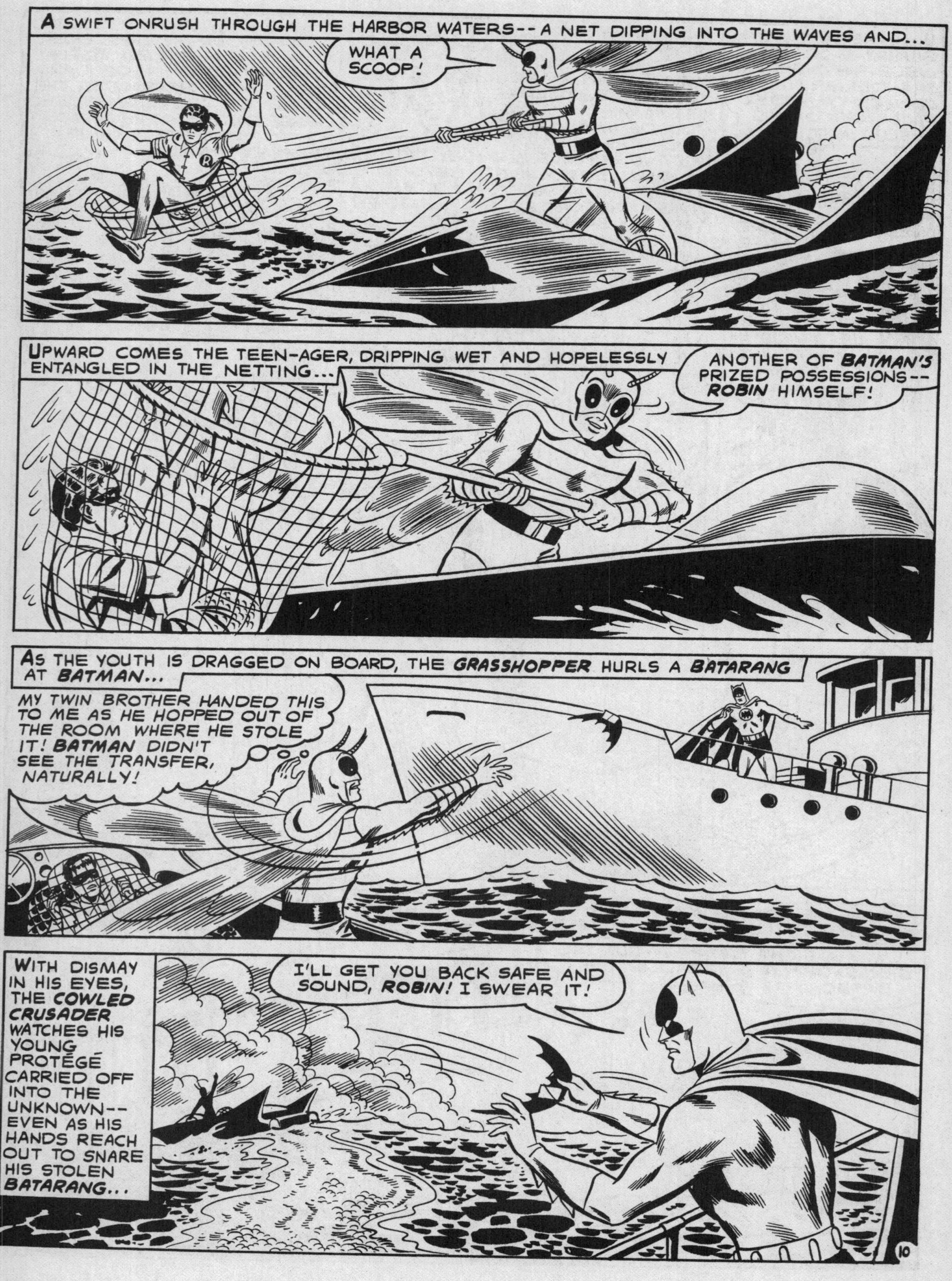
A SWIFT ONRUSH THROUGH THE HARBOR WATERS--A NET DIPPING INTO THE WAVES AND...
WHAT A SCOOP!
UPWARD COMES THE TEEN-AGER, DRIPPING WET AND HOPELESSLY ENTANGLED IN THE NETTING...
ANOTHER OF BATMAN'S PRIZED POSSESSIONS--ROBIN HIMSELF!
AS THE YOUTH IS DRAGGED ON BOARD, THE GRASSHOPPER HURLS A BATARANG AT BATMAN...
MY TWIN BROTHER HANDED THIS TO ME AS HE HOPPED OUT OF THE ROOM WHERE HE STOLE IT! BATMAN DIDN'T SEE THE TRANSFER, NATURALLY!
WITH DISMAY IN HIS EYES, THE COWLED CRUSADER WATCHES HIS YOUNG PROTÉGÉ CARRIED OFF INTO THE UNKNOWN--EVEN AS HIS HANDS REACH OUT TO SNARE HIS STOLEN BATARANG...
I'LL GET YOU BACK SAFE AND SOUND, ROBIN! I SWEAR IT!
10

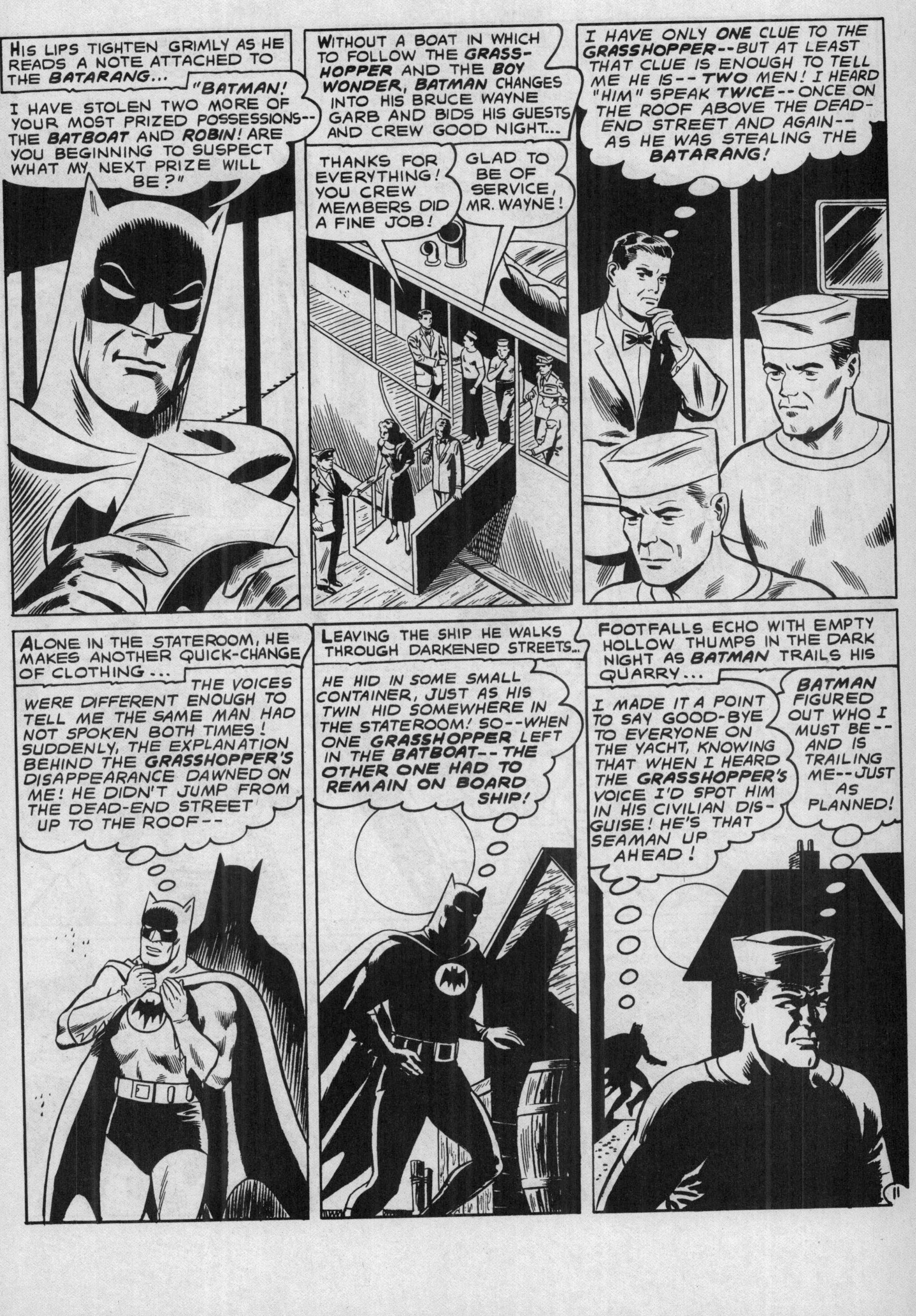
HIS LIPS TIGHTEN GRIMLY AS HE READS A NOTE ATTACHED TO THE BATARANG...
"BATMAN! I HAVE STOLEN TWO MORE OF YOUR MOST PRIZED POSSESSIONS-- THE BATBOAT AND ROBIN! ARE YOU BEGINNING TO SUSPECT WHAT MY NEXT PRIZE WILL BE?"
WITHOUT A BOAT IN WHICH TO FOLLOW THE GRASSHOPPER AND THE BOY WONDER, BATMAN CHANGES INTO HIS BRUCE WAYNE GARB AND BIDS HIS GUESTS AND CREW GOOD NIGHT...
THANKS FOR EVERYTHING! YOU CREW MEMBERS DID A FINE JOB!
GLAD TO BE OF SERVICE, MR. WAYNE!
I HAVE ONLY ONE CLUE TO THE GRASSHOPPER--BUT AT LEAST THAT CLUE IS ENOUGH TO TELL ME HE IS-- TWO MEN! I HEARD "HIM" SPEAK TWICE-- ONCE ON THE ROOF ABOVE THE DEAD-END STREET AND AGAIN-- AS HE WAS STEALING THE BATARANG!
ALONE IN THE STATEROOM, HE MAKES ANOTHER QUICK-CHANGE OF CLOTHING...
THE VOICES WERE DIFFERENT ENOUGH TO TELL ME THE SAME MAN HAD NOT SPOKEN BOTH TIMES! SUDDENLY, THE EXPLANATION BEHIND THE GRASSHOPPER'S DISAPPEARANCE DAWNED ON ME! HE DIDN'T JUMP FROM THE DEAD-END STREET UP TO THE ROOF--
LEAVING THE SHIP HE WALKS THROUGH DARKENED STREETS...
HE HID IN SOME SMALL CONTAINER, JUST AS HIS TWIN HID SOMEWHERE IN THE STATEROOM! SO--WHEN ONE GRASSHOPPER LEFT IN THE BATBOAT-- THE OTHER ONE HAD TO REMAIN ON BOARD SHIP!
FOOTFALLS ECHO WITH EMPTY HOLLOW THUMPS IN THE DARK NIGHT AS BATMAN TRAILS HIS QUARRY...
I MADE IT A POINT TO SAY GOOD-BYE TO EVERYONE ON THE YACHT, KNOWING THAT WHEN I HEARD THE GRASSHOPPER'S VOICE I'D SPOT HIM IN HIS CIVILIAN DISGUISE! HE'S THAT SEAMAN UP AHEAD!
BATMAN FIGURED OUT WHO I MUST BE-- AND IS TRAILING ME--JUST AS PLANNED!
11

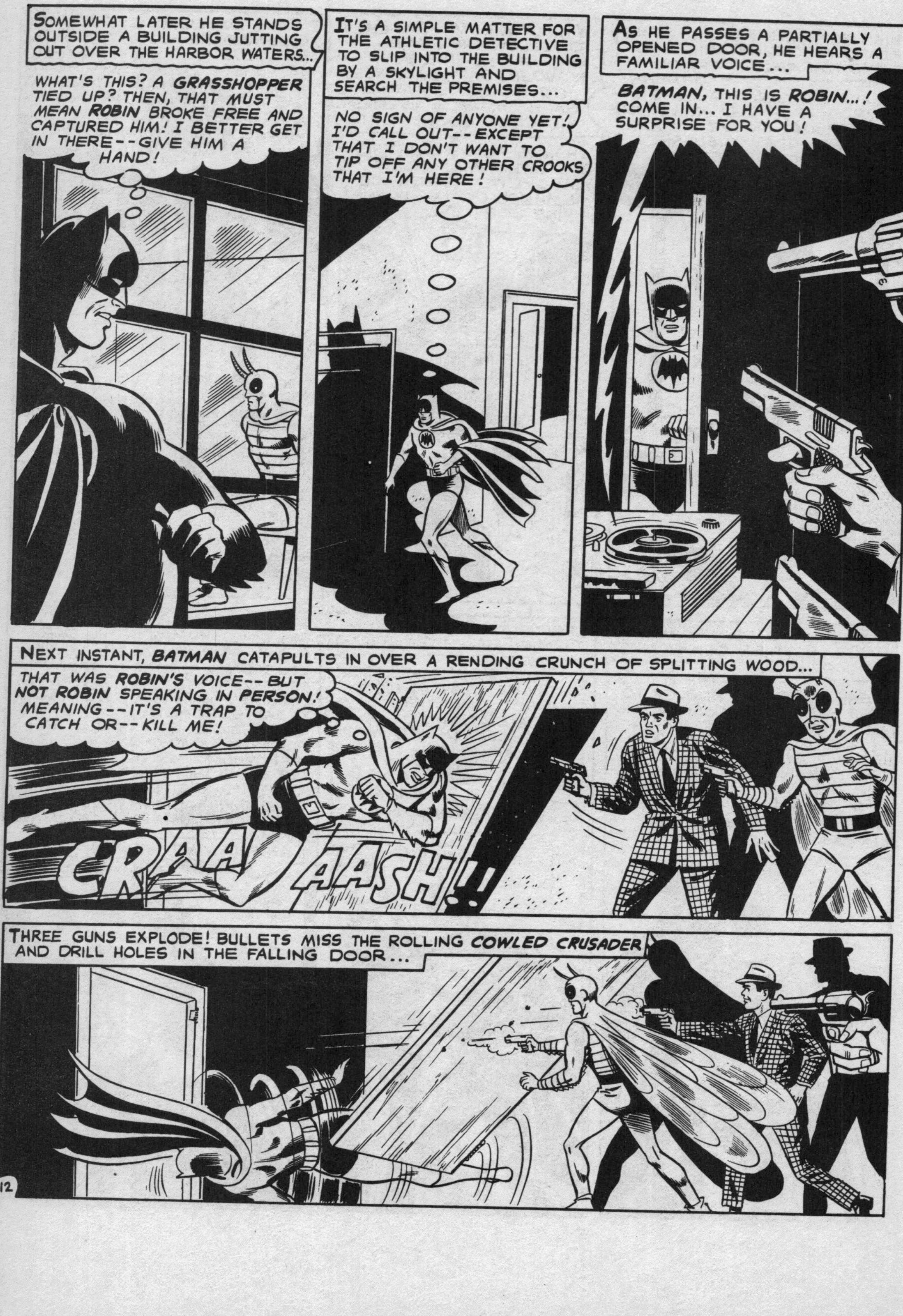
SOMEWHAT LATER HE STANDS OUTSIDE A BUILDING JUTTING OUT OVER THE HARBOR WATERS...
WHAT'S THIS? A GRASSHOPPER TIED UP? THEN, THAT MUST MEAN ROBIN BROKE FREE AND CAPTURED HIM! I BETTER GET IN THERE--GIVE HIM A HAND!
IT'S A SIMPLE MATTER FOR THE ATHLETIC DETECTIVE TO SLIP INTO THE BUILDING BY A SKYLIGHT AND SEARCH THE PREMISES...
NO SIGN OF ANYONE YET! I'D CALL OUT--EXCEPT THAT I DON'T WANT TO TIP OFF ANY OTHER CROOKS THAT I'M HERE!
AS HE PASSES A PARTIALLY OPENED DOOR, HE HEARS A FAMILIAR VOICE...
BATMAN, THIS IS ROBIN...! COME IN... I HAVE A SURPRISE FOR YOU!
NEXT INSTANT, BATMAN CATAPULTS IN OVER A RENDING CRUNCH OF SPLITTING WOOD...
THAT WAS ROBIN'S VOICE--BUT NOT ROBIN SPEAKING IN PERSON! MEANING--IT'S A TRAP TO CATCH OR--KILL ME!
CRAAAASH!!
THREE GUNS EXPLODE! BULLETS MISS THE ROLLING COWLED CRUSADER AND DRILL HOLES IN THE FALLING DOOR...
12

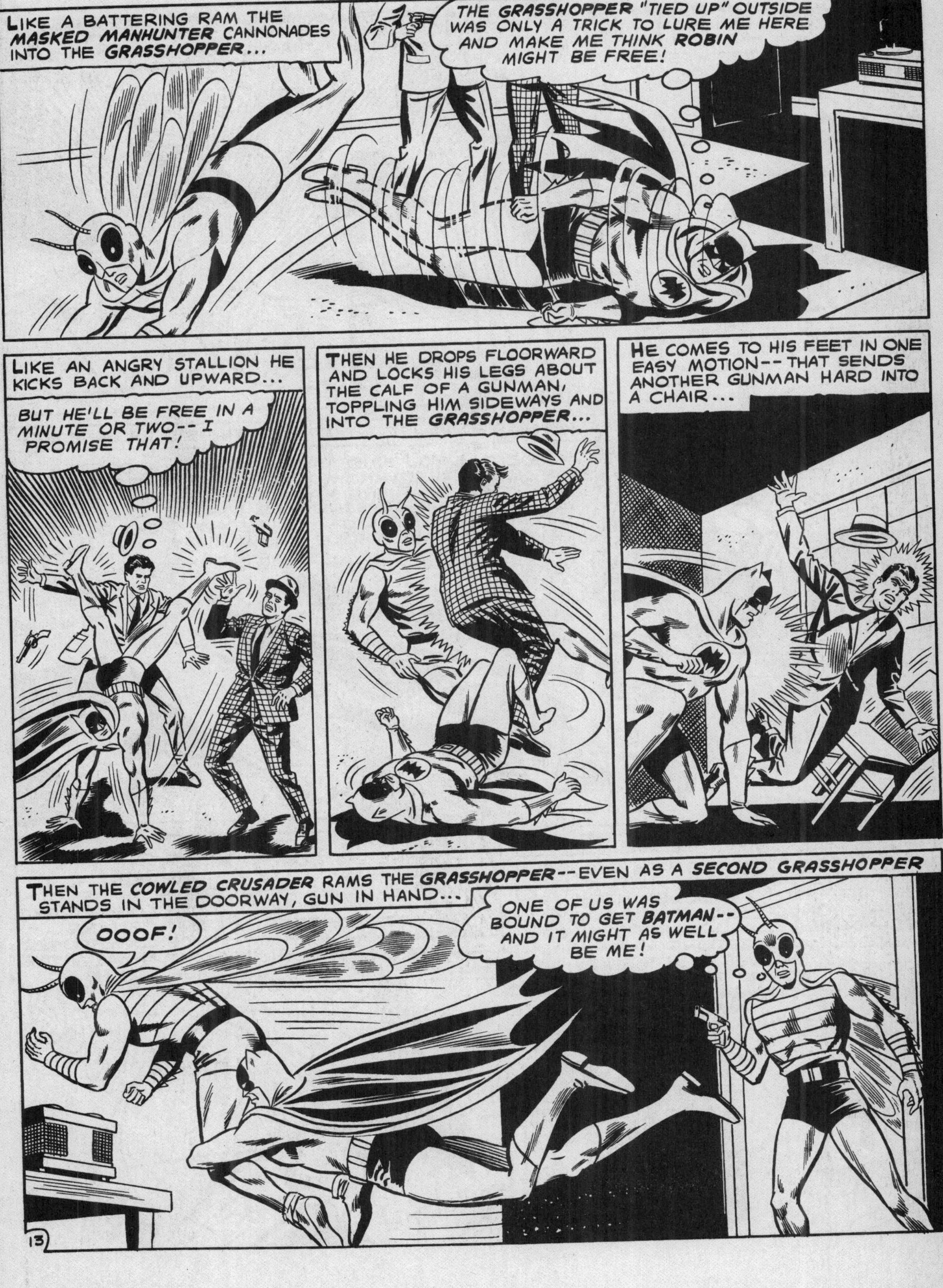
LIKE A BATTERING RAM THE MASKED MANHUNTER CANNONADES INTO THE GRASSHOPPER...
THE GRASSHOPPER "TIED UP" OUTSIDE WAS ONLY A TRICK TO LURE ME HERE AND MAKE ME THINK ROBIN MIGHT BE FREE!
LIKE AN ANGRY STALLION HE KICKS BACK AND UPWARD...
BUT HE'LL BE FREE IN A MINUTE OR TWO-- I PROMISE THAT!
THEN HE DROPS FLOORWARD AND LOCKS HIS LEGS ABOUT THE CALF OF A GUNMAN, TOPPLING HIM SIDEWAYS AND INTO THE GRASSHOPPER...
HE COMES TO HIS FEET IN ONE EASY MOTION-- THAT SENDS ANOTHER GUNMAN HARD INTO A CHAIR...
THEN THE COWLED CRUSADER RAMS THE GRASSHOPPER--EVEN AS A SECOND GRASSHOPPER STANDS IN THE DOORWAY, GUN IN HAND...
OOOF!
ONE OF US WAS BOUND TO GET BATMAN-- AND IT MIGHT AS WELL BE ME!
13

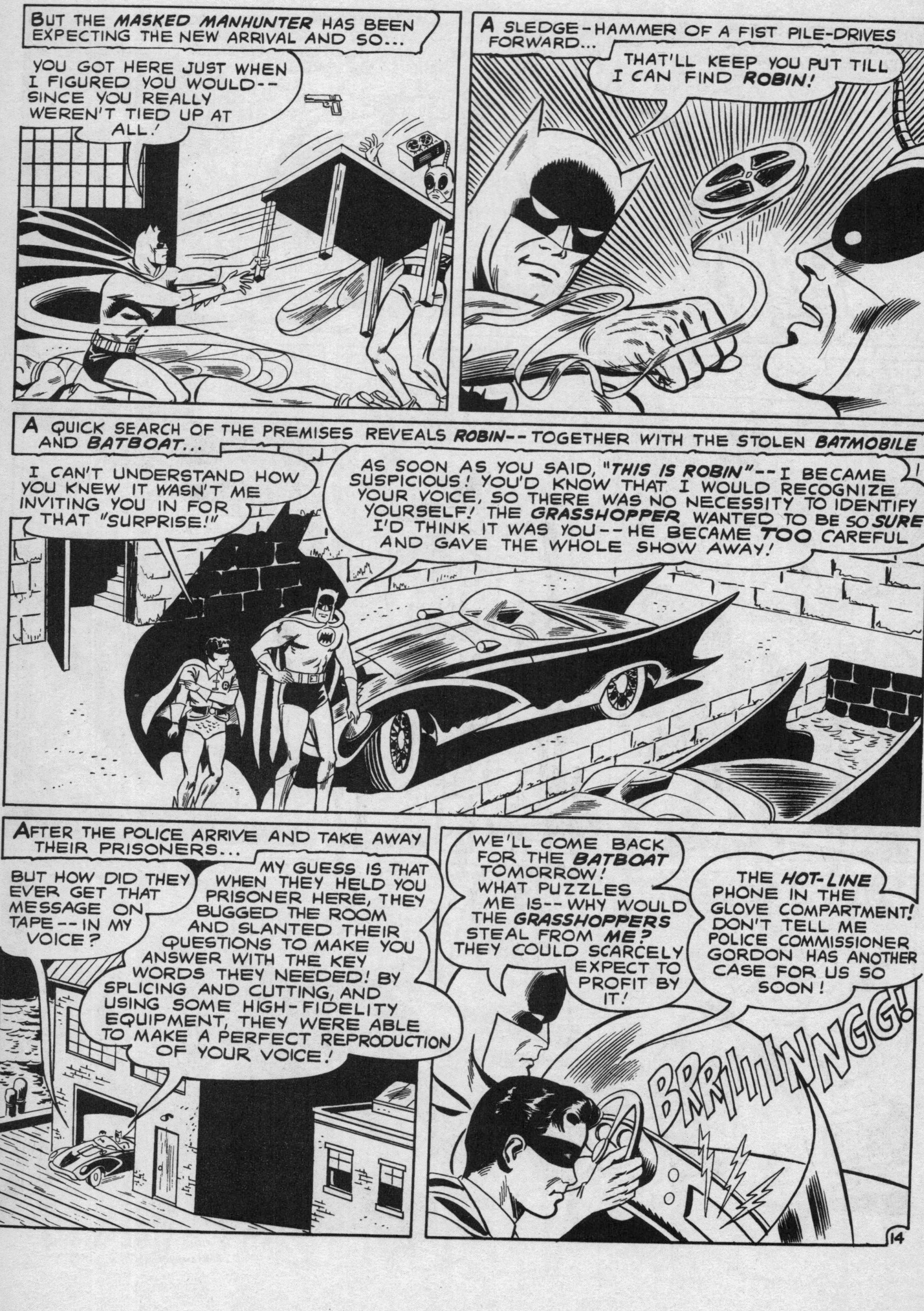
BUT THE MASKED MANHUNTER HAS BEEN EXPECTING THE NEW ARRIVAL AND SO...
YOU GOT HERE JUST WHEN I FIGURED YOU WOULD-- SINCE YOU REALLY WEREN'T TIED UP AT ALL!
A SLEDGE-HAMMER OF A FIST PILE-DRIVES FORWARD...
THAT'LL KEEP YOU PUT TILL I CAN FIND ROBIN!
A QUICK SEARCH OF THE PREMISES REVEALS ROBIN--TOGETHER WITH THE STOLEN BATMOBILE AND BATBOAT...
I CAN'T UNDERSTAND HOW YOU KNEW IT WASN'T ME INVITING YOU IN FOR THAT "SURPRISE!"
AS SOON AS YOU SAID, "THIS IS ROBIN"--I BECAME SUSPICIOUS! YOU'D KNOW THAT I WOULD RECOGNIZE YOUR VOICE, SO THERE WAS NO NECESSITY TO IDENTIFY YOURSELF! THE GRASSHOPPER WANTED TO BE SO SURE I'D THINK IT WAS YOU--HE BECAME TOO CAREFUL AND GAVE THE WHOLE SHOW AWAY!
AFTER THE POLICE ARRIVE AND TAKE AWAY THEIR PRISONERS...
BUT HOW DID THEY EVER GET THAT MESSAGE ON TAPE--IN MY VOICE?
MY GUESS IS THAT WHEN THEY HELD YOU PRISONER HERE, THEY BUGGED THE ROOM AND SLANTED THEIR QUESTIONS TO MAKE YOU ANSWER WITH THE KEY WORDS THEY NEEDED! BY SPLICING AND CUTTING, AND USING SOME HIGH-FIDELITY EQUIPMENT, THEY WERE ABLE TO MAKE A PERFECT REPRODUCTION OF YOUR VOICE!
WE'LL COME BACK FOR THE BATBOAT TOMORROW! WHAT PUZZLES ME IS--WHY WOULD THE GRASSHOPPERS STEAL FROM ME? THEY COULD SCARCELY EXPECT TO PROFIT BY IT!
THE HOT-LINE PHONE IN THE GLOVE COMPARTMENT! DON'T TELL ME POLICE COMMISSIONER GORDON HAS ANOTHER CASE FOR US SO SOON!
BRRIIIINNGG!
14

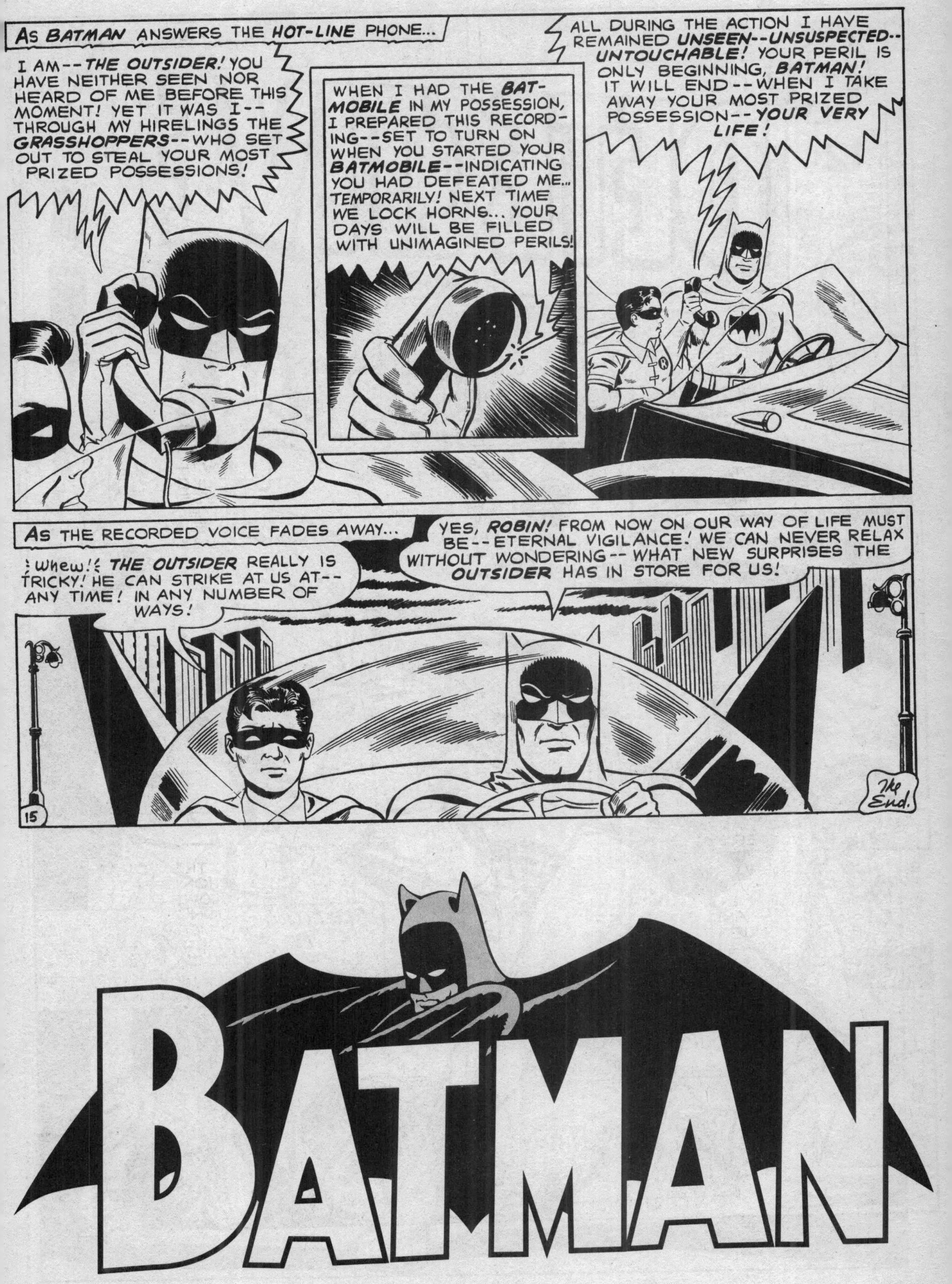
AS BATMAN ANSWERS THE HOT-LINE PHONE...
I AM--THE OUTSIDER! YOU HAVE NEITHER SEEN NOR HEARD OF ME BEFORE THIS MOMENT! YET IT WAS I--THROUGH MY HIRELINGS THE GRASSHOPPERS--WHO SET OUT TO STEAL YOUR MOST PRIZED POSSESSIONS!
WHEN I HAD THE BAT-MOBILE IN MY POSSESSION, I PREPARED THIS RECORD-ING--SET TO TURN ON WHEN YOU STARTED YOUR BATMOBILE--INDICATING YOU HAD DEFEATED ME... TEMPORARILY! NEXT TIME WE LOCK HORNS... YOUR DAYS WILL BE FILLED WITH UNIMAGINED PERILS!
ALL DURING THE ACTION I HAVE REMAINED UNSEEN--UNSUSPECTED--UNTOUCHABLE! YOUR PERIL IS ONLY BEGINNING, BATMAN! IT WILL END--WHEN I TAKE AWAY YOUR MOST PRIZED POSSESSION--YOUR VERY LIFE!
AS THE RECORDED VOICE FADES AWAY...
!WHEW!! THE OUTSIDER REALLY IS TRICKY! HE CAN STRIKE AT US AT--ANY TIME! IN ANY NUMBER OF WAYS!
YES, ROBIN! FROM NOW ON OUR WAY OF LIFE MUST BE--ETERNAL VIGILANCE! WE CAN NEVER RELAX WITHOUT WONDERING--WHAT NEW SURPRISES THE OUTSIDER HAS IN STORE FOR US!
15
The End.

BATMAN

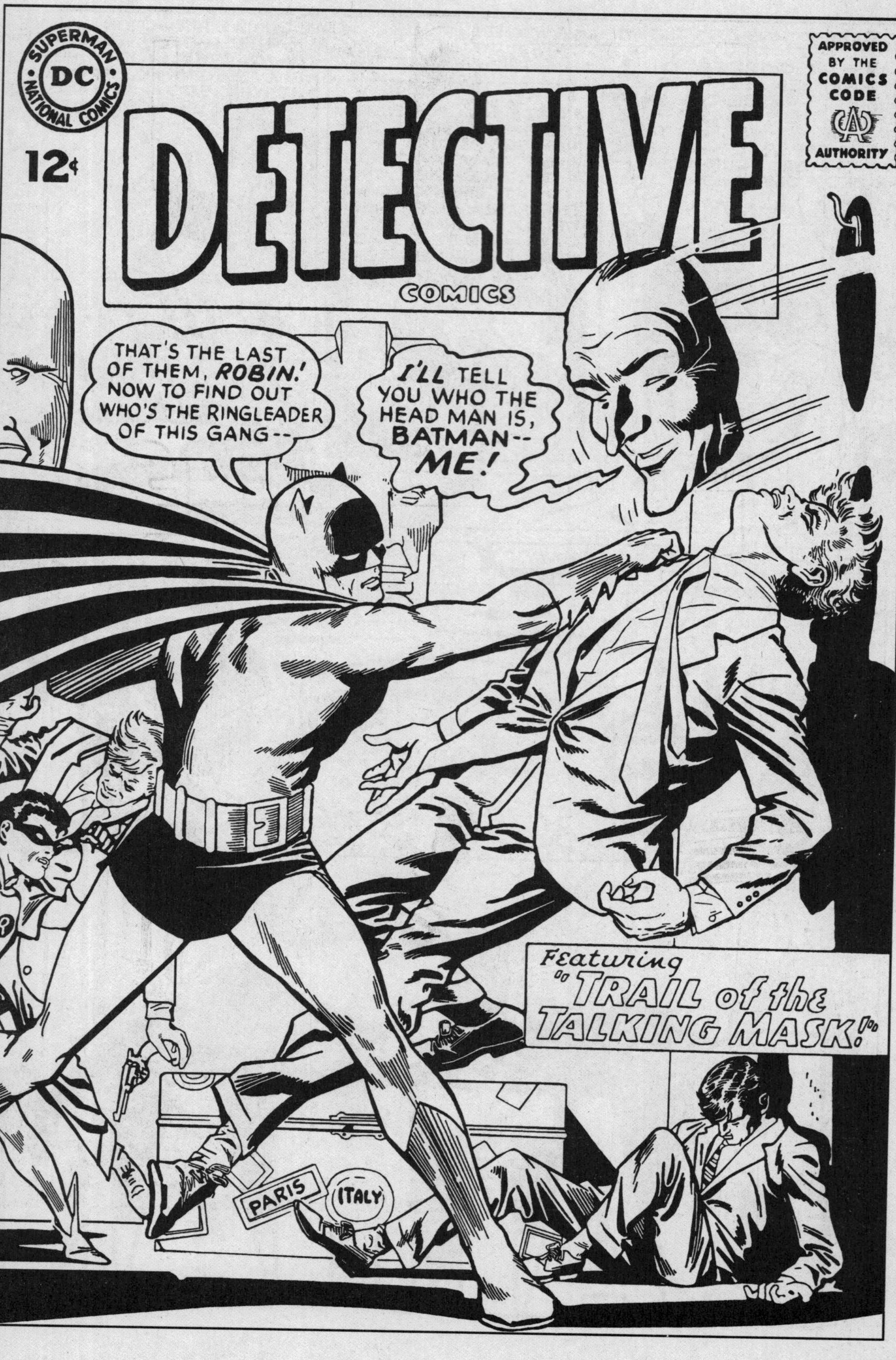
SUPERMAN DC NATIONAL COMICS
12¢
APPROVED BY THE COMICS CODE AUTHORITY
DETECTIVE COMICS
THAT'S THE LAST OF THEM, ROBIN! NOW TO FIND OUT WHO'S THE RINGLEADER OF THIS GANG--
I'LL TELL YOU WHO THE HEAD MAN IS, BATMAN-- ME!
Featuring "TRAIL of the TALKING MASK!"
PARIS
ITALY

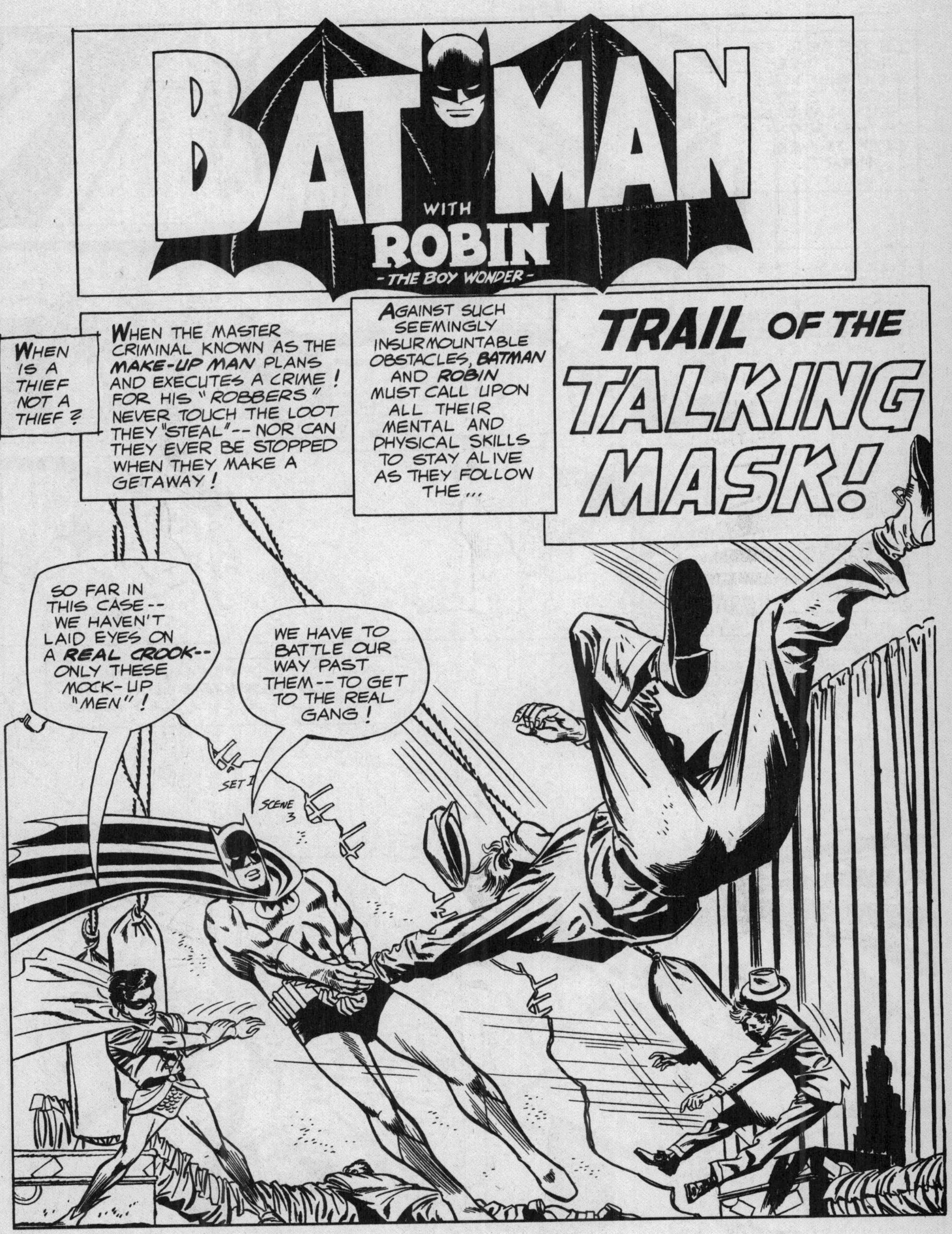
BATMAN
WITH
ROBIN
-THE BOY WONDER-
WHEN IS A THIEF NOT A THIEF ?
WHEN THE MASTER CRIMINAL KNOWN AS THE MAKE-UP MAN PLANS AND EXECUTES A CRIME ! FOR HIS "ROBBERS" NEVER TOUCH THE LOOT THEY "STEAL" -- NOR CAN THEY EVER BE STOPPED WHEN THEY MAKE A GETAWAY !
AGAINST SUCH SEEMINGLY INSURMOUNTABLE OBSTACLES, BATMAN AND ROBIN MUST CALL UPON ALL THEIR MENTAL AND PHYSICAL SKILLS TO STAY ALIVE AS THEY FOLLOW THE ...
TRAIL OF THE TALKING MASK!
SO FAR IN THIS CASE -- WE HAVEN'T LAID EYES ON A REAL CROOK -- ONLY THESE MOCK-UP "MEN" !
WE HAVE TO BATTLE OUR WAY PAST THEM -- TO GET TO THE REAL GANG !
SET 1
SCENE 3

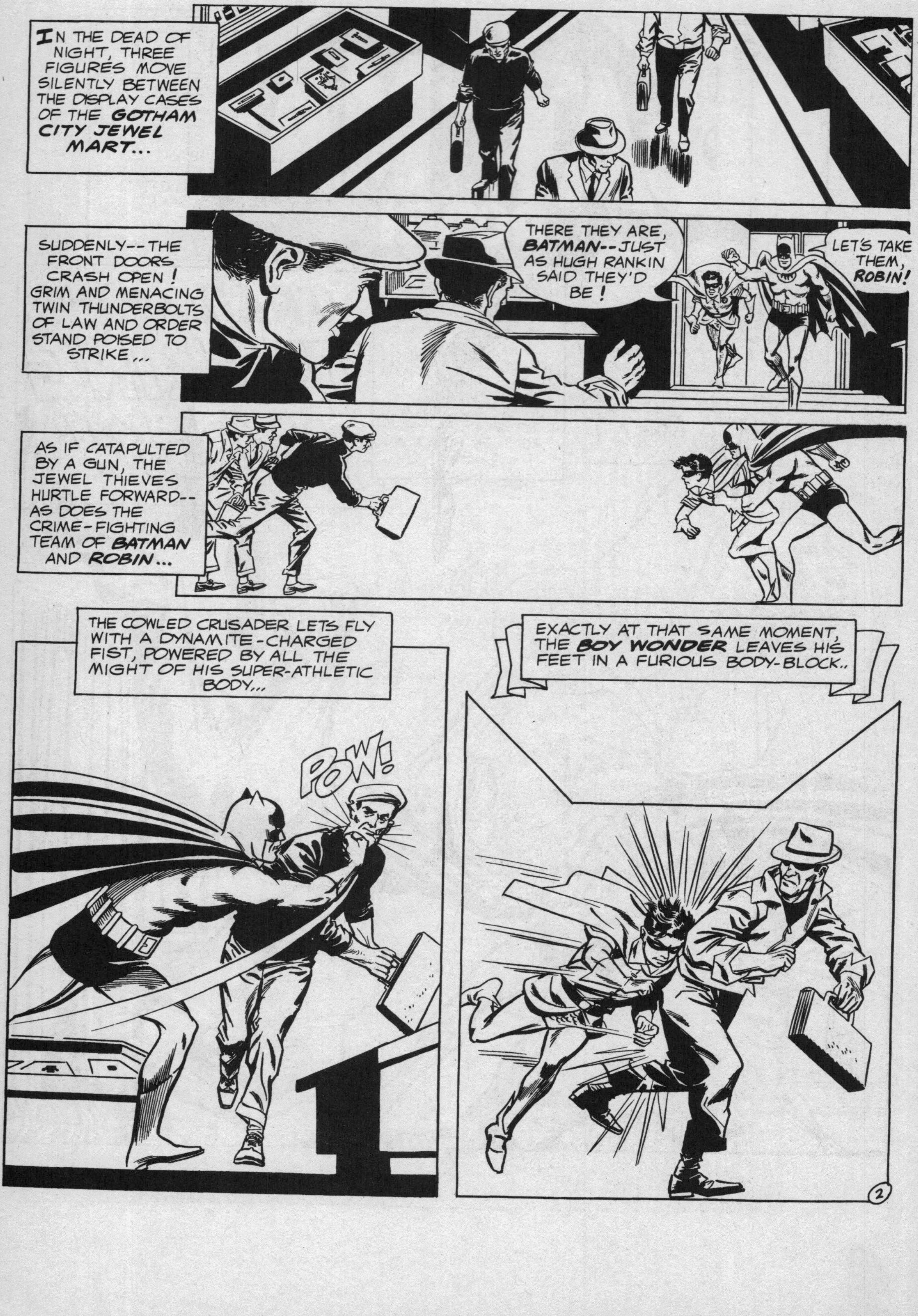
IN THE DEAD OF NIGHT, THREE FIGURES MOVE SILENTLY BETWEEN THE DISPLAY CASES OF THE GOTHAM CITY JEWEL MART...
SUDDENLY--THE FRONT DOORS CRASH OPEN! GRIM AND MENACING TWIN THUNDERBOLTS OF LAW AND ORDER STAND POISED TO STRIKE...
THERE THEY ARE, BATMAN--JUST AS HUGH RANKIN SAID THEY'D BE!
LET'S TAKE THEM, ROBIN!
AS IF CATAPULTED BY A GUN, THE JEWEL THIEVES HURTLE FORWARD--AS DOES THE CRIME-FIGHTING TEAM OF BATMAN AND ROBIN...
THE COWLED CRUSADER LETS FLY WITH A DYNAMITE-CHARGED FIST, POWERED BY ALL THE MIGHT OF HIS SUPER-ATHLETIC BODY...
POW!
EXACTLY AT THAT SAME MOMENT, THE BOY WONDER LEAVES HIS FEET IN A FURIOUS BODY-BLOCK..
2

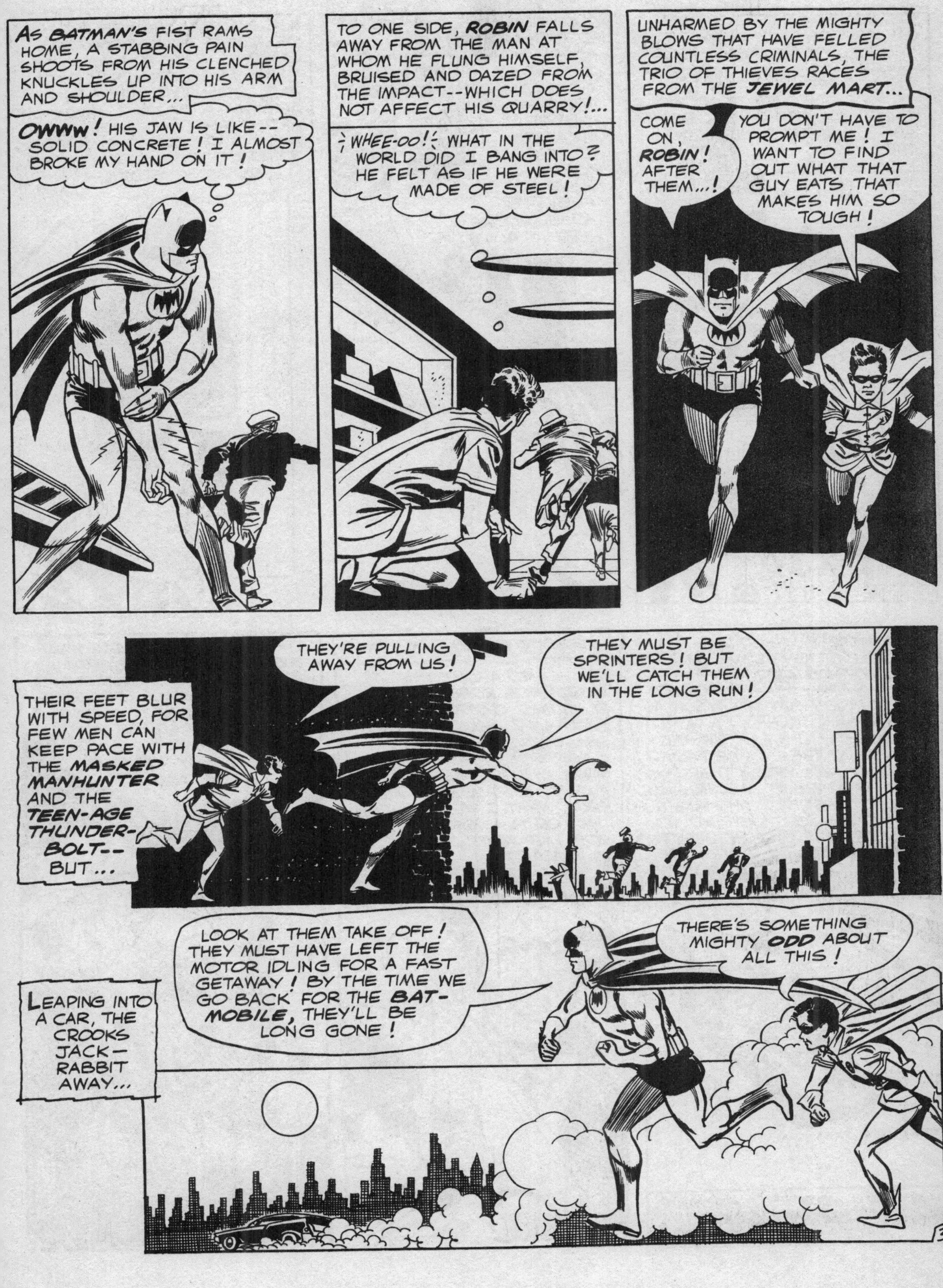
AS BATMAN'S FIST RAMS HOME, A STABBING PAIN SHOOTS FROM HIS CLENCHED KNUCKLES UP INTO HIS ARM AND SHOULDER...
OWWW! HIS JAW IS LIKE-- SOLID CONCRETE! I ALMOST BROKE MY HAND ON IT!
TO ONE SIDE, ROBIN FALLS AWAY FROM THE MAN AT WHOM HE FLUNG HIMSELF, BRUISED AND DAZED FROM THE IMPACT--WHICH DOES NOT AFFECT HIS QUARRY!...
WHEE-OO! WHAT IN THE WORLD DID I BANG INTO? HE FELT AS IF HE WERE MADE OF STEEL!
UNHARMED BY THE MIGHTY BLOWS THAT HAVE FELLED COUNTLESS CRIMINALS, THE TRIO OF THIEVES RACES FROM THE JEWEL MART...
COME ON, ROBIN! AFTER THEM...!
YOU DON'T HAVE TO PROMPT ME! I WANT TO FIND OUT WHAT THAT GUY EATS THAT MAKES HIM SO TOUGH!
THEIR FEET BLUR WITH SPEED, FOR FEW MEN CAN KEEP PACE WITH THE MASKED MANHUNTER AND THE TEEN-AGE THUNDER-BOLT-- BUT...
THEY'RE PULLING AWAY FROM US!
THEY MUST BE SPRINTERS! BUT WE'LL CATCH THEM IN THE LONG RUN!
LEAPING INTO A CAR, THE CROOKS JACK-RABBIT AWAY...
LOOK AT THEM TAKE OFF! THEY MUST HAVE LEFT THE MOTOR IDLING FOR A FAST GETAWAY! BY THE TIME WE GO BACK FOR THE BAT-MOBILE, THEY'LL BE LONG GONE!
THERE'S SOMETHING MIGHTY ODD ABOUT ALL THIS!
3

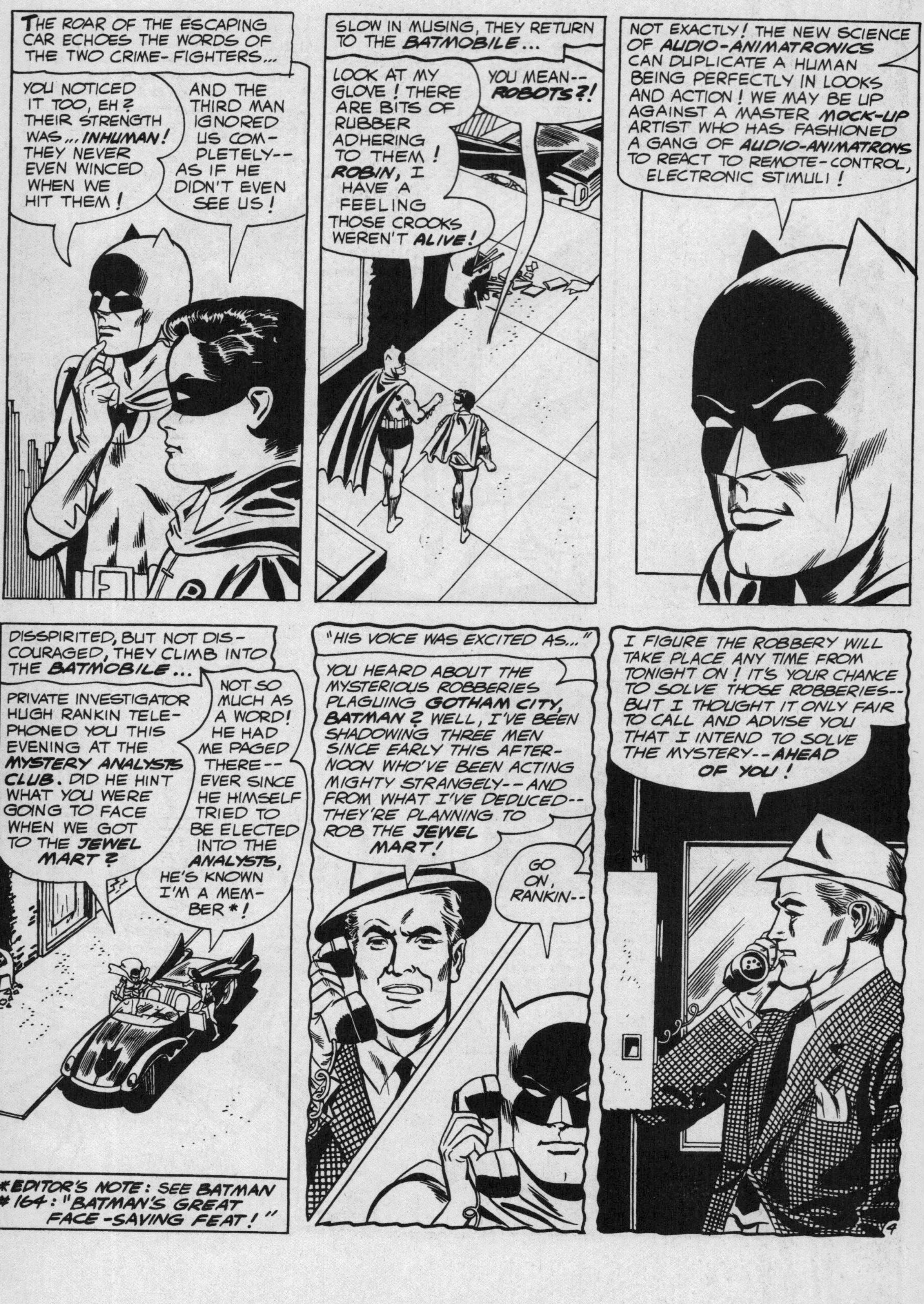
THE ROAR OF THE ESCAPING CAR ECHOES THE WORDS OF THE TWO CRIME-FIGHTERS...
YOU NOTICED IT TOO, EH? THEIR STRENGTH WAS... INHUMAN! THEY NEVER EVEN WINCED WHEN WE HIT THEM!
AND THE THIRD MAN IGNORED US COMPLETELY-- AS IF HE DIDN'T EVEN SEE US!
SLOW IN MUSING, THEY RETURN TO THE BATMOBILE...
LOOK AT MY GLOVE! THERE ARE BITS OF RUBBER ADHERING TO THEM! ROBIN, I HAVE A FEELING THOSE CROOKS WEREN'T ALIVE!
YOU MEAN-- ROBOTS?!
NOT EXACTLY! THE NEW SCIENCE OF AUDIO-ANIMATRONICS CAN DUPLICATE A HUMAN BEING PERFECTLY IN LOOKS AND ACTION! WE MAY BE UP AGAINST A MASTER MOCK-UP ARTIST WHO HAS FASHIONED A GANG OF AUDIO-ANIMATRONS TO REACT TO REMOTE-CONTROL, ELECTRONIC STIMULI!
DISSPIRITED, BUT NOT DISCOURAGED, THEY CLIMB INTO THE BATMOBILE...
PRIVATE INVESTIGATOR HUGH RANKIN TELEPHONED YOU THIS EVENING AT THE MYSTERY ANALYSTS CLUB. DID HE HINT WHAT YOU WERE GOING TO FACE WHEN WE GOT TO THE JEWEL MART?
NOT SO MUCH AS A WORD! HE HAD ME PAGED THERE-- EVER SINCE HE HIMSELF TRIED TO BE ELECTED INTO THE ANALYSTS, HE'S KNOWN I'M A MEMBER*!
*EDITOR'S NOTE: SEE BATMAN #164: "BATMAN'S GREAT FACE-SAVING FEAT!"
"HIS VOICE WAS EXCITED AS..."
YOU HEARD ABOUT THE MYSTERIOUS ROBBERIES PLAGUING GOTHAM CITY, BATMAN? WELL, I'VE BEEN SHADOWING THREE MEN SINCE EARLY THIS AFTERNOON WHO'VE BEEN ACTING MIGHTY STRANGELY-- AND FROM WHAT I'VE DEDUCED-- THEY'RE PLANNING TO ROB THE JEWEL MART!
GO ON, RANKIN--
I FIGURE THE ROBBERY WILL TAKE PLACE ANY TIME FROM TONIGHT ON! IT'S YOUR CHANCE TO SOLVE THOSE ROBBERIES-- BUT I THOUGHT IT ONLY FAIR TO CALL AND ADVISE YOU THAT I INTEND TO SOLVE THE MYSTERY-- AHEAD OF YOU!
4

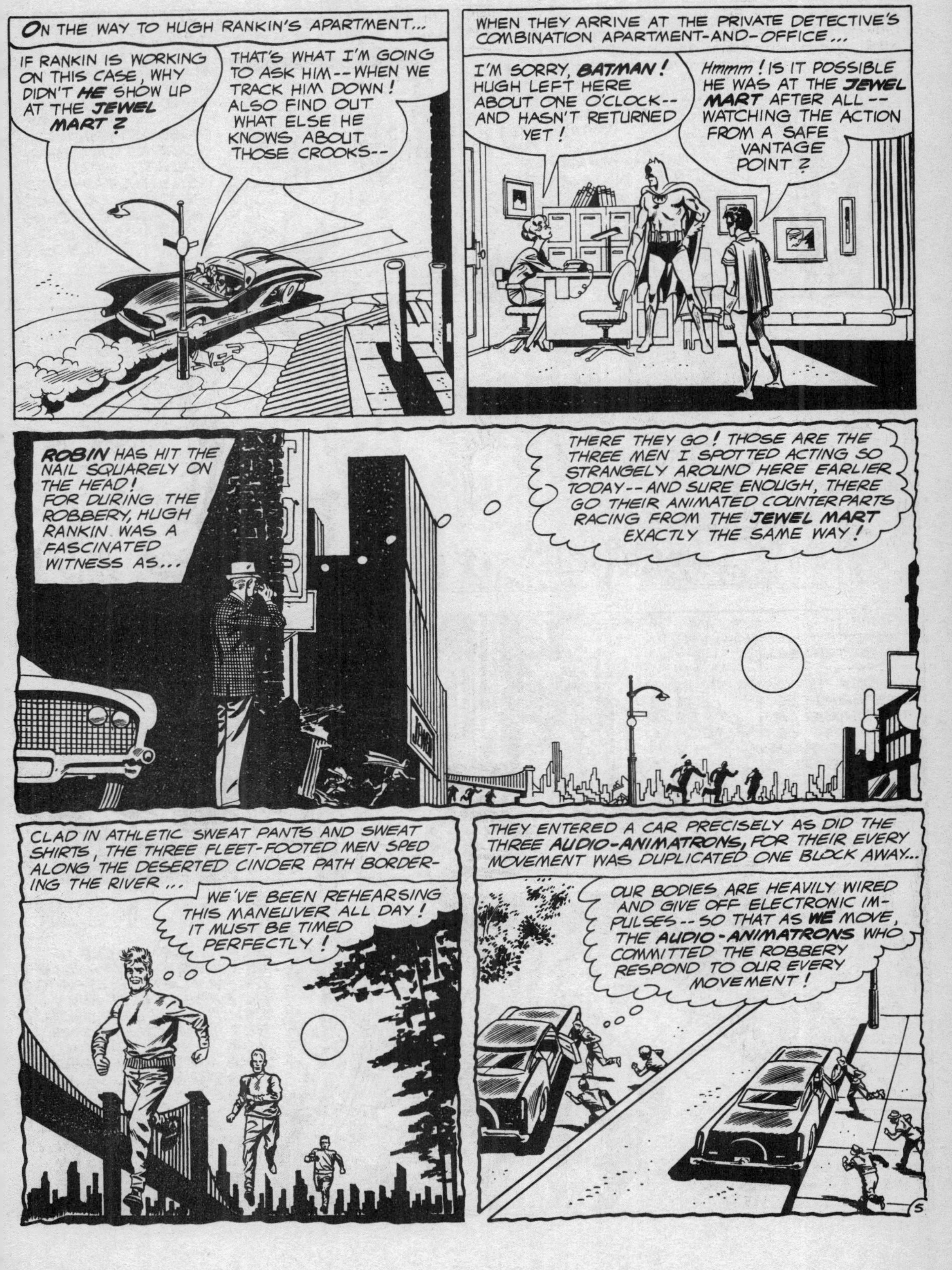
ON THE WAY TO HUGH RANKIN'S APARTMENT...
IF RANKIN IS WORKING ON THIS CASE, WHY DIDN'T HE SHOW UP AT THE JEWEL MART ?
THAT'S WHAT I'M GOING TO ASK HIM--WHEN WE TRACK HIM DOWN! ALSO FIND OUT WHAT ELSE HE KNOWS ABOUT THOSE CROOKS--
WHEN THEY ARRIVE AT THE PRIVATE DETECTIVE'S COMBINATION APARTMENT-AND-OFFICE...
I'M SORRY, BATMAN! HUGH LEFT HERE ABOUT ONE O'CLOCK--AND HASN'T RETURNED YET!
Hmmm! IS IT POSSIBLE HE WAS AT THE JEWEL MART AFTER ALL--WATCHING THE ACTION FROM A SAFE VANTAGE POINT ?
ROBIN HAS HIT THE NAIL SQUARELY ON THE HEAD! FOR DURING THE ROBBERY, HUGH RANKIN WAS A FASCINATED WITNESS AS...
THERE THEY GO! THOSE ARE THE THREE MEN I SPOTTED ACTING SO STRANGELY AROUND HERE EARLIER TODAY--AND SURE ENOUGH, THERE GO THEIR ANIMATED COUNTERPARTS RACING FROM THE JEWEL MART EXACTLY THE SAME WAY!
CLAD IN ATHLETIC SWEAT PANTS AND SWEAT SHIRTS, THE THREE FLEET-FOOTED MEN SPED ALONG THE DESERTED CINDER PATH BORDERING THE RIVER...
WE'VE BEEN REHEARSING THIS MANEUVER ALL DAY! IT MUST BE TIMED PERFECTLY!
THEY ENTERED A CAR PRECISELY AS DID THE THREE AUDIO-ANIMATRONS, FOR THEIR EVERY MOVEMENT WAS DUPLICATED ONE BLOCK AWAY...
OUR BODIES ARE HEAVILY WIRED AND GIVE OFF ELECTRONIC IMPULSES--SO THAT AS WE MOVE, THE AUDIO-ANIMATRONS WHO COMMITTED THE ROBBERY RESPOND TO OUR EVERY MOVEMENT!
5

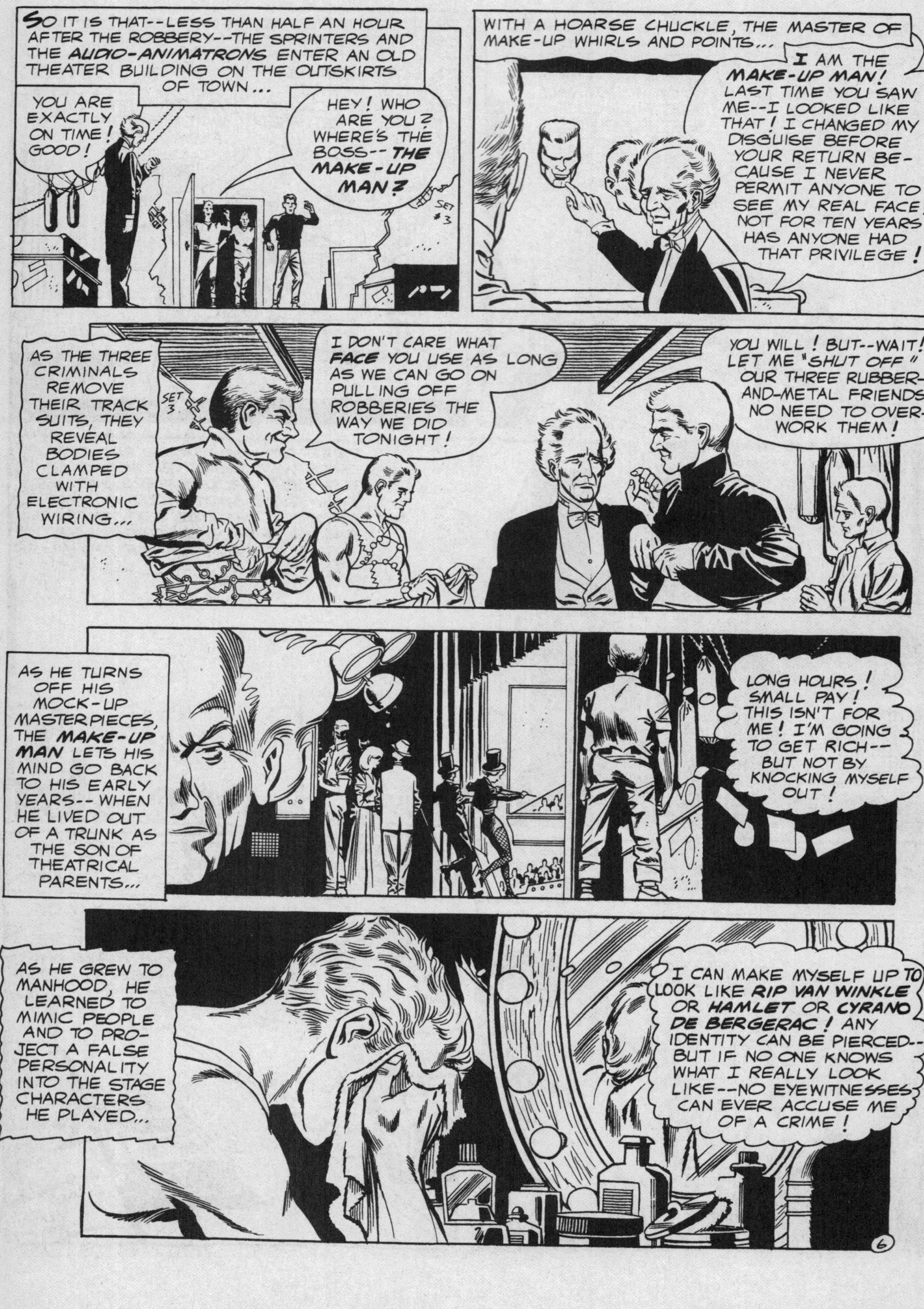
SO IT IS THAT--LESS THAN HALF AN HOUR AFTER THE ROBBERY--THE SPRINTERS AND THE AUDIO-ANIMATRONS ENTER AN OLD THEATER BUILDING ON THE OUTSKIRTS OF TOWN...
YOU ARE EXACTLY ON TIME! GOOD!
HEY! WHO ARE YOU? WHERE'S THE BOSS--THE MAKE-UP MAN?
WITH A HOARSE CHUCKLE, THE MASTER OF MAKE-UP WHIRLS AND POINTS...
I AM THE MAKE-UP MAN! LAST TIME YOU SAW ME--I LOOKED LIKE THAT! I CHANGED MY DISGUISE BEFORE YOUR RETURN BECAUSE I NEVER PERMIT ANYONE TO SEE MY REAL FACE! NOT FOR TEN YEARS HAS ANYONE HAD THAT PRIVILEGE!
AS THE THREE CRIMINALS REMOVE THEIR TRACK SUITS, THEY REVEAL BODIES CLAMPED WITH ELECTRONIC WIRING...
I DON'T CARE WHAT FACE YOU USE AS LONG AS WE CAN GO ON PULLING OFF ROBBERIES THE WAY WE DID TONIGHT!
YOU WILL! BUT--WAIT! LET ME "SHUT OFF" OUR THREE RUBBER-AND-METAL FRIENDS! NO NEED TO OVERWORK THEM!
AS HE TURNS OFF HIS MOCK-UP MASTERPIECES, THE MAKE-UP MAN LETS HIS MIND GO BACK TO HIS EARLY YEARS--WHEN HE LIVED OUT OF A TRUNK AS THE SON OF THEATRICAL PARENTS...
LONG HOURS! SMALL PAY! THIS ISN'T FOR ME! I'M GOING TO GET RICH--BUT NOT BY KNOCKING MYSELF OUT!
AS HE GREW TO MANHOOD, HE LEARNED TO MIMIC PEOPLE AND TO PROJECT A FALSE PERSONALITY INTO THE STAGE CHARACTERS HE PLAYED...
I CAN MAKE MYSELF UP TO LOOK LIKE RIP VAN WINKLE OR HAMLET OR CYRANO DE BERGERAC! ANY IDENTITY CAN BE PIERCED--BUT IF NO ONE KNOWS WHAT I REALLY LOOK LIKE--NO EYEWITNESSES CAN EVER ACCUSE ME OF A CRIME!
6

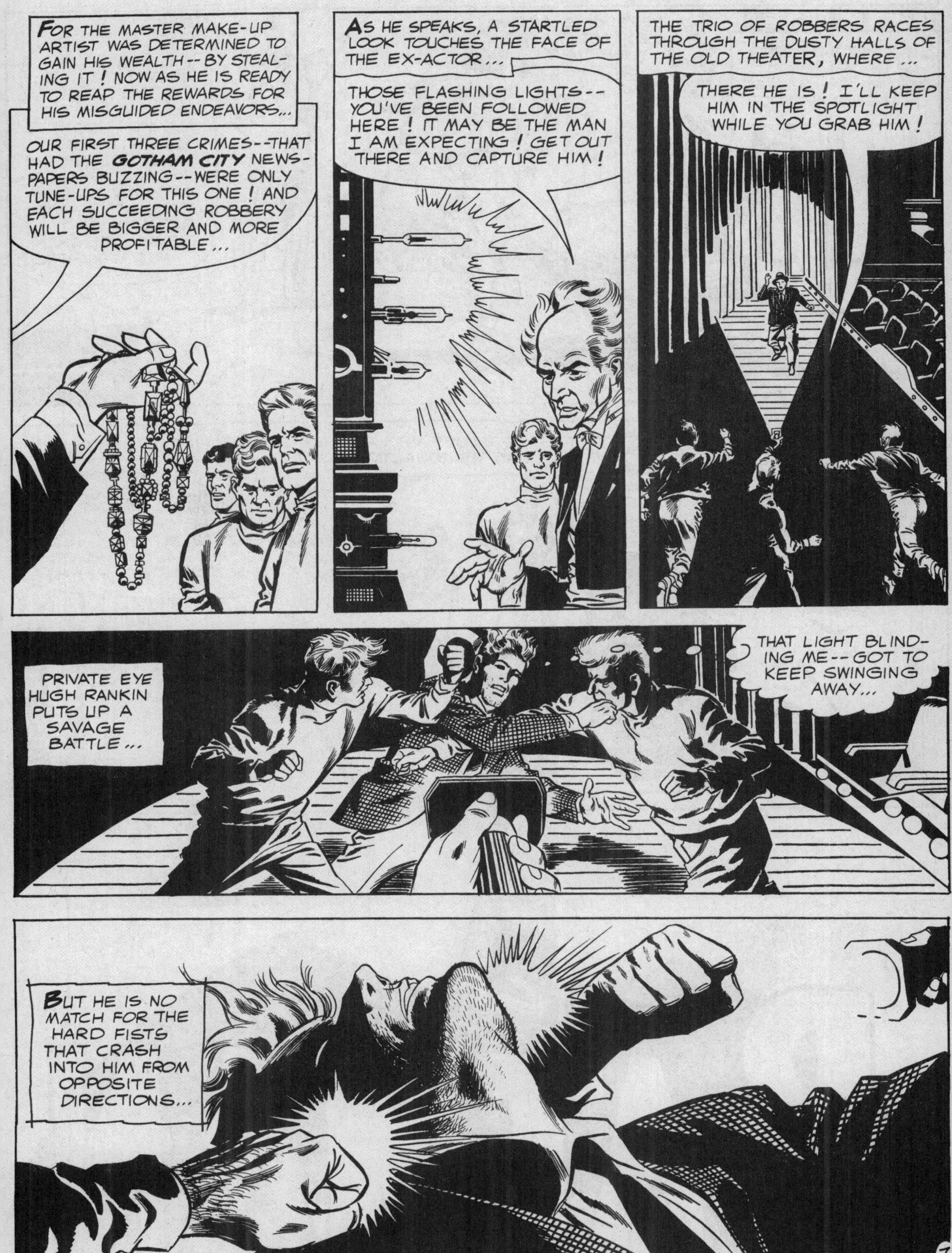
FOR THE MASTER MAKE-UP ARTIST WAS DETERMINED TO GAIN HIS WEALTH -- BY STEALING IT ! NOW AS HE IS READY TO REAP THE REWARDS FOR HIS MISGUIDED ENDEAVORS...
OUR FIRST THREE CRIMES--THAT HAD THE GOTHAM CITY NEWSPAPERS BUZZING--WERE ONLY TUNE-UPS FOR THIS ONE ! AND EACH SUCCEEDING ROBBERY WILL BE BIGGER AND MORE PROFITABLE...
AS HE SPEAKS, A STARTLED LOOK TOUCHES THE FACE OF THE EX-ACTOR...
THOSE FLASHING LIGHTS--YOU'VE BEEN FOLLOWED HERE ! IT MAY BE THE MAN I AM EXPECTING ! GET OUT THERE AND CAPTURE HIM !
THE TRIO OF ROBBERS RACES THROUGH THE DUSTY HALLS OF THE OLD THEATER, WHERE ...
THERE HE IS ! I'LL KEEP HIM IN THE SPOTLIGHT WHILE YOU GRAB HIM !
PRIVATE EYE HUGH RANKIN PUTS UP A SAVAGE BATTLE...
THAT LIGHT BLINDING ME--GOT TO KEEP SWINGING AWAY...
BUT HE IS NO MATCH FOR THE HARD FISTS THAT CRASH INTO HIM FROM OPPOSITE DIRECTIONS...
7

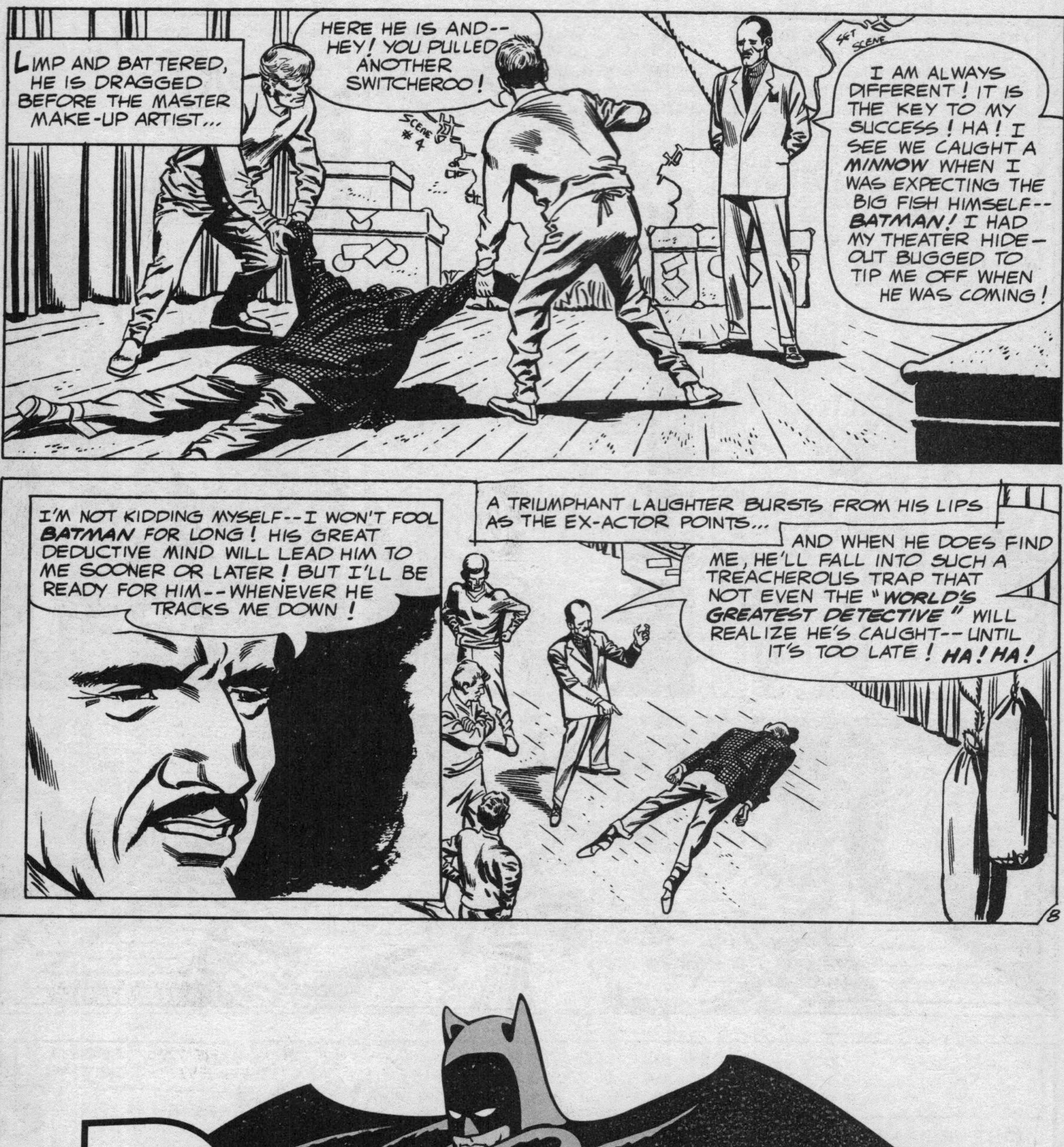
LIMP AND BATTERED, HE IS DRAGGED BEFORE THE MASTER MAKE-UP ARTIST...
HERE HE IS AND-- HEY! YOU PULLED ANOTHER SWITCHEROO!
SCENE #4
SET SCENE
I AM ALWAYS DIFFERENT! IT IS THE KEY TO MY SUCCESS! HA! I SEE WE CAUGHT A MINNOW WHEN I WAS EXPECTING THE BIG FISH HIMSELF-- BATMAN! I HAD MY THEATER HIDE-OUT BUGGED TO TIP ME OFF WHEN HE WAS COMING!
I'M NOT KIDDING MYSELF--I WON'T FOOL BATMAN FOR LONG! HIS GREAT DEDUCTIVE MIND WILL LEAD HIM TO ME SOONER OR LATER! BUT I'LL BE READY FOR HIM--WHENEVER HE TRACKS ME DOWN!
A TRIUMPHANT LAUGHTER BURSTS FROM HIS LIPS AS THE EX-ACTOR POINTS...
AND WHEN HE DOES FIND ME, HE'LL FALL INTO SUCH A TREACHEROUS TRAP THAT NOT EVEN THE "WORLD'S GREATEST DETECTIVE" WILL REALIZE HE'S CAUGHT--UNTIL IT'S TOO LATE! HA! HA!
8

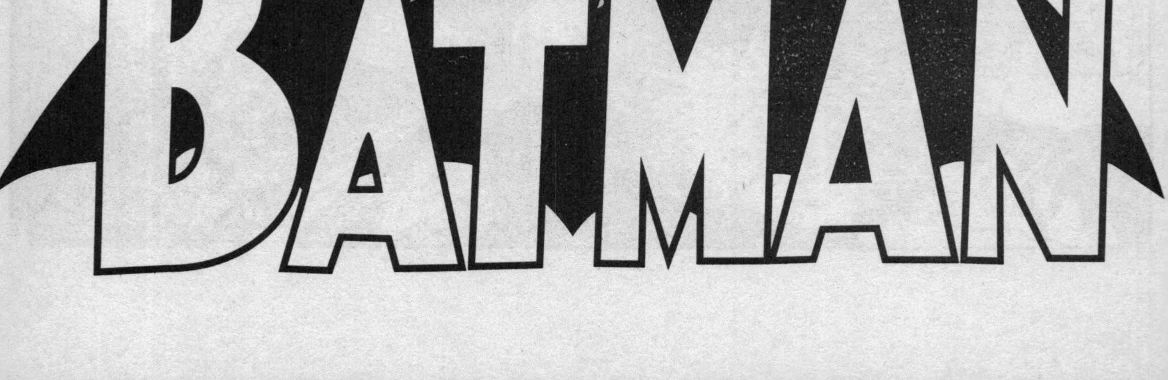
BATMAN

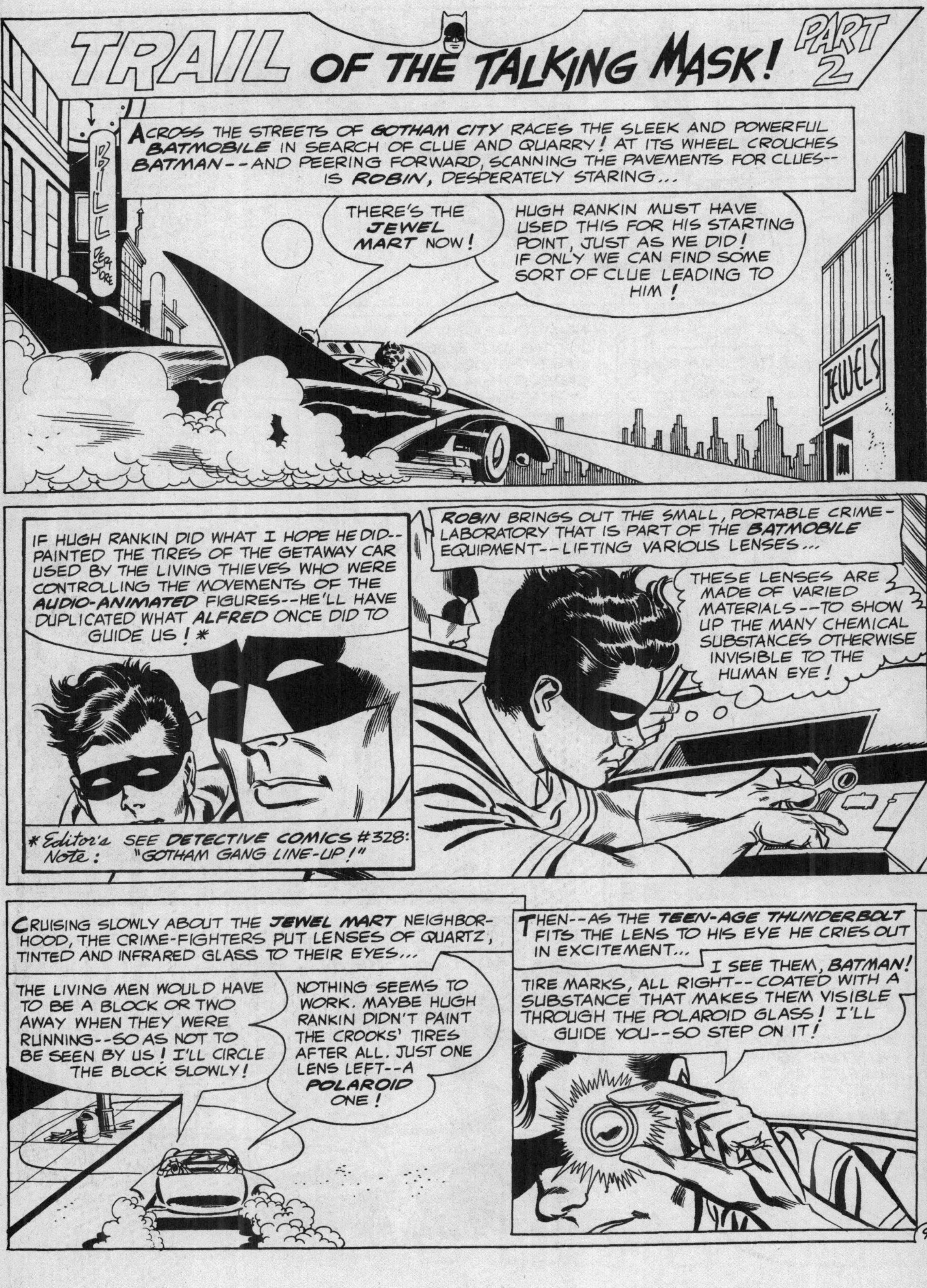
TRAIL OF THE TALKING MASK! PART 2
ACROSS THE STREETS OF GOTHAM CITY RACES THE SLEEK AND POWERFUL BATMOBILE IN SEARCH OF CLUE AND QUARRY! AT ITS WHEEL CROUCHES BATMAN--AND PEERING FORWARD, SCANNING THE PAVEMENTS FOR CLUES--IS ROBIN, DESPERATELY STARING...
BILL DEPT. STORE
THERE'S THE JEWEL MART NOW!
HUGH RANKIN MUST HAVE USED THIS FOR HIS STARTING POINT, JUST AS WE DID! IF ONLY WE CAN FIND SOME SORT OF CLUE LEADING TO HIM!
JEWELS
IF HUGH RANKIN DID WHAT I HOPE HE DID--PAINTED THE TIRES OF THE GETAWAY CAR USED BY THE LIVING THIEVES WHO WERE CONTROLLING THE MOVEMENTS OF THE AUDIO-ANIMATED FIGURES--HE'LL HAVE DUPLICATED WHAT ALFRED ONCE DID TO GUIDE US! *
* Editor's Note: SEE DETECTIVE COMICS #328: "GOTHAM GANG LINE-UP!"
ROBIN BRINGS OUT THE SMALL, PORTABLE CRIME-LABORATORY THAT IS PART OF THE BATMOBILE EQUIPMENT--LIFTING VARIOUS LENSES...
THESE LENSES ARE MADE OF VARIED MATERIALS--TO SHOW UP THE MANY CHEMICAL SUBSTANCES OTHERWISE INVISIBLE TO THE HUMAN EYE!
CRUISING SLOWLY ABOUT THE JEWEL MART NEIGHBORHOOD, THE CRIME-FIGHTERS PUT LENSES OF QUARTZ, TINTED AND INFRARED GLASS TO THEIR EYES...
THE LIVING MEN WOULD HAVE TO BE A BLOCK OR TWO AWAY WHEN THEY WERE RUNNING--SO AS NOT TO BE SEEN BY US! I'LL CIRCLE THE BLOCK SLOWLY!
NOTHING SEEMS TO WORK. MAYBE HUGH RANKIN DIDN'T PAINT THE CROOKS' TIRES AFTER ALL. JUST ONE LENS LEFT--A POLAROID ONE!
THEN--AS THE TEEN-AGE THUNDERBOLT FITS THE LENS TO HIS EYE HE CRIES OUT IN EXCITEMENT...
I SEE THEM, BATMAN! TIRE MARKS, ALL RIGHT--COATED WITH A SUBSTANCE THAT MAKES THEM VISIBLE THROUGH THE POLAROID GLASS! I'LL GUIDE YOU--SO STEP ON IT!
9

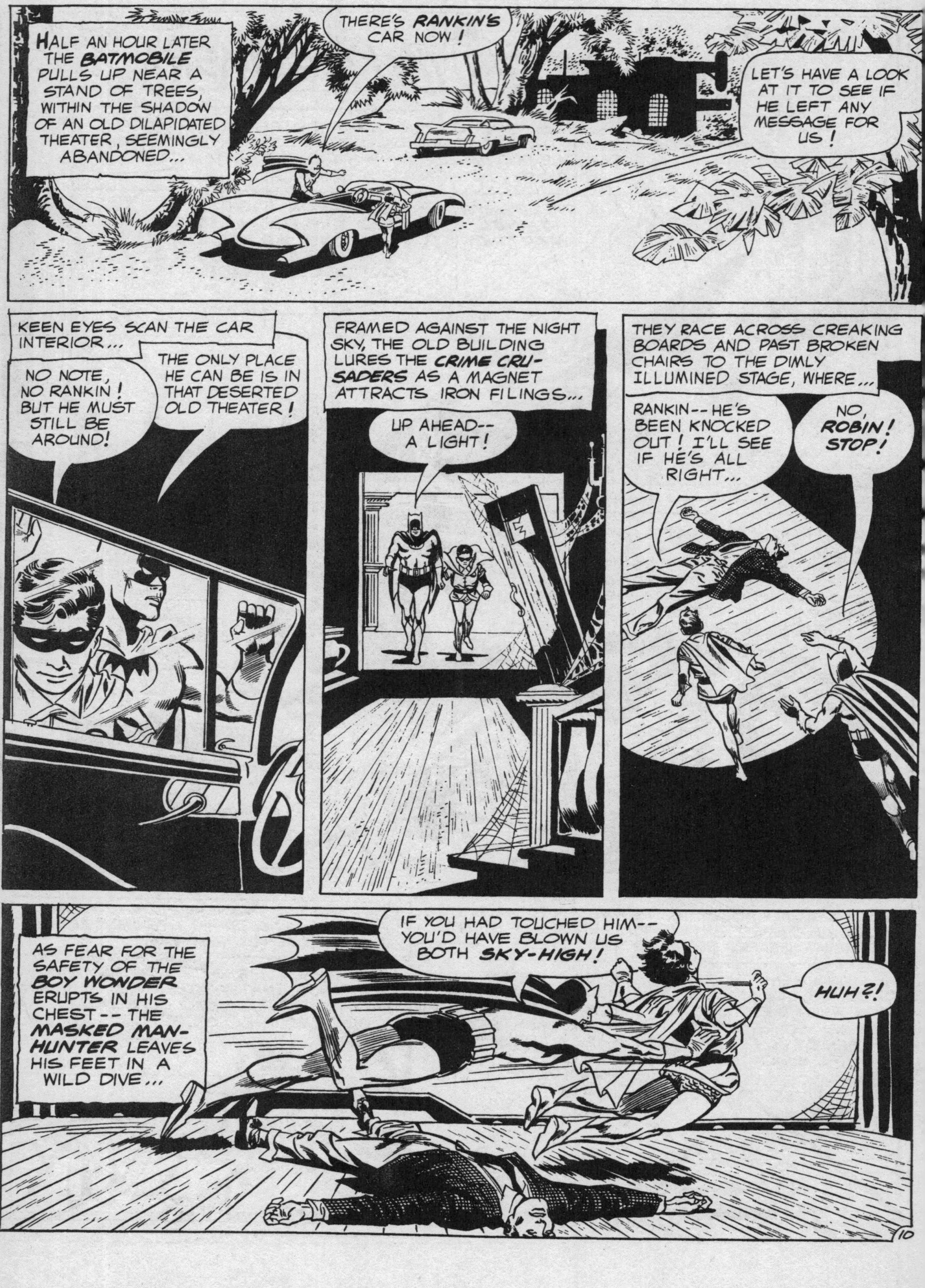
HALF AN HOUR LATER THE BATMOBILE PULLS UP NEAR A STAND OF TREES, WITHIN THE SHADOW OF AN OLD DILAPIDATED THEATER, SEEMINGLY ABANDONED...
THERE'S RANKIN'S CAR NOW!
LET'S HAVE A LOOK AT IT TO SEE IF HE LEFT ANY MESSAGE FOR US!
KEEN EYES SCAN THE CAR INTERIOR...
NO NOTE, NO RANKIN! BUT HE MUST STILL BE AROUND!
THE ONLY PLACE HE CAN BE IS IN THAT DESERTED OLD THEATER!
FRAMED AGAINST THE NIGHT SKY, THE OLD BUILDING LURES THE CRIME CRUSADERS AS A MAGNET ATTRACTS IRON FILINGS...
UP AHEAD-- A LIGHT!
THEY RACE ACROSS CREAKING BOARDS AND PAST BROKEN CHAIRS TO THE DIMLY ILLUMINED STAGE, WHERE...
RANKIN--HE'S BEEN KNOCKED OUT! I'LL SEE IF HE'S ALL RIGHT...
NO, ROBIN! STOP!
AS FEAR FOR THE SAFETY OF THE BOY WONDER ERUPTS IN HIS CHEST-- THE MASKED MAN-HUNTER LEAVES HIS FEET IN A WILD DIVE...
IF YOU HAD TOUCHED HIM-- YOU'D HAVE BLOWN US BOTH SKY-HIGH!
HUH?!
10

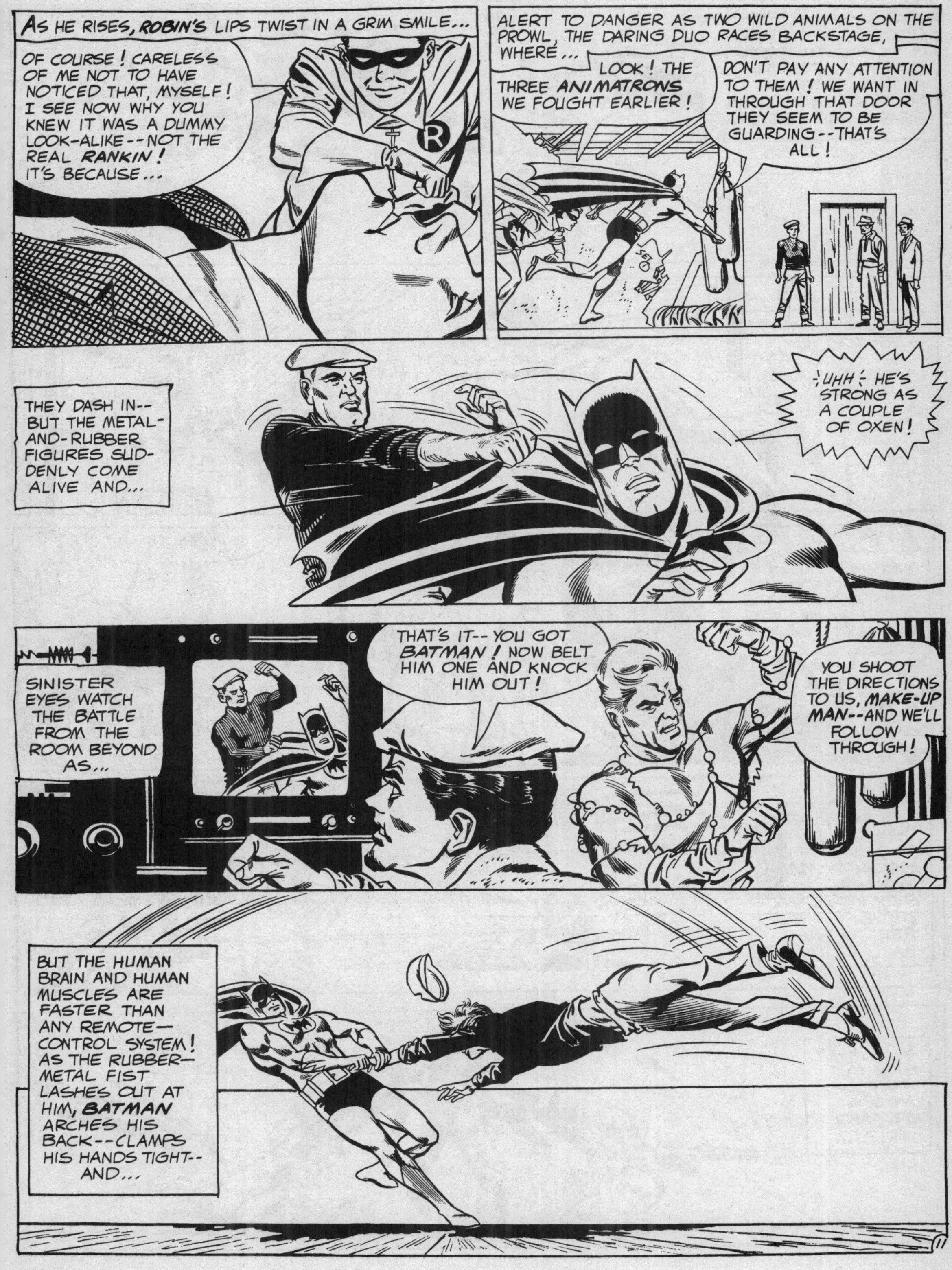
AS HE RISES, ROBIN'S LIPS TWIST IN A GRIM SMILE...
OF COURSE! CARELESS OF ME NOT TO HAVE NOTICED THAT, MYSELF! I SEE NOW WHY YOU KNEW IT WAS A DUMMY LOOK-ALIKE--NOT THE REAL RANKIN! IT'S BECAUSE...
ALERT TO DANGER AS TWO WILD ANIMALS ON THE PROWL, THE DARING DUO RACES BACKSTAGE, WHERE...
LOOK! THE THREE ANIMATRONS WE FOUGHT EARLIER!
DON'T PAY ANY ATTENTION TO THEM! WE WANT IN THROUGH THAT DOOR THEY SEEM TO BE GUARDING--THAT'S ALL!
THEY DASH IN--BUT THE METAL-AND-RUBBER FIGURES SUDDENLY COME ALIVE AND...
-UHH- HE'S STRONG AS A COUPLE OF OXEN!
SINISTER EYES WATCH THE BATTLE FROM THE ROOM BEYOND AS...
THAT'S IT--YOU GOT BATMAN! NOW BELT HIM ONE AND KNOCK HIM OUT!
YOU SHOOT THE DIRECTIONS TO US, MAKE-UP MAN--AND WE'LL FOLLOW THROUGH!
BUT THE HUMAN BRAIN AND HUMAN MUSCLES ARE FASTER THAN ANY REMOTE-CONTROL SYSTEM! AS THE RUBBER-METAL FIST LASHES OUT AT HIM, BATMAN ARCHES HIS BACK--CLAMPS HIS HANDS TIGHT--AND...

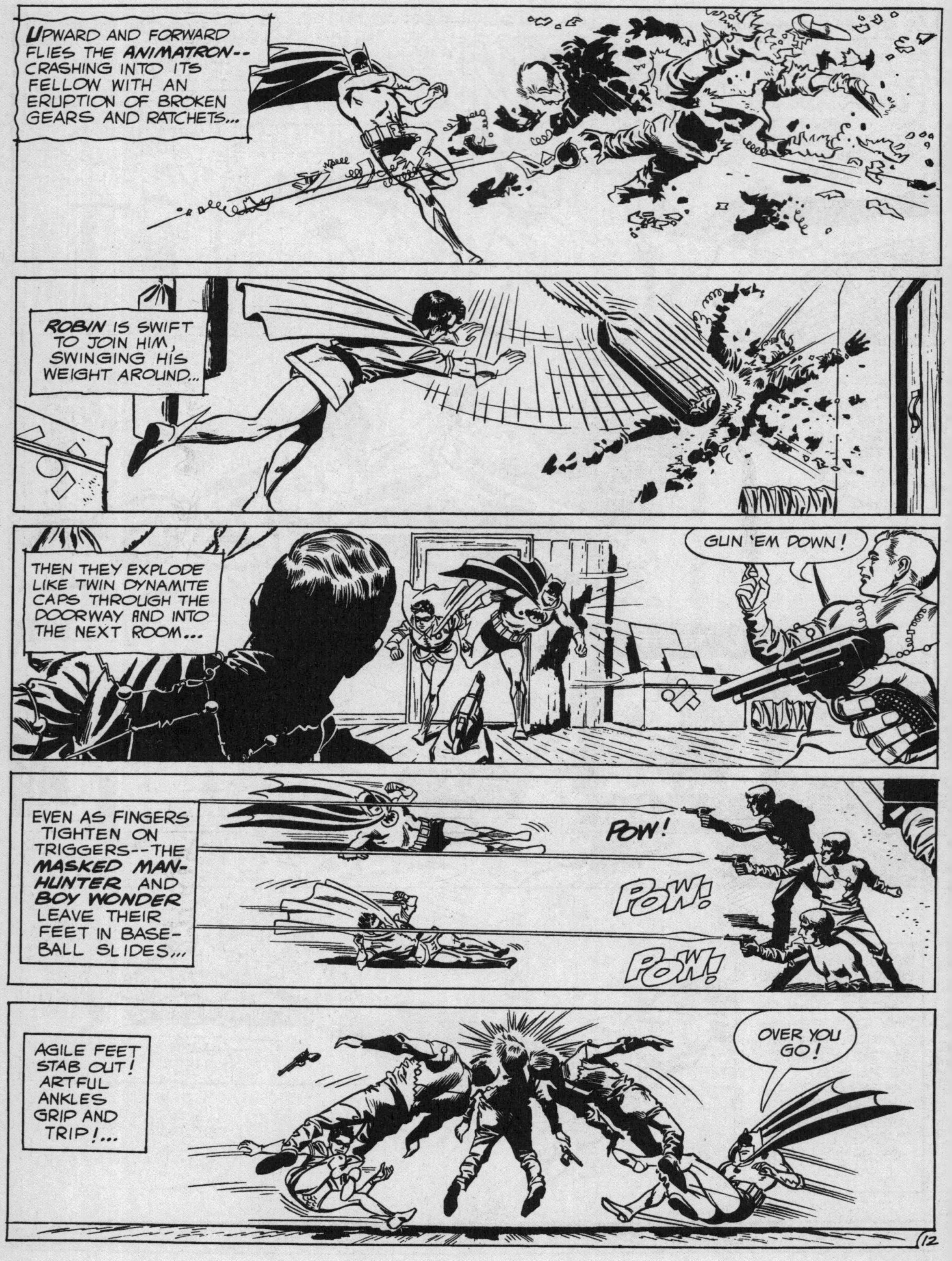
UPWARD AND FORWARD FLIES THE ANIMATRON--CRASHING INTO ITS FELLOW WITH AN ERUPTION OF BROKEN GEARS AND RATCHETS...
ROBIN IS SWIFT TO JOIN HIM, SWINGING HIS WEIGHT AROUND...
THEN THEY EXPLODE LIKE TWIN DYNAMITE CAPS THROUGH THE DOORWAY AND INTO THE NEXT ROOM...
GUN 'EM DOWN!
EVEN AS FINGERS TIGHTEN ON TRIGGERS--THE MASKED MAN-HUNTER AND BOY WONDER LEAVE THEIR FEET IN BASE-BALL SLIDES...
POW!
POW!
POW!
AGILE FEET STAB OUT! ARTFUL ANKLES GRIP AND TRIP!...
OVER YOU GO!
12

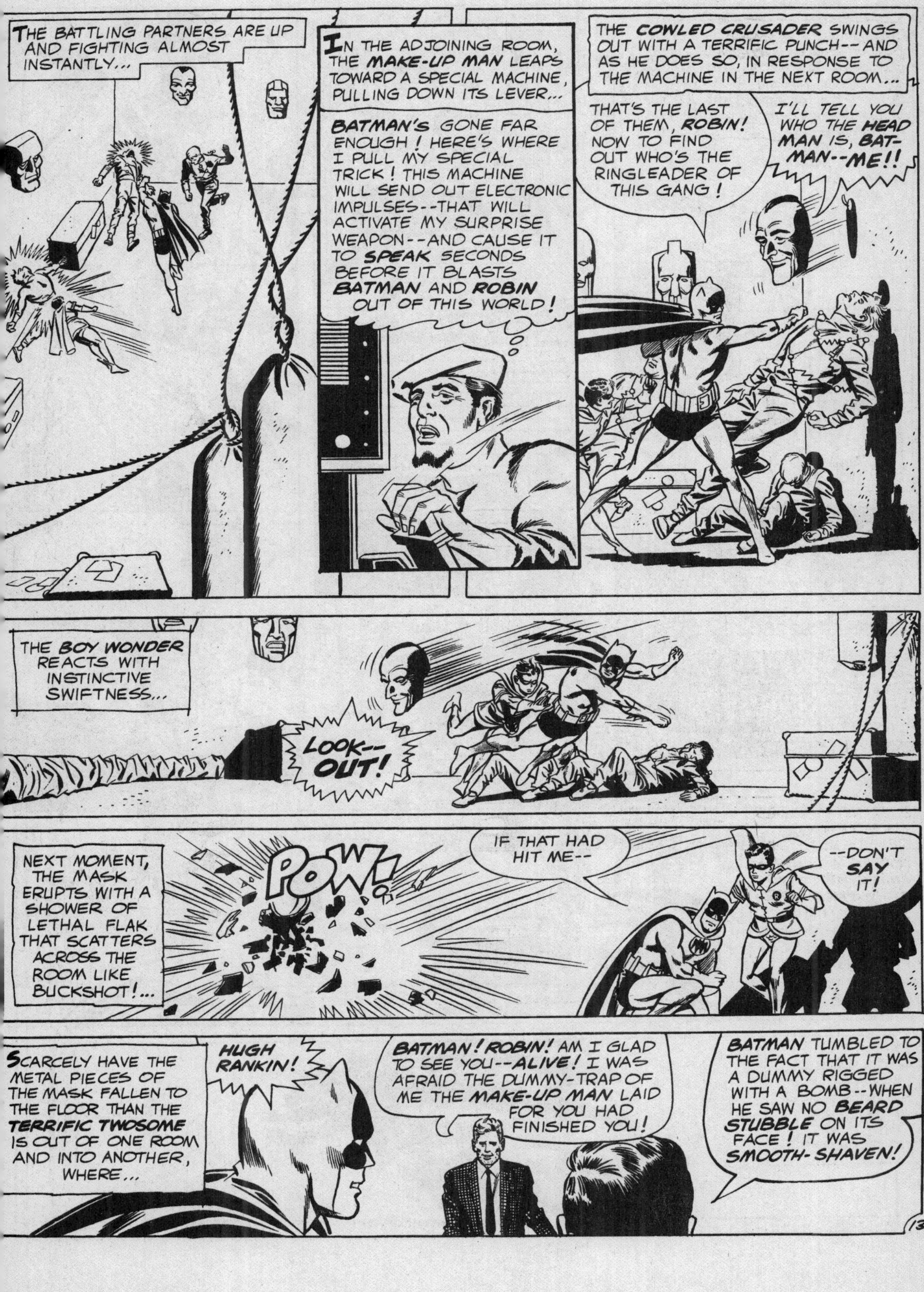
THE BATTLING PARTNERS ARE UP AND FIGHTING ALMOST INSTANTLY...
IN THE ADJOINING ROOM, THE MAKE-UP MAN LEAPS TOWARD A SPECIAL MACHINE, PULLING DOWN ITS LEVER...
BATMAN'S GONE FAR ENOUGH! HERE'S WHERE I PULL MY SPECIAL TRICK! THIS MACHINE WILL SEND OUT ELECTRONIC IMPULSES--THAT WILL ACTIVATE MY SURPRISE WEAPON--AND CAUSE IT TO SPEAK SECONDS BEFORE IT BLASTS BATMAN AND ROBIN OUT OF THIS WORLD!
THE COWLED CRUSADER SWINGS OUT WITH A TERRIFIC PUNCH--AND AS HE DOES SO, IN RESPONSE TO THE MACHINE IN THE NEXT ROOM...
THAT'S THE LAST OF THEM, ROBIN! NOW TO FIND OUT WHO'S THE RINGLEADER OF THIS GANG!
I'LL TELL YOU WHO THE HEAD MAN IS, BATMAN--ME!!
THE BOY WONDER REACTS WITH INSTINCTIVE SWIFTNESS...
LOOK--OUT!
NEXT MOMENT, THE MASK ERUPTS WITH A SHOWER OF LETHAL FLAK THAT SCATTERS ACROSS THE ROOM LIKE BUCKSHOT!...
POW!
IF THAT HAD HIT ME--
--DON'T SAY IT!
SCARCELY HAVE THE METAL PIECES OF THE MASK FALLEN TO THE FLOOR THAN THE TERRIFIC TWOSOME IS OUT OF ONE ROOM AND INTO ANOTHER, WHERE...
HUGH RANKIN!
BATMAN! ROBIN! AM I GLAD TO SEE YOU--ALIVE! I WAS AFRAID THE DUMMY-TRAP OF ME THE MAKE-UP MAN LAID FOR YOU HAD FINISHED YOU!
BATMAN TUMBLED TO THE FACT THAT IT WAS A DUMMY RIGGED WITH A BOMB--WHEN HE SAW NO BEARD STUBBLE ON ITS FACE! IT WAS SMOOTH-SHAVEN!
13

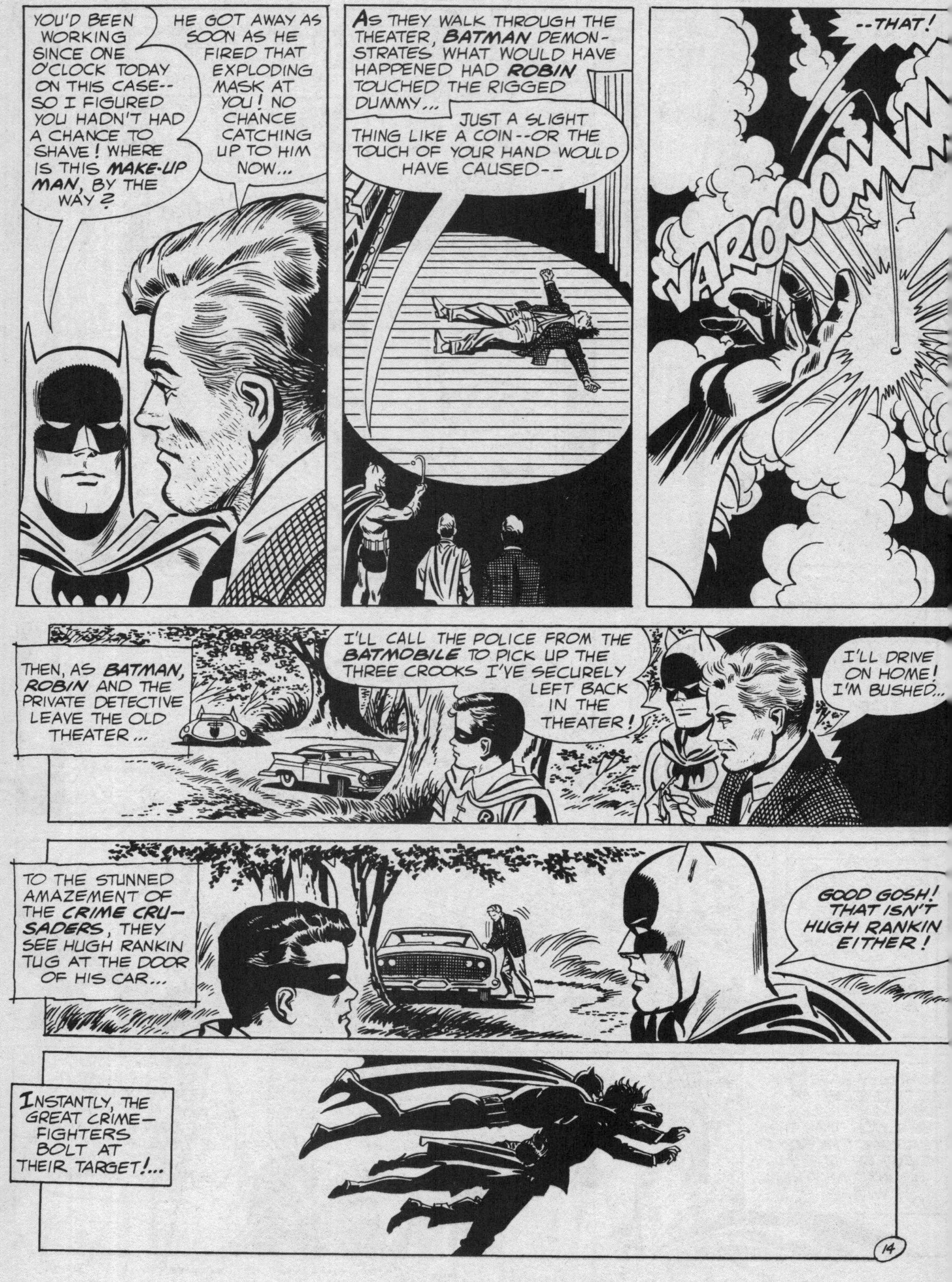
YOU'D BEEN WORKING SINCE ONE O'CLOCK TODAY ON THIS CASE-- SO I FIGURED YOU HADN'T HAD A CHANCE TO SHAVE! WHERE IS THIS MAKE-UP MAN, BY THE WAY?
HE GOT AWAY AS SOON AS HE FIRED THAT EXPLODING MASK AT YOU! NO CHANCE CATCHING UP TO HIM NOW...
AS THEY WALK THROUGH THE THEATER, BATMAN DEMONSTRATES WHAT WOULD HAVE HAPPENED HAD ROBIN TOUCHED THE RIGGED DUMMY...
JUST A SLIGHT THING LIKE A COIN--OR THE TOUCH OF YOUR HAND WOULD HAVE CAUSED--
--THAT!
VAROOOM
THEN, AS BATMAN, ROBIN AND THE PRIVATE DETECTIVE LEAVE THE OLD THEATER...
I'LL CALL THE POLICE FROM THE BATMOBILE TO PICK UP THE THREE CROOKS I'VE SECURELY LEFT BACK IN THE THEATER!
I'LL DRIVE ON HOME! I'M BUSHED...
TO THE STUNNED AMAZEMENT OF THE CRIME CRUSADERS, THEY SEE HUGH RANKIN TUG AT THE DOOR OF HIS CAR...
GOOD GOSH! THAT ISN'T HUGH RANKIN EITHER!
INSTANTLY, THE GREAT CRIME-FIGHTERS BOLT AT THEIR TARGET!...
14

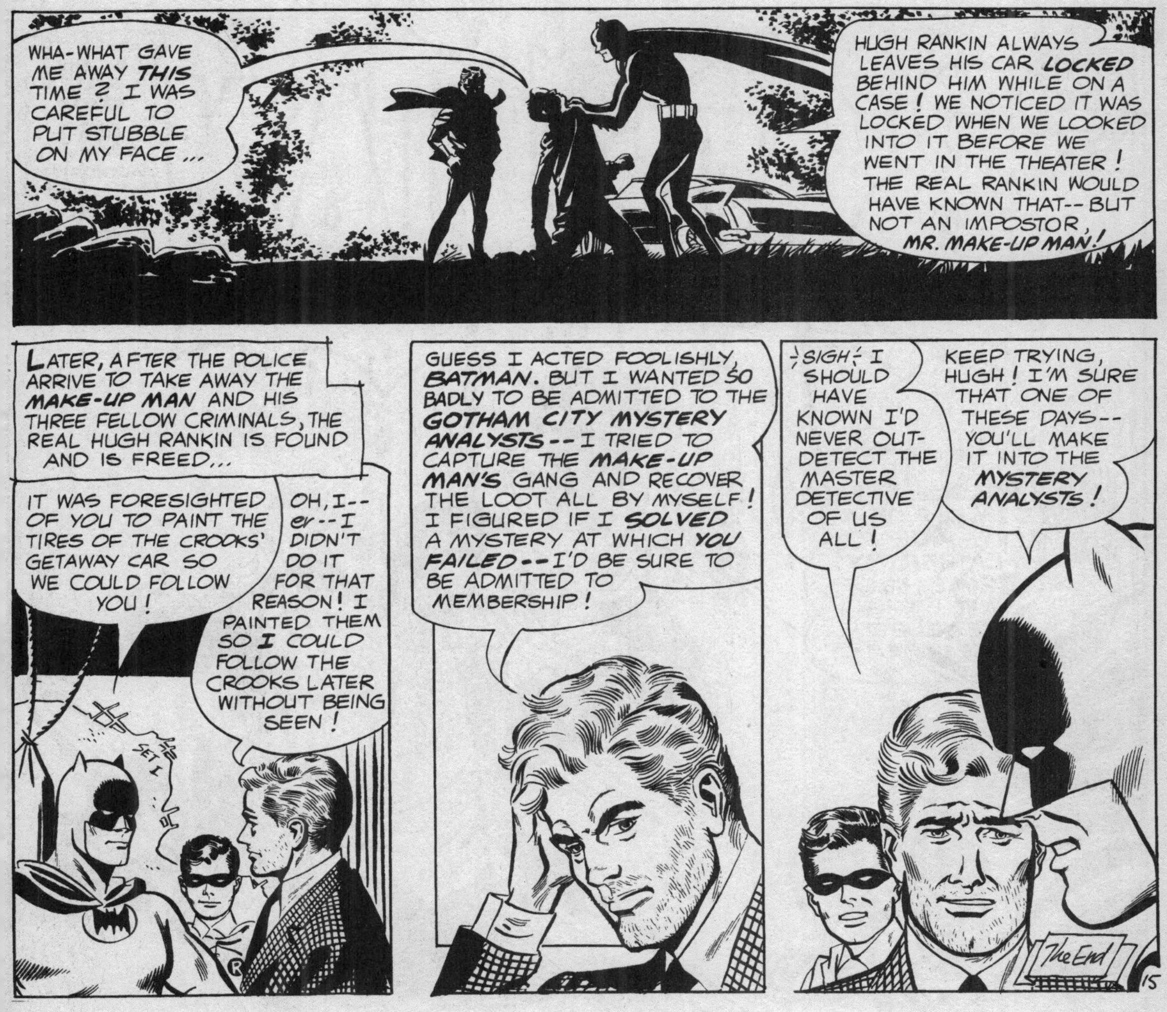
WHA-WHAT GAVE ME AWAY THIS TIME? I WAS CAREFUL TO PUT STUBBLE ON MY FACE...
HUGH RANKIN ALWAYS LEAVES HIS CAR LOCKED BEHIND HIM WHILE ON A CASE! WE NOTICED IT WAS LOCKED WHEN WE LOOKED INTO IT BEFORE WE WENT IN THE THEATER! THE REAL RANKIN WOULD HAVE KNOWN THAT--BUT NOT AN IMPOSTOR, MR. MAKE-UP MAN!
LATER, AFTER THE POLICE ARRIVE TO TAKE AWAY THE MAKE-UP MAN AND HIS THREE FELLOW CRIMINALS, THE REAL HUGH RANKIN IS FOUND AND IS FREED...
IT WAS FORESIGHTED OF YOU TO PAINT THE TIRES OF THE CROOKS' GETAWAY CAR SO WE COULD FOLLOW YOU!
OH, I-- er--I DIDN'T DO IT FOR THAT REASON! I PAINTED THEM SO I COULD FOLLOW THE CROOKS LATER WITHOUT BEING SEEN!
GUESS I ACTED FOOLISHLY, BATMAN. BUT I WANTED SO BADLY TO BE ADMITTED TO THE GOTHAM CITY MYSTERY ANALYSTS--I TRIED TO CAPTURE THE MAKE-UP MAN'S GANG AND RECOVER THE LOOT ALL BY MYSELF! I FIGURED IF I SOLVED A MYSTERY AT WHICH YOU FAILED--I'D BE SURE TO BE ADMITTED TO MEMBERSHIP!
-SIGH- I SHOULD HAVE KNOWN I'D NEVER OUT-DETECT THE MASTER DETECTIVE OF US ALL!
KEEP TRYING, HUGH! I'M SURE THAT ONE OF THESE DAYS--YOU'LL MAKE IT INTO THE MYSTERY ANALYSTS!
The End
15

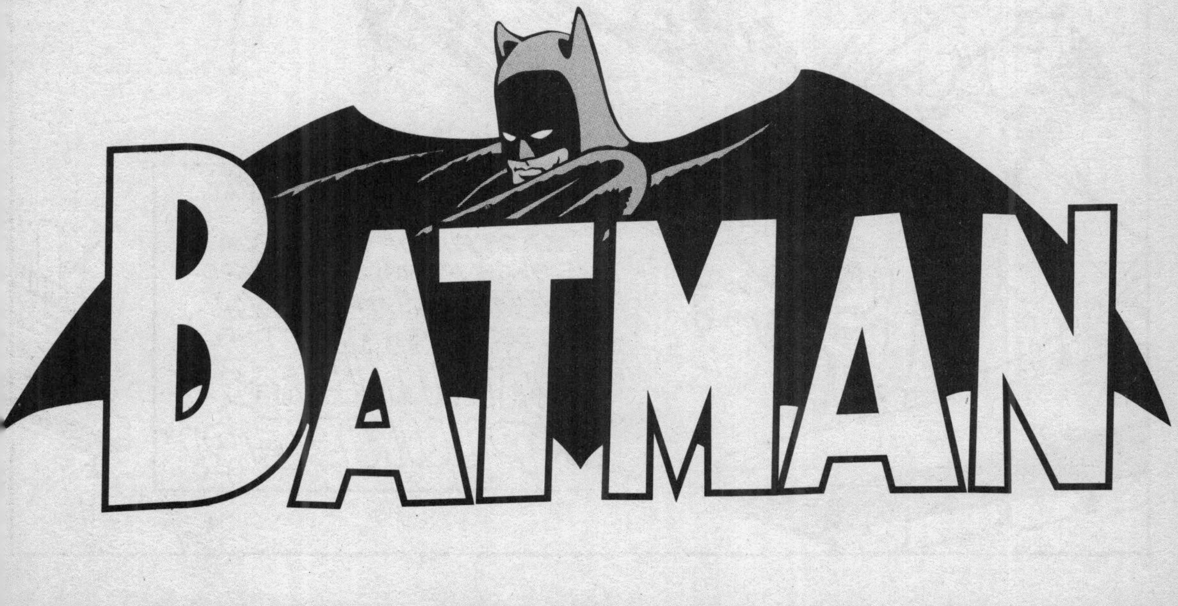
BATMAN

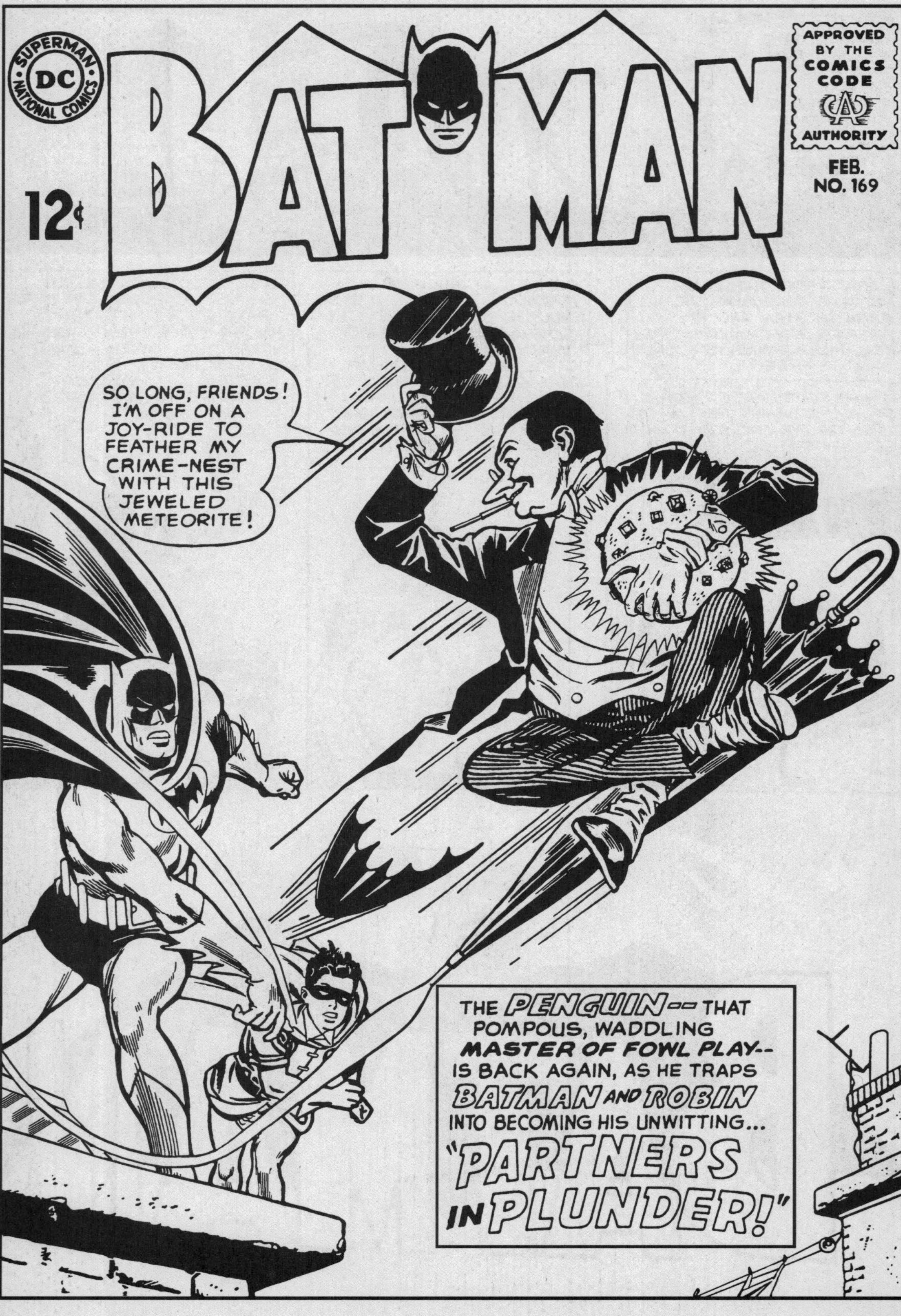
SUPERMAN DC NATIONAL COMICS
BATMAN
APPROVED BY THE COMICS CODE AUTHORITY
FEB. NO. 169
12¢
SO LONG, FRIENDS! I'M OFF ON A JOY-RIDE TO FEATHER MY CRIME-NEST WITH THIS JEWELED METEORITE!
THE PENGUIN-- THAT POMPOUS, WADDLING MASTER OF FOWL PLAY-- IS BACK AGAIN, AS HE TRAPS BATMAN AND ROBIN INTO BECOMING HIS UNWITTING... "PARTNERS IN PLUNDER!"

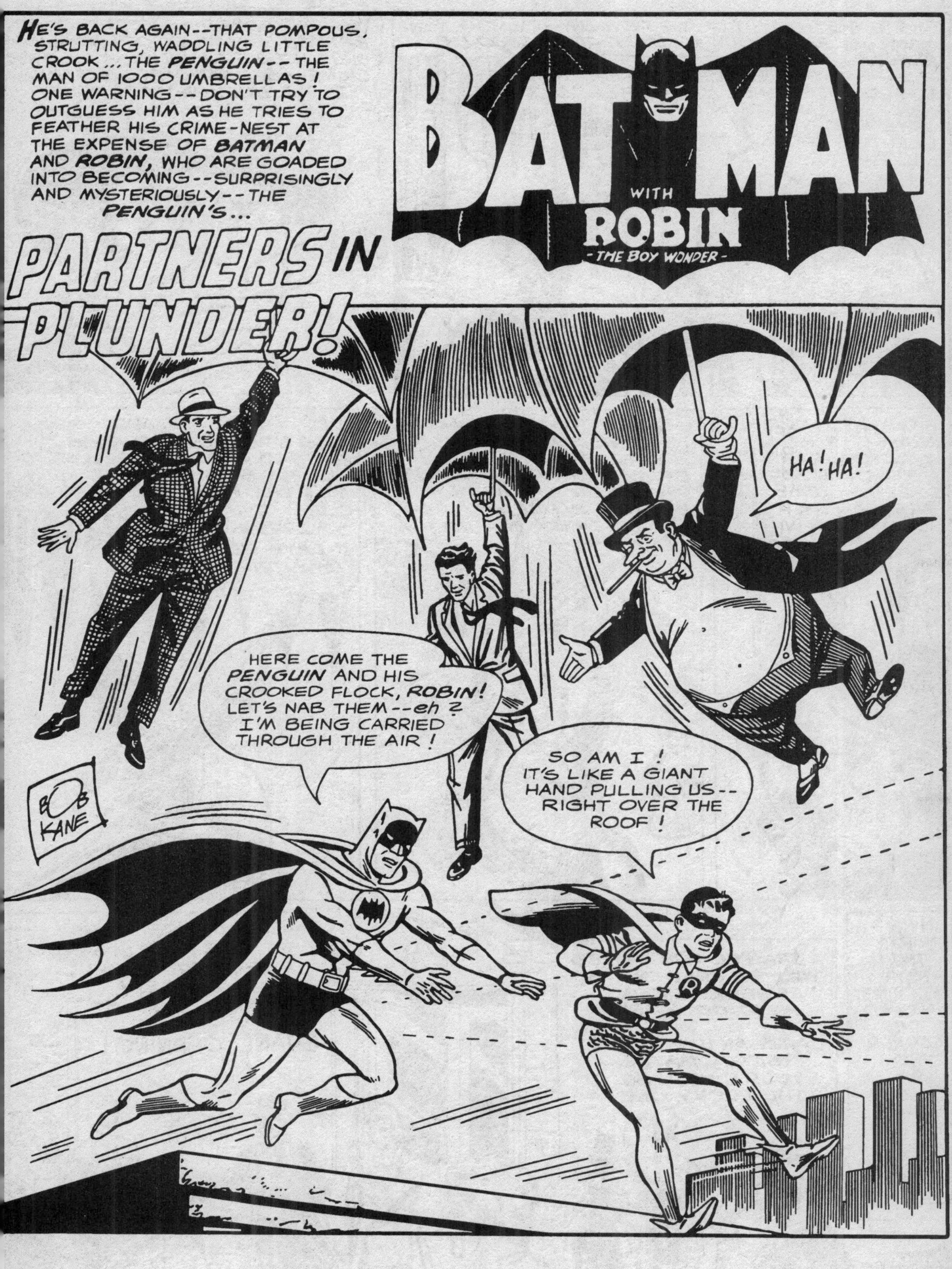
HE'S BACK AGAIN--THAT POMPOUS, STRUTTING, WADDLING LITTLE CROOK... THE PENGUIN--THE MAN OF 1000 UMBRELLAS! ONE WARNING--DON'T TRY TO OUTGUESS HIM AS HE TRIES TO FEATHER HIS CRIME-NEST AT THE EXPENSE OF BATMAN AND ROBIN, WHO ARE GOADED INTO BECOMING--SURPRISINGLY AND MYSTERIOUSLY--THE PENGUIN'S...
PARTNERS IN PLUNDER!
BATMAN
WITH ROBIN
-THE BOY WONDER-
HA! HA!
HERE COME THE PENGUIN AND HIS CROOKED FLOCK, ROBIN! LET'S NAB THEM--eh? I'M BEING CARRIED THROUGH THE AIR!
SO AM I! IT'S LIKE A GIANT HAND PULLING US--RIGHT OVER THE ROOF!
BOB KANE

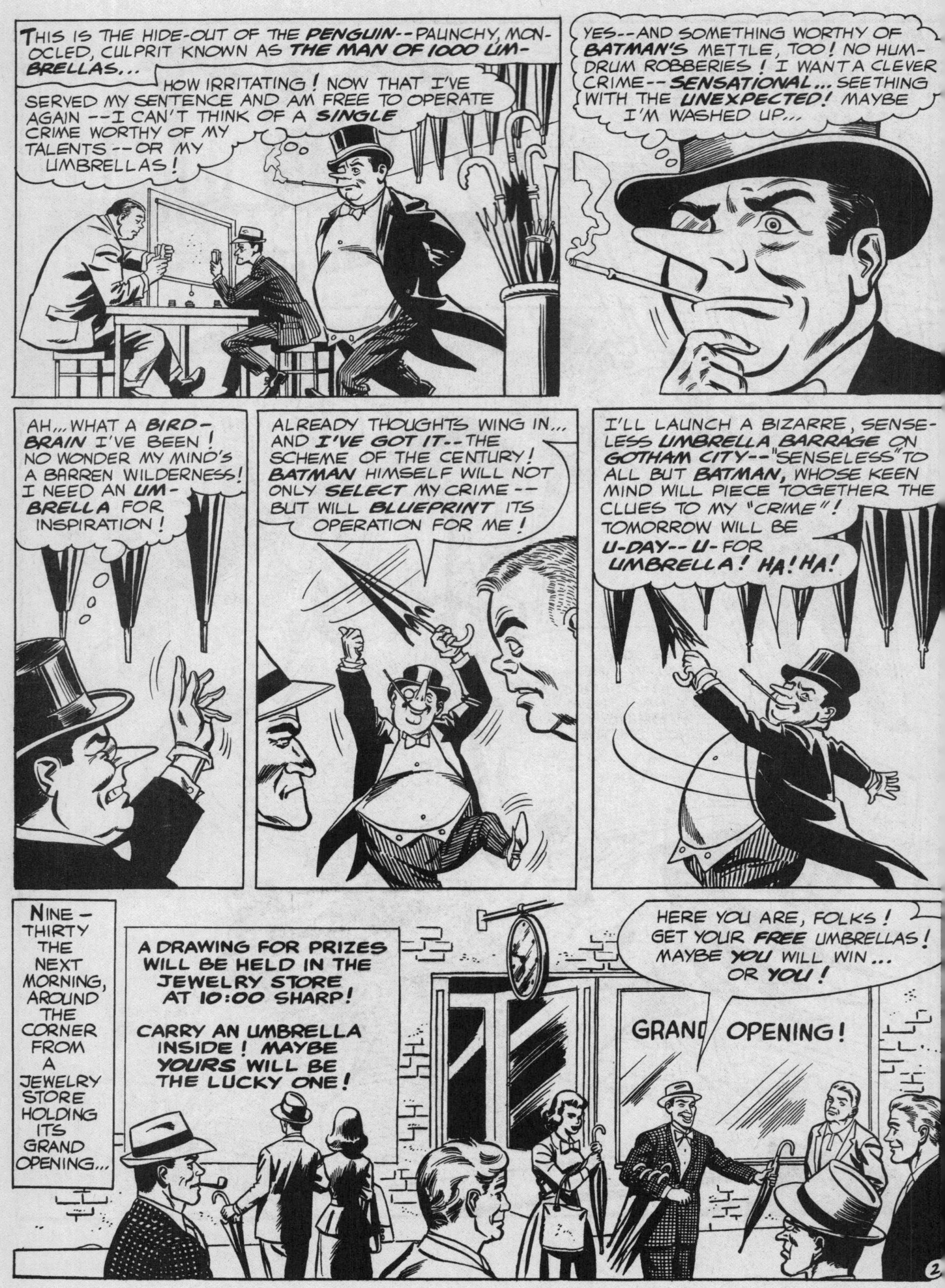
THIS IS THE HIDE-OUT OF THE PENGUIN--PAUNCHY, MONOCLED, CULPRIT KNOWN AS THE MAN OF 1000 UMBRELLAS...
HOW IRRITATING! NOW THAT I'VE SERVED MY SENTENCE AND AM FREE TO OPERATE AGAIN --I CAN'T THINK OF A SINGLE CRIME WORTHY OF MY TALENTS --OR MY UMBRELLAS!
YES--AND SOMETHING WORTHY OF BATMAN'S METTLE, TOO! NO HUMDRUM ROBBERIES! I WANT A CLEVER CRIME--SENSATIONAL... SEETHING WITH THE UNEXPECTED! MAYBE I'M WASHED UP...
AH... WHAT A BIRD-BRAIN I'VE BEEN! NO WONDER MY MIND'S A BARREN WILDERNESS! I NEED AN UMBRELLA FOR INSPIRATION!
ALREADY THOUGHTS WING IN... AND I'VE GOT IT--THE SCHEME OF THE CENTURY! BATMAN HIMSELF WILL NOT ONLY SELECT MY CRIME--BUT WILL BLUEPRINT ITS OPERATION FOR ME!
I'LL LAUNCH A BIZARRE, SENSELESS UMBRELLA BARRAGE ON GOTHAM CITY--"SENSELESS" TO ALL BUT BATMAN, WHOSE KEEN MIND WILL PIECE TOGETHER THE CLUES TO MY "CRIME"! TOMORROW WILL BE U-DAY--U-FOR UMBRELLA! HA! HA!
NINE-THIRTY THE NEXT MORNING, AROUND THE CORNER FROM A JEWELRY STORE HOLDING ITS GRAND OPENING...
A DRAWING FOR PRIZES WILL BE HELD IN THE JEWELRY STORE AT 10:00 SHARP!
CARRY AN UMBRELLA INSIDE! MAYBE YOURS WILL BE THE LUCKY ONE!
GRAND OPENING!
HERE YOU ARE, FOLKS! GET YOUR FREE UMBRELLAS! MAYBE YOU WILL WIN... OR YOU!
2

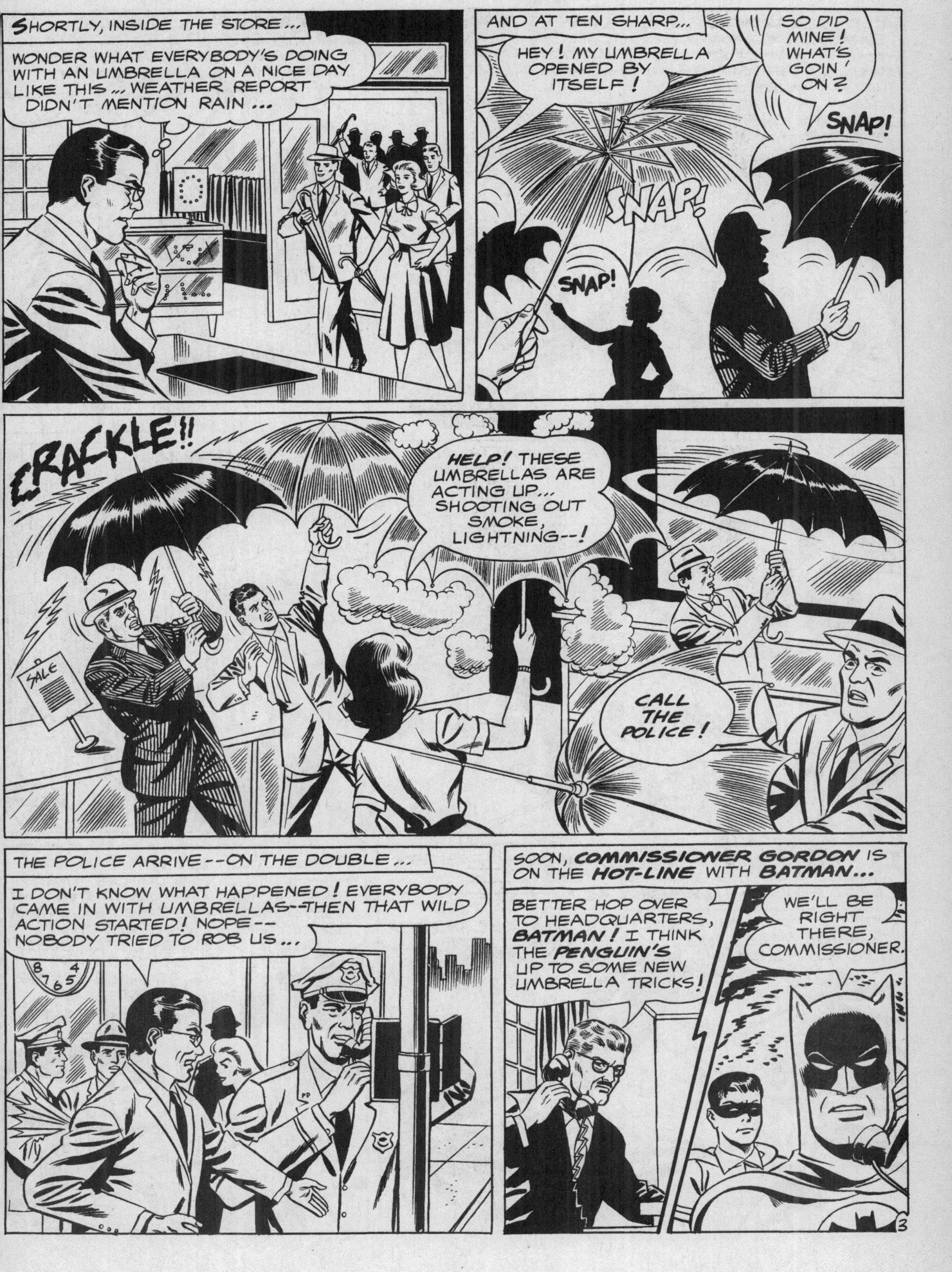
SHORTLY, INSIDE THE STORE...
WONDER WHAT EVERYBODY'S DOING WITH AN UMBRELLA ON A NICE DAY LIKE THIS... WEATHER REPORT DIDN'T MENTION RAIN...
AND AT TEN SHARP...
HEY! MY UMBRELLA OPENED BY ITSELF!
SO DID MINE! WHAT'S GOIN' ON?
SNAP!
SNAP!
SNAP!
CRACKLE!!
HELP! THESE UMBRELLAS ARE ACTING UP... SHOOTING OUT SMOKE, LIGHTNING--!
SALE
CALL THE POLICE!
THE POLICE ARRIVE--ON THE DOUBLE...
I DON'T KNOW WHAT HAPPENED! EVERYBODY CAME IN WITH UMBRELLAS--THEN THAT WILD ACTION STARTED! NOPE-- NOBODY TRIED TO ROB US...
SOON, COMMISSIONER GORDON IS ON THE HOT-LINE WITH BATMAN...
BETTER HOP OVER TO HEADQUARTERS, BATMAN! I THINK THE PENGUIN'S UP TO SOME NEW UMBRELLA TRICKS!
WE'LL BE RIGHT THERE, COMMISSIONER.
3

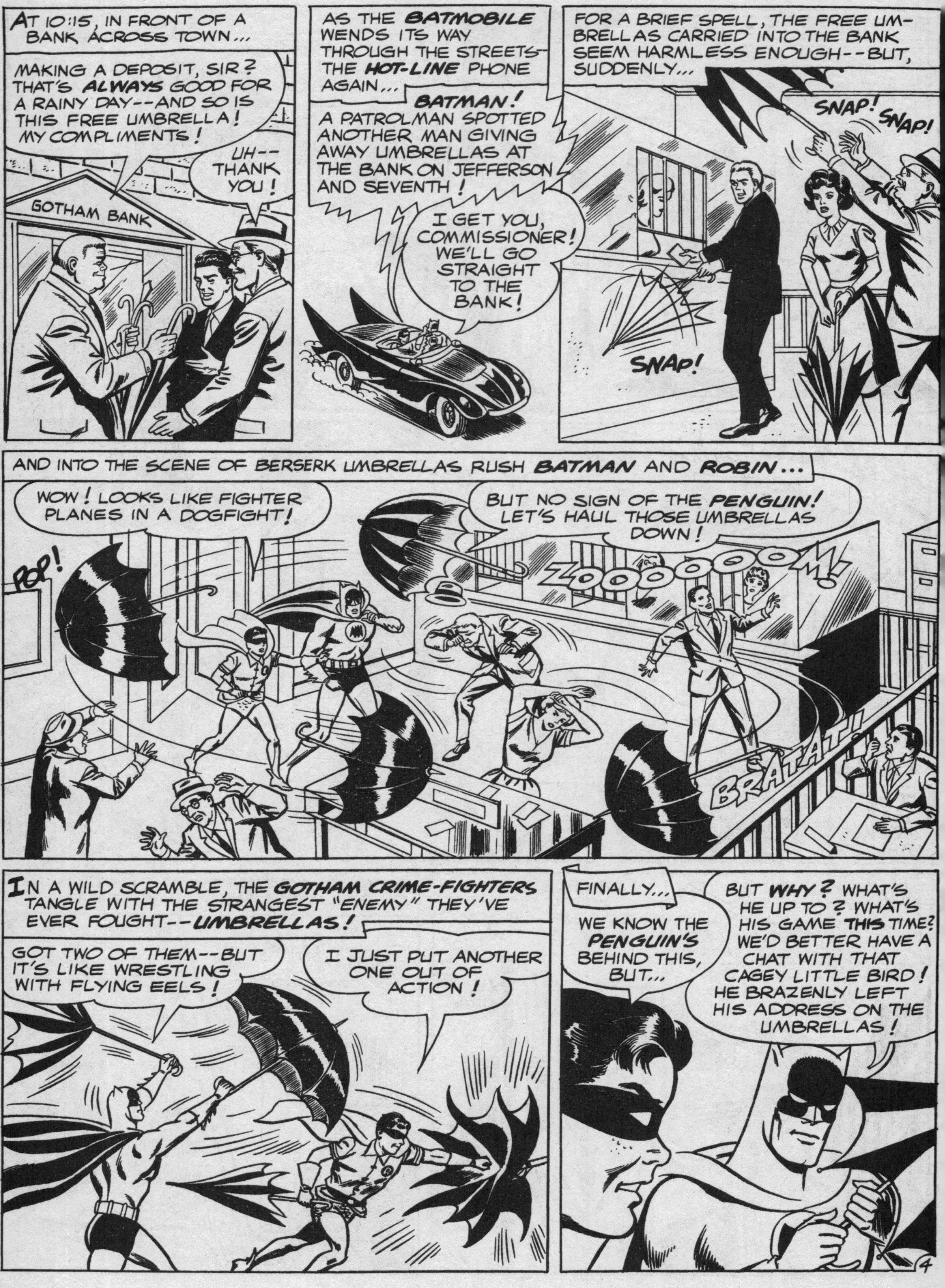
AT 10:15, IN FRONT OF A BANK ACROSS TOWN...
MAKING A DEPOSIT, SIR? THAT'S ALWAYS GOOD FOR A RAINY DAY--AND SO IS THIS FREE UMBRELLA! MY COMPLIMENTS!
UH--THANK YOU!
GOTHAM BANK
AS THE BATMOBILE WENDS ITS WAY THROUGH THE STREETS-THE HOT-LINE PHONE AGAIN...
BATMAN! A PATROLMAN SPOTTED ANOTHER MAN GIVING AWAY UMBRELLAS AT THE BANK ON JEFFERSON AND SEVENTH!
I GET YOU, COMMISSIONER! WE'LL GO STRAIGHT TO THE BANK!
FOR A BRIEF SPELL, THE FREE UMBRELLAS CARRIED INTO THE BANK SEEM HARMLESS ENOUGH--BUT, SUDDENLY...
SNAP! SNAP!
SNAP!
AND INTO THE SCENE OF BERSERK UMBRELLAS RUSH BATMAN AND ROBIN...
WOW! LOOKS LIKE FIGHTER PLANES IN A DOGFIGHT!
BUT NO SIGN OF THE PENGUIN! LET'S HAUL THOSE UMBRELLAS DOWN!
POP!
ZOOOOOOOM!
BRATAT!
IN A WILD SCRAMBLE, THE GOTHAM CRIME-FIGHTERS TANGLE WITH THE STRANGEST "ENEMY" THEY'VE EVER FOUGHT--UMBRELLAS!
GOT TWO OF THEM--BUT IT'S LIKE WRESTLING WITH FLYING EELS!
I JUST PUT ANOTHER ONE OUT OF ACTION!
FINALLY...
WE KNOW THE PENGUIN'S BEHIND THIS, BUT...
BUT WHY? WHAT'S HE UP TO? WHAT'S HIS GAME THIS TIME? WE'D BETTER HAVE A CHAT WITH THAT CAGEY LITTLE BIRD! HE BRAZENLY LEFT HIS ADDRESS ON THE UMBRELLAS!
4

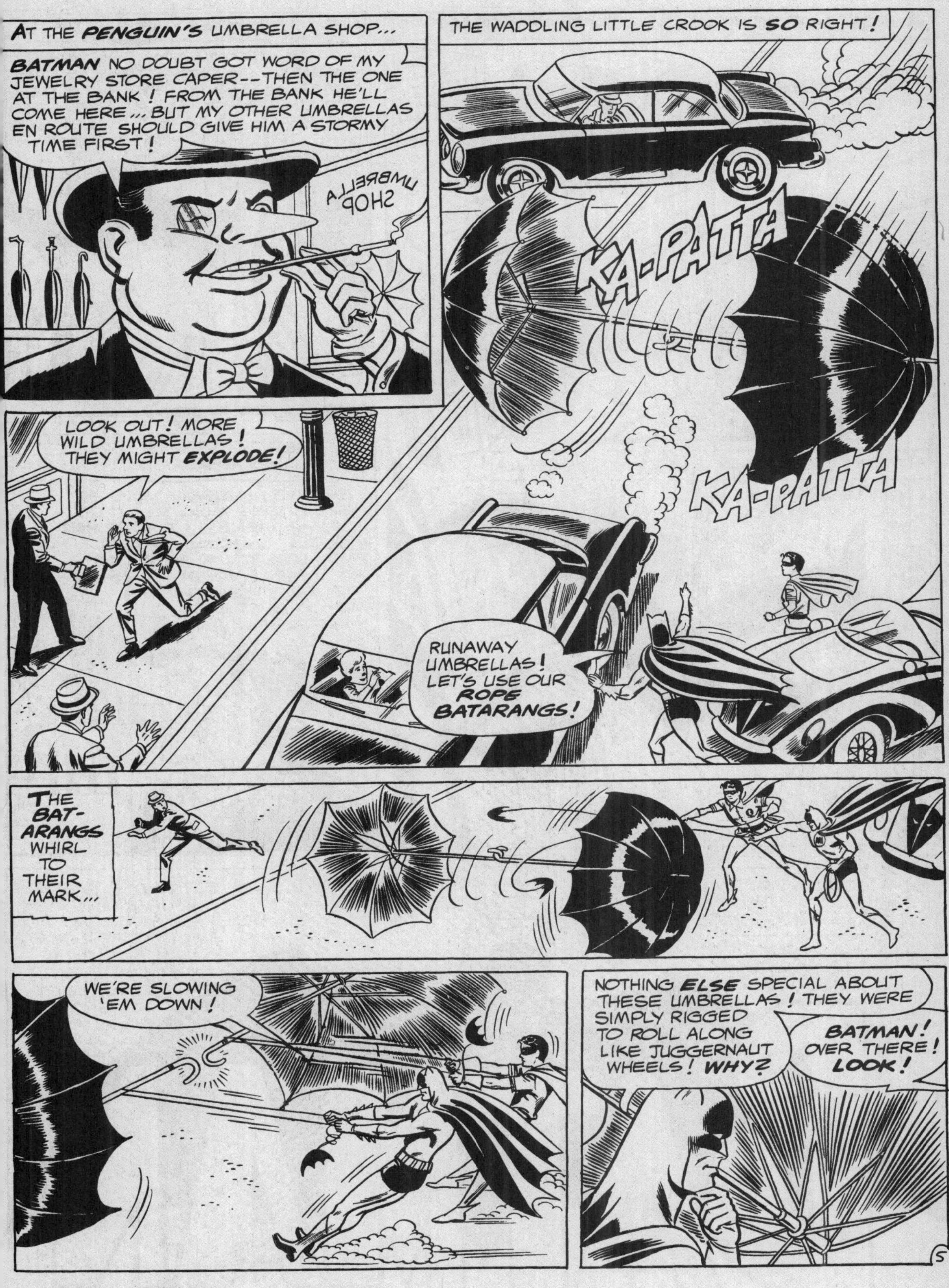
AT THE PENGUIN'S UMBRELLA SHOP...
BATMAN NO DOUBT GOT WORD OF MY JEWELRY STORE CAPER--THEN THE ONE AT THE BANK! FROM THE BANK HE'LL COME HERE... BUT MY OTHER UMBRELLAS EN ROUTE SHOULD GIVE HIM A STORMY TIME FIRST!
UMBRELLA SHOP
THE WADDLING LITTLE CROOK IS SO RIGHT!
KA-PATTA
KA-PATTA
LOOK OUT! MORE WILD UMBRELLAS! THEY MIGHT EXPLODE!
RUNAWAY UMBRELLAS! LET'S USE OUR ROPE BATARANGS!
THE BAT-ARANGS WHIRL TO THEIR MARK...
WE'RE SLOWING 'EM DOWN!
NOTHING ELSE SPECIAL ABOUT THESE UMBRELLAS! THEY WERE SIMPLY RIGGED TO ROLL ALONG LIKE JUGGERNAUT WHEELS! WHY?
BATMAN! OVER THERE! LOOK!
5

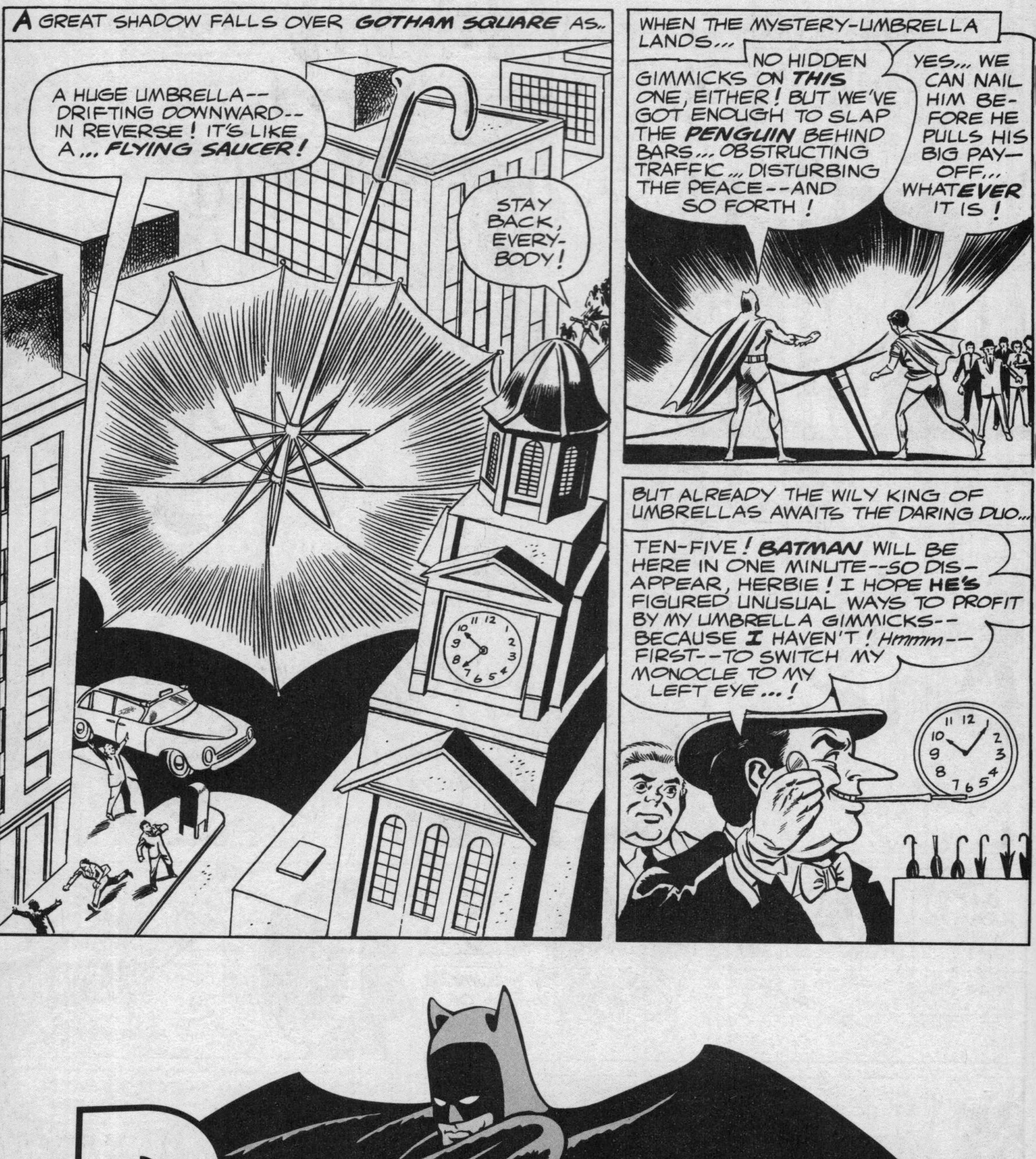
A GREAT SHADOW FALLS OVER GOTHAM SQUARE AS..
A HUGE UMBRELLA-- DRIFTING DOWNWARD-- IN REVERSE! IT'S LIKE A... FLYING SAUCER!
STAY BACK, EVERYBODY!
WHEN THE MYSTERY-UMBRELLA LANDS...
NO HIDDEN GIMMICKS ON THIS ONE, EITHER! BUT WE'VE GOT ENOUGH TO SLAP THE PENGUIN BEHIND BARS... OBSTRUCTING TRAFFIC... DISTURBING THE PEACE--AND SO FORTH!
YES... WE CAN NAIL HIM BEFORE HE PULLS HIS BIG PAY-OFF... WHATEVER IT IS!
BUT ALREADY THE WILY KING OF UMBRELLAS AWAITS THE DARING DUO...
TEN-FIVE! BATMAN WILL BE HERE IN ONE MINUTE--SO DISAPPEAR, HERBIE! I HOPE HE'S FIGURED UNUSUAL WAYS TO PROFIT BY MY UMBRELLA GIMMICKS--BECAUSE I HAVEN'T! Hmmm--FIRST--TO SWITCH MY MONOCLE TO MY LEFT EYE...!

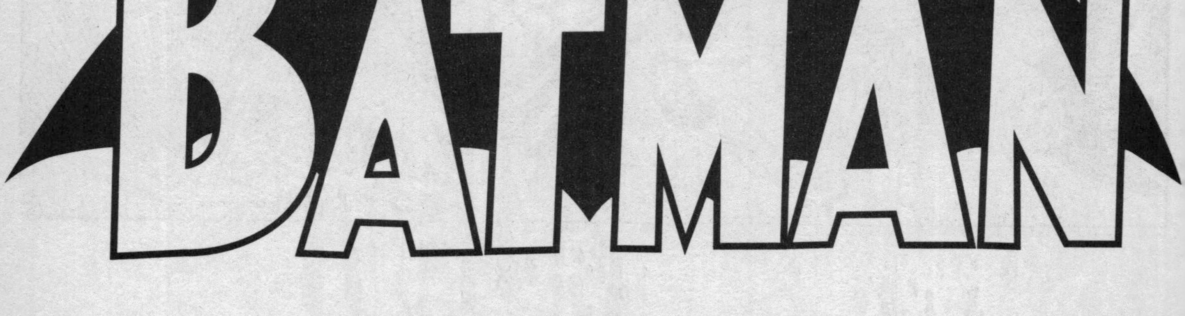
BATMAN

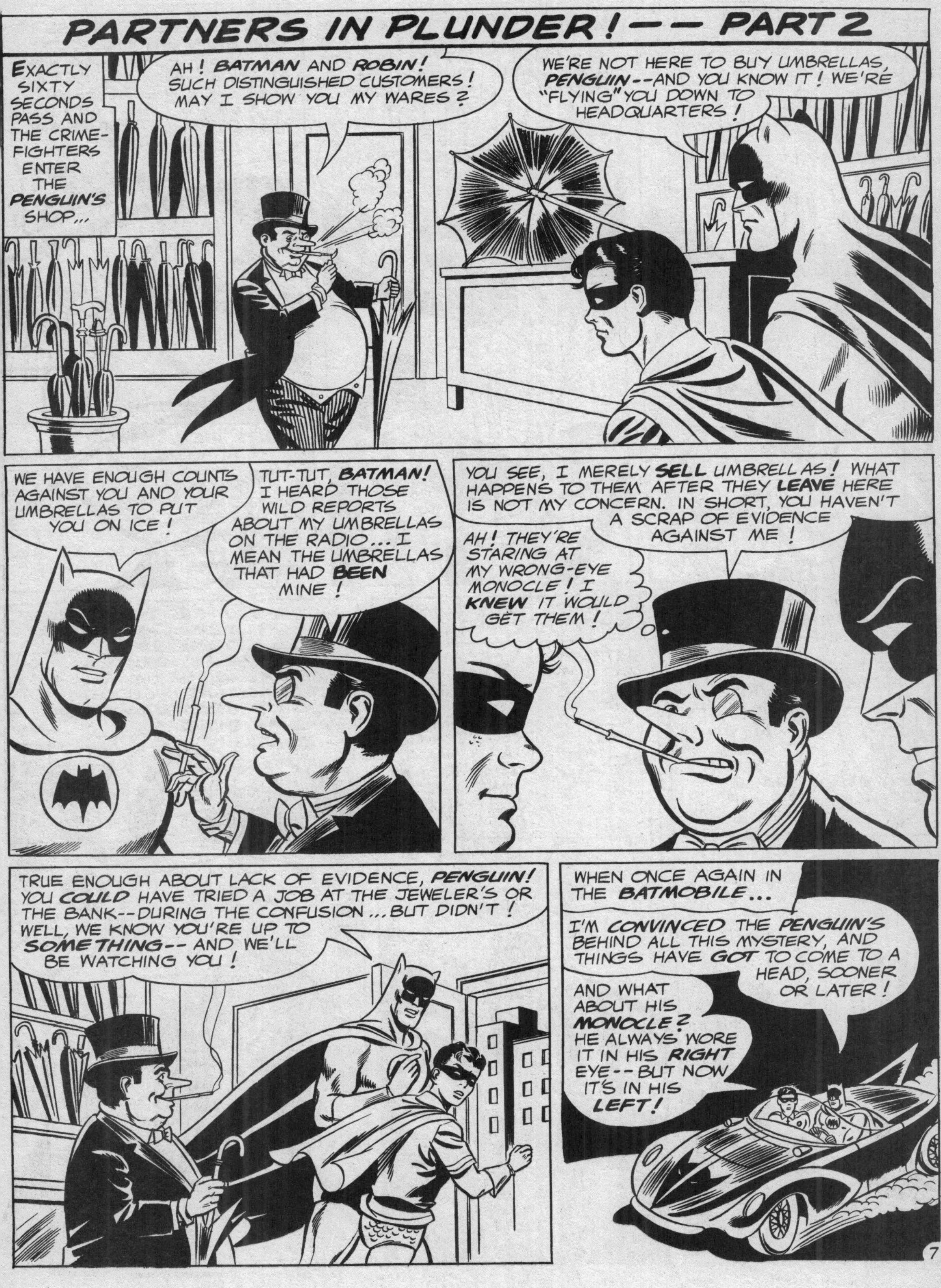
PARTNERS IN PLUNDER! -- PART 2
EXACTLY SIXTY SECONDS PASS AND THE CRIME-FIGHTERS ENTER THE PENGUIN'S SHOP...
AH! BATMAN AND ROBIN! SUCH DISTINGUISHED CUSTOMERS! MAY I SHOW YOU MY WARES?
WE'RE NOT HERE TO BUY UMBRELLAS, PENGUIN--AND YOU KNOW IT! WE'RE "FLYING" YOU DOWN TO HEADQUARTERS!
WE HAVE ENOUGH COUNTS AGAINST YOU AND YOUR UMBRELLAS TO PUT YOU ON ICE!
TUT-TUT, BATMAN! I HEARD THOSE WILD REPORTS ABOUT MY UMBRELLAS ON THE RADIO... I MEAN THE UMBRELLAS THAT HAD BEEN MINE!
YOU SEE, I MERELY SELL UMBRELLAS! WHAT HAPPENS TO THEM AFTER THEY LEAVE HERE IS NOT MY CONCERN. IN SHORT, YOU HAVEN'T A SCRAP OF EVIDENCE AGAINST ME!
AH! THEY'RE STARING AT MY WRONG-EYE MONOCLE! I KNEW IT WOULD GET THEM!
TRUE ENOUGH ABOUT LACK OF EVIDENCE, PENGUIN! YOU COULD HAVE TRIED A JOB AT THE JEWELER'S OR THE BANK--DURING THE CONFUSION... BUT DIDN'T! WELL, WE KNOW YOU'RE UP TO SOMETHING-- AND WE'LL BE WATCHING YOU!
WHEN ONCE AGAIN IN THE BATMOBILE...
I'M CONVINCED THE PENGUIN'S BEHIND ALL THIS MYSTERY, AND THINGS HAVE GOT TO COME TO A HEAD, SOONER OR LATER!
AND WHAT ABOUT HIS MONOCLE? HE ALWAYS WORE IT IN HIS RIGHT EYE--BUT NOW IT'S IN HIS LEFT!
7

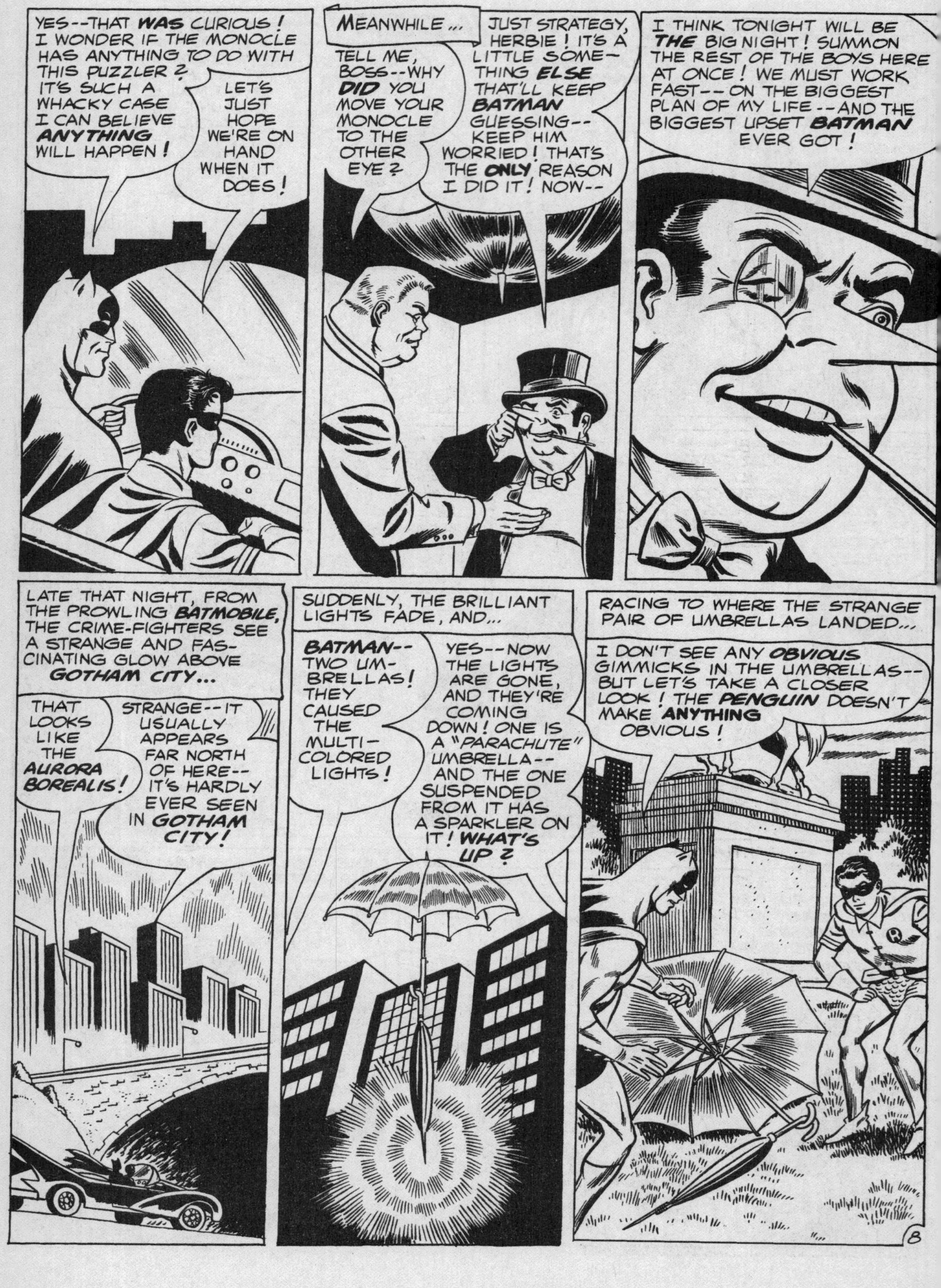
YES--THAT WAS CURIOUS! I WONDER IF THE MONOCLE HAS ANYTHING TO DO WITH THIS PUZZLER? IT'S SUCH A WHACKY CASE I CAN BELIEVE ANYTHING WILL HAPPEN!
LET'S JUST HOPE WE'RE ON HAND WHEN IT DOES!
MEANWHILE...
TELL ME, BOSS--WHY DID YOU MOVE YOUR MONOCLE TO THE OTHER EYE?
JUST STRATEGY, HERBIE! IT'S A LITTLE SOMETHING ELSE THAT'LL KEEP BATMAN GUESSING--KEEP HIM WORRIED! THAT'S THE ONLY REASON I DID IT! NOW--
I THINK TONIGHT WILL BE THE BIG NIGHT! SUMMON THE REST OF THE BOYS HERE AT ONCE! WE MUST WORK FAST--ON THE BIGGEST PLAN OF MY LIFE--AND THE BIGGEST UPSET BATMAN EVER GOT!
LATE THAT NIGHT, FROM THE PROWLING BATMOBILE, THE CRIME-FIGHTERS SEE A STRANGE AND FASCINATING GLOW ABOVE GOTHAM CITY...
THAT LOOKS LIKE THE AURORA BOREALIS!
STRANGE--IT USUALLY APPEARS FAR NORTH OF HERE--IT'S HARDLY EVER SEEN IN GOTHAM CITY!
SUDDENLY, THE BRILLIANT LIGHTS FADE, AND...
BATMAN--TWO UMBRELLAS! THEY CAUSED THE MULTI-COLORED LIGHTS!
YES--NOW THE LIGHTS ARE GONE, AND THEY'RE COMING DOWN! ONE IS A "PARACHUTE" UMBRELLA--AND THE ONE SUSPENDED FROM IT HAS A SPARKLER ON IT! WHAT'S UP?
RACING TO WHERE THE STRANGE PAIR OF UMBRELLAS LANDED...
I DON'T SEE ANY OBVIOUS GIMMICKS IN THE UMBRELLAS--BUT LET'S TAKE A CLOSER LOOK! THE PENGUIN DOESN'T MAKE ANYTHING OBVIOUS!
8

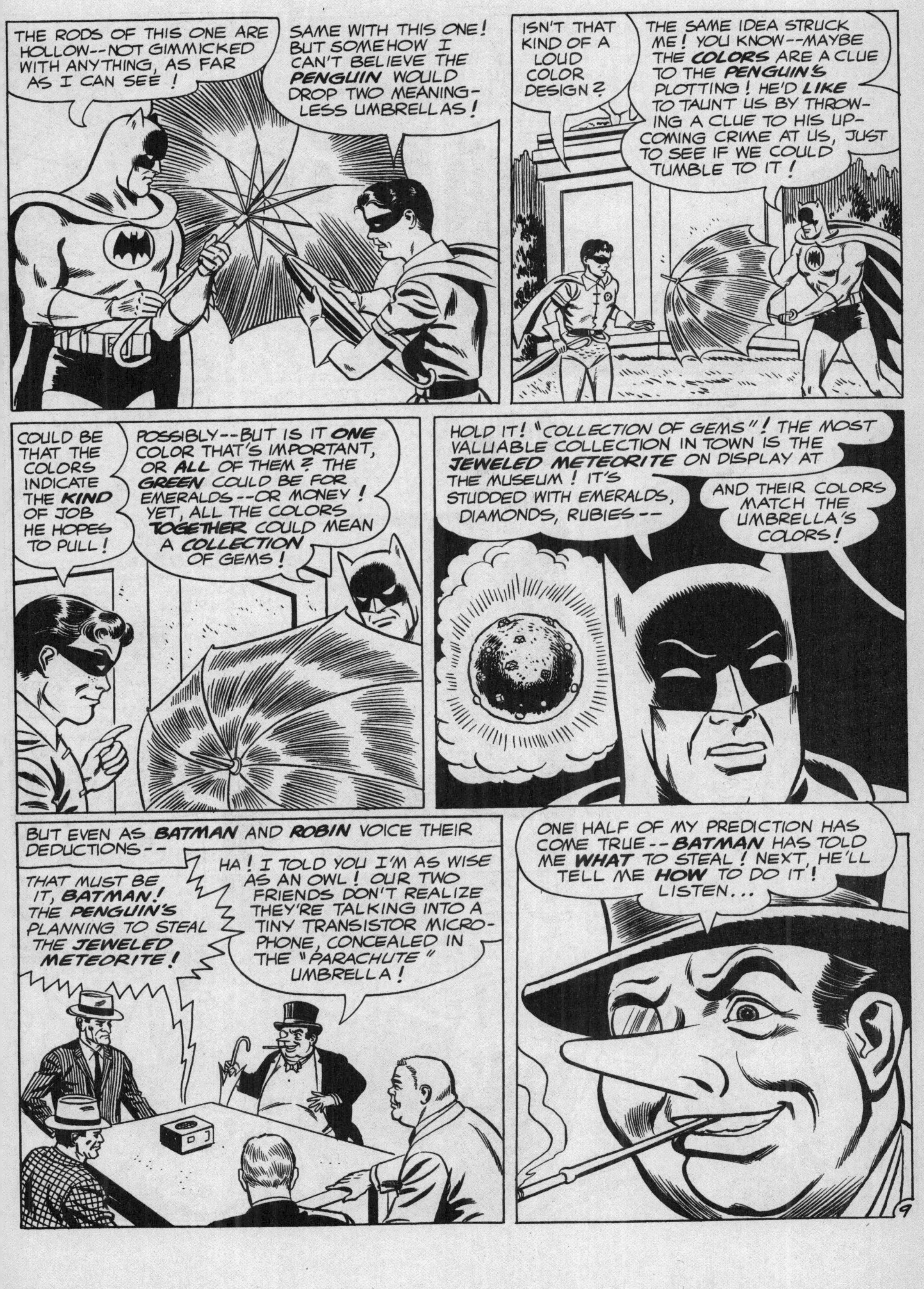
THE RODS OF THIS ONE ARE HOLLOW--NOT GIMMICKED WITH ANYTHING, AS FAR AS I CAN SEE!
SAME WITH THIS ONE! BUT SOMEHOW I CAN'T BELIEVE THE PENGUIN WOULD DROP TWO MEANINGLESS UMBRELLAS!
ISN'T THAT KIND OF A LOUD COLOR DESIGN?
THE SAME IDEA STRUCK ME! YOU KNOW--MAYBE THE COLORS ARE A CLUE TO THE PENGUIN'S PLOTTING! HE'D LIKE TO TAUNT US BY THROWING A CLUE TO HIS UPCOMING CRIME AT US, JUST TO SEE IF WE COULD TUMBLE TO IT!
COULD BE THAT THE COLORS INDICATE THE KIND OF JOB HE HOPES TO PULL!
POSSIBLY--BUT IS IT ONE COLOR THAT'S IMPORTANT, OR ALL OF THEM? THE GREEN COULD BE FOR EMERALDS--OR MONEY! YET, ALL THE COLORS TOGETHER COULD MEAN A COLLECTION OF GEMS!
HOLD IT! "COLLECTION OF GEMS"! THE MOST VALUABLE COLLECTION IN TOWN IS THE JEWELED METEORITE ON DISPLAY AT THE MUSEUM! IT'S STUDDED WITH EMERALDS, DIAMONDS, RUBIES--
AND THEIR COLORS MATCH THE UMBRELLA'S COLORS!
BUT EVEN AS BATMAN AND ROBIN VOICE THEIR DEDUCTIONS--
THAT MUST BE IT, BATMAN! THE PENGUIN'S PLANNING TO STEAL THE JEWELED METEORITE!
HA! I TOLD YOU I'M AS WISE AS AN OWL! OUR TWO FRIENDS DON'T REALIZE THEY'RE TALKING INTO A TINY TRANSISTOR MICROPHONE, CONCEALED IN THE "PARACHUTE" UMBRELLA!
ONE HALF OF MY PREDICTION HAS COME TRUE--BATMAN HAS TOLD ME WHAT TO STEAL! NEXT, HE'LL TELL ME HOW TO DO IT! LISTEN...
9

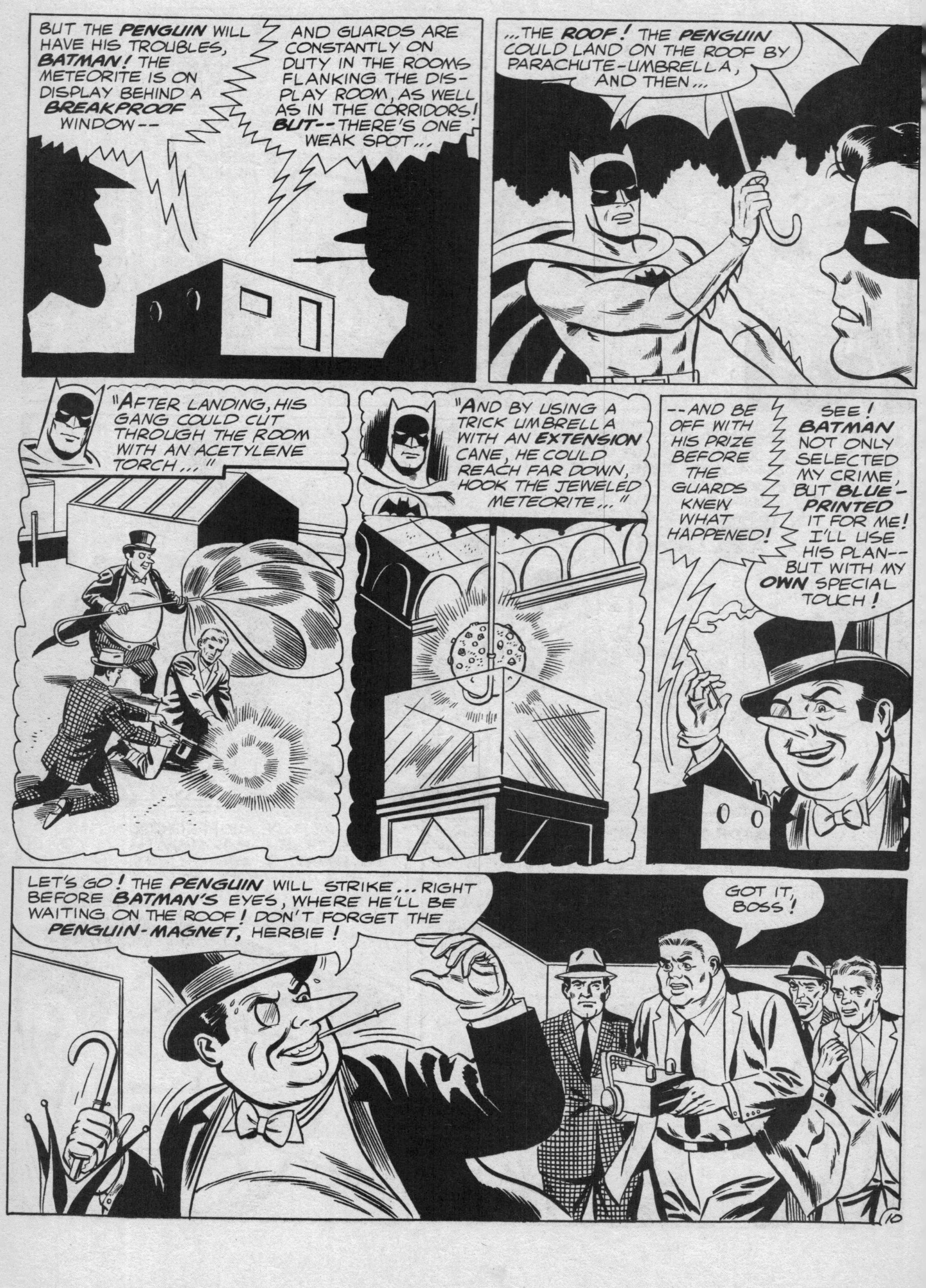
BUT THE PENGUIN WILL HAVE HIS TROUBLES, BATMAN! THE METEORITE IS ON DISPLAY BEHIND A BREAKPROOF WINDOW--
AND GUARDS ARE CONSTANTLY ON DUTY IN THE ROOMS FLANKING THE DISPLAY ROOM, AS WELL AS IN THE CORRIDORS! BUT--THERE'S ONE WEAK SPOT...
...THE ROOF! THE PENGUIN COULD LAND ON THE ROOF BY PARACHUTE-UMBRELLA, AND THEN...
"AFTER LANDING, HIS GANG COULD CUT THROUGH THE ROOM WITH AN ACETYLENE TORCH..."
"AND BY USING A TRICK UMBRELLA WITH AN EXTENSION CANE, HE COULD REACH FAR DOWN, HOOK THE JEWELED METEORITE..."
--AND BE OFF WITH HIS PRIZE BEFORE THE GUARDS KNEW WHAT HAPPENED!
SEE! BATMAN NOT ONLY SELECTED MY CRIME, BUT BLUE-PRINTED IT FOR ME! I'LL USE HIS PLAN--BUT WITH MY OWN SPECIAL TOUCH!
LET'S GO! THE PENGUIN WILL STRIKE... RIGHT BEFORE BATMAN'S EYES, WHERE HE'LL BE WAITING ON THE ROOF! DON'T FORGET THE PENGUIN-MAGNET, HERBIE!
GOT IT, BOSS!
10

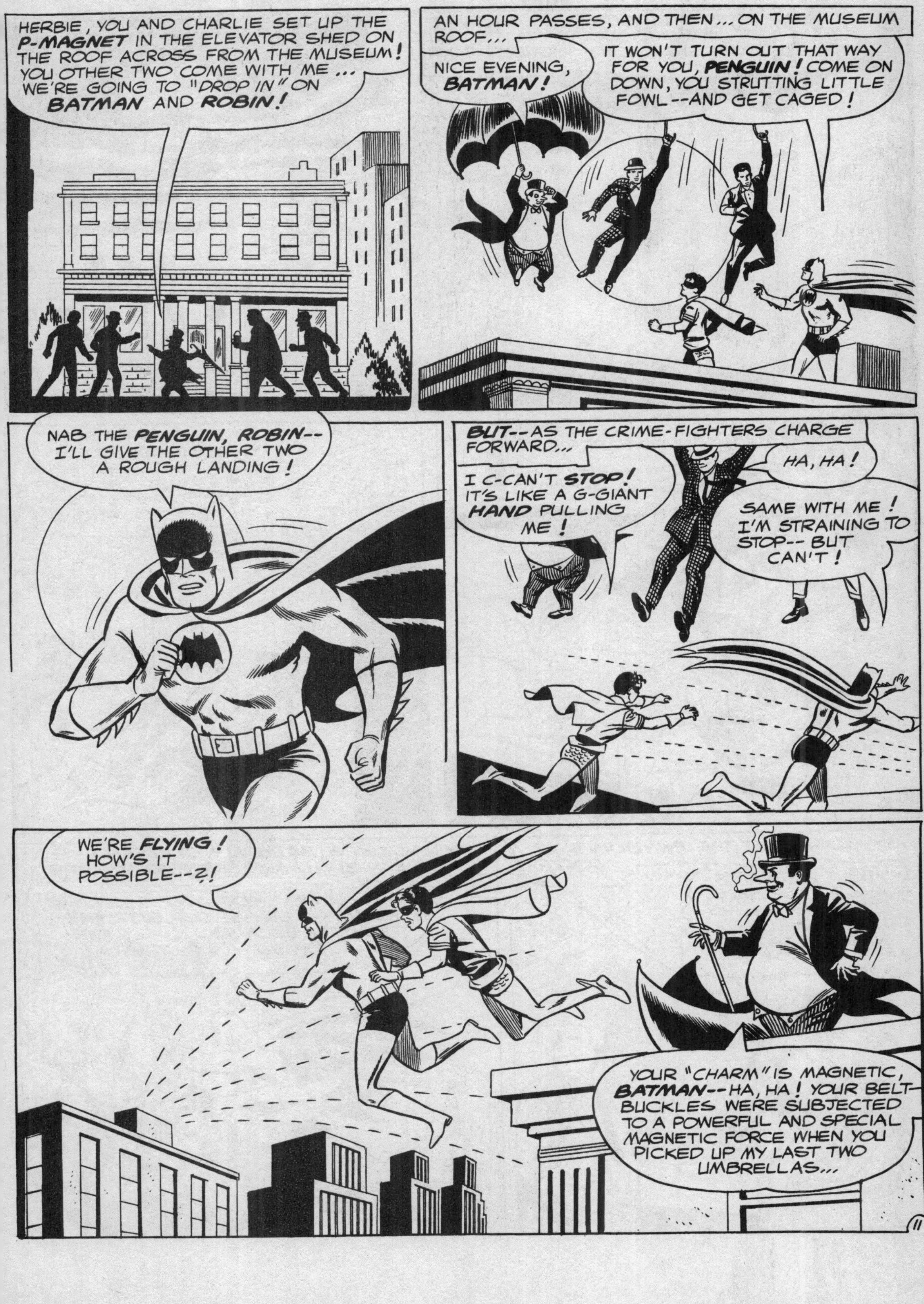
HERBIE, YOU AND CHARLIE SET UP THE P-MAGNET IN THE ELEVATOR SHED ON THE ROOF ACROSS FROM THE MUSEUM! YOU OTHER TWO COME WITH ME ... WE'RE GOING TO "DROP IN" ON BATMAN AND ROBIN!
AN HOUR PASSES, AND THEN... ON THE MUSEUM ROOF...
NICE EVENING, BATMAN!
IT WON'T TURN OUT THAT WAY FOR YOU, PENGUIN! COME ON DOWN, YOU STRUTTING LITTLE FOWL--AND GET CAGED!
NAB THE PENGUIN, ROBIN-- I'LL GIVE THE OTHER TWO A ROUGH LANDING!
BUT--AS THE CRIME-FIGHTERS CHARGE FORWARD...
HA, HA!
I C-CAN'T STOP! IT'S LIKE A G-GIANT HAND PULLING ME!
SAME WITH ME! I'M STRAINING TO STOP-- BUT CAN'T!
WE'RE FLYING! HOW'S IT POSSIBLE--?!
YOUR "CHARM" IS MAGNETIC, BATMAN--HA, HA! YOUR BELT-BUCKLES WERE SUBJECTED TO A POWERFUL AND SPECIAL MAGNETIC FORCE WHEN YOU PICKED UP MY LAST TWO UMBRELLAS...
11

WE WERE ABLE TO TURN ON MY *P-MAGNET* AT ANY TIME, DRAWING YOU TO IT! IT'S INSIDE THE ELEVATOR SHED ACROSS YONDER ROOF!

THAT PESKY *PENGUIN*-- ONE STEP AHEAD OF US AGAIN!

STUCK--LIKE FLIES IN FLYPAPER!

JUST AS WE DEDUCED, THE *PENGUIN'S* USED AN ACETYLENE TORCH TO CUT THROUGH THE ROOF, AND MUST BE PULLING THE JEWELED METEORITE OUT BY NOW! WE'VE *GOT* TO GET LOOSE-- BUT NOT WITH THOSE TWO WATCHING US LIKE HAWKS!

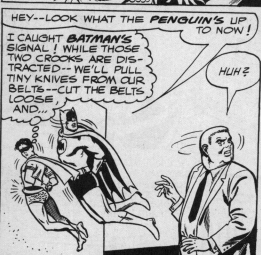

HEY--LOOK WHAT THE *PENGUIN'S* UP TO NOW!

I CAUGHT *BATMAN'S* SIGNAL! WHILE THOSE TWO CROOKS ARE DIS-TRACTED--WE'LL PULL TINY KNIVES FROM OUR BELTS--CUT THE BELTS LOOSE, AND...

HUH?

WITHIN MOMENTS, *BATMAN* AND *ROBIN* HAVE FREED THEMSELVES AND SLAMMED INTO THE TWO CROOKS...

WE'LL COOL OFF THESE TWO, *ROBIN*--THEN GET OUR *BATROPES* FROM THE BELTS AND RUFFLE THE *PENGUIN'S* FEATHERS!

12

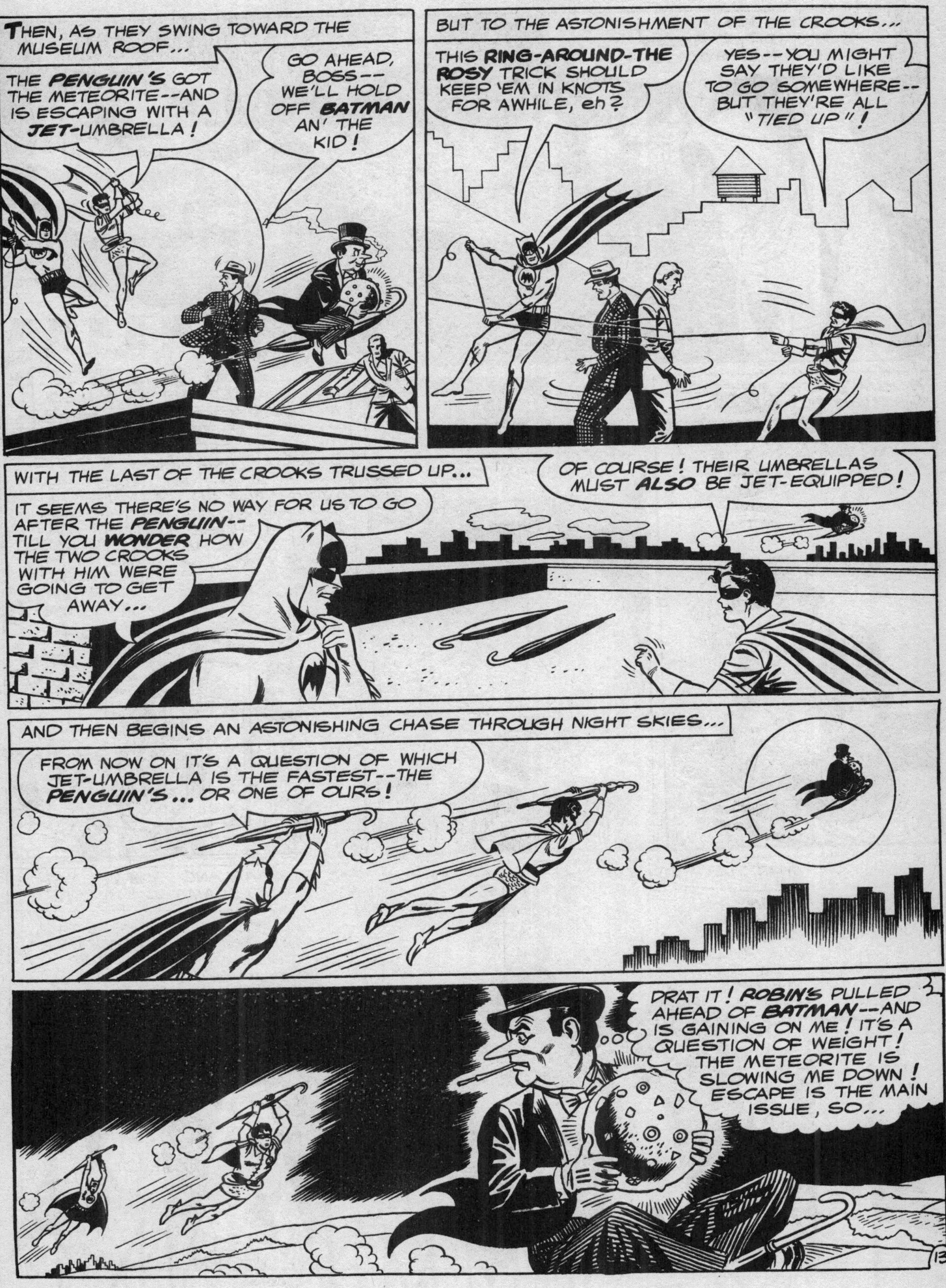
THEN, AS THEY SWING TOWARD THE MUSEUM ROOF...
THE PENGUIN'S GOT THE METEORITE--AND IS ESCAPING WITH A JET-UMBRELLA!
GO AHEAD, BOSS--WE'LL HOLD OFF BATMAN AN' THE KID!
BUT TO THE ASTONISHMENT OF THE CROOKS...
THIS RING-AROUND-THE ROSY TRICK SHOULD KEEP 'EM IN KNOTS FOR AWHILE, eh?
YES--YOU MIGHT SAY THEY'D LIKE TO GO SOMEWHERE--BUT THEY'RE ALL "TIED UP"!
WITH THE LAST OF THE CROOKS TRUSSED UP...
IT SEEMS THERE'S NO WAY FOR US TO GO AFTER THE PENGUIN--TILL YOU WONDER HOW THE TWO CROOKS WITH HIM WERE GOING TO GET AWAY...
OF COURSE! THEIR UMBRELLAS MUST ALSO BE JET-EQUIPPED!
AND THEN BEGINS AN ASTONISHING CHASE THROUGH NIGHT SKIES...
FROM NOW ON IT'S A QUESTION OF WHICH JET-UMBRELLA IS THE FASTEST--THE PENGUIN'S... OR ONE OF OURS!
DRAT IT! ROBIN'S PULLED AHEAD OF BATMAN--AND IS GAINING ON ME! IT'S A QUESTION OF WEIGHT! THE METEORITE IS SLOWING ME DOWN! ESCAPE IS THE MAIN ISSUE, SO...
13

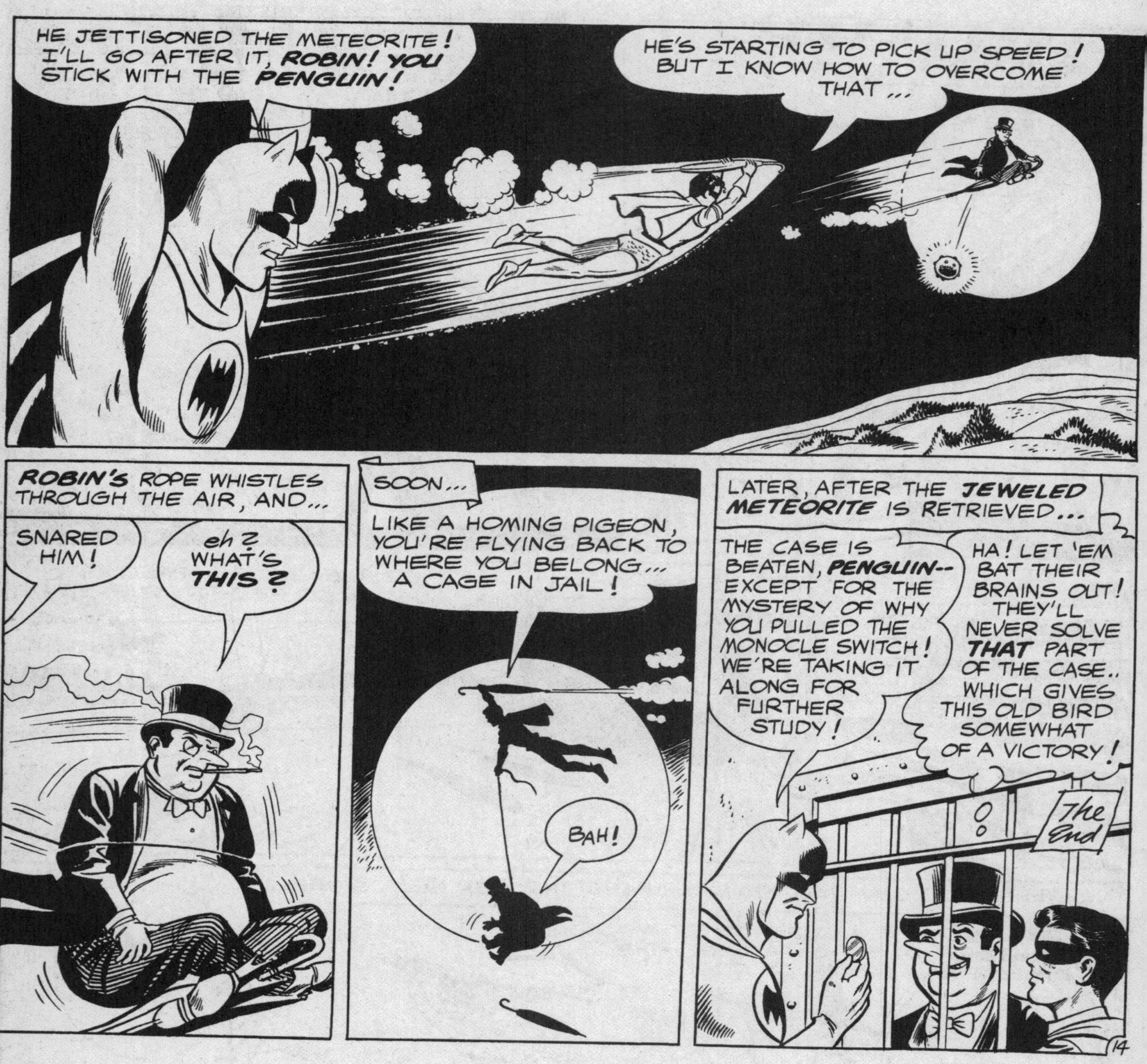
HE JETTISONED THE METEORITE! I'LL GO AFTER IT, ROBIN! YOU STICK WITH THE PENGUIN!
HE'S STARTING TO PICK UP SPEED! BUT I KNOW HOW TO OVERCOME THAT...
ROBIN'S ROPE WHISTLES THROUGH THE AIR, AND...
SNARED HIM!
eh? WHAT'S THIS?
SOON...
LIKE A HOMING PIGEON, YOU'RE FLYING BACK TO WHERE YOU BELONG... A CAGE IN JAIL!
BAH!
LATER, AFTER THE JEWELED METEORITE IS RETRIEVED...
THE CASE IS BEATEN, PENGUIN-- EXCEPT FOR THE MYSTERY OF WHY YOU PULLED THE MONOCLE SWITCH! WE'RE TAKING IT ALONG FOR FURTHER STUDY!
HA! LET 'EM BAT THEIR BRAINS OUT! THEY'LL NEVER SOLVE THAT PART OF THE CASE.. WHICH GIVES THIS OLD BIRD SOMEWHAT OF A VICTORY!
The End
14

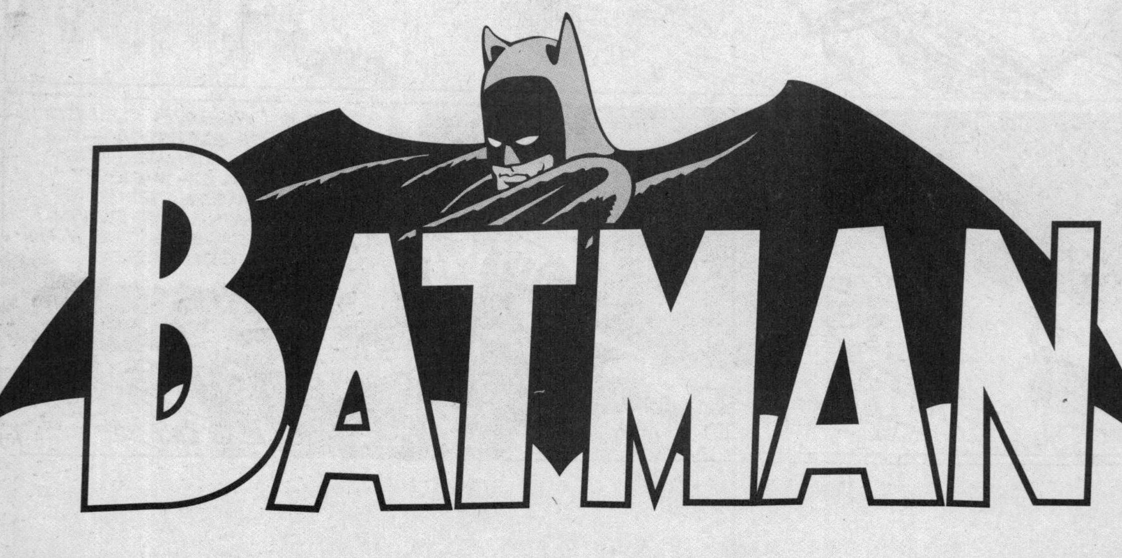
BATMAN

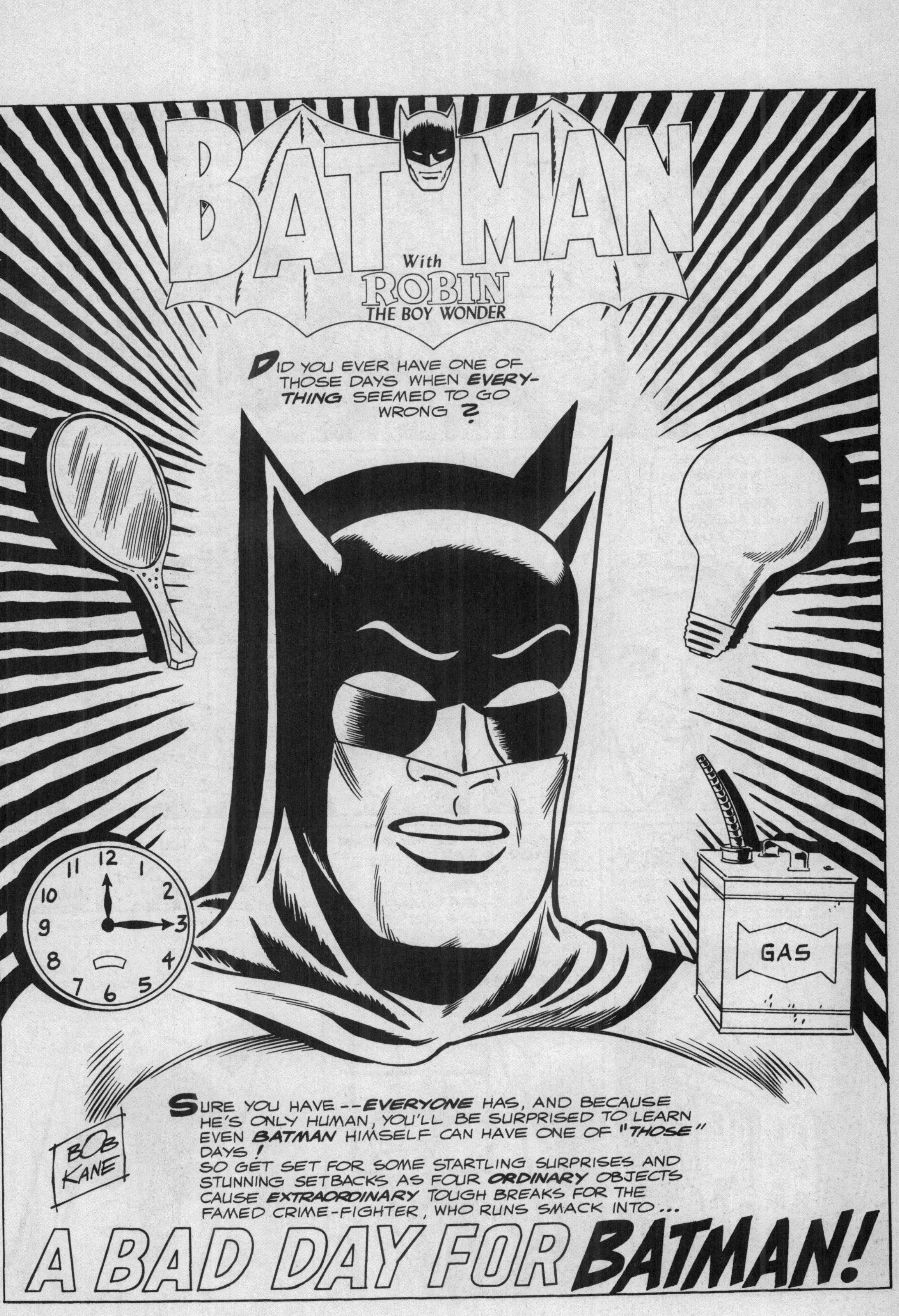
BATMAN
With
ROBIN
THE BOY WONDER
DID YOU EVER HAVE ONE OF THOSE DAYS WHEN EVERYTHING SEEMED TO GO WRONG ?
GAS
SURE YOU HAVE--EVERYONE HAS, AND BECAUSE HE'S ONLY HUMAN, YOU'LL BE SURPRISED TO LEARN EVEN BATMAN HIMSELF CAN HAVE ONE OF "THOSE" DAYS ! SO GET SET FOR SOME STARTLING SURPRISES AND STUNNING SETBACKS AS FOUR ORDINARY OBJECTS CAUSE EXTRAORDINARY TOUGH BREAKS FOR THE FAMED CRIME-FIGHTER, WHO RUNS SMACK INTO...
BOB KANE
A BAD DAY FOR BATMAN!

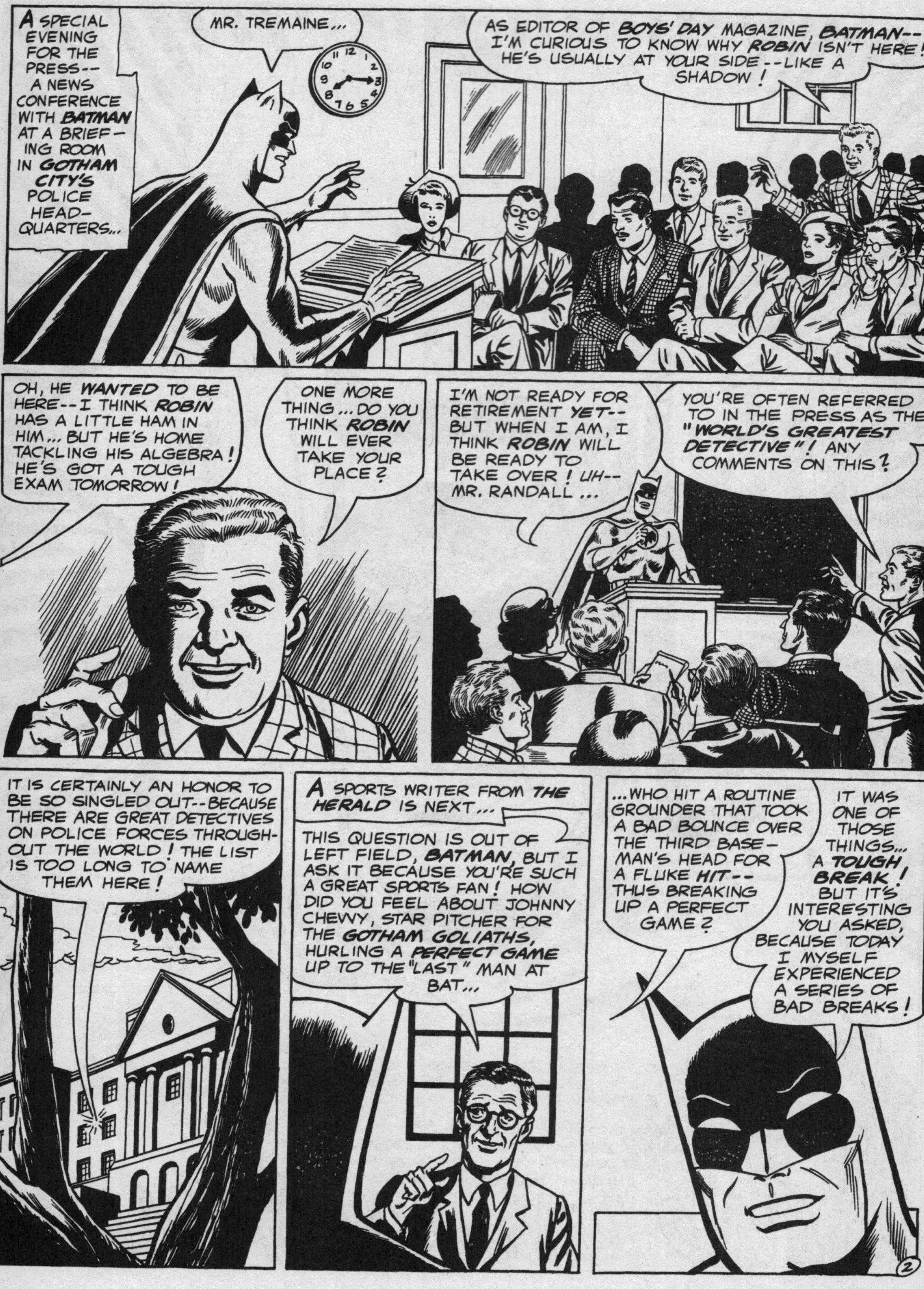
A SPECIAL EVENING FOR THE PRESS-- A NEWS CONFERENCE WITH BATMAN AT A BRIEFING ROOM IN GOTHAM CITY'S POLICE HEADQUARTERS...
MR. TREMAINE...
AS EDITOR OF BOYS' DAY MAGAZINE, BATMAN-- I'M CURIOUS TO KNOW WHY ROBIN ISN'T HERE! HE'S USUALLY AT YOUR SIDE--LIKE A SHADOW!
OH, HE WANTED TO BE HERE--I THINK ROBIN HAS A LITTLE HAM IN HIM... BUT HE'S HOME TACKLING HIS ALGEBRA! HE'S GOT A TOUGH EXAM TOMORROW!
ONE MORE THING... DO YOU THINK ROBIN WILL EVER TAKE YOUR PLACE?
I'M NOT READY FOR RETIREMENT YET-- BUT WHEN I AM, I THINK ROBIN WILL BE READY TO TAKE OVER! UH-- MR. RANDALL...
YOU'RE OFTEN REFERRED TO IN THE PRESS AS THE "WORLD'S GREATEST DETECTIVE"! ANY COMMENTS ON THIS?
IT IS CERTAINLY AN HONOR TO BE SO SINGLED OUT--BECAUSE THERE ARE GREAT DETECTIVES ON POLICE FORCES THROUGHOUT THE WORLD! THE LIST IS TOO LONG TO NAME THEM HERE!
A SPORTS WRITER FROM THE HERALD IS NEXT...
THIS QUESTION IS OUT OF LEFT FIELD, BATMAN, BUT I ASK IT BECAUSE YOU'RE SUCH A GREAT SPORTS FAN! HOW DID YOU FEEL ABOUT JOHNNY CHEVVY, STAR PITCHER FOR THE GOTHAM GOLIATHS, HURLING A PERFECT GAME UP TO THE "LAST" MAN AT BAT...
...WHO HIT A ROUTINE GROUNDER THAT TOOK A BAD BOUNCE OVER THE THIRD BASEMAN'S HEAD FOR A FLUKE HIT-- THUS BREAKING UP A PERFECT GAME?
IT WAS ONE OF THOSE THINGS... A TOUGH BREAK! BUT IT'S INTERESTING YOU ASKED, BECAUSE TODAY I MYSELF EXPERIENCED A SERIES OF BAD BREAKS!
2

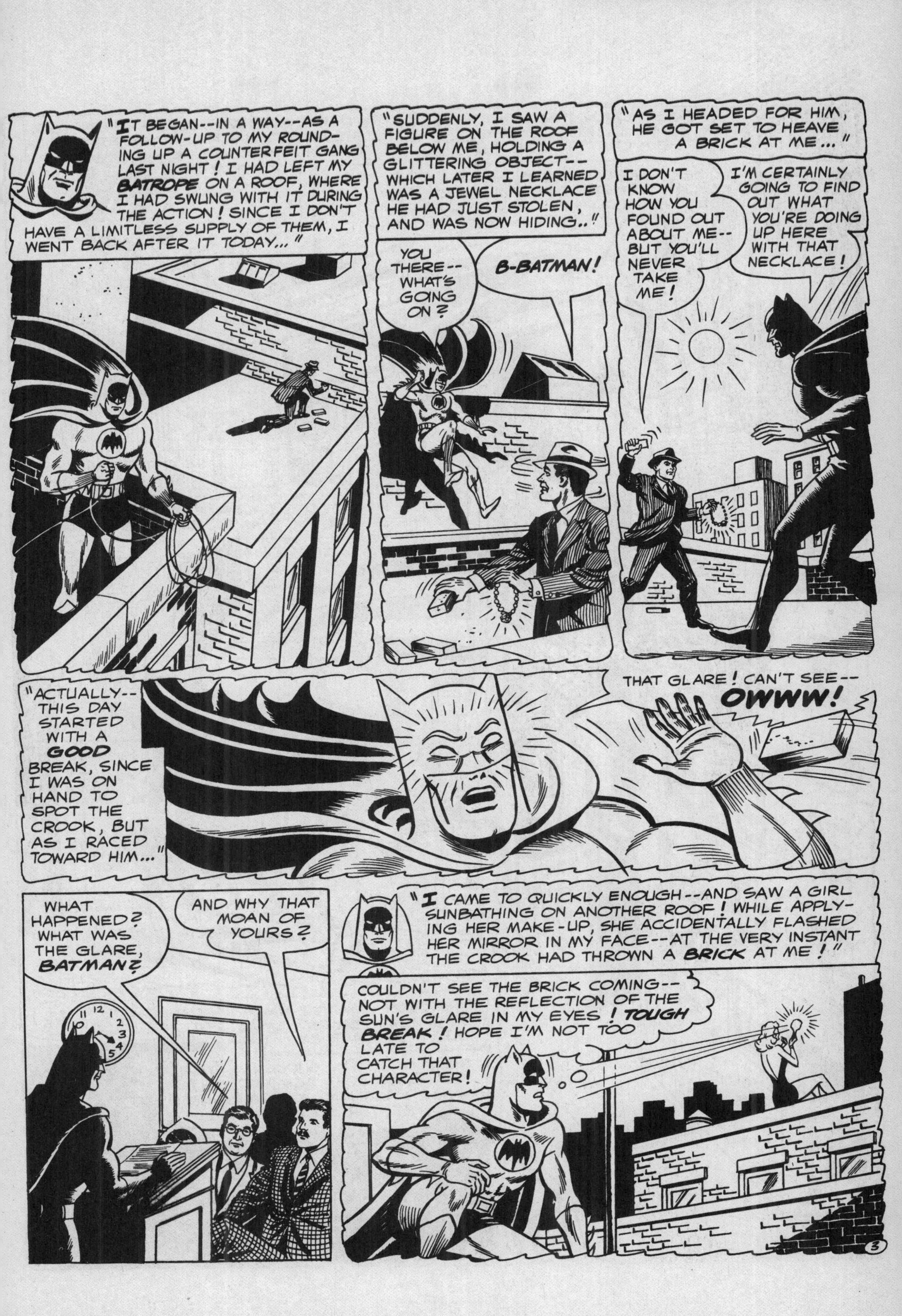
"IT BEGAN--IN A WAY--AS A FOLLOW-UP TO MY ROUNDING UP A COUNTERFEIT GANG LAST NIGHT! I HAD LEFT MY BATROPE ON A ROOF, WHERE I HAD SWUNG WITH IT DURING THE ACTION! SINCE I DON'T HAVE A LIMITLESS SUPPLY OF THEM, I WENT BACK AFTER IT TODAY..."
"SUDDENLY, I SAW A FIGURE ON THE ROOF BELOW ME, HOLDING A GLITTERING OBJECT--WHICH LATER I LEARNED WAS A JEWEL NECKLACE HE HAD JUST STOLEN, AND WAS NOW HIDING.."
YOU THERE--WHAT'S GOING ON?
B-BATMAN!
"AS I HEADED FOR HIM, HE GOT SET TO HEAVE A BRICK AT ME..."
I DON'T KNOW HOW YOU FOUND OUT ABOUT ME--BUT YOU'LL NEVER TAKE ME!
I'M CERTAINLY GOING TO FIND OUT WHAT YOU'RE DOING UP HERE WITH THAT NECKLACE!
"ACTUALLY--THIS DAY STARTED WITH A GOOD BREAK, SINCE I WAS ON HAND TO SPOT THE CROOK, BUT AS I RACED TOWARD HIM..."
THAT GLARE! CAN'T SEE--
OWWW!
WHAT HAPPENED? WHAT WAS THE GLARE, BATMAN?
AND WHY THAT MOAN OF YOURS?
"I CAME TO QUICKLY ENOUGH--AND SAW A GIRL SUNBATHING ON ANOTHER ROOF! WHILE APPLYING HER MAKE-UP, SHE ACCIDENTALLY FLASHED HER MIRROR IN MY FACE--AT THE VERY INSTANT THE CROOK HAD THROWN A BRICK AT ME!"
COULDN'T SEE THE BRICK COMING--NOT WITH THE REFLECTION OF THE SUN'S GLARE IN MY EYES! TOUGH BREAK! HOPE I'M NOT TOO LATE TO CATCH THAT CHARACTER!
3

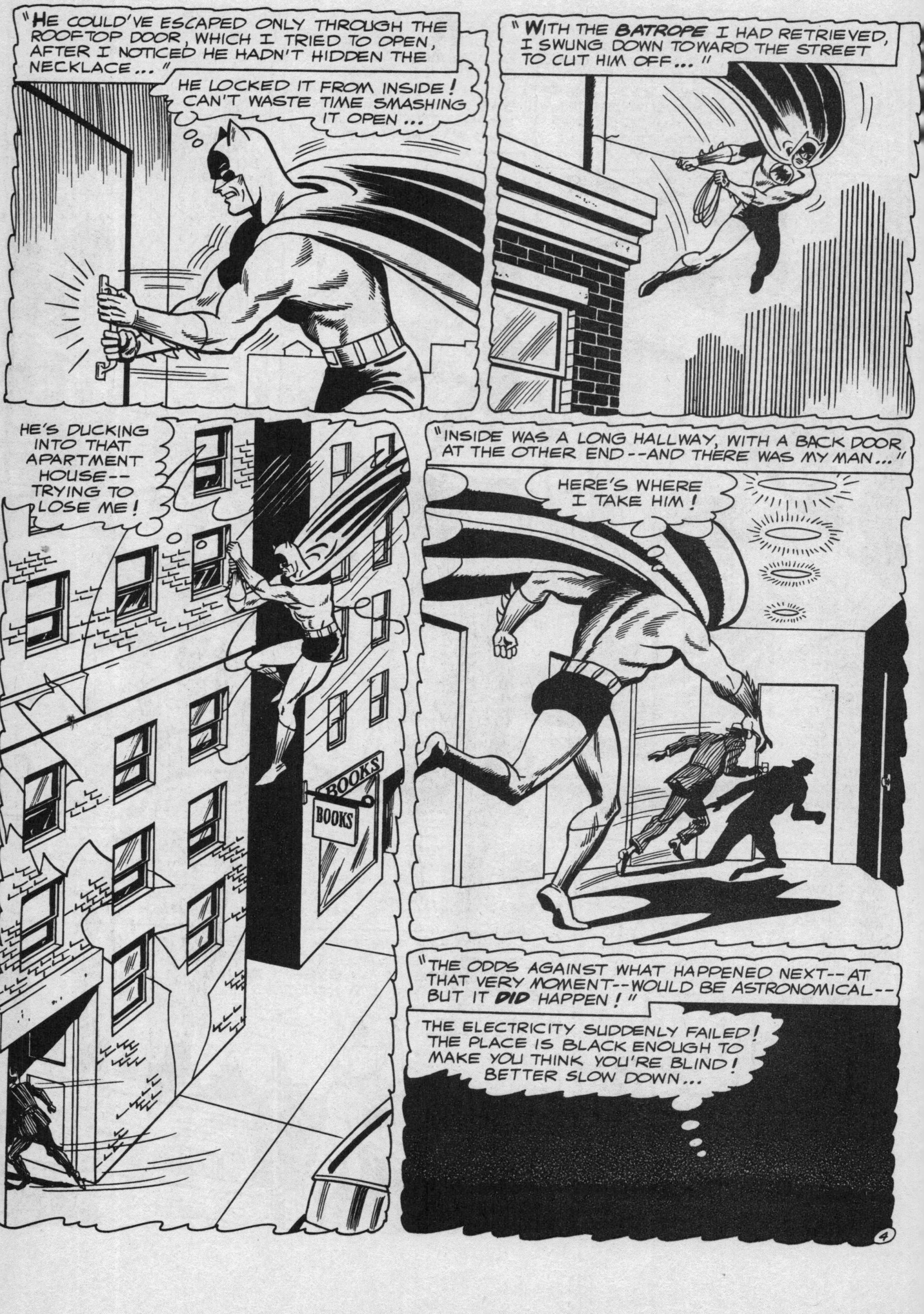
"HE COULD'VE ESCAPED ONLY THROUGH THE ROOFTOP DOOR, WHICH I TRIED TO OPEN, AFTER I NOTICED HE HADN'T HIDDEN THE NECKLACE..."
HE LOCKED IT FROM INSIDE! CAN'T WASTE TIME SMASHING IT OPEN...
"WITH THE BATROPE I HAD RETRIEVED, I SWUNG DOWN TOWARD THE STREET TO CUT HIM OFF..."
HE'S DUCKING INTO THAT APARTMENT HOUSE--TRYING TO LOSE ME!
BOOKS
BOOKS
"INSIDE WAS A LONG HALLWAY, WITH A BACK DOOR AT THE OTHER END--AND THERE WAS MY MAN..."
HERE'S WHERE I TAKE HIM!
"THE ODDS AGAINST WHAT HAPPENED NEXT--AT THAT VERY MOMENT--WOULD BE ASTRONOMICAL--BUT IT DID HAPPEN!"
THE ELECTRICITY SUDDENLY FAILED! THE PLACE IS BLACK ENOUGH TO MAKE YOU THINK YOU'RE BLIND! BETTER SLOW DOWN...
4

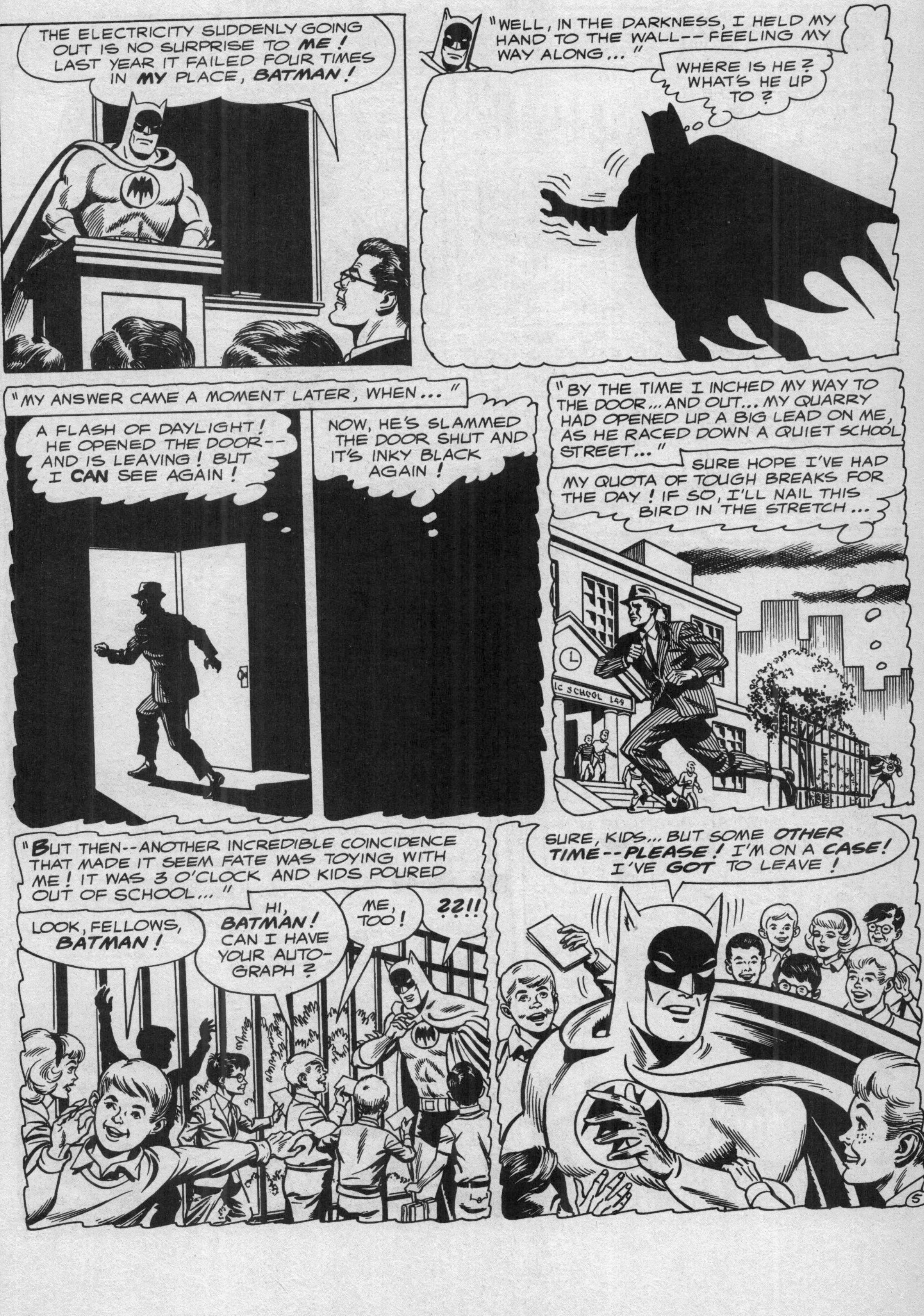
THE ELECTRICITY SUDDENLY GOING OUT IS NO SURPRISE TO ME! LAST YEAR IT FAILED FOUR TIMES IN MY PLACE, BATMAN!
"WELL, IN THE DARKNESS, I HELD MY HAND TO THE WALL-- FEELING MY WAY ALONG..."
WHERE IS HE? WHAT'S HE UP TO?
"MY ANSWER CAME A MOMENT LATER, WHEN..."
A FLASH OF DAYLIGHT! HE OPENED THE DOOR-- AND IS LEAVING! BUT I CAN SEE AGAIN!
NOW, HE'S SLAMMED THE DOOR SHUT AND IT'S INKY BLACK AGAIN!
"BY THE TIME I INCHED MY WAY TO THE DOOR... AND OUT... MY QUARRY HAD OPENED UP A BIG LEAD ON ME, AS HE RACED DOWN A QUIET SCHOOL STREET..."
SURE HOPE I'VE HAD MY QUOTA OF TOUGH BREAKS FOR THE DAY! IF SO, I'LL NAIL THIS BIRD IN THE STRETCH...
LC SCHOOL 149
"BUT THEN--ANOTHER INCREDIBLE COINCIDENCE THAT MADE IT SEEM FATE WAS TOYING WITH ME! IT WAS 3 O'CLOCK AND KIDS POURED OUT OF SCHOOL..."
LOOK, FELLOWS, BATMAN!
HI, BATMAN! CAN I HAVE YOUR AUTOGRAPH?
ME, TOO!
??!!
SURE, KIDS... BUT SOME OTHER TIME--PLEASE! I'M ON A CASE! I'VE GOT TO LEAVE!
5

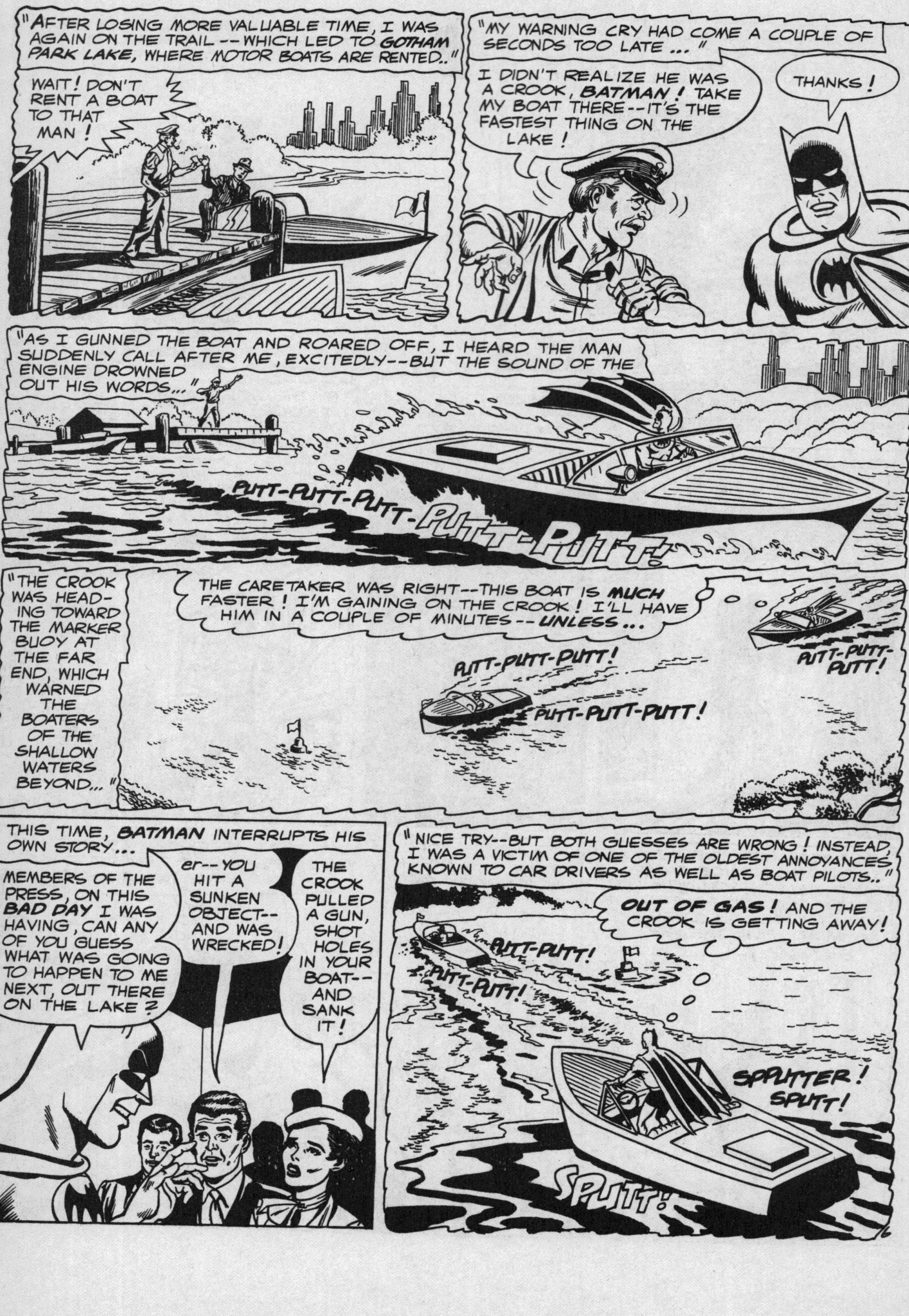
"AFTER LOSING MORE VALUABLE TIME, I WAS AGAIN ON THE TRAIL -- WHICH LED TO GOTHAM PARK LAKE, WHERE MOTOR BOATS ARE RENTED.."
WAIT! DON'T RENT A BOAT TO THAT MAN!
"MY WARNING CRY HAD COME A COUPLE OF SECONDS TOO LATE ..."
I DIDN'T REALIZE HE WAS A CROOK, BATMAN! TAKE MY BOAT THERE--IT'S THE FASTEST THING ON THE LAKE!
THANKS!
"AS I GUNNED THE BOAT AND ROARED OFF, I HEARD THE MAN SUDDENLY CALL AFTER ME, EXCITEDLY--BUT THE SOUND OF THE ENGINE DROWNED OUT HIS WORDS..."
PUTT-PUTT-PUTT-PUTT-PUTT!
"THE CROOK WAS HEADING TOWARD THE MARKER BUOY AT THE FAR END, WHICH WARNED THE BOATERS OF THE SHALLOW WATERS BEYOND..."
THE CARETAKER WAS RIGHT--THIS BOAT IS MUCH FASTER! I'M GAINING ON THE CROOK! I'LL HAVE HIM IN A COUPLE OF MINUTES -- UNLESS...
PUTT-PUTT-PUTT!
PUTT-PUTT-PUTT!
PUTT-PUTT-PUTT!
THIS TIME, BATMAN INTERRUPTS HIS OWN STORY...
MEMBERS OF THE PRESS, ON THIS BAD DAY I WAS HAVING, CAN ANY OF YOU GUESS WHAT WAS GOING TO HAPPEN TO ME NEXT, OUT THERE ON THE LAKE?
er--YOU HIT A SUNKEN OBJECT--AND WAS WRECKED!
THE CROOK PULLED A GUN, SHOT HOLES IN YOUR BOAT--AND SANK IT!
"NICE TRY--BUT BOTH GUESSES ARE WRONG! INSTEAD, I WAS A VICTIM OF ONE OF THE OLDEST ANNOYANCES KNOWN TO CAR DRIVERS AS WELL AS BOAT PILOTS.."
OUT OF GAS! AND THE CROOK IS GETTING AWAY!
PUTT-PUTT!
PUTT-PUTT!
SPPUTTER! SPUTT!
SPUTT!
16

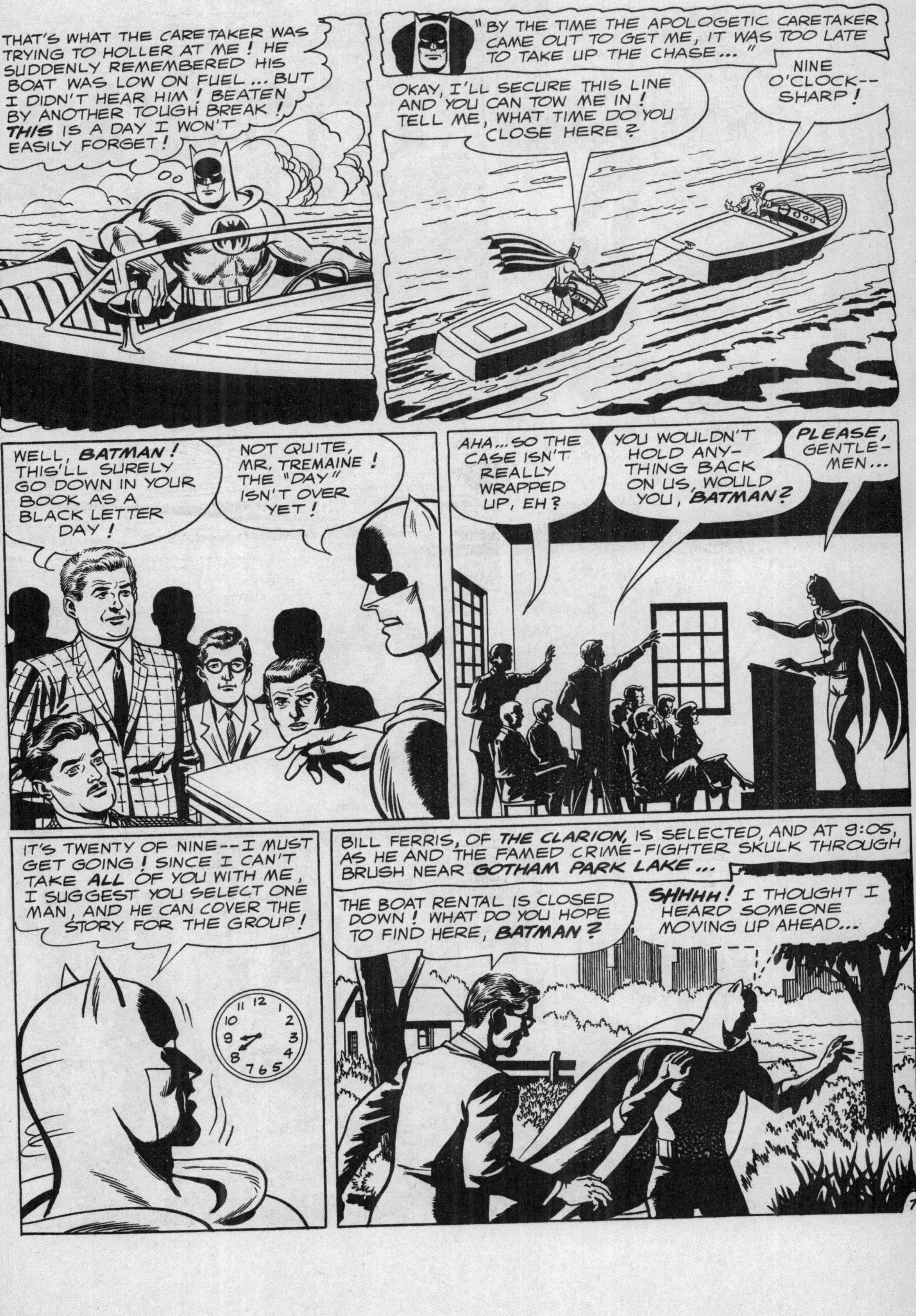
THAT'S WHAT THE CARETAKER WAS TRYING TO HOLLER AT ME! HE SUDDENLY REMEMBERED HIS BOAT WAS LOW ON FUEL ... BUT I DIDN'T HEAR HIM! BEATEN BY ANOTHER TOUGH BREAK! THIS IS A DAY I WON'T EASILY FORGET!
"BY THE TIME THE APOLOGETIC CARETAKER CAME OUT TO GET ME, IT WAS TOO LATE TO TAKE UP THE CHASE..."
OKAY, I'LL SECURE THIS LINE AND YOU CAN TOW ME IN! TELL ME, WHAT TIME DO YOU CLOSE HERE?
NINE O'CLOCK--SHARP!
WELL, BATMAN! THIS'LL SURELY GO DOWN IN YOUR BOOK AS A BLACK LETTER DAY!
NOT QUITE, MR. TREMAINE! THE "DAY" ISN'T OVER YET!
AHA... SO THE CASE ISN'T REALLY WRAPPED UP, EH?
YOU WOULDN'T HOLD ANYTHING BACK ON US, WOULD YOU, BATMAN?
PLEASE, GENTLEMEN...
IT'S TWENTY OF NINE--I MUST GET GOING! SINCE I CAN'T TAKE ALL OF YOU WITH ME, I SUGGEST YOU SELECT ONE MAN, AND HE CAN COVER THE STORY FOR THE GROUP!
BILL FERRIS, OF THE CLARION, IS SELECTED, AND AT 9:05, AS HE AND THE FAMED CRIME-FIGHTER SKULK THROUGH BRUSH NEAR GOTHAM PARK LAKE...
THE BOAT RENTAL IS CLOSED DOWN! WHAT DO YOU HOPE TO FIND HERE, BATMAN?
SHHHH! I THOUGHT I HEARD SOMEONE MOVING UP AHEAD...
7

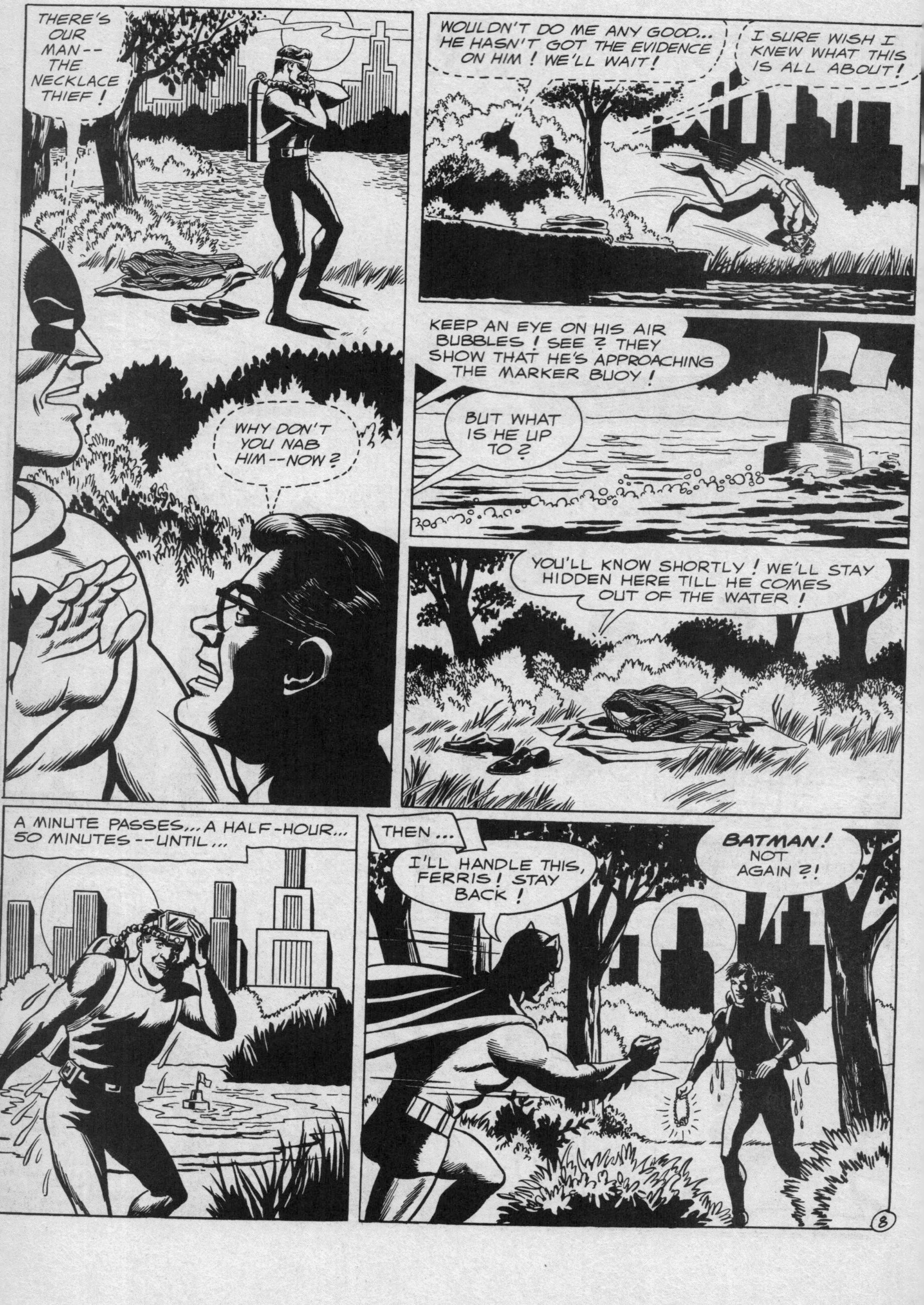
THERE'S OUR MAN-- THE NECKLACE THIEF!
WHY DON'T YOU NAB HIM--NOW?
WOULDN'T DO ME ANY GOOD... HE HASN'T GOT THE EVIDENCE ON HIM! WE'LL WAIT!
I SURE WISH I KNEW WHAT THIS IS ALL ABOUT!
KEEP AN EYE ON HIS AIR BUBBLES! SEE? THEY SHOW THAT HE'S APPROACHING THE MARKER BUOY!
BUT WHAT IS HE UP TO?
YOU'LL KNOW SHORTLY! WE'LL STAY HIDDEN HERE TILL HE COMES OUT OF THE WATER!
A MINUTE PASSES... A HALF-HOUR... 50 MINUTES--UNTIL...
THEN...
I'LL HANDLE THIS, FERRIS! STAY BACK!
BATMAN! NOT AGAIN?!
8

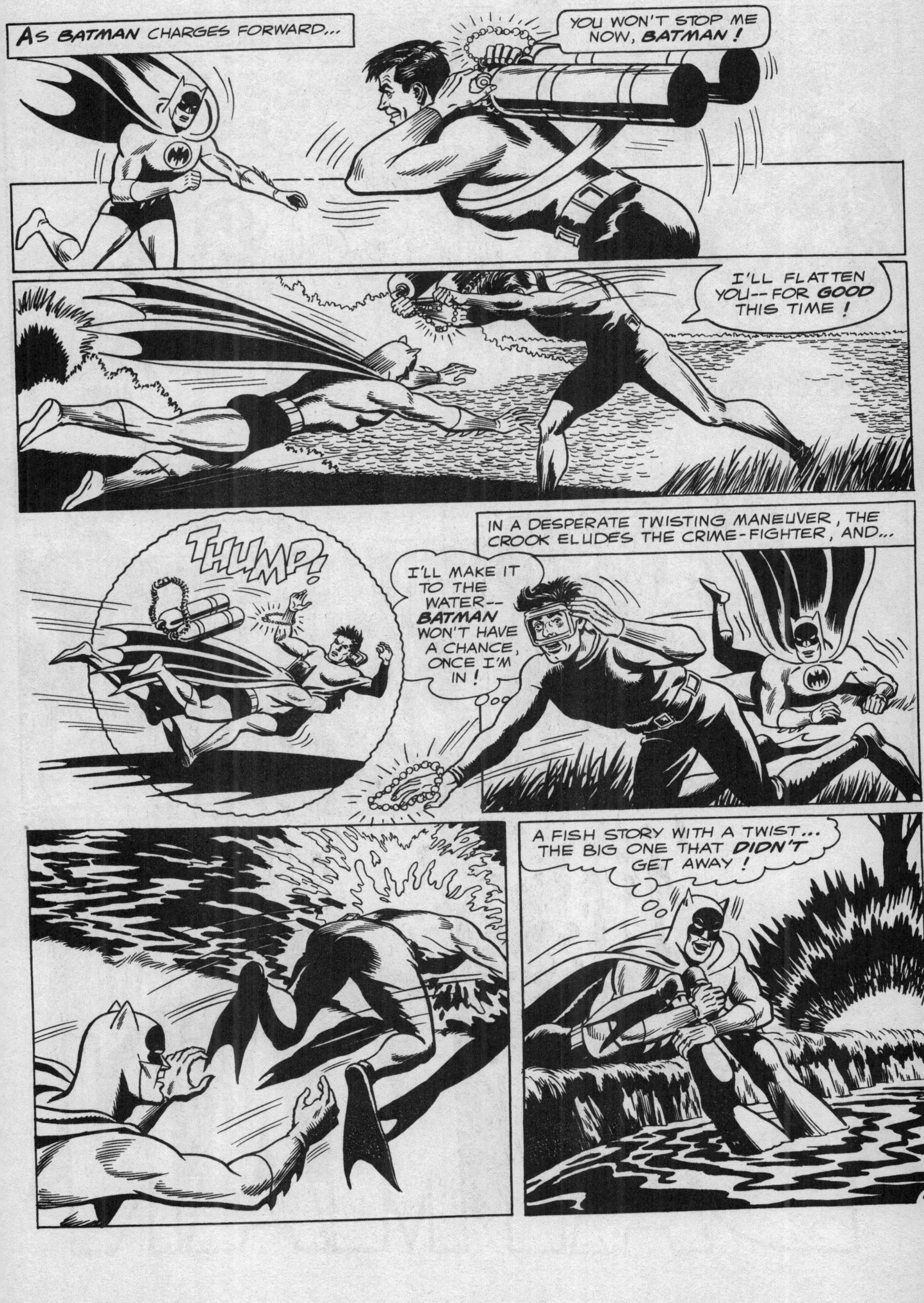
AS BATMAN CHARGES FORWARD...
YOU WON'T STOP ME NOW, BATMAN!
I'LL FLATTEN YOU--FOR GOOD THIS TIME!
THUMP!
IN A DESPERATE TWISTING MANEUVER, THE CROOK ELUDES THE CRIME-FIGHTER, AND...
I'LL MAKE IT TO THE WATER-- BATMAN WON'T HAVE A CHANCE, ONCE I'M IN!
A FISH STORY WITH A TWIST... THE BIG ONE THAT DIDN'T GET AWAY!
9

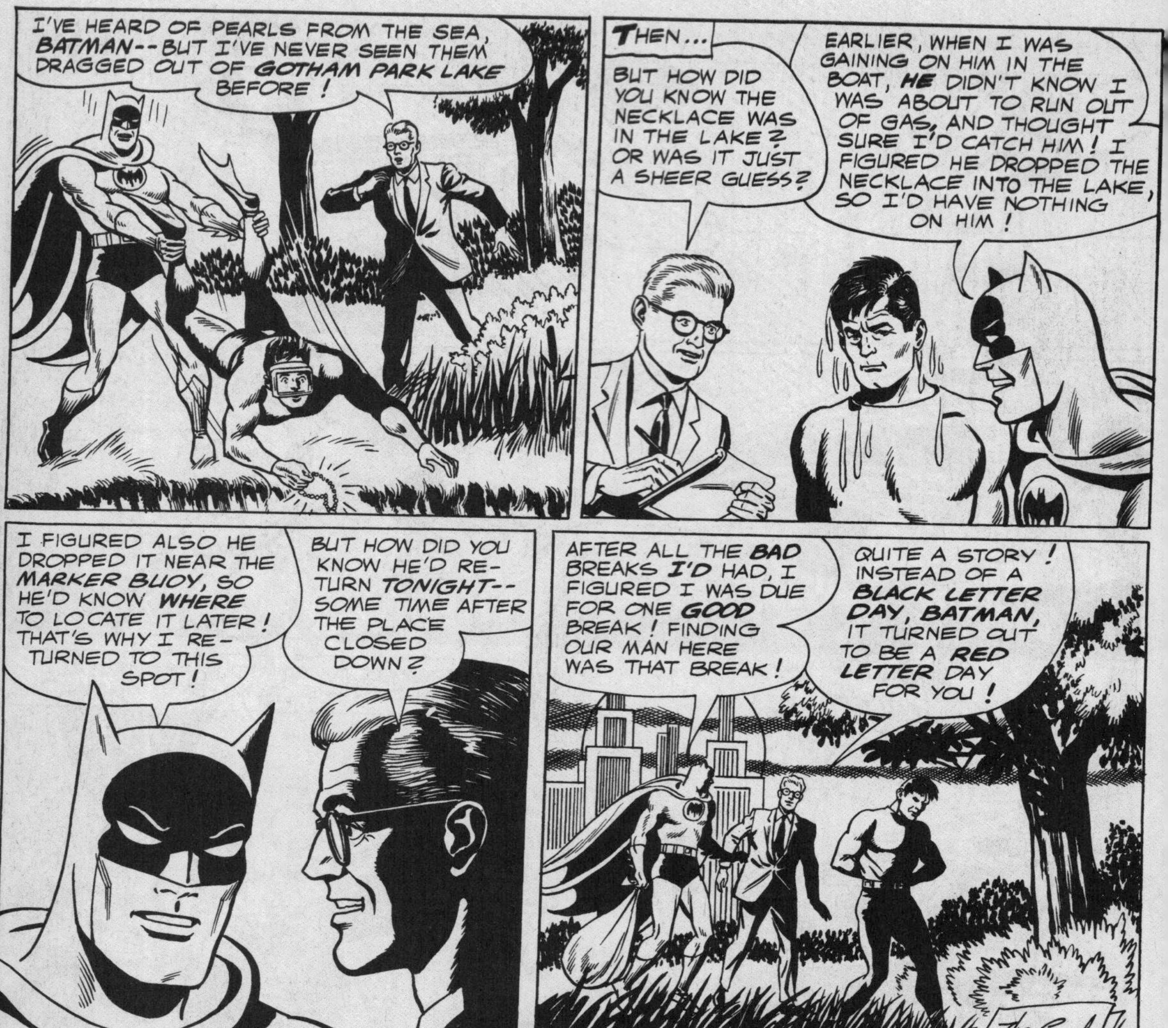
I'VE HEARD OF PEARLS FROM THE SEA, BATMAN--BUT I'VE NEVER SEEN THEM DRAGGED OUT OF GOTHAM PARK LAKE BEFORE!
THEN...
BUT HOW DID YOU KNOW THE NECKLACE WAS IN THE LAKE? OR WAS IT JUST A SHEER GUESS?
EARLIER, WHEN I WAS GAINING ON HIM IN THE BOAT, HE DIDN'T KNOW I WAS ABOUT TO RUN OUT OF GAS, AND THOUGHT SURE I'D CATCH HIM! I FIGURED HE DROPPED THE NECKLACE INTO THE LAKE, SO I'D HAVE NOTHING ON HIM!
I FIGURED ALSO HE DROPPED IT NEAR THE MARKER BUOY, SO HE'D KNOW WHERE TO LOCATE IT LATER! THAT'S WHY I RETURNED TO THIS SPOT!
BUT HOW DID YOU KNOW HE'D RETURN TONIGHT--SOME TIME AFTER THE PLACE CLOSED DOWN?
AFTER ALL THE BAD BREAKS I'D HAD, I FIGURED I WAS DUE FOR ONE GOOD BREAK! FINDING OUR MAN HERE WAS THAT BREAK!
QUITE A STORY! INSTEAD OF A BLACK LETTER DAY, BATMAN, IT TURNED OUT TO BE A RED LETTER DAY FOR YOU!
The End
10

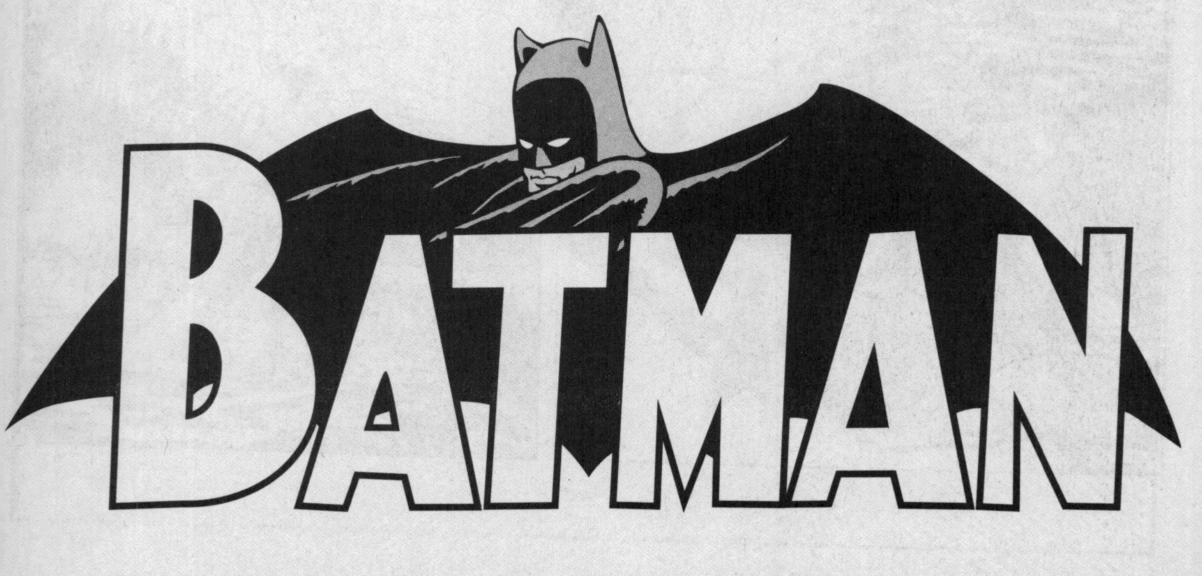
BATMAN

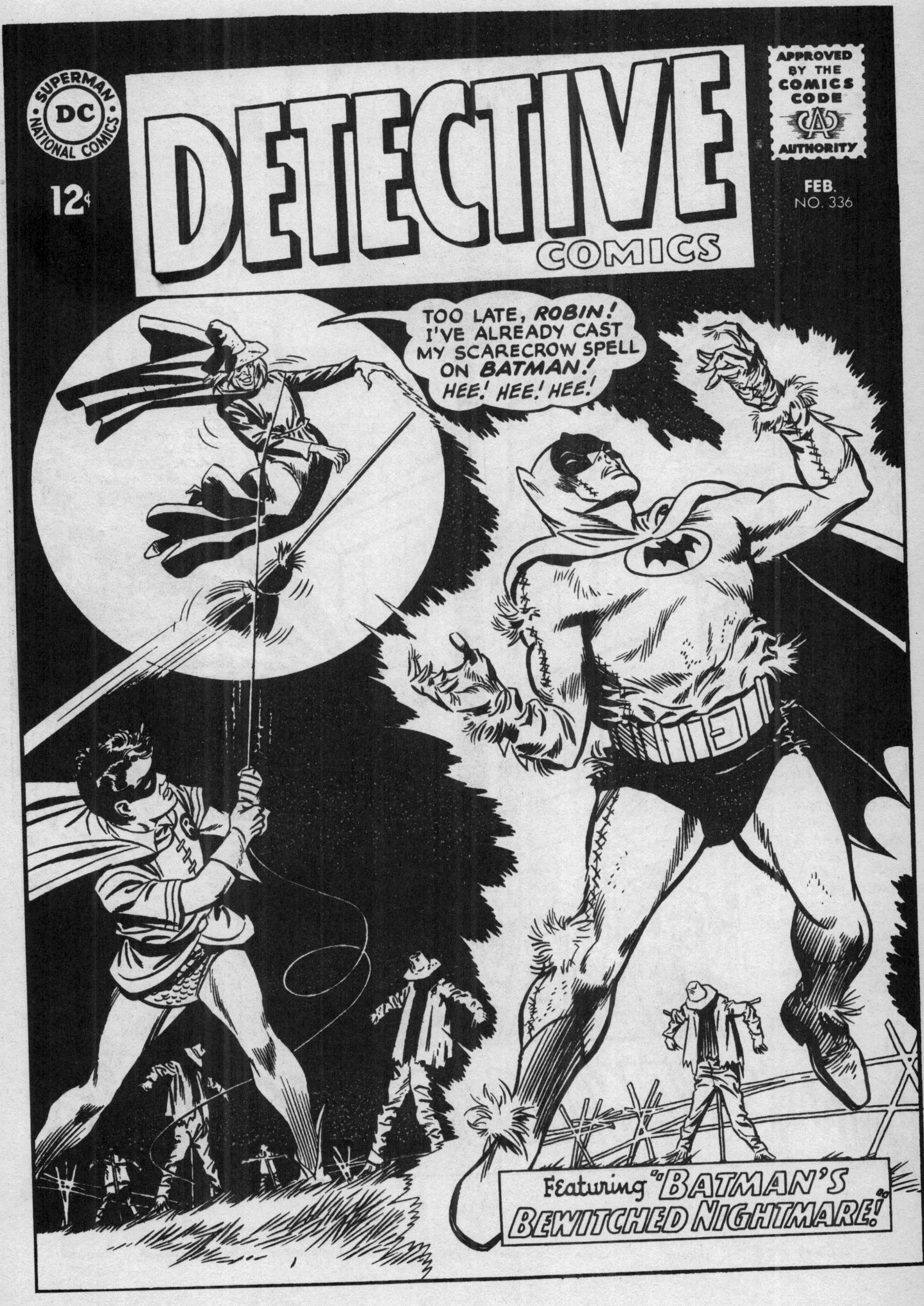
SUPERMAN DC NATIONAL COMICS
12¢
DETECTIVE COMICS
APPROVED BY THE COMICS CODE AUTHORITY
FEB. NO. 336
TOO LATE, ROBIN! I'VE ALREADY CAST MY SCARECROW SPELL ON BATMAN! HEE! HEE! HEE!
Featuring "BATMAN'S BEWITCHED NIGHTMARE!"

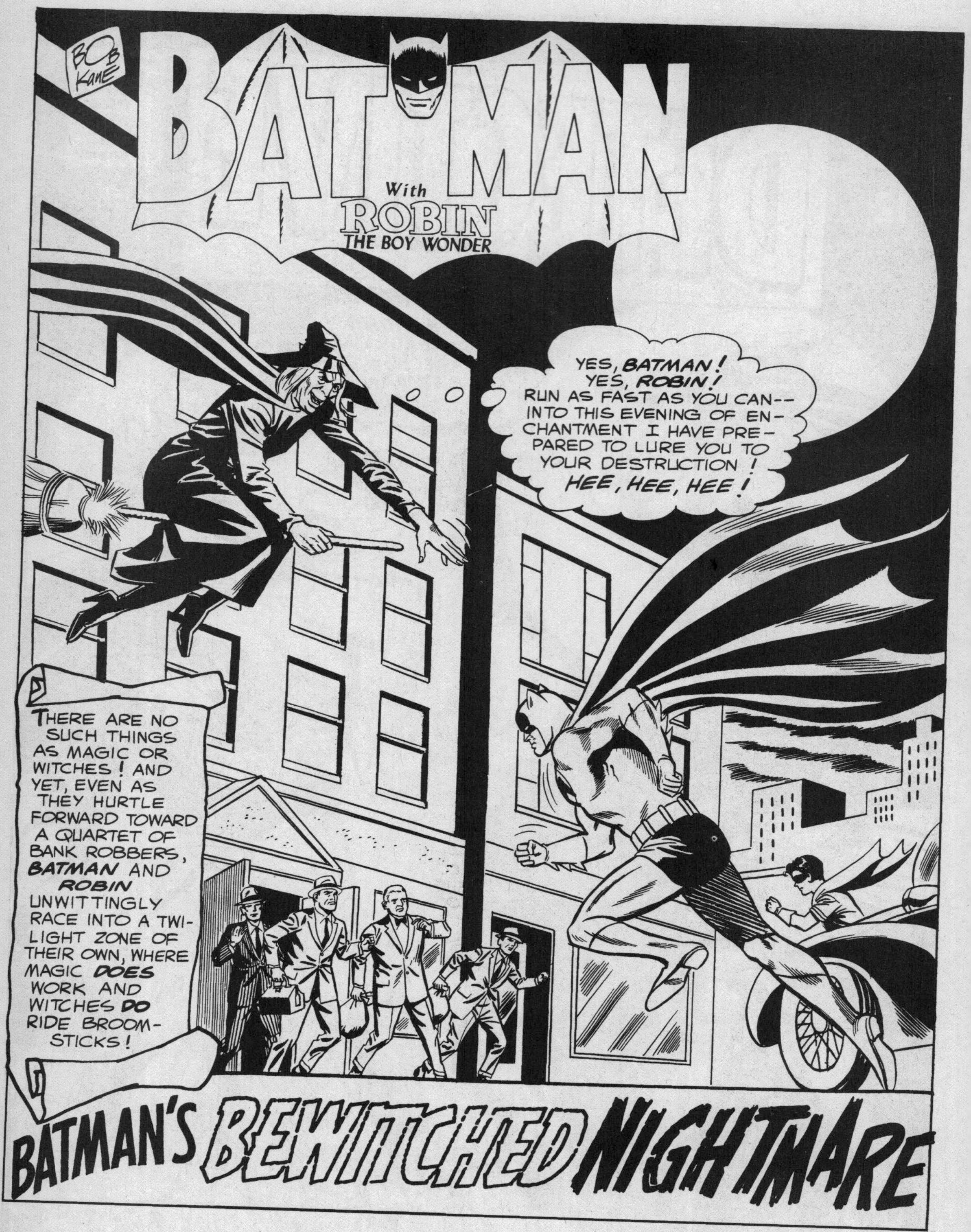
BOB KANE
BATMAN
With ROBIN THE BOY WONDER
YES, BATMAN! YES, ROBIN! RUN AS FAST AS YOU CAN-- INTO THIS EVENING OF ENCHANTMENT I HAVE PREPARED TO LURE YOU TO YOUR DESTRUCTION! HEE, HEE, HEE!
THERE ARE NO SUCH THINGS AS MAGIC OR WITCHES! AND YET, EVEN AS THEY HURTLE FORWARD TOWARD A QUARTET OF BANK ROBBERS, BATMAN AND ROBIN UNWITTINGLY RACE INTO A TWILIGHT ZONE OF THEIR OWN, WHERE MAGIC DOES WORK AND WITCHES DO RIDE BROOMSTICKS!
BATMAN'S BEWITCHED NIGHTMARE

MOVING ACROSS A SIDEWALK IN *GOTHAM CITY* IS A TINY PUMPKIN COACH--DRAWN BY FOUR WHITE MICE...

EVEN MORE STARTLING IS THE EERIE FIGURE OUTLINED AGAINST THE FULL MOON AS IT SWOOPS ABOVE THE ROOF TOPS...

THE WITCH LEANS DOWN AND FROM HER HAND STREAK TINY SPURTS OF ENCHANTED ENERGY...

BY MOON, BY RUNE, BY MAGIC OLD-- I ORDER YOU TO CHANGE YOUR MOLD!

INSTANTLY THE PUMPKIN COACH TURNS INTO AN--*AUTOMOBILE*, AND THE FOUR WHITE MICE TURN INTO --GANGSTERS...

THERE'S THE BANK AHEAD OF US!

WITH THE WITCH TO PROTECT US, WE HAVEN'T A THING TO FEAR--NOT EVEN FROM *BATMAN* AND *ROBIN!*

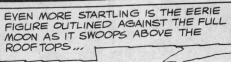

THEN, AS THE SHADOW OF THE FLYING WITCH FALLS ACROSS THE BANK DOORS...

LOOK AT THAT! SHE CAN OPEN LOCKED DOORS-- LIKE MAGIC!

COME ON! *BATMAN'S* DUE HERE ANY MINUTE! WE WANT TO GET OUR HANDS ON THE LOOT BEFORE HE APPEARS!

BANK

2

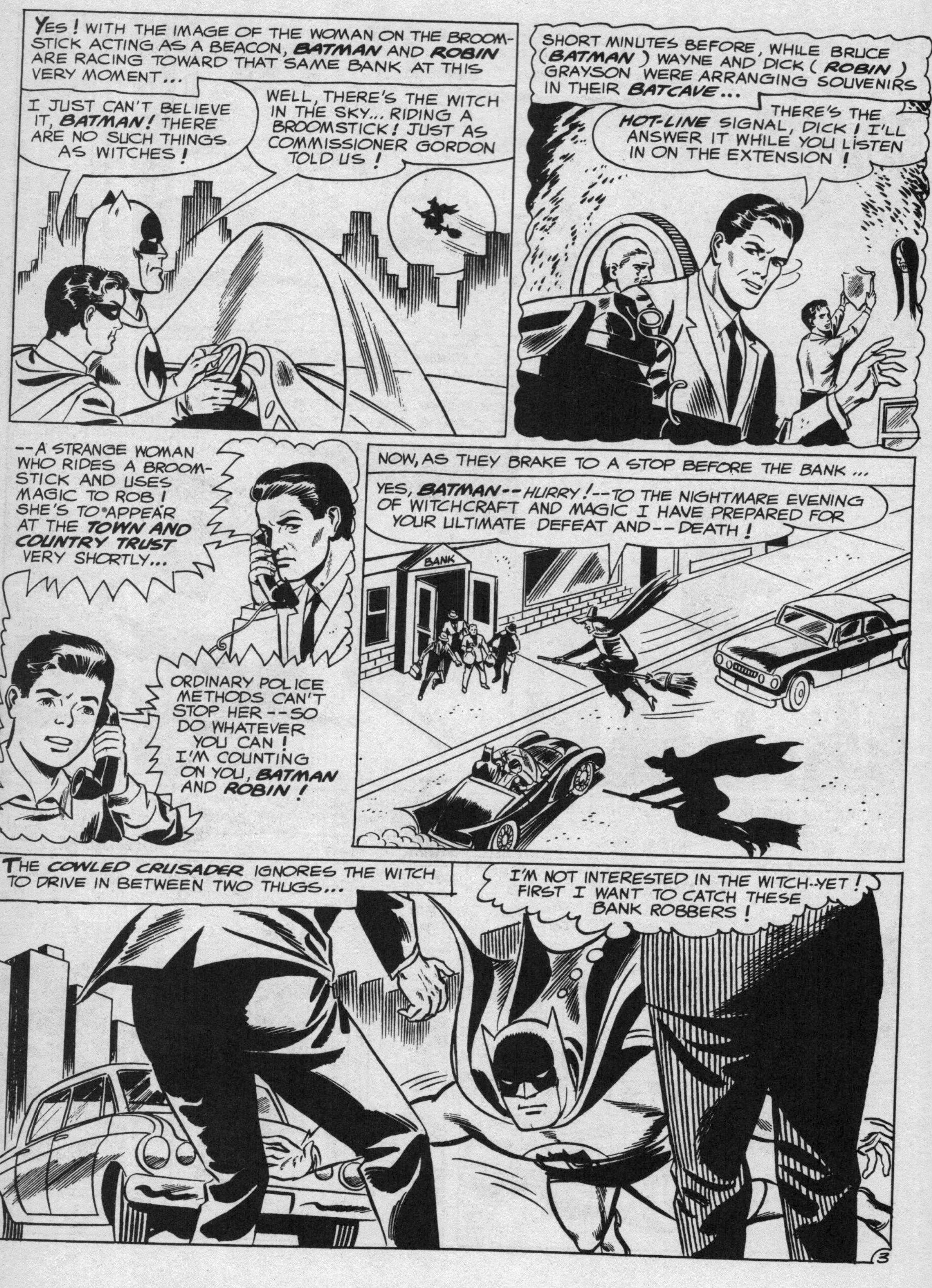
YES! WITH THE IMAGE OF THE WOMAN ON THE BROOMSTICK ACTING AS A BEACON, BATMAN AND ROBIN ARE RACING TOWARD THAT SAME BANK AT THIS VERY MOMENT...
I JUST CAN'T BELIEVE IT, BATMAN! THERE ARE NO SUCH THINGS AS WITCHES!
WELL, THERE'S THE WITCH IN THE SKY... RIDING A BROOMSTICK! JUST AS COMMISSIONER GORDON TOLD US!
SHORT MINUTES BEFORE, WHILE BRUCE (BATMAN) WAYNE AND DICK (ROBIN) GRAYSON WERE ARRANGING SOUVENIRS IN THEIR BATCAVE...
THERE'S THE HOT-LINE SIGNAL, DICK! I'LL ANSWER IT WHILE YOU LISTEN IN ON THE EXTENSION!
--A STRANGE WOMAN WHO RIDES A BROOMSTICK AND USES MAGIC TO ROB! SHE'S TO APPEAR AT THE TOWN AND COUNTRY TRUST VERY SHORTLY...
ORDINARY POLICE METHODS CAN'T STOP HER--SO DO WHATEVER YOU CAN! I'M COUNTING ON YOU, BATMAN AND ROBIN!
NOW, AS THEY BRAKE TO A STOP BEFORE THE BANK...
YES, BATMAN--HURRY!--TO THE NIGHTMARE EVENING OF WITCHCRAFT AND MAGIC I HAVE PREPARED FOR YOUR ULTIMATE DEFEAT AND--DEATH!
BANK
THE COWLED CRUSADER IGNORES THE WITCH TO DRIVE IN BETWEEN TWO THUGS...
I'M NOT INTERESTED IN THE WITCH--YET! FIRST I WANT TO CATCH THESE BANK ROBBERS!
3

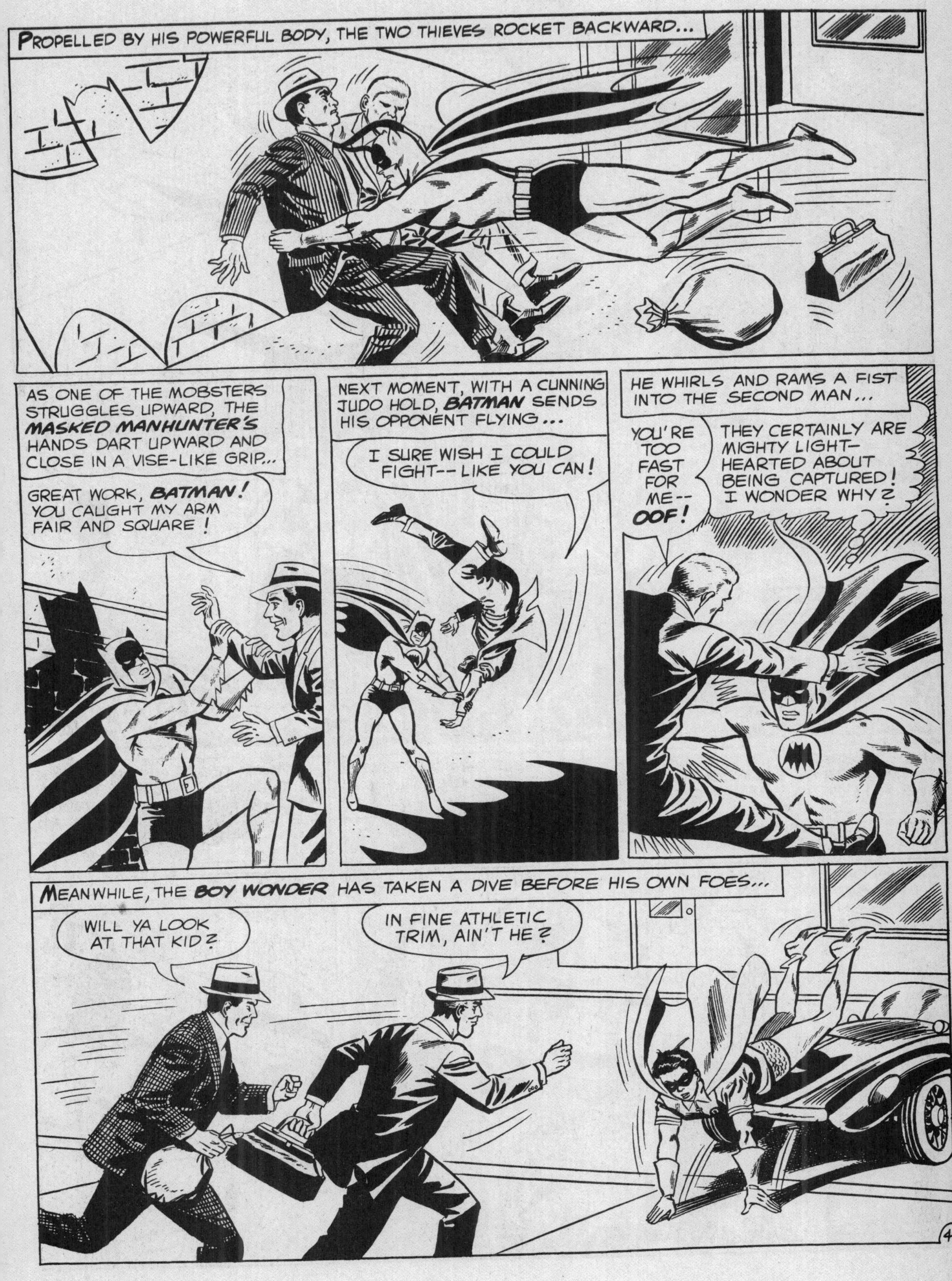
PROPELLED BY HIS POWERFUL BODY, THE TWO THIEVES ROCKET BACKWARD...
AS ONE OF THE MOBSTERS STRUGGLES UPWARD, THE **MASKED MANHUNTER'S** HANDS DART UPWARD AND CLOSE IN A VISE-LIKE GRIP...
GREAT WORK, **BATMAN**! YOU CAUGHT MY ARM FAIR AND SQUARE!
NEXT MOMENT, WITH A CUNNING JUDO HOLD, **BATMAN** SENDS HIS OPPONENT FLYING...
I SURE WISH I COULD FIGHT-- LIKE YOU CAN!
HE WHIRLS AND RAMS A FIST INTO THE SECOND MAN...
YOU'RE TOO FAST FOR ME-- **OOF**!
THEY CERTAINLY ARE MIGHTY LIGHT-HEARTED ABOUT BEING CAPTURED! I WONDER WHY?
MEANWHILE, THE **BOY WONDER** HAS TAKEN A DIVE BEFORE HIS OWN FOES...
WILL YA LOOK AT THAT KID?
IN FINE ATHLETIC TRIM, AIN'T HE?
4

AS HIS HANDS TOUCH THE GROUND HE BACKFLIPS UPWARD AND...

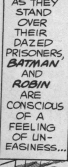

AS THEY STAND OVER THEIR DAZED PRISONERS, *BATMAN* AND *ROBIN* ARE CONSCIOUS OF A FEELING OF UNEASINESS...

WHAT'S GOING ON, *BATMAN?* THEY ACT AS IF THIS WERE ALL A BIG JOKE!

THEY'LL SING A DIFFERENT TUNE IN THE POLICE STATION!

WITH A BURST OF LAUGHTER, THE MOBSTERS LEAP TO THEIR FEET AND BRUSH THEMSELVES OFF CALMLY...

HAW, HAW! KNOCKING US OUT IS ONE THING, *BATMAN!* TAKING US TO JAIL IS ANOTHER!

THE WITCH WON'T LET YOU NAB US! SHE WAS TOYIN' WITH YOU!

THE *TEEN-AGE THUNDERBOLT* REACHES OUT TO COLLAR HIS TWO PRISONERS, WHEN...

THEY STILL HAVEN'T LEARNED THEIR LESSON! WE'LL HAVE TO DRAG THEM OFF TO... HUH? MY HANDS WENT RIGHT THROUGH THEM!

BATMAN TESTS HIS OWN SENSE OF TOUCH BY THROWING A HARD RIGHT STRAIGHT THROUGH THE FACE OF A BANK ROBBER...

¡GASP! I CAN'T MAKE CONTACT EITHER!

5

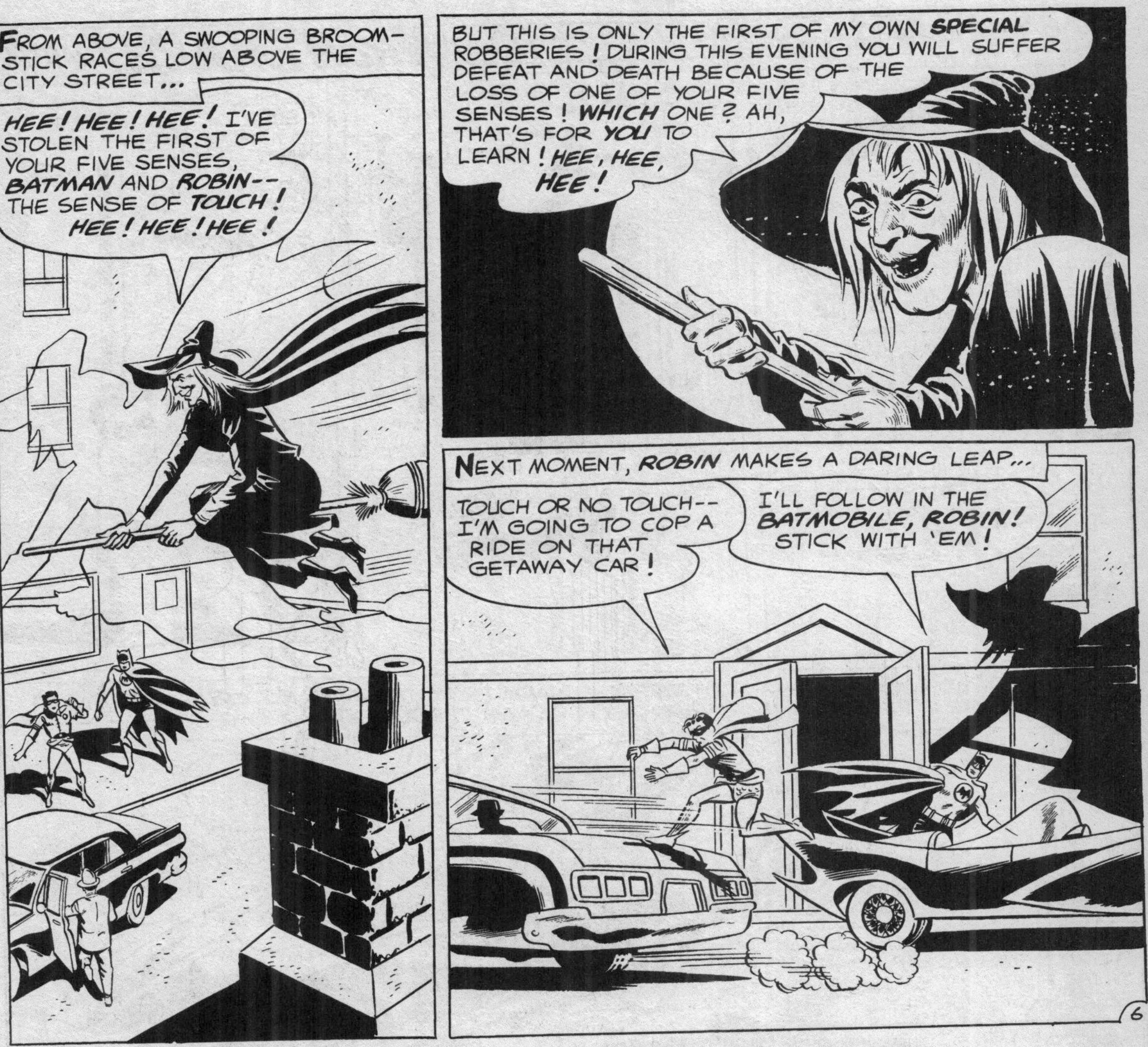
FROM ABOVE, A SWOOPING BROOM-STICK RACES LOW ABOVE THE CITY STREET...
HEE! HEE! HEE! I'VE STOLEN THE FIRST OF YOUR FIVE SENSES, BATMAN AND ROBIN-- THE SENSE OF TOUCH! HEE! HEE! HEE!
BUT THIS IS ONLY THE FIRST OF MY OWN SPECIAL ROBBERIES! DURING THIS EVENING YOU WILL SUFFER DEFEAT AND DEATH BECAUSE OF THE LOSS OF ONE OF YOUR FIVE SENSES! WHICH ONE? AH, THAT'S FOR YOU TO LEARN! HEE, HEE, HEE!
NEXT MOMENT, ROBIN MAKES A DARING LEAP...
TOUCH OR NO TOUCH-- I'M GOING TO COP A RIDE ON THAT GETAWAY CAR!
I'LL FOLLOW IN THE BATMOBILE, ROBIN! STICK WITH 'EM!
6

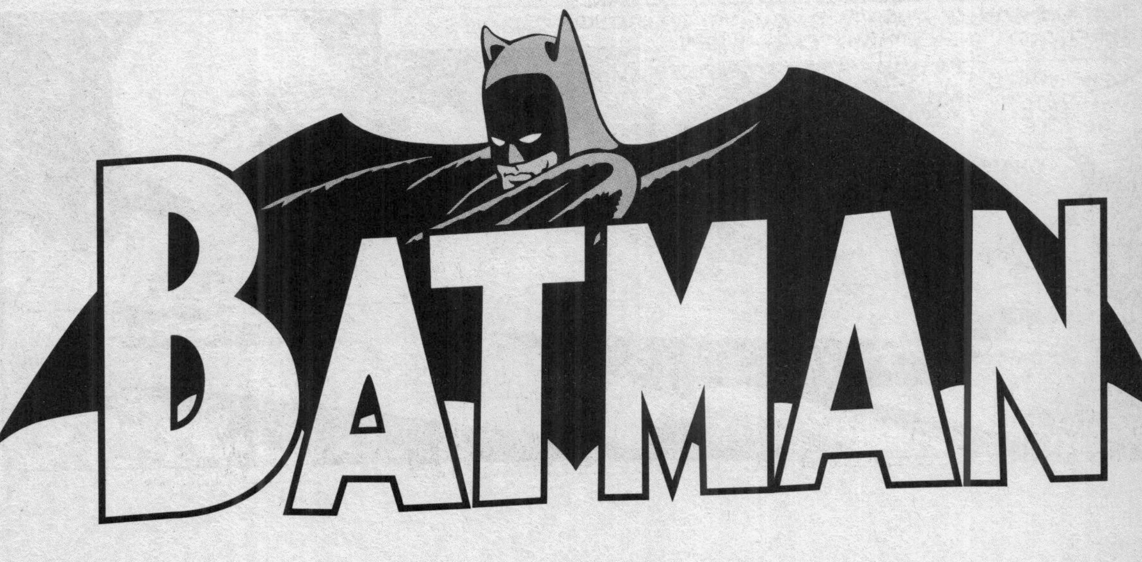
BATMAN

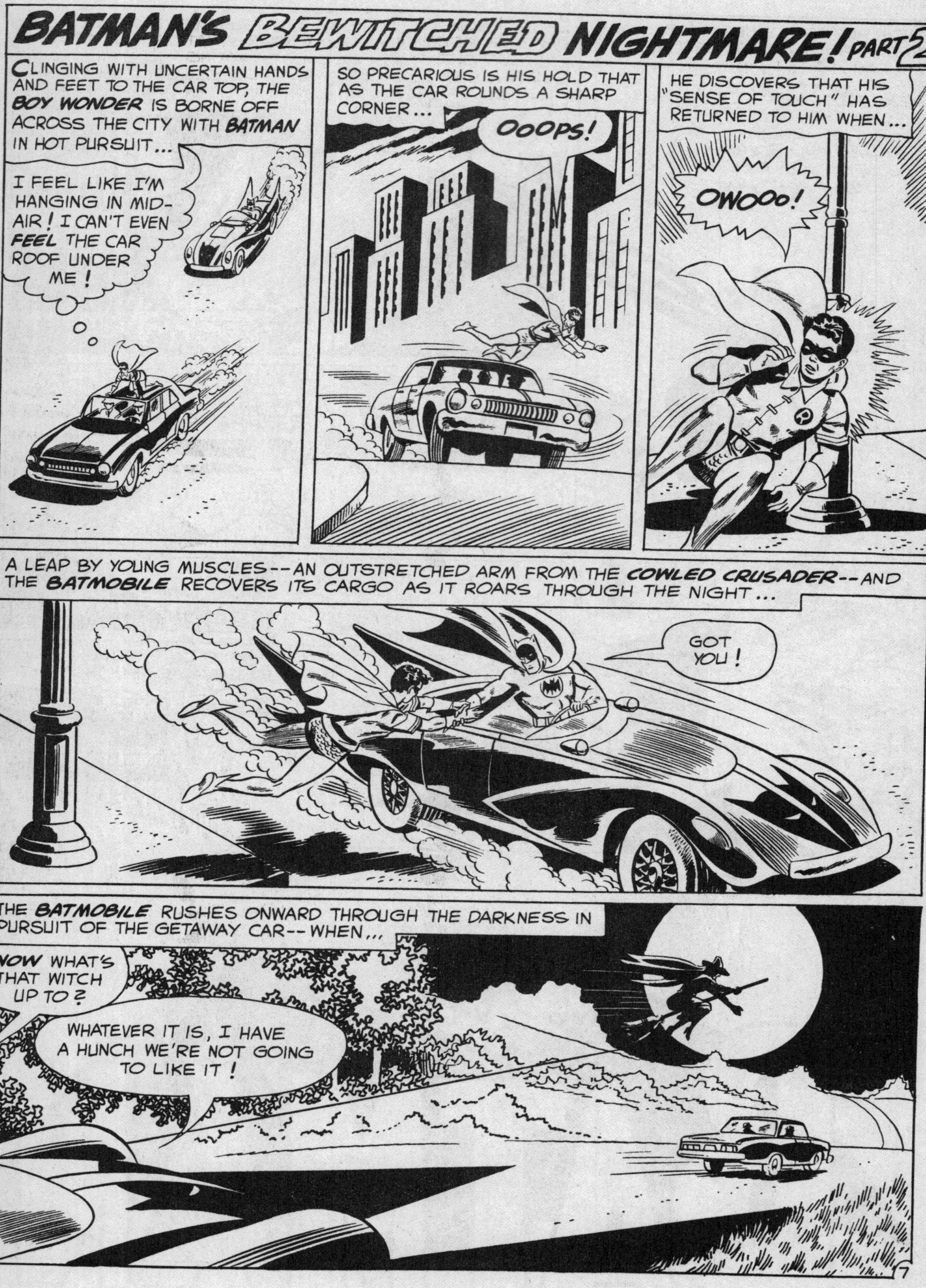
BATMAN'S BEWITCHED NIGHTMARE! PART 2
CLINGING WITH UNCERTAIN HANDS AND FEET TO THE CAR TOP, THE BOY WONDER IS BORNE OFF ACROSS THE CITY WITH BATMAN IN HOT PURSUIT...
I FEEL LIKE I'M HANGING IN MID-AIR! I CAN'T EVEN FEEL THE CAR ROOF UNDER ME!
SO PRECARIOUS IS HIS HOLD THAT AS THE CAR ROUNDS A SHARP CORNER...
OOOPS!
HE DISCOVERS THAT HIS "SENSE OF TOUCH" HAS RETURNED TO HIM WHEN...
OWOOO!
A LEAP BY YOUNG MUSCLES--AN OUTSTRETCHED ARM FROM THE COWLED CRUSADER--AND THE BATMOBILE RECOVERS ITS CARGO AS IT ROARS THROUGH THE NIGHT...
GOT YOU!
THE BATMOBILE RUSHES ONWARD THROUGH THE DARKNESS IN PURSUIT OF THE GETAWAY CAR--WHEN...
NOW WHAT'S THAT WITCH UP TO?
WHATEVER IT IS, I HAVE A HUNCH WE'RE NOT GOING TO LIKE IT!
7

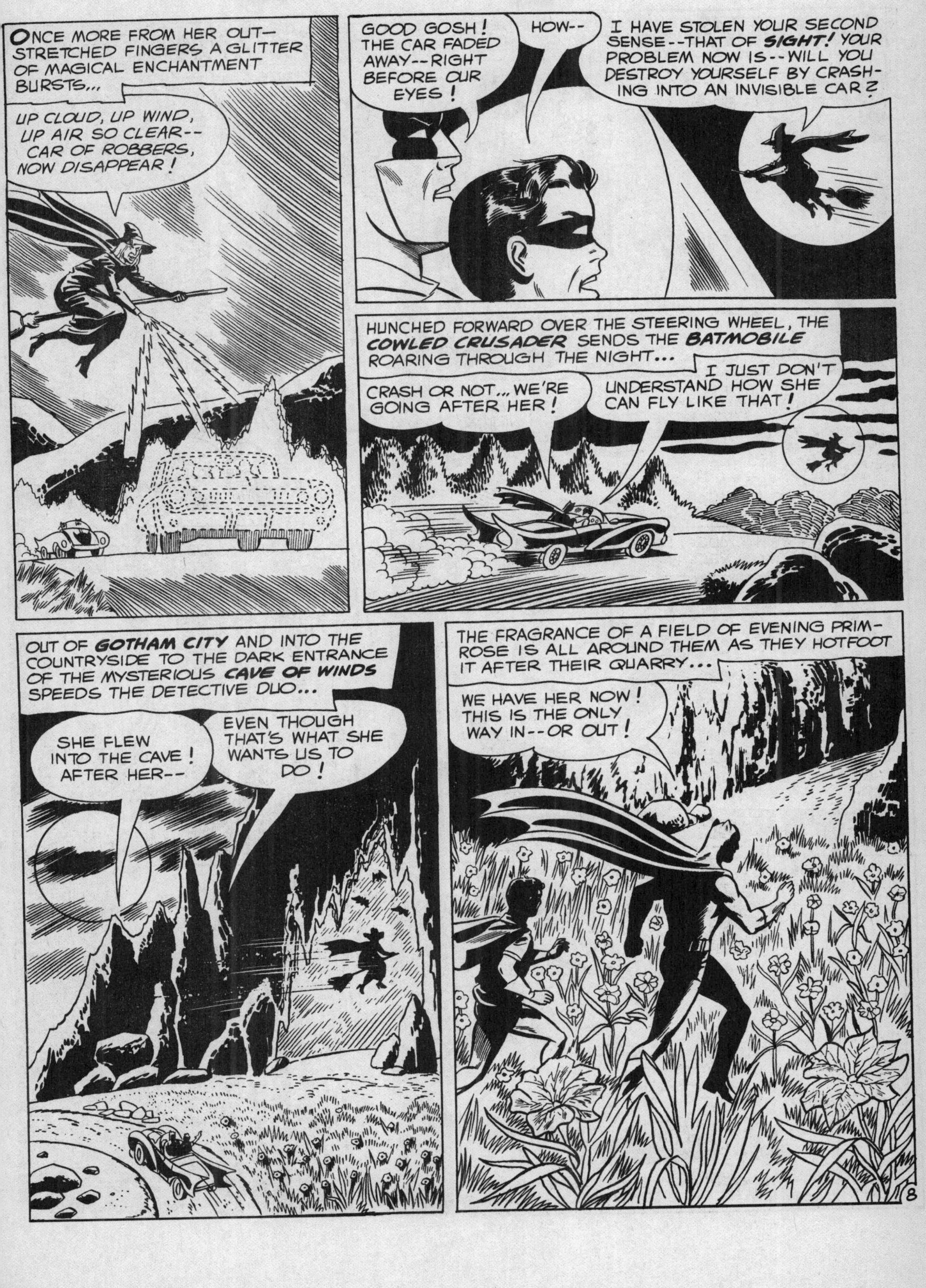
ONCE MORE FROM HER OUT-STRETCHED FINGERS A GLITTER OF MAGICAL ENCHANTMENT BURSTS...
UP CLOUD, UP WIND, UP AIR SO CLEAR-- CAR OF ROBBERS, NOW DISAPPEAR!
GOOD GOSH! THE CAR FADED AWAY--RIGHT BEFORE OUR EYES!
HOW--
I HAVE STOLEN YOUR SECOND SENSE--THAT OF SIGHT! YOUR PROBLEM NOW IS--WILL YOU DESTROY YOURSELF BY CRASHING INTO AN INVISIBLE CAR?
HUNCHED FORWARD OVER THE STEERING WHEEL, THE COWLED CRUSADER SENDS THE BATMOBILE ROARING THROUGH THE NIGHT...
CRASH OR NOT... WE'RE GOING AFTER HER!
I JUST DON'T UNDERSTAND HOW SHE CAN FLY LIKE THAT!
OUT OF GOTHAM CITY AND INTO THE COUNTRYSIDE TO THE DARK ENTRANCE OF THE MYSTERIOUS CAVE OF WINDS SPEEDS THE DETECTIVE DUO...
SHE FLEW INTO THE CAVE! AFTER HER--
EVEN THOUGH THAT'S WHAT SHE WANTS US TO DO!
THE FRAGRANCE OF A FIELD OF EVENING PRIMROSE IS ALL AROUND THEM AS THEY HOTFOOT IT AFTER THEIR QUARRY...
WE HAVE HER NOW! THIS IS THE ONLY WAY IN--OR OUT!
8

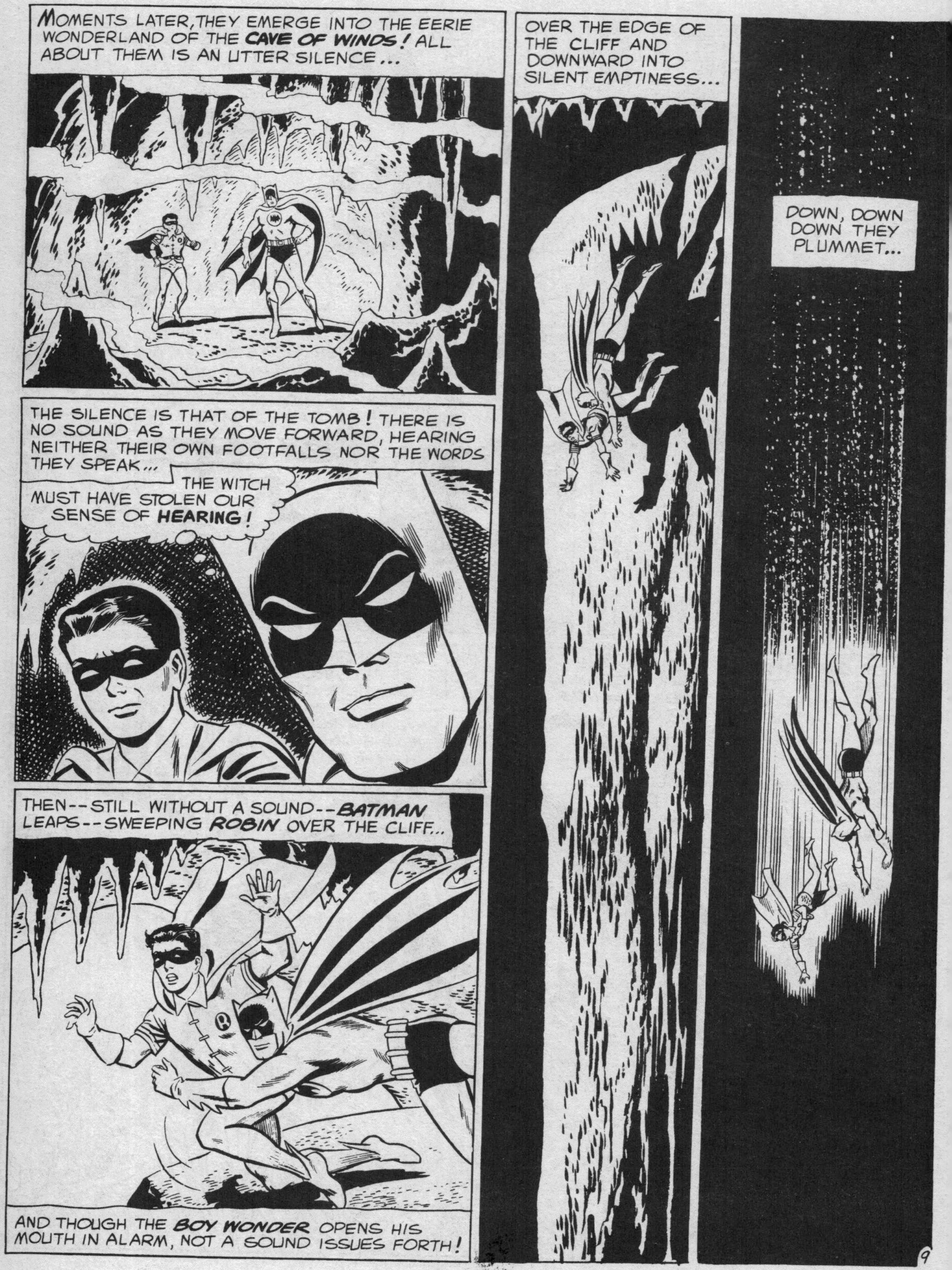
MOMENTS LATER, THEY EMERGE INTO THE EERIE WONDERLAND OF THE CAVE OF WINDS! ALL ABOUT THEM IS AN UTTER SILENCE...
THE SILENCE IS THAT OF THE TOMB! THERE IS NO SOUND AS THEY MOVE FORWARD, HEARING NEITHER THEIR OWN FOOTFALLS NOR THE WORDS THEY SPEAK...
THE WITCH MUST HAVE STOLEN OUR SENSE OF HEARING!
THEN--STILL WITHOUT A SOUND--BATMAN LEAPS--SWEEPING ROBIN OVER THE CLIFF...
AND THOUGH THE BOY WONDER OPENS HIS MOUTH IN ALARM, NOT A SOUND ISSUES FORTH!
OVER THE EDGE OF THE CLIFF AND DOWNWARD INTO SILENT EMPTINESS...
DOWN, DOWN DOWN THEY PLUMMET...
9

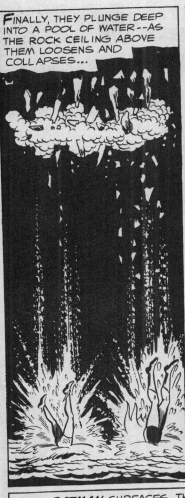

FINALLY, THEY PLUNGE DEEP INTO A POOL OF WATER--AS THE ROCK CEILING ABOVE THEM LOOSENS AND COLLAPSES...

IT IS *ROBIN* WHO COMES TO THE SURFACE FIRST AND SEES...

NO WONDER *BATMAN* TACKLED ME! IF THOSE FALLING ROCKS HAD HIT US, WE'D HAVE BEEN CRUSHED!

DESPERATELY, THE WITCH STRADDLES HER BROOM-STICK AND RISES UPWARD-- THE ROCKS PARTING ON EITHER SIDE OF HER TO ALLOW HER TO FLY BETWEEN THEM...

SHE STOLE OUR SENSE OF *HEARING*--SO WE WOULDN'T BE ALERTED BY THE RUMBLE OF THE COLLAPSING CEILING! THAT WAY, SHE HOPED TO DESTROY US!

WHEN *BATMAN* SURFACES, THEY DISCOVER THEIR ABILITY TO HEAR HAS RETURNED...

LUCKILY YOU SPOTTED THOSE ROCKS FALLING, *BATMAN*--AND REALIZED WHAT THEY MEANT!

I TRIED TO WARN YOU BUT YOU COULDN'T HEAR ME!

THEIR FEET BARELY TOUCH THE GROUND AS THEY HURTLE TOWARD THE CAVE ENTRANCE AND OUT INTO THE AUTUMNAL DARKNESS...

SOMETHING'S WRONG! WE'RE SURROUNDED BY--*DANGER!*

10

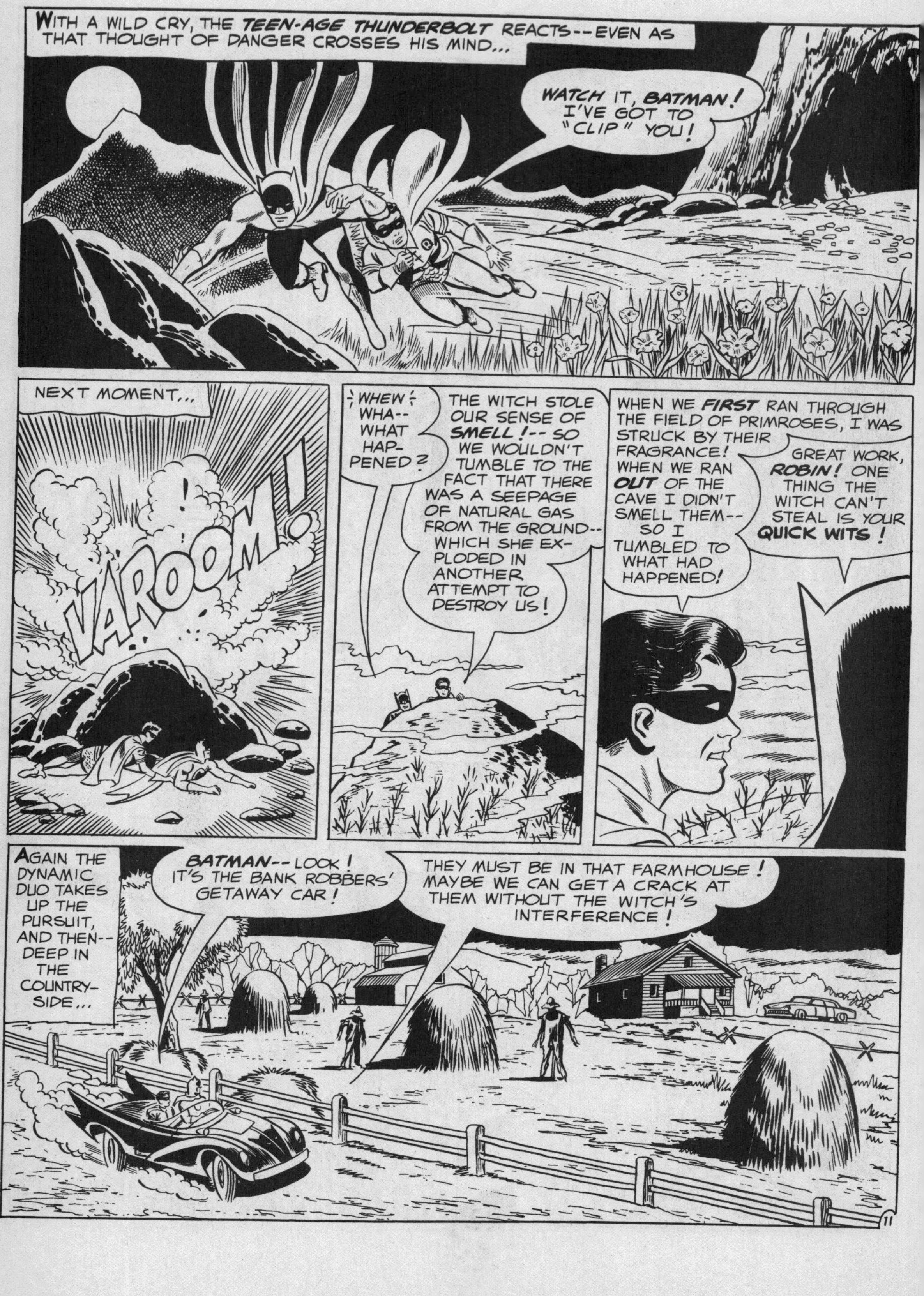
WITH A WILD CRY, THE TEEN-AGE THUNDERBOLT REACTS--EVEN AS THAT THOUGHT OF DANGER CROSSES HIS MIND...
WATCH IT, BATMAN! I'VE GOT TO "CLIP" YOU!
NEXT MOMENT...
VAROOM!
WHEW! WHA--WHAT HAPPENED?
THE WITCH STOLE OUR SENSE OF SMELL!--SO WE WOULDN'T TUMBLE TO THE FACT THAT THERE WAS A SEEPAGE OF NATURAL GAS FROM THE GROUND--WHICH SHE EXPLODED IN ANOTHER ATTEMPT TO DESTROY US!
WHEN WE FIRST RAN THROUGH THE FIELD OF PRIMROSES, I WAS STRUCK BY THEIR FRAGRANCE! WHEN WE RAN OUT OF THE CAVE I DIDN'T SMELL THEM--SO I TUMBLED TO WHAT HAD HAPPENED!
GREAT WORK, ROBIN! ONE THING THE WITCH CAN'T STEAL IS YOUR QUICK WITS!
AGAIN THE DYNAMIC DUO TAKES UP THE PURSUIT, AND THEN--DEEP IN THE COUNTRY-SIDE...
BATMAN--LOOK! IT'S THE BANK ROBBERS' GETAWAY CAR!
THEY MUST BE IN THAT FARMHOUSE! MAYBE WE CAN GET A CRACK AT THEM WITHOUT THE WITCH'S INTERFERENCE!
11

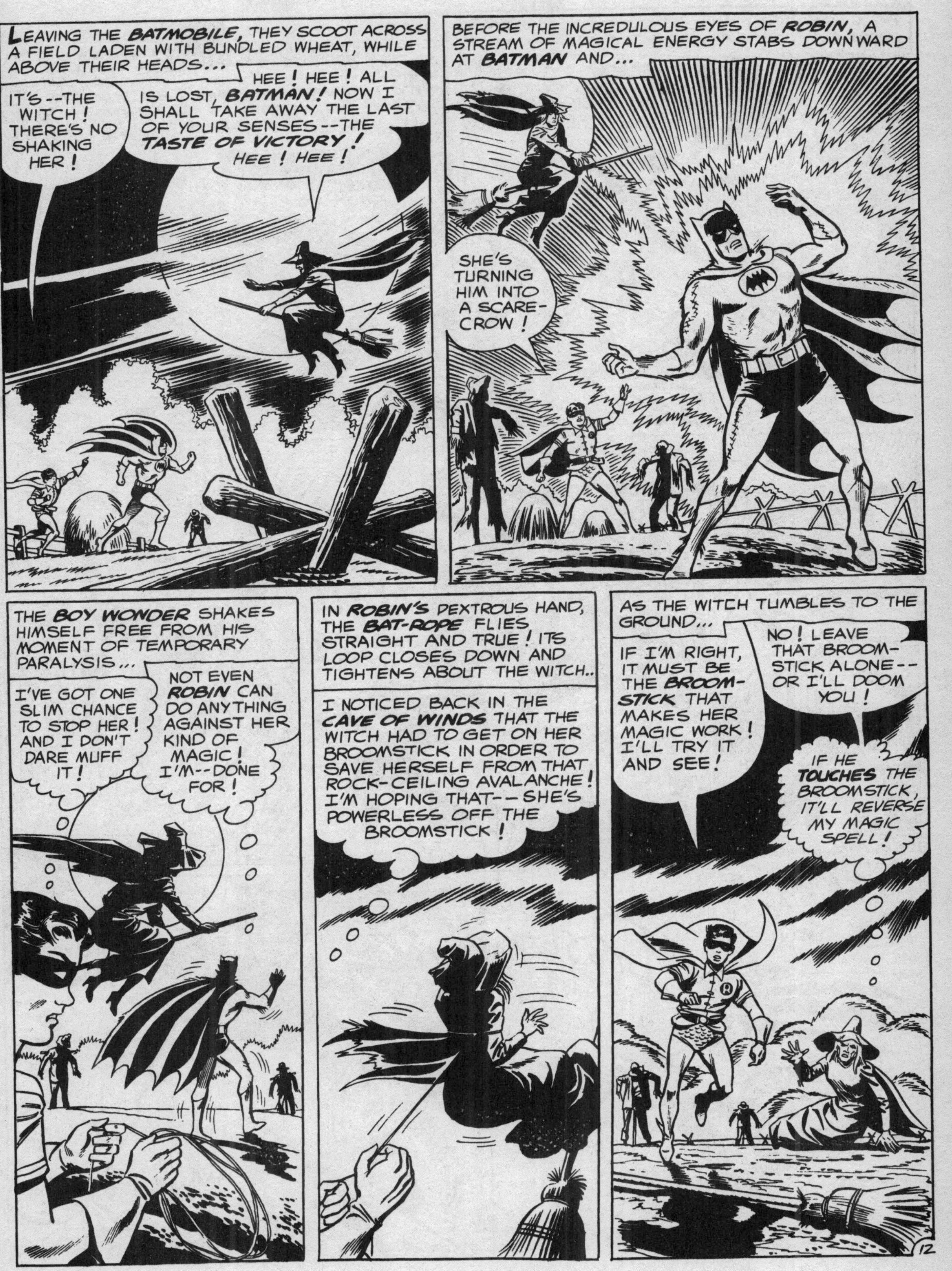
LEAVING THE BATMOBILE, THEY SCOOT ACROSS A FIELD LADEN WITH BUNDLED WHEAT, WHILE ABOVE THEIR HEADS...
IT'S--THE WITCH! THERE'S NO SHAKING HER!
HEE! HEE! ALL IS LOST, BATMAN! NOW I SHALL TAKE AWAY THE LAST OF YOUR SENSES--THE TASTE OF VICTORY! HEE! HEE!
BEFORE THE INCREDULOUS EYES OF ROBIN, A STREAM OF MAGICAL ENERGY STABS DOWNWARD AT BATMAN AND...
SHE'S TURNING HIM INTO A SCARE-CROW!
THE BOY WONDER SHAKES HIMSELF FREE FROM HIS MOMENT OF TEMPORARY PARALYSIS...
I'VE GOT ONE SLIM CHANCE TO STOP HER! AND I DON'T DARE MUFF IT!
NOT EVEN ROBIN CAN DO ANYTHING AGAINST HER KIND OF MAGIC! I'M--DONE FOR!
IN ROBIN'S DEXTROUS HAND, THE BAT-ROPE FLIES STRAIGHT AND TRUE! ITS LOOP CLOSES DOWN AND TIGHTENS ABOUT THE WITCH..
I NOTICED BACK IN THE CAVE OF WINDS THAT THE WITCH HAD TO GET ON HER BROOMSTICK IN ORDER TO SAVE HERSELF FROM THAT ROCK-CEILING AVALANCHE! I'M HOPING THAT--SHE'S POWERLESS OFF THE BROOMSTICK!
AS THE WITCH TUMBLES TO THE GROUND...
IF I'M RIGHT, IT MUST BE THE BROOMSTICK THAT MAKES HER MAGIC WORK! I'LL TRY IT AND SEE!
NO! LEAVE THAT BROOM-STICK ALONE--OR I'LL DOOM YOU!
IF HE TOUCHES THE BROOMSTICK, IT'LL REVERSE MY MAGIC SPELL!
12

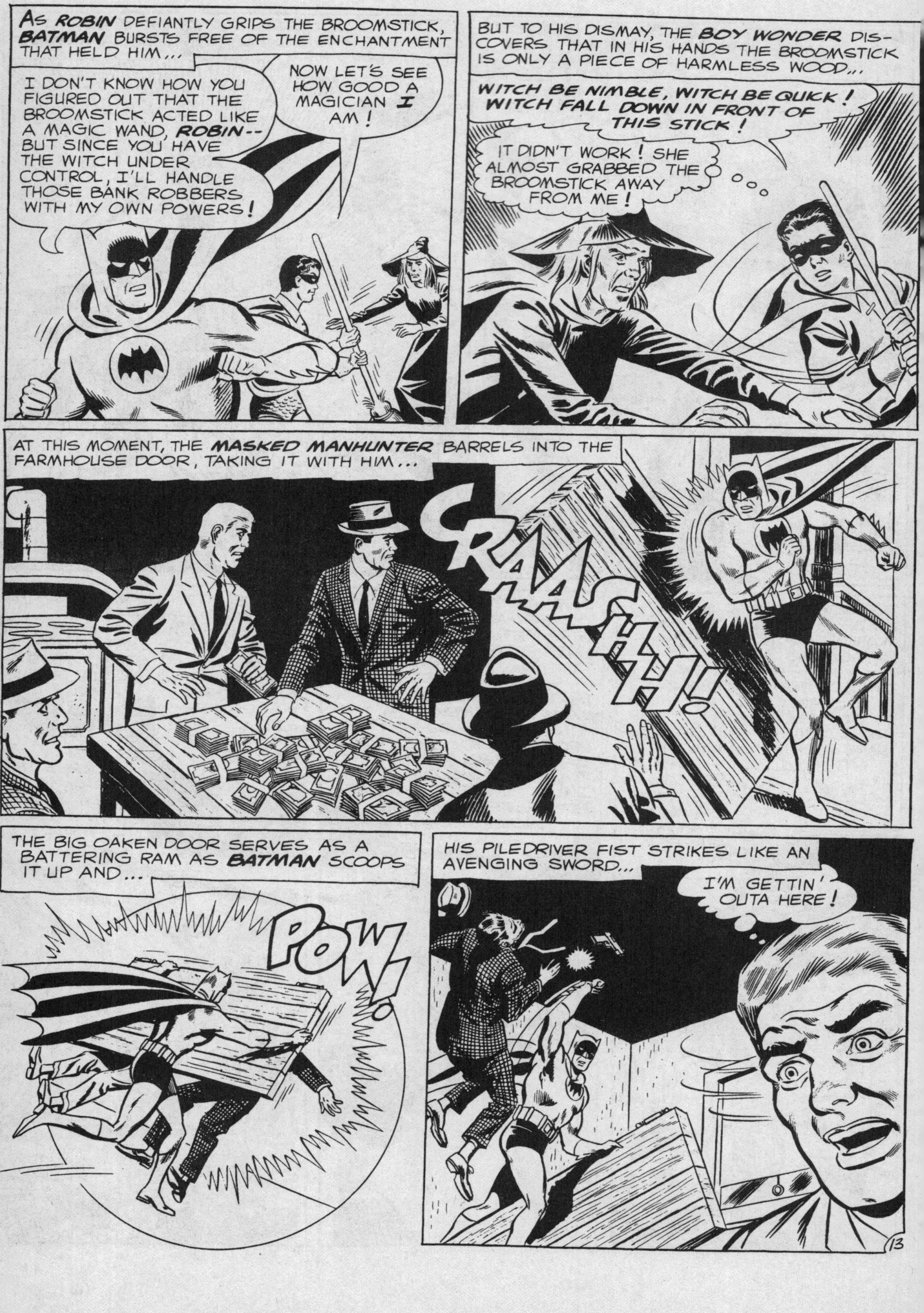
AS ROBIN DEFIANTLY GRIPS THE BROOMSTICK, BATMAN BURSTS FREE OF THE ENCHANTMENT THAT HELD HIM...
I DON'T KNOW HOW YOU FIGURED OUT THAT THE BROOMSTICK ACTED LIKE A MAGIC WAND, ROBIN-- BUT SINCE YOU HAVE THE WITCH UNDER CONTROL, I'LL HANDLE THOSE BANK ROBBERS WITH MY OWN POWERS!
NOW LET'S SEE HOW GOOD A MAGICIAN I AM!
BUT TO HIS DISMAY, THE BOY WONDER DISCOVERS THAT IN HIS HANDS THE BROOMSTICK IS ONLY A PIECE OF HARMLESS WOOD...
WITCH BE NIMBLE, WITCH BE QUICK! WITCH FALL DOWN IN FRONT OF THIS STICK!
IT DIDN'T WORK! SHE ALMOST GRABBED THE BROOMSTICK AWAY FROM ME!
AT THIS MOMENT, THE MASKED MANHUNTER BARRELS INTO THE FARMHOUSE DOOR, TAKING IT WITH HIM...
CRAASHH!
THE BIG OAKEN DOOR SERVES AS A BATTERING RAM AS BATMAN SCOOPS IT UP AND...
POW!
HIS PILEDRIVER FIST STRIKES LIKE AN AVENGING SWORD...
I'M GETTIN' OUTA HERE!
13

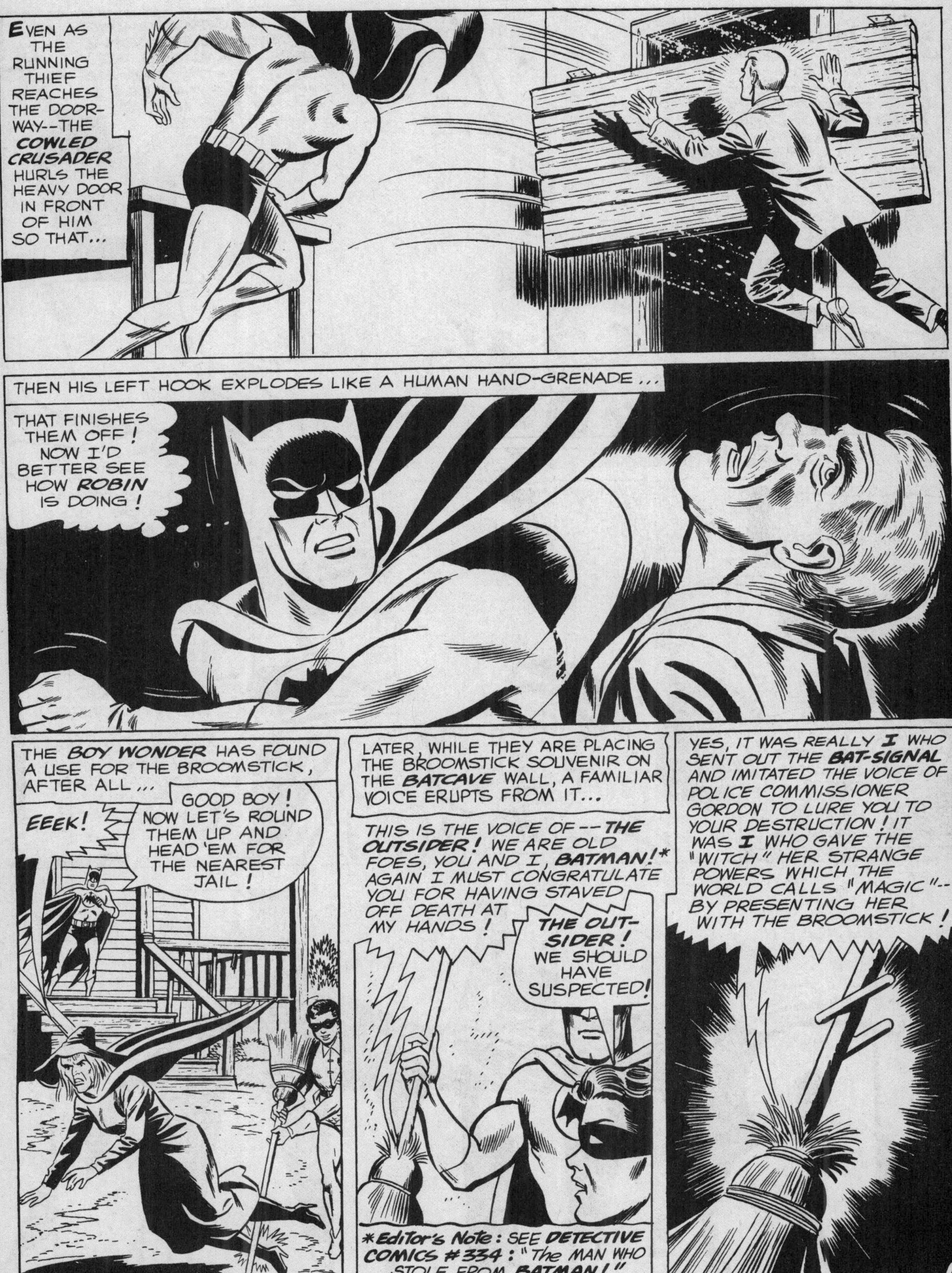
EVEN AS THE RUNNING THIEF REACHES THE DOORWAY--THE COWLED CRUSADER HURLS THE HEAVY DOOR IN FRONT OF HIM SO THAT...
THEN HIS LEFT HOOK EXPLODES LIKE A HUMAN HAND-GRENADE...
THAT FINISHES THEM OFF! NOW I'D BETTER SEE HOW ROBIN IS DOING!
THE BOY WONDER HAS FOUND A USE FOR THE BROOMSTICK, AFTER ALL...
EEEK!
GOOD BOY! NOW LET'S ROUND THEM UP AND HEAD 'EM FOR THE NEAREST JAIL!
LATER, WHILE THEY ARE PLACING THE BROOMSTICK SOUVENIR ON THE BATCAVE WALL, A FAMILIAR VOICE ERUPTS FROM IT...
THIS IS THE VOICE OF --THE OUTSIDER! WE ARE OLD FOES, YOU AND I, BATMAN!* AGAIN I MUST CONGRATULATE YOU FOR HAVING STAVED OFF DEATH AT MY HANDS!
THE OUTSIDER! WE SHOULD HAVE SUSPECTED!
*Editor's Note: SEE DETECTIVE COMICS #334: "The MAN WHO STOLE FROM BATMAN!"
YES, IT WAS REALLY I WHO SENT OUT THE BAT-SIGNAL AND IMITATED THE VOICE OF POLICE COMMISSIONER GORDON TO LURE YOU TO YOUR DESTRUCTION! IT WAS I WHO GAVE THE "WITCH" HER STRANGE POWERS WHICH THE WORLD CALLS "MAGIC"--BY PRESENTING HER WITH THE BROOMSTICK!
14

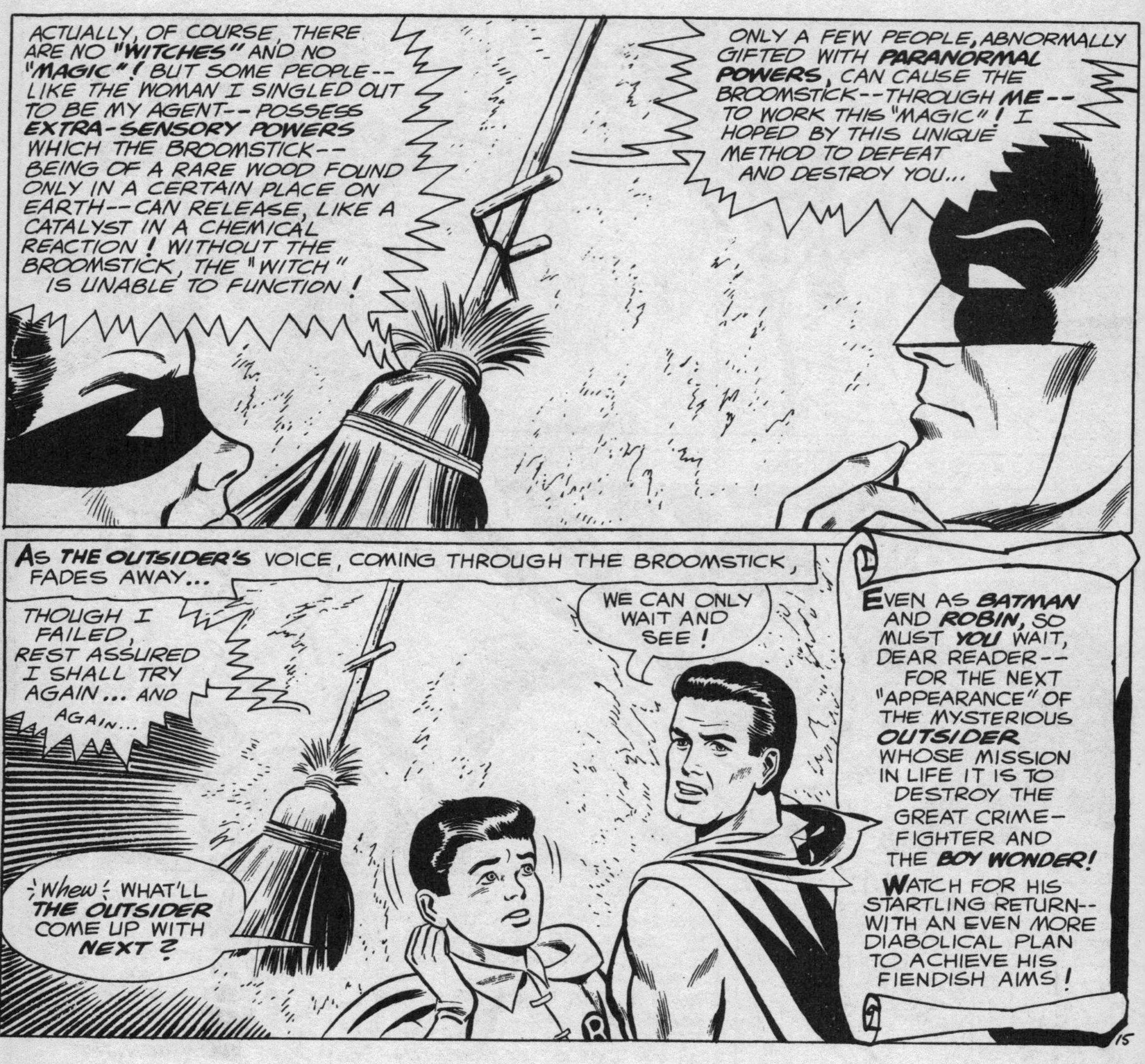
ACTUALLY, OF COURSE, THERE ARE NO "WITCHES" AND NO "MAGIC"! BUT SOME PEOPLE-- LIKE THE WOMAN I SINGLED OUT TO BE MY AGENT-- POSSESS EXTRA-SENSORY POWERS WHICH THE BROOMSTICK-- BEING OF A RARE WOOD FOUND ONLY IN A CERTAIN PLACE ON EARTH--CAN RELEASE, LIKE A CATALYST IN A CHEMICAL REACTION! WITHOUT THE BROOMSTICK, THE "WITCH" IS UNABLE TO FUNCTION!
ONLY A FEW PEOPLE, ABNORMALLY GIFTED WITH PARANORMAL POWERS, CAN CAUSE THE BROOMSTICK--THROUGH ME-- TO WORK THIS "MAGIC"! I HOPED BY THIS UNIQUE METHOD TO DEFEAT AND DESTROY YOU...
AS THE OUTSIDER'S VOICE, COMING THROUGH THE BROOMSTICK, FADES AWAY...
THOUGH I FAILED, REST ASSURED I SHALL TRY AGAIN... AND AGAIN...
WE CAN ONLY WAIT AND SEE!
WHEW! WHAT'LL THE OUTSIDER COME UP WITH NEXT?
EVEN AS BATMAN AND ROBIN, SO MUST YOU WAIT, DEAR READER-- FOR THE NEXT "APPEARANCE" OF THE MYSTERIOUS OUTSIDER WHOSE MISSION IN LIFE IT IS TO DESTROY THE GREAT CRIME-FIGHTER AND THE BOY WONDER!
WATCH FOR HIS STARTLING RETURN-- WITH AN EVEN MORE DIABOLICAL PLAN TO ACHIEVE HIS FIENDISH AIMS!
15

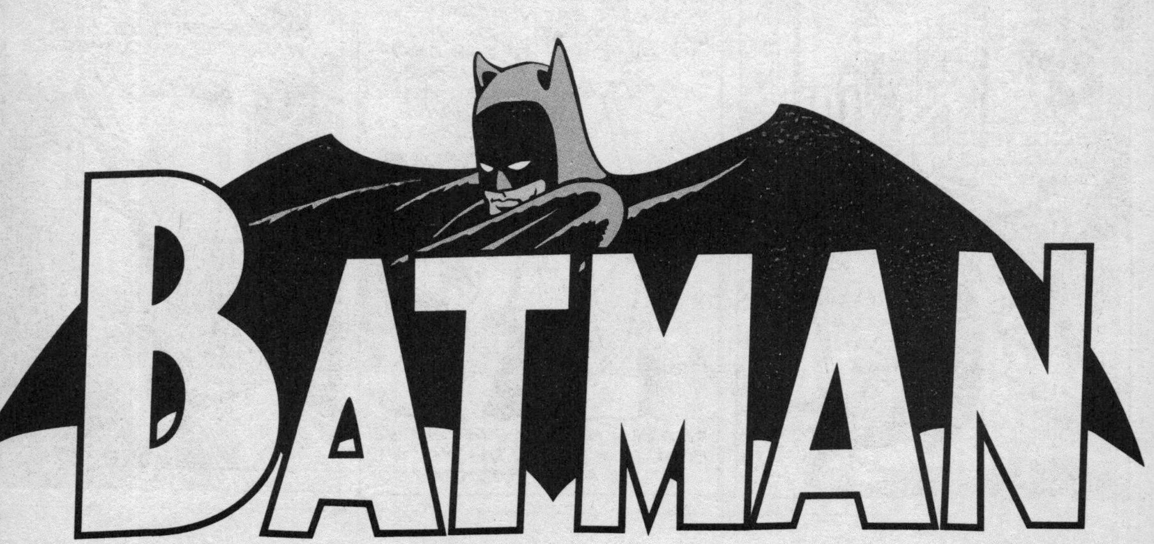
BATMAN

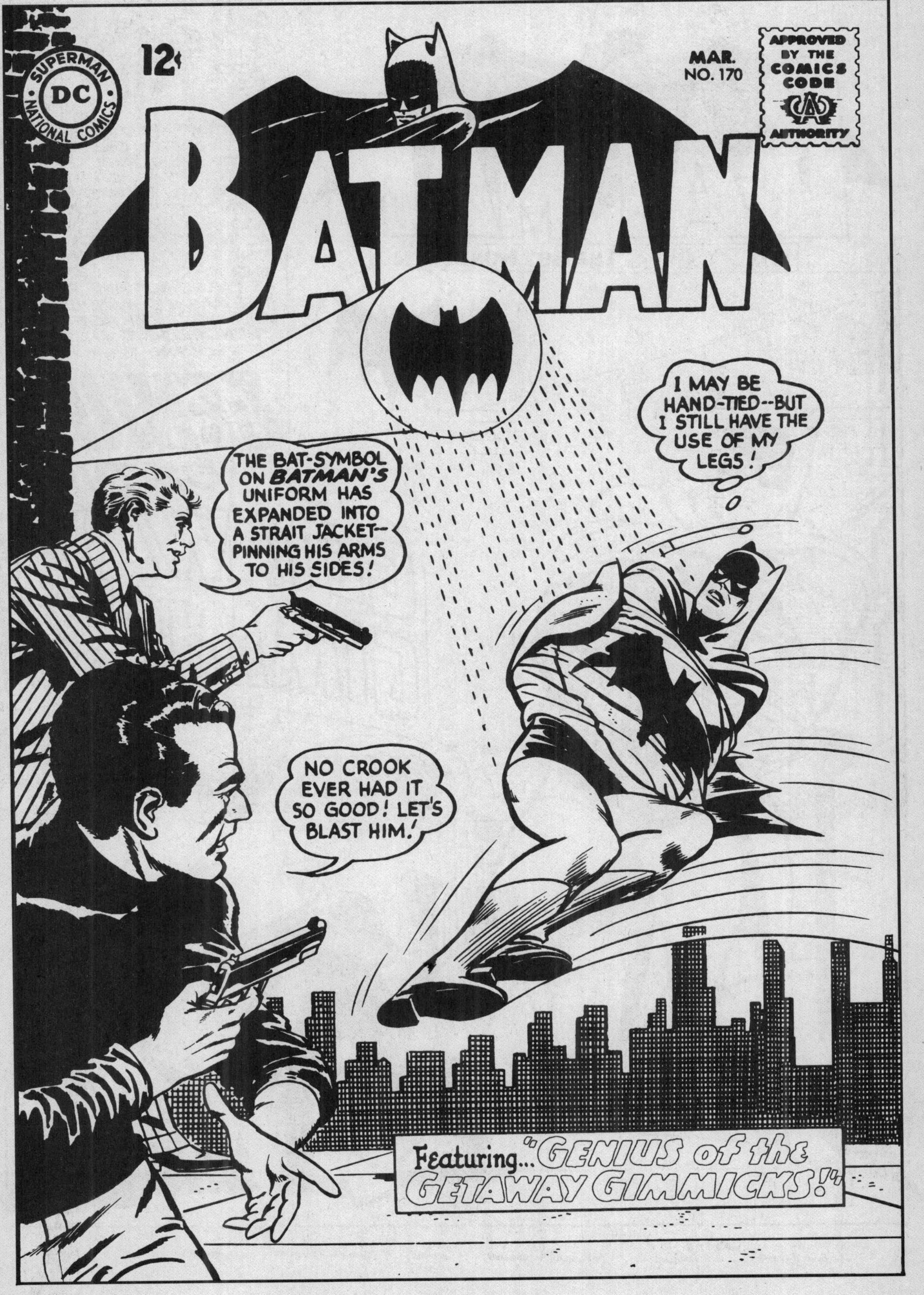
12¢
SUPERMAN DC NATIONAL COMICS
MAR. NO. 170
APPROVED BY THE COMICS CODE AUTHORITY
BATMAN
I MAY BE HAND-TIED--BUT I STILL HAVE THE USE OF MY LEGS!
THE BAT-SYMBOL ON BATMAN'S UNIFORM HAS EXPANDED INTO A STRAIT JACKET-- PINNING HIS ARMS TO HIS SIDES!
NO CROOK EVER HAD IT SO GOOD! LET'S BLAST HIM!
Featuring... "GENIUS of the GETAWAY GIMMICKS!"

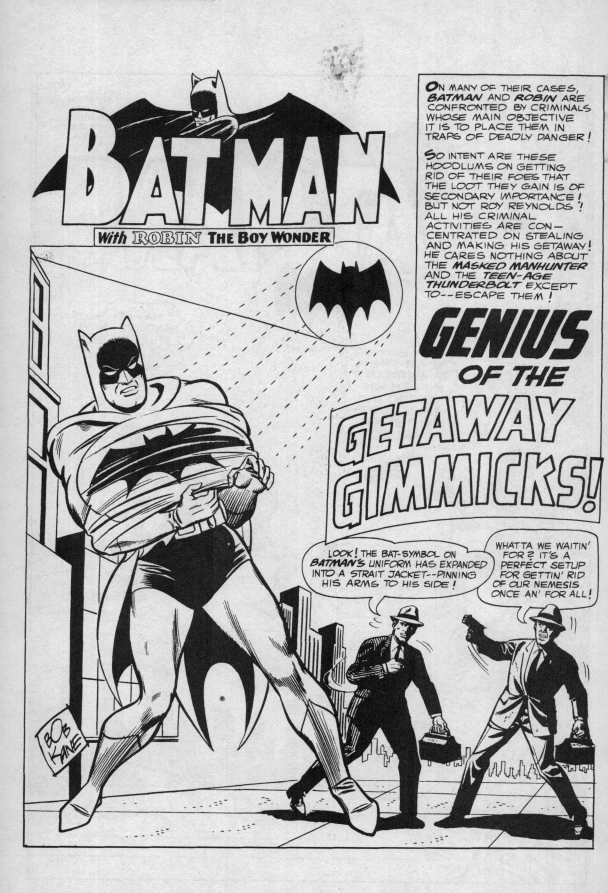

BATMAN
with ROBIN THE BOY WONDER

On many of their cases, **BATMAN** and **ROBIN** are confronted by criminals whose main objective it is to place them in traps of deadly danger!

So intent are these hoodlums on getting rid of their foes that the loot they gain is of secondary importance! But not ROY REYNOLDS! All his criminal activities are concentrated on stealing and making his getaway! He cares nothing about the **MASKED MANHUNTER** and the **TEEN-AGE THUNDERBOLT** except to -- escape them!

GENIUS OF THE GETAWAY GIMMICKS!

LOOK! THE BAT-SYMBOL ON **BATMAN'S** UNIFORM HAS EXPANDED INTO A STRAIT JACKET--PINNING HIS ARMS TO HIS SIDE!

WHATTA WE WAITIN' FOR? IT'S A PERFECT SETUP FOR GETTIN' RID OF OUR NEMESIS ONCE AN' FOR ALL!

BOB KANE

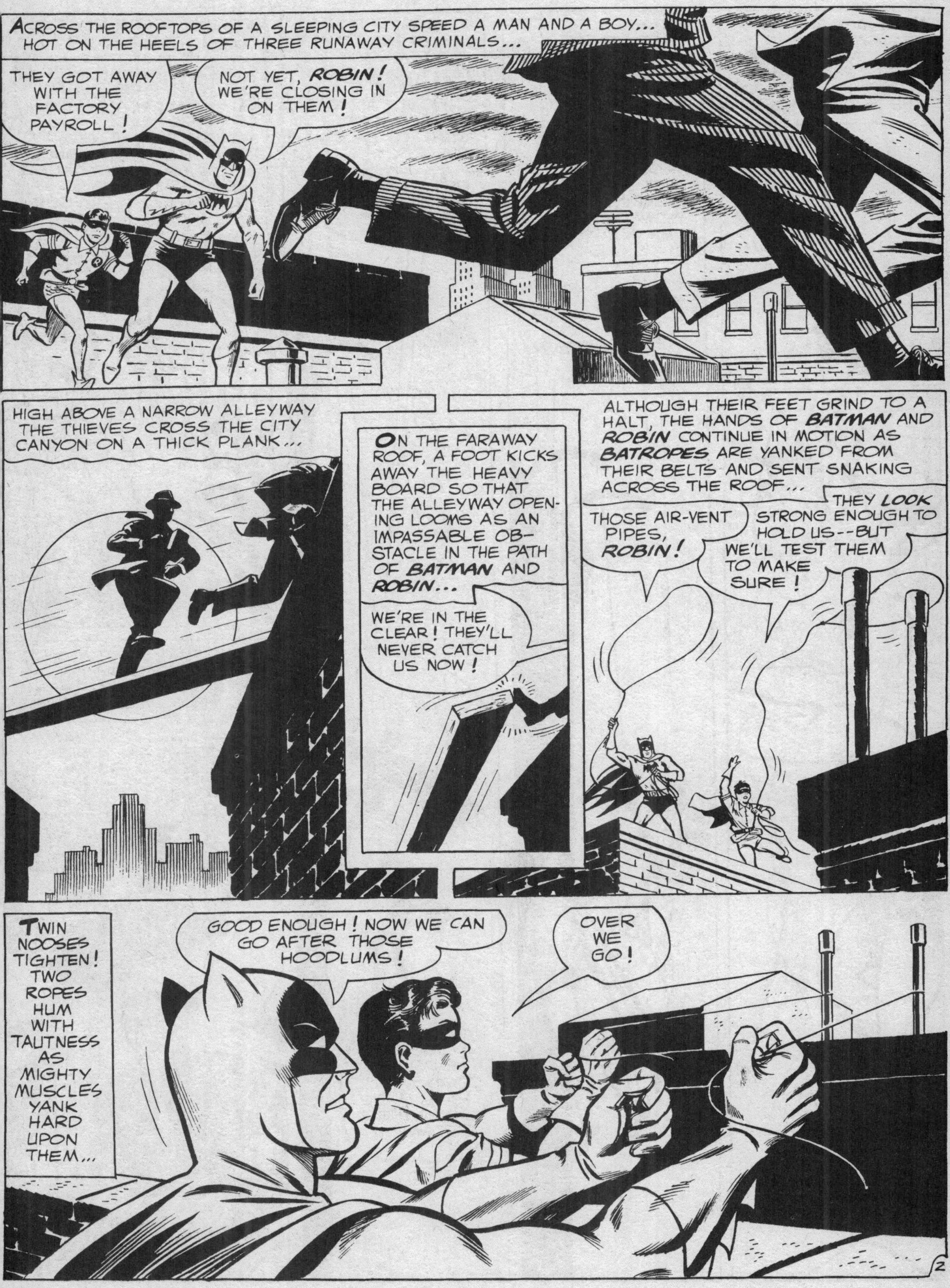
ACROSS THE ROOFTOPS OF A SLEEPING CITY SPEED A MAN AND A BOY... HOT ON THE HEELS OF THREE RUNAWAY CRIMINALS...
THEY GOT AWAY WITH THE FACTORY PAYROLL!
NOT YET, ROBIN! WE'RE CLOSING IN ON THEM!
HIGH ABOVE A NARROW ALLEYWAY THE THIEVES CROSS THE CITY CANYON ON A THICK PLANK...
ON THE FARAWAY ROOF, A FOOT KICKS AWAY THE HEAVY BOARD SO THAT THE ALLEYWAY OPENING LOOMS AS AN IMPASSABLE OBSTACLE IN THE PATH OF BATMAN AND ROBIN...
WE'RE IN THE CLEAR! THEY'LL NEVER CATCH US NOW!
ALTHOUGH THEIR FEET GRIND TO A HALT, THE HANDS OF BATMAN AND ROBIN CONTINUE IN MOTION AS BATROPES ARE YANKED FROM THEIR BELTS AND SENT SNAKING ACROSS THE ROOF...
THOSE AIR-VENT PIPES, ROBIN!
THEY LOOK STRONG ENOUGH TO HOLD US--BUT WE'LL TEST THEM TO MAKE SURE!
TWIN NOOSES TIGHTEN! TWO ROPES HUM WITH TAUTNESS AS MIGHTY MUSCLES YANK HARD UPON THEM...
GOOD ENOUGH! NOW WE CAN GO AFTER THOSE HOODLUMS!
OVER WE GO!
2

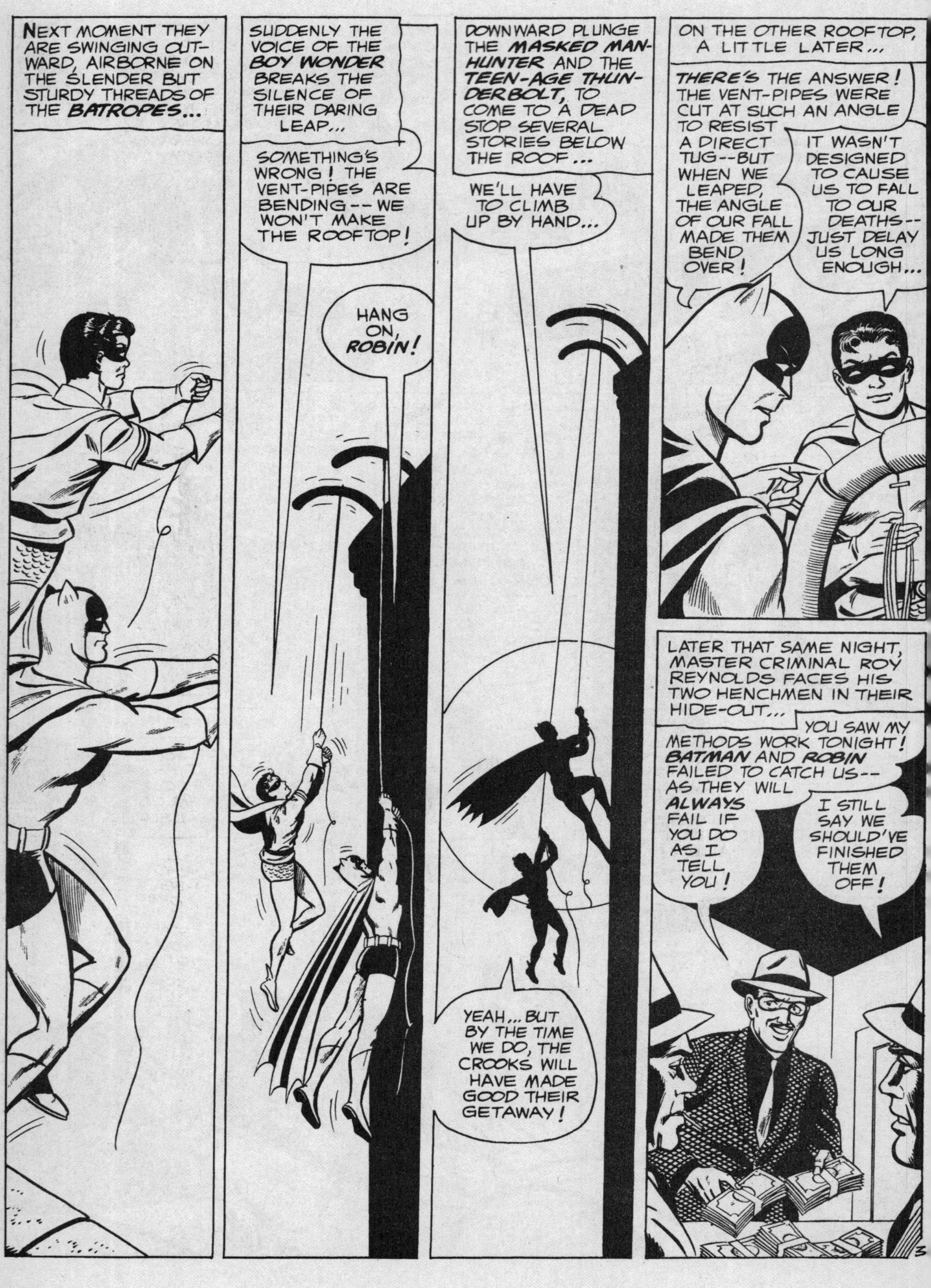
NEXT MOMENT THEY ARE SWINGING OUTWARD, AIRBORNE ON THE SLENDER BUT STURDY THREADS OF THE BATROPES...
SUDDENLY THE VOICE OF THE BOY WONDER BREAKS THE SILENCE OF THEIR DARING LEAP...
SOMETHING'S WRONG! THE VENT-PIPES ARE BENDING -- WE WON'T MAKE THE ROOFTOP!
HANG ON, ROBIN!
DOWNWARD PLUNGE THE MASKED MAN-HUNTER AND THE TEEN-AGE THUNDERBOLT, TO COME TO A DEAD STOP SEVERAL STORIES BELOW THE ROOF...
WE'LL HAVE TO CLIMB UP BY HAND...
YEAH,.. BUT BY THE TIME WE DO, THE CROOKS WILL HAVE MADE GOOD THEIR GETAWAY!
ON THE OTHER ROOFTOP, A LITTLE LATER...
THERE'S THE ANSWER! THE VENT-PIPES WERE CUT AT SUCH AN ANGLE TO RESIST A DIRECT TUG--BUT WHEN WE LEAPED, THE ANGLE OF OUR FALL MADE THEM BEND OVER!
IT WASN'T DESIGNED TO CAUSE US TO FALL TO OUR DEATHS-- JUST DELAY US LONG ENOUGH...
LATER THAT SAME NIGHT, MASTER CRIMINAL ROY REYNOLDS FACES HIS TWO HENCHMEN IN THEIR HIDE-OUT...
YOU SAW MY METHODS WORK TONIGHT! BATMAN AND ROBIN FAILED TO CATCH US-- AS THEY WILL ALWAYS FAIL IF YOU DO AS I TELL YOU!
I STILL SAY WE SHOULD'VE FINISHED THEM OFF!
3

ANGER CONTORTS THE FACE OF ROY REYNOLDS INTO HARSH LINES...

NO! I ABSOLUTELY FORBID IT! THIS IS ONE THING YOU MUST *NOT* TRY TO DO! FAR SMARTER CROOKS THAN YOU OR I HAVE TRIED TO CAPTURE *BATMAN*--AND ALWAYS THEY FAILED! IT'S THE ONE WAY TO COURT DISASTER!

I TELL YOU THIS: IF YOUR OBJECTIVE IS TO GET RID OF *BATMAN* AND *ROBIN*-- FORGET IT! IT CAN'T BE DONE! THEIR RECORD PROVES THEY ALWAYS MANAGE TO ESCAPE EVERY TRAP LAID FOR THEM! BESIDES--I'M A THIEF-- NOT AN EXECUTIONER!

ALL MY EFFORTS ARE DIRECTED TO COMMITTING A CRIME AND GETTING AWAY SAFELY! THE MINUTE I CONCENTRATE ON TRYING TO GET RID OF *BATMAN* AND *ROBIN*-- IT'LL BOOMERANG ON ME AND CAUSE MY OWN DOOM!

IN THE DAYS THAT FOLLOW, THE PAPERS ARE FILLED WITH THE AMAZING ESCAPES OF *BATMAN* FROM AWESOME TRAPS--WITH THE RESULTANT *CAPTURE* OF THE CRIMINALS WHO LAID THEM...

TWO MORE FOOLHARDY CROOKS WHO SOUGHT TO OUTWIT *BATMAN*--AND FAILED!

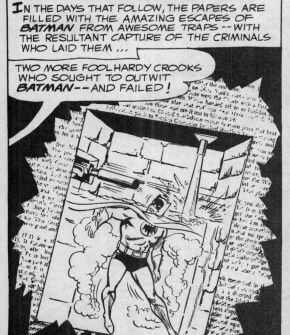

AGAIN, WHEN *THE JOKER* HAS CHALLENGED HIS ARCH-FOES...

THAT *JOKER* WILL NEVER LEARN! HE THOUGHT HE HAD *BATMAN* AND *ROBIN* IN A FOOLPROOF TRAP--ONLY TO HAVE THEM ESCAPE AND PUT HIM IN JAIL--AS USUAL!

YOU TWO ARE WASHED UP! YOU'LL NEVER GET OUT OF HERE ALIVE--BECAUSE ONLY *THIS KEY* CAN *SAFELY* OPEN THE DOOR--AND I'M TAKING IT WITH ME! ANY *OTHER* MEANS OF ESCAPE WILL BLOW THE CELL--AND *YOU*--TO SMITHEREENS!

4

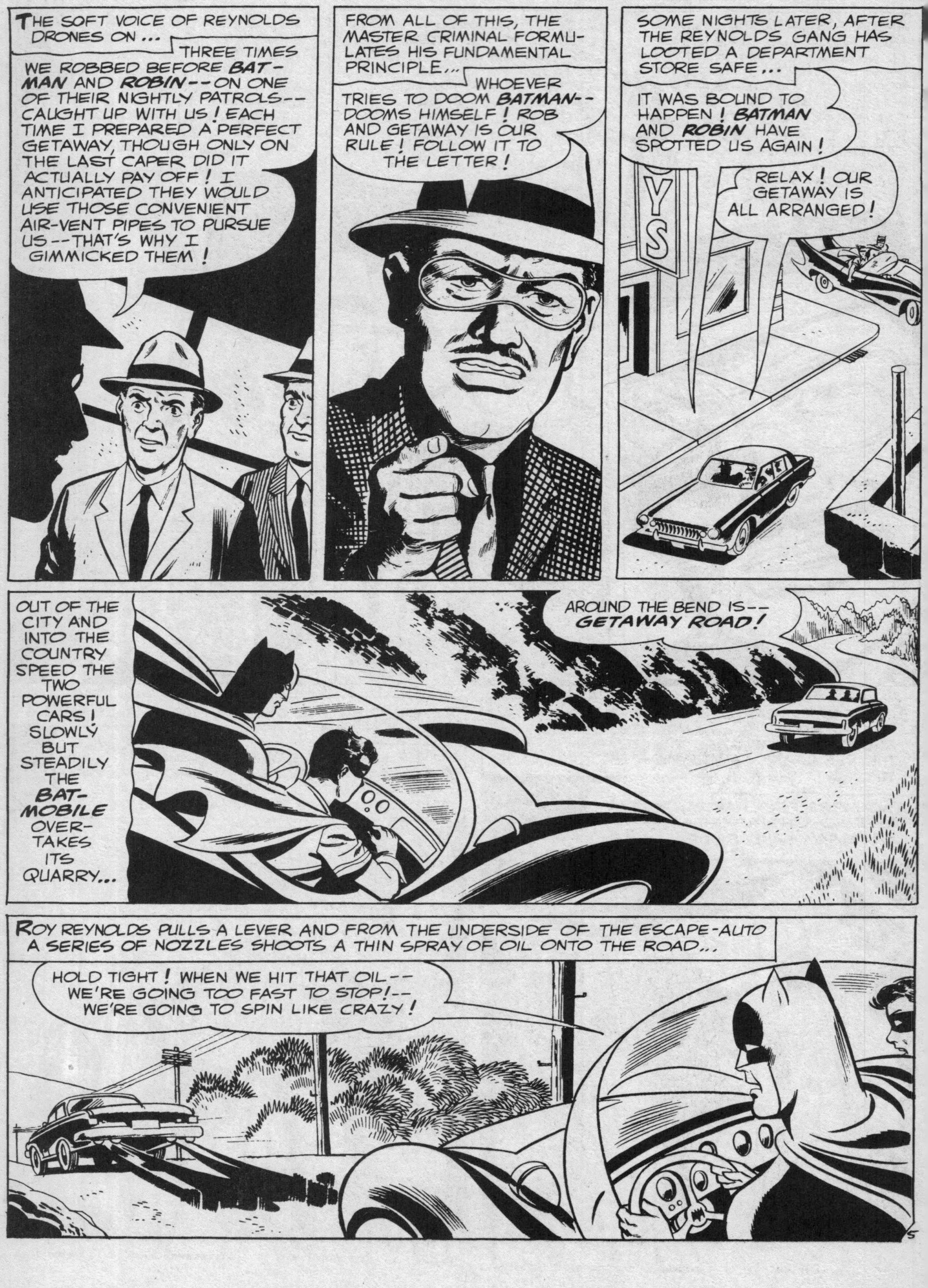
THE SOFT VOICE OF REYNOLDS DRONES ON...
THREE TIMES WE ROBBED BEFORE BATMAN AND ROBIN--ON ONE OF THEIR NIGHTLY PATROLS--CAUGHT UP WITH US! EACH TIME I PREPARED A PERFECT GETAWAY, THOUGH ONLY ON THE LAST CAPER DID IT ACTUALLY PAY OFF! I ANTICIPATED THEY WOULD USE THOSE CONVENIENT AIR-VENT PIPES TO PURSUE US--THAT'S WHY I GIMMICKED THEM!
FROM ALL OF THIS, THE MASTER CRIMINAL FORMULATES HIS FUNDAMENTAL PRINCIPLE...
WHOEVER TRIES TO DOOM BATMAN--DOOMS HIMSELF! ROB AND GETAWAY IS OUR RULE! FOLLOW IT TO THE LETTER!
SOME NIGHTS LATER, AFTER THE REYNOLDS GANG HAS LOOTED A DEPARTMENT STORE SAFE...
IT WAS BOUND TO HAPPEN! BATMAN AND ROBIN HAVE SPOTTED US AGAIN!
RELAX! OUR GETAWAY IS ALL ARRANGED!
OUT OF THE CITY AND INTO THE COUNTRY SPEED THE TWO POWERFUL CARS! SLOWLY BUT STEADILY THE BATMOBILE OVERTAKES ITS QUARRY...
AROUND THE BEND IS--GETAWAY ROAD!
ROY REYNOLDS PULLS A LEVER AND FROM THE UNDERSIDE OF THE ESCAPE-AUTO A SERIES OF NOZZLES SHOOTS A THIN SPRAY OF OIL ONTO THE ROAD...
HOLD TIGHT! WHEN WE HIT THAT OIL--WE'RE GOING TOO FAST TO STOP!--WE'RE GOING TO SPIN LIKE CRAZY!
5

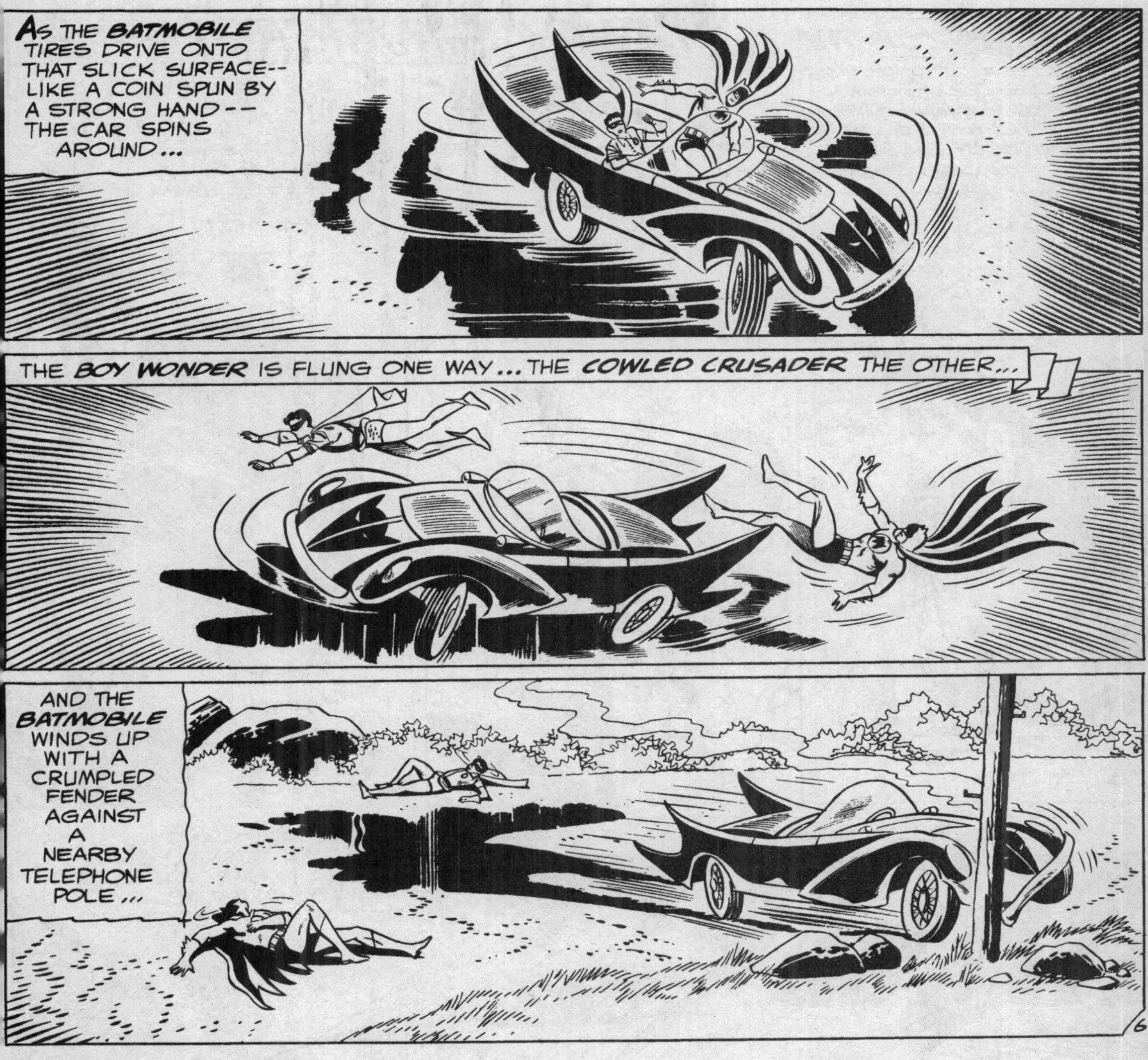
AS THE BATMOBILE TIRES DRIVE ONTO THAT SLICK SURFACE-- LIKE A COIN SPUN BY A STRONG HAND-- THE CAR SPINS AROUND...
THE BOY WONDER IS FLUNG ONE WAY... THE COWLED CRUSADER THE OTHER...
AND THE BATMOBILE WINDS UP WITH A CRUMPLED FENDER AGAINST A NEARBY TELEPHONE POLE...

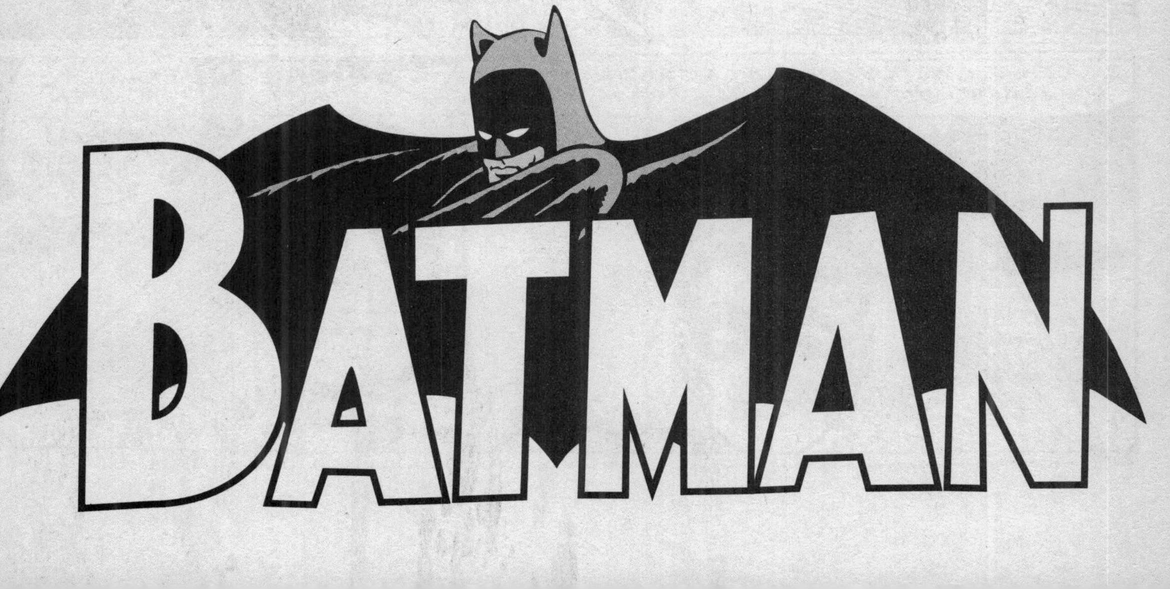
BATMAN

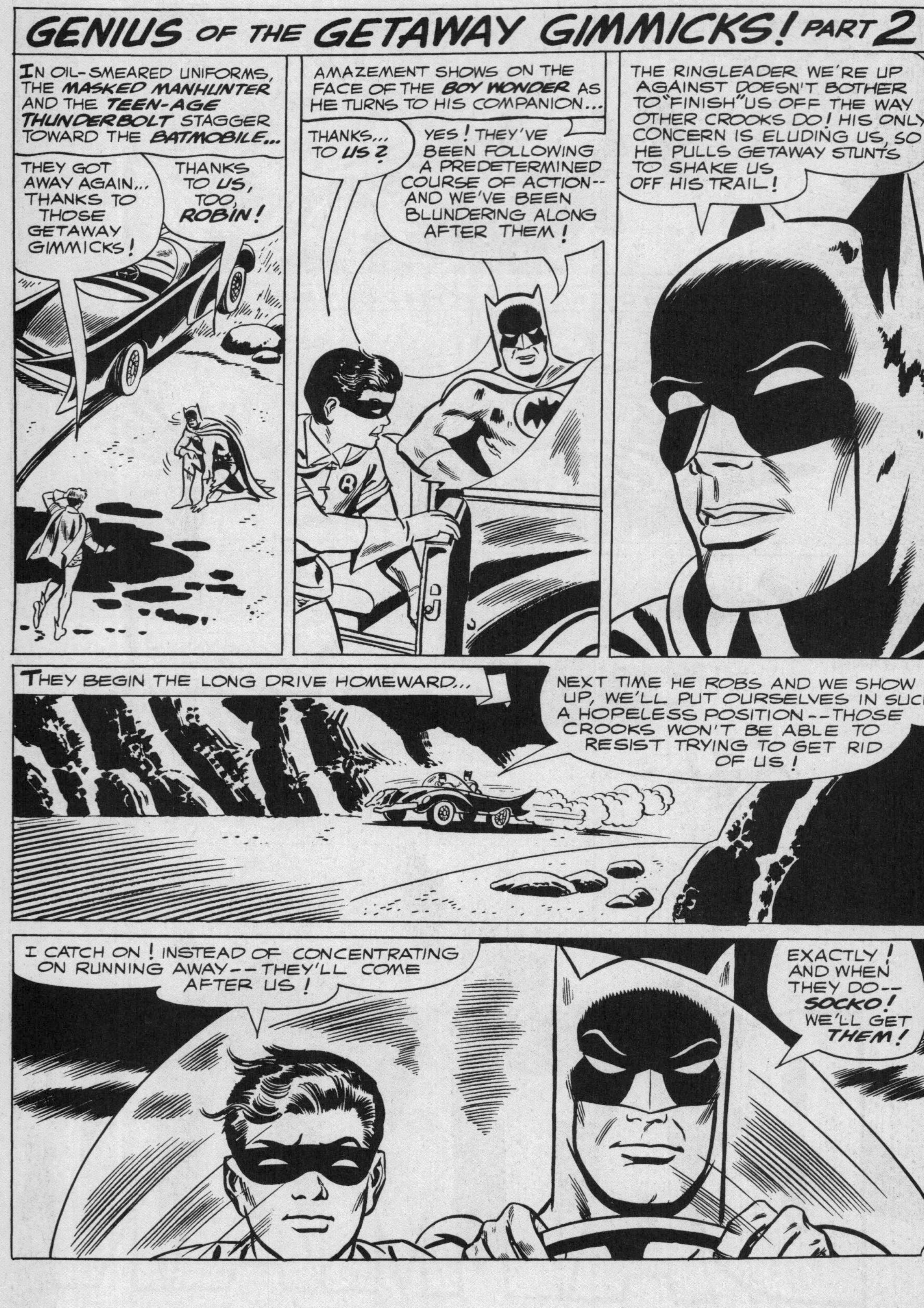
GENIUS OF THE GETAWAY GIMMICKS! PART 2
IN OIL-SMEARED UNIFORMS, THE MASKED MANHUNTER AND THE TEEN-AGE THUNDERBOLT STAGGER TOWARD THE BATMOBILE...
THEY GOT AWAY AGAIN... THANKS TO THOSE GETAWAY GIMMICKS!
THANKS TO US, TOO, ROBIN!
AMAZEMENT SHOWS ON THE FACE OF THE BOY WONDER AS HE TURNS TO HIS COMPANION...
THANKS... TO US?
YES! THEY'VE BEEN FOLLOWING A PREDETERMINED COURSE OF ACTION-- AND WE'VE BEEN BLUNDERING ALONG AFTER THEM!
THE RINGLEADER WE'RE UP AGAINST DOESN'T BOTHER TO "FINISH" US OFF THE WAY OTHER CROOKS DO! HIS ONLY CONCERN IS ELUDING US, SO HE PULLS GETAWAY STUNTS TO SHAKE US OFF HIS TRAIL!
THEY BEGIN THE LONG DRIVE HOMEWARD...
NEXT TIME HE ROBS AND WE SHOW UP, WE'LL PUT OURSELVES IN SUCH A HOPELESS POSITION --THOSE CROOKS WON'T BE ABLE TO RESIST TRYING TO GET RID OF US!
I CATCH ON! INSTEAD OF CONCENTRATING ON RUNNING AWAY--THEY'LL COME AFTER US!
EXACTLY! AND WHEN THEY DO-- SOCKO! WE'LL GET THEM!
7

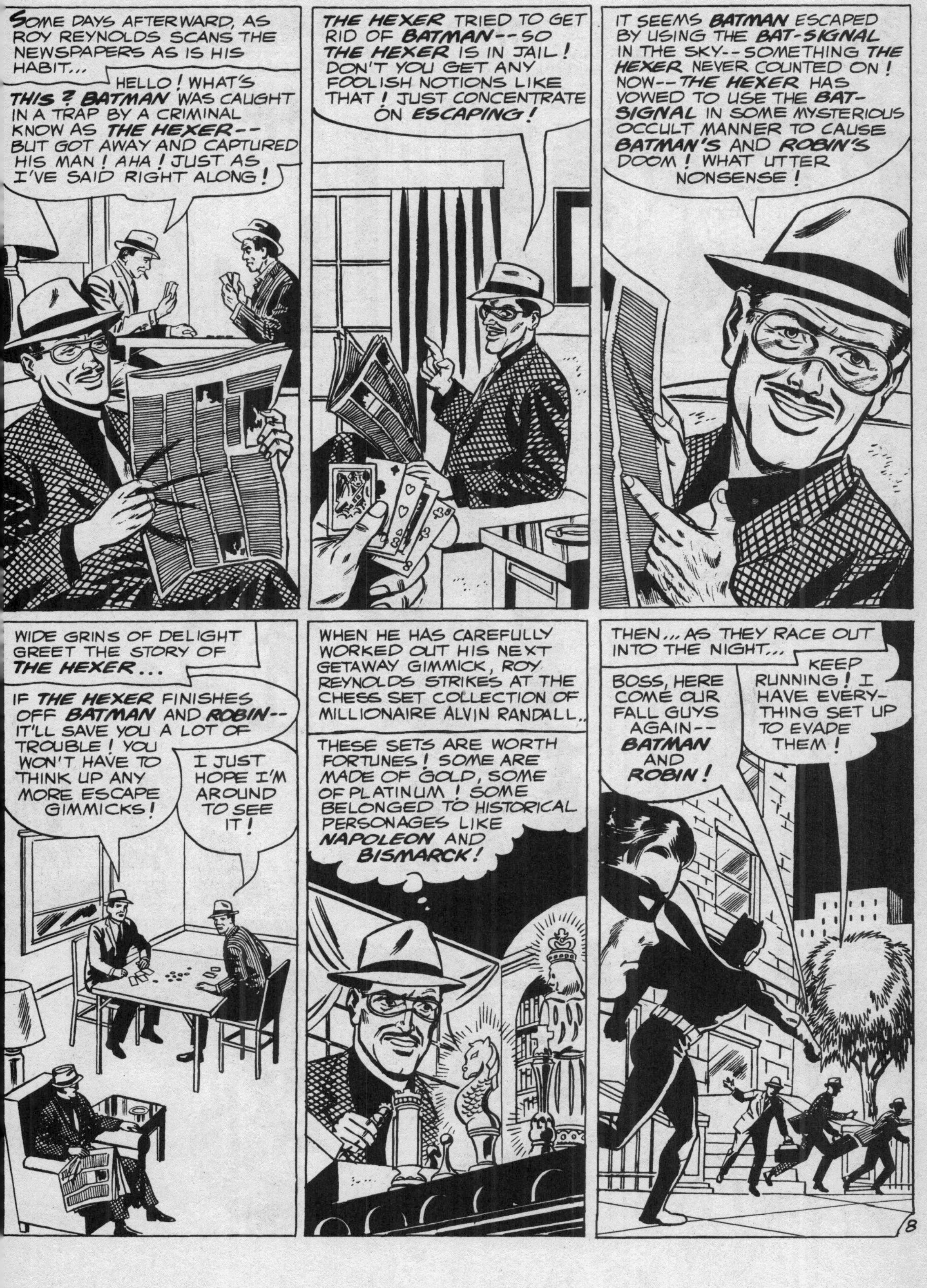
SOME DAYS AFTERWARD, AS ROY REYNOLDS SCANS THE NEWSPAPERS AS IS HIS HABIT...
HELLO! WHAT'S THIS? BATMAN WAS CAUGHT IN A TRAP BY A CRIMINAL KNOW AS THE HEXER-- BUT GOT AWAY AND CAPTURED HIS MAN! AHA! JUST AS I'VE SAID RIGHT ALONG!
THE HEXER TRIED TO GET RID OF BATMAN--SO THE HEXER IS IN JAIL! DON'T YOU GET ANY FOOLISH NOTIONS LIKE THAT! JUST CONCENTRATE ON ESCAPING!
IT SEEMS BATMAN ESCAPED BY USING THE BAT-SIGNAL IN THE SKY--SOMETHING THE HEXER NEVER COUNTED ON! NOW--THE HEXER HAS VOWED TO USE THE BAT-SIGNAL IN SOME MYSTERIOUS OCCULT MANNER TO CAUSE BATMAN'S AND ROBIN'S DOOM! WHAT UTTER NONSENSE!
WIDE GRINS OF DELIGHT GREET THE STORY OF THE HEXER...
IF THE HEXER FINISHES OFF BATMAN AND ROBIN-- IT'LL SAVE YOU A LOT OF TROUBLE! YOU WON'T HAVE TO THINK UP ANY MORE ESCAPE GIMMICKS!
I JUST HOPE I'M AROUND TO SEE IT!
WHEN HE HAS CAREFULLY WORKED OUT HIS NEXT GETAWAY GIMMICK, ROY REYNOLDS STRIKES AT THE CHESS SET COLLECTION OF MILLIONAIRE ALVIN RANDALL..
THESE SETS ARE WORTH FORTUNES! SOME ARE MADE OF GOLD, SOME OF PLATINUM! SOME BELONGED TO HISTORICAL PERSONAGES LIKE NAPOLEON AND BISMARCK!
THEN... AS THEY RACE OUT INTO THE NIGHT...
BOSS, HERE COME OUR FALL GUYS AGAIN-- BATMAN AND ROBIN!
KEEP RUNNING! I HAVE EVERY-THING SET UP TO EVADE THEM!
8

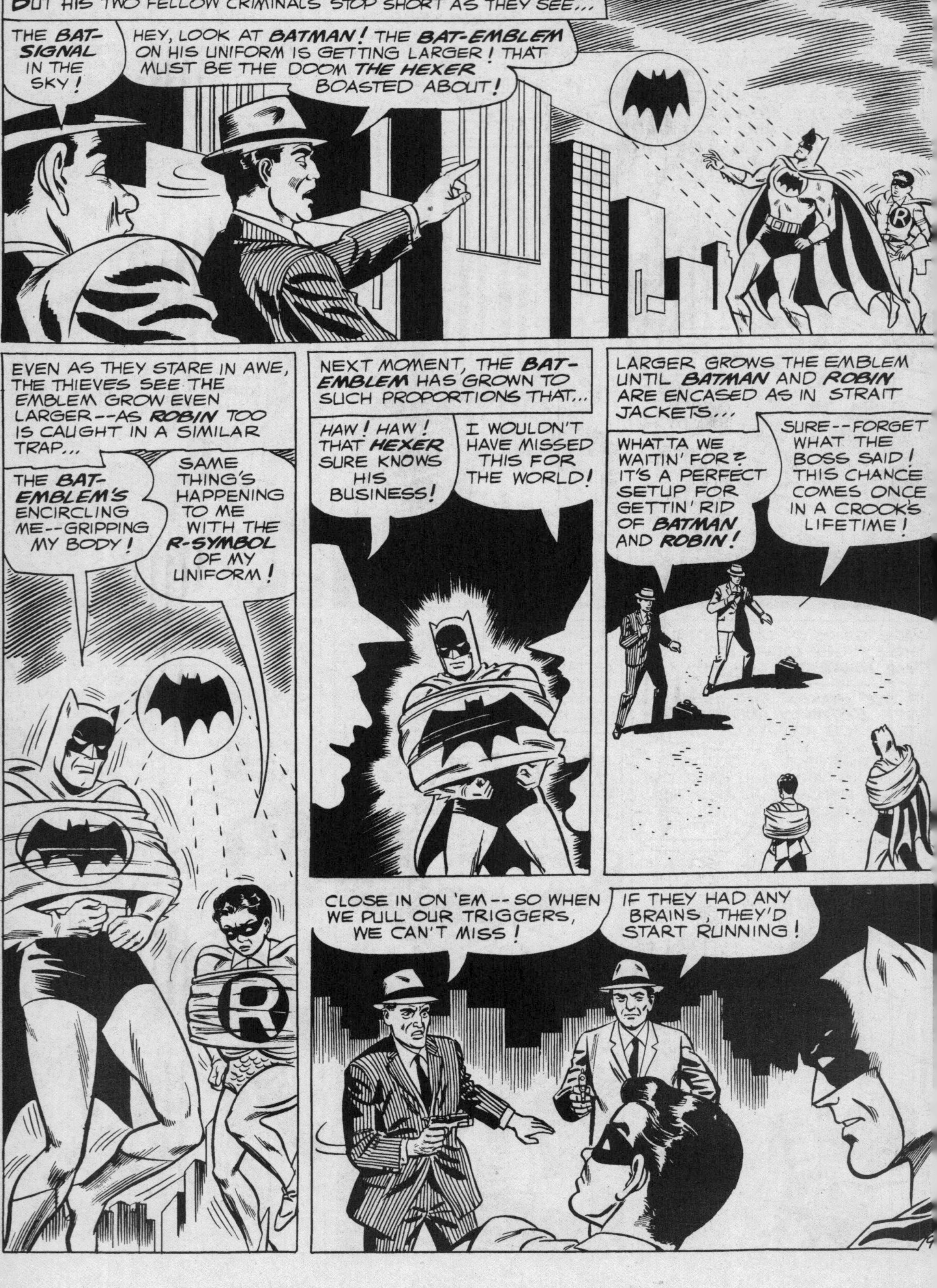
BUT HIS TWO FELLOW CRIMINALS STOP SHORT AS THEY SEE...
THE BAT-SIGNAL IN THE SKY!
HEY, LOOK AT BATMAN! THE BAT-EMBLEM ON HIS UNIFORM IS GETTING LARGER! THAT MUST BE THE DOOM THE HEXER BOASTED ABOUT!
EVEN AS THEY STARE IN AWE, THE THIEVES SEE THE EMBLEM GROW EVEN LARGER--AS ROBIN TOO IS CAUGHT IN A SIMILAR TRAP...
THE BAT-EMBLEM'S ENCIRCLING ME--GRIPPING MY BODY!
SAME THING'S HAPPENING TO ME WITH THE R-SYMBOL OF MY UNIFORM!
NEXT MOMENT, THE BAT-EMBLEM HAS GROWN TO SUCH PROPORTIONS THAT...
HAW! HAW! THAT HEXER SURE KNOWS HIS BUSINESS!
I WOULDN'T HAVE MISSED THIS FOR THE WORLD!
LARGER GROWS THE EMBLEM UNTIL BATMAN AND ROBIN ARE ENCASED AS IN STRAIT JACKETS...
WHATTA WE WAITIN' FOR? IT'S A PERFECT SETUP FOR GETTIN' RID OF BATMAN AND ROBIN!
SURE--FORGET WHAT THE BOSS SAID! THIS CHANCE COMES ONCE IN A CROOK'S LIFETIME!
CLOSE IN ON 'EM--SO WHEN WE PULL OUR TRIGGERS, WE CAN'T MISS!
IF THEY HAD ANY BRAINS, THEY'D START RUNNING!

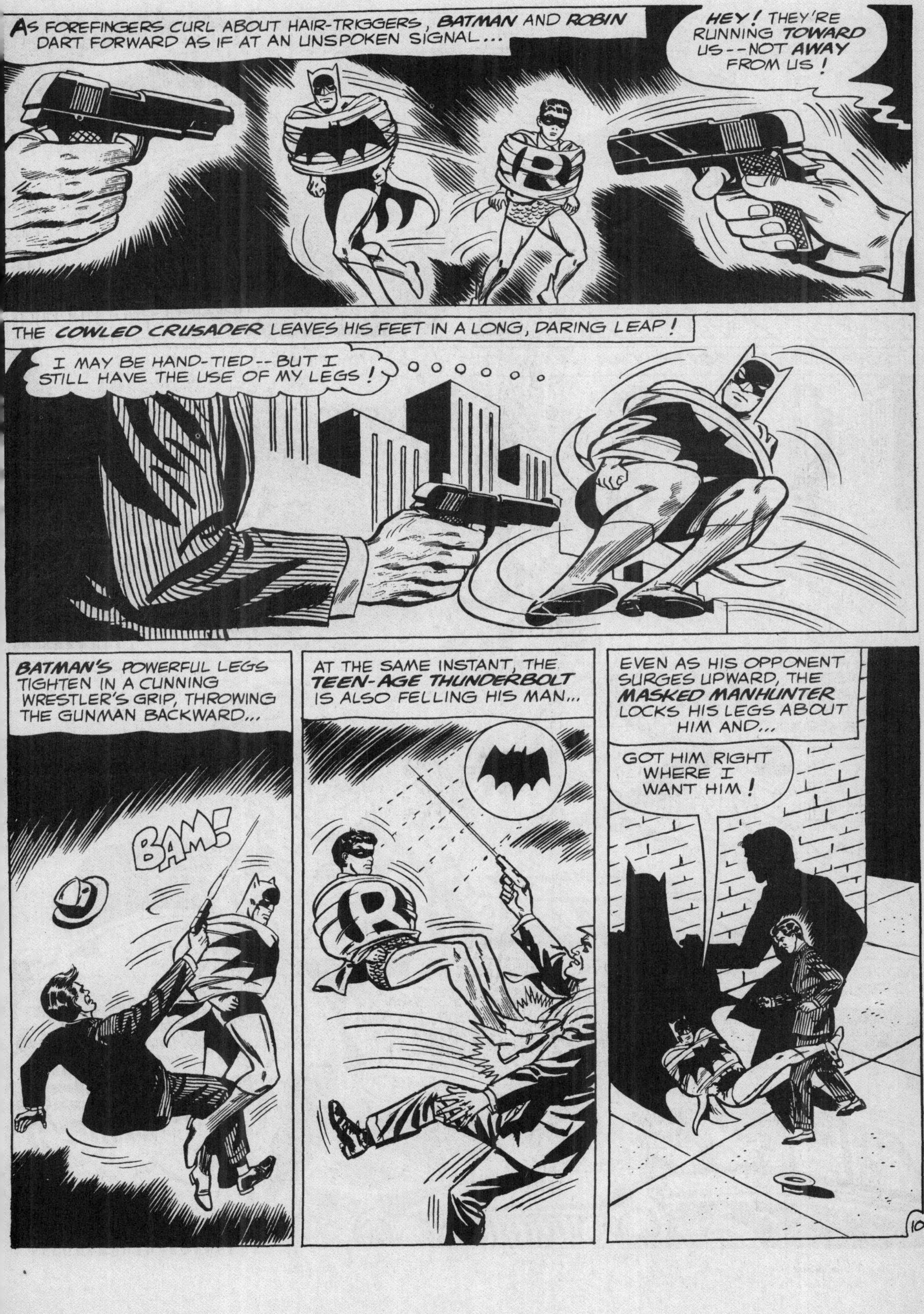
AS FOREFINGERS CURL ABOUT HAIR-TRIGGERS, BATMAN AND ROBIN DART FORWARD AS IF AT AN UNSPOKEN SIGNAL...
HEY! THEY'RE RUNNING TOWARD US--NOT AWAY FROM US!
THE COWLED CRUSADER LEAVES HIS FEET IN A LONG, DARING LEAP!
I MAY BE HAND-TIED--BUT I STILL HAVE THE USE OF MY LEGS!
BATMAN'S POWERFUL LEGS TIGHTEN IN A CUNNING WRESTLER'S GRIP, THROWING THE GUNMAN BACKWARD...
BAM!
AT THE SAME INSTANT, THE TEEN-AGE THUNDERBOLT IS ALSO FELLING HIS MAN...
EVEN AS HIS OPPONENT SURGES UPWARD, THE MASKED MANHUNTER LOCKS HIS LEGS ABOUT HIM AND...
GOT HIM RIGHT WHERE I WANT HIM!
10

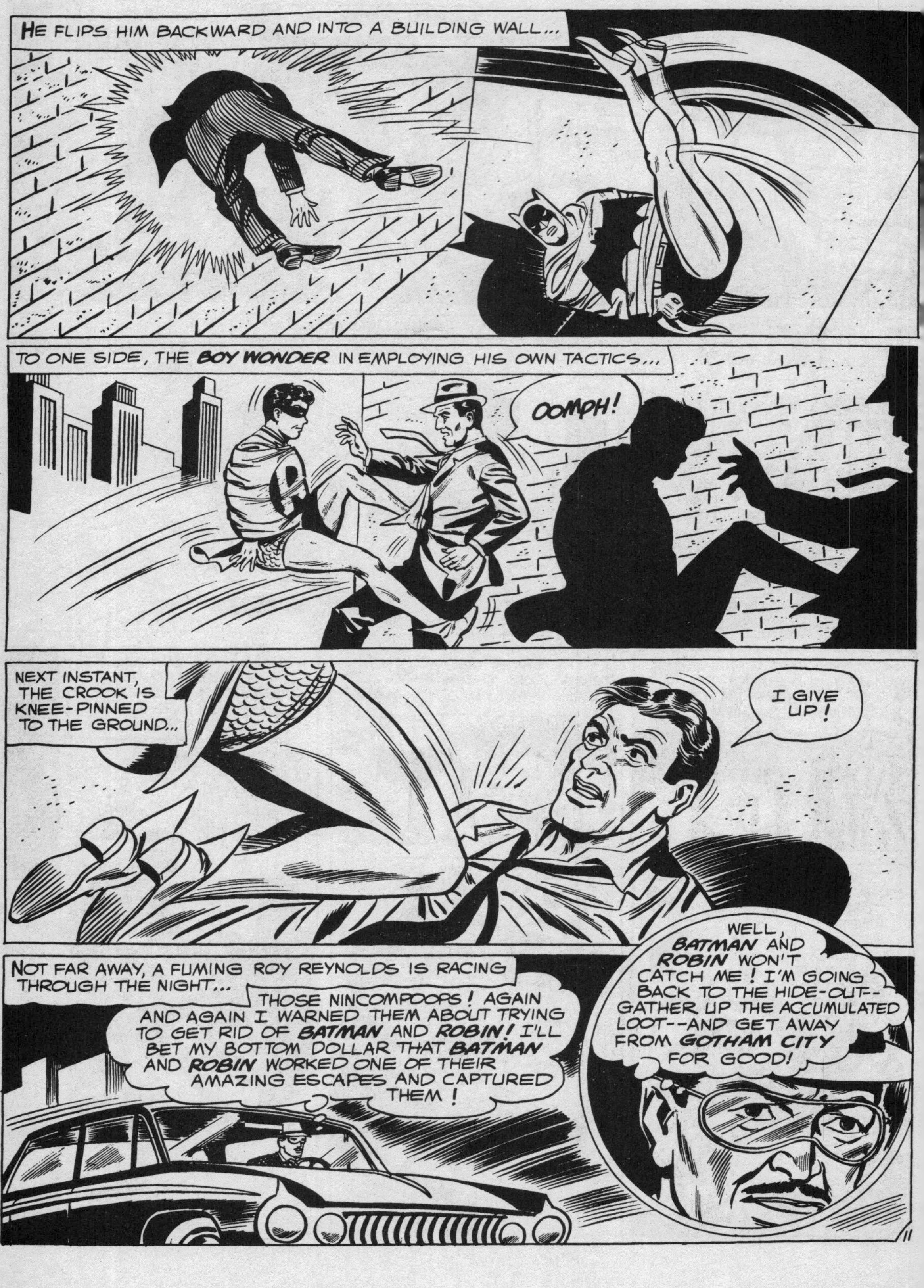
HE FLIPS HIM BACKWARD AND INTO A BUILDING WALL...
TO ONE SIDE, THE BOY WONDER IN EMPLOYING HIS OWN TACTICS...
OOMPH!
NEXT INSTANT, THE CROOK IS KNEE-PINNED TO THE GROUND...
I GIVE UP!
NOT FAR AWAY, A FUMING ROY REYNOLDS IS RACING THROUGH THE NIGHT...
THOSE NINCOMPOOPS! AGAIN AND AGAIN I WARNED THEM ABOUT TRYING TO GET RID OF BATMAN AND ROBIN! I'LL BET MY BOTTOM DOLLAR THAT BATMAN AND ROBIN WORKED ONE OF THEIR AMAZING ESCAPES AND CAPTURED THEM!
WELL, BATMAN AND ROBIN WON'T CATCH ME! I'M GOING BACK TO THE HIDE-OUT--GATHER UP THE ACCUMULATED LOOT--AND GET AWAY FROM GOTHAM CITY FOR GOOD!
11

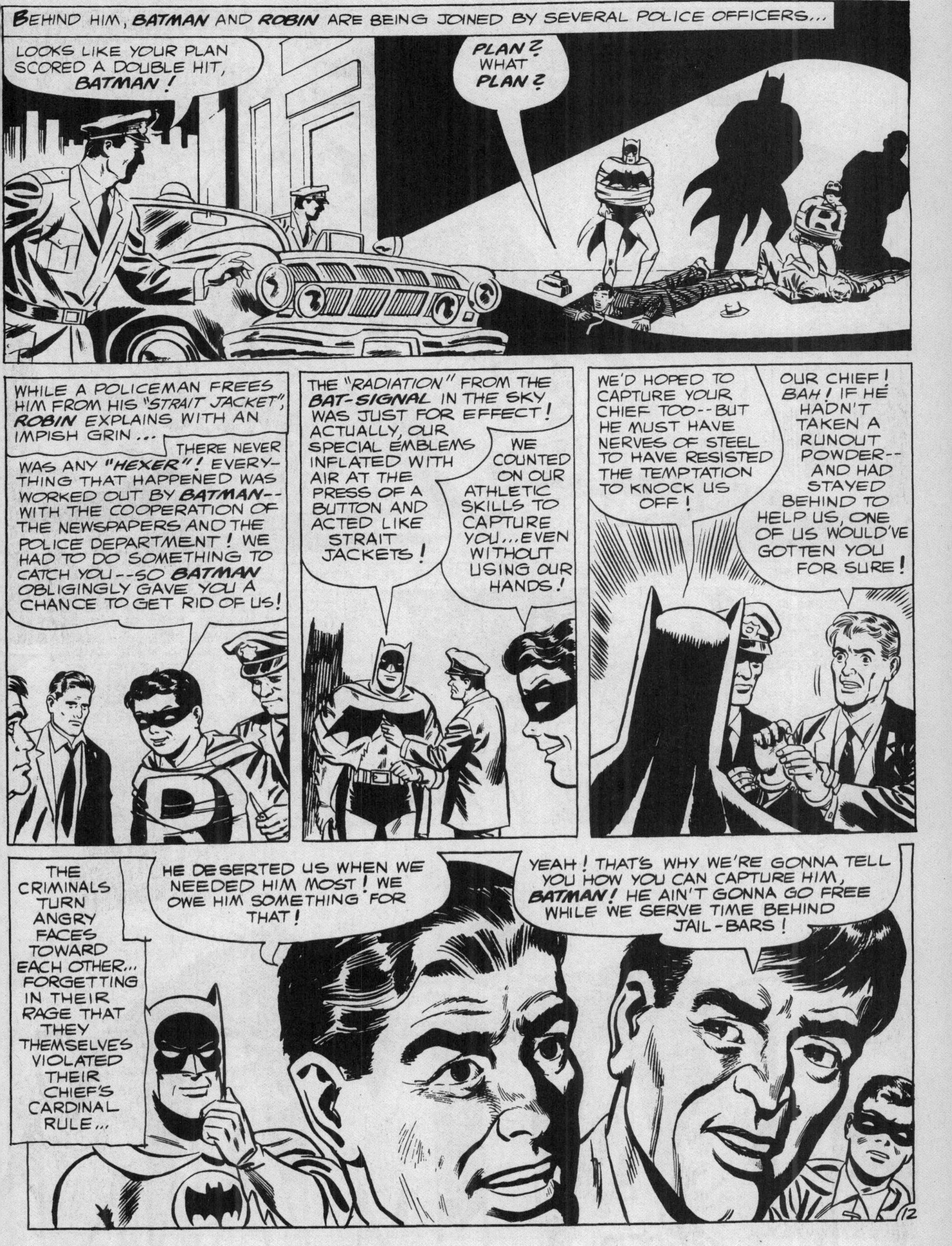
BEHIND HIM, BATMAN AND ROBIN ARE BEING JOINED BY SEVERAL POLICE OFFICERS...
LOOKS LIKE YOUR PLAN SCORED A DOUBLE HIT, BATMAN!
PLAN? WHAT PLAN?
WHILE A POLICEMAN FREES HIM FROM HIS "STRAIT JACKET", ROBIN EXPLAINS WITH AN IMPISH GRIN...
THERE NEVER WAS ANY "HEXER"! EVERYTHING THAT HAPPENED WAS WORKED OUT BY BATMAN--WITH THE COOPERATION OF THE NEWSPAPERS AND THE POLICE DEPARTMENT! WE HAD TO DO SOMETHING TO CATCH YOU--SO BATMAN OBLIGINGLY GAVE YOU A CHANCE TO GET RID OF US!
THE "RADIATION" FROM THE BAT-SIGNAL IN THE SKY WAS JUST FOR EFFECT! ACTUALLY, OUR SPECIAL EMBLEMS INFLATED WITH AIR AT THE PRESS OF A BUTTON AND ACTED LIKE STRAIT JACKETS!
WE COUNTED ON OUR ATHLETIC SKILLS TO CAPTURE YOU...EVEN WITHOUT USING OUR HANDS!
WE'D HOPED TO CAPTURE YOUR CHIEF TOO--BUT HE MUST HAVE NERVES OF STEEL TO HAVE RESISTED THE TEMPTATION TO KNOCK US OFF!
OUR CHIEF! BAH! IF HE HADN'T TAKEN A RUNOUT POWDER--AND HAD STAYED BEHIND TO HELP US, ONE OF US WOULD'VE GOTTEN YOU FOR SURE!
THE CRIMINALS TURN ANGRY FACES TOWARD EACH OTHER... FORGETTING IN THEIR RAGE THAT THEY THEMSELVES VIOLATED THEIR CHIEF'S CARDINAL RULE...
HE DESERTED US WHEN WE NEEDED HIM MOST! WE OWE HIM SOMETHING FOR THAT!
YEAH! THAT'S WHY WE'RE GONNA TELL YOU HOW YOU CAN CAPTURE HIM, BATMAN! HE AIN'T GONNA GO FREE WHILE WE SERVE TIME BEHIND JAIL-BARS!
12

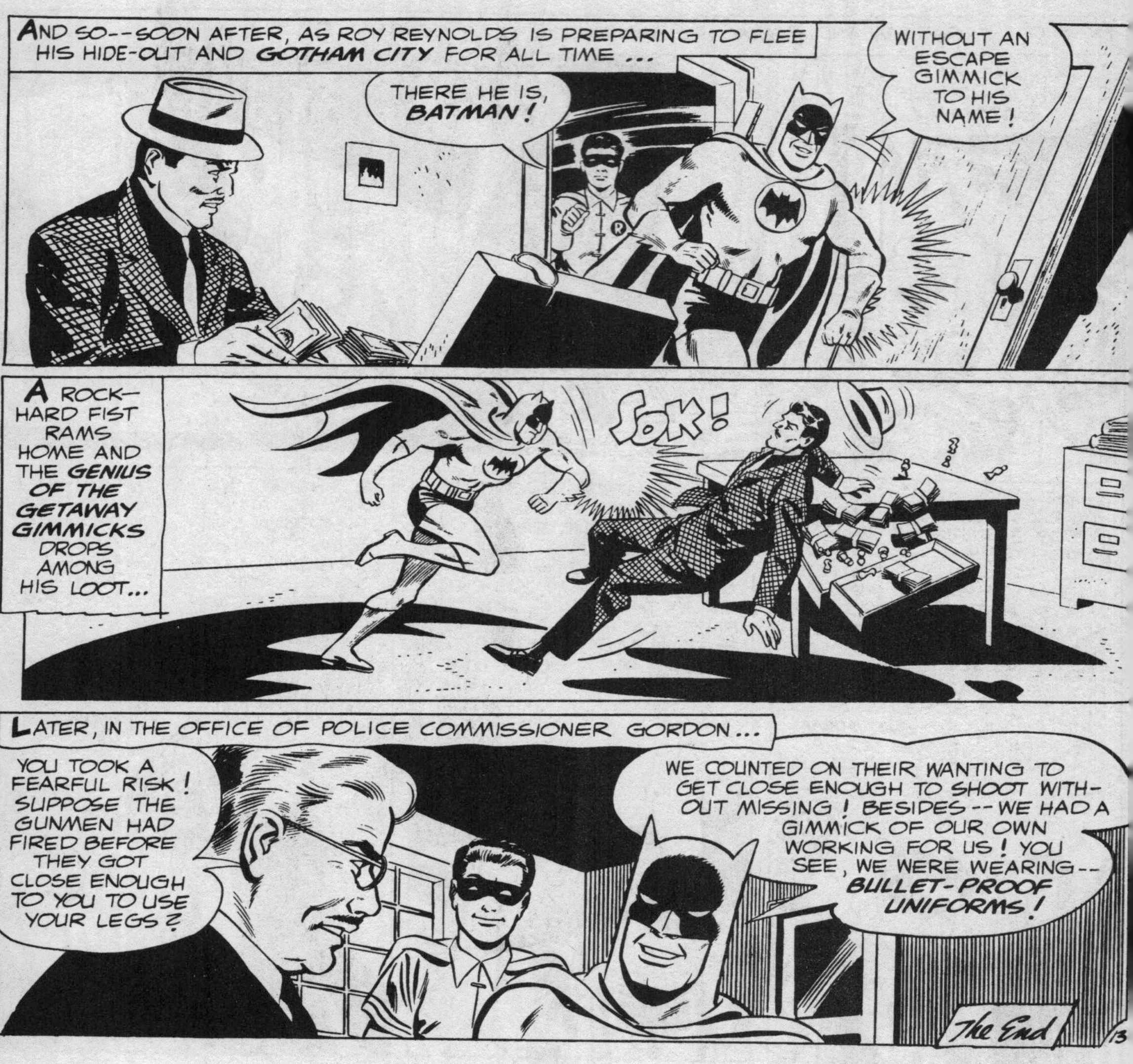
AND SO--SOON AFTER, AS ROY REYNOLDS IS PREPARING TO FLEE HIS HIDE-OUT AND GOTHAM CITY FOR ALL TIME ...
THERE HE IS, BATMAN!
WITHOUT AN ESCAPE GIMMICK TO HIS NAME!
A ROCK-HARD FIST RAMS HOME AND THE GENIUS OF THE GETAWAY GIMMICKS DROPS AMONG HIS LOOT...
SOK!
LATER, IN THE OFFICE OF POLICE COMMISSIONER GORDON...
YOU TOOK A FEARFUL RISK! SUPPOSE THE GUNMEN HAD FIRED BEFORE THEY GOT CLOSE ENOUGH TO YOU TO USE YOUR LEGS?
WE COUNTED ON THEIR WANTING TO GET CLOSE ENOUGH TO SHOOT WITH-OUT MISSING! BESIDES--WE HAD A GIMMICK OF OUR OWN WORKING FOR US! YOU SEE, WE WERE WEARING--BULLET-PROOF UNIFORMS!
The End
13

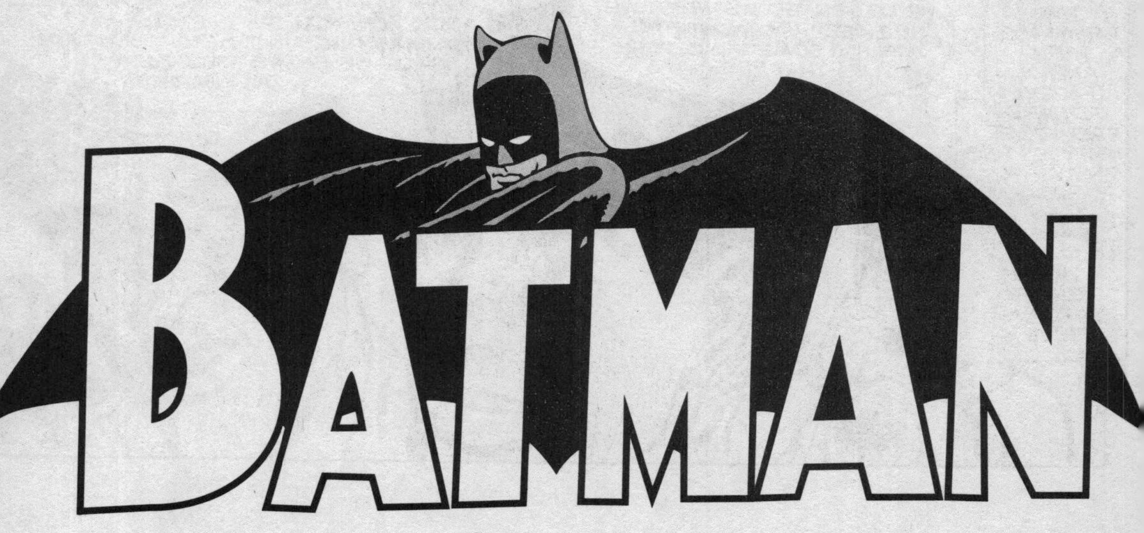
BATMAN

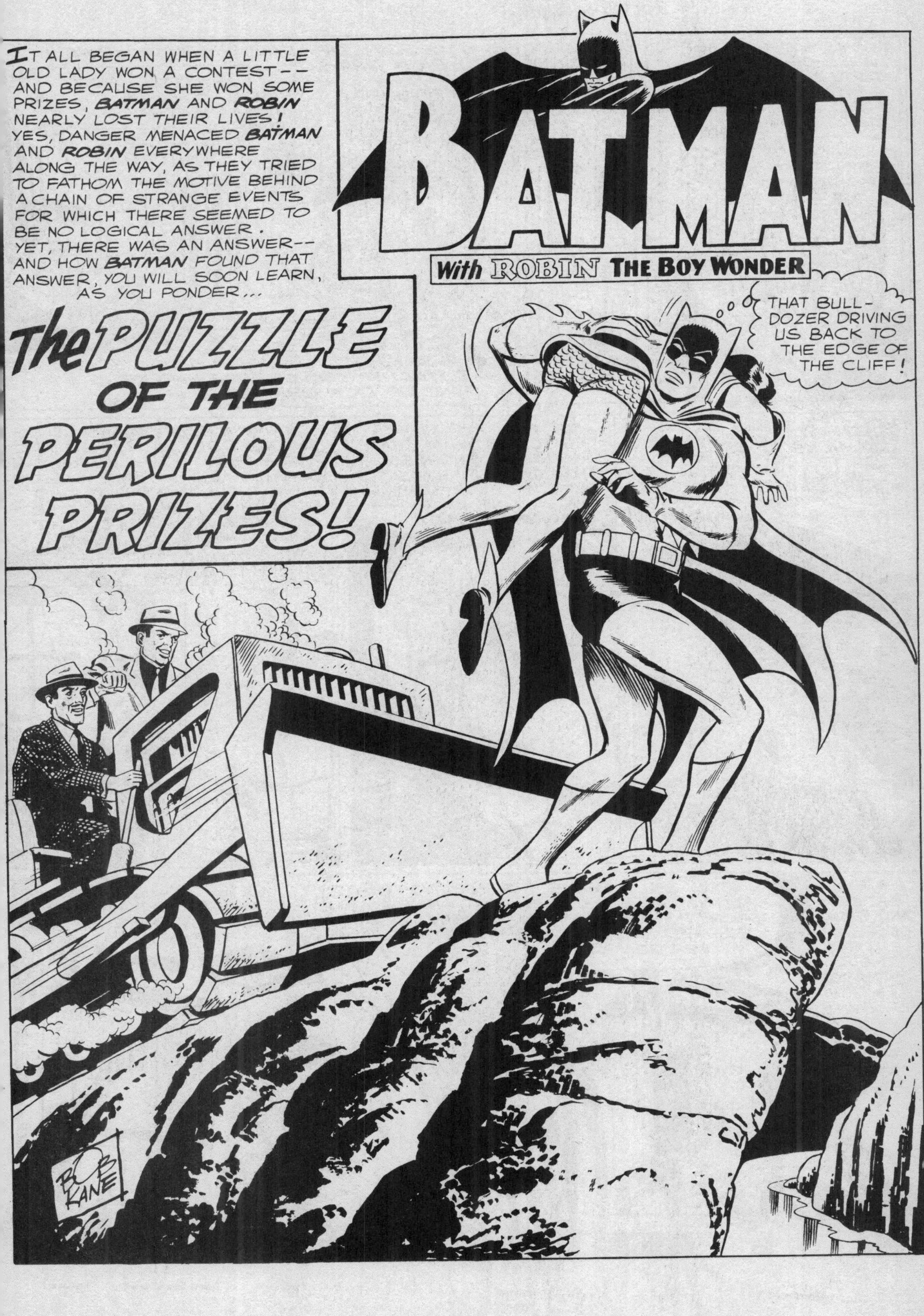
IT ALL BEGAN WHEN A LITTLE OLD LADY WON A CONTEST -- AND BECAUSE SHE WON SOME PRIZES, BATMAN AND ROBIN NEARLY LOST THEIR LIVES! YES, DANGER MENACED BATMAN AND ROBIN EVERYWHERE ALONG THE WAY, AS THEY TRIED TO FATHOM THE MOTIVE BEHIND A CHAIN OF STRANGE EVENTS FOR WHICH THERE SEEMED TO BE NO LOGICAL ANSWER. YET, THERE WAS AN ANSWER-- AND HOW BATMAN FOUND THAT ANSWER, YOU WILL SOON LEARN, AS YOU PONDER...
BATMAN
With ROBIN THE BOY WONDER
The PUZZLE OF THE PERILOUS PRIZES!
THAT BULL-DOZER DRIVING US BACK TO THE EDGE OF THE CLIFF!
BOB KANE

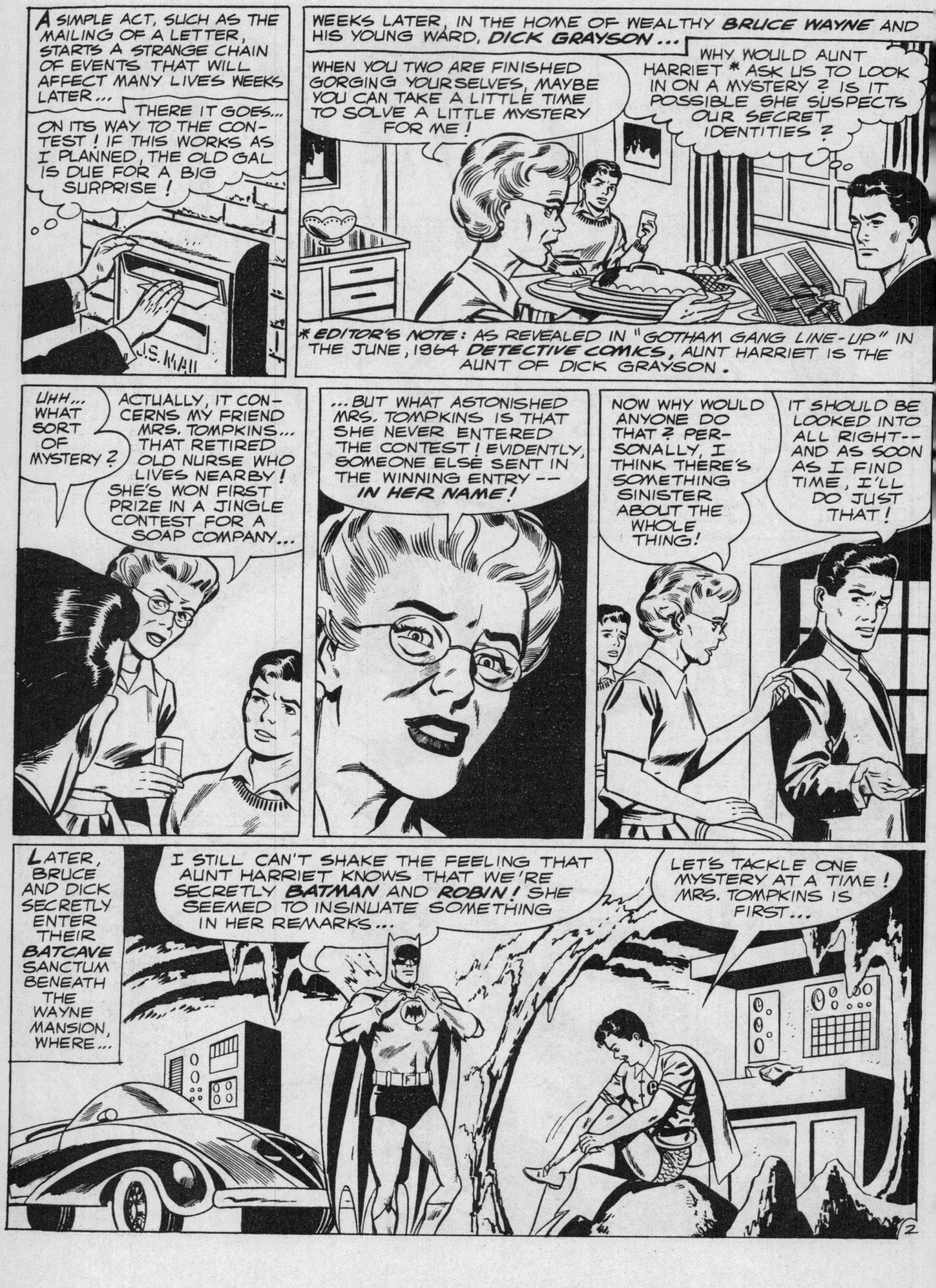
A SIMPLE ACT, SUCH AS THE MAILING OF A LETTER, STARTS A STRANGE CHAIN OF EVENTS THAT WILL AFFECT MANY LIVES WEEKS LATER...
THERE IT GOES... ON ITS WAY TO THE CONTEST! IF THIS WORKS AS I PLANNED, THE OLD GAL IS DUE FOR A BIG SURPRISE!
U.S. MAIL
WEEKS LATER, IN THE HOME OF WEALTHY BRUCE WAYNE AND HIS YOUNG WARD, DICK GRAYSON...
WHEN YOU TWO ARE FINISHED GORGING YOURSELVES, MAYBE YOU CAN TAKE A LITTLE TIME TO SOLVE A LITTLE MYSTERY FOR ME!
WHY WOULD AUNT HARRIET * ASK US TO LOOK IN ON A MYSTERY? IS IT POSSIBLE SHE SUSPECTS OUR SECRET IDENTITIES?
* EDITOR'S NOTE: AS REVEALED IN "GOTHAM GANG LINE-UP" IN THE JUNE, 1964 DETECTIVE COMICS, AUNT HARRIET IS THE AUNT OF DICK GRAYSON.
UHH... WHAT SORT OF MYSTERY?
ACTUALLY, IT CONCERNS MY FRIEND MRS. TOMPKINS... THAT RETIRED OLD NURSE WHO LIVES NEARBY! SHE'S WON FIRST PRIZE IN A JINGLE CONTEST FOR A SOAP COMPANY...
...BUT WHAT ASTONISHED MRS. TOMPKINS IS THAT SHE NEVER ENTERED THE CONTEST! EVIDENTLY, SOMEONE ELSE SENT IN THE WINNING ENTRY -- IN HER NAME!
NOW WHY WOULD ANYONE DO THAT? PERSONALLY, I THINK THERE'S SOMETHING SINISTER ABOUT THE WHOLE THING!
IT SHOULD BE LOOKED INTO ALL RIGHT-- AND AS SOON AS I FIND TIME, I'LL DO JUST THAT!
LATER, BRUCE AND DICK SECRETLY ENTER THEIR BATCAVE SANCTUM BENEATH THE WAYNE MANSION, WHERE...
I STILL CAN'T SHAKE THE FEELING THAT AUNT HARRIET KNOWS THAT WE'RE SECRETLY BATMAN AND ROBIN! SHE SEEMED TO INSINUATE SOMETHING IN HER REMARKS...
LET'S TACKLE ONE MYSTERY AT A TIME! MRS. TOMPKINS IS FIRST...
2

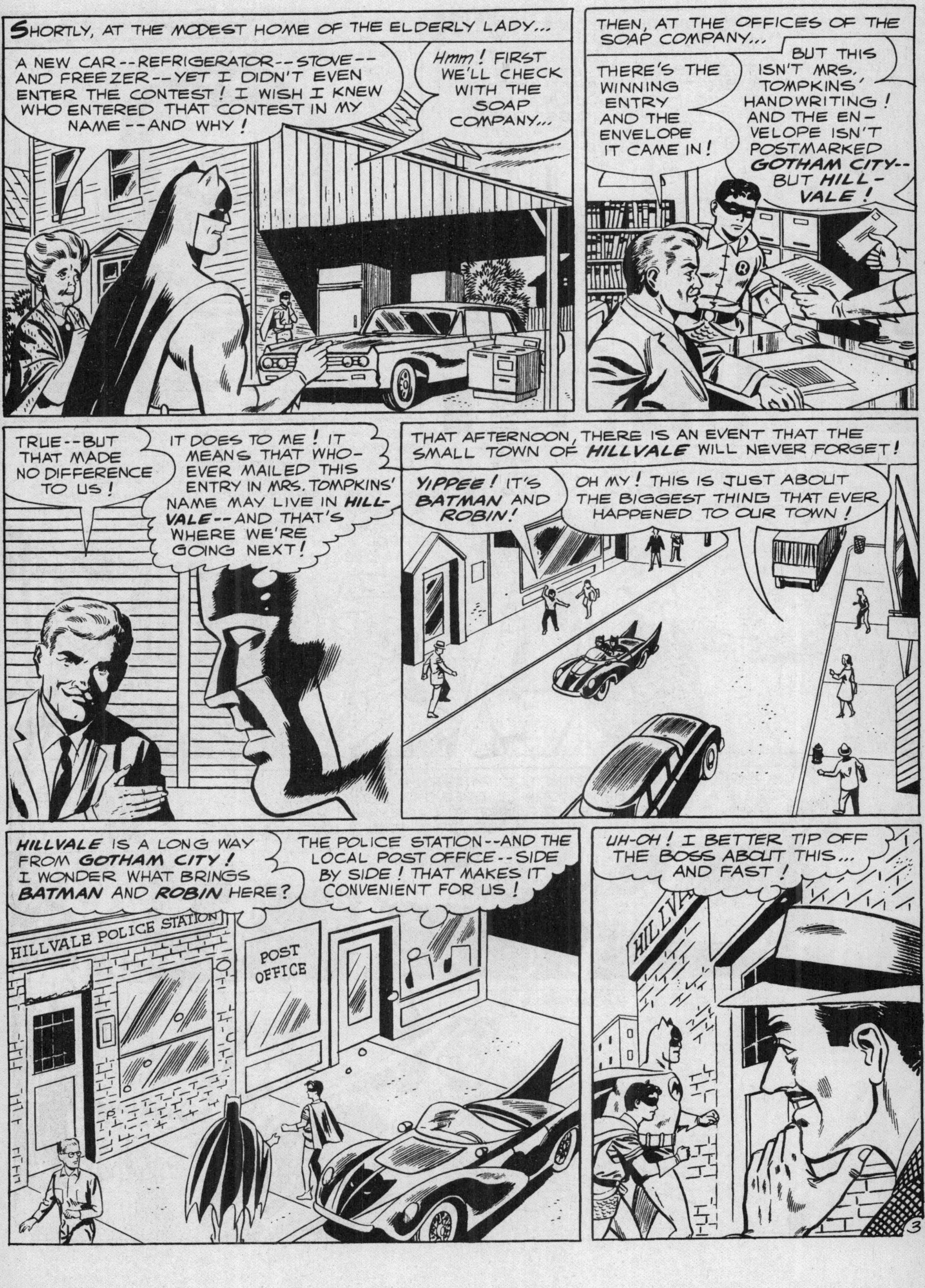
SHORTLY, AT THE MODEST HOME OF THE ELDERLY LADY...
A NEW CAR--REFRIGERATOR--STOVE--AND FREEZER--YET I DIDN'T EVEN ENTER THE CONTEST! I WISH I KNEW WHO ENTERED THAT CONTEST IN MY NAME--AND WHY!
Hmm! FIRST WE'LL CHECK WITH THE SOAP COMPANY...
THEN, AT THE OFFICES OF THE SOAP COMPANY...
THERE'S THE WINNING ENTRY AND THE ENVELOPE IT CAME IN!
BUT THIS ISN'T MRS. TOMPKINS' HANDWRITING! AND THE ENVELOPE ISN'T POSTMARKED GOTHAM CITY--BUT HILL-VALE!
TRUE--BUT THAT MADE NO DIFFERENCE TO US!
IT DOES TO ME! IT MEANS THAT WHO-EVER MAILED THIS ENTRY IN MRS. TOMPKINS' NAME MAY LIVE IN HILL-VALE--AND THAT'S WHERE WE'RE GOING NEXT!
THAT AFTERNOON, THERE IS AN EVENT THAT THE SMALL TOWN OF HILLVALE WILL NEVER FORGET!
YIPPEE! IT'S BATMAN AND ROBIN!
OH MY! THIS IS JUST ABOUT THE BIGGEST THING THAT EVER HAPPENED TO OUR TOWN!
HILLVALE IS A LONG WAY FROM GOTHAM CITY! I WONDER WHAT BRINGS BATMAN AND ROBIN HERE?
THE POLICE STATION--AND THE LOCAL POST OFFICE--SIDE BY SIDE! THAT MAKES IT CONVENIENT FOR US!
HILLVALE POLICE STATION
POST OFFICE
UH-OH! I BETTER TIP OFF THE BOSS ABOUT THIS... AND FAST!
3

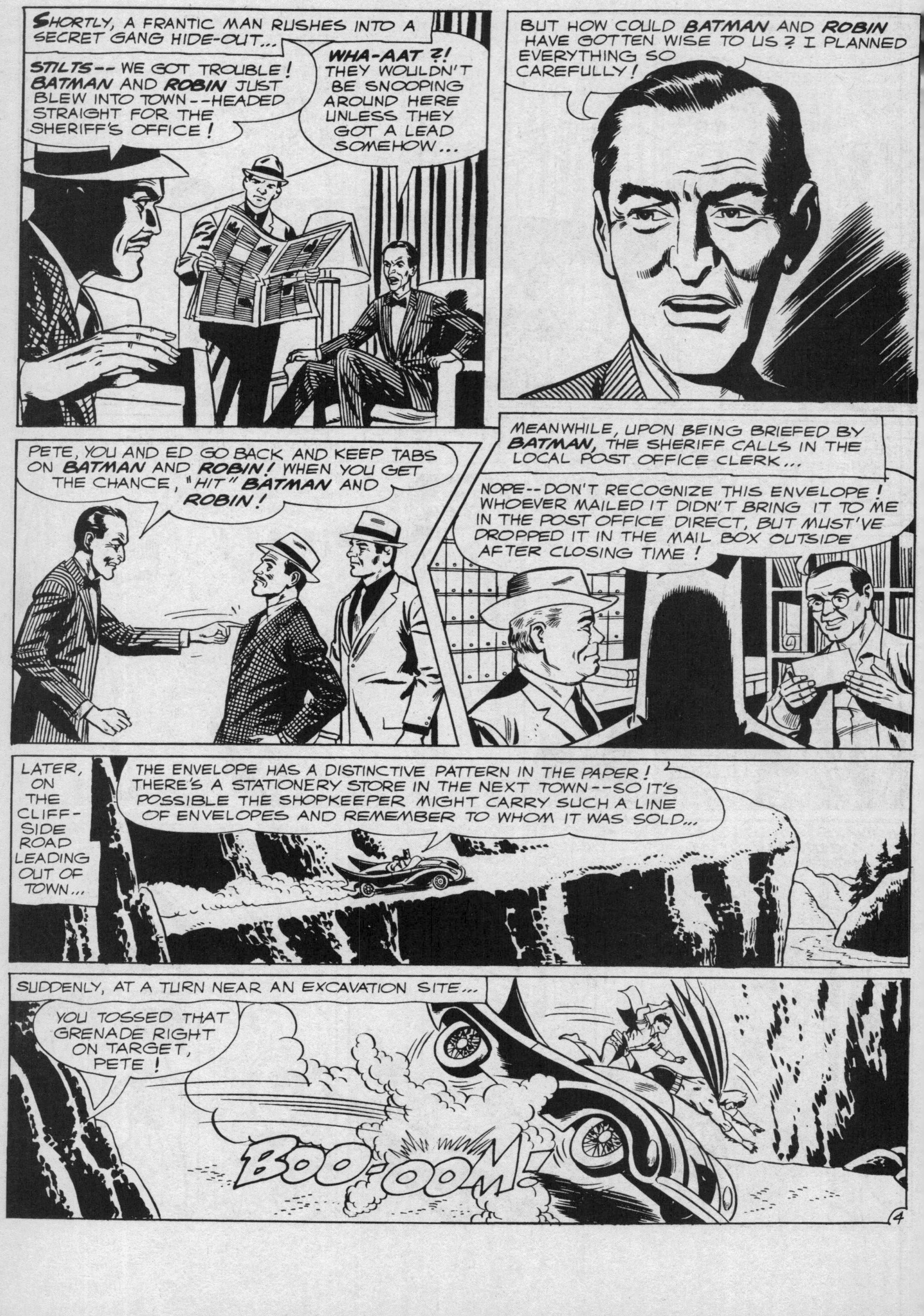
SHORTLY, A FRANTIC MAN RUSHES INTO A SECRET GANG HIDE-OUT...
STILTS-- WE GOT TROUBLE! BATMAN AND ROBIN JUST BLEW INTO TOWN--HEADED STRAIGHT FOR THE SHERIFF'S OFFICE!
WHA-AAT ?! THEY WOULDN'T BE SNOOPING AROUND HERE UNLESS THEY GOT A LEAD SOMEHOW...
BUT HOW COULD BATMAN AND ROBIN HAVE GOTTEN WISE TO US? I PLANNED EVERYTHING SO CAREFULLY!
PETE, YOU AND ED GO BACK AND KEEP TABS ON BATMAN AND ROBIN! WHEN YOU GET THE CHANCE, "HIT" BATMAN AND ROBIN!
MEANWHILE, UPON BEING BRIEFED BY BATMAN, THE SHERIFF CALLS IN THE LOCAL POST OFFICE CLERK...
NOPE--DON'T RECOGNIZE THIS ENVELOPE! WHOEVER MAILED IT DIDN'T BRING IT TO ME IN THE POST OFFICE DIRECT, BUT MUST'VE DROPPED IT IN THE MAIL BOX OUTSIDE AFTER CLOSING TIME!
LATER, ON THE CLIFF-SIDE ROAD LEADING OUT OF TOWN...
THE ENVELOPE HAS A DISTINCTIVE PATTERN IN THE PAPER! THERE'S A STATIONERY STORE IN THE NEXT TOWN--SO IT'S POSSIBLE THE SHOPKEEPER MIGHT CARRY SUCH A LINE OF ENVELOPES AND REMEMBER TO WHOM IT WAS SOLD...
SUDDENLY, AT A TURN NEAR AN EXCAVATION SITE...
YOU TOSSED THAT GRENADE RIGHT ON TARGET, PETE!
BOO-OOM!
4

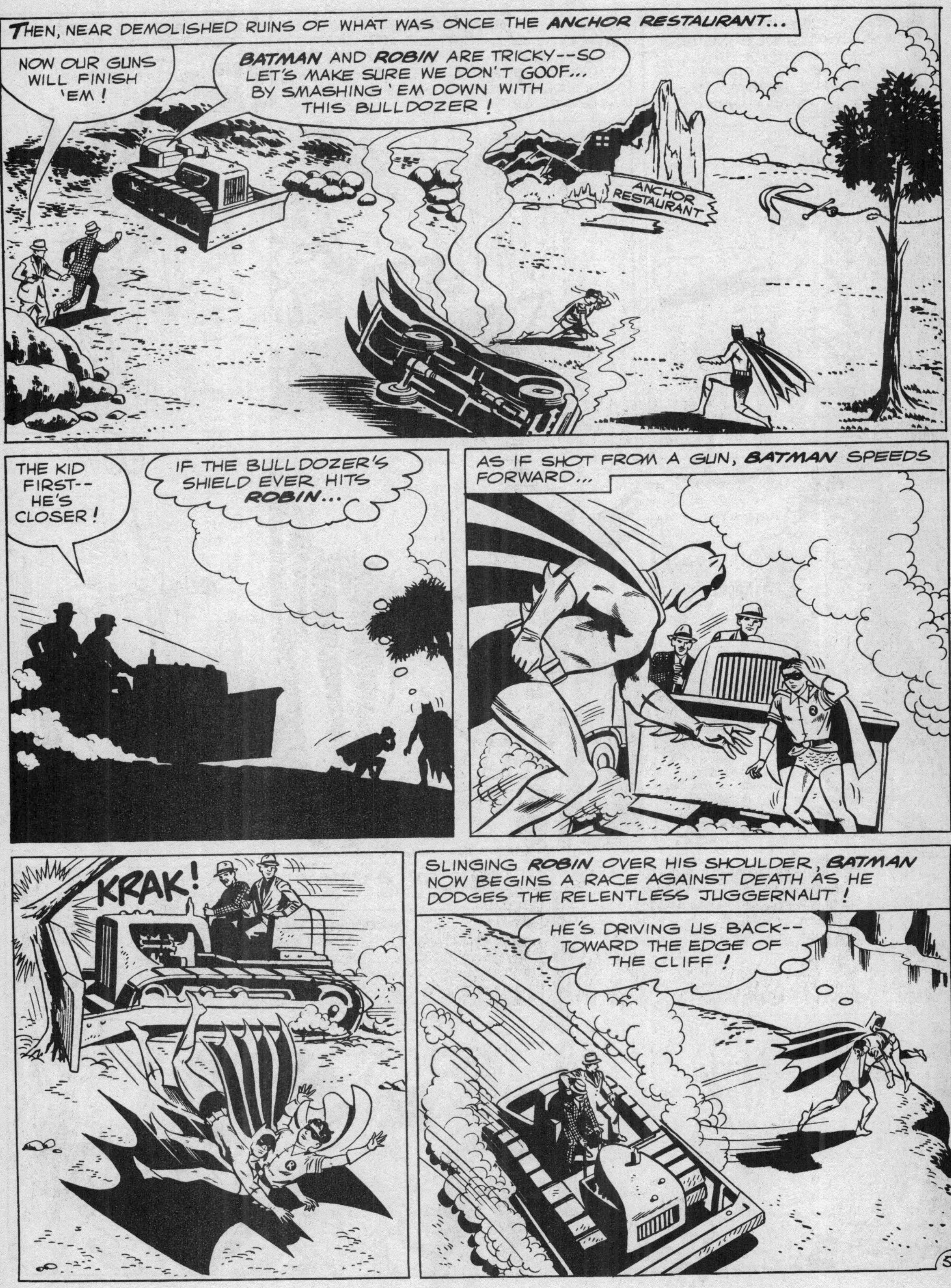
THEN, NEAR DEMOLISHED RUINS OF WHAT WAS ONCE THE ANCHOR RESTAURANT...
NOW OUR GUNS WILL FINISH 'EM!
BATMAN AND ROBIN ARE TRICKY--SO LET'S MAKE SURE WE DON'T GOOF... BY SMASHING 'EM DOWN WITH THIS BULLDOZER!
ANCHOR RESTAURANT
THE KID FIRST--HE'S CLOSER!
IF THE BULLDOZER'S SHIELD EVER HITS ROBIN...
AS IF SHOT FROM A GUN, BATMAN SPEEDS FORWARD...
KRAK!
SLINGING ROBIN OVER HIS SHOULDER, BATMAN NOW BEGINS A RACE AGAINST DEATH AS HE DODGES THE RELENTLESS JUGGERNAUT!
HE'S DRIVING US BACK--TOWARD THE EDGE OF THE CLIFF!
5

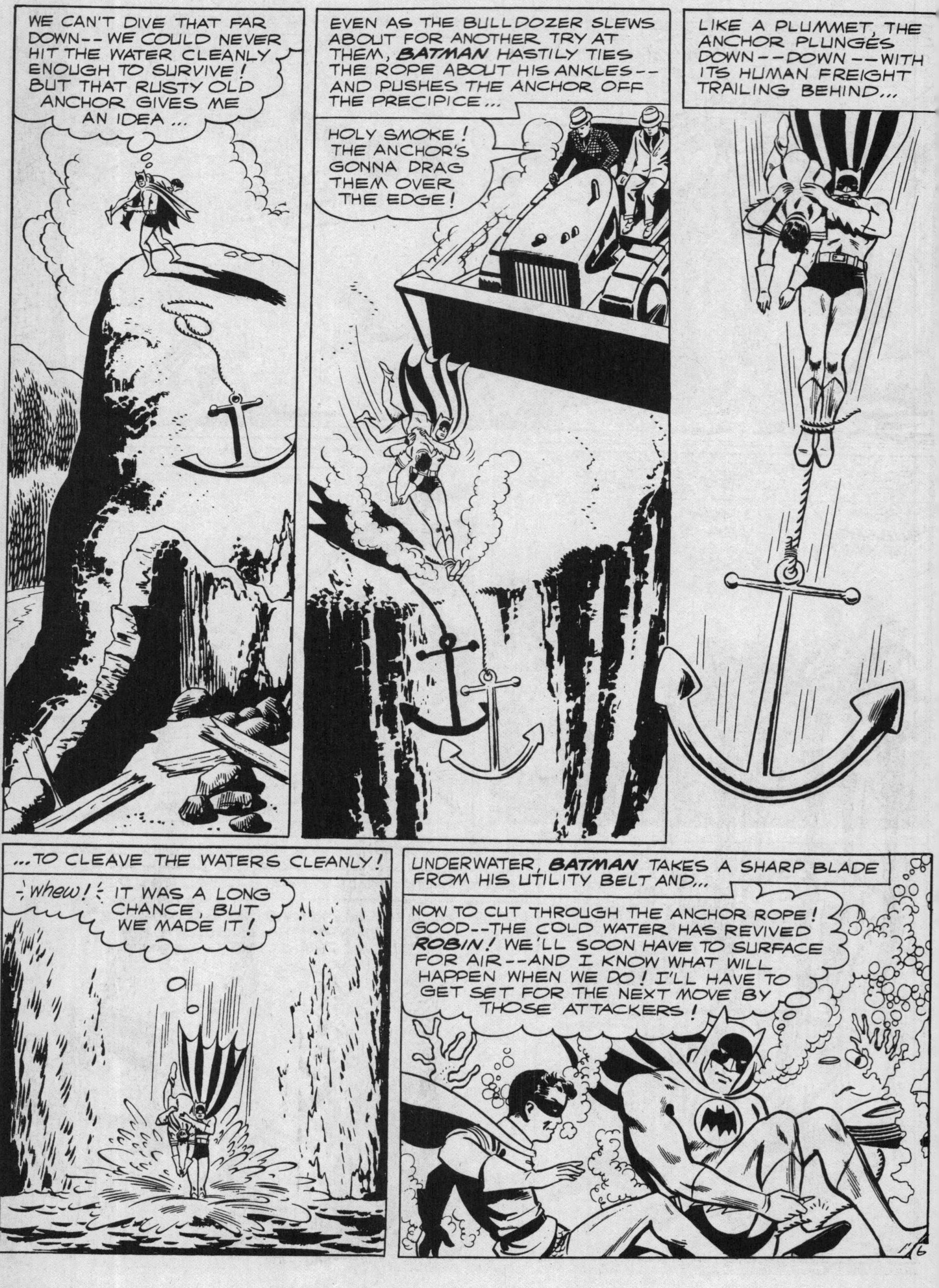
WE CAN'T DIVE THAT FAR DOWN--WE COULD NEVER HIT THE WATER CLEANLY ENOUGH TO SURVIVE! BUT THAT RUSTY OLD ANCHOR GIVES ME AN IDEA...
EVEN AS THE BULLDOZER SLEWS ABOUT FOR ANOTHER TRY AT THEM, BATMAN HASTILY TIES THE ROPE ABOUT HIS ANKLES--AND PUSHES THE ANCHOR OFF THE PRECIPICE...
HOLY SMOKE! THE ANCHOR'S GONNA DRAG THEM OVER THE EDGE!
LIKE A PLUMMET, THE ANCHOR PLUNGES DOWN--DOWN--WITH ITS HUMAN FREIGHT TRAILING BEHIND...
...TO CLEAVE THE WATERS CLEANLY!
-WHEW!- IT WAS A LONG CHANCE, BUT WE MADE IT!
UNDERWATER, BATMAN TAKES A SHARP BLADE FROM HIS UTILITY BELT AND...
NOW TO CUT THROUGH THE ANCHOR ROPE! GOOD--THE COLD WATER HAS REVIVED ROBIN! WE'LL SOON HAVE TO SURFACE FOR AIR--AND I KNOW WHAT WILL HAPPEN WHEN WE DO! I'LL HAVE TO GET SET FOR THE NEXT MOVE BY THOSE ATTACKERS!
6

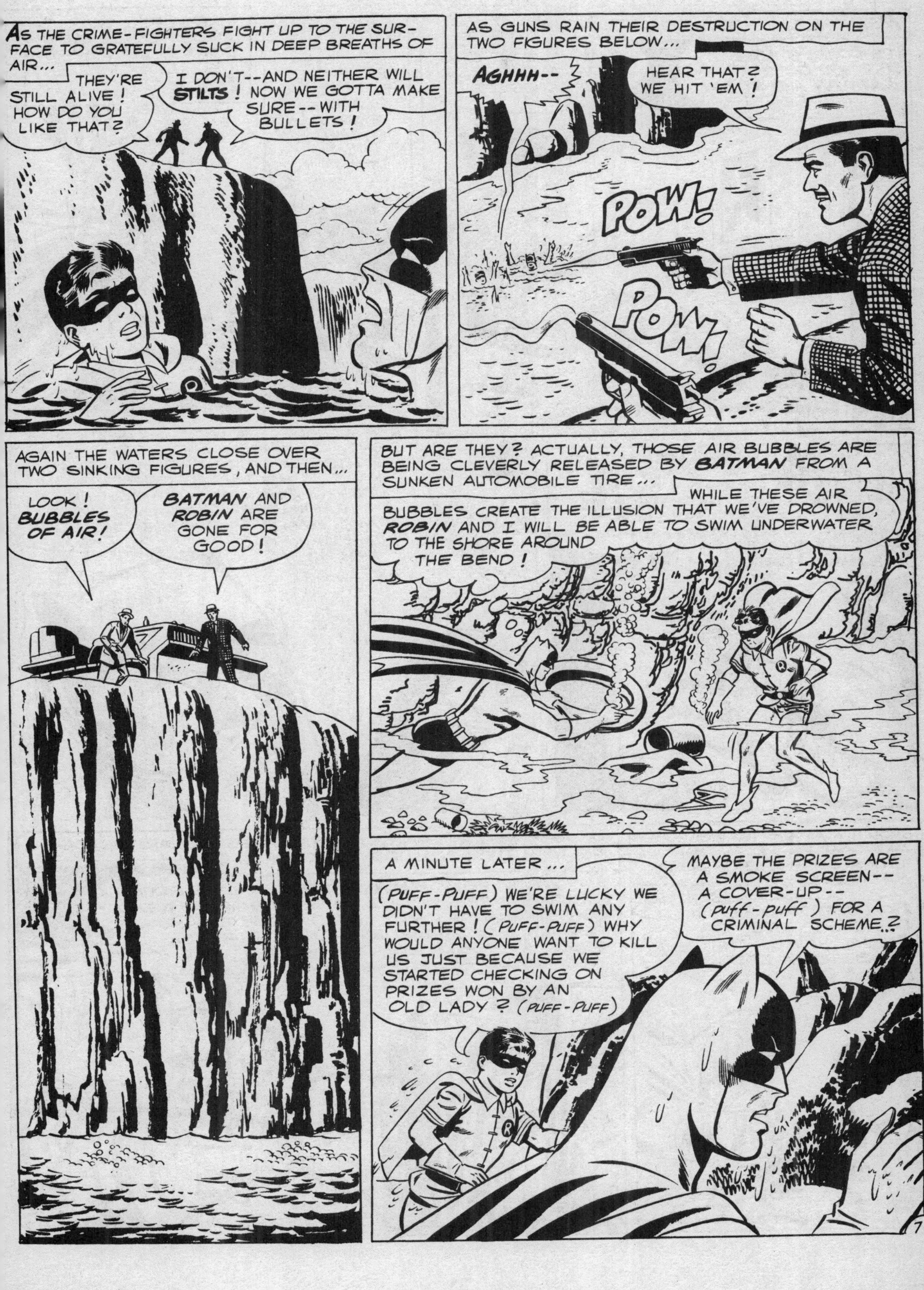
AS THE CRIME-FIGHTERS FIGHT UP TO THE SURFACE TO GRATEFULLY SUCK IN DEEP BREATHS OF AIR...
THEY'RE STILL ALIVE! HOW DO YOU LIKE THAT?
I DON'T--AND NEITHER WILL STILTS! NOW WE GOTTA MAKE SURE--WITH BULLETS!
AS GUNS RAIN THEIR DESTRUCTION ON THE TWO FIGURES BELOW...
AGHHH--
HEAR THAT? WE HIT 'EM!
POW!
POW!
AGAIN THE WATERS CLOSE OVER TWO SINKING FIGURES, AND THEN...
LOOK! BUBBLES OF AIR!
BATMAN AND ROBIN ARE GONE FOR GOOD!
BUT ARE THEY? ACTUALLY, THOSE AIR BUBBLES ARE BEING CLEVERLY RELEASED BY BATMAN FROM A SUNKEN AUTOMOBILE TIRE...
WHILE THESE AIR BUBBLES CREATE THE ILLUSION THAT WE'VE DROWNED, ROBIN AND I WILL BE ABLE TO SWIM UNDERWATER TO THE SHORE AROUND THE BEND!
A MINUTE LATER...
(PUFF-PUFF) WE'RE LUCKY WE DIDN'T HAVE TO SWIM ANY FURTHER! (PUFF-PUFF) WHY WOULD ANYONE WANT TO KILL US JUST BECAUSE WE STARTED CHECKING ON PRIZES WON BY AN OLD LADY? (PUFF-PUFF)
MAYBE THE PRIZES ARE A SMOKE SCREEN--A COVER-UP--(puff-puff) FOR A CRIMINAL SCHEME...?
7

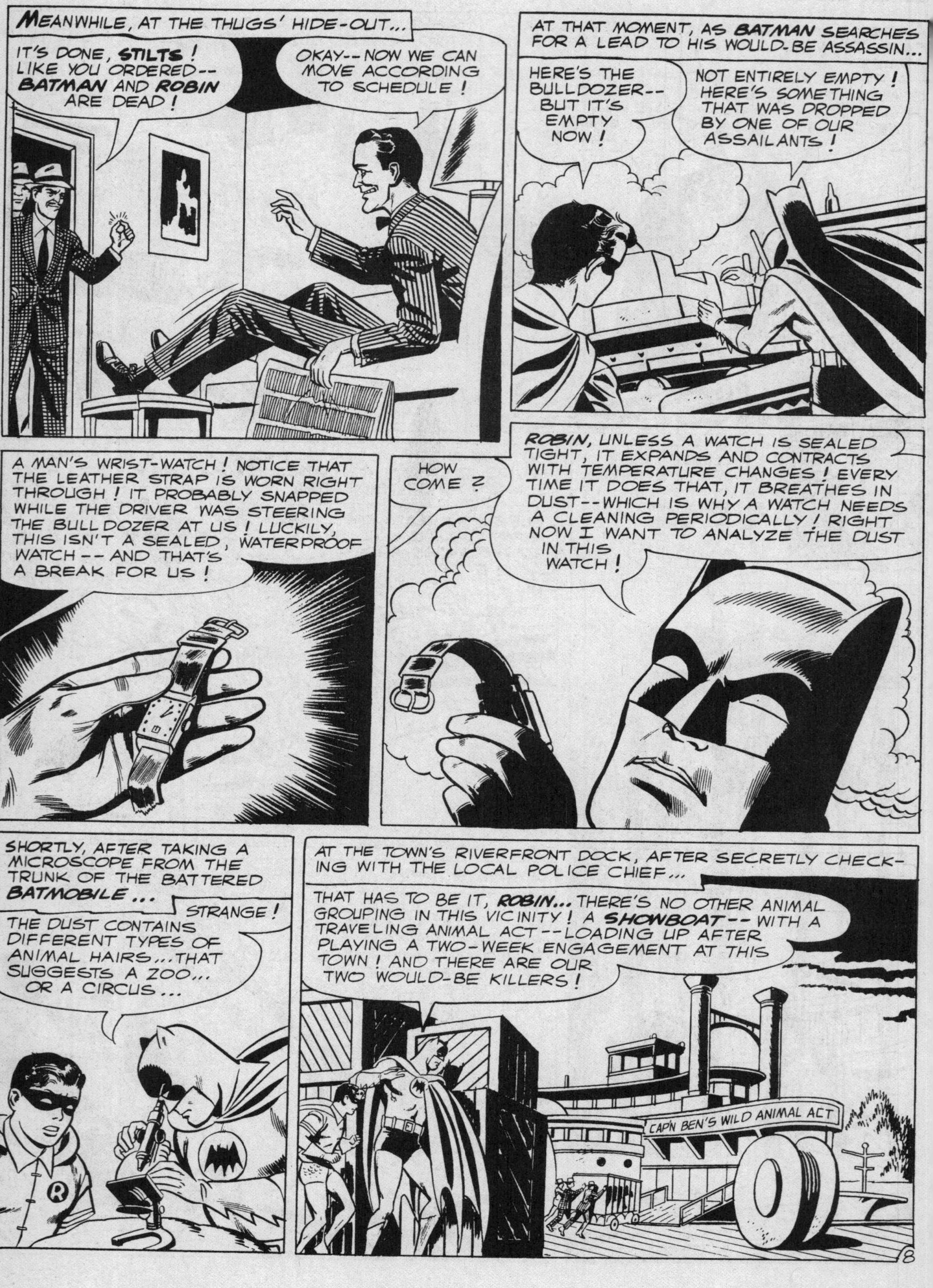
MEANWHILE, AT THE THUGS' HIDE-OUT...
IT'S DONE, STILTS! LIKE YOU ORDERED-- BATMAN AND ROBIN ARE DEAD!
OKAY--NOW WE CAN MOVE ACCORDING TO SCHEDULE!
AT THAT MOMENT, AS BATMAN SEARCHES FOR A LEAD TO HIS WOULD-BE ASSASSIN...
HERE'S THE BULLDOZER-- BUT IT'S EMPTY NOW!
NOT ENTIRELY EMPTY! HERE'S SOMETHING THAT WAS DROPPED BY ONE OF OUR ASSAILANTS!
A MAN'S WRIST-WATCH! NOTICE THAT THE LEATHER STRAP IS WORN RIGHT THROUGH! IT PROBABLY SNAPPED WHILE THE DRIVER WAS STEERING THE BULLDOZER AT US! LUCKILY, THIS ISN'T A SEALED, WATERPROOF WATCH -- AND THAT'S A BREAK FOR US!
HOW COME?
ROBIN, UNLESS A WATCH IS SEALED TIGHT, IT EXPANDS AND CONTRACTS WITH TEMPERATURE CHANGES! EVERY TIME IT DOES THAT, IT BREATHES IN DUST--WHICH IS WHY A WATCH NEEDS A CLEANING PERIODICALLY! RIGHT NOW I WANT TO ANALYZE THE DUST IN THIS WATCH!
SHORTLY, AFTER TAKING A MICROSCOPE FROM THE TRUNK OF THE BATTERED BATMOBILE...
STRANGE! THE DUST CONTAINS DIFFERENT TYPES OF ANIMAL HAIRS... THAT SUGGESTS A ZOO... OR A CIRCUS...
AT THE TOWN'S RIVERFRONT DOCK, AFTER SECRETLY CHECKING WITH THE LOCAL POLICE CHIEF...
THAT HAS TO BE IT, ROBIN... THERE'S NO OTHER ANIMAL GROUPING IN THIS VICINITY! A SHOWBOAT--WITH A TRAVELING ANIMAL ACT--LOADING UP AFTER PLAYING A TWO-WEEK ENGAGEMENT AT THIS TOWN! AND THERE ARE OUR TWO WOULD-BE KILLERS!
CAP'N BEN'S WILD ANIMAL ACT
8

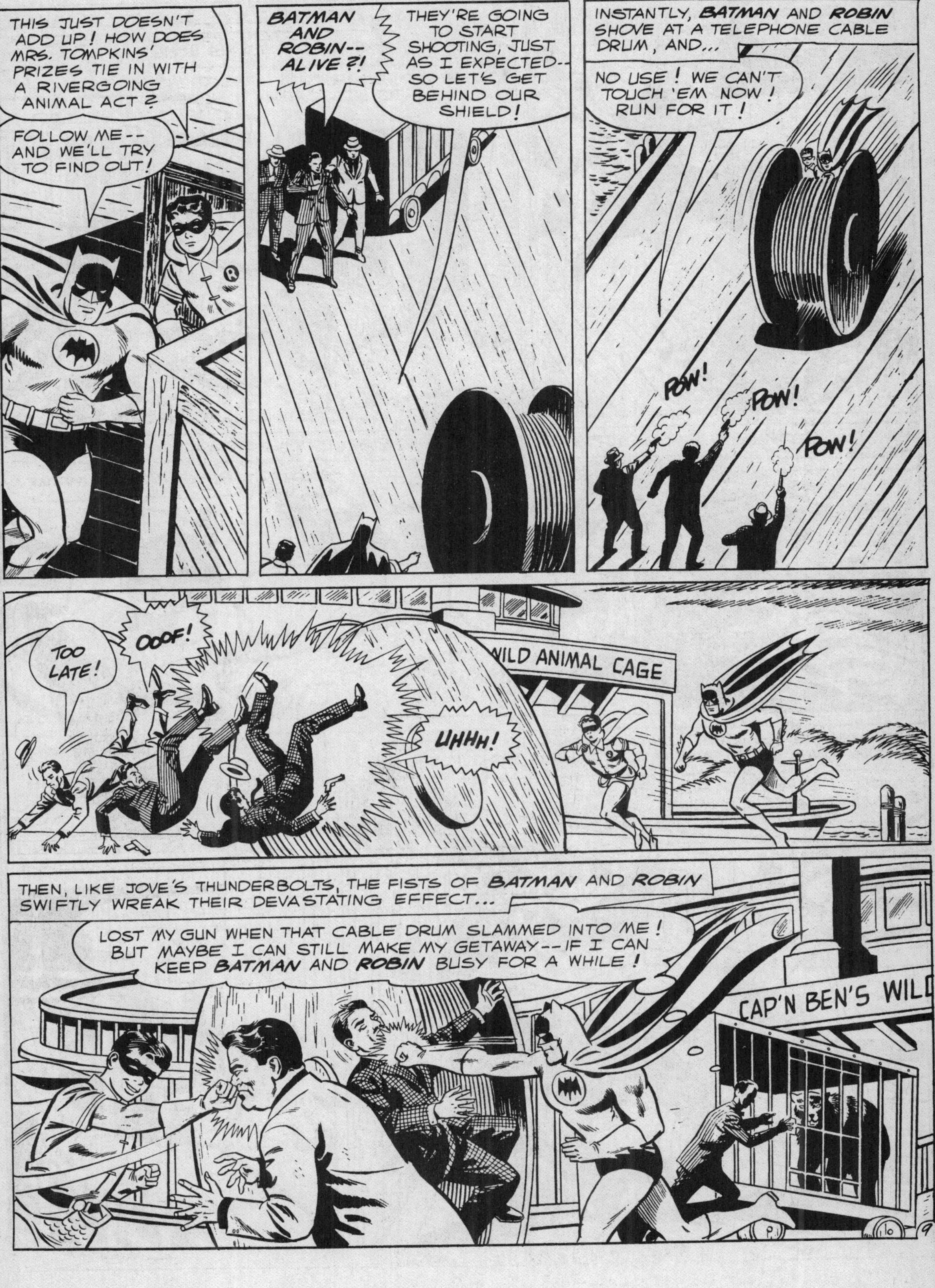
THIS JUST DOESN'T ADD UP! HOW DOES MRS. TOMPKINS' PRIZES TIE IN WITH A RIVERGOING ANIMAL ACT?
FOLLOW ME-- AND WE'LL TRY TO FIND OUT!
BATMAN AND ROBIN-- ALIVE?!
THEY'RE GOING TO START SHOOTING, JUST AS I EXPECTED-- SO LET'S GET BEHIND OUR SHIELD!
INSTANTLY, BATMAN AND ROBIN SHOVE AT A TELEPHONE CABLE DRUM, AND...
NO USE! WE CAN'T TOUCH 'EM NOW! RUN FOR IT!
POW!
POW!
POW!
TOO LATE!
OOOF!
UHHH!
WILD ANIMAL CAGE
THEN, LIKE JOVE'S THUNDERBOLTS, THE FISTS OF BATMAN AND ROBIN SWIFTLY WREAK THEIR DEVASTATING EFFECT...
LOST MY GUN WHEN THAT CABLE DRUM SLAMMED INTO ME! BUT MAYBE I CAN STILL MAKE MY GETAWAY--IF I CAN KEEP BATMAN AND ROBIN BUSY FOR A WHILE!
CAP'N BEN'S WILD
9

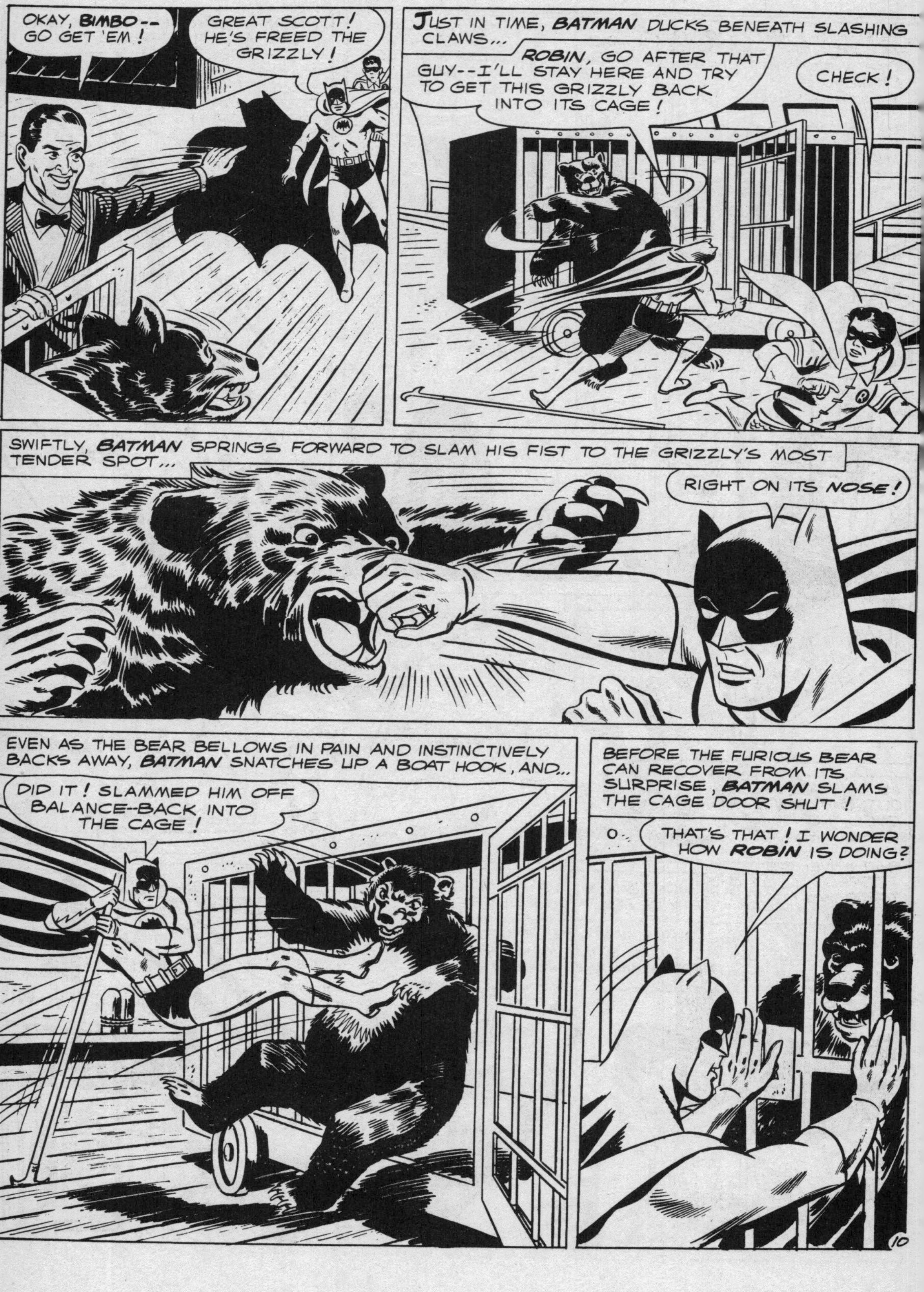

OKAY, BIMBO-- GO GET 'EM!
GREAT SCOTT! HE'S FREED THE GRIZZLY!
JUST IN TIME, BATMAN DUCKS BENEATH SLASHING CLAWS...
ROBIN, GO AFTER THAT GUY--I'LL STAY HERE AND TRY TO GET THIS GRIZZLY BACK INTO ITS CAGE!
CHECK!
SWIFTLY, BATMAN SPRINGS FORWARD TO SLAM HIS FIST TO THE GRIZZLY'S MOST TENDER SPOT...
RIGHT ON ITS NOSE!
EVEN AS THE BEAR BELLOWS IN PAIN AND INSTINCTIVELY BACKS AWAY, BATMAN SNATCHES UP A BOAT HOOK, AND...
DID IT! SLAMMED HIM OFF BALANCE--BACK INTO THE CAGE!
BEFORE THE FURIOUS BEAR CAN RECOVER FROM ITS SURPRISE, BATMAN SLAMS THE CAGE DOOR SHUT!
THAT'S THAT! I WONDER HOW ROBIN IS DOING?
10

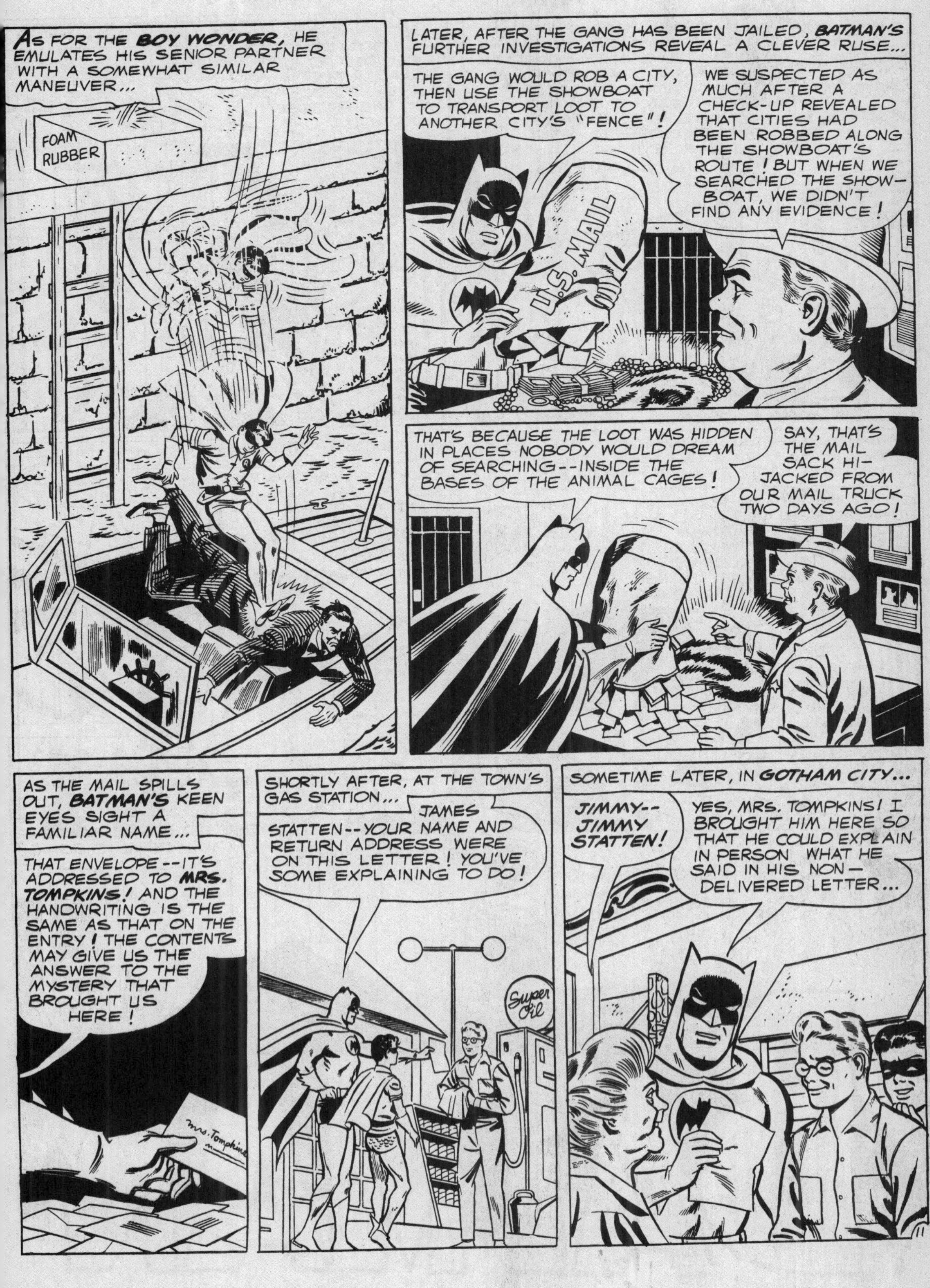
AS FOR THE BOY WONDER, HE EMULATES HIS SENIOR PARTNER WITH A SOMEWHAT SIMILAR MANEUVER...
FOAM RUBBER
LATER, AFTER THE GANG HAS BEEN JAILED, BATMAN'S FURTHER INVESTIGATIONS REVEAL A CLEVER RUSE...
THE GANG WOULD ROB A CITY, THEN USE THE SHOWBOAT TO TRANSPORT LOOT TO ANOTHER CITY'S "FENCE"!
WE SUSPECTED AS MUCH AFTER A CHECK-UP REVEALED THAT CITIES HAD BEEN ROBBED ALONG THE SHOWBOAT'S ROUTE! BUT WHEN WE SEARCHED THE SHOW-BOAT, WE DIDN'T FIND ANY EVIDENCE!
U.S. MAIL
THAT'S BECAUSE THE LOOT WAS HIDDEN IN PLACES NOBODY WOULD DREAM OF SEARCHING--INSIDE THE BASES OF THE ANIMAL CAGES!
SAY, THAT'S THE MAIL SACK HI-JACKED FROM OUR MAIL TRUCK TWO DAYS AGO!
AS THE MAIL SPILLS OUT, BATMAN'S KEEN EYES SIGHT A FAMILIAR NAME...
THAT ENVELOPE--IT'S ADDRESSED TO MRS. TOMPKINS! AND THE HANDWRITING IS THE SAME AS THAT ON THE ENTRY! THE CONTENTS MAY GIVE US THE ANSWER TO THE MYSTERY THAT BROUGHT US HERE!
Mrs. Tompkins
SHORTLY AFTER, AT THE TOWN'S GAS STATION...
JAMES STATTEN--YOUR NAME AND RETURN ADDRESS WERE ON THIS LETTER! YOU'VE SOME EXPLAINING TO DO!
Super Oil
SOMETIME LATER, IN GOTHAM CITY...
JIMMY--JIMMY STATTEN!
YES, MRS. TOMPKINS! I BROUGHT HIM HERE SO THAT HE COULD EXPLAIN IN PERSON WHAT HE SAID IN HIS NON-DELIVERED LETTER...
11

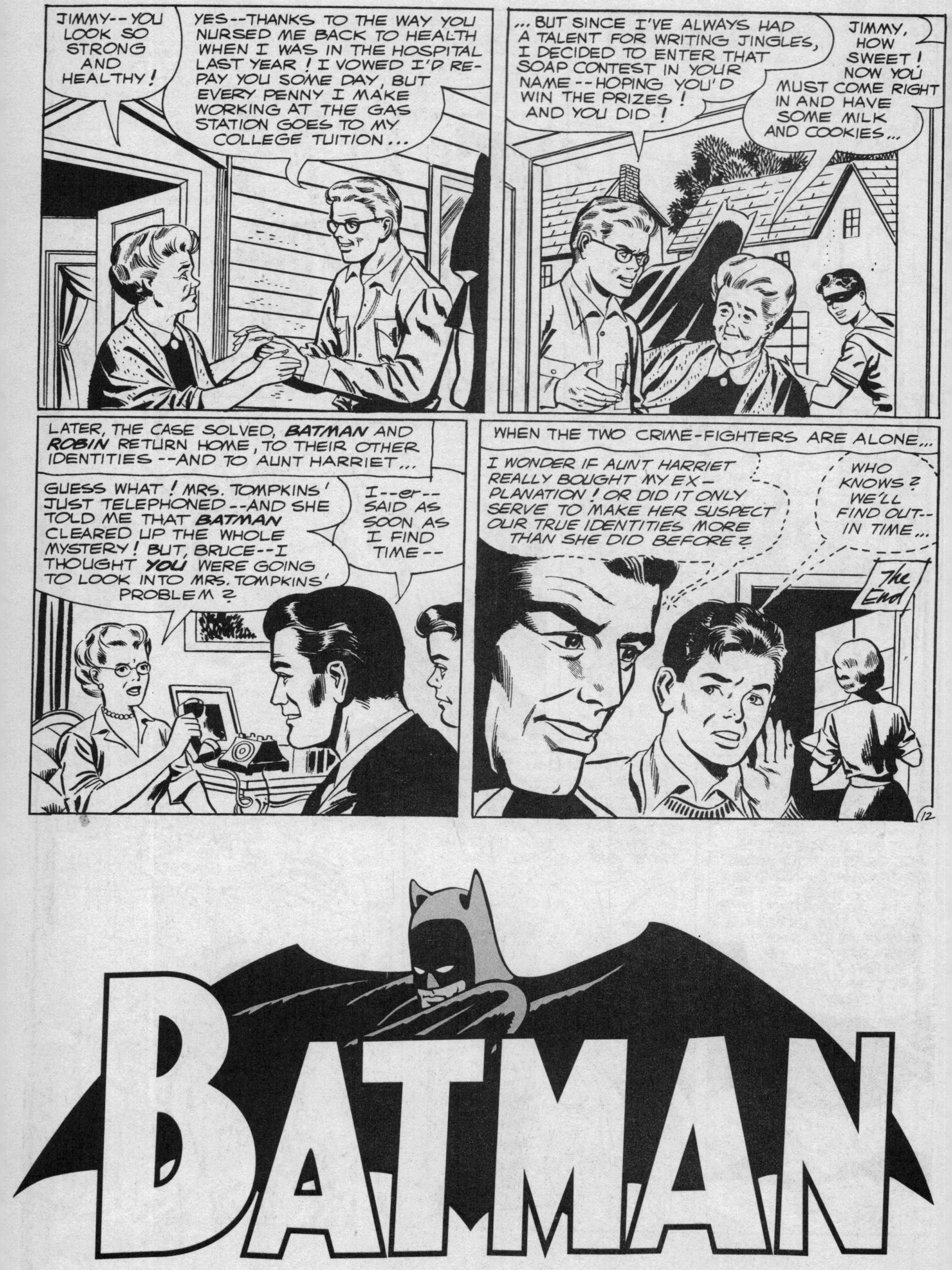
JIMMY--YOU LOOK SO STRONG AND HEALTHY!
YES--THANKS TO THE WAY YOU NURSED ME BACK TO HEALTH WHEN I WAS IN THE HOSPITAL LAST YEAR! I VOWED I'D RE-PAY YOU SOME DAY, BUT EVERY PENNY I MAKE WORKING AT THE GAS STATION GOES TO MY COLLEGE TUITION...
...BUT SINCE I'VE ALWAYS HAD A TALENT FOR WRITING JINGLES, I DECIDED TO ENTER THAT SOAP CONTEST IN YOUR NAME--HOPING YOU'D WIN THE PRIZES! AND YOU DID!
JIMMY, HOW SWEET! NOW YOU MUST COME RIGHT IN AND HAVE SOME MILK AND COOKIES...
LATER, THE CASE SOLVED, BATMAN AND ROBIN RETURN HOME, TO THEIR OTHER IDENTITIES--AND TO AUNT HARRIET...
GUESS WHAT! MRS. TOMPKINS' JUST TELEPHONED--AND SHE TOLD ME THAT BATMAN CLEARED UP THE WHOLE MYSTERY! BUT, BRUCE--I THOUGHT YOU WERE GOING TO LOOK INTO MRS. TOMPKINS' PROBLEM?
I--er--SAID AS SOON AS I FIND TIME--
WHEN THE TWO CRIME-FIGHTERS ARE ALONE...
I WONDER IF AUNT HARRIET REALLY BOUGHT MY EX-PLANATION! OR DID IT ONLY SERVE TO MAKE HER SUSPECT OUR TRUE IDENTITIES MORE THAN SHE DID BEFORE?
WHO KNOWS? WE'LL FIND OUT--IN TIME...
The End
12

BATMAN

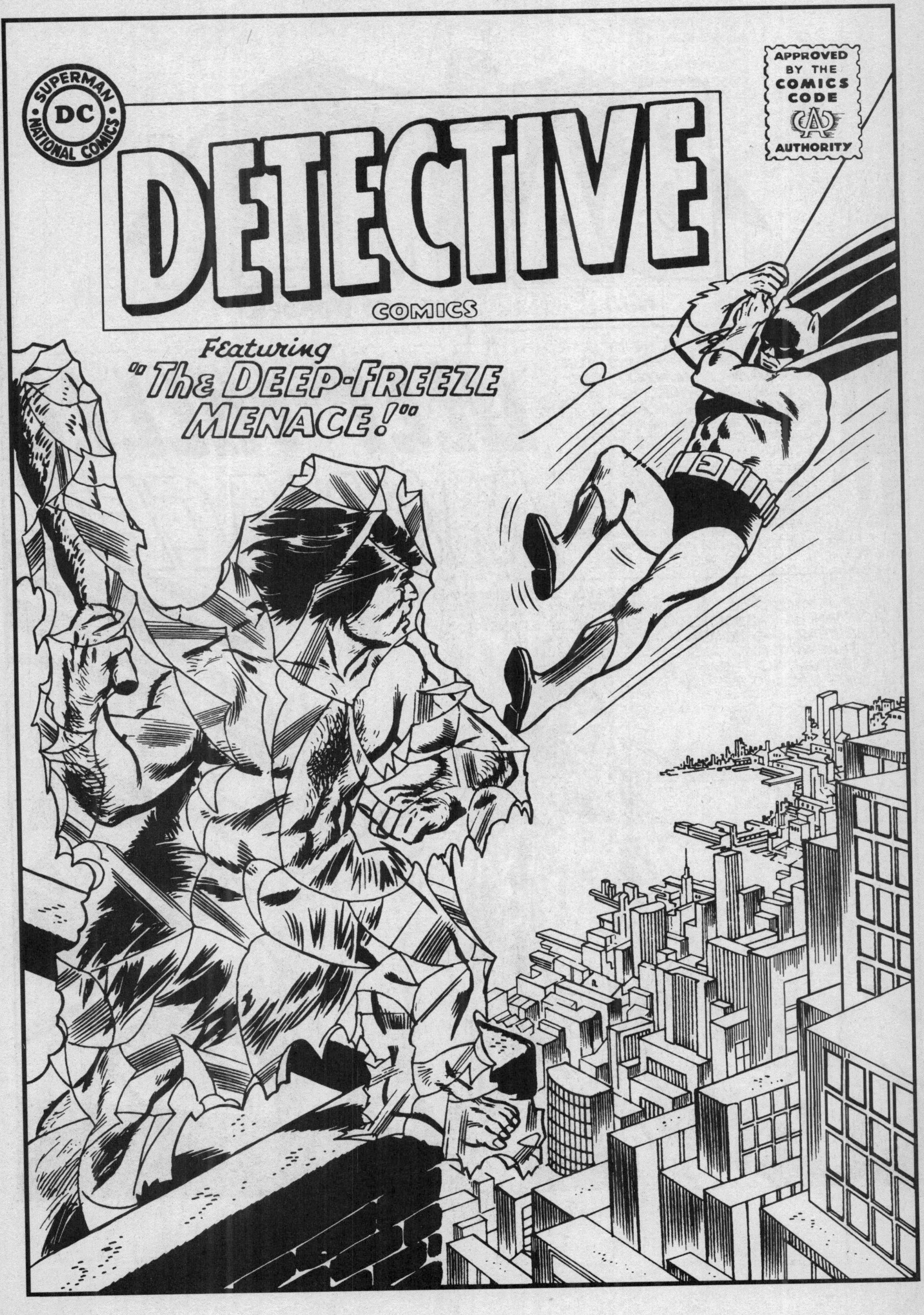
SUPERMAN DC NATIONAL COMICS
DETECTIVE
COMICS
APPROVED BY THE COMICS CODE AUTHORITY
Featuring "The DEEP-FREEZE MENACE!"

BATMAN

With ROBIN The Boy Wonder

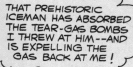

OUT OF THE LOST EONS OF EARTH'S PAST HE COMES--KLAG, THE *CRO-MAGNON HUNTER*, THE CAVEMAN CLUB-WIELDER WHO SEEKS ONE MAN IN ALL EARTH'S TEEMING MILLIONS! SHEATHED IN THE ICE WHICH GIVES HIM FANTASTIC POWERS-- MASTER OF THE EARTH'S NATURAL FORCES--INVULNERABLE TO BULLETS OR BOMBS--KLAG STANDS LIKE A COLOSSUS, DEFYING *BATMAN* AND *ROBIN* TO MATCH THEIR MIGHTIEST BLOWS AGAINST THE...

DEEP-FREEZE MENACE!

THAT PREHISTORIC ICEMAN HAS ABSORBED THE TEAR-GAS BOMBS I THREW AT HIM--AND IS EXPELLING THE GAS BACK AT ME!

ROBIN'S DIVERSIONARY MOVE HAS GIVEN ME A CHANCE TO COME TO GRIPS WITH THAT CAVEMAN!

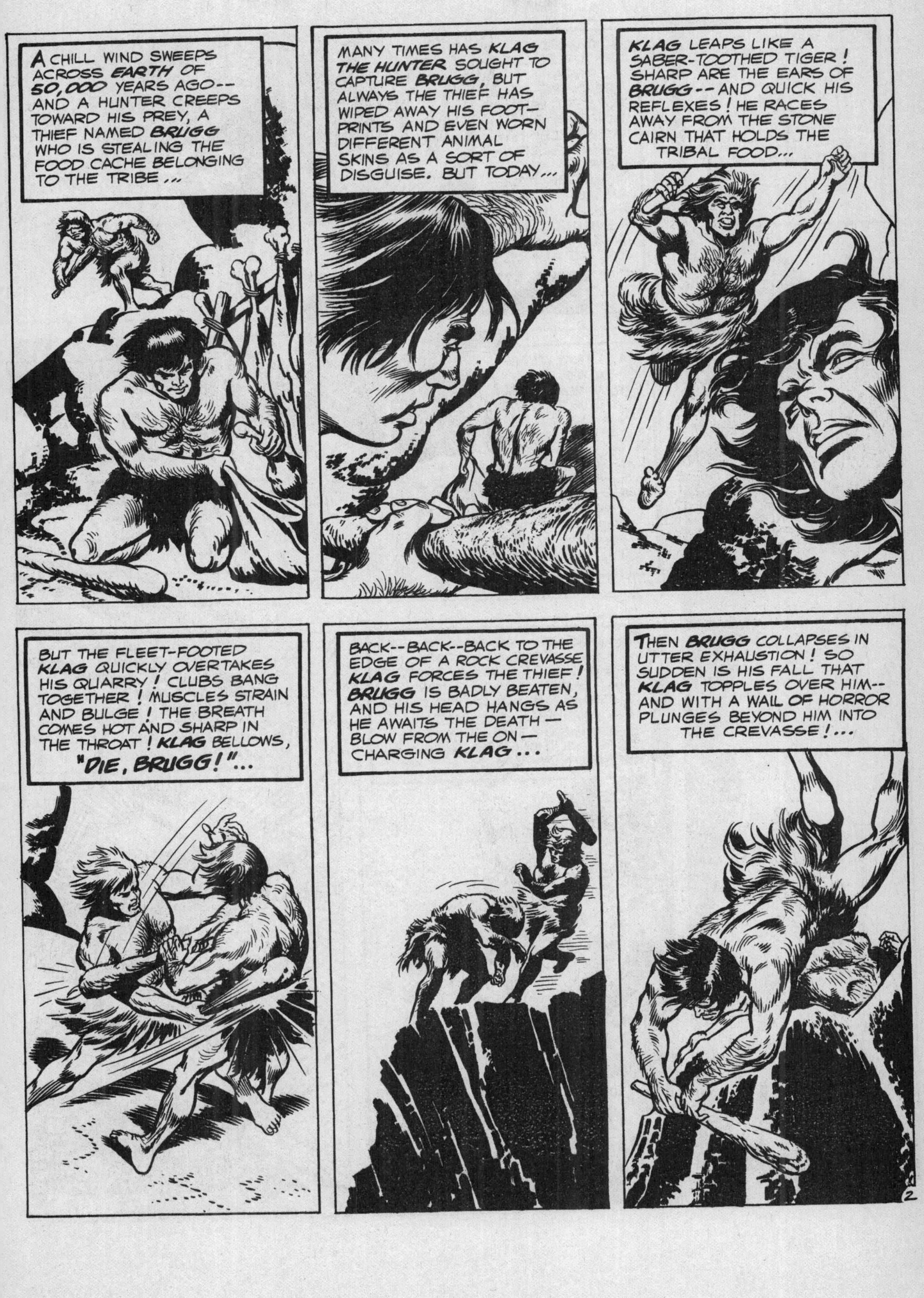
A CHILL WIND SWEEPS ACROSS EARTH OF 50,000 YEARS AGO-- AND A HUNTER CREEPS TOWARD HIS PREY, A THIEF NAMED BRUGG WHO IS STEALING THE FOOD CACHE BELONGING TO THE TRIBE...
MANY TIMES HAS KLAG THE HUNTER SOUGHT TO CAPTURE BRUGG, BUT ALWAYS THE THIEF HAS WIPED AWAY HIS FOOT-PRINTS AND EVEN WORN DIFFERENT ANIMAL SKINS AS A SORT OF DISGUISE. BUT TODAY...
KLAG LEAPS LIKE A SABER-TOOTHED TIGER! SHARP ARE THE EARS OF BRUGG-- AND QUICK HIS REFLEXES! HE RACES AWAY FROM THE STONE CAIRN THAT HOLDS THE TRIBAL FOOD...
BUT THE FLEET-FOOTED KLAG QUICKLY OVERTAKES HIS QUARRY! CLUBS BANG TOGETHER! MUSCLES STRAIN AND BULGE! THE BREATH COMES HOT AND SHARP IN THE THROAT! KLAG BELLOWS, "DIE, BRUGG!"...
BACK--BACK--BACK TO THE EDGE OF A ROCK CREVASSE KLAG FORCES THE THIEF! BRUGG IS BADLY BEATEN, AND HIS HEAD HANGS AS HE AWAITS THE DEATH—BLOW FROM THE ON—CHARGING KLAG...
THEN BRUGG COLLAPSES IN UTTER EXHAUSTION! SO SUDDEN IS HIS FALL THAT KLAG TOPPLES OVER HIM-- AND WITH A WAIL OF HORROR PLUNGES BEYOND HIM INTO THE CREVASSE!...
2

KLAG BEGINS HIS LONG DOWNWARD FALL INTO THE ROCK TOMB FROM WHICH THERE IS NO ESCAPE! A SINGLE SOUND-- A LONG DRAWN OUT *"AIIEEEEEEE!"* ECHOES UPWARD! THEN THERE IS ONLY SILENCE...

NOW--*500* CENTURIES LATER-- A CERTAIN DESOLATE AREA IN NORTHERN EUROPE EX- PERIENCES A GREAT EARTH- QUAKE--AND IN A HIDDEN CAVE AN EERIE FIGURE IS REVEALED AS A CLIFFWALL SPLITS APART...

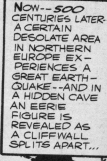

ALL THAT TIME *KLAG THE HUNTER* HAS LAIN IN THIS CAVE IN A DEEP-FREEZE STATE OF SUSPENDED ANIMATION, HIS ICE-SHEATHED BODY DRIPPED ON BY THE MINERALS FROM THE STALACTITE CEILING ABOVE...

THE EARTHQUAKE SHAKES HIM VIOLENTLY--CAUSING TINY OPENINGS TO FORM IN THE ICE THAT SHEATHED HIS BODY, JARRING HIS HEART TO PUMP- ING AND HIS LUNGS TO BREATHING! THE FLOOR TILTS AS THE EARTH HEAVES BENEATH HIM AND...

THE ICE-SHEATHING IS FLEXIBLE AND SLOWLY *KLAG* RISES AND STARES ABOUT HIM. THE WORLD IS DIFFERENT--STRANGE--AND YET FAMILIAR. AS OF YORE HIS MIND KNOWS ONLY ONE THOUGHT: *FIND BRUGG-- AND KILL HIM!*...

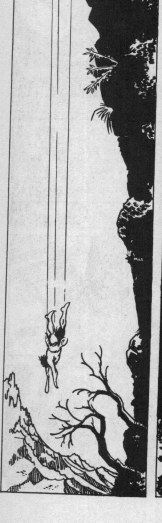

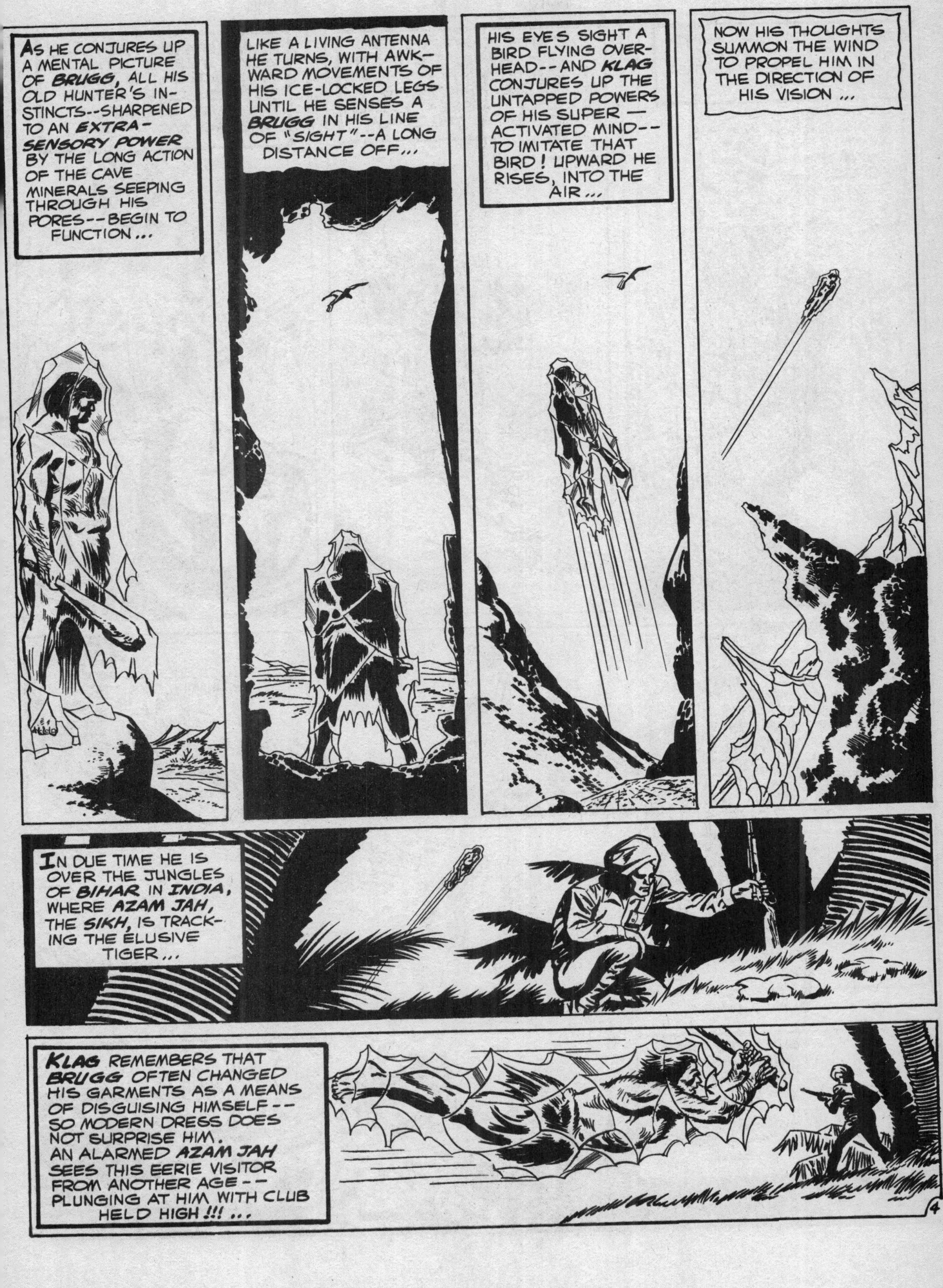
AS HE CONJURES UP A MENTAL PICTURE OF BRUGG, ALL HIS OLD HUNTER'S IN-STINCTS--SHARPENED TO AN EXTRA-SENSORY POWER BY THE LONG ACTION OF THE CAVE MINERALS SEEPING THROUGH HIS PORES--BEGIN TO FUNCTION...
LIKE A LIVING ANTENNA HE TURNS, WITH AWK-WARD MOVEMENTS OF HIS ICE-LOCKED LEGS UNTIL HE SENSES A BRUGG IN HIS LINE OF "SIGHT"--A LONG DISTANCE OFF...
HIS EYES SIGHT A BIRD FLYING OVER-HEAD--AND KLAG CONJURES UP THE UNTAPPED POWERS OF HIS SUPER — ACTIVATED MIND-- TO IMITATE THAT BIRD! UPWARD HE RISES, INTO THE AIR...
NOW HIS THOUGHTS SUMMON THE WIND TO PROPEL HIM IN THE DIRECTION OF HIS VISION...
IN DUE TIME HE IS OVER THE JUNGLES OF BIHAR IN INDIA, WHERE AZAM JAH, THE SIKH, IS TRACK-ING THE ELUSIVE TIGER...
KLAG REMEMBERS THAT BRUGG OFTEN CHANGED HIS GARMENTS AS A MEANS OF DISGUISING HIMSELF-- SO MODERN DRESS DOES NOT SURPRISE HIM.
AN ALARMED AZAM JAH SEES THIS EERIE VISITOR FROM ANOTHER AGE-- PLUNGING AT HIM WITH CLUB HELD HIGH!!!...
4

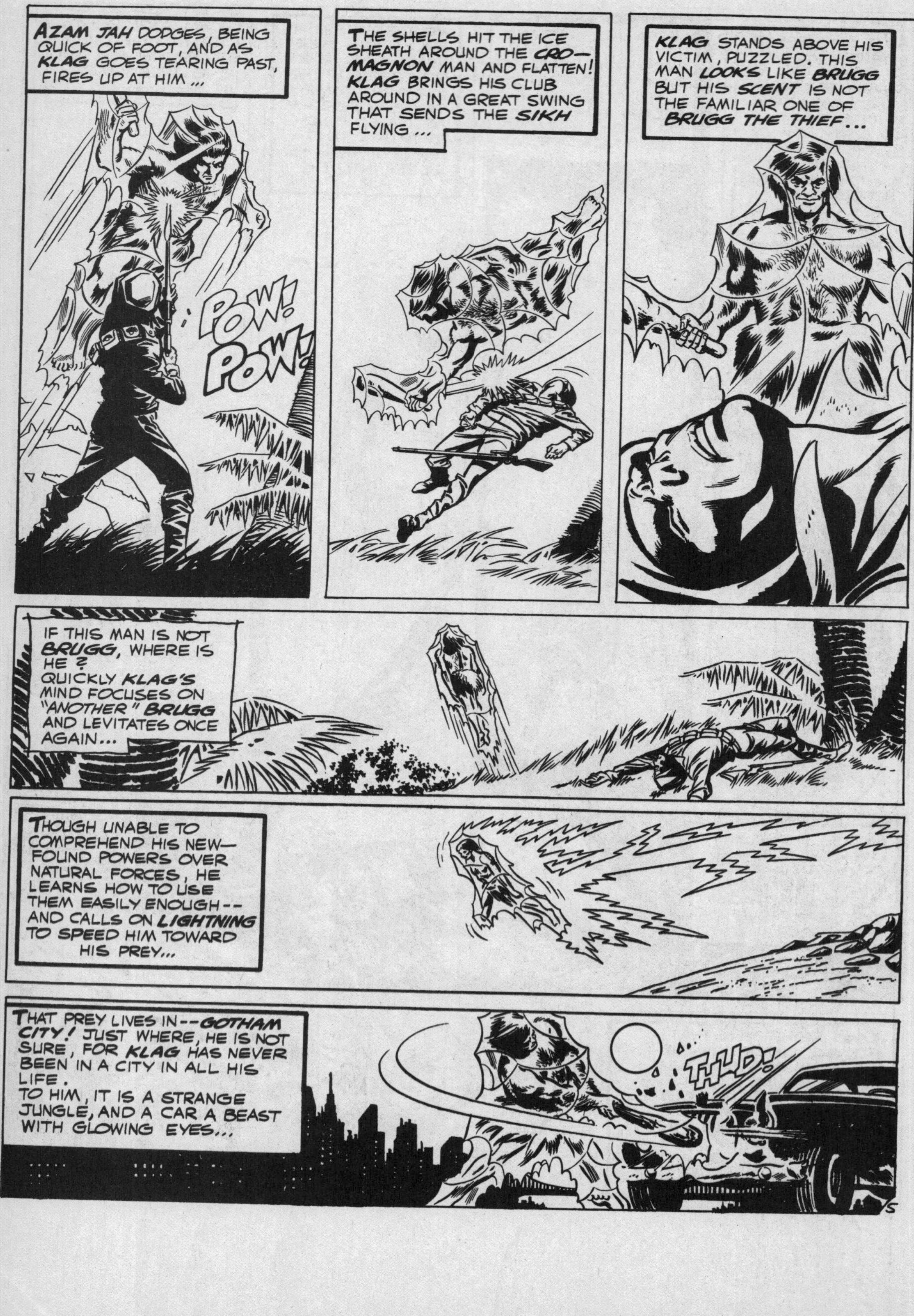
AZAM JAH DODGES, BEING QUICK OF FOOT, AND AS KLAG GOES TEARING PAST, FIRES UP AT HIM ...
POW! POW!
THE SHELLS HIT THE ICE SHEATH AROUND THE CRO-MAGNON MAN AND FLATTEN! KLAG BRINGS HIS CLUB AROUND IN A GREAT SWING THAT SENDS THE SIKH FLYING ...
KLAG STANDS ABOVE HIS VICTIM, PUZZLED. THIS MAN LOOKS LIKE BRUGG BUT HIS SCENT IS NOT THE FAMILIAR ONE OF BRUGG THE THIEF ...
IF THIS MAN IS NOT BRUGG, WHERE IS HE? QUICKLY KLAG'S MIND FOCUSES ON "ANOTHER" BRUGG AND LEVITATES ONCE AGAIN...
THOUGH UNABLE TO COMPREHEND HIS NEW-FOUND POWERS OVER NATURAL FORCES, HE LEARNS HOW TO USE THEM EASILY ENOUGH-- AND CALLS ON LIGHTNING TO SPEED HIM TOWARD HIS PREY...
THAT PREY LIVES IN--GOTHAM CITY! JUST WHERE, HE IS NOT SURE, FOR KLAG HAS NEVER BEEN IN A CITY IN ALL HIS LIFE. TO HIM, IT IS A STRANGE JUNGLE, AND A CAR A BEAST WITH GLOWING EYES...
THUD!
15

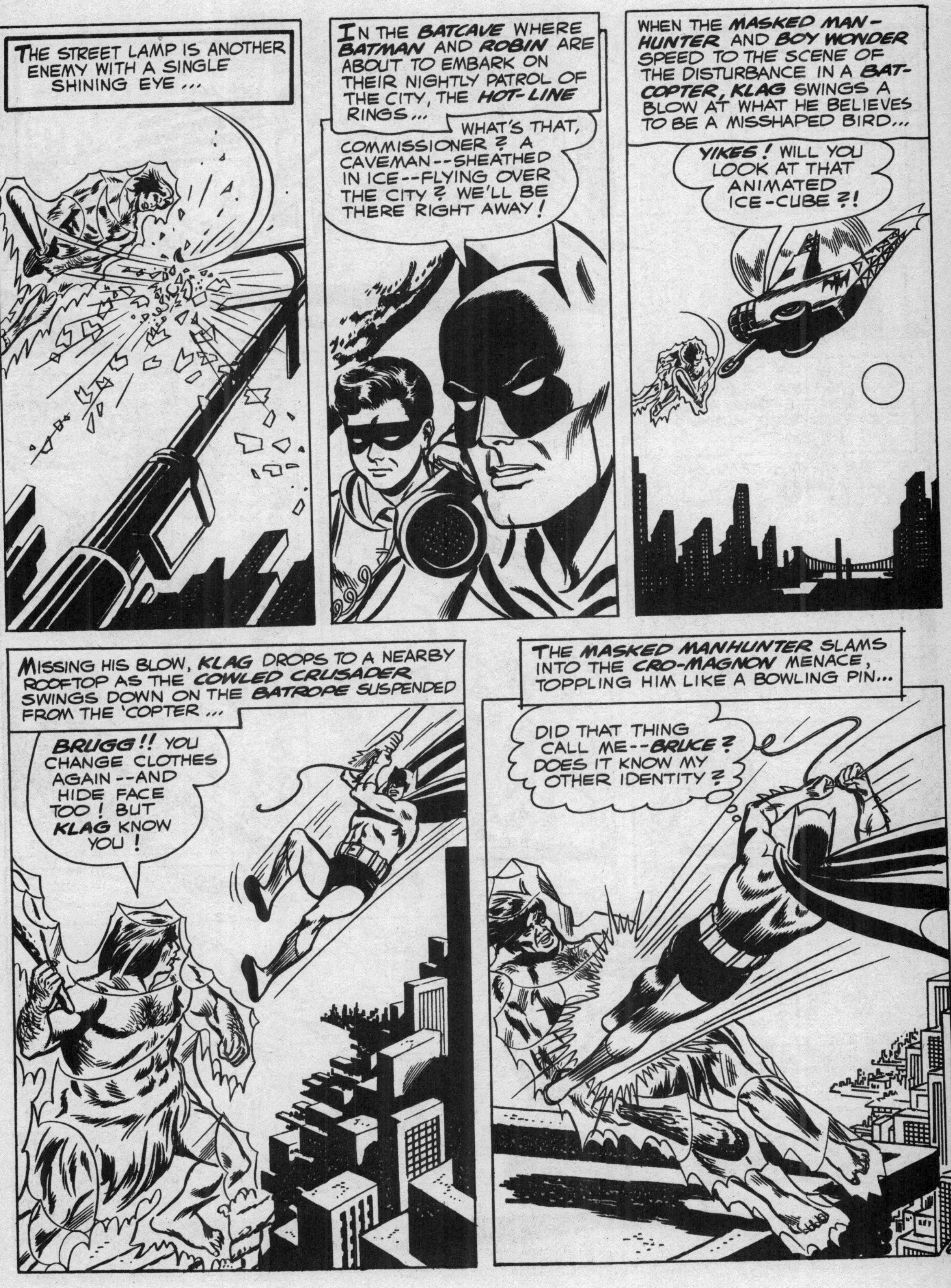
THE STREET LAMP IS ANOTHER ENEMY WITH A SINGLE SHINING EYE ...
IN THE BATCAVE WHERE BATMAN AND ROBIN ARE ABOUT TO EMBARK ON THEIR NIGHTLY PATROL OF THE CITY, THE HOT-LINE RINGS ...
WHAT'S THAT, COMMISSIONER ? A CAVEMAN--SHEATHED IN ICE--FLYING OVER THE CITY ? WE'LL BE THERE RIGHT AWAY !
WHEN THE MASKED MAN-HUNTER AND BOY WONDER SPEED TO THE SCENE OF THE DISTURBANCE IN A BAT-COPTER, KLAG SWINGS A BLOW AT WHAT HE BELIEVES TO BE A MISSHAPED BIRD...
YIKES ! WILL YOU LOOK AT THAT ANIMATED ICE-CUBE ?!
MISSING HIS BLOW, KLAG DROPS TO A NEARBY ROOFTOP AS THE COWLED CRUSADER SWINGS DOWN ON THE BATROPE SUSPENDED FROM THE 'COPTER ...
BRUGG !! YOU CHANGE CLOTHES AGAIN --AND HIDE FACE TOO ! BUT KLAG KNOW YOU !
THE MASKED MANHUNTER SLAMS INTO THE CRO-MAGNON MENACE, TOPPLING HIM LIKE A BOWLING PIN...
DID THAT THING CALL ME--BRUCE ? DOES IT KNOW MY OTHER IDENTITY ?
6

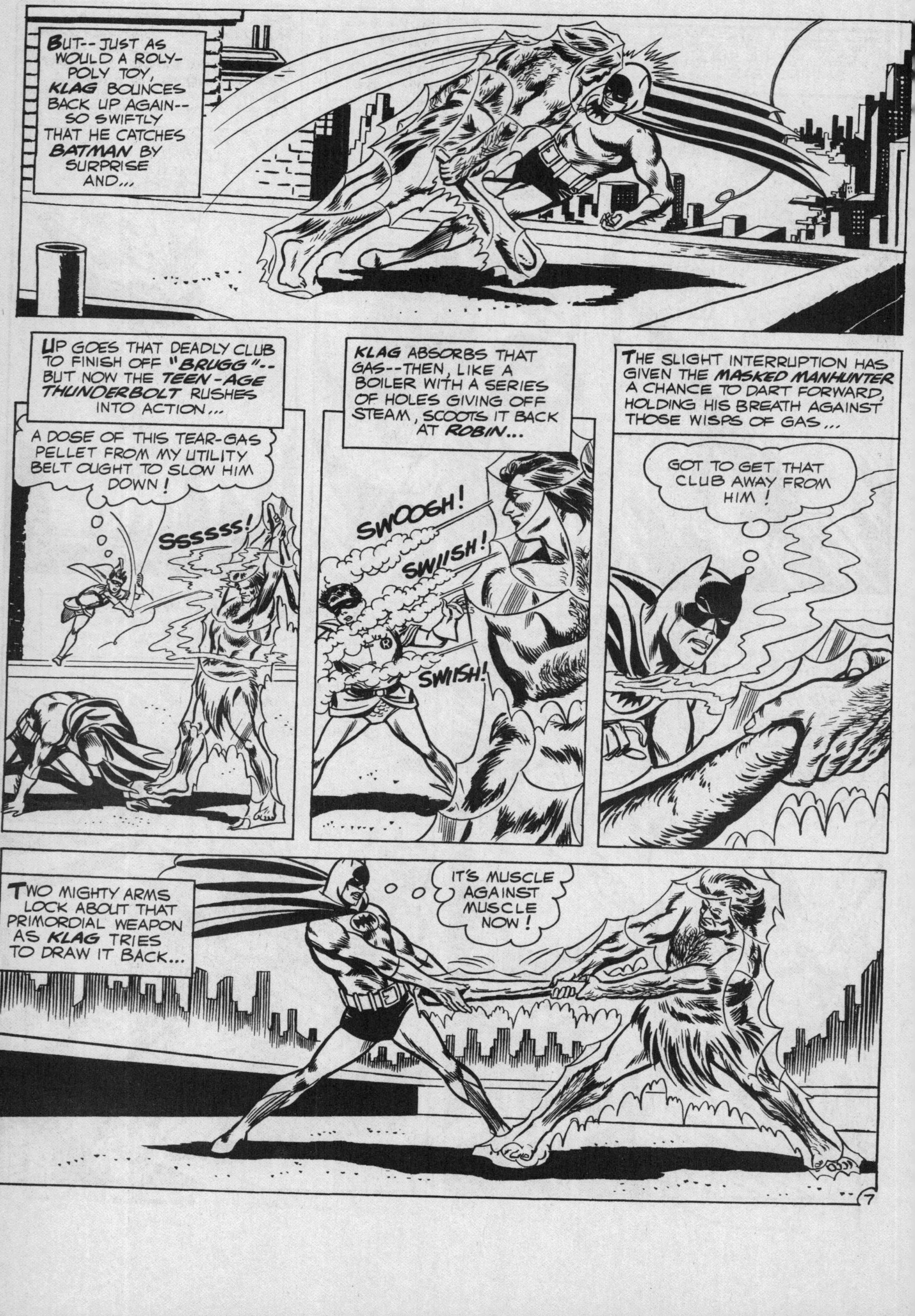
BUT--JUST AS WOULD A ROLY-POLY TOY, KLAG BOUNCES BACK UP AGAIN--SO SWIFTLY THAT HE CATCHES BATMAN BY SURPRISE AND...
UP GOES THAT DEADLY CLUB TO FINISH OFF "BRUGG"--BUT NOW THE TEEN-AGE THUNDERBOLT RUSHES INTO ACTION...
A DOSE OF THIS TEAR-GAS PELLET FROM MY UTILITY BELT OUGHT TO SLOW HIM DOWN!
SSSSSS!
KLAG ABSORBS THAT GAS--THEN, LIKE A BOILER WITH A SERIES OF HOLES GIVING OFF STEAM, SCOOTS IT BACK AT ROBIN...
SWOOSH!
SWISH!
SWISH!
THE SLIGHT INTERRUPTION HAS GIVEN THE MASKED MANHUNTER A CHANCE TO DART FORWARD, HOLDING HIS BREATH AGAINST THOSE WISPS OF GAS...
GOT TO GET THAT CLUB AWAY FROM HIM!
TWO MIGHTY ARMS LOCK ABOUT THAT PRIMORDIAL WEAPON AS KLAG TRIES TO DRAW IT BACK...
IT'S MUSCLE AGAINST MUSCLE NOW!
7

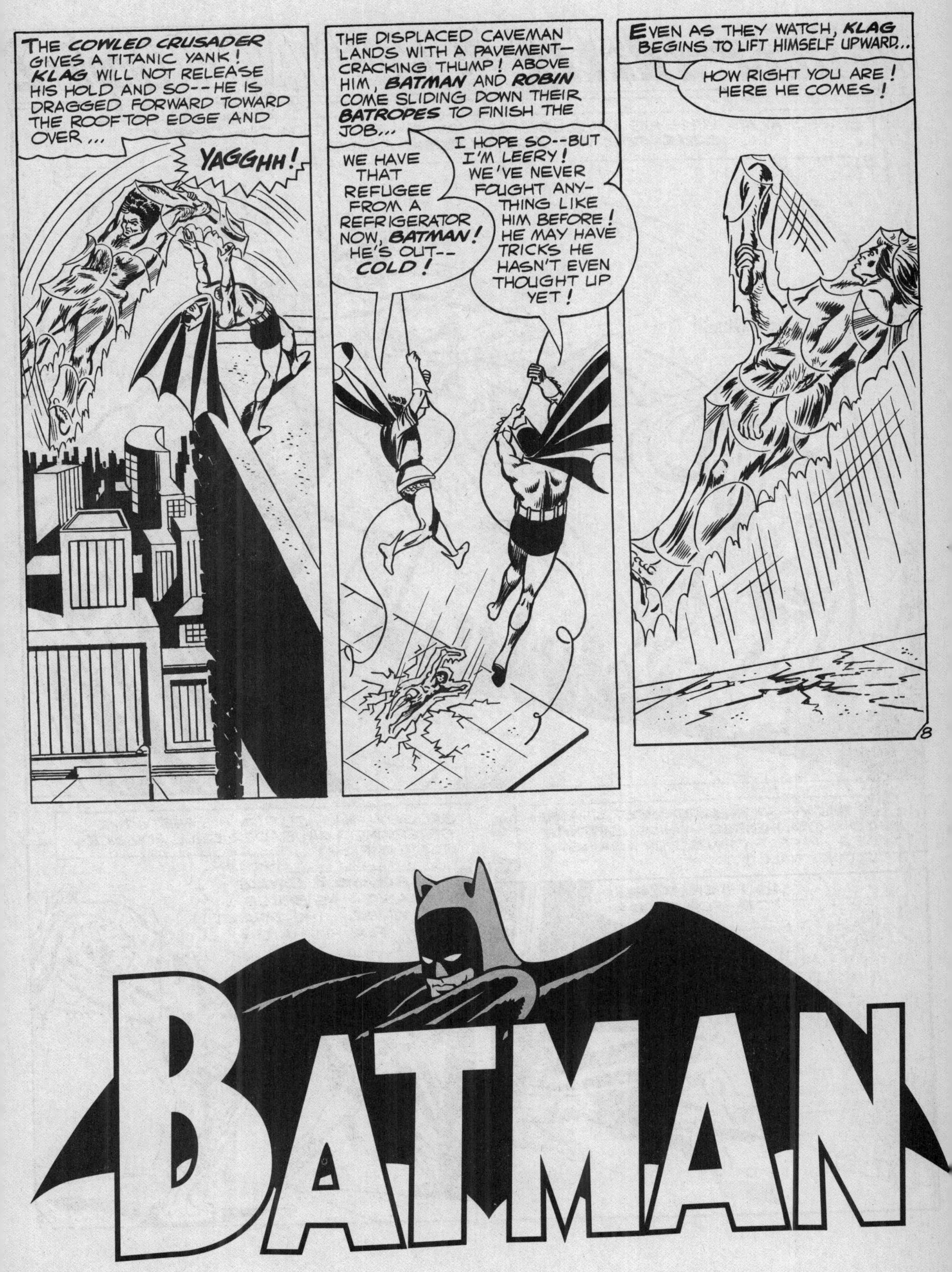
THE COWLED CRUSADER GIVES A TITANIC YANK! KLAG WILL NOT RELEASE HIS HOLD AND SO-- HE IS DRAGGED FORWARD TOWARD THE ROOFTOP EDGE AND OVER...
YAGGHH!
THE DISPLACED CAVEMAN LANDS WITH A PAVEMENT-CRACKING THUMP! ABOVE HIM, BATMAN AND ROBIN COME SLIDING DOWN THEIR BATROPES TO FINISH THE JOB...
WE HAVE THAT REFUGEE FROM A REFRIGERATOR NOW, BATMAN! HE'S OUT-- COLD!
I HOPE SO--BUT I'M LEERY! WE'VE NEVER FOUGHT ANY-THING LIKE HIM BEFORE! HE MAY HAVE TRICKS HE HASN'T EVEN THOUGHT UP YET!
EVEN AS THEY WATCH, KLAG BEGINS TO LIFT HIMSELF UPWARD...
HOW RIGHT YOU ARE! HERE HE COMES!
8

BATMAN

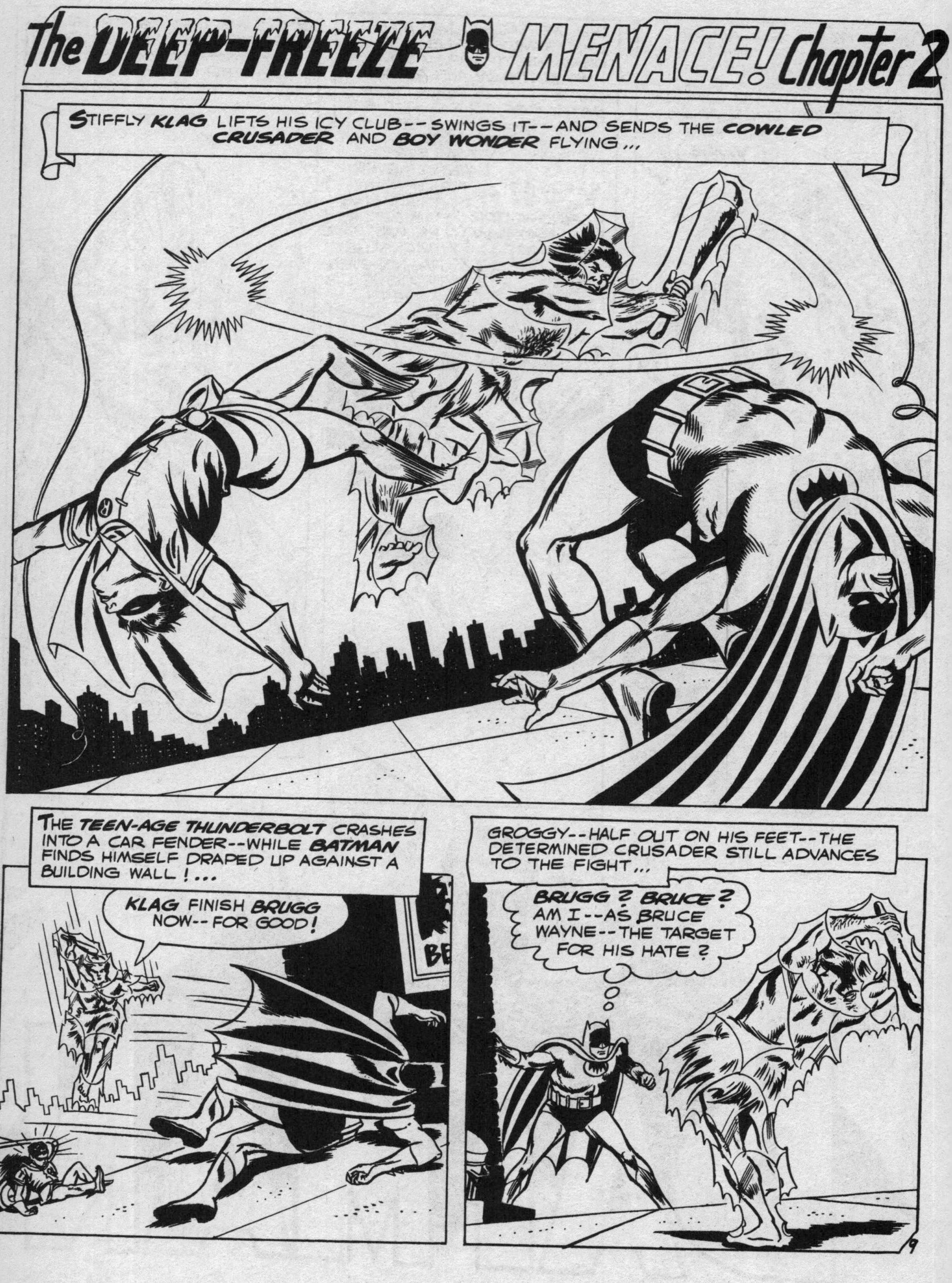
The DEEP-FREEZE MENACE! Chapter 2
STIFFLY KLAG LIFTS HIS ICY CLUB--SWINGS IT--AND SENDS THE COWLED CRUSADER AND BOY WONDER FLYING...
THE TEEN-AGE THUNDERBOLT CRASHES INTO A CAR FENDER--WHILE BATMAN FINDS HIMSELF DRAPED UP AGAINST A BUILDING WALL!...
KLAG FINISH BRUGG NOW--FOR GOOD!
GROGGY--HALF OUT ON HIS FEET--THE DETERMINED CRUSADER STILL ADVANCES TO THE FIGHT...
BRUGG? BRUCE? AM I--AS BRUCE WAYNE--THE TARGET FOR HIS HATE?
9

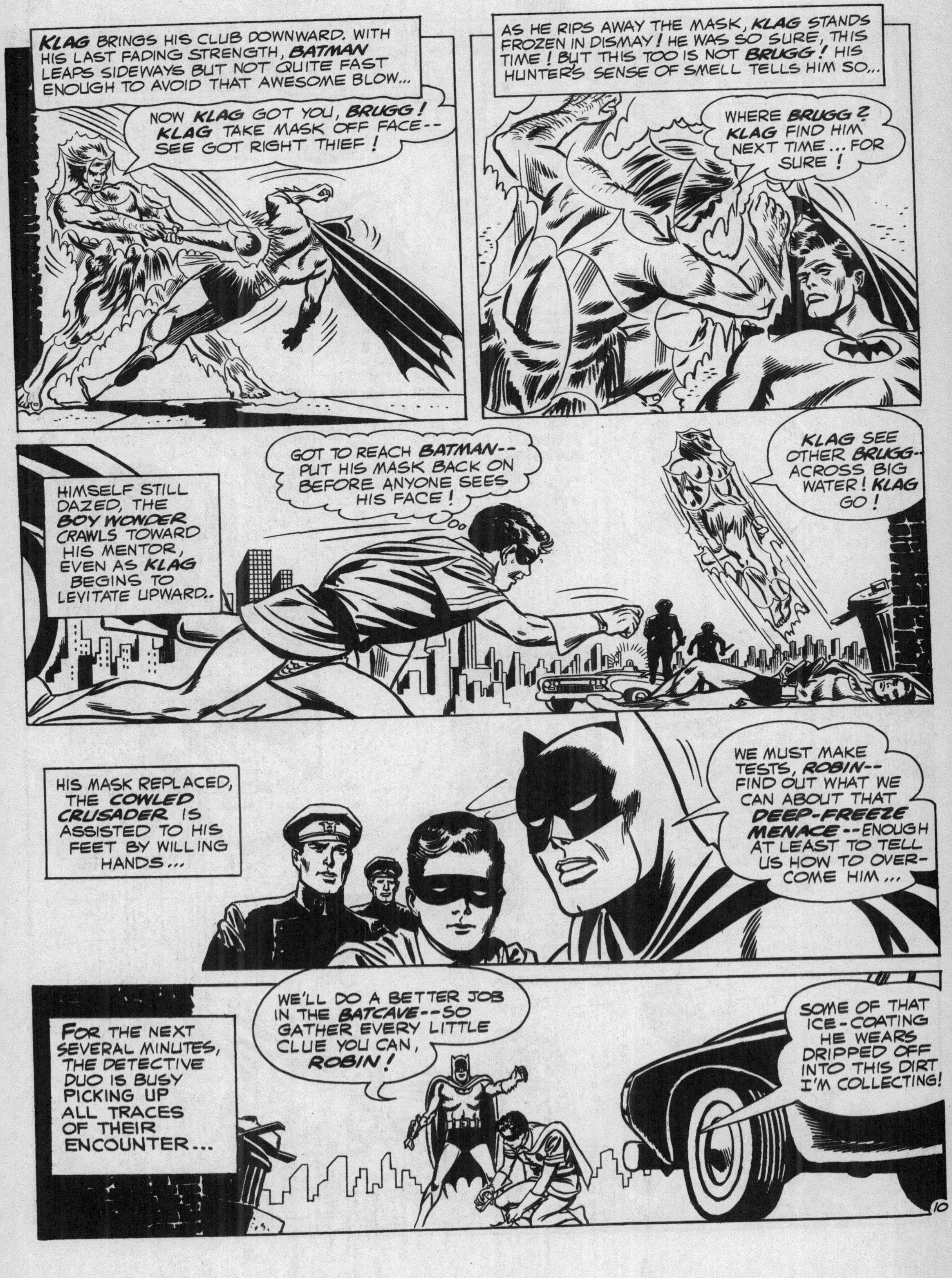
KLAG BRINGS HIS CLUB DOWNWARD. WITH HIS LAST FADING STRENGTH, BATMAN LEAPS SIDEWAYS BUT NOT QUITE FAST ENOUGH TO AVOID THAT AWESOME BLOW...
NOW KLAG GOT YOU, BRUGG! KLAG TAKE MASK OFF FACE-- SEE GOT RIGHT THIEF!
AS HE RIPS AWAY THE MASK, KLAG STANDS FROZEN IN DISMAY! HE WAS SO SURE, THIS TIME! BUT THIS TOO IS NOT BRUGG! HIS HUNTER'S SENSE OF SMELL TELLS HIM SO...
WHERE BRUGG? KLAG FIND HIM NEXT TIME... FOR SURE!
HIMSELF STILL DAZED, THE BOY WONDER CRAWLS TOWARD HIS MENTOR, EVEN AS KLAG BEGINS TO LEVITATE UPWARD..
GOT TO REACH BATMAN-- PUT HIS MASK BACK ON BEFORE ANYONE SEES HIS FACE!
KLAG SEE OTHER BRUGG-- ACROSS BIG WATER! KLAG GO!
HIS MASK REPLACED, THE COWLED CRUSADER IS ASSISTED TO HIS FEET BY WILLING HANDS...
WE MUST MAKE TESTS, ROBIN-- FIND OUT WHAT WE CAN ABOUT THAT DEEP-FREEZE MENACE--ENOUGH AT LEAST TO TELL US HOW TO OVER-COME HIM...
FOR THE NEXT SEVERAL MINUTES, THE DETECTIVE DUO IS BUSY PICKING UP ALL TRACES OF THEIR ENCOUNTER...
WE'LL DO A BETTER JOB IN THE BATCAVE--SO GATHER EVERY LITTLE CLUE YOU CAN, ROBIN!
SOME OF THAT ICE-COATING HE WEARS DRIPPED OFF INTO THIS DIRT I'M COLLECTING!
10

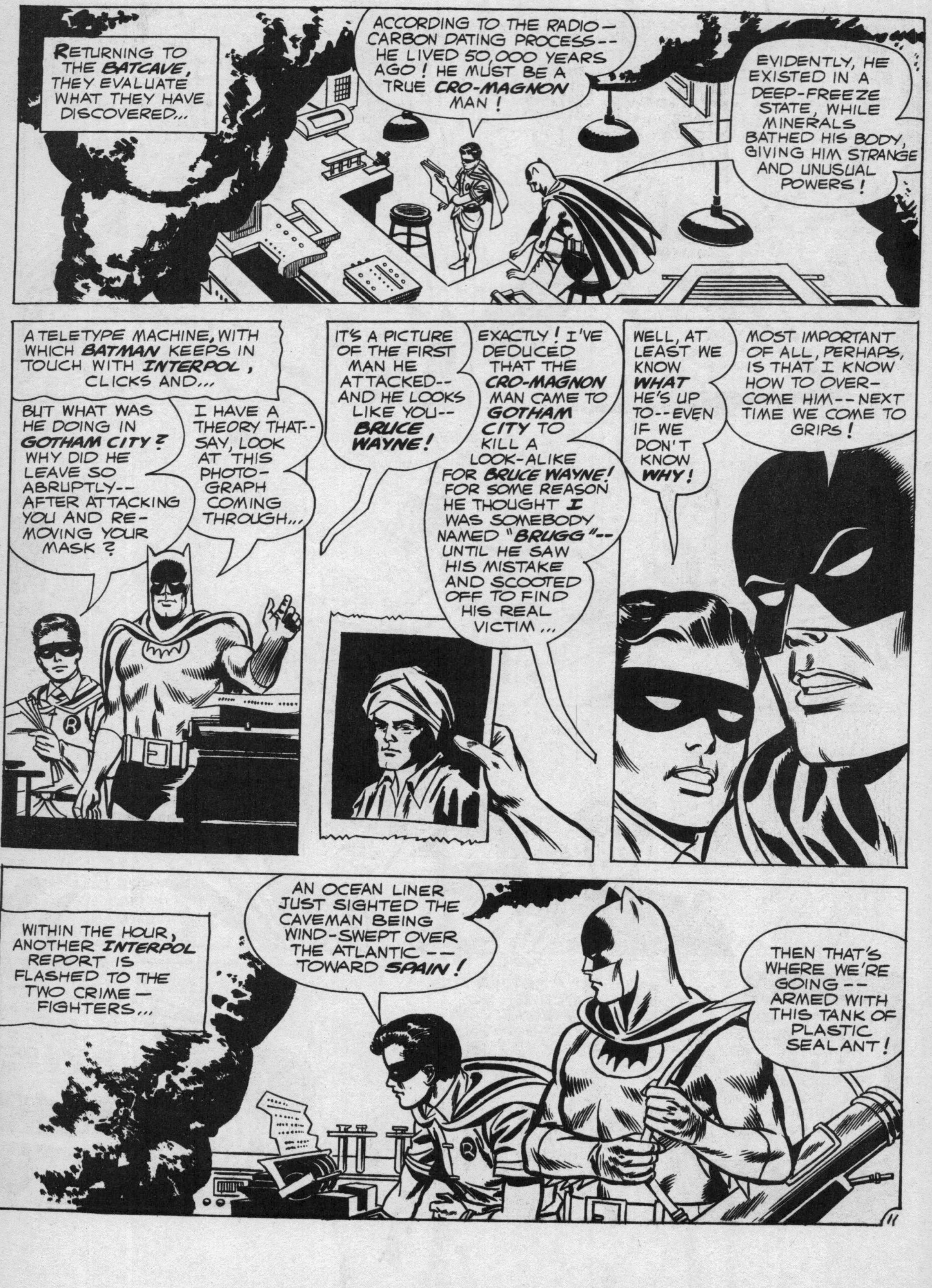
RETURNING TO THE BATCAVE, THEY EVALUATE WHAT THEY HAVE DISCOVERED...
ACCORDING TO THE RADIO-CARBON DATING PROCESS-- HE LIVED 50,000 YEARS AGO! HE MUST BE A TRUE CRO-MAGNON MAN!
EVIDENTLY, HE EXISTED IN A DEEP-FREEZE STATE, WHILE MINERALS BATHED HIS BODY, GIVING HIM STRANGE AND UNUSUAL POWERS!
A TELETYPE MACHINE, WITH WHICH BATMAN KEEPS IN TOUCH WITH INTERPOL, CLICKS AND...
BUT WHAT WAS HE DOING IN GOTHAM CITY? WHY DID HE LEAVE SO ABRUPTLY-- AFTER ATTACKING YOU AND RE-MOVING YOUR MASK?
I HAVE A THEORY THAT-- SAY, LOOK AT THIS PHOTO-GRAPH COMING THROUGH...
IT'S A PICTURE OF THE FIRST MAN HE ATTACKED-- AND HE LOOKS LIKE YOU-- BRUCE WAYNE!
EXACTLY! I'VE DEDUCED THAT THE CRO-MAGNON MAN CAME TO GOTHAM CITY TO KILL A LOOK-ALIKE FOR BRUCE WAYNE! FOR SOME REASON HE THOUGHT I WAS SOMEBODY NAMED "BRUGG"-- UNTIL HE SAW HIS MISTAKE AND SCOOTED OFF TO FIND HIS REAL VICTIM...
WELL, AT LEAST WE KNOW WHAT HE'S UP TO--EVEN IF WE DON'T KNOW WHY!
MOST IMPORTANT OF ALL, PERHAPS, IS THAT I KNOW HOW TO OVER-COME HIM--NEXT TIME WE COME TO GRIPS!
WITHIN THE HOUR, ANOTHER INTERPOL REPORT IS FLASHED TO THE TWO CRIME-FIGHTERS...
AN OCEAN LINER JUST SIGHTED THE CAVEMAN BEING WIND-SWEPT OVER THE ATLANTIC -- TOWARD SPAIN!
THEN THAT'S WHERE WE'RE GOING -- ARMED WITH THIS TANK OF PLASTIC SEALANT!
11

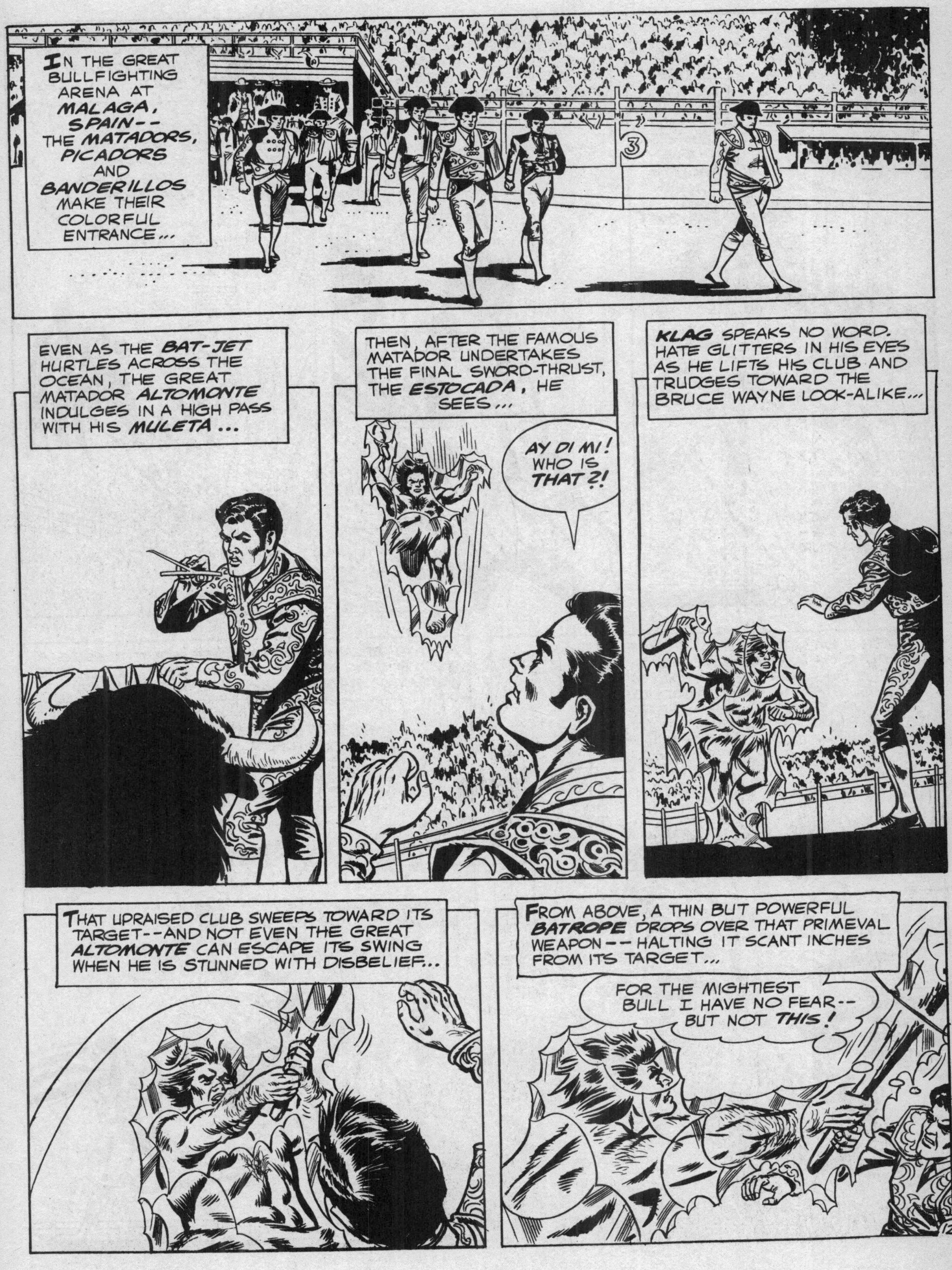
IN THE GREAT BULLFIGHTING ARENA AT MALAGA, SPAIN-- THE MATADORS, PICADORS AND BANDERILLOS MAKE THEIR COLORFUL ENTRANCE...
3
EVEN AS THE BAT-JET HURTLES ACROSS THE OCEAN, THE GREAT MATADOR ALTOMONTE INDULGES IN A HIGH PASS WITH HIS MULETA...
THEN, AFTER THE FAMOUS MATADOR UNDERTAKES THE FINAL SWORD-THRUST, THE ESTOCADA, HE SEES...
AY DI MI! WHO IS THAT?!
KLAG SPEAKS NO WORD. HATE GLITTERS IN HIS EYES AS HE LIFTS HIS CLUB AND TRUDGES TOWARD THE BRUCE WAYNE LOOK-ALIKE...
THAT UPRAISED CLUB SWEEPS TOWARD ITS TARGET--AND NOT EVEN THE GREAT ALTOMONTE CAN ESCAPE ITS SWING WHEN HE IS STUNNED WITH DISBELIEF...
FROM ABOVE, A THIN BUT POWERFUL BATROPE DROPS OVER THAT PRIMEVAL WEAPON -- HALTING IT SCANT INCHES FROM ITS TARGET...
FOR THE MIGHTIEST BULL I HAVE NO FEAR-- BUT NOT THIS!
12

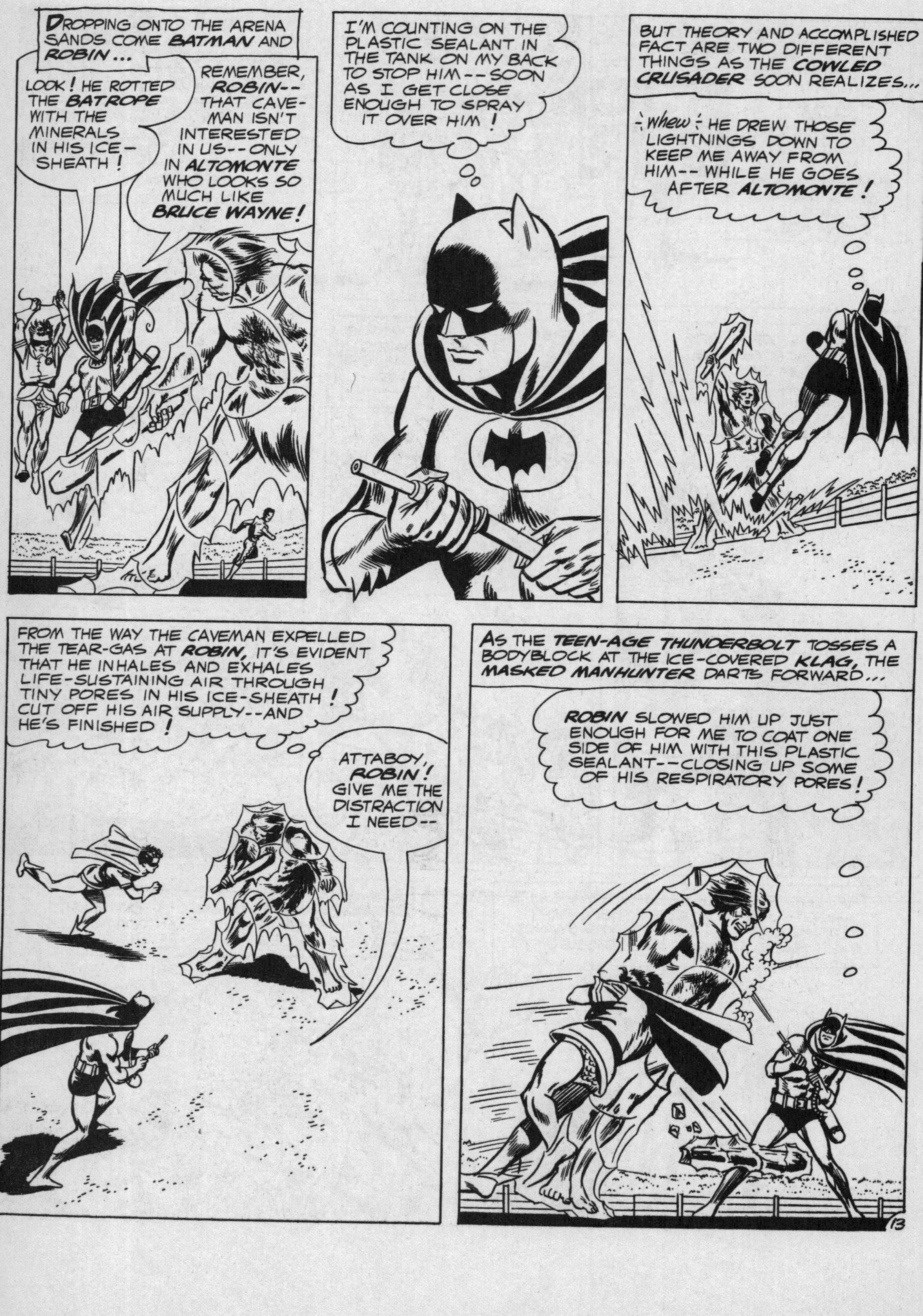
DROPPING ONTO THE ARENA SANDS COME BATMAN AND ROBIN...
LOOK! HE ROTTED THE BATROPE WITH THE MINERALS IN HIS ICE-SHEATH!
REMEMBER, ROBIN-- THAT CAVEMAN ISN'T INTERESTED IN US--ONLY IN ALTOMONTE WHO LOOKS SO MUCH LIKE BRUCE WAYNE!
I'M COUNTING ON THE PLASTIC SEALANT IN THE TANK ON MY BACK TO STOP HIM--SOON AS I GET CLOSE ENOUGH TO SPRAY IT OVER HIM!
BUT THEORY AND ACCOMPLISHED FACT ARE TWO DIFFERENT THINGS AS THE COWLED CRUSADER SOON REALIZES...
-whew- HE DREW THOSE LIGHTNINGS DOWN TO KEEP ME AWAY FROM HIM-- WHILE HE GOES AFTER ALTOMONTE!
FROM THE WAY THE CAVEMAN EXPELLED THE TEAR-GAS AT ROBIN, IT'S EVIDENT THAT HE INHALES AND EXHALES LIFE-SUSTAINING AIR THROUGH TINY PORES IN HIS ICE-SHEATH! CUT OFF HIS AIR SUPPLY--AND HE'S FINISHED!
ATTABOY, ROBIN! GIVE ME THE DISTRACTION I NEED--
AS THE TEEN-AGE THUNDERBOLT TOSSES A BODYBLOCK AT THE ICE-COVERED KLAG, THE MASKED MANHUNTER DARTS FORWARD...
ROBIN SLOWED HIM UP JUST ENOUGH FOR ME TO COAT ONE SIDE OF HIM WITH THIS PLASTIC SEALANT--CLOSING UP SOME OF HIS RESPIRATORY PORES!
13

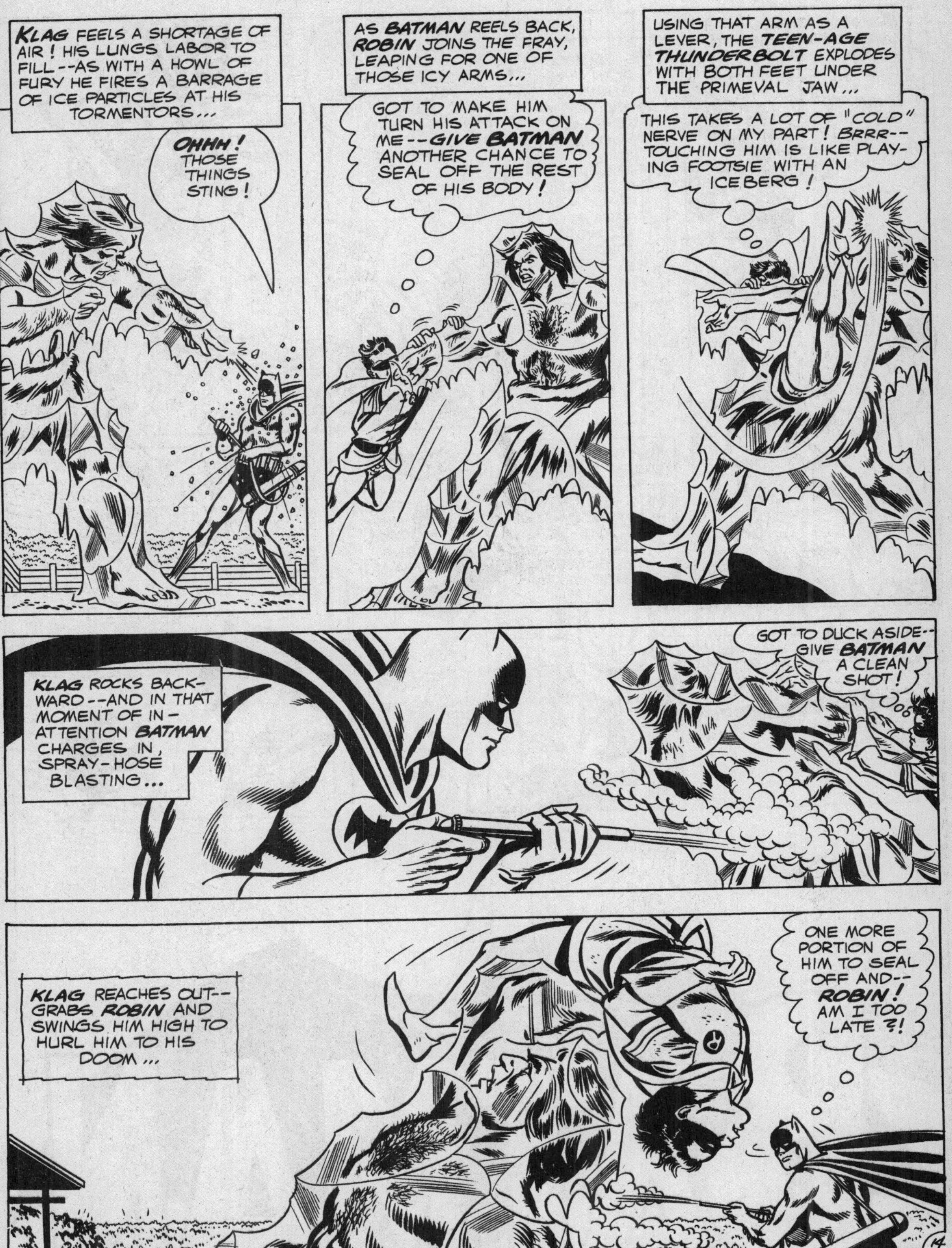
KLAG FEELS A SHORTAGE OF AIR! HIS LUNGS LABOR TO FILL--AS WITH A HOWL OF FURY HE FIRES A BARRAGE OF ICE PARTICLES AT HIS TORMENTORS...
OHHH! THOSE THINGS STING!
AS BATMAN REELS BACK, ROBIN JOINS THE FRAY, LEAPING FOR ONE OF THOSE ICY ARMS...
GOT TO MAKE HIM TURN HIS ATTACK ON ME--GIVE BATMAN ANOTHER CHANCE TO SEAL OFF THE REST OF HIS BODY!
USING THAT ARM AS A LEVER, THE TEEN-AGE THUNDERBOLT EXPLODES WITH BOTH FEET UNDER THE PRIMEVAL JAW...
THIS TAKES A LOT OF "COLD" NERVE ON MY PART! BRRR--TOUCHING HIM IS LIKE PLAYING FOOTSIE WITH AN ICEBERG!
KLAG ROCKS BACKWARD--AND IN THAT MOMENT OF INATTENTION BATMAN CHARGES IN, SPRAY-HOSE BLASTING...
GOT TO DUCK ASIDE--GIVE BATMAN A CLEAN SHOT!
KLAG REACHES OUT--GRABS ROBIN AND SWINGS HIM HIGH TO HURL HIM TO HIS DOOM...
ONE MORE PORTION OF HIM TO SEAL OFF AND--ROBIN! AM I TOO LATE ?!
14

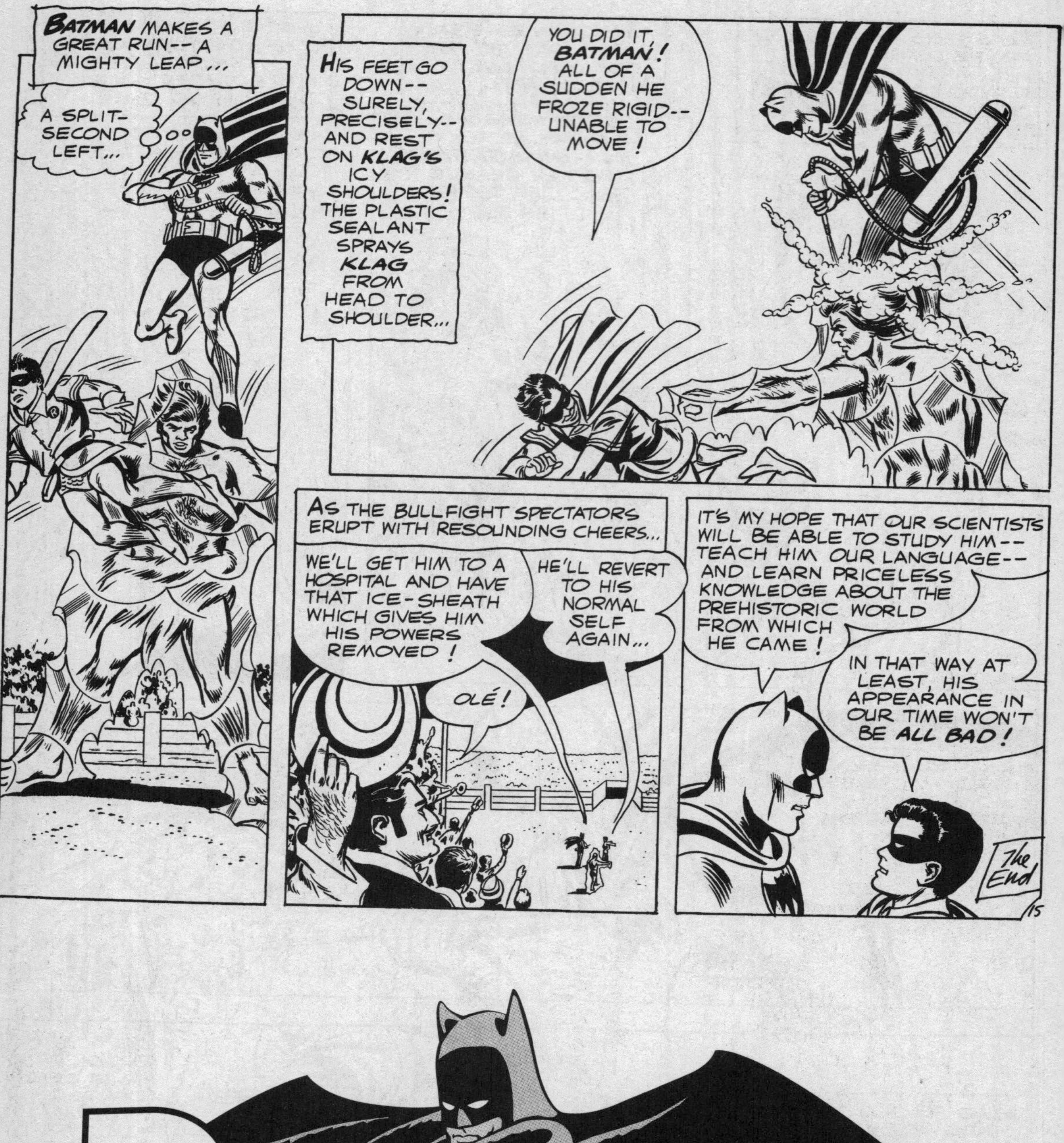
BATMAN MAKES A GREAT RUN-- A MIGHTY LEAP ...
A SPLIT-SECOND LEFT...
HIS FEET GO DOWN-- SURELY, PRECISELY-- AND REST ON KLAG'S ICY SHOULDERS! THE PLASTIC SEALANT SPRAYS KLAG FROM HEAD TO SHOULDER...
YOU DID IT, BATMAN! ALL OF A SUDDEN HE FROZE RIGID-- UNABLE TO MOVE!
AS THE BULLFIGHT SPECTATORS ERUPT WITH RESOUNDING CHEERS...
WE'LL GET HIM TO A HOSPITAL AND HAVE THAT ICE-SHEATH WHICH GIVES HIM HIS POWERS REMOVED!
HE'LL REVERT TO HIS NORMAL SELF AGAIN...
OLÉ!
IT'S MY HOPE THAT OUR SCIENTISTS WILL BE ABLE TO STUDY HIM-- TEACH HIM OUR LANGUAGE-- AND LEARN PRICELESS KNOWLEDGE ABOUT THE PREHISTORIC WORLD FROM WHICH HE CAME!
IN THAT WAY AT LEAST, HIS APPEARANCE IN OUR TIME WON'T BE ALL BAD!
The End
15

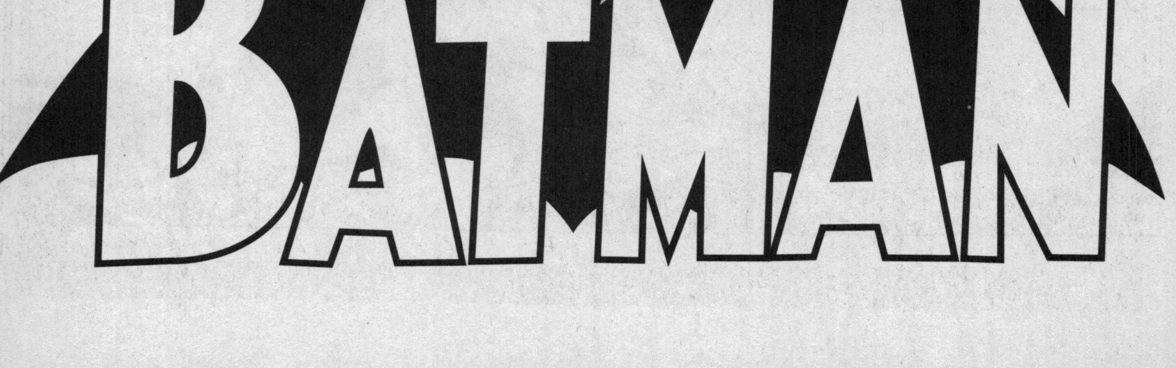
BATMAN

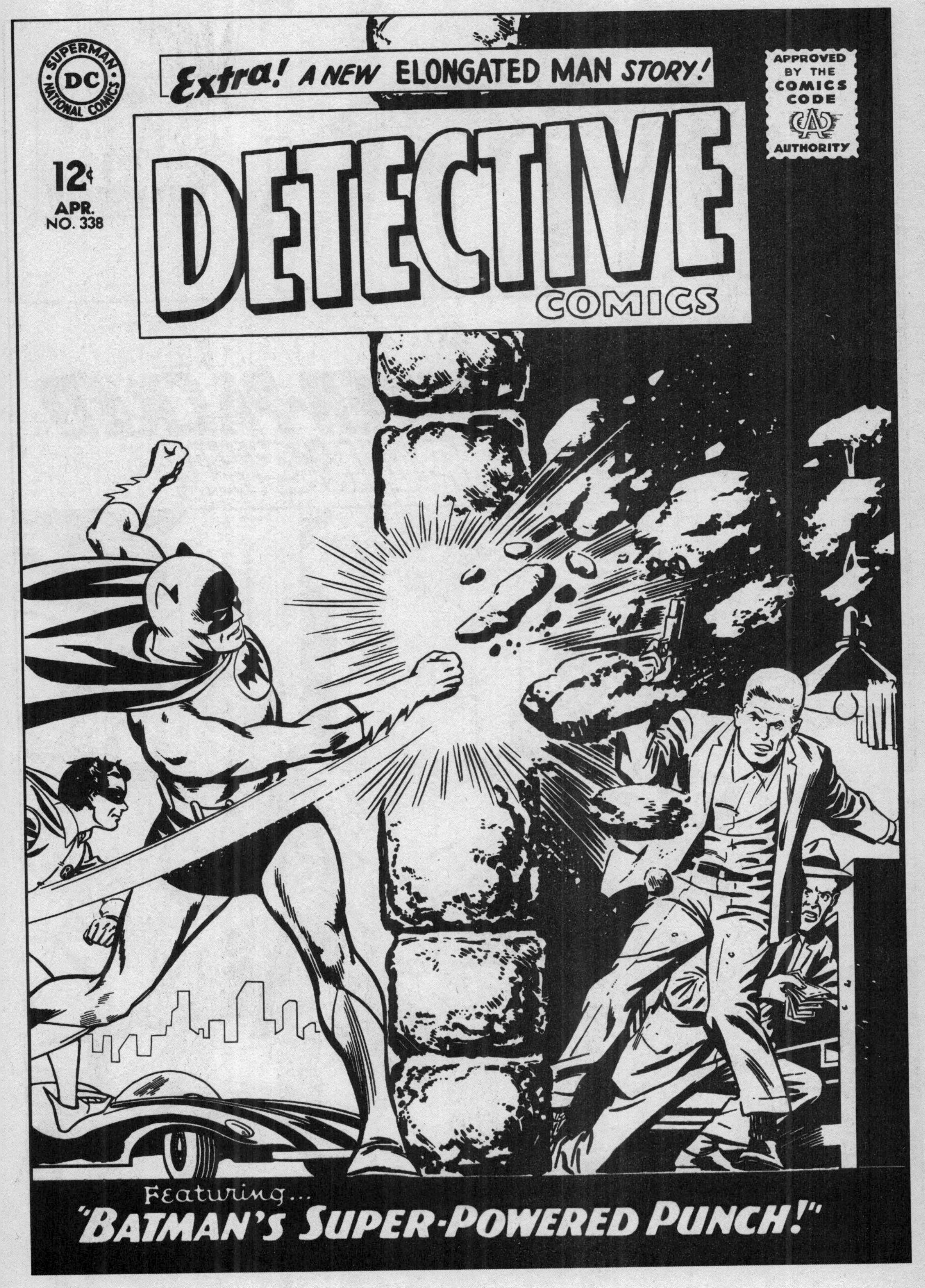
SUPERMAN DC NATIONAL COMICS
Extra! A NEW ELONGATED MAN STORY!
APPROVED BY THE COMICS CODE AUTHORITY
12¢
APR.
NO. 338
DETECTIVE COMICS
Featuring...
"BATMAN'S SUPER-POWERED PUNCH!"

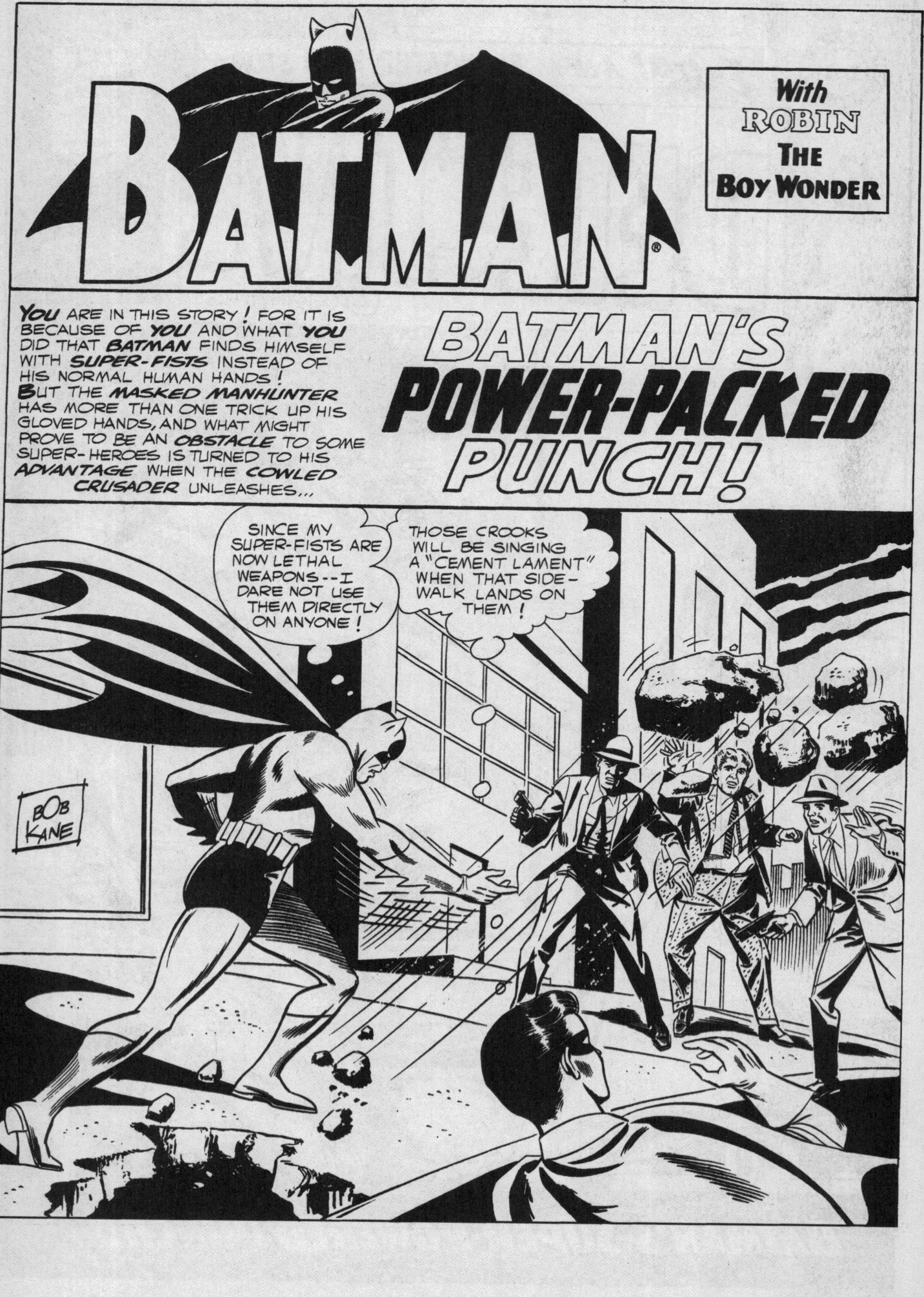
BATMAN
With ROBIN THE BOY WONDER
YOU ARE IN THIS STORY! FOR IT IS BECAUSE OF YOU AND WHAT YOU DID THAT BATMAN FINDS HIMSELF WITH SUPER-FISTS INSTEAD OF HIS NORMAL HUMAN HANDS! BUT THE MASKED MANHUNTER HAS MORE THAN ONE TRICK UP HIS GLOVED HANDS, AND WHAT MIGHT PROVE TO BE AN OBSTACLE TO SOME SUPER-HEROES IS TURNED TO HIS ADVANTAGE WHEN THE COWLED CRUSADER UNLEASHES...
BATMAN'S POWER-PACKED PUNCH!
SINCE MY SUPER-FISTS ARE NOW LETHAL WEAPONS--I DARE NOT USE THEM DIRECTLY ON ANYONE!
THOSE CROOKS WILL BE SINGING A "CEMENT LAMENT" WHEN THAT SIDE-WALK LANDS ON THEM!
BOB KANE

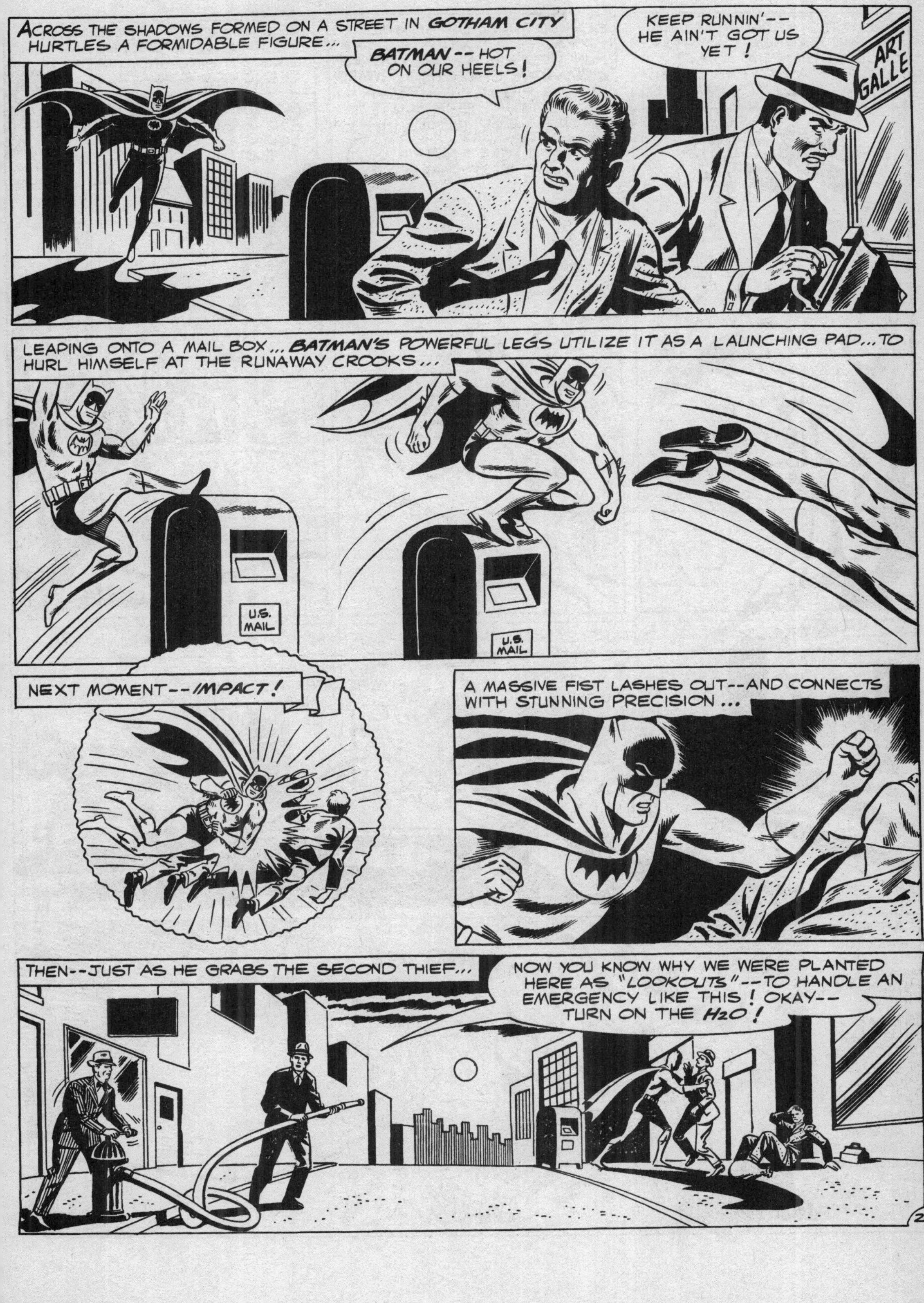
ACROSS THE SHADOWS FORMED ON A STREET IN GOTHAM CITY HURTLES A FORMIDABLE FIGURE...
BATMAN -- HOT ON OUR HEELS!
KEEP RUNNIN'-- HE AIN'T GOT US YET!
ART GALLE
LEAPING ONTO A MAIL BOX... BATMAN'S POWERFUL LEGS UTILIZE IT AS A LAUNCHING PAD... TO HURL HIMSELF AT THE RUNAWAY CROOKS...
U.S. MAIL
U.S. MAIL
NEXT MOMENT--IMPACT!
A MASSIVE FIST LASHES OUT--AND CONNECTS WITH STUNNING PRECISION...
THEN--JUST AS HE GRABS THE SECOND THIEF...
NOW YOU KNOW WHY WE WERE PLANTED HERE AS "LOOKOUTS"--TO HANDLE AN EMERGENCY LIKE THIS! OKAY-- TURN ON THE H2O!
2

FROM THE METAL NOZZLE OF THE FIREHOSE A WATERY COLUMN WITH THE IMPACT FORCE OF A BATTERING RAM IS DIRECTED AT ITS TARGET...

WHA...?

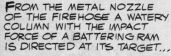

SOAKED THROUGH WITH ICY WATER--POUNDED AS IF BY A HUNDRED FISTS--THE *COWLED CRUSADER* CHARGES FORWARD, PITTING HIS MIGHTY FRAME AGAINST THAT TERRIBLE CANNONADE...

CAN'T NOTHIN' STOP THAT GUY?

TO ONE SIDE OF HIM, *ROBIN*, THE *BOY WONDER*, RUSHES IN LIKE A WHIRLWIND, FISTS CLENCHED FOR ACTION...

BATMAN HAD *HIS* LOOKOUT TOO!

LET'S CLEAR OUTTA HERE!

THE MOBSTERS DROP THE HOSE! RELEASED FROM GRIPPING HANDS, IT SNAKES EERILY IN THE AIR...

IT'S THOSE CROOKS WHO ARE ALL WASHED UP--

AS FATE AND ILL LUCK WILL HAVE IT, THE "*SNAKING*" HOSE UNCOILS ITS WATERY COLUMN RIGHT AT *ROBIN*, DRIVING HIS LEGS OUT FROM UNDER HIM...SMACK INTO *BATMAN!*...

WHOOPS!

3

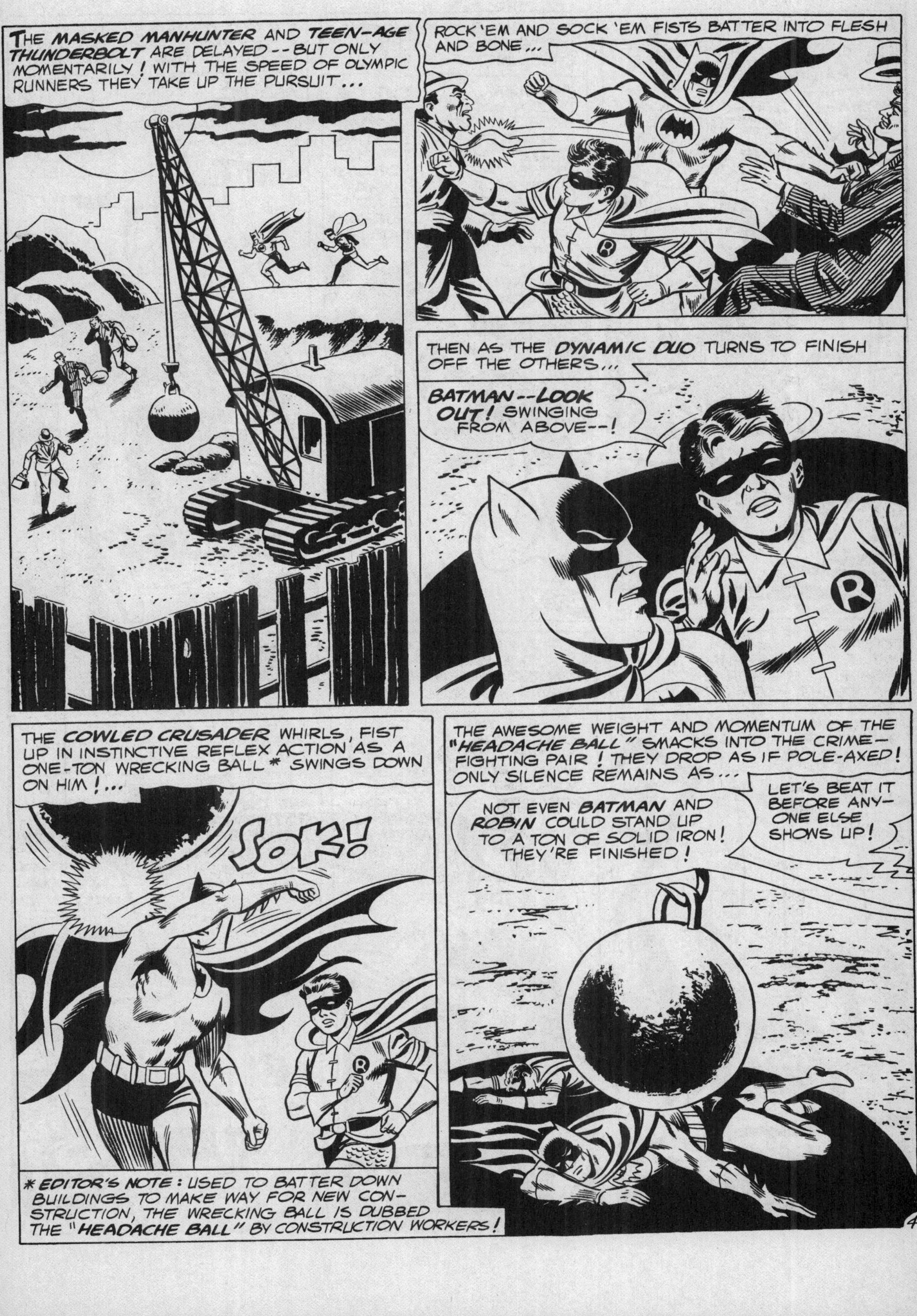
THE MASKED MANHUNTER AND TEEN-AGE THUNDERBOLT ARE DELAYED--BUT ONLY MOMENTARILY! WITH THE SPEED OF OLYMPIC RUNNERS THEY TAKE UP THE PURSUIT...
ROCK 'EM AND SOCK 'EM FISTS BATTER INTO FLESH AND BONE...
THEN AS THE DYNAMIC DUO TURNS TO FINISH OFF THE OTHERS...
BATMAN--LOOK OUT! SWINGING FROM ABOVE--!
THE COWLED CRUSADER WHIRLS, FIST UP IN INSTINCTIVE REFLEX ACTION AS A ONE-TON WRECKING BALL * SWINGS DOWN ON HIM!...
SOK!
* EDITOR'S NOTE: USED TO BATTER DOWN BUILDINGS TO MAKE WAY FOR NEW CONSTRUCTION, THE WRECKING BALL IS DUBBED THE "HEADACHE BALL" BY CONSTRUCTION WORKERS!
THE AWESOME WEIGHT AND MOMENTUM OF THE "HEADACHE BALL" SMACKS INTO THE CRIME-FIGHTING PAIR! THEY DROP AS IF POLE-AXED! ONLY SILENCE REMAINS AS...
NOT EVEN BATMAN AND ROBIN COULD STAND UP TO A TON OF SOLID IRON! THEY'RE FINISHED!
LET'S BEAT IT BEFORE ANY-ONE ELSE SHOWS UP!
4

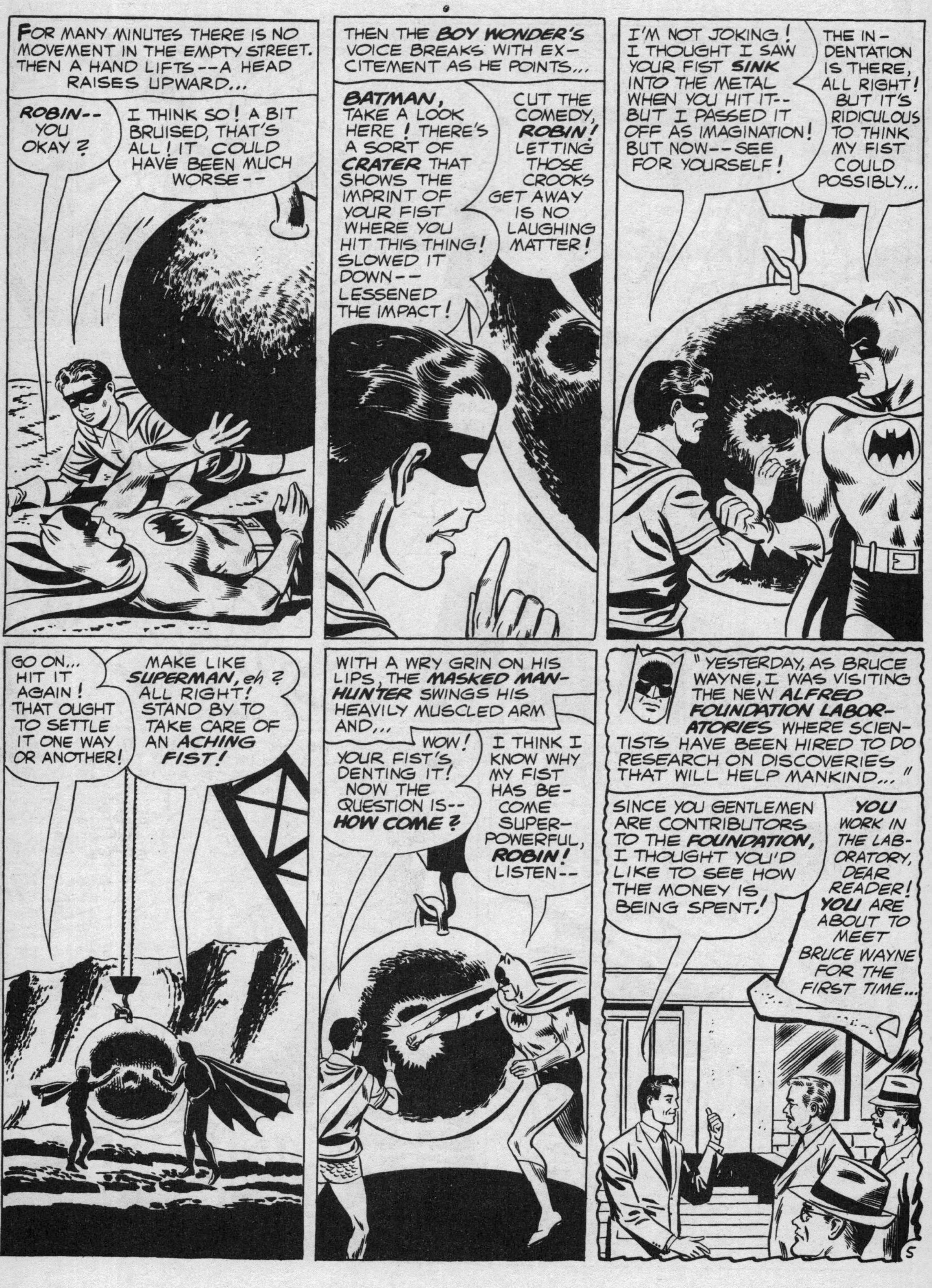
FOR MANY MINUTES THERE IS NO MOVEMENT IN THE EMPTY STREET. THEN A HAND LIFTS--A HEAD RAISES UPWARD...
ROBIN--YOU OKAY?
I THINK SO! A BIT BRUISED, THAT'S ALL! IT COULD HAVE BEEN MUCH WORSE--
THEN THE BOY WONDER'S VOICE BREAKS WITH EXCITEMENT AS HE POINTS...
BATMAN, TAKE A LOOK HERE! THERE'S A SORT OF CRATER THAT SHOWS THE IMPRINT OF YOUR FIST WHERE YOU HIT THIS THING! SLOWED IT DOWN--LESSENED THE IMPACT!
CUT THE COMEDY, ROBIN! LETTING THOSE CROOKS GET AWAY IS NO LAUGHING MATTER!
I'M NOT JOKING! I THOUGHT I SAW YOUR FIST SINK INTO THE METAL WHEN YOU HIT IT--BUT I PASSED IT OFF AS IMAGINATION! BUT NOW--SEE FOR YOURSELF!
THE INDENTATION IS THERE, ALL RIGHT! BUT IT'S RIDICULOUS TO THINK MY FIST COULD POSSIBLY...
GO ON... HIT IT AGAIN! THAT OUGHT TO SETTLE IT ONE WAY OR ANOTHER!
MAKE LIKE SUPERMAN, eh? ALL RIGHT! STAND BY TO TAKE CARE OF AN ACHING FIST!
WITH A WRY GRIN ON HIS LIPS, THE MASKED MAN-HUNTER SWINGS HIS HEAVILY MUSCLED ARM AND...
WOW! YOUR FIST'S DENTING IT! NOW THE QUESTION IS--HOW COME?
I THINK I KNOW WHY MY FIST HAS BECOME SUPER-POWERFUL, ROBIN! LISTEN--
"YESTERDAY, AS BRUCE WAYNE, I WAS VISITING THE NEW ALFRED FOUNDATION LABORATORIES WHERE SCIENTISTS HAVE BEEN HIRED TO DO RESEARCH ON DISCOVERIES THAT WILL HELP MANKIND..."
SINCE YOU GENTLEMEN ARE CONTRIBUTORS TO THE FOUNDATION, I THOUGHT YOU'D LIKE TO SEE HOW THE MONEY IS BEING SPENT!
YOU WORK IN THE LABORATORY, DEAR READER! YOU ARE ABOUT TO MEET BRUCE WAYNE FOR THE FIRST TIME...
5

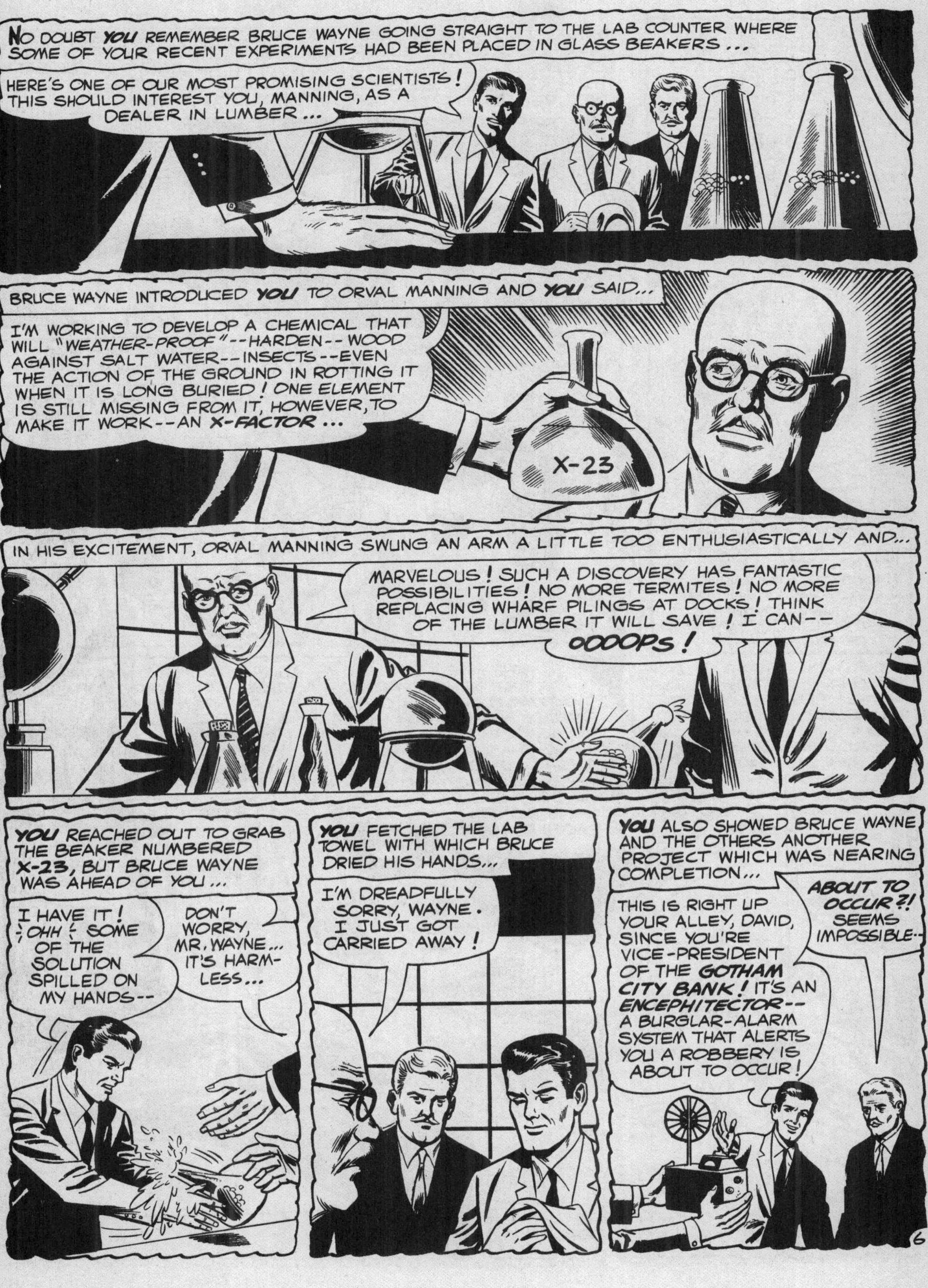
NO DOUBT YOU REMEMBER BRUCE WAYNE GOING STRAIGHT TO THE LAB COUNTER WHERE SOME OF YOUR RECENT EXPERIMENTS HAD BEEN PLACED IN GLASS BEAKERS ...
HERE'S ONE OF OUR MOST PROMISING SCIENTISTS! THIS SHOULD INTEREST YOU, MANNING, AS A DEALER IN LUMBER ...
BRUCE WAYNE INTRODUCED YOU TO ORVAL MANNING AND YOU SAID...
I'M WORKING TO DEVELOP A CHEMICAL THAT WILL "WEATHER-PROOF"--HARDEN--WOOD AGAINST SALT WATER--INSECTS--EVEN THE ACTION OF THE GROUND IN ROTTING IT WHEN IT IS LONG BURIED! ONE ELEMENT IS STILL MISSING FROM IT, HOWEVER, TO MAKE IT WORK--AN X-FACTOR ...
X-23
IN HIS EXCITEMENT, ORVAL MANNING SWUNG AN ARM A LITTLE TOO ENTHUSIASTICALLY AND...
MARVELOUS! SUCH A DISCOVERY HAS FANTASTIC POSSIBILITIES! NO MORE TERMITES! NO MORE REPLACING WHARF PILINGS AT DOCKS! THINK OF THE LUMBER IT WILL SAVE! I CAN-- OOOOPS!
YOU REACHED OUT TO GRAB THE BEAKER NUMBERED X-23, BUT BRUCE WAYNE WAS AHEAD OF YOU ...
I HAVE IT! OHH! SOME OF THE SOLUTION SPILLED ON MY HANDS--
DON'T WORRY, MR. WAYNE... IT'S HARMLESS...
YOU FETCHED THE LAB TOWEL WITH WHICH BRUCE DRIED HIS HANDS...
I'M DREADFULLY SORRY, WAYNE. I JUST GOT CARRIED AWAY!
YOU ALSO SHOWED BRUCE WAYNE AND THE OTHERS ANOTHER PROJECT WHICH WAS NEARING COMPLETION...
THIS IS RIGHT UP YOUR ALLEY, DAVID, SINCE YOU'RE VICE-PRESIDENT OF THE GOTHAM CITY BANK! IT'S AN ENCEPHITECTOR--A BURGLAR-ALARM SYSTEM THAT ALERTS YOU A ROBBERY IS ABOUT TO OCCUR!
ABOUT TO OCCUR?! SEEMS IMPOSSIBLE--
6

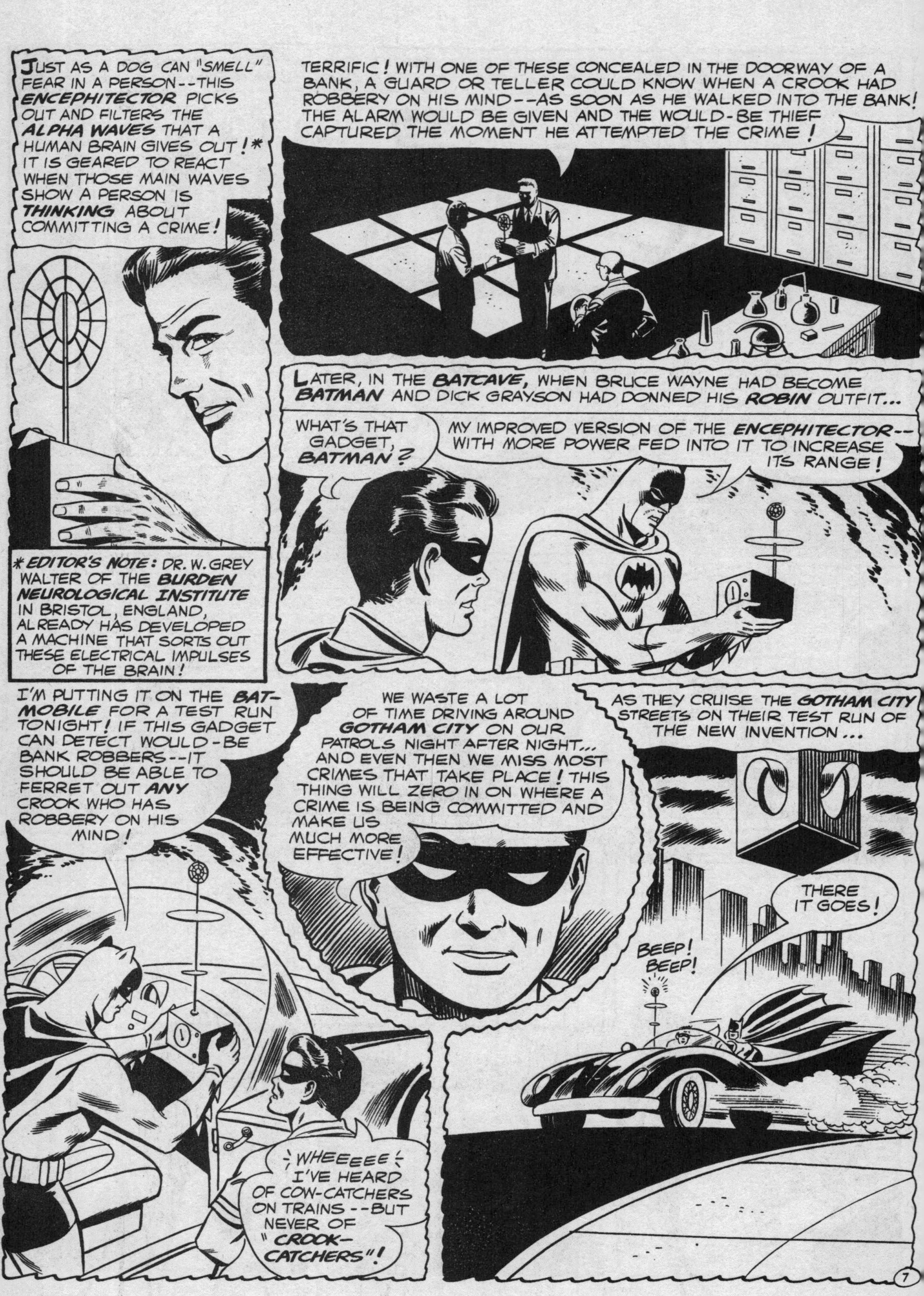
JUST AS A DOG CAN "SMELL" FEAR IN A PERSON--THIS ENCEPHITECTOR PICKS OUT AND FILTERS THE ALPHA WAVES THAT A HUMAN BRAIN GIVES OUT!* IT IS GEARED TO REACT WHEN THOSE MAIN WAVES SHOW A PERSON IS THINKING ABOUT COMMITTING A CRIME!
*EDITOR'S NOTE: DR. W. GREY WALTER OF THE BURDEN NEUROLOGICAL INSTITUTE IN BRISTOL, ENGLAND, ALREADY HAS DEVELOPED A MACHINE THAT SORTS OUT THESE ELECTRICAL IMPULSES OF THE BRAIN!
TERRIFIC! WITH ONE OF THESE CONCEALED IN THE DOORWAY OF A BANK, A GUARD OR TELLER COULD KNOW WHEN A CROOK HAD ROBBERY ON HIS MIND--AS SOON AS HE WALKED INTO THE BANK! THE ALARM WOULD BE GIVEN AND THE WOULD-BE THIEF CAPTURED THE MOMENT HE ATTEMPTED THE CRIME!
LATER, IN THE BATCAVE, WHEN BRUCE WAYNE HAD BECOME BATMAN AND DICK GRAYSON HAD DONNED HIS ROBIN OUTFIT...
WHAT'S THAT GADGET, BATMAN?
MY IMPROVED VERSION OF THE ENCEPHITECTOR--WITH MORE POWER FED INTO IT TO INCREASE ITS RANGE!
I'M PUTTING IT ON THE BAT-MOBILE FOR A TEST RUN TONIGHT! IF THIS GADGET CAN DETECT WOULD-BE BANK ROBBERS--IT SHOULD BE ABLE TO FERRET OUT ANY CROOK WHO HAS ROBBERY ON HIS MIND!
WE WASTE A LOT OF TIME DRIVING AROUND GOTHAM CITY ON OUR PATROLS NIGHT AFTER NIGHT... AND EVEN THEN WE MISS MOST CRIMES THAT TAKE PLACE! THIS THING WILL ZERO IN ON WHERE A CRIME IS BEING COMMITTED AND MAKE US MUCH MORE EFFECTIVE!
WHEEEEE I'VE HEARD OF COW-CATCHERS ON TRAINS--BUT NEVER OF "CROOK-CATCHERS"!
AS THEY CRUISE THE GOTHAM CITY STREETS ON THEIR TEST RUN OF THE NEW INVENTION...
THERE IT GOES!
BEEP! BEEP!
7

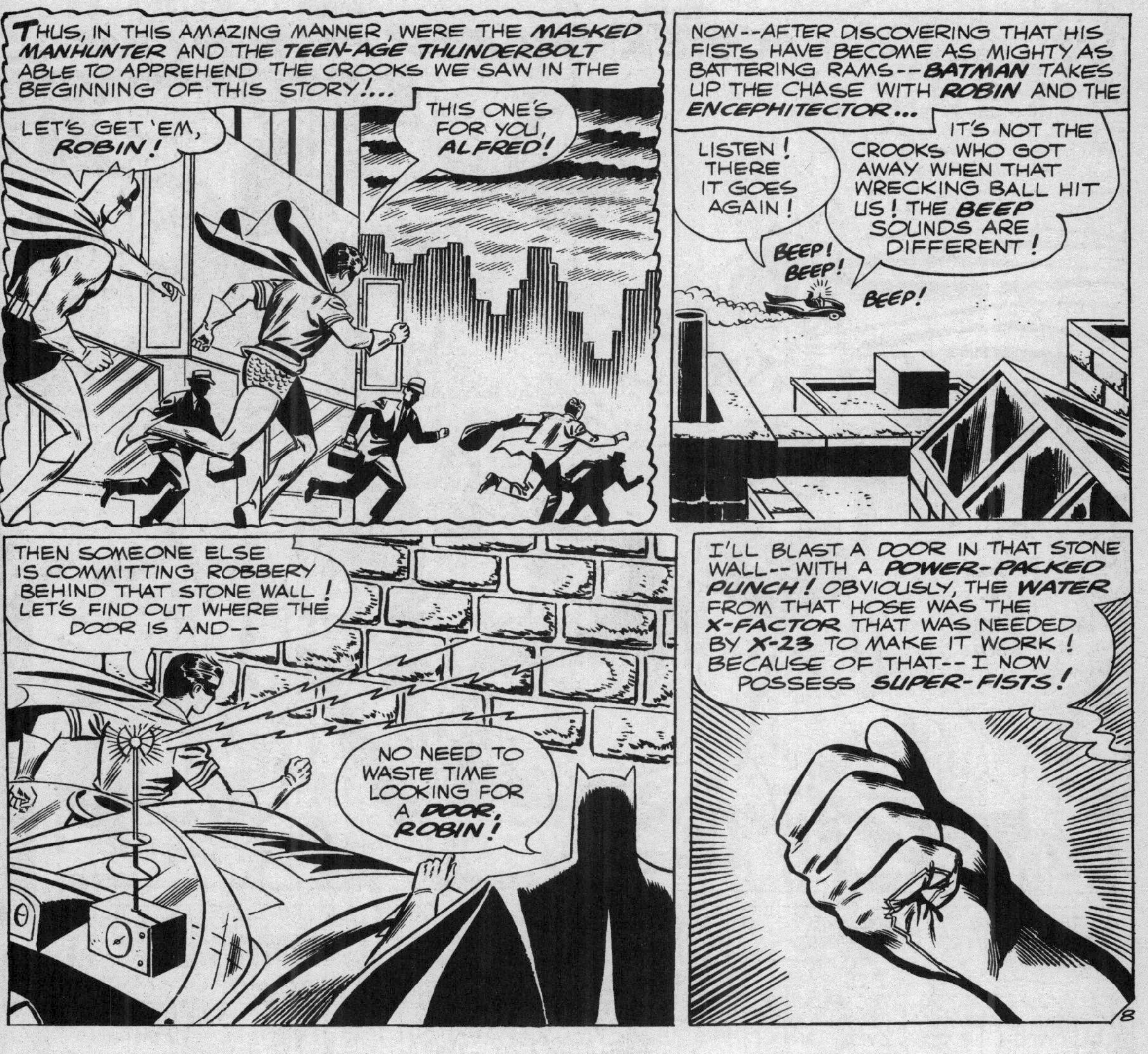
THUS, IN THIS AMAZING MANNER, WERE THE MASKED MANHUNTER AND THE TEEN-AGE THUNDERBOLT ABLE TO APPREHEND THE CROOKS WE SAW IN THE BEGINNING OF THIS STORY!...
LET'S GET 'EM, ROBIN!
THIS ONE'S FOR YOU, ALFRED!
NOW--AFTER DISCOVERING THAT HIS FISTS HAVE BECOME AS MIGHTY AS BATTERING RAMS--BATMAN TAKES UP THE CHASE WITH ROBIN AND THE ENCEPHITECTOR...
LISTEN! THERE IT GOES AGAIN!
IT'S NOT THE CROOKS WHO GOT AWAY WHEN THAT WRECKING BALL HIT US! THE BEEP SOUNDS ARE DIFFERENT!
BEEP! BEEP!
BEEP!
THEN SOMEONE ELSE IS COMMITTING ROBBERY BEHIND THAT STONE WALL! LET'S FIND OUT WHERE THE DOOR IS AND--
NO NEED TO WASTE TIME LOOKING FOR A DOOR, ROBIN!
I'LL BLAST A DOOR IN THAT STONE WALL--WITH A POWER-PACKED PUNCH! OBVIOUSLY, THE WATER FROM THAT HOSE WAS THE X-FACTOR THAT WAS NEEDED BY X-23 TO MAKE IT WORK! BECAUSE OF THAT--I NOW POSSESS SUPER-FISTS!
8

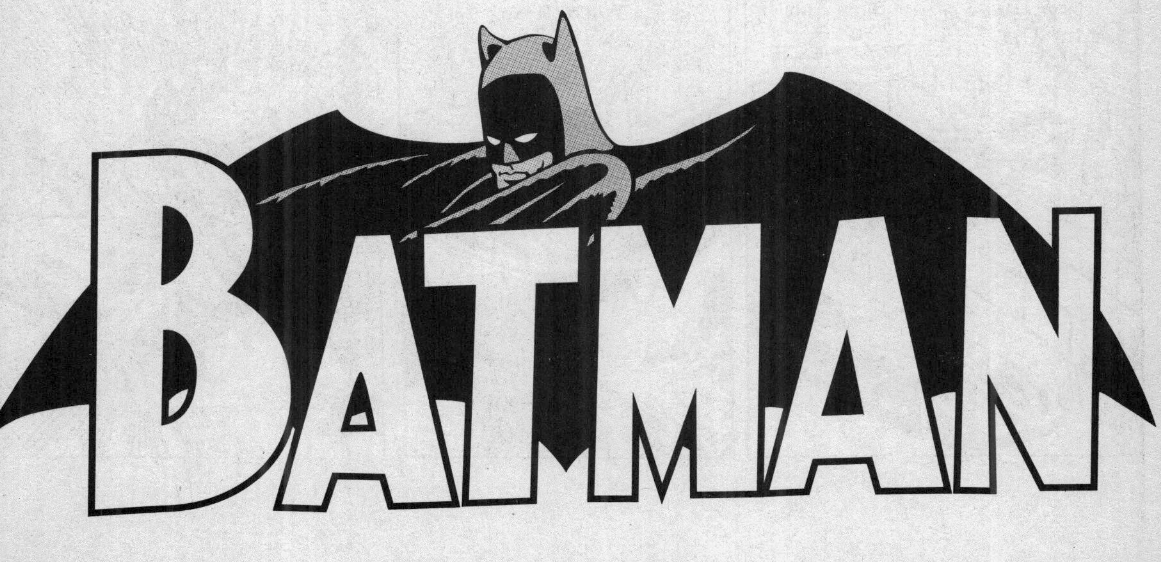
BATMAN

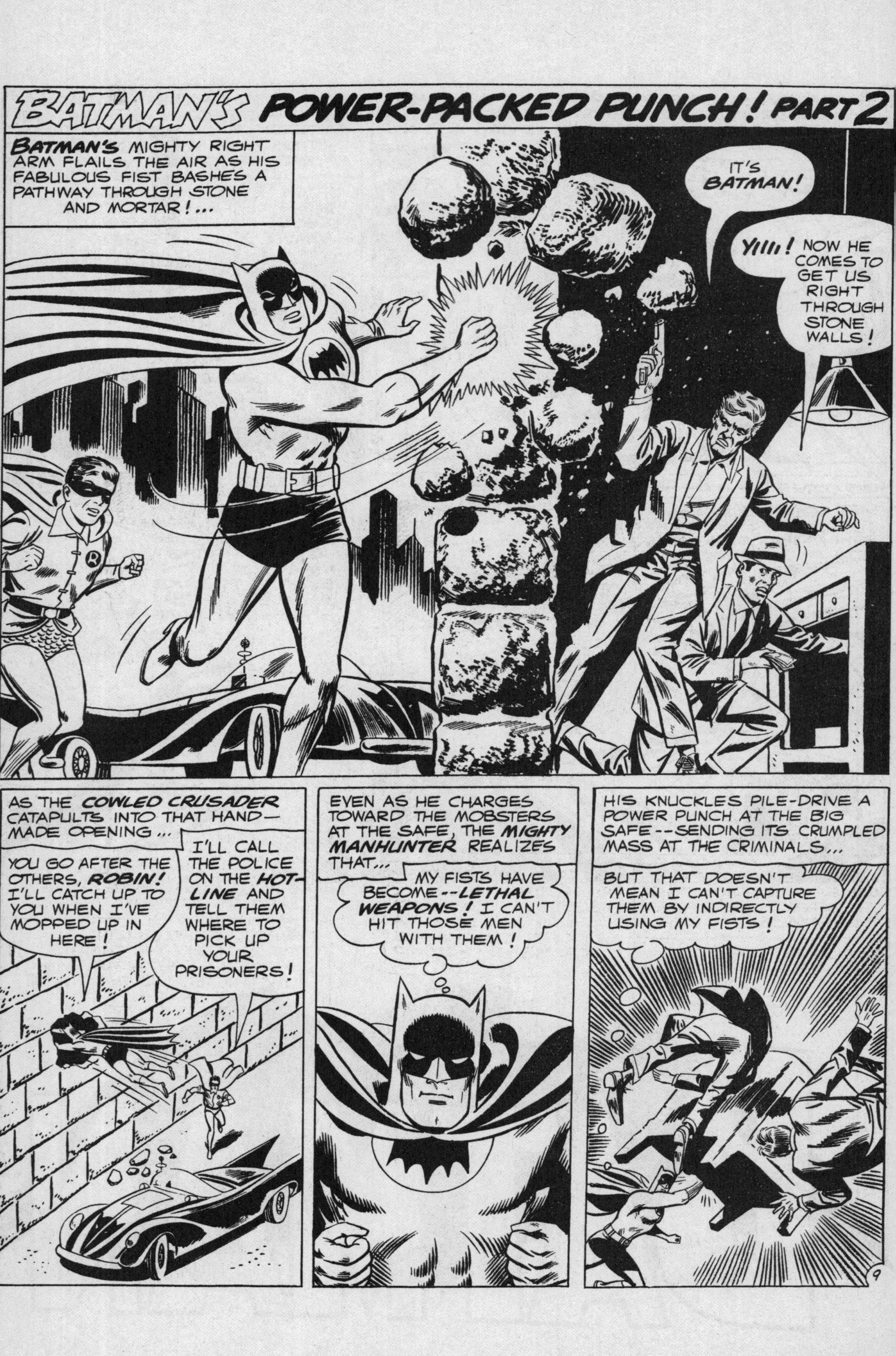
BATMAN'S POWER-PACKED PUNCH! PART 2
BATMAN'S MIGHTY RIGHT ARM FLAILS THE AIR AS HIS FABULOUS FIST BASHES A PATHWAY THROUGH STONE AND MORTAR!...
IT'S BATMAN!
YIII! NOW HE COMES TO GET US RIGHT THROUGH STONE WALLS!
AS THE COWLED CRUSADER CATAPULTS INTO THAT HAND-MADE OPENING...
YOU GO AFTER THE OTHERS, ROBIN! I'LL CATCH UP TO YOU WHEN I'VE MOPPED UP IN HERE!
I'LL CALL THE POLICE ON THE HOT-LINE AND TELL THEM WHERE TO PICK UP YOUR PRISONERS!
EVEN AS HE CHARGES TOWARD THE MOBSTERS AT THE SAFE, THE MIGHTY MANHUNTER REALIZES THAT...
MY FISTS HAVE BECOME--LETHAL WEAPONS! I CAN'T HIT THOSE MEN WITH THEM!
HIS KNUCKLES PILE-DRIVE A POWER PUNCH AT THE BIG SAFE--SENDING ITS CRUMPLED MASS AT THE CRIMINALS...
BUT THAT DOESN'T MEAN I CAN'T CAPTURE THEM BY INDIRECTLY USING MY FISTS!
9

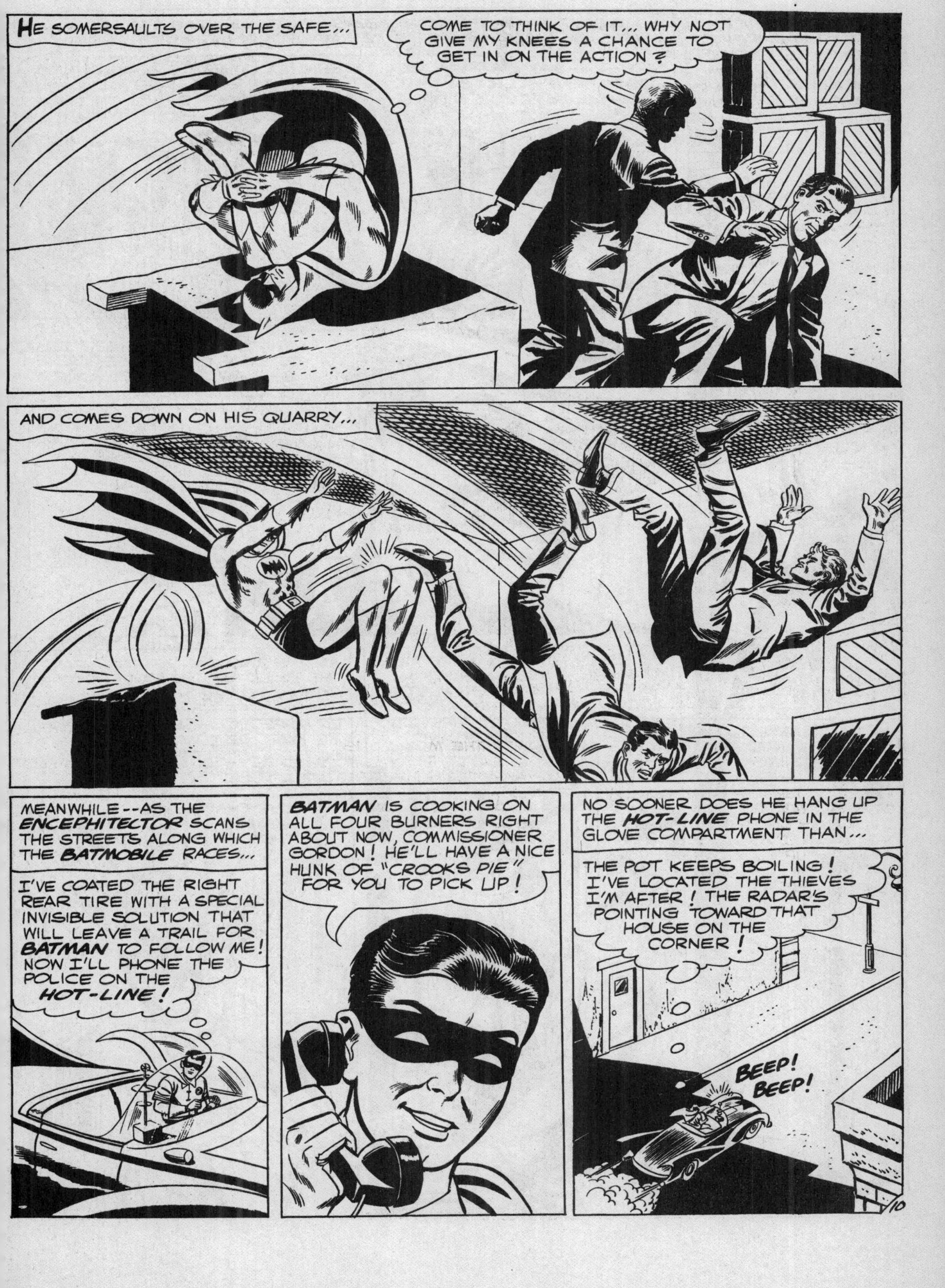
HE SOMERSAULTS OVER THE SAFE...
COME TO THINK OF IT... WHY NOT GIVE MY KNEES A CHANCE TO GET IN ON THE ACTION?
AND COMES DOWN ON HIS QUARRY...
MEANWHILE--AS THE ENCEPHITECTOR SCANS THE STREETS ALONG WHICH THE BATMOBILE RACES...
I'VE COATED THE RIGHT REAR TIRE WITH A SPECIAL INVISIBLE SOLUTION THAT WILL LEAVE A TRAIL FOR BATMAN TO FOLLOW ME! NOW I'LL PHONE THE POLICE ON THE HOT-LINE!
BATMAN IS COOKING ON ALL FOUR BURNERS RIGHT ABOUT NOW, COMMISSIONER GORDON! HE'LL HAVE A NICE HUNK OF "CROOKS PIE" FOR YOU TO PICK UP!
NO SOONER DOES HE HANG UP THE HOT-LINE PHONE IN THE GLOVE COMPARTMENT THAN...
THE POT KEEPS BOILING! I'VE LOCATED THE THIEVES I'M AFTER! THE RADAR'S POINTING TOWARD THAT HOUSE ON THE CORNER!
BEEP! BEEP!
10

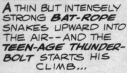

A THIN BUT INTENSELY STRONG *BAT-ROPE* SNAKES UPWARD INTO THE AIR--AND THE *TEEN-AGE THUNDER-BOLT* STARTS HIS CLIMB...

IN A BRIGHTLY LIGHTED ROOM ABOVE HIM, GANG BOSS *"BULL"* FLEMING SNARLS HIS DISBELIEF AS HIS MEN MAKE THEIR REPORT...

SURE--YOU *SAY BATMAN* AND *ROBIN* WERE KILLED BY THAT SWINGING DEMOLITION BALL-- BUT I GOT MY DOUBTS!

BOSS, CHUCK HERE SNEAKED INTO THE CAB OF THAT CRANE AND SWUNG THE *"HEADACHE BALL"* ON THEM TWO! TELL HIM ABOUT IT, CHUCK!

THAT'S RIGHT, *"BULL"*! I USED TO BE A CRANE OPERATOR BEFORE I JOINED YOUR BUNCH. BELIEVE ME, THEY'RE DONE FOR! THAT BALL WEIGHS A *TON*! NOT EVEN *BATMAN* AND *ROBIN* COULD STAND UP UNDER IT!

I'LL BET MY SHARE OF THE LOOT WE'LL NEVER HEAR FROM THEM AGAIN!

WELL, I HOPE YOU'RE RIGHT, CHUCK! COME ON--LET'S GET THIS LOOT OVER TO FREDDY THE FENCE AND TURN IT INTO COLD CASH!

AS THE TWO GANGSTERS LEAVE THE BUILDING, THE EAVESDROPPING *ROBIN* MAKES HIS MOVE...

I'D HOPED TO HAVE *BATMAN* JOIN ME BEFORE I WENT INTO ACTION-- BUT I CAN'T LET THOSE TWO SCOOT OFF WITH THAT LOOT!

11

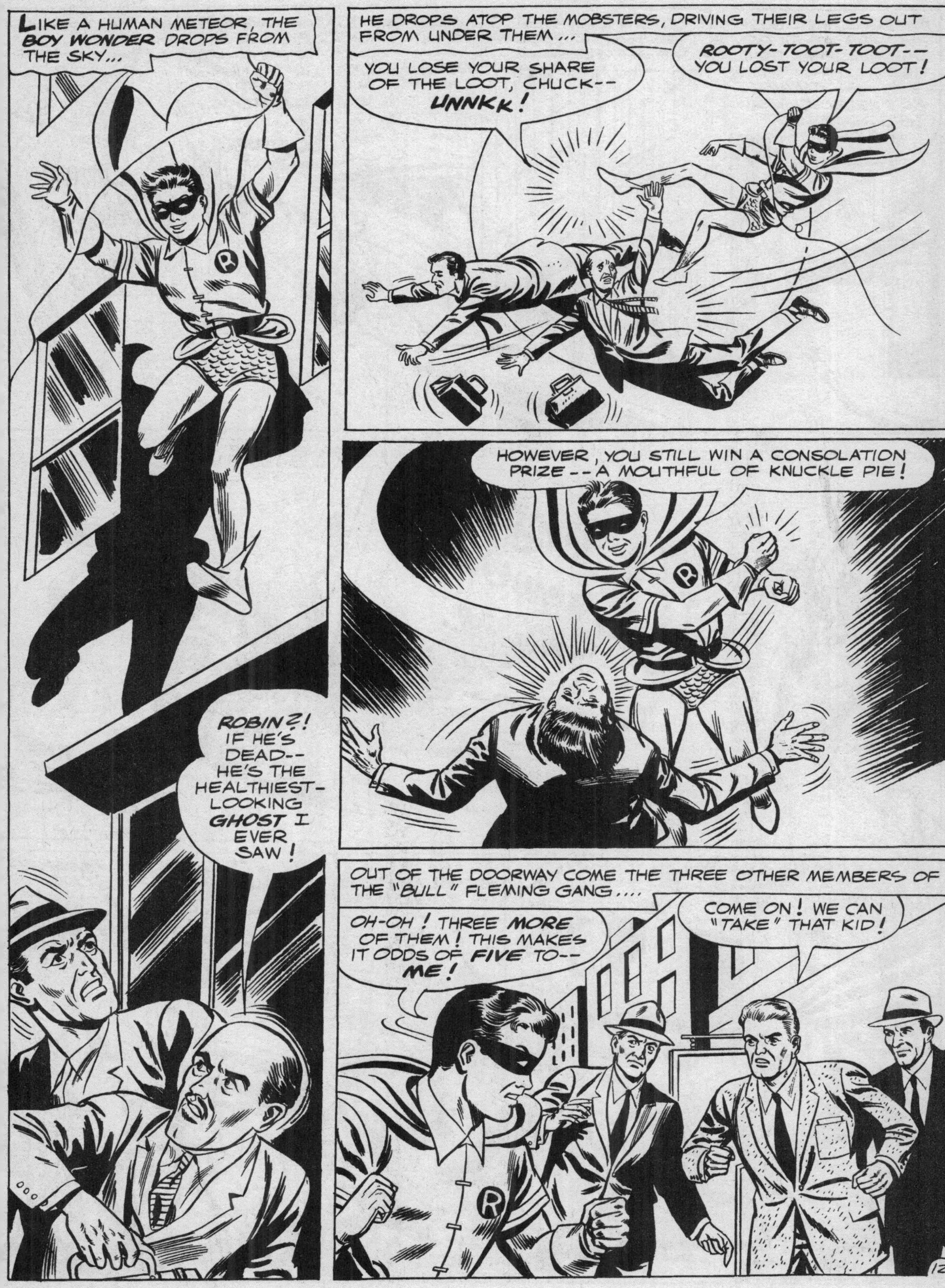
LIKE A HUMAN METEOR, THE BOY WONDER DROPS FROM THE SKY...
HE DROPS ATOP THE MOBSTERS, DRIVING THEIR LEGS OUT FROM UNDER THEM...
YOU LOSE YOUR SHARE OF THE LOOT, CHUCK-- UNNKK!
ROOTY-TOOT-TOOT-- YOU LOST YOUR LOOT!
HOWEVER, YOU STILL WIN A CONSOLATION PRIZE--A MOUTHFUL OF KNUCKLE PIE!
ROBIN?! IF HE'S DEAD-- HE'S THE HEALTHIEST-LOOKING GHOST I EVER SAW!
OUT OF THE DOORWAY COME THE THREE OTHER MEMBERS OF THE "BULL" FLEMING GANG....
OH-OH! THREE MORE OF THEM! THIS MAKES IT ODDS OF FIVE TO-- ME!
COME ON! WE CAN "TAKE" THAT KID!
12

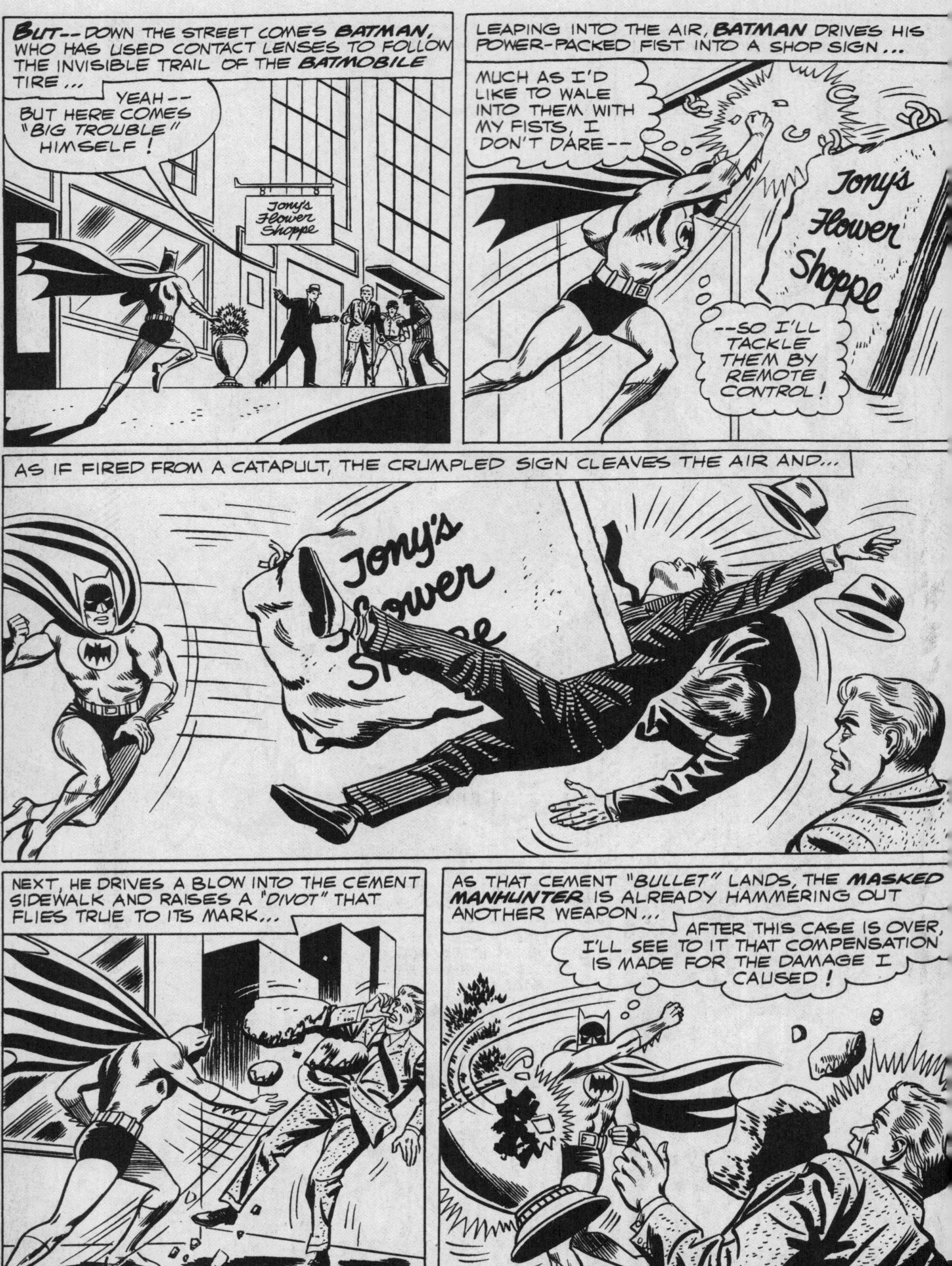
BUT--DOWN THE STREET COMES BATMAN, WHO HAS USED CONTACT LENSES TO FOLLOW THE INVISIBLE TRAIL OF THE BATMOBILE TIRE...
YEAH-- BUT HERE COMES "BIG TROUBLE" HIMSELF!
Jony's Flower Shoppe
LEAPING INTO THE AIR, BATMAN DRIVES HIS POWER-PACKED FIST INTO A SHOP SIGN...
MUCH AS I'D LIKE TO WALE INTO THEM WITH MY FISTS, I DON'T DARE--
Jony's Flower Shoppe
--SO I'LL TACKLE THEM BY REMOTE CONTROL!
AS IF FIRED FROM A CATAPULT, THE CRUMPLED SIGN CLEAVES THE AIR AND...
NEXT, HE DRIVES A BLOW INTO THE CEMENT SIDEWALK AND RAISES A "DIVOT" THAT FLIES TRUE TO ITS MARK...
AS THAT CEMENT "BULLET" LANDS, THE MASKED MANHUNTER IS ALREADY HAMMERING OUT ANOTHER WEAPON...
AFTER THIS CASE IS OVER, I'LL SEE TO IT THAT COMPENSATION IS MADE FOR THE DAMAGE I CAUSED!
13

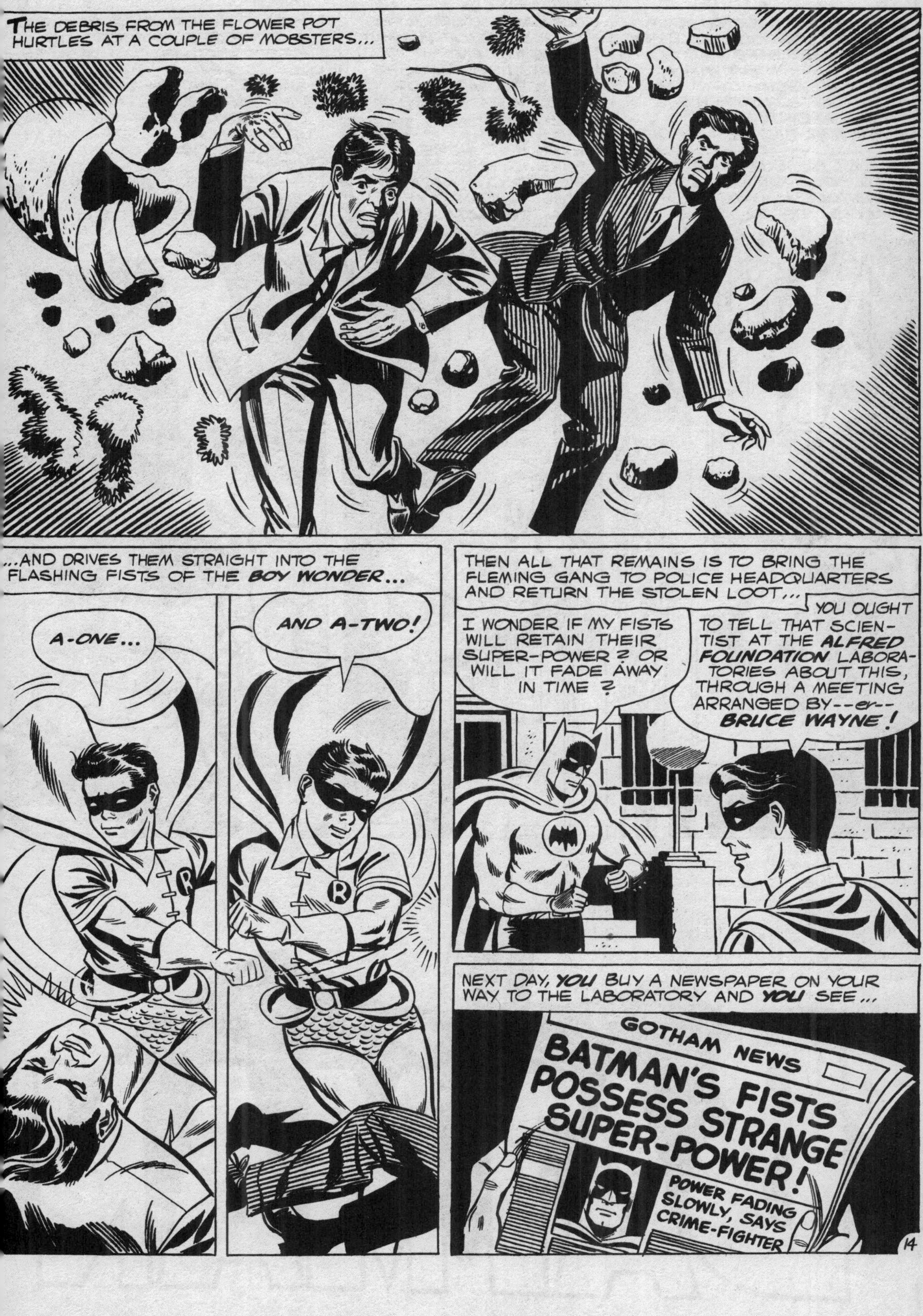
THE DEBRIS FROM THE FLOWER POT HURTLES AT A COUPLE OF MOBSTERS...
...AND DRIVES THEM STRAIGHT INTO THE FLASHING FISTS OF THE BOY WONDER...
A-ONE...
AND A-TWO!
THEN ALL THAT REMAINS IS TO BRING THE FLEMING GANG TO POLICE HEADQUARTERS AND RETURN THE STOLEN LOOT...
I WONDER IF MY FISTS WILL RETAIN THEIR SUPER-POWER ? OR WILL IT FADE AWAY IN TIME ?
YOU OUGHT TO TELL THAT SCIENTIST AT THE ALFRED FOUNDATION LABORATORIES ABOUT THIS, THROUGH A MEETING ARRANGED BY--er--BRUCE WAYNE!
NEXT DAY, YOU BUY A NEWSPAPER ON YOUR WAY TO THE LABORATORY AND YOU SEE...
GOTHAM NEWS
BATMAN'S FISTS POSSESS STRANGE SUPER-POWER!
POWER FADING SLOWLY, SAYS CRIME-FIGHTER
14

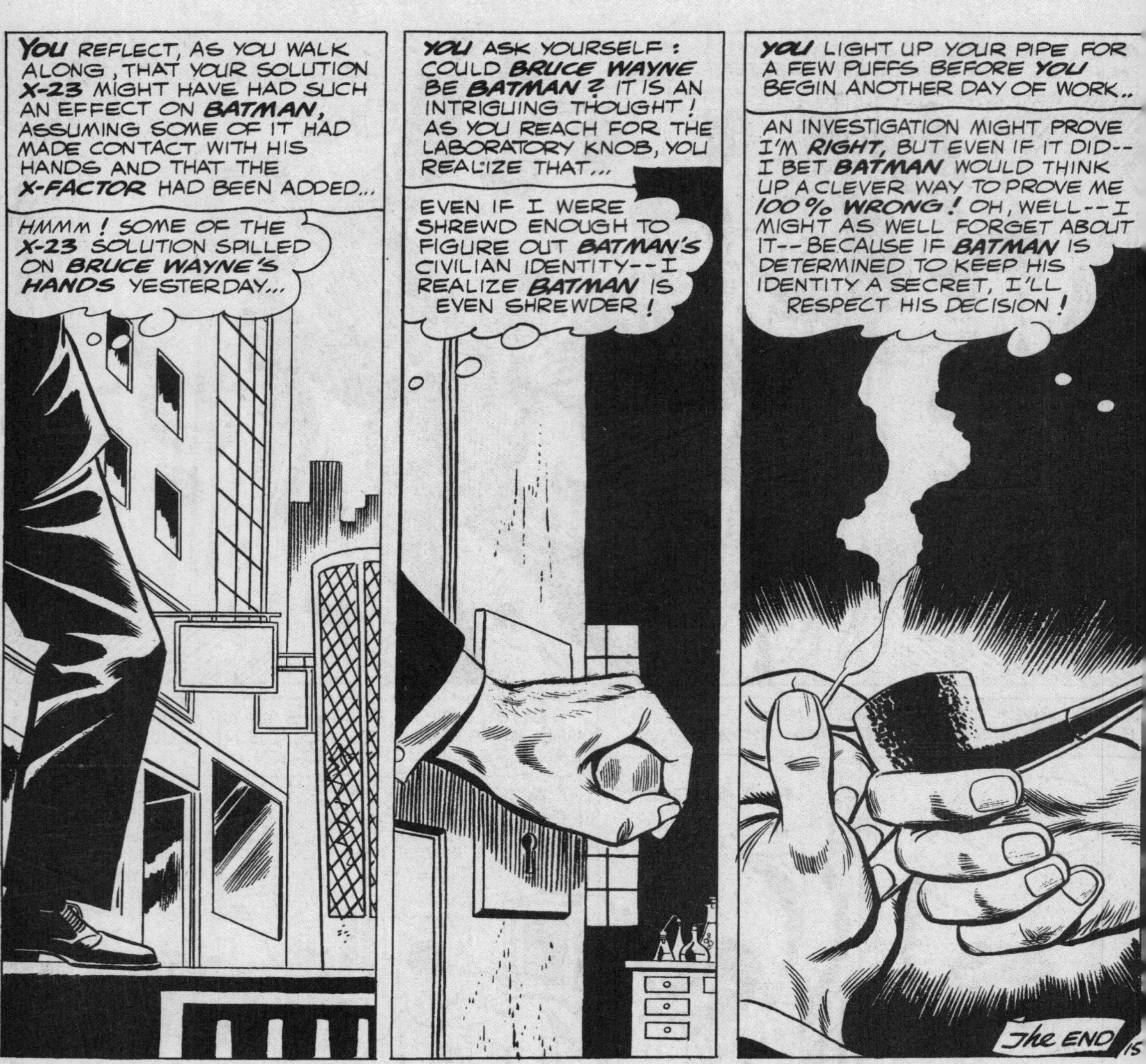
YOU REFLECT, AS YOU WALK ALONG, THAT YOUR SOLUTION X-23 MIGHT HAVE HAD SUCH AN EFFECT ON BATMAN, ASSUMING SOME OF IT HAD MADE CONTACT WITH HIS HANDS AND THAT THE X-FACTOR HAD BEEN ADDED...
HMMM! SOME OF THE X-23 SOLUTION SPILLED ON BRUCE WAYNE'S HANDS YESTERDAY...
YOU ASK YOURSELF: COULD BRUCE WAYNE BE BATMAN? IT IS AN INTRIGUING THOUGHT! AS YOU REACH FOR THE LABORATORY KNOB, YOU REALIZE THAT...
EVEN IF I WERE SHREWD ENOUGH TO FIGURE OUT BATMAN'S CIVILIAN IDENTITY--I REALIZE BATMAN IS EVEN SHREWDER!
YOU LIGHT UP YOUR PIPE FOR A FEW PUFFS BEFORE YOU BEGIN ANOTHER DAY OF WORK...
AN INVESTIGATION MIGHT PROVE I'M RIGHT, BUT EVEN IF IT DID-- I BET BATMAN WOULD THINK UP A CLEVER WAY TO PROVE ME 100% WRONG! OH, WELL--I MIGHT AS WELL FORGET ABOUT IT--BECAUSE IF BATMAN IS DETERMINED TO KEEP HIS IDENTITY A SECRET, I'LL RESPECT HIS DECISION!
The END
15

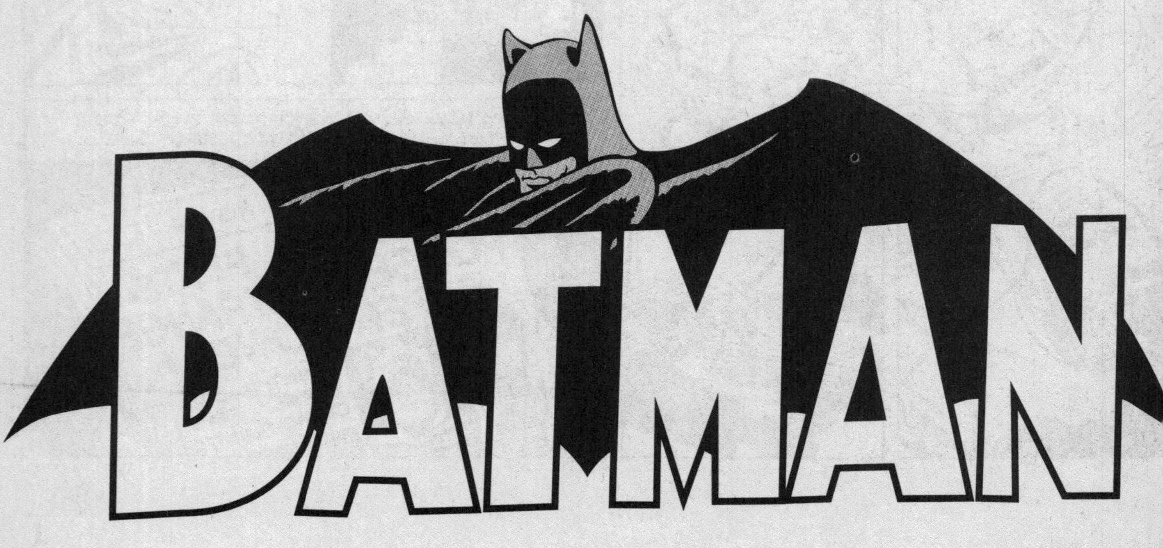
BATMAN

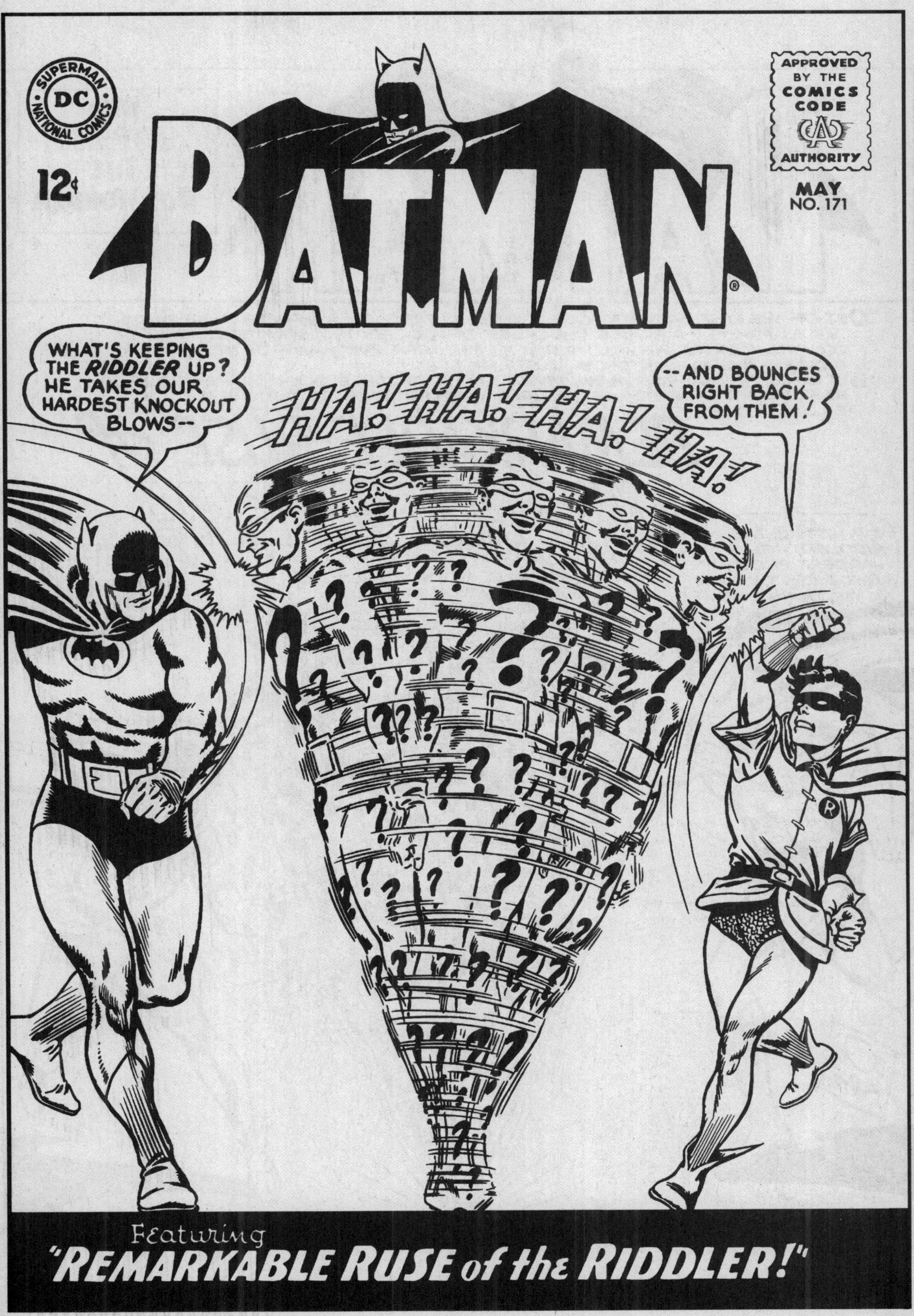
SUPERMAN DC NATIONAL COMICS
12¢
BATMAN®
APPROVED BY THE COMICS CODE AUTHORITY
MAY NO. 171
WHAT'S KEEPING THE RIDDLER UP? HE TAKES OUR HARDEST KNOCKOUT BLOWS--
HA! HA! HA! HA!
--AND BOUNCES RIGHT BACK FROM THEM!
Featuring "REMARKABLE RUSE of the RIDDLER!"

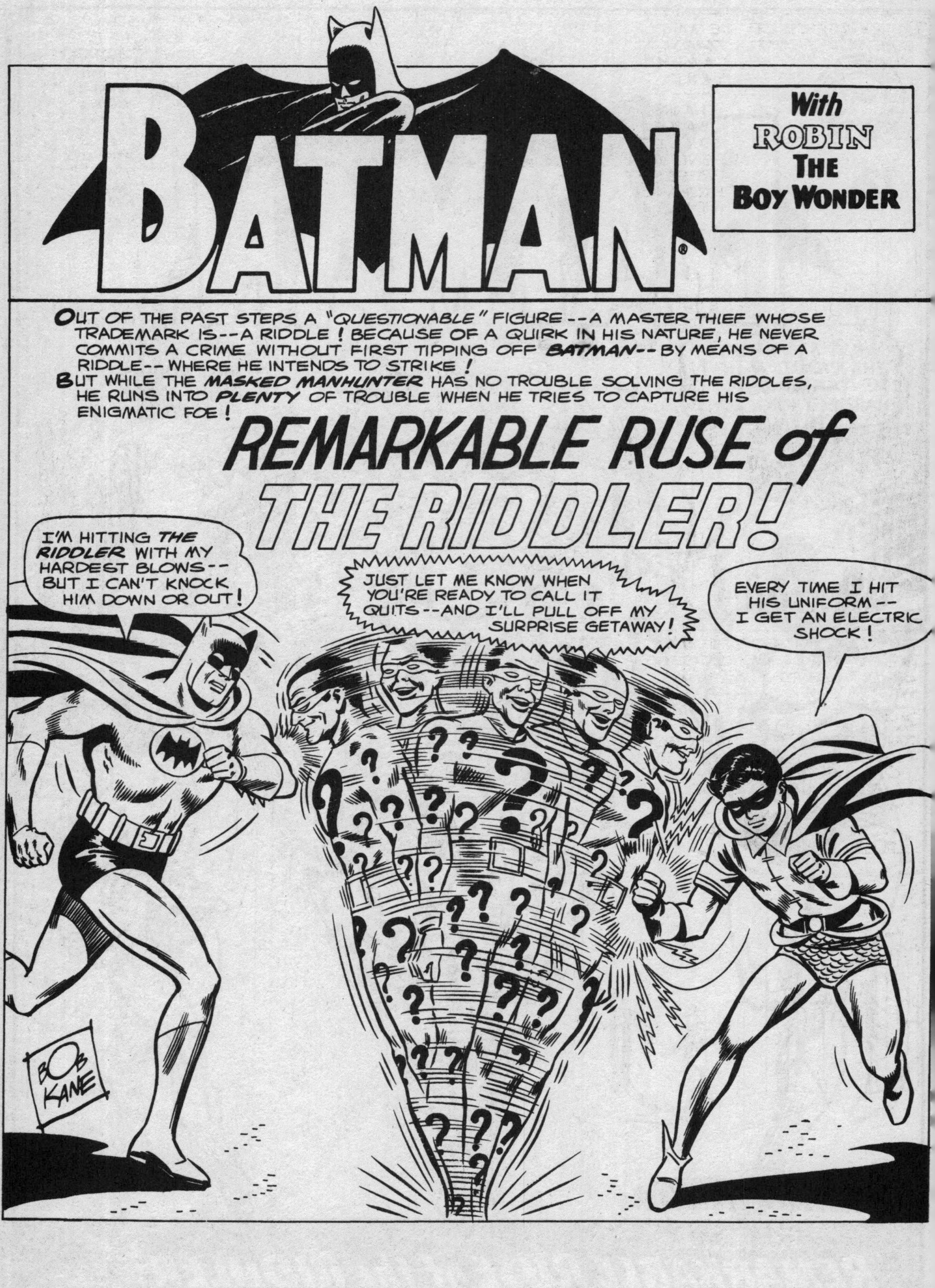
BATMAN
With ROBIN THE BOY WONDER
OUT OF THE PAST STEPS A "QUESTIONABLE" FIGURE--A MASTER THIEF WHOSE TRADEMARK IS--A RIDDLE! BECAUSE OF A QUIRK IN HIS NATURE, HE NEVER COMMITS A CRIME WITHOUT FIRST TIPPING OFF BATMAN--BY MEANS OF A RIDDLE--WHERE HE INTENDS TO STRIKE!
BUT WHILE THE MASKED MANHUNTER HAS NO TROUBLE SOLVING THE RIDDLES, HE RUNS INTO PLENTY OF TROUBLE WHEN HE TRIES TO CAPTURE HIS ENIGMATIC FOE!
REMARKABLE RUSE of THE RIDDLER!
I'M HITTING THE RIDDLER WITH MY HARDEST BLOWS--BUT I CAN'T KNOCK HIM DOWN OR OUT!
JUST LET ME KNOW WHEN YOU'RE READY TO CALL IT QUITS--AND I'LL PULL OFF MY SURPRISE GETAWAY!
EVERY TIME I HIT HIS UNIFORM--I GET AN ELECTRIC SHOCK!
BOB KANE

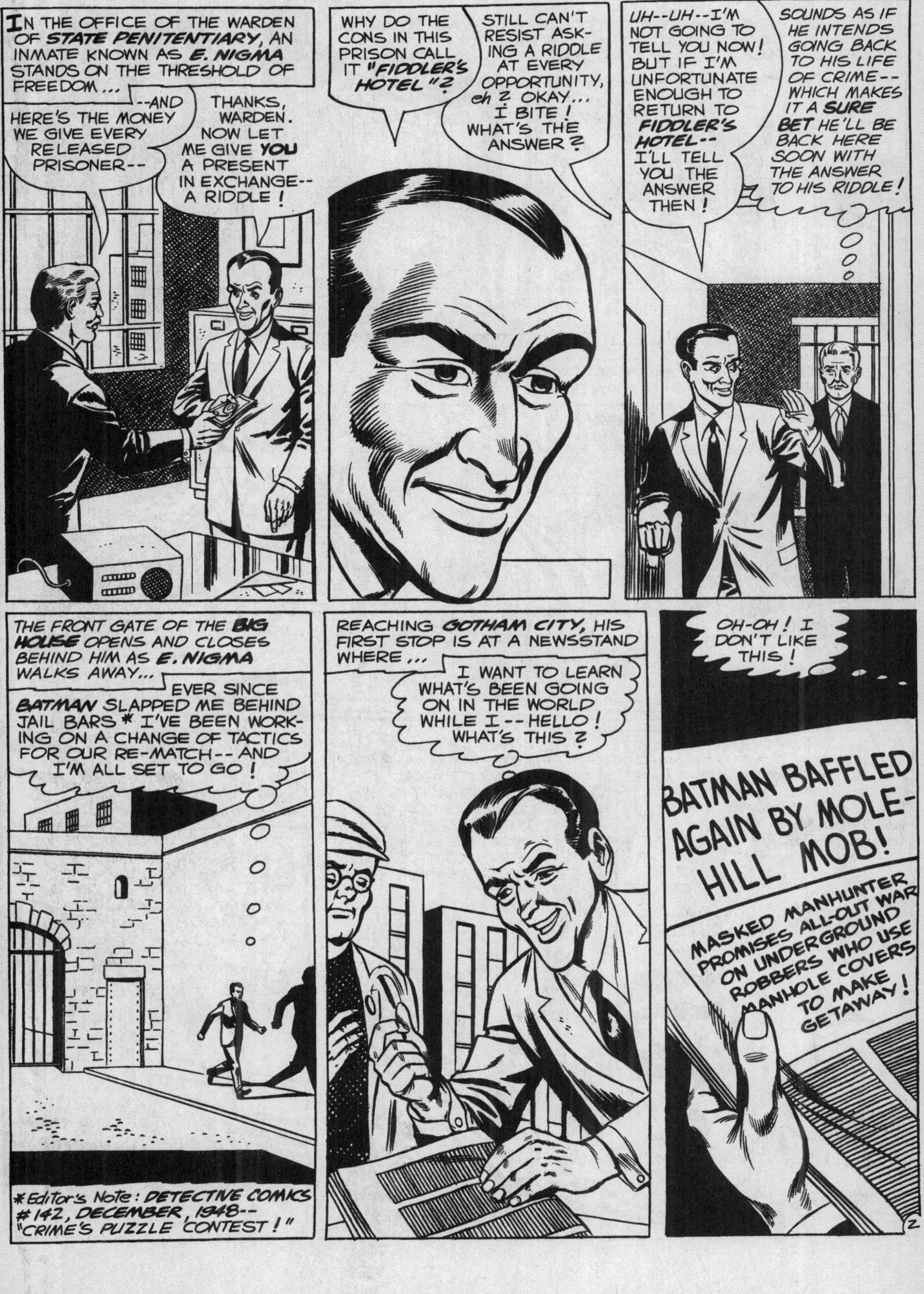
IN THE OFFICE OF THE WARDEN OF STATE PENITENTIARY, AN INMATE KNOWN AS E. NIGMA STANDS ON THE THRESHOLD OF FREEDOM ...
--AND HERE'S THE MONEY WE GIVE EVERY RELEASED PRISONER--
THANKS, WARDEN. NOW LET ME GIVE YOU A PRESENT IN EXCHANGE-- A RIDDLE!
WHY DO THE CONS IN THIS PRISON CALL IT "FIDDLER'S HOTEL"?
STILL CAN'T RESIST ASKING A RIDDLE AT EVERY OPPORTUNITY, eh? OKAY... I BITE! WHAT'S THE ANSWER?
UH--UH--I'M NOT GOING TO TELL YOU NOW! BUT IF I'M UNFORTUNATE ENOUGH TO RETURN TO FIDDLER'S HOTEL-- I'LL TELL YOU THE ANSWER THEN!
SOUNDS AS IF HE INTENDS GOING BACK TO HIS LIFE OF CRIME-- WHICH MAKES IT A SURE BET HE'LL BE BACK HERE SOON WITH THE ANSWER TO HIS RIDDLE!
THE FRONT GATE OF THE BIG HOUSE OPENS AND CLOSES BEHIND HIM AS E. NIGMA WALKS AWAY...
EVER SINCE BATMAN SLAPPED ME BEHIND JAIL BARS * I'VE BEEN WORKING ON A CHANGE OF TACTICS FOR OUR RE-MATCH-- AND I'M ALL SET TO GO!
*Editor's Note: DETECTIVE COMICS #142, DECEMBER, 1948-- "CRIME'S PUZZLE CONTEST!"
REACHING GOTHAM CITY, HIS FIRST STOP IS AT A NEWSSTAND WHERE ...
I WANT TO LEARN WHAT'S BEEN GOING ON IN THE WORLD WHILE I--HELLO! WHAT'S THIS?
OH-OH! I DON'T LIKE THIS!
BATMAN BAFFLED AGAIN BY MOLE-HILL MOB!
MASKED MANHUNTER PROMISES ALL-OUT WAR ON UNDERGROUND ROBBERS WHO USE MANHOLE COVERS TO MAKE GETAWAY!
2

I WANT **ALL** OF **BATMAN'S** ATTENTION WHEN I MAKE MY MOVE! BUT HE CAN'T CONCENTRATE ON ME -- IF HE'S OUT CHASING SOMEBODY ELSE! GOT TO DO SOMETHING ABOUT THIS!

THE FOLLOWING DAY, AS **BATMAN** AND **ROBIN** STEP TOWARD POLICE HEADQUARTERS...

HI THERE, **BATMAN!** HELLO, **ROBIN!** I WAS HOPING YOU'D SHOW UP HERE! REMEMBER ME?

THE FACE IS FAMILIAR -- BUT --

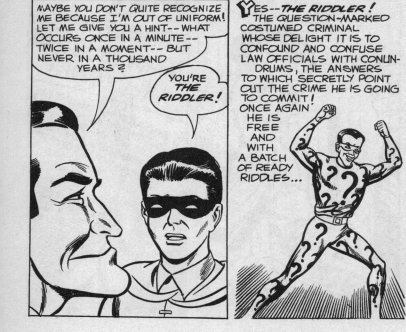

MAYBE YOU DON'T QUITE RECOGNIZE ME BECAUSE I'M OUT OF UNIFORM! LET ME GIVE YOU A HINT -- WHAT OCCURS ONCE IN A MINUTE -- TWICE IN A MOMENT -- BUT NEVER IN A THOUSAND YEARS?

YOU'RE **THE RIDDLER!**

YES -- **THE RIDDLER!** THE QUESTION-MARKED COSTUMED CRIMINAL WHOSE DELIGHT IT IS TO CONFOUND AND CONFUSE LAW OFFICIALS WITH CONUNDRUMS, THE ANSWERS TO WHICH SECRETLY POINT OUT THE CRIME HE IS GOING TO COMMIT! ONCE AGAIN HE IS FREE AND WITH A BATCH OF READY RIDDLES...

LONG AGO AS A BOY -- **EDWARD NIGMA** WAS HIS FULL NAME -- HE WON AN HISTORICAL JIG-SAW PUZZLE IN SCHOOL -- BY **CHEATING**...

SO THAT'S WHAT THE COMPLETED PUZZLE LOOKS LIKE -- COLUMBUS DISCOVERING AMERICA! I'LL TAKE A PICTURE OF IT WITH MY FLASH CAMERA!

3

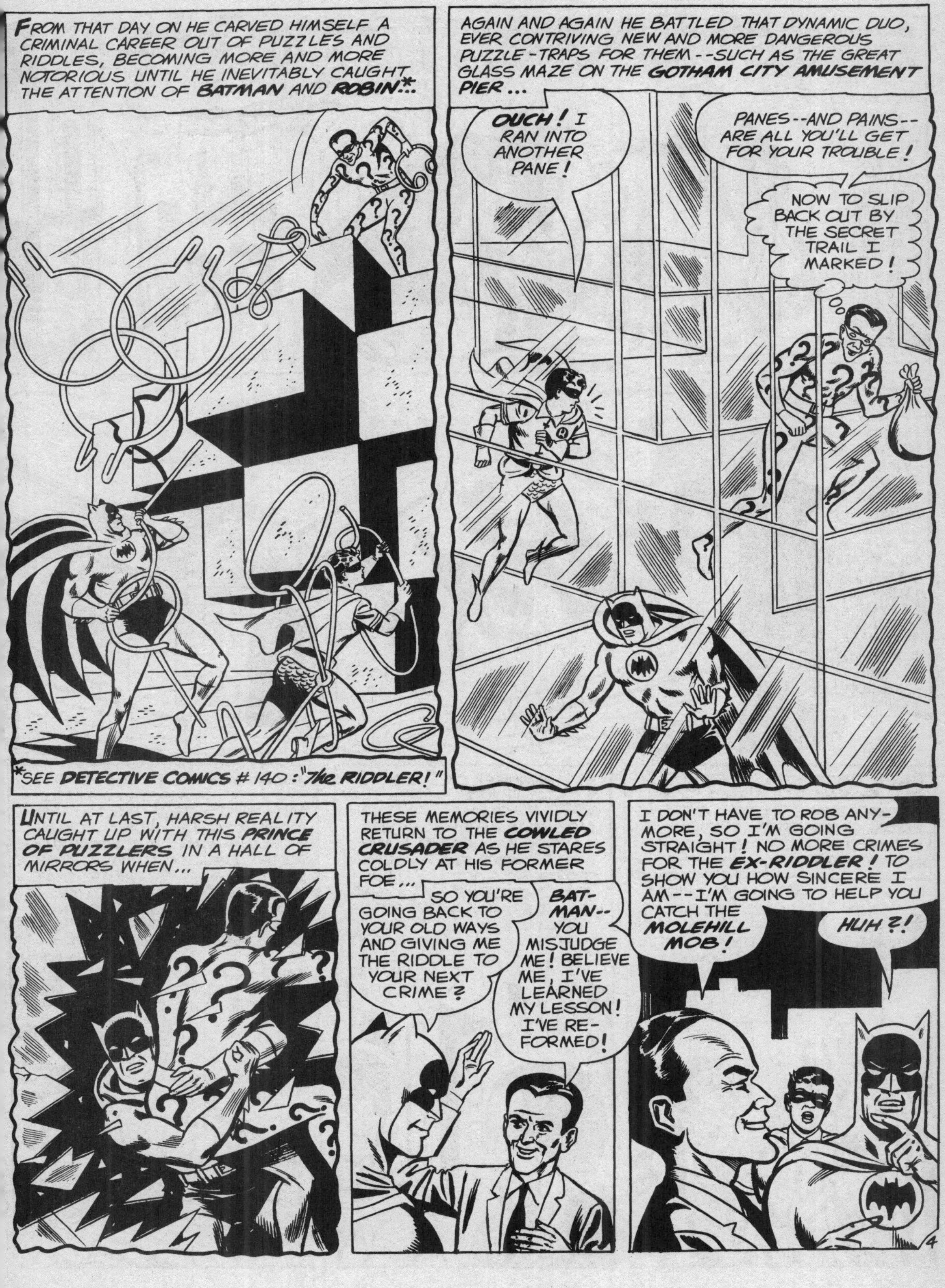
FROM THAT DAY ON HE CARVED HIMSELF A CRIMINAL CAREER OUT OF PUZZLES AND RIDDLES, BECOMING MORE AND MORE NOTORIOUS UNTIL HE INEVITABLY CAUGHT THE ATTENTION OF BATMAN AND ROBIN*...
*SEE DETECTIVE COMICS # 140: "The RIDDLER!"
AGAIN AND AGAIN HE BATTLED THAT DYNAMIC DUO, EVER CONTRIVING NEW AND MORE DANGEROUS PUZZLE-TRAPS FOR THEM--SUCH AS THE GREAT GLASS MAZE ON THE GOTHAM CITY AMUSEMENT PIER...
OUCH! I RAN INTO ANOTHER PANE!
PANES--AND PAINS--ARE ALL YOU'LL GET FOR YOUR TROUBLE!
NOW TO SLIP BACK OUT BY THE SECRET TRAIL I MARKED!
UNTIL AT LAST, HARSH REALITY CAUGHT UP WITH THIS PRINCE OF PUZZLERS IN A HALL OF MIRRORS WHEN...
THESE MEMORIES VIVIDLY RETURN TO THE COWLED CRUSADER AS HE STARES COLDLY AT HIS FORMER FOE...
SO YOU'RE GOING BACK TO YOUR OLD WAYS AND GIVING ME THE RIDDLE TO YOUR NEXT CRIME?
BATMAN--YOU MISJUDGE ME! BELIEVE ME, I'VE LEARNED MY LESSON! I'VE REFORMED!
I DON'T HAVE TO ROB ANYMORE, SO I'M GOING STRAIGHT! NO MORE CRIMES FOR THE EX-RIDDLER! TO SHOW YOU HOW SINCERE I AM--I'M GOING TO HELP YOU CATCH THE MOLEHILL MOB!
HUH?!
4

BATMAN REFLECTS A MOMENT ON THE *MOLEHILL MOB*-- GANGSTERS THAT COME *OUT* OF MANHOLES TO STRIKE SWIFTLY AT THEIR TARGETS-- AND CRAWL *INTO* THEM TO FLEE WITH THEIR LOOT...

THEY'RE GETTING AWAY!

ONCE INSIDE THOSE UNDERGROUND TUNNELS-- THEY'LL GIVE US THE SLIP!

FOR IN THAT SUB-TERRANEAN WORLD BENEATH THE GREAT METROPOLIS THERE ARE MILES AND MILES OF TUNNELS AND STRANGE BYWAYS, CONDUITS AND CABLES...

WE'VE DUG OUR OWN SECRET ENTRANCES AND EXITS DOWN HERE! NO ONE CAN EVER CATCH UP TO US!

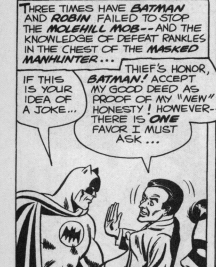

THREE TIMES HAVE *BATMAN* AND *ROBIN* FAILED TO STOP THE *MOLEHILL MOB*--AND THE KNOWLEDGE OF DEFEAT RANKLES IN THE CHEST OF THE *MASKED MANHUNTER* ...

IF THIS IS YOUR IDEA OF A JOKE...

THIEF'S HONOR, *BATMAN!* ACCEPT MY GOOD DEED AS PROOF OF MY "*NEW*" HONESTY! HOWEVER-- THERE IS *ONE* FAVOR I MUST ASK ...

;er; WOULD IT BE ALL RIGHT IF I WORE MY OLD UNIFORM? AFTER ALL, YOU AND *ROBIN* WEAR "*WORKING CLOTHES*"-- SO WHY SHOULDN'T I? HOW ABOUT IT?

I DON'T SEE HOW IT CAN DO ANY HARM! ALL RIGHT, MEET US TONIGHT AT EIGHT O'CLOCK NEAR THE SQUARE!

AS *E. NIGMA* DRIVES OFF...

WAIT--WHAT'S THE ANSWER TO THE RIDDLE? WHAT OCCURS ONCE IN EVERY MINUTE-- TWICE IN A MOMENT-- BUT NEVER IN A THOU-SAND YEARS?

THE LETTER "*M*", ROBIN! I WISH *ALL* HIS PUZZLES WERE THAT EASY! I HAVE THE FEELING THAT WE'RE BEING CON-FRONTED WITH THE TRICKIEST ONE OF ALL!

5

LATER THAT SAME DAY, IN THE STATELY WAYNE MANSION, BRUCE (*BATMAN*) WAYNE AND DICK (*ROBIN*) GRAYSON ARE SHARPENING THEIR MENTAL FACULTIES...

I'M GETTING RID OF ALL SEVEN LETTERS, *BRUCE!*

R-I-D-D-L-E-R! : Hmm : I CAN SEE WHAT'S ON *YOUR* MIND, DICK, EVEN WHILE PLAYING THIS GAME OF *SCRABBLE!*

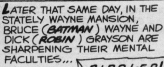

THAT EVENING AS THE TOWN CLOCK PEALS OUT THE HOUR OF EIGHT, CRIME-FIGHTERS MEET WITH CRIMINAL IN A COMMON CAUSE...

NOW TO SEE IF THE *RIDDLER'S* REALLY REFORMED!

I WONDER! I DON'T THINK HE CAN CHANGE HIS NATURE ANY MORE THAN A LEOPARD CAN CHANGE ITS SPOTS!

BONG

BONG

LEADING THE DUO DOWN THE STREET, *THE RIDDLER* PROPS UP A MANHOLE COVER...

FROM THE GRAPE-VINE AT THE *BIG HOUSE*, I LEARNED ENOUGH TO FIGURE OUT WHERE THE *MOLEHILL MOB* HAS ITS HIDE-OUT!

WHAT CAN HE BE UP TO? IF HE'S LEAD-ING US INTO A TRAP-- I'M SURE WE CAN GET OUT OF IT--

MOMENTS LATER, THE *CONUN-DRUM CHAMPION* LEADS THE WAY PAST MILES OF CABLES, DOWN INTO THE SUB-TERRANEAN PASSAGE-WAYS OF *GOTHAM CITY*...

WE'RE ALMOST THERE--

THEN IN A BRIGHTLY LIGHTED ROOM WHICH ONCE WAS A SUBWAY WORK-CREW'S TOOLHOUSE...

AS ADVERTISED--THE *MOLEHILL GANG!* TAKE 'EM, *BATMAN!*

6

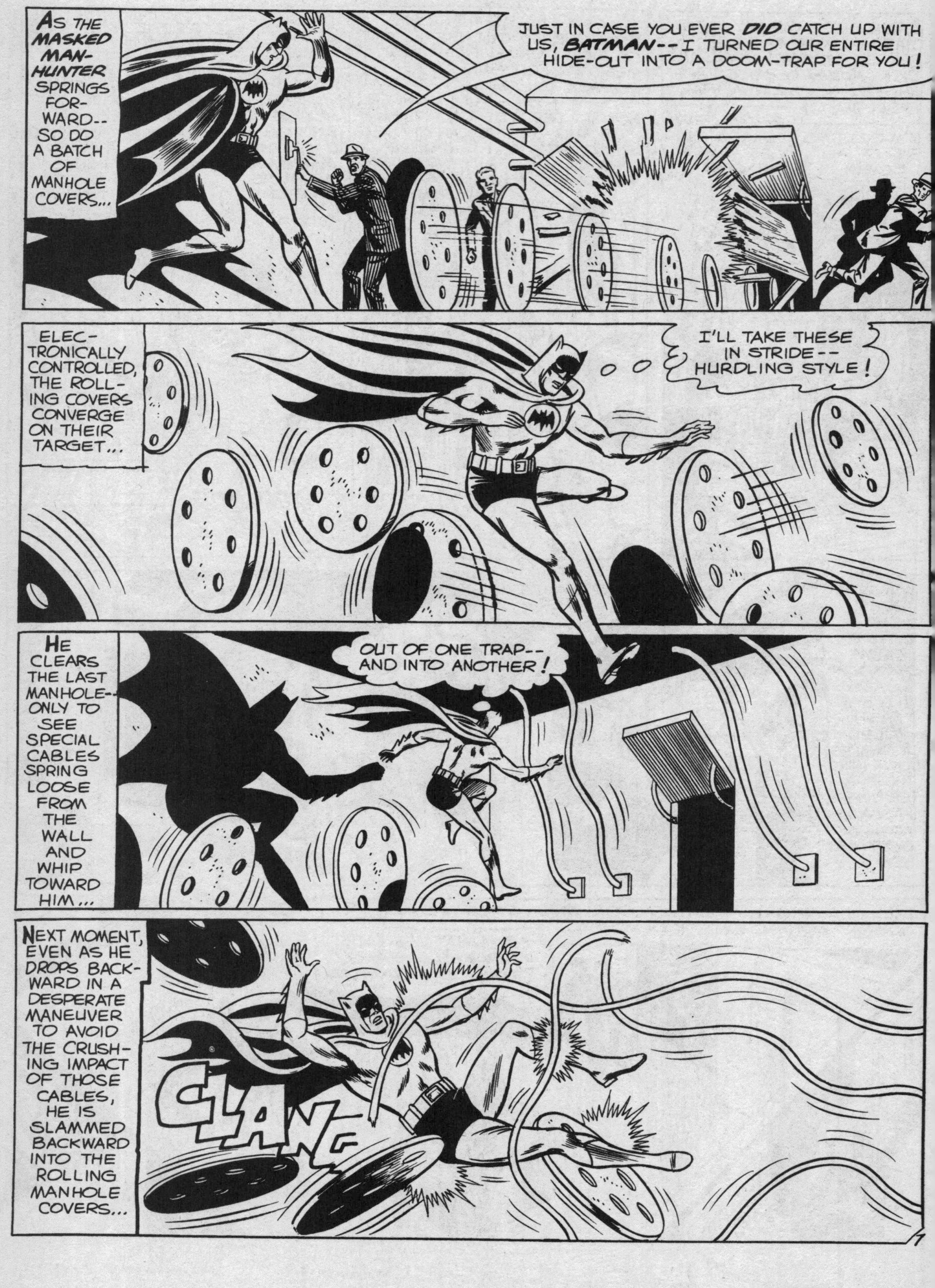
AS THE MASKED MAN-HUNTER SPRINGS FOR-WARD-- SO DO A BATCH OF MANHOLE COVERS...
JUST IN CASE YOU EVER DID CATCH UP WITH US, BATMAN-- I TURNED OUR ENTIRE HIDE-OUT INTO A DOOM-TRAP FOR YOU!
ELEC-TRONICALLY CONTROLLED, THE ROLL-ING COVERS CONVERGE ON THEIR TARGET...
I'LL TAKE THESE IN STRIDE-- HURDLING STYLE!
HE CLEARS THE LAST MANHOLE-- ONLY TO SEE SPECIAL CABLES SPRING LOOSE FROM THE WALL AND WHIP TOWARD HIM...
OUT OF ONE TRAP-- AND INTO ANOTHER!
NEXT MOMENT, EVEN AS HE DROPS BACK-WARD IN A DESPERATE MANEUVER TO AVOID THE CRUSH-ING IMPACT OF THOSE CABLES, HE IS SLAMMED BACKWARD INTO THE ROLLING MANHOLE COVERS...
CLANG
7

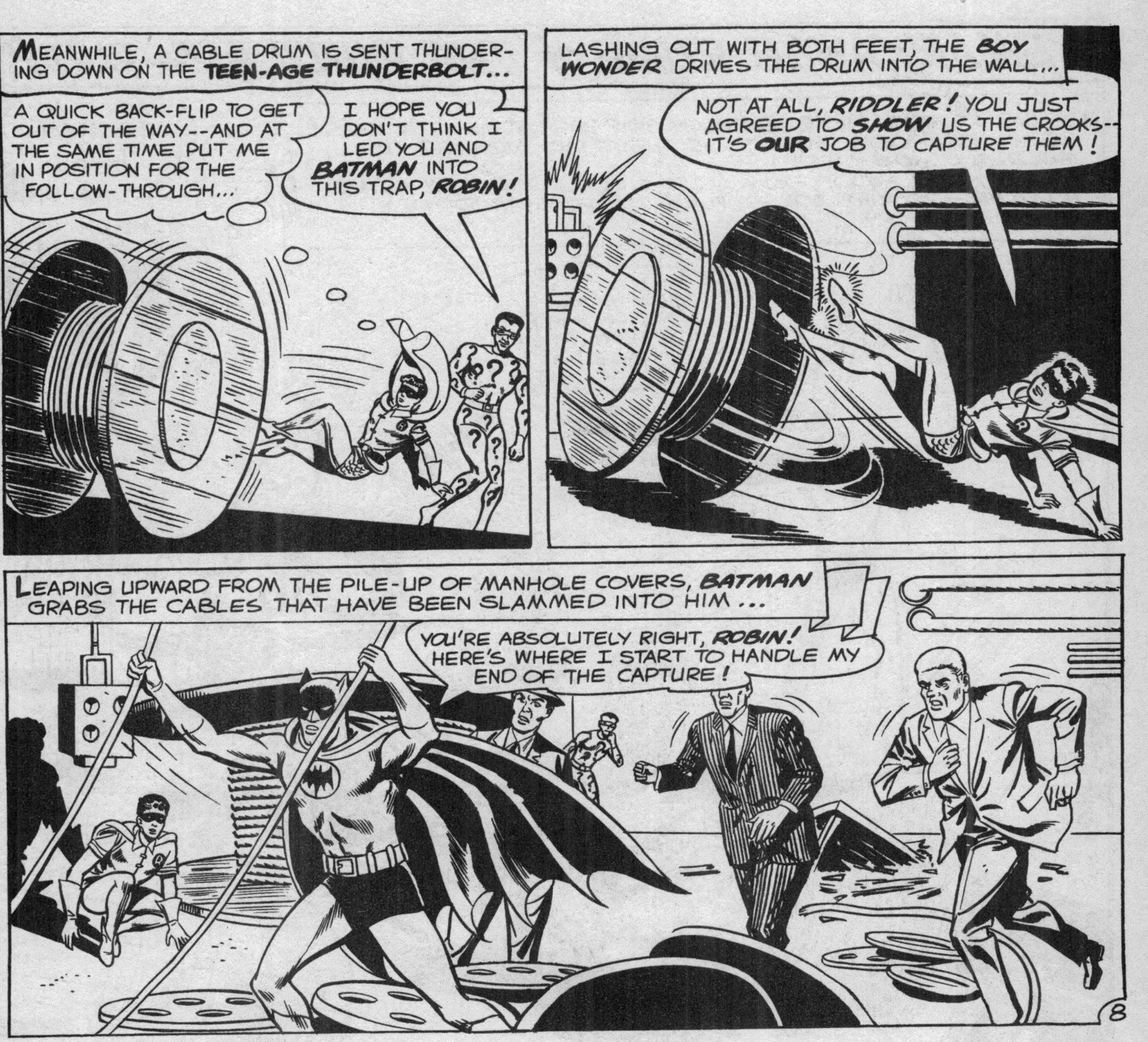
MEANWHILE, A CABLE DRUM IS SENT THUNDERING DOWN ON THE TEEN-AGE THUNDERBOLT...
A QUICK BACK-FLIP TO GET OUT OF THE WAY--AND AT THE SAME TIME PUT ME IN POSITION FOR THE FOLLOW-THROUGH...
I HOPE YOU DON'T THINK I LED YOU AND BATMAN INTO THIS TRAP, ROBIN!
LASHING OUT WITH BOTH FEET, THE BOY WONDER DRIVES THE DRUM INTO THE WALL...
NOT AT ALL, RIDDLER! YOU JUST AGREED TO SHOW US THE CROOKS--IT'S OUR JOB TO CAPTURE THEM!
LEAPING UPWARD FROM THE PILE-UP OF MANHOLE COVERS, BATMAN GRABS THE CABLES THAT HAVE BEEN SLAMMED INTO HIM...
YOU'RE ABSOLUTELY RIGHT, ROBIN! HERE'S WHERE I START TO HANDLE MY END OF THE CAPTURE!
8

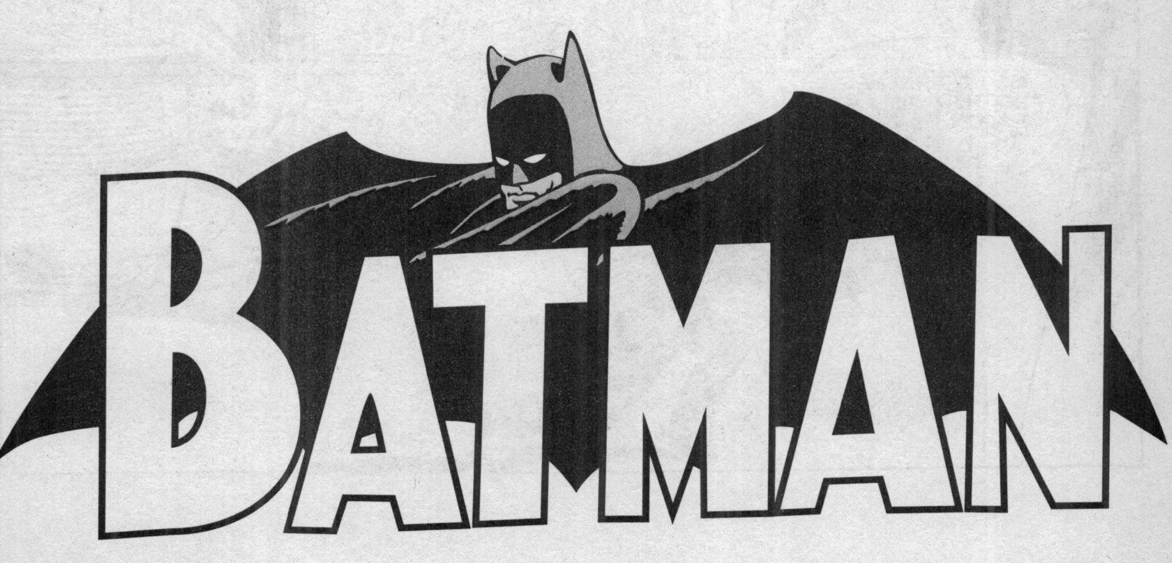
BATMAN

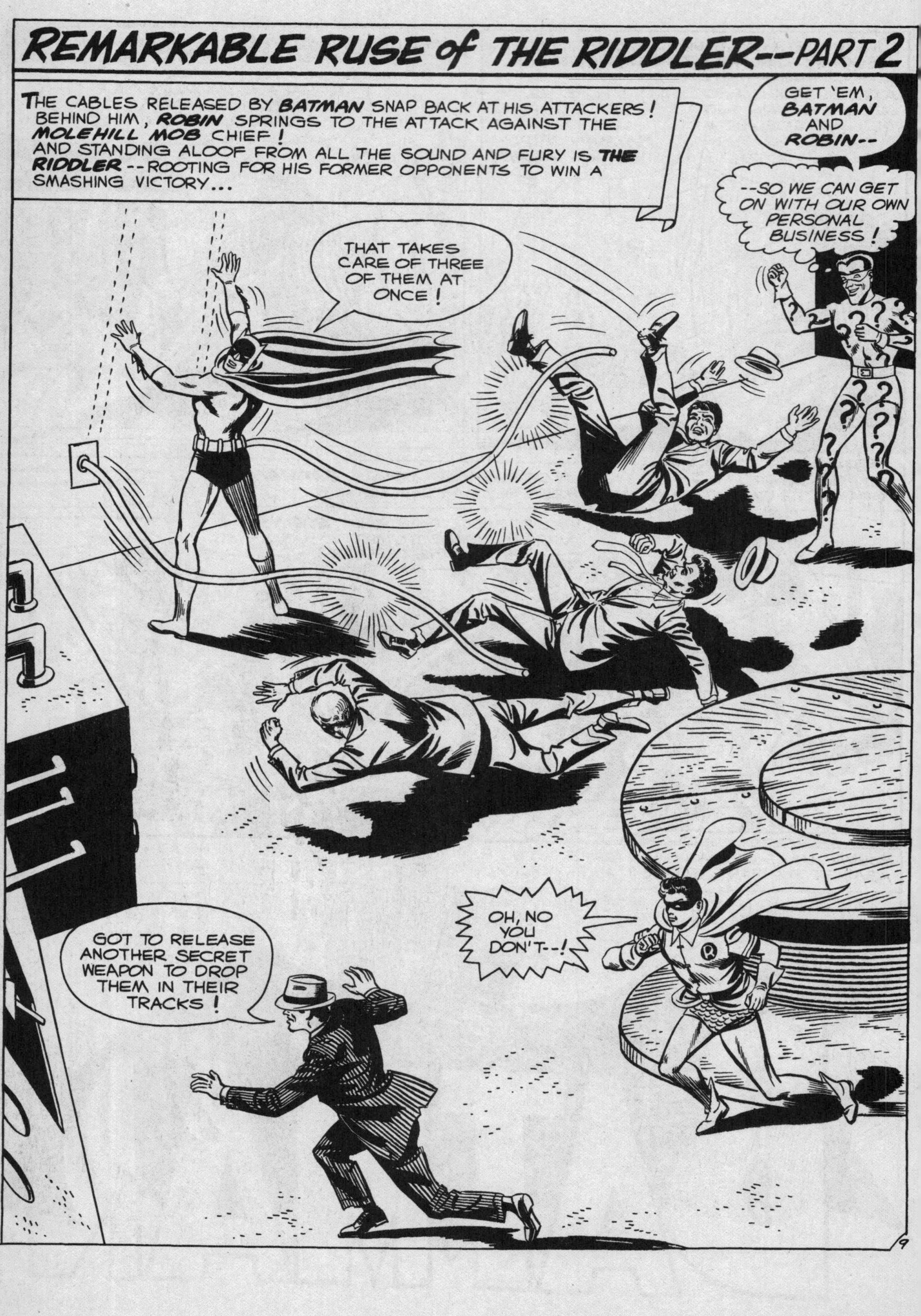
REMARKABLE RUSE of THE RIDDLER--PART 2
THE CABLES RELEASED BY BATMAN SNAP BACK AT HIS ATTACKERS! BEHIND HIM, ROBIN SPRINGS TO THE ATTACK AGAINST THE MOLEHILL MOB CHIEF! AND STANDING ALOOF FROM ALL THE SOUND AND FURY IS THE RIDDLER--ROOTING FOR HIS FORMER OPPONENTS TO WIN A SMASHING VICTORY...
GET 'EM, BATMAN AND ROBIN--
--SO WE CAN GET ON WITH OUR OWN PERSONAL BUSINESS!
THAT TAKES CARE OF THREE OF THEM AT ONCE!
OH, NO YOU DON'T--!
GOT TO RELEASE ANOTHER SECRET WEAPON TO DROP THEM IN THEIR TRACKS!
9

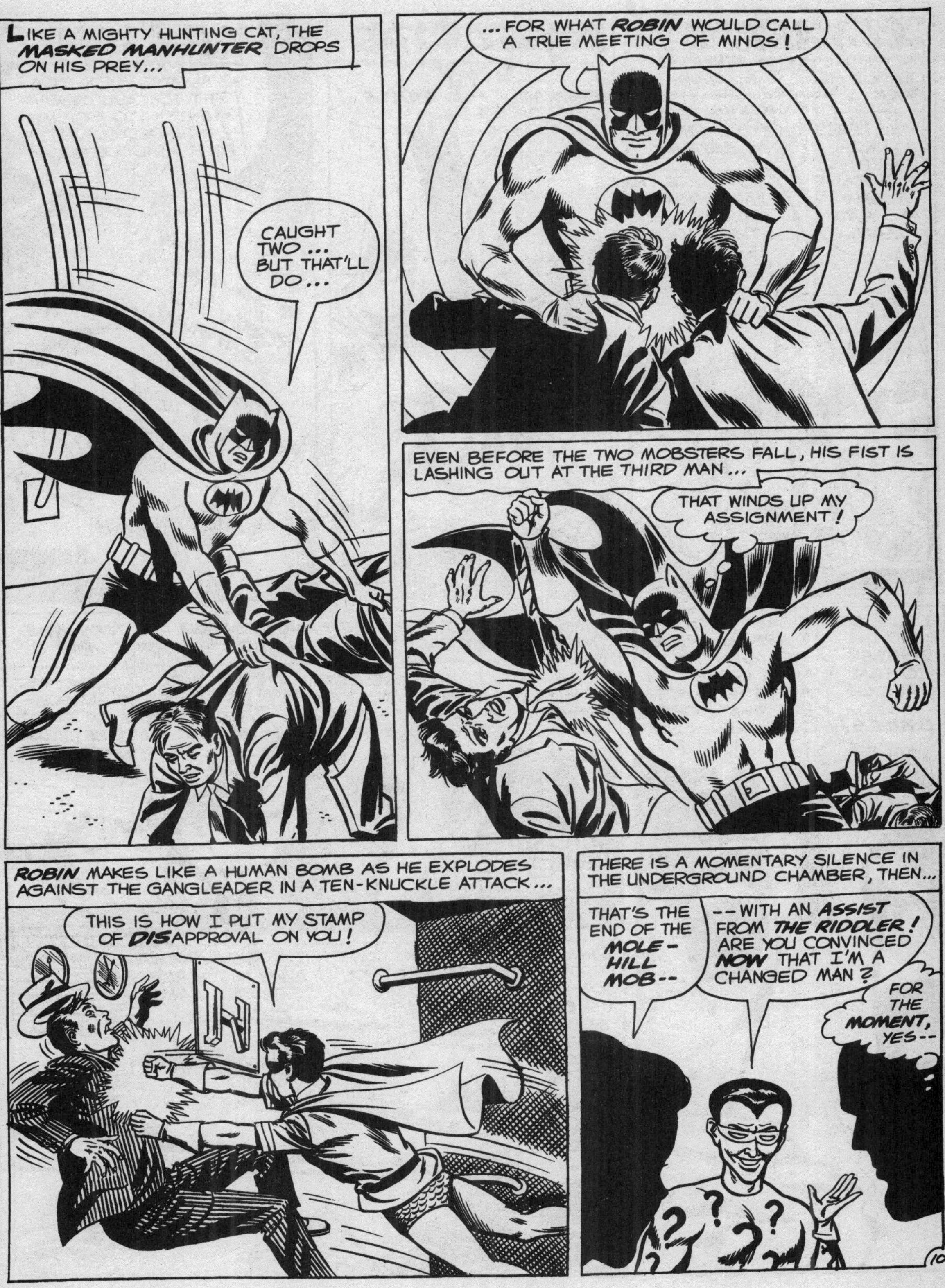
LIKE A MIGHTY HUNTING CAT, THE MASKED MANHUNTER DROPS ON HIS PREY...
CAUGHT TWO... BUT THAT'LL DO...
...FOR WHAT ROBIN WOULD CALL A TRUE MEETING OF MINDS!
EVEN BEFORE THE TWO MOBSTERS FALL, HIS FIST IS LASHING OUT AT THE THIRD MAN...
THAT WINDS UP MY ASSIGNMENT!
ROBIN MAKES LIKE A HUMAN BOMB AS HE EXPLODES AGAINST THE GANGLEADER IN A TEN-KNUCKLE ATTACK...
THIS IS HOW I PUT MY STAMP OF DISAPPROVAL ON YOU!
THERE IS A MOMENTARY SILENCE IN THE UNDERGROUND CHAMBER, THEN...
THAT'S THE END OF THE MOLE-HILL MOB--
--WITH AN ASSIST FROM THE RIDDLER! ARE YOU CONVINCED NOW THAT I'M A CHANGED MAN?
FOR THE MOMENT, YES--
10

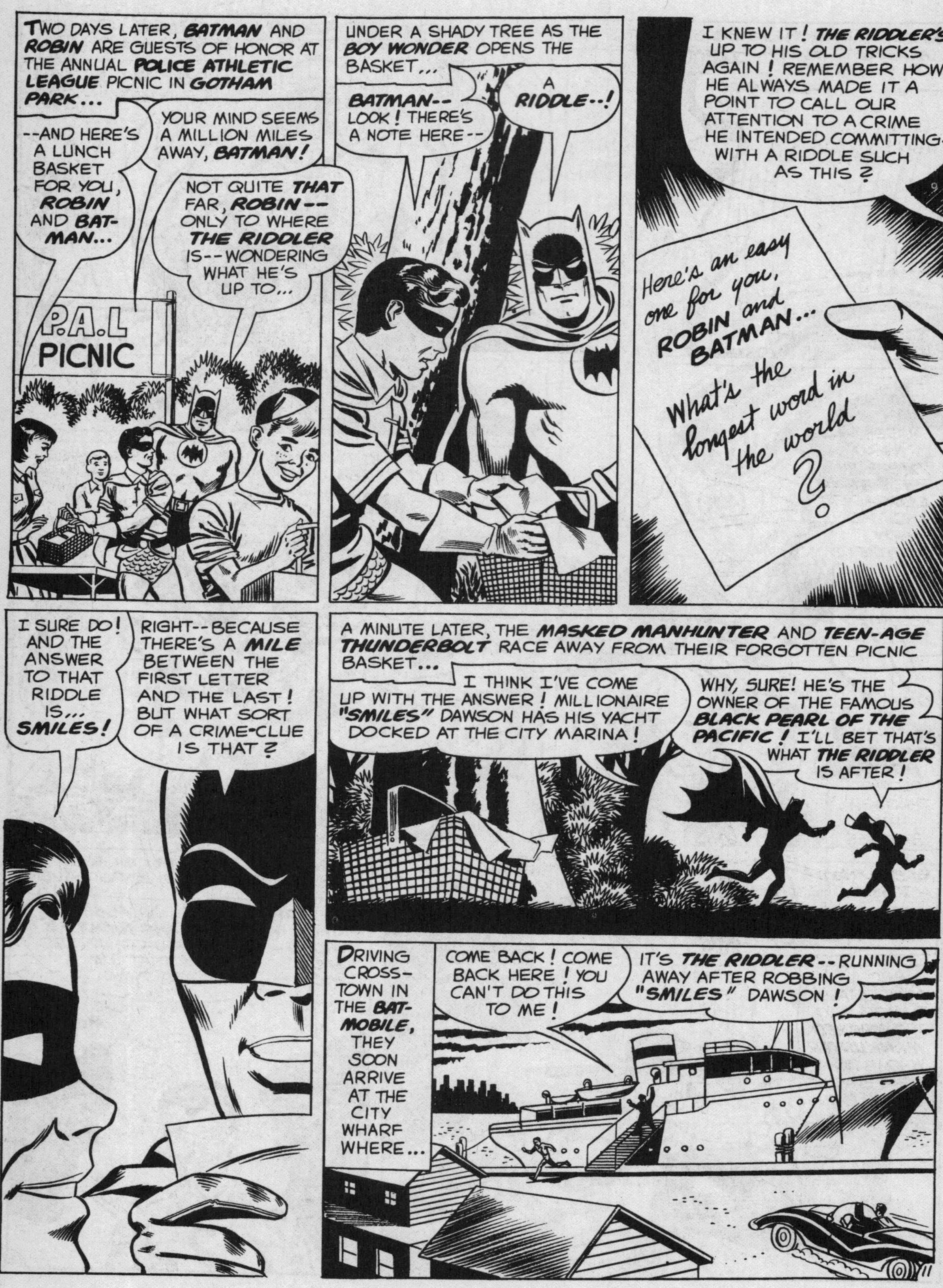
TWO DAYS LATER, BATMAN AND ROBIN ARE GUESTS OF HONOR AT THE ANNUAL POLICE ATHLETIC LEAGUE PICNIC IN GOTHAM PARK...
--AND HERE'S A LUNCH BASKET FOR YOU, ROBIN AND BATMAN...
YOUR MIND SEEMS A MILLION MILES AWAY, BATMAN!
NOT QUITE THAT FAR, ROBIN-- ONLY TO WHERE THE RIDDLER IS--WONDERING WHAT HE'S UP TO...
P.A.L PICNIC
UNDER A SHADY TREE AS THE BOY WONDER OPENS THE BASKET...
BATMAN-- LOOK! THERE'S A NOTE HERE--
A RIDDLE--!
I KNEW IT! THE RIDDLER'S UP TO HIS OLD TRICKS AGAIN! REMEMBER HOW HE ALWAYS MADE IT A POINT TO CALL OUR ATTENTION TO A CRIME HE INTENDED COMMITTING-- WITH A RIDDLE SUCH AS THIS?
Here's an easy one for you, ROBIN and BATMAN... What's the longest word in the world ?
I SURE DO! AND THE ANSWER TO THAT RIDDLE IS... SMILES!
RIGHT--BECAUSE THERE'S A MILE BETWEEN THE FIRST LETTER AND THE LAST! BUT WHAT SORT OF A CRIME-CLUE IS THAT?
A MINUTE LATER, THE MASKED MANHUNTER AND TEEN-AGE THUNDERBOLT RACE AWAY FROM THEIR FORGOTTEN PICNIC BASKET...
I THINK I'VE COME UP WITH THE ANSWER! MILLIONAIRE "SMILES" DAWSON HAS HIS YACHT DOCKED AT THE CITY MARINA!
WHY, SURE! HE'S THE OWNER OF THE FAMOUS BLACK PEARL OF THE PACIFIC! I'LL BET THAT'S WHAT THE RIDDLER IS AFTER!
DRIVING CROSS-TOWN IN THE BATMOBILE, THEY SOON ARRIVE AT THE CITY WHARF WHERE...
COME BACK! COME BACK HERE! YOU CAN'T DO THIS TO ME!
IT'S THE RIDDLER--RUNNING AWAY AFTER ROBBING "SMILES" DAWSON!
11

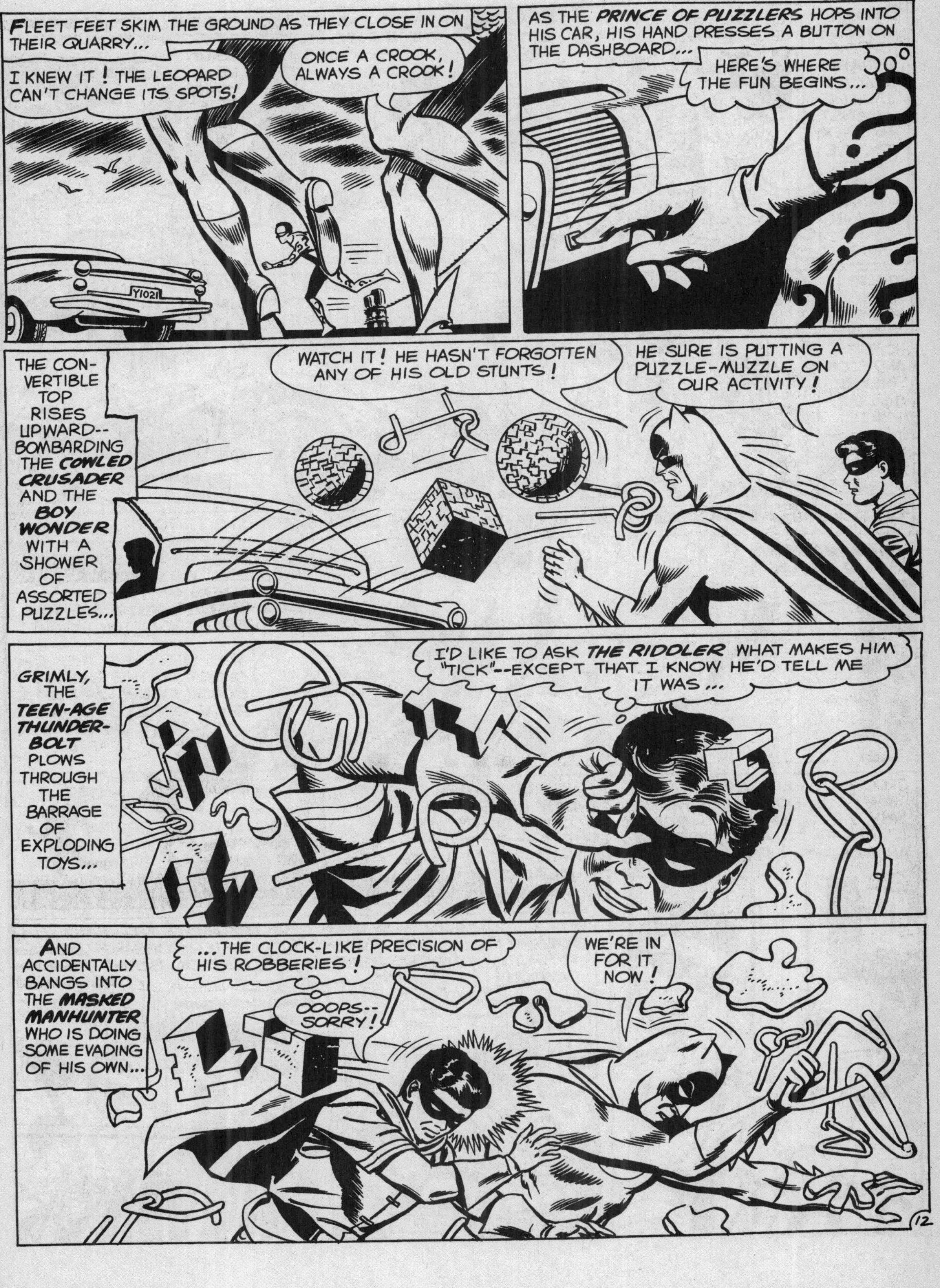
FLEET FEET SKIM THE GROUND AS THEY CLOSE IN ON THEIR QUARRY...
I KNEW IT! THE LEOPARD CAN'T CHANGE ITS SPOTS!
ONCE A CROOK, ALWAYS A CROOK!
Y1021
AS THE PRINCE OF PUZZLERS HOPS INTO HIS CAR, HIS HAND PRESSES A BUTTON ON THE DASHBOARD...
HERE'S WHERE THE FUN BEGINS...
THE CONVERTIBLE TOP RISES UPWARD--BOMBARDING THE COWLED CRUSADER AND THE BOY WONDER WITH A SHOWER OF ASSORTED PUZZLES...
WATCH IT! HE HASN'T FORGOTTEN ANY OF HIS OLD STUNTS!
HE SURE IS PUTTING A PUZZLE-MUZZLE ON OUR ACTIVITY!
GRIMLY, THE TEEN-AGE THUNDERBOLT PLOWS THROUGH THE BARRAGE OF EXPLODING TOYS...
I'D LIKE TO ASK THE RIDDLER WHAT MAKES HIM "TICK"--EXCEPT THAT I KNOW HE'D TELL ME IT WAS...
AND ACCIDENTALLY BANGS INTO THE MASKED MANHUNTER WHO IS DOING SOME EVADING OF HIS OWN...
...THE CLOCK-LIKE PRECISION OF HIS ROBBERIES!
OOOPS--SORRY!
WE'RE IN FOR IT NOW!
12

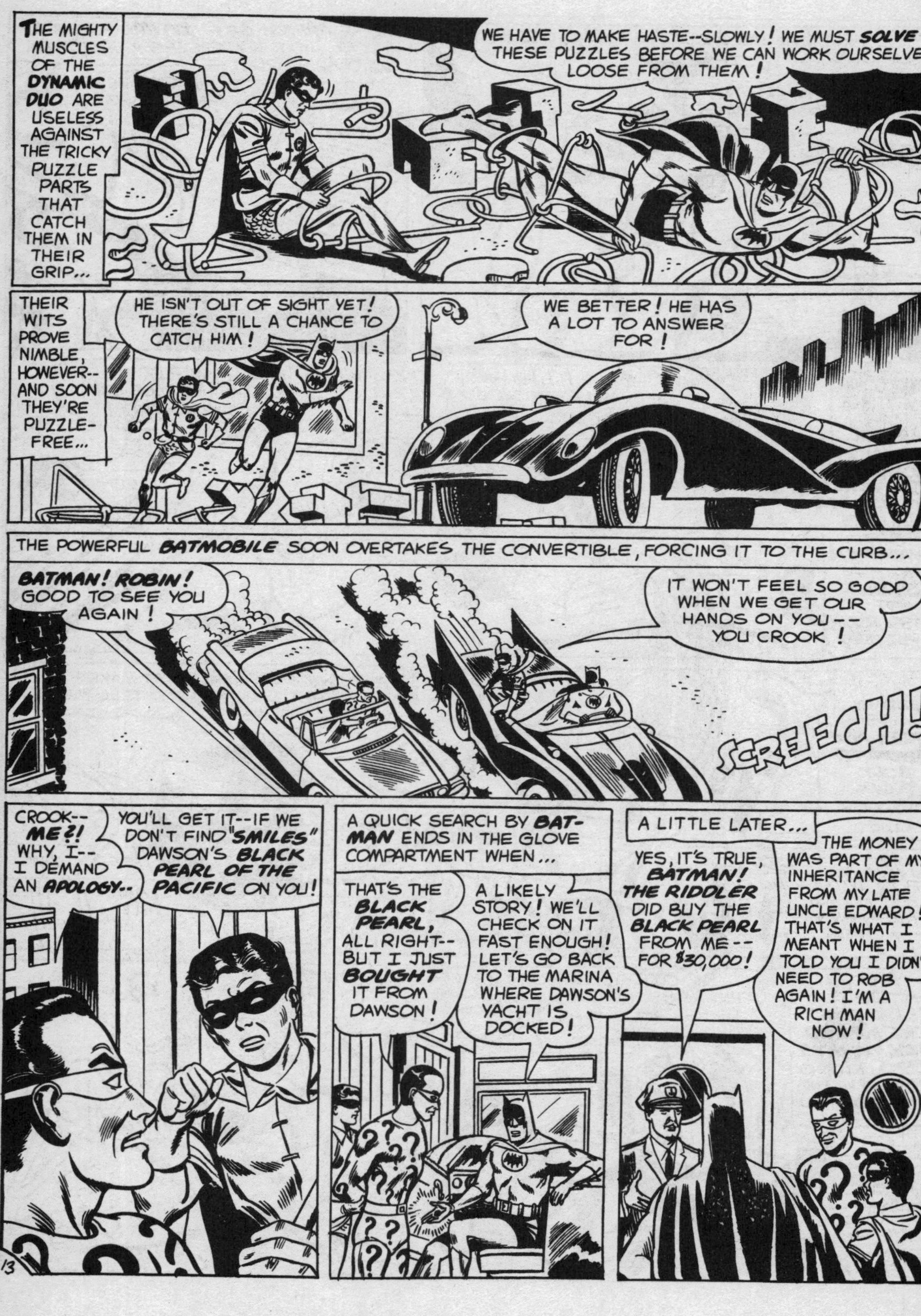
THE MIGHTY MUSCLES OF THE DYNAMIC DUO ARE USELESS AGAINST THE TRICKY PUZZLE PARTS THAT CATCH THEM IN THEIR GRIP...
WE HAVE TO MAKE HASTE--SLOWLY! WE MUST SOLVE THESE PUZZLES BEFORE WE CAN WORK OURSELVES LOOSE FROM THEM!
THEIR WITS PROVE NIMBLE, HOWEVER-- AND SOON THEY'RE PUZZLE-FREE...
HE ISN'T OUT OF SIGHT YET! THERE'S STILL A CHANCE TO CATCH HIM!
WE BETTER! HE HAS A LOT TO ANSWER FOR!
THE POWERFUL BATMOBILE SOON OVERTAKES THE CONVERTIBLE, FORCING IT TO THE CURB...
BATMAN! ROBIN! GOOD TO SEE YOU AGAIN!
IT WON'T FEEL SO GOOD WHEN WE GET OUR HANDS ON YOU -- YOU CROOK!
SCREECH!
CROOK-- ME?! WHY, I-- I DEMAND AN APOLOGY..
YOU'LL GET IT--IF WE DON'T FIND "SMILES" DAWSON'S BLACK PEARL OF THE PACIFIC ON YOU!
13
A QUICK SEARCH BY BATMAN ENDS IN THE GLOVE COMPARTMENT WHEN...
THAT'S THE BLACK PEARL, ALL RIGHT-- BUT I JUST BOUGHT IT FROM DAWSON!
A LIKELY STORY! WE'LL CHECK ON IT FAST ENOUGH! LET'S GO BACK TO THE MARINA WHERE DAWSON'S YACHT IS DOCKED!
A LITTLE LATER...
YES, IT'S TRUE, BATMAN! THE RIDDLER DID BUY THE BLACK PEARL FROM ME -- FOR $30,000!
THE MONEY WAS PART OF MY INHERITANCE FROM MY LATE UNCLE EDWARD! THAT'S WHAT I MEANT WHEN I TOLD YOU I DIDN'T NEED TO ROB AGAIN! I'M A RICH MAN NOW!

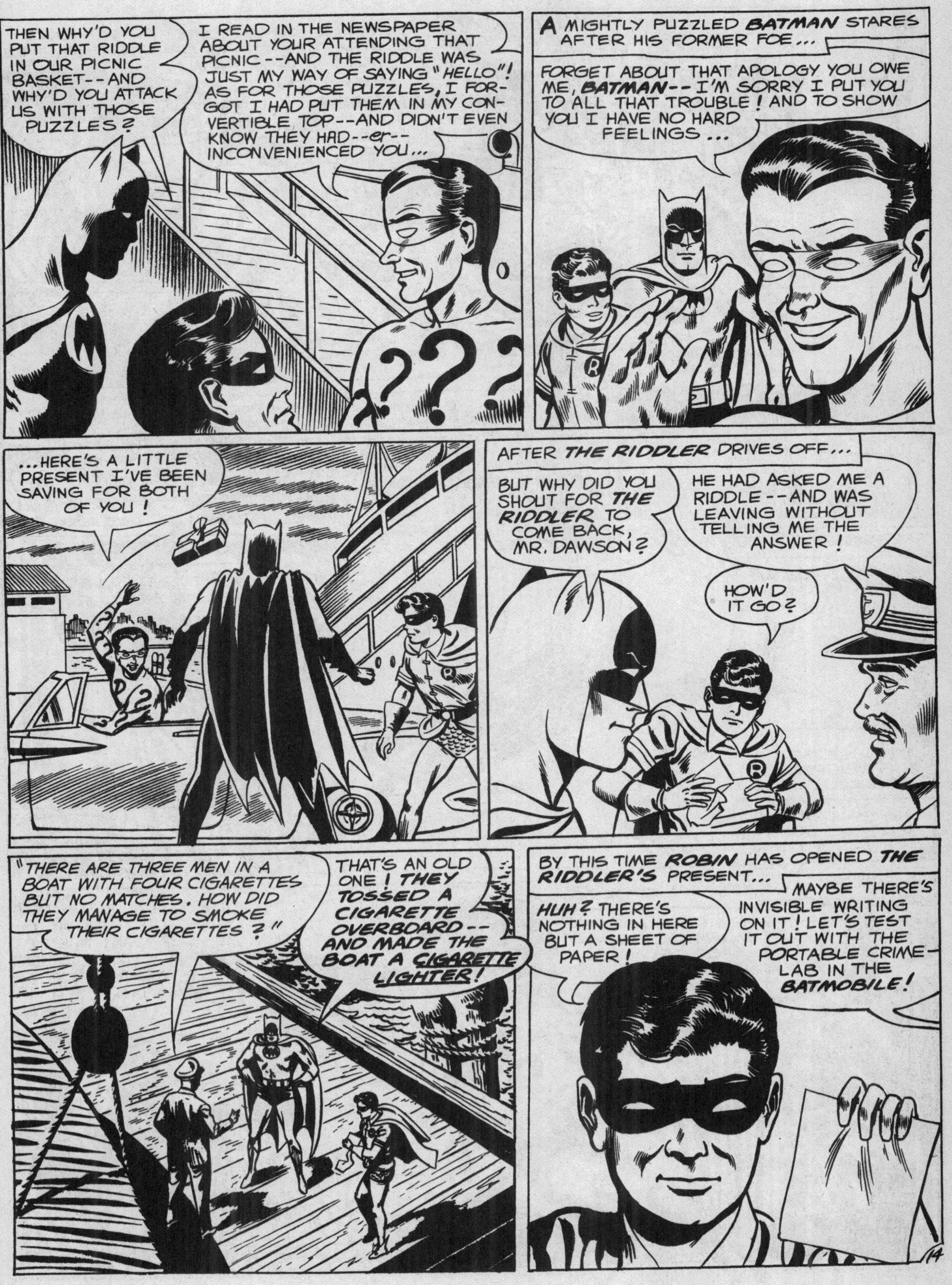
THEN WHY'D YOU PUT THAT RIDDLE IN OUR PICNIC BASKET--AND WHY'D YOU ATTACK US WITH THOSE PUZZLES?
I READ IN THE NEWSPAPER ABOUT YOUR ATTENDING THAT PICNIC--AND THE RIDDLE WAS JUST MY WAY OF SAYING "HELLO"! AS FOR THOSE PUZZLES, I FORGOT I HAD PUT THEM IN MY CONVERTIBLE TOP--AND DIDN'T EVEN KNOW THEY HAD--er--INCONVENIENCED YOU...
A MIGHTLY PUZZLED BATMAN STARES AFTER HIS FORMER FOE...
FORGET ABOUT THAT APOLOGY YOU OWE ME, BATMAN--I'M SORRY I PUT YOU TO ALL THAT TROUBLE! AND TO SHOW YOU I HAVE NO HARD FEELINGS...
...HERE'S A LITTLE PRESENT I'VE BEEN SAVING FOR BOTH OF YOU!
AFTER THE RIDDLER DRIVES OFF...
BUT WHY DID YOU SHOUT FOR THE RIDDLER TO COME BACK, MR. DAWSON?
HE HAD ASKED ME A RIDDLE--AND WAS LEAVING WITHOUT TELLING ME THE ANSWER!
HOW'D IT GO?
"THERE ARE THREE MEN IN A BOAT WITH FOUR CIGARETTES BUT NO MATCHES. HOW DID THEY MANAGE TO SMOKE THEIR CIGARETTES?"
THAT'S AN OLD ONE! THEY TOSSED A CIGARETTE OVERBOARD--AND MADE THE BOAT A CIGARETTE LIGHTER!
BY THIS TIME ROBIN HAS OPENED THE RIDDLER'S PRESENT...
HUH? THERE'S NOTHING IN HERE BUT A SHEET OF PAPER!
MAYBE THERE'S INVISIBLE WRITING ON IT! LET'S TEST IT OUT WITH THE PORTABLE CRIME-LAB IN THE BATMOBILE!
14

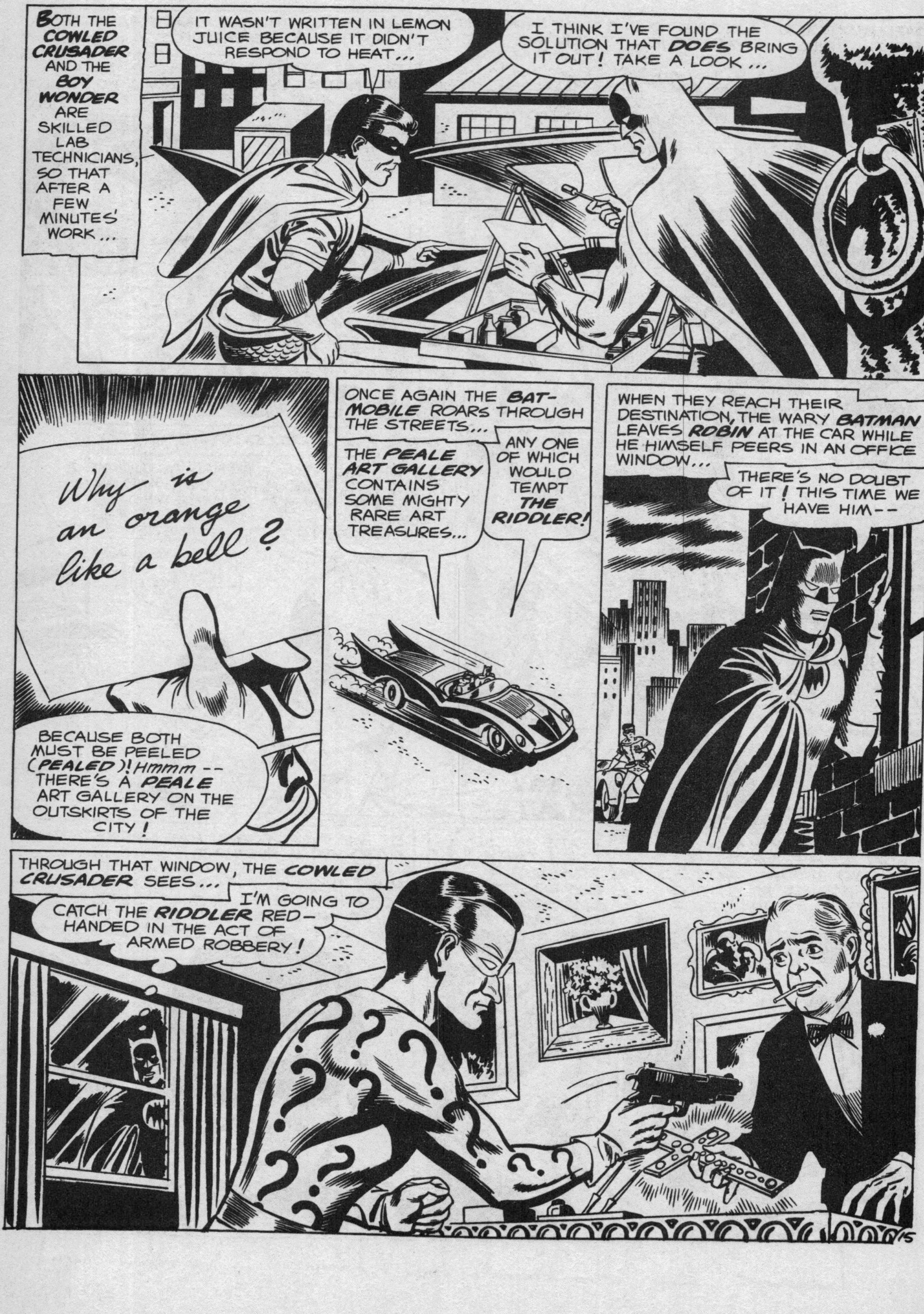

BOTH THE COWLED CRUSADER AND THE BOY WONDER ARE SKILLED LAB TECHNICIANS, SO THAT AFTER A FEW MINUTES' WORK...
IT WASN'T WRITTEN IN LEMON JUICE BECAUSE IT DIDN'T RESPOND TO HEAT...
I THINK I'VE FOUND THE SOLUTION THAT DOES BRING IT OUT! TAKE A LOOK...
Why is an orange like a bell?
BECAUSE BOTH MUST BE PEELED (PEALED)! Hmmm -- THERE'S A PEALE ART GALLERY ON THE OUTSKIRTS OF THE CITY!
ONCE AGAIN THE BAT-MOBILE ROARS THROUGH THE STREETS...
THE PEALE ART GALLERY CONTAINS SOME MIGHTY RARE ART TREASURES...
ANY ONE OF WHICH WOULD TEMPT THE RIDDLER!
WHEN THEY REACH THEIR DESTINATION, THE WARY BATMAN LEAVES ROBIN AT THE CAR WHILE HE HIMSELF PEERS IN AN OFFICE WINDOW...
THERE'S NO DOUBT OF IT! THIS TIME WE HAVE HIM--
THROUGH THAT WINDOW, THE COWLED CRUSADER SEES...
I'M GOING TO CATCH THE RIDDLER RED-HANDED IN THE ACT OF ARMED ROBBERY!
15

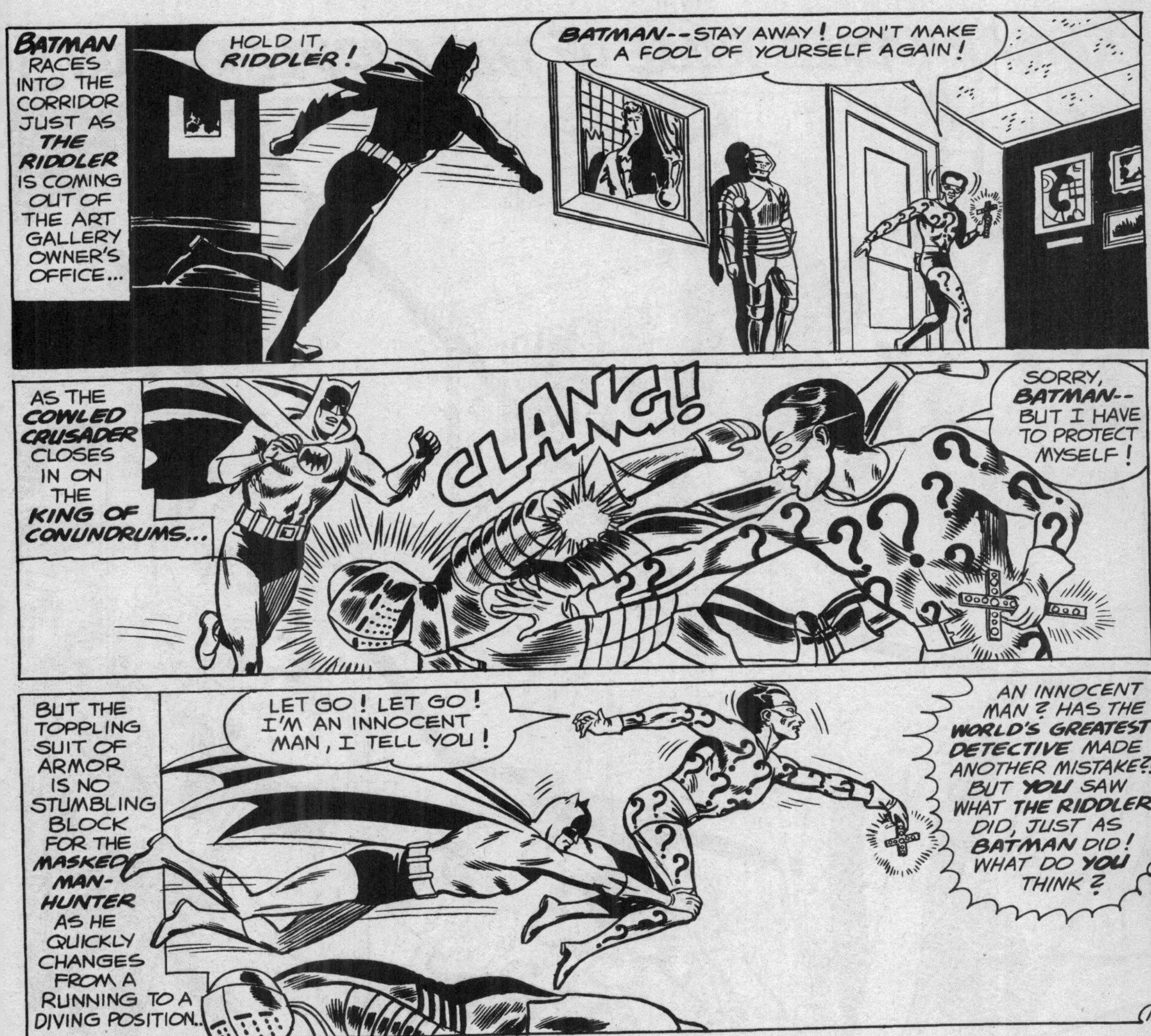
BATMAN RACES INTO THE CORRIDOR JUST AS THE RIDDLER IS COMING OUT OF THE ART GALLERY OWNER'S OFFICE...
HOLD IT, RIDDLER!
BATMAN--STAY AWAY! DON'T MAKE A FOOL OF YOURSELF AGAIN!
AS THE COWLED CRUSADER CLOSES IN ON THE KING OF CONUNDRUMS...
CLANG!
SORRY, BATMAN-- BUT I HAVE TO PROTECT MYSELF!
BUT THE TOPPLING SUIT OF ARMOR IS NO STUMBLING BLOCK FOR THE MASKED MAN-HUNTER AS HE QUICKLY CHANGES FROM A RUNNING TO A DIVING POSITION...
LET GO! LET GO! I'M AN INNOCENT MAN, I TELL YOU!
AN INNOCENT MAN? HAS THE WORLD'S GREATEST DETECTIVE MADE ANOTHER MISTAKE?! BUT YOU SAW WHAT THE RIDDLER DID, JUST AS BATMAN DID! WHAT DO YOU THINK?
16

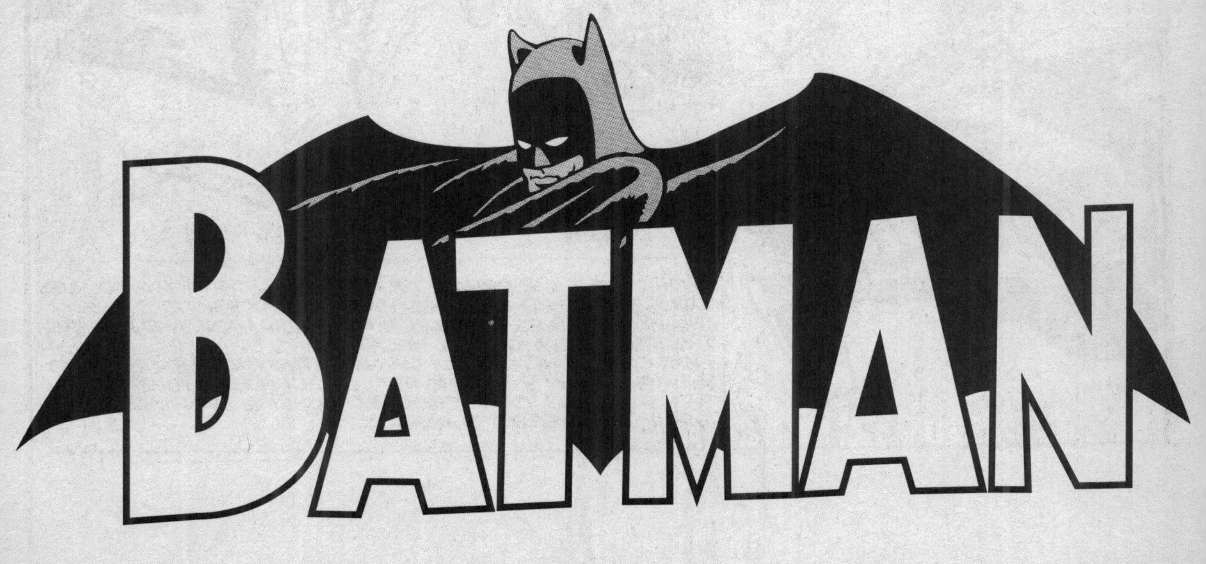
BATMAN

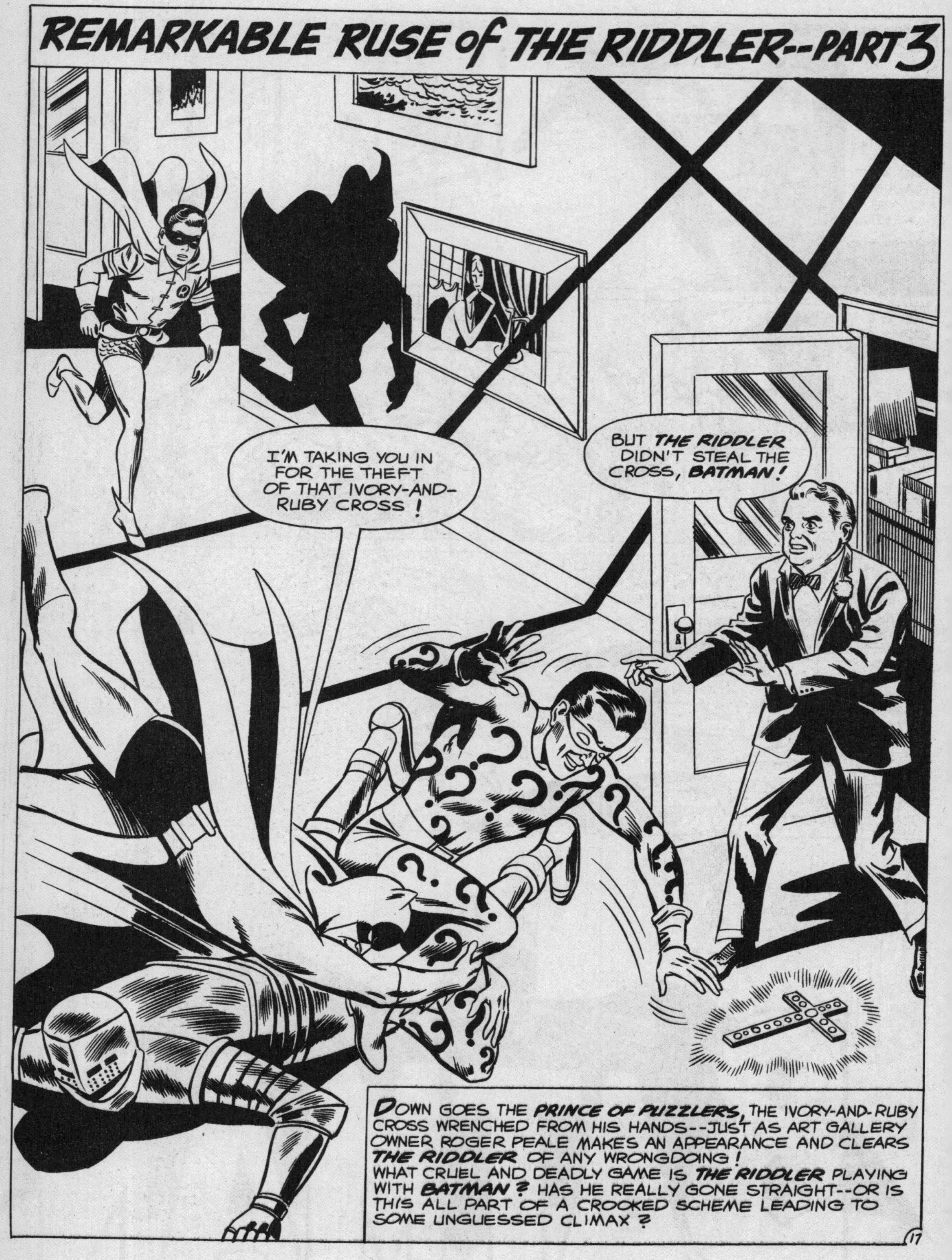
REMARKABLE RUSE of THE RIDDLER--PART 3
I'M TAKING YOU IN FOR THE THEFT OF THAT IVORY-AND-RUBY CROSS!
BUT THE RIDDLER DIDN'T STEAL THE CROSS, BATMAN!
DOWN GOES THE PRINCE OF PUZZLERS, THE IVORY-AND-RUBY CROSS WRENCHED FROM HIS HANDS--JUST AS ART GALLERY OWNER ROGER PEALE MAKES AN APPEARANCE AND CLEARS THE RIDDLER OF ANY WRONGDOING!
WHAT CRUEL AND DEADLY GAME IS THE RIDDLER PLAYING WITH BATMAN? HAS HE REALLY GONE STRAIGHT--OR IS THIS ALL PART OF A CROOKED SCHEME LEADING TO SOME UNGUESSED CLIMAX?
17

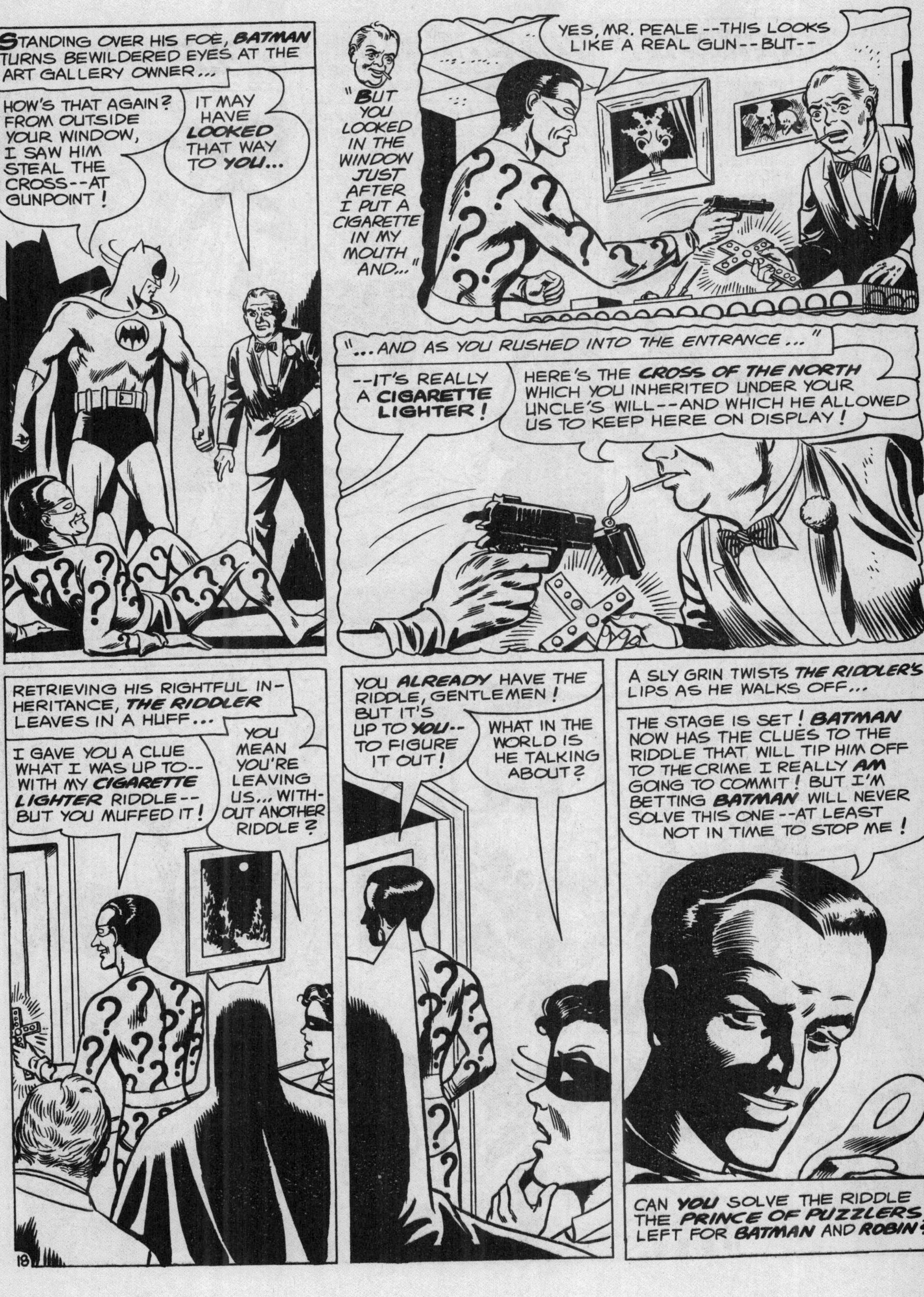
STANDING OVER HIS FOE, BATMAN TURNS BEWILDERED EYES AT THE ART GALLERY OWNER...
HOW'S THAT AGAIN? FROM OUTSIDE YOUR WINDOW, I SAW HIM STEAL THE CROSS--AT GUNPOINT!
IT MAY HAVE LOOKED THAT WAY TO YOU...
"BUT YOU LOOKED IN THE WINDOW JUST AFTER I PUT A CIGARETTE IN MY MOUTH AND..."
YES, MR. PEALE--THIS LOOKS LIKE A REAL GUN--BUT--
"...AND AS YOU RUSHED INTO THE ENTRANCE..."
--IT'S REALLY A CIGARETTE LIGHTER!
HERE'S THE CROSS OF THE NORTH WHICH YOU INHERITED UNDER YOUR UNCLE'S WILL--AND WHICH HE ALLOWED US TO KEEP HERE ON DISPLAY!
RETRIEVING HIS RIGHTFUL INHERITANCE, THE RIDDLER LEAVES IN A HUFF...
I GAVE YOU A CLUE WHAT I WAS UP TO--WITH MY CIGARETTE LIGHTER RIDDLE--BUT YOU MUFFED IT!
YOU MEAN YOU'RE LEAVING US... WITHOUT ANOTHER RIDDLE?
YOU ALREADY HAVE THE RIDDLE, GENTLEMEN! BUT IT'S UP TO YOU--TO FIGURE IT OUT!
WHAT IN THE WORLD IS HE TALKING ABOUT?
A SLY GRIN TWISTS THE RIDDLER'S LIPS AS HE WALKS OFF...
THE STAGE IS SET! BATMAN NOW HAS THE CLUES TO THE RIDDLE THAT WILL TIP HIM OFF TO THE CRIME I REALLY AM GOING TO COMMIT! BUT I'M BETTING BATMAN WILL NEVER SOLVE THIS ONE--AT LEAST NOT IN TIME TO STOP ME!
CAN YOU SOLVE THE RIDDLE THE PRINCE OF PUZZLERS LEFT FOR BATMAN AND ROBIN?
18

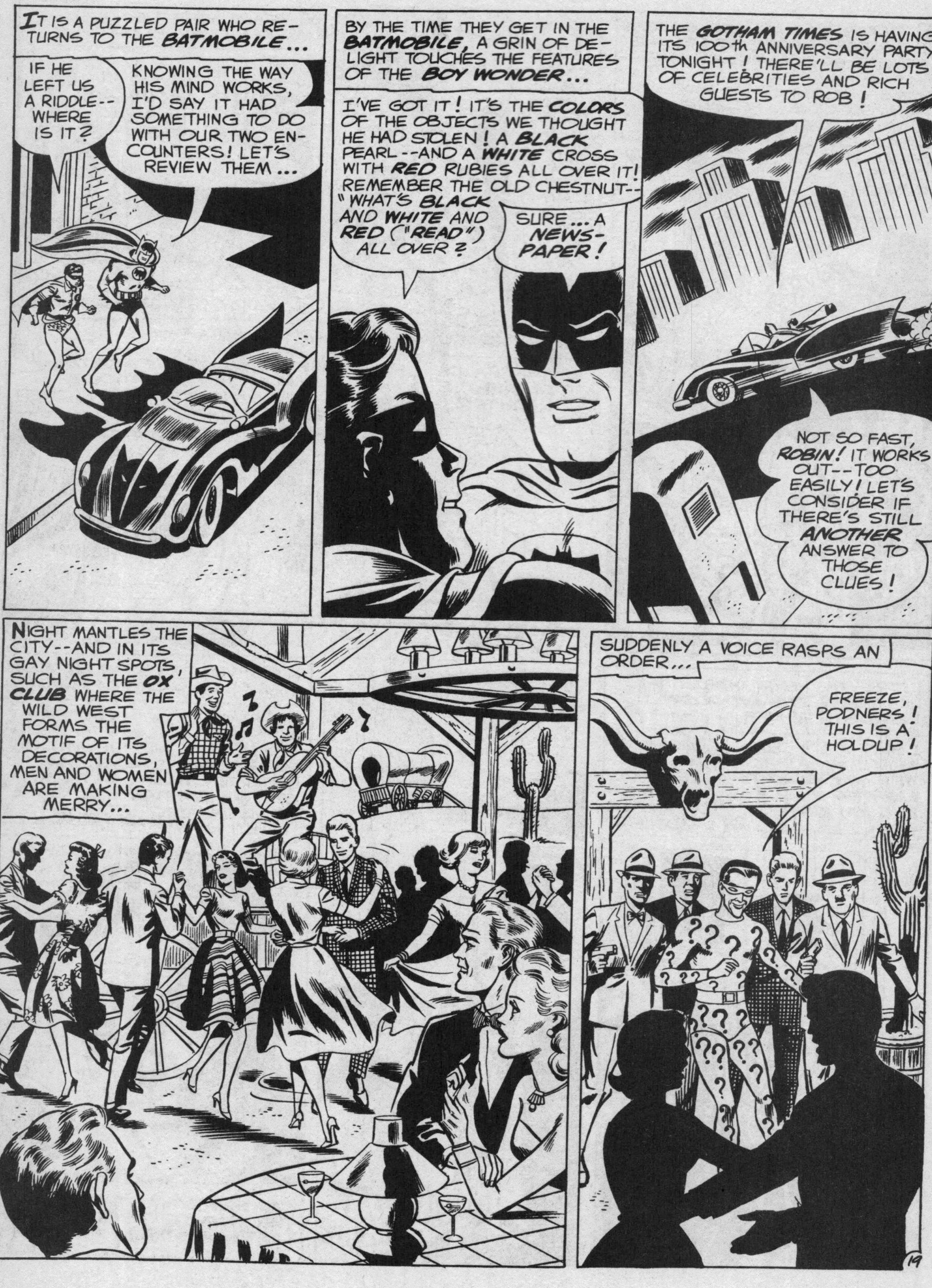
IT IS A PUZZLED PAIR WHO RETURNS TO THE BATMOBILE...
IF HE LEFT US A RIDDLE--WHERE IS IT?
KNOWING THE WAY HIS MIND WORKS, I'D SAY IT HAD SOMETHING TO DO WITH OUR TWO ENCOUNTERS! LET'S REVIEW THEM...
BY THE TIME THEY GET IN THE BATMOBILE, A GRIN OF DELIGHT TOUCHES THE FEATURES OF THE BOY WONDER...
I'VE GOT IT! IT'S THE COLORS OF THE OBJECTS WE THOUGHT HE HAD STOLEN! A BLACK PEARL--AND A WHITE CROSS WITH RED RUBIES ALL OVER IT! REMEMBER THE OLD CHESTNUT--"WHAT'S BLACK AND WHITE AND RED ("READ") ALL OVER?
SURE... A NEWSPAPER!
THE GOTHAM TIMES IS HAVING ITS 100th ANNIVERSARY PARTY TONIGHT! THERE'LL BE LOTS OF CELEBRITIES AND RICH GUESTS TO ROB!
NOT SO FAST, ROBIN! IT WORKS OUT--TOO EASILY! LET'S CONSIDER IF THERE'S STILL ANOTHER ANSWER TO THOSE CLUES!
NIGHT MANTLES THE CITY--AND IN ITS GAY NIGHT SPOTS, SUCH AS THE OX CLUB WHERE THE WILD WEST FORMS THE MOTIF OF ITS DECORATIONS, MEN AND WOMEN ARE MAKING MERRY...
SUDDENLY A VOICE RASPS AN ORDER...
FREEZE, PODNERS! THIS IS A HOLDUP!
19

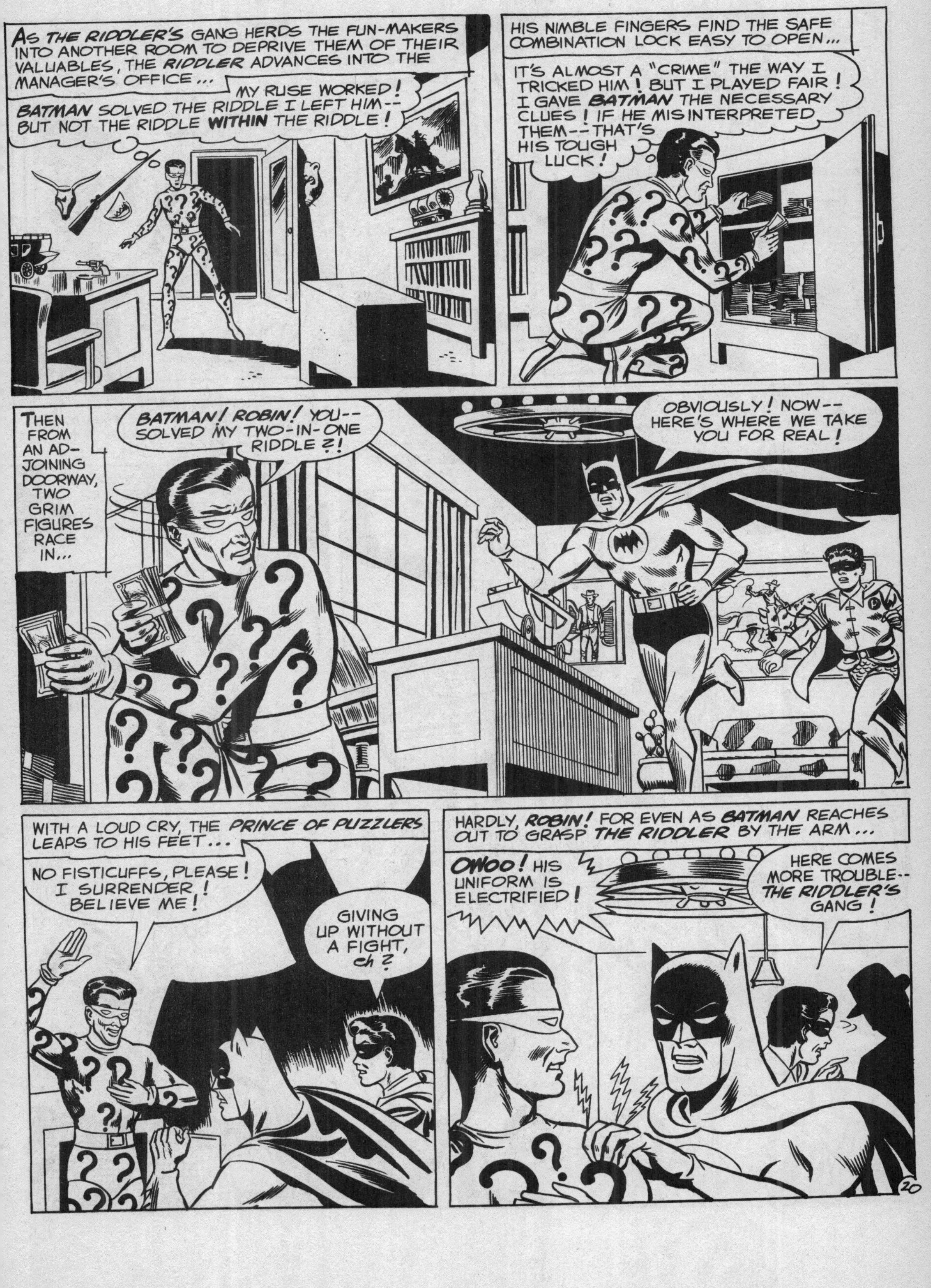
AS THE RIDDLER'S GANG HERDS THE FUN-MAKERS INTO ANOTHER ROOM TO DEPRIVE THEM OF THEIR VALUABLES, THE RIDDLER ADVANCES INTO THE MANAGER'S OFFICE...
MY RUSE WORKED! BATMAN SOLVED THE RIDDLE I LEFT HIM-- BUT NOT THE RIDDLE WITHIN THE RIDDLE!
HIS NIMBLE FINGERS FIND THE SAFE COMBINATION LOCK EASY TO OPEN...
IT'S ALMOST A "CRIME" THE WAY I TRICKED HIM! BUT I PLAYED FAIR! I GAVE BATMAN THE NECESSARY CLUES! IF HE MISINTERPRETED THEM--THAT'S HIS TOUGH LUCK!
THEN FROM AN AD-JOINING DOORWAY, TWO GRIM FIGURES RACE IN...
BATMAN! ROBIN! YOU-- SOLVED MY TWO-IN-ONE RIDDLE?!
OBVIOUSLY! NOW-- HERE'S WHERE WE TAKE YOU FOR REAL!
WITH A LOUD CRY, THE PRINCE OF PUZZLERS LEAPS TO HIS FEET...
NO FISTICUFFS, PLEASE! I SURRENDER! BELIEVE ME!
GIVING UP WITHOUT A FIGHT, eh?
HARDLY, ROBIN! FOR EVEN AS BATMAN REACHES OUT TO GRASP THE RIDDLER BY THE ARM...
OWOO! HIS UNIFORM IS ELECTRIFIED!
HERE COMES MORE TROUBLE-- THE RIDDLER'S GANG!
20

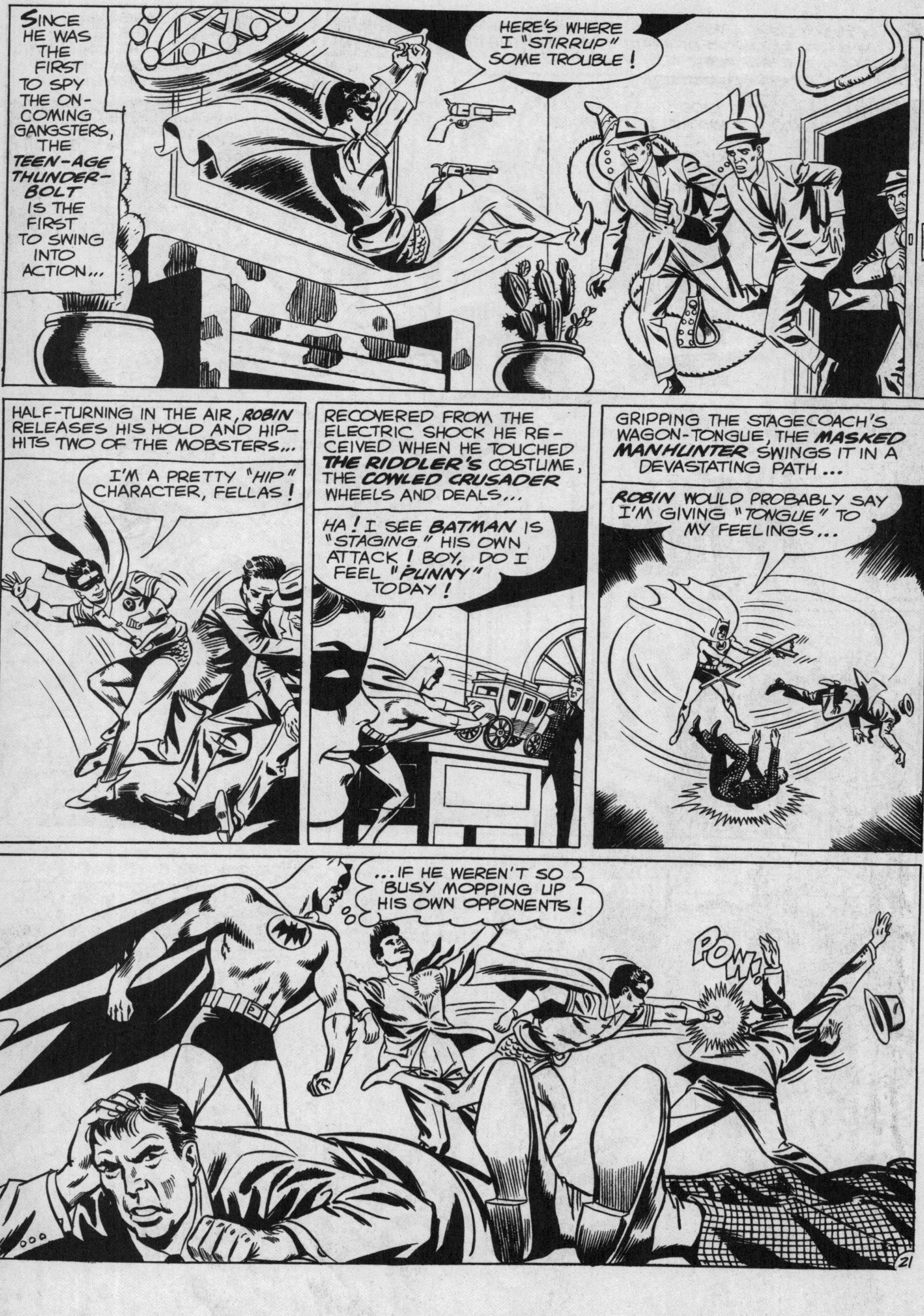
SINCE HE WAS THE FIRST TO SPY THE ON-COMING GANGSTERS, THE TEEN-AGE THUNDER-BOLT IS THE FIRST TO SWING INTO ACTION...
HERE'S WHERE I "STIRRUP" SOME TROUBLE!
HALF-TURNING IN THE AIR, ROBIN RELEASES HIS HOLD AND HIP-HITS TWO OF THE MOBSTERS...
I'M A PRETTY "HIP" CHARACTER, FELLAS!
RECOVERED FROM THE ELECTRIC SHOCK HE RE-CEIVED WHEN HE TOUCHED THE RIDDLER'S COSTUME, THE COWLED CRUSADER WHEELS AND DEALS...
HA! I SEE BATMAN IS "STAGING" HIS OWN ATTACK! BOY, DO I FEEL "PUNNY" TODAY!
GRIPPING THE STAGECOACH'S WAGON-TONGUE, THE MASKED MANHUNTER SWINGS IT IN A DEVASTATING PATH...
ROBIN WOULD PROBABLY SAY I'M GIVING "TONGUE" TO MY FEELINGS...
...IF HE WEREN'T SO BUSY MOPPING UP HIS OWN OPPONENTS!
POW!
21

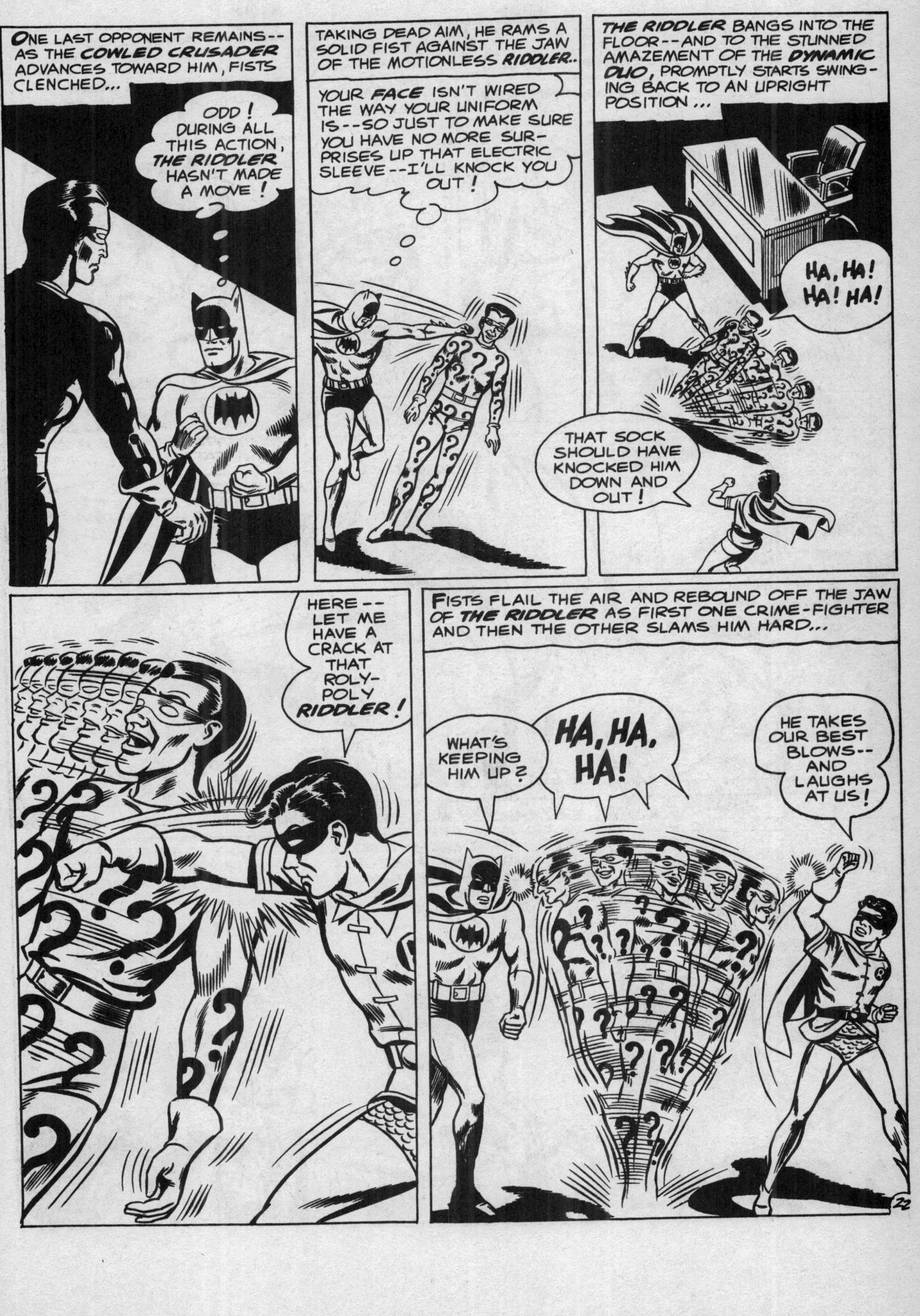
ONE LAST OPPONENT REMAINS-- AS THE COWLED CRUSADER ADVANCES TOWARD HIM, FISTS CLENCHED...
ODD! DURING ALL THIS ACTION, THE RIDDLER HASN'T MADE A MOVE!
TAKING DEAD AIM, HE RAMS A SOLID FIST AGAINST THE JAW OF THE MOTIONLESS RIDDLER..
YOUR FACE ISN'T WIRED THE WAY YOUR UNIFORM IS--SO JUST TO MAKE SURE YOU HAVE NO MORE SURPRISES UP THAT ELECTRIC SLEEVE--I'LL KNOCK YOU OUT!
THE RIDDLER BANGS INTO THE FLOOR--AND TO THE STUNNED AMAZEMENT OF THE DYNAMIC DUO, PROMPTLY STARTS SWINGING BACK TO AN UPRIGHT POSITION...
HA, HA! HA! HA!
THAT SOCK SHOULD HAVE KNOCKED HIM DOWN AND OUT!
HERE-- LET ME HAVE A CRACK AT THAT ROLY-POLY RIDDLER!
FISTS FLAIL THE AIR AND REBOUND OFF THE JAW OF THE RIDDLER AS FIRST ONE CRIME-FIGHTER AND THEN THE OTHER SLAMS HIM HARD...
WHAT'S KEEPING HIM UP?
HA, HA, HA!
HE TAKES OUR BEST BLOWS-- AND LAUGHS AT US!
22

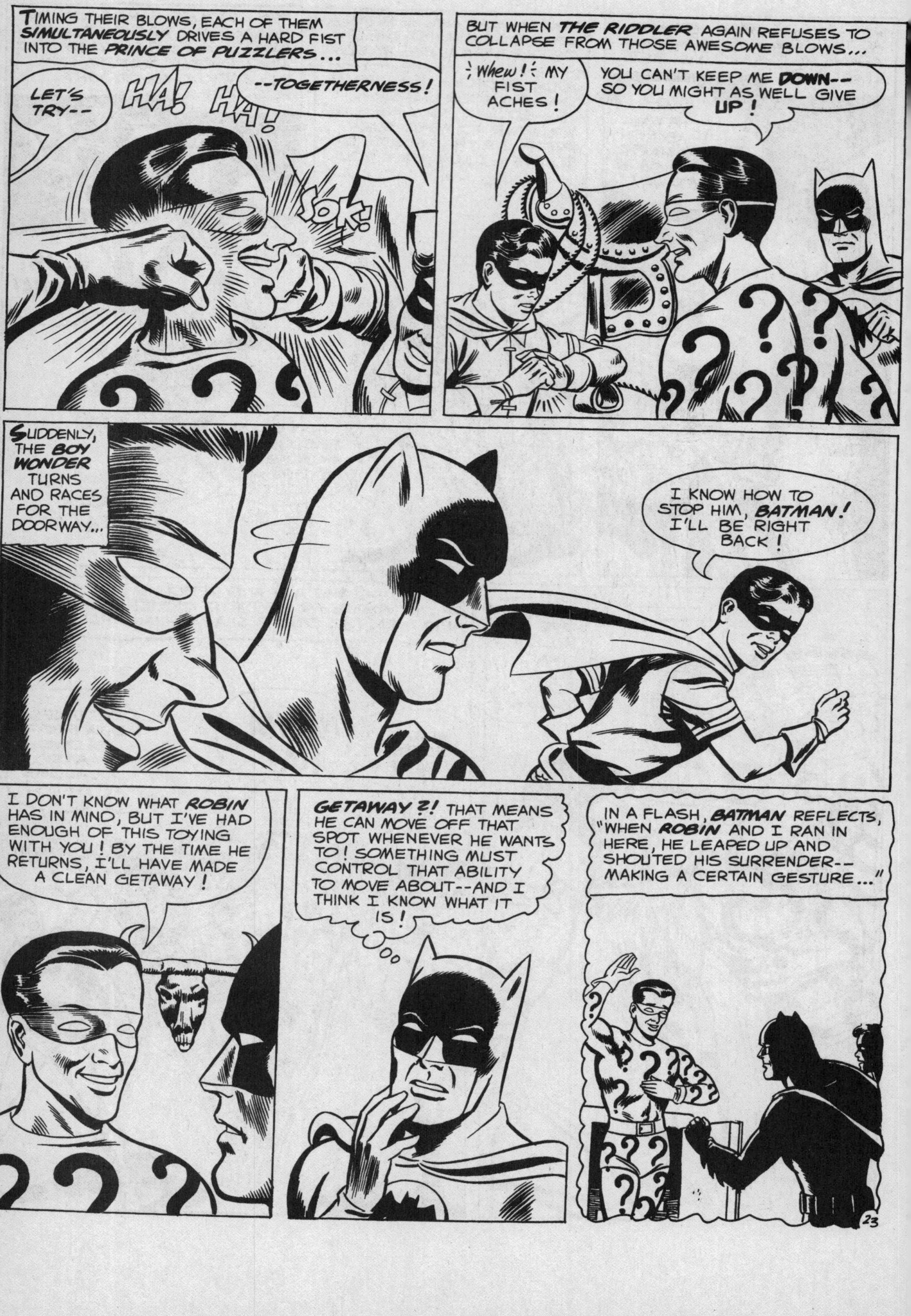
TIMING THEIR BLOWS, EACH OF THEM SIMULTANEOUSLY DRIVES A HARD FIST INTO THE PRINCE OF PUZZLERS...
LET'S TRY--
--TOGETHERNESS!
HA! HA!
SOK!
BUT WHEN THE RIDDLER AGAIN REFUSES TO COLLAPSE FROM THOSE AWESOME BLOWS...
Whew! MY FIST ACHES!
YOU CAN'T KEEP ME DOWN-- SO YOU MIGHT AS WELL GIVE UP!
SUDDENLY, THE BOY WONDER TURNS AND RACES FOR THE DOORWAY...
I KNOW HOW TO STOP HIM, BATMAN! I'LL BE RIGHT BACK!
I DON'T KNOW WHAT ROBIN HAS IN MIND, BUT I'VE HAD ENOUGH OF THIS TOYING WITH YOU! BY THE TIME HE RETURNS, I'LL HAVE MADE A CLEAN GETAWAY!
GETAWAY?! THAT MEANS HE CAN MOVE OFF THAT SPOT WHENEVER HE WANTS TO! SOMETHING MUST CONTROL THAT ABILITY TO MOVE ABOUT--AND I THINK I KNOW WHAT IT IS!
IN A FLASH, BATMAN REFLECTS, "WHEN ROBIN AND I RAN IN HERE, HE LEAPED UP AND SHOUTED HIS SURRENDER-- MAKING A CERTAIN GESTURE..."
23

WHEN *ROBIN* RETURNS, HE SEES *THE RIDDLER* DRAPED OVER THE SAFE...

MY BLUFF WORKED! I FIGURED IF I TOLD HIM I KNEW HOW TO OVERCOME HIM, HE'D DO--OR SAY--SOMETHING TO GIVE YOU A CLUE HOW TO DEAL WITH HIM!

HE SURE DID--BY BOASTING HE WAS ABOUT TO MAKE HIS GETAWAY!

I RECALLED THAT HE TOUCHED THE *DOT PART* OF THE LARGE QUESTION MARK ON HIS CHEST WHEN WE RAN IN! IMMEDIATELY AFTER THAT-- HE NEVER MOVED FROM THAT SPOT ON THE FLOOR HE WAS ON! I DEDUCED THAT DOT ACTIVATED HIS ELECTRIC SUIT AND HIS ROLY-POLY DEFENSE!

"*SO ALL I HAD TO DO WAS REACH OUT AND PRESS THAT DOT--THE ONLY PART OF HIS UNIFORM THAT WAS NOT ELECTRIFIED--TO DEACTIVATE THE CONTROLS...*"

NO, *BATMAN--* DON'T!

"THEN I REALLY LET HIM HAVE IT!..."

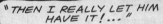

AS THE *MASKED MAN-HUNTER* LIFTS THE DAZED *RIDDLER* TO HIS FEET...

CON--GRATULATIONS, *BATMAN--* ON FIGURING OUT-- THE RIGHT RIDDLE--

IT WASN'T A *NEWS-PAPER* YOU MEANT-- THOUGH *ROBIN* AND I WENT THERE TO MAKE YOU THINK WE'D FALLEN FOR YOUR TRICK!

BATMAN FIGURED OUT THAT YOUR RIDDLE REFERRED TO THE *SHAPES* OF THE OBJECTS, NOT THEIR *COLORS!* THERE-FORE THE RIDDLE WAS: "MY FIRST IS A *CIRCLE* (the pearl), MY SECOND IS A *CROSS* (the ivory relic). JOIN THEM TO-GETHER--OR BE AT A LOSS!" JOINING A CIRCLE TO A CROSS MAKES THE WORD *OX*-- MEANING YOU INTENDED TO ROB THE PLUSH *OX CLUB!*

24

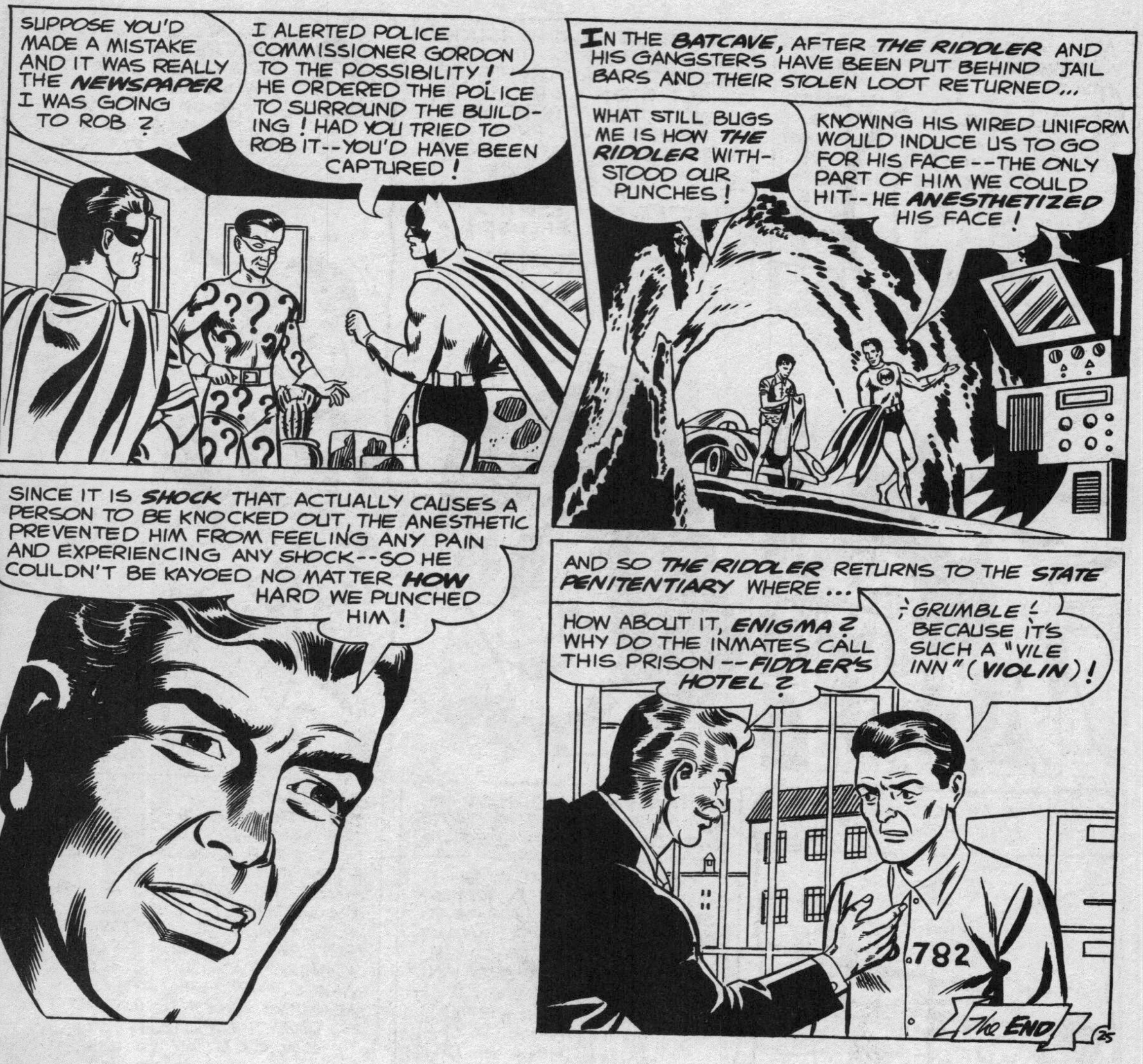
SUPPOSE YOU'D MADE A MISTAKE AND IT WAS REALLY THE NEWSPAPER I WAS GOING TO ROB ?
I ALERTED POLICE COMMISSIONER GORDON TO THE POSSIBILITY! HE ORDERED THE POLICE TO SURROUND THE BUILDING! HAD YOU TRIED TO ROB IT--YOU'D HAVE BEEN CAPTURED!
IN THE BATCAVE, AFTER THE RIDDLER AND HIS GANGSTERS HAVE BEEN PUT BEHIND JAIL BARS AND THEIR STOLEN LOOT RETURNED...
WHAT STILL BUGS ME IS HOW THE RIDDLER WITHSTOOD OUR PUNCHES!
KNOWING HIS WIRED UNIFORM WOULD INDUCE US TO GO FOR HIS FACE--THE ONLY PART OF HIM WE COULD HIT--HE ANESTHETIZED HIS FACE!
SINCE IT IS SHOCK THAT ACTUALLY CAUSES A PERSON TO BE KNOCKED OUT, THE ANESTHETIC PREVENTED HIM FROM FEELING ANY PAIN AND EXPERIENCING ANY SHOCK--SO HE COULDN'T BE KAYOED NO MATTER HOW HARD WE PUNCHED HIM!
AND SO THE RIDDLER RETURNS TO THE STATE PENITENTIARY WHERE...
HOW ABOUT IT, ENIGMA? WHY DO THE INMATES CALL THIS PRISON--FIDDLER'S HOTEL?
¡GRUMBLE! BECAUSE IT'S SUCH A "VILE INN" (VIOLIN)!
782
The END
25

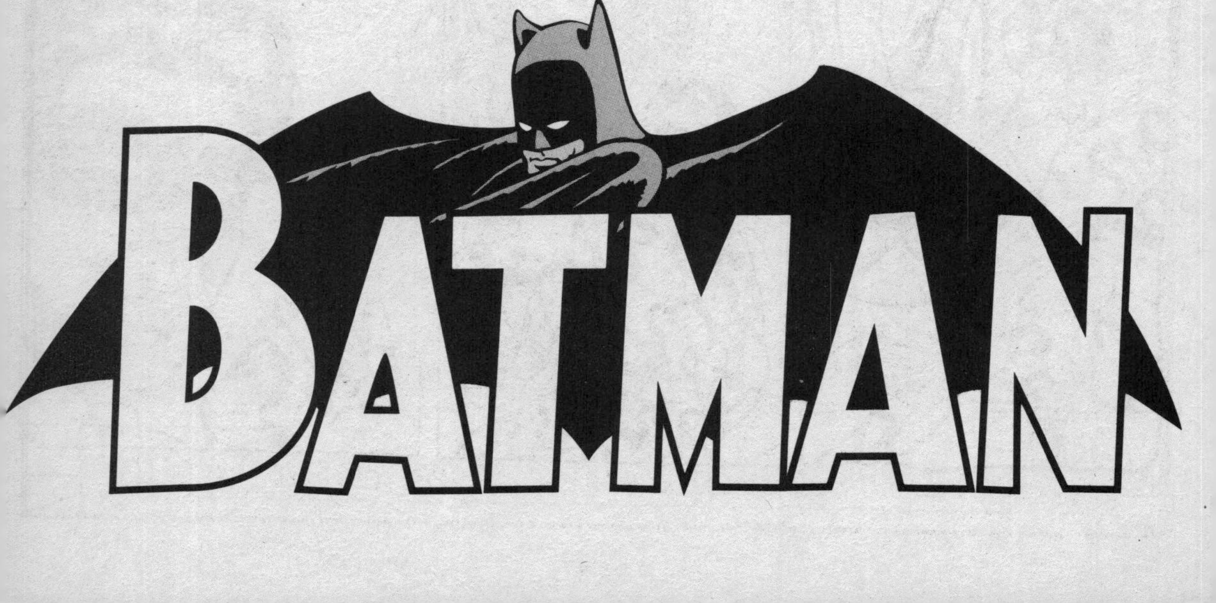
BATMAN

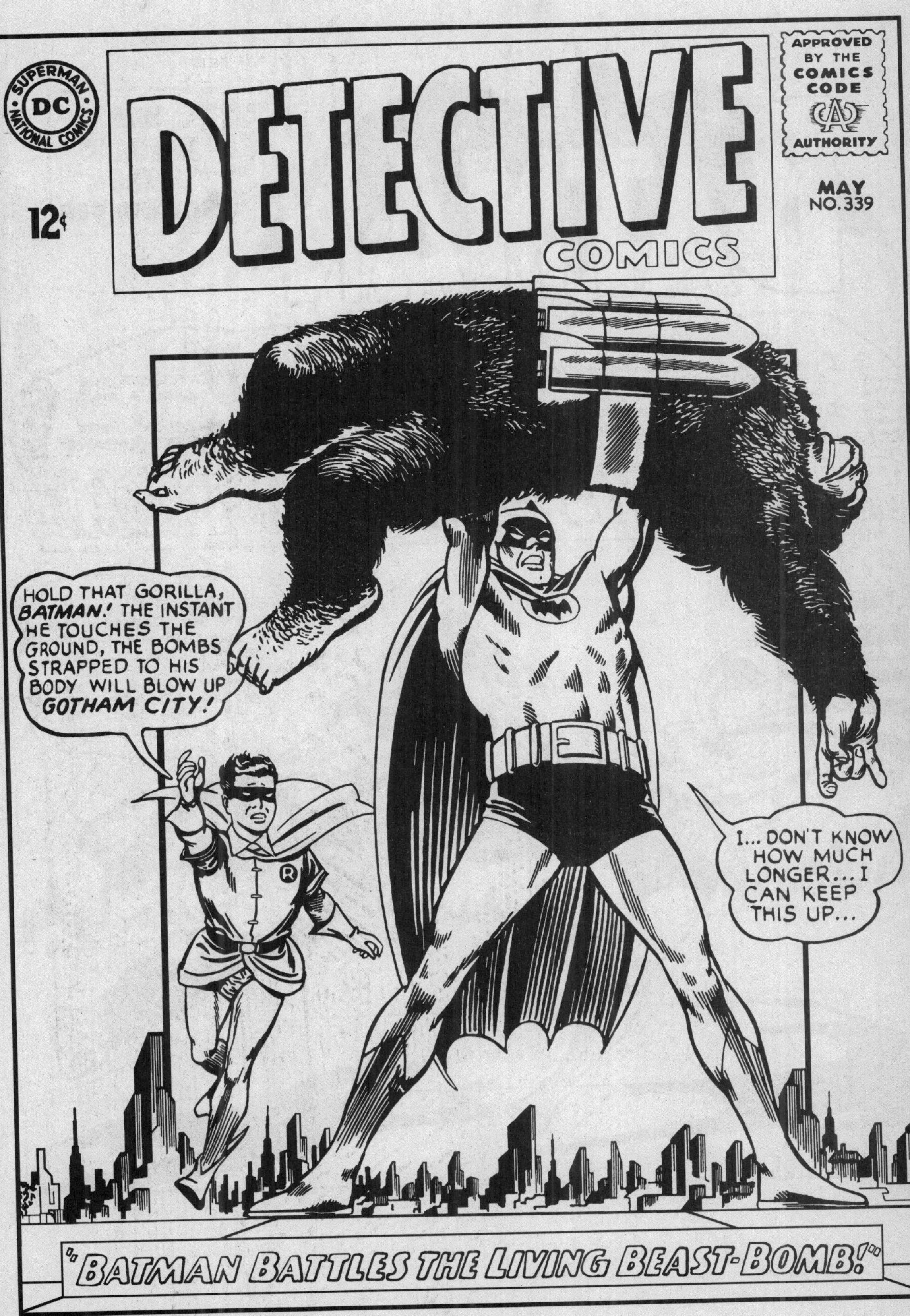
SUPERMAN DC NATIONAL COMICS
DETECTIVE COMICS
APPROVED BY THE COMICS CODE AUTHORITY
12¢
MAY NO. 339
HOLD THAT GORILLA, BATMAN! THE INSTANT HE TOUCHES THE GROUND, THE BOMBS STRAPPED TO HIS BODY WILL BLOW UP GOTHAM CITY!
I... DON'T KNOW HOW MUCH LONGER... I CAN KEEP THIS UP...
"BATMAN BATTLES THE LIVING BEAST-BOMB!"

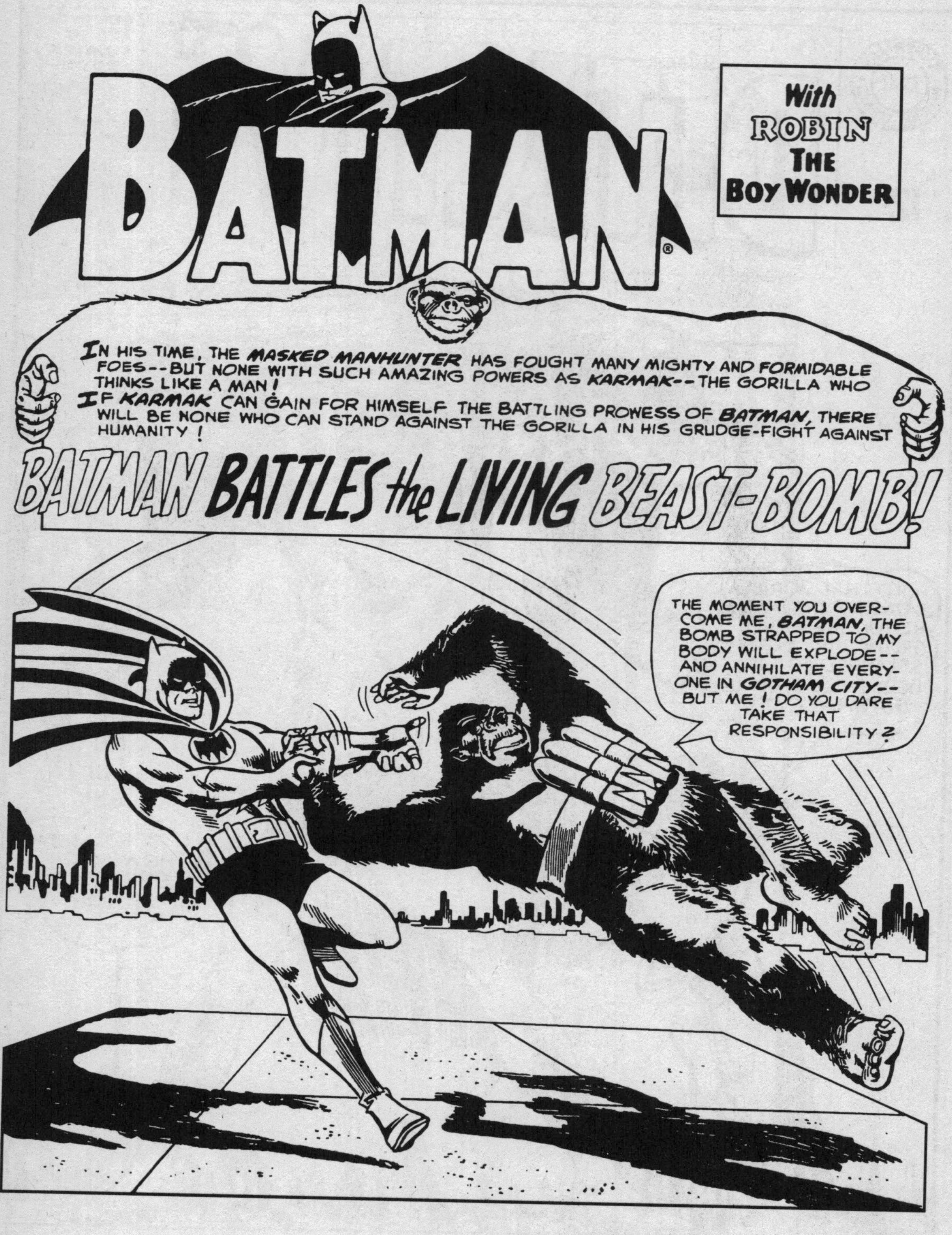
BATMAN®
With ROBIN THE BOY WONDER
IN HIS TIME, THE MASKED MANHUNTER HAS FOUGHT MANY MIGHTY AND FORMIDABLE FOES--BUT NONE WITH SUCH AMAZING POWERS AS KARMAK--THE GORILLA WHO THINKS LIKE A MAN!
IF KARMAK CAN GAIN FOR HIMSELF THE BATTLING PROWESS OF BATMAN, THERE WILL BE NONE WHO CAN STAND AGAINST THE GORILLA IN HIS GRUDGE-FIGHT AGAINST HUMANITY!
BATMAN BATTLES the LIVING BEAST-BOMB!
THE MOMENT YOU OVER-COME ME, BATMAN, THE BOMB STRAPPED TO MY BODY WILL EXPLODE--AND ANNIHILATE EVERY-ONE IN GOTHAM CITY--BUT ME! DO YOU DARE TAKE THAT RESPONSIBILITY?

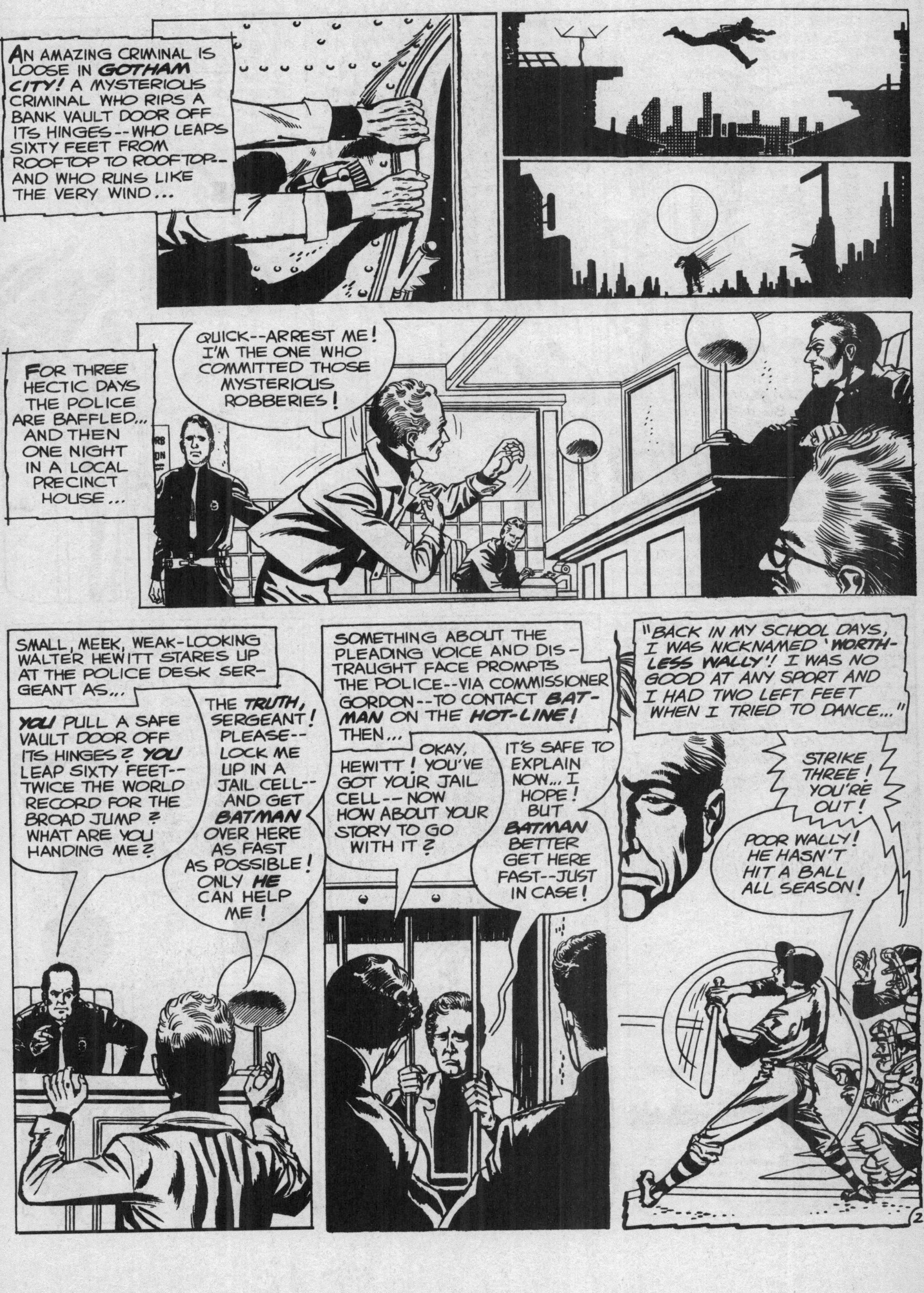
AN AMAZING CRIMINAL IS LOOSE IN GOTHAM CITY! A MYSTERIOUS CRIMINAL WHO RIPS A BANK VAULT DOOR OFF ITS HINGES--WHO LEAPS SIXTY FEET FROM ROOFTOP TO ROOFTOP--AND WHO RUNS LIKE THE VERY WIND...
FOR THREE HECTIC DAYS THE POLICE ARE BAFFLED... AND THEN ONE NIGHT IN A LOCAL PRECINCT HOUSE...
QUICK--ARREST ME! I'M THE ONE WHO COMMITTED THOSE MYSTERIOUS ROBBERIES!
SMALL, MEEK, WEAK-LOOKING WALTER HEWITT STARES UP AT THE POLICE DESK SERGEANT AS...
YOU! PULL A SAFE VAULT DOOR OFF ITS HINGES? YOU LEAP SIXTY FEET--TWICE THE WORLD RECORD FOR THE BROAD JUMP? WHAT ARE YOU HANDING ME?
THE TRUTH, SERGEANT! PLEASE--LOCK ME UP IN A JAIL CELL--AND GET BATMAN OVER HERE AS FAST AS POSSIBLE! ONLY HE CAN HELP ME!
SOMETHING ABOUT THE PLEADING VOICE AND DISTRAUGHT FACE PROMPTS THE POLICE--VIA COMMISSIONER GORDON--TO CONTACT BATMAN ON THE HOT-LINE! THEN...
OKAY, HEWITT! YOU'VE GOT YOUR JAIL CELL--NOW HOW ABOUT YOUR STORY TO GO WITH IT?
IT'S SAFE TO EXPLAIN NOW... I HOPE! BUT BATMAN BETTER GET HERE FAST--JUST IN CASE!
"BACK IN MY SCHOOL DAYS, I WAS NICKNAMED 'WORTHLESS WALLY'! I WAS NO GOOD AT ANY SPORT AND I HAD TWO LEFT FEET WHEN I TRIED TO DANCE..."
STRIKE THREE! YOU'RE OUT!
POOR WALLY! HE HASN'T HIT A BALL ALL SEASON!
2

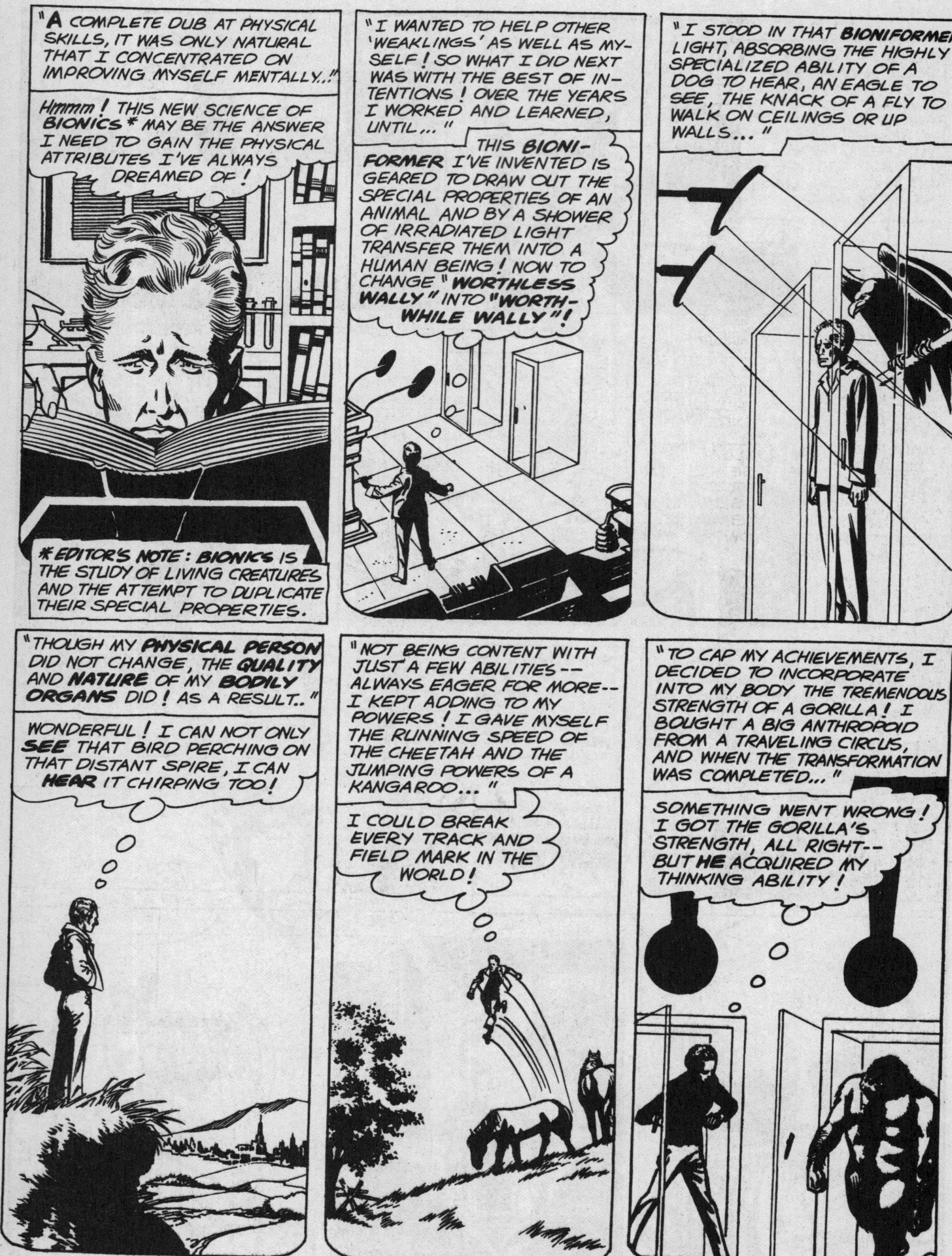
"A COMPLETE DUB AT PHYSICAL SKILLS, IT WAS ONLY NATURAL THAT I CONCENTRATED ON IMPROVING MYSELF MENTALLY..!"
Hmmm! THIS NEW SCIENCE OF BIONICS* MAY BE THE ANSWER I NEED TO GAIN THE PHYSICAL ATTRIBUTES I'VE ALWAYS DREAMED OF!
*EDITOR'S NOTE: BIONICS IS THE STUDY OF LIVING CREATURES AND THE ATTEMPT TO DUPLICATE THEIR SPECIAL PROPERTIES.
"I WANTED TO HELP OTHER 'WEAKLINGS' AS WELL AS MYSELF! SO WHAT I DID NEXT WAS WITH THE BEST OF INTENTIONS! OVER THE YEARS I WORKED AND LEARNED, UNTIL..."
THIS BIONIFORMER I'VE INVENTED IS GEARED TO DRAW OUT THE SPECIAL PROPERTIES OF AN ANIMAL AND BY A SHOWER OF IRRADIATED LIGHT TRANSFER THEM INTO A HUMAN BEING! NOW TO CHANGE "WORTHLESS WALLY" INTO "WORTHWHILE WALLY"!
"I STOOD IN THAT BIONIFORMER LIGHT, ABSORBING THE HIGHLY SPECIALIZED ABILITY OF A DOG TO HEAR, AN EAGLE TO SEE, THE KNACK OF A FLY TO WALK ON CEILINGS OR UP WALLS..."
"THOUGH MY PHYSICAL PERSON DID NOT CHANGE, THE QUALITY AND NATURE OF MY BODILY ORGANS DID! AS A RESULT.."
WONDERFUL! I CAN NOT ONLY SEE THAT BIRD PERCHING ON THAT DISTANT SPIRE, I CAN HEAR IT CHIRPING TOO!
"NOT BEING CONTENT WITH JUST A FEW ABILITIES -- ALWAYS EAGER FOR MORE -- I KEPT ADDING TO MY POWERS! I GAVE MYSELF THE RUNNING SPEED OF THE CHEETAH AND THE JUMPING POWERS OF A KANGAROO..."
I COULD BREAK EVERY TRACK AND FIELD MARK IN THE WORLD!
"TO CAP MY ACHIEVEMENTS, I DECIDED TO INCORPORATE INTO MY BODY THE TREMENDOUS STRENGTH OF A GORILLA! I BOUGHT A BIG ANTHROPOID FROM A TRAVELING CIRCUS, AND WHEN THE TRANSFORMATION WAS COMPLETED..."
SOMETHING WENT WRONG! I GOT THE GORILLA'S STRENGTH, ALL RIGHT-- BUT HE ACQUIRED MY THINKING ABILITY!
3

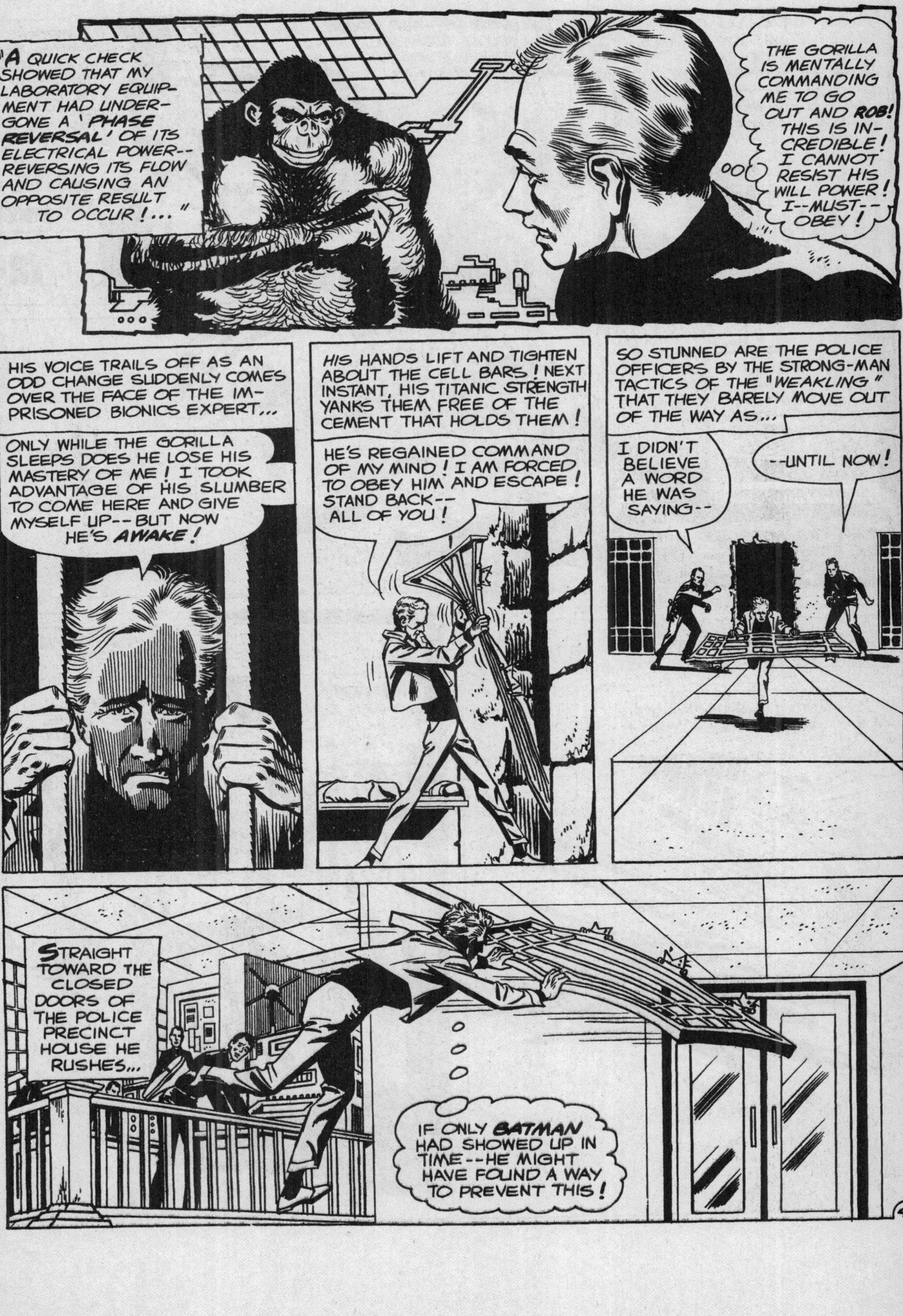
"A QUICK CHECK SHOWED THAT MY LABORATORY EQUIPMENT HAD UNDERGONE A 'PHASE REVERSAL' OF ITS ELECTRICAL POWER--REVERSING ITS FLOW AND CAUSING AN OPPOSITE RESULT TO OCCUR!..."
THE GORILLA IS MENTALLY COMMANDING ME TO GO OUT AND ROB! THIS IS INCREDIBLE! I CANNOT RESIST HIS WILL POWER! I--MUST--OBEY!
HIS VOICE TRAILS OFF AS AN ODD CHANGE SUDDENLY COMES OVER THE FACE OF THE IMPRISONED BIONICS EXPERT...
ONLY WHILE THE GORILLA SLEEPS DOES HE LOSE HIS MASTERY OF ME! I TOOK ADVANTAGE OF HIS SLUMBER TO COME HERE AND GIVE MYSELF UP--BUT NOW HE'S AWAKE!
HIS HANDS LIFT AND TIGHTEN ABOUT THE CELL BARS! NEXT INSTANT, HIS TITANIC STRENGTH YANKS THEM FREE OF THE CEMENT THAT HOLDS THEM!
HE'S REGAINED COMMAND OF MY MIND! I AM FORCED TO OBEY HIM AND ESCAPE! STAND BACK--ALL OF YOU!
SO STUNNED ARE THE POLICE OFFICERS BY THE STRONG-MAN TACTICS OF THE "WEAKLING" THAT THEY BARELY MOVE OUT OF THE WAY AS...
I DIDN'T BELIEVE A WORD HE WAS SAYING--
--UNTIL NOW!
STRAIGHT TOWARD THE CLOSED DOORS OF THE POLICE PRECINCT HOUSE HE RUSHES...
IF ONLY BATMAN HAD SHOWED UP IN TIME--HE MIGHT HAVE FOUND A WAY TO PREVENT THIS!
4

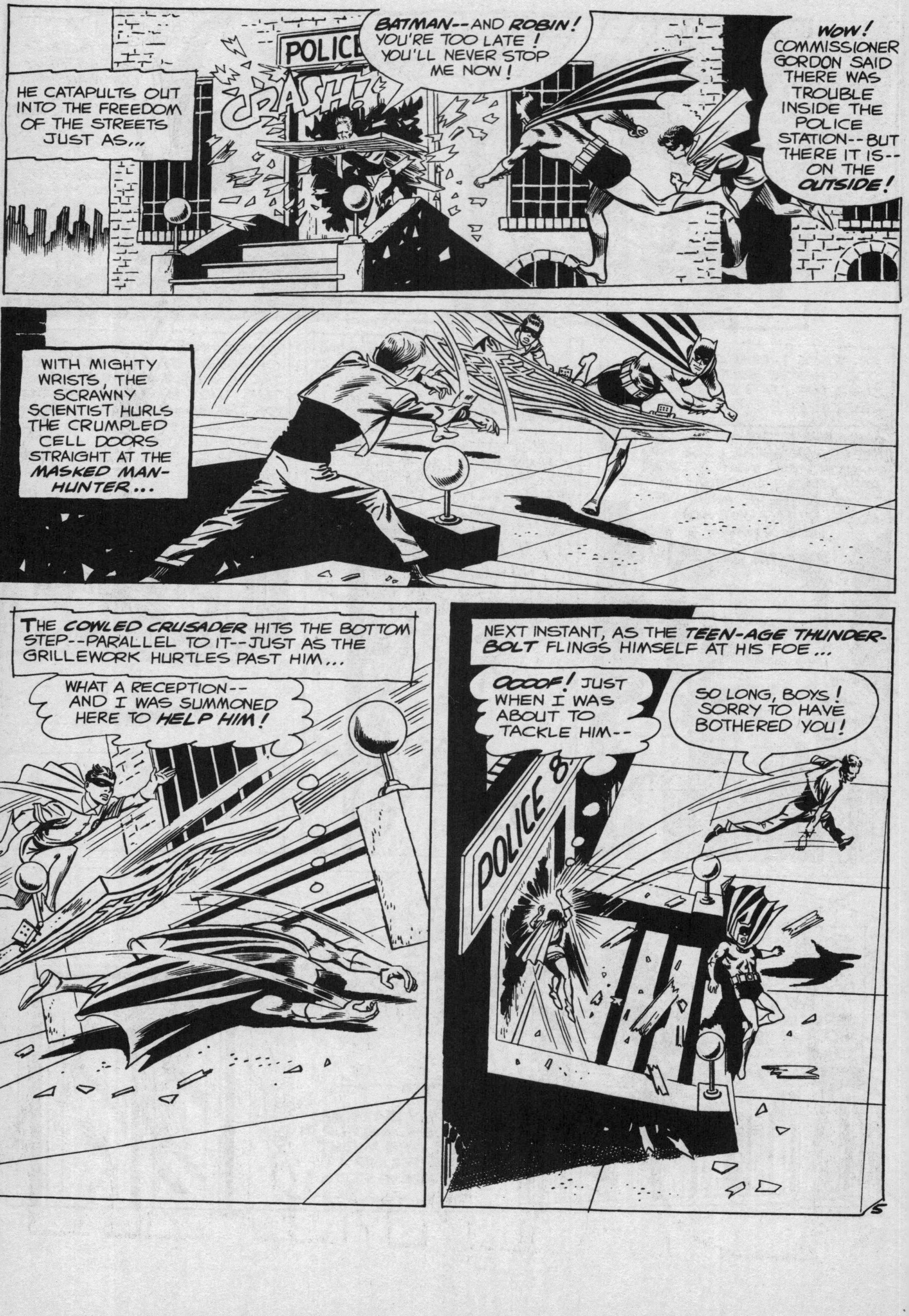
HE CATAPULTS OUT INTO THE FREEDOM OF THE STREETS JUST AS,...
POLICE
CRASH!
BATMAN--AND ROBIN! YOU'RE TOO LATE! YOU'LL NEVER STOP ME NOW!
WOW! COMMISSIONER GORDON SAID THERE WAS TROUBLE INSIDE THE POLICE STATION--BUT THERE IT IS--ON THE OUTSIDE!
WITH MIGHTY WRISTS, THE SCRAWNY SCIENTIST HURLS THE CRUMPLED CELL DOORS STRAIGHT AT THE MASKED MAN-HUNTER...
THE COWLED CRUSADER HITS THE BOTTOM STEP--PARALLEL TO IT--JUST AS THE GRILLEWORK HURTLES PAST HIM...
WHAT A RECEPTION--AND I WAS SUMMONED HERE TO HELP HIM!
NEXT INSTANT, AS THE TEEN-AGE THUNDER-BOLT FLINGS HIMSELF AT HIS FOE...
OOOOF! JUST WHEN I WAS ABOUT TO TACKLE HIM--
SO LONG, BOYS! SORRY TO HAVE BOTHERED YOU!
POLICE 8
5

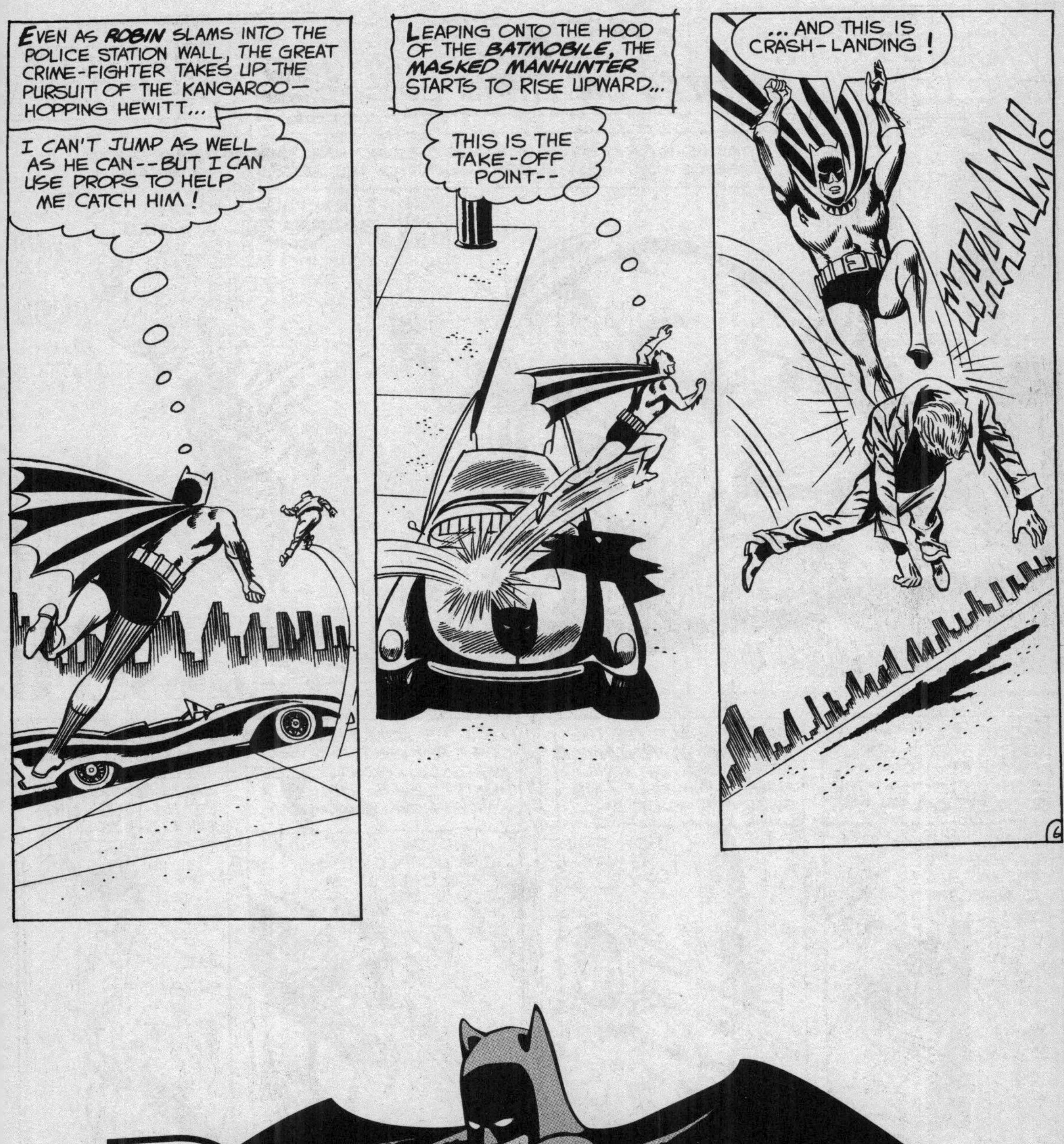
EVEN AS ROBIN SLAMS INTO THE POLICE STATION WALL, THE GREAT CRIME-FIGHTER TAKES UP THE PURSUIT OF THE KANGAROO-HOPPING HEWITT...
I CAN'T JUMP AS WELL AS HE CAN--BUT I CAN USE PROPS TO HELP ME CATCH HIM!
LEAPING ONTO THE HOOD OF THE BATMOBILE, THE MASKED MANHUNTER STARTS TO RISE UPWARD...
THIS IS THE TAKE-OFF POINT--
...AND THIS IS CRASH-LANDING!
6

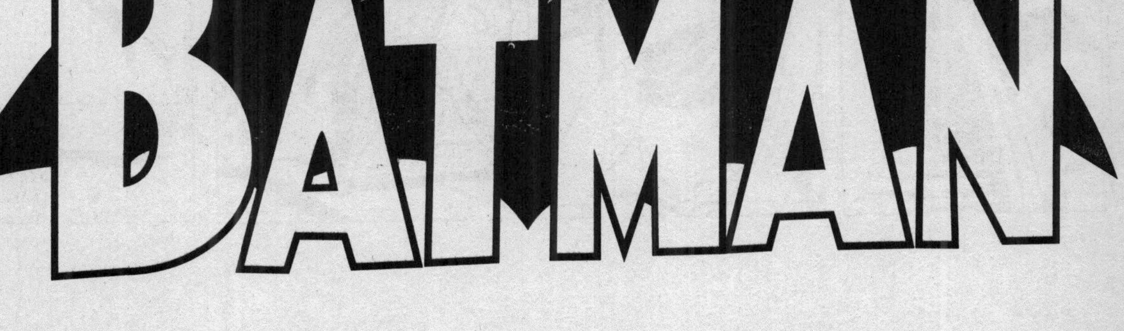
BATMAN

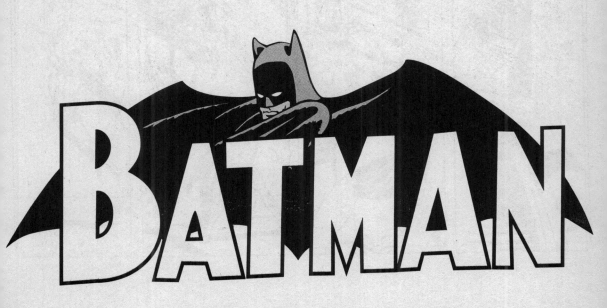

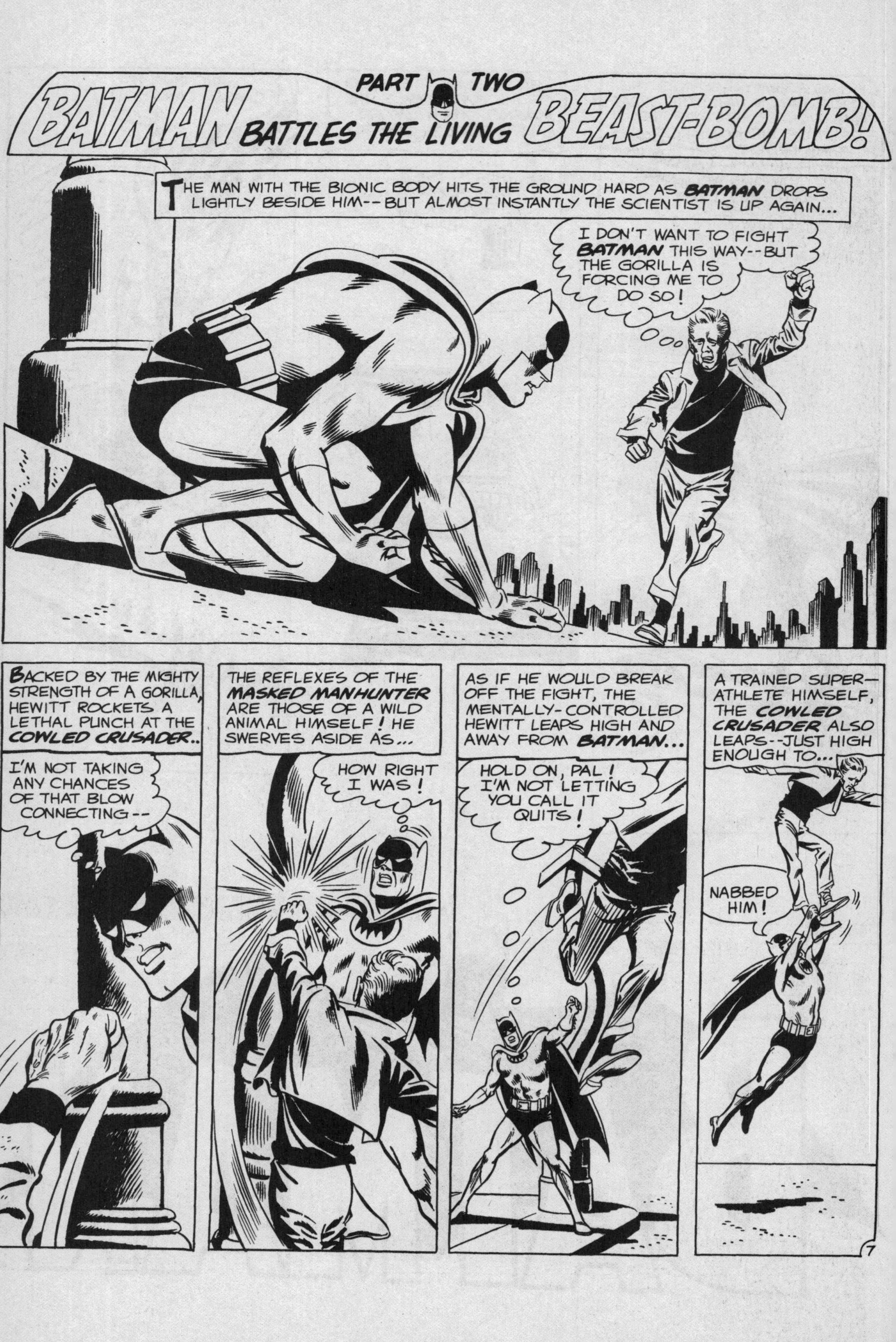
PART TWO
BATMAN BATTLES THE LIVING BEAST-BOMB!
THE MAN WITH THE BIONIC BODY HITS THE GROUND HARD AS BATMAN DROPS LIGHTLY BESIDE HIM-- BUT ALMOST INSTANTLY THE SCIENTIST IS UP AGAIN...
I DON'T WANT TO FIGHT BATMAN THIS WAY--BUT THE GORILLA IS FORCING ME TO DO SO!
BACKED BY THE MIGHTY STRENGTH OF A GORILLA, HEWITT ROCKETS A LETHAL PUNCH AT THE COWLED CRUSADER..
I'M NOT TAKING ANY CHANCES OF THAT BLOW CONNECTING--
THE REFLEXES OF THE MASKED MANHUNTER ARE THOSE OF A WILD ANIMAL HIMSELF! HE SWERVES ASIDE AS...
HOW RIGHT I WAS!
AS IF HE WOULD BREAK OFF THE FIGHT, THE MENTALLY-CONTROLLED HEWITT LEAPS HIGH AND AWAY FROM BATMAN...
HOLD ON, PAL! I'M NOT LETTING YOU CALL IT QUITS!
A TRAINED SUPER-ATHLETE HIMSELF, THE COWLED CRUSADER ALSO LEAPS--JUST HIGH ENOUGH TO...
NABBED HIM!
7

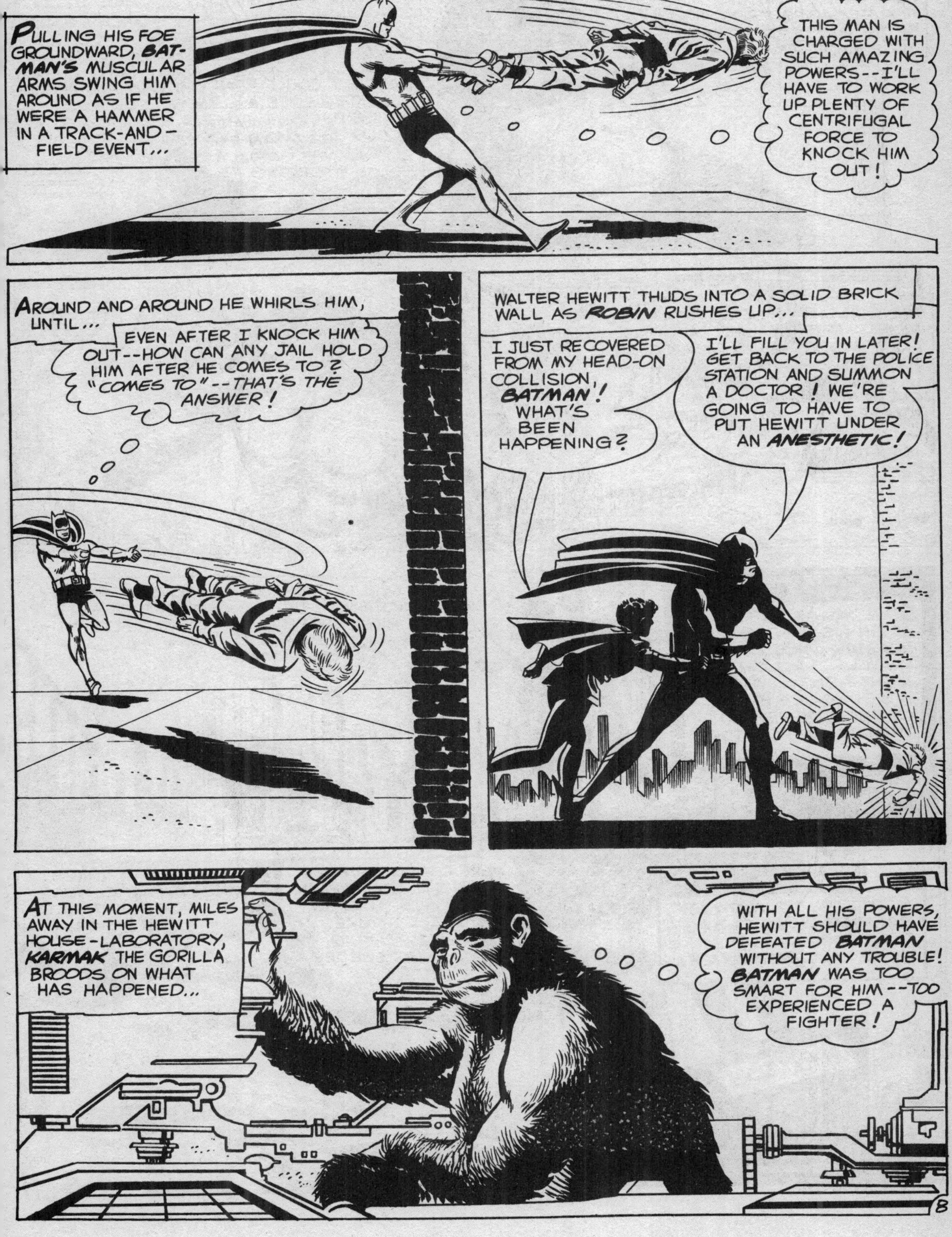
PULLING HIS FOE GROUNDWARD, BATMAN'S MUSCULAR ARMS SWING HIM AROUND AS IF HE WERE A HAMMER IN A TRACK-AND-FIELD EVENT...
THIS MAN IS CHARGED WITH SUCH AMAZING POWERS--I'LL HAVE TO WORK UP PLENTY OF CENTRIFUGAL FORCE TO KNOCK HIM OUT!
AROUND AND AROUND HE WHIRLS HIM, UNTIL...
EVEN AFTER I KNOCK HIM OUT--HOW CAN ANY JAIL HOLD HIM AFTER HE COMES TO? "COMES TO"--THAT'S THE ANSWER!
WALTER HEWITT THUDS INTO A SOLID BRICK WALL AS ROBIN RUSHES UP...
I JUST RECOVERED FROM MY HEAD-ON COLLISION, BATMAN! WHAT'S BEEN HAPPENING?
I'LL FILL YOU IN LATER! GET BACK TO THE POLICE STATION AND SUMMON A DOCTOR! WE'RE GOING TO HAVE TO PUT HEWITT UNDER AN ANESTHETIC!
AT THIS MOMENT, MILES AWAY IN THE HEWITT HOUSE-LABORATORY, KARMAK THE GORILLA BROODS ON WHAT HAS HAPPENED...
WITH ALL HIS POWERS, HEWITT SHOULD HAVE DEFEATED BATMAN WITHOUT ANY TROUBLE! BATMAN WAS TOO SMART FOR HIM--TOO EXPERIENCED A FIGHTER!
8

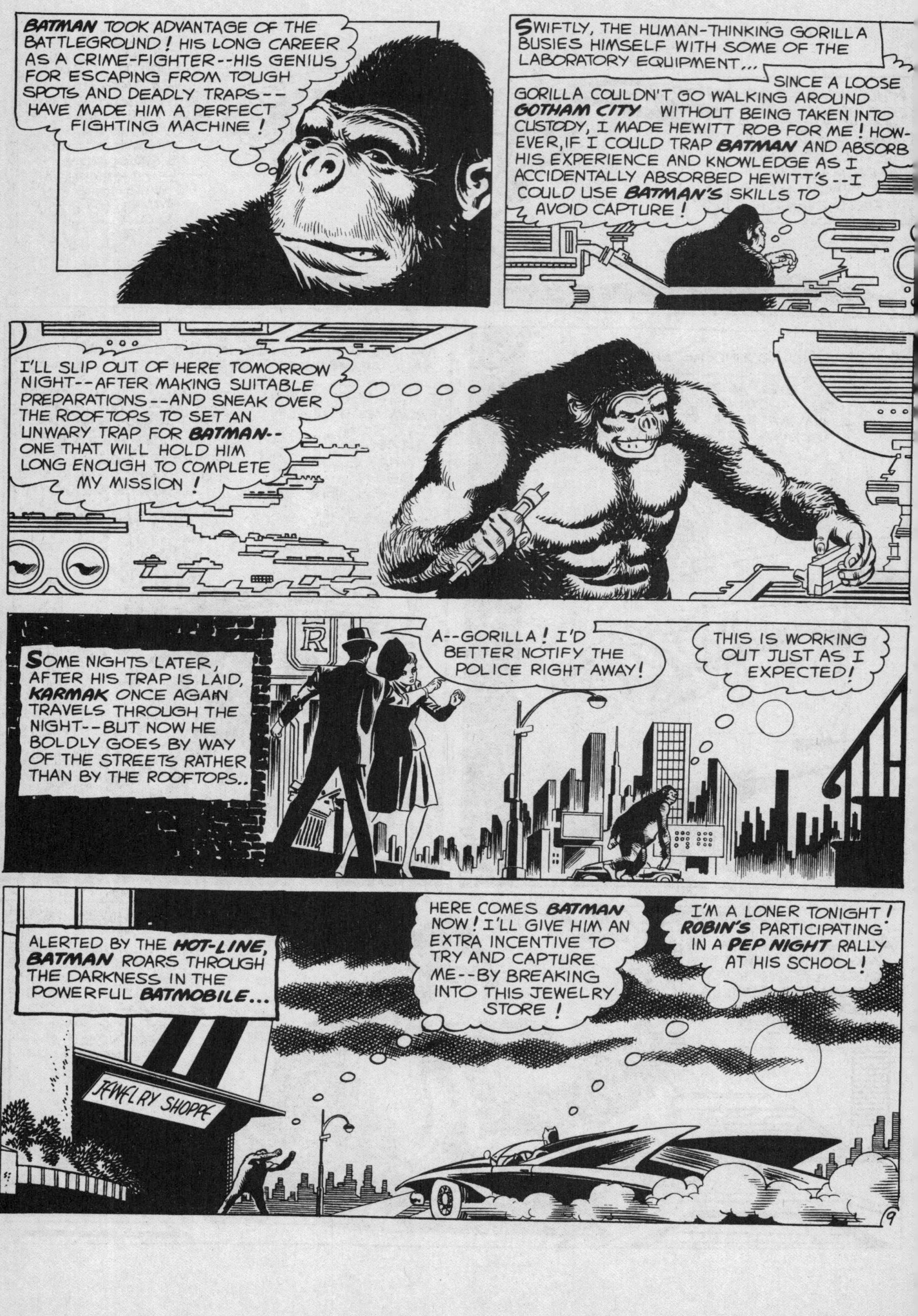
BATMAN TOOK ADVANTAGE OF THE BATTLEGROUND! HIS LONG CAREER AS A CRIME-FIGHTER--HIS GENIUS FOR ESCAPING FROM TOUGH SPOTS AND DEADLY TRAPS--HAVE MADE HIM A PERFECT FIGHTING MACHINE!
SWIFTLY, THE HUMAN-THINKING GORILLA BUSIES HIMSELF WITH SOME OF THE LABORATORY EQUIPMENT...
SINCE A LOOSE GORILLA COULDN'T GO WALKING AROUND GOTHAM CITY WITHOUT BEING TAKEN INTO CUSTODY, I MADE HEWITT ROB FOR ME! HOWEVER, IF I COULD TRAP BATMAN AND ABSORB HIS EXPERIENCE AND KNOWLEDGE AS I ACCIDENTALLY ABSORBED HEWITT'S--I COULD USE BATMAN'S SKILLS TO AVOID CAPTURE!
I'LL SLIP OUT OF HERE TOMORROW NIGHT--AFTER MAKING SUITABLE PREPARATIONS--AND SNEAK OVER THE ROOFTOPS TO SET AN UNWARY TRAP FOR BATMAN--ONE THAT WILL HOLD HIM LONG ENOUGH TO COMPLETE MY MISSION!
SOME NIGHTS LATER, AFTER HIS TRAP IS LAID, KARMAK ONCE AGAIN TRAVELS THROUGH THE NIGHT--BUT NOW HE BOLDLY GOES BY WAY OF THE STREETS RATHER THAN BY THE ROOFTOPS..
A--GORILLA! I'D BETTER NOTIFY THE POLICE RIGHT AWAY!
THIS IS WORKING OUT JUST AS I EXPECTED!
ALERTED BY THE HOT-LINE, BATMAN ROARS THROUGH THE DARKNESS IN THE POWERFUL BATMOBILE...
HERE COMES BATMAN NOW! I'LL GIVE HIM AN EXTRA INCENTIVE TO TRY AND CAPTURE ME--BY BREAKING INTO THIS JEWELRY STORE!
I'M A LONER TONIGHT! ROBIN'S PARTICIPATING IN A PEP NIGHT RALLY AT HIS SCHOOL!
JEWELRY SHOPPE
9

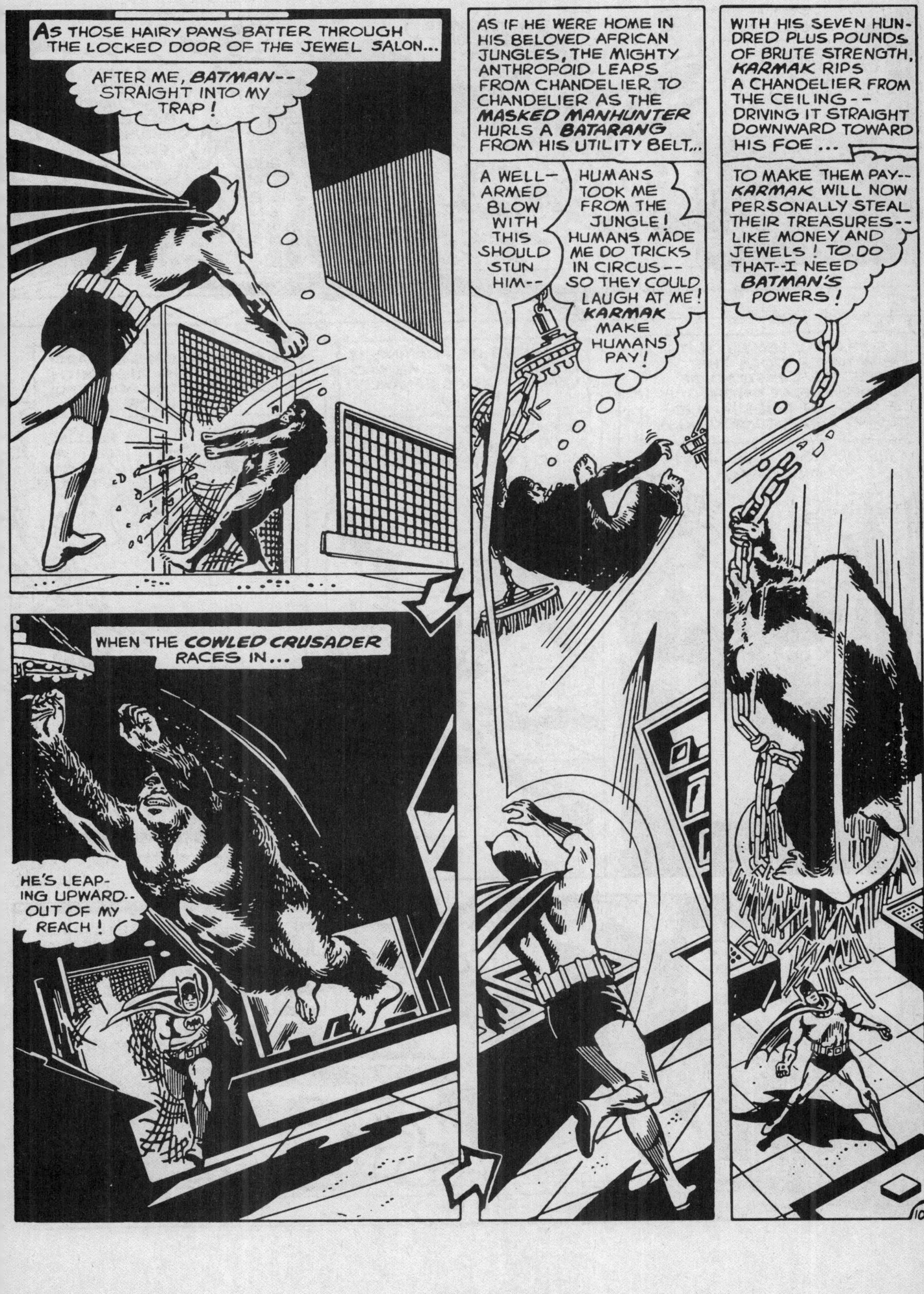
AS THOSE HAIRY PAWS BATTER THROUGH THE LOCKED DOOR OF THE JEWEL SALON...
AFTER ME, BATMAN-- STRAIGHT INTO MY TRAP!
WHEN THE COWLED CRUSADER RACES IN...
HE'S LEAPING UPWARD-- OUT OF MY REACH!
AS IF HE WERE HOME IN HIS BELOVED AFRICAN JUNGLES, THE MIGHTY ANTHROPOID LEAPS FROM CHANDELIER TO CHANDELIER AS THE MASKED MANHUNTER HURLS A BATARANG FROM HIS UTILITY BELT...
A WELL-ARMED BLOW WITH THIS SHOULD STUN HIM--
HUMANS TOOK ME FROM THE JUNGLE! HUMANS MADE ME DO TRICKS IN CIRCUS-- SO THEY COULD LAUGH AT ME! KARMAK MAKE HUMANS PAY!
WITH HIS SEVEN HUNDRED PLUS POUNDS OF BRUTE STRENGTH, KARMAK RIPS A CHANDELIER FROM THE CEILING-- DRIVING IT STRAIGHT DOWNWARD TOWARD HIS FOE...
TO MAKE THEM PAY-- KARMAK WILL NOW PERSONALLY STEAL THEIR TREASURES-- LIKE MONEY AND JEWELS! TO DO THAT--I NEED BATMAN'S POWERS!
10

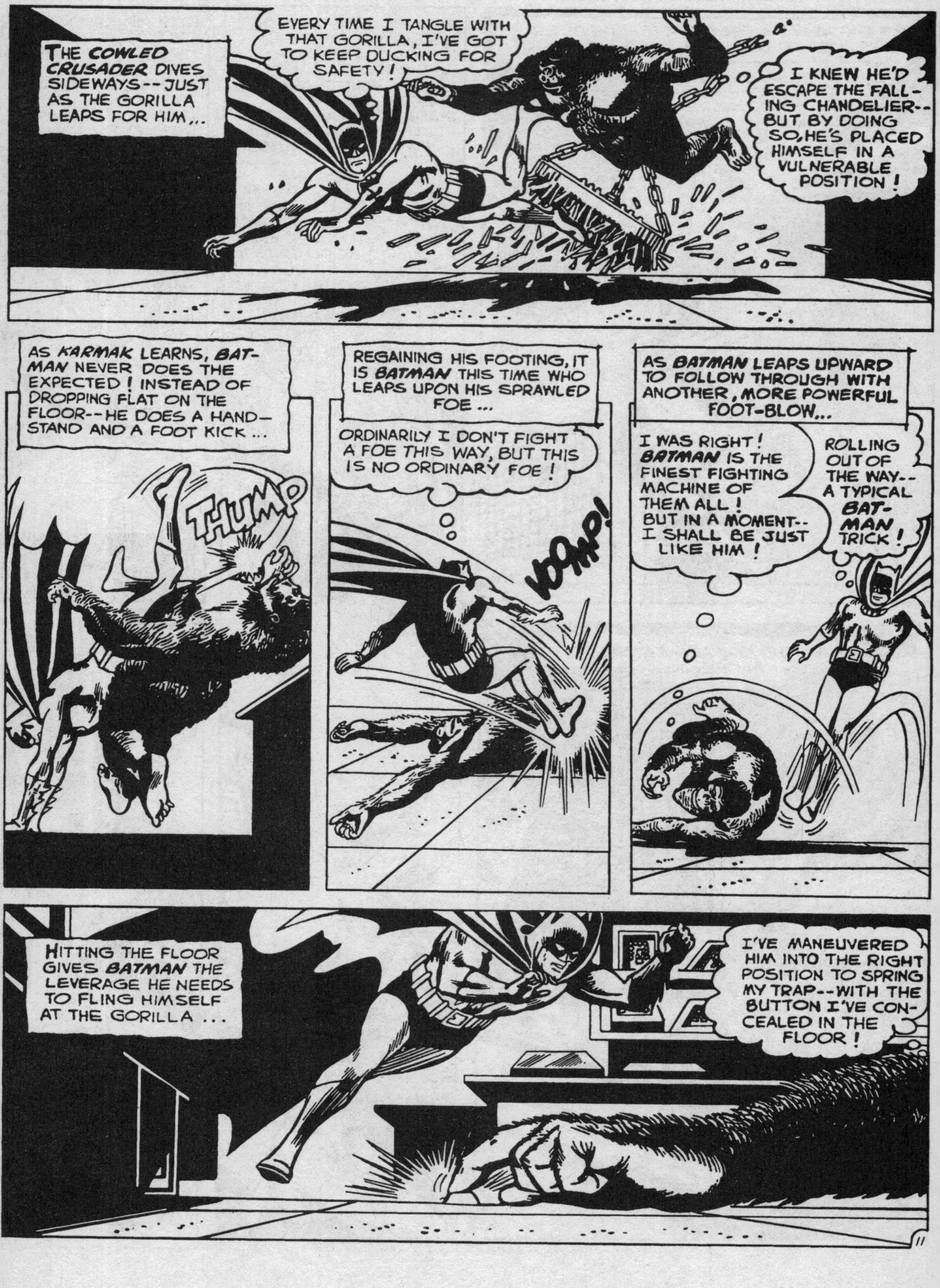
THE COWLED CRUSADER DIVES SIDEWAYS--JUST AS THE GORILLA LEAPS FOR HIM,...
EVERY TIME I TANGLE WITH THAT GORILLA, I'VE GOT TO KEEP DUCKING FOR SAFETY!
I KNEW HE'D ESCAPE THE FALLING CHANDELIER--BUT BY DOING SO, HE'S PLACED HIMSELF IN A VULNERABLE POSITION!
AS KARMAK LEARNS, BATMAN NEVER DOES THE EXPECTED! INSTEAD OF DROPPING FLAT ON THE FLOOR--HE DOES A HANDSTAND AND A FOOT KICK...
THUMP
REGAINING HIS FOOTING, IT IS BATMAN THIS TIME WHO LEAPS UPON HIS SPRAWLED FOE...
ORDINARILY I DON'T FIGHT A FOE THIS WAY, BUT THIS IS NO ORDINARY FOE!
VOOMP!
AS BATMAN LEAPS UPWARD TO FOLLOW THROUGH WITH ANOTHER, MORE POWERFUL FOOT-BLOW...
I WAS RIGHT! BATMAN IS THE FINEST FIGHTING MACHINE OF THEM ALL! BUT IN A MOMENT--I SHALL BE JUST LIKE HIM!
ROLLING OUT OF THE WAY--A TYPICAL BAT-MAN TRICK!
HITTING THE FLOOR GIVES BATMAN THE LEVERAGE HE NEEDS TO FLING HIMSELF AT THE GORILLA...
I'VE MANEUVERED HIM INTO THE RIGHT POSITION TO SPRING MY TRAP--WITH THE BUTTON I'VE CONCEALED IN THE FLOOR!
11

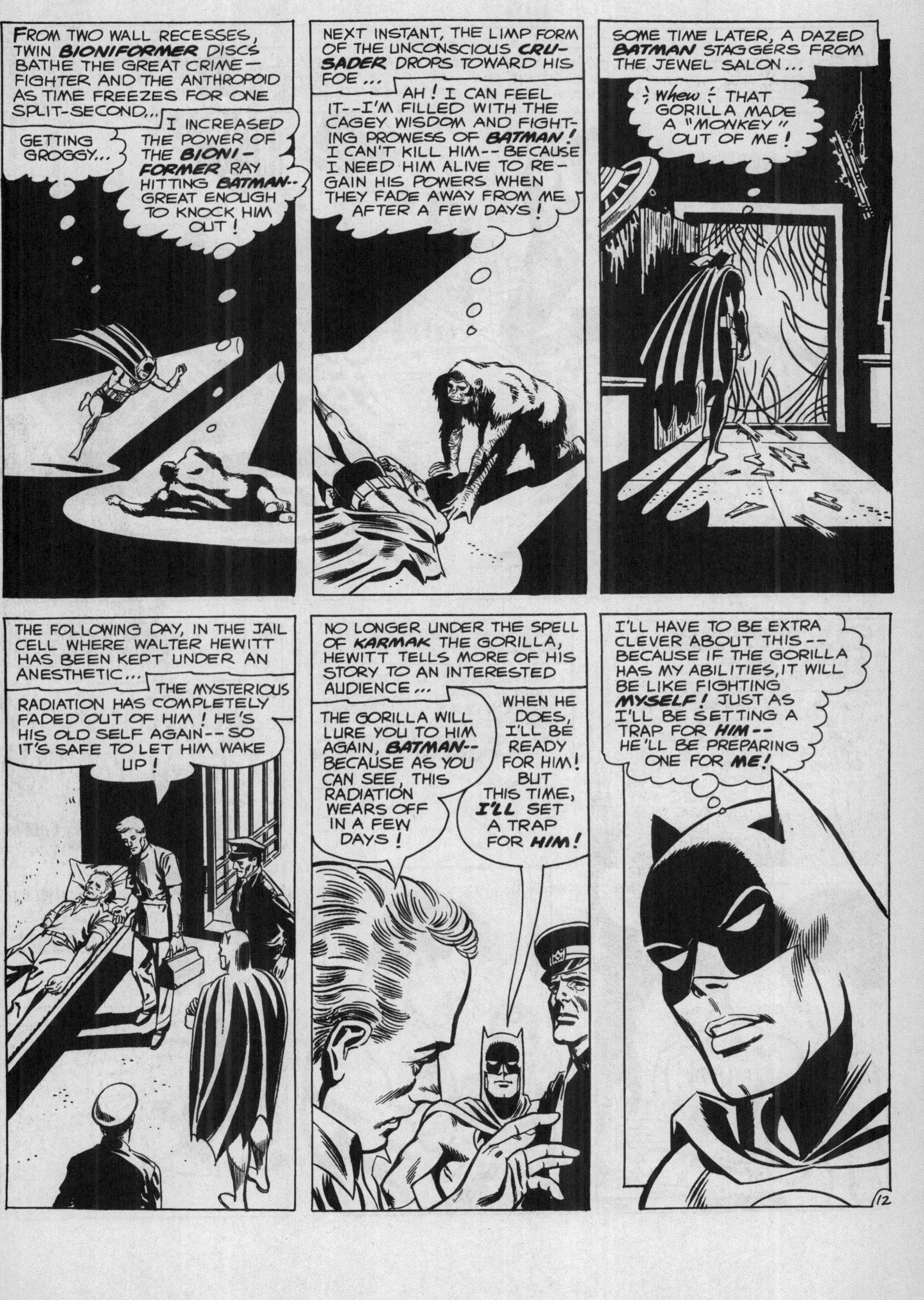
FROM TWO WALL RECESSES, TWIN BIONIFORMER DISCS BATHE THE GREAT CRIME-FIGHTER AND THE ANTHROPOID AS TIME FREEZES FOR ONE SPLIT-SECOND...
GETTING GROGGY...
I INCREASED THE POWER OF THE BIONI-FORMER RAY HITTING BATMAN-- GREAT ENOUGH TO KNOCK HIM OUT!
NEXT INSTANT, THE LIMP FORM OF THE UNCONSCIOUS CRUSADER DROPS TOWARD HIS FOE...
AH! I CAN FEEL IT--I'M FILLED WITH THE CAGEY WISDOM AND FIGHTING PROWESS OF BATMAN! I CAN'T KILL HIM-- BECAUSE I NEED HIM ALIVE TO REGAIN HIS POWERS WHEN THEY FADE AWAY FROM ME AFTER A FEW DAYS!
SOME TIME LATER, A DAZED BATMAN STAGGERS FROM THE JEWEL SALON...
WHEW - THAT GORILLA MADE A "MONKEY" OUT OF ME!
THE FOLLOWING DAY, IN THE JAIL CELL WHERE WALTER HEWITT HAS BEEN KEPT UNDER AN ANESTHETIC...
THE MYSTERIOUS RADIATION HAS COMPLETELY FADED OUT OF HIM! HE'S HIS OLD SELF AGAIN-- SO IT'S SAFE TO LET HIM WAKE UP!
NO LONGER UNDER THE SPELL OF KARMAK THE GORILLA, HEWITT TELLS MORE OF HIS STORY TO AN INTERESTED AUDIENCE...
THE GORILLA WILL LURE YOU TO HIM AGAIN, BATMAN-- BECAUSE AS YOU CAN SEE, THIS RADIATION WEARS OFF IN A FEW DAYS!
WHEN HE DOES, I'LL BE READY FOR HIM! BUT THIS TIME, I'LL SET A TRAP FOR HIM!
I'LL HAVE TO BE EXTRA CLEVER ABOUT THIS-- BECAUSE IF THE GORILLA HAS MY ABILITIES, IT WILL BE LIKE FIGHTING MYSELF! JUST AS I'LL BE SETTING A TRAP FOR HIM-- HE'LL BE PREPARING ONE FOR ME!
12

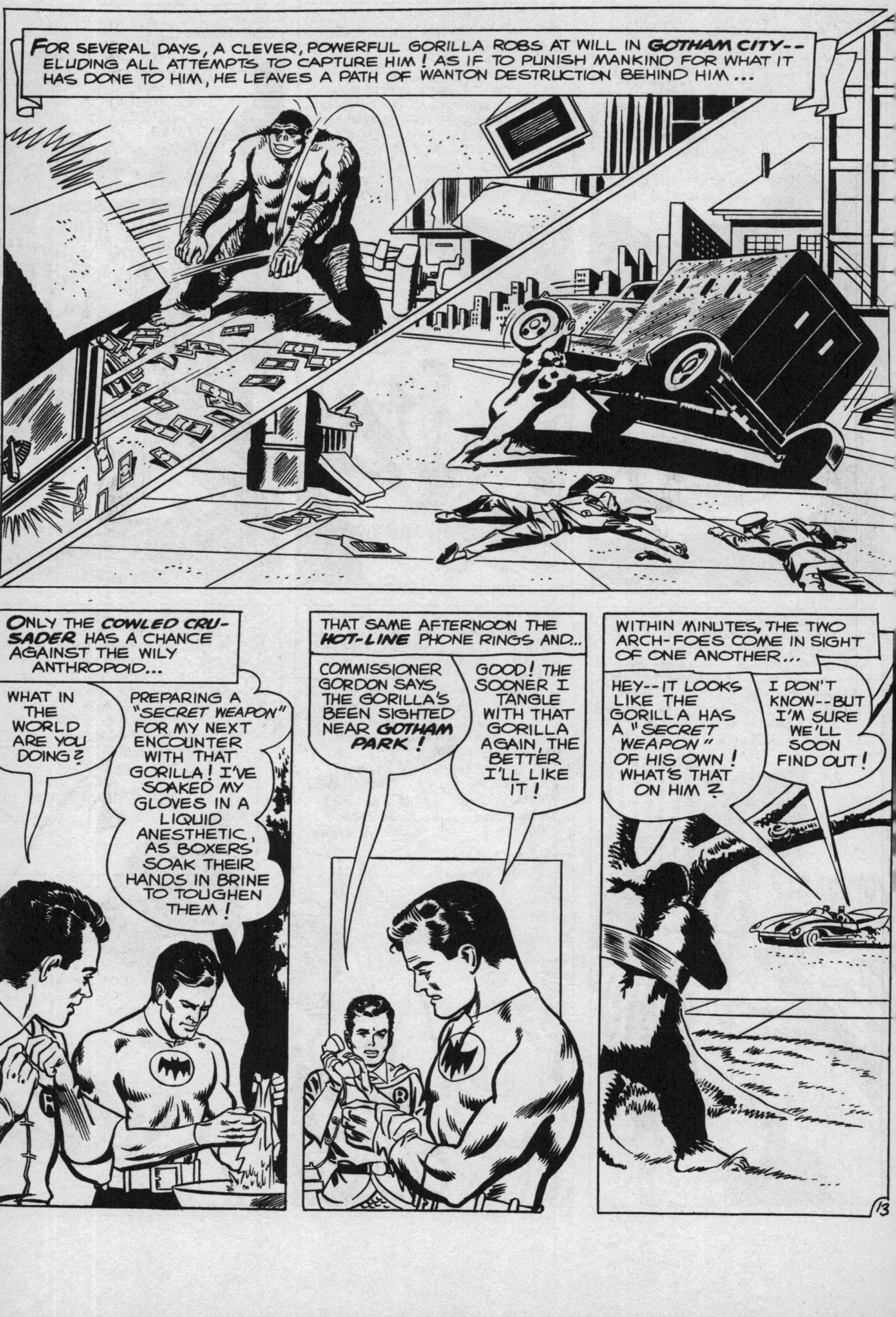
FOR SEVERAL DAYS, A CLEVER, POWERFUL GORILLA ROBS AT WILL IN GOTHAM CITY-- ELUDING ALL ATTEMPTS TO CAPTURE HIM! AS IF TO PUNISH MANKIND FOR WHAT IT HAS DONE TO HIM, HE LEAVES A PATH OF WANTON DESTRUCTION BEHIND HIM...
ONLY THE COWLED CRUSADER HAS A CHANCE AGAINST THE WILY ANTHROPOID...
WHAT IN THE WORLD ARE YOU DOING?
PREPARING A "SECRET WEAPON" FOR MY NEXT ENCOUNTER WITH THAT GORILLA! I'VE SOAKED MY GLOVES IN A LIQUID ANESTHETIC, AS BOXERS SOAK THEIR HANDS IN BRINE TO TOUGHEN THEM!
THAT SAME AFTERNOON THE HOT-LINE PHONE RINGS AND...
COMMISSIONER GORDON SAYS THE GORILLA'S BEEN SIGHTED NEAR GOTHAM PARK!
GOOD! THE SOONER I TANGLE WITH THAT GORILLA AGAIN, THE BETTER I'LL LIKE IT!
WITHIN MINUTES, THE TWO ARCH-FOES COME IN SIGHT OF ONE ANOTHER...
HEY--IT LOOKS LIKE THE GORILLA HAS A "SECRET WEAPON" OF HIS OWN! WHAT'S THAT ON HIM?
I DON'T KNOW--BUT I'M SURE WE'LL SOON FIND OUT!
13

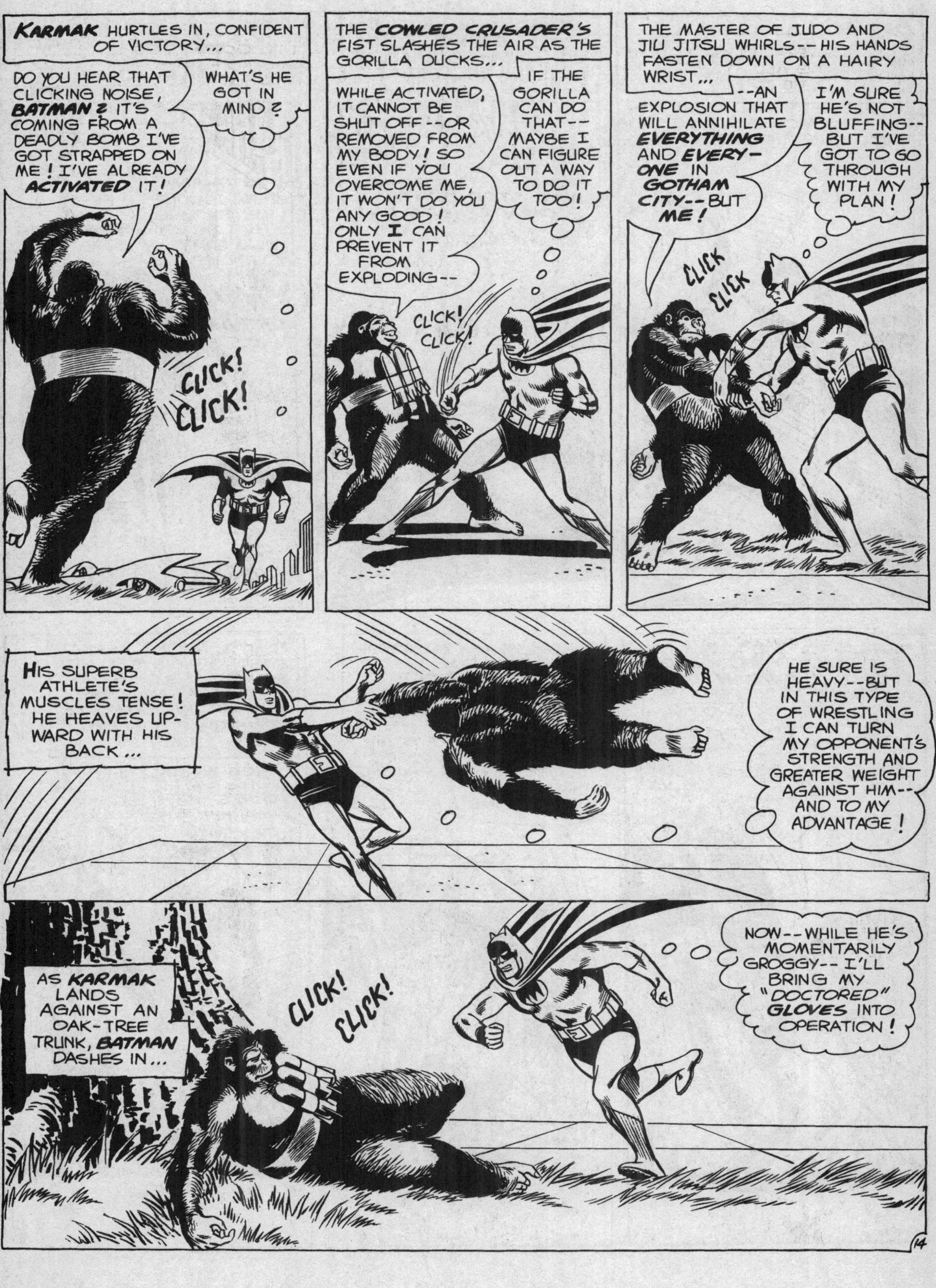
KARMAK HURTLES IN, CONFIDENT OF VICTORY...
DO YOU HEAR THAT CLICKING NOISE, BATMAN? IT'S COMING FROM A DEADLY BOMB I'VE GOT STRAPPED ON ME! I'VE ALREADY ACTIVATED IT!
WHAT'S HE GOT IN MIND?
CLICK! CLICK!
THE COWLED CRUSADER'S FIST SLASHES THE AIR AS THE GORILLA DUCKS...
WHILE ACTIVATED, IT CANNOT BE SHUT OFF--OR REMOVED FROM MY BODY! SO EVEN IF YOU OVERCOME ME, IT WON'T DO YOU ANY GOOD! ONLY I CAN PREVENT IT FROM EXPLODING--
IF THE GORILLA CAN DO THAT--MAYBE I CAN FIGURE OUT A WAY TO DO IT TOO!
CLICK! CLICK!
THE MASTER OF JUDO AND JIU JITSU WHIRLS--HIS HANDS FASTEN DOWN ON A HAIRY WRIST...
--AN EXPLOSION THAT WILL ANNIHILATE EVERYTHING AND EVERY-ONE IN GOTHAM CITY--BUT ME!
I'M SURE HE'S NOT BLUFFING--BUT I'VE GOT TO GO THROUGH WITH MY PLAN!
CLICK CLICK
HIS SUPERB ATHLETE'S MUSCLES TENSE! HE HEAVES UPWARD WITH HIS BACK...
HE SURE IS HEAVY--BUT IN THIS TYPE OF WRESTLING I CAN TURN MY OPPONENT'S STRENGTH AND GREATER WEIGHT AGAINST HIM--AND TO MY ADVANTAGE!
AS KARMAK LANDS AGAINST AN OAK-TREE TRUNK, BATMAN DASHES IN...
CLICK! CLICK!
NOW--WHILE HE'S MOMENTARILY GROGGY--I'LL BRING MY "DOCTORED" GLOVES INTO OPERATION!
14

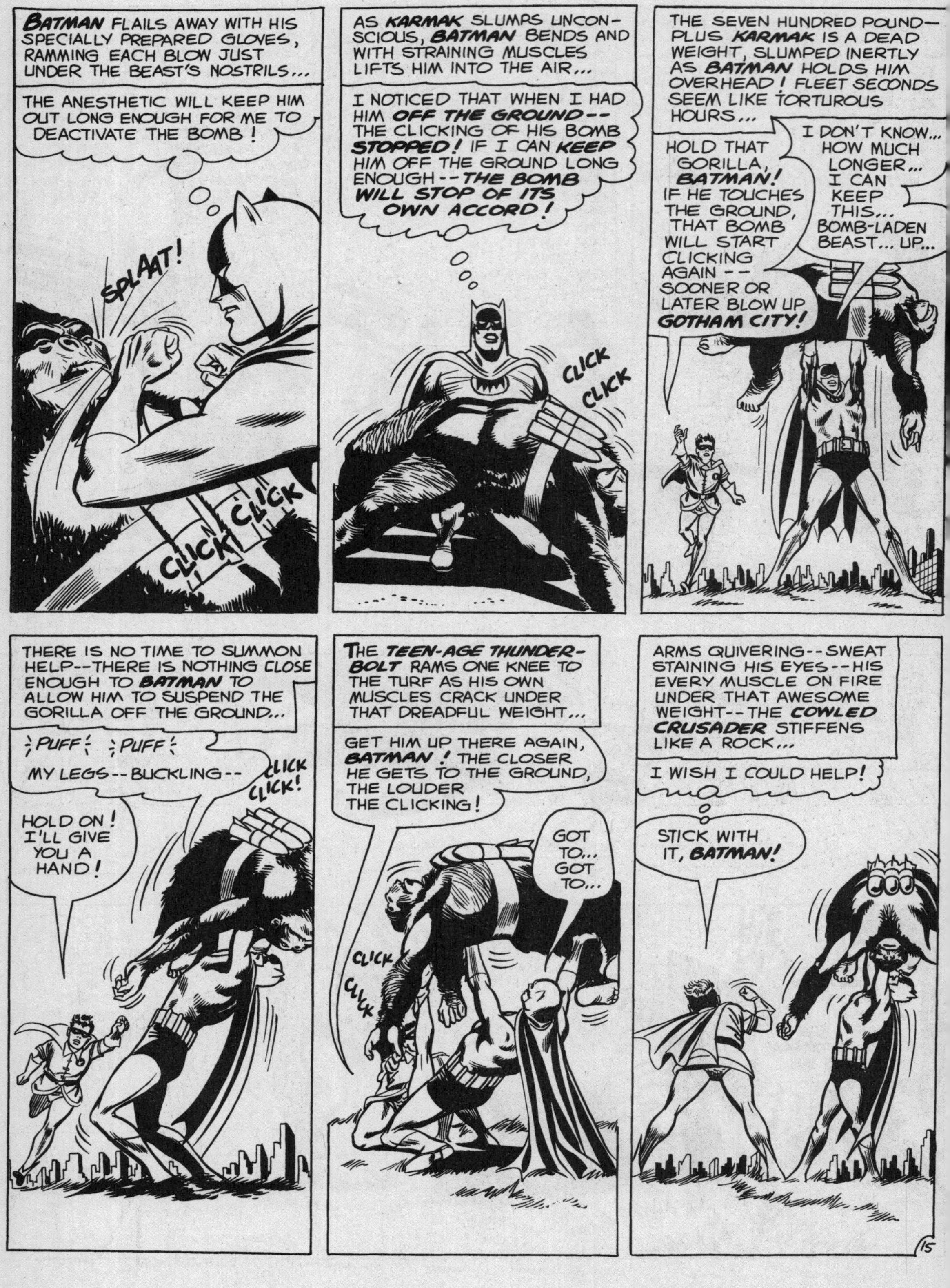
BATMAN FLAILS AWAY WITH HIS SPECIALLY PREPARED GLOVES, RAMMING EACH BLOW JUST UNDER THE BEAST'S NOSTRILS...
THE ANESTHETIC WILL KEEP HIM OUT LONG ENOUGH FOR ME TO DEACTIVATE THE BOMB!
SPLAAT!
CLICK CLICK
AS KARMAK SLUMPS UNCONSCIOUS, BATMAN BENDS AND WITH STRAINING MUSCLES LIFTS HIM INTO THE AIR...
I NOTICED THAT WHEN I HAD HIM OFF THE GROUND-- THE CLICKING OF HIS BOMB STOPPED! IF I CAN KEEP HIM OFF THE GROUND LONG ENOUGH--THE BOMB WILL STOP OF ITS OWN ACCORD!
CLICK CLICK
THE SEVEN HUNDRED POUND-PLUS KARMAK IS A DEAD WEIGHT, SLUMPED INERTLY AS BATMAN HOLDS HIM OVERHEAD! FLEET SECONDS SEEM LIKE TORTUROUS HOURS...
HOLD THAT GORILLA, BATMAN! IF HE TOUCHES THE GROUND, THAT BOMB WILL START CLICKING AGAIN -- SOONER OR LATER BLOW UP GOTHAM CITY!
I DON'T KNOW... HOW MUCH LONGER... I CAN KEEP THIS... BOMB-LADEN BEAST... UP...
THERE IS NO TIME TO SUMMON HELP--THERE IS NOTHING CLOSE ENOUGH TO BATMAN TO ALLOW HIM TO SUSPEND THE GORILLA OFF THE GROUND...
PUFF PUFF
MY LEGS--BUCKLING--
CLICK CLICK!
HOLD ON! I'LL GIVE YOU A HAND!
THE TEEN-AGE THUNDERBOLT RAMS ONE KNEE TO THE TURF AS HIS OWN MUSCLES CRACK UNDER THAT DREADFUL WEIGHT...
GET HIM UP THERE AGAIN, BATMAN! THE CLOSER HE GETS TO THE GROUND, THE LOUDER THE CLICKING!
GOT TO... GOT TO...
CLICK CLICK
ARMS QUIVERING--SWEAT STAINING HIS EYES--HIS EVERY MUSCLE ON FIRE UNDER THAT AWESOME WEIGHT--THE COWLED CRUSADER STIFFENS LIKE A ROCK...
I WISH I COULD HELP!
STICK WITH IT, BATMAN!
15

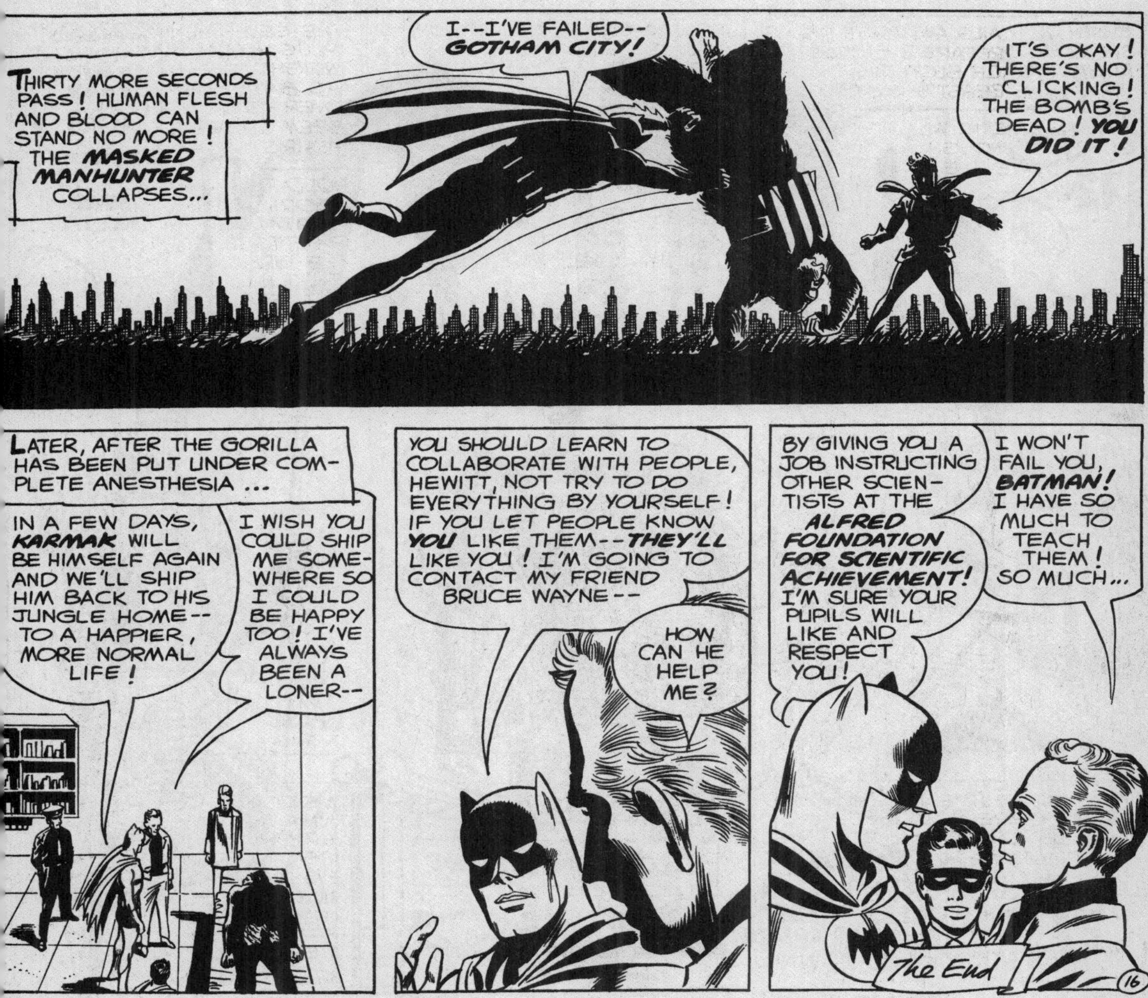
THIRTY MORE SECONDS PASS! HUMAN FLESH AND BLOOD CAN STAND NO MORE! THE MASKED MANHUNTER COLLAPSES...
I--I'VE FAILED-- GOTHAM CITY!
IT'S OKAY! THERE'S NO CLICKING! THE BOMB'S DEAD! YOU DID IT!
LATER, AFTER THE GORILLA HAS BEEN PUT UNDER COMPLETE ANESTHESIA ...
IN A FEW DAYS, KARMAK WILL BE HIMSELF AGAIN AND WE'LL SHIP HIM BACK TO HIS JUNGLE HOME-- TO A HAPPIER, MORE NORMAL LIFE!
I WISH YOU COULD SHIP ME SOMEWHERE SO I COULD BE HAPPY TOO! I'VE ALWAYS BEEN A LONER--
YOU SHOULD LEARN TO COLLABORATE WITH PEOPLE, HEWITT, NOT TRY TO DO EVERYTHING BY YOURSELF! IF YOU LET PEOPLE KNOW YOU LIKE THEM--THEY'LL LIKE YOU! I'M GOING TO CONTACT MY FRIEND BRUCE WAYNE--
HOW CAN HE HELP ME?
BY GIVING YOU A JOB INSTRUCTING OTHER SCIENTISTS AT THE ALFRED FOUNDATION FOR SCIENTIFIC ACHIEVEMENT! I'M SURE YOUR PUPILS WILL LIKE AND RESPECT YOU!
I WON'T FAIL YOU, BATMAN! I HAVE SO MUCH TO TEACH THEM! SO MUCH...
The End
16

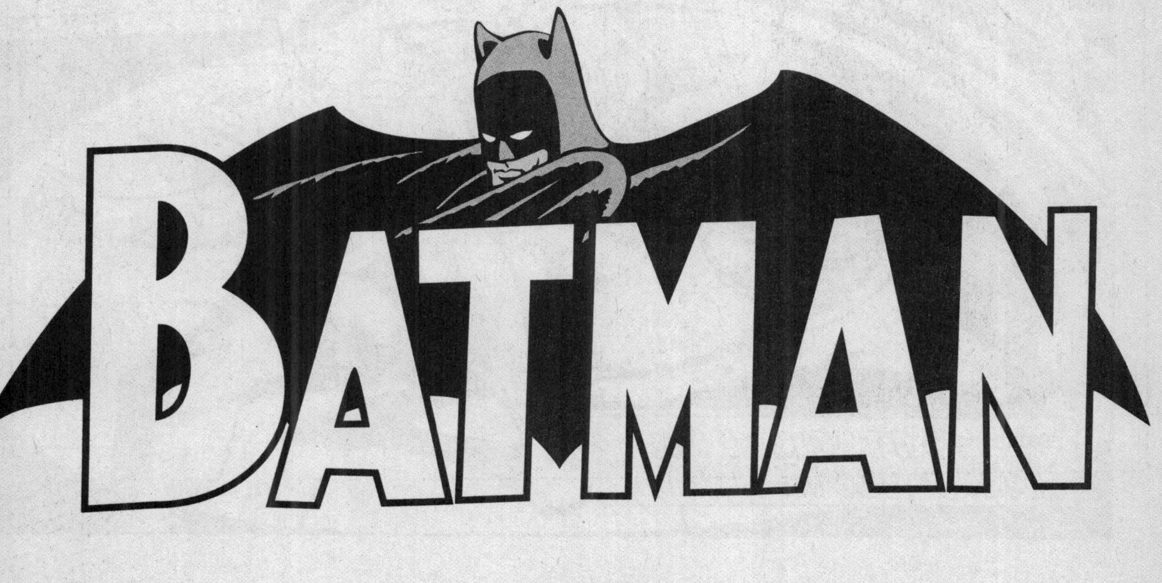
BATMAN

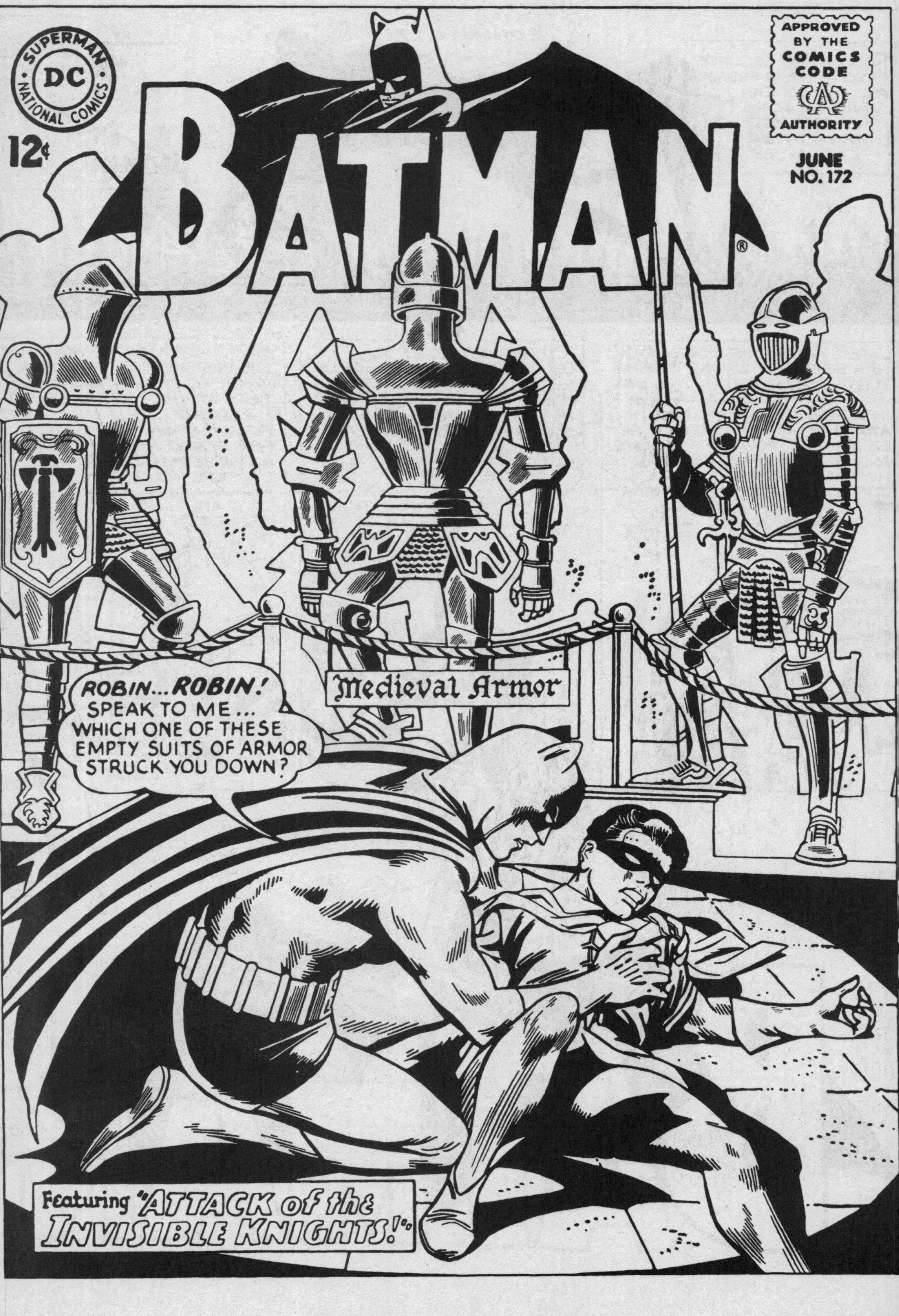
SUPERMAN DC NATIONAL COMICS
12¢
BATMAN
APPROVED BY THE COMICS CODE AUTHORITY
JUNE NO. 172
Medieval Armor
ROBIN... ROBIN! SPEAK TO ME... WHICH ONE OF THESE EMPTY SUITS OF ARMOR STRUCK YOU DOWN?
Featuring "ATTACK of the INVISIBLE KNIGHTS!"

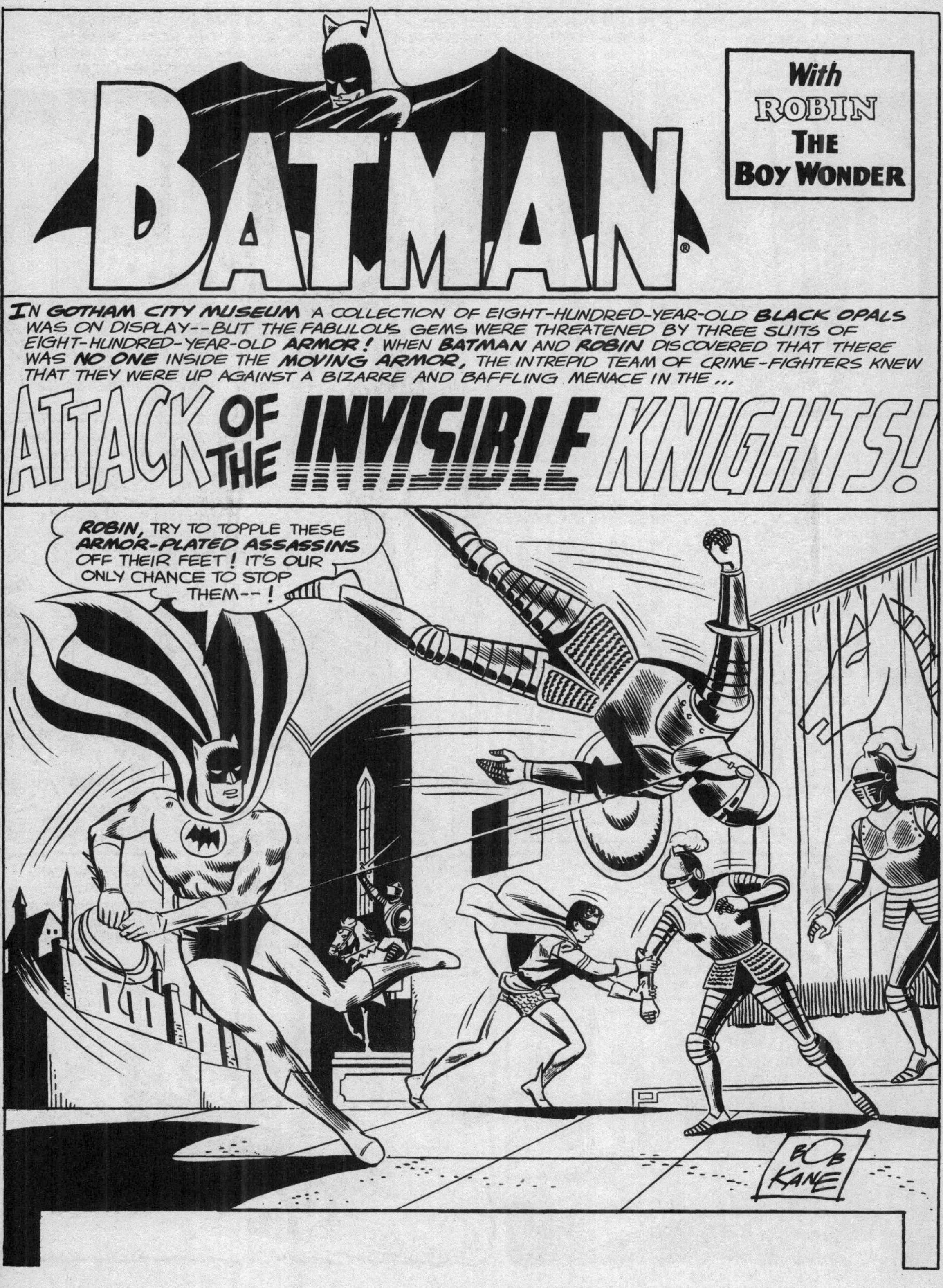
BATMAN®
With ROBIN THE BOY WONDER
IN GOTHAM CITY MUSEUM A COLLECTION OF EIGHT-HUNDRED-YEAR-OLD BLACK OPALS WAS ON DISPLAY--BUT THE FABULOUS GEMS WERE THREATENED BY THREE SUITS OF EIGHT-HUNDRED-YEAR-OLD ARMOR! WHEN BATMAN AND ROBIN DISCOVERED THAT THERE WAS NO ONE INSIDE THE MOVING ARMOR, THE INTREPID TEAM OF CRIME-FIGHTERS KNEW THAT THEY WERE UP AGAINST A BIZARRE AND BAFFLING MENACE IN THE ...
ATTACK OF THE INVISIBLE KNIGHTS!
ROBIN, TRY TO TOPPLE THESE ARMOR-PLATED ASSASSINS OFF THEIR FEET! IT'S OUR ONLY CHANCE TO STOP THEM--!
BOB KANE

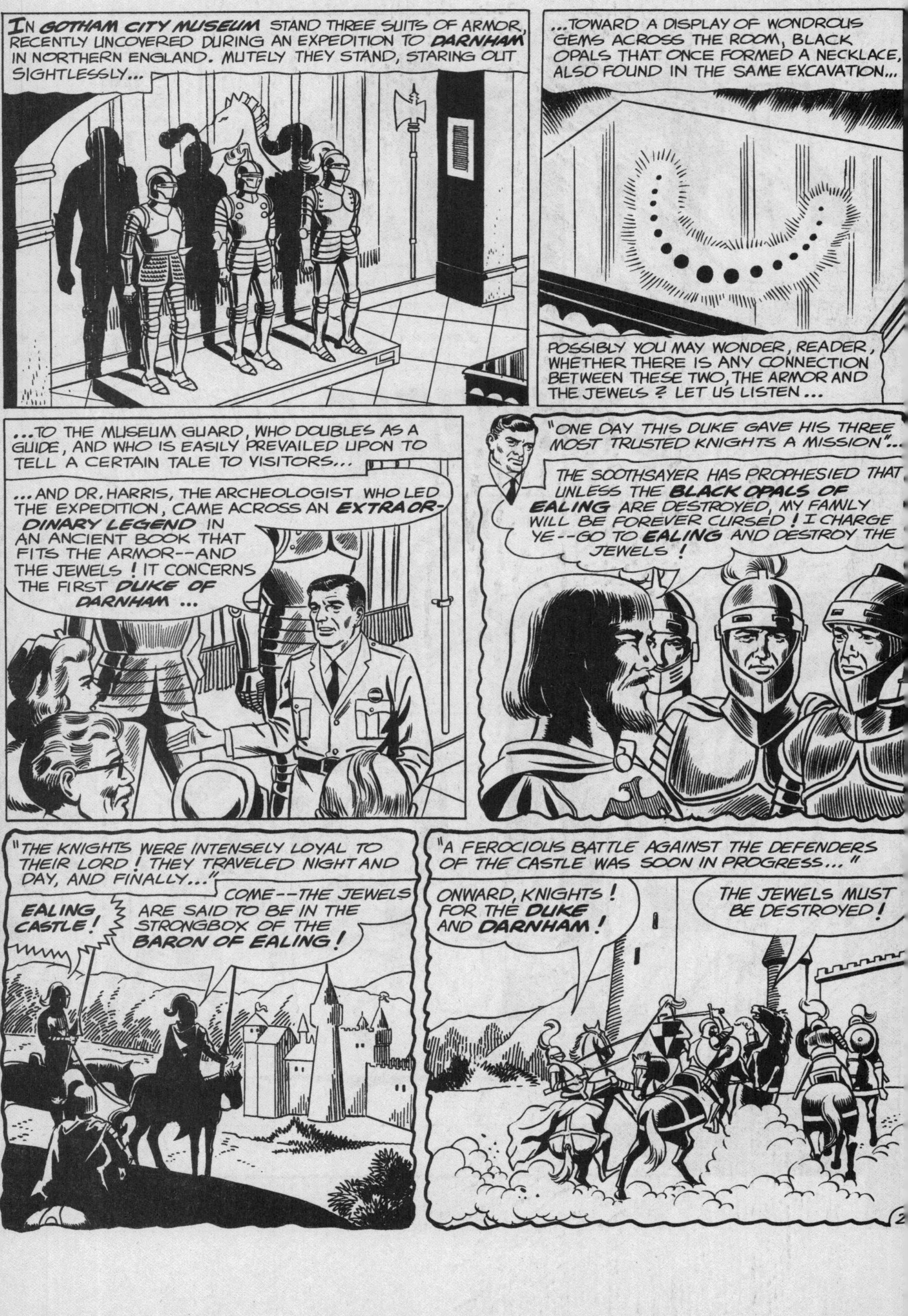
IN GOTHAM CITY MUSEUM STAND THREE SUITS OF ARMOR, RECENTLY UNCOVERED DURING AN EXPEDITION TO DARNHAM IN NORTHERN ENGLAND. MUTELY THEY STAND, STARING OUT SIGHTLESSLY...
...TOWARD A DISPLAY OF WONDROUS GEMS ACROSS THE ROOM, BLACK OPALS THAT ONCE FORMED A NECKLACE, ALSO FOUND IN THE SAME EXCAVATION...
POSSIBLY YOU MAY WONDER, READER, WHETHER THERE IS ANY CONNECTION BETWEEN THESE TWO, THE ARMOR AND THE JEWELS? LET US LISTEN...
...TO THE MUSEUM GUARD, WHO DOUBLES AS A GUIDE, AND WHO IS EASILY PREVAILED UPON TO TELL A CERTAIN TALE TO VISITORS...
...AND DR. HARRIS, THE ARCHEOLOGIST WHO LED THE EXPEDITION, CAME ACROSS AN EXTRAORDINARY LEGEND IN AN ANCIENT BOOK THAT FITS THE ARMOR--AND THE JEWELS! IT CONCERNS THE FIRST DUKE OF DARNHAM...
"ONE DAY THIS DUKE GAVE HIS THREE MOST TRUSTED KNIGHTS A MISSION"...
THE SOOTHSAYER HAS PROPHESIED THAT UNLESS THE BLACK OPALS OF EALING ARE DESTROYED, MY FAMILY WILL BE FOREVER CURSED! I CHARGE YE--GO TO EALING AND DESTROY THE JEWELS!
"THE KNIGHTS WERE INTENSELY LOYAL TO THEIR LORD! THEY TRAVELED NIGHT AND DAY, AND FINALLY..."
EALING CASTLE!
COME--THE JEWELS ARE SAID TO BE IN THE STRONGBOX OF THE BARON OF EALING!
"A FEROCIOUS BATTLE AGAINST THE DEFENDERS OF THE CASTLE WAS SOON IN PROGRESS..."
ONWARD, KNIGHTS! FOR THE DUKE AND DARNHAM!
THE JEWELS MUST BE DESTROYED!
2

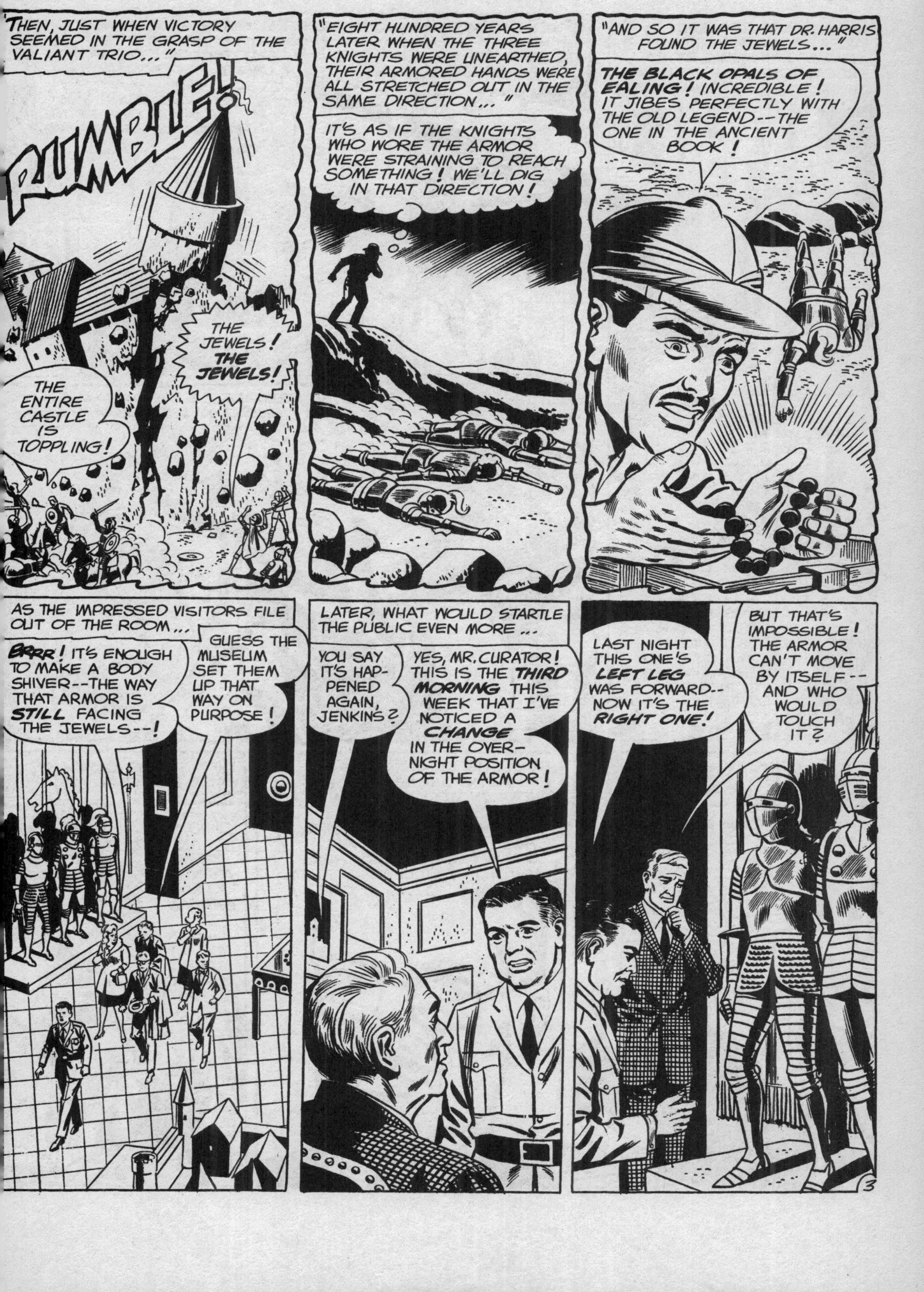
"THEN, JUST WHEN VICTORY SEEMED IN THE GRASP OF THE VALIANT TRIO..."
RUMBLE!
THE JEWELS! THE JEWELS!
THE ENTIRE CASTLE IS TOPPLING!
"EIGHT HUNDRED YEARS LATER WHEN THE THREE KNIGHTS WERE UNEARTHED, THEIR ARMORED HANDS WERE ALL STRETCHED OUT IN THE SAME DIRECTION..."
IT'S AS IF THE KNIGHTS WHO WORE THE ARMOR WERE STRAINING TO REACH SOMETHING! WE'LL DIG IN THAT DIRECTION!
"AND SO IT WAS THAT DR. HARRIS FOUND THE JEWELS..."
THE BLACK OPALS OF EALING! INCREDIBLE! IT JIBES PERFECTLY WITH THE OLD LEGEND--THE ONE IN THE ANCIENT BOOK!
AS THE IMPRESSED VISITORS FILE OUT OF THE ROOM...
BRRR! IT'S ENOUGH TO MAKE A BODY SHIVER--THE WAY THAT ARMOR IS STILL FACING THE JEWELS--!
GUESS THE MUSEUM SET THEM UP THAT WAY ON PURPOSE!
LATER, WHAT WOULD STARTLE THE PUBLIC EVEN MORE...
YOU SAY IT'S HAPPENED AGAIN, JENKINS?
YES, MR. CURATOR! THIS IS THE THIRD MORNING THIS WEEK THAT I'VE NOTICED A CHANGE IN THE OVERNIGHT POSITION OF THE ARMOR!
LAST NIGHT THIS ONE'S LEFT LEG WAS FORWARD-- NOW IT'S THE RIGHT ONE!
BUT THAT'S IMPOSSIBLE! THE ARMOR CAN'T MOVE BY ITSELF--AND WHO WOULD TOUCH IT?
3

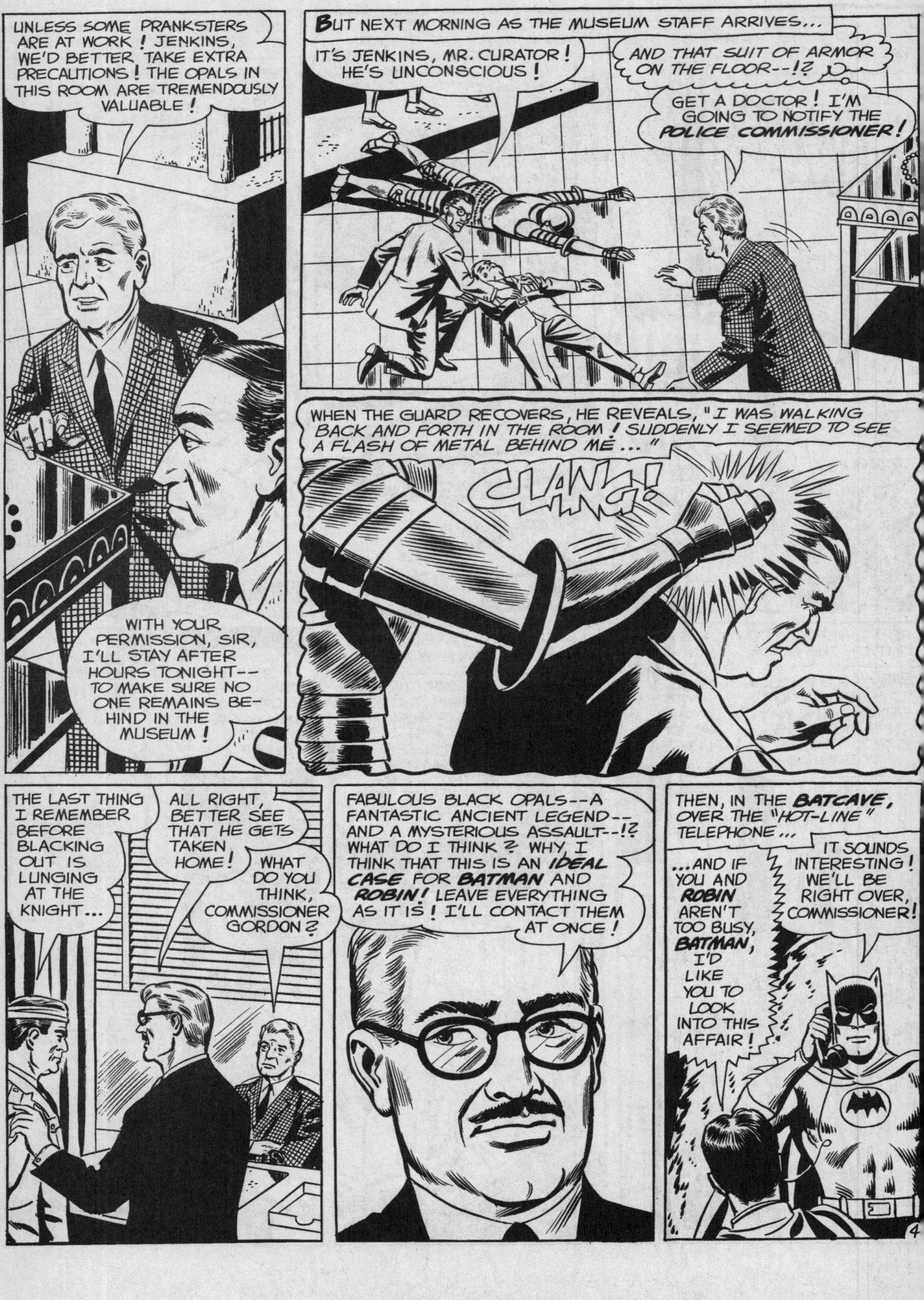
UNLESS SOME PRANKSTERS ARE AT WORK! JENKINS, WE'D BETTER TAKE EXTRA PRECAUTIONS! THE OPALS IN THIS ROOM ARE TREMENDOUSLY VALUABLE!
WITH YOUR PERMISSION, SIR, I'LL STAY AFTER HOURS TONIGHT--TO MAKE SURE NO ONE REMAINS BEHIND IN THE MUSEUM!
BUT NEXT MORNING AS THE MUSEUM STAFF ARRIVES...
IT'S JENKINS, MR. CURATOR! HE'S UNCONSCIOUS!
AND THAT SUIT OF ARMOR ON THE FLOOR--!?
GET A DOCTOR! I'M GOING TO NOTIFY THE POLICE COMMISSIONER!
WHEN THE GUARD RECOVERS, HE REVEALS, "I WAS WALKING BACK AND FORTH IN THE ROOM! SUDDENLY I SEEMED TO SEE A FLASH OF METAL BEHIND ME..."
CLANG!
THE LAST THING I REMEMBER BEFORE BLACKING OUT IS LUNGING AT THE KNIGHT...
ALL RIGHT, BETTER SEE THAT HE GETS TAKEN HOME!
WHAT DO YOU THINK, COMMISSIONER GORDON?
FABULOUS BLACK OPALS--A FANTASTIC ANCIENT LEGEND--AND A MYSTERIOUS ASSAULT--!? WHAT DO I THINK? WHY, I THINK THAT THIS IS AN IDEAL CASE FOR BATMAN AND ROBIN! LEAVE EVERYTHING AS IT IS! I'LL CONTACT THEM AT ONCE!
THEN, IN THE BATCAVE, OVER THE "HOT-LINE" TELEPHONE...
...AND IF YOU AND ROBIN AREN'T TOO BUSY, BATMAN, I'D LIKE YOU TO LOOK INTO THIS AFFAIR!
IT SOUNDS INTERESTING! WE'LL BE RIGHT OVER, COMMISSIONER!
4

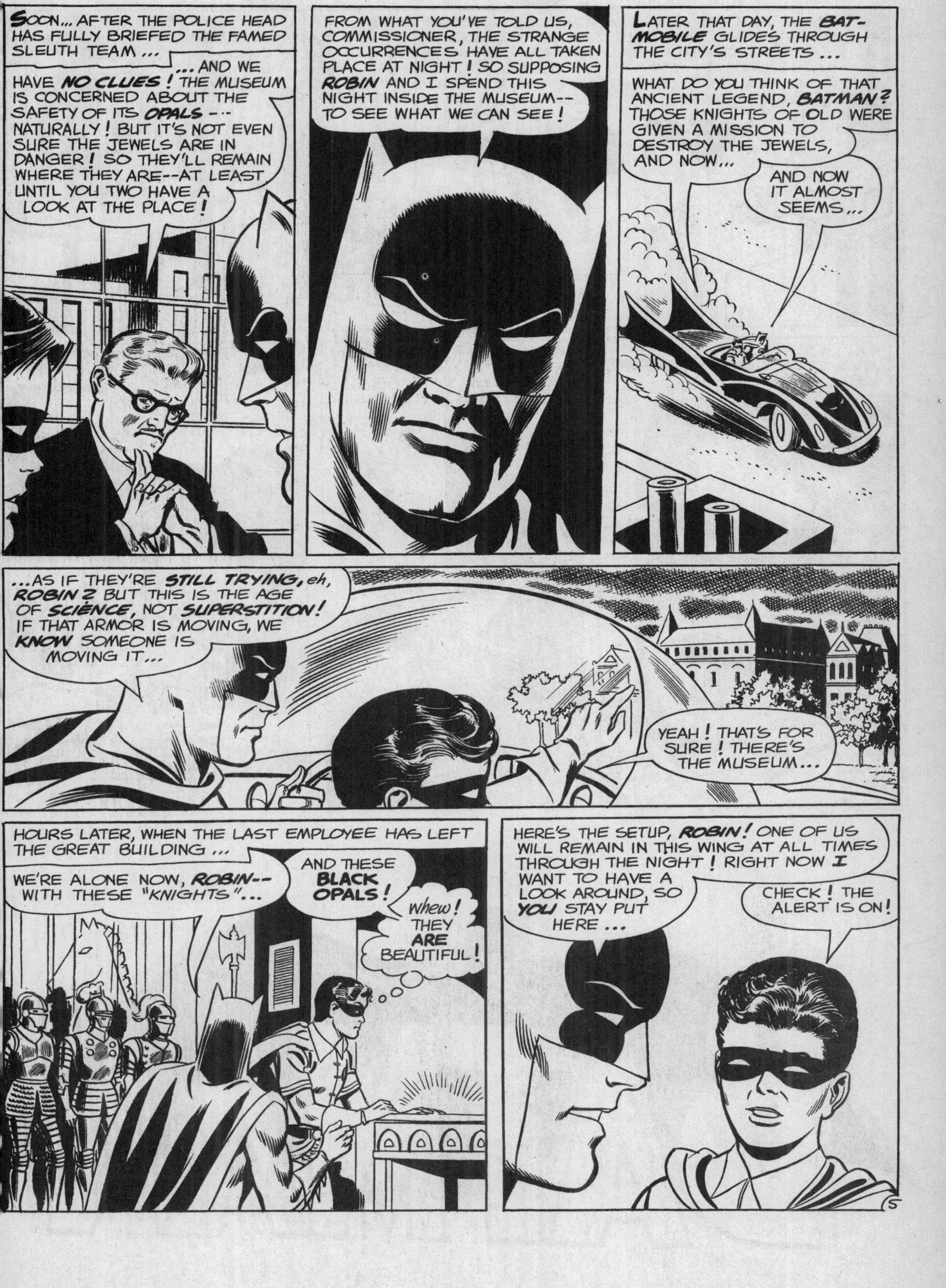
SOON... AFTER THE POLICE HEAD HAS FULLY BRIEFED THE FAMED SLEUTH TEAM ...
... AND WE HAVE NO CLUES! THE MUSEUM IS CONCERNED ABOUT THE SAFETY OF ITS OPALS --- NATURALLY! BUT IT'S NOT EVEN SURE THE JEWELS ARE IN DANGER! SO THEY'LL REMAIN WHERE THEY ARE--AT LEAST UNTIL YOU TWO HAVE A LOOK AT THE PLACE!
FROM WHAT YOU'VE TOLD US, COMMISSIONER, THE STRANGE OCCURRENCES HAVE ALL TAKEN PLACE AT NIGHT! SO SUPPOSING ROBIN AND I SPEND THIS NIGHT INSIDE THE MUSEUM-- TO SEE WHAT WE CAN SEE!
LATER THAT DAY, THE BATMOBILE GLIDES THROUGH THE CITY'S STREETS ...
WHAT DO YOU THINK OF THAT ANCIENT LEGEND, BATMAN? THOSE KNIGHTS OF OLD WERE GIVEN A MISSION TO DESTROY THE JEWELS, AND NOW...
AND NOW IT ALMOST SEEMS...
...AS IF THEY'RE STILL TRYING, eh, ROBIN? BUT THIS IS THE AGE OF SCIENCE, NOT SUPERSTITION! IF THAT ARMOR IS MOVING, WE KNOW SOMEONE IS MOVING IT...
YEAH! THAT'S FOR SURE! THERE'S THE MUSEUM...
HOURS LATER, WHEN THE LAST EMPLOYEE HAS LEFT THE GREAT BUILDING ...
WE'RE ALONE NOW, ROBIN-- WITH THESE "KNIGHTS"...
AND THESE BLACK OPALS!
Whew! THEY ARE BEAUTIFUL!
HERE'S THE SETUP, ROBIN! ONE OF US WILL REMAIN IN THIS WING AT ALL TIMES THROUGH THE NIGHT! RIGHT NOW I WANT TO HAVE A LOOK AROUND, SO YOU STAY PUT HERE ...
CHECK! THE ALERT IS ON!
5

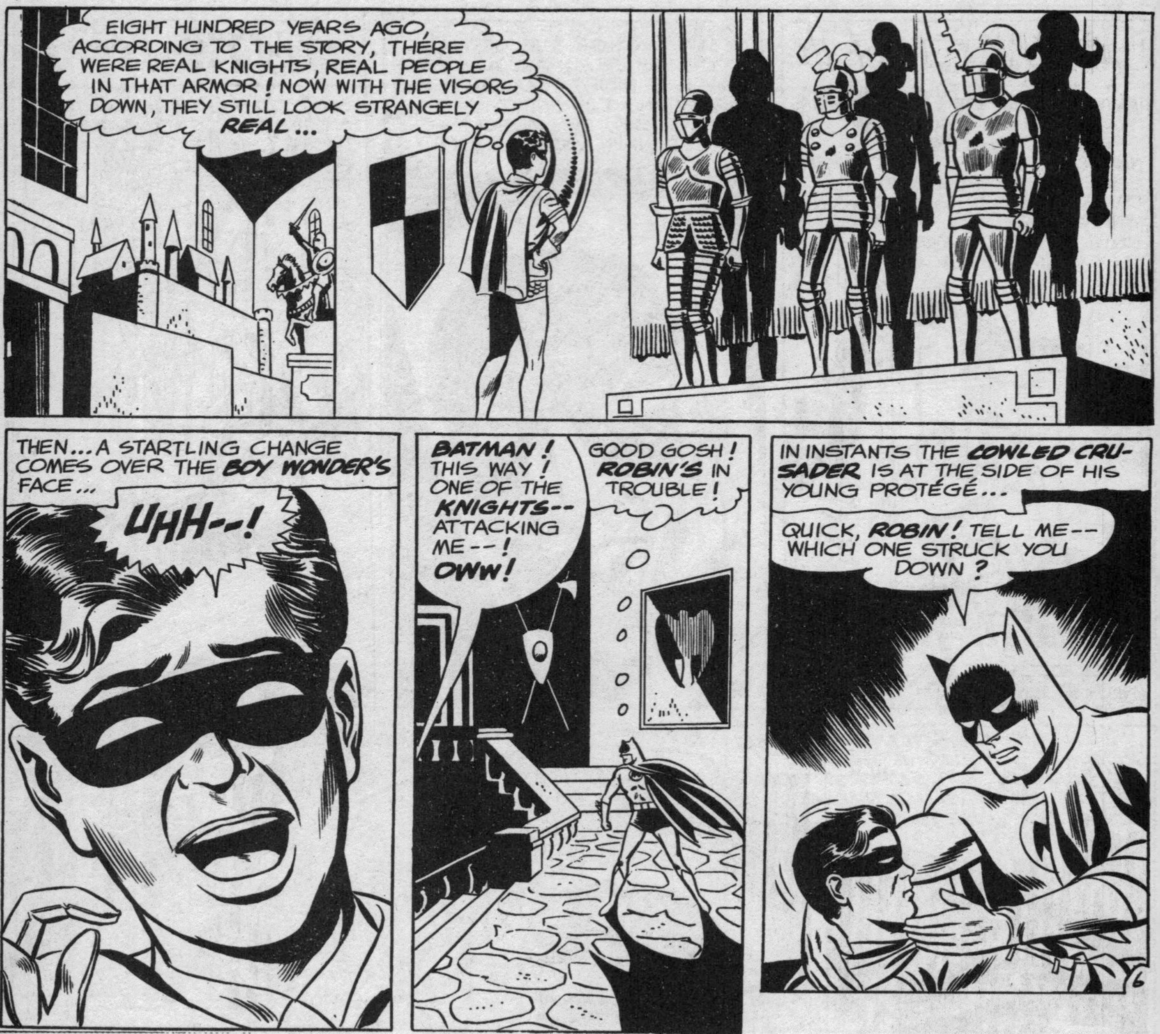
EIGHT HUNDRED YEARS AGO, ACCORDING TO THE STORY, THERE WERE REAL KNIGHTS, REAL PEOPLE IN THAT ARMOR! NOW WITH THE VISORS DOWN, THEY STILL LOOK STRANGELY REAL...
THEN... A STARTLING CHANGE COMES OVER THE BOY WONDER'S FACE...
UHH--!
BATMAN! THIS WAY! ONE OF THE KNIGHTS-- ATTACKING ME--! OWW!
GOOD GOSH! ROBIN'S IN TROUBLE!
IN INSTANTS THE COWLED CRUSADER IS AT THE SIDE OF HIS YOUNG PROTÉGÉ...
QUICK, ROBIN! TELL ME-- WHICH ONE STRUCK YOU DOWN?
6

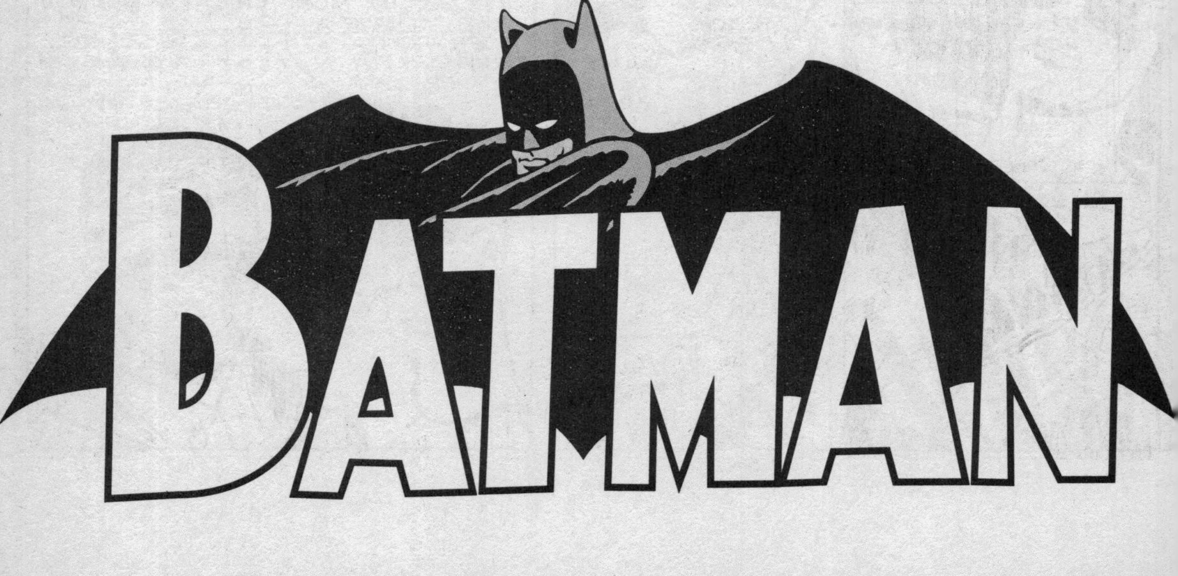
BATMAN

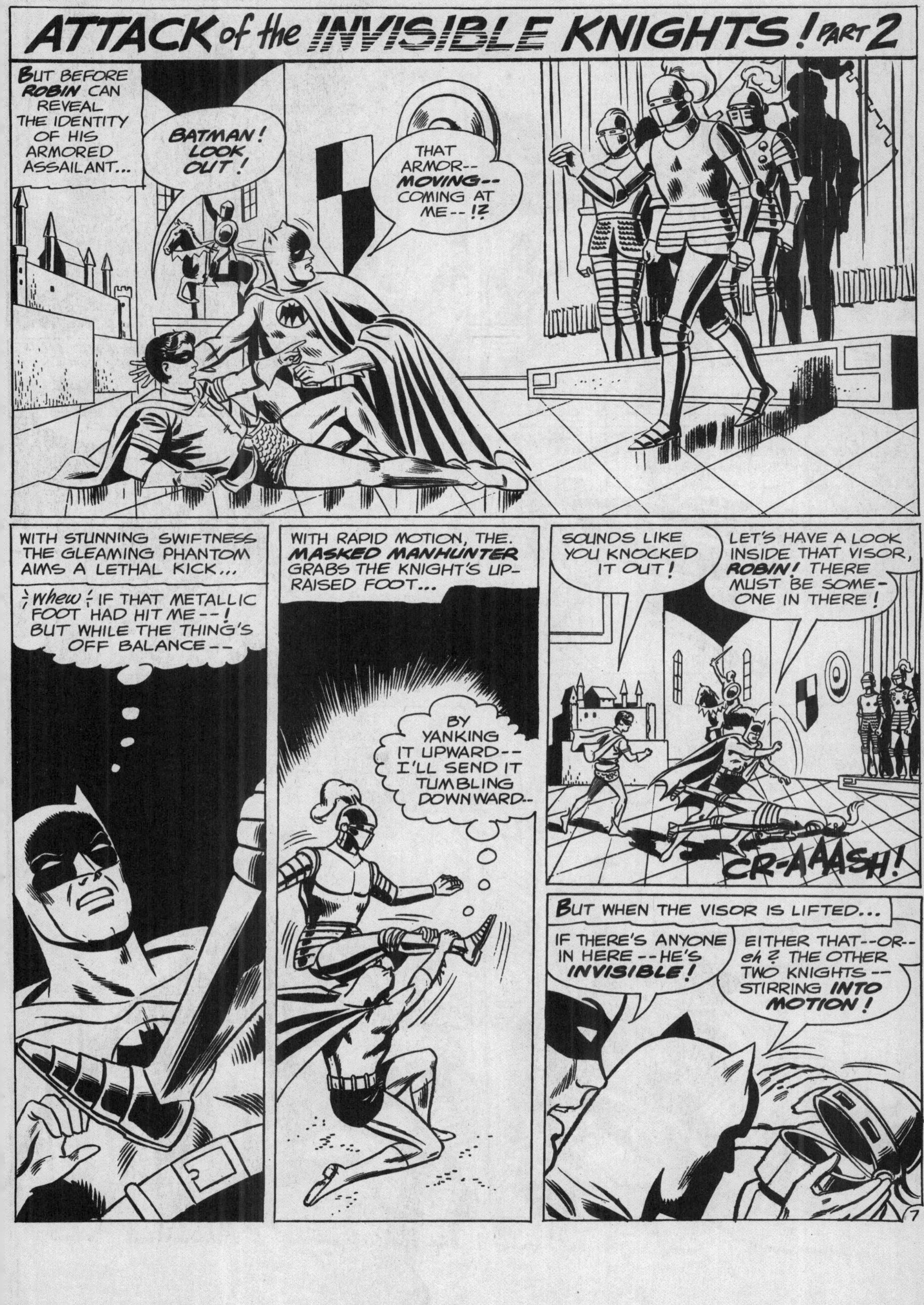
ATTACK of the INVISIBLE KNIGHTS! PART 2
BUT BEFORE ROBIN CAN REVEAL THE IDENTITY OF HIS ARMORED ASSAILANT...
BATMAN! LOOK OUT!
THAT ARMOR-- MOVING-- COMING AT ME--!?
WITH STUNNING SWIFTNESS THE GLEAMING PHANTOM AIMS A LETHAL KICK...
-WHEW- IF THAT METALLIC FOOT HAD HIT ME--! BUT WHILE THE THING'S OFF BALANCE--
WITH RAPID MOTION, THE. MASKED MANHUNTER GRABS THE KNIGHT'S UPRAISED FOOT...
BY YANKING IT UPWARD-- I'LL SEND IT TUMBLING DOWNWARD--
SOUNDS LIKE YOU KNOCKED IT OUT!
LET'S HAVE A LOOK INSIDE THAT VISOR, ROBIN! THERE MUST BE SOMEONE IN THERE!
CR-AAASH!
BUT WHEN THE VISOR IS LIFTED...
IF THERE'S ANYONE IN HERE--HE'S INVISIBLE!
EITHER THAT--OR--eh? THE OTHER TWO KNIGHTS-- STIRRING INTO MOTION!
7

A STRANGE, GRIM BATTLE ENVELOPS THE DAUNTLESS DUO...

CAREFUL, *ROBIN!* IF ONE OF THEM HITS YOU--

HE'S TELLING ME! I STILL FEEL THE EFFECTS OF THAT FIRST SURPRISE ATTACK! BUT THIS TIME I'M PREPARED...

BUT DESPITE ALL OF THE *BOY WONDER'S* EFFORTS...

UHHH!

THAT *KNIGHT* KNOCKED OUT *ROBIN!*

GETTING NOWHERE USING MY FISTS ON THESE ARMOR-PLATED ATTACKERS!

CLANG!

OUT OF *BATMAN'S* UTILITY BELT KIT COMES HIS SILKEN ROPE AND...

MANAGED TO LOOP THE *BATROPE* AROUND THAT KNIGHT-- SWINGING HIM--

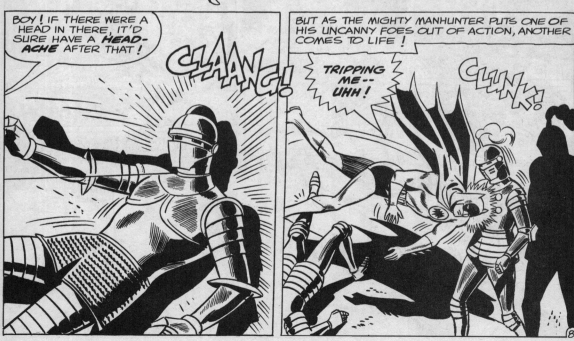

BOY! IF THERE WERE A HEAD IN THERE, IT'D SURE HAVE A *HEAD-ACHE* AFTER THAT!

CLAAANG!

BUT AS THE MIGHTY MANHUNTER PUTS ONE OF HIS UNCANNY FOES OUT OF ACTION, ANOTHER COMES TO LIFE!

TRIPPING ME-- UHH!

CLUNK!

8

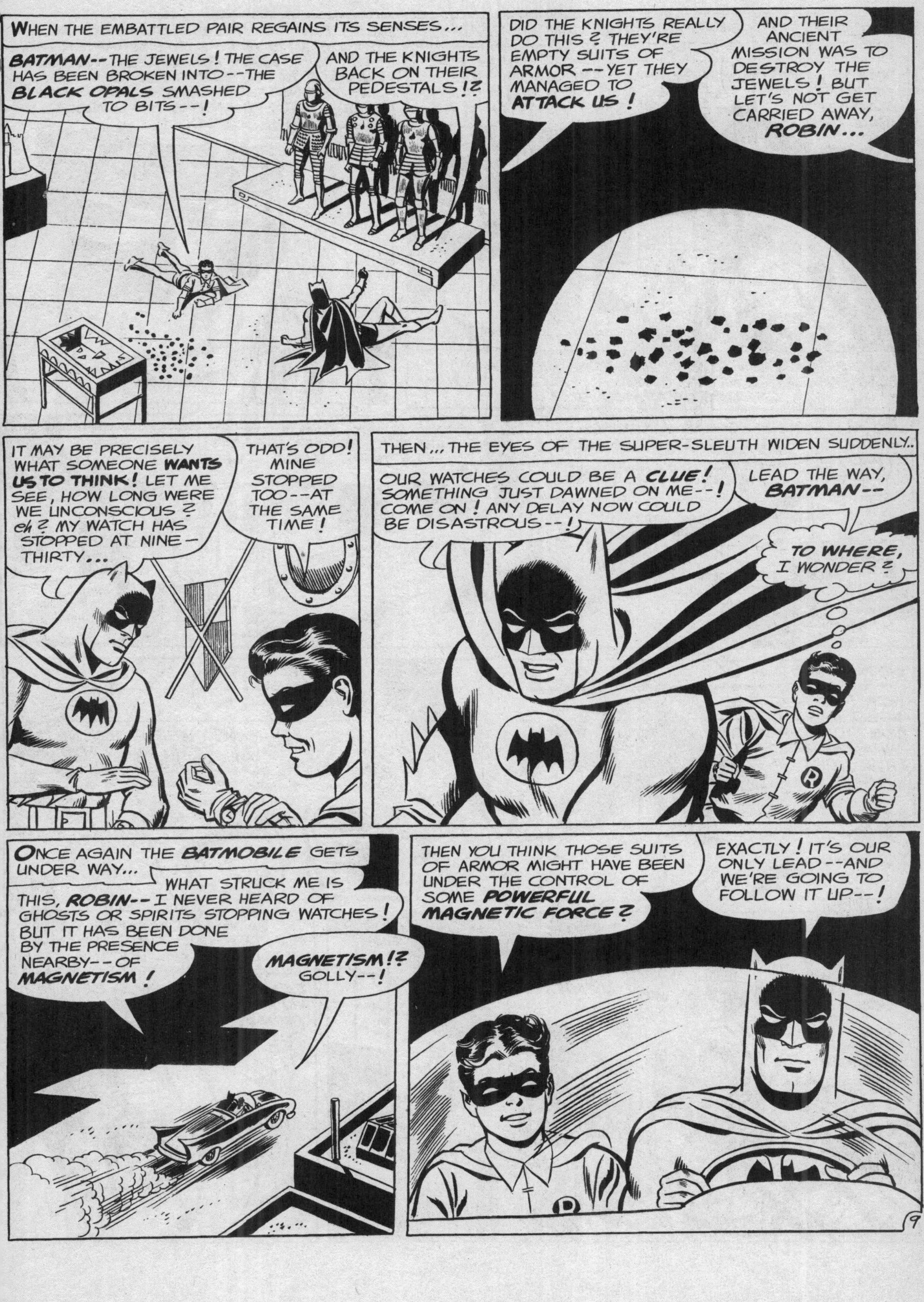
WHEN THE EMBATTLED PAIR REGAINS ITS SENSES...
BATMAN--THE JEWELS! THE CASE HAS BEEN BROKEN INTO--THE BLACK OPALS SMASHED TO BITS--!
AND THE KNIGHTS BACK ON THEIR PEDESTALS!?
DID THE KNIGHTS REALLY DO THIS? THEY'RE EMPTY SUITS OF ARMOR--YET THEY MANAGED TO ATTACK US!
AND THEIR ANCIENT MISSION WAS TO DESTROY THE JEWELS! BUT LET'S NOT GET CARRIED AWAY, ROBIN...
IT MAY BE PRECISELY WHAT SOMEONE WANTS US TO THINK! LET ME SEE, HOW LONG WERE WE UNCONSCIOUS? eh? MY WATCH HAS STOPPED AT NINE-THIRTY...
THAT'S ODD! MINE STOPPED TOO--AT THE SAME TIME!
THEN... THE EYES OF THE SUPER-SLEUTH WIDEN SUDDENLY..
OUR WATCHES COULD BE A CLUE! SOMETHING JUST DAWNED ON ME--! COME ON! ANY DELAY NOW COULD BE DISASTROUS--!
LEAD THE WAY, BATMAN--
TO WHERE, I WONDER?
ONCE AGAIN THE BATMOBILE GETS UNDER WAY...
WHAT STRUCK ME IS THIS, ROBIN--I NEVER HEARD OF GHOSTS OR SPIRITS STOPPING WATCHES! BUT IT HAS BEEN DONE BY THE PRESENCE NEARBY--OF MAGNETISM!
MAGNETISM!? GOLLY--!
THEN YOU THINK THOSE SUITS OF ARMOR MIGHT HAVE BEEN UNDER THE CONTROL OF SOME POWERFUL MAGNETIC FORCE?
EXACTLY! IT'S OUR ONLY LEAD--AND WE'RE GOING TO FOLLOW IT UP--!
9

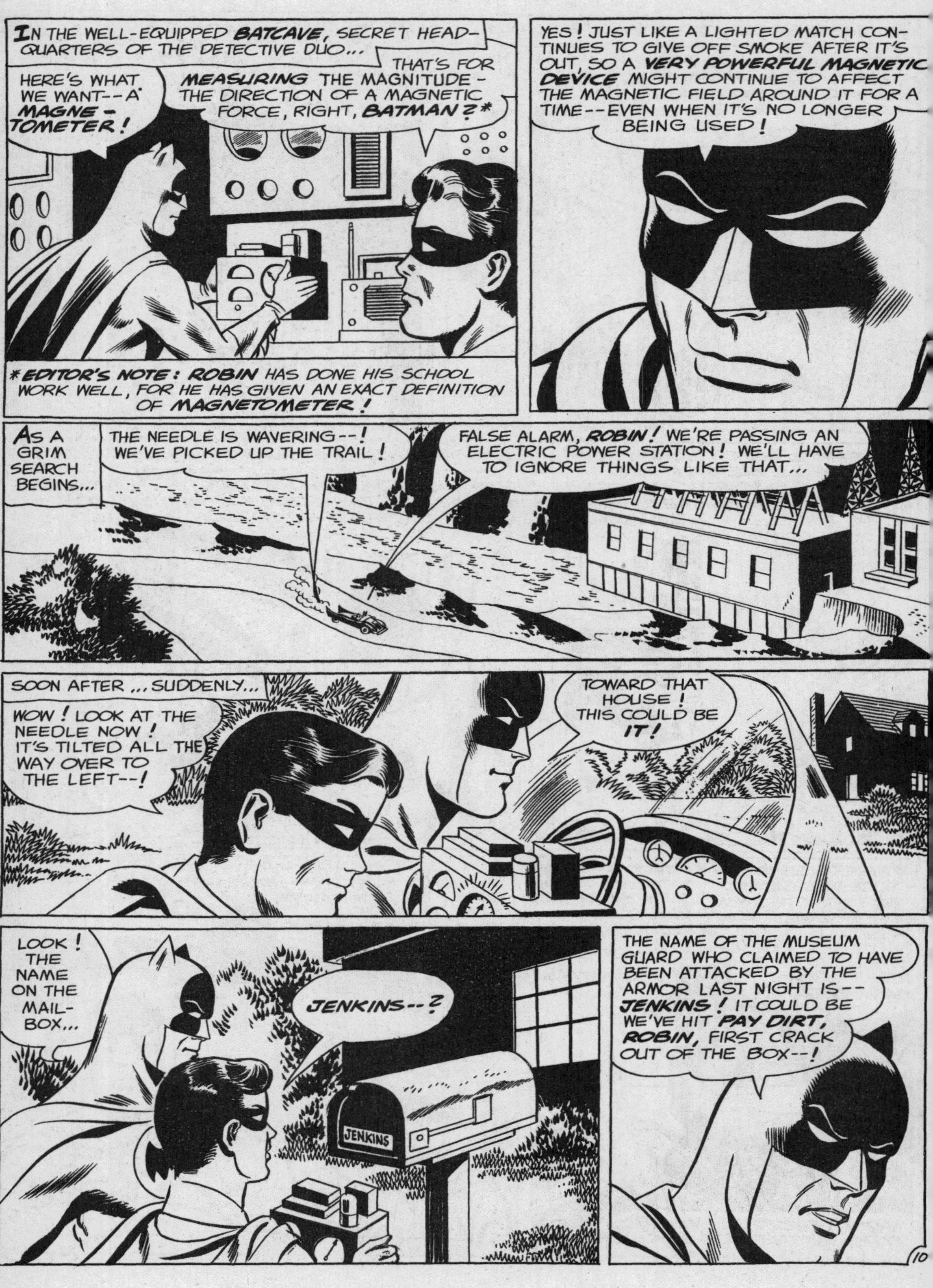
IN THE WELL-EQUIPPED BATCAVE, SECRET HEADQUARTERS OF THE DETECTIVE DUO...
HERE'S WHAT WE WANT--A MAGNE-TOMETER!
THAT'S FOR MEASURING THE MAGNITUDE - THE DIRECTION OF A MAGNETIC FORCE, RIGHT, BATMAN?*
*EDITOR'S NOTE: ROBIN HAS DONE HIS SCHOOL WORK WELL, FOR HE HAS GIVEN AN EXACT DEFINITION OF MAGNETOMETER!
YES! JUST LIKE A LIGHTED MATCH CONTINUES TO GIVE OFF SMOKE AFTER IT'S OUT, SO A VERY POWERFUL MAGNETIC DEVICE MIGHT CONTINUE TO AFFECT THE MAGNETIC FIELD AROUND IT FOR A TIME--EVEN WHEN IT'S NO LONGER BEING USED!
AS A GRIM SEARCH BEGINS...
THE NEEDLE IS WAVERING--! WE'VE PICKED UP THE TRAIL!
FALSE ALARM, ROBIN! WE'RE PASSING AN ELECTRIC POWER STATION! WE'LL HAVE TO IGNORE THINGS LIKE THAT...
SOON AFTER... SUDDENLY...
WOW! LOOK AT THE NEEDLE NOW! IT'S TILTED ALL THE WAY OVER TO THE LEFT--!
TOWARD THAT HOUSE! THIS COULD BE IT!
LOOK! THE NAME ON THE MAIL-BOX...
JENKINS--?
JENKINS
THE NAME OF THE MUSEUM GUARD WHO CLAIMED TO HAVE BEEN ATTACKED BY THE ARMOR LAST NIGHT IS--JENKINS! IT COULD BE WE'VE HIT PAY DIRT, ROBIN, FIRST CRACK OUT OF THE BOX--!
10

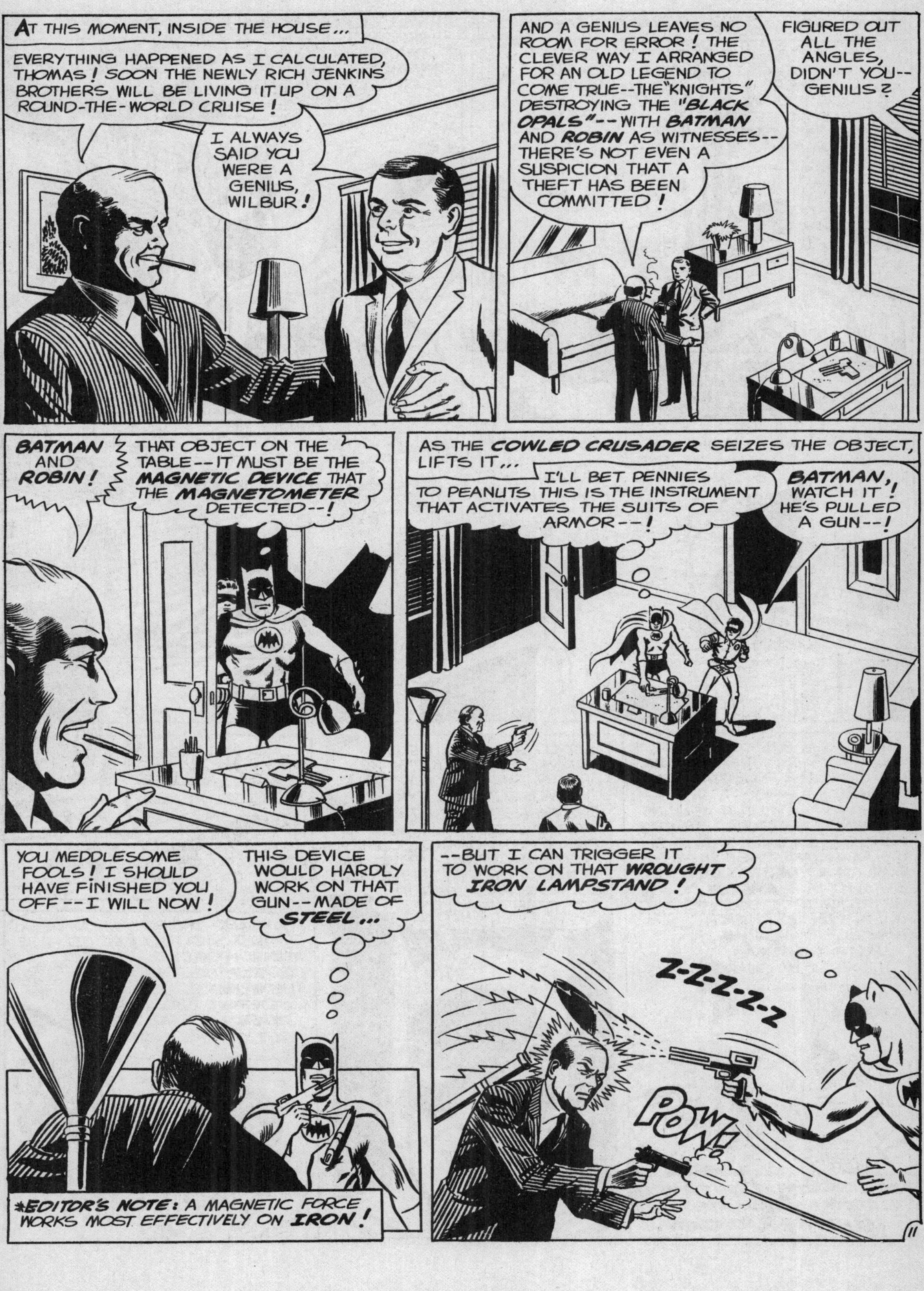
AT THIS MOMENT, INSIDE THE HOUSE...
EVERYTHING HAPPENED AS I CALCULATED, THOMAS! SOON THE NEWLY RICH JENKINS BROTHERS WILL BE LIVING IT UP ON A ROUND-THE-WORLD CRUISE!
I ALWAYS SAID YOU WERE A GENIUS, WILBUR!
AND A GENIUS LEAVES NO ROOM FOR ERROR! THE CLEVER WAY I ARRANGED FOR AN OLD LEGEND TO COME TRUE--THE "KNIGHTS" DESTROYING THE "BLACK OPALS"--WITH BATMAN AND ROBIN AS WITNESSES--THERE'S NOT EVEN A SUSPICION THAT A THEFT HAS BEEN COMMITTED!
FIGURED OUT ALL THE ANGLES, DIDN'T YOU--GENIUS?
BATMAN AND ROBIN!
THAT OBJECT ON THE TABLE--IT MUST BE THE MAGNETIC DEVICE THAT THE MAGNETOMETER DETECTED--!
AS THE COWLED CRUSADER SEIZES THE OBJECT, LIFTS IT...
I'LL BET PENNIES TO PEANUTS THIS IS THE INSTRUMENT THAT ACTIVATES THE SUITS OF ARMOR--!
BATMAN, WATCH IT! HE'S PULLED A GUN--!
YOU MEDDLESOME FOOLS! I SHOULD HAVE FINISHED YOU OFF--I WILL NOW!
THIS DEVICE WOULD HARDLY WORK ON THAT GUN--MADE OF STEEL...
*EDITOR'S NOTE: A MAGNETIC FORCE WORKS MOST EFFECTIVELY ON IRON!
--BUT I CAN TRIGGER IT TO WORK ON THAT WROUGHT IRON LAMPSTAND!
Z-Z-Z-Z-Z
POW!
11

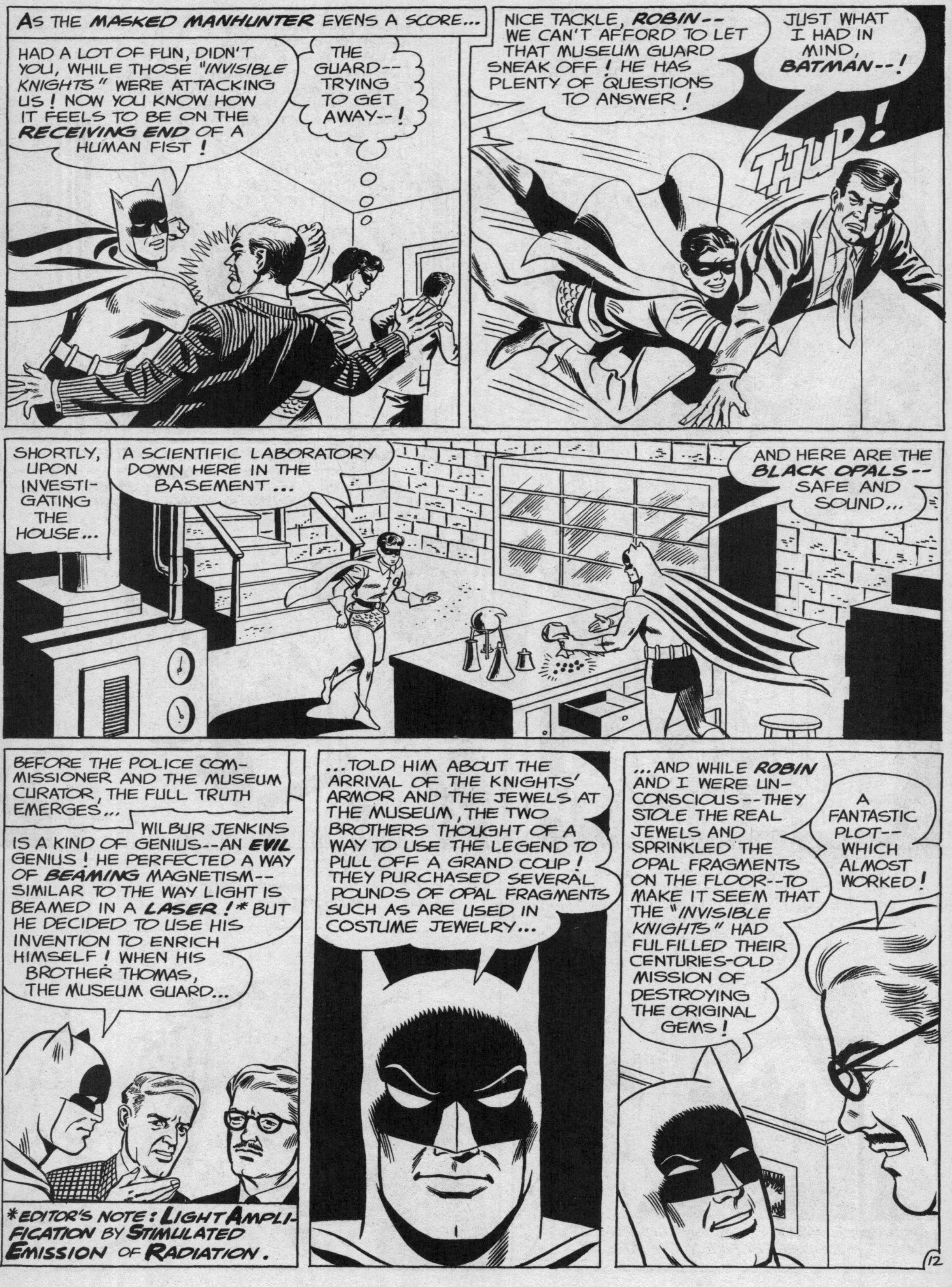
AS THE MASKED MANHUNTER EVENS A SCORE...
HAD A LOT OF FUN, DIDN'T YOU, WHILE THOSE "INVISIBLE KNIGHTS" WERE ATTACKING US! NOW YOU KNOW HOW IT FEELS TO BE ON THE RECEIVING END OF A HUMAN FIST!
THE GUARD-- TRYING TO GET AWAY--!
NICE TACKLE, ROBIN-- WE CAN'T AFFORD TO LET THAT MUSEUM GUARD SNEAK OFF! HE HAS PLENTY OF QUESTIONS TO ANSWER!
JUST WHAT I HAD IN MIND, BATMAN--!
THUD!
SHORTLY, UPON INVESTIGATING THE HOUSE...
A SCIENTIFIC LABORATORY DOWN HERE IN THE BASEMENT...
AND HERE ARE THE BLACK OPALS-- SAFE AND SOUND...
BEFORE THE POLICE COMMISSIONER AND THE MUSEUM CURATOR, THE FULL TRUTH EMERGES...
WILBUR JENKINS IS A KIND OF GENIUS--AN EVIL GENIUS! HE PERFECTED A WAY OF BEAMING MAGNETISM-- SIMILAR TO THE WAY LIGHT IS BEAMED IN A LASER!* BUT HE DECIDED TO USE HIS INVENTION TO ENRICH HIMSELF! WHEN HIS BROTHER THOMAS, THE MUSEUM GUARD...
*EDITOR'S NOTE: LIGHT AMPLIFICATION BY STIMULATED EMISSION OF RADIATION.
...TOLD HIM ABOUT THE ARRIVAL OF THE KNIGHTS' ARMOR AND THE JEWELS AT THE MUSEUM, THE TWO BROTHERS THOUGHT OF A WAY TO USE THE LEGEND TO PULL OFF A GRAND COUP! THEY PURCHASED SEVERAL POUNDS OF OPAL FRAGMENTS SUCH AS ARE USED IN COSTUME JEWELRY...
...AND WHILE ROBIN AND I WERE UNCONSCIOUS--THEY STOLE THE REAL JEWELS AND SPRINKLED THE OPAL FRAGMENTS ON THE FLOOR--TO MAKE IT SEEM THAT THE "INVISIBLE KNIGHTS" HAD FULFILLED THEIR CENTURIES-OLD MISSION OF DESTROYING THE ORIGINAL GEMS!
A FANTASTIC PLOT-- WHICH ALMOST WORKED!
12

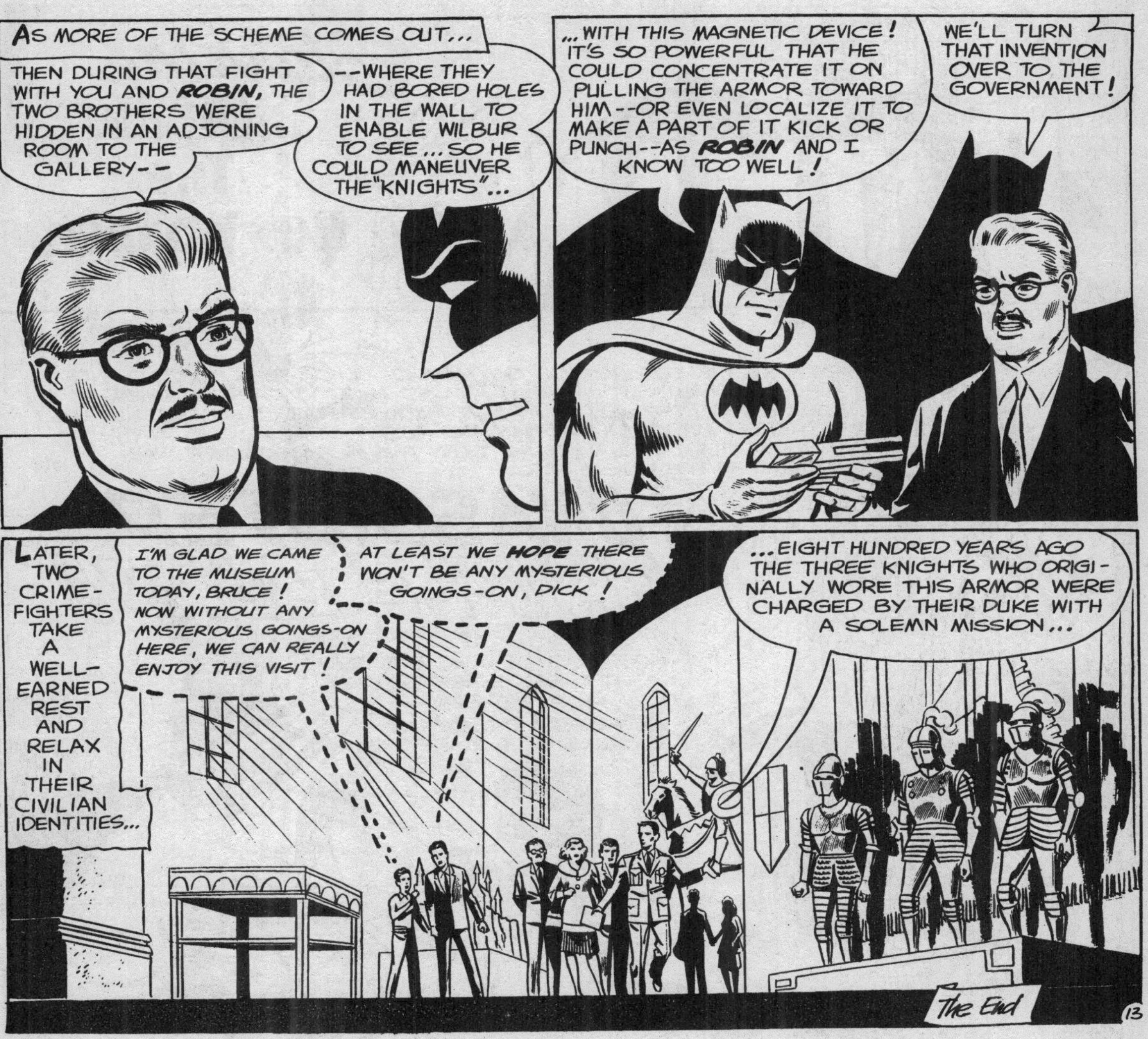
AS MORE OF THE SCHEME COMES OUT...
THEN DURING THAT FIGHT WITH YOU AND ROBIN, THE TWO BROTHERS WERE HIDDEN IN AN ADJOINING ROOM TO THE GALLERY--
--WHERE THEY HAD BORED HOLES IN THE WALL TO ENABLE WILBUR TO SEE... SO HE COULD MANEUVER THE "KNIGHTS"...
...WITH THIS MAGNETIC DEVICE! IT'S SO POWERFUL THAT HE COULD CONCENTRATE IT ON PULLING THE ARMOR TOWARD HIM--OR EVEN LOCALIZE IT TO MAKE A PART OF IT KICK OR PUNCH--AS ROBIN AND I KNOW TOO WELL!
WE'LL TURN THAT INVENTION OVER TO THE GOVERNMENT!
LATER, TWO CRIME-FIGHTERS TAKE A WELL-EARNED REST AND RELAX IN THEIR CIVILIAN IDENTITIES...
I'M GLAD WE CAME TO THE MUSEUM TODAY, BRUCE! NOW WITHOUT ANY MYSTERIOUS GOINGS-ON HERE, WE CAN REALLY ENJOY THIS VISIT!
AT LEAST WE HOPE THERE WON'T BE ANY MYSTERIOUS GOINGS-ON, DICK!
...EIGHT HUNDRED YEARS AGO THE THREE KNIGHTS WHO ORIGINALLY WORE THIS ARMOR WERE CHARGED BY THEIR DUKE WITH A SOLEMN MISSION...
The End
13

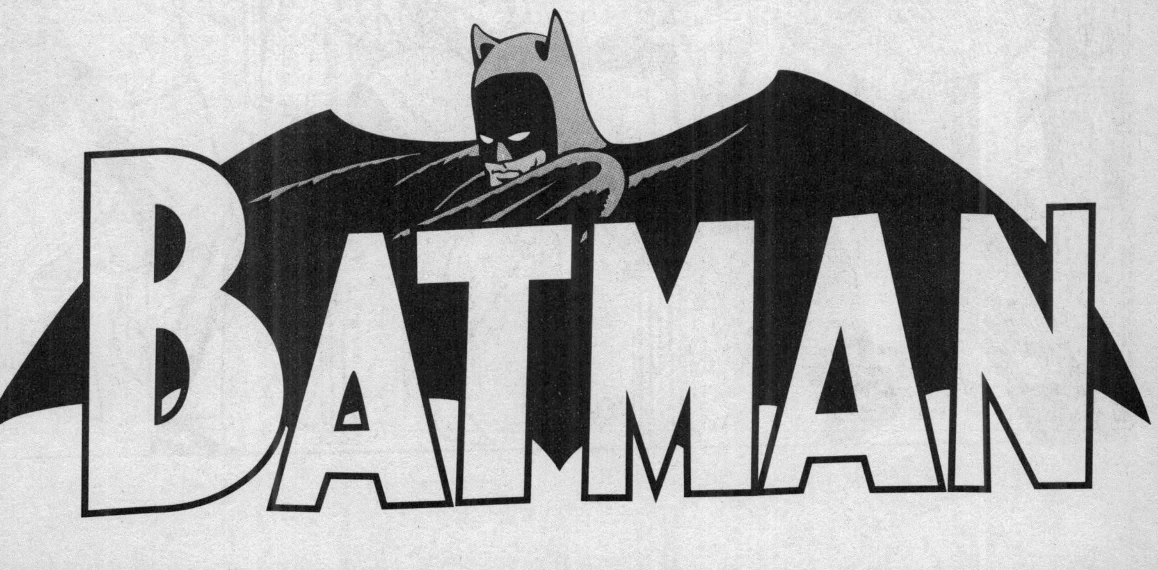
BATMAN

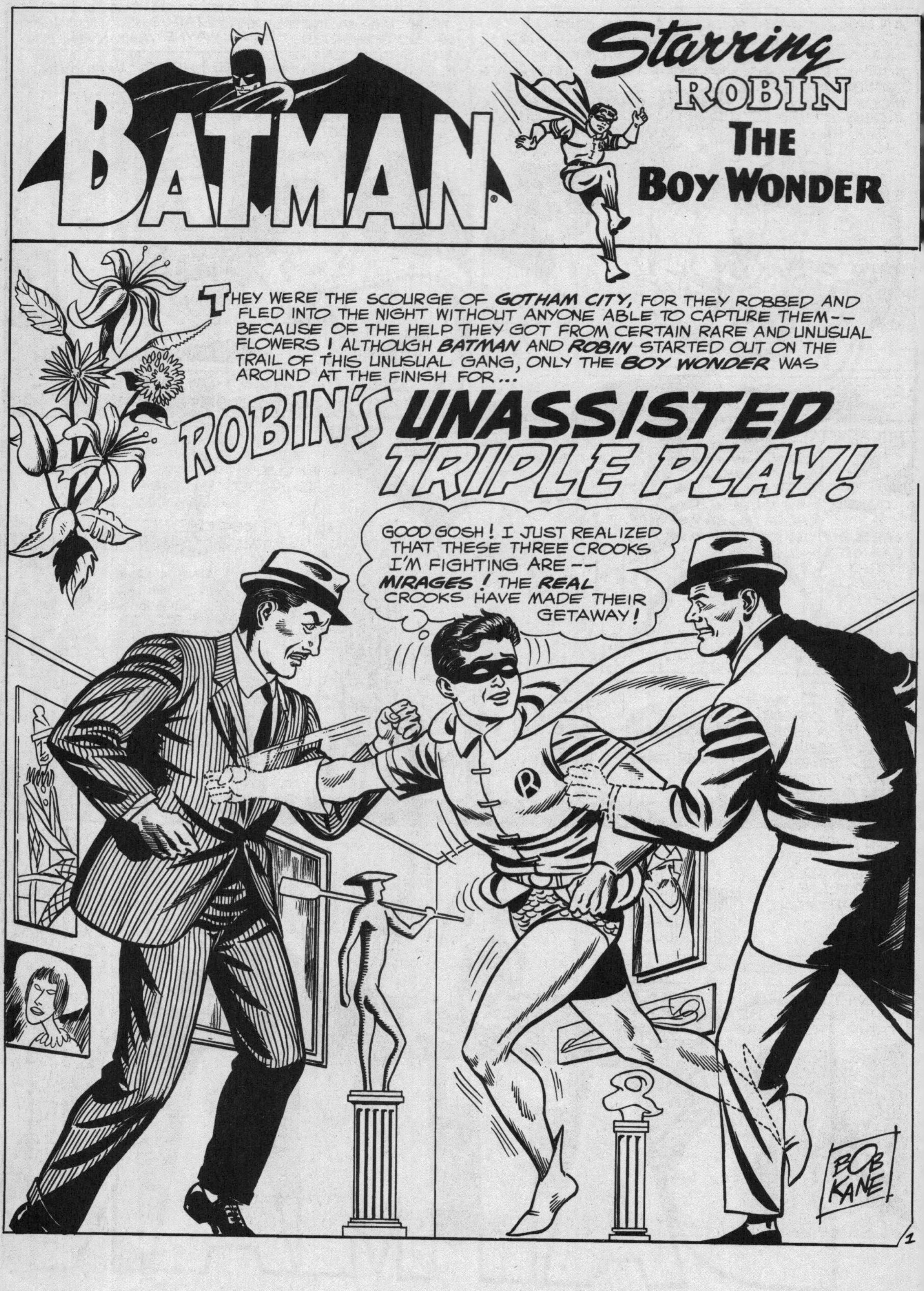
BATMAN
Starring ROBIN THE BOY WONDER
THEY WERE THE SCOURGE OF GOTHAM CITY, FOR THEY ROBBED AND FLED INTO THE NIGHT WITHOUT ANYONE ABLE TO CAPTURE THEM-- BECAUSE OF THE HELP THEY GOT FROM CERTAIN RARE AND UNUSUAL FLOWERS! ALTHOUGH BATMAN AND ROBIN STARTED OUT ON THE TRAIL OF THIS UNUSUAL GANG, ONLY THE BOY WONDER WAS AROUND AT THE FINISH FOR...
ROBIN'S UNASSISTED TRIPLE PLAY!
GOOD GOSH! I JUST REALIZED THAT THESE THREE CROOKS I'M FIGHTING ARE -- MIRAGES! THE REAL CROOKS HAVE MADE THEIR GETAWAY!
BOB KANE
1

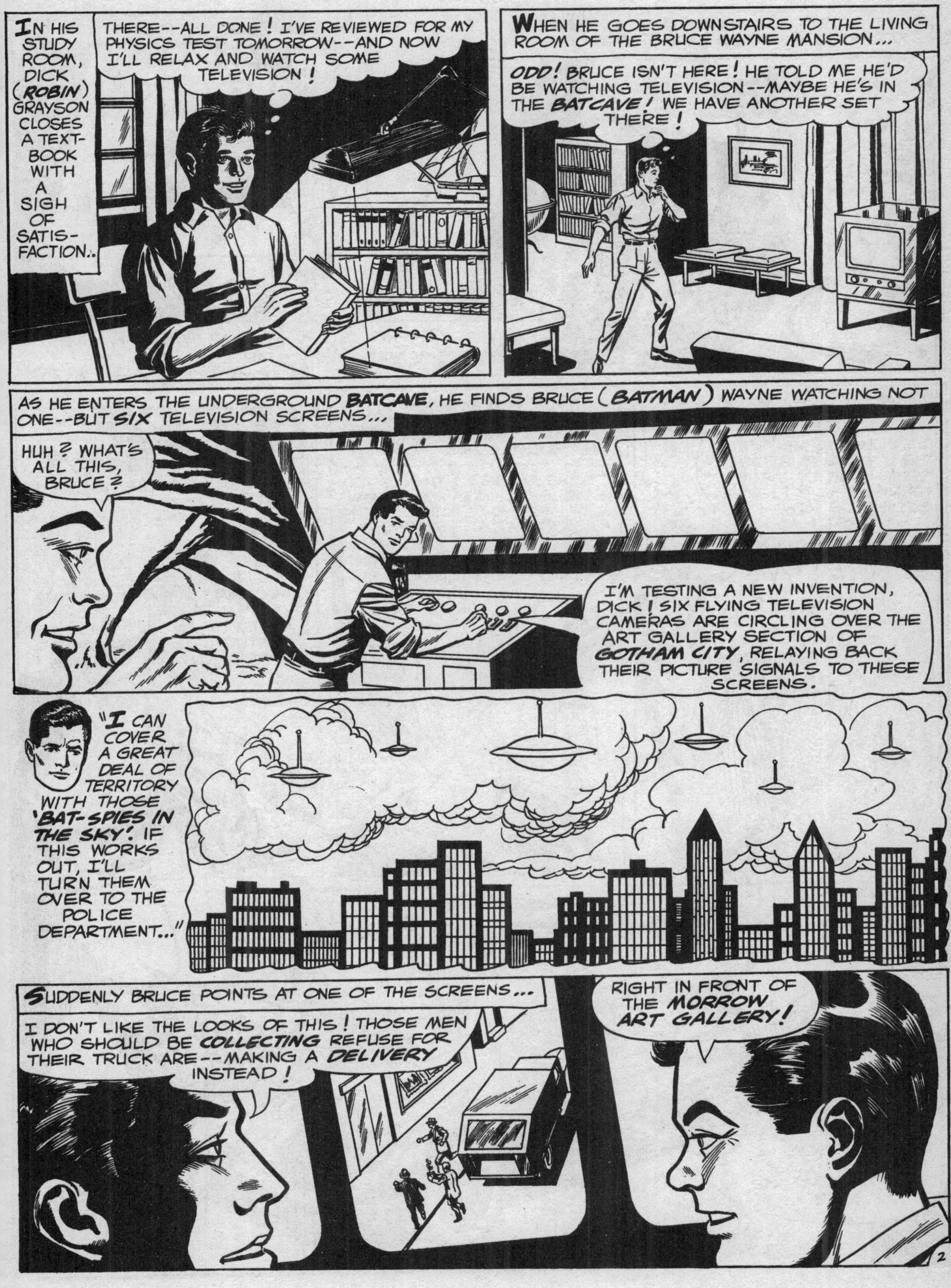
IN HIS STUDY ROOM, DICK (ROBIN) GRAYSON CLOSES A TEXT-BOOK WITH A SIGH OF SATIS-FACTION..
THERE--ALL DONE! I'VE REVIEWED FOR MY PHYSICS TEST TOMORROW--AND NOW I'LL RELAX AND WATCH SOME TELEVISION!
WHEN HE GOES DOWNSTAIRS TO THE LIVING ROOM OF THE BRUCE WAYNE MANSION...
ODD! BRUCE ISN'T HERE! HE TOLD ME HE'D BE WATCHING TELEVISION--MAYBE HE'S IN THE BATCAVE! WE HAVE ANOTHER SET THERE!
AS HE ENTERS THE UNDERGROUND BATCAVE, HE FINDS BRUCE (BATMAN) WAYNE WATCHING NOT ONE--BUT SIX TELEVISION SCREENS...
HUH? WHAT'S ALL THIS, BRUCE?
I'M TESTING A NEW INVENTION, DICK! SIX FLYING TELEVISION CAMERAS ARE CIRCLING OVER THE ART GALLERY SECTION OF GOTHAM CITY, RELAYING BACK THEIR PICTURE SIGNALS TO THESE SCREENS.
"I CAN COVER A GREAT DEAL OF TERRITORY WITH THOSE 'BAT-SPIES IN THE SKY'! IF THIS WORKS OUT, I'LL TURN THEM OVER TO THE POLICE DEPARTMENT..."
SUDDENLY BRUCE POINTS AT ONE OF THE SCREENS...
I DON'T LIKE THE LOOKS OF THIS! THOSE MEN WHO SHOULD BE COLLECTING REFUSE FOR THEIR TRUCK ARE--MAKING A DELIVERY INSTEAD!
RIGHT IN FRONT OF THE MORROW ART GALLERY!
2

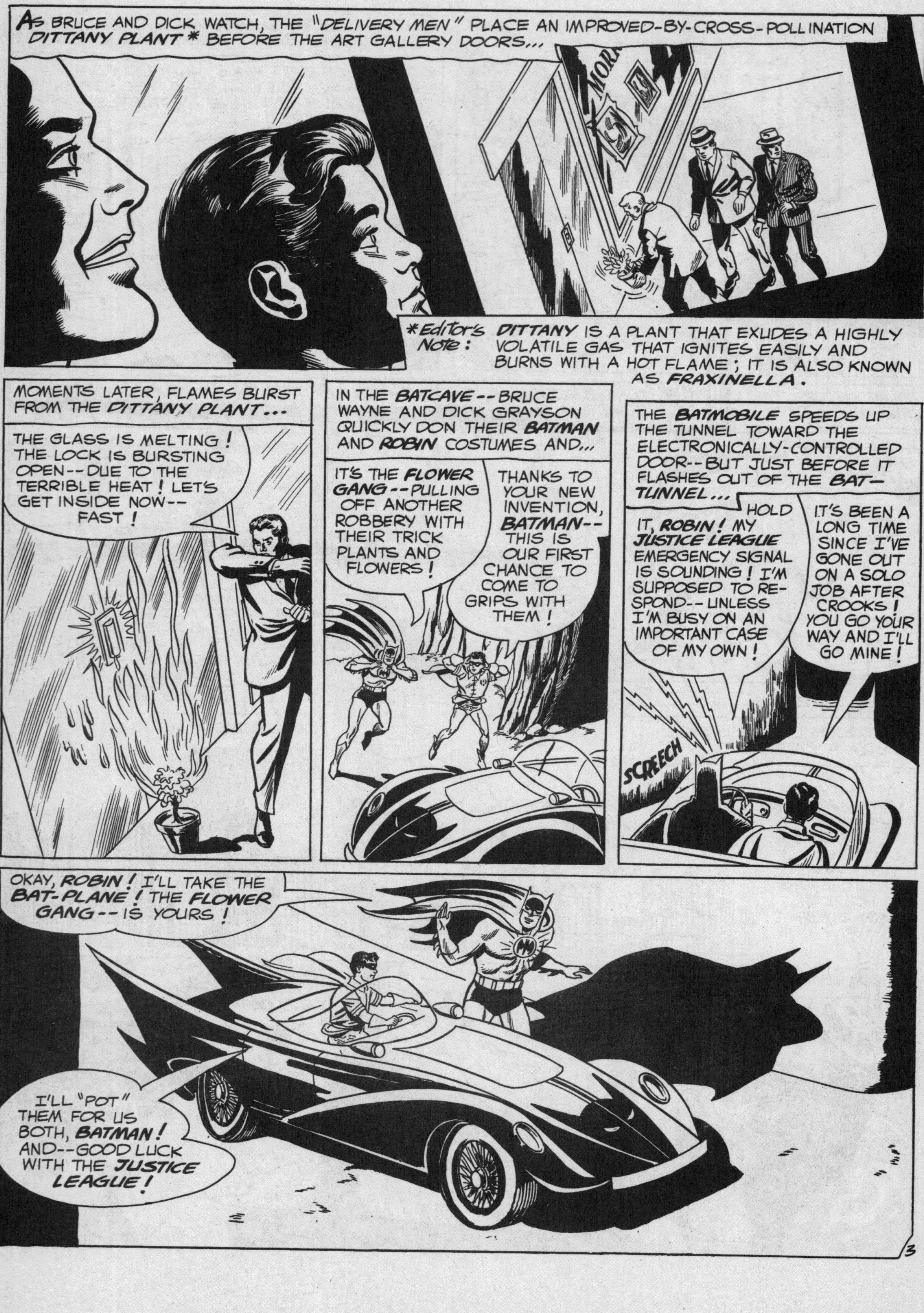
AS BRUCE AND DICK WATCH, THE "DELIVERY MEN" PLACE AN IMPROVED-BY-CROSS-POLLINATION DITTANY PLANT* BEFORE THE ART GALLERY DOORS...
*Editor's Note: DITTANY IS A PLANT THAT EXUDES A HIGHLY VOLATILE GAS THAT IGNITES EASILY AND BURNS WITH A HOT FLAME; IT IS ALSO KNOWN AS FRAXINELLA.
MOMENTS LATER, FLAMES BURST FROM THE DITTANY PLANT...
THE GLASS IS MELTING! THE LOCK IS BURSTING OPEN--DUE TO THE TERRIBLE HEAT! LET'S GET INSIDE NOW--FAST!
IN THE BATCAVE--BRUCE WAYNE AND DICK GRAYSON QUICKLY DON THEIR BATMAN AND ROBIN COSTUMES AND...
IT'S THE FLOWER GANG--PULLING OFF ANOTHER ROBBERY WITH THEIR TRICK PLANTS AND FLOWERS!
THANKS TO YOUR NEW INVENTION, BATMAN--THIS IS OUR FIRST CHANCE TO COME TO GRIPS WITH THEM!
THE BATMOBILE SPEEDS UP THE TUNNEL TOWARD THE ELECTRONICALLY-CONTROLLED DOOR--BUT JUST BEFORE IT FLASHES OUT OF THE BAT-TUNNEL...
HOLD IT, ROBIN! MY JUSTICE LEAGUE EMERGENCY SIGNAL IS SOUNDING! I'M SUPPOSED TO RESPOND--UNLESS I'M BUSY ON AN IMPORTANT CASE OF MY OWN!
IT'S BEEN A LONG TIME SINCE I'VE GONE OUT ON A SOLO JOB AFTER CROOKS! YOU GO YOUR WAY AND I'LL GO MINE!
SCREECH
OKAY, ROBIN! I'LL TAKE THE BAT-PLANE! THE FLOWER GANG--IS YOURS!
I'LL "POT" THEM FOR US BOTH, BATMAN! AND--GOOD LUCK WITH THE JUSTICE LEAGUE!
3

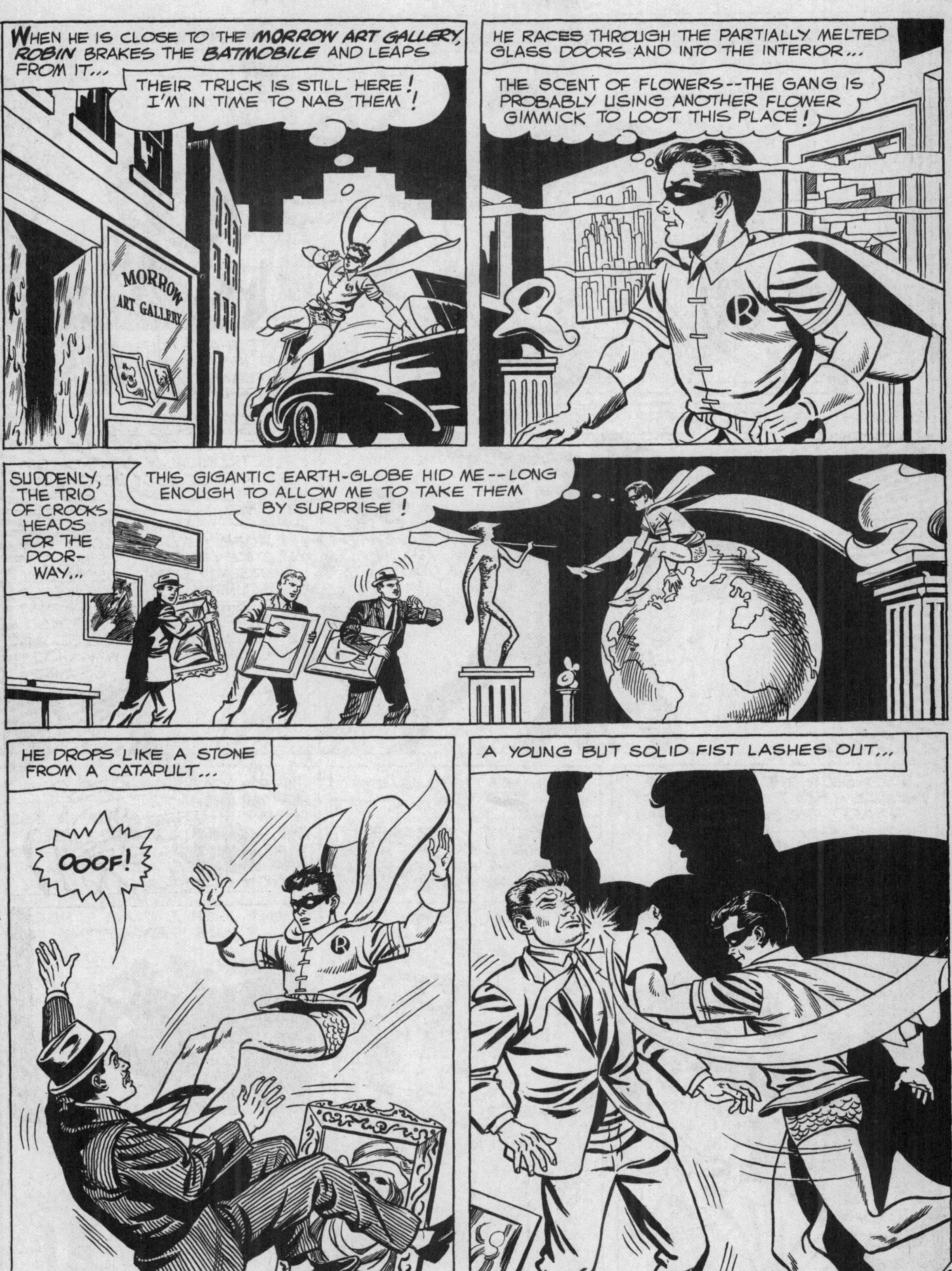
WHEN HE IS CLOSE TO THE MORROW ART GALLERY, ROBIN BRAKES THE BATMOBILE AND LEAPS FROM IT...
THEIR TRUCK IS STILL HERE! I'M IN TIME TO NAB THEM!
MORROW ART GALLERY
HE RACES THROUGH THE PARTIALLY MELTED GLASS DOORS AND INTO THE INTERIOR...
THE SCENT OF FLOWERS--THE GANG IS PROBABLY USING ANOTHER FLOWER GIMMICK TO LOOT THIS PLACE!
SUDDENLY, THE TRIO OF CROOKS HEADS FOR THE DOORWAY...
THIS GIGANTIC EARTH-GLOBE HID ME--LONG ENOUGH TO ALLOW ME TO TAKE THEM BY SURPRISE!
HE DROPS LIKE A STONE FROM A CATAPULT...
OOOF!
A YOUNG BUT SOLID FIST LASHES OUT...
4

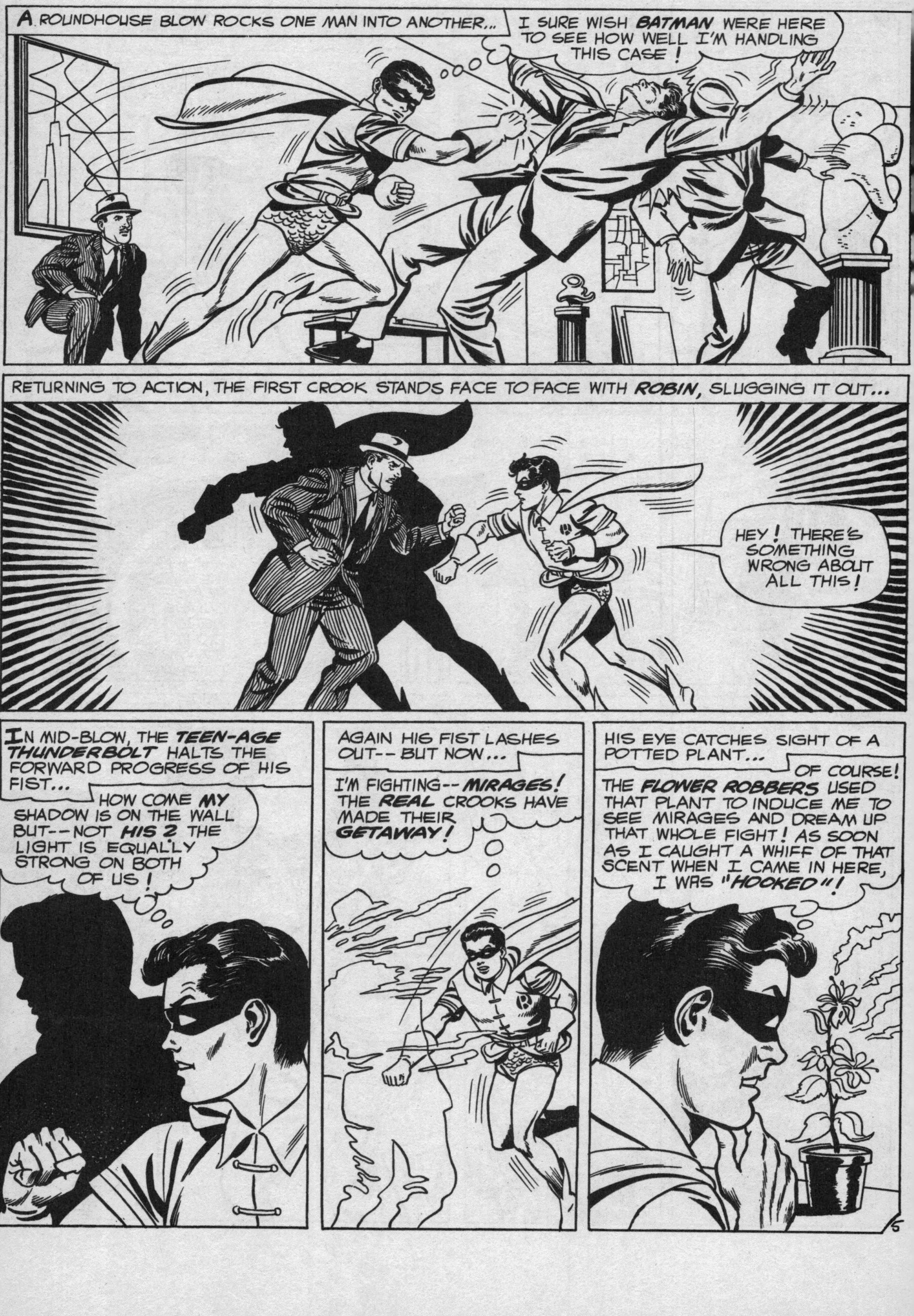
A ROUNDHOUSE BLOW ROCKS ONE MAN INTO ANOTHER...
I SURE WISH BATMAN WERE HERE TO SEE HOW WELL I'M HANDLING THIS CASE!
RETURNING TO ACTION, THE FIRST CROOK STANDS FACE TO FACE WITH ROBIN, SLUGGING IT OUT...
HEY! THERE'S SOMETHING WRONG ABOUT ALL THIS!
IN MID-BLOW, THE TEEN-AGE THUNDERBOLT HALTS THE FORWARD PROGRESS OF HIS FIST...
HOW COME MY SHADOW IS ON THE WALL BUT--NOT HIS? THE LIGHT IS EQUALLY STRONG ON BOTH OF US!
AGAIN HIS FIST LASHES OUT-- BUT NOW...
I'M FIGHTING--MIRAGES! THE REAL CROOKS HAVE MADE THEIR GETAWAY!
HIS EYE CATCHES SIGHT OF A POTTED PLANT...
OF COURSE! THE FLOWER ROBBERS USED THAT PLANT TO INDUCE ME TO SEE MIRAGES AND DREAM UP THAT WHOLE FIGHT! AS SOON AS I CAUGHT A WHIFF OF THAT SCENT WHEN I CAME IN HERE, I WAS "HOOKED"!
5

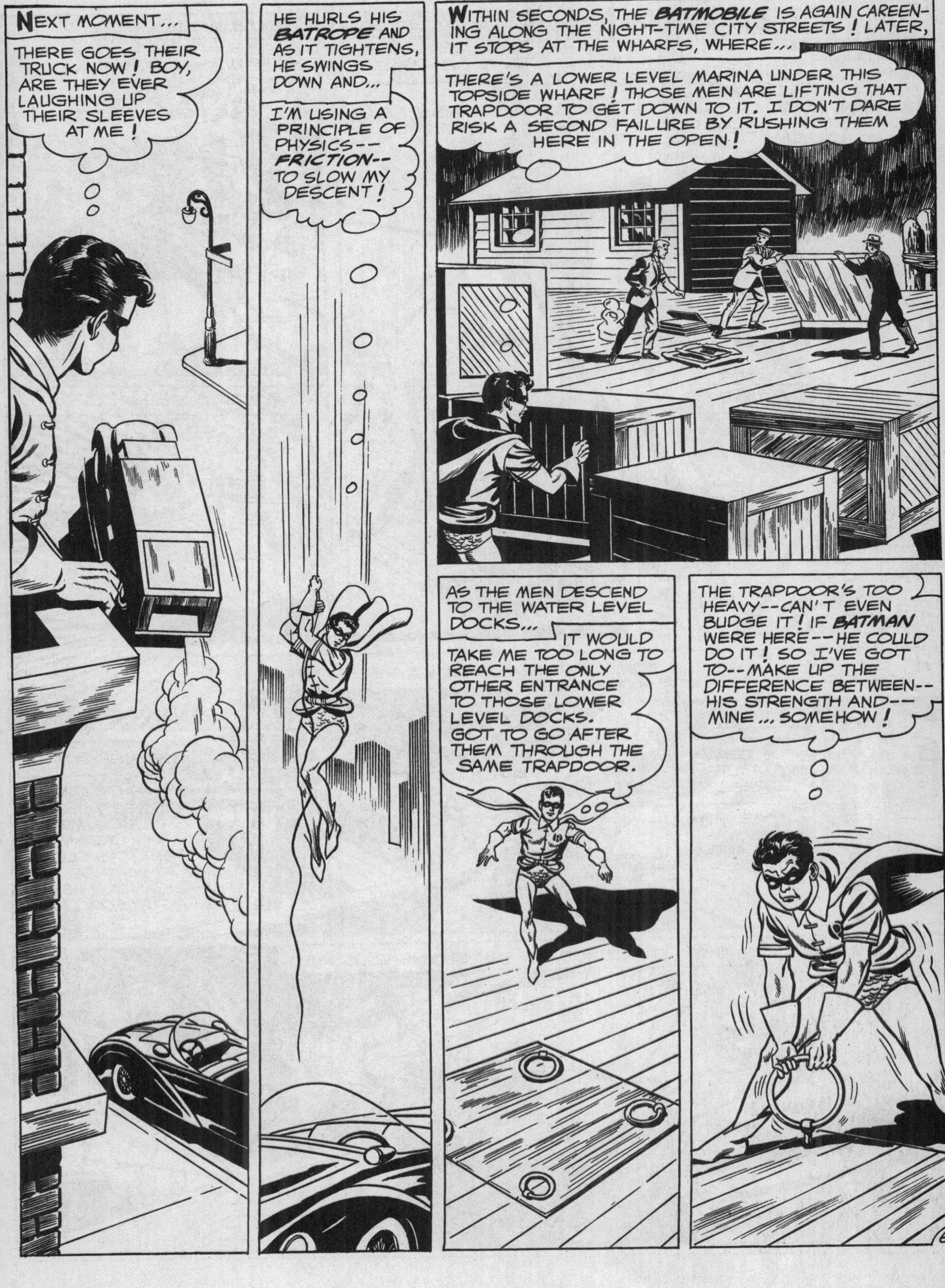
NEXT MOMENT...
THERE GOES THEIR TRUCK NOW! BOY, ARE THEY EVER LAUGHING UP THEIR SLEEVES AT ME!
HE HURLS HIS BATROPE AND AS IT TIGHTENS, HE SWINGS DOWN AND...
I'M USING A PRINCIPLE OF PHYSICS--FRICTION--TO SLOW MY DESCENT!
WITHIN SECONDS, THE BATMOBILE IS AGAIN CAREENING ALONG THE NIGHT-TIME CITY STREETS! LATER, IT STOPS AT THE WHARFS, WHERE...
THERE'S A LOWER LEVEL MARINA UNDER THIS TOPSIDE WHARF! THOSE MEN ARE LIFTING THAT TRAPDOOR TO GET DOWN TO IT. I DON'T DARE RISK A SECOND FAILURE BY RUSHING THEM HERE IN THE OPEN!
AS THE MEN DESCEND TO THE WATER LEVEL DOCKS...
IT WOULD TAKE ME TOO LONG TO REACH THE ONLY OTHER ENTRANCE TO THOSE LOWER LEVEL DOCKS. GOT TO GO AFTER THEM THROUGH THE SAME TRAPDOOR.
THE TRAPDOOR'S TOO HEAVY--CAN'T EVEN BUDGE IT! IF BATMAN WERE HERE--HE COULD DO IT! SO I'VE GOT TO--MAKE UP THE DIFFERENCE BETWEEN--HIS STRENGTH AND--MINE... SOMEHOW!
6

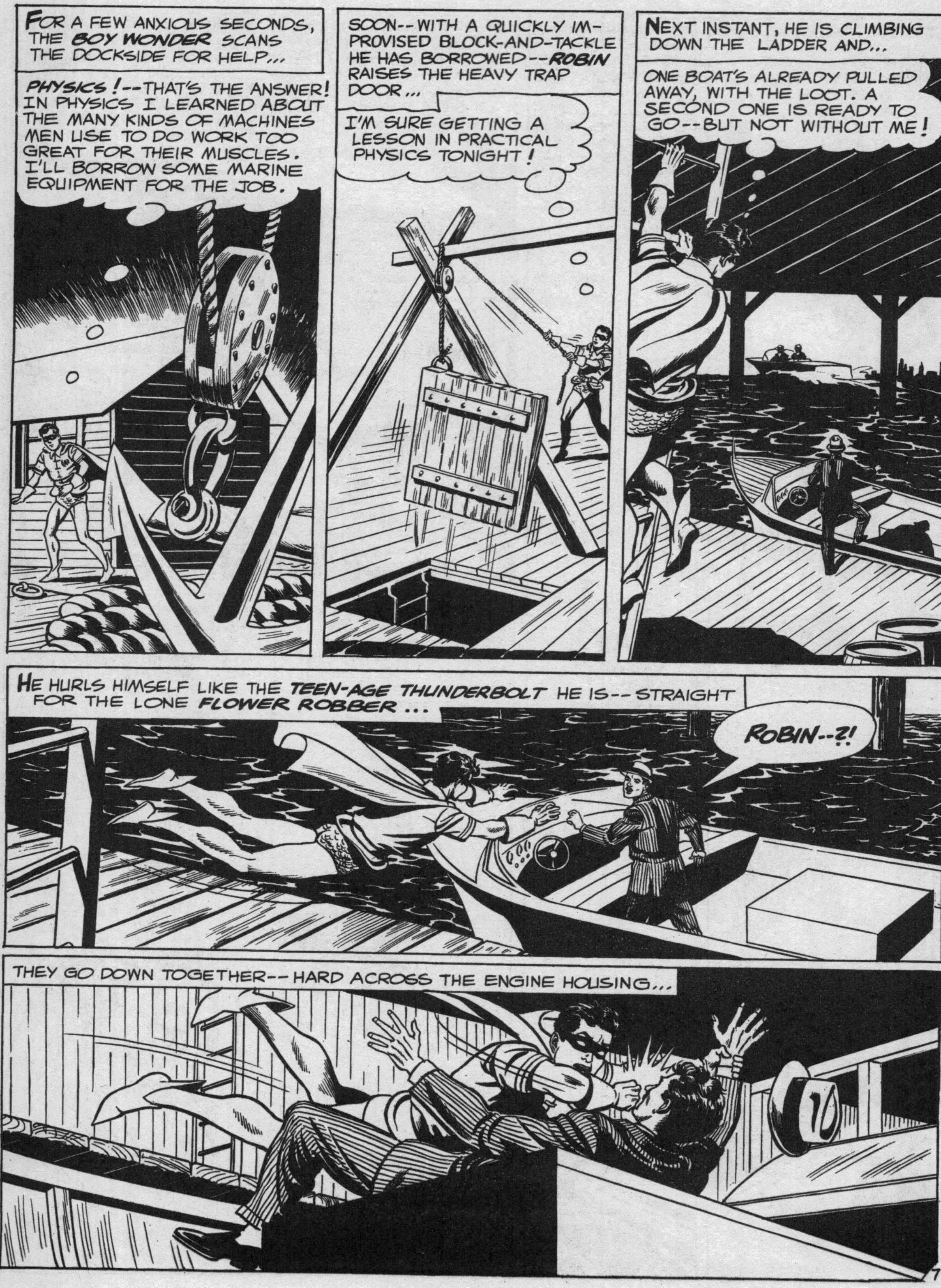

FOR A FEW ANXIOUS SECONDS, THE BOY WONDER SCANS THE DOCKSIDE FOR HELP...
PHYSICS!--THAT'S THE ANSWER! IN PHYSICS I LEARNED ABOUT THE MANY KINDS OF MACHINES MEN USE TO DO WORK TOO GREAT FOR THEIR MUSCLES. I'LL BORROW SOME MARINE EQUIPMENT FOR THE JOB.
SOON--WITH A QUICKLY IMPROVISED BLOCK-AND-TACKLE HE HAS BORROWED--ROBIN RAISES THE HEAVY TRAP DOOR...
I'M SURE GETTING A LESSON IN PRACTICAL PHYSICS TONIGHT!
NEXT INSTANT, HE IS CLIMBING DOWN THE LADDER AND...
ONE BOAT'S ALREADY PULLED AWAY, WITH THE LOOT. A SECOND ONE IS READY TO GO--BUT NOT WITHOUT ME!
HE HURLS HIMSELF LIKE THE TEEN-AGE THUNDERBOLT HE IS--STRAIGHT FOR THE LONE FLOWER ROBBER...
ROBIN--?!
THEY GO DOWN TOGETHER--HARD ACROSS THE ENGINE HOUSING...
7

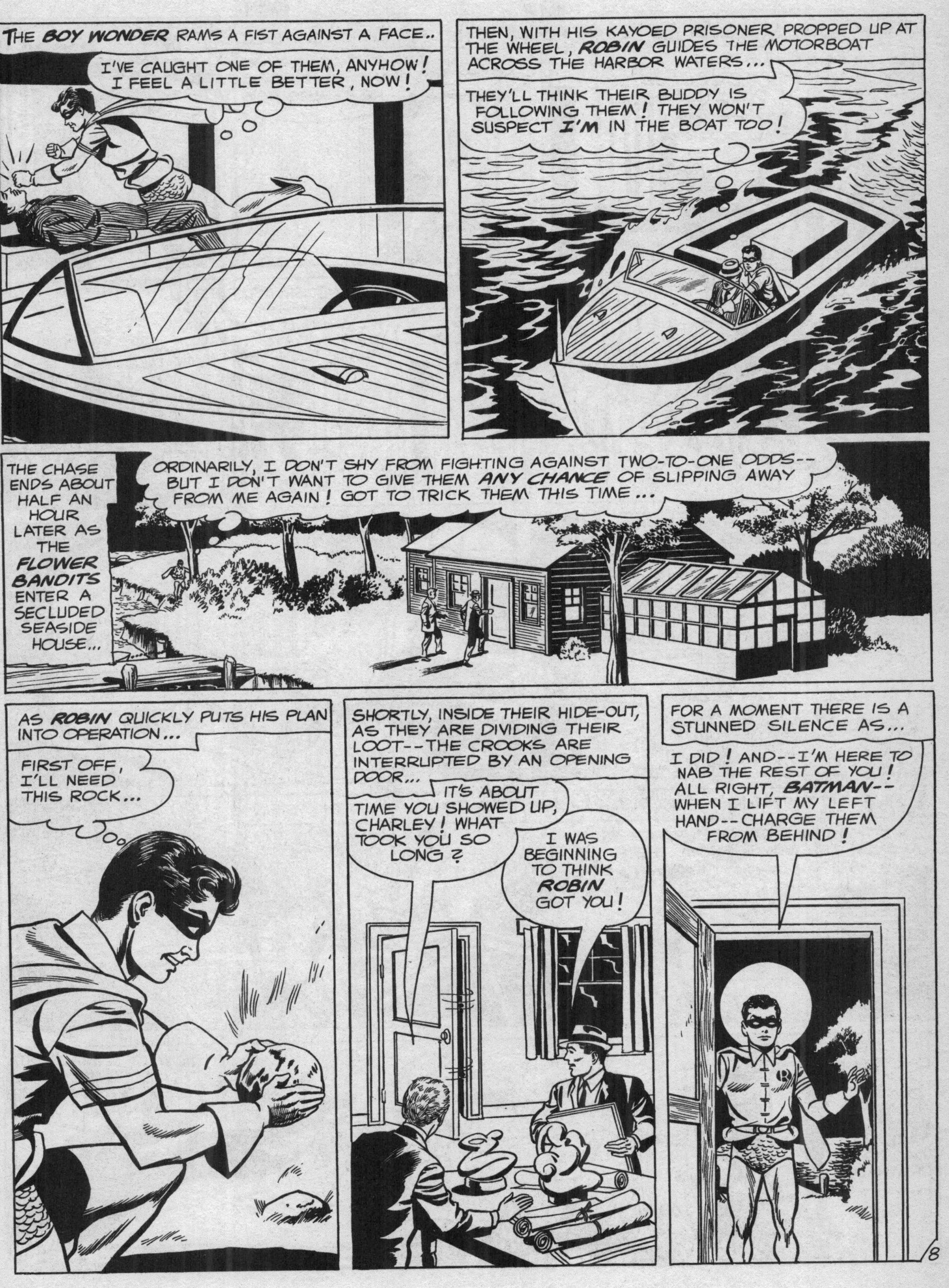
THE BOY WONDER RAMS A FIST AGAINST A FACE..
I'VE CAUGHT ONE OF THEM, ANYHOW! I FEEL A LITTLE BETTER, NOW!
THEN, WITH HIS KAYOED PRISONER PROPPED UP AT THE WHEEL, ROBIN GUIDES THE MOTORBOAT ACROSS THE HARBOR WATERS...
THEY'LL THINK THEIR BUDDY IS FOLLOWING THEM! THEY WON'T SUSPECT I'M IN THE BOAT TOO!
THE CHASE ENDS ABOUT HALF AN HOUR LATER AS THE FLOWER BANDITS ENTER A SECLUDED SEASIDE HOUSE...
ORDINARILY, I DON'T SHY FROM FIGHTING AGAINST TWO-TO-ONE ODDS-- BUT I DON'T WANT TO GIVE THEM ANY CHANCE OF SLIPPING AWAY FROM ME AGAIN! GOT TO TRICK THEM THIS TIME...
AS ROBIN QUICKLY PUTS HIS PLAN INTO OPERATION...
FIRST OFF, I'LL NEED THIS ROCK...
SHORTLY, INSIDE THEIR HIDE-OUT, AS THEY ARE DIVIDING THEIR LOOT--THE CROOKS ARE INTERRUPTED BY AN OPENING DOOR...
IT'S ABOUT TIME YOU SHOWED UP, CHARLEY! WHAT TOOK YOU SO LONG?
I WAS BEGINNING TO THINK ROBIN GOT YOU!
FOR A MOMENT THERE IS A STUNNED SILENCE AS...
I DID! AND--I'M HERE TO NAB THE REST OF YOU! ALL RIGHT, BATMAN-- WHEN I LIFT MY LEFT HAND--CHARGE THEM FROM BEHIND!
8

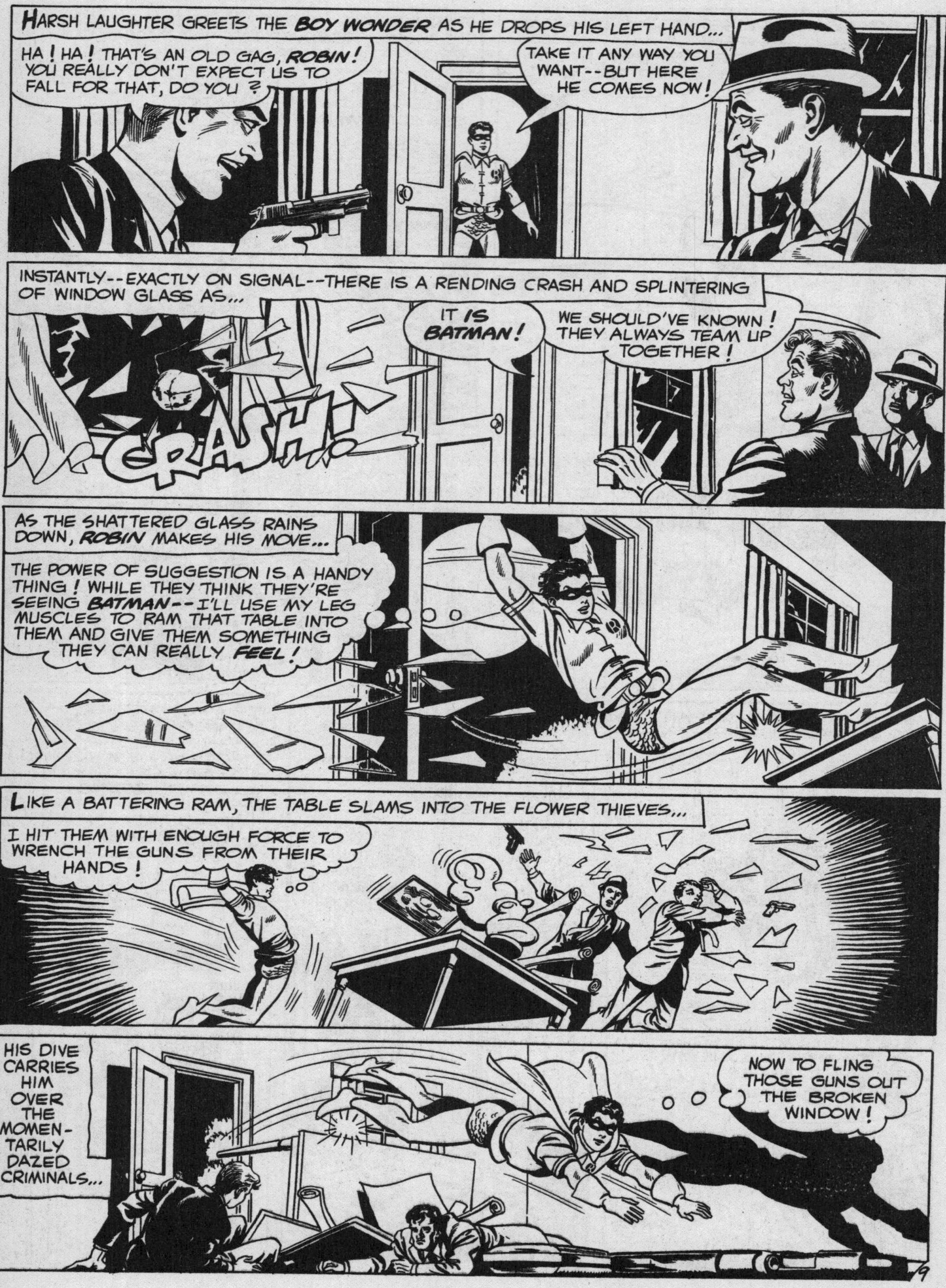
HARSH LAUGHTER GREETS THE BOY WONDER AS HE DROPS HIS LEFT HAND...
HA! HA! THAT'S AN OLD GAG, ROBIN! YOU REALLY DON'T EXPECT US TO FALL FOR THAT, DO YOU?
TAKE IT ANY WAY YOU WANT--BUT HERE HE COMES NOW!
INSTANTLY--EXACTLY ON SIGNAL--THERE IS A RENDING CRASH AND SPLINTERING OF WINDOW GLASS AS...
CRASH!
IT IS BATMAN!
WE SHOULD'VE KNOWN! THEY ALWAYS TEAM UP TOGETHER!
AS THE SHATTERED GLASS RAINS DOWN, ROBIN MAKES HIS MOVE...
THE POWER OF SUGGESTION IS A HANDY THING! WHILE THEY THINK THEY'RE SEEING BATMAN--I'LL USE MY LEG MUSCLES TO RAM THAT TABLE INTO THEM AND GIVE THEM SOMETHING THEY CAN REALLY FEEL!
LIKE A BATTERING RAM, THE TABLE SLAMS INTO THE FLOWER THIEVES...
I HIT THEM WITH ENOUGH FORCE TO WRENCH THE GUNS FROM THEIR HANDS!
HIS DIVE CARRIES HIM OVER THE MOMENTARILY DAZED CRIMINALS...
NOW TO FLING THOSE GUNS OUT THE BROKEN WINDOW!
9

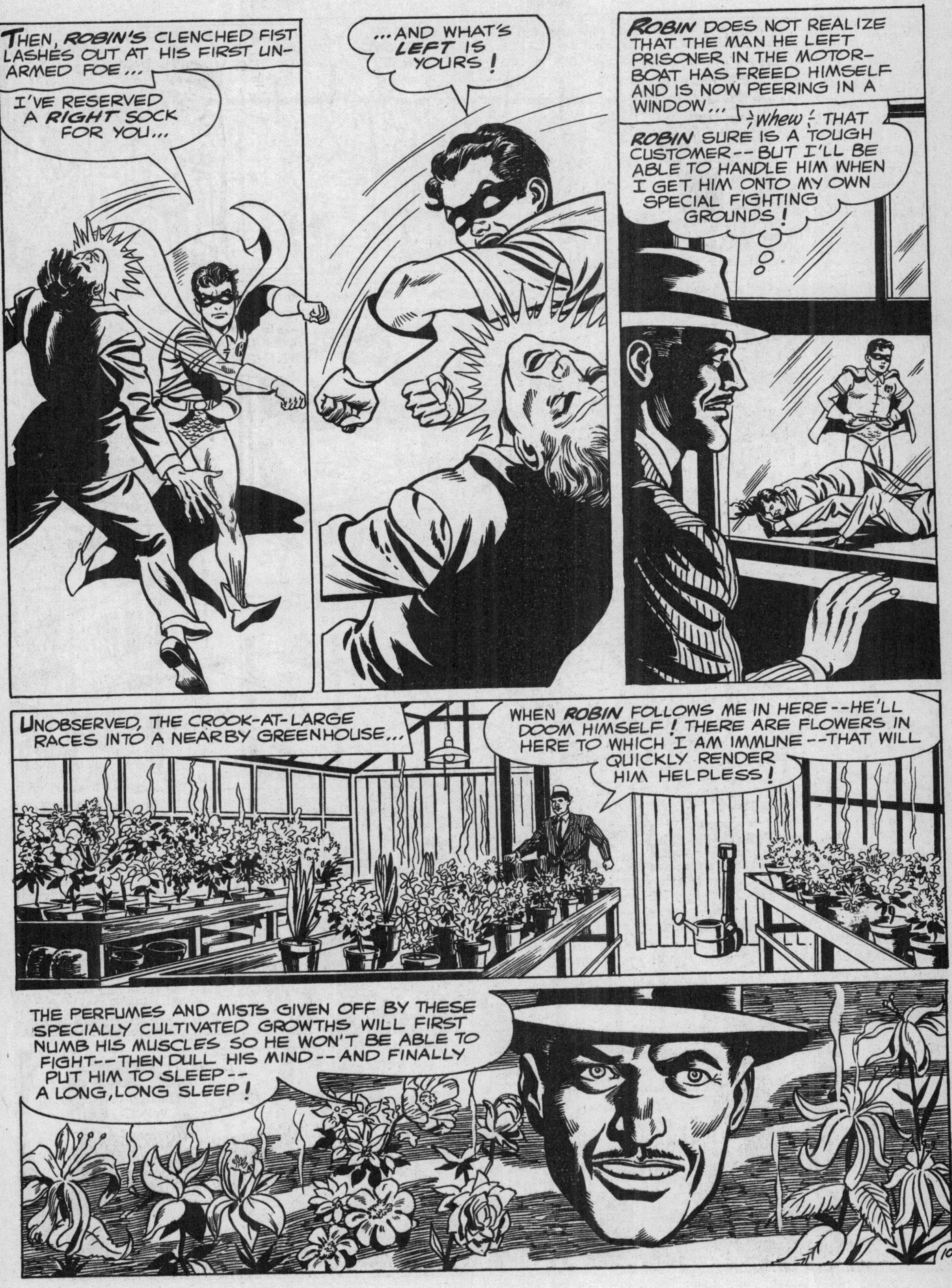
THEN, ROBIN'S CLENCHED FIST LASHES OUT AT HIS FIRST UN-ARMED FOE...
I'VE RESERVED A RIGHT SOCK FOR YOU...
...AND WHAT'S LEFT IS YOURS!
ROBIN DOES NOT REALIZE THAT THE MAN HE LEFT PRISONER IN THE MOTOR-BOAT HAS FREED HIMSELF AND IS NOW PEERING IN A WINDOW...
-WHEW!- THAT ROBIN SURE IS A TOUGH CUSTOMER--BUT I'LL BE ABLE TO HANDLE HIM WHEN I GET HIM ONTO MY OWN SPECIAL FIGHTING GROUNDS!
UNOBSERVED, THE CROOK-AT-LARGE RACES INTO A NEARBY GREENHOUSE...
WHEN ROBIN FOLLOWS ME IN HERE--HE'LL DOOM HIMSELF! THERE ARE FLOWERS IN HERE TO WHICH I AM IMMUNE--THAT WILL QUICKLY RENDER HIM HELPLESS!
THE PERFUMES AND MISTS GIVEN OFF BY THESE SPECIALLY CULTIVATED GROWTHS WILL FIRST NUMB HIS MUSCLES SO HE WON'T BE ABLE TO FIGHT--THEN DULL HIS MIND--AND FINALLY PUT HIM TO SLEEP--A LONG, LONG SLEEP!
10

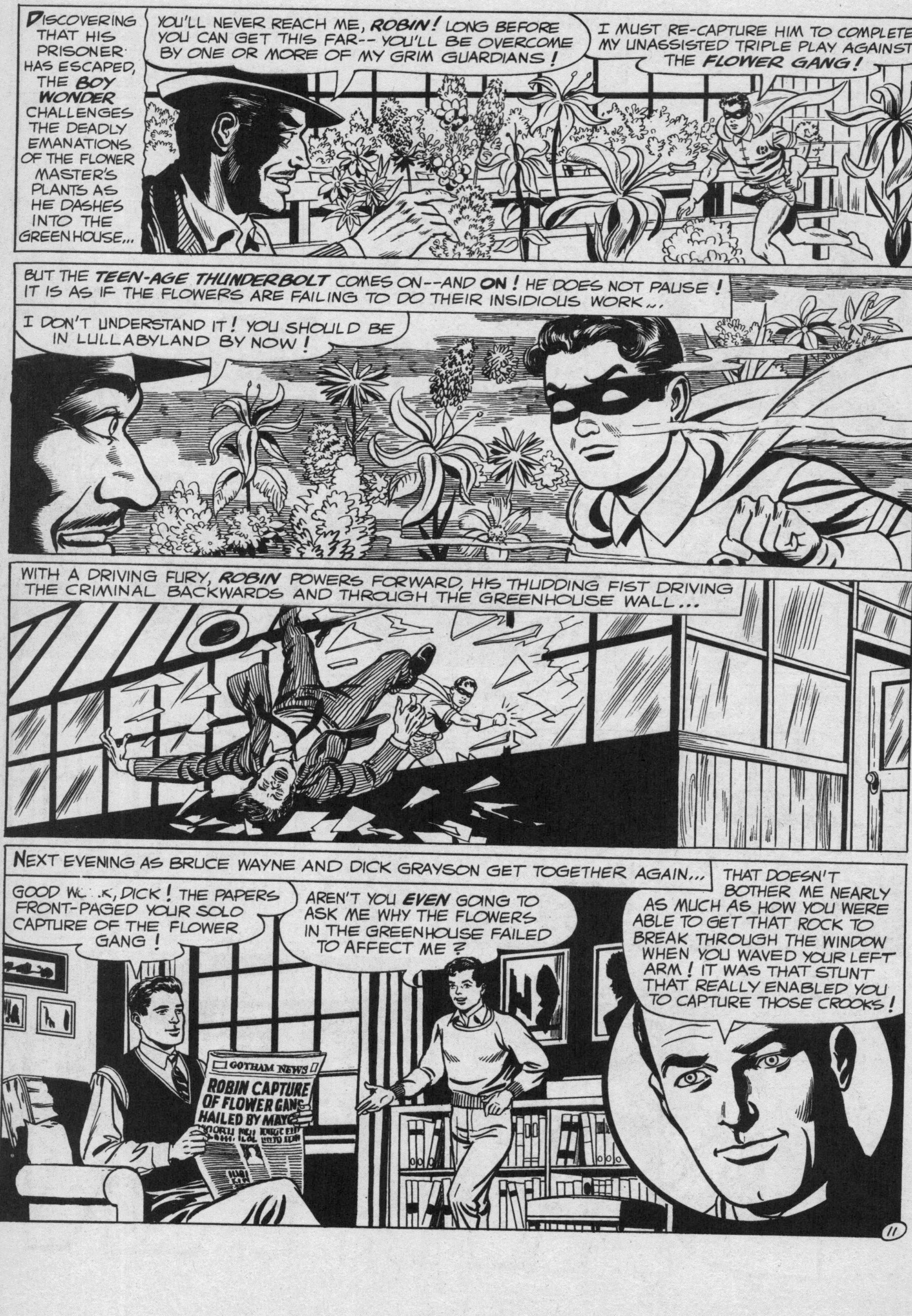
DISCOVERING THAT HIS PRISONER HAS ESCAPED, THE BOY WONDER CHALLENGES THE DEADLY EMANATIONS OF THE FLOWER MASTER'S PLANTS AS HE DASHES INTO THE GREENHOUSE...
YOU'LL NEVER REACH ME, ROBIN! LONG BEFORE YOU CAN GET THIS FAR-- YOU'LL BE OVERCOME BY ONE OR MORE OF MY GRIM GUARDIANS!
I MUST RE-CAPTURE HIM TO COMPLETE MY UNASSISTED TRIPLE PLAY AGAINST THE FLOWER GANG!
BUT THE TEEN-AGE THUNDERBOLT COMES ON--AND ON! HE DOES NOT PAUSE! IT IS AS IF THE FLOWERS ARE FAILING TO DO THEIR INSIDIOUS WORK...
I DON'T UNDERSTAND IT! YOU SHOULD BE IN LULLABYLAND BY NOW!
WITH A DRIVING FURY, ROBIN POWERS FORWARD, HIS THUDDING FIST DRIVING THE CRIMINAL BACKWARDS AND THROUGH THE GREENHOUSE WALL...
NEXT EVENING AS BRUCE WAYNE AND DICK GRAYSON GET TOGETHER AGAIN...
GOOD WORK, DICK! THE PAPERS FRONT-PAGED YOUR SOLO CAPTURE OF THE FLOWER GANG!
GOTHAM NEWS
ROBIN CAPTURE OF FLOWER GANG HAILED BY MAY
AREN'T YOU EVEN GOING TO ASK ME WHY THE FLOWERS IN THE GREENHOUSE FAILED TO AFFECT ME?
THAT DOESN'T BOTHER ME NEARLY AS MUCH AS HOW YOU WERE ABLE TO GET THAT ROCK TO BREAK THROUGH THE WINDOW WHEN YOU WAVED YOUR LEFT ARM! IT WAS THAT STUNT THAT REALLY ENABLED YOU TO CAPTURE THOSE CROOKS!
11

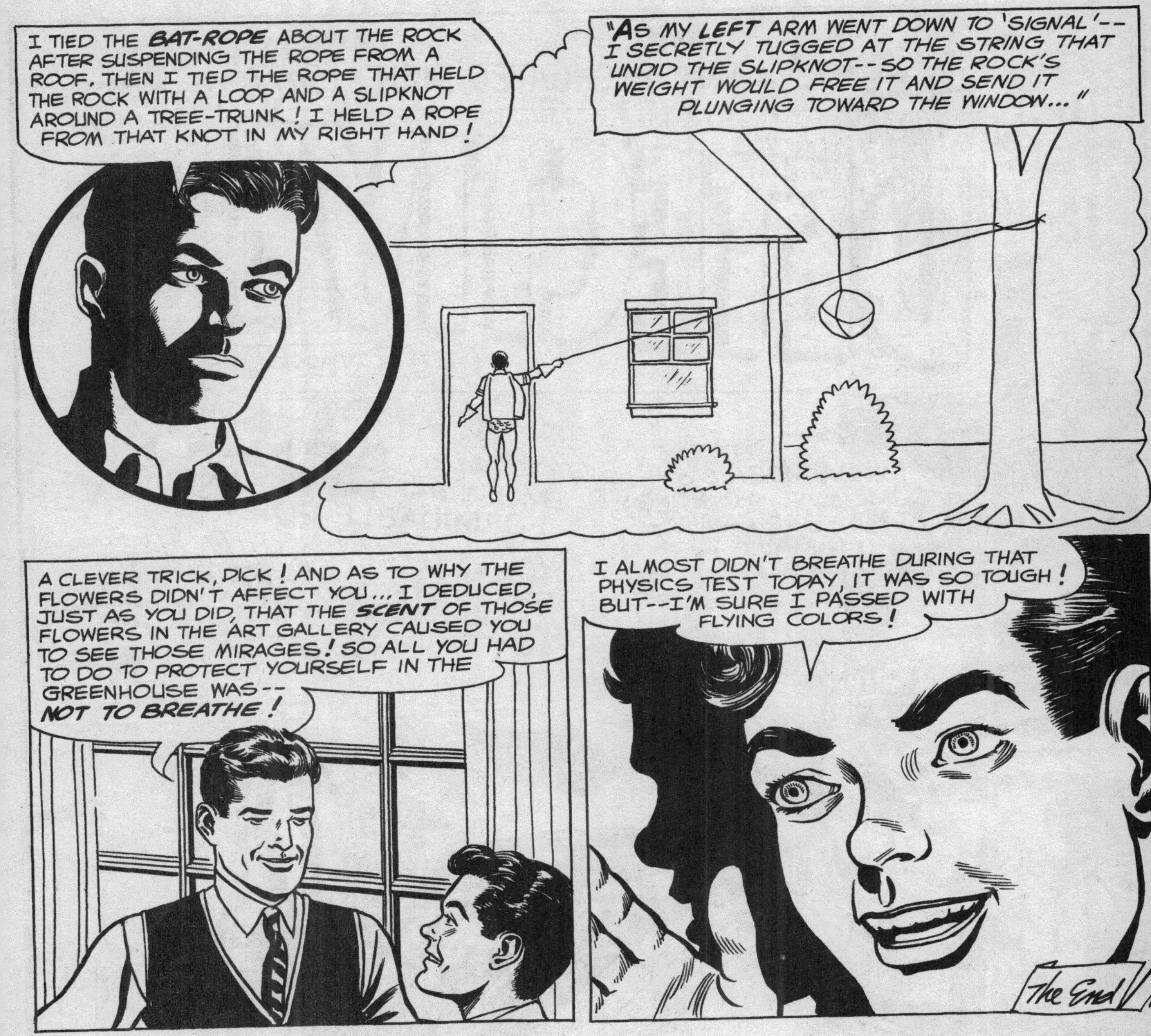
I TIED THE BAT-ROPE ABOUT THE ROCK AFTER SUSPENDING THE ROPE FROM A ROOF. THEN I TIED THE ROPE THAT HELD THE ROCK WITH A LOOP AND A SLIPKNOT AROUND A TREE-TRUNK! I HELD A ROPE FROM THAT KNOT IN MY RIGHT HAND!
"AS MY LEFT ARM WENT DOWN TO 'SIGNAL'-- I SECRETLY TUGGED AT THE STRING THAT UNDID THE SLIPKNOT--SO THE ROCK'S WEIGHT WOULD FREE IT AND SEND IT PLUNGING TOWARD THE WINDOW..."
A CLEVER TRICK, DICK! AND AS TO WHY THE FLOWERS DIDN'T AFFECT YOU... I DEDUCED, JUST AS YOU DID, THAT THE SCENT OF THOSE FLOWERS IN THE ART GALLERY CAUSED YOU TO SEE THOSE MIRAGES! SO ALL YOU HAD TO DO TO PROTECT YOURSELF IN THE GREENHOUSE WAS-- NOT TO BREATHE!
I ALMOST DIDN'T BREATHE DURING THAT PHYSICS TEST TODAY, IT WAS SO TOUGH! BUT--I'M SURE I PASSED WITH FLYING COLORS!
The End
12

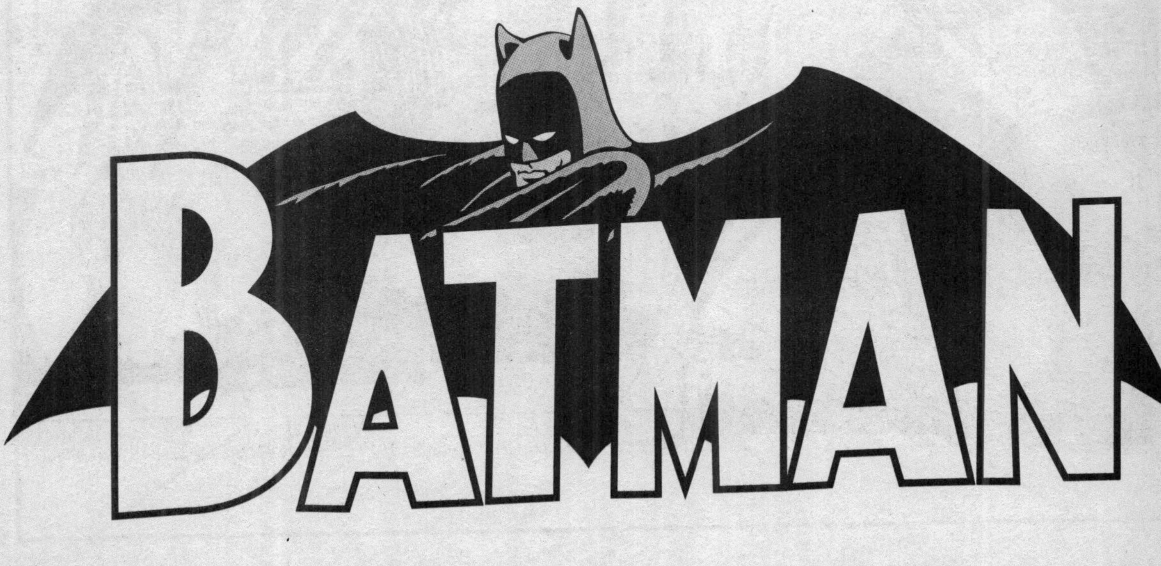
BATMAN

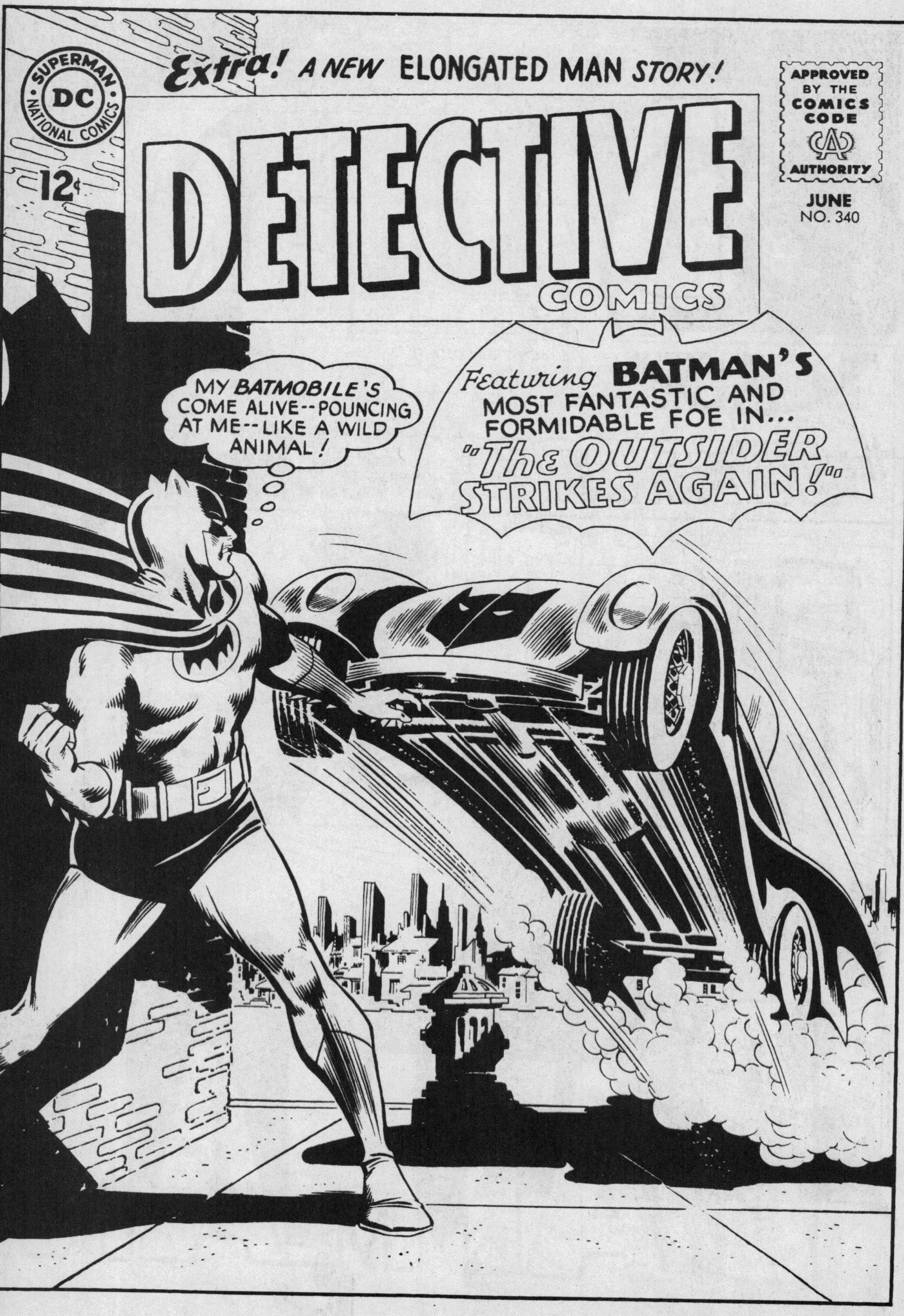
SUPERMAN DC NATIONAL COMICS
12¢
Extra! A NEW ELONGATED MAN STORY!
APPROVED BY THE COMICS CODE AUTHORITY
DETECTIVE COMICS
JUNE
NO. 340
MY BATMOBILE'S COME ALIVE--POUNCING AT ME--LIKE A WILD ANIMAL!
Featuring BATMAN'S MOST FANTASTIC AND FORMIDABLE FOE IN... "The OUTSIDER STRIKES AGAIN!"

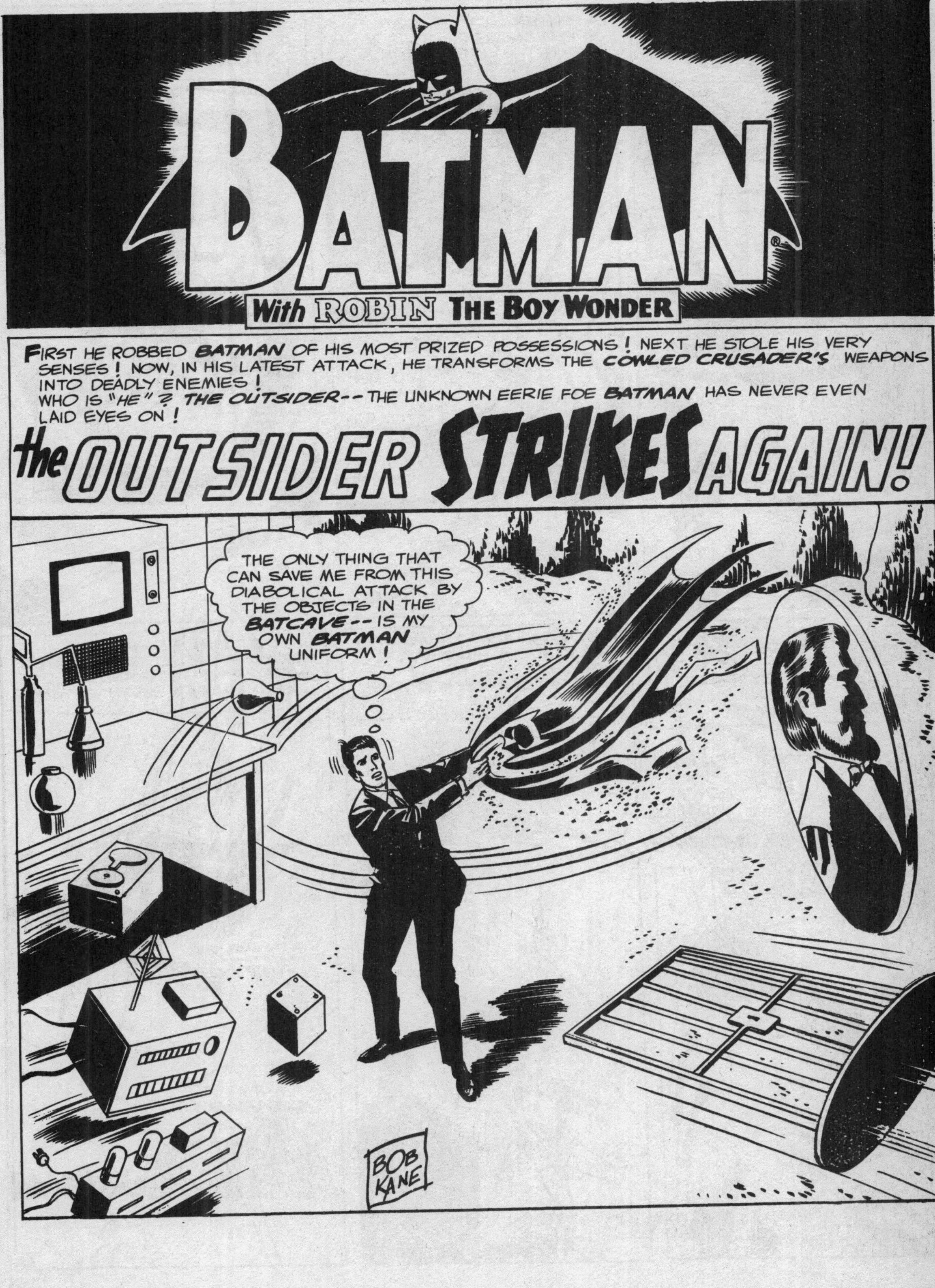
BATMAN
With ROBIN THE BOY WONDER
FIRST HE ROBBED BATMAN OF HIS MOST PRIZED POSSESSIONS! NEXT HE STOLE HIS VERY SENSES! NOW, IN HIS LATEST ATTACK, HE TRANSFORMS THE COWLED CRUSADER'S WEAPONS INTO DEADLY ENEMIES!
WHO IS "HE"? THE OUTSIDER-- THE UNKNOWN EERIE FOE BATMAN HAS NEVER EVEN LAID EYES ON!
the OUTSIDER STRIKES AGAIN!
THE ONLY THING THAT CAN SAVE ME FROM THIS DIABOLICAL ATTACK BY THE OBJECTS IN THE BATCAVE-- IS MY OWN BATMAN UNIFORM!
BOB KANE

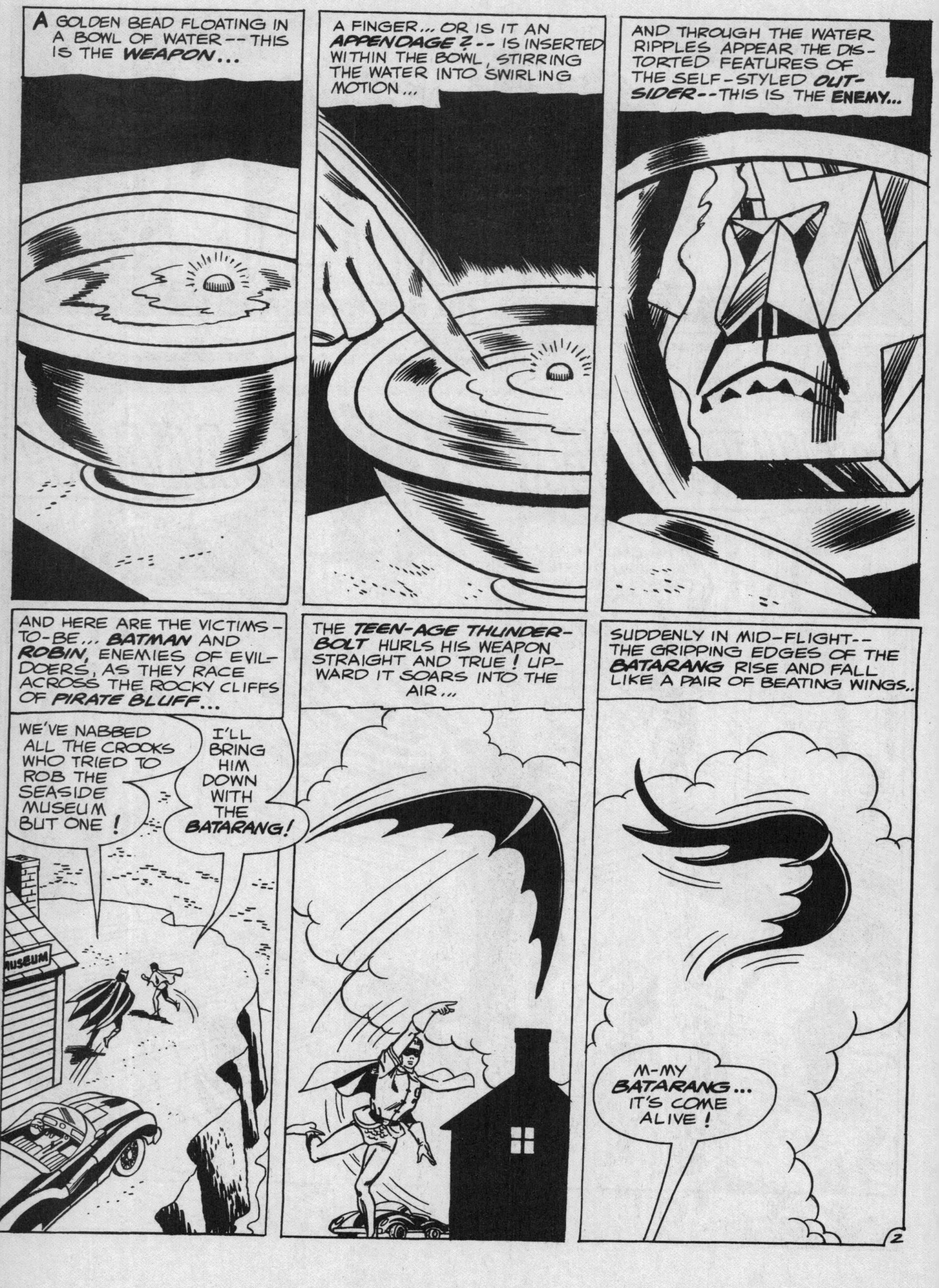

A GOLDEN BEAD FLOATING IN A BOWL OF WATER -- THIS IS THE WEAPON...
A FINGER... OR IS IT AN APPENDAGE ? -- IS INSERTED WITHIN THE BOWL, STIRRING THE WATER INTO SWIRLING MOTION...
AND THROUGH THE WATER RIPPLES APPEAR THE DISTORTED FEATURES OF THE SELF-STYLED OUTSIDER -- THIS IS THE ENEMY...
AND HERE ARE THE VICTIMS-TO-BE... BATMAN AND ROBIN, ENEMIES OF EVIL-DOERS, AS THEY RACE ACROSS THE ROCKY CLIFFS OF PIRATE BLUFF...
WE'VE NABBED ALL THE CROOKS WHO TRIED TO ROB THE SEASIDE MUSEUM BUT ONE !
I'LL BRING HIM DOWN WITH THE BATARANG!
MUSEUM
THE TEEN-AGE THUNDERBOLT HURLS HIS WEAPON STRAIGHT AND TRUE ! UPWARD IT SOARS INTO THE AIR...
SUDDENLY IN MID-FLIGHT-- THE GRIPPING EDGES OF THE BATARANG RISE AND FALL LIKE A PAIR OF BEATING WINGS..
M-MY BATARANG... IT'S COME ALIVE !
2

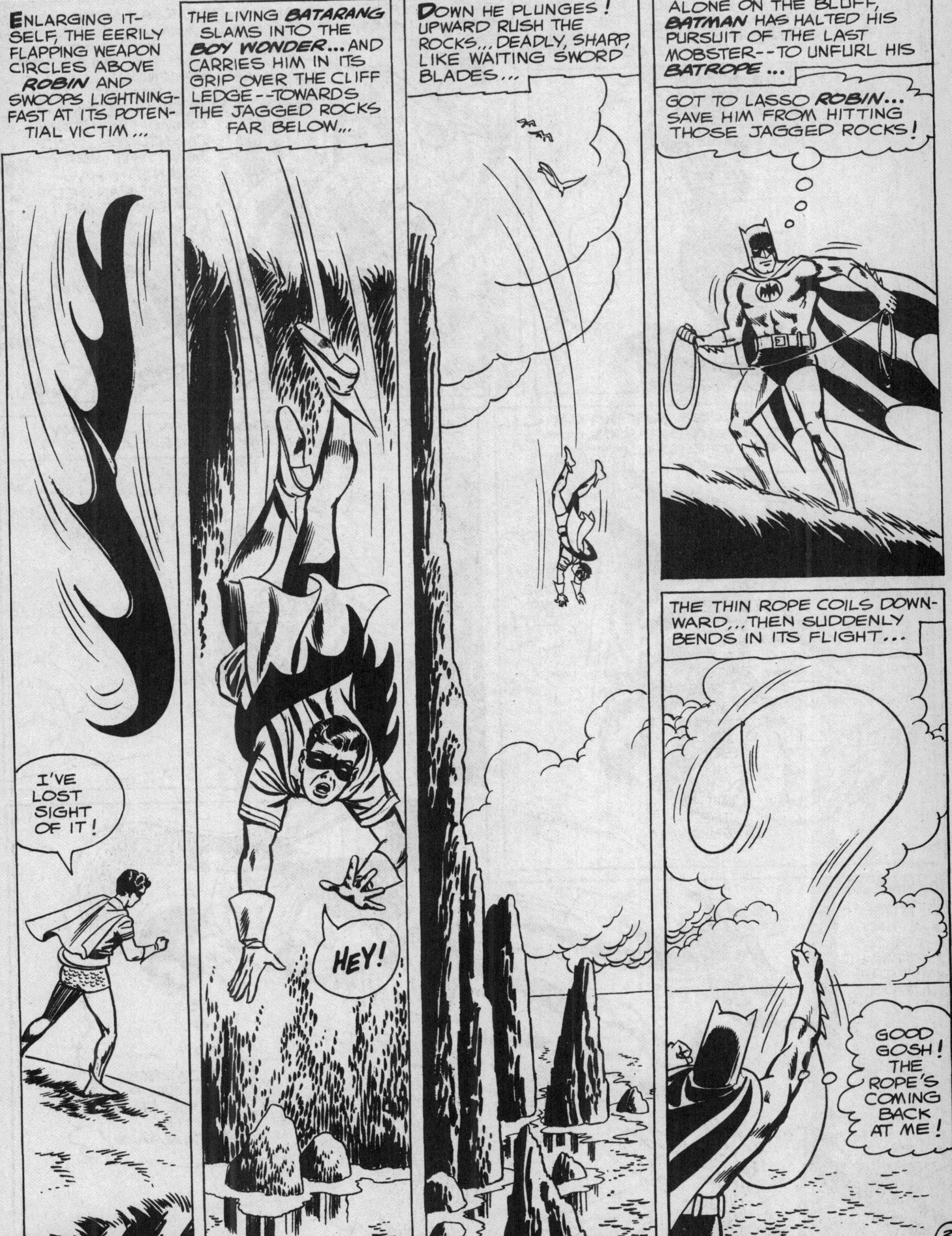
ENLARGING IT-SELF, THE EERILY FLAPPING WEAPON CIRCLES ABOVE ROBIN AND SWOOPS LIGHTNING-FAST AT ITS POTENTIAL VICTIM...
I'VE LOST SIGHT OF IT!
THE LIVING BATARANG SLAMS INTO THE BOY WONDER... AND CARRIES HIM IN ITS GRIP OVER THE CLIFF LEDGE--TOWARDS THE JAGGED ROCKS FAR BELOW...
HEY!
DOWN HE PLUNGES! UPWARD RUSH THE ROCKS... DEADLY, SHARP, LIKE WAITING SWORD BLADES...
ALONE ON THE BLUFF, BATMAN HAS HALTED HIS PURSUIT OF THE LAST MOBSTER--TO UNFURL HIS BATROPE...
GOT TO LASSO ROBIN... SAVE HIM FROM HITTING THOSE JAGGED ROCKS!
THE THIN ROPE COILS DOWNWARD... THEN SUDDENLY BENDS IN ITS FLIGHT...
GOOD GOSH! THE ROPE'S COMING BACK AT ME!
3

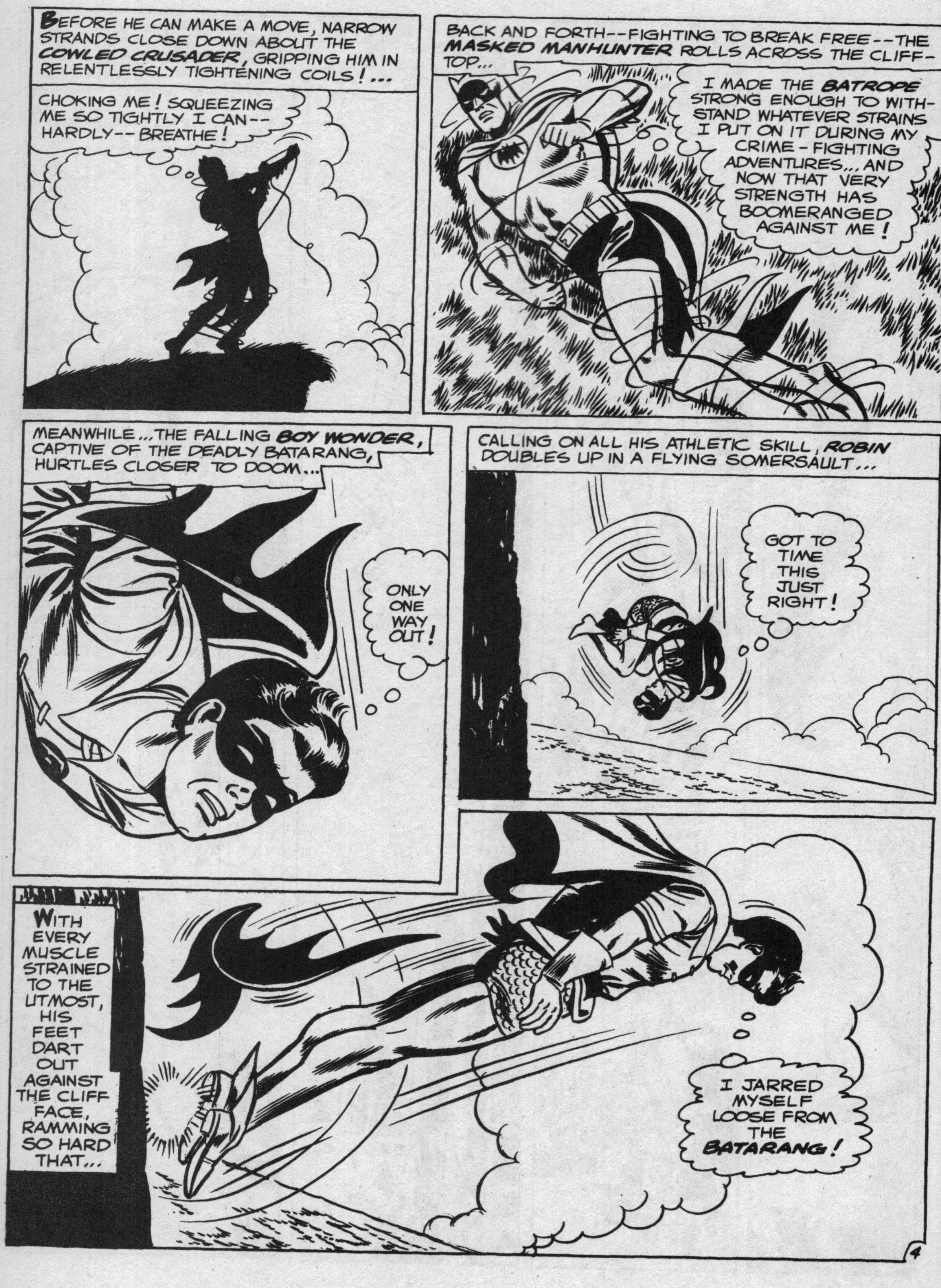
BEFORE HE CAN MAKE A MOVE, NARROW STRANDS CLOSE DOWN ABOUT THE COWLED CRUSADER, GRIPPING HIM IN RELENTLESSLY TIGHTENING COILS!...
CHOKING ME! SQUEEZING ME SO TIGHTLY I CAN-- HARDLY-- BREATHE!
BACK AND FORTH--FIGHTING TO BREAK FREE--THE MASKED MANHUNTER ROLLS ACROSS THE CLIFF-TOP...
I MADE THE BATROPE STRONG ENOUGH TO WITHSTAND WHATEVER STRAINS I PUT ON IT DURING MY CRIME-FIGHTING ADVENTURES... AND NOW THAT VERY STRENGTH HAS BOOMERANGED AGAINST ME!
MEANWHILE... THE FALLING BOY WONDER, CAPTIVE OF THE DEADLY BATARANG, HURTLES CLOSER TO DOOM...
ONLY ONE WAY OUT!
CALLING ON ALL HIS ATHLETIC SKILL, ROBIN DOUBLES UP IN A FLYING SOMERSAULT...
GOT TO TIME THIS JUST RIGHT!
WITH EVERY MUSCLE STRAINED TO THE UTMOST, HIS FEET DART OUT AGAINST THE CLIFF FACE, RAMMING SO HARD THAT...
I JARRED MYSELF LOOSE FROM THE BATARANG!
4

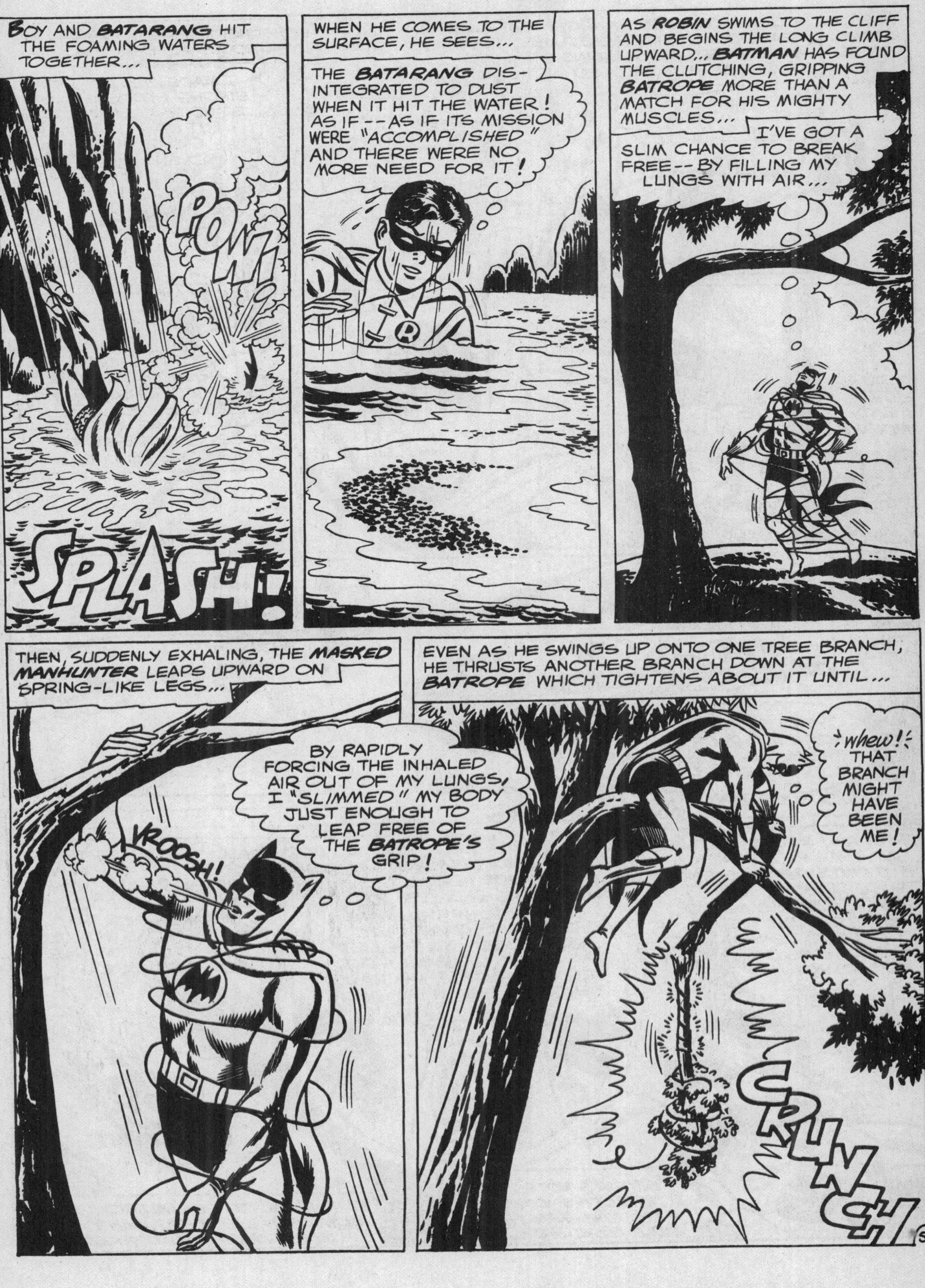
BOY AND BATARANG HIT THE FOAMING WATERS TOGETHER...
POW!
SPLASH!
WHEN HE COMES TO THE SURFACE, HE SEES...
THE BATARANG DIS-INTEGRATED TO DUST WHEN IT HIT THE WATER! AS IF--AS IF ITS MISSION WERE "ACCOMPLISHED" AND THERE WERE NO MORE NEED FOR IT!
AS ROBIN SWIMS TO THE CLIFF AND BEGINS THE LONG CLIMB UPWARD... BATMAN HAS FOUND THE CLUTCHING, GRIPPING BATROPE MORE THAN A MATCH FOR HIS MIGHTY MUSCLES...
I'VE GOT A SLIM CHANCE TO BREAK FREE--BY FILLING MY LUNGS WITH AIR...
THEN, SUDDENLY EXHALING, THE MASKED MANHUNTER LEAPS UPWARD ON SPRING-LIKE LEGS...
VROOSH!
BY RAPIDLY FORCING THE INHALED AIR OUT OF MY LUNGS, I "SLIMMED" MY BODY JUST ENOUGH TO LEAP FREE OF THE BATROPE'S GRIP!
EVEN AS HE SWINGS UP ONTO ONE TREE BRANCH, HE THRUSTS ANOTHER BRANCH DOWN AT THE BATROPE WHICH TIGHTENS ABOUT IT UNTIL...
whew! THAT BRANCH MIGHT HAVE BEEN ME!
CRUNCH
5

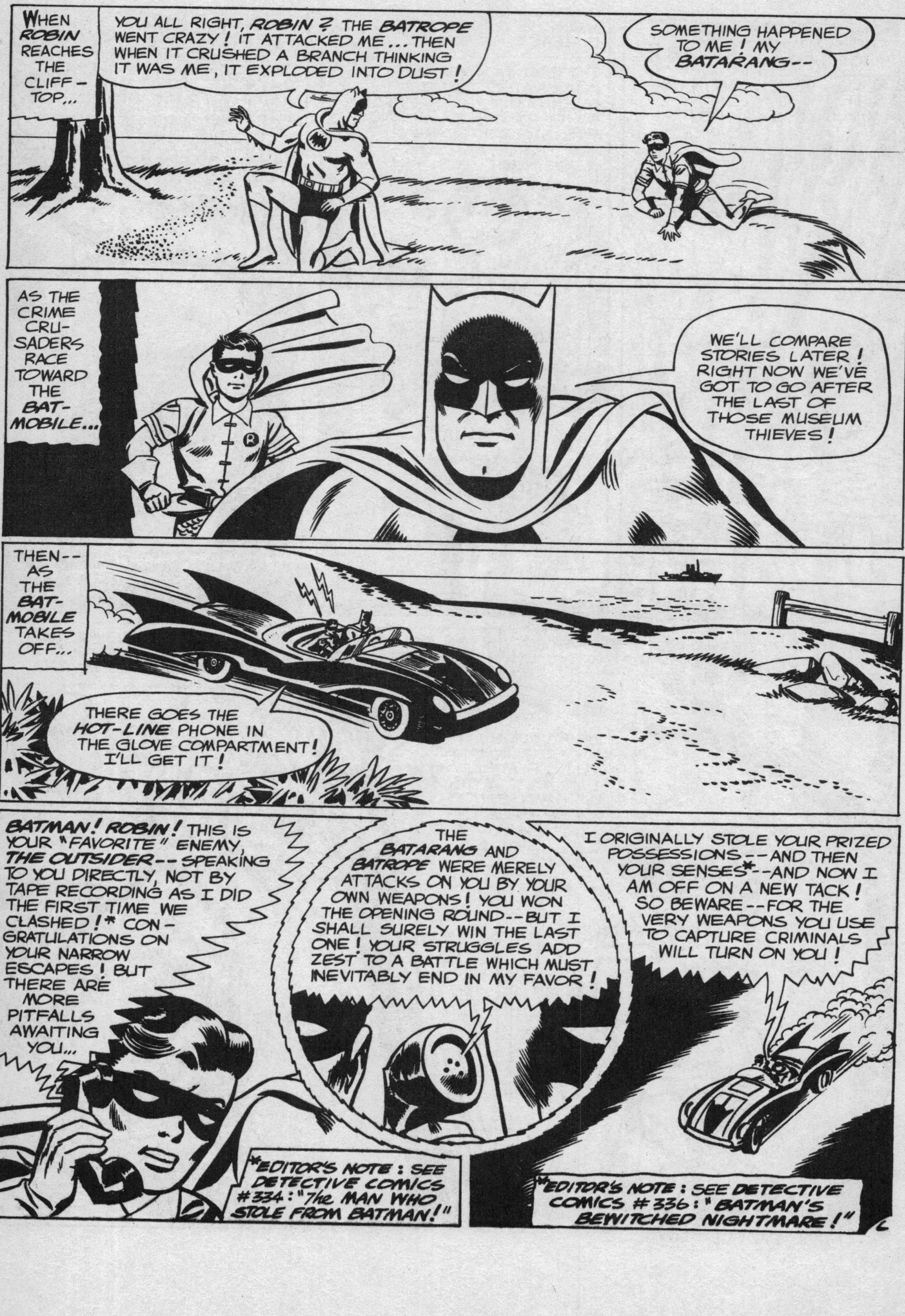
WHEN ROBIN REACHES THE CLIFF-TOP...
YOU ALL RIGHT, ROBIN? THE BATROPE WENT CRAZY! IT ATTACKED ME... THEN WHEN IT CRUSHED A BRANCH THINKING IT WAS ME, IT EXPLODED INTO DUST!
SOMETHING HAPPENED TO ME! MY BATARANG--
AS THE CRIME CRUSADERS RACE TOWARD THE BATMOBILE...
WE'LL COMPARE STORIES LATER! RIGHT NOW WE'VE GOT TO GO AFTER THE LAST OF THOSE MUSEUM THIEVES!
THEN--AS THE BATMOBILE TAKES OFF...
THERE GOES THE HOT-LINE PHONE IN THE GLOVE COMPARTMENT! I'LL GET IT!
BATMAN! ROBIN! THIS IS YOUR "FAVORITE" ENEMY, THE OUTSIDER--SPEAKING TO YOU DIRECTLY, NOT BY TAPE RECORDING AS I DID THE FIRST TIME WE CLASHED!* CONGRATULATIONS ON YOUR NARROW ESCAPES! BUT THERE ARE MORE PITFALLS AWAITING YOU...
THE BATARANG AND BATROPE WERE MERELY ATTACKS ON YOU BY YOUR OWN WEAPONS! YOU WON THE OPENING ROUND--BUT I SHALL SURELY WIN THE LAST ONE! YOUR STRUGGLES ADD ZEST TO A BATTLE WHICH MUST INEVITABLY END IN MY FAVOR!
I ORIGINALLY STOLE YOUR PRIZED POSSESSIONS--AND THEN YOUR SENSES*--AND NOW I AM OFF ON A NEW TACK! SO BEWARE--FOR THE VERY WEAPONS YOU USE TO CAPTURE CRIMINALS WILL TURN ON YOU!
*EDITOR'S NOTE: SEE DETECTIVE COMICS #334: "The MAN WHO STOLE FROM BATMAN!"
*EDITOR'S NOTE: SEE DETECTIVE COMICS #336: "BATMAN'S BEWITCHED NIGHTMARE!"
6

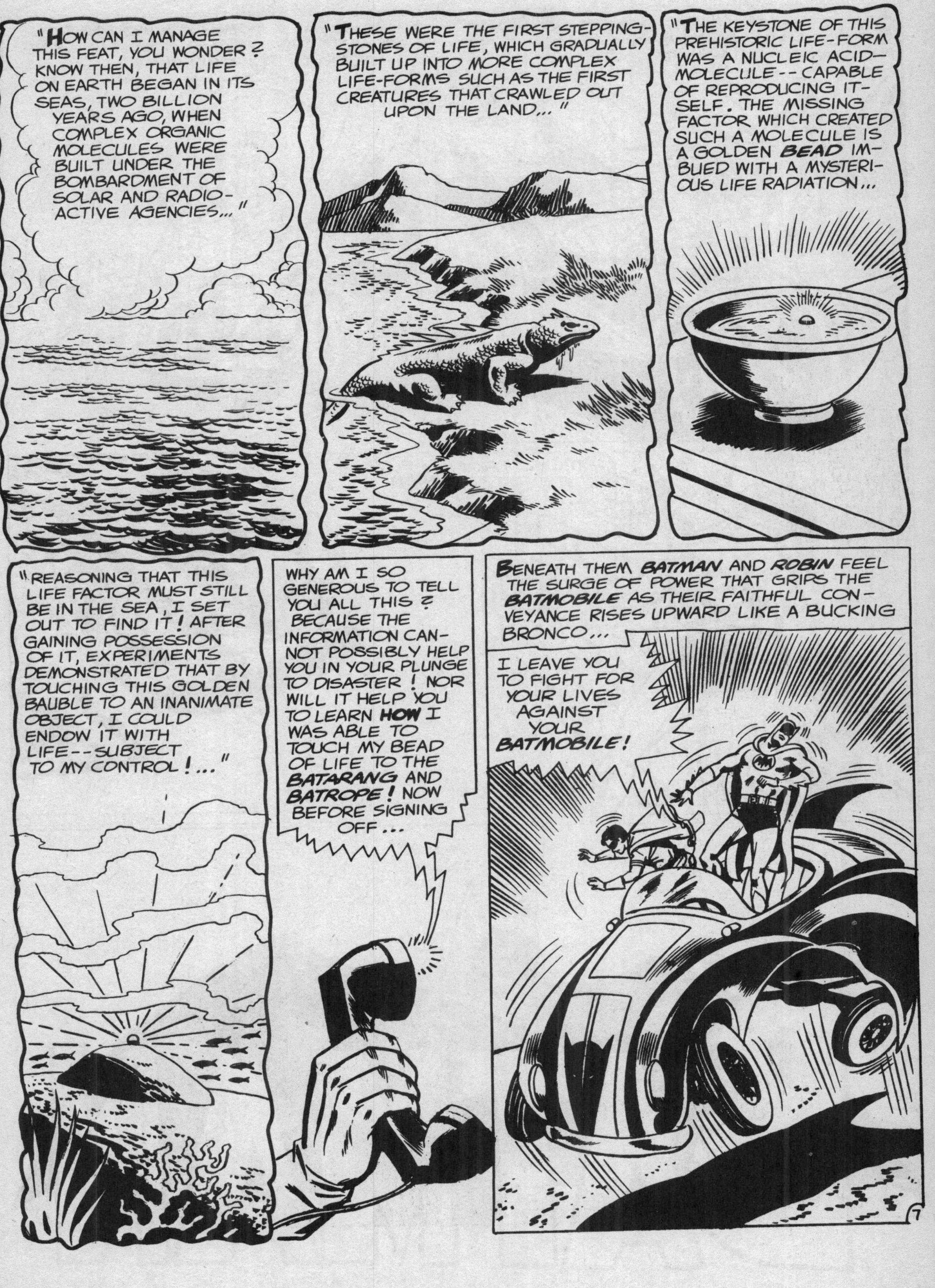
"HOW CAN I MANAGE THIS FEAT, YOU WONDER? KNOW THEN, THAT LIFE ON EARTH BEGAN IN ITS SEAS, TWO BILLION YEARS AGO, WHEN COMPLEX ORGANIC MOLECULES WERE BUILT UNDER THE BOMBARDMENT OF SOLAR AND RADIO-ACTIVE AGENCIES..."
"THESE WERE THE FIRST STEPPING-STONES OF LIFE, WHICH GRADUALLY BUILT UP INTO MORE COMPLEX LIFE-FORMS SUCH AS THE FIRST CREATURES THAT CRAWLED OUT UPON THE LAND..."
"THE KEYSTONE OF THIS PREHISTORIC LIFE-FORM WAS A NUCLEIC ACID-MOLECULE -- CAPABLE OF REPRODUCING IT-SELF. THE MISSING FACTOR WHICH CREATED SUCH A MOLECULE IS A GOLDEN BEAD IMBUED WITH A MYSTERIOUS LIFE RADIATION...
"REASONING THAT THIS LIFE FACTOR MUST STILL BE IN THE SEA, I SET OUT TO FIND IT! AFTER GAINING POSSESSION OF IT, EXPERIMENTS DEMONSTRATED THAT BY TOUCHING THIS GOLDEN BAUBLE TO AN INANIMATE OBJECT, I COULD ENDOW IT WITH LIFE--SUBJECT TO MY CONTROL!..."
WHY AM I SO GENEROUS TO TELL YOU ALL THIS? BECAUSE THE INFORMATION CANNOT POSSIBLY HELP YOU IN YOUR PLUNGE TO DISASTER! NOR WILL IT HELP YOU TO LEARN HOW I WAS ABLE TO TOUCH MY BEAD OF LIFE TO THE BATARANG AND BATROPE! NOW BEFORE SIGNING OFF...
BENEATH THEM BATMAN AND ROBIN FEEL THE SURGE OF POWER THAT GRIPS THE BATMOBILE AS THEIR FAITHFUL CONVEYANCE RISES UPWARD LIKE A BUCKING BRONCO...
I LEAVE YOU TO FIGHT FOR YOUR LIVES AGAINST YOUR BATMOBILE!
7

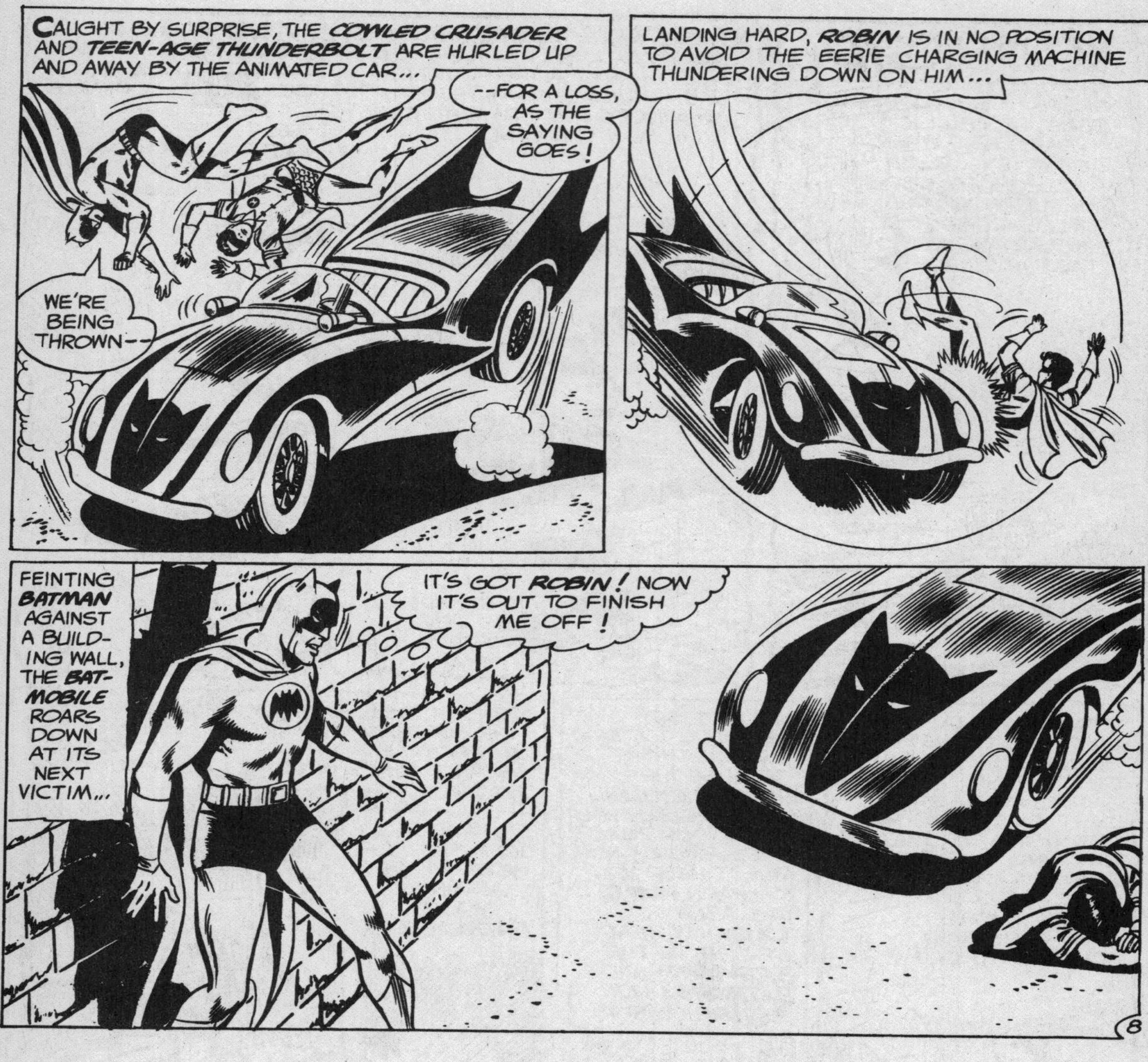
CAUGHT BY SURPRISE, THE COWLED CRUSADER AND TEEN-AGE THUNDERBOLT ARE HURLED UP AND AWAY BY THE ANIMATED CAR...
WE'RE BEING THROWN--
--FOR A LOSS, AS THE SAYING GOES!
LANDING HARD, ROBIN IS IN NO POSITION TO AVOID THE EERIE CHARGING MACHINE THUNDERING DOWN ON HIM...
FEINTING BATMAN AGAINST A BUILD-ING WALL, THE BAT-MOBILE ROARS DOWN AT ITS NEXT VICTIM...
IT'S GOT ROBIN! NOW IT'S OUT TO FINISH ME OFF!
8

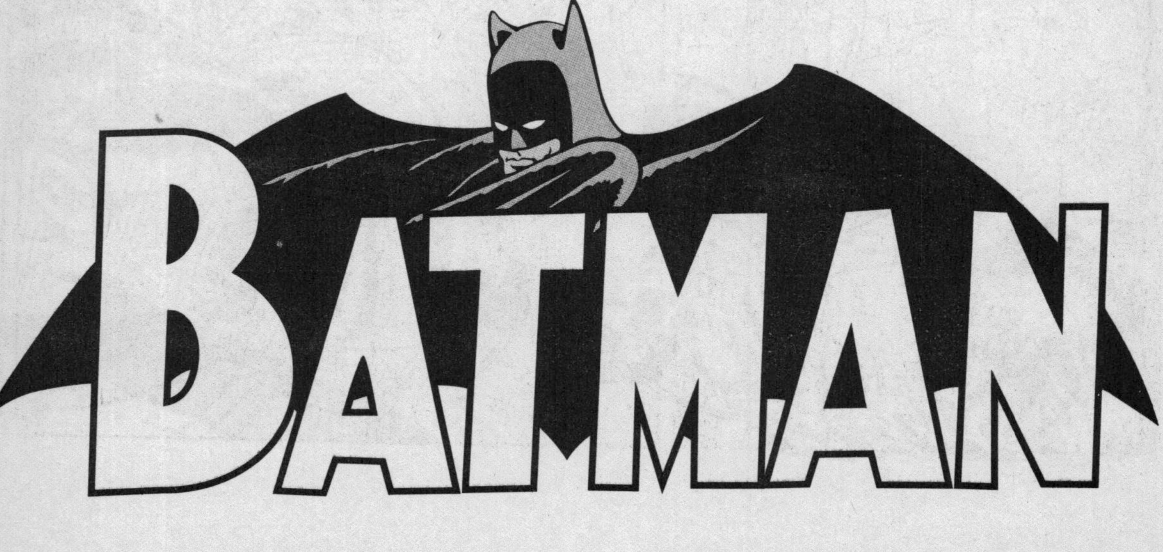
BATMAN

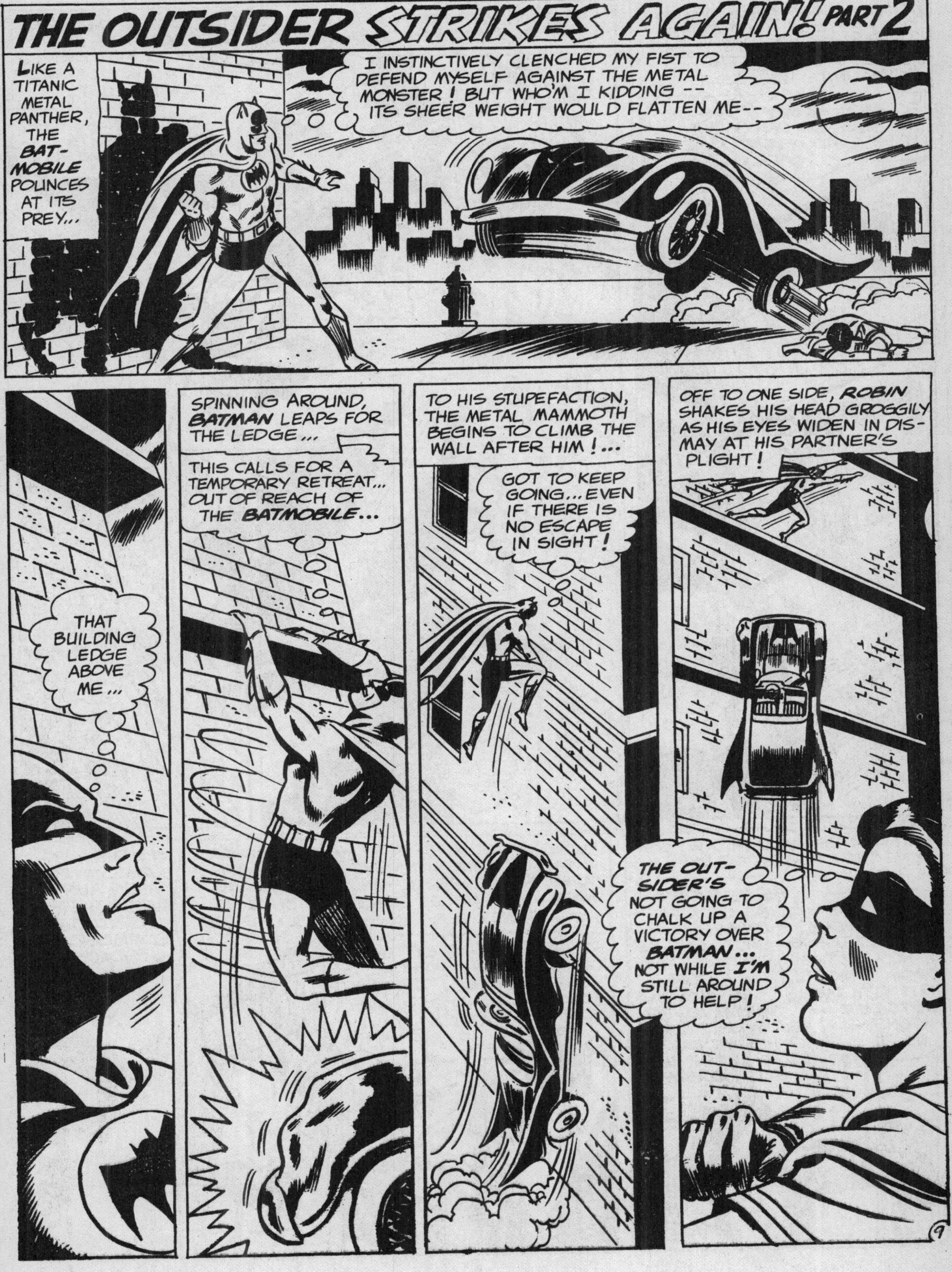
THE OUTSIDER STRIKES AGAIN! PART 2
LIKE A TITANIC METAL PANTHER, THE BATMOBILE POUNCES AT ITS PREY...
I INSTINCTIVELY CLENCHED MY FIST TO DEFEND MYSELF AGAINST THE METAL MONSTER! BUT WHO'M I KIDDING -- ITS SHEER WEIGHT WOULD FLATTEN ME--
THAT BUILDING LEDGE ABOVE ME...
SPINNING AROUND, BATMAN LEAPS FOR THE LEDGE...
THIS CALLS FOR A TEMPORARY RETREAT... OUT OF REACH OF THE BATMOBILE...
TO HIS STUPEFACTION, THE METAL MAMMOTH BEGINS TO CLIMB THE WALL AFTER HIM!...
GOT TO KEEP GOING... EVEN IF THERE IS NO ESCAPE IN SIGHT!
OFF TO ONE SIDE, ROBIN SHAKES HIS HEAD GROGGILY AS HIS EYES WIDEN IN DISMAY AT HIS PARTNER'S PLIGHT!
THE OUTSIDER'S NOT GOING TO CHALK UP A VICTORY OVER BATMAN... NOT WHILE I'M STILL AROUND TO HELP!
9

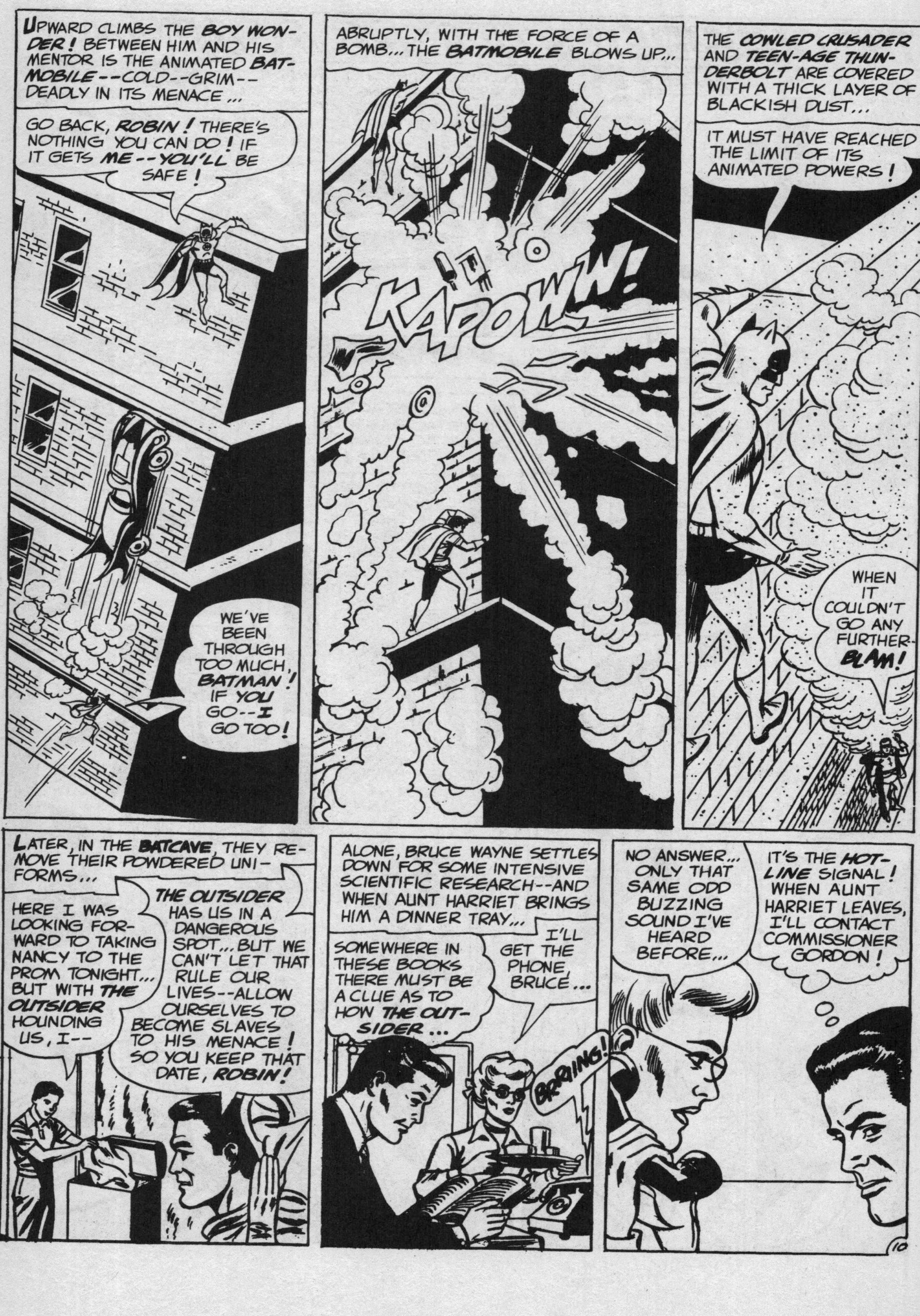
UPWARD CLIMBS THE BOY WONDER! BETWEEN HIM AND HIS MENTOR IS THE ANIMATED BATMOBILE--COLD--GRIM--DEADLY IN ITS MENACE...
GO BACK, ROBIN! THERE'S NOTHING YOU CAN DO! IF IT GETS ME--YOU'LL BE SAFE!
WE'VE BEEN THROUGH TOO MUCH, BATMAN! IF YOU GO--I GO TOO!
ABRUPTLY, WITH THE FORCE OF A BOMB... THE BATMOBILE BLOWS UP...
KAPOWW!
THE COWLED CRUSADER AND TEEN-AGE THUNDERBOLT ARE COVERED WITH A THICK LAYER OF BLACKISH DUST...
IT MUST HAVE REACHED THE LIMIT OF ITS ANIMATED POWERS!
WHEN IT COULDN'T GO ANY FURTHER-BLAM!
LATER, IN THE BATCAVE, THEY REMOVE THEIR POWDERED UNIFORMS...
HERE I WAS LOOKING FORWARD TO TAKING NANCY TO THE PROM TONIGHT... BUT WITH THE OUTSIDER HOUNDING US, I--
THE OUTSIDER HAS US IN A DANGEROUS SPOT... BUT WE CAN'T LET THAT RULE OUR LIVES--ALLOW OURSELVES TO BECOME SLAVES TO HIS MENACE! SO YOU KEEP THAT DATE, ROBIN!
ALONE, BRUCE WAYNE SETTLES DOWN FOR SOME INTENSIVE SCIENTIFIC RESEARCH--AND WHEN AUNT HARRIET BRINGS HIM A DINNER TRAY...
SOMEWHERE IN THESE BOOKS THERE MUST BE A CLUE AS TO HOW THE OUTSIDER...
I'LL GET THE PHONE, BRUCE...
BRRING!
NO ANSWER... ONLY THAT SAME ODD BUZZING SOUND I'VE HEARD BEFORE...
IT'S THE HOT-LINE SIGNAL! WHEN AUNT HARRIET LEAVES, I'LL CONTACT COMMISSIONER GORDON!
10

PRESSING A CONCEALED BUTTON IN THE PHONE, HE IS SOON SPEAKING WITH THE *GOTHAM CITY* POLICE COMMISSIONER...

AN EMERGENCY HAS JUST COME UP, *BATMAN!* WE NEED YOUR HELP!

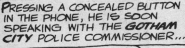

¿er¿ I'M BUSY ON ANOTHER CASE! CAN'T YOU HANDLE IT WITH-OUT ME?

"*NOT* WHEN YOU HEAR THIS! MY MEN SPOTTED SOME CROOKS IN THE *ATHLETIC HALL OF FAME* -- AND WHEN THEY TRIED TO GO IN AFTER THEM,..."

WE HAD THE *HALL* UNDER CONSTANT GUARD! HOW COULD THEY HAVE SNEAKED IN WITHOUT OUR SEEING THEM?

THE DOOR IS WIDE OPEN... BUT SOMETHING IS PRE-VENTING US FROM ENTERING!

"SUDDENLY, ABOVE THE DOOR-WAY, FLAMING LETTERS APPEARED..."

IF THE CROOKS HAD A SECRET WAY TO GET IN, THEY MUST HAVE A SECRET WAY TO GET OUT!

THIS ENTRANCE RESERVED FOR BATMAN ONLY!

WE'D BETTER SEND FOR *BATMAN* RIGHT AWAY!

YOU SEE NOW WHY WE CAN'T HANDLE THIS WITHOUT YOU, *BATMAN!*

I'LL BE RIGHT OVER!

A MOMENT LATER, BRUCE WAYNE STEPS INTO THE SECRET ELEVATOR LEADING TO THE *BATCAVE*...

THIS *WOULD* HAPPEN... JUST WHEN I WAS ON THE VERGE OF FIGURING OUT HOW TO DEAL WITH *THE OUTSIDER--!*

SUDDENLY, HIS FEET GO OUT FROM UNDER HIM AS...

THE ELEVATOR IS -- OUT OF CONTROL! IT'S DROPPING AT FULL SPEED TO THE *BAT-CAVE!* THE *OUTSIDER* IS STRIKING AT ME AGAIN!

11

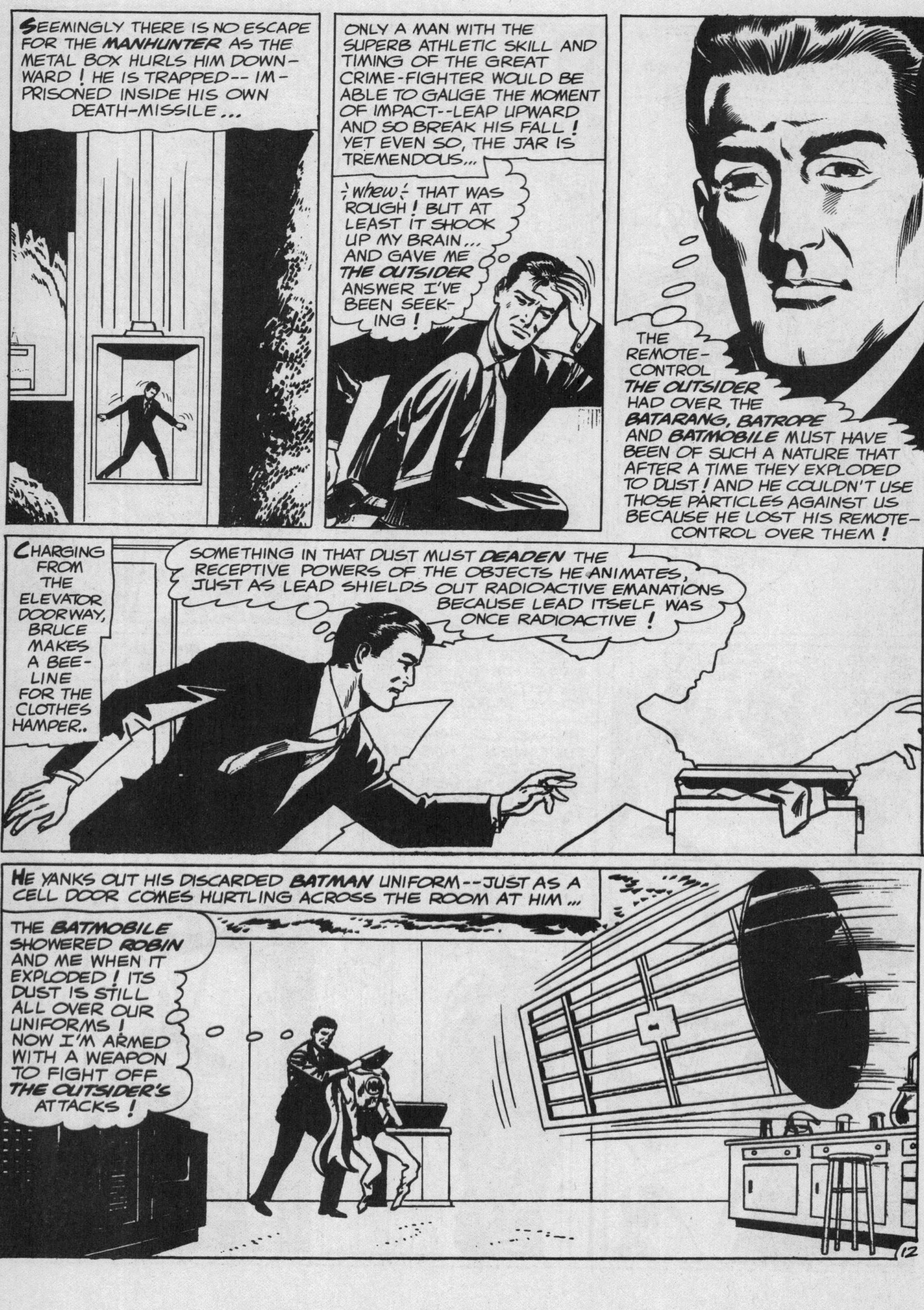
SEEMINGLY THERE IS NO ESCAPE FOR THE MANHUNTER AS THE METAL BOX HURLS HIM DOWNWARD! HE IS TRAPPED-- IMPRISONED INSIDE HIS OWN DEATH-MISSILE...
ONLY A MAN WITH THE SUPERB ATHLETIC SKILL AND TIMING OF THE GREAT CRIME-FIGHTER WOULD BE ABLE TO GAUGE THE MOMENT OF IMPACT--LEAP UPWARD AND SO BREAK HIS FALL! YET EVEN SO, THE JAR IS TREMENDOUS...
-WHEW- THAT WAS ROUGH! BUT AT LEAST IT SHOOK UP MY BRAIN... AND GAVE ME THE OUTSIDER ANSWER I'VE BEEN SEEKING!
THE REMOTE-CONTROL THE OUTSIDER HAD OVER THE BATARANG, BATROPE AND BATMOBILE MUST HAVE BEEN OF SUCH A NATURE THAT AFTER A TIME THEY EXPLODED TO DUST! AND HE COULDN'T USE THOSE PARTICLES AGAINST US BECAUSE HE LOST HIS REMOTE-CONTROL OVER THEM!
CHARGING FROM THE ELEVATOR DOORWAY, BRUCE MAKES A BEE-LINE FOR THE CLOTHES HAMPER..
SOMETHING IN THAT DUST MUST DEADEN THE RECEPTIVE POWERS OF THE OBJECTS HE ANIMATES, JUST AS LEAD SHIELDS OUT RADIOACTIVE EMANATIONS BECAUSE LEAD ITSELF WAS ONCE RADIOACTIVE!
HE YANKS OUT HIS DISCARDED BATMAN UNIFORM--JUST AS A CELL DOOR COMES HURTLING ACROSS THE ROOM AT HIM...
THE BATMOBILE SHOWERED ROBIN AND ME WHEN IT EXPLODED! ITS DUST IS STILL ALL OVER OUR UNIFORMS! NOW I'M ARMED WITH A WEAPON TO FIGHT OFF THE OUTSIDER'S ATTACKS!
12

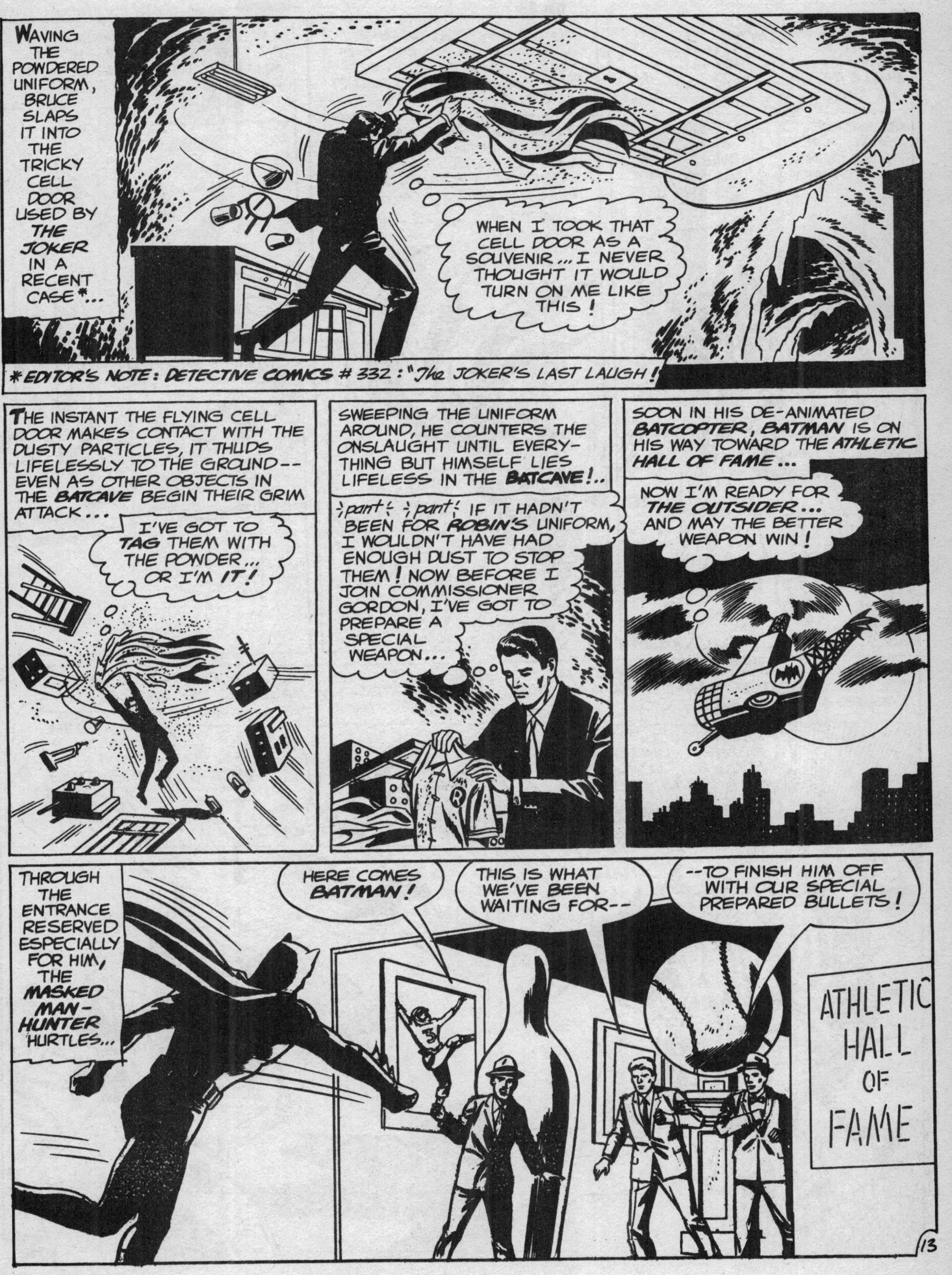
WAVING THE POWDERED UNIFORM, BRUCE SLAPS IT INTO THE TRICKY CELL DOOR USED BY THE JOKER IN A RECENT CASE*...
WHEN I TOOK THAT CELL DOOR AS A SOUVENIR... I NEVER THOUGHT IT WOULD TURN ON ME LIKE THIS!
*EDITOR'S NOTE: DETECTIVE COMICS # 332: "The JOKER'S LAST LAUGH!"
THE INSTANT THE FLYING CELL DOOR MAKES CONTACT WITH THE DUSTY PARTICLES, IT THUDS LIFELESSLY TO THE GROUND-- EVEN AS OTHER OBJECTS IN THE BATCAVE BEGIN THEIR GRIM ATTACK...
I'VE GOT TO TAG THEM WITH THE POWDER... OR I'M IT!
SWEEPING THE UNIFORM AROUND, HE COUNTERS THE ONSLAUGHT UNTIL EVERY-THING BUT HIMSELF LIES LIFELESS IN THE BATCAVE!..
¦pant¦ ¦pant¦ IF IT HADN'T BEEN FOR ROBIN'S UNIFORM, I WOULDN'T HAVE HAD ENOUGH DUST TO STOP THEM! NOW BEFORE I JOIN COMMISSIONER GORDON, I'VE GOT TO PREPARE A SPECIAL WEAPON...
SOON IN HIS DE-ANIMATED BATCOPTER, BATMAN IS ON HIS WAY TOWARD THE ATHLETIC HALL OF FAME...
NOW I'M READY FOR THE OUTSIDER... AND MAY THE BETTER WEAPON WIN!
THROUGH THE ENTRANCE RESERVED ESPECIALLY FOR HIM, THE MASKED MAN-HUNTER HURTLES...
HERE COMES BATMAN!
THIS IS WHAT WE'VE BEEN WAITING FOR--
--TO FINISH HIM OFF WITH OUR SPECIAL PREPARED BULLETS!
ATHLETIC HALL OF FAME
13

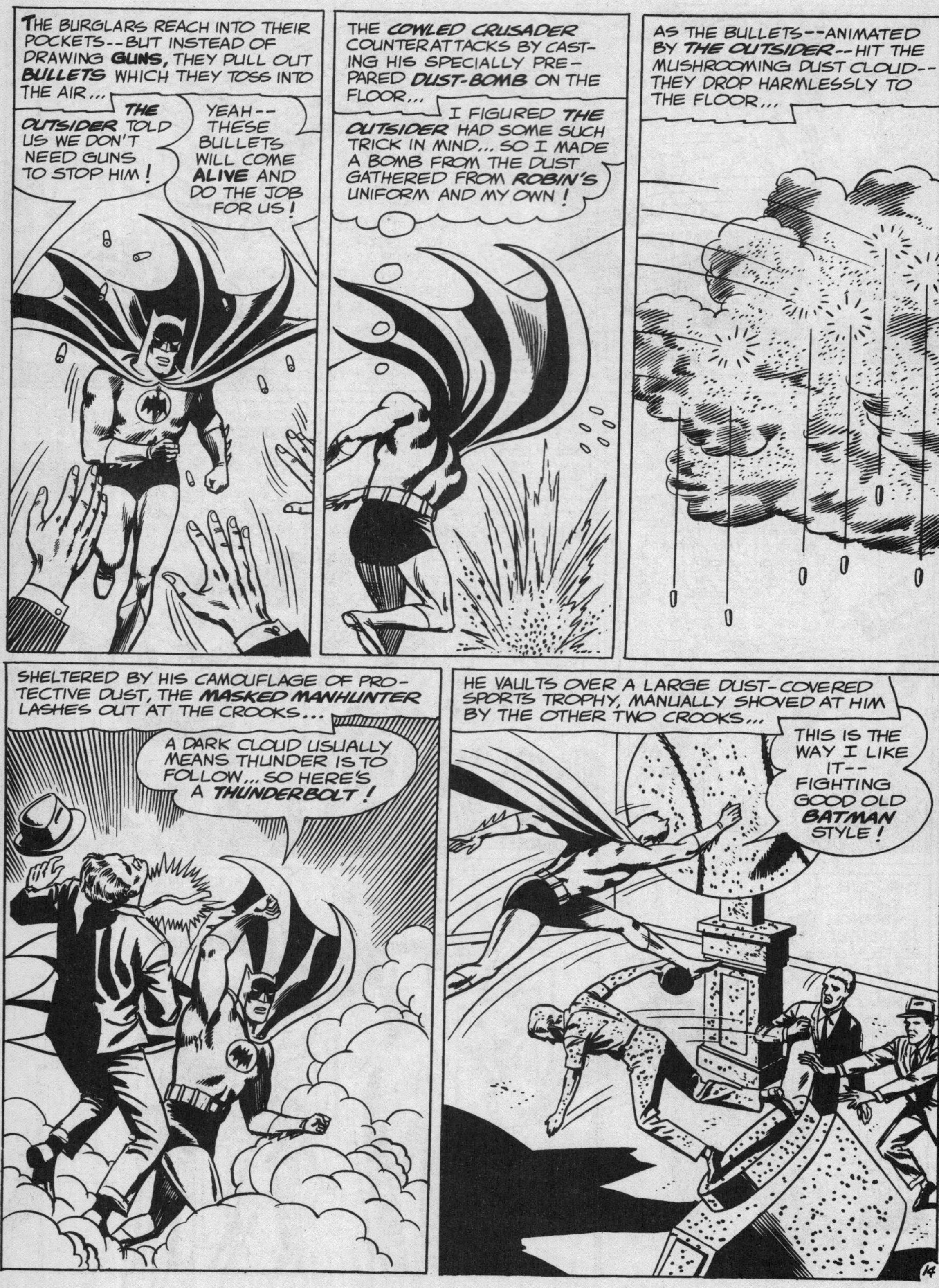
THE BURGLARS REACH INTO THEIR POCKETS--BUT INSTEAD OF DRAWING GUNS, THEY PULL OUT BULLETS WHICH THEY TOSS INTO THE AIR...
THE OUTSIDER TOLD US WE DON'T NEED GUNS TO STOP HIM!
YEAH--THESE BULLETS WILL COME ALIVE AND DO THE JOB FOR US!
THE COWLED CRUSADER COUNTERATTACKS BY CASTING HIS SPECIALLY PREPARED DUST-BOMB ON THE FLOOR...
I FIGURED THE OUTSIDER HAD SOME SUCH TRICK IN MIND... SO I MADE A BOMB FROM THE DUST GATHERED FROM ROBIN'S UNIFORM AND MY OWN!
AS THE BULLETS--ANIMATED BY THE OUTSIDER--HIT THE MUSHROOMING DUST CLOUD--THEY DROP HARMLESSLY TO THE FLOOR...
SHELTERED BY HIS CAMOUFLAGE OF PROTECTIVE DUST, THE MASKED MANHUNTER LASHES OUT AT THE CROOKS...
A DARK CLOUD USUALLY MEANS THUNDER IS TO FOLLOW... SO HERE'S A THUNDERBOLT!
HE VAULTS OVER A LARGE DUST-COVERED SPORTS TROPHY, MANUALLY SHOVED AT HIM BY THE OTHER TWO CROOKS...
THIS IS THE WAY I LIKE IT--FIGHTING GOOD OLD BATMAN STYLE!
14

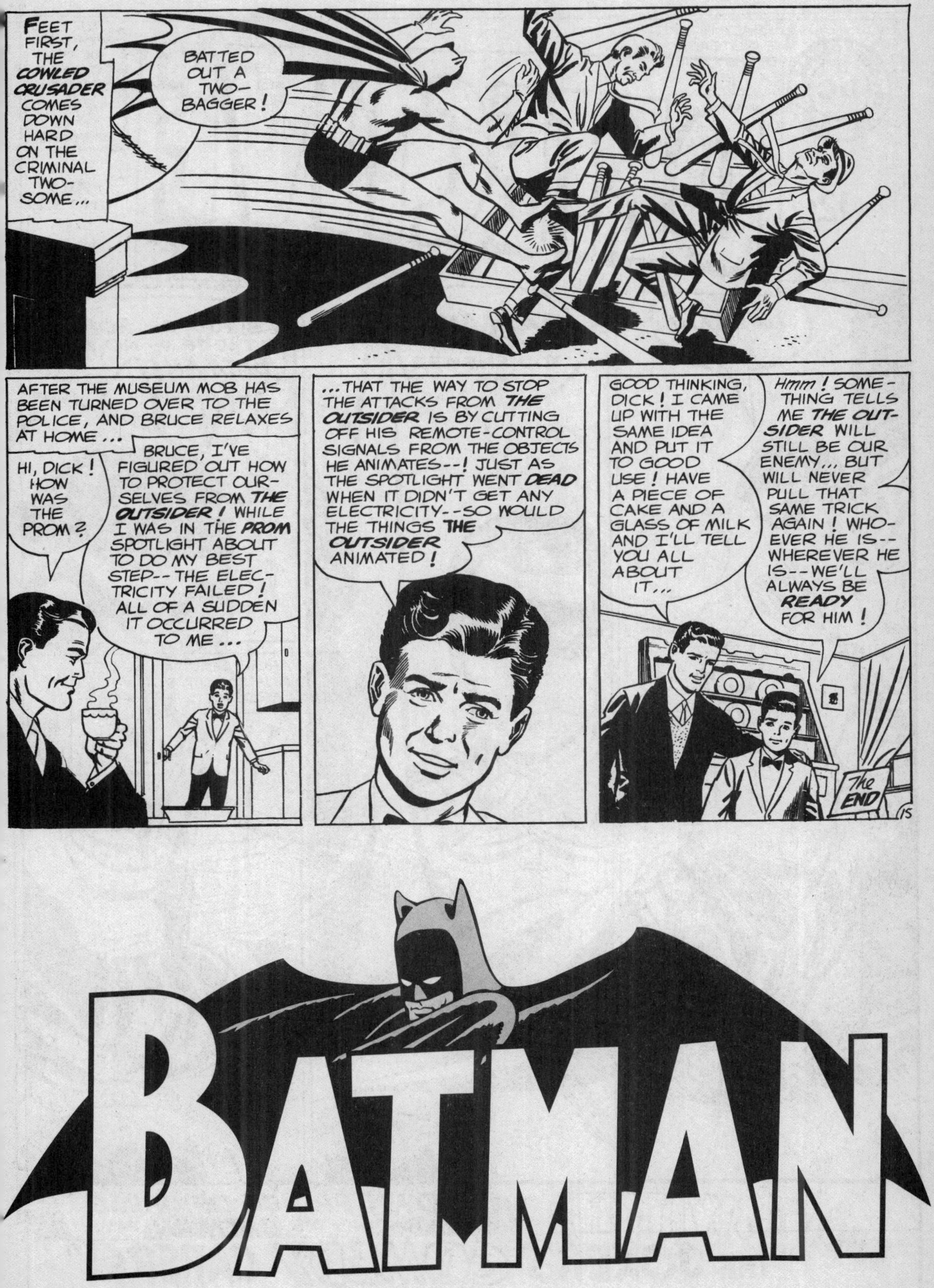
FEET FIRST, THE COWLED CRUSADER COMES DOWN HARD ON THE CRIMINAL TWO-SOME...
BATTED OUT A TWO-BAGGER!
AFTER THE MUSEUM MOB HAS BEEN TURNED OVER TO THE POLICE, AND BRUCE RELAXES AT HOME...
HI, DICK! HOW WAS THE PROM?
BRUCE, I'VE FIGURED OUT HOW TO PROTECT OURSELVES FROM THE OUTSIDER! WHILE I WAS IN THE PROM SPOTLIGHT ABOUT TO DO MY BEST STEP-- THE ELECTRICITY FAILED! ALL OF A SUDDEN IT OCCURRED TO ME...
...THAT THE WAY TO STOP THE ATTACKS FROM THE OUTSIDER IS BY CUTTING OFF HIS REMOTE-CONTROL SIGNALS FROM THE OBJECTS HE ANIMATES--! JUST AS THE SPOTLIGHT WENT DEAD WHEN IT DIDN'T GET ANY ELECTRICITY--SO WOULD THE THINGS THE OUTSIDER ANIMATED!
GOOD THINKING, DICK! I CAME UP WITH THE SAME IDEA AND PUT IT TO GOOD USE! HAVE A PIECE OF CAKE AND A GLASS OF MILK AND I'LL TELL YOU ALL ABOUT IT...
Hmm! SOMETHING TELLS ME THE OUTSIDER WILL STILL BE OUR ENEMY... BUT WILL NEVER PULL THAT SAME TRICK AGAIN! WHOEVER HE IS--WHEREVER HE IS--WE'LL ALWAYS BE READY FOR HIM!
The END
15

BATMAN

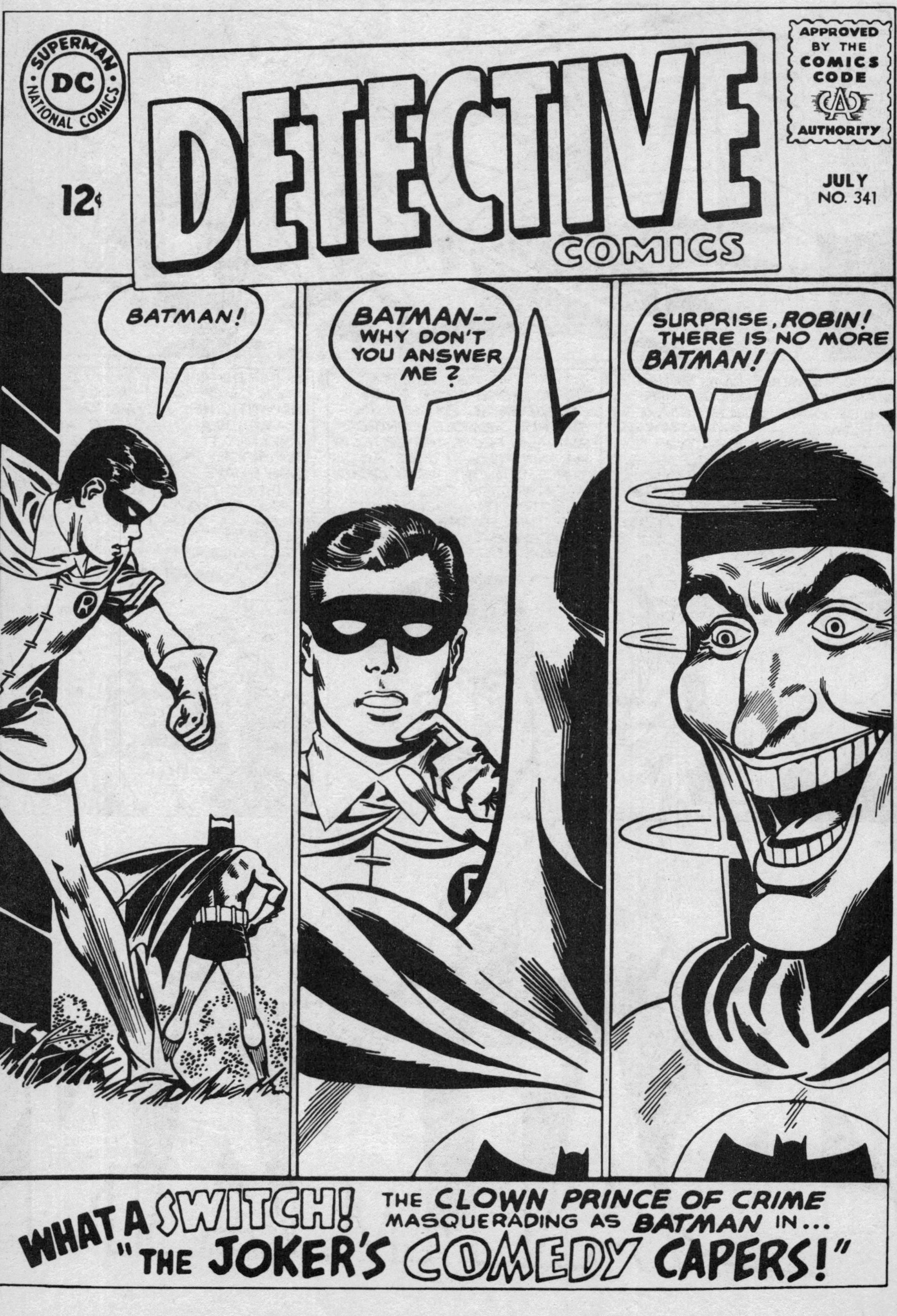
SUPERMAN DC NATIONAL COMICS
APPROVED BY THE COMICS CODE AUTHORITY
12¢
DETECTIVE COMICS
JULY NO. 341
BATMAN!
BATMAN-- WHY DON'T YOU ANSWER ME?
SURPRISE, ROBIN! THERE IS NO MORE BATMAN!
WHAT A SWITCH! THE CLOWN PRINCE OF CRIME MASQUERADING AS BATMAN IN...
"THE JOKER'S COMEDY CAPERS!"

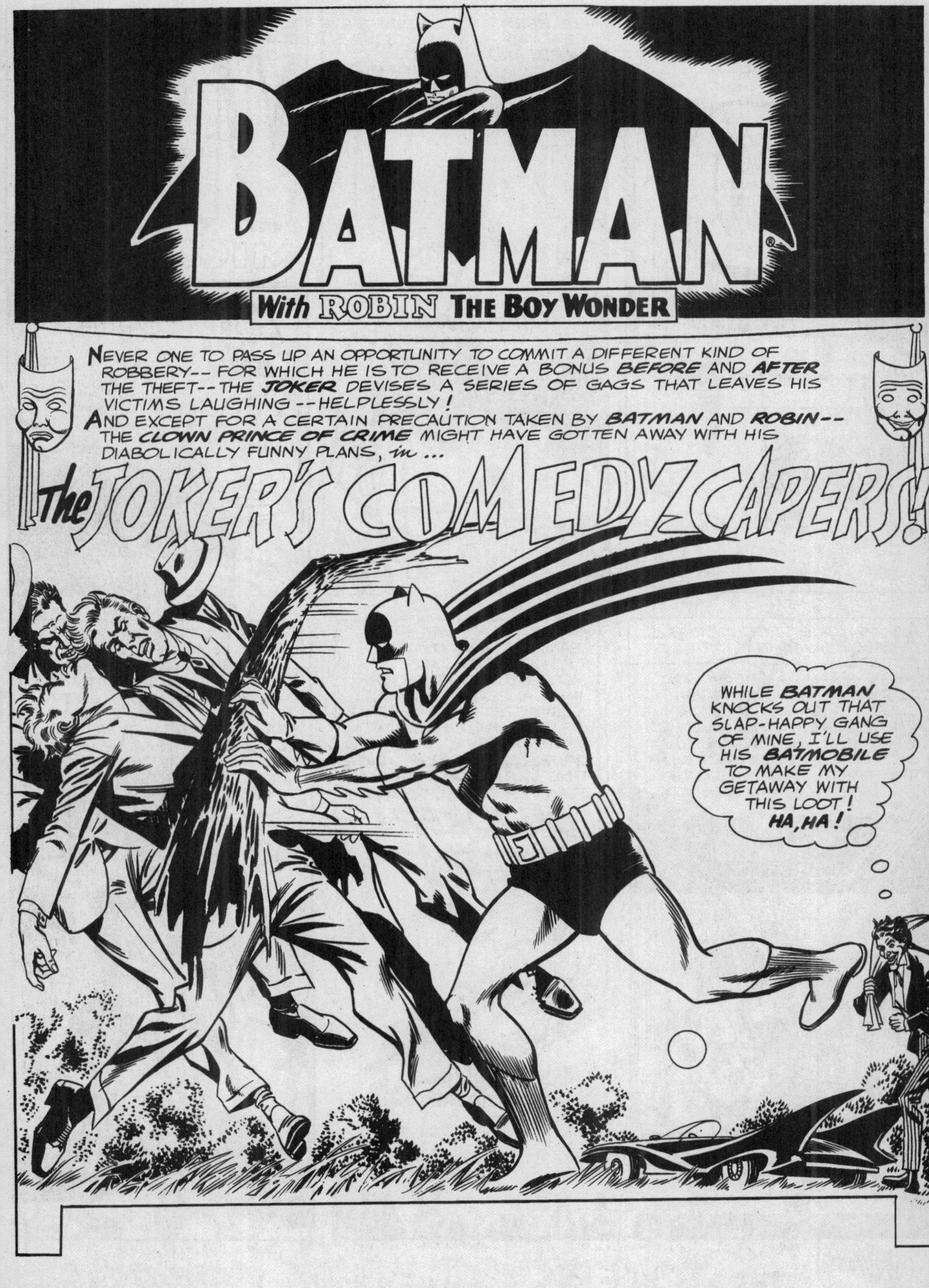
BATMAN®
With ROBIN THE BOY WONDER
NEVER ONE TO PASS UP AN OPPORTUNITY TO COMMIT A DIFFERENT KIND OF ROBBERY-- FOR WHICH HE IS TO RECEIVE A BONUS BEFORE AND AFTER THE THEFT--THE JOKER DEVISES A SERIES OF GAGS THAT LEAVES HIS VICTIMS LAUGHING --HELPLESSLY!
AND EXCEPT FOR A CERTAIN PRECAUTION TAKEN BY BATMAN AND ROBIN-- THE CLOWN PRINCE OF CRIME MIGHT HAVE GOTTEN AWAY WITH HIS DIABOLICALLY FUNNY PLANS, in ...
The JOKER'S COMEDY CAPERS!
WHILE BATMAN KNOCKS OUT THAT SLAP-HAPPY GANG OF MINE, I'LL USE HIS BATMOBILE TO MAKE MY GETAWAY WITH THIS LOOT! HA, HA!

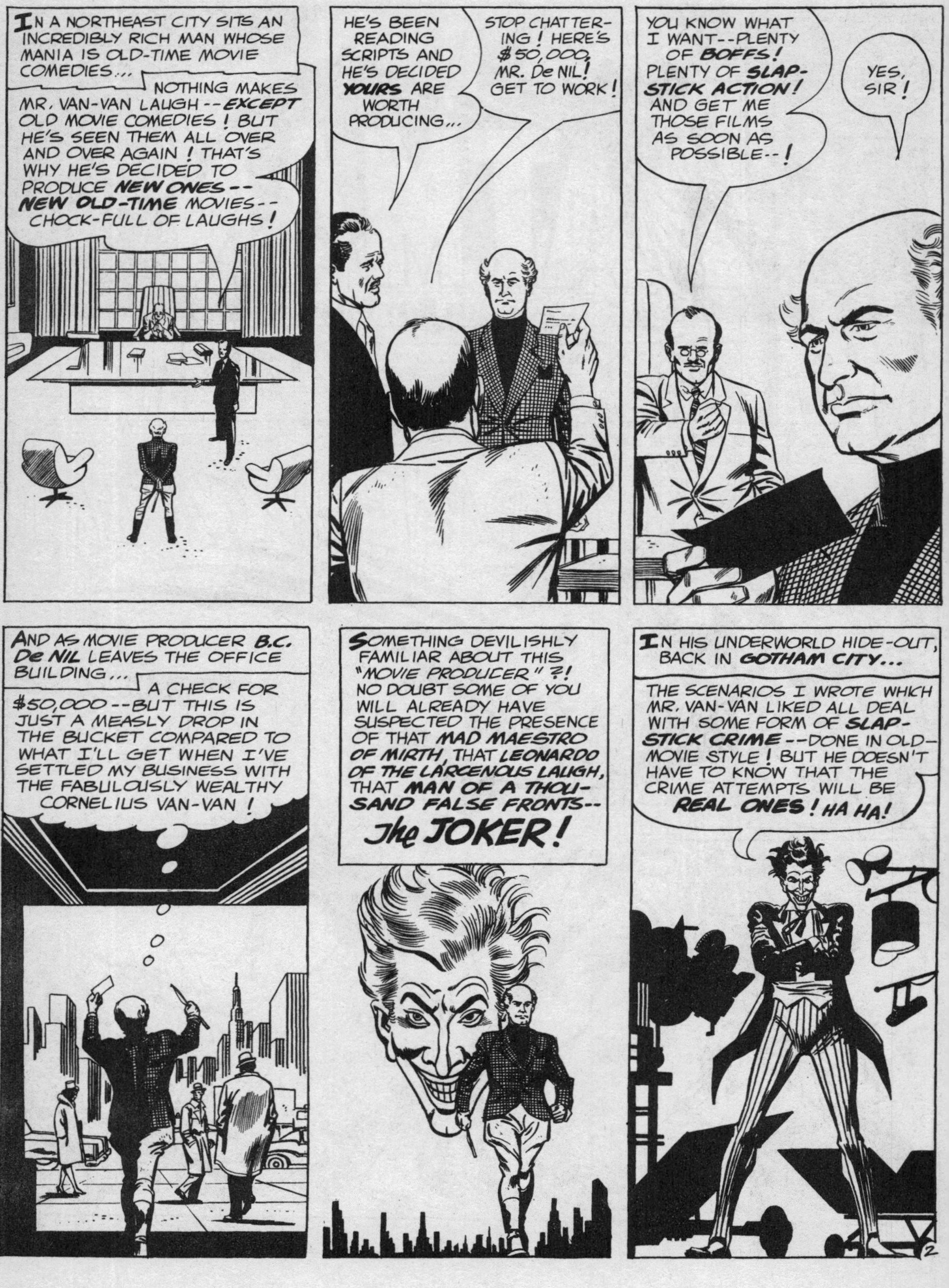
IN A NORTHEAST CITY SITS AN INCREDIBLY RICH MAN WHOSE MANIA IS OLD-TIME MOVIE COMEDIES...
NOTHING MAKES MR. VAN-VAN LAUGH -- EXCEPT OLD MOVIE COMEDIES! BUT HE'S SEEN THEM ALL OVER AND OVER AGAIN! THAT'S WHY HE'S DECIDED TO PRODUCE NEW ONES -- NEW OLD-TIME MOVIES -- CHOCK-FULL OF LAUGHS!
HE'S BEEN READING SCRIPTS AND HE'S DECIDED YOURS ARE WORTH PRODUCING...
STOP CHATTERING! HERE'S $50,000, MR. De NIL! GET TO WORK!
YOU KNOW WHAT I WANT--PLENTY OF BOFFS! PLENTY OF SLAPSTICK ACTION! AND GET ME THOSE FILMS AS SOON AS POSSIBLE--!
YES, SIR!
AND AS MOVIE PRODUCER B.C. De NIL LEAVES THE OFFICE BUILDING...
A CHECK FOR $50,000 -- BUT THIS IS JUST A MEASLY DROP IN THE BUCKET COMPARED TO WHAT I'LL GET WHEN I'VE SETTLED MY BUSINESS WITH THE FABULOUSLY WEALTHY CORNELIUS VAN-VAN!
SOMETHING DEVILISHLY FAMILIAR ABOUT THIS "MOVIE PRODUCER"?! NO DOUBT SOME OF YOU WILL ALREADY HAVE SUSPECTED THE PRESENCE OF THAT MAD MAESTRO OF MIRTH, THAT LEONARDO OF THE LARCENOUS LAUGH, THAT MAN OF A THOUSAND FALSE FRONTS -- The JOKER!
IN HIS UNDERWORLD HIDE-OUT, BACK IN GOTHAM CITY...
THE SCENARIOS I WROTE WHICH MR. VAN-VAN LIKED ALL DEAL WITH SOME FORM OF SLAPSTICK CRIME -- DONE IN OLD-MOVIE STYLE! BUT HE DOESN'T HAVE TO KNOW THAT THE CRIME ATTEMPTS WILL BE REAL ONES! HA HA!
2

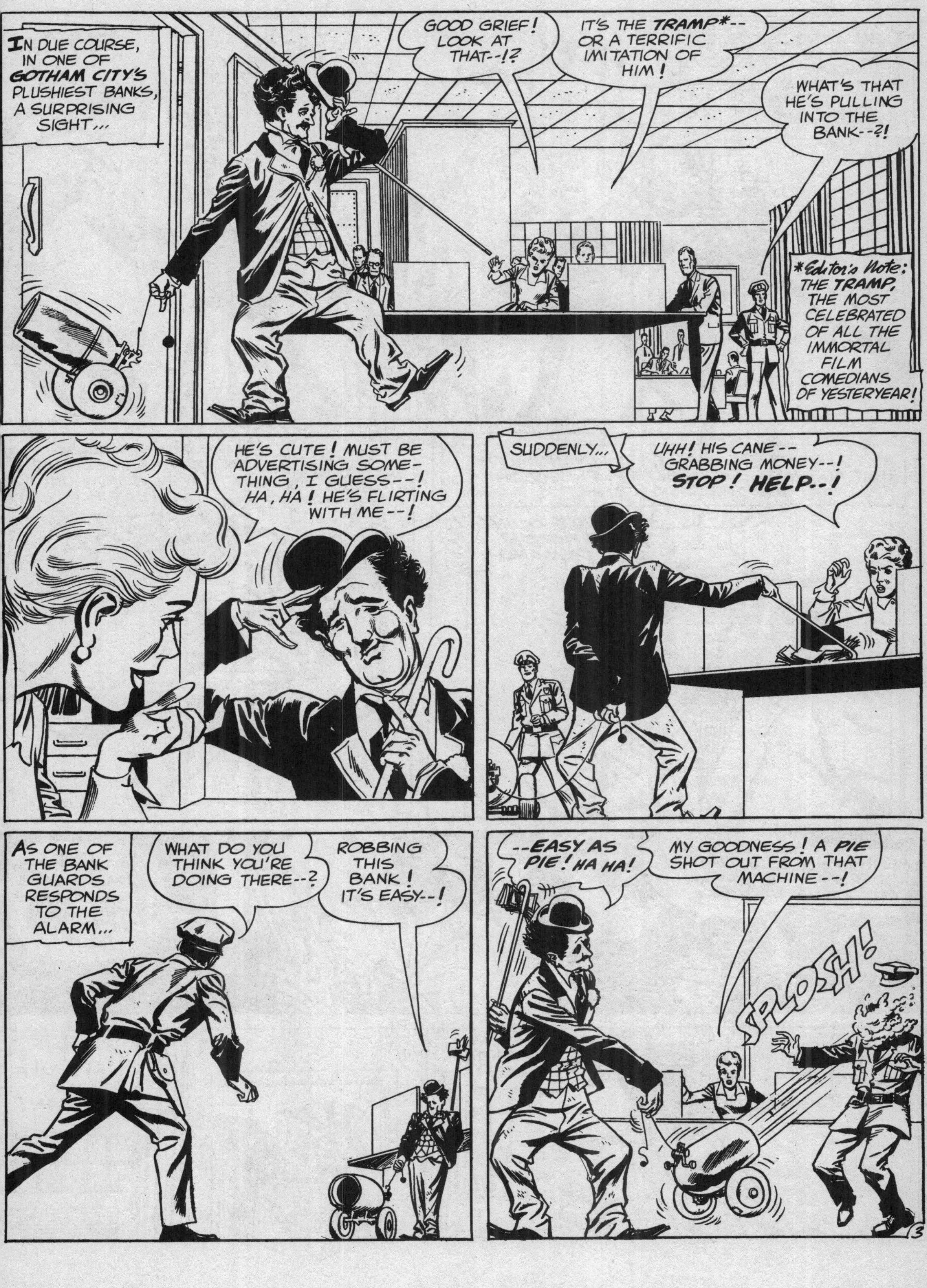
IN DUE COURSE, IN ONE OF GOTHAM CITY'S PLUSHIEST BANKS, A SURPRISING SIGHT...
GOOD GRIEF! LOOK AT THAT--!?
IT'S THE TRAMP*-- OR A TERRIFIC IMITATION OF HIM!
WHAT'S THAT HE'S PULLING INTO THE BANK--?!
*Editor's Note: THE TRAMP, THE MOST CELEBRATED OF ALL THE IMMORTAL FILM COMEDIANS OF YESTERYEAR!
HE'S CUTE! MUST BE ADVERTISING SOME-THING, I GUESS--! HA, HA! HE'S FLIRTING WITH ME--!
SUDDENLY...
UHH! HIS CANE-- GRABBING MONEY--! STOP! HELP..!
AS ONE OF THE BANK GUARDS RESPONDS TO THE ALARM...
WHAT DO YOU THINK YOU'RE DOING THERE--?
ROBBING THIS BANK! IT'S EASY--!
--EASY AS PIE! HA HA!
MY GOODNESS! A PIE SHOT OUT FROM THAT MACHINE--!
SPLOSH!
3

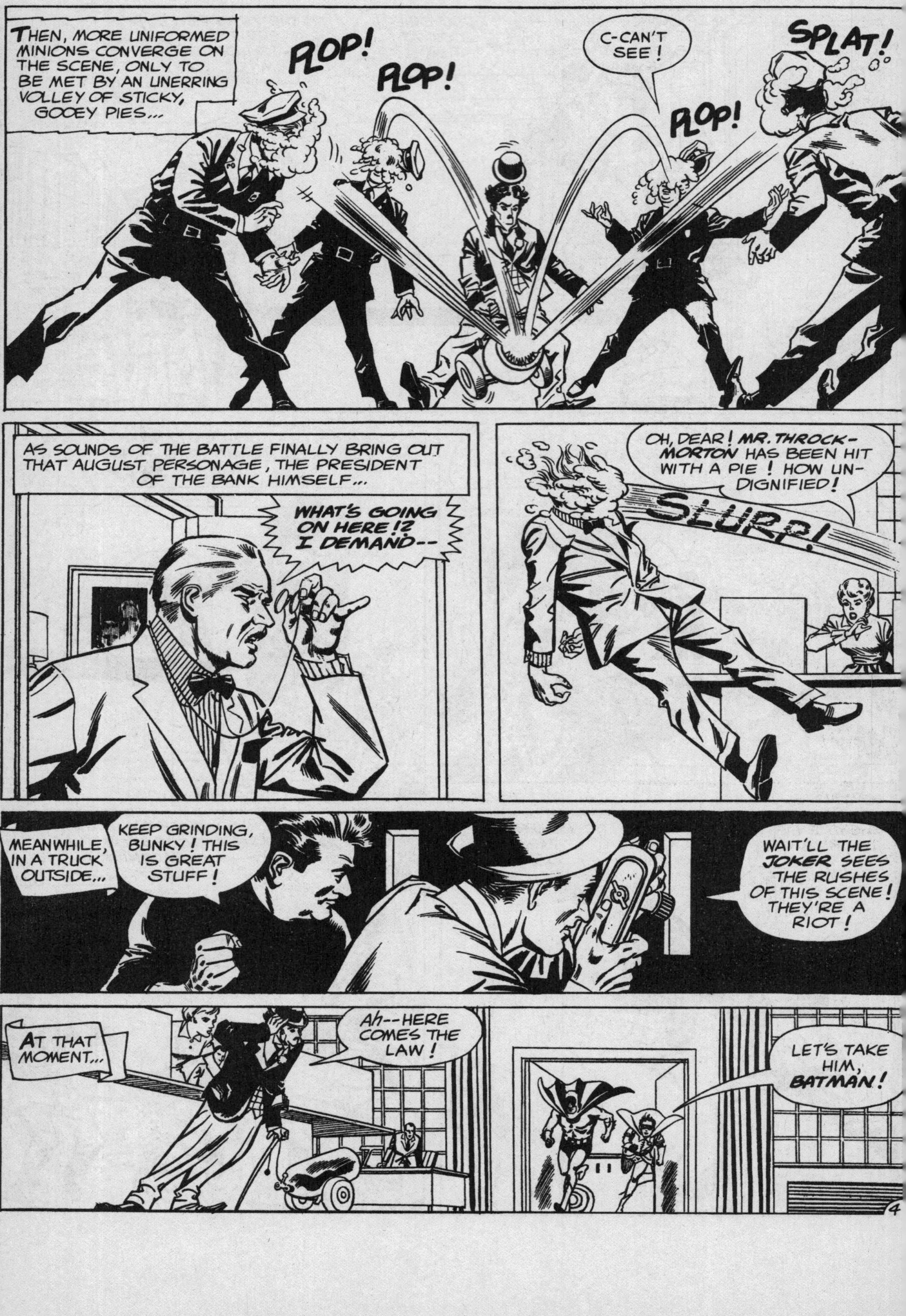
THEN, MORE UNIFORMED MINIONS CONVERGE ON THE SCENE, ONLY TO BE MET BY AN UNERRING VOLLEY OF STICKY, GOOEY PIES...
PLOP!
PLOP!
C-CAN'T SEE!
PLOP!
SPLAT!
AS SOUNDS OF THE BATTLE FINALLY BRING OUT THAT AUGUST PERSONAGE, THE PRESIDENT OF THE BANK HIMSELF...
WHAT'S GOING ON HERE!? I DEMAND--
OH, DEAR! MR. THROCK-MORTON HAS BEEN HIT WITH A PIE! HOW UN-DIGNIFIED!
SLURP!
MEANWHILE, IN A TRUCK OUTSIDE...
KEEP GRINDING, BUNKY! THIS IS GREAT STUFF!
WAIT'LL THE JOKER SEES THE RUSHES OF THIS SCENE! THEY'RE A RIOT!
AT THAT MOMENT...
Ah--HERE COMES THE LAW!
LET'S TAKE HIM, BATMAN!
4

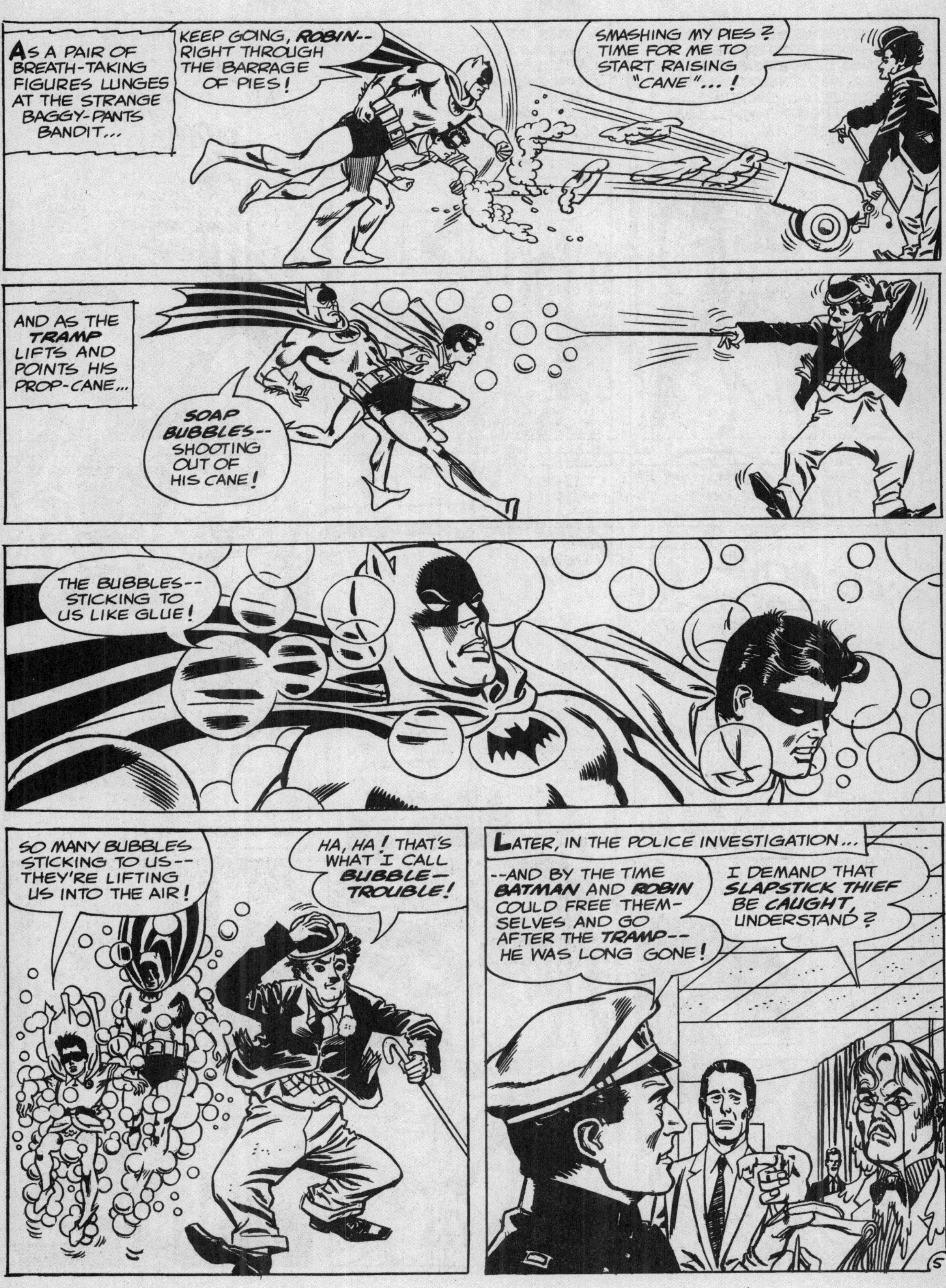
AS A PAIR OF BREATH-TAKING FIGURES LUNGES AT THE STRANGE BAGGY-PANTS BANDIT...
KEEP GOING, ROBIN-- RIGHT THROUGH THE BARRAGE OF PIES!
SMASHING MY PIES? TIME FOR ME TO START RAISING "CANE"...!
AND AS THE TRAMP LIFTS AND POINTS HIS PROP-CANE...
SOAP BUBBLES-- SHOOTING OUT OF HIS CANE!
THE BUBBLES-- STICKING TO US LIKE GLUE!
SO MANY BUBBLES STICKING TO US-- THEY'RE LIFTING US INTO THE AIR!
HA, HA! THAT'S WHAT I CALL BUBBLE-TROUBLE!
LATER, IN THE POLICE INVESTIGATION...
--AND BY THE TIME BATMAN AND ROBIN COULD FREE THEMSELVES AND GO AFTER THE TRAMP-- HE WAS LONG GONE!
I DEMAND THAT SLAPSTICK THIEF BE CAUGHT, UNDERSTAND?
5

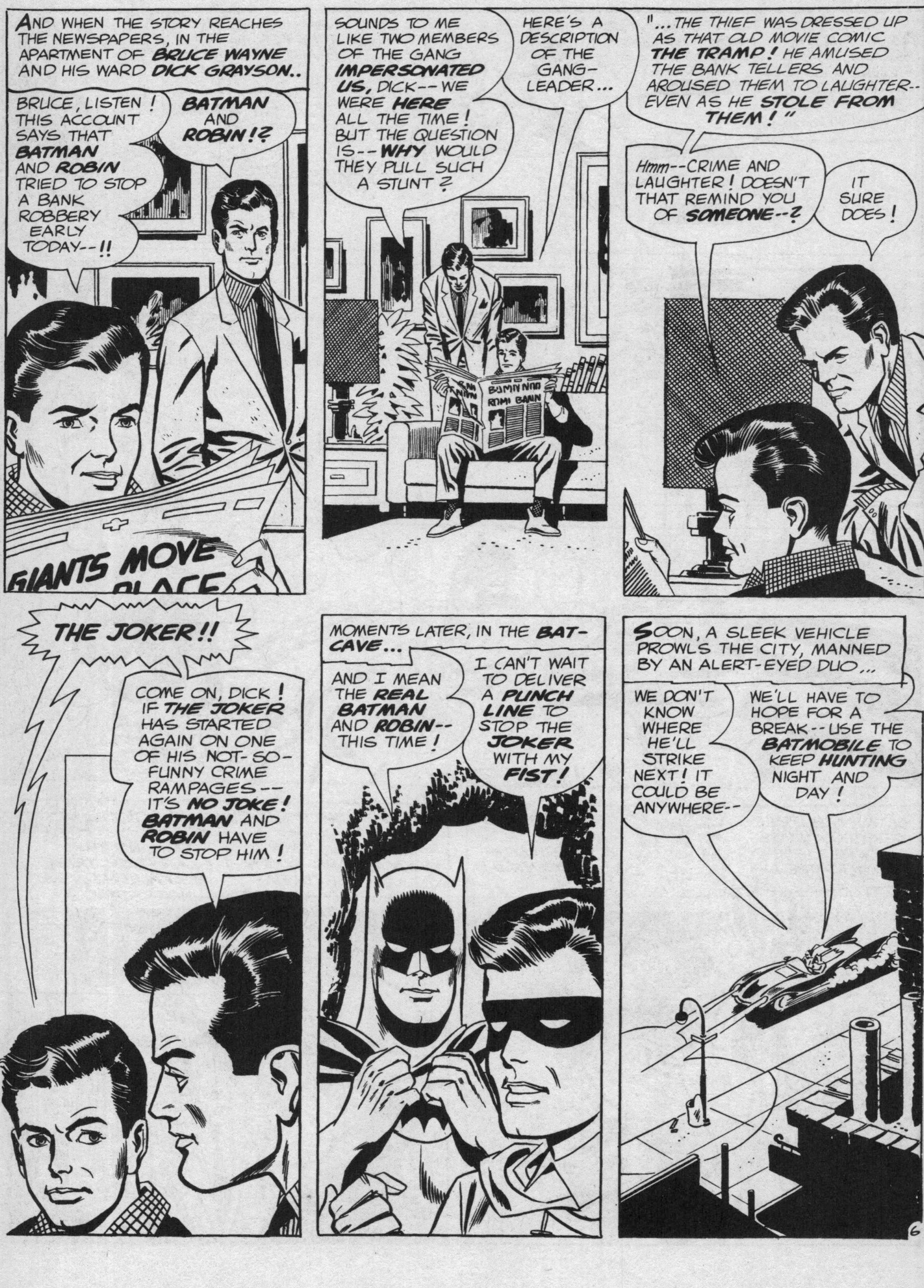
AND WHEN THE STORY REACHES THE NEWSPAPERS, IN THE APARTMENT OF BRUCE WAYNE AND HIS WARD DICK GRAYSON..
BRUCE, LISTEN! THIS ACCOUNT SAYS THAT BATMAN AND ROBIN TRIED TO STOP A BANK ROBBERY EARLY TODAY--!!
BATMAN AND ROBIN!?
GIANTS MOVE
SOUNDS TO ME LIKE TWO MEMBERS OF THE GANG IMPERSONATED US, DICK-- WE WERE HERE ALL THE TIME! BUT THE QUESTION IS--WHY WOULD THEY PULL SUCH A STUNT?
HERE'S A DESCRIPTION OF THE GANG-LEADER...
"...THE THIEF WAS DRESSED UP AS THAT OLD MOVIE COMIC THE TRAMP! HE AMUSED THE BANK TELLERS AND AROUSED THEM TO LAUGHTER-- EVEN AS HE STOLE FROM THEM!"
Hmm--CRIME AND LAUGHTER! DOESN'T THAT REMIND YOU OF SOMEONE--?
IT SURE DOES!
THE JOKER!!
COME ON, DICK! IF THE JOKER HAS STARTED AGAIN ON ONE OF HIS NOT-SO-FUNNY CRIME RAMPAGES-- IT'S NO JOKE! BATMAN AND ROBIN HAVE TO STOP HIM!
MOMENTS LATER, IN THE BAT-CAVE...
AND I MEAN THE REAL BATMAN AND ROBIN-- THIS TIME!
I CAN'T WAIT TO DELIVER A PUNCH LINE TO STOP THE JOKER WITH MY FIST!
SOON, A SLEEK VEHICLE PROWLS THE CITY, MANNED BY AN ALERT-EYED DUO...
WE DON'T KNOW WHERE HE'LL STRIKE NEXT! IT COULD BE ANYWHERE--
WE'LL HAVE TO HOPE FOR A BREAK--USE THE BATMOBILE TO KEEP HUNTING NIGHT AND DAY!
6

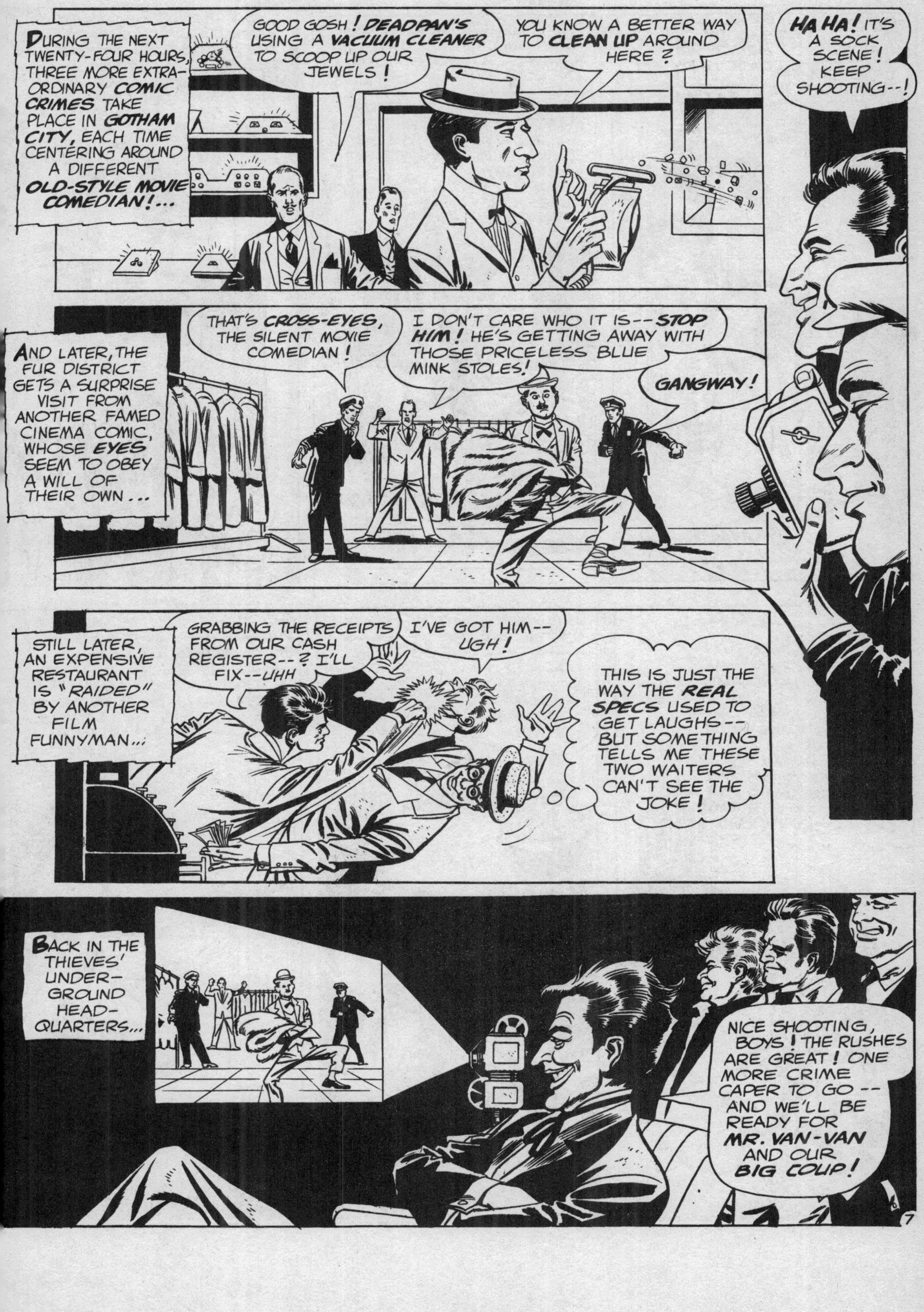
DURING THE NEXT TWENTY-FOUR HOURS, THREE MORE EXTRA-ORDINARY COMIC CRIMES TAKE PLACE IN GOTHAM CITY, EACH TIME CENTERING AROUND A DIFFERENT OLD-STYLE MOVIE COMEDIAN!...
GOOD GOSH! DEADPAN'S USING A VACUUM CLEANER TO SCOOP UP OUR JEWELS!
YOU KNOW A BETTER WAY TO CLEAN UP AROUND HERE?
HA HA! IT'S A SOCK SCENE! KEEP SHOOTING--!
AND LATER, THE FUR DISTRICT GETS A SURPRISE VISIT FROM ANOTHER FAMED CINEMA COMIC, WHOSE EYES SEEM TO OBEY A WILL OF THEIR OWN...
THAT'S CROSS-EYES, THE SILENT MOVIE COMEDIAN!
I DON'T CARE WHO IT IS--STOP HIM! HE'S GETTING AWAY WITH THOSE PRICELESS BLUE MINK STOLES!
GANGWAY!
STILL LATER, AN EXPENSIVE RESTAURANT IS "RAIDED" BY ANOTHER FILM FUNNYMAN...
GRABBING THE RECEIPTS FROM OUR CASH REGISTER--? I'LL FIX--UHH
I'VE GOT HIM-- UGH!
THIS IS JUST THE WAY THE REAL SPECS USED TO GET LAUGHS--BUT SOMETHING TELLS ME THESE TWO WAITERS CAN'T SEE THE JOKE!
BACK IN THE THIEVES' UNDER-GROUND HEAD-QUARTERS...
NICE SHOOTING, BOYS! THE RUSHES ARE GREAT! ONE MORE CRIME CAPER TO GO--AND WE'LL BE READY FOR MR. VAN-VAN AND OUR BIG COUP!
7

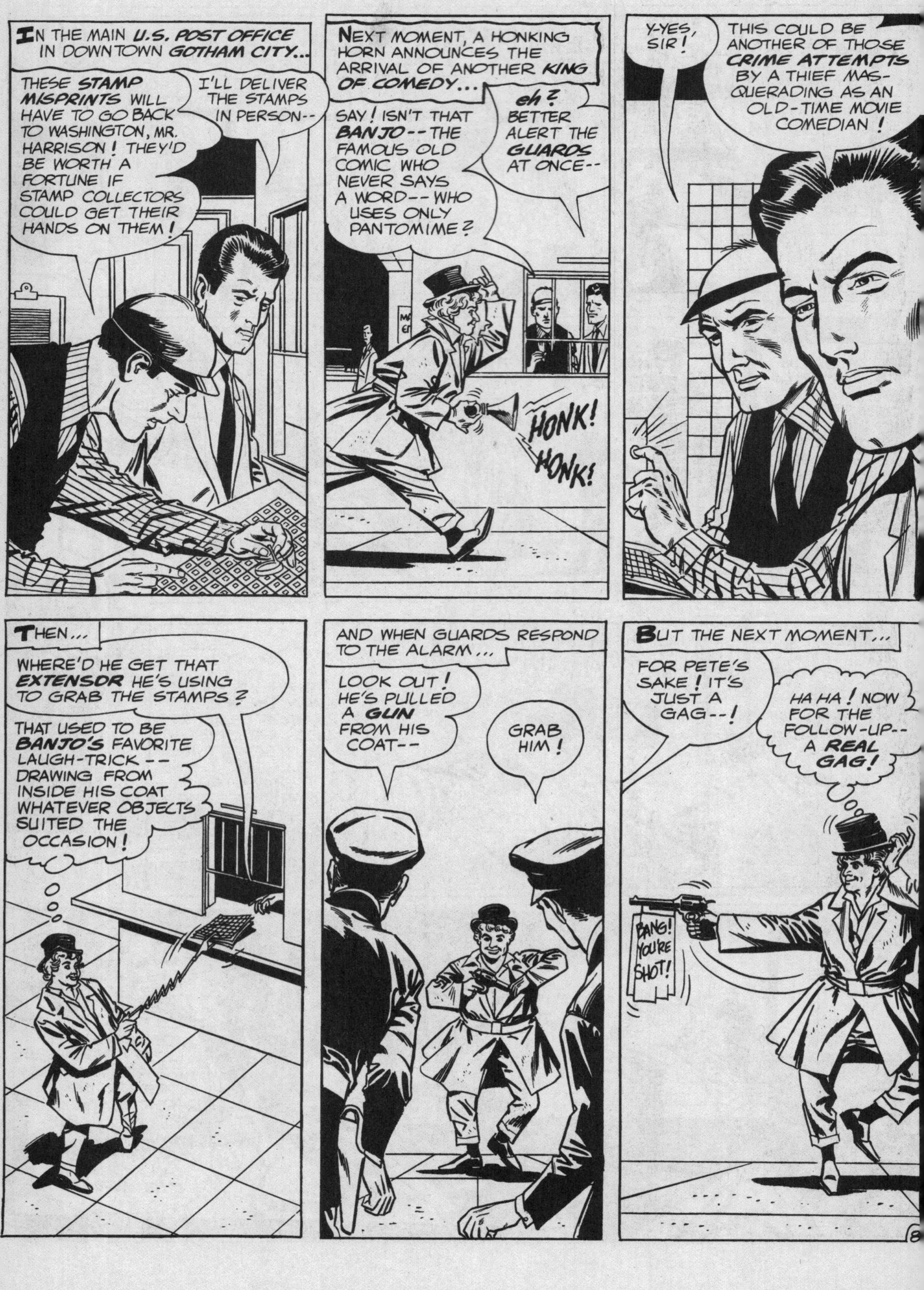
IN THE MAIN U.S. POST OFFICE IN DOWNTOWN GOTHAM CITY...
THESE STAMP MISPRINTS WILL HAVE TO GO BACK TO WASHINGTON, MR. HARRISON! THEY'D BE WORTH A FORTUNE IF STAMP COLLECTORS COULD GET THEIR HANDS ON THEM!
I'LL DELIVER THE STAMPS IN PERSON--
NEXT MOMENT, A HONKING HORN ANNOUNCES THE ARRIVAL OF ANOTHER KING OF COMEDY...
SAY! ISN'T THAT BANJO--THE FAMOUS OLD COMIC WHO NEVER SAYS A WORD--WHO USES ONLY PANTOMIME?
eh? BETTER ALERT THE GUARDS AT ONCE--
HONK! HONK!
Y-YES, SIR!
THIS COULD BE ANOTHER OF THOSE CRIME ATTEMPTS BY A THIEF MASQUERADING AS AN OLD-TIME MOVIE COMEDIAN!
THEN...
WHERE'D HE GET THAT EXTENSOR HE'S USING TO GRAB THE STAMPS?
THAT USED TO BE BANJO'S FAVORITE LAUGH-TRICK--DRAWING FROM INSIDE HIS COAT WHATEVER OBJECTS SUITED THE OCCASION!
AND WHEN GUARDS RESPOND TO THE ALARM...
LOOK OUT! HE'S PULLED A GUN FROM HIS COAT--
GRAB HIM!
BUT THE NEXT MOMENT...
FOR PETE'S SAKE! IT'S JUST A GAG--!
HA HA! NOW FOR THE FOLLOW-UP--A REAL GAG!
BANG! YOU'RE SHOT!
8

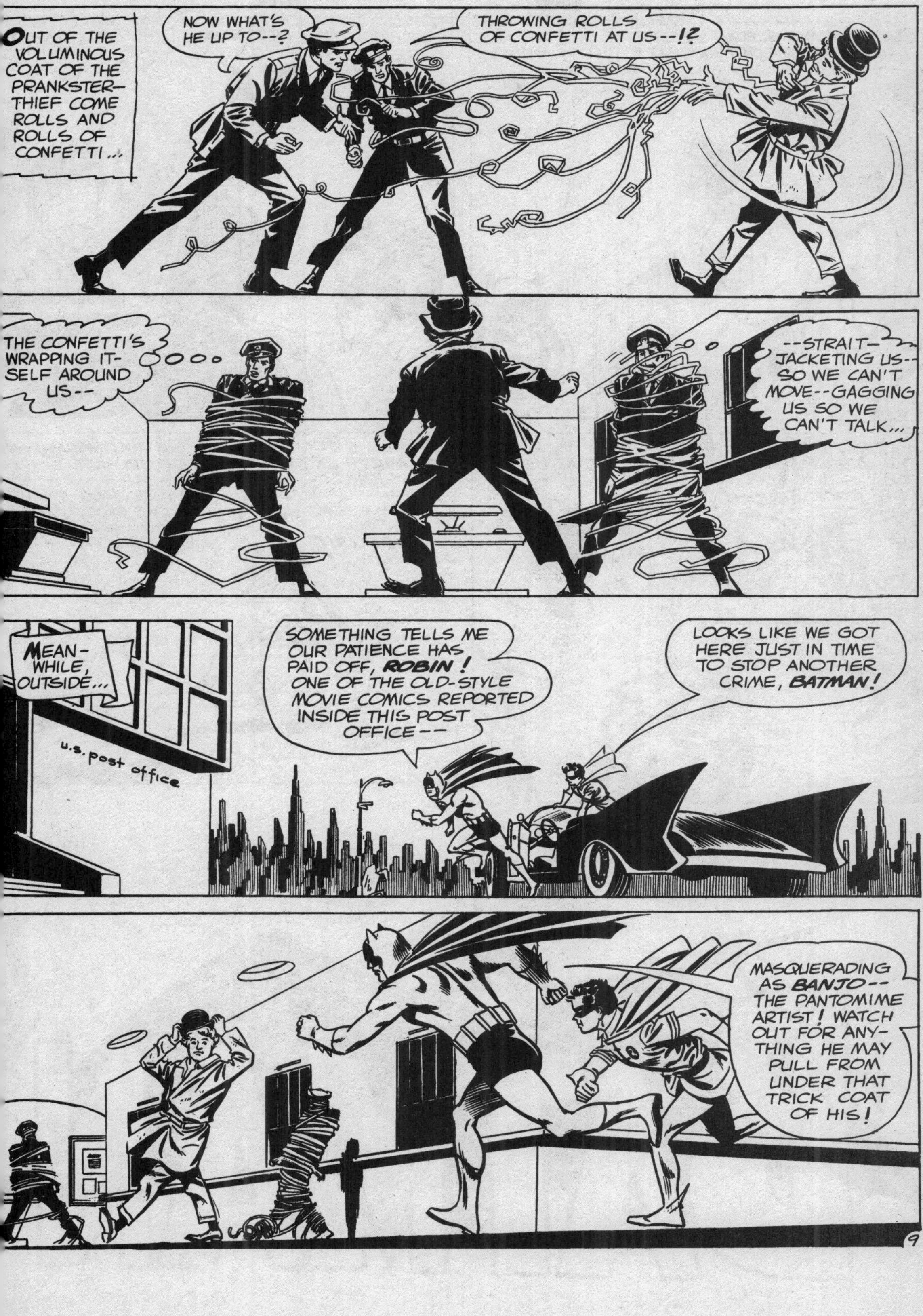
OUT OF THE VOLUMINOUS COAT OF THE PRANKSTER-THIEF COME ROLLS AND ROLLS OF CONFETTI...
NOW WHAT'S HE UP TO--?
THROWING ROLLS OF CONFETTI AT US--!?
THE CONFETTI'S WRAPPING IT-SELF AROUND US--
--STRAIT-JACKETING US--SO WE CAN'T MOVE--GAGGING US SO WE CAN'T TALK...
MEAN-WHILE, OUTSIDE...
SOMETHING TELLS ME OUR PATIENCE HAS PAID OFF, ROBIN! ONE OF THE OLD-STYLE MOVIE COMICS REPORTED INSIDE THIS POST OFFICE--
LOOKS LIKE WE GOT HERE JUST IN TIME TO STOP ANOTHER CRIME, BATMAN!
u.s. post office
MASQUERADING AS BANJO--THE PANTOMIME ARTIST! WATCH OUT FOR ANY-THING HE MAY PULL FROM UNDER THAT TRICK COAT OF HIS!
9

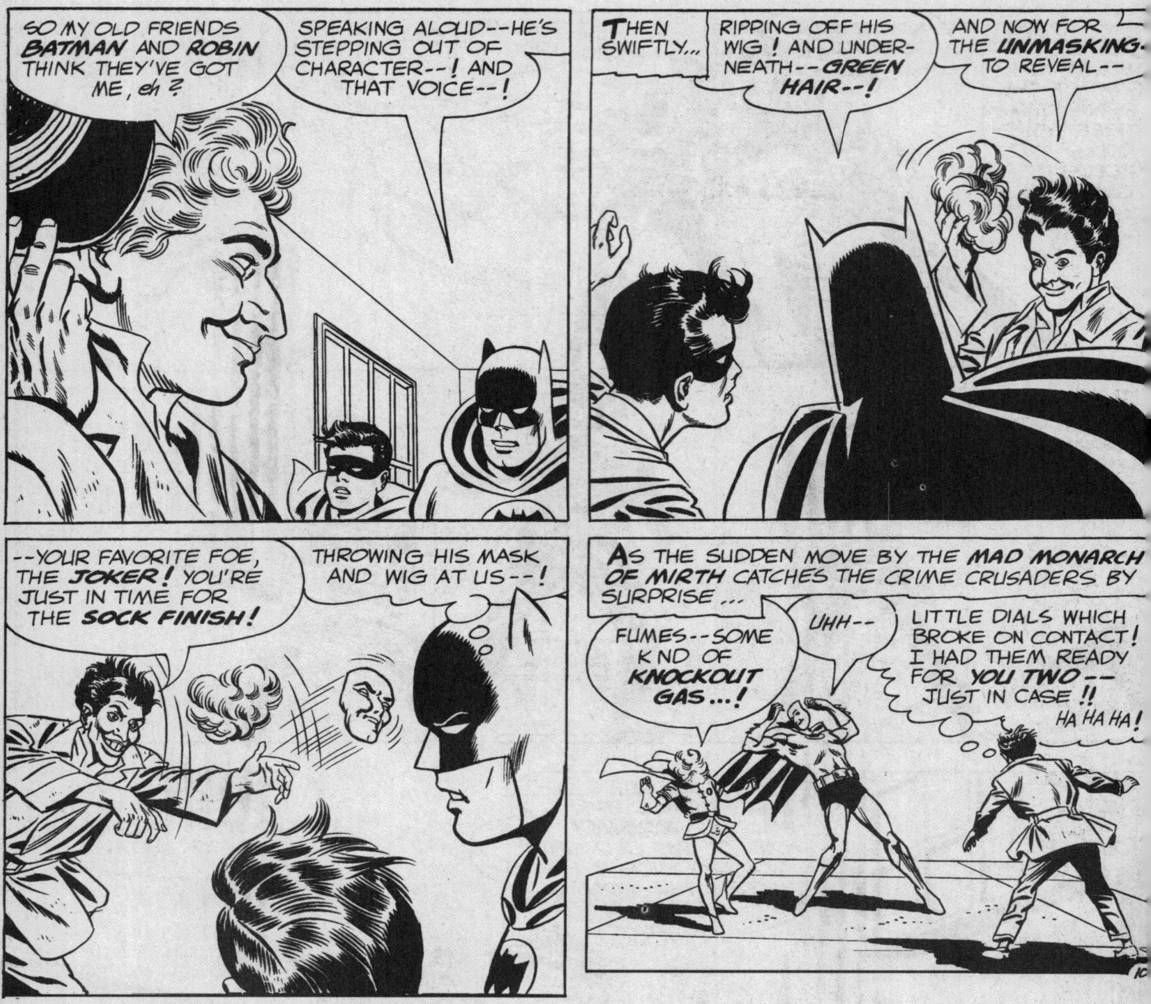
SO MY OLD FRIENDS BATMAN AND ROBIN THINK THEY'VE GOT ME, eh ?
SPEAKING ALOUD--HE'S STEPPING OUT OF CHARACTER--! AND THAT VOICE--!
THEN SWIFTLY...
RIPPING OFF HIS WIG ! AND UNDERNEATH--GREEN HAIR--!
AND NOW FOR THE UNMASKING-TO REVEAL--
--YOUR FAVORITE FOE, THE JOKER! YOU'RE JUST IN TIME FOR THE SOCK FINISH!
THROWING HIS MASK AND WIG AT US--!
AS THE SUDDEN MOVE BY THE MAD MONARCH OF MIRTH CATCHES THE CRIME CRUSADERS BY SURPRISE...
FUMES--SOME KND OF KNOCKOUT GAS...!
UHH--
LITTLE DIALS WHICH BROKE ON CONTACT! I HAD THEM READY FOR YOU TWO--JUST IN CASE !!
HA HA HA!
10

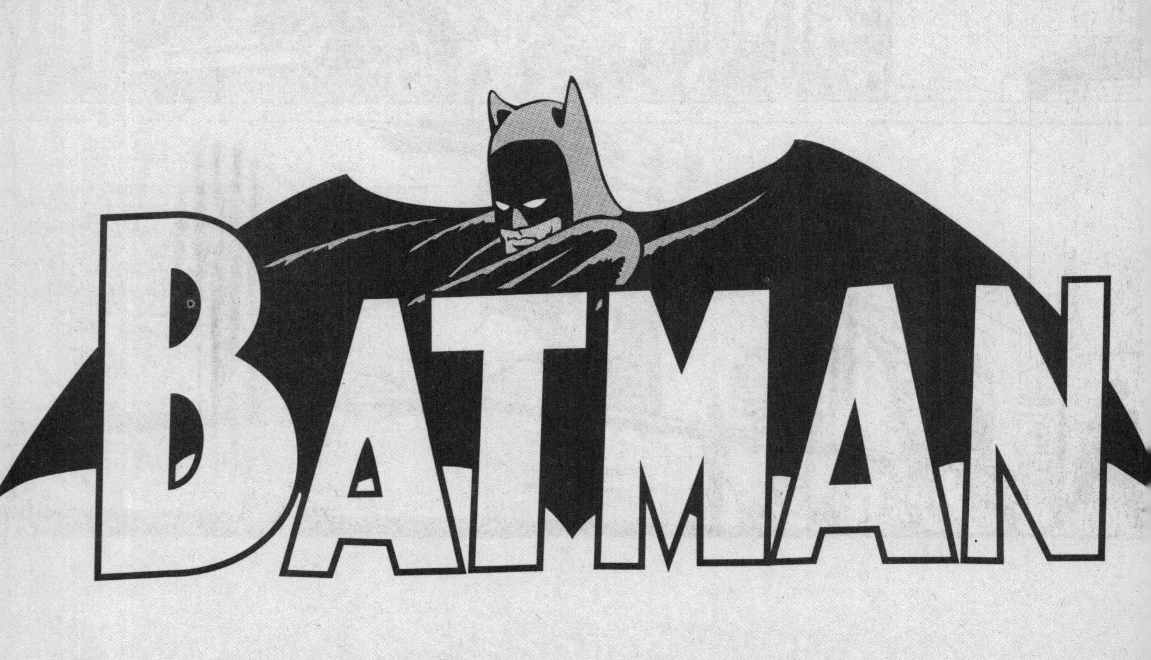
BATMAN

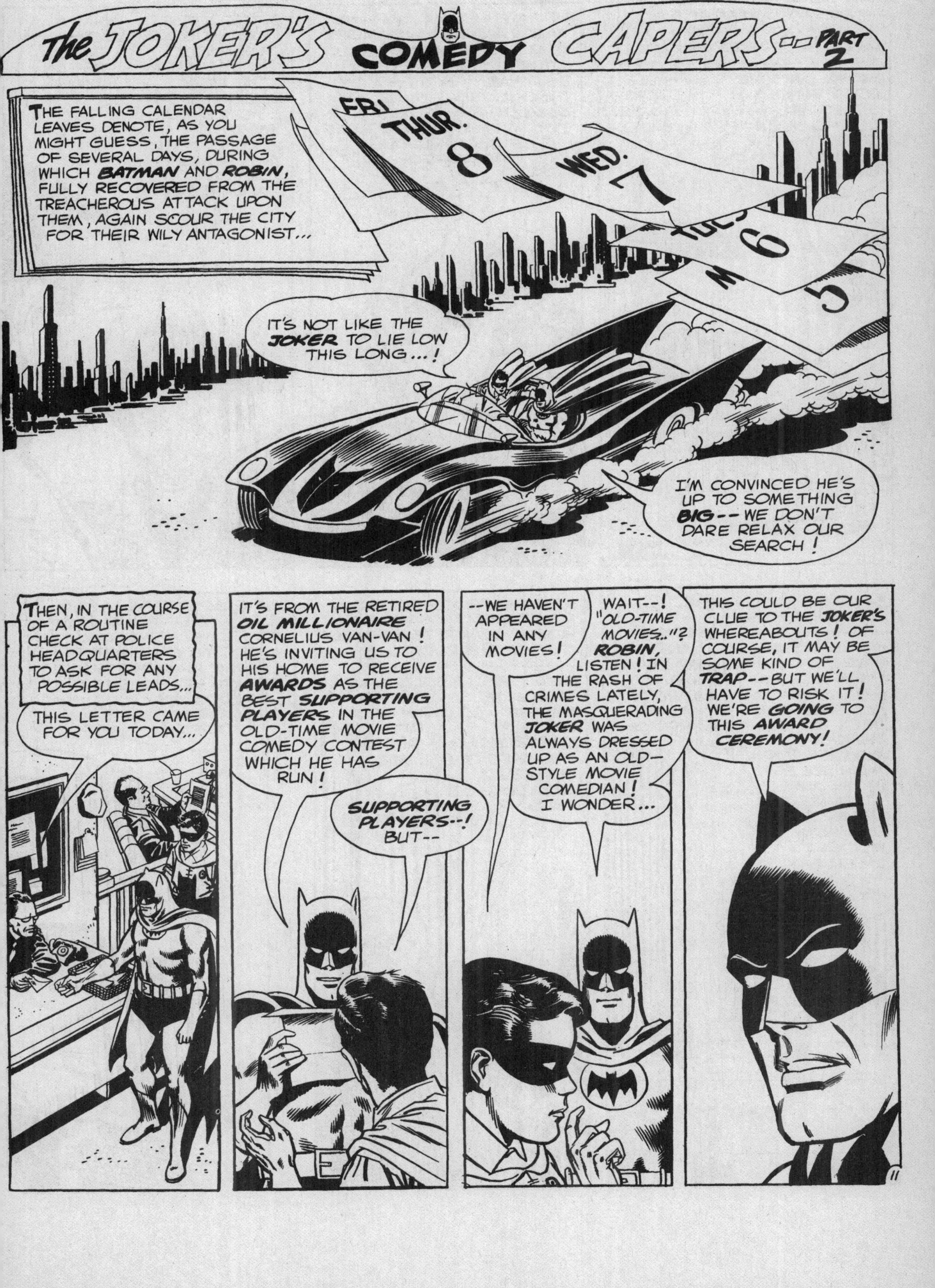
The JOKER'S COMEDY CAPERS -- PART 2
THE FALLING CALENDAR LEAVES DENOTE, AS YOU MIGHT GUESS, THE PASSAGE OF SEVERAL DAYS, DURING WHICH BATMAN AND ROBIN, FULLY RECOVERED FROM THE TREACHEROUS ATTACK UPON THEM, AGAIN SCOUR THE CITY FOR THEIR WILY ANTAGONIST...
FRI
THUR. 8
WED. 7
6
M 5
IT'S NOT LIKE THE JOKER TO LIE LOW THIS LONG...!
I'M CONVINCED HE'S UP TO SOMETHING BIG -- WE DON'T DARE RELAX OUR SEARCH!
THEN, IN THE COURSE OF A ROUTINE CHECK AT POLICE HEADQUARTERS TO ASK FOR ANY POSSIBLE LEADS...
THIS LETTER CAME FOR YOU TODAY...
IT'S FROM THE RETIRED OIL MILLIONAIRE CORNELIUS VAN-VAN! HE'S INVITING US TO HIS HOME TO RECEIVE AWARDS AS THE BEST SUPPORTING PLAYERS IN THE OLD-TIME MOVIE COMEDY CONTEST WHICH HE HAS RUN!
SUPPORTING PLAYERS--! BUT--
--WE HAVEN'T APPEARED IN ANY MOVIES!
WAIT--! "OLD-TIME MOVIES..."? ROBIN, LISTEN! IN THE RASH OF CRIMES LATELY, THE MASQUERADING JOKER WAS ALWAYS DRESSED UP AS AN OLD-STYLE MOVIE COMEDIAN! I WONDER...
THIS COULD BE OUR CLUE TO THE JOKER'S WHEREABOUTS! OF COURSE, IT MAY BE SOME KIND OF TRAP-- BUT WE'LL HAVE TO RISK IT! WE'RE GOING TO THIS AWARD CEREMONY!
11

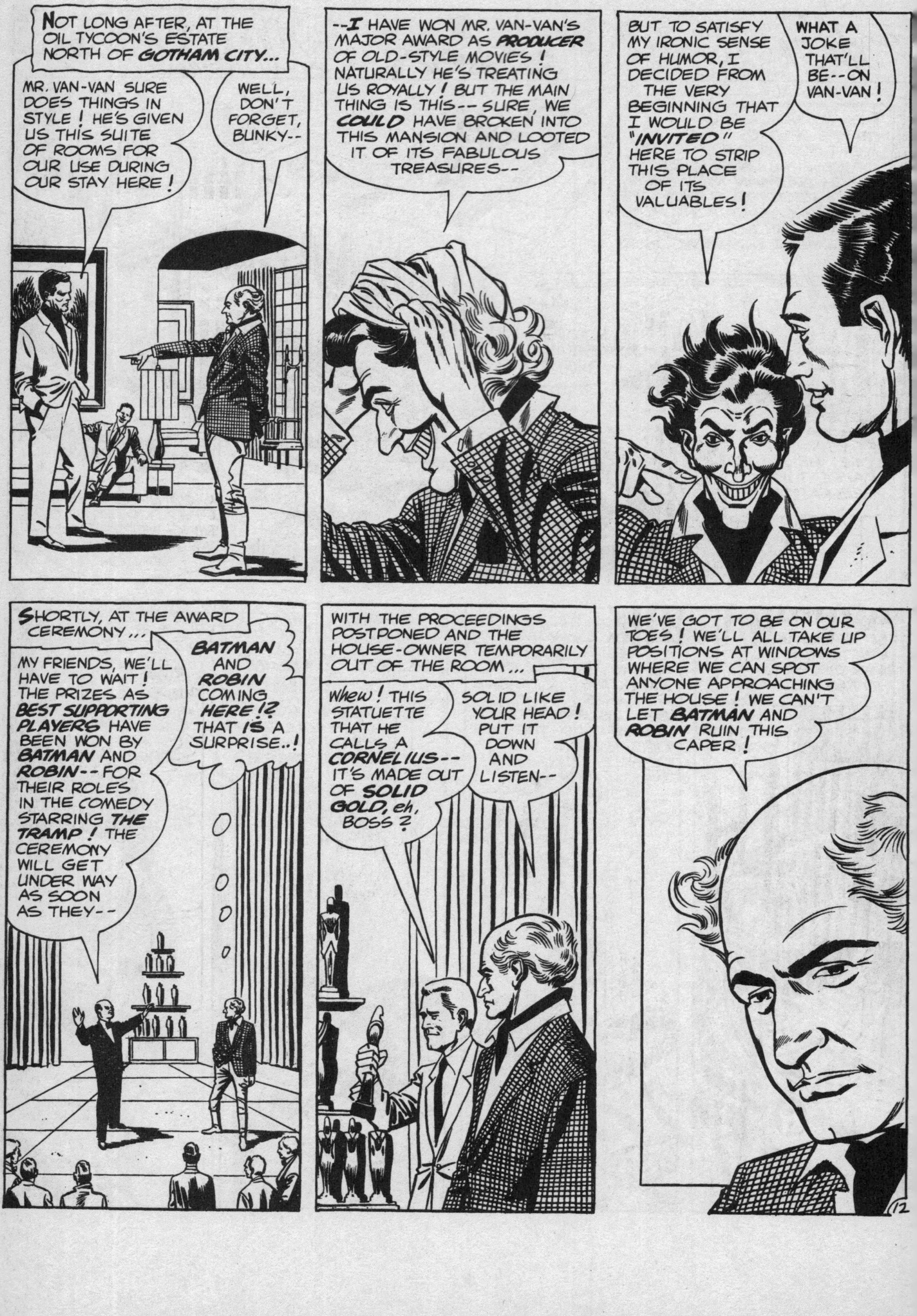
NOT LONG AFTER, AT THE OIL TYCOON'S ESTATE NORTH OF GOTHAM CITY...
MR. VAN-VAN SURE DOES THINGS IN STYLE! HE'S GIVEN US THIS SUITE OF ROOMS FOR OUR USE DURING OUR STAY HERE!
WELL, DON'T FORGET, BUNKY--
--I HAVE WON MR. VAN-VAN'S MAJOR AWARD AS PRODUCER OF OLD-STYLE MOVIES! NATURALLY HE'S TREATING US ROYALLY! BUT THE MAIN THING IS THIS-- SURE, WE COULD HAVE BROKEN INTO THIS MANSION AND LOOTED IT OF ITS FABULOUS TREASURES--
BUT TO SATISFY MY IRONIC SENSE OF HUMOR, I DECIDED FROM THE VERY BEGINNING THAT I WOULD BE "INVITED" HERE TO STRIP THIS PLACE OF ITS VALUABLES!
WHAT A JOKE THAT'LL BE--ON VAN-VAN!
SHORTLY, AT THE AWARD CEREMONY...
MY FRIENDS, WE'LL HAVE TO WAIT! THE PRIZES AS BEST SUPPORTING PLAYERS HAVE BEEN WON BY BATMAN AND ROBIN--FOR THEIR ROLES IN THE COMEDY STARRING THE TRAMP! THE CEREMONY WILL GET UNDER WAY AS SOON AS THEY--
BATMAN AND ROBIN COMING HERE!? THAT IS A SURPRISE..!
WITH THE PROCEEDINGS POSTPONED AND THE HOUSE-OWNER TEMPORARILY OUT OF THE ROOM...
Whew! THIS STATUETTE THAT HE CALLS A CORNELIUS-- IT'S MADE OUT OF SOLID GOLD, eh, BOSS?
SOLID LIKE YOUR HEAD! PUT IT DOWN AND LISTEN--
WE'VE GOT TO BE ON OUR TOES! WE'LL ALL TAKE UP POSITIONS AT WINDOWS WHERE WE CAN SPOT ANYONE APPROACHING THE HOUSE! WE CAN'T LET BATMAN AND ROBIN RUIN THIS CAPER!
12

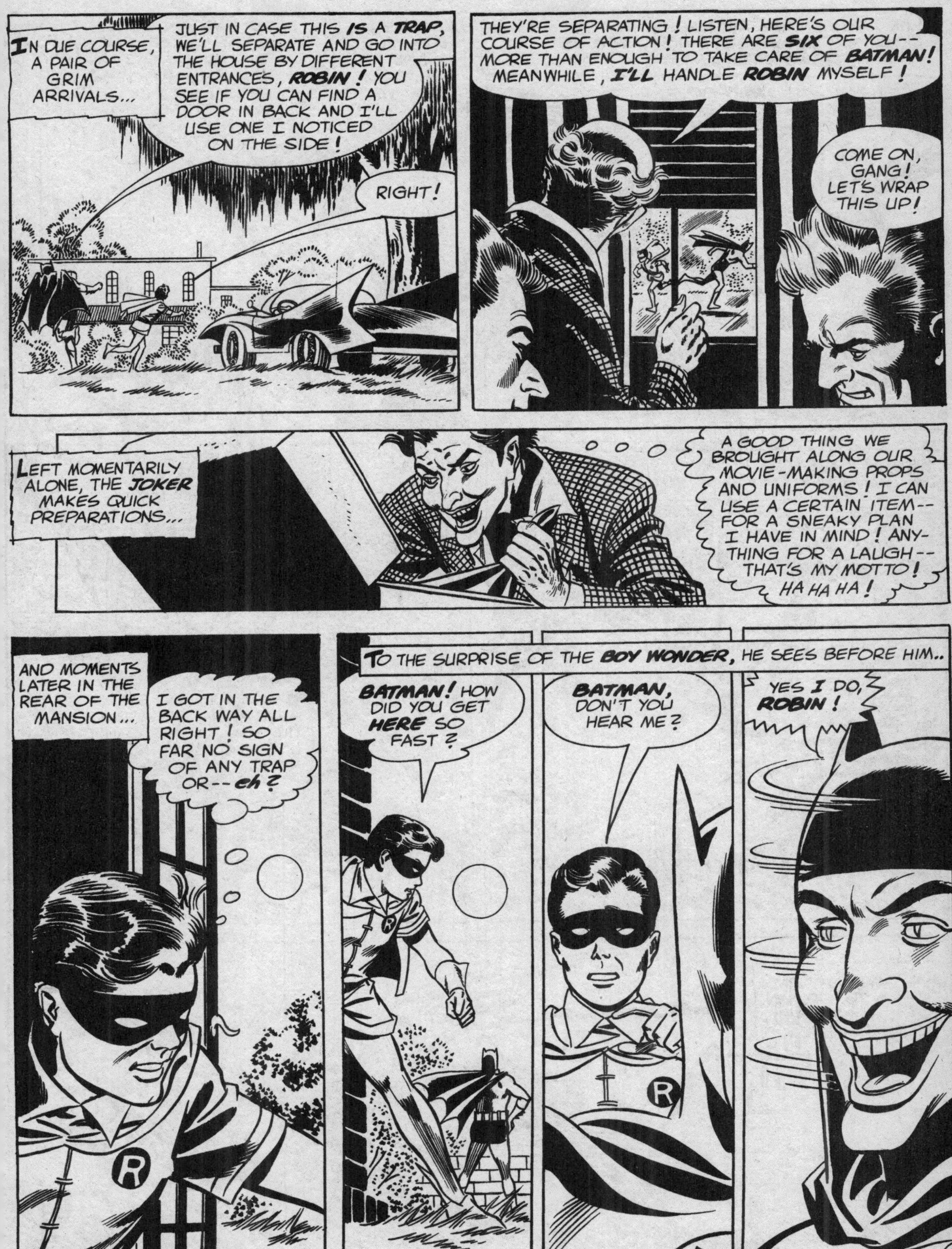
IN DUE COURSE, A PAIR OF GRIM ARRIVALS...
JUST IN CASE THIS IS A TRAP, WE'LL SEPARATE AND GO INTO THE HOUSE BY DIFFERENT ENTRANCES, ROBIN! YOU SEE IF YOU CAN FIND A DOOR IN BACK AND I'LL USE ONE I NOTICED ON THE SIDE!
RIGHT!
THEY'RE SEPARATING! LISTEN, HERE'S OUR COURSE OF ACTION! THERE ARE SIX OF YOU-- MORE THAN ENOUGH TO TAKE CARE OF BATMAN! MEANWHILE, I'LL HANDLE ROBIN MYSELF!
COME ON, GANG! LET'S WRAP THIS UP!
LEFT MOMENTARILY ALONE, THE JOKER MAKES QUICK PREPARATIONS...
A GOOD THING WE BROUGHT ALONG OUR MOVIE-MAKING PROPS AND UNIFORMS! I CAN USE A CERTAIN ITEM-- FOR A SNEAKY PLAN I HAVE IN MIND! ANYTHING FOR A LAUGH-- THAT'S MY MOTTO! HA HA HA!
AND MOMENTS LATER IN THE REAR OF THE MANSION...
I GOT IN THE BACK WAY ALL RIGHT! SO FAR NO SIGN OF ANY TRAP OR-- eh?
TO THE SURPRISE OF THE BOY WONDER, HE SEES BEFORE HIM..
BATMAN! HOW DID YOU GET HERE SO FAST?
BATMAN, DON'T YOU HEAR ME?
YES I DO, ROBIN!
13

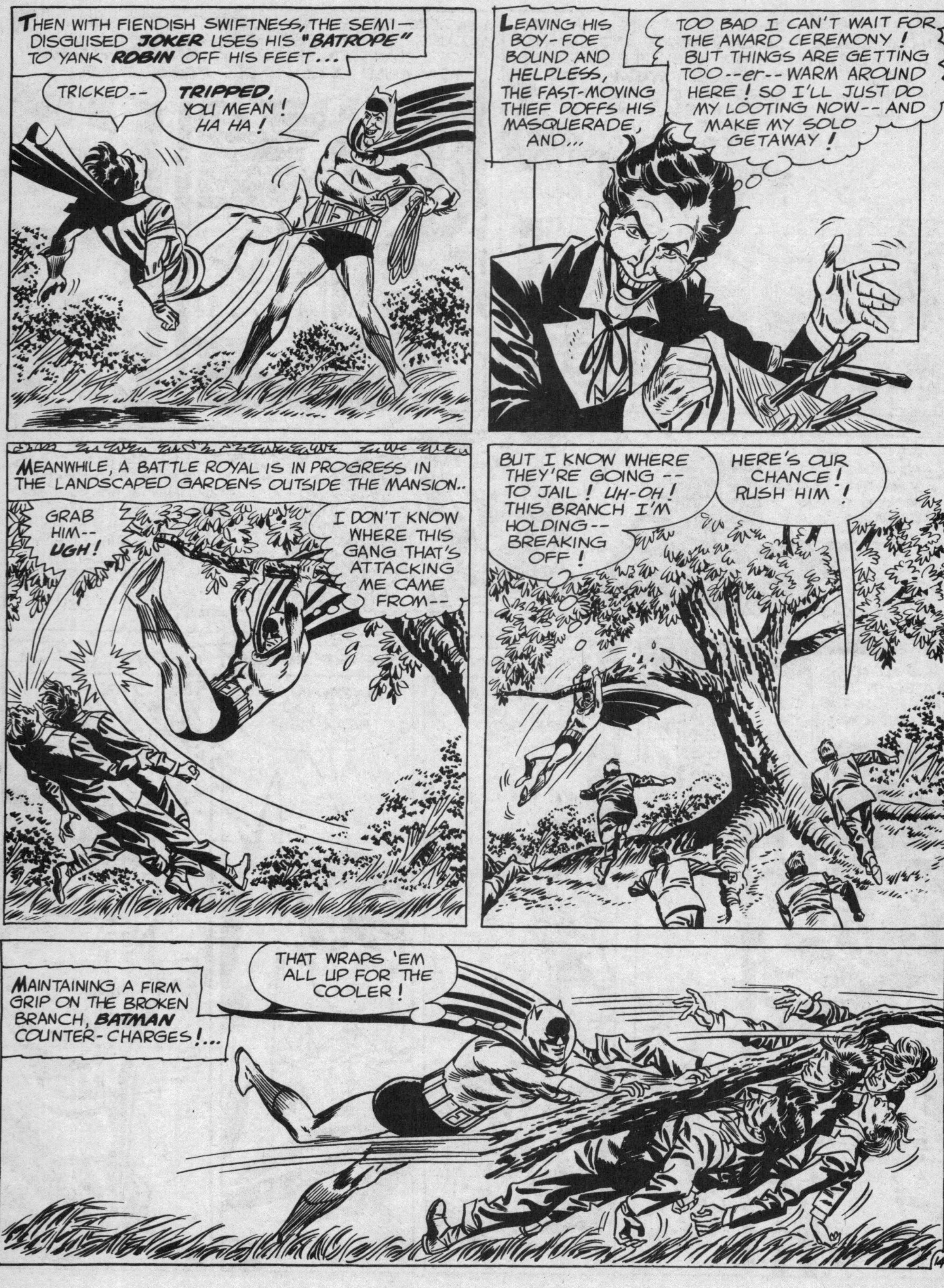
THEN WITH FIENDISH SWIFTNESS, THE SEMI-DISGUISED JOKER USES HIS "BATROPE" TO YANK ROBIN OFF HIS FEET...
TRICKED--
TRIPPED, YOU MEAN! HA HA!
LEAVING HIS BOY-FOE BOUND AND HELPLESS, THE FAST-MOVING THIEF DOFFS HIS MASQUERADE, AND...
TOO BAD I CAN'T WAIT FOR THE AWARD CEREMONY! BUT THINGS ARE GETTING TOO--er--WARM AROUND HERE! SO I'LL JUST DO MY LOOTING NOW--AND MAKE MY SOLO GETAWAY!
MEANWHILE, A BATTLE ROYAL IS IN PROGRESS IN THE LANDSCAPED GARDENS OUTSIDE THE MANSION..
GRAB HIM--UGH!
I DON'T KNOW WHERE THIS GANG THAT'S ATTACKING ME CAME FROM--
BUT I KNOW WHERE THEY'RE GOING--TO JAIL! UH-OH! THIS BRANCH I'M HOLDING--BREAKING OFF!
HERE'S OUR CHANCE! RUSH HIM!
MAINTAINING A FIRM GRIP ON THE BROKEN BRANCH, BATMAN COUNTER-CHARGES!...
THAT WRAPS 'EM ALL UP FOR THE COOLER!
14

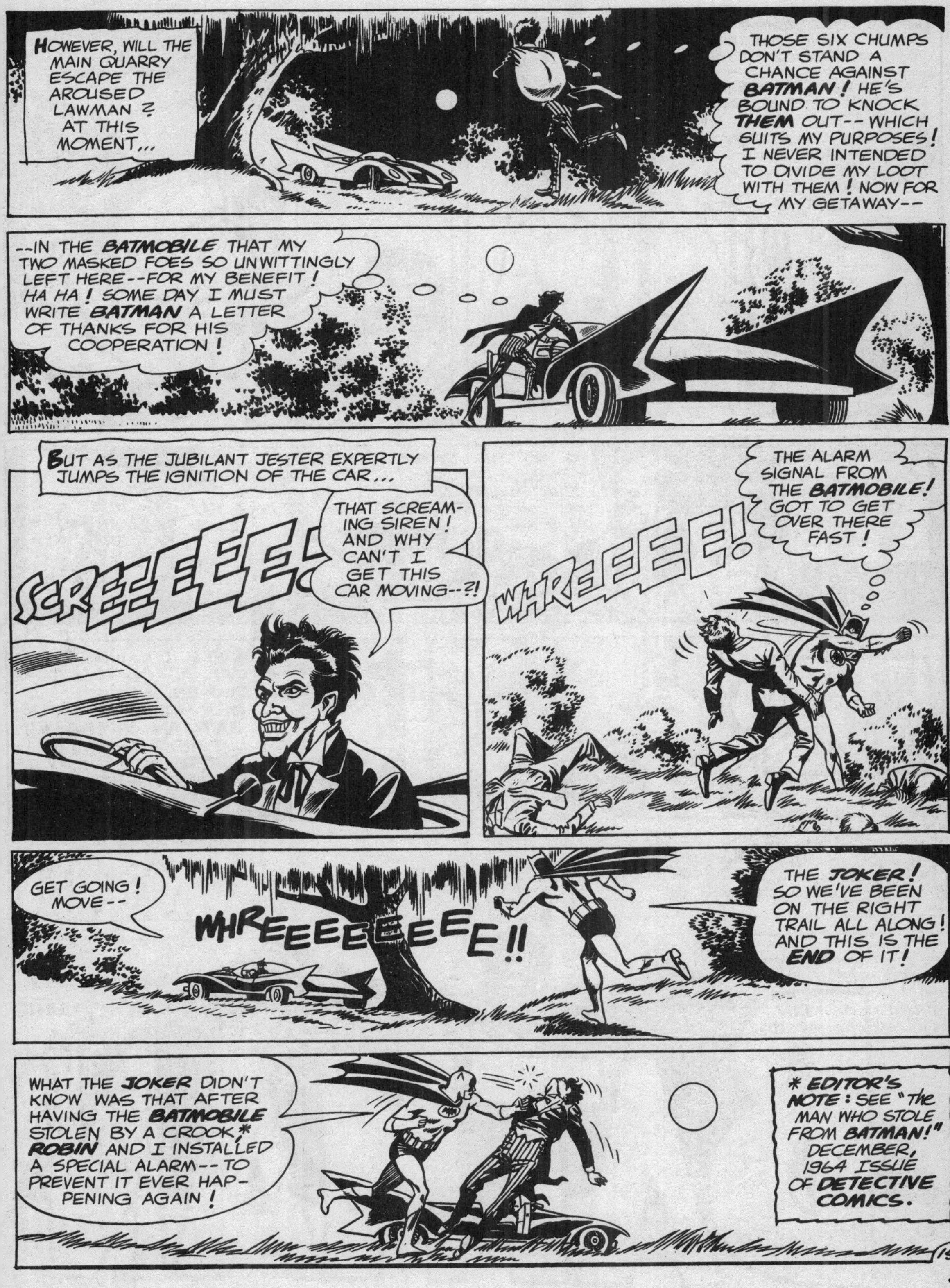
HOWEVER, WILL THE MAIN QUARRY ESCAPE THE AROUSED LAWMAN ? AT THIS MOMENT...
THOSE SIX CHUMPS DON'T STAND A CHANCE AGAINST BATMAN ! HE'S BOUND TO KNOCK THEM OUT-- WHICH SUITS MY PURPOSES! I NEVER INTENDED TO DIVIDE MY LOOT WITH THEM ! NOW FOR MY GETAWAY--
--IN THE BATMOBILE THAT MY TWO MASKED FOES SO UNWITTINGLY LEFT HERE--FOR MY BENEFIT ! HA HA ! SOME DAY I MUST WRITE BATMAN A LETTER OF THANKS FOR HIS COOPERATION !
BUT AS THE JUBILANT JESTER EXPERTLY JUMPS THE IGNITION OF THE CAR...
SCREEEEEE!
THAT SCREAMING SIREN ! AND WHY CAN'T I GET THIS CAR MOVING--?!
THE ALARM SIGNAL FROM THE BATMOBILE! GOT TO GET OVER THERE FAST !
WHREEEEE!
GET GOING ! MOVE--
WHREEEEEEEEE!!
THE JOKER! SO WE'VE BEEN ON THE RIGHT TRAIL ALL ALONG! AND THIS IS THE END OF IT!
WHAT THE JOKER DIDN'T KNOW WAS THAT AFTER HAVING THE BATMOBILE STOLEN BY A CROOK,* ROBIN AND I INSTALLED A SPECIAL ALARM-- TO PREVENT IT EVER HAPPENING AGAIN !
* EDITOR'S NOTE : SEE "The MAN WHO STOLE FROM BATMAN!" DECEMBER, 1964 ISSUE OF DETECTIVE COMICS.
15

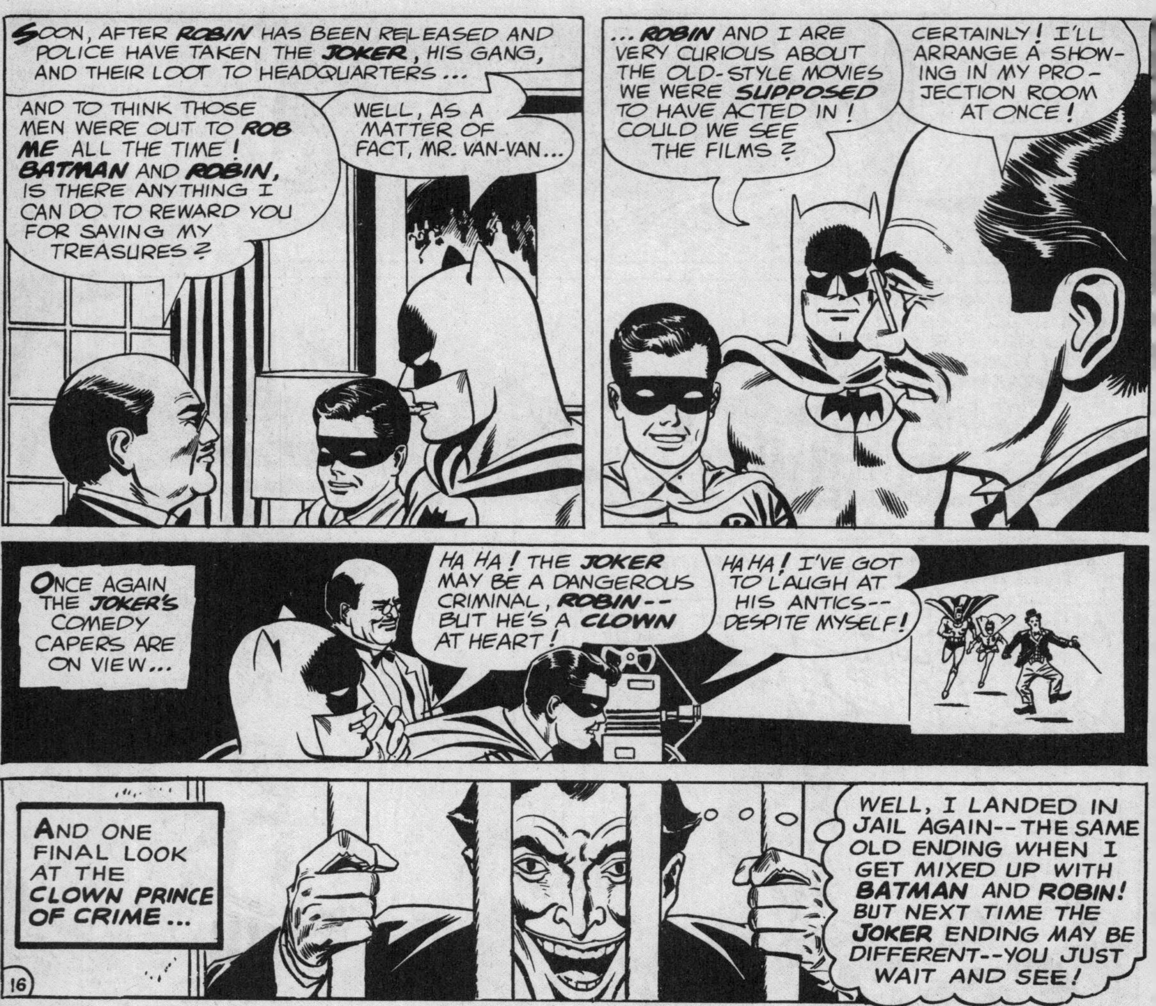
SOON, AFTER ROBIN HAS BEEN RELEASED AND POLICE HAVE TAKEN THE JOKER, HIS GANG, AND THEIR LOOT TO HEADQUARTERS ...
AND TO THINK THOSE MEN WERE OUT TO ROB ME ALL THE TIME! BATMAN AND ROBIN, IS THERE ANYTHING I CAN DO TO REWARD YOU FOR SAVING MY TREASURES?
WELL, AS A MATTER OF FACT, MR. VAN-VAN...
... ROBIN AND I ARE VERY CURIOUS ABOUT THE OLD-STYLE MOVIES WE WERE SUPPOSED TO HAVE ACTED IN! COULD WE SEE THE FILMS?
CERTAINLY! I'LL ARRANGE A SHOWING IN MY PROJECTION ROOM AT ONCE!
ONCE AGAIN THE JOKER'S COMEDY CAPERS ARE ON VIEW...
HA HA! THE JOKER MAY BE A DANGEROUS CRIMINAL, ROBIN-- BUT HE'S A CLOWN AT HEART!
HA HA! I'VE GOT TO LAUGH AT HIS ANTICS-- DESPITE MYSELF!
AND ONE FINAL LOOK AT THE CLOWN PRINCE OF CRIME ...
WELL, I LANDED IN JAIL AGAIN--THE SAME OLD ENDING WHEN I GET MIXED UP WITH BATMAN AND ROBIN! BUT NEXT TIME THE JOKER ENDING MAY BE DIFFERENT--YOU JUST WAIT AND SEE!
16

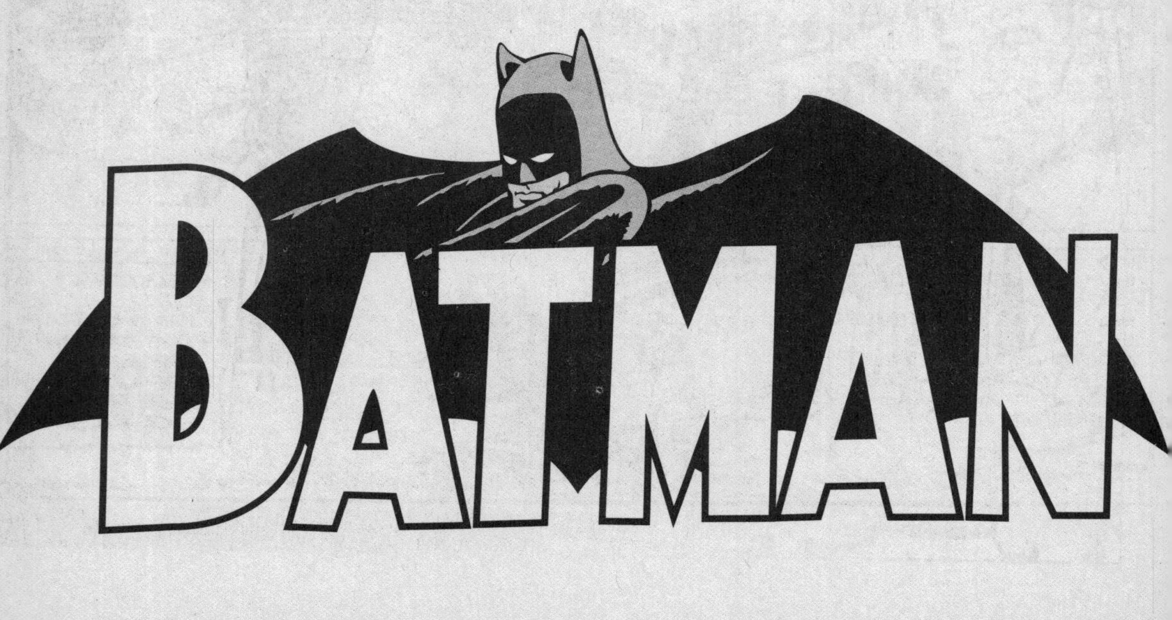
BATMAN

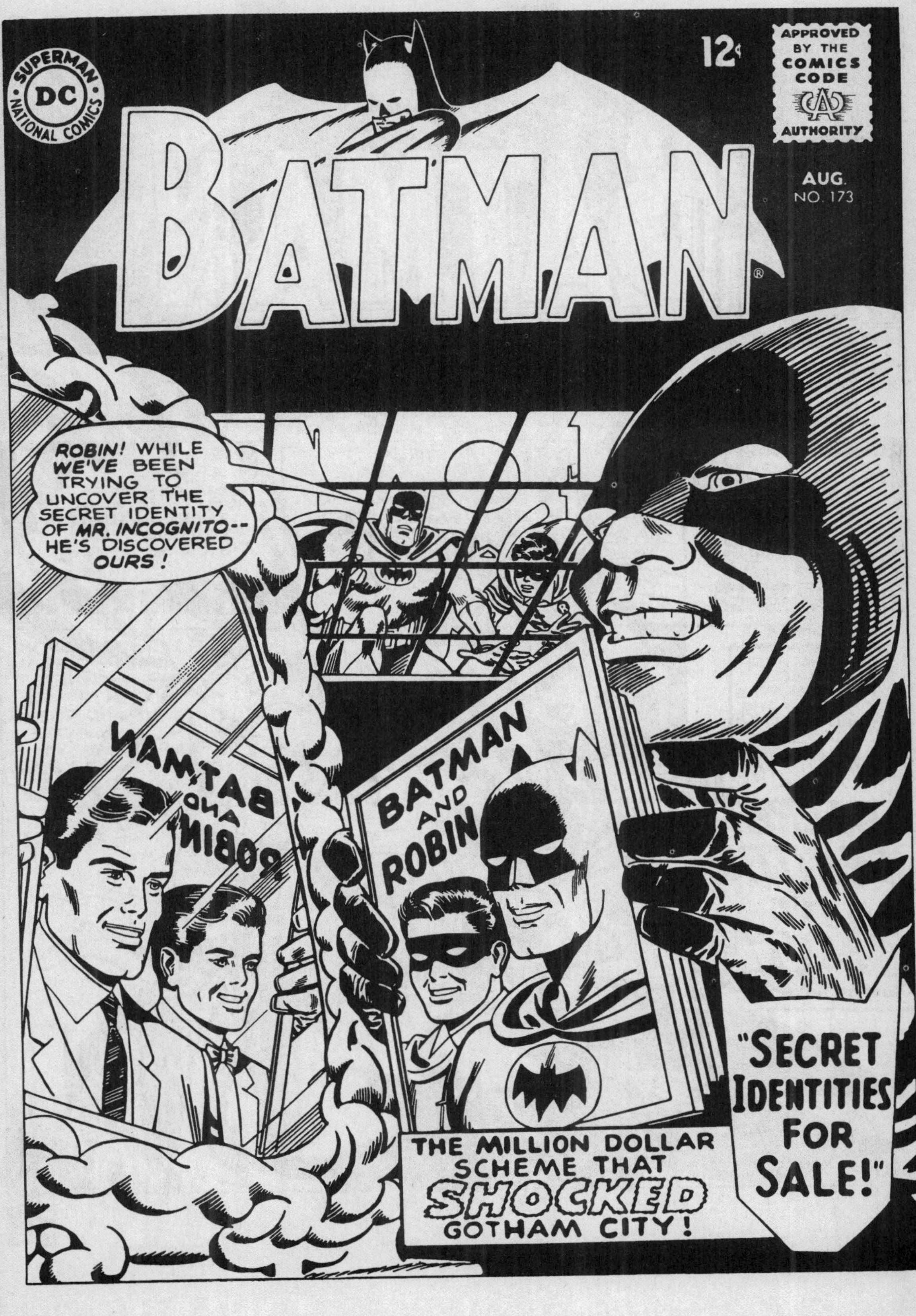
SUPERMAN DC NATIONAL COMICS
12¢
APPROVED BY THE COMICS CODE AUTHORITY
BATMAN®
AUG. NO. 173
ROBIN! WHILE WE'VE BEEN TRYING TO UNCOVER THE SECRET IDENTITY OF MR. INCOGNITO-- HE'S DISCOVERED OURS!
BATMAN AND ROBIN
BATMAN AND ROBIN
THE MILLION DOLLAR SCHEME THAT SHOCKED GOTHAM CITY!
"SECRET IDENTITIES FOR SALE!"

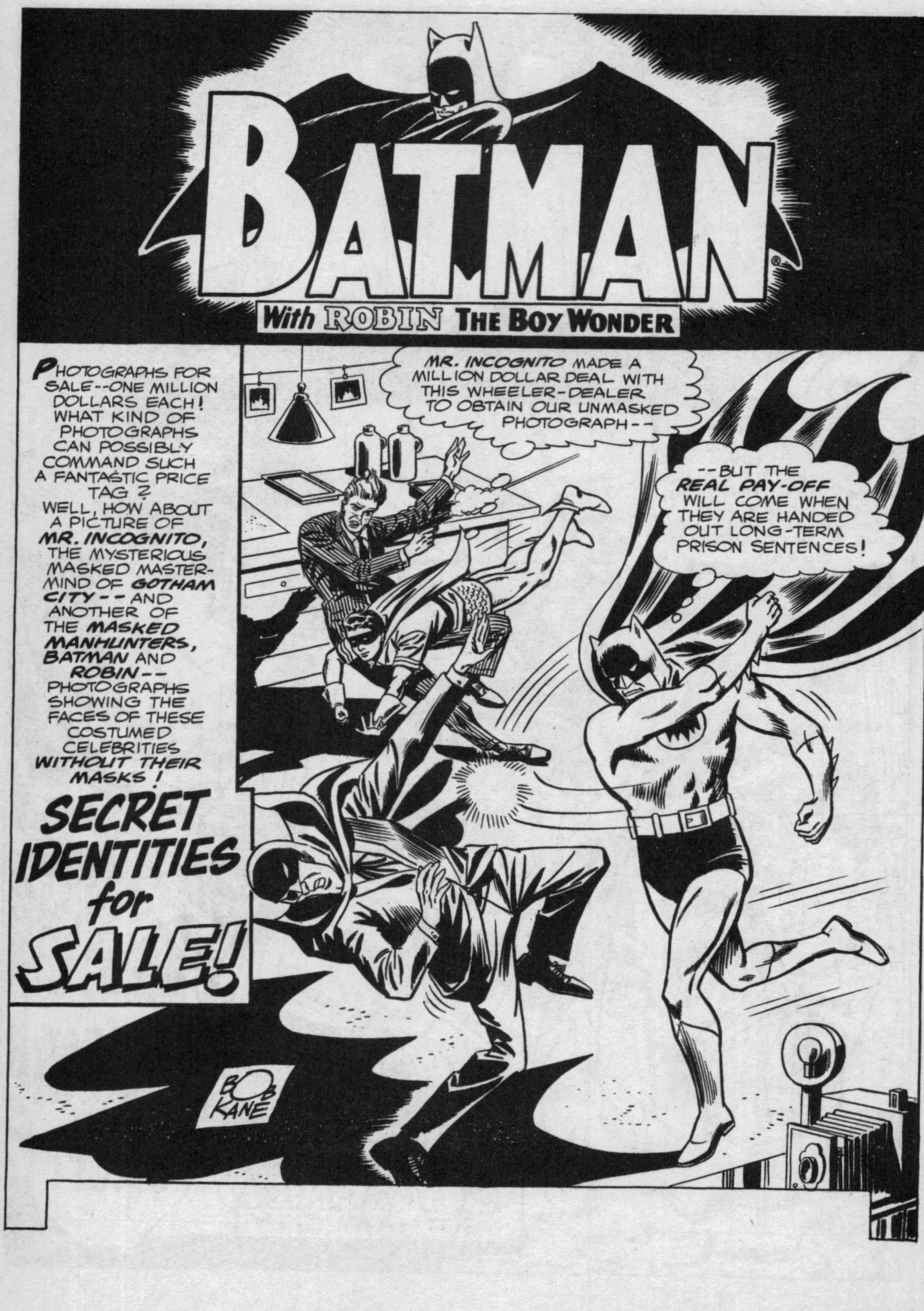
BATMAN®
With ROBIN THE BOY WONDER
PHOTOGRAPHS FOR SALE--ONE MILLION DOLLARS EACH! WHAT KIND OF PHOTOGRAPHS CAN POSSIBLY COMMAND SUCH A FANTASTIC PRICE TAG ? WELL, HOW ABOUT A PICTURE OF MR. INCOGNITO, THE MYSTERIOUS MASKED MASTER-MIND OF GOTHAM CITY -- AND ANOTHER OF THE MASKED MANHUNTERS, BATMAN AND ROBIN -- PHOTOGRAPHS SHOWING THE FACES OF THESE COSTUMED CELEBRITIES WITHOUT THEIR MASKS !
SECRET IDENTITIES for SALE!
MR. INCOGNITO MADE A MILLION DOLLAR DEAL WITH THIS WHEELER-DEALER TO OBTAIN OUR UNMASKED PHOTOGRAPH --
-- BUT THE REAL PAY-OFF WILL COME WHEN THEY ARE HANDED OUT LONG-TERM PRISON SENTENCES!
BOB KANE

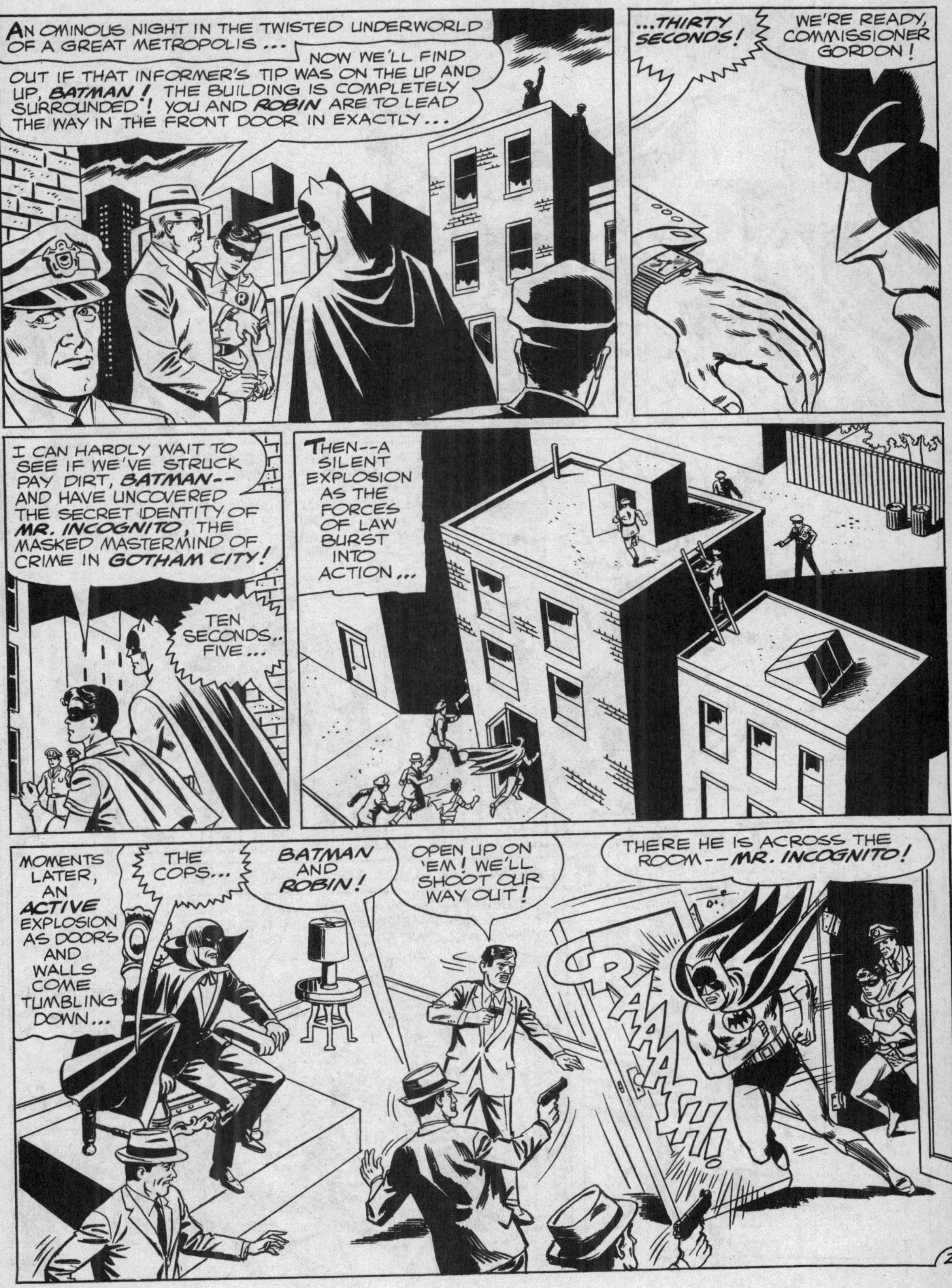
AN OMINOUS NIGHT IN THE TWISTED UNDERWORLD OF A GREAT METROPOLIS ...
NOW WE'LL FIND OUT IF THAT INFORMER'S TIP WAS ON THE UP AND UP, BATMAN! THE BUILDING IS COMPLETELY SURROUNDED! YOU AND ROBIN ARE TO LEAD THE WAY IN THE FRONT DOOR IN EXACTLY...
...THIRTY SECONDS!
WE'RE READY, COMMISSIONER GORDON!
I CAN HARDLY WAIT TO SEE IF WE'VE STRUCK PAY DIRT, BATMAN-- AND HAVE UNCOVERED THE SECRET IDENTITY OF MR. INCOGNITO, THE MASKED MASTERMIND OF CRIME IN GOTHAM CITY!
TEN SECONDS.. FIVE...
THEN--A SILENT EXPLOSION AS THE FORCES OF LAW BURST INTO ACTION...
MOMENTS LATER, AN ACTIVE EXPLOSION AS DOORS AND WALLS COME TUMBLING DOWN...
THE COPS...
BATMAN AND ROBIN!
OPEN UP ON 'EM! WE'LL SHOOT OUR WAY OUT!
THERE HE IS ACROSS THE ROOM--MR. INCOGNITO!
CRAAAASH!
2

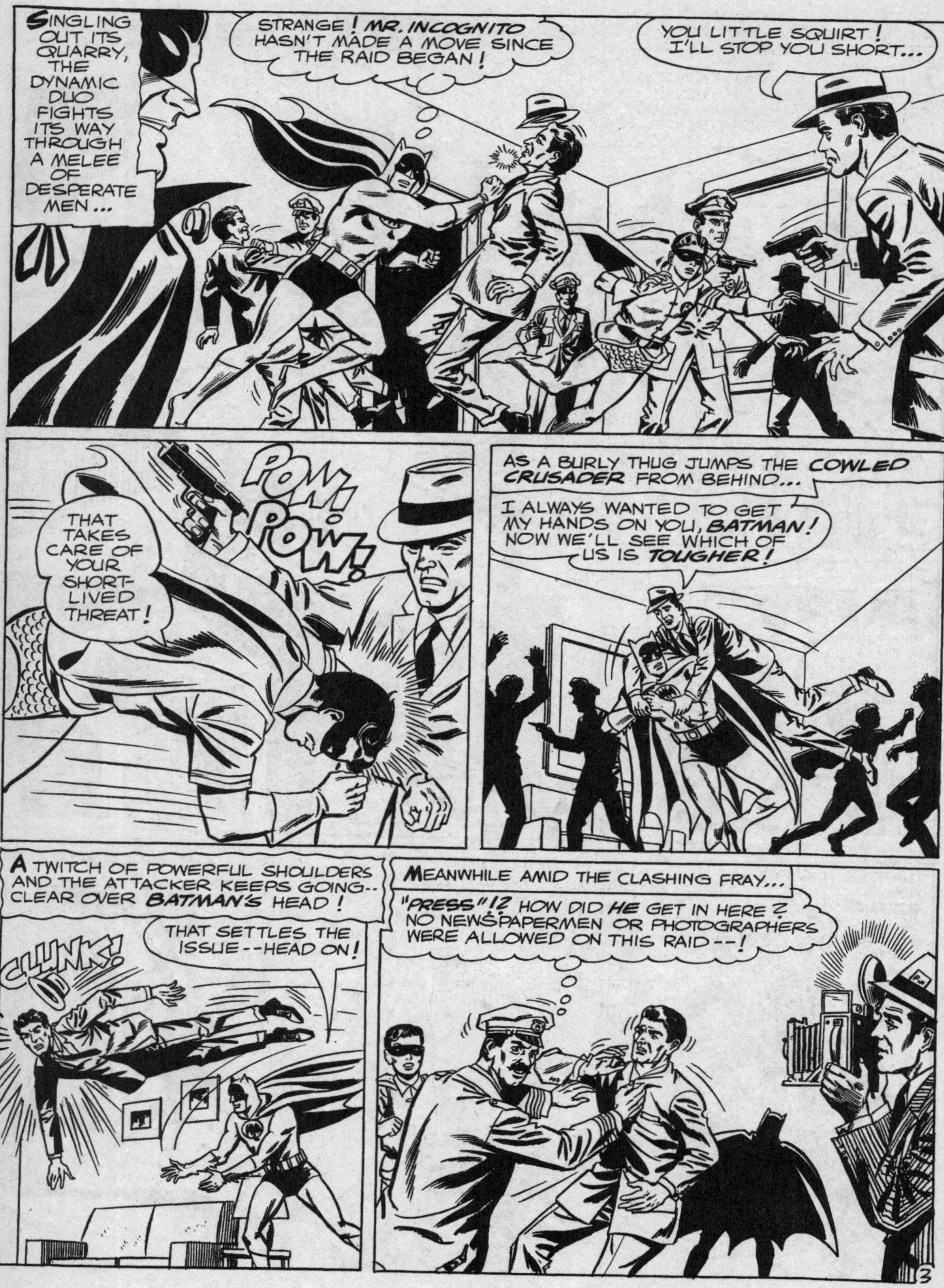
SINGLING OUT ITS QUARRY, THE DYNAMIC DUO FIGHTS ITS WAY THROUGH A MELEE OF DESPERATE MEN...
STRANGE! MR. INCOGNITO HASN'T MADE A MOVE SINCE THE RAID BEGAN!
YOU LITTLE SQUIRT! I'LL STOP YOU SHORT...
THAT TAKES CARE OF YOUR SHORT-LIVED THREAT!
POW! POW!
AS A BURLY THUG JUMPS THE COWLED CRUSADER FROM BEHIND...
I ALWAYS WANTED TO GET MY HANDS ON YOU, BATMAN! NOW WE'LL SEE WHICH OF US IS TOUGHER!
A TWITCH OF POWERFUL SHOULDERS AND THE ATTACKER KEEPS GOING--CLEAR OVER BATMAN'S HEAD!
THAT SETTLES THE ISSUE--HEAD ON!
CLUNK!
MEANWHILE AMID THE CLASHING FRAY...
"PRESS"!? HOW DID HE GET IN HERE? NO NEWSPAPERMEN OR PHOTOGRAPHERS WERE ALLOWED ON THIS RAID--!
3

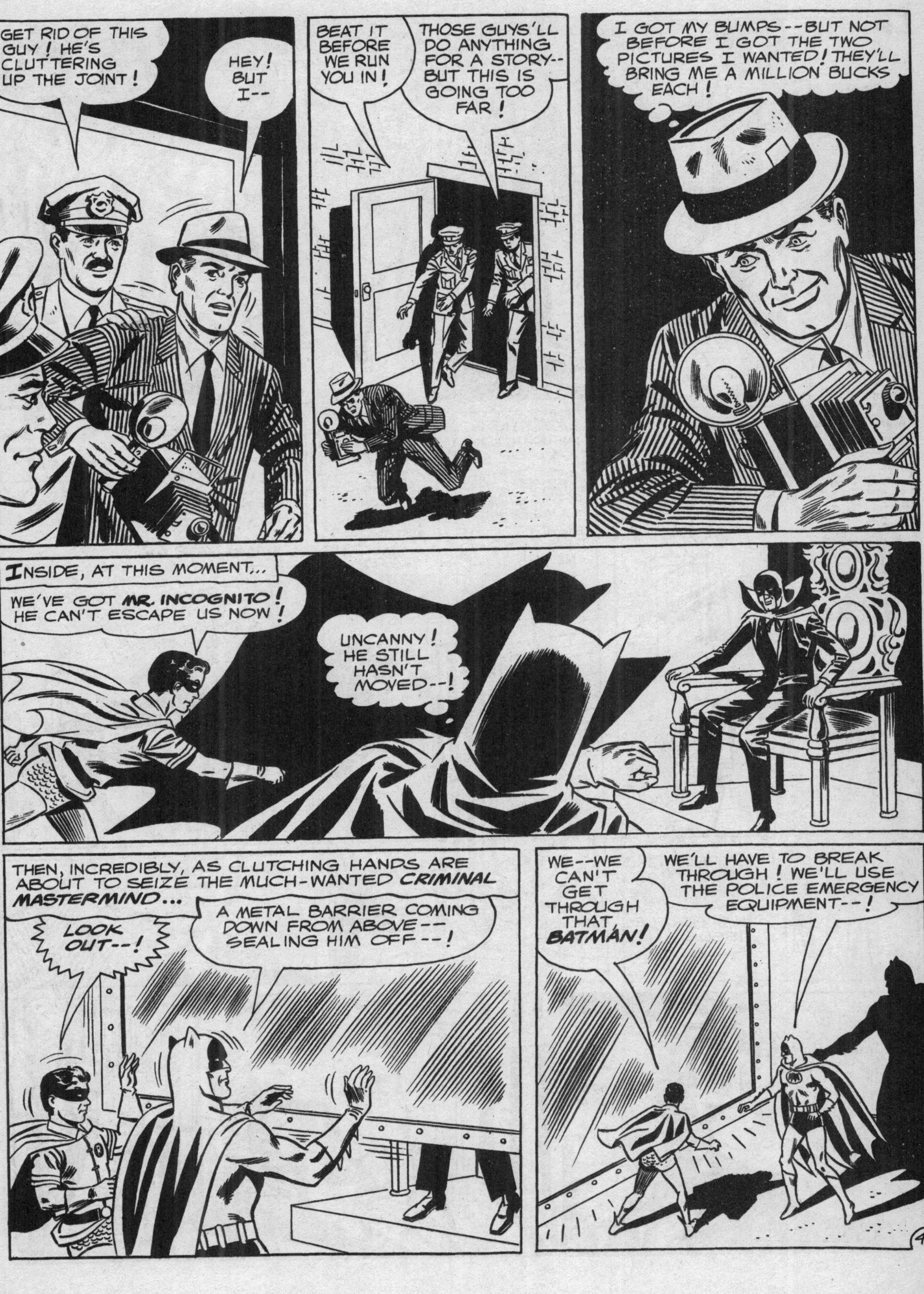
GET RID OF THIS GUY! HE'S CLUTTERING UP THE JOINT!
HEY! BUT I--
BEAT IT BEFORE WE RUN YOU IN!
THOSE GUYS'LL DO ANYTHING FOR A STORY-- BUT THIS IS GOING TOO FAR!
I GOT MY BUMPS--BUT NOT BEFORE I GOT THE TWO PICTURES I WANTED! THEY'LL BRING ME A MILLION BUCKS EACH!
INSIDE, AT THIS MOMENT...
WE'VE GOT MR. INCOGNITO! HE CAN'T ESCAPE US NOW!
UNCANNY! HE STILL HASN'T MOVED--!
THEN, INCREDIBLY, AS CLUTCHING HANDS ARE ABOUT TO SEIZE THE MUCH-WANTED CRIMINAL MASTERMIND...
LOOK OUT--!
A METAL BARRIER COMING DOWN FROM ABOVE-- SEALING HIM OFF--!
WE--WE CAN'T GET THROUGH THAT, BATMAN!
WE'LL HAVE TO BREAK THROUGH! WE'LL USE THE POLICE EMERGENCY EQUIPMENT--!
4

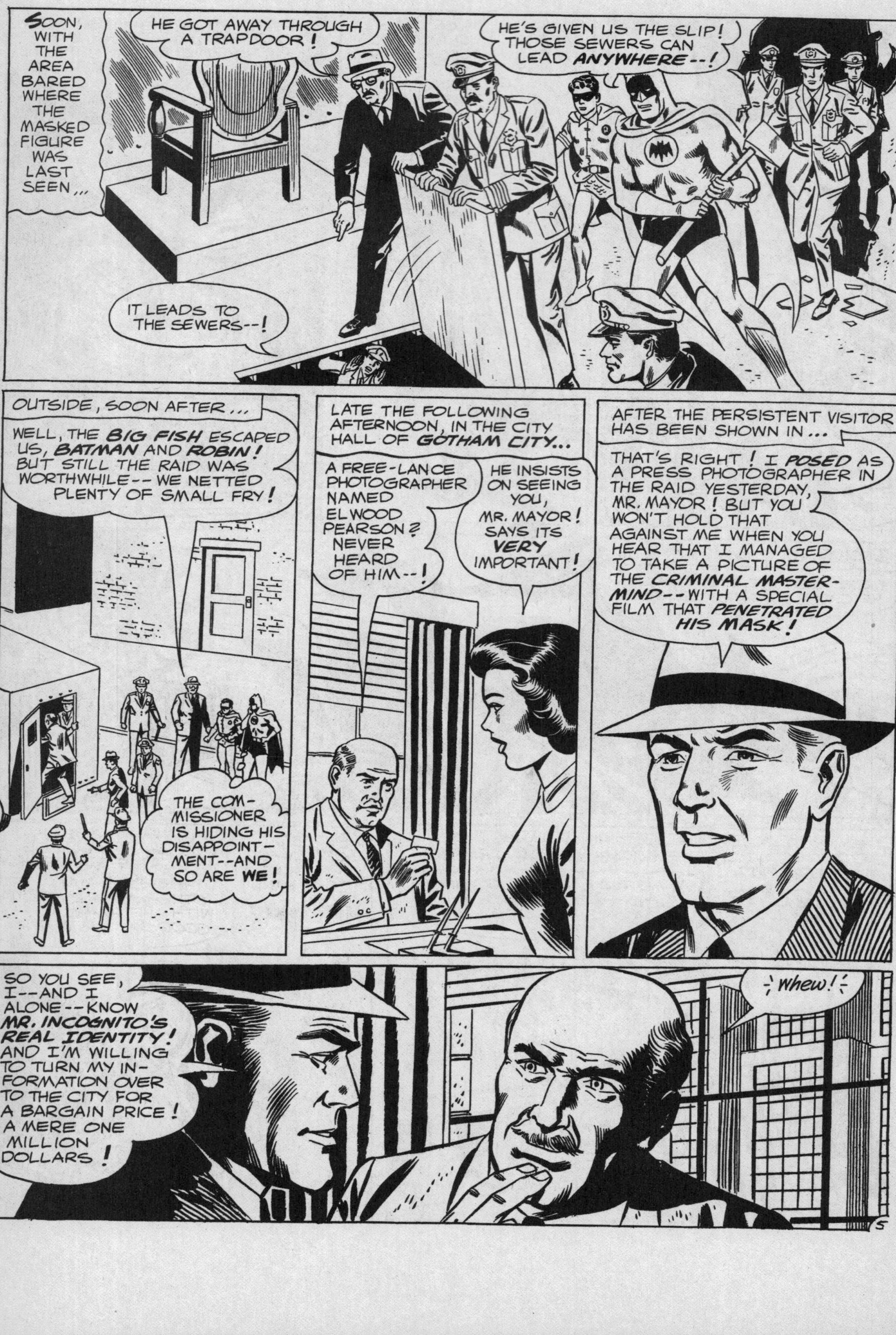
SOON, WITH THE AREA BARED WHERE THE MASKED FIGURE WAS LAST SEEN,...
HE GOT AWAY THROUGH A TRAPDOOR!
IT LEADS TO THE SEWERS--!
HE'S GIVEN US THE SLIP! THOSE SEWERS CAN LEAD ANYWHERE--!
OUTSIDE, SOON AFTER...
WELL, THE BIG FISH ESCAPED US, BATMAN AND ROBIN! BUT STILL THE RAID WAS WORTHWHILE-- WE NETTED PLENTY OF SMALL FRY!
THE COMMISSIONER IS HIDING HIS DISAPPOINTMENT--AND SO ARE WE!
LATE THE FOLLOWING AFTERNOON, IN THE CITY HALL OF GOTHAM CITY...
A FREE-LANCE PHOTOGRAPHER NAMED ELWOOD PEARSON? NEVER HEARD OF HIM--!
HE INSISTS ON SEEING YOU, MR. MAYOR! SAYS ITS VERY IMPORTANT!
AFTER THE PERSISTENT VISITOR HAS BEEN SHOWN IN...
THAT'S RIGHT! I POSED AS A PRESS PHOTOGRAPHER IN THE RAID YESTERDAY, MR. MAYOR! BUT YOU WON'T HOLD THAT AGAINST ME WHEN YOU HEAR THAT I MANAGED TO TAKE A PICTURE OF THE CRIMINAL MASTER-MIND--WITH A SPECIAL FILM THAT PENETRATED HIS MASK!
SO YOU SEE, I--AND I ALONE--KNOW MR. INCOGNITO'S REAL IDENTITY! AND I'M WILLING TO TURN MY INFORMATION OVER TO THE CITY FOR A BARGAIN PRICE! A MERE ONE MILLION DOLLARS!
Whew!
5

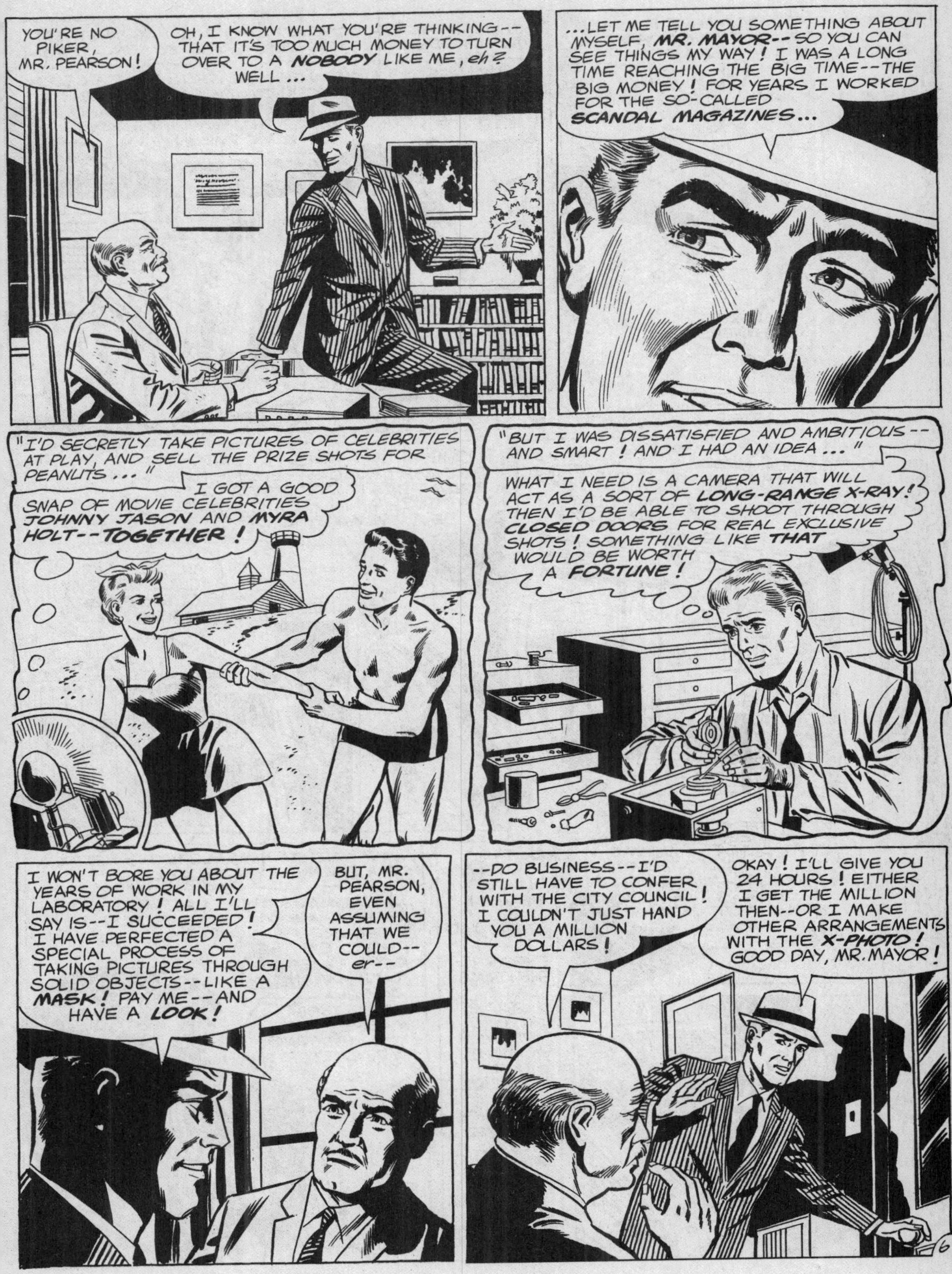
YOU'RE NO PIKER, MR. PEARSON!
OH, I KNOW WHAT YOU'RE THINKING-- THAT IT'S TOO MUCH MONEY TO TURN OVER TO A NOBODY LIKE ME, eh? WELL ...
...LET ME TELL YOU SOMETHING ABOUT MYSELF, MR. MAYOR-- SO YOU CAN SEE THINGS MY WAY! I WAS A LONG TIME REACHING THE BIG TIME--THE BIG MONEY! FOR YEARS I WORKED FOR THE SO-CALLED SCANDAL MAGAZINES...
"I'D SECRETLY TAKE PICTURES OF CELEBRITIES AT PLAY, AND SELL THE PRIZE SHOTS FOR PEANUTS ..."
I GOT A GOOD SNAP OF MOVIE CELEBRITIES JOHNNY JASON AND MYRA HOLT--TOGETHER!
"BUT I WAS DISSATISFIED AND AMBITIOUS-- AND SMART! AND I HAD AN IDEA ..."
WHAT I NEED IS A CAMERA THAT WILL ACT AS A SORT OF LONG-RANGE X-RAY! THEN I'D BE ABLE TO SHOOT THROUGH CLOSED DOORS FOR REAL EXCLUSIVE SHOTS! SOMETHING LIKE THAT WOULD BE WORTH A FORTUNE!
I WON'T BORE YOU ABOUT THE YEARS OF WORK IN MY LABORATORY! ALL I'LL SAY IS--I SUCCEEDED! I HAVE PERFECTED A SPECIAL PROCESS OF TAKING PICTURES THROUGH SOLID OBJECTS--LIKE A MASK! PAY ME--AND HAVE A LOOK!
BUT, MR. PEARSON, EVEN ASSUMING THAT WE COULD-- er--
--DO BUSINESS--I'D STILL HAVE TO CONFER WITH THE CITY COUNCIL! I COULDN'T JUST HAND YOU A MILLION DOLLARS!
OKAY! I'LL GIVE YOU 24 HOURS! EITHER I GET THE MILLION THEN--OR I MAKE OTHER ARRANGEMENTS WITH THE X-PHOTO! GOOD DAY, MR. MAYOR!
6

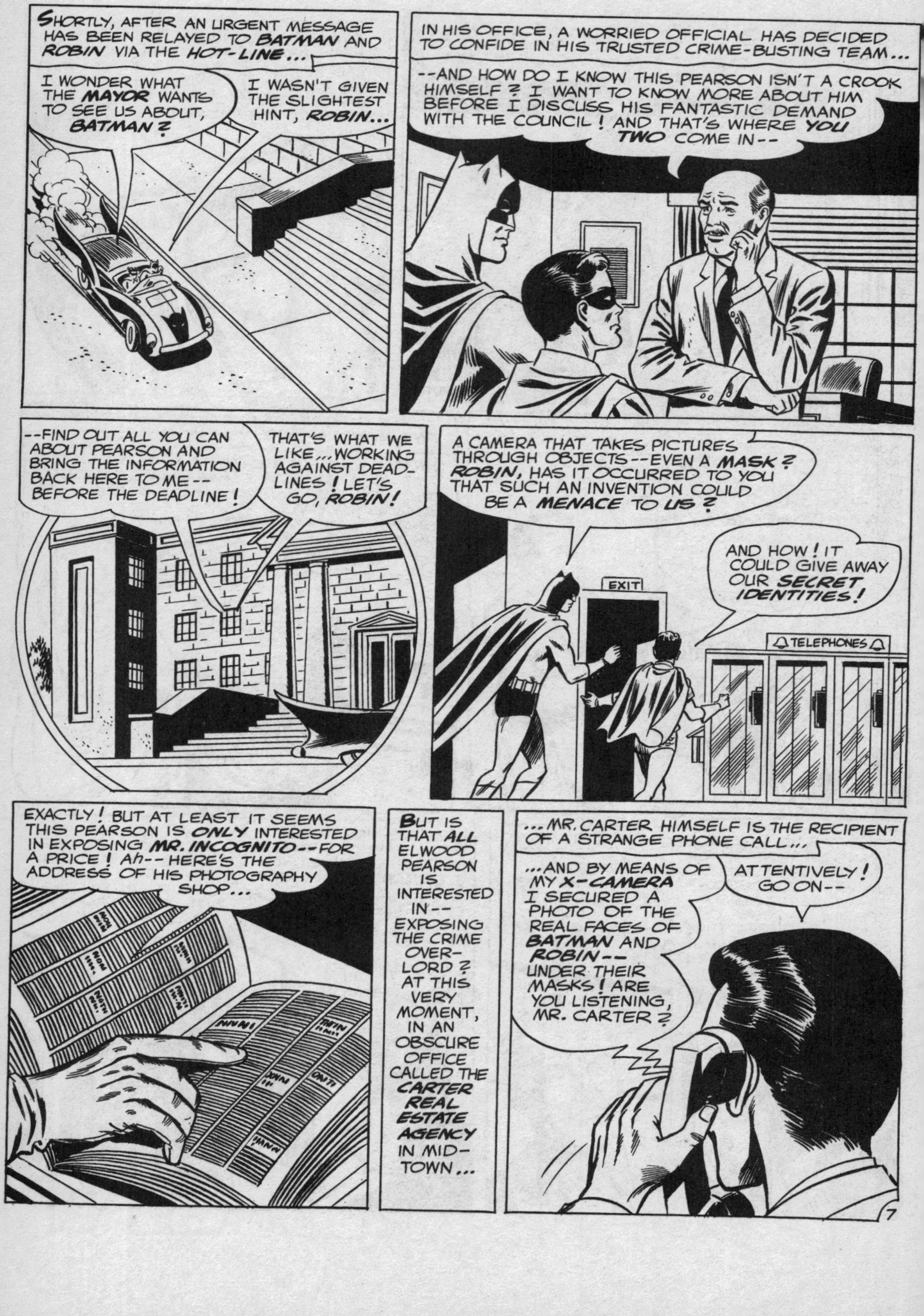
SHORTLY, AFTER AN URGENT MESSAGE HAS BEEN RELAYED TO BATMAN AND ROBIN VIA THE HOT-LINE...
I WONDER WHAT THE MAYOR WANTS TO SEE US ABOUT, BATMAN?
I WASN'T GIVEN THE SLIGHTEST HINT, ROBIN...
IN HIS OFFICE, A WORRIED OFFICIAL HAS DECIDED TO CONFIDE IN HIS TRUSTED CRIME-BUSTING TEAM...
--AND HOW DO I KNOW THIS PEARSON ISN'T A CROOK HIMSELF? I WANT TO KNOW MORE ABOUT HIM BEFORE I DISCUSS HIS FANTASTIC DEMAND WITH THE COUNCIL! AND THAT'S WHERE YOU TWO COME IN--
--FIND OUT ALL YOU CAN ABOUT PEARSON AND BRING THE INFORMATION BACK HERE TO ME-- BEFORE THE DEADLINE!
THAT'S WHAT WE LIKE,...WORKING AGAINST DEAD-LINES! LET'S GO, ROBIN!
A CAMERA THAT TAKES PICTURES THROUGH OBJECTS--EVEN A MASK? ROBIN, HAS IT OCCURRED TO YOU THAT SUCH AN INVENTION COULD BE A MENACE TO US?
AND HOW! IT COULD GIVE AWAY OUR SECRET IDENTITIES!
EXIT
TELEPHONES
EXACTLY! BUT AT LEAST IT SEEMS THIS PEARSON IS ONLY INTERESTED IN EXPOSING MR. INCOGNITO--FOR A PRICE! Ah--HERE'S THE ADDRESS OF HIS PHOTOGRAPHY SHOP...
BUT IS THAT ALL ELWOOD PEARSON IS INTERESTED IN--EXPOSING THE CRIME OVER-LORD? AT THIS VERY MOMENT, IN AN OBSCURE OFFICE CALLED THE CARTER REAL ESTATE AGENCY IN MID-TOWN...
...MR. CARTER HIMSELF IS THE RECIPIENT OF A STRANGE PHONE CALL...
...AND BY MEANS OF MY X-CAMERA I SECURED A PHOTO OF THE REAL FACES OF BATMAN AND ROBIN-- UNDER THEIR MASKS! ARE YOU LISTENING, MR. CARTER?
ATTENTIVELY! GO ON--
7

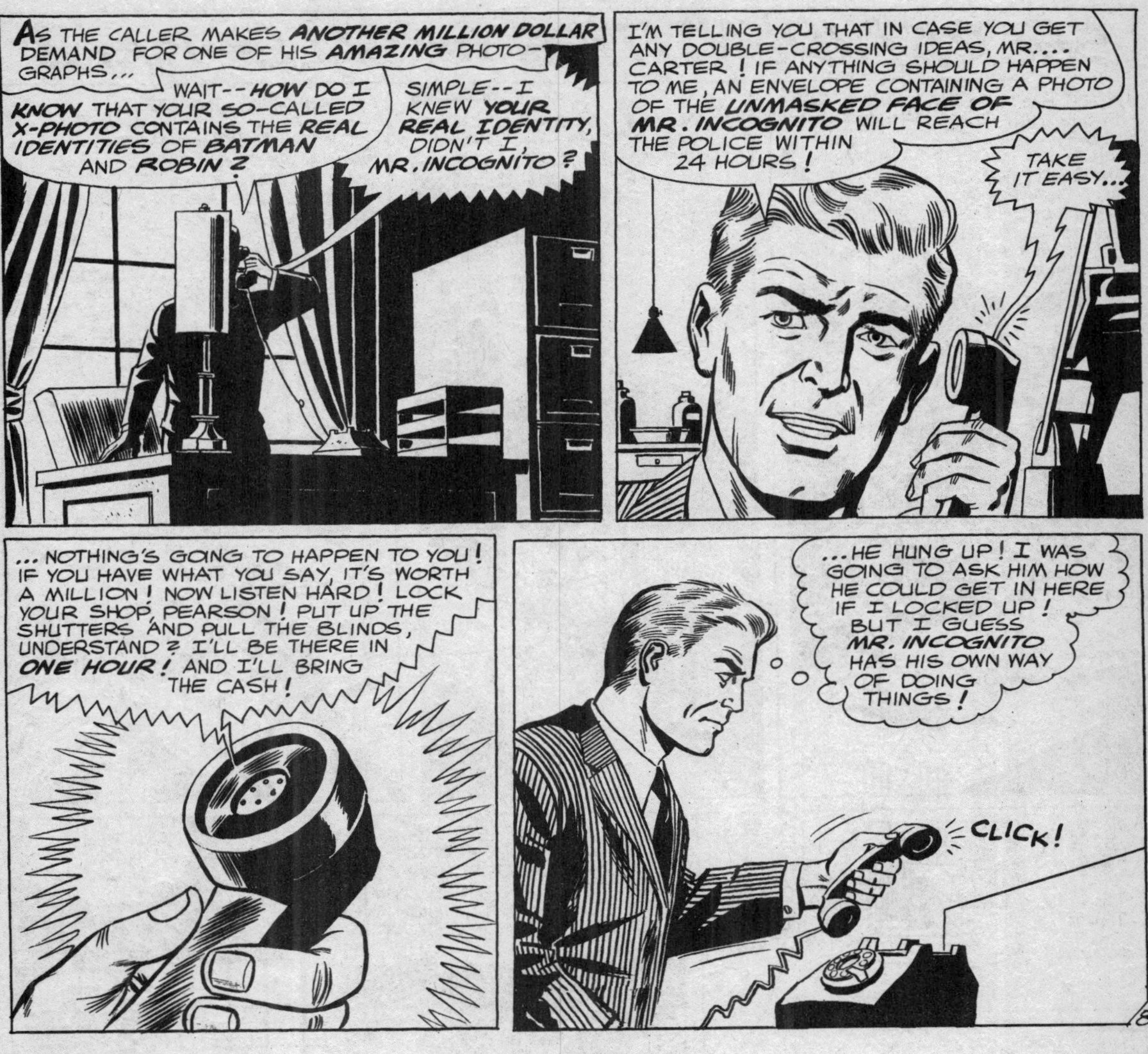
AS THE CALLER MAKES ANOTHER MILLION DOLLAR DEMAND FOR ONE OF HIS AMAZING PHOTOGRAPHS ...
WAIT-- HOW DO I KNOW THAT YOUR SO-CALLED X-PHOTO CONTAINS THE REAL IDENTITIES OF BATMAN AND ROBIN ?
SIMPLE-- I KNEW YOUR REAL IDENTITY, DIDN'T I, MR. INCOGNITO ?
I'M TELLING YOU THAT IN CASE YOU GET ANY DOUBLE-CROSSING IDEAS, MR.... CARTER ! IF ANYTHING SHOULD HAPPEN TO ME, AN ENVELOPE CONTAINING A PHOTO OF THE UNMASKED FACE OF MR. INCOGNITO WILL REACH THE POLICE WITHIN 24 HOURS !
TAKE IT EASY...
... NOTHING'S GOING TO HAPPEN TO YOU ! IF YOU HAVE WHAT YOU SAY, IT'S WORTH A MILLION ! NOW LISTEN HARD ! LOCK YOUR SHOP, PEARSON ! PUT UP THE SHUTTERS AND PULL THE BLINDS, UNDERSTAND ? I'LL BE THERE IN ONE HOUR ! AND I'LL BRING THE CASH !
... HE HUNG UP ! I WAS GOING TO ASK HIM HOW HE COULD GET IN HERE IF I LOCKED UP ! BUT I GUESS MR. INCOGNITO HAS HIS OWN WAY OF DOING THINGS !
CLICK !
8

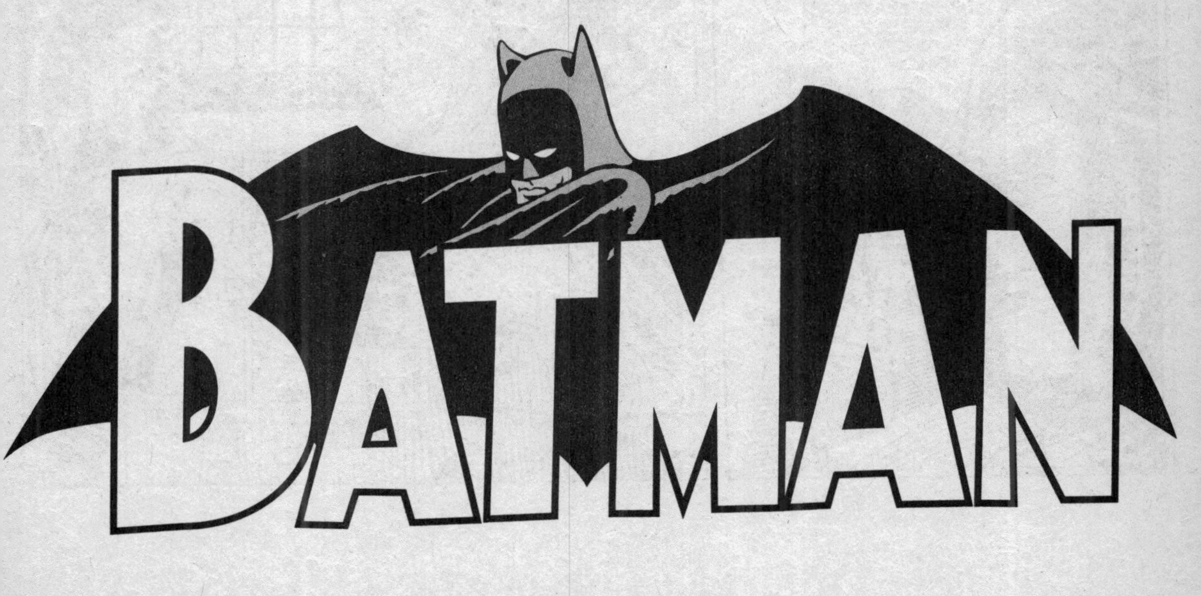
BATMAN

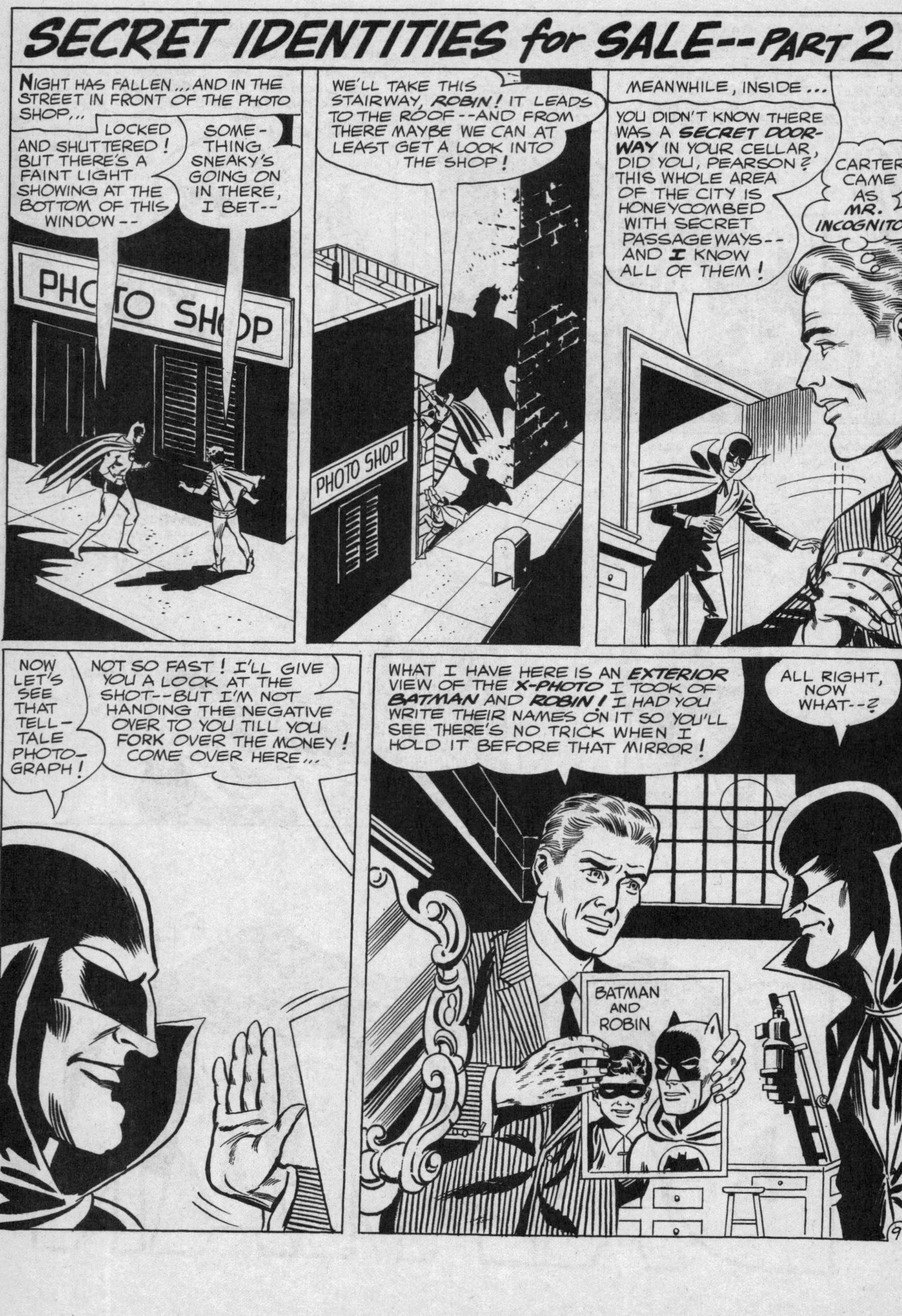
SECRET IDENTITIES for SALE--PART 2
NIGHT HAS FALLEN ... AND IN THE STREET IN FRONT OF THE PHOTO SHOP...
LOCKED AND SHUTTERED! BUT THERE'S A FAINT LIGHT SHOWING AT THE BOTTOM OF THIS WINDOW--
SOME-THING SNEAKY'S GOING ON IN THERE, I BET--
PHOTO SHOP
WE'LL TAKE THIS STAIRWAY, ROBIN! IT LEADS TO THE ROOF--AND FROM THERE MAYBE WE CAN AT LEAST GET A LOOK INTO THE SHOP!
PHOTO SHOP
MEANWHILE, INSIDE...
YOU DIDN'T KNOW THERE WAS A SECRET DOORWAY IN YOUR CELLAR, DID YOU, PEARSON? THIS WHOLE AREA OF THE CITY IS HONEYCOMBED WITH SECRET PASSAGEWAYS--AND I KNOW ALL OF THEM!
CARTER CAME AS MR. INCOGNITO--
NOW LET'S SEE THAT TELL-TALE PHOTO-GRAPH!
NOT SO FAST! I'LL GIVE YOU A LOOK AT THE SHOT--BUT I'M NOT HANDING THE NEGATIVE OVER TO YOU TILL YOU FORK OVER THE MONEY! COME OVER HERE...
WHAT I HAVE HERE IS AN EXTERIOR VIEW OF THE X-PHOTO I TOOK OF BATMAN AND ROBIN! I HAD YOU WRITE THEIR NAMES ON IT SO YOU'LL SEE THERE'S NO TRICK WHEN I HOLD IT BEFORE THAT MIRROR!
ALL RIGHT, NOW WHAT--?
BATMAN AND ROBIN
9

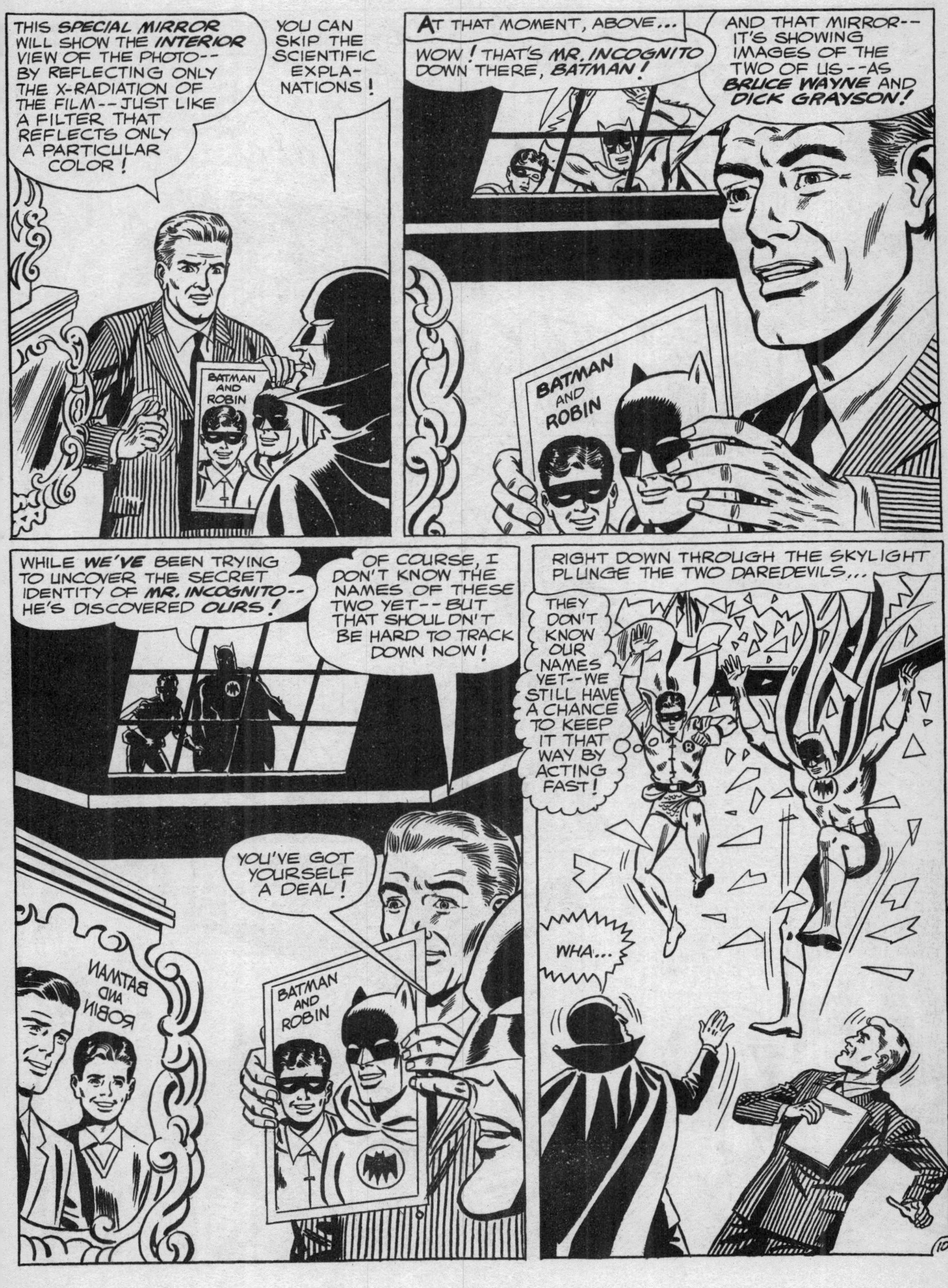
THIS SPECIAL MIRROR WILL SHOW THE INTERIOR VIEW OF THE PHOTO-- BY REFLECTING ONLY THE X-RADIATION OF THE FILM--JUST LIKE A FILTER THAT REFLECTS ONLY A PARTICULAR COLOR!
YOU CAN SKIP THE SCIENTIFIC EXPLA-NATIONS!
BATMAN AND ROBIN
AT THAT MOMENT, ABOVE...
WOW! THAT'S MR. INCOGNITO DOWN THERE, BATMAN!
AND THAT MIRROR-- IT'S SHOWING IMAGES OF THE TWO OF US--AS BRUCE WAYNE AND DICK GRAYSON!
BATMAN AND ROBIN
WHILE WE'VE BEEN TRYING TO UNCOVER THE SECRET IDENTITY OF MR. INCOGNITO-- HE'S DISCOVERED OURS!
OF COURSE, I DON'T KNOW THE NAMES OF THESE TWO YET--BUT THAT SHOULDN'T BE HARD TO TRACK DOWN NOW!
YOU'VE GOT YOURSELF A DEAL!
BATMAN AND ROBIN
BATMAN AND ROBIN
RIGHT DOWN THROUGH THE SKYLIGHT PLUNGE THE TWO DAREDEVILS...
THEY DON'T KNOW OUR NAMES YET--WE STILL HAVE A CHANCE TO KEEP IT THAT WAY BY ACTING FAST!
WHA...
10

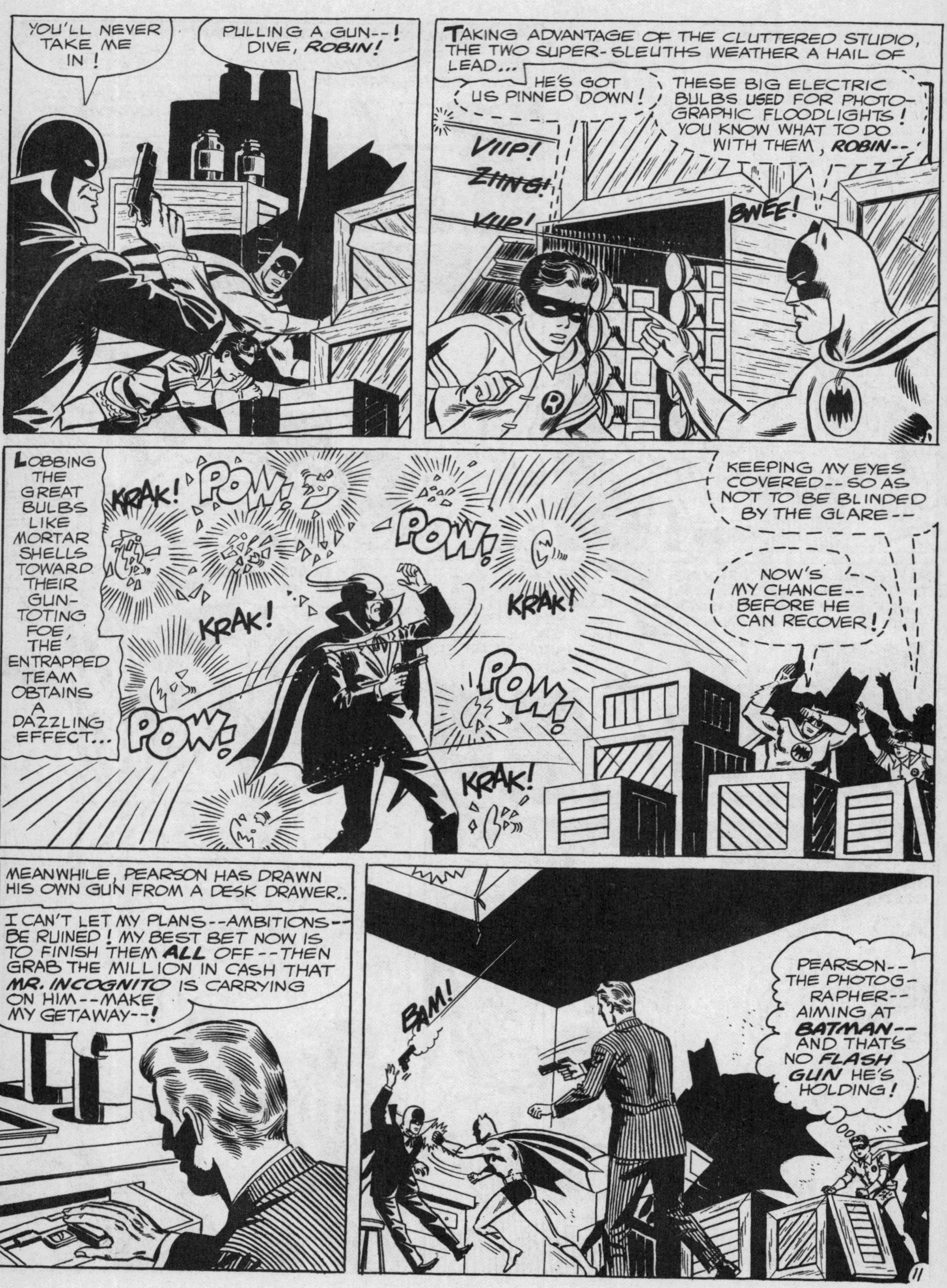
YOU'LL NEVER TAKE ME IN!
PULLING A GUN--! DIVE, ROBIN!
TAKING ADVANTAGE OF THE CLUTTERED STUDIO, THE TWO SUPER-SLEUTHS WEATHER A HAIL OF LEAD...
HE'S GOT US PINNED DOWN!
THESE BIG ELECTRIC BULBS USED FOR PHOTOGRAPHIC FLOODLIGHTS! YOU KNOW WHAT TO DO WITH THEM, ROBIN--
VIIP!
ZHING!
VIIP!
BWEE!
LOBBING THE GREAT BULBS LIKE MORTAR SHELLS TOWARD THEIR GUN-TOTING FOE, THE ENTRAPPED TEAM OBTAINS A DAZZLING EFFECT...
KRAK!
POW!
POW!
KRAK!
KRAK!
POW!
POW!
KRAK!
KEEPING MY EYES COVERED--SO AS NOT TO BE BLINDED BY THE GLARE--
NOW'S MY CHANCE--BEFORE HE CAN RECOVER!
MEANWHILE, PEARSON HAS DRAWN HIS OWN GUN FROM A DESK DRAWER..
I CAN'T LET MY PLANS--AMBITIONS--BE RUINED! MY BEST BET NOW IS TO FINISH THEM ALL OFF--THEN GRAB THE MILLION IN CASH THAT MR. INCOGNITO IS CARRYING ON HIM--MAKE MY GETAWAY--!
BAM!
PEARSON--THE PHOTOGRAPHER--AIMING AT BATMAN--AND THAT'S NO FLASH GUN HE'S HOLDING!
11

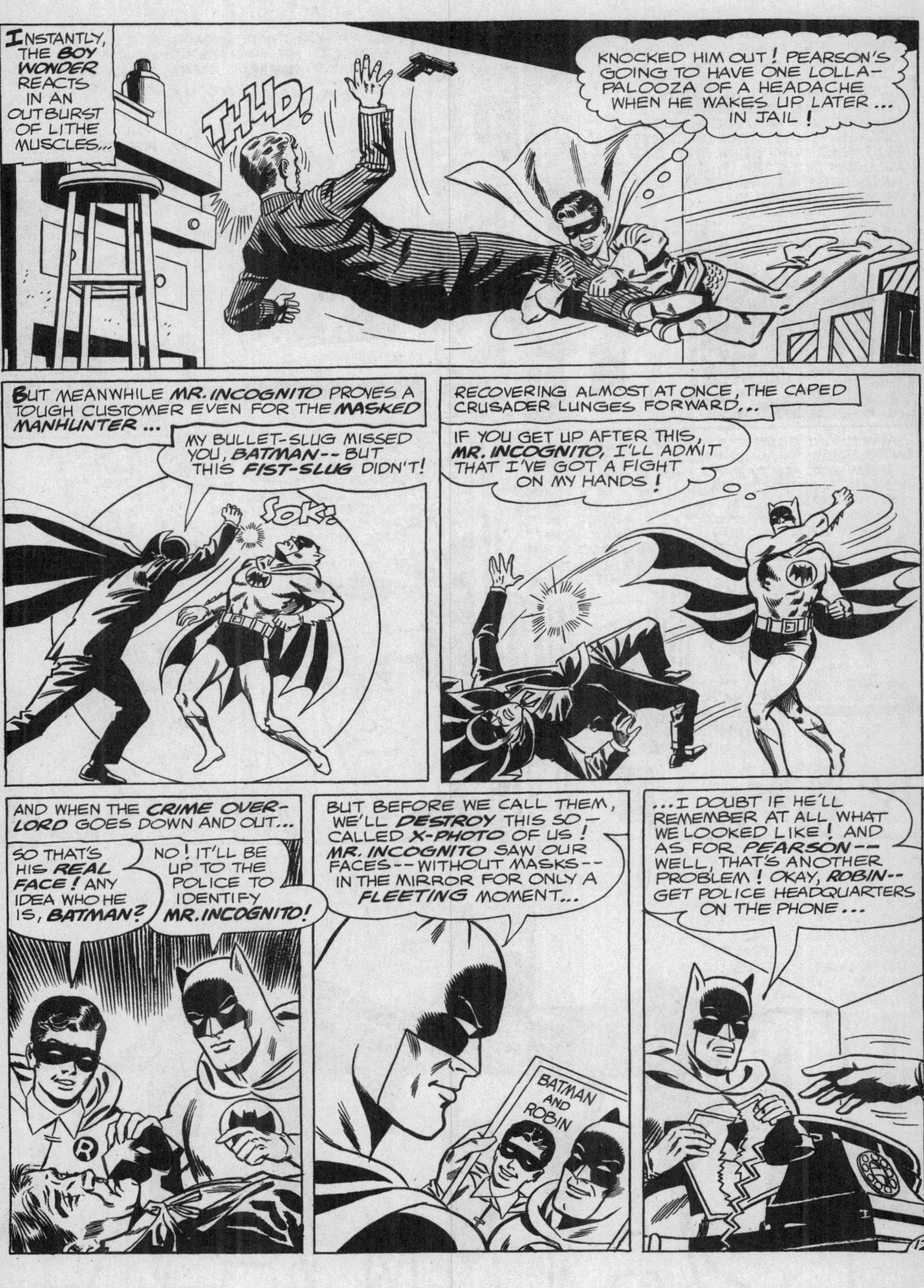
INSTANTLY, THE BOY WONDER REACTS IN AN OUTBURST OF LITHE MUSCLES...
THUD!
KNOCKED HIM OUT! PEARSON'S GOING TO HAVE ONE LOLLA-PALOOZA OF A HEADACHE WHEN HE WAKES UP LATER... IN JAIL!
BUT MEANWHILE MR. INCOGNITO PROVES A TOUGH CUSTOMER EVEN FOR THE MASKED MANHUNTER...
MY BULLET-SLUG MISSED YOU, BATMAN-- BUT THIS FIST-SLUG DIDN'T!
SOK!
RECOVERING ALMOST AT ONCE, THE CAPED CRUSADER LUNGES FORWARD...
IF YOU GET UP AFTER THIS, MR. INCOGNITO, I'LL ADMIT THAT I'VE GOT A FIGHT ON MY HANDS!
AND WHEN THE CRIME OVER-LORD GOES DOWN AND OUT...
SO THAT'S HIS REAL FACE! ANY IDEA WHO HE IS, BATMAN?
NO! IT'LL BE UP TO THE POLICE TO IDENTIFY MR. INCOGNITO!
BUT BEFORE WE CALL THEM, WE'LL DESTROY THIS SO-CALLED X-PHOTO OF US! MR. INCOGNITO SAW OUR FACES--WITHOUT MASKS-- IN THE MIRROR FOR ONLY A FLEETING MOMENT...
BATMAN AND ROBIN
...I DOUBT IF HE'LL REMEMBER AT ALL WHAT WE LOOKED LIKE! AND AS FOR PEARSON-- WELL, THAT'S ANOTHER PROBLEM! OKAY, ROBIN-- GET POLICE HEADQUARTERS ON THE PHONE...
12

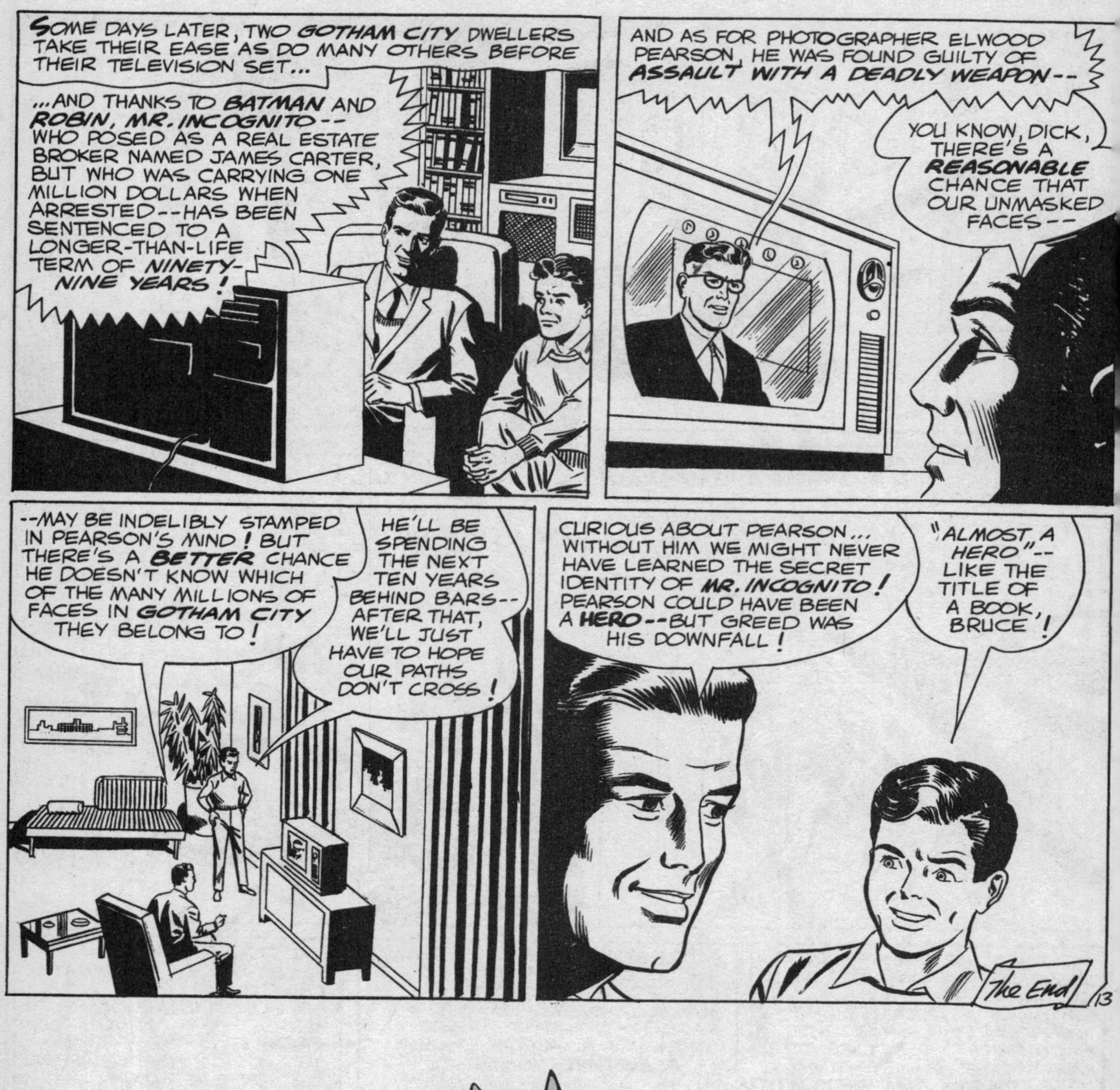
SOME DAYS LATER, TWO GOTHAM CITY DWELLERS TAKE THEIR EASE AS DO MANY OTHERS BEFORE THEIR TELEVISION SET...
...AND THANKS TO BATMAN AND ROBIN, MR. INCOGNITO-- WHO POSED AS A REAL ESTATE BROKER NAMED JAMES CARTER, BUT WHO WAS CARRYING ONE MILLION DOLLARS WHEN ARRESTED--HAS BEEN SENTENCED TO A LONGER-THAN-LIFE TERM OF NINETY-NINE YEARS!
AND AS FOR PHOTOGRAPHER ELWOOD PEARSON, HE WAS FOUND GUILTY OF ASSAULT WITH A DEADLY WEAPON--
YOU KNOW, DICK, THERE'S A REASONABLE CHANCE THAT OUR UNMASKED FACES--
--MAY BE INDELIBLY STAMPED IN PEARSON'S MIND! BUT THERE'S A BETTER CHANCE HE DOESN'T KNOW WHICH OF THE MANY MILLIONS OF FACES IN GOTHAM CITY THEY BELONG TO!
HE'LL BE SPENDING THE NEXT TEN YEARS BEHIND BARS-- AFTER THAT, WE'LL JUST HAVE TO HOPE OUR PATHS DON'T CROSS!
CURIOUS ABOUT PEARSON... WITHOUT HIM WE MIGHT NEVER HAVE LEARNED THE SECRET IDENTITY OF MR. INCOGNITO! PEARSON COULD HAVE BEEN A HERO--BUT GREED WAS HIS DOWNFALL!
"ALMOST A HERO"-- LIKE THE TITLE OF A BOOK, BRUCE!
The End
13

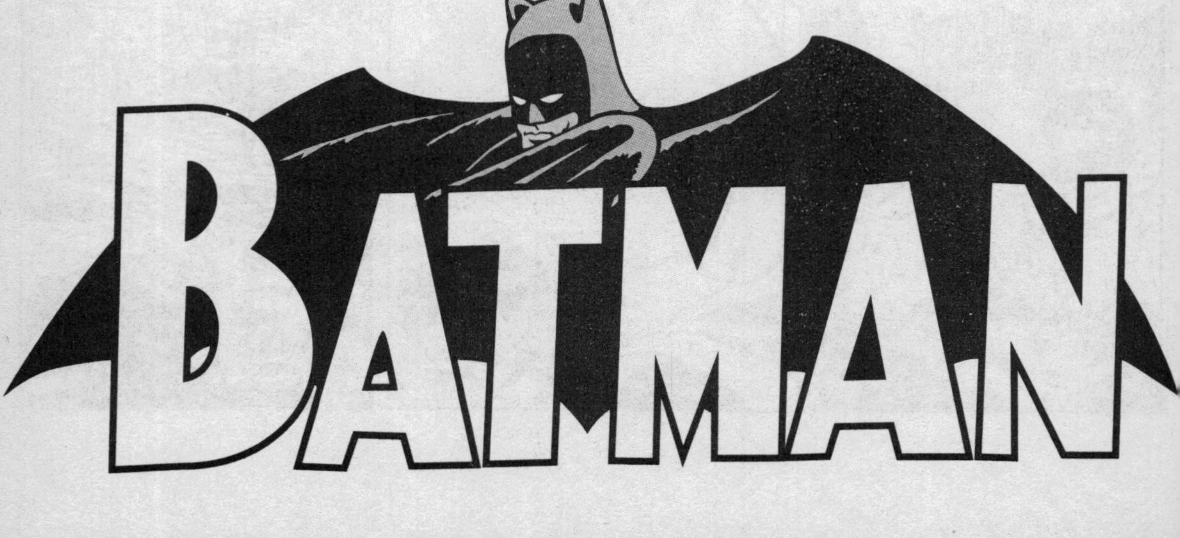
BATMAN

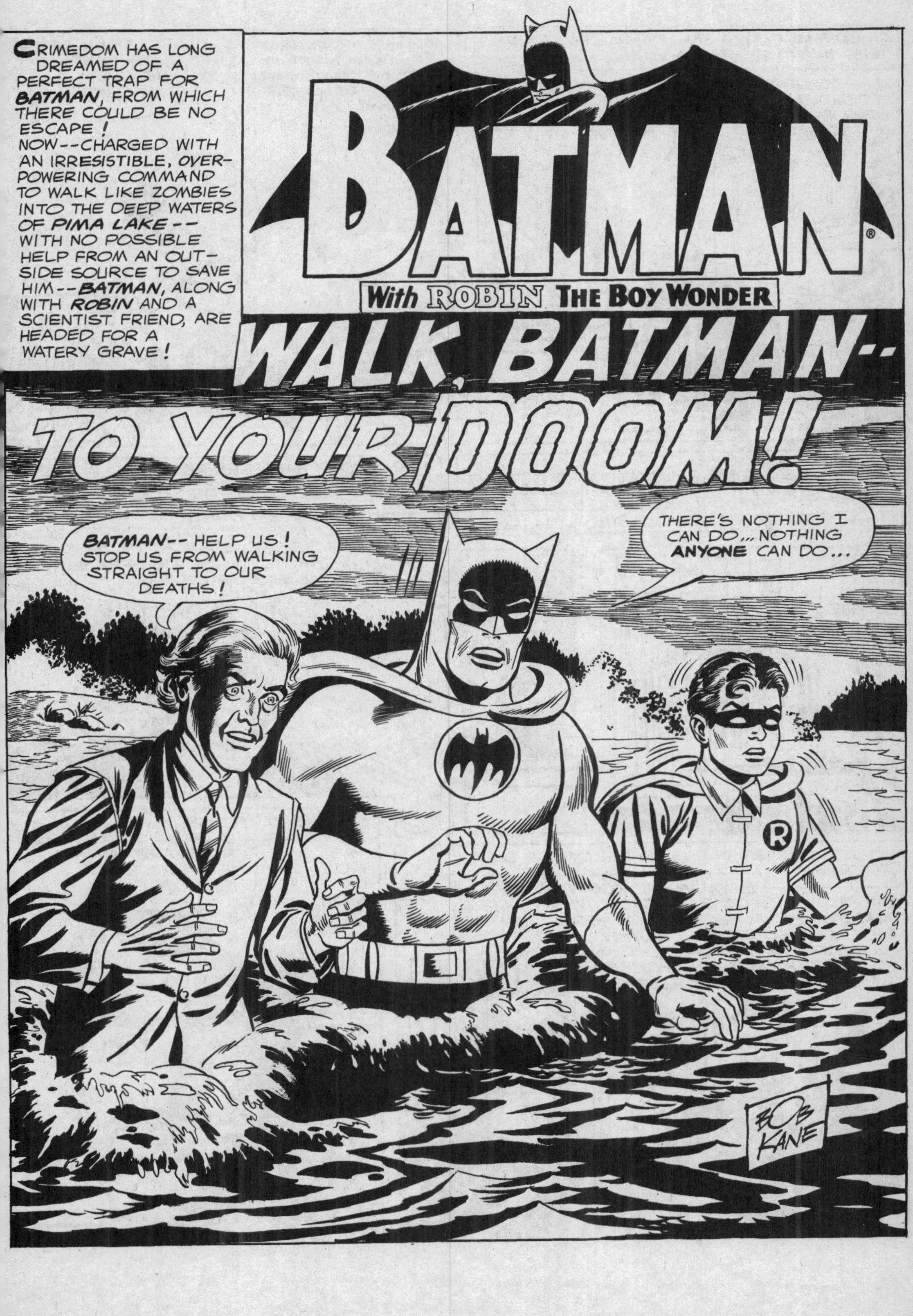
CRIMEDOM HAS LONG DREAMED OF A PERFECT TRAP FOR BATMAN, FROM WHICH THERE COULD BE NO ESCAPE! NOW--CHARGED WITH AN IRRESISTIBLE, OVER-POWERING COMMAND TO WALK LIKE ZOMBIES INTO THE DEEP WATERS OF PIMA LAKE--WITH NO POSSIBLE HELP FROM AN OUT-SIDE SOURCE TO SAVE HIM--BATMAN, ALONG WITH ROBIN AND A SCIENTIST FRIEND, ARE HEADED FOR A WATERY GRAVE!
BATMAN®
With ROBIN THE BOY WONDER
WALK, BATMAN--TO YOUR DOOM!
BATMAN-- HELP US! STOP US FROM WALKING STRAIGHT TO OUR DEATHS!
THERE'S NOTHING I CAN DO... NOTHING ANYONE CAN DO...
BOB KANE

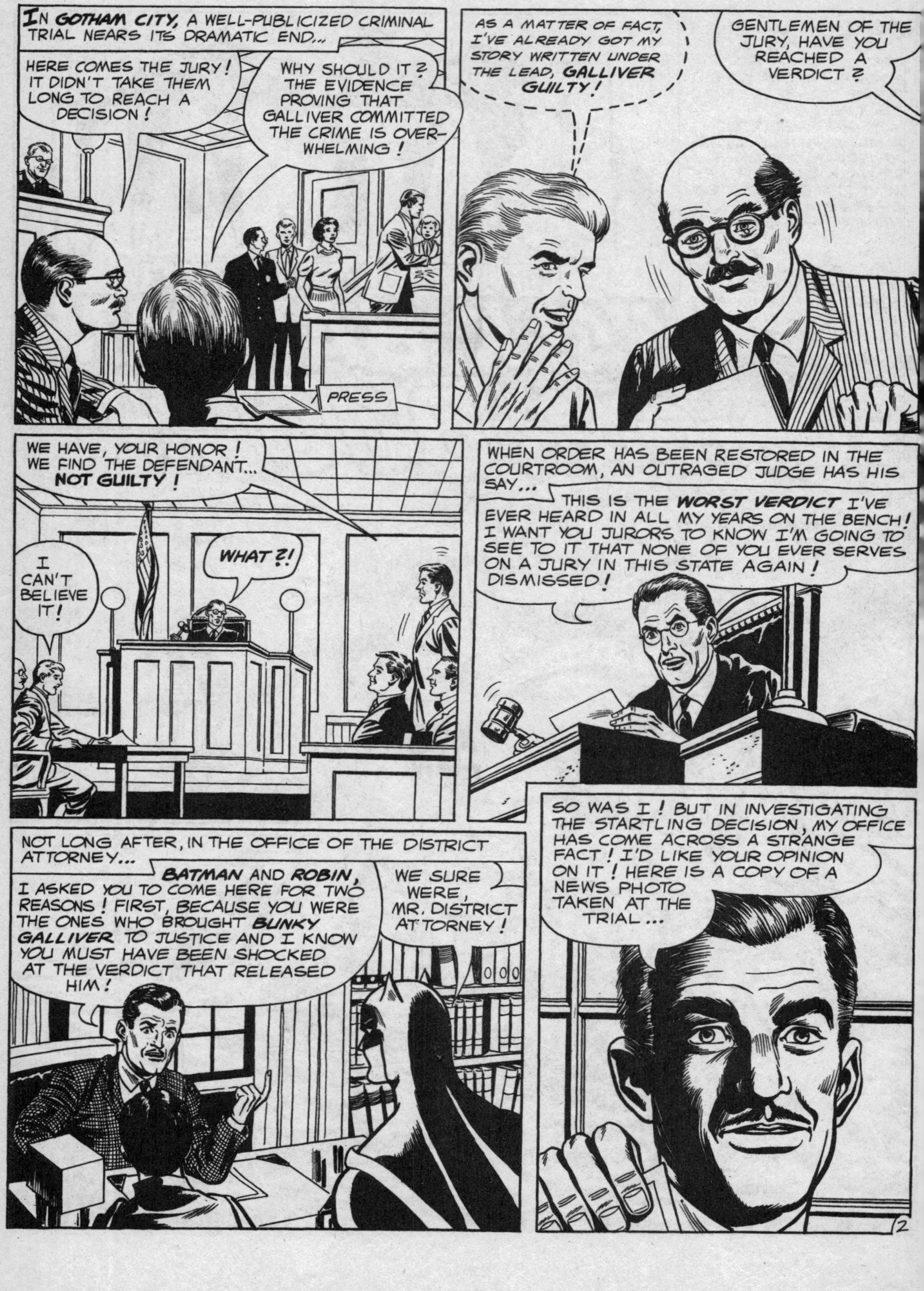

IN GOTHAM CITY, A WELL-PUBLICIZED CRIMINAL TRIAL NEARS ITS DRAMATIC END...
HERE COMES THE JURY! IT DIDN'T TAKE THEM LONG TO REACH A DECISION!
WHY SHOULD IT? THE EVIDENCE PROVING THAT GALLIVER COMMITTED THE CRIME IS OVERWHELMING!
PRESS
AS A MATTER OF FACT, I'VE ALREADY GOT MY STORY WRITTEN UNDER THE LEAD, GALLIVER GUILTY!
GENTLEMEN OF THE JURY, HAVE YOU REACHED A VERDICT?
WE HAVE, YOUR HONOR! WE FIND THE DEFENDANT... NOT GUILTY!
WHAT?!
I CAN'T BELIEVE IT!
WHEN ORDER HAS BEEN RESTORED IN THE COURTROOM, AN OUTRAGED JUDGE HAS HIS SAY...
THIS IS THE WORST VERDICT I'VE EVER HEARD IN ALL MY YEARS ON THE BENCH! I WANT YOU JURORS TO KNOW I'M GOING TO SEE TO IT THAT NONE OF YOU EVER SERVES ON A JURY IN THIS STATE AGAIN! DISMISSED!
NOT LONG AFTER, IN THE OFFICE OF THE DISTRICT ATTORNEY...
BATMAN AND ROBIN, I ASKED YOU TO COME HERE FOR TWO REASONS! FIRST, BECAUSE YOU WERE THE ONES WHO BROUGHT BUNKY GALLIVER TO JUSTICE AND I KNOW YOU MUST HAVE BEEN SHOCKED AT THE VERDICT THAT RELEASED HIM!
WE SURE WERE, MR. DISTRICT ATTORNEY!
SO WAS I! BUT IN INVESTIGATING THE STARTLING DECISION, MY OFFICE HAS COME ACROSS A STRANGE FACT! I'D LIKE YOUR OPINION ON IT! HERE IS A COPY OF A NEWS PHOTO TAKEN AT THE TRIAL...
2

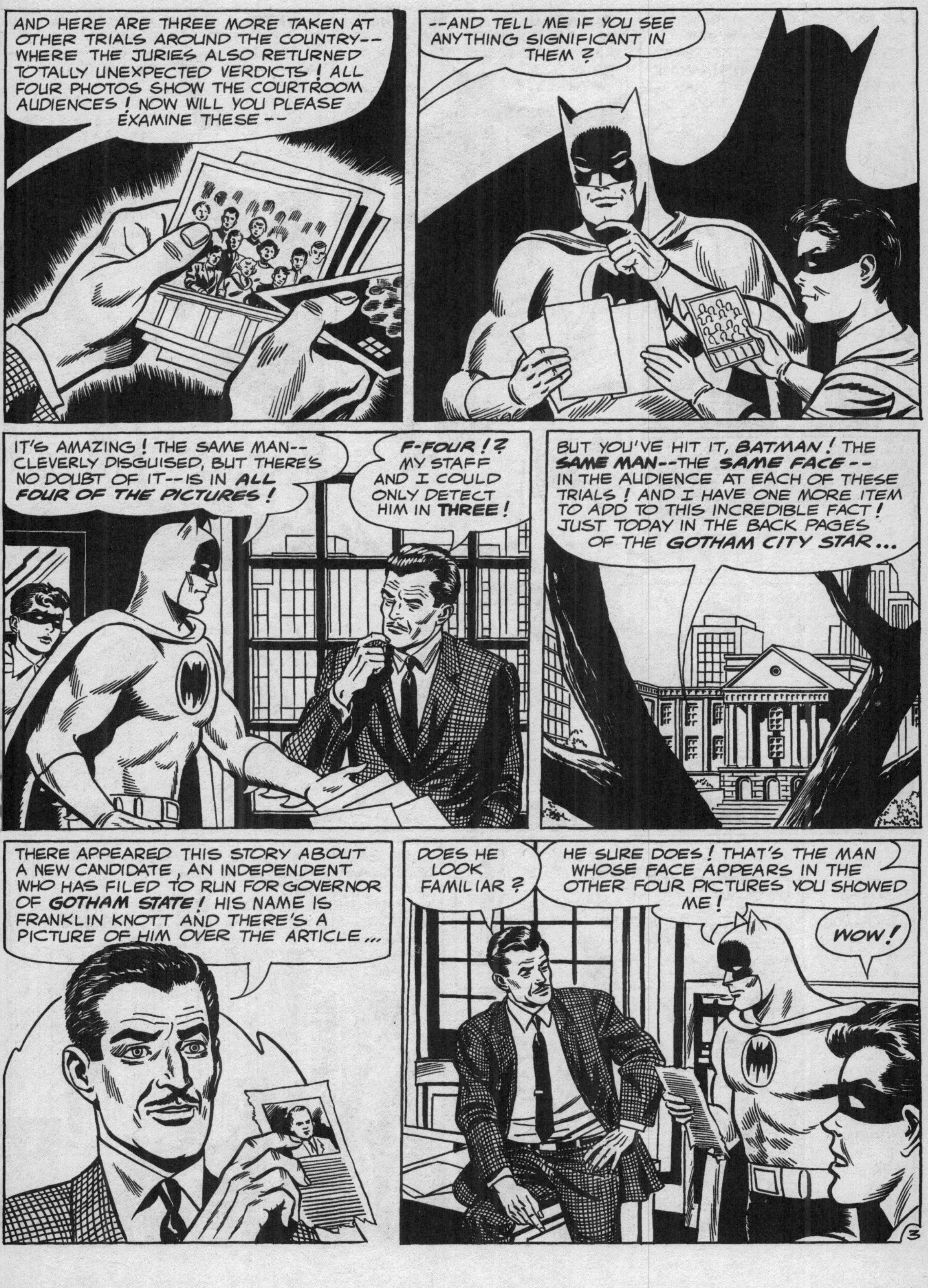
AND HERE ARE THREE MORE TAKEN AT OTHER TRIALS AROUND THE COUNTRY-- WHERE THE JURIES ALSO RETURNED TOTALLY UNEXPECTED VERDICTS! ALL FOUR PHOTOS SHOW THE COURTROOM AUDIENCES! NOW WILL YOU PLEASE EXAMINE THESE --
--AND TELL ME IF YOU SEE ANYTHING SIGNIFICANT IN THEM?
IT'S AMAZING! THE SAME MAN-- CLEVERLY DISGUISED, BUT THERE'S NO DOUBT OF IT--IS IN ALL FOUR OF THE PICTURES!
F-FOUR!? MY STAFF AND I COULD ONLY DETECT HIM IN THREE!
BUT YOU'VE HIT IT, BATMAN! THE SAME MAN--THE SAME FACE-- IN THE AUDIENCE AT EACH OF THESE TRIALS! AND I HAVE ONE MORE ITEM TO ADD TO THIS INCREDIBLE FACT! JUST TODAY IN THE BACK PAGES OF THE GOTHAM CITY STAR...
THERE APPEARED THIS STORY ABOUT A NEW CANDIDATE, AN INDEPENDENT WHO HAS FILED TO RUN FOR GOVERNOR OF GOTHAM STATE! HIS NAME IS FRANKLIN KNOTT AND THERE'S A PICTURE OF HIM OVER THE ARTICLE...
DOES HE LOOK FAMILIAR?
HE SURE DOES! THAT'S THE MAN WHOSE FACE APPEARS IN THE OTHER FOUR PICTURES YOU SHOWED ME!
WOW!
3

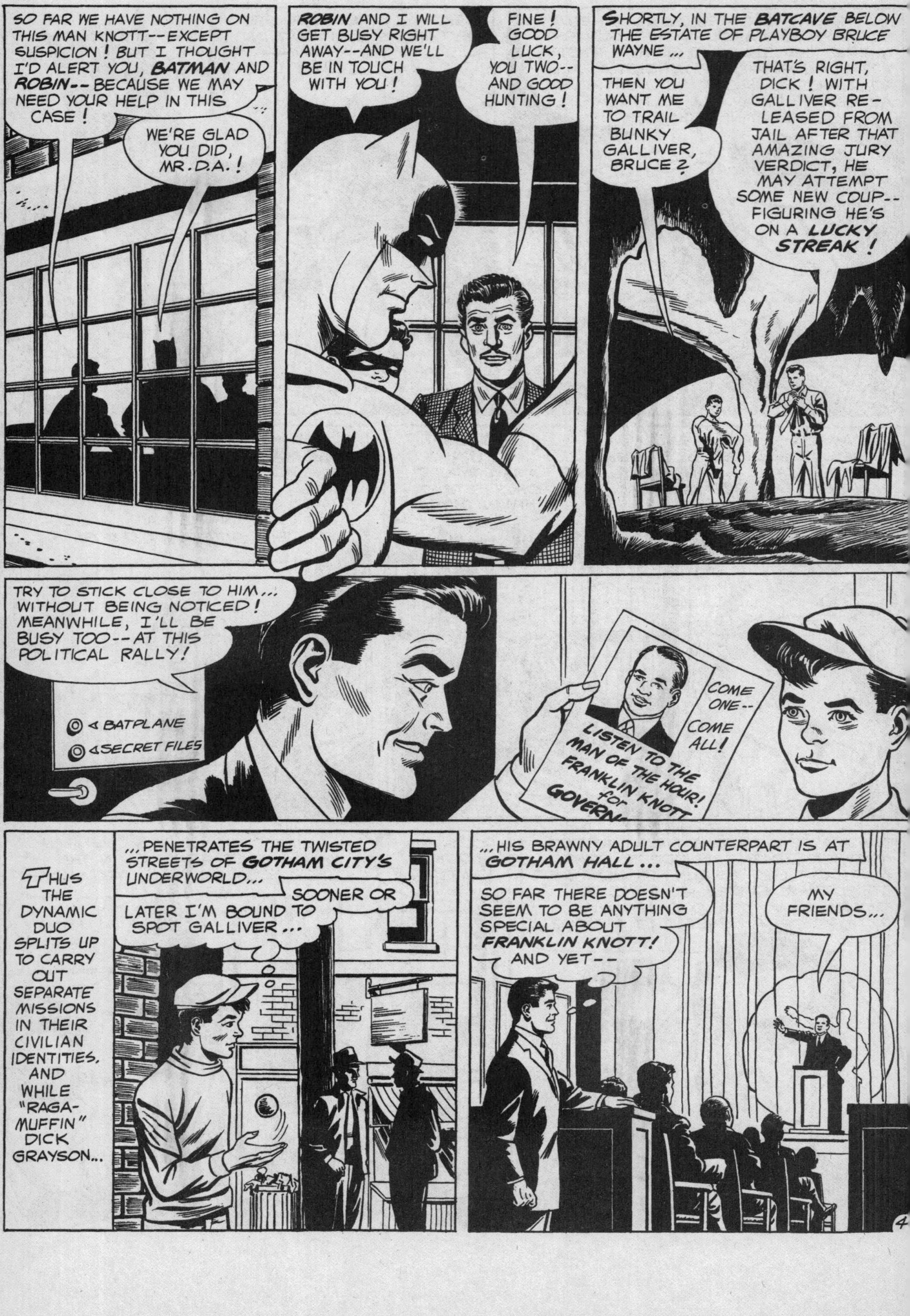
SO FAR WE HAVE NOTHING ON THIS MAN KNOTT--EXCEPT SUSPICION! BUT I THOUGHT I'D ALERT YOU, BATMAN AND ROBIN--BECAUSE WE MAY NEED YOUR HELP IN THIS CASE!
WE'RE GLAD YOU DID, MR. D.A.!
ROBIN AND I WILL GET BUSY RIGHT AWAY--AND WE'LL BE IN TOUCH WITH YOU!
FINE! GOOD LUCK, YOU TWO--AND GOOD HUNTING!
SHORTLY, IN THE BATCAVE BELOW THE ESTATE OF PLAYBOY BRUCE WAYNE ...
THEN YOU WANT ME TO TRAIL BUNKY GALLIVER, BRUCE?
THAT'S RIGHT, DICK! WITH GALLIVER RE-LEASED FROM JAIL AFTER THAT AMAZING JURY VERDICT, HE MAY ATTEMPT SOME NEW COUP-FIGURING HE'S ON A LUCKY STREAK!
TRY TO STICK CLOSE TO HIM... WITHOUT BEING NOTICED! MEANWHILE, I'LL BE BUSY TOO--AT THIS POLITICAL RALLY!
◎ ◁ BATPLANE
◎ ◁ SECRET FILES
COME ONE--COME ALL!
LISTEN TO THE MAN OF THE HOUR! FRANKLIN KNOTT for GOVERN
THUS THE DYNAMIC DUO SPLITS UP TO CARRY OUT SEPARATE MISSIONS IN THEIR CIVILIAN IDENTITIES. AND WHILE "RAGA-MUFFIN" DICK GRAYSON...
...PENETRATES THE TWISTED STREETS OF GOTHAM CITY'S UNDERWORLD...
SOONER OR LATER I'M BOUND TO SPOT GALLIVER...
...HIS BRAWNY ADULT COUNTERPART IS AT GOTHAM HALL...
SO FAR THERE DOESN'T SEEM TO BE ANYTHING SPECIAL ABOUT FRANKLIN KNOTT! AND YET--
MY FRIENDS...
4

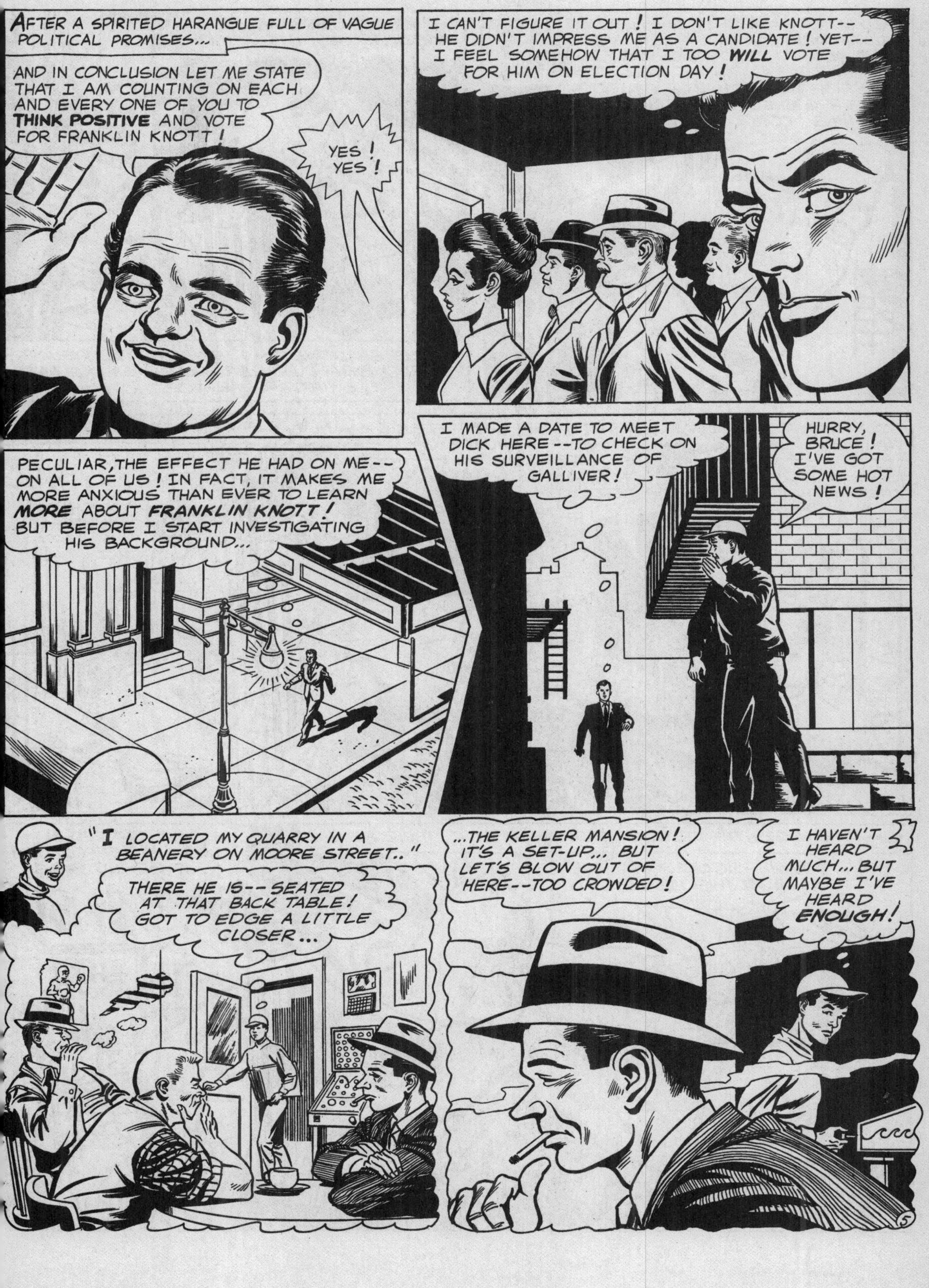
AFTER A SPIRITED HARANGUE FULL OF VAGUE POLITICAL PROMISES...
AND IN CONCLUSION LET ME STATE THAT I AM COUNTING ON EACH AND EVERY ONE OF YOU TO **THINK POSITIVE** AND VOTE FOR FRANKLIN KNOTT!
YES! YES!
I CAN'T FIGURE IT OUT! I DON'T LIKE KNOTT-- HE DIDN'T IMPRESS ME AS A CANDIDATE! YET-- I FEEL SOMEHOW THAT I TOO **WILL** VOTE FOR HIM ON ELECTION DAY!
PECULIAR, THE EFFECT HE HAD ON ME-- ON ALL OF US! IN FACT, IT MAKES ME MORE ANXIOUS THAN EVER TO LEARN **MORE** ABOUT **FRANKLIN KNOTT!** BUT BEFORE I START INVESTIGATING HIS BACKGROUND...
I MADE A DATE TO MEET DICK HERE--TO CHECK ON HIS SURVEILLANCE OF GALLIVER!
HURRY, BRUCE! I'VE GOT SOME HOT NEWS!
"I LOCATED MY QUARRY IN A BEANERY ON MOORE STREET.."
THERE HE IS--SEATED AT THAT BACK TABLE! GOT TO EDGE A LITTLE CLOSER...
...THE KELLER MANSION! IT'S A SET-UP... BUT LET'S BLOW OUT OF HERE--TOO CROWDED!
I HAVEN'T HEARD MUCH... BUT MAYBE I'VE HEARD **ENOUGH!**
5

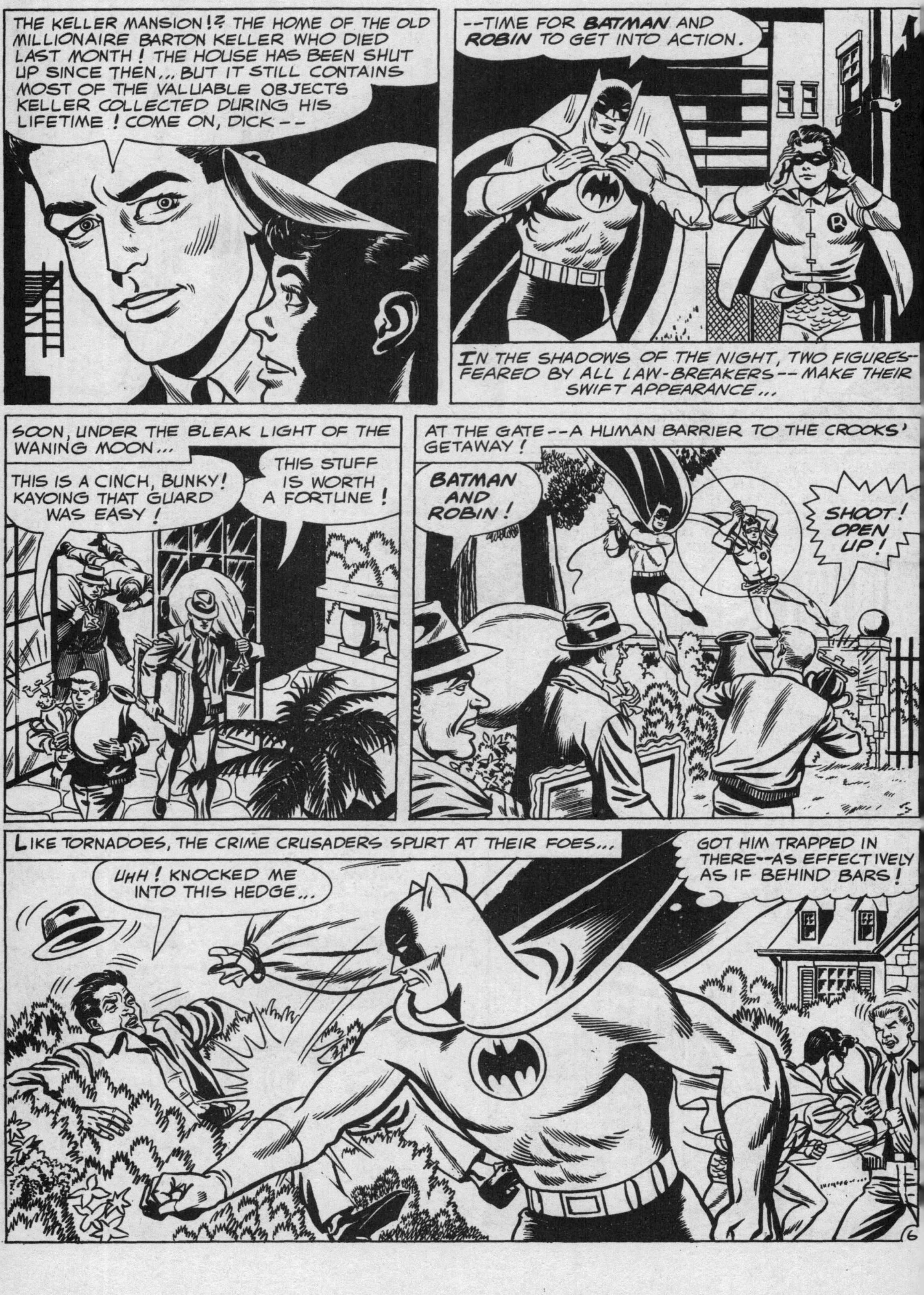
THE KELLER MANSION!? THE HOME OF THE OLD MILLIONAIRE BARTON KELLER WHO DIED LAST MONTH! THE HOUSE HAS BEEN SHUT UP SINCE THEN... BUT IT STILL CONTAINS MOST OF THE VALUABLE OBJECTS KELLER COLLECTED DURING HIS LIFETIME! COME ON, DICK--
--TIME FOR BATMAN AND ROBIN TO GET INTO ACTION.
IN THE SHADOWS OF THE NIGHT, TWO FIGURES--FEARED BY ALL LAW-BREAKERS--MAKE THEIR SWIFT APPEARANCE...
SOON, UNDER THE BLEAK LIGHT OF THE WANING MOON...
THIS IS A CINCH, BUNKY! KAYOING THAT GUARD WAS EASY!
THIS STUFF IS WORTH A FORTUNE!
AT THE GATE--A HUMAN BARRIER TO THE CROOKS' GETAWAY!
BATMAN AND ROBIN!
SHOOT! OPEN UP!
LIKE TORNADOES, THE CRIME CRUSADERS SPURT AT THEIR FOES...
UHH! KNOCKED ME INTO THIS HEDGE...
GOT HIM TRAPPED IN THERE--AS EFFECTIVELY AS IF BEHIND BARS!
6

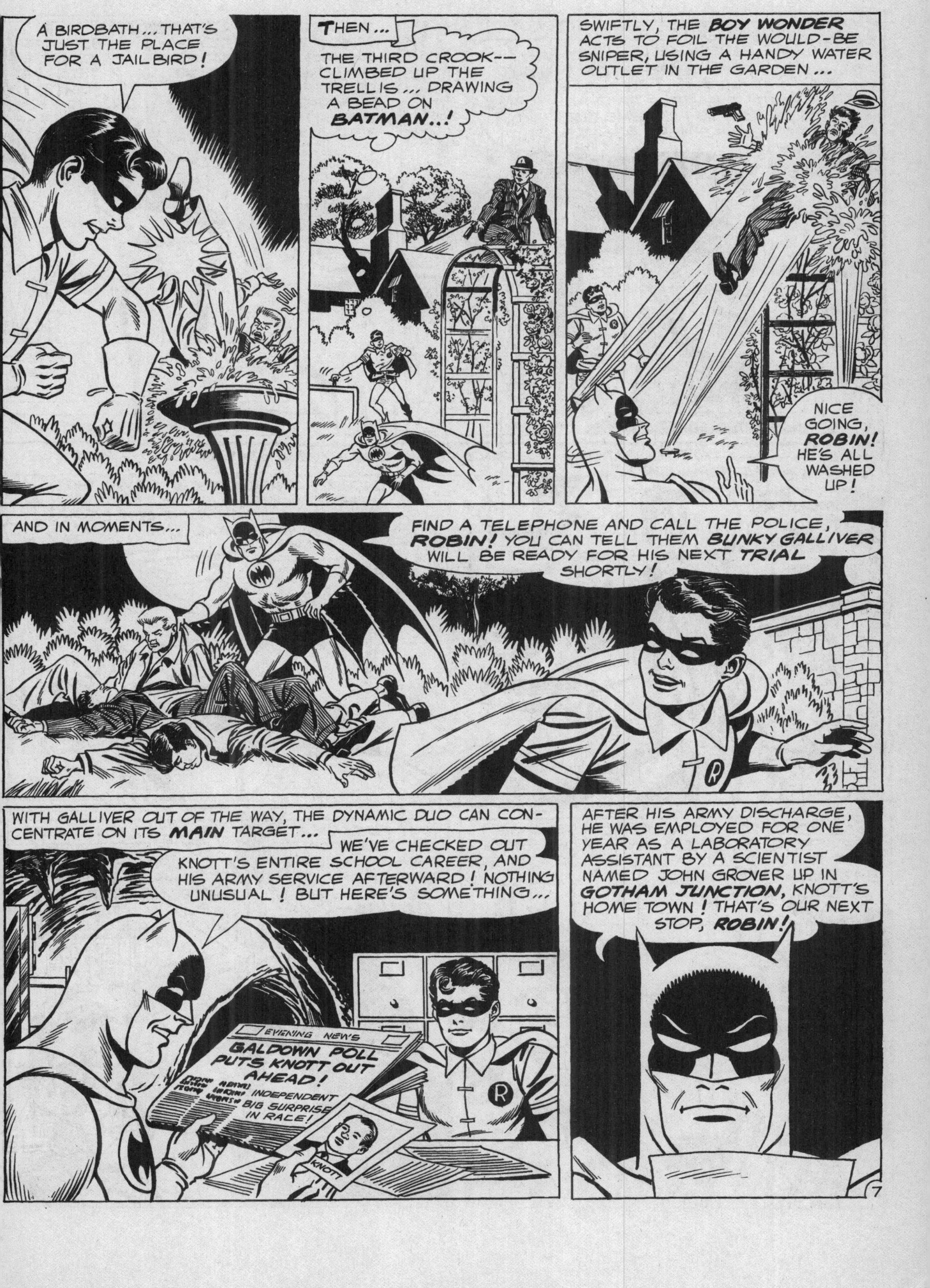
A BIRDBATH... THAT'S JUST THE PLACE FOR A JAILBIRD!
THEN...
THE THIRD CROOK-- CLIMBED UP THE TRELLIS... DRAWING A BEAD ON BATMAN...!
SWIFTLY, THE BOY WONDER ACTS TO FOIL THE WOULD-BE SNIPER, USING A HANDY WATER OUTLET IN THE GARDEN...
NICE GOING, ROBIN! HE'S ALL WASHED UP!
AND IN MOMENTS...
FIND A TELEPHONE AND CALL THE POLICE, ROBIN! YOU CAN TELL THEM BUNKY GALLIVER WILL BE READY FOR HIS NEXT TRIAL SHORTLY!
WITH GALLIVER OUT OF THE WAY, THE DYNAMIC DUO CAN CONCENTRATE ON ITS MAIN TARGET...
WE'VE CHECKED OUT KNOTT'S ENTIRE SCHOOL CAREER, AND HIS ARMY SERVICE AFTERWARD! NOTHING UNUSUAL! BUT HERE'S SOMETHING...
EVENING NEWS
GALDOWN POLL PUTS KNOTT OUT AHEAD!
INDEPENDENT BIG SURPRISE IN RACE!
KNOTT
AFTER HIS ARMY DISCHARGE, HE WAS EMPLOYED FOR ONE YEAR AS A LABORATORY ASSISTANT BY A SCIENTIST NAMED JOHN GROVER UP IN GOTHAM JUNCTION, KNOTT'S HOME TOWN! THAT'S OUR NEXT STOP, ROBIN!
7

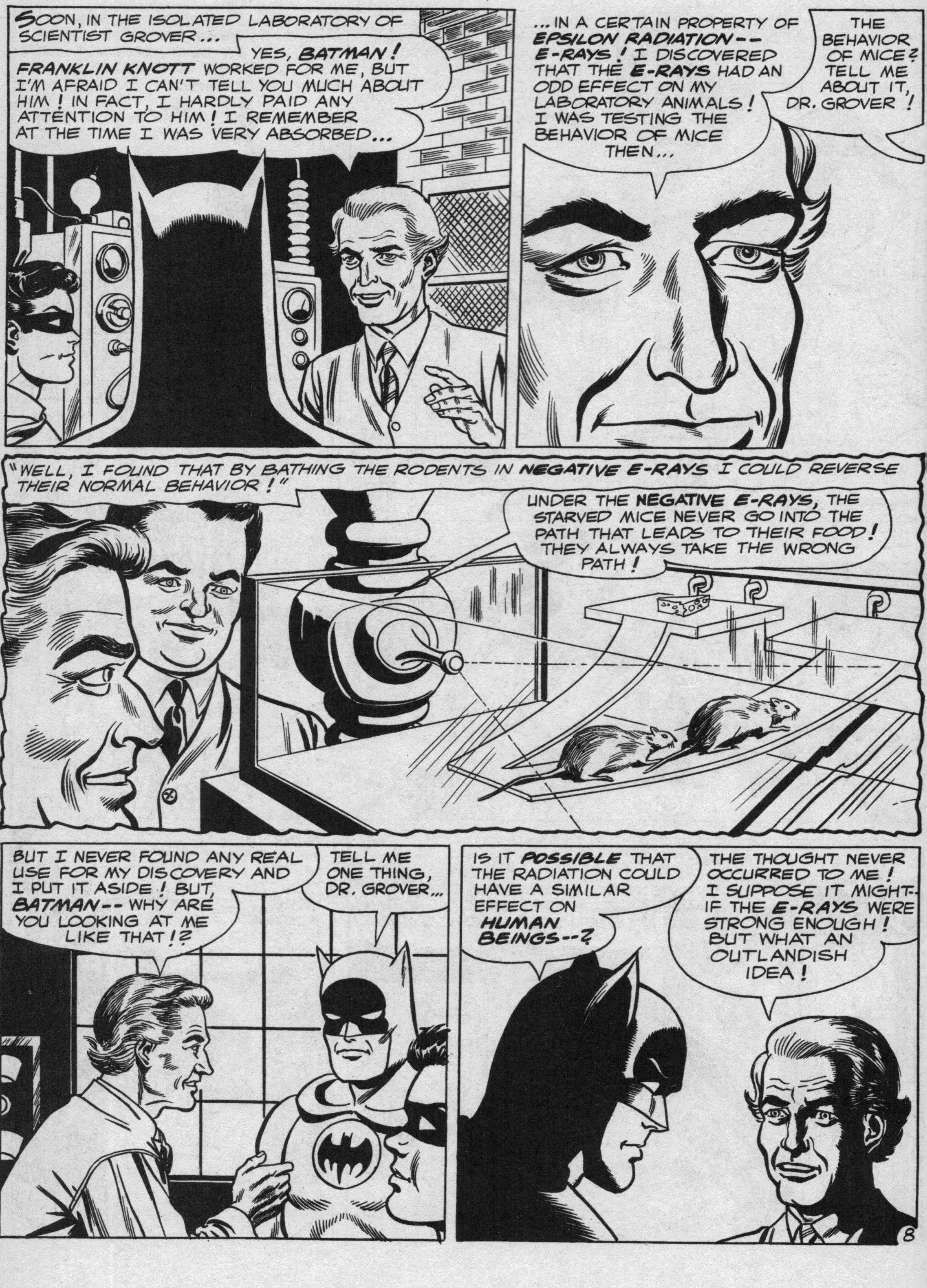
SOON, IN THE ISOLATED LABORATORY OF SCIENTIST GROVER...
YES, BATMAN! FRANKLIN KNOTT WORKED FOR ME, BUT I'M AFRAID I CAN'T TELL YOU MUCH ABOUT HIM! IN FACT, I HARDLY PAID ANY ATTENTION TO HIM! I REMEMBER AT THE TIME I WAS VERY ABSORBED...
...IN A CERTAIN PROPERTY OF EPSILON RADIATION-- E-RAYS! I DISCOVERED THAT THE E-RAYS HAD AN ODD EFFECT ON MY LABORATORY ANIMALS! I WAS TESTING THE BEHAVIOR OF MICE THEN...
THE BEHAVIOR OF MICE? TELL ME ABOUT IT, DR. GROVER!
"WELL, I FOUND THAT BY BATHING THE RODENTS IN NEGATIVE E-RAYS I COULD REVERSE THEIR NORMAL BEHAVIOR!"
UNDER THE NEGATIVE E-RAYS, THE STARVED MICE NEVER GO INTO THE PATH THAT LEADS TO THEIR FOOD! THEY ALWAYS TAKE THE WRONG PATH!
BUT I NEVER FOUND ANY REAL USE FOR MY DISCOVERY AND I PUT IT ASIDE! BUT, BATMAN-- WHY ARE YOU LOOKING AT ME LIKE THAT!?
TELL ME ONE THING, DR. GROVER...
IS IT POSSIBLE THAT THE RADIATION COULD HAVE A SIMILAR EFFECT ON HUMAN BEINGS--?
THE THOUGHT NEVER OCCURRED TO ME! I SUPPOSE IT MIGHT-- IF THE E-RAYS WERE STRONG ENOUGH! BUT WHAT AN OUTLANDISH IDEA!
8

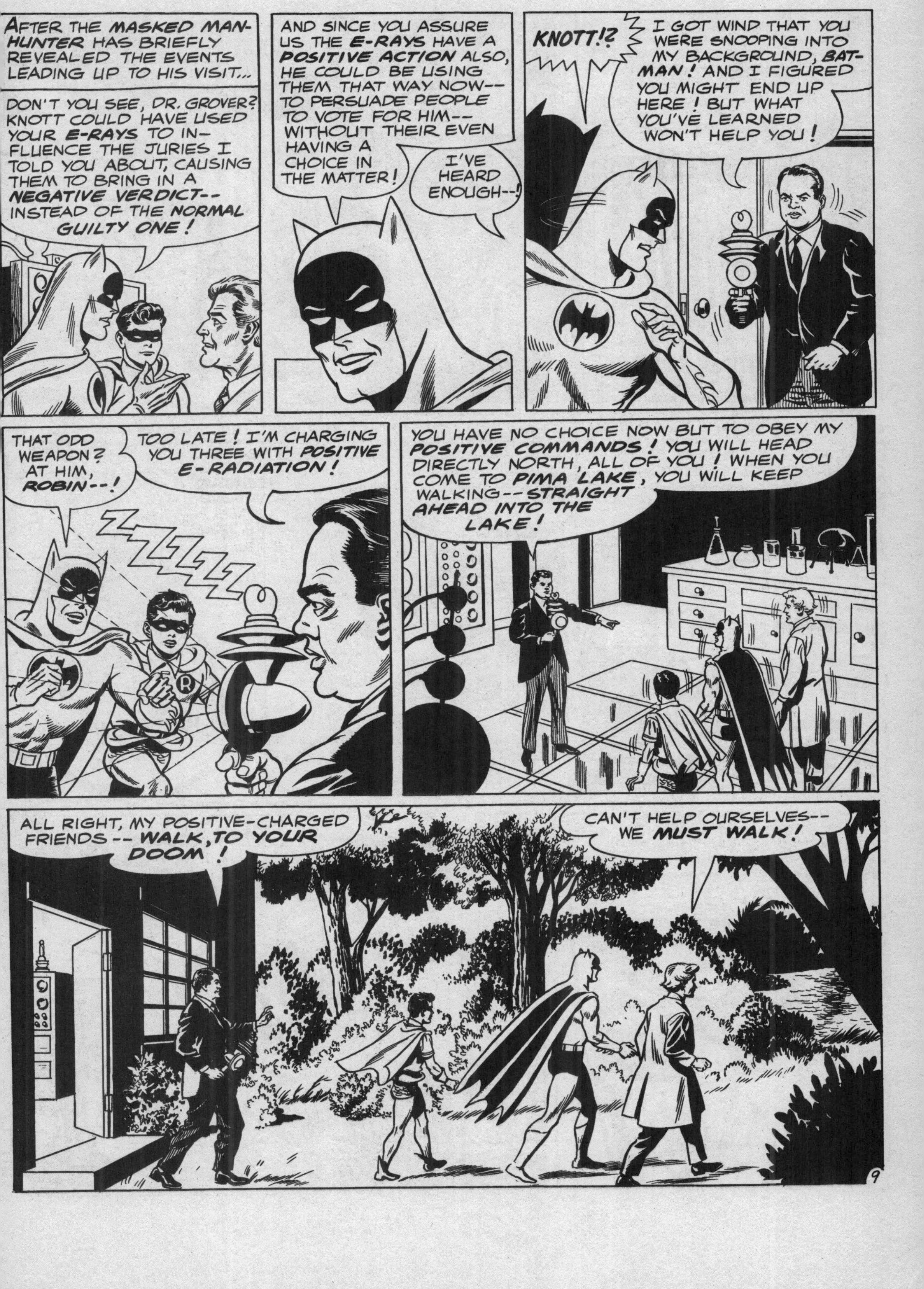
AFTER THE MASKED MAN-HUNTER HAS BRIEFLY REVEALED THE EVENTS LEADING UP TO HIS VISIT...
DON'T YOU SEE, DR. GROVER? KNOTT COULD HAVE USED YOUR E-RAYS TO INFLUENCE THE JURIES I TOLD YOU ABOUT, CAUSING THEM TO BRING IN A NEGATIVE VERDICT--INSTEAD OF THE NORMAL GUILTY ONE!
AND SINCE YOU ASSURE US THE E-RAYS HAVE A POSITIVE ACTION ALSO, HE COULD BE USING THEM THAT WAY NOW--TO PERSUADE PEOPLE TO VOTE FOR HIM--WITHOUT THEIR EVEN HAVING A CHOICE IN THE MATTER!
I'VE HEARD ENOUGH--!
KNOTT!?
I GOT WIND THAT YOU WERE SNOOPING INTO MY BACKGROUND, BATMAN! AND I FIGURED YOU MIGHT END UP HERE! BUT WHAT YOU'VE LEARNED WON'T HELP YOU!
THAT ODD WEAPON? AT HIM, ROBIN--!
TOO LATE! I'M CHARGING YOU THREE WITH POSITIVE E-RADIATION!
YOU HAVE NO CHOICE NOW BUT TO OBEY MY POSITIVE COMMANDS! YOU WILL HEAD DIRECTLY NORTH, ALL OF YOU! WHEN YOU COME TO PIMA LAKE, YOU WILL KEEP WALKING--STRAIGHT AHEAD INTO THE LAKE!
ALL RIGHT, MY POSITIVE-CHARGED FRIENDS--WALK, TO YOUR DOOM!
CAN'T HELP OURSELVES--WE MUST WALK!
9

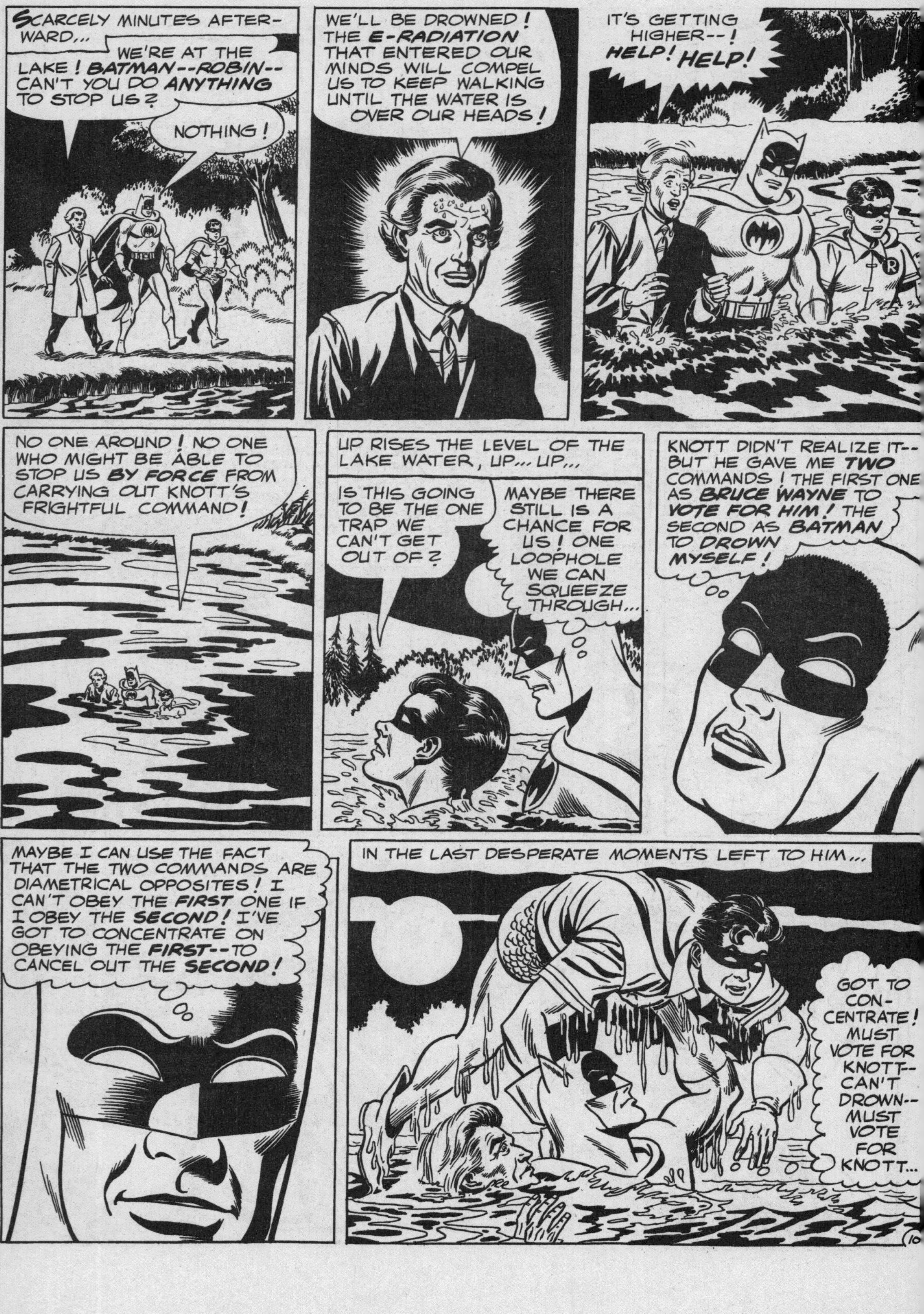
SCARCELY MINUTES AFTERWARD...
WE'RE AT THE LAKE! BATMAN--ROBIN--CAN'T YOU DO ANYTHING TO STOP US?
NOTHING!
WE'LL BE DROWNED! THE E-RADIATION THAT ENTERED OUR MINDS WILL COMPEL US TO KEEP WALKING UNTIL THE WATER IS OVER OUR HEADS!
IT'S GETTING HIGHER--! HELP! HELP!
NO ONE AROUND! NO ONE WHO MIGHT BE ABLE TO STOP US BY FORCE FROM CARRYING OUT KNOTT'S FRIGHTFUL COMMAND!
UP RISES THE LEVEL OF THE LAKE WATER, UP... UP...
IS THIS GOING TO BE THE ONE TRAP WE CAN'T GET OUT OF?
MAYBE THERE STILL IS A CHANCE FOR US! ONE LOOPHOLE WE CAN SQUEEZE THROUGH...
KNOTT DIDN'T REALIZE IT--BUT HE GAVE ME TWO COMMANDS! THE FIRST ONE AS BRUCE WAYNE TO VOTE FOR HIM! THE SECOND AS BATMAN TO DROWN MYSELF!
MAYBE I CAN USE THE FACT THAT THE TWO COMMANDS ARE DIAMETRICAL OPPOSITES! I CAN'T OBEY THE FIRST ONE IF I OBEY THE SECOND! I'VE GOT TO CONCENTRATE ON OBEYING THE FIRST--TO CANCEL OUT THE SECOND!
IN THE LAST DESPERATE MOMENTS LEFT TO HIM...
GOT TO CONCENTRATE! MUST VOTE FOR KNOTT--CAN'T DROWN--MUST VOTE FOR KNOTT...
10

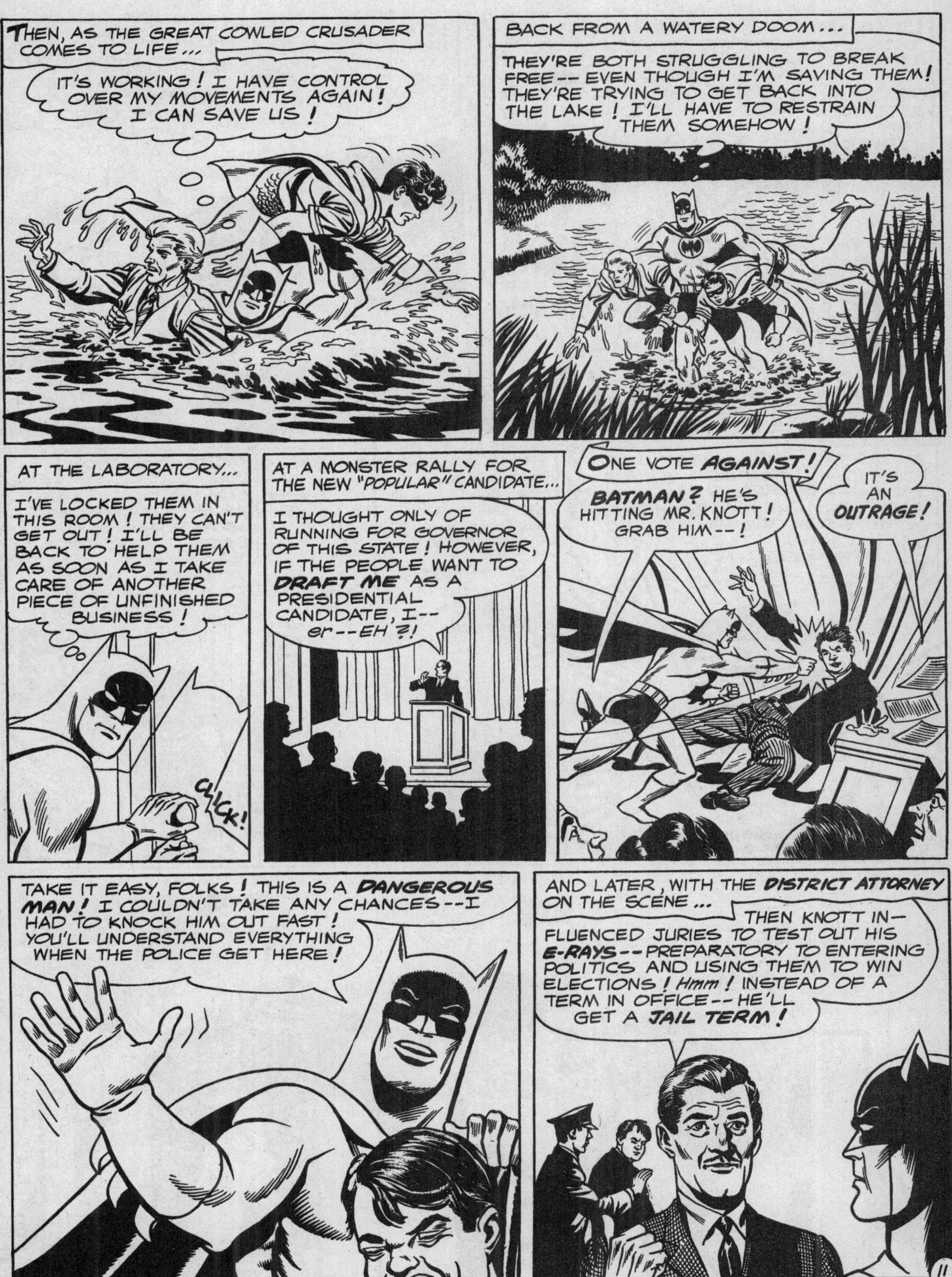
THEN, AS THE GREAT COWLED CRUSADER COMES TO LIFE...
IT'S WORKING! I HAVE CONTROL OVER MY MOVEMENTS AGAIN! I CAN SAVE US!
BACK FROM A WATERY DOOM...
THEY'RE BOTH STRUGGLING TO BREAK FREE-- EVEN THOUGH I'M SAVING THEM! THEY'RE TRYING TO GET BACK INTO THE LAKE! I'LL HAVE TO RESTRAIN THEM SOMEHOW!
AT THE LABORATORY...
I'VE LOCKED THEM IN THIS ROOM! THEY CAN'T GET OUT! I'LL BE BACK TO HELP THEM AS SOON AS I TAKE CARE OF ANOTHER PIECE OF UNFINISHED BUSINESS!
CLICK!
AT A MONSTER RALLY FOR THE NEW "POPULAR" CANDIDATE...
I THOUGHT ONLY OF RUNNING FOR GOVERNOR OF THIS STATE! HOWEVER, IF THE PEOPLE WANT TO DRAFT ME AS A PRESIDENTIAL CANDIDATE, I-- er--EH?!
ONE VOTE AGAINST!
BATMAN? HE'S HITTING MR. KNOTT! GRAB HIM--!
IT'S AN OUTRAGE!
TAKE IT EASY, FOLKS! THIS IS A DANGEROUS MAN! I COULDN'T TAKE ANY CHANCES--I HAD TO KNOCK HIM OUT FAST! YOU'LL UNDERSTAND EVERYTHING WHEN THE POLICE GET HERE!
AND LATER, WITH THE DISTRICT ATTORNEY ON THE SCENE...
THEN KNOTT INFLUENCED JURIES TO TEST OUT HIS E-RAYS--PREPARATORY TO ENTERING POLITICS AND USING THEM TO WIN ELECTIONS! Hmm! INSTEAD OF A TERM IN OFFICE--HE'LL GET A JAIL TERM!
11

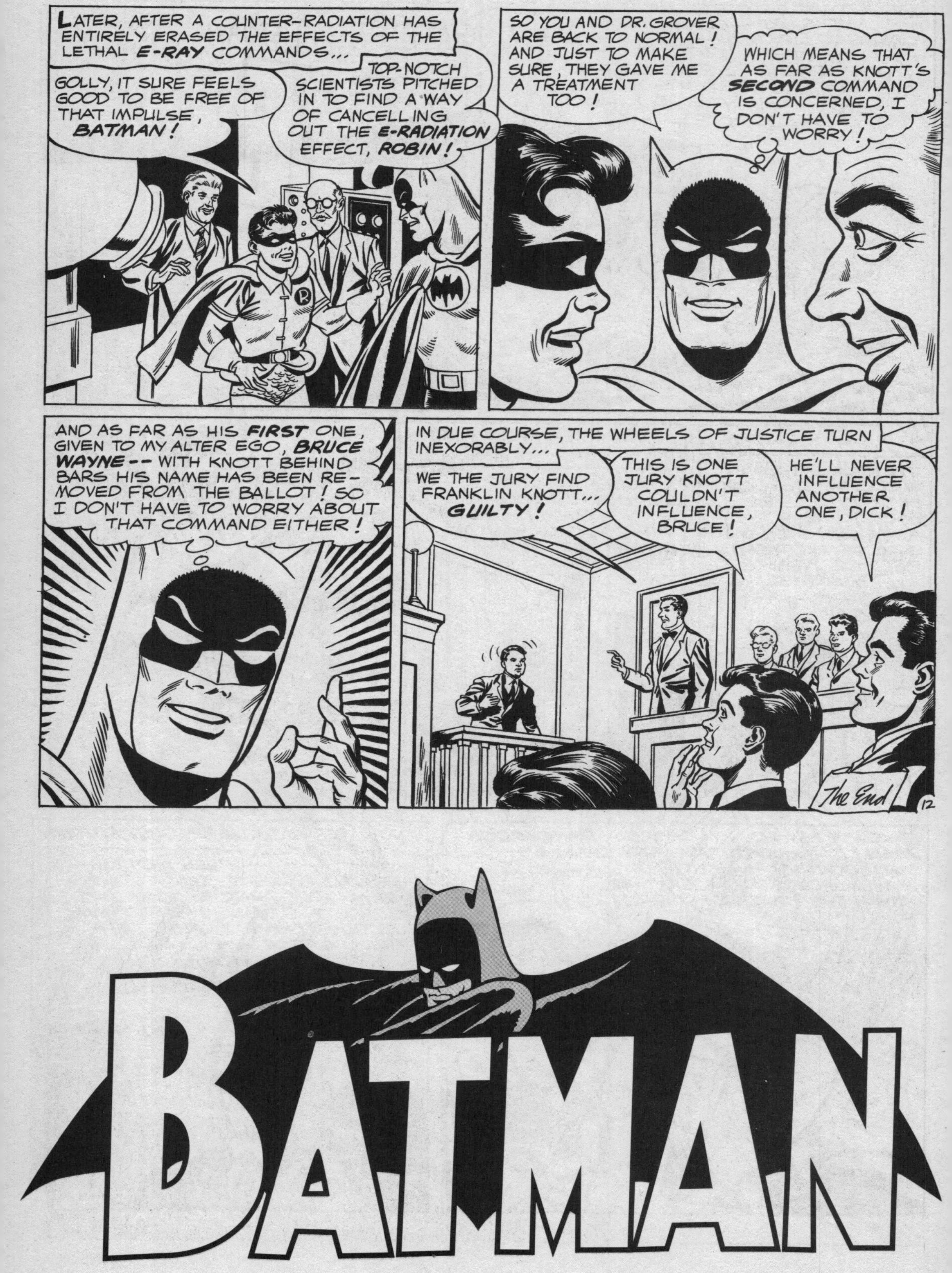
LATER, AFTER A COUNTER-RADIATION HAS ENTIRELY ERASED THE EFFECTS OF THE LETHAL E-RAY COMMANDS...
GOLLY, IT SURE FEELS GOOD TO BE FREE OF THAT IMPULSE, BATMAN!
TOP-NOTCH SCIENTISTS PITCHED IN TO FIND A WAY OF CANCELLING OUT THE E-RADIATION EFFECT, ROBIN!
SO YOU AND DR. GROVER ARE BACK TO NORMAL! AND JUST TO MAKE SURE, THEY GAVE ME A TREATMENT TOO!
WHICH MEANS THAT AS FAR AS KNOTT'S SECOND COMMAND IS CONCERNED, I DON'T HAVE TO WORRY!
AND AS FAR AS HIS FIRST ONE, GIVEN TO MY ALTER EGO, BRUCE WAYNE -- WITH KNOTT BEHIND BARS HIS NAME HAS BEEN REMOVED FROM THE BALLOT! SO I DON'T HAVE TO WORRY ABOUT THAT COMMAND EITHER!
IN DUE COURSE, THE WHEELS OF JUSTICE TURN INEXORABLY...
WE THE JURY FIND FRANKLIN KNOTT... GUILTY!
THIS IS ONE JURY KNOTT COULDN'T INFLUENCE, BRUCE!
HE'LL NEVER INFLUENCE ANOTHER ONE, DICK!
The End
12

BATMAN

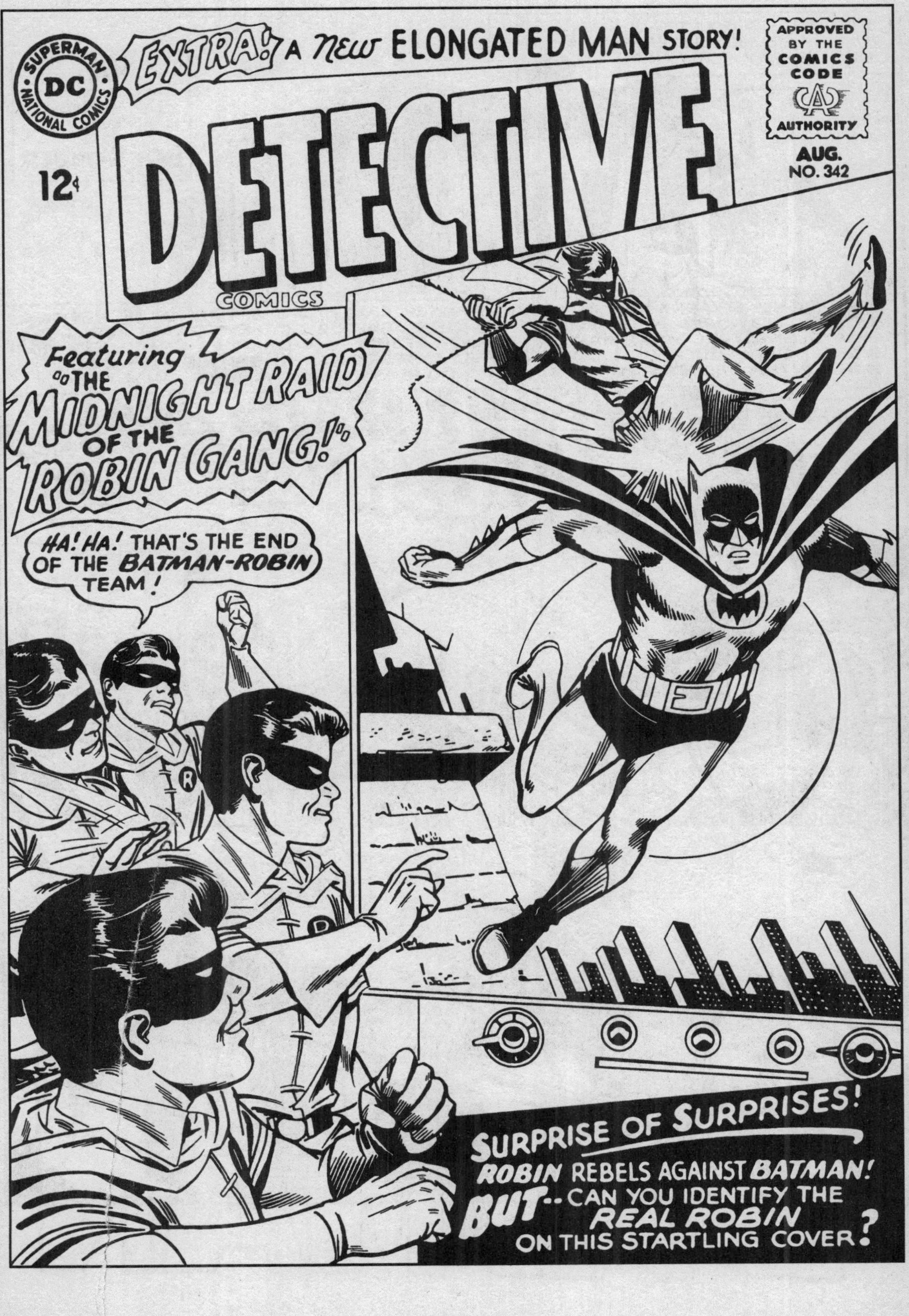
EXTRA! A NEW ELONGATED MAN STORY!
SUPERMAN DC NATIONAL COMICS
APPROVED BY THE COMICS CODE AUTHORITY
12¢
DETECTIVE COMICS
AUG. NO. 342
Featuring "THE MIDNIGHT RAID OF THE ROBIN GANG!"
HA! HA! THAT'S THE END OF THE BATMAN-ROBIN TEAM!
SURPRISE OF SURPRISES!
ROBIN REBELS AGAINST BATMAN!
BUT.. CAN YOU IDENTIFY THE REAL ROBIN ON THIS STARTLING COVER?

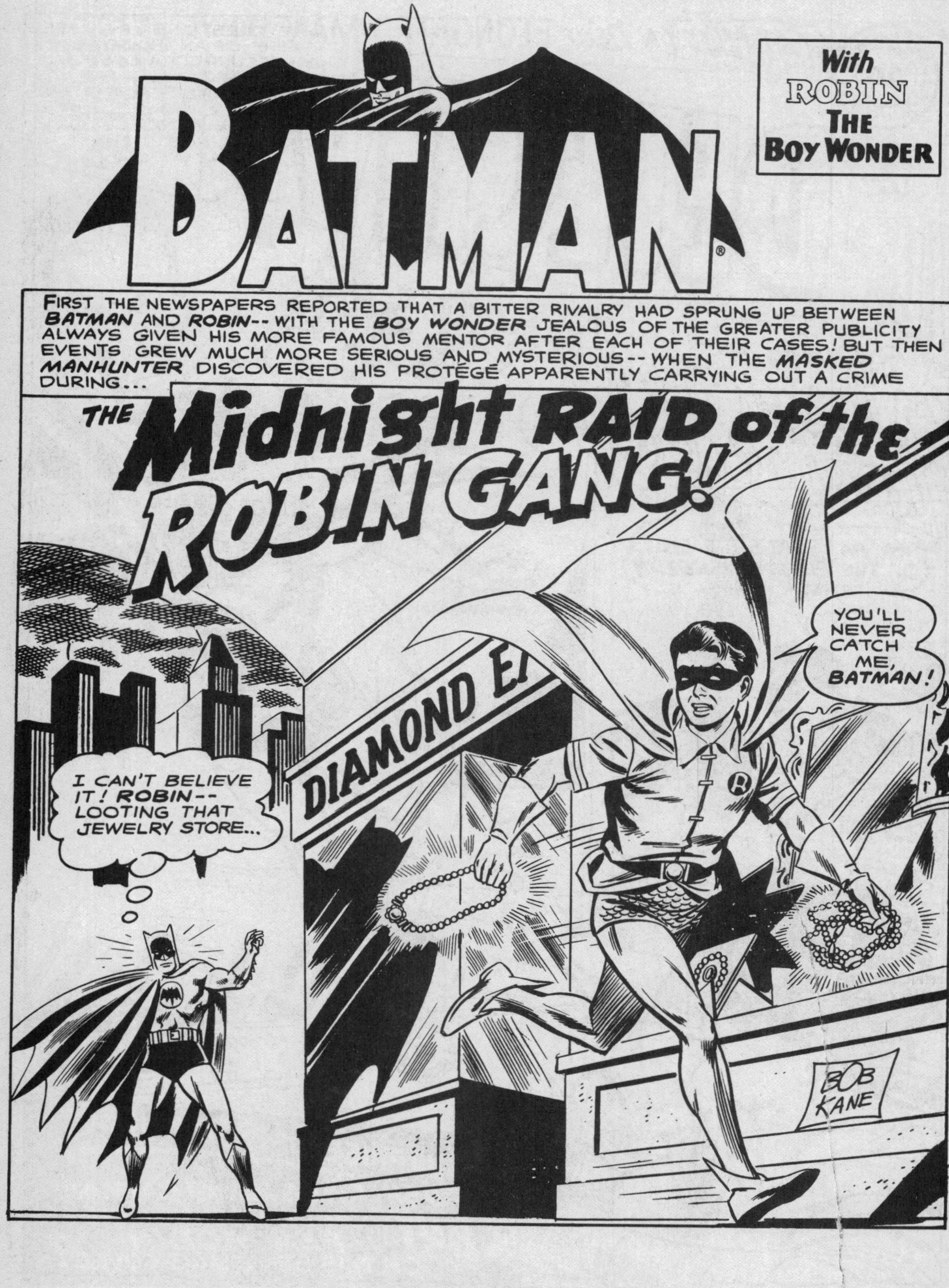

With ROBIN THE BOY WONDER
BATMAN®
FIRST THE NEWSPAPERS REPORTED THAT A BITTER RIVALRY HAD SPRUNG UP BETWEEN BATMAN AND ROBIN-- WITH THE BOY WONDER JEALOUS OF THE GREATER PUBLICITY ALWAYS GIVEN HIS MORE FAMOUS MENTOR AFTER EACH OF THEIR CASES! BUT THEN EVENTS GREW MUCH MORE SERIOUS AND MYSTERIOUS-- WHEN THE MASKED MANHUNTER DISCOVERED HIS PROTÉGÉ APPARENTLY CARRYING OUT A CRIME DURING...
THE Midnight RAID of the ROBIN GANG!
YOU'LL NEVER CATCH ME, BATMAN!
I CAN'T BELIEVE IT! ROBIN-- LOOTING THAT JEWELRY STORE...
DIAMOND E
BOB KANE

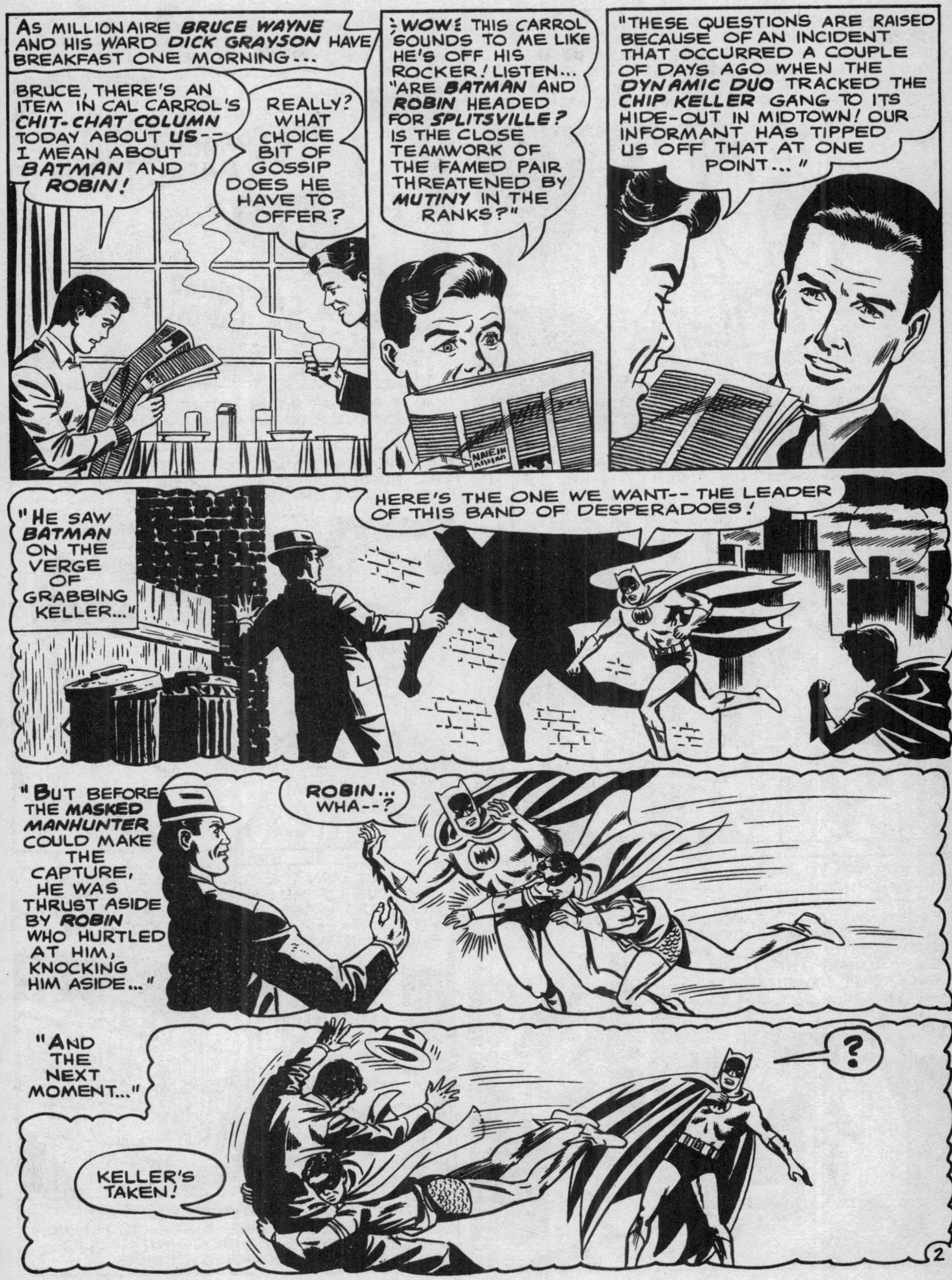
AS MILLIONAIRE BRUCE WAYNE AND HIS WARD DICK GRAYSON HAVE BREAKFAST ONE MORNING...
BRUCE, THERE'S AN ITEM IN CAL CARROL'S CHIT-CHAT COLUMN TODAY ABOUT US-- I MEAN ABOUT BATMAN AND ROBIN!
REALLY? WHAT CHOICE BIT OF GOSSIP DOES HE HAVE TO OFFER?
WOW! THIS CARROL SOUNDS TO ME LIKE HE'S OFF HIS ROCKER! LISTEN... "ARE BATMAN AND ROBIN HEADED FOR SPLITSVILLE? IS THE CLOSE TEAMWORK OF THE FAMED PAIR THREATENED BY MUTINY IN THE RANKS?"
"THESE QUESTIONS ARE RAISED BECAUSE OF AN INCIDENT THAT OCCURRED A COUPLE OF DAYS AGO WHEN THE DYNAMIC DUO TRACKED THE CHIP KELLER GANG TO ITS HIDE-OUT IN MIDTOWN! OUR INFORMANT HAS TIPPED US OFF THAT AT ONE POINT..."
"HE SAW BATMAN ON THE VERGE OF GRABBING KELLER..."
HERE'S THE ONE WE WANT-- THE LEADER OF THIS BAND OF DESPERADOES!
"BUT BEFORE THE MASKED MANHUNTER COULD MAKE THE CAPTURE, HE WAS THRUST ASIDE BY ROBIN WHO HURTLED AT HIM, KNOCKING HIM ASIDE..."
ROBIN... WHA--?
"AND THE NEXT MOMENT..."
?
KELLER'S TAKEN!
2

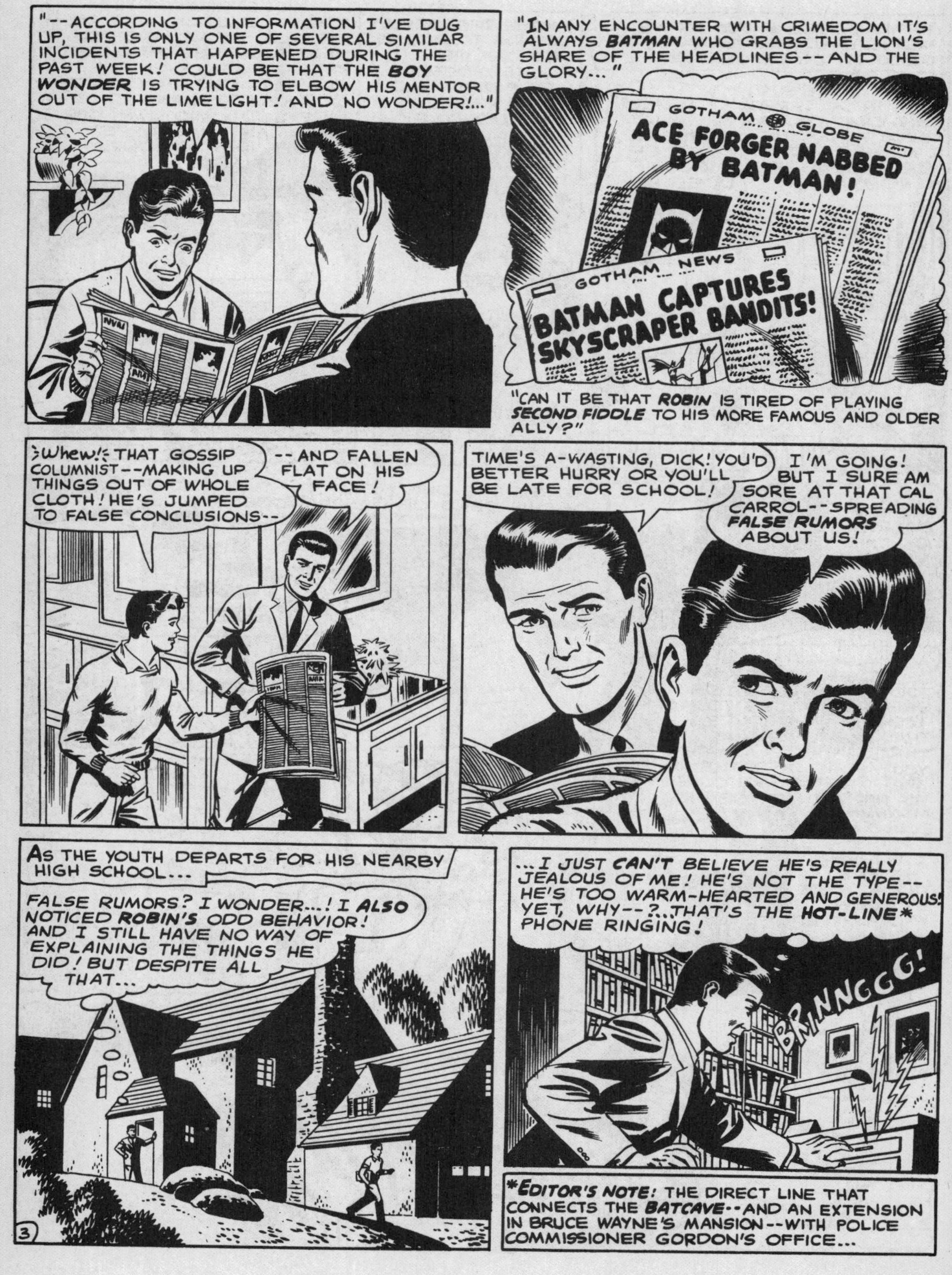
"--ACCORDING TO INFORMATION I'VE DUG UP, THIS IS ONLY ONE OF SEVERAL SIMILAR INCIDENTS THAT HAPPENED DURING THE PAST WEEK! COULD BE THAT THE BOY WONDER IS TRYING TO ELBOW HIS MENTOR OUT OF THE LIMELIGHT! AND NO WONDER!..."
"IN ANY ENCOUNTER WITH CRIMEDOM IT'S ALWAYS BATMAN WHO GRABS THE LION'S SHARE OF THE HEADLINES--AND THE GLORY..."
GOTHAM GLOBE
ACE FORGER NABBED BY BATMAN!
GOTHAM NEWS
BATMAN CAPTURES SKYSCRAPER BANDITS!
"CAN IT BE THAT ROBIN IS TIRED OF PLAYING SECOND FIDDLE TO HIS MORE FAMOUS AND OLDER ALLY?"
Whew! THAT GOSSIP COLUMNIST--MAKING UP THINGS OUT OF WHOLE CLOTH! HE'S JUMPED TO FALSE CONCLUSIONS--
--AND FALLEN FLAT ON HIS FACE!
TIME'S A-WASTING, DICK! YOU'D BETTER HURRY OR YOU'LL BE LATE FOR SCHOOL!
I'M GOING! BUT I SURE AM SORE AT THAT CAL CARROL--SPREADING FALSE RUMORS ABOUT US!
AS THE YOUTH DEPARTS FOR HIS NEARBY HIGH SCHOOL...
FALSE RUMORS? I WONDER...! I ALSO NOTICED ROBIN'S ODD BEHAVIOR! AND I STILL HAVE NO WAY OF EXPLAINING THE THINGS HE DID! BUT DESPITE ALL THAT...
...I JUST CAN'T BELIEVE HE'S REALLY JEALOUS OF ME! HE'S NOT THE TYPE--HE'S TOO WARM-HEARTED AND GENEROUS! YET, WHY--?..THAT'S THE HOT-LINE* PHONE RINGING!
BRRNNGGG!
*EDITOR'S NOTE: THE DIRECT LINE THAT CONNECTS THE BATCAVE--AND AN EXTENSION IN BRUCE WAYNE'S MANSION--WITH POLICE COMMISSIONER GORDON'S OFFICE...
3

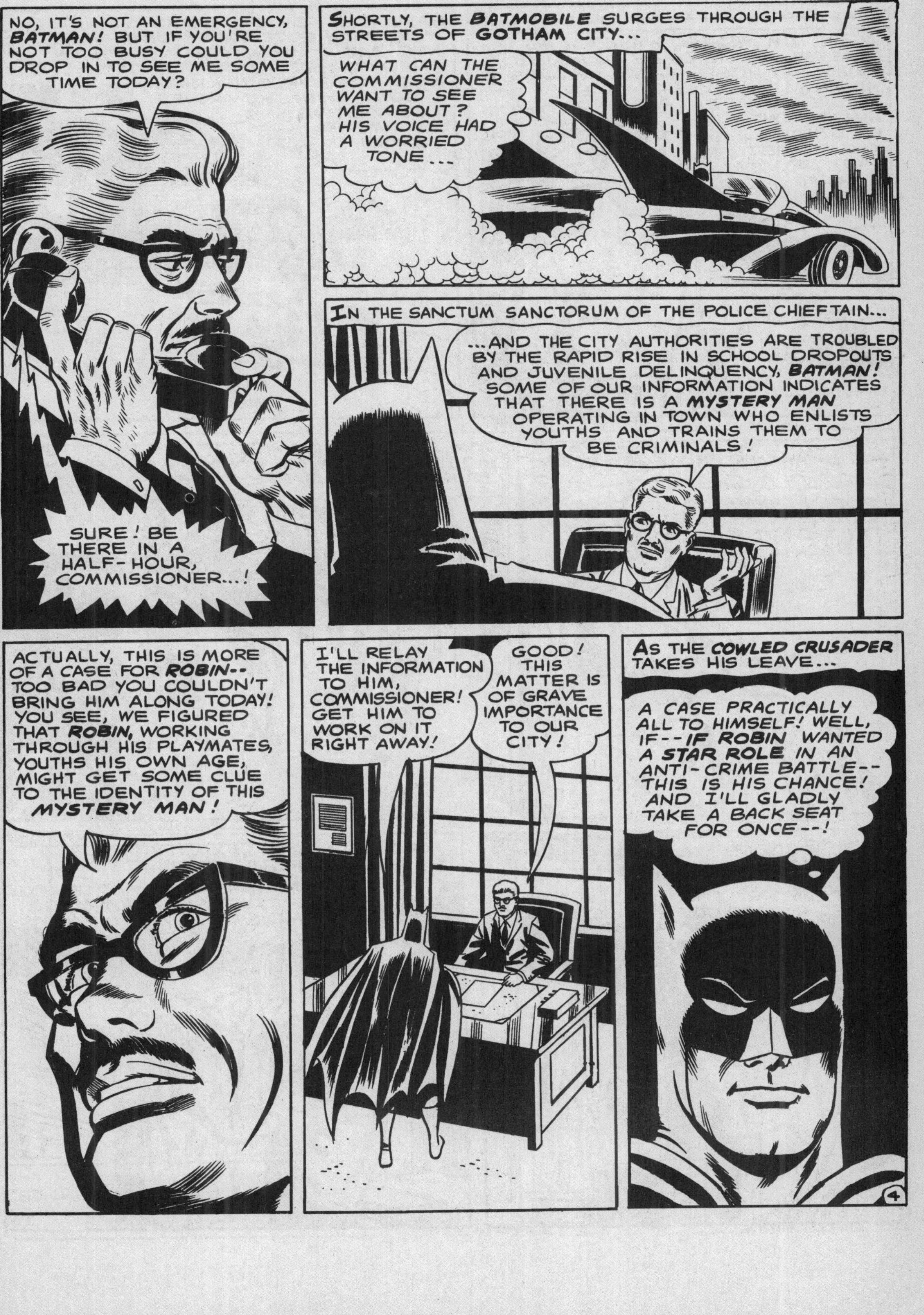
NO, IT'S NOT AN EMERGENCY, BATMAN! BUT IF YOU'RE NOT TOO BUSY COULD YOU DROP IN TO SEE ME SOME TIME TODAY?
SURE! BE THERE IN A HALF-HOUR, COMMISSIONER...!
SHORTLY, THE BATMOBILE SURGES THROUGH THE STREETS OF GOTHAM CITY...
WHAT CAN THE COMMISSIONER WANT TO SEE ME ABOUT? HIS VOICE HAD A WORRIED TONE...
IN THE SANCTUM SANCTORUM OF THE POLICE CHIEFTAIN...
...AND THE CITY AUTHORITIES ARE TROUBLED BY THE RAPID RISE IN SCHOOL DROPOUTS AND JUVENILE DELINQUENCY, BATMAN! SOME OF OUR INFORMATION INDICATES THAT THERE IS A MYSTERY MAN OPERATING IN TOWN WHO ENLISTS YOUTHS AND TRAINS THEM TO BE CRIMINALS!
ACTUALLY, THIS IS MORE OF A CASE FOR ROBIN-- TOO BAD YOU COULDN'T BRING HIM ALONG TODAY! YOU SEE, WE FIGURED THAT ROBIN, WORKING THROUGH HIS PLAYMATES, YOUTHS HIS OWN AGE, MIGHT GET SOME CLUE TO THE IDENTITY OF THIS MYSTERY MAN!
I'LL RELAY THE INFORMATION TO HIM, COMMISSIONER! GET HIM TO WORK ON IT RIGHT AWAY!
GOOD! THIS MATTER IS OF GRAVE IMPORTANCE TO OUR CITY!
AS THE COWLED CRUSADER TAKES HIS LEAVE...
A CASE PRACTICALLY ALL TO HIMSELF! WELL, IF--IF ROBIN WANTED A STAR ROLE IN AN ANTI-CRIME BATTLE-- THIS IS HIS CHANCE! AND I'LL GLADLY TAKE A BACK SEAT FOR ONCE--!
4

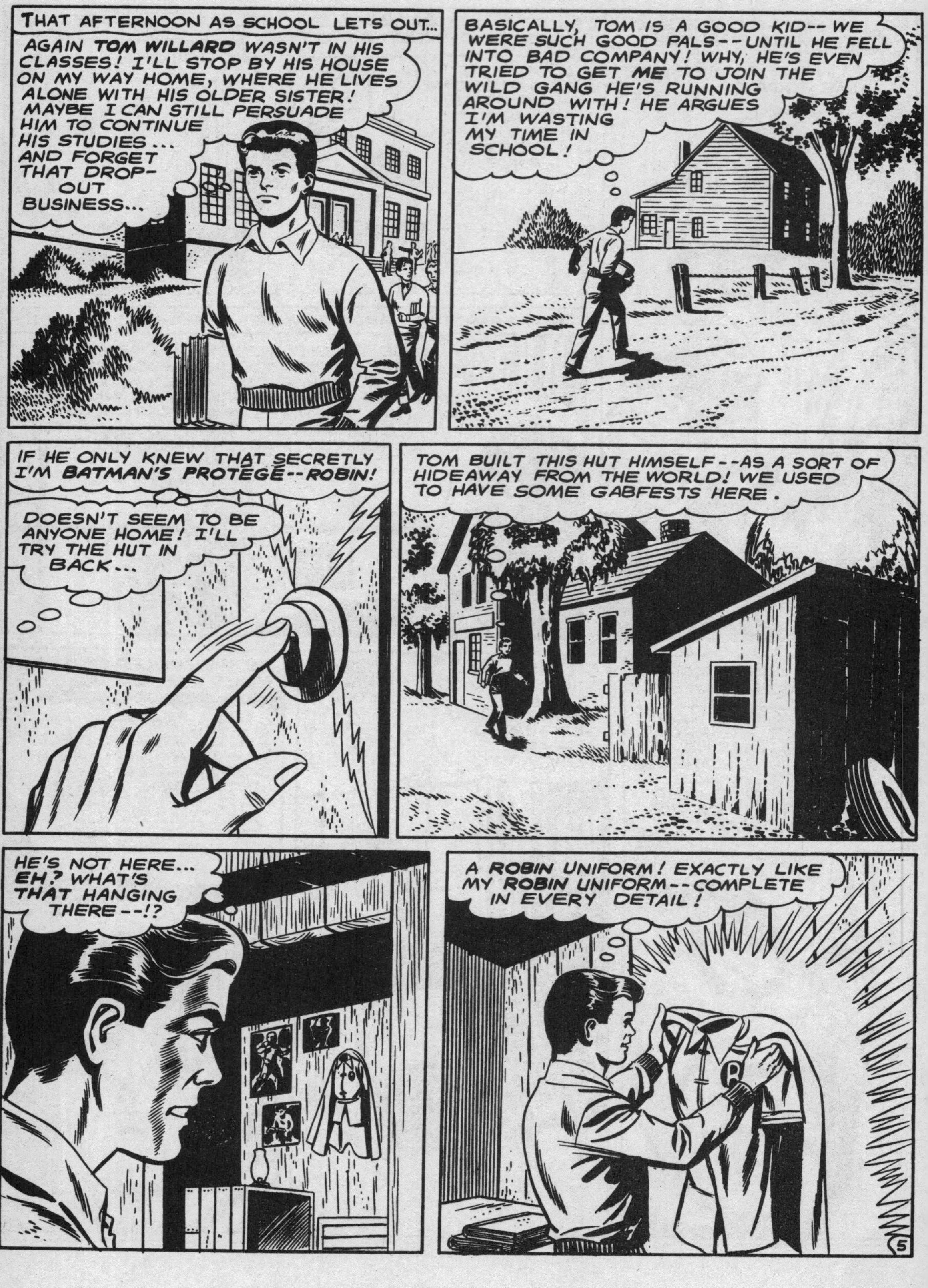
THAT AFTERNOON AS SCHOOL LETS OUT...
AGAIN TOM WILLARD WASN'T IN HIS CLASSES! I'LL STOP BY HIS HOUSE ON MY WAY HOME, WHERE HE LIVES ALONE WITH HIS OLDER SISTER! MAYBE I CAN STILL PERSUADE HIM TO CONTINUE HIS STUDIES... AND FORGET THAT DROP-OUT BUSINESS...
BASICALLY, TOM IS A GOOD KID-- WE WERE SUCH GOOD PALS--UNTIL HE FELL INTO BAD COMPANY! WHY, HE'S EVEN TRIED TO GET ME TO JOIN THE WILD GANG HE'S RUNNING AROUND WITH! HE ARGUES I'M WASTING MY TIME IN SCHOOL!
IF HE ONLY KNEW THAT SECRETLY I'M BATMAN'S PROTÉGÉ--ROBIN!
DOESN'T SEEM TO BE ANYONE HOME! I'LL TRY THE HUT IN BACK...
TOM BUILT THIS HUT HIMSELF--AS A SORT OF HIDEAWAY FROM THE WORLD! WE USED TO HAVE SOME GABFESTS HERE.
HE'S NOT HERE... EH? WHAT'S THAT HANGING THERE--!?
A ROBIN UNIFORM! EXACTLY LIKE MY ROBIN UNIFORM--COMPLETE IN EVERY DETAIL!
5

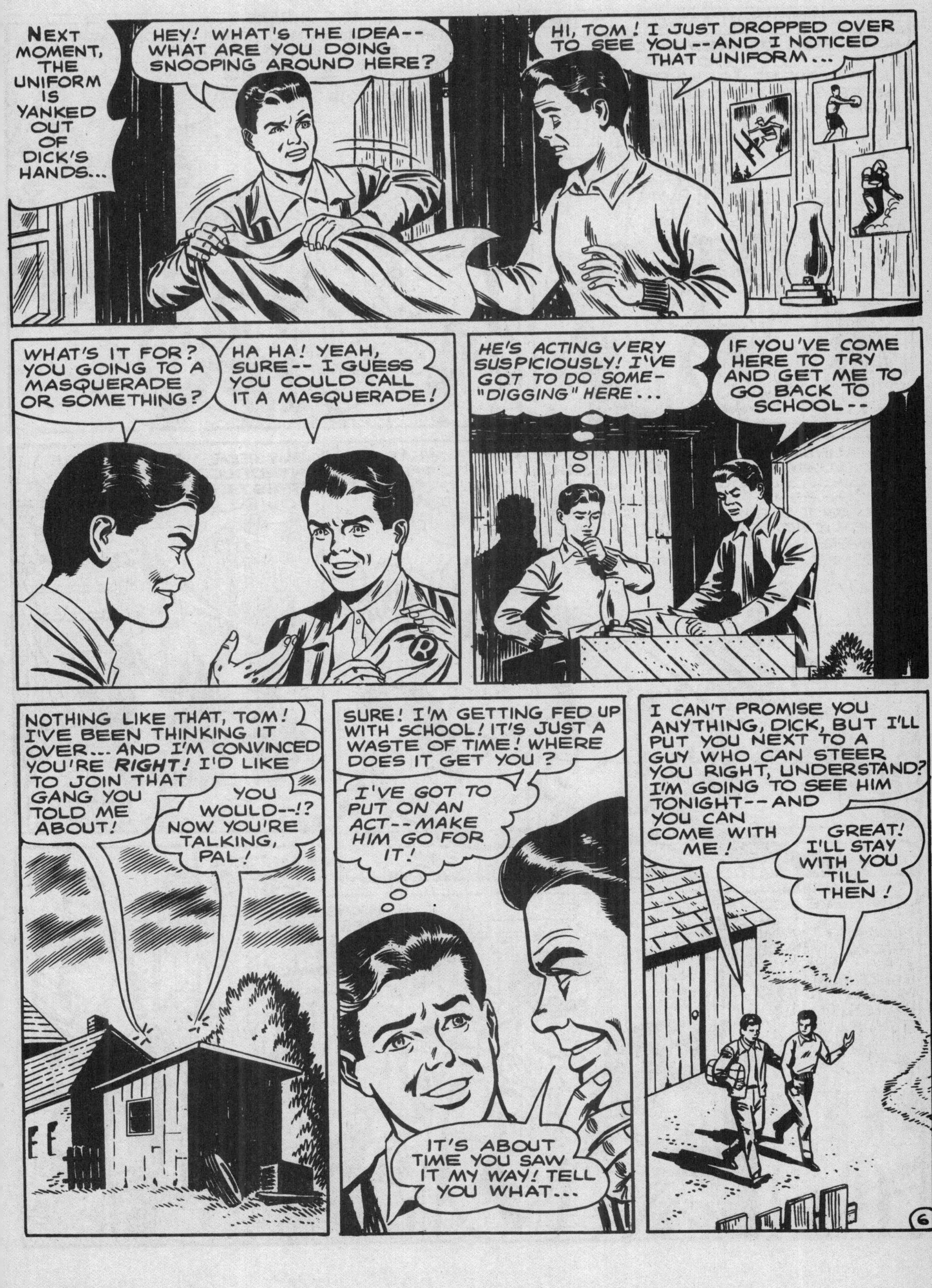
NEXT MOMENT, THE UNIFORM IS YANKED OUT OF DICK'S HANDS...
HEY! WHAT'S THE IDEA-- WHAT ARE YOU DOING SNOOPING AROUND HERE?
HI, TOM! I JUST DROPPED OVER TO SEE YOU--AND I NOTICED THAT UNIFORM...
WHAT'S IT FOR? YOU GOING TO A MASQUERADE OR SOMETHING?
HA HA! YEAH, SURE-- I GUESS YOU COULD CALL IT A MASQUERADE!
HE'S ACTING VERY SUSPICIOUSLY! I'VE GOT TO DO SOME-"DIGGING" HERE...
IF YOU'VE COME HERE TO TRY AND GET ME TO GO BACK TO SCHOOL--
NOTHING LIKE THAT, TOM! I'VE BEEN THINKING IT OVER... AND I'M CONVINCED YOU'RE RIGHT! I'D LIKE TO JOIN THAT GANG YOU TOLD ME ABOUT!
YOU WOULD--!? NOW YOU'RE TALKING, PAL!
SURE! I'M GETTING FED UP WITH SCHOOL! IT'S JUST A WASTE OF TIME! WHERE DOES IT GET YOU?
I'VE GOT TO PUT ON AN ACT--MAKE HIM GO FOR IT!
IT'S ABOUT TIME YOU SAW IT MY WAY! TELL YOU WHAT...
I CAN'T PROMISE YOU ANYTHING, DICK, BUT I'LL PUT YOU NEXT TO A GUY WHO CAN STEER YOU RIGHT, UNDERSTAND? I'M GOING TO SEE HIM TONIGHT--AND YOU CAN COME WITH ME!
GREAT! I'LL STAY WITH YOU TILL THEN!
6

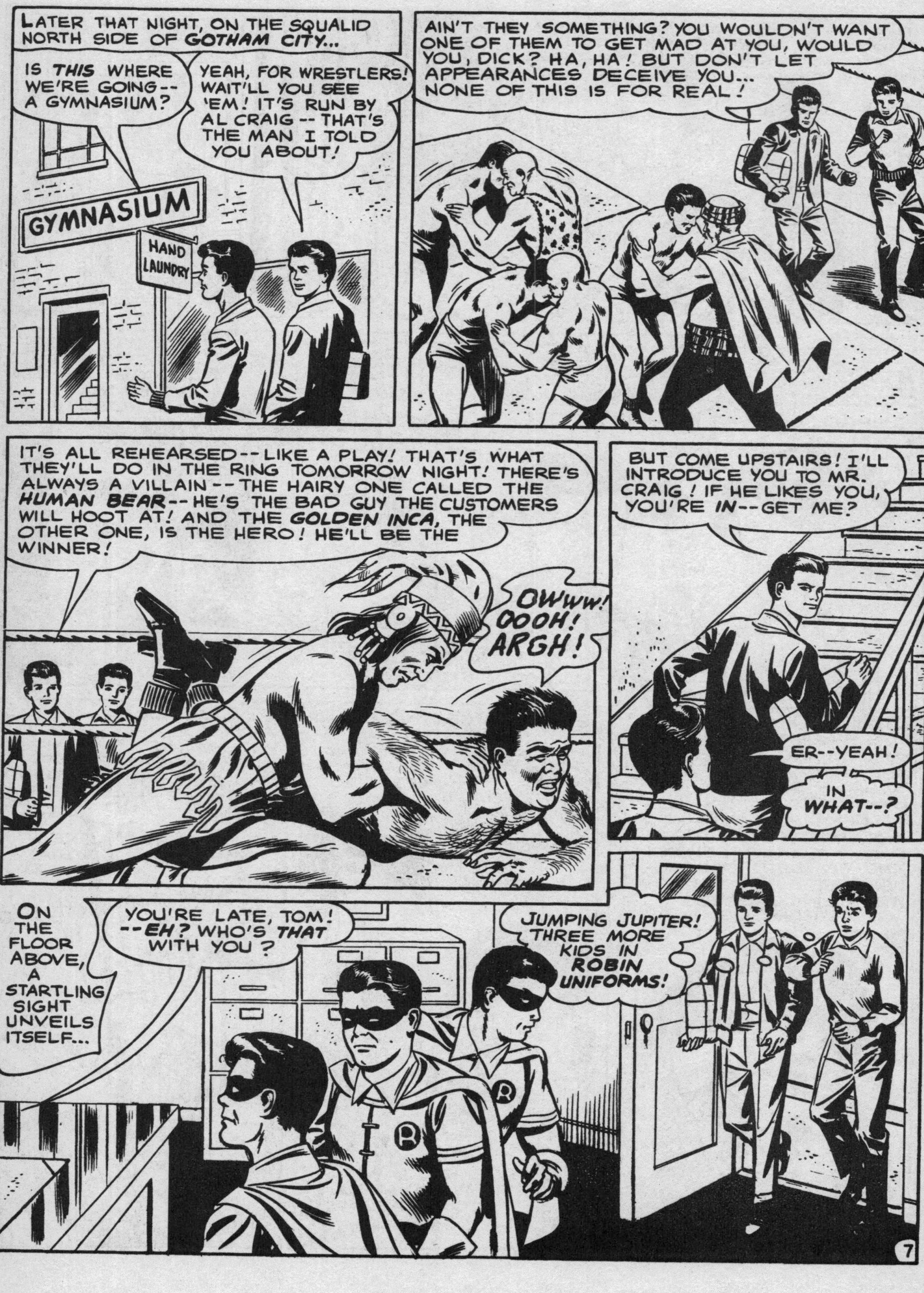
LATER THAT NIGHT, ON THE SQUALID NORTH SIDE OF GOTHAM CITY...
IS THIS WHERE WE'RE GOING-- A GYMNASIUM?
YEAH, FOR WRESTLERS! WAIT'LL YOU SEE 'EM! IT'S RUN BY AL CRAIG -- THAT'S THE MAN I TOLD YOU ABOUT!
GYMNASIUM
HAND LAUNDRY
AIN'T THEY SOMETHING? YOU WOULDN'T WANT ONE OF THEM TO GET MAD AT YOU, WOULD YOU, DICK? HA, HA! BUT DON'T LET APPEARANCES DECEIVE YOU... NONE OF THIS IS FOR REAL!
IT'S ALL REHEARSED--LIKE A PLAY! THAT'S WHAT THEY'LL DO IN THE RING TOMORROW NIGHT! THERE'S ALWAYS A VILLAIN -- THE HAIRY ONE CALLED THE HUMAN BEAR--HE'S THE BAD GUY THE CUSTOMERS WILL HOOT AT! AND THE GOLDEN INCA, THE OTHER ONE, IS THE HERO! HE'LL BE THE WINNER!
OWWW! OOOH! ARGH!
BUT COME UPSTAIRS! I'LL INTRODUCE YOU TO MR. CRAIG! IF HE LIKES YOU, YOU'RE IN--GET ME?
ER--YEAH!
IN WHAT--?
ON THE FLOOR ABOVE, A STARTLING SIGHT UNVEILS ITSELF...
YOU'RE LATE, TOM! --EH? WHO'S THAT WITH YOU?
JUMPING JUPITER! THREE MORE KIDS IN ROBIN UNIFORMS!
7

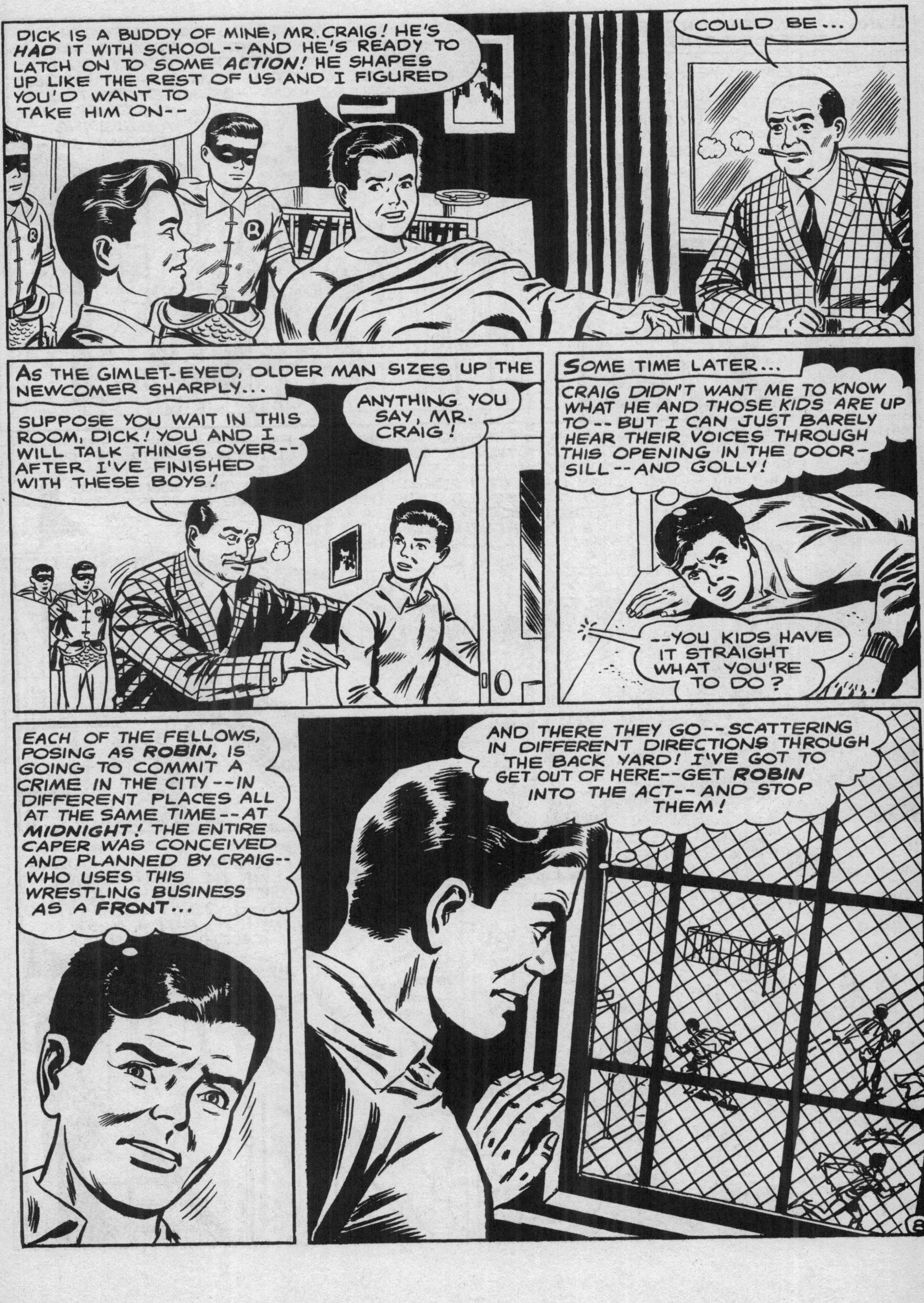
DICK IS A BUDDY OF MINE, MR. CRAIG! HE'S HAD IT WITH SCHOOL--AND HE'S READY TO LATCH ON TO SOME ACTION! HE SHAPES UP LIKE THE REST OF US AND I FIGURED YOU'D WANT TO TAKE HIM ON--
COULD BE...
AS THE GIMLET-EYED, OLDER MAN SIZES UP THE NEWCOMER SHARPLY...
SUPPOSE YOU WAIT IN THIS ROOM, DICK! YOU AND I WILL TALK THINGS OVER--AFTER I'VE FINISHED WITH THESE BOYS!
ANYTHING YOU SAY, MR. CRAIG!
SOME TIME LATER...
CRAIG DIDN'T WANT ME TO KNOW WHAT HE AND THOSE KIDS ARE UP TO--BUT I CAN JUST BARELY HEAR THEIR VOICES THROUGH THIS OPENING IN THE DOOR-SILL--AND GOLLY!
--YOU KIDS HAVE IT STRAIGHT WHAT YOU'RE TO DO?
EACH OF THE FELLOWS, POSING AS ROBIN, IS GOING TO COMMIT A CRIME IN THE CITY--IN DIFFERENT PLACES ALL AT THE SAME TIME--AT MIDNIGHT! THE ENTIRE CAPER WAS CONCEIVED AND PLANNED BY CRAIG--WHO USES THIS WRESTLING BUSINESS AS A FRONT...
AND THERE THEY GO--SCATTERING IN DIFFERENT DIRECTIONS THROUGH THE BACK YARD! I'VE GOT TO GET OUT OF HERE--GET ROBIN INTO THE ACT--AND STOP THEM!
8

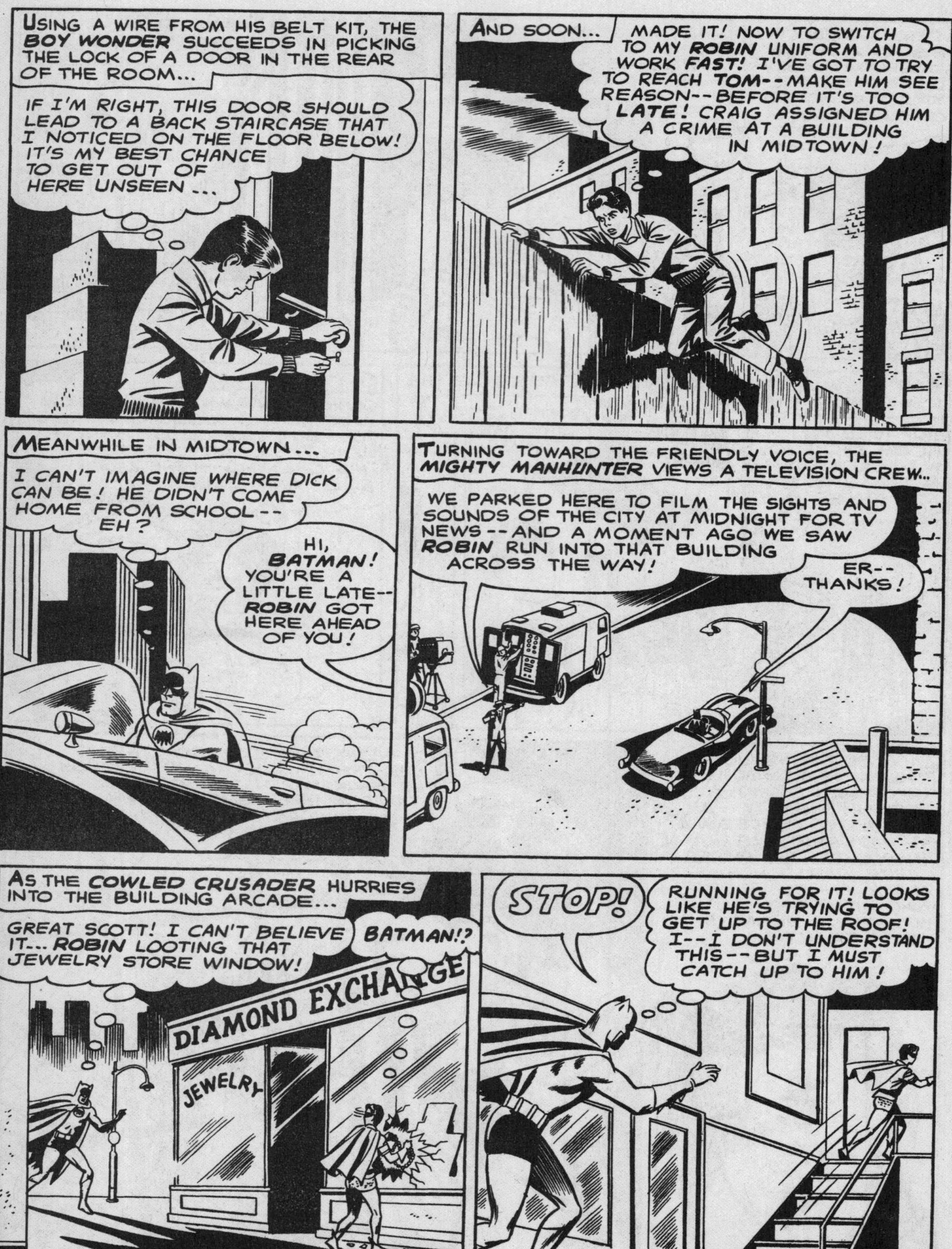
USING A WIRE FROM HIS BELT KIT, THE BOY WONDER SUCCEEDS IN PICKING THE LOCK OF A DOOR IN THE REAR OF THE ROOM...
IF I'M RIGHT, THIS DOOR SHOULD LEAD TO A BACK STAIRCASE THAT I NOTICED ON THE FLOOR BELOW! IT'S MY BEST CHANCE TO GET OUT OF HERE UNSEEN ...
AND SOON...
MADE IT! NOW TO SWITCH TO MY ROBIN UNIFORM AND WORK FAST! I'VE GOT TO TRY TO REACH TOM--MAKE HIM SEE REASON--BEFORE IT'S TOO LATE! CRAIG ASSIGNED HIM A CRIME AT A BUILDING IN MIDTOWN!
MEANWHILE IN MIDTOWN...
I CAN'T IMAGINE WHERE DICK CAN BE! HE DIDN'T COME HOME FROM SCHOOL-- EH?
HI, BATMAN! YOU'RE A LITTLE LATE-- ROBIN GOT HERE AHEAD OF YOU!
TURNING TOWARD THE FRIENDLY VOICE, THE MIGHTY MANHUNTER VIEWS A TELEVISION CREW...
WE PARKED HERE TO FILM THE SIGHTS AND SOUNDS OF THE CITY AT MIDNIGHT FOR TV NEWS--AND A MOMENT AGO WE SAW ROBIN RUN INTO THAT BUILDING ACROSS THE WAY!
ER-- THANKS!
AS THE COWLED CRUSADER HURRIES INTO THE BUILDING ARCADE...
GREAT SCOTT! I CAN'T BELIEVE IT... ROBIN LOOTING THAT JEWELRY STORE WINDOW!
BATMAN!?
DIAMOND EXCHANGE
JEWELRY
STOP!
RUNNING FOR IT! LOOKS LIKE HE'S TRYING TO GET UP TO THE ROOF! I--I DON'T UNDERSTAND THIS--BUT I MUST CATCH UP TO HIM!
9

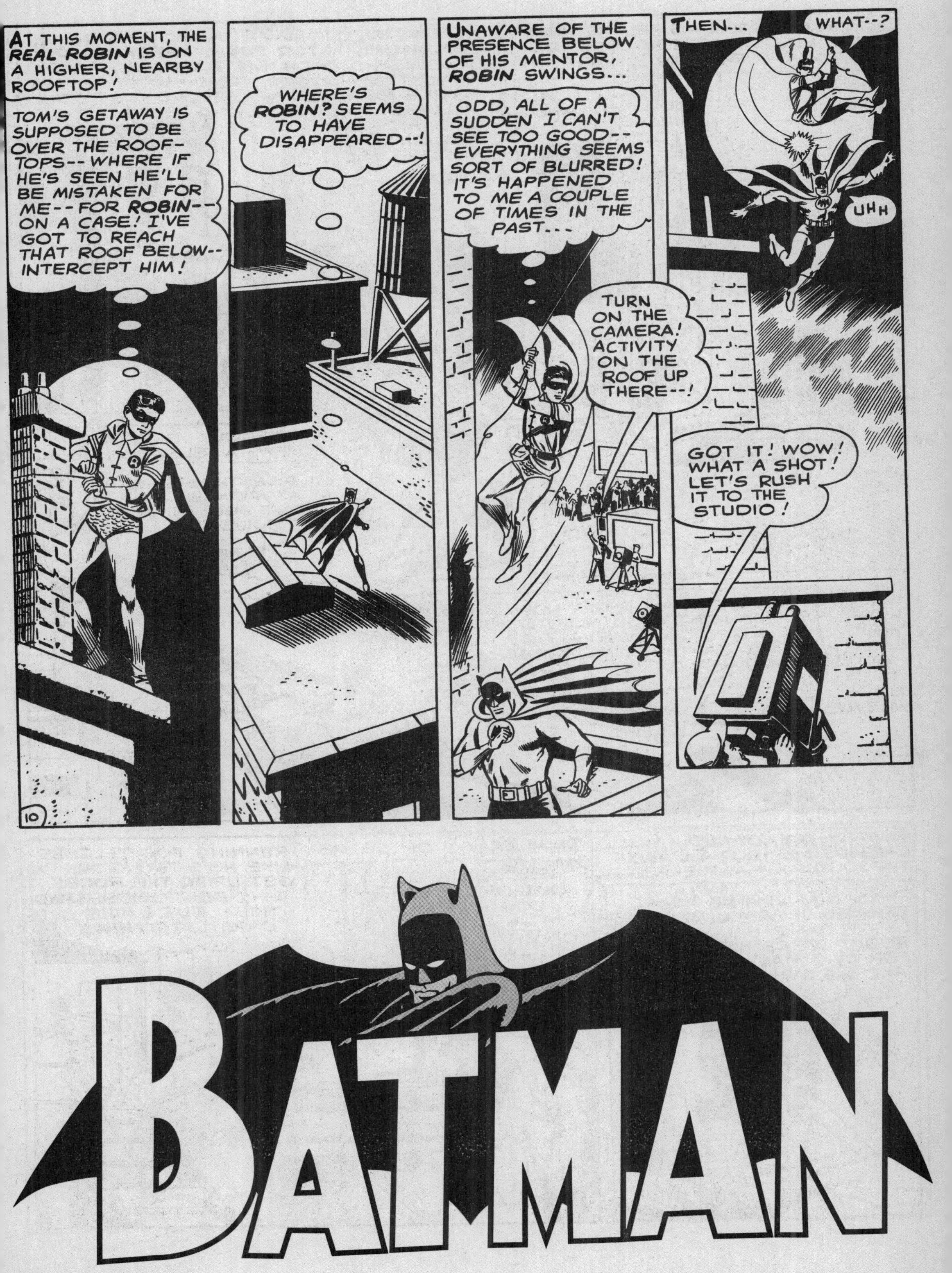
AT THIS MOMENT, THE REAL ROBIN IS ON A HIGHER, NEARBY ROOFTOP!
TOM'S GETAWAY IS SUPPOSED TO BE OVER THE ROOF-TOPS-- WHERE IF HE'S SEEN HE'LL BE MISTAKEN FOR ME-- FOR ROBIN-- ON A CASE! I'VE GOT TO REACH THAT ROOF BELOW-- INTERCEPT HIM!
10
WHERE'S ROBIN? SEEMS TO HAVE DISAPPEARED--!
UNAWARE OF THE PRESENCE BELOW OF HIS MENTOR, ROBIN SWINGS...
ODD, ALL OF A SUDDEN I CAN'T SEE TOO GOOD-- EVERYTHING SEEMS SORT OF BLURRED! IT'S HAPPENED TO ME A COUPLE OF TIMES IN THE PAST...
TURN ON THE CAMERA! ACTIVITY ON THE ROOF UP THERE--!
THEN...
WHAT--?
UHH
GOT IT! WOW! WHAT A SHOT! LET'S RUSH IT TO THE STUDIO!

BATMAN

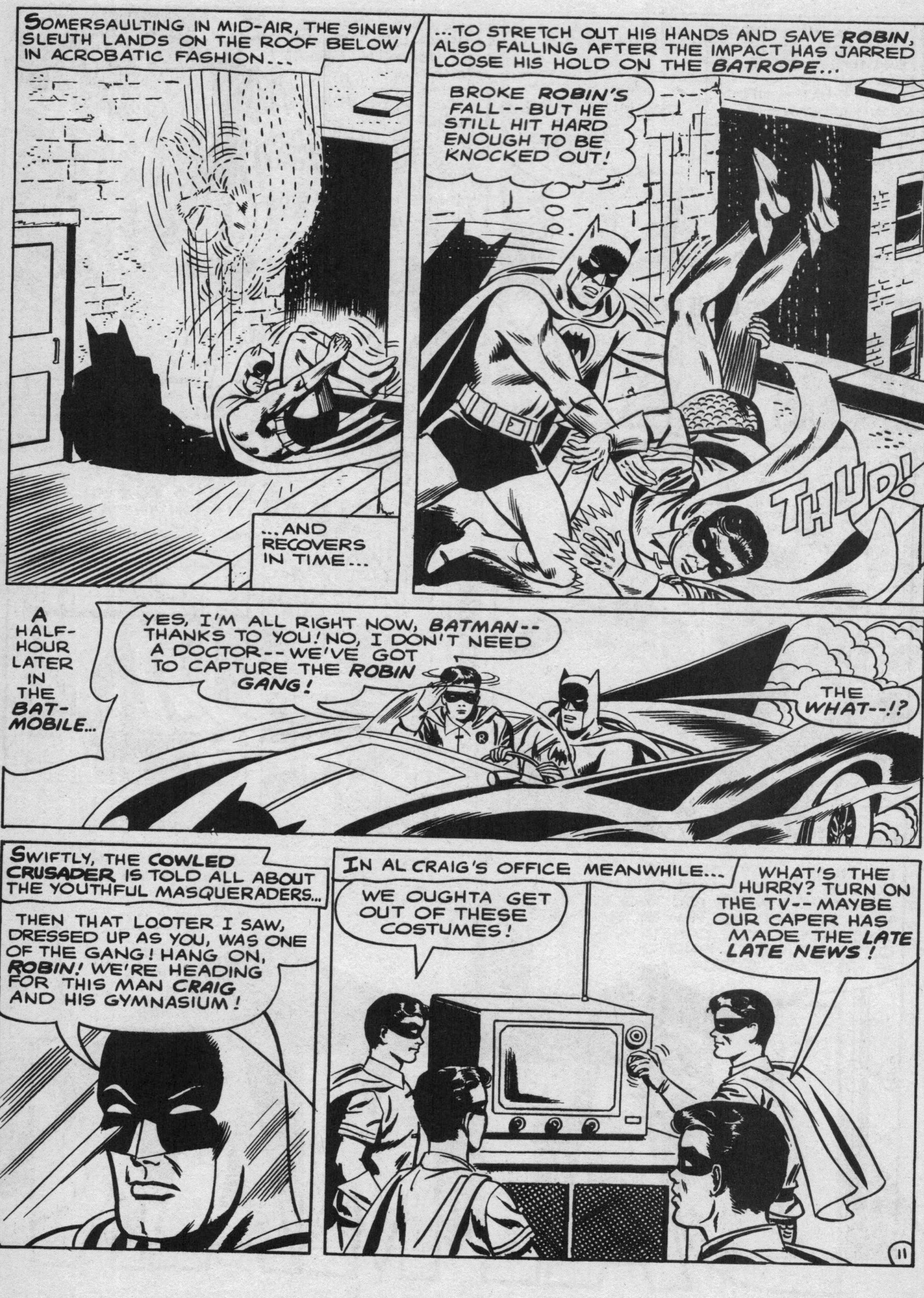
SOMERSAULTING IN MID-AIR, THE SINEWY SLEUTH LANDS ON THE ROOF BELOW IN ACROBATIC FASHION...
...AND RECOVERS IN TIME...
...TO STRETCH OUT HIS HANDS AND SAVE ROBIN, ALSO FALLING AFTER THE IMPACT HAS JARRED LOOSE HIS HOLD ON THE BATROPE...
BROKE ROBIN'S FALL--BUT HE STILL HIT HARD ENOUGH TO BE KNOCKED OUT!
THUD!
A HALF-HOUR LATER IN THE BAT-MOBILE...
YES, I'M ALL RIGHT NOW, BATMAN--THANKS TO YOU! NO, I DON'T NEED A DOCTOR--WE'VE GOT TO CAPTURE THE ROBIN GANG!
THE WHAT--!?
SWIFTLY, THE COWLED CRUSADER IS TOLD ALL ABOUT THE YOUTHFUL MASQUERADERS...
THEN THAT LOOTER I SAW, DRESSED UP AS YOU, WAS ONE OF THE GANG! HANG ON, ROBIN! WE'RE HEADING FOR THIS MAN CRAIG AND HIS GYMNASIUM!
IN AL CRAIG'S OFFICE MEANWHILE...
WE OUGHTA GET OUT OF THESE COSTUMES!
WHAT'S THE HURRY? TURN ON THE TV--MAYBE OUR CAPER HAS MADE THE LATE LATE NEWS!
11

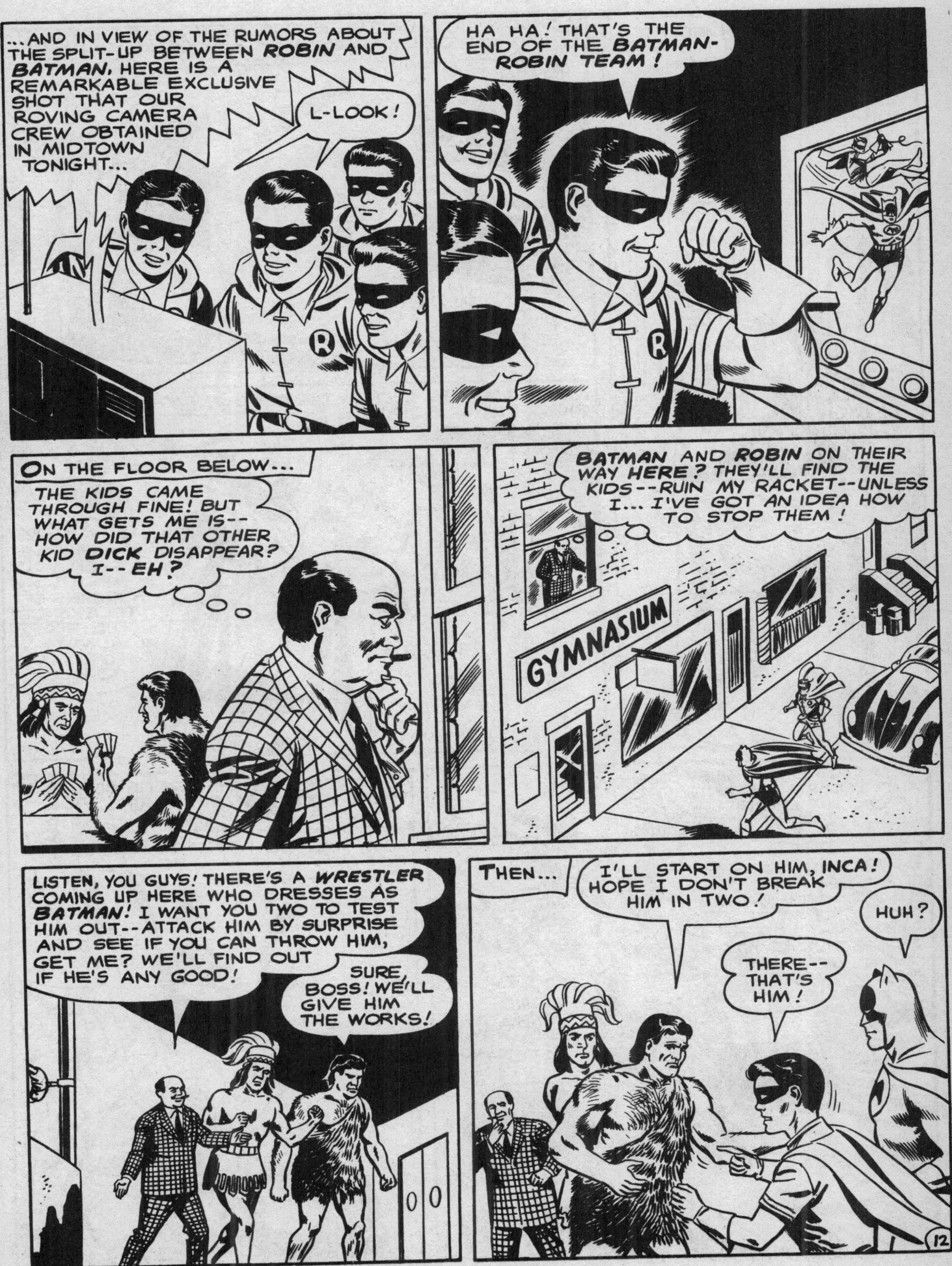
...AND IN VIEW OF THE RUMORS ABOUT THE SPLIT-UP BETWEEN ROBIN AND BATMAN, HERE IS A REMARKABLE EXCLUSIVE SHOT THAT OUR ROVING CAMERA CREW OBTAINED IN MIDTOWN TONIGHT...
L-LOOK!
HA HA! THAT'S THE END OF THE BATMAN-ROBIN TEAM!
ON THE FLOOR BELOW...
THE KIDS CAME THROUGH FINE! BUT WHAT GETS ME IS-- HOW DID THAT OTHER KID DICK DISAPPEAR? I--EH?
BATMAN AND ROBIN ON THEIR WAY HERE? THEY'LL FIND THE KIDS--RUIN MY RACKET--UNLESS I... I'VE GOT AN IDEA HOW TO STOP THEM!
GYMNASIUM
LISTEN, YOU GUYS! THERE'S A WRESTLER COMING UP HERE WHO DRESSES AS BATMAN! I WANT YOU TWO TO TEST HIM OUT--ATTACK HIM BY SURPRISE AND SEE IF YOU CAN THROW HIM, GET ME? WE'LL FIND OUT IF HE'S ANY GOOD!
SURE, BOSS! WE'LL GIVE HIM THE WORKS!
THEN...
I'LL START ON HIM, INCA! HOPE I DON'T BREAK HIM IN TWO!
HUH?
THERE-- THAT'S HIM!
12

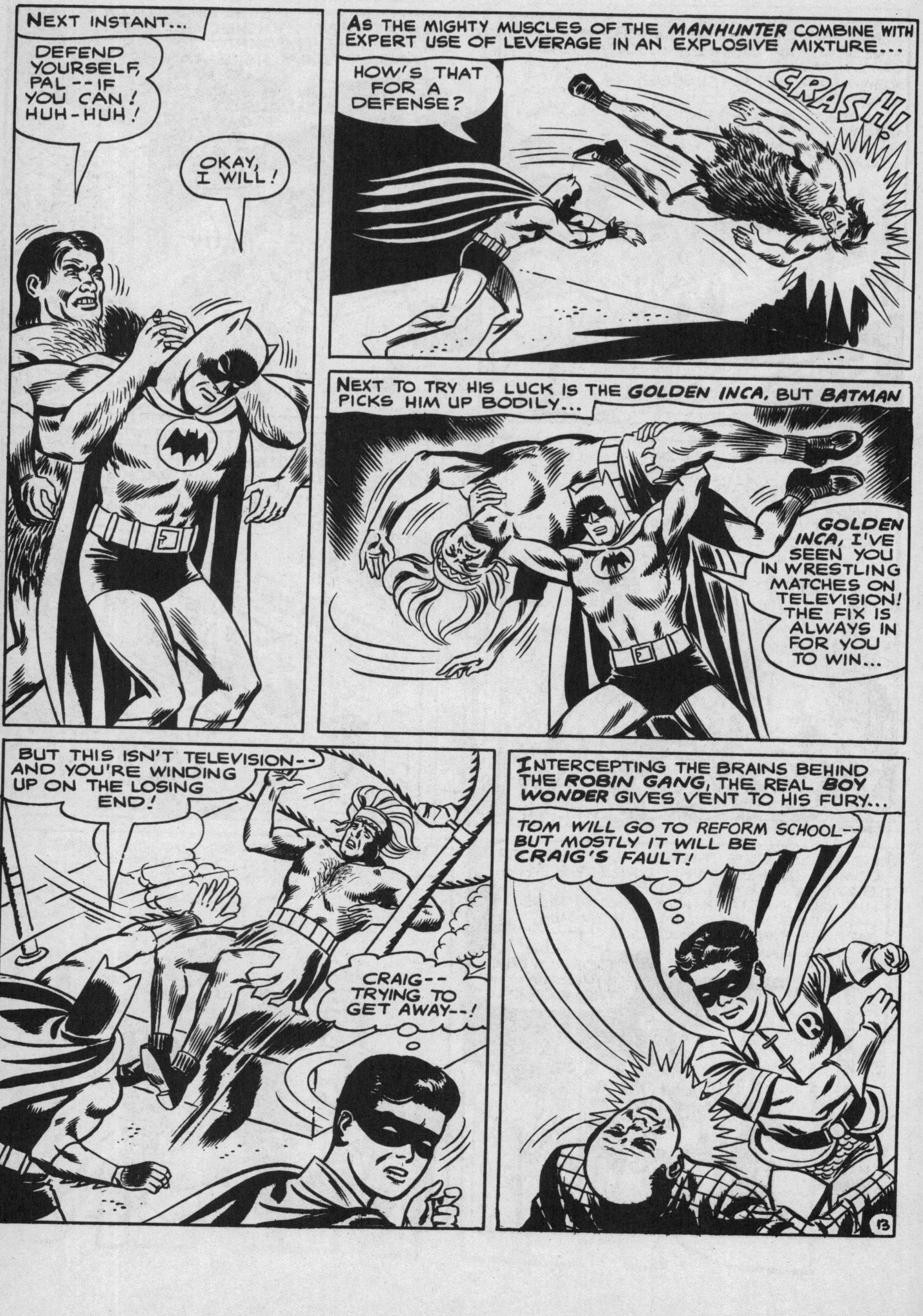
NEXT INSTANT...
DEFEND YOURSELF, PAL--IF YOU CAN! HUH-HUH!
OKAY, I WILL!
AS THE MIGHTY MUSCLES OF THE MANHUNTER COMBINE WITH EXPERT USE OF LEVERAGE IN AN EXPLOSIVE MIXTURE...
HOW'S THAT FOR A DEFENSE?
CRASH!
NEXT TO TRY HIS LUCK IS THE GOLDEN INCA, BUT BATMAN PICKS HIM UP BODILY...
GOLDEN INCA, I'VE SEEN YOU IN WRESTLING MATCHES ON TELEVISION! THE FIX IS ALWAYS IN FOR YOU TO WIN...
BUT THIS ISN'T TELEVISION--AND YOU'RE WINDING UP ON THE LOSING END!
CRAIG--TRYING TO GET AWAY--!
INTERCEPTING THE BRAINS BEHIND THE ROBIN GANG, THE REAL BOY WONDER GIVES VENT TO HIS FURY...
TOM WILL GO TO REFORM SCHOOL--BUT MOSTLY IT WILL BE CRAIG'S FAULT!
13

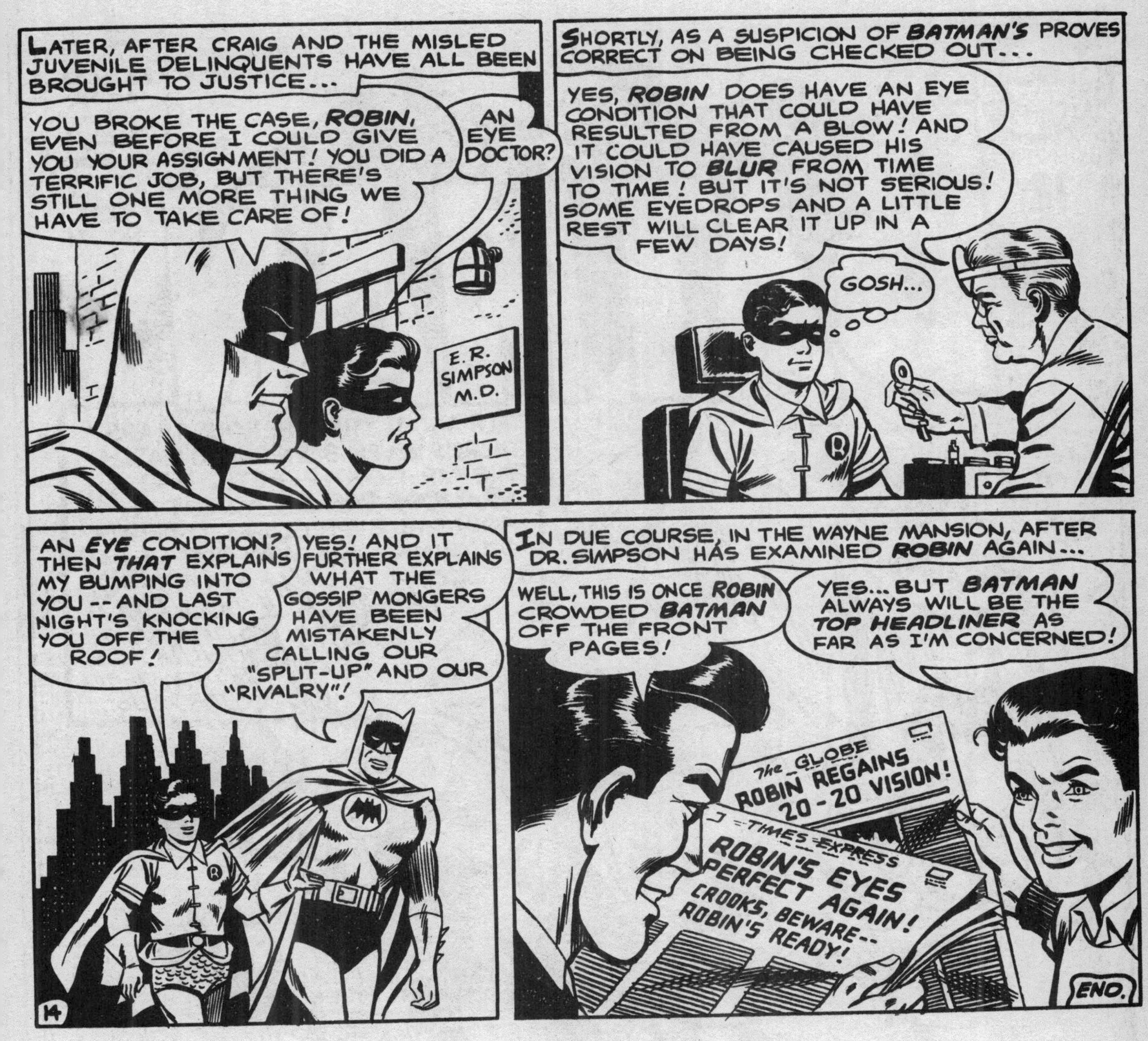
LATER, AFTER CRAIG AND THE MISLED JUVENILE DELINQUENTS HAVE ALL BEEN BROUGHT TO JUSTICE...
YOU BROKE THE CASE, ROBIN, EVEN BEFORE I COULD GIVE YOU YOUR ASSIGNMENT! YOU DID A TERRIFIC JOB, BUT THERE'S STILL ONE MORE THING WE HAVE TO TAKE CARE OF!
AN EYE DOCTOR?
E.R. SIMPSON M.D.
SHORTLY, AS A SUSPICION OF BATMAN'S PROVES CORRECT ON BEING CHECKED OUT...
YES, ROBIN DOES HAVE AN EYE CONDITION THAT COULD HAVE RESULTED FROM A BLOW! AND IT COULD HAVE CAUSED HIS VISION TO BLUR FROM TIME TO TIME! BUT IT'S NOT SERIOUS! SOME EYEDROPS AND A LITTLE REST WILL CLEAR IT UP IN A FEW DAYS!
GOSH...
AN EYE CONDITION? THEN THAT EXPLAINS MY BUMPING INTO YOU -- AND LAST NIGHT'S KNOCKING YOU OFF THE ROOF!
YES! AND IT FURTHER EXPLAINS WHAT THE GOSSIP MONGERS HAVE BEEN MISTAKENLY CALLING OUR "SPLIT-UP" AND OUR "RIVALRY"!
14
IN DUE COURSE, IN THE WAYNE MANSION, AFTER DR. SIMPSON HAS EXAMINED ROBIN AGAIN...
WELL, THIS IS ONCE ROBIN CROWDED BATMAN OFF THE FRONT PAGES!
YES... BUT BATMAN ALWAYS WILL BE THE TOP HEADLINER AS FAR AS I'M CONCERNED!
The GLOBE
ROBIN REGAINS 20-20 VISION!
TIMES-EXPRESS
ROBIN'S EYES PERFECT AGAIN!
CROOKS, BEWARE-- ROBIN'S READY!
END.

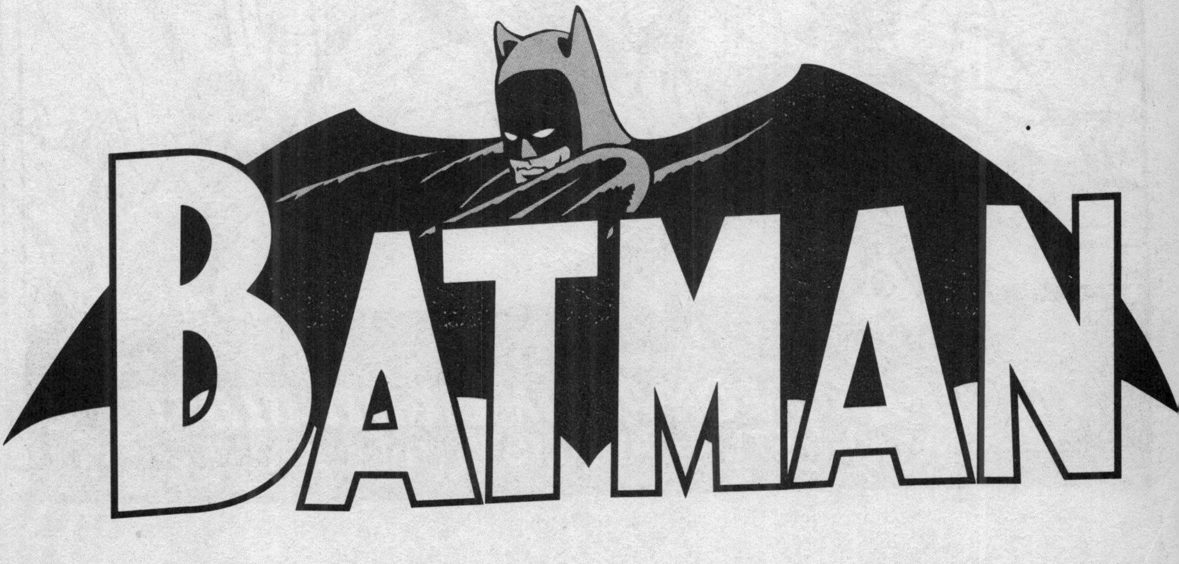
BATMAN

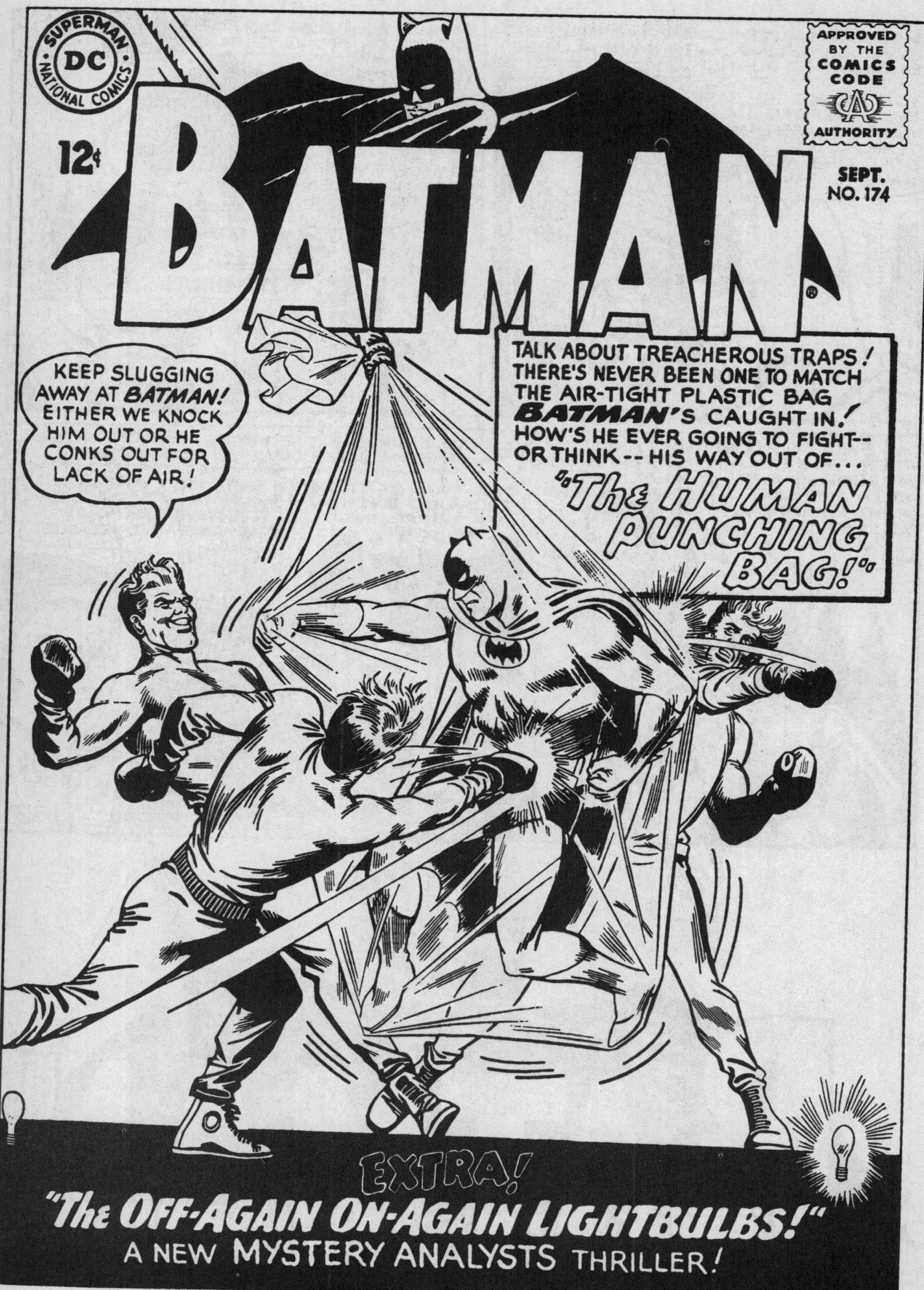
SUPERMAN DC NATIONAL COMICS
12¢
APPROVED BY THE COMICS CODE AUTHORITY
BATMAN
SEPT. NO. 174
KEEP SLUGGING AWAY AT BATMAN! EITHER WE KNOCK HIM OUT OR HE CONKS OUT FOR LACK OF AIR!
TALK ABOUT TREACHEROUS TRAPS! THERE'S NEVER BEEN ONE TO MATCH THE AIR-TIGHT PLASTIC BAG BATMAN'S CAUGHT IN! HOW'S HE EVER GOING TO FIGHT-- OR THINK -- HIS WAY OUT OF... "The HUMAN PUNCHING BAG!"
EXTRA!
"The OFF-AGAIN ON-AGAIN LIGHTBULBS!"
A NEW MYSTERY ANALYSTS THRILLER!

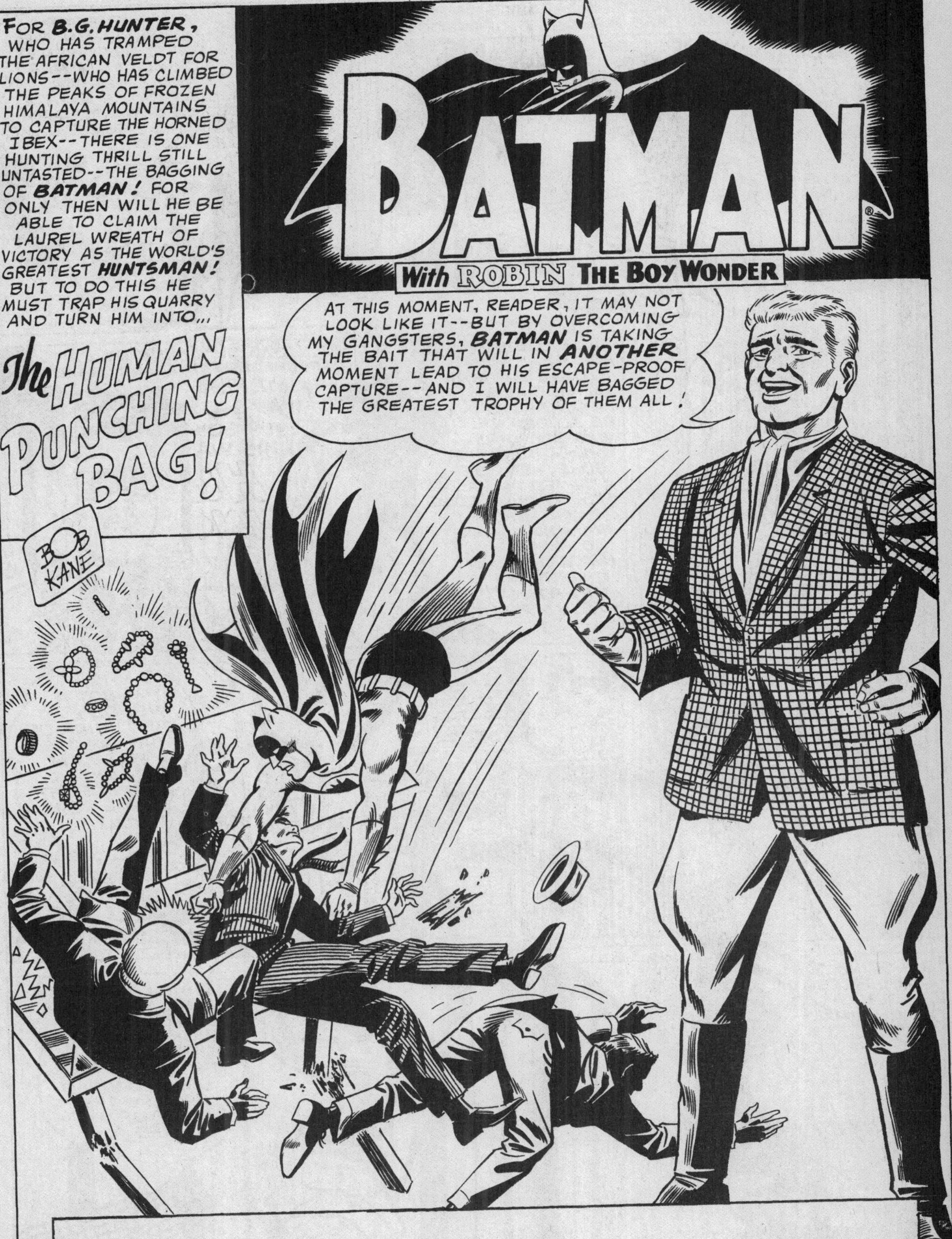
FOR B.G. HUNTER, WHO HAS TRAMPED THE AFRICAN VELDT FOR LIONS--WHO HAS CLIMBED THE PEAKS OF FROZEN HIMALAYA MOUNTAINS TO CAPTURE THE HORNED IBEX--THERE IS ONE HUNTING THRILL STILL UNTASTED--THE BAGGING OF BATMAN! FOR ONLY THEN WILL HE BE ABLE TO CLAIM THE LAUREL WREATH OF VICTORY AS THE WORLD'S GREATEST HUNTSMAN! BUT TO DO THIS HE MUST TRAP HIS QUARRY AND TURN HIM INTO...
The HUMAN PUNCHING BAG!
BOB KANE
BATMAN®
With ROBIN THE BOY WONDER
AT THIS MOMENT, READER, IT MAY NOT LOOK LIKE IT--BUT BY OVERCOMING MY GANGSTERS, BATMAN IS TAKING THE BAIT THAT WILL IN ANOTHER MOMENT LEAD TO HIS ESCAPE-PROOF CAPTURE--AND I WILL HAVE BAGGED THE GREATEST TROPHY OF THEM ALL!

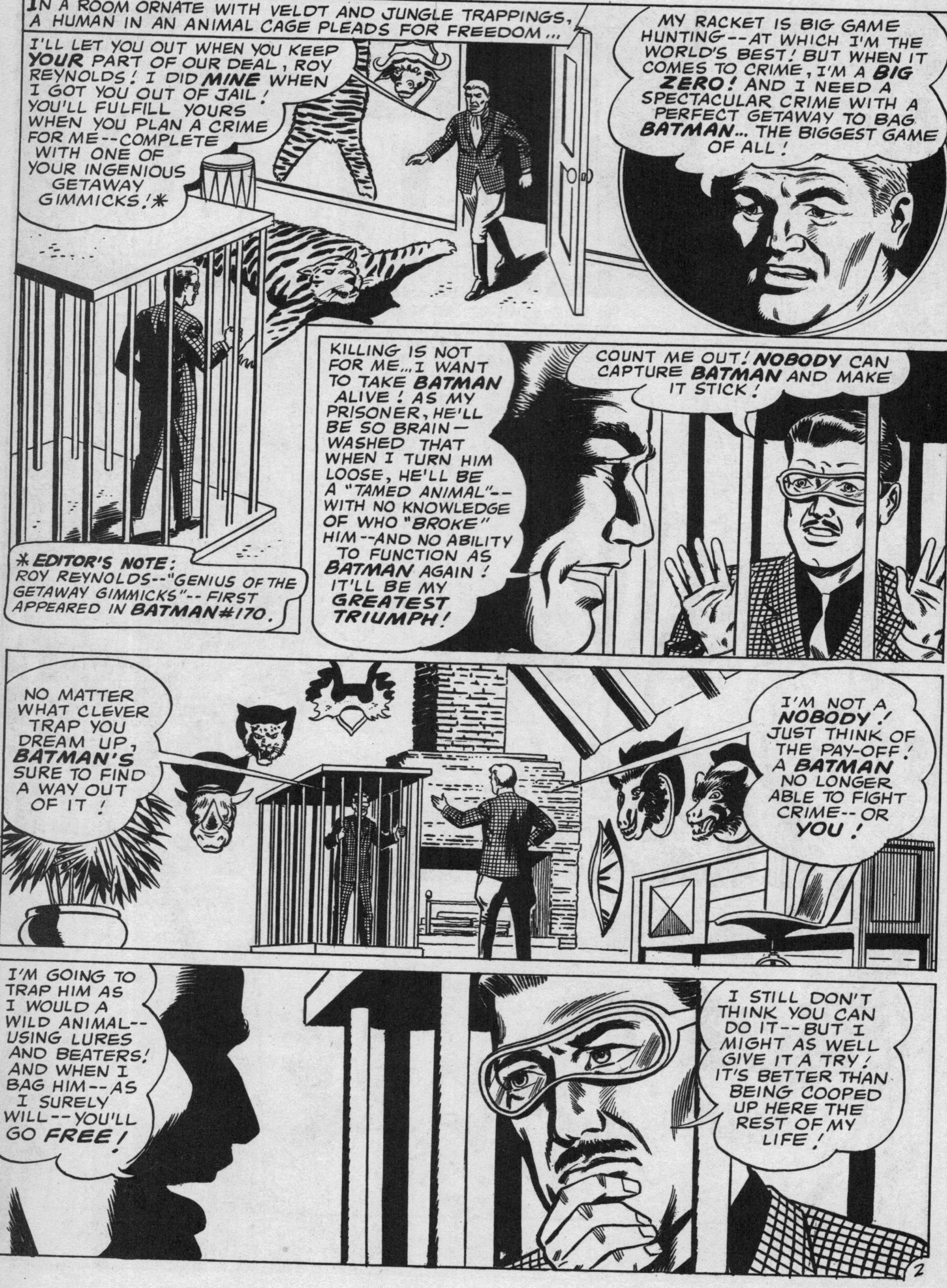
IN A ROOM ORNATE WITH VELDT AND JUNGLE TRAPPINGS, A HUMAN IN AN ANIMAL CAGE PLEADS FOR FREEDOM...
I'LL LET YOU OUT WHEN YOU KEEP YOUR PART OF OUR DEAL, ROY REYNOLDS! I DID MINE WHEN I GOT YOU OUT OF JAIL! YOU'LL FULFILL YOURS WHEN YOU PLAN A CRIME FOR ME--COMPLETE WITH ONE OF YOUR INGENIOUS GETAWAY GIMMICKS!*
*EDITOR'S NOTE: ROY REYNOLDS--"GENIUS OF THE GETAWAY GIMMICKS"-- FIRST APPEARED IN BATMAN #170.
MY RACKET IS BIG GAME HUNTING--AT WHICH I'M THE WORLD'S BEST! BUT WHEN IT COMES TO CRIME, I'M A BIG ZERO! AND I NEED A SPECTACULAR CRIME WITH A PERFECT GETAWAY TO BAG BATMAN... THE BIGGEST GAME OF ALL!
KILLING IS NOT FOR ME...I WANT TO TAKE BATMAN ALIVE! AS MY PRISONER, HE'LL BE SO BRAIN-WASHED THAT WHEN I TURN HIM LOOSE, HE'LL BE A "TAMED ANIMAL"--WITH NO KNOWLEDGE OF WHO "BROKE" HIM--AND NO ABILITY TO FUNCTION AS BATMAN AGAIN! IT'LL BE MY GREATEST TRIUMPH!
COUNT ME OUT! NOBODY CAN CAPTURE BATMAN AND MAKE IT STICK!
NO MATTER WHAT CLEVER TRAP YOU DREAM UP, BATMAN'S SURE TO FIND A WAY OUT OF IT!
I'M NOT A NOBODY! JUST THINK OF THE PAY-OFF! A BATMAN NO LONGER ABLE TO FIGHT CRIME--OR YOU!
I'M GOING TO TRAP HIM AS I WOULD A WILD ANIMAL--USING LURES AND BEATERS! AND WHEN I BAG HIM--AS I SURELY WILL--YOU'LL GO FREE!
I STILL DON'T THINK YOU CAN DO IT--BUT I MIGHT AS WELL GIVE IT A TRY! IT'S BETTER THAN BEING COOPED UP HERE THE REST OF MY LIFE!
2

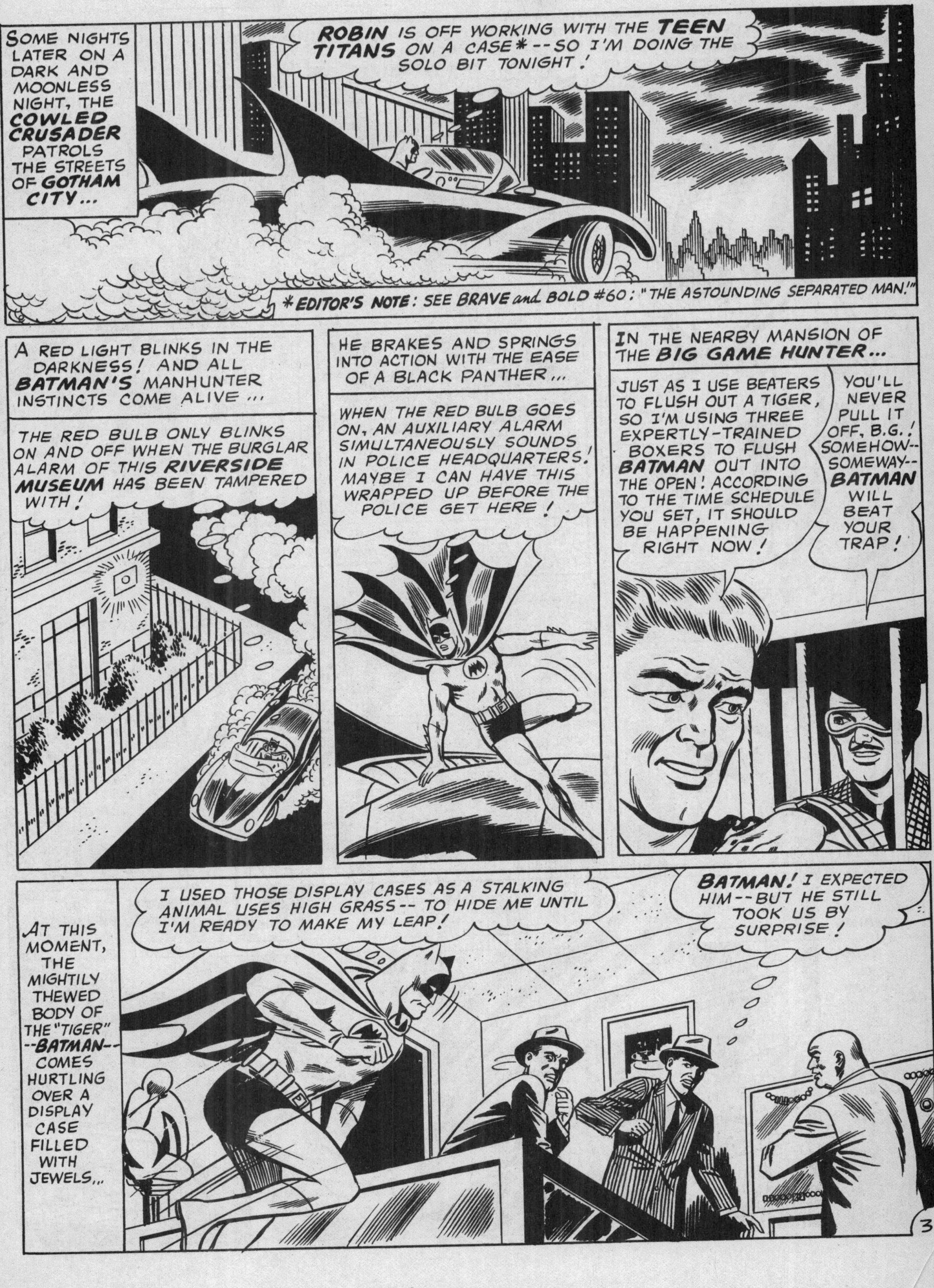
SOME NIGHTS LATER ON A DARK AND MOONLESS NIGHT, THE COWLED CRUSADER PATROLS THE STREETS OF GOTHAM CITY...
ROBIN IS OFF WORKING WITH THE TEEN TITANS ON A CASE* --SO I'M DOING THE SOLO BIT TONIGHT!
*EDITOR'S NOTE: SEE BRAVE and BOLD #60: "THE ASTOUNDING SEPARATED MAN!"
A RED LIGHT BLINKS IN THE DARKNESS! AND ALL BATMAN'S MANHUNTER INSTINCTS COME ALIVE...
THE RED BULB ONLY BLINKS ON AND OFF WHEN THE BURGLAR ALARM OF THIS RIVERSIDE MUSEUM HAS BEEN TAMPERED WITH!
HE BRAKES AND SPRINGS INTO ACTION WITH THE EASE OF A BLACK PANTHER...
WHEN THE RED BULB GOES ON, AN AUXILIARY ALARM SIMULTANEOUSLY SOUNDS IN POLICE HEADQUARTERS! MAYBE I CAN HAVE THIS WRAPPED UP BEFORE THE POLICE GET HERE!
IN THE NEARBY MANSION OF THE BIG GAME HUNTER...
JUST AS I USE BEATERS TO FLUSH OUT A TIGER, SO I'M USING THREE EXPERTLY-TRAINED BOXERS TO FLUSH BATMAN OUT INTO THE OPEN! ACCORDING TO THE TIME SCHEDULE YOU SET, IT SHOULD BE HAPPENING RIGHT NOW!
YOU'LL NEVER PULL IT OFF, B.G.! SOMEHOW--SOMEWAY--BATMAN WILL BEAT YOUR TRAP!
AT THIS MOMENT, THE MIGHTILY THEWED BODY OF THE "TIGER" --BATMAN-- COMES HURTLING OVER A DISPLAY CASE FILLED WITH JEWELS...
I USED THOSE DISPLAY CASES AS A STALKING ANIMAL USES HIGH GRASS-- TO HIDE ME UNTIL I'M READY TO MAKE MY LEAP!
BATMAN! I EXPECTED HIM--BUT HE STILL TOOK US BY SURPRISE!
3

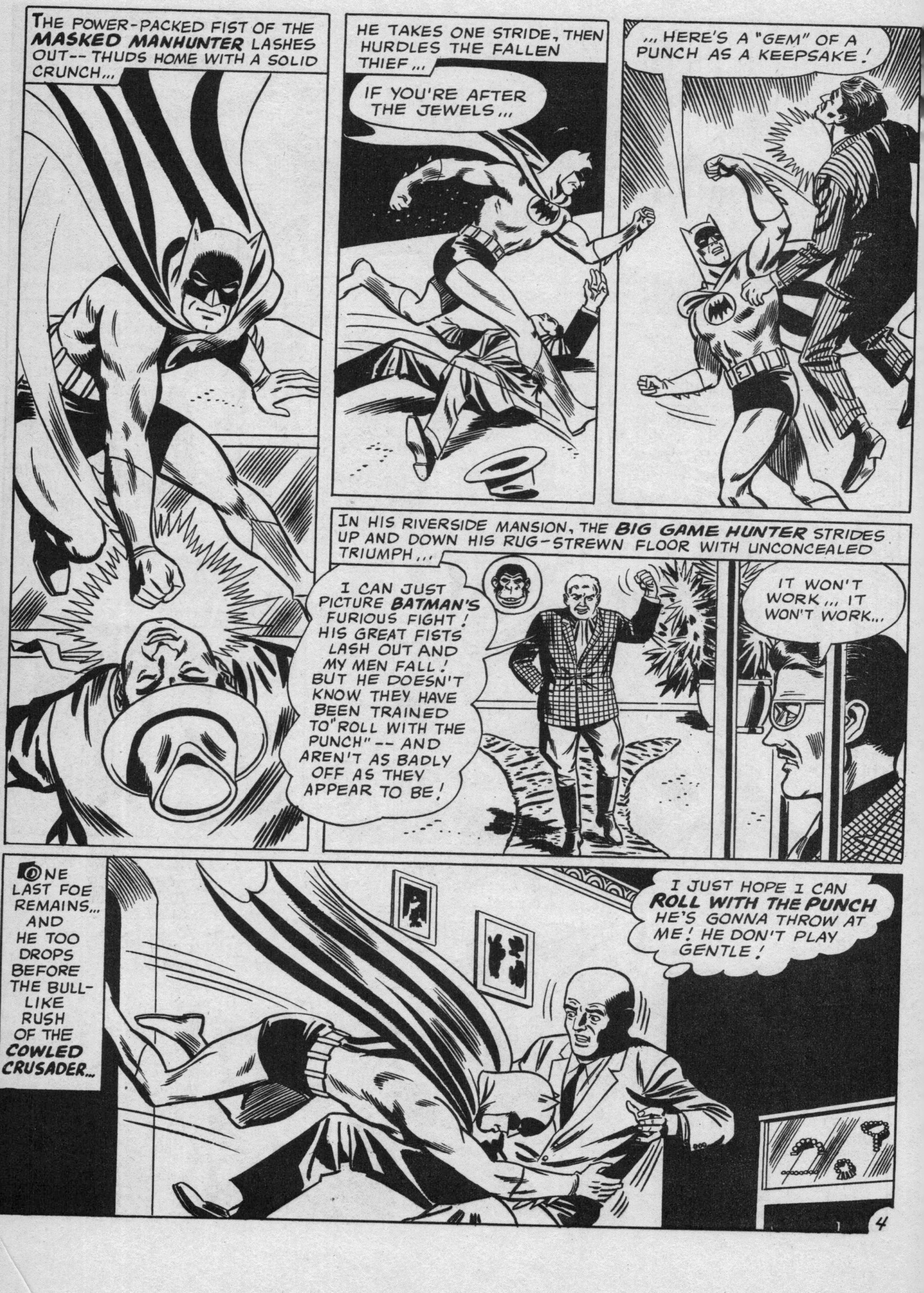
THE POWER-PACKED FIST OF THE MASKED MANHUNTER LASHES OUT-- THUDS HOME WITH A SOLID CRUNCH...
HE TAKES ONE STRIDE, THEN HURDLES THE FALLEN THIEF...
IF YOU'RE AFTER THE JEWELS...
... HERE'S A "GEM" OF A PUNCH AS A KEEPSAKE!
IN HIS RIVERSIDE MANSION, THE BIG GAME HUNTER STRIDES UP AND DOWN HIS RUG-STREWN FLOOR WITH UNCONCEALED TRIUMPH...
I CAN JUST PICTURE BATMAN'S FURIOUS FIGHT! HIS GREAT FISTS LASH OUT AND MY MEN FALL! BUT HE DOESN'T KNOW THEY HAVE BEEN TRAINED TO "ROLL WITH THE PUNCH" -- AND AREN'T AS BADLY OFF AS THEY APPEAR TO BE!
IT WON'T WORK... IT WON'T WORK...
ONE LAST FOE REMAINS... AND HE TOO DROPS BEFORE THE BULL-LIKE RUSH OF THE COWLED CRUSADER...
I JUST HOPE I CAN ROLL WITH THE PUNCH HE'S GONNA THROW AT ME! HE DON'T PLAY GENTLE!
4

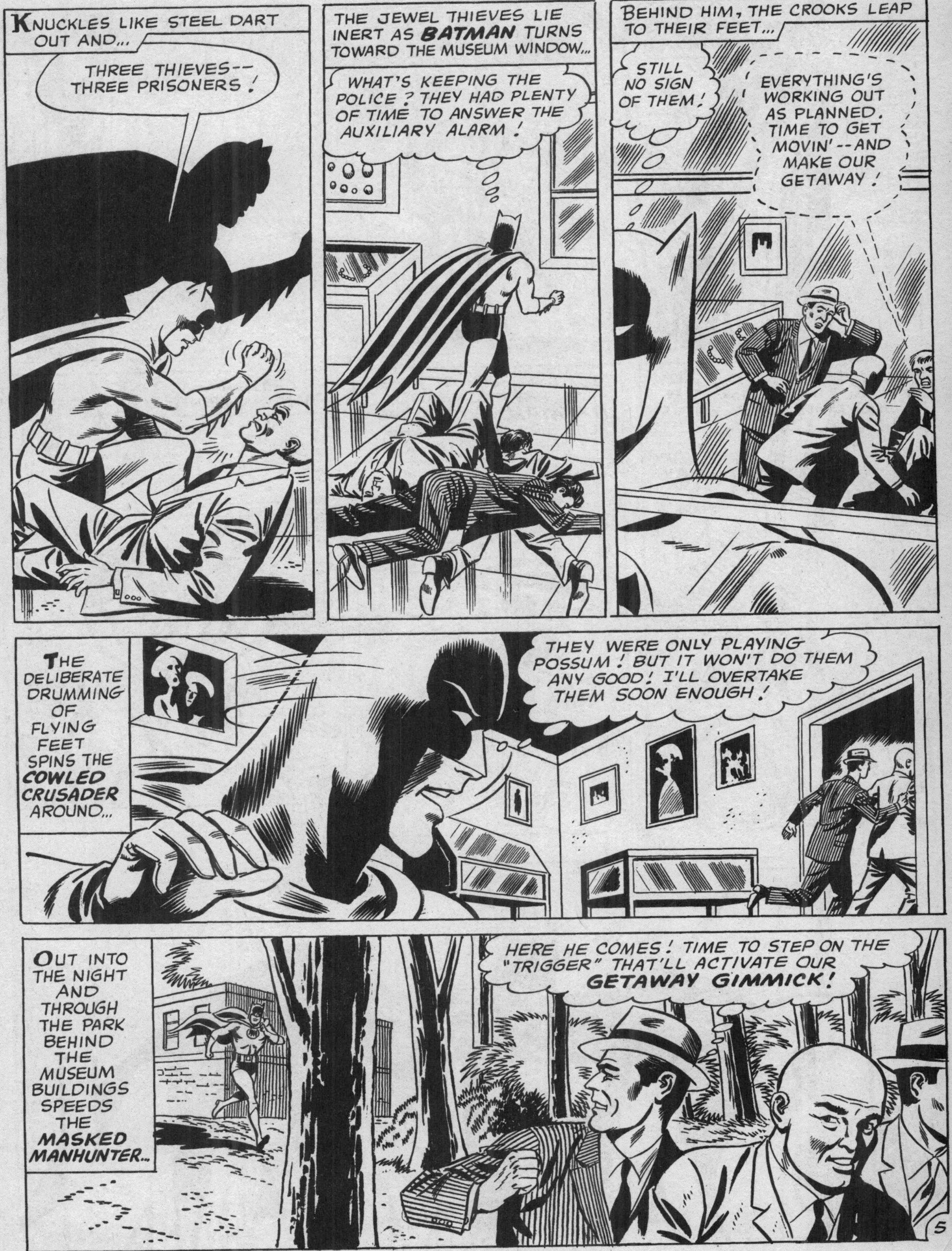
KNUCKLES LIKE STEEL DART OUT AND...
THREE THIEVES-- THREE PRISONERS!
THE JEWEL THIEVES LIE INERT AS BATMAN TURNS TOWARD THE MUSEUM WINDOW...
WHAT'S KEEPING THE POLICE? THEY HAD PLENTY OF TIME TO ANSWER THE AUXILIARY ALARM!
BEHIND HIM, THE CROOKS LEAP TO THEIR FEET...
STILL NO SIGN OF THEM!
EVERYTHING'S WORKING OUT AS PLANNED. TIME TO GET MOVIN' --AND MAKE OUR GETAWAY!
THE DELIBERATE DRUMMING OF FLYING FEET SPINS THE COWLED CRUSADER AROUND...
THEY WERE ONLY PLAYING POSSUM! BUT IT WON'T DO THEM ANY GOOD! I'LL OVERTAKE THEM SOON ENOUGH!
OUT INTO THE NIGHT AND THROUGH THE PARK BEHIND THE MUSEUM BUILDINGS SPEEDS THE MASKED MANHUNTER...
HERE HE COMES! TIME TO STEP ON THE "TRIGGER" THAT'LL ACTIVATE OUR GETAWAY GIMMICK!
5

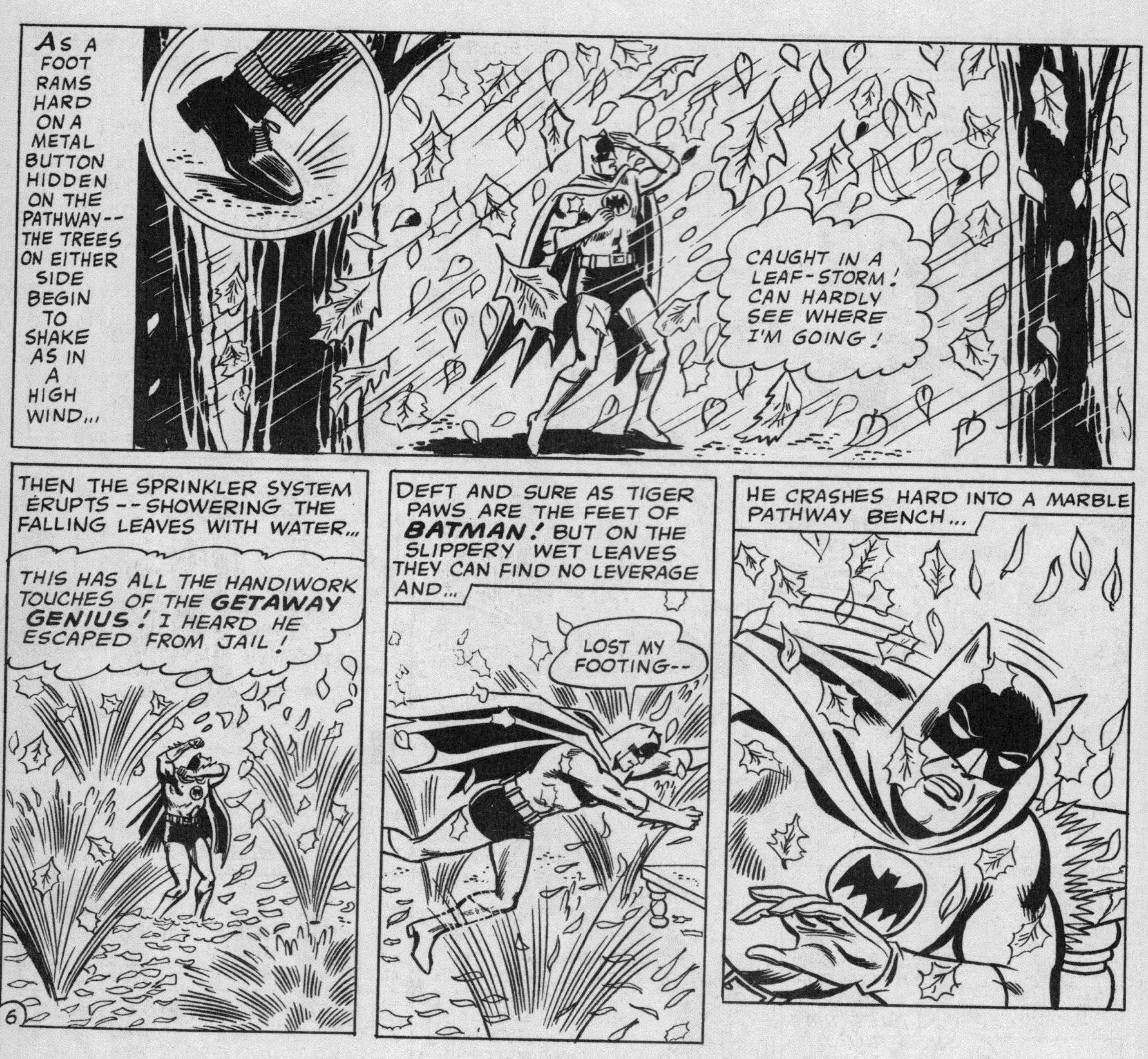
AS A FOOT RAMS HARD ON A METAL BUTTON HIDDEN ON THE PATHWAY-- THE TREES ON EITHER SIDE BEGIN TO SHAKE AS IN A HIGH WIND...
CAUGHT IN A LEAF-STORM! CAN HARDLY SEE WHERE I'M GOING!
THEN THE SPRINKLER SYSTEM ERUPTS -- SHOWERING THE FALLING LEAVES WITH WATER...
THIS HAS ALL THE HANDIWORK TOUCHES OF THE GETAWAY GENIUS! I HEARD HE ESCAPED FROM JAIL!
6
DEFT AND SURE AS TIGER PAWS ARE THE FEET OF BATMAN! BUT ON THE SLIPPERY WET LEAVES THEY CAN FIND NO LEVERAGE AND...
LOST MY FOOTING--
HE CRASHES HARD INTO A MARBLE PATHWAY BENCH...

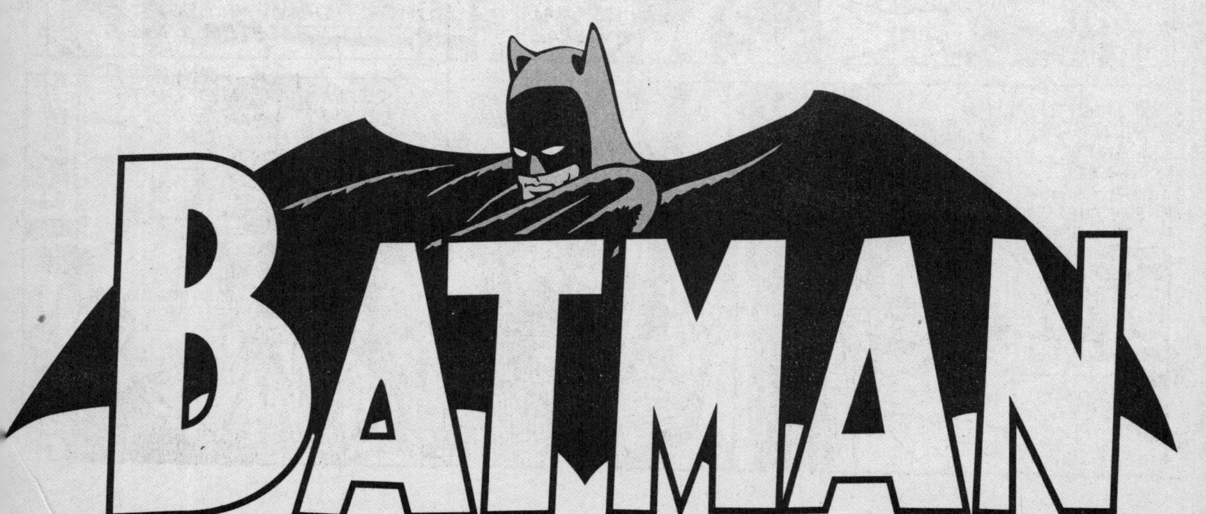
BATMAN

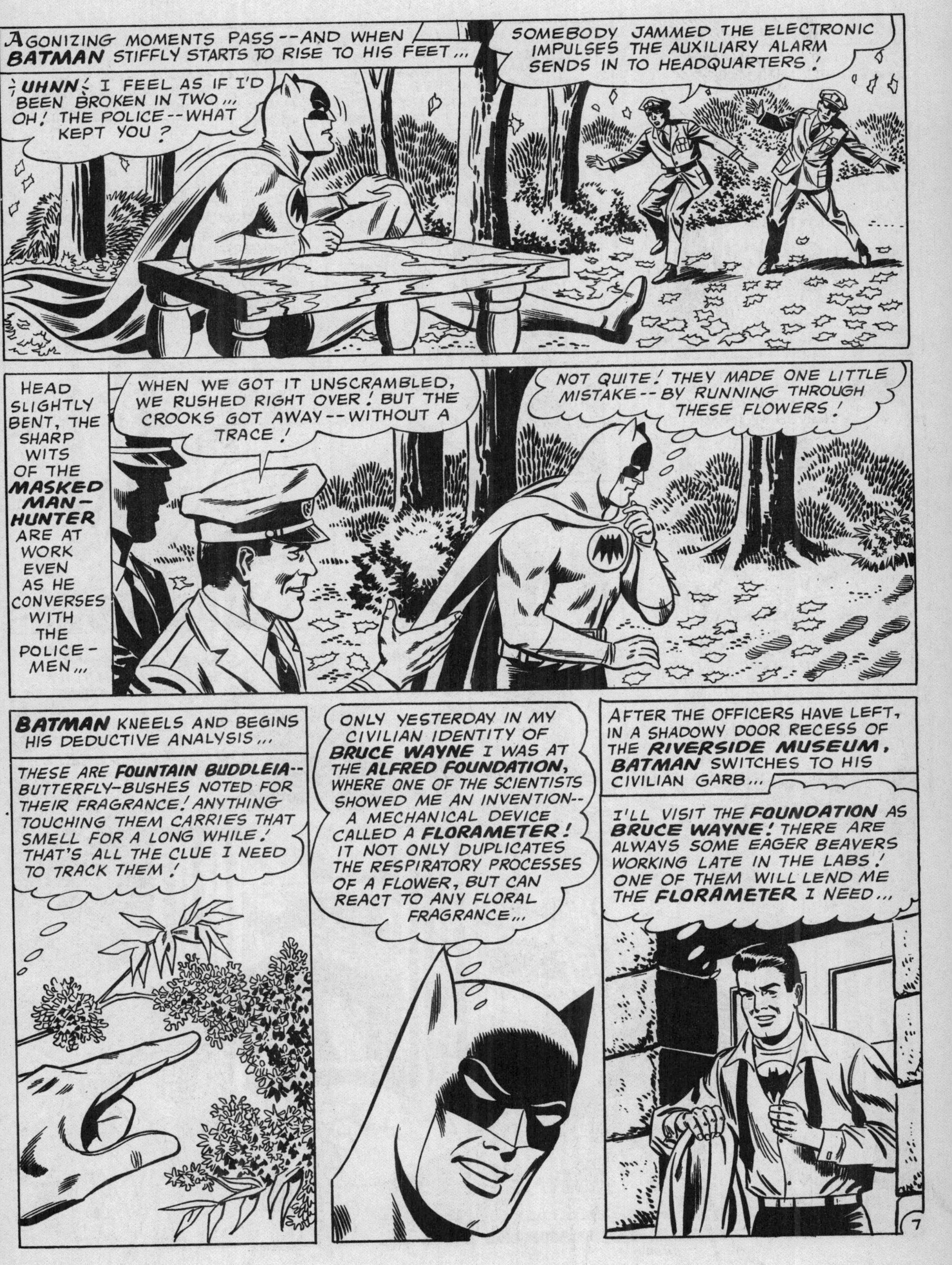
AGONIZING MOMENTS PASS--AND WHEN BATMAN STIFFLY STARTS TO RISE TO HIS FEET,,,
UHNN! I FEEL AS IF I'D BEEN BROKEN IN TWO,,, OH! THE POLICE--WHAT KEPT YOU?
SOMEBODY JAMMED THE ELECTRONIC IMPULSES THE AUXILIARY ALARM SENDS IN TO HEADQUARTERS!
HEAD SLIGHTLY BENT, THE SHARP WITS OF THE MASKED MAN-HUNTER ARE AT WORK EVEN AS HE CONVERSES WITH THE POLICE-MEN,,,
WHEN WE GOT IT UNSCRAMBLED, WE RUSHED RIGHT OVER! BUT THE CROOKS GOT AWAY--WITHOUT A TRACE!
NOT QUITE! THEY MADE ONE LITTLE MISTAKE--BY RUNNING THROUGH THESE FLOWERS!
BATMAN KNEELS AND BEGINS HIS DEDUCTIVE ANALYSIS,,,
THESE ARE FOUNTAIN BUDDLEIA--BUTTERFLY-BUSHES NOTED FOR THEIR FRAGRANCE! ANYTHING TOUCHING THEM CARRIES THAT SMELL FOR A LONG WHILE! THAT'S ALL THE CLUE I NEED TO TRACK THEM!
ONLY YESTERDAY IN MY CIVILIAN IDENTITY OF BRUCE WAYNE I WAS AT THE ALFRED FOUNDATION, WHERE ONE OF THE SCIENTISTS SHOWED ME AN INVENTION--A MECHANICAL DEVICE CALLED A FLORAMETER! IT NOT ONLY DUPLICATES THE RESPIRATORY PROCESSES OF A FLOWER, BUT CAN REACT TO ANY FLORAL FRAGRANCE,,,
AFTER THE OFFICERS HAVE LEFT, IN A SHADOWY DOOR RECESS OF THE RIVERSIDE MUSEUM, BATMAN SWITCHES TO HIS CIVILIAN GARB...
I'LL VISIT THE FOUNDATION AS BRUCE WAYNE! THERE ARE ALWAYS SOME EAGER BEAVERS WORKING LATE IN THE LABS! ONE OF THEM WILL LEND ME THE FLORAMETER I NEED,,,
7

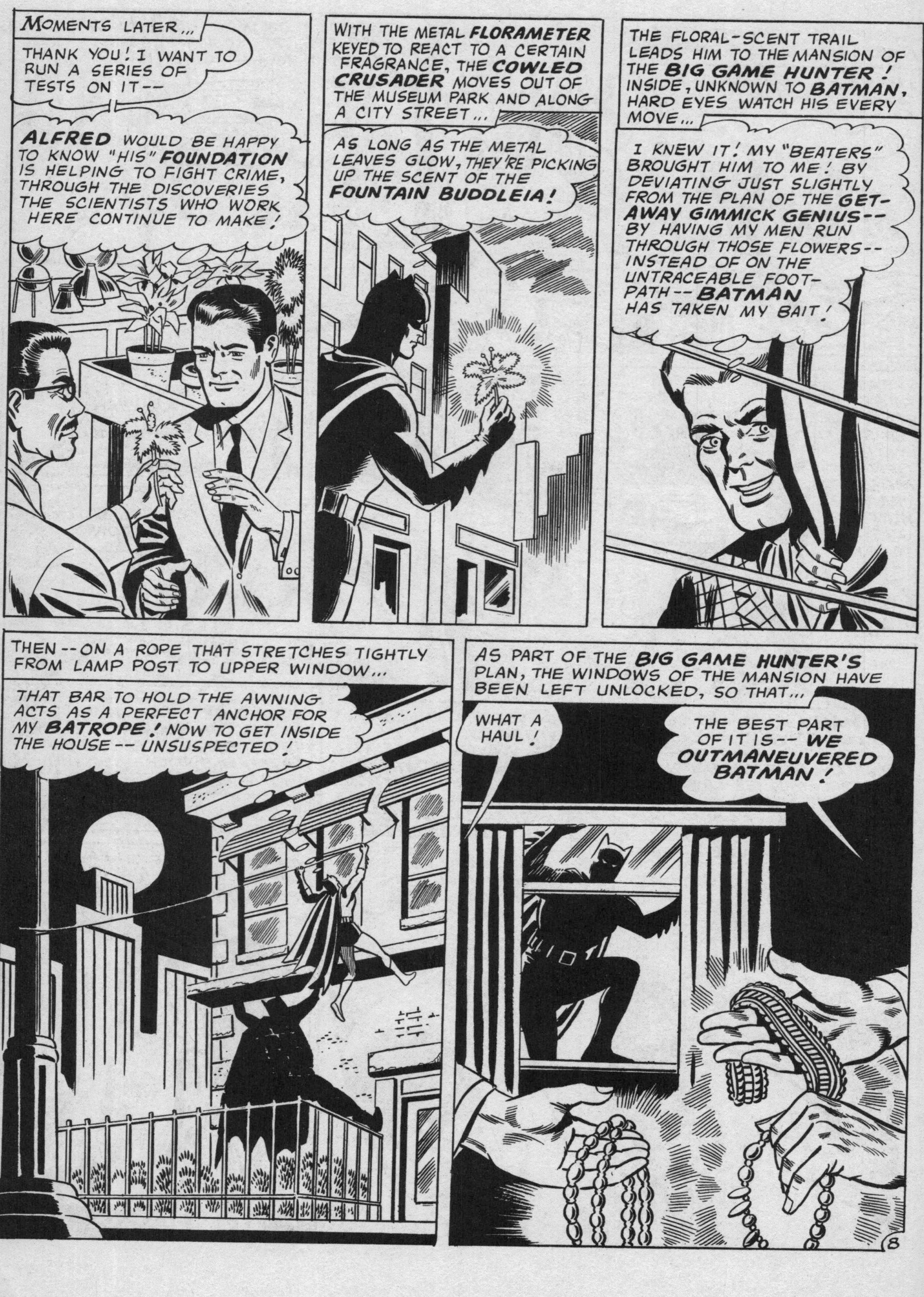
MOMENTS LATER...
THANK YOU! I WANT TO RUN A SERIES OF TESTS ON IT--
ALFRED WOULD BE HAPPY TO KNOW "HIS" FOUNDATION IS HELPING TO FIGHT CRIME, THROUGH THE DISCOVERIES THE SCIENTISTS WHO WORK HERE CONTINUE TO MAKE!
WITH THE METAL FLORAMETER KEYED TO REACT TO A CERTAIN FRAGRANCE, THE COWLED CRUSADER MOVES OUT OF THE MUSEUM PARK AND ALONG A CITY STREET...
AS LONG AS THE METAL LEAVES GLOW, THEY'RE PICKING UP THE SCENT OF THE FOUNTAIN BUDDLEIA!
THE FLORAL-SCENT TRAIL LEADS HIM TO THE MANSION OF THE BIG GAME HUNTER! INSIDE, UNKNOWN TO BATMAN, HARD EYES WATCH HIS EVERY MOVE...
I KNEW IT! MY "BEATERS" BROUGHT HIM TO ME! BY DEVIATING JUST SLIGHTLY FROM THE PLAN OF THE GET-AWAY GIMMICK GENIUS-- BY HAVING MY MEN RUN THROUGH THOSE FLOWERS-- INSTEAD OF ON THE UNTRACEABLE FOOT-PATH-- BATMAN HAS TAKEN MY BAIT!
THEN--ON A ROPE THAT STRETCHES TIGHTLY FROM LAMP POST TO UPPER WINDOW...
THAT BAR TO HOLD THE AWNING ACTS AS A PERFECT ANCHOR FOR MY BATROPE! NOW TO GET INSIDE THE HOUSE-- UNSUSPECTED!
AS PART OF THE BIG GAME HUNTER'S PLAN, THE WINDOWS OF THE MANSION HAVE BEEN LEFT UNLOCKED, SO THAT...
WHAT A HAUL!
THE BEST PART OF IT IS-- WE OUTMANEUVERED BATMAN!
8

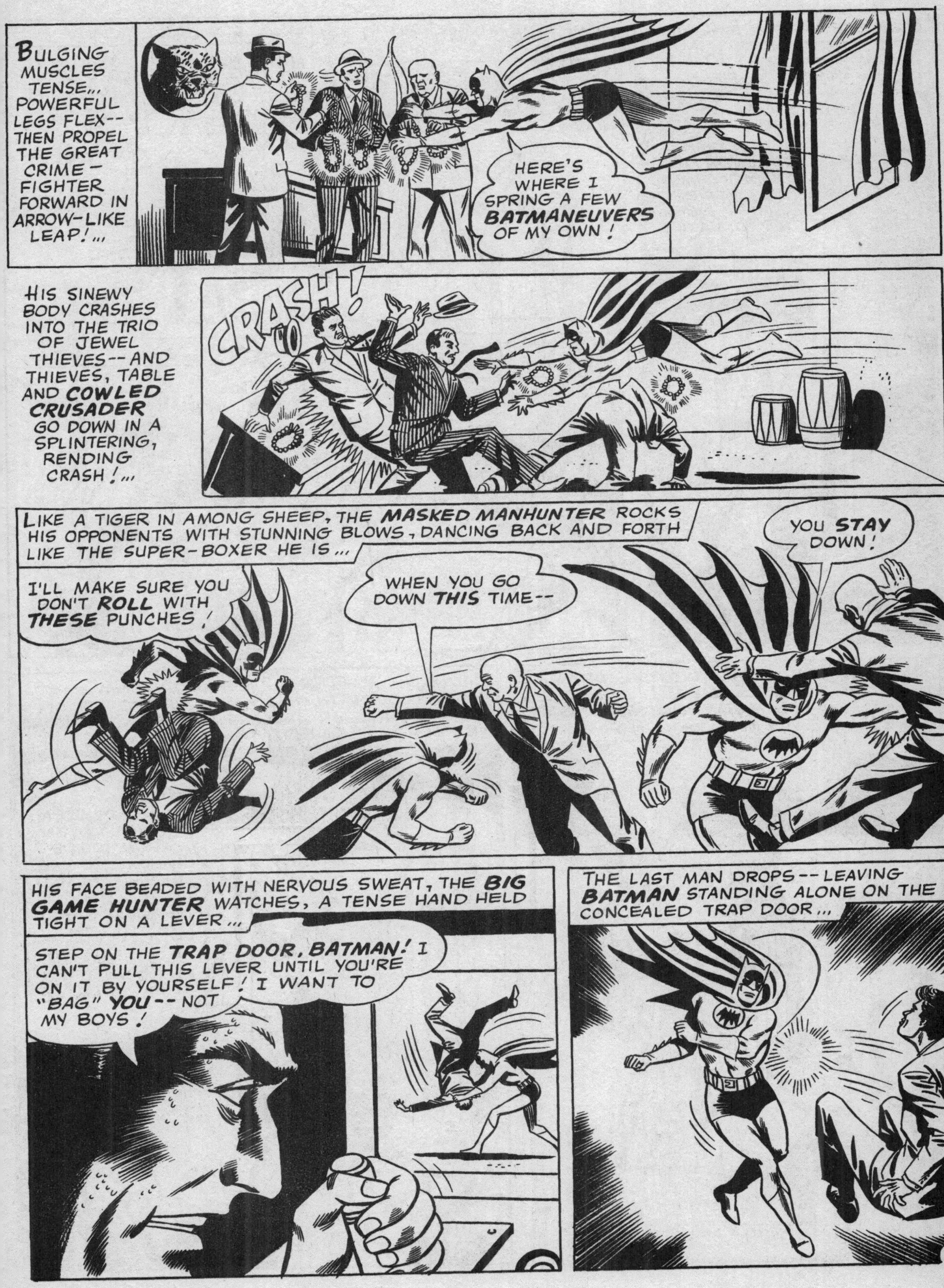
BULGING MUSCLES TENSE... POWERFUL LEGS FLEX-- THEN PROPEL THE GREAT CRIME-FIGHTER FORWARD IN ARROW-LIKE LEAP!...
HERE'S WHERE I SPRING A FEW BATMANEUVERS OF MY OWN!
HIS SINEWY BODY CRASHES INTO THE TRIO OF JEWEL THIEVES--AND THIEVES, TABLE AND COWLED CRUSADER GO DOWN IN A SPLINTERING, RENDING CRASH!...
CRASH!
LIKE A TIGER IN AMONG SHEEP, THE MASKED MANHUNTER ROCKS HIS OPPONENTS WITH STUNNING BLOWS, DANCING BACK AND FORTH LIKE THE SUPER-BOXER HE IS...
I'LL MAKE SURE YOU DON'T ROLL WITH THESE PUNCHES!
WHEN YOU GO DOWN THIS TIME--
YOU STAY DOWN!
HIS FACE BEADED WITH NERVOUS SWEAT, THE BIG GAME HUNTER WATCHES, A TENSE HAND HELD TIGHT ON A LEVER...
STEP ON THE TRAP DOOR, BATMAN! I CAN'T PULL THIS LEVER UNTIL YOU'RE ON IT BY YOURSELF! I WANT TO "BAG" YOU--NOT MY BOYS!
THE LAST MAN DROPS--LEAVING BATMAN STANDING ALONE ON THE CONCEALED TRAP DOOR...
9

NEXT INSTANT -- HIS FEET GO OUT INTO SPACE! HIS HEAVILY THEWED BODY FALLS LIKE A STONE...

THE FLOOR GAVE WAY UNDER ME...

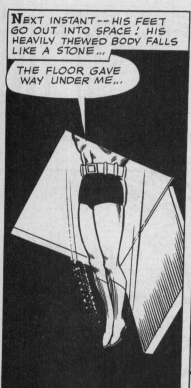

HIS FALL IS INTERCEPTED BY A SUPER-PLASTIC BAG SPECIALLY DESIGNED TO HOLD HIM!...

THERE HE IS, JUST LIKE THE **BIG GAME HUNTER** PROMISED!

OUR INSTRUCTIONS ARE TO KEEP HIM SO BUSY HE'LL QUICKLY USE UP THE SMALL SUPPLY OF OXYGEN IN THE SEALED BAG--

--GIVING HIM NO CHANCE TO **THINK** OF A WAY OUT!

WHEN THE TOP OF THE BAG IS DRAWN TIGHT, GLOVED HANDS BEGIN A RAPID-FIRE BOMBARDMENT...

THUD!

THUD!

THUD!

AN ANGRY SNARL RISES INTO THE THROAT OF THE **COWLED CRUSADER**! HE REFUSES TO SERVE AS A **HUMAN PUNCHING BAG**! HIS BODY ERUPTS INTO RETURN-FIRE ACTION...

SUDDENLY HE FLINGS HIMSELF SIDEWAYS-- BACK AND FORTH -- CAUSING THE BAG TO ROTATE! FASTER AND FASTER IT SWINGS AROUND IN RESPONSE TO **BATMAN'S** MOVEMENTS...

HEY! WHAT'S HE UP TO?

AW, WHAT'S THE DIFF? IN THAT BAG-- HE CAN'T HURT US!

YEAH -- AND THERE'S NO WAY FOR **BATMAN** TO CUT IT OPEN FROM INSIDE-- EVEN IF HE HAS A KNIFE ON HIM!

10

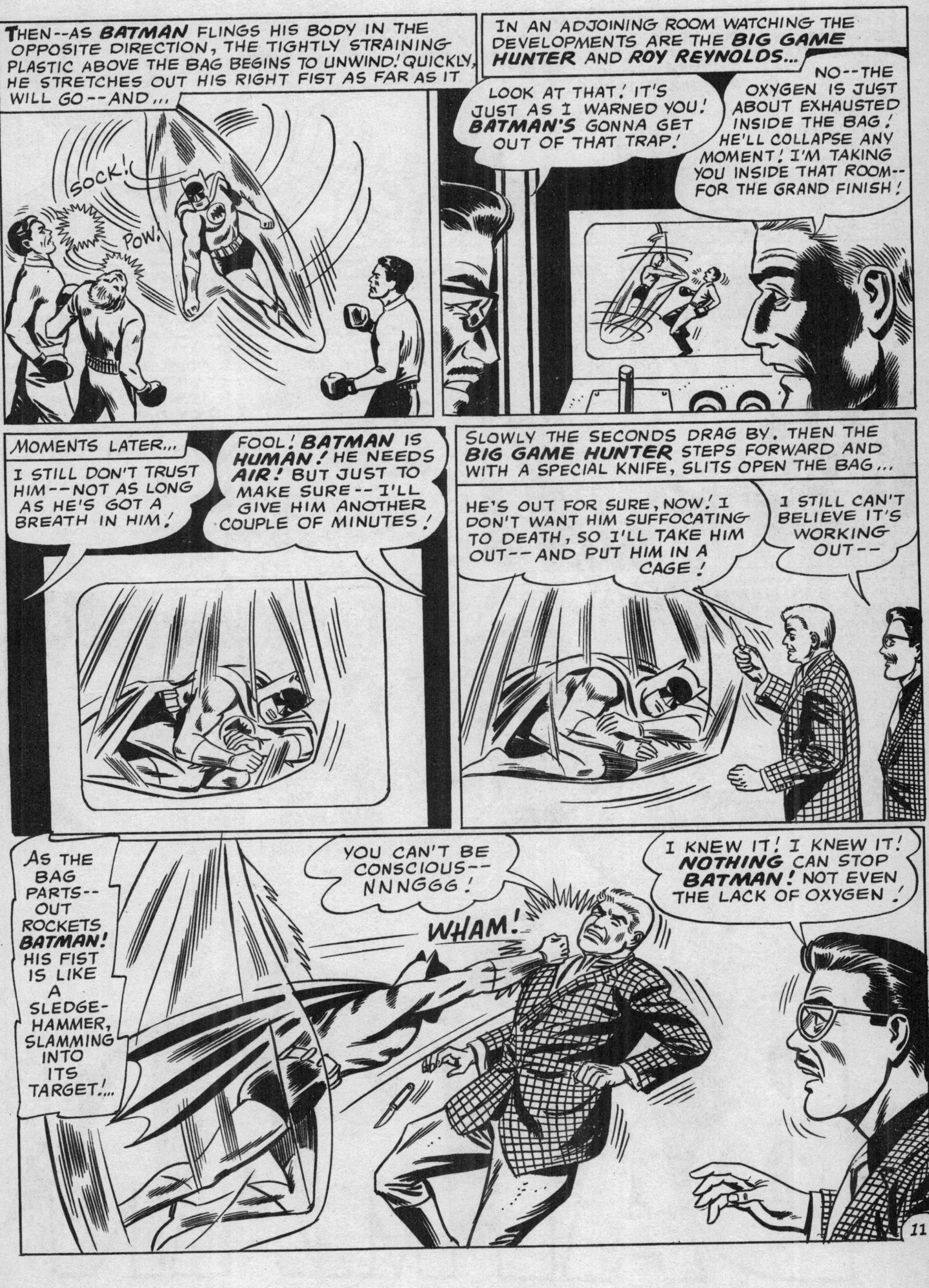
THEN--AS BATMAN FLINGS HIS BODY IN THE OPPOSITE DIRECTION, THE TIGHTLY STRAINING PLASTIC ABOVE THE BAG BEGINS TO UNWIND! QUICKLY, HE STRETCHES OUT HIS RIGHT FIST AS FAR AS IT WILL GO--AND...
SOCK!
POW!
IN AN ADJOINING ROOM WATCHING THE DEVELOPMENTS ARE THE BIG GAME HUNTER AND ROY REYNOLDS...
LOOK AT THAT! IT'S JUST AS I WARNED YOU! BATMAN'S GONNA GET OUT OF THAT TRAP!
NO--THE OXYGEN IS JUST ABOUT EXHAUSTED INSIDE THE BAG! HE'LL COLLAPSE ANY MOMENT! I'M TAKING YOU INSIDE THAT ROOM--FOR THE GRAND FINISH!
MOMENTS LATER...
I STILL DON'T TRUST HIM--NOT AS LONG AS HE'S GOT A BREATH IN HIM!
FOOL! BATMAN IS HUMAN! HE NEEDS AIR! BUT JUST TO MAKE SURE--I'LL GIVE HIM ANOTHER COUPLE OF MINUTES!
SLOWLY THE SECONDS DRAG BY. THEN THE BIG GAME HUNTER STEPS FORWARD AND WITH A SPECIAL KNIFE, SLITS OPEN THE BAG...
HE'S OUT FOR SURE, NOW! I DON'T WANT HIM SUFFOCATING TO DEATH, SO I'LL TAKE HIM OUT--AND PUT HIM IN A CAGE!
I STILL CAN'T BELIEVE IT'S WORKING OUT--
AS THE BAG PARTS--OUT ROCKETS BATMAN! HIS FIST IS LIKE A SLEDGE-HAMMER, SLAMMING INTO ITS TARGET!...
YOU CAN'T BE CONSCIOUS--NNNGGG!
WHAM!
I KNEW IT! I KNEW IT! NOTHING CAN STOP BATMAN! NOT EVEN THE LACK OF OXYGEN!
11

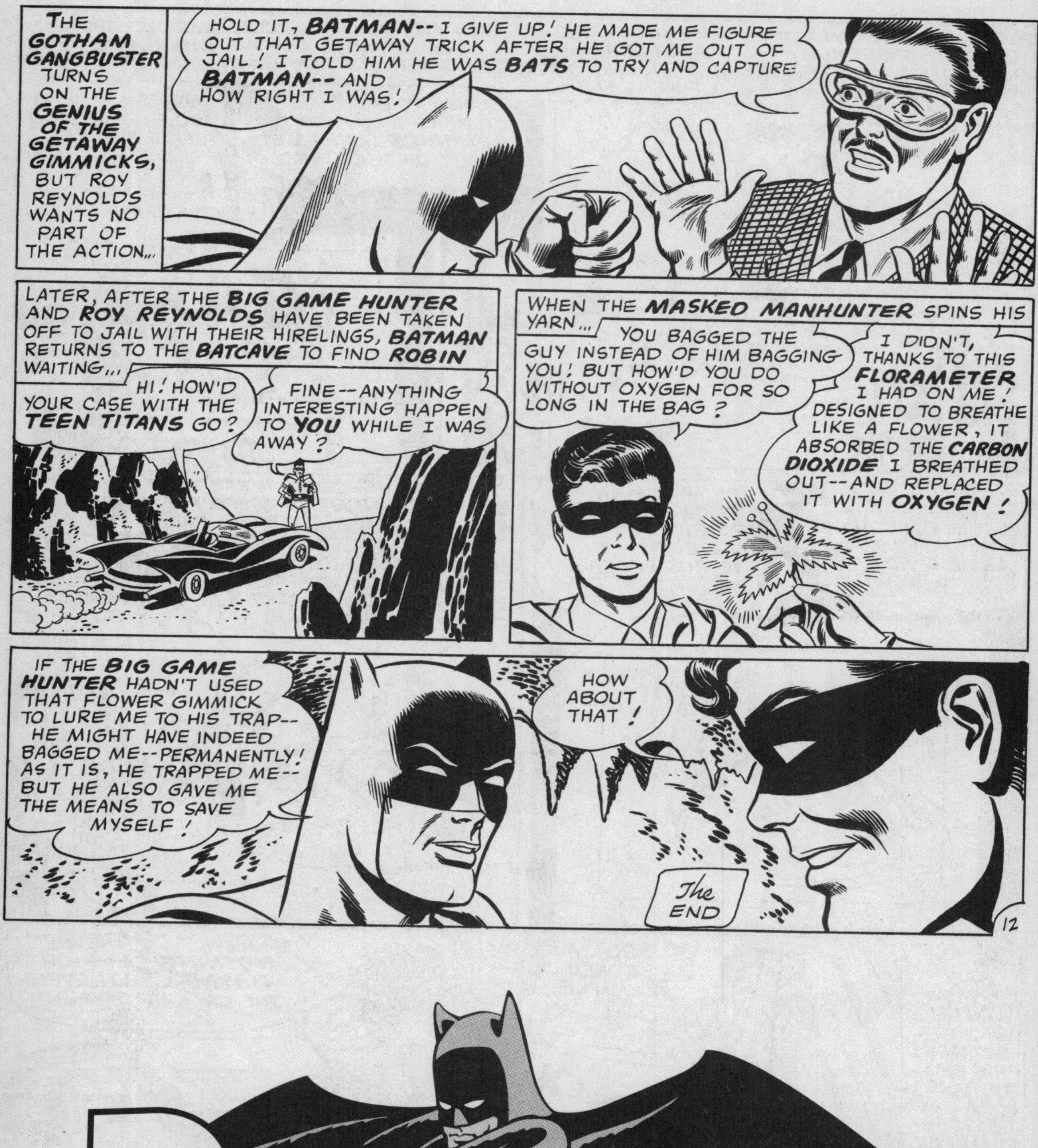
THE GOTHAM GANGBUSTER TURNS ON THE GENIUS OF THE GETAWAY GIMMICKS, BUT ROY REYNOLDS WANTS NO PART OF THE ACTION...
HOLD IT, BATMAN-- I GIVE UP! HE MADE ME FIGURE OUT THAT GETAWAY TRICK AFTER HE GOT ME OUT OF JAIL! I TOLD HIM HE WAS BATS TO TRY AND CAPTURE BATMAN-- AND HOW RIGHT I WAS!
LATER, AFTER THE BIG GAME HUNTER AND ROY REYNOLDS HAVE BEEN TAKEN OFF TO JAIL WITH THEIR HIRELINGS, BATMAN RETURNS TO THE BATCAVE TO FIND ROBIN WAITING...
HI! HOW'D YOUR CASE WITH THE TEEN TITANS GO?
FINE--ANYTHING INTERESTING HAPPEN TO YOU WHILE I WAS AWAY?
WHEN THE MASKED MANHUNTER SPINS HIS YARN...
YOU BAGGED THE GUY INSTEAD OF HIM BAGGING YOU! BUT HOW'D YOU DO WITHOUT OXYGEN FOR SO LONG IN THE BAG?
I DIDN'T, THANKS TO THIS FLORAMETER I HAD ON ME! DESIGNED TO BREATHE LIKE A FLOWER, IT ABSORBED THE CARBON DIOXIDE I BREATHED OUT--AND REPLACED IT WITH OXYGEN!
IF THE BIG GAME HUNTER HADN'T USED THAT FLOWER GIMMICK TO LURE ME TO HIS TRAP-- HE MIGHT HAVE INDEED BAGGED ME--PERMANENTLY! AS IT IS, HE TRAPPED ME-- BUT HE ALSO GAVE ME THE MEANS TO SAVE MYSELF!
HOW ABOUT THAT!
The END
12

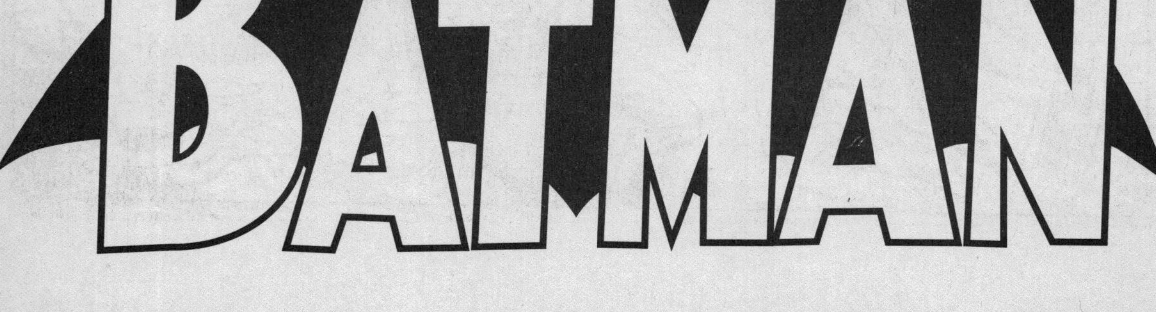
BATMAN

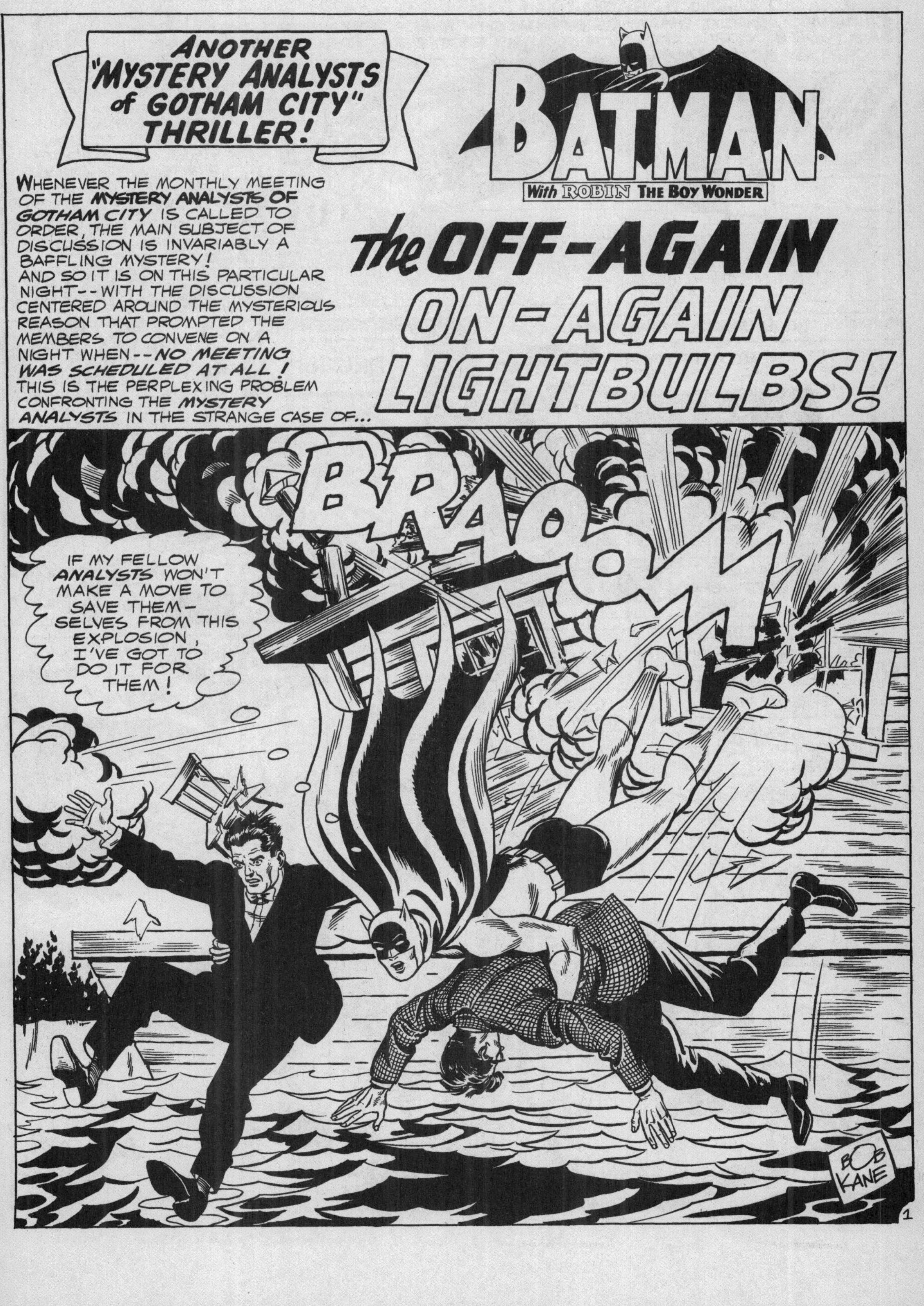
ANOTHER "MYSTERY ANALYSTS of GOTHAM CITY" THRILLER!
BATMAN
With ROBIN THE BOY WONDER
WHENEVER THE MONTHLY MEETING OF THE MYSTERY ANALYSTS OF GOTHAM CITY IS CALLED TO ORDER, THE MAIN SUBJECT OF DISCUSSION IS INVARIABLY A BAFFLING MYSTERY! AND SO IT IS ON THIS PARTICULAR NIGHT--WITH THE DISCUSSION CENTERED AROUND THE MYSTERIOUS REASON THAT PROMPTED THE MEMBERS TO CONVENE ON A NIGHT WHEN--NO MEETING WAS SCHEDULED AT ALL! THIS IS THE PERPLEXING PROBLEM CONFRONTING THE MYSTERY ANALYSTS IN THE STRANGE CASE OF...
the OFF-AGAIN ON-AGAIN LIGHTBULBS!
BRAAOOM
IF MY FELLOW ANALYSTS WON'T MAKE A MOVE TO SAVE THEMSELVES FROM THIS EXPLOSION, I'VE GOT TO DO IT FOR THEM!
BOB KANE
1

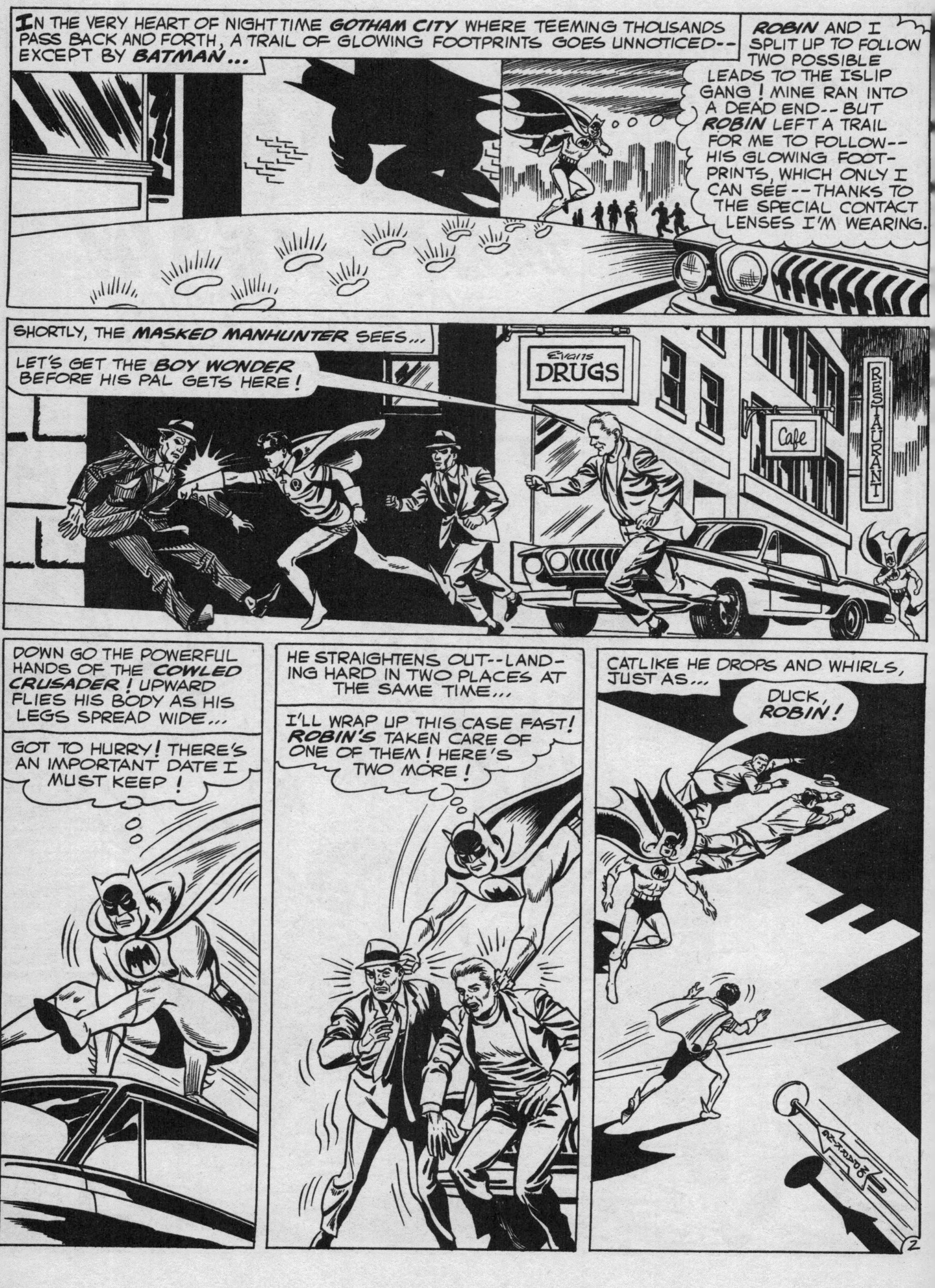
IN THE VERY HEART OF NIGHTTIME GOTHAM CITY WHERE TEEMING THOUSANDS PASS BACK AND FORTH, A TRAIL OF GLOWING FOOTPRINTS GOES UNNOTICED-- EXCEPT BY BATMAN...
ROBIN AND I SPLIT UP TO FOLLOW TWO POSSIBLE LEADS TO THE ISLIP GANG! MINE RAN INTO A DEAD END--BUT ROBIN LEFT A TRAIL FOR ME TO FOLLOW--HIS GLOWING FOOT-PRINTS, WHICH ONLY I CAN SEE--THANKS TO THE SPECIAL CONTACT LENSES I'M WEARING.
SHORTLY, THE MASKED MANHUNTER SEES...
LET'S GET THE BOY WONDER BEFORE HIS PAL GETS HERE!
Evans DRUGS
RESTAURANT
Cafe
DOWN GO THE POWERFUL HANDS OF THE COWLED CRUSADER! UPWARD FLIES HIS BODY AS HIS LEGS SPREAD WIDE...
GOT TO HURRY! THERE'S AN IMPORTANT DATE I MUST KEEP!
HE STRAIGHTENS OUT--LANDING HARD IN TWO PLACES AT THE SAME TIME...
I'LL WRAP UP THIS CASE FAST! ROBIN'S TAKEN CARE OF ONE OF THEM! HERE'S TWO MORE!
CATLIKE HE DROPS AND WHIRLS, JUST AS...
DUCK, ROBIN!
2

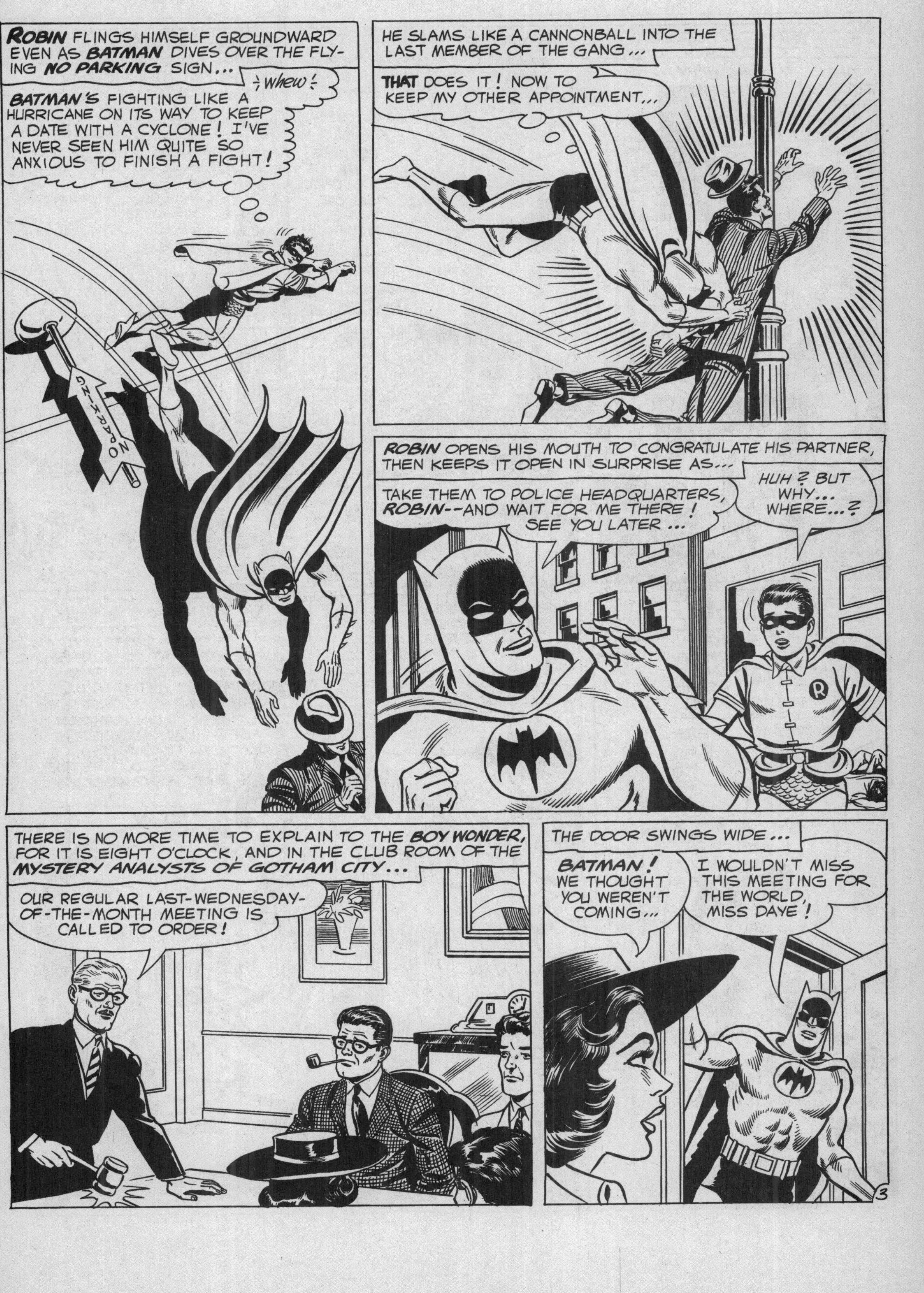
ROBIN FLINGS HIMSELF GROUNDWARD EVEN AS BATMAN DIVES OVER THE FLYING NO PARKING SIGN...
-whew!- BATMAN'S FIGHTING LIKE A HURRICANE ON ITS WAY TO KEEP A DATE WITH A CYCLONE! I'VE NEVER SEEN HIM QUITE SO ANXIOUS TO FINISH A FIGHT!
NO PARKING
HE SLAMS LIKE A CANNONBALL INTO THE LAST MEMBER OF THE GANG...
THAT DOES IT! NOW TO KEEP MY OTHER APPOINTMENT...
ROBIN OPENS HIS MOUTH TO CONGRATULATE HIS PARTNER, THEN KEEPS IT OPEN IN SURPRISE AS...
TAKE THEM TO POLICE HEADQUARTERS, ROBIN--AND WAIT FOR ME THERE! SEE YOU LATER...
HUH? BUT WHY... WHERE...?
THERE IS NO MORE TIME TO EXPLAIN TO THE BOY WONDER, FOR IT IS EIGHT O'CLOCK, AND IN THE CLUB ROOM OF THE MYSTERY ANALYSTS OF GOTHAM CITY...
OUR REGULAR LAST-WEDNESDAY-OF-THE-MONTH MEETING IS CALLED TO ORDER!
THE DOOR SWINGS WIDE...
BATMAN! WE THOUGHT YOU WEREN'T COMING...
I WOULDN'T MISS THIS MEETING FOR THE WORLD, MISS DAYE!
3

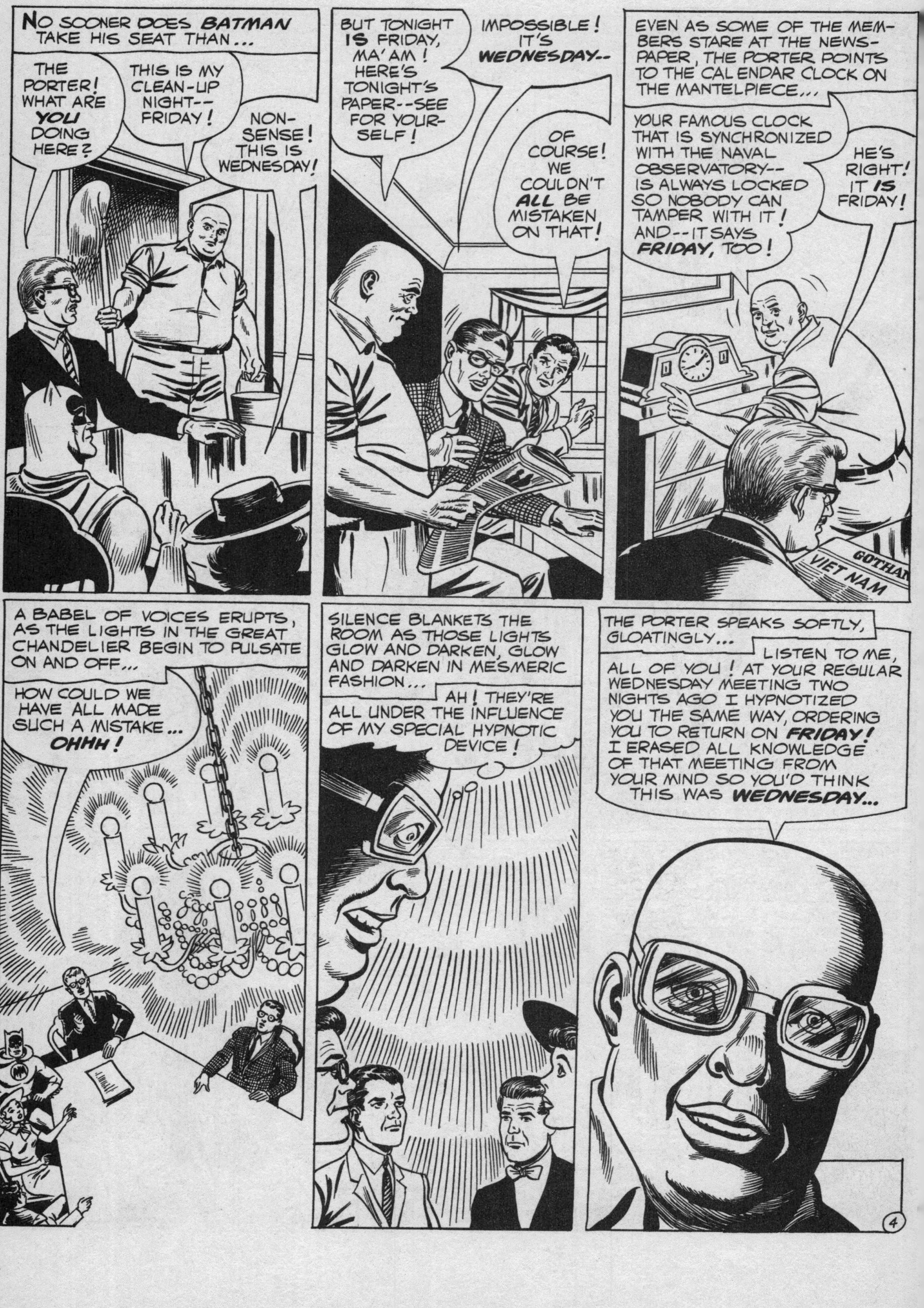
NO SOONER DOES BATMAN TAKE HIS SEAT THAN...
THE PORTER! WHAT ARE YOU DOING HERE?
THIS IS MY CLEAN-UP NIGHT-- FRIDAY!
NON-SENSE! THIS IS WEDNESDAY!
BUT TONIGHT IS FRIDAY, MA'AM! HERE'S TONIGHT'S PAPER--SEE FOR YOURSELF!
IMPOSSIBLE! IT'S WEDNESDAY--
OF COURSE! WE COULDN'T ALL BE MISTAKEN ON THAT!
EVEN AS SOME OF THE MEMBERS STARE AT THE NEWSPAPER, THE PORTER POINTS TO THE CALENDAR CLOCK ON THE MANTELPIECE...
YOUR FAMOUS CLOCK THAT IS SYNCHRONIZED WITH THE NAVAL OBSERVATORY-- IS ALWAYS LOCKED SO NOBODY CAN TAMPER WITH IT! AND--IT SAYS FRIDAY, TOO!
HE'S RIGHT! IT IS FRIDAY!
GOTHAM
VIET NAM
A BABEL OF VOICES ERUPTS, AS THE LIGHTS IN THE GREAT CHANDELIER BEGIN TO PULSATE ON AND OFF...
HOW COULD WE HAVE ALL MADE SUCH A MISTAKE... OHHH!
SILENCE BLANKETS THE ROOM AS THOSE LIGHTS GLOW AND DARKEN, GLOW AND DARKEN IN MESMERIC FASHION...
AH! THEY'RE ALL UNDER THE INFLUENCE OF MY SPECIAL HYPNOTIC DEVICE!
THE PORTER SPEAKS SOFTLY, GLOATINGLY...
LISTEN TO ME, ALL OF YOU! AT YOUR REGULAR WEDNESDAY MEETING TWO NIGHTS AGO I HYPNOTIZED YOU THE SAME WAY, ORDERING YOU TO RETURN ON FRIDAY! I ERASED ALL KNOWLEDGE OF THAT MEETING FROM YOUR MIND SO YOU'D THINK THIS WAS WEDNESDAY...
4

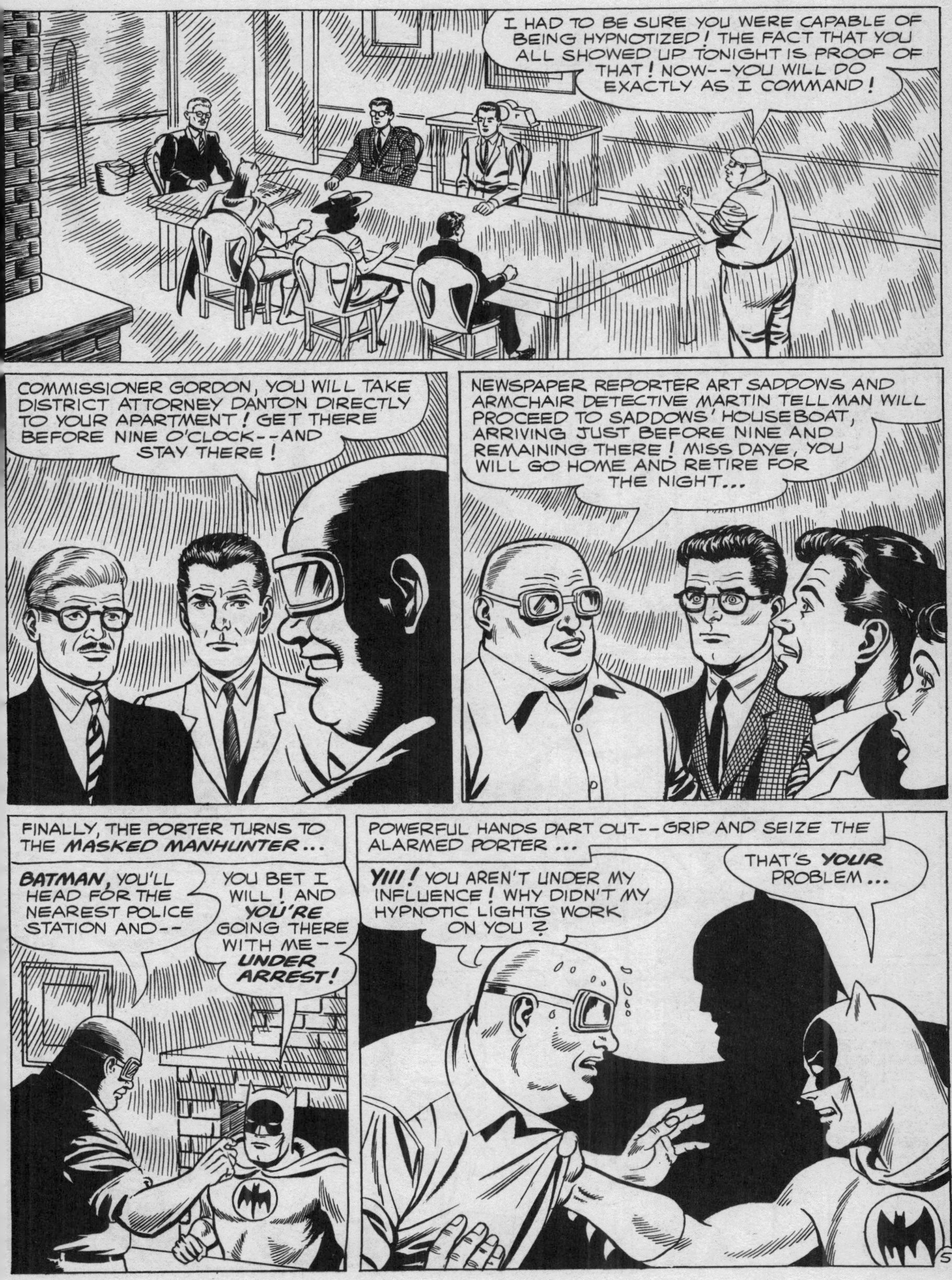
I HAD TO BE SURE YOU WERE CAPABLE OF BEING HYPNOTIZED! THE FACT THAT YOU ALL SHOWED UP TONIGHT IS PROOF OF THAT! NOW--YOU WILL DO EXACTLY AS I COMMAND!
COMMISSIONER GORDON, YOU WILL TAKE DISTRICT ATTORNEY DANTON DIRECTLY TO YOUR APARTMENT! GET THERE BEFORE NINE O'CLOCK--AND STAY THERE!
NEWSPAPER REPORTER ART SADDOWS AND ARMCHAIR DETECTIVE MARTIN TELLMAN WILL PROCEED TO SADDOWS' HOUSEBOAT, ARRIVING JUST BEFORE NINE AND REMAINING THERE! MISS DAYE, YOU WILL GO HOME AND RETIRE FOR THE NIGHT...
FINALLY, THE PORTER TURNS TO THE MASKED MANHUNTER...
BATMAN, YOU'LL HEAD FOR THE NEAREST POLICE STATION AND--
YOU BET I WILL! AND YOU'RE GOING THERE WITH ME--UNDER ARREST!
POWERFUL HANDS DART OUT--GRIP AND SEIZE THE ALARMED PORTER...
YIII! YOU AREN'T UNDER MY INFLUENCE! WHY DIDN'T MY HYPNOTIC LIGHTS WORK ON YOU?
THAT'S YOUR PROBLEM...
5

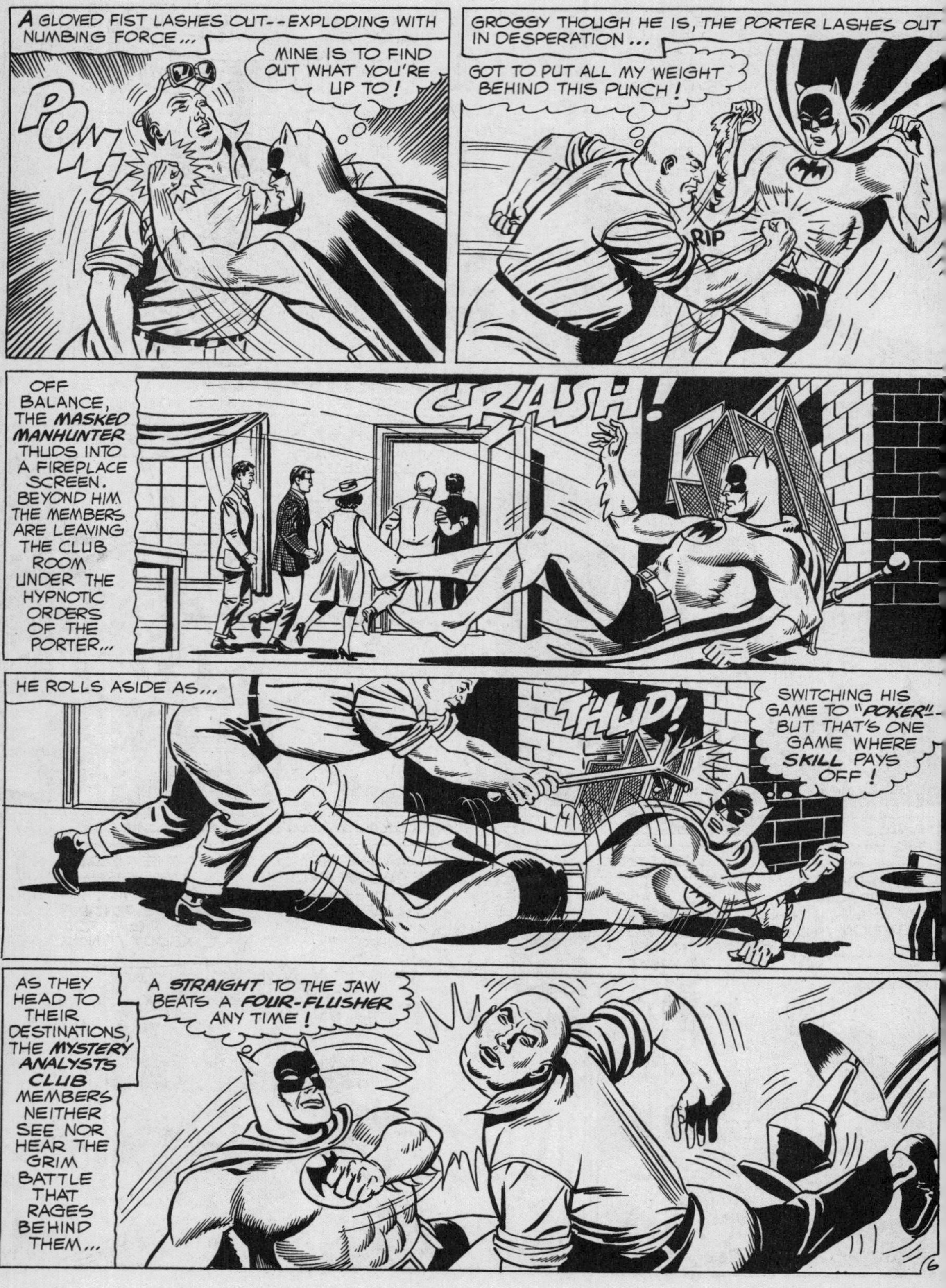
A GLOVED FIST LASHES OUT--EXPLODING WITH NUMBING FORCE...
MINE IS TO FIND OUT WHAT YOU'RE UP TO!
POW!
GROGGY THOUGH HE IS, THE PORTER LASHES OUT IN DESPERATION...
GOT TO PUT ALL MY WEIGHT BEHIND THIS PUNCH!
RIP
OFF BALANCE, THE **MASKED MANHUNTER** THUDS INTO A FIREPLACE SCREEN. BEYOND HIM THE MEMBERS ARE LEAVING THE CLUB ROOM UNDER THE HYPNOTIC ORDERS OF THE PORTER...
CRASH!
HE ROLLS ASIDE AS...
THUD!
SWITCHING HIS GAME TO "**POKER**"!-- BUT THAT'S ONE GAME WHERE **SKILL** PAYS OFF!
AS THEY HEAD TO THEIR DESTINATIONS, THE **MYSTERY ANALYSTS CLUB** MEMBERS NEITHER SEE NOR HEAR THE GRIM BATTLE THAT RAGES BEHIND THEM...
A **STRAIGHT** TO THE JAW BEATS A **FOUR-FLUSHER** ANY TIME!
6

LIKE A GREASED PIG, THE HYPNOTIST TWISTS AWAY AND YANKS OUT A SNUB-NOSED REVOLVER....

YOU PLAYED NO PARTICULAR ROLE IN MY SCHEME, *BATMAN*-- BUT SINCE YOU'RE DETERMINED TO SMASH IT--

--YOU'RE GOING TO WIND UP JUST LIKE THE OTHERS -- DEAD AS A--

THE GUN SPITS FLAME AND THUNDER--BUT THE *COWLED CRUSADER* HAS LIFTED THE HEAVY COAL SCUTTLE AND....

POW!

CLANG!!

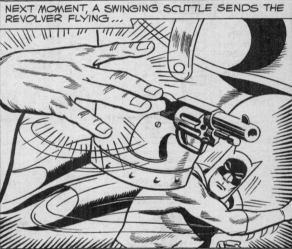

NEXT MOMENT, A SWINGING SCUTTLE SENDS THE REVOLVER FLYING....

FOLLOWED DIRECTLY BY A SWINGING ROUND-HOUSE....

GNNNG!!

FROM THE WRECKAGE OF THE ROOM, HE LIFTS HIS PRISONER....

NOW YOU CAN TELL ME WHAT THIS IS ALL ABOUT!

NOT--ME! YOU CAN'T MAKE ME TALK, *BATMAN!* I'VE PLANNED THIS NIGHT TOO LONG TO PANIC ABOUT IT NOW!

7

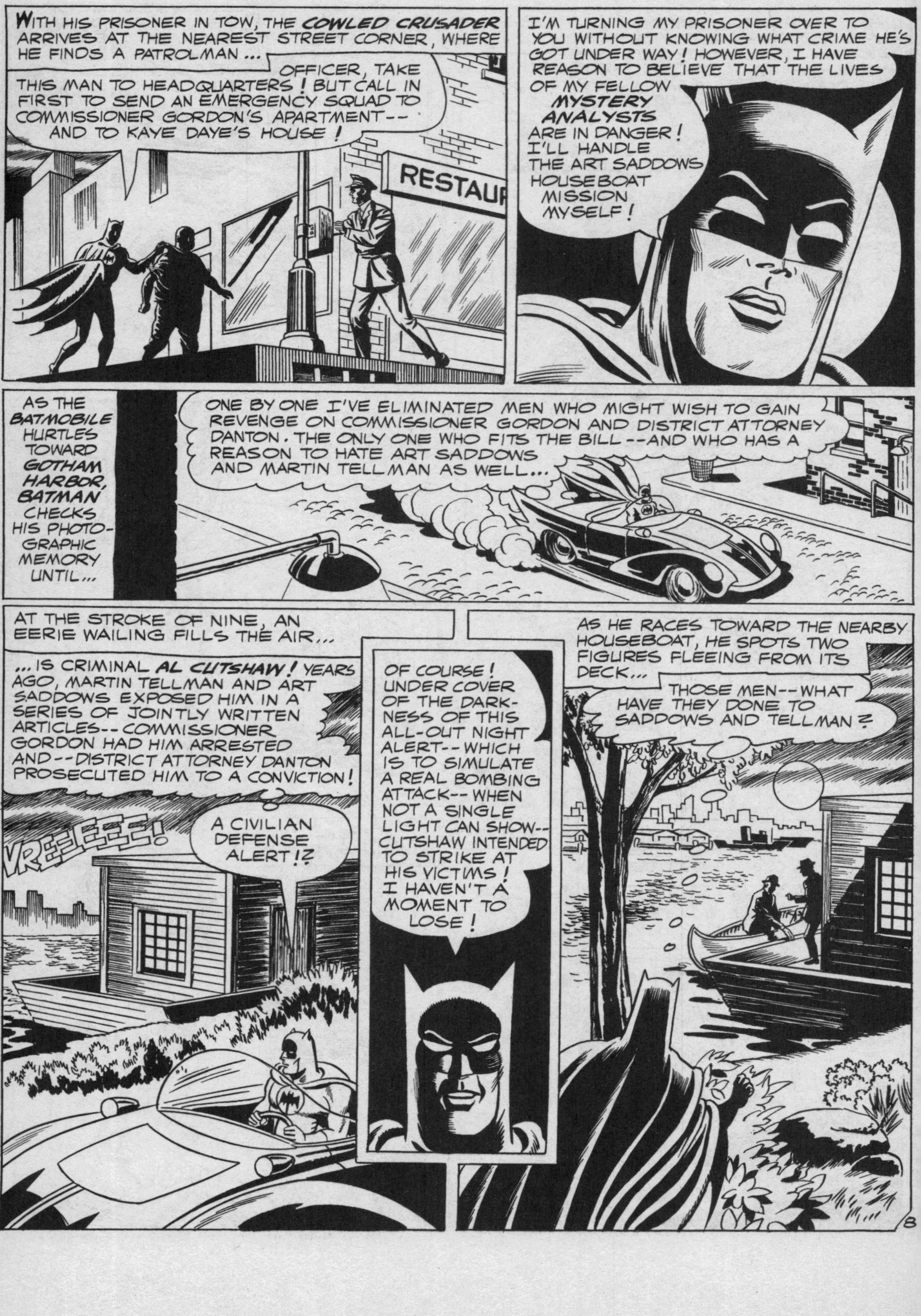
WITH HIS PRISONER IN TOW, THE COWLED CRUSADER ARRIVES AT THE NEAREST STREET CORNER, WHERE HE FINDS A PATROLMAN ...
OFFICER, TAKE THIS MAN TO HEADQUARTERS! BUT CALL IN FIRST TO SEND AN EMERGENCY SQUAD TO COMMISSIONER GORDON'S APARTMENT-- AND TO KAYE DAYE'S HOUSE!
RESTAU
I'M TURNING MY PRISONER OVER TO YOU WITHOUT KNOWING WHAT CRIME HE'S GOT UNDER WAY! HOWEVER, I HAVE REASON TO BELIEVE THAT THE LIVES OF MY FELLOW MYSTERY ANALYSTS ARE IN DANGER! I'LL HANDLE THE ART SADDOWS HOUSEBOAT MISSION MYSELF!
AS THE BATMOBILE HURTLES TOWARD GOTHAM HARBOR, BATMAN CHECKS HIS PHOTOGRAPHIC MEMORY UNTIL...
ONE BY ONE I'VE ELIMINATED MEN WHO MIGHT WISH TO GAIN REVENGE ON COMMISSIONER GORDON AND DISTRICT ATTORNEY DANTON. THE ONLY ONE WHO FITS THE BILL--AND WHO HAS A REASON TO HATE ART SADDOWS AND MARTIN TELLMAN AS WELL...
...IS CRIMINAL AL CUTSHAW! YEARS AGO, MARTIN TELLMAN AND ART SADDOWS EXPOSED HIM IN A SERIES OF JOINTLY WRITTEN ARTICLES-- COMMISSIONER GORDON HAD HIM ARRESTED AND--DISTRICT ATTORNEY DANTON PROSECUTED HIM TO A CONVICTION!
AT THE STROKE OF NINE, AN EERIE WAILING FILLS THE AIR...
VREEEEE!
A CIVILIAN DEFENSE ALERT!?
OF COURSE! UNDER COVER OF THE DARKNESS OF THIS ALL-OUT NIGHT ALERT--WHICH IS TO SIMULATE A REAL BOMBING ATTACK--WHEN NOT A SINGLE LIGHT CAN SHOW--CUTSHAW INTENDED TO STRIKE AT HIS VICTIMS! I HAVEN'T A MOMENT TO LOSE!
AS HE RACES TOWARD THE NEARBY HOUSEBOAT, HE SPOTS TWO FIGURES FLEEING FROM ITS DECK...
THOSE MEN--WHAT HAVE THEY DONE TO SADDOWS AND TELLMAN?
8

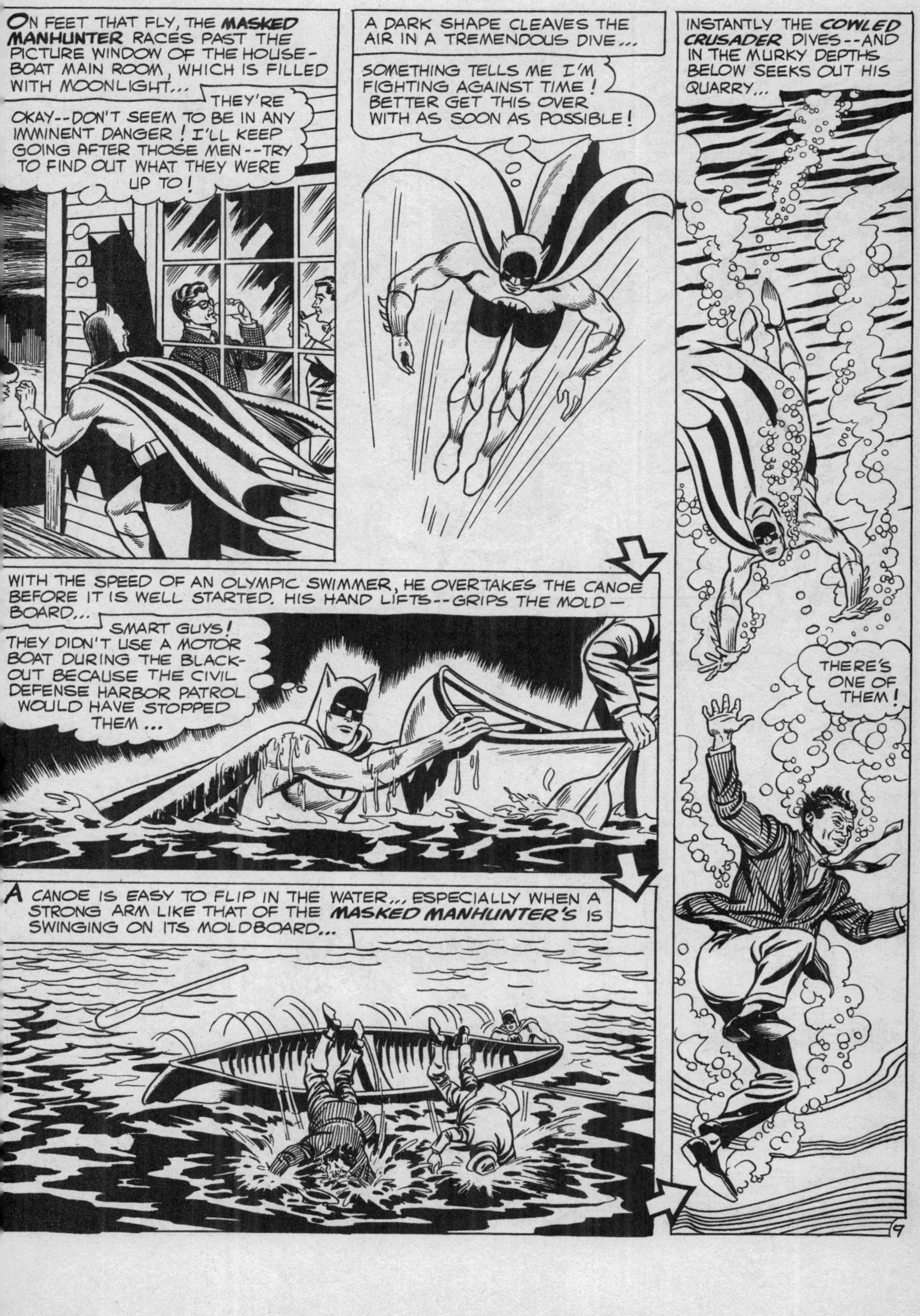
ON FEET THAT FLY, THE MASKED MANHUNTER RACES PAST THE PICTURE WINDOW OF THE HOUSE-BOAT MAIN ROOM, WHICH IS FILLED WITH MOONLIGHT...
THEY'RE OKAY--DON'T SEEM TO BE IN ANY IMMINENT DANGER! I'LL KEEP GOING AFTER THOSE MEN--TRY TO FIND OUT WHAT THEY WERE UP TO!
A DARK SHAPE CLEAVES THE AIR IN A TREMENDOUS DIVE...
SOMETHING TELLS ME I'M FIGHTING AGAINST TIME! BETTER GET THIS OVER WITH AS SOON AS POSSIBLE!
INSTANTLY THE COWLED CRUSADER DIVES--AND IN THE MURKY DEPTHS BELOW SEEKS OUT HIS QUARRY...
THERE'S ONE OF THEM!
WITH THE SPEED OF AN OLYMPIC SWIMMER, HE OVERTAKES THE CANOE BEFORE IT IS WELL STARTED. HIS HAND LIFTS--GRIPS THE MOLD-BOARD...
SMART GUYS! THEY DIDN'T USE A MOTOR BOAT DURING THE BLACK-OUT BECAUSE THE CIVIL DEFENSE HARBOR PATROL WOULD HAVE STOPPED THEM...
A CANOE IS EASY TO FLIP IN THE WATER... ESPECIALLY WHEN A STRONG ARM LIKE THAT OF THE MASKED MANHUNTER'S IS SWINGING ON ITS MOLDBOARD...
9

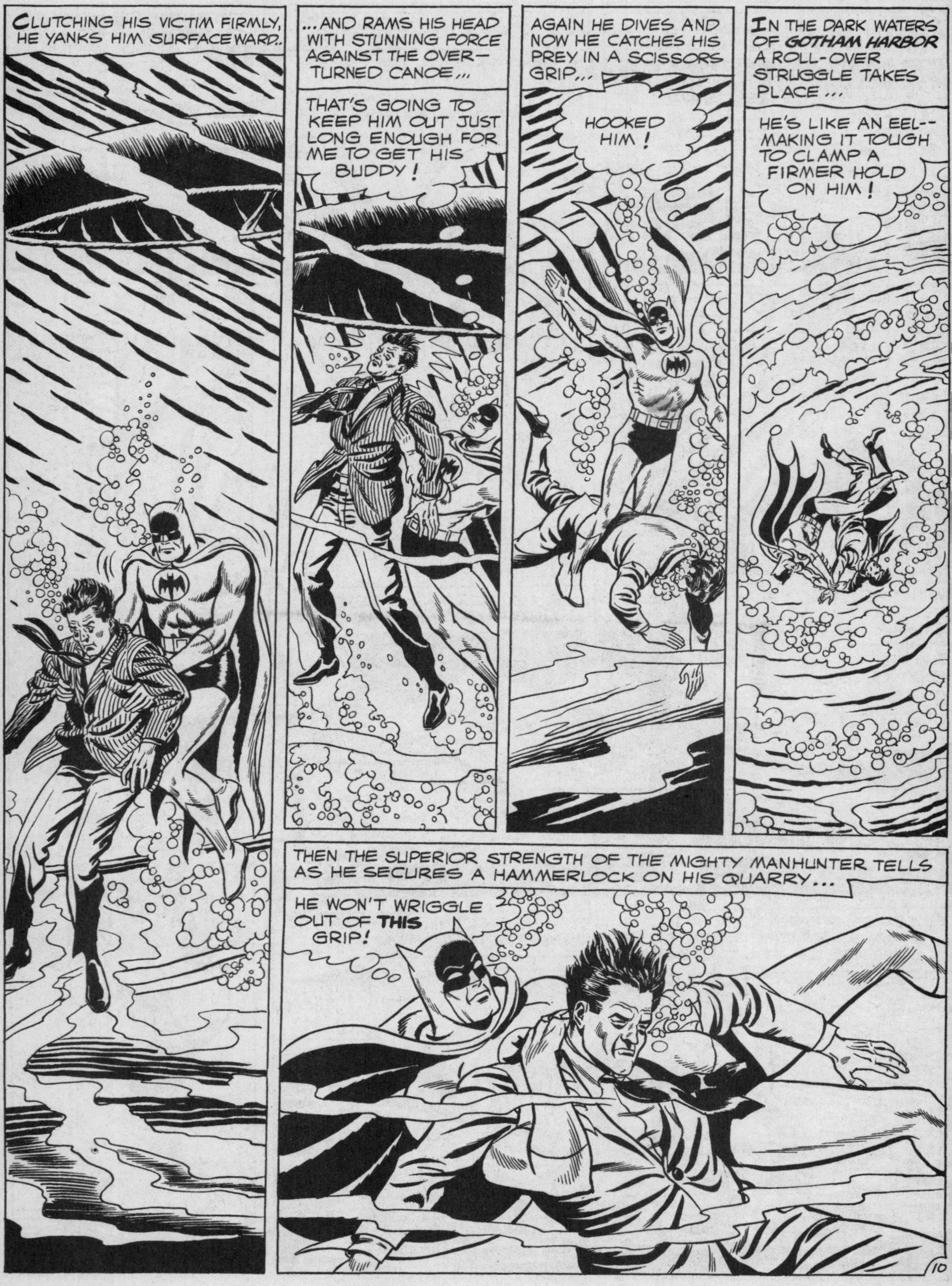

CLUTCHING HIS VICTIM FIRMLY, HE YANKS HIM SURFACEWARD..
...AND RAMS HIS HEAD WITH STUNNING FORCE AGAINST THE OVER-TURNED CANOE,,,
THAT'S GOING TO KEEP HIM OUT JUST LONG ENOUGH FOR ME TO GET HIS BUDDY!
AGAIN HE DIVES AND NOW HE CATCHES HIS PREY IN A SCISSORS GRIP,,,
HOOKED HIM!
IN THE DARK WATERS OF GOTHAM HARBOR A ROLL-OVER STRUGGLE TAKES PLACE...
HE'S LIKE AN EEL-- MAKING IT TOUGH TO CLAMP A FIRMER HOLD ON HIM!
THEN THE SUPERIOR STRENGTH OF THE MIGHTY MANHUNTER TELLS AS HE SECURES A HAMMERLOCK ON HIS QUARRY...
HE WON'T WRIGGLE OUT OF THIS GRIP!
10

DUMPING HIS HARD-BREATHING PRISONERS ACROSS THE OVERTURNED CANOE, *BATMAN* PROPELS THE CRAFT BACK TO THE HOUSEBOAT...

NOW TO CHECK WITH SADDOWS AND TELLMAN...

AS HE BURSTS INTO THE HOUSE-BOAT LIVING ROOM...

ART! MARTY! THOSE TELLTALE SOUNDS! LET'S GET OUT OF HERE--FAST!

NO! WE'VE GOT TO REMAIN HERE!

TICK-TOC!

HEAD DOWN, THE *MASKED MANHUNTER* GRABS UP HIS FRIENDS AND CARRIES THEM THROUGH THE WINDOW...

CRASH!

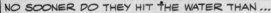

NO SOONER DO THEY HIT THE WATER THAN...

NOW I KNOW WHAT CRIME CUTSHAW INTENDED TO COMMIT!

BARROOM

LATER, AT POLICE HEADQUARTERS, *BATMAN* MAKES EXPLANATIONS TO HIS FELLOW MEMBERS AFTER THEIR HYPNOTIC SPELL HAS BEEN REMOVED...

I UNDERSTAND THE POLICE CAUGHT TWO MEN AND A TIME BOMB IN YOUR APARTMENT, COMMISSIONER, BEFORE YOU AND DENTON ARRIVED! IT'S OBVIOUS THEY WERE WAITING FOR YOU TO GET THERE BEFORE SWITCHING IT ON!

11

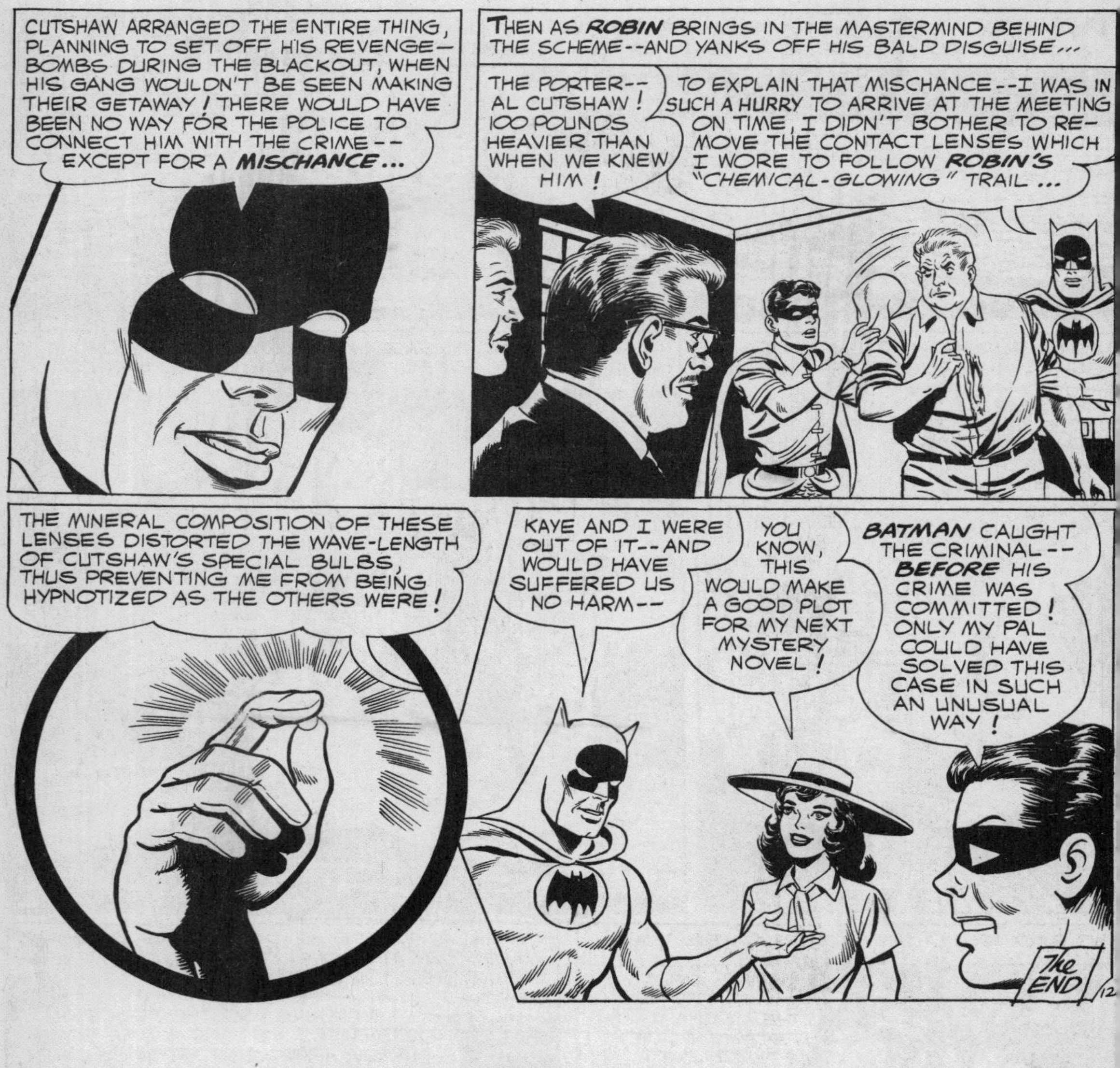
CUTSHAW ARRANGED THE ENTIRE THING, PLANNING TO SET OFF HIS REVENGE-BOMBS DURING THE BLACKOUT, WHEN HIS GANG WOULDN'T BE SEEN MAKING THEIR GETAWAY! THERE WOULD HAVE BEEN NO WAY FOR THE POLICE TO CONNECT HIM WITH THE CRIME--EXCEPT FOR A MISCHANCE...
THEN AS ROBIN BRINGS IN THE MASTERMIND BEHIND THE SCHEME--AND YANKS OFF HIS BALD DISGUISE...
THE PORTER--AL CUTSHAW! 100 POUNDS HEAVIER THAN WHEN WE KNEW HIM!
TO EXPLAIN THAT MISCHANCE--I WAS IN SUCH A HURRY TO ARRIVE AT THE MEETING ON TIME, I DIDN'T BOTHER TO REMOVE THE CONTACT LENSES WHICH I WORE TO FOLLOW ROBIN'S "CHEMICAL-GLOWING" TRAIL...
THE MINERAL COMPOSITION OF THESE LENSES DISTORTED THE WAVE-LENGTH OF CUTSHAW'S SPECIAL BULBS, THUS PREVENTING ME FROM BEING HYPNOTIZED AS THE OTHERS WERE!
KAYE AND I WERE OUT OF IT--AND WOULD HAVE SUFFERED US NO HARM--
YOU KNOW, THIS WOULD MAKE A GOOD PLOT FOR MY NEXT MYSTERY NOVEL!
BATMAN CAUGHT THE CRIMINAL--BEFORE HIS CRIME WAS COMMITTED! ONLY MY PAL COULD HAVE SOLVED THIS CASE IN SUCH AN UNUSUAL WAY!
The END
12

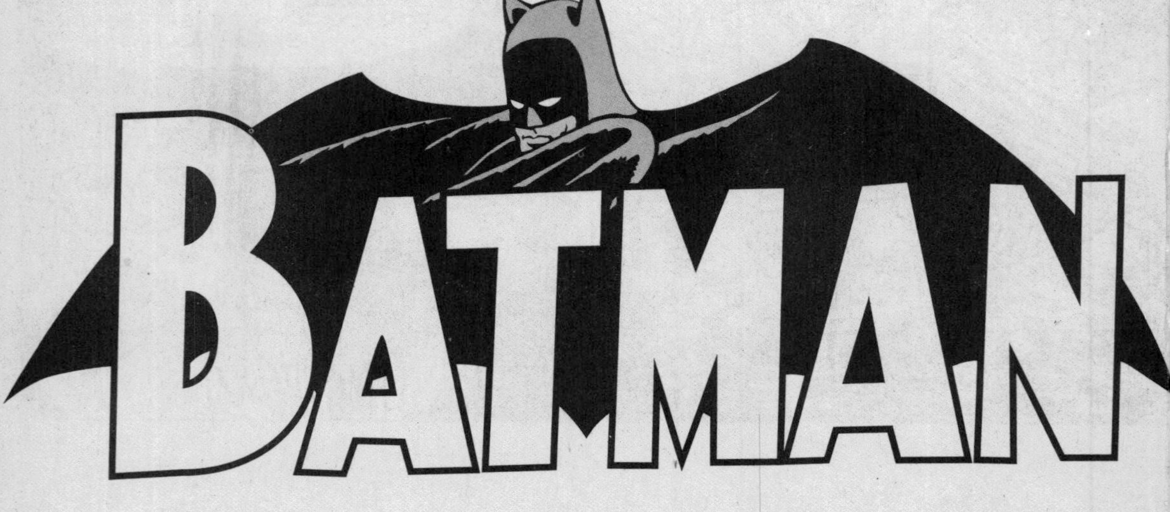
BATMAN